BUSINESS & SOCIETY

A Strategic Approach to Social Responsibility and Ethics

4TH EDITION

Debbie M. Thorne
Texas State University-San Marcos

O. C. Ferrell
University of New Mexico

Linda Ferrell
University of New Mexico

SOUTH-WESTERN
CENGAGE Learning

Australia • Brazil • Japan • Korea • Mexico • Singapore • Spain • United Kingdom • United States

SOUTH-WESTERN
CENGAGE Learning

Business and Society: A Strategic Approach to Social Responsibility and Ethics, 4th Edition

Debbie M. Thorne, O.C. Ferrell, Linda Ferrell

Vice President of Editorial, Business: Jack W. Calhoun

Acquisitions Editor: Michele Rhoades

Sr. Developmental Editor: Joanne Dauksewicz

Marketing Manager: Nathan Anderson

Marketing Communications Manager: Jim Overly

Content Project Manager: Corey Geissler

Media Editor: Danny Bolan

Sr. Manufacturing Coordinator: Kevin Kluck

Production Service: Integra

Sr. Art Director: Tippy McIntosh

Permission Editor Text: Mardell Glinski Schultz

Permission Editor Images: Deanna Ettinger

Internal Designer: Craig Ramsdell, Ramsdell Design

Cover Designer: Craig Ramsdell, Ramsdell Design

Cover Image: iStock

For product information and technology assistance, contact us at **Cengage Learning Customer & Sales Support, 1-800-354-9706**

For permission to use material from this text or product, submit all requests online at **www.cengage.com/permissions** Further permissions questions can be emailed to **permissionrequest@cengage.com**

Library of Congress Control Number: 2009939855

ISBN-13: 978-1-4390-4231-1
ISBN-10: 1-4390-4231-4

South-Western Cengage Learning
5191 Natorp Boulevard
Mason, OH 45040
USA

Cengage Learning products are represented in Canada by Nelson Education, Ltd.

For your course and learning solutions, visit **www.cengage.com**

Purchase any of our products at your local college store or at our preferred online store **www.ichapters.com**

Printed in the United States of America
3 4 5 6 7 13 12

This book is dedicated to:

My students-past, present, and future
– *Debbie M. Thorne*

Kathlene C. Ferrell
– *O. C. Ferrell*

Alleen and Newell Henderson
– *Linda Ferrell*

BRIEF CONTENTS

CONTENTS

CASES

PREFACE

Business and Society: A Strategic Approach to Social Responsibility and Ethics introduces a strategic social responsibility framework for courses that address the role of business in society. Social responsibility is concerned with issues related to values and expectations, as well as the rights of members of society. We view social responsibility as the extent to which a business adopts a strategic focus for fulfilling the economic, legal, ethical, and philanthropic responsibilities expected by all its stakeholders.

The Fourth Edition has been completely updated to capture the dynamic nature of today's environment as well as the evolving strategic approaches to managing the societal interface with business. This revision reflects the challenges faced by the deepest recession in the last eighty years. A collapse of major world financial institutions resulted from excessive risk-taking, ethical misconduct, and the failure to consider stakeholder interests. Most agree that questionable ethical and social decision making, exploiting legal and regulatory loopholes, and avoiding stakeholder transparency caused the recent series of economic disasters. Legendary companies such as Lehman Brothers, Bear Stearns, Merrill Lynch, Countrywide Financial, and AIG no longer exist as independent companies. Their stakeholders lost most, if not all, of their investments. On the other hand, during the same period of time, companies recognized for being ethically and socially responsible—such as IBM, Motorola, General Mills, and Texas Instruments—recovered quickly after the recession.

We have been diligent in this revision about discussing the most up-to-date findings and describing best practices related to social responsibility. The innovative text, cutting-edge cases, and comprehensive teaching and learning package ensure that business students understand and appreciate concerns about business ethics, social auditing, corporate social responsibility, corporate governance, sustainability, and a host of other factors involving a global perspective for today's business leaders. The soft cover format is affordable to students and provides more opportunities for instructors to supplement the course content or to further customize the content to meet their needs.

PHILOSOPHY OF THIS TEXT

In this text, we demonstrate and help the instructor prove that social responsibility is a theoretically grounded yet highly actionable and practical field of interest. The relationship between business and society is inherently controversial and complex, yet the intersection of its components, such as corporate governance, workplace ethics, the natural environment, government institutions, business objectives, community needs, and technology, is experienced in every organization. For this reason, we developed this text to effectively assist decision making and inspire the application of social responsibility principles to a variety of situations and organizations.

IMPORTANT CHANGES TO THE FOURTH EDITION

The Fourth Edition has been completely revised to include two new chapters focusing on key concerns for businesses and their stakeholders. Sustainability includes assessment and improvement of business strategies, economic sectors, work practices, technologies, and lifestyles. Chapter 11, "Sustainability Issues," focuses on strategic approaches for ensuring the long-range well-being of the natural environment. Chapter 12, "Social Responsibility in a Global Environment," examines the unique nature of business and social responsibility in a global environment. We discuss the importance of cultural intelligence, global stakeholders, national competitiveness, and global standards of social reporting.

Each chapter in the text has been updated to include recent social responsibility issues related to the economy, ethical decision making, and concerns about corporate governance. New opening cases at the start of each chapter address a variety of issues related to the chapter content. Two new inserts entitled "Ethical Responsibilities in Finance" and "Earth in the Balance" focus on social responsibility related to the recent financial crisis and on emerging sustainability issues. The "Responsible Business Debate" feature at the end of each chapter introduces a real-world issue and presents two competing perspectives. The debate is positioned so that class teams can defend a position and analyze topics, giving students the opportunity to engage in active learning. We also have provided sixteen cutting-edge cases, eight of which are completely new and all of which are updated.

CONTENT AND ORGANIZATION

Professors who teach business and society courses come from diverse backgrounds, including law, management, marketing, philosophy, and many others. Such diversity affords great opportunities to the field of business and society and showcases the central role that social responsibility occupies within various academic, professional, work, and community circles. Because of the widespread interest and multiplicity of stakeholders, the philosophy and practice of social responsibility is both exciting and debatable; it is in a constant state of discussion and refinement—just like all important business concepts and practices.

We define social responsibility in Chapter 1, "Social Responsibility Framework," as *the adoption by a business of a strategic focus for fulfilling the economic, legal, ethical, and philanthropic responsibilities expected of it by its stakeholders*. To gain the benefits of social responsibility, effective and mutually beneficial relationships must be developed with customers, employees, investors, competitors, government, the community, and others who have a stake in the company. We believe that social responsibility must be fully valued and championed by top managers and granted the same planning time, priority, and management attention as any company initiative. Therefore, the framework for the text reflects a process that begins with the social responsibility philosophy, includes the four types of responsibilities, involves many types of stakeholders, and ultimately results in both short- and long-term performance gains. We also provide a strategic orientation, so students will develop the knowledge, skills, and attitudes for understanding how organizations achieve many benefits through social responsibility.

Chapter 2, "Strategic Management of Stakeholder Relationships," examines the types and attributes of stakeholders, how stakeholders become influential, and the processes for integrating and managing their influence on a firm. The chapter introduces the stakeholder interaction model and examines the impact of global business, corporate reputation, and crisis situations on stakeholder relationships.

Because both daily and strategic decisions affect a variety of stakeholders, companies must maintain a governance structure for ensuring proper control and responsibility for their actions. Chapter 3, "Corporate Governance," examines the rights of shareholders, the accountability of top management for corporate actions, executive compensation, and strategic-level processes for ensuring that economic, legal, ethical, and philanthropic responsibilities are satisfied. Corporate governance is an integral element for social responsibility, which, until the recent scandals, had not received the same level of emphasis as issues such as the environment and human rights.

Chapter 4, "Legal, Regulatory, and Political Issues," explores the complex relationship between business and government. Every business must be aware of and abide by the laws and regulations that dictate required business conduct. This chapter also examines how business can participate in the public policy process to influence government. A strategic approach for legal compliance, based on the Federal Sentencing Guidelines for Organizations, is also provided.

Chapter 5, "Business Ethics and Ethical Decision Making," and Chapter 6, "Strategic Approaches to Improving Ethical Behavior," are devoted to exploring the role of ethics in business decision making. Business ethics relates to responsibilities and expectations that exist beyond legally prescribed levels. We examine the factors that influence ethical decision making and consider how companies can apply this understanding to improve ethical conduct. We fully describe the components of an organizational ethics program and detail the implementation plans needed for effectiveness.

Chapter 7, "Employee Relations," and Chapter 8, "Consumer Relations," explore relationships with two pivotal stakeholders, consumers and employees. These constituencies, although different by definition, have similar expectations of the economic, legal, ethical, and philanthropic responsibilities that must be addressed by business.

Chapter 9, "Community Relations and Strategic Philanthropy," examines companies' synergistic use of organizational core competencies and resources to address key stakeholders' interests and achieve both organizational and social benefits. While traditional benevolent philanthropy involves donating a percentage of sales to social causes, a strategic approach aligns employees and organizational resources and expertise with the needs and concerns of stakeholders. Strategic philanthropy involves both financial and nonfinancial contributions (employee time, goods and services, technology and equipment, as well as facilities) to stakeholders, but it also directly benefits the company.

Due to the Internet and other technological advances, communication is faster than ever, information is readily available, people are living longer and healthier lives, and consumer expectations of businesses continue to rise. Chapter 10, "Technology Issues," provides cutting-edge information on the unique issues that arise as a result of enhanced technology in the workplace and business environment, including its effects on privacy, intellectual property, and health. The strategic direction for technology depends on the government's and businesses' ability to plan, implement, and audit the influence of technology on society.

Chapter 11, "Sustainability Issues," explores the significant environmental issues business and society face today, including air pollution, global warming, water pollution and water quantity, land pollution, waste management, deforestation, urban sprawl, biodiversity, genetically modified foods, and alternative energy. This chapter also considers the impact of government environmental policy and regulation, and examines how some companies are going beyond these laws to address environmental issues and act in an environmentally responsible manner.

Chapter 12, "Social Responsibility in a Global Environment," is a new chapter that addresses the unique issues found in a global business environment. Emerging trends and standards are placed in a global context.

A new appendix, "The Social Audit," describes an auditing procedure that can be used to measure and improve the social responsibility effort. This appendix takes a complete strategic perspective on social responsibility, including stakeholder relations, legal and ethical issues, and philanthropy. This audit is important for demonstrating commitment and ensuring the continuous improvement of the social responsibility effort. An example of a company's social responsibility or social audit is included on the book's companion website. Since many instructors use the audit as a class project or organizing mechanism for the course, the appendix and website serve as important additions to instructor resources.

SPECIAL FEATURES

Examples. Company examples and anecdotes from all over the world are found throughout the text. The purpose of these tools is to take students through a complete strategic planning and implementation perspective on business and society concerns by incorporating an active and team-based learning perspective.

Every chapter opens with a vignette and includes numerous examples that shed more light on how social responsibility works in today's business. In this edition, all boxed features focus on the financial and global dimensions of social responsibility. Chapter opening objectives, a chapter summary, boldfaced key terms, and discussion questions at the end of each chapter help direct students' attention to key points.

Experiential Exercises. Experiential exercises at the end of each chapter help students apply social responsibility concepts and ideas to business practice. Most of the exercises involve research on the activities, programs, and philosophies that companies and organizations are using to implement social responsibility today. These exercises are designed for higher-level learning and require students to apply, analyze, synthesize, and evaluate knowledge, concepts, practices, and possibilities for social responsibility. At the same time, the instructor can generate rich and complex discussions from student responses to the exercises. For example, the experiential exercise for Chapter 1 asks students to examine *Fortune* magazine's annual list of the Most Admired Companies. This exercise sets the stage for a discussion on the broad context in which stakeholders, business objectives, and responsibilities converge. The experiential exercise for the technology chapter requires students to visit websites targeted at children. In visiting the site, students take on the perspective of a child and then assess the site for any persuasion, potentially worrisome content, privacy issues, and guidelines of the Children's Online Privacy Protection Act.

"What Would You Do?" exercises depict people in real-world scenarios who are faced with decisions about social responsibility in the workplace. One exercise (Chapter 9) discusses the dilemma of a newly named Vice President of Corporate Philanthropy. His charge over the next year is to develop a stronger reputation for philanthropy and social responsibility with the company's stakeholders, including employees, customers, and the community. At the end of the scenario, students are asked to help the VP develop a plan for gaining internal support for the office and its philanthropic efforts. Another exercise (Chapter 5) describes an ethical conflict that occurs when an employee discovers that a coworker is using company resources for personal consulting jobs. He confronts his coworker and learns that she is using the resources after normal work hours and on the weekends. He is also concerned that the intellectual capital generated by company projects is getting used in these consulting jobs. Students are asked to help the employee decide what to do with this information.

A new debate issue is located at the end of each chapter. The topic of each debate deals with a real-world company or dilemma that is both current and controversial. Many students have not had the opportunity to engage in a debate and to defend a position related to social responsibility. This feature highlights the complexity of ethical issues by creating a dialog on advantages and disadvantages surrounding issues. The debates also help students develop their critical-thinking, research, and communication skills.

Cases. So that students learn more about specific practices, problems, and opportunities in social responsibility, sixteen cases are provided at the end of this book. The cases represent a comprehensive collection for examining social responsibility in a multidimensional way. The recent trials and tribulations of high-profile companies and people are covered in new cases on Countrywide Financial, AIG (American International Group), Bernard Madoff, the American Red Cross, BP (Beyond Petroleum), and Mattel. The sixteen cases allow students to consider the effects of stakeholders and responsibility expectations on larger and well-known businesses. These cases represent the most up-to-date and compelling issues in social responsibility. Students will find these cases to be pivotal to their understanding of the complexity of social responsibility in practice. Additional cases on the text website give professors more resources to use for testing and other course projects.

Role-Play Exercises. In addition to many examples, end-of-chapter exercises, and the cases, several role-play exercises are provided in the *Instructor's Resource Manual*. The role-play exercises are built around a fictitious yet plausible scenario or case, support higher-level learning objectives, require group decision-making skills, and can be used in classes of any size. Implementation of the exercises can be customized to the time frame, course objectives, student population, and other unique characteristics of a course. These exercises are aligned with trends in higher education toward teamwork, active learning, and student experiences in handling real-world business issues. For example, the National Farm & Garden exercise places students in a crisis situation that requires an immediate response and consideration of changes over the long term. The role-play simulations (1) give students the opportunity to practice making decisions that have consequences for social responsibility, (2) utilize a team-based approach, (3) recreate the pressures, power, information flows, and other factors that affect decision making in the workplace, and (4) incorporate a debriefing and feedback period for maximum learning and linkages to course objectives. We developed the role-play exercises to enhance more traditional learning tools and to complement the array of resources provided to users of this text. Few textbooks offer this level of teaching support and proprietary learning devices.

A COMPLETE SUPPLEMENTS PACKAGE

Instructor's Resource CD-ROM. This instructor's CD provides a variety of teaching resources in electronic format, allowing for easy customization to meet specific instructional needs. Files include Lecture PowerPoint® slides, Word files from the Instructor's Manual, and the Test Bank, along with its computerized version.

The comprehensive *Instructor's Resource Manual* includes chapter outlines, answers to the discussion questions at the end of each chapter, comments on the experiential exercises at the end of each chapter, comments on each case, a sample syllabus, and Video Guide. Special role-play exercises are included in the manual, along with specific suggestions for using and implementing them in class. The *Test Bank* provides multiple-choice and essay questions for each chapter and includes a mix of objective and application questions. *ExamView*, a computerized version of the Test Bank, provides instructors with all the tools they need to create, author/edit, customize, and deliver multiple types of tests. Instructors can import questions directly from the test bank, create their own questions, or edit existing questions.

Videos. A DVD is also available to support the Fourth Edition. The seventeen segments can be used across several chapters, and the Video Guide (which appears at the end of the Instructor Manual) contains a matrix intended to show the closest relationships between the videos and chapter topics. The Video Guide also includes summaries of each video as well as teaching guidelines and issues for discussion.

Instructor Companion Site. The Instructor Companion Site can be found at http://www.cengage.com/management/thorne. It includes a complete Instructor Manual, Word files from both the Instructor Manual and Test Bank, and PowerPoint slides for easy downloading.

Student Companion Site. The Student Companion Site can also be found at http://www.cengage.com/management/thorne. It includes interactive quizzes, a glossary, company links, role-play scenarios, and experiential exercises. A *Premium Companion Site* is also available with a number of online study tools, including flashcards, additional interactive quizzes, student PowerPoint slides, crossword puzzles, and games.

WebTutor™. Whether you want to Web-enable your class or teach entirely online, WebTutor provides customizable text-specific content within your course system. This content-rich, Web-based teaching and learning aid reinforces chapter concepts and acts as an electronic student study guide. WebTutor provides students with interactive chapter review quizzes, critical-thinking and writing-improvement exercises, flashcards, PowerPoints, and links to online videos.

ACKNOWLEDGMENTS

A number of individuals provided reviews and suggestions that helped improve the text and related materials. We sincerely appreciate their time, expertise, and interest in the project.

We wish to acknowledge the many people who played an important role in the development of this book. Jennifer Jackson played a key role in research, writing, editing, and project management. Jennifer Sawayda assisted with research and provided support in revising much of this material. Melanie Drever also assisted with previous drafts of some of the cases. Ashli Lane assisted with research and writing and suggested revisions to meet students' key interests. Holly Tipton provided project management support. Finally, we express much appreciation to our colleagues and the administration at Texas State University–San Marcos and the University of New Mexico.

Our goal is to provide materials and resources that enhance and strengthen both teaching and learning and thinking about social responsibility. We invite your comments, concerns, and questions. Your suggestions will be sincerely appreciated and utilized.

Debbie M. Thorne
O. C. Ferrell
Linda Ferrell

Social Responsibility Framework

Chapter Objectives

- To define the concept of social responsibility

- To trace the development of social responsibility

- To examine the global nature of social responsibility

- To discuss the benefits of social responsibility

- To discuss the framework for understanding social responsibility

Chapter Outline

Social Responsibility Defined

Development of Social Responsibility

Global Nature of Social Responsibility

Benefits of Social Responsibility

Framework for Studying Social Responsibility

© Tom Tomczyk

Going Public, Maintaining Values at Huntsman

Huntsman is a global manufacturer and marketer of a wide variety of chemicals. Originally founded in 1970, this Salt Lake City–based corporation employs 11,300 individuals in 100 locations as diverse as São Paulo, Brazil; Cairo, Egypt; Chocolate Bayou, Texas; and Kobe, Japan. The company supplies chemicals and related materials to global industries. Huntsman recently launched its green chemistry business unit to ensure the firm remains a leader in environmentally sound engineering and manufacturing processes. The company still bears the name of its founder and chairman, Jon M. Huntsman, and the company's mission statement articulates a clear dedication to corporate responsibility:

> We will operate safe, clean, efficient facilities in an environmentally and socially responsible manner.
>
> We will provide a work environment that fosters teamwork, innovation, accountability, and open communication.
>
> We will place into society assistance for those who suffer, hope for those who may need inspiration and education for those who may feel the challenge but do not have the means.
>
> We have an aggressive growth philosophy which reflects the spirit of free enterprise and maximization of long term profits, the best motives for creating mutual benefits for customers, employees, suppliers, and the communities in which we are located.

Peter R. Huntsman, Jon's son, became President and CEO of Huntsman in 2000 and has led the company through an increasingly tumultuous business environment. Huntsman, a privately held firm until 2005, has gone through the difficult transition to a public ownership structure. Now subject to heightened Wall Street scrutiny, short-term investors, increased reporting, and new compliance structures, the company is faced with decisions and actions that still need to align with its mission, including the maximization of long-term profits, environmental responsibility, philanthropy, and benefits for multiple stakeholders.

During the first decade of 2000s, the company achieved its lowest rate ever of occupational injuries as measured by the Occupational Safety and Health Administration (OSHA), gained recognition for outstanding environmental performance, and weathered the effects of Hurricane Ike on operations in the Texas Gulf Coast region. By 2009, however, Huntsman had posted significant losses amidst a halting global economy and vowed to recover via cost-cutting mechanisms and new business opportunities in China. Huntsman was also embroiled in a lawsuit against Credit Suisse and Deutsche Bank, alleging fraud and conspiracy over a failed merger agreement.

Even in the face of a disruptive business environment and pressures of public ownership, Huntsman's website clearly outlines expectations for corporate governance, business conduct, and other policies designed to meet and exceed legal standards. The company also elaborates on its philanthropic orientation and efforts to assist society via cancer research and programs combating homelessness and domestic violence. Although some of these responsibilities are mandatory, others are discretionary and were built over time as the Huntsman business grew, the economy changed, and new societal expectations emerged.[1]

Businesses today must cope with increasingly complex, and often competing, motives and incentives in their decision making. In a *Business Week*–Harris Poll survey of the general population, 95 percent of respondents agreed with the following statement: "U.S. corporations should have more than one purpose. They also owe something to their workers and the communities in which they operate, and they should sometimes sacrifice some profit for the sake of making things better for their workers and communities."[2] In an era of intense global competition and increasing media scrutiny, consumer activism, and government regulation, all types of organizations need to become adept at fulfilling these expectations. Like Huntsman, many companies are trying, with varying results, to meet the many economic, legal, ethical, and philanthropic responsibilities they now face. Satisfying the expectations of social responsibility is a never-ending process of continuous improvement that requires leadership from top management, buy-in from employees, and good relationships across the community, industry, market, and government. Companies must properly plan, allocate, and use resources to satisfy the demands placed on them by investors, employees, customers, business partners, the government, the community, and others.

"The general population believes that U.S. corporations owe something to their workers and the communities in which they operate, and should sometimes sacrifice some profit to make things better for their workers and communities."

In this chapter, we examine the concept of social responsibility and how it relates to today's complex business environment. First, we define social responsibility. Next, we consider the development of social responsibility, its benefits to organizations, and the changing nature of expectations in our increasingly global economy. Finally, we introduce the framework for studying social responsibility used by this text, which includes such elements as strategic management for stakeholder relations; legal, regulatory, and political issues; business ethics; corporate governance; consumer relations; employee relations; philanthropy and community relations; environmental issues; technology issues; and the social audit.

SOCIAL RESPONSIBILITY DEFINED

Business ethics, corporate volunteerism, compliance, corporate citizenship, reputation management—these are terms you may have heard used, or even used yourself, to describe the various rights and responsibilities of business organizations. You may have thought about what these terms actually mean for business practice. You may also have wondered what expectations of business these phrases describe. In this chapter, we clarify some of the confusion that exists in the terminology that people use when they talk about expectations for business conduct. To this end, we begin by defining social responsibility.

In most societies, businesses are granted a license to operate and the right to exist through a combination of social and legal mechanisms. Businesses are expected to pay taxes, abide by laws and regulations, treat employees fairly, follow through on contracts, protect the natural environment, meet warranty obligations, and adhere to many other standards. Companies that continuously meet and exceed these standards are rewarded with customer satisfaction, employee dedication, investor loyalty, strong relationships in the community, and the time and energy to continue focusing on business-related concerns. Firms that fail to meet these responsibilities can face penalties, both formal and informal, and may have their attention diverted away from core business issues. For example, a restaurant that delivers poor-quality food and shoddy service may be informally sanctioned by customers who decide to take their business elsewhere. These same customers often tell friends and family to avoid the restaurant, thus creating a spiral of effects that eventually shutters the restaurant's doors. On the other hand, a large multinational corporation may be faced with protestors who use physical means to destroy or deface one of its retail stores. In this case, the company is not permanently harmed, but it must allocate resources to remodel the store and answer criticism.

Finally, a company engaged in deceptive practices may face formal investigation by a government agency. This investigation could lead to legal charges and penalties, perhaps severe enough to significantly alter the company's products and practices or close the business. For example, Conseco Inc., a large insurance and finance company, filed for Chapter 11 bankruptcy protection amid a federal investigation into its accounting practices and investor lawsuits. Before the filing, Conseco reported $52.3 billion in assets, making its bankruptcy one of the largest in U.S. history. Although the firm eventually emerged from bankruptcy, investors and analysts continued to be critical of Conseco's executive management and strategic direction. After a literal revolving door of executives, the company failed to file its annual report in a timely manner in 2009, prompting concerns about a looming second bankruptcy.[3]

Businesses today are expected to look beyond self-interest and recognize that they belong to a larger group, or society, that expects responsible participation. Thus, if any group, society, or institution is to function, there must be a delicate interplay between rights (i.e., what people expect to get) and responsibilities (i.e., what people are expected to contribute) for the common good.

A Starbucks barista proudly makes and serves drinks in downtown Seattle

© AP Photo/Ted S. Warren

The adage "no man is an island" describes the relational and integrative nature of society. Although businesses are not human beings, they plan, develop goals, allocate resources, and act and behave purposefully. Thus, society grants them both benefits and responsibilities.

The term *social responsibility* came into widespread use in the business world during the 1970s, but there remains some confusion over the term's exact meaning. Table 1.1 lists some of the different ways people commonly use the term to describe business responsibilities. Many of these characterizations have elements in common, such as focusing on the achievement of both corporate and social goals and recognizing the broad groups to which business has an obligation. Only the sixth characterization, which describes social responsibility as an oxymoron, is distinctly different from the others. This view of social responsibility, articulated in the famous economist Milton Friedman's 1962 *Capitalism and Freedom*, asserts that business has one purpose, satisfying its investors or stockholders, and that any other considerations are outside its scope.[4] Although this view still exists today, it has lost some credence as more and more companies have assumed the social responsibility orientation.[5]

Table 1.1 Characterizations of Social Responsibility

Characterization	Description
1. License to operate	Social responsibility is a condition for doing business, and as with customer requirements, a firm should find the most efficient way to meet requirements from the government and other external groups.
2. Long-term business investment	Like research and development, social responsibility is designed to improve the business environment for future progress.
3. Vehicle for achieving goals and reputation	Companies that focus on social responsibility will have stronger customer loyalty, more committed employees, better government relations, and ultimately, stronger reputations.
4. Activity to avoid exposure and risk	Responsible activities help companies avoid being singled out or exposed to unnecessary outsider intrusion.
5. Economic and constructive	Companies should reinforce the economic foundation and viability of the communities in which they operate.
6. Relationship	Business and society are interwoven and interdependent, rather than distinct entities.
7. Responsibility to stakeholders	Management should act responsibly in its relationships with other stakeholders who have a legitimate interest in the business.
8. Oxymoron	Companies are designed to increase shareholder wealth.

Sources: Archie Carroll, "A Three-Dimensional Conceptual Model of Corporate Social Performance," *Academy of Management Review* 4 (1979): 497–505; Kim Davenport, "Corporate Citizenship: A Stakeholder Approach for Defining Corporate Social Performance and Identifying Measures for Assessing It," *Business and Society* 39 (June 2000): 210–219; Lance Moir, "What Do We Mean by Social Responsibility?," *Corporate Governance: The International Journal for Effective Board Performance* 1 (2001), 16–22.

We define **social responsibility** as the adoption by a business of a strategic focus for fulfilling the economic, legal, ethical, and philanthropic responsibilities expected of it by its stakeholders. This definition encompasses a wide range of objectives and activities, including both historical views of business and perceptions that have emerged in the last decade. Let's take a closer look at the parts of this definition.

Social Responsibility Applies to All Types of Businesses

It is important to recognize that all types of businesses—small and large, sole proprietorships and partnerships, as well as large corporations—implement social responsibility initiatives to further their relationships with their customers, their employees, and their community at large. For example, RunTex, a store in Austin, Texas, which sells athletic shoes, clothing, and accessories, donates used shoes (which customers have traded in for discounts on new shoes) to the community's poor and homeless. The company also cosponsors walk/run events that generate funds for local and national social causes. Thus, the ideas advanced in this book are equally relevant and applicable across a broad spectrum of business firms.

Although the social responsibility efforts of large corporations usually receive the most attention, the activities of small businesses may have a greater impact on local communities.[6] Owners of small businesses often serve as community leaders, provide goods and services for customers in smaller markets that larger corporations are not interested in serving, create jobs, and donate resources to local community causes. Medium-sized businesses and their employees have similar roles and functions on both a local and a regional level. Although larger firms produce a substantial portion of the gross national output of the United States, small businesses employ about half of the private sector workforce and produce roughly half of the private sector output. In addition to these economic outcomes, small business presents an entrepreneurial opportunity to many people, some of whom have been shut out of the traditional labor force. Women, minorities, and veterans are increasingly interested in self-employment and other forms of small business activity.[7] It is vital that all businesses consider the relationships and expectations that our definition of social responsibility suggests.

Social Responsibility Adopts a Strategic Focus

Social responsibility is not just an academic term; it involves action and measurement, or the "extent" to which a firm embraces the philosophy of social responsibility and then follows through with the implementation of initiatives. Our definition of social responsibility requires a formal commitment, or way of communicating the company's social responsibility philosophy and commitment. For example, Herman Miller, a multinational provider of office, residential, and health-care furniture and services, crafted a statement that describes the company's commitment to core values (shown in Figure 1.1). This statement declares Herman Miller's philosophy and the way it will fulfill its responsibilities to its customers, its shareholders, its employees, the community, and the natural environment. Because this statement takes into account all of Herman Miller's

social responsibility the adoption by a business of a strategic focus for fulfilling the economic, legal, ethical, and philanthropic responsibilities expected of it by its stakeholders

Figure 1.1 Herman Miller Inc.'s Blueprint for Corporate Community

- Curiosity and Exploration
- Performance
- Engagement
- Design
- Relationships
- Inclusiveness
- A Better World
- Transparency
- Foundations

Source: "What We Believe," Herman Miller, Inc., http://www.hermanmiller.com/About-Us/What-We-Believe, accessed July 9, 2009. Courtesy of Herman Miller, Inc.

constituents and applies directly to all of the company's operations, products, markets, and business relationships, it demonstrates the company's strategic focus on social responsibility. Other companies that embrace social responsibility have incorporated similar elements into their strategic communications, including mission and vision statements, annual reports, and websites. For example, the website and annual report of the Shimizu Corporation of Japan highlight a companywide commitment to constructing high-quality buildings that create social and cultural value and are in harmony with the environment. The company refers to this commitment as "Total Eco-Construction."[8]

In addition to a company's verbal and written commitment to social responsibility, our definition requires action and results. To implement its social responsibility philosophy, Herman Miller has developed and implemented several corporate-wide strategic initiatives, including research on improving work furniture and environments, innovation in the area of ergonomically correct products, progressive employee development opportunities, and an environmental stewardship program. These efforts have earned the company many accolades, such as being named the "Most Admired" furniture manufacturer in America by *Fortune* magazine, and a place on numerous prestigious lists, including *Fortune* magazine's "100 Best Companies to Work for in America," *Forbes* magazine's "Platinum List" of America's 400 best-managed large companies, *Business Ethics* magazine's "100 Best Corporate Citizens," *Diversity Inc.* magazine's "Top 10 Corporations for Supplier Diversity," the "2007 Wastewise Gold Achievement Award for Smart Packaging," and *The Progressive Investor's* "Sustainable Business Top 20."[9] As this example demonstrates, effective social responsibility requires both words and action.

If any such initiative is to have strategic importance, it must be fully valued and championed by top management. Executives must believe in and support the integration of constituent interests and economic, legal, ethical, and philanthropic responsibilities into every corporate decision. For example, company objectives for brand awareness and loyalty can be developed and measured from both a marketing and a social responsibility standpoint because researchers have documented a relationship between consumers' perceptions of a firm's social responsibility and their intentions to purchase that company's brands.[10] Likewise, engineers can integrate consumers' desires for reduced negative environmental impact in product designs, and marketers can ensure that a brand's advertising campaign incorporates this product benefit. Finally, consumers' desires for an environmentally sound product may stimulate a stronger company interest in assuming environmental leadership in all aspects of its operations. Home Depot, for example, responded to demands by consumers and environmentalists for environmentally friendly wood products by launching a new initiative that gives preference to wood products certified as having been harvested responsibly over those taken from endangered forests.[11] With this action, the company, which has long touted its environmental principles, has chosen to take a leadership role in the campaign for environmental responsibility in the home-improvement industry. Although social responsibility depends on collaboration and coordination across many parts of the business and among its constituencies, it also produces effects throughout these same groups. We discuss some of these benefits in a later section of this chapter.

Because of the need for coordination, a large company that is committed to social responsibility often creates specific positions or departments to spearhead the various components of its program. For example, Target, the national retailer, uses a decentralized approach to manage employee volunteerism. Each Target store has a "good neighbor captain" who coordinates employees' efforts with a local charity or cause. The Sara Lee Corporation, whose brands include Bryan Meats, L'eggs, Coach, Kiwi, and Champion, has established an office of public responsibility to oversee its citizenship efforts.[12] The Japanese firm TOTO Ltd., the world's largest manufacturer of plumbing-related products, has created an explicit management structure for its social responsibility effort. TOTO's new president recently initiated a focus on becoming an excellent, more vibrant, and dynamic company. The major theme linking these three areas is corporate social responsibility, TOTO style. Upon opening a luxury showroom in New York, a TOTO executive commented, "It will provide an educational environment where they . . . may learn more about TOTO, its progressive social and environmental philosophies and innovative products." TOTO uses a variety of tools to communicate about its social responsibility efforts, including the following chart from a recent annual report (see Figure 1.2). In the table of contents page of the company's annual report, CSR (corporate social responsibility) is listed as a key feature.[13]

A smaller firm may give an executive, perhaps in human resources or corporate communications, the additional task of overseeing social responsibility. In a very small

"Social responsibility must be given the same planning time, priority, and management attention that is given to any other company initiative."

Figure 1.2 TOTO Corporate Social Responsibility Committee Structure

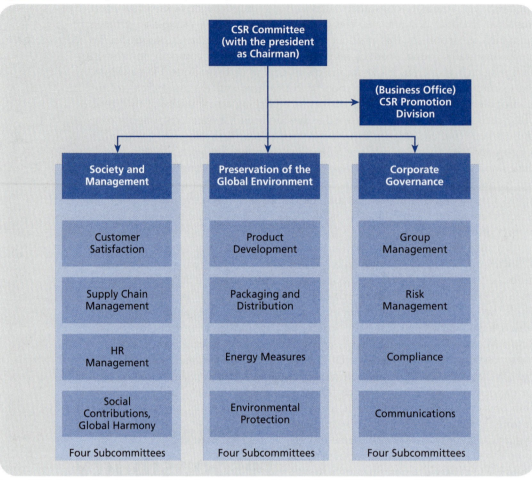

Source: TOTO, "Annual Report 2008," p. 17, http://www.toto.co.jp/en/ir/annual/pdf/annu2008.pdf, accessed May 5, 2009.

business, the owner is likely to make decisions regarding community involvement, ethical standards, philanthropy, and other areas. Regardless of the formal or informal nature of the structure, this department or executive should ensure that social responsibility initiatives are aligned with the company's corporate culture, integrated with companywide goals and plans, fully communicated within and outside the company, and measured to determine their effectiveness and strategic impact. In sum, social responsibility must be given the same planning time, priority, and management attention that is given to any other company initiative, such as continuous improvement, cost management, investor relations, research and development, human resources, or marketing research.

Social Responsibility Fulfills Society's Expectations

Another element of our definition of social responsibility involves society's expectations of business conduct. Many people believe that businesses should

Figure 1.3 Pyramid of Responsibility

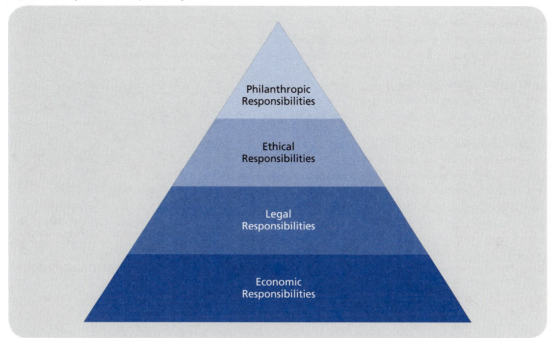

Source: Reprinted with permission from *Business Horizons* 34 (July–August 1991): 42. Archie B. Carroll, "The Pyramid of Corporate Social Responsibility: Toward the Moral Management of Organizational Stakeholders." Copyright © 1991 by the Board of Trustees of Indiana State University, Kelley School of Business.

accept and abide by four types of responsibility: economic, legal, ethical, and philanthropic (see Figure 1.3). To varying degrees, the four types are required, expected, and/or desired by society.[14]

At the lowest level of the pyramid, businesses have a responsibility to be economically viable so that they can provide a return on investment for their owners, create jobs for the community, and contribute goods and services to the economy. The economy is influenced by the ways organizations relate to their stockholders, their customers, their employees, their suppliers, their competitors, their community, and even the natural environment. For example, in nations with corrupt businesses and industries, the negative effects often pervade the entire society. Transparency International, a German organization dedicated to curbing national and international corruption, conducts an annual survey on the effects of business and government corruption on a country's economic growth and prospects. The organization reports that corruption reduces economic growth, inhibits foreign investment, and often channels investment and funds into "pet projects" that may create little benefit other than high returns to the corrupt decision makers. For example, many of the countries with the highest levels of perceived corruption also report the highest levels of poverty in the world. These countries include Somalia, Chad, Iraq, Haiti, Afghanistan, and Myanmar. Transparency International also notes that some relatively poor

Figure 1.4 Recommendations for Countering Corruption

By lower income countries
- Increase resources and political will for anticorruption efforts.
- Enable greater public access to information about budgets, revenue, and expenditure.

By higher income countries
- Combine increased aid with support for recipient-led reforms.
- Reduce tied aid, which limits local opportunities and ownership of aid programs.

By all countries
- Promote strong coordination among governments, the private sector, and civil society to increase efficiency and sustainability in anticorruption and good governance efforts.
- Ratify, implement, and monitor existing anticorruption conventions in all countries to establish international norms. These include the UN Convention Against Corruption, the OECD Anti-Bribery Convention, and the regional conventions of the African Union and the Organization of American States.

Source: "Corruption Perceptions Index 2005," Transparency International, http://www.transparency.org/policy_research/surveys_indices/cpi/2005/media_pack, accessed May 2, 2009.

counties, including Bulgaria, Colombia, and Estonia, have made positive strides in curbing corruption. However, Canada and Ireland have started to experience higher levels of perceived corruption, yet maintain relatively strong economies. The organization encourages governments, consumers, and nonprofit groups to take action in the fight against corruption (see Figure 1.4).[15] Although business and society may be theoretically distinct, there are a host of practical implications for the four levels of social responsibility, business, and its effects on society.

At the next level of the pyramid, companies are required to obey laws and regulations that specify the nature of responsible business conduct. Society enforces its expectations regarding the behavior of businesses through the legal system. If a business chooses to behave in a way that customers, special-interest groups, or other businesses perceive as irresponsible, these groups may ask their elected representatives to draft legislation to regulate the firm's behavior, or they may sue the firm in a court of law in an effort to force it to "play by the rules." For example, many businesses have complained that Microsoft Corporation effectively had a monopoly in the computer operating system and Web browser markets and that the company acted illegally to maintain this dominance. Their complaints were validated when a U.S. district judge ruled in a federal lawsuit that Microsoft had indeed used anticompetitive tactics to maintain its Windows monopoly in operating-system software and to attempt to dominate the Web browser market by illegally bundling its Internet Explorer Web browser into its Windows operating system. Microsoft, which vehemently denied the charges, appealed that decision. The election of George W. Bush and a court of appeal's ruling to overturn the judge's decision shifted the focus to settlement talks, away from an earlier suggestion to break up the company. Microsoft began implementing the provisions of the antitrust settlement agreement in late 2002, including hiring a compliance officer.[16]

Beyond the economic and legal dimensions of social responsibility, companies must decide what they consider to be just, fair, and right—the realm of business ethics. Business ethics refers to the principles and standards that guide behavior in the world of business. These principles are determined and expected by the public, government regulators, special-interest groups, consumers, industry, and individual organizations. The most basic of these principles have been codified into laws and regulations to require that companies conduct themselves in ways that conform to society's expectations. Many firms and industries have chosen to go beyond these basic laws in an effort to act responsibly. The Direct Selling Association (DSA), for example, has established a code of ethics that applies to all individual and company members of the association. Because direct selling, such as door-to-door selling, involves personal contact with consumers, many ethical issues can arise. For this reason, the DSA code directs the association's members to go beyond legal standards of conduct in areas such as product representation, appropriate ways of contacting consumers, and warranties and guarantees. In addition, the DSA actively works with government agencies and consumer groups to ensure that ethical standards are pervasive in the direct-selling industry. The World Federation of Direct Selling Associations (WFDSA) also maintains two codes of conduct, one for dealing with consumers and the other for interactions within the industry, that provide guidance for direct sellers around the world in countries as diverse as Argentina, Canada, Finland, Taiwan, and Poland.[17]

At the top of the pyramid are philanthropic activities, which promote human welfare and goodwill. By making voluntary donations of money, time, and other resources, companies can contribute to their communities and society and improve the quality of life. For example, Hitachi, Ltd., of Tokyo, Japan, established the Hitachi Foundation, a nonprofit philanthropic organization that invests in increasing the well-being of underserved people and communities. This Japanese company recognizes the foundation as a "tool for helping the Hitachi corporation move from being a major Japanese corporation to being a major global citizen . . . by providing opportunities for Hitachi to interact with American communities on issues that cut across national boundaries, such as the increasing diversity and multiculturalism of society, and to help Hitachi practice good corporate citizenship

© AP Photo/Andrew Milligan/PA Wire

Auto manufacturers are responding to environmental concerns by building electric cars, including Peugeot

Figure 1.5 Social Responsibility Continuum

Source: Based on ideas presented in Malcolm McIntosh, Deborah Leipziger, Keith Jones, and Gill Coleman, *Corporate Citizenship: Successful Strategies for Responsible Companies* (London: Financial Times Management, 2000); Linda S. Munilla and Morgan P. Miles, "The Corporate Social Responsibility Continuum as a Component of Stakeholder Theory," *Business and Society Review* 110 (December 2005): 371–387.

with integrity." With over two decades of existence and annual contributions of $4 million, the foundation is considered a pioneer of global social responsibility.[18] Although Hitachi is not required to support the community, similar corporate actions are increasingly desired and expected by people around the world.

When the pyramid was first introduced, many people assumed that there was a natural progression from economic to philanthropic responsibilities, meaning that a firm had to be economically viable before it could properly consider the other three elements. Today, the pyramid is viewed in a more holistic fashion, with all four responsibilities seen as related and integrated, and this is the view we will use in this book.[19] In fact, companies demonstrate varying degrees of social responsibility at different points in time. Figure 1.5 depicts the social responsibility continuum. Companies' fulfillment of their economic, legal, ethical, and philanthropic responsibilities can range from minimal to strategic. Firms that focus only on the expectations required by laws and contracts demonstrate minimal responsibility or a compliance orientation. Firms that take minimal responsibility view such activities as a "cost of doing business." Some critics believe that pharmaceutical manufacturers take the minimal approach with respect to the advertising and sale of certain drugs. A recent situation involving two pain medicines known as Cox-2 inhibitors demonstrates this point. After safety concerns were expressed about Cox-2 inhibitors, Merck voluntarily withdrew Vioxx from the market while Pfizer began an advertising campaign focused on the safety record of Celebrex, a major competitor to Vioxx. The Food and Drug Administration soon advised Pfizer to discontinue the advertising. While Celebrex remained on the market, some critics assessed Merck's decision to withdraw Vioxx as overreactionary. Combined, the two companies eventually settled over $5 billion in lawsuits over the aggressive consumer marketing of Cox-2 inhibitors, although Celebrex is still prescribed.[20]

Strategic responsibility is realized when a company has integrated a range of expectations, desires, and constituencies into its strategic direction and planning processes. In this case, an organization considers social responsibility an essential component of its vision, mission, values, and practices. BT, formerly known as British Telecom, is communicating its commitment to strategic responsibility with the theme of "Responsible Business," where BT is focused on tackling climate change, helping create a more inclusive society, and enabling sustainable economic growth. BT has been reporting on its social responsibility activities for fifteen years, which makes the company a leader in accountability disclosure. Finally, firms may operate outside the continuum by taking the approach that social responsibility is being forced by government, nongovernmental organizations, consumer groups, and other stakeholders. In this case, any expenditures are considered a "tax" that occurs outside the firm's strategic direction and resource allocation process. Executives with this philosophy often maintain that customers will be lost, employees will become dissatisfied, and other detrimental effects will occur because of forced social responsibility.[21]

In this book, we will give many examples of firms that are at different places along this continuum to show how the pursuit of social responsibility is never ending. For example, Coca-Cola, the world's largest beverage firm, dropped out of the top ten in *Fortune* magazine's annual list of "America's Most Admired Companies" in 2000 and out of the top 100 in *Business Ethics* magazine's annual list of "100 Best Corporate Citizens" in 2001. For a company that had spent years on both lists, this was disappointing, but perhaps it was not unexpected, as the company was planning to eliminate 6,000 jobs, was facing a racial discrimination lawsuit, was still recovering from a product contamination scare in Europe, and was trying to salvage its relationships with its bottlers. Then, in 2002, Coca-Cola scored highest in the beverage industry on *Fortune* magazine's measure of social responsibility, and the *Business Ethics* magazine survey highlighted Coca-Cola's relationships with stakeholders. By a few years later, Coca-Cola lost most of the gains it had experienced in the U.S. rankings but upheld a top-twenty-five ranking in *Fortune* magazine's list of globally admired corporations. As with most multinational firms, Coca-Cola must continuously monitor a number of social responsibility issues and determine the most appropriate corporate response and action.[22] Figure 1.6 outlines the complexity of managing corporate citizenship in both host and home country environments.

Figure 1.6 Managing Social Responsibility in Home and Host Markets

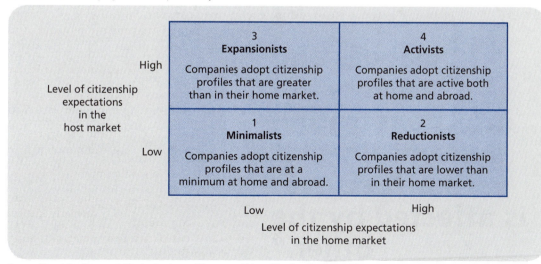

Source: Naomi Gardberg and Charles Fombrun, "Corporate Citizenship: Creating Intangible Assets Across Institutional Environments," *Academy of Management Review* 31 (April 2006): 329–336.

Social Responsibility Requires a Stakeholder Orientation

The final element of our definition involves those to whom an organization is responsible, including customers, employees, investors and shareholders, suppliers, governments, communities, and many others. These constituents have a stake in, or claim on, some aspect of a company's products, operations, markets, industry, and outcomes and thus are known as **stakeholders.** We explore the roles and expectations of stakeholders in Chapter 2. Companies that consider the diverse perspectives of these constituents in their daily operations and strategic planning are said to have a stakeholder orientation, meaning that they are focused on stakeholders' concerns. Adopting this orientation is part of the social responsibility philosophy, which implies that business is fundamentally connected to other parts of society and must take responsibility for its effects in those areas. Table 1.2 examines the relationship between stakeholder perspectives and strategic, minimal/compliance, and forced responsibility.[23]

R. E. Freeman, one of the earliest writers on stakeholder theory, maintains that business and society are "interpenetrating systems," in that each affects and is affected by the other.[24] For example, Kingfisher, the operator of more than 600 home-improvement retail stores in Europe and Asia, developed a formal process for securing stakeholder input on a variety of issues, including child labor, fair wages, environmental impact, and equal opportunity. To develop a vision and key objectives in these areas, Kingfisher confers with suppliers, store managers, employees, customers, government representatives, and other relevant stakeholders. For example, the firm recently met with seventy suppliers in China to discuss factory working conditions and conducted focus groups in the United Kingdom to discover customers' main social responsibility concerns. Every quarter, Kingfisher's eleven operating companies complete a 165-point questionnaire over the firm's social responsibility focus areas, including product stewardship, energy management, sustainable operation, supply chain management, equality and diversity, and community investment. Health and safety issues are handled by a separate function. The survey results enable Kingfisher to rate its progress on the six issues from (1) minimum action to (3) leadership position in the industry and community.[25] Kingfisher largely strengthened its dedication and efforts in the 1990s, when social responsibility and the requisite stakeholder orientation became more popular and more generally accepted within the corporate community. Many events have led to this era of increasing accountability and responsibility.

stakeholders constituents that have a stake in, or claim on, some aspect of a company's products, operations, markets, industry, and outcomes

> **"Business and society are interpenetrating systems, in that each affects and is affected by the other."**

Table 1.2 Stakeholder Perspectives Along the Social Responsibility Continuum

Stakeholder group	Compliance CSR perspective	Strategic CSR perspective	Forced CSR perspective
Owners	Perceives CSR as a cost or tax to do business	Perceives CSR as a mechanism to potentially create value more effectively and efficiently, create competitive advantage, hence enhance the economic value of the firm	Result in lower returns to the owners due to the potentially higher cost structure and damage to the corporation's reputation
Creditors	No impact on cost of credit	Credit ratings are impacted by social and environmental risks and how the firm manages these risks. Superior CSR management tends to lower levels of social and environmental risks and lowers the probability of default, therefore reducing the cost of capital	Cost of credit may be adversely impacted if creditors perceive that firm costs are increased or revenues reduced due to a "forced" CSR—may be associated with higher financial risk
Customers	No impact on target market, marketing mix, or marketing strategy	A superior environmental and social reputation could allow the firm to target more socially and/or environmentally oriented market segments, creating additional value for the customers and superior returns for the firm	May result in alienation of specific customer segments, loss of brand equity, and negative impact on corporate reputation
Regional/national community	No impact	May become a corporate citizen "role model"—may enhance regional/national reputation for social and environmental management. SA 8000. Emas, and ISO 14000 have become standards for global market access.	May result in an increase in regulatory scrutiny
Local community	No impact	Tends to result in a superior reputation in the community, with many positive consequences	Tends to result in a very negative reputation in the community, with many negative consequences

Source: Linda S. Munilla and Morgan P. Miles, "The Corporate Social Responsibility Continuum as a Component of Stakeholder Theory," *Business and Society Review* 110 (December 2005): 371–387.

DEVELOPMENT OF SOCIAL RESPONSIBILITY

In 1959, Harvard economist Edward Mason asserted that business corporations are "the most important economic institutions."[26] His declaration implied that companies probably affect the community and society as much, or perhaps more, in social terms as in monetary, or financial, terms. For example, most businesses use advertising to convey messages that have an economic impact but also have a social meaning. As an extreme example, when Benetton decided to use convicted felons who had been given death sentences in an advertising campaign, many people were outraged. The Italian clothier had a history of using cutting-edge advertising to comment on social ideas and political issues, but some people felt that this campaign went too far. Other controversies surrounded campaigns that included photographs of a dead soldier's bloody uniform, three human hearts, condoms, and victims of HIV/AIDS. Benetton's original goal was to open a dialog on the controversial issue of the death penalty, but criticism of the campaign was rampant and at least one major retailer dropped its contract with Benetton as a result. While Benetton's sales have continued to be challenged by other European clothiers, the retailer has diminished the shock value of its advertising. However, the company continues to focus on cultural and social issues through its advertising, often partnering with nonprofit organizations. Benetton has promoted a wide variety of causes, including protecting endangered species and reducing world hunger and poverty.[27]

Although most companies do not go to the extremes that Benetton does, companies do influence many aspects of our lives, from the workplace to the natural environment. This influence has led many people to conclude that companies' actions should be designed to benefit employees, customers, business partners, and the community as well as shareholders. Social responsibility has become a benchmark for companies today.[28] However, these expectations have changed over time. For example, the first corporations in the United States were granted charters by various state governments because they were needed to serve an important function in society, such as transportation, insurance, water, or banking services. In addition to serving as a "license to operate," these charters specified the internal structure of these firms, allowing their actions to be more closely monitored.[29] During this period, corporate charters were often granted for a limited period of time because many people, including legislators, feared the power that corporations could potentially wield. It was not until the mid-1800s that profit and responsibility to stockholders became major corporate goals.[30]

After World War II, as many large U.S. firms came to dominate the global economy, their actions inspired imitation in other nations. The definitive external characteristic of these firms was their economic dominance. Internally, they were marked by the virtually unlimited autonomy afforded to their top managers. This total discretion meant that these firms' top managers had the luxury of not having to answer much for their actions.[31] In the current business mind-set, such total autonomy would be viewed as a hindrance to social responsibility because there is no effective system of checks and balances. In Chapter 3, we elaborate on corporate governance, the process of control and accountability in organizations that is necessary for social responsibility.

In the 1950s, the 130 or so largest companies in the United States provided more than half of the country's manufacturing output. The top 500 firms accounted for almost two-thirds of the country's nonagricultural economic activity.[32] United States productivity and technological advancements also dramatically outpaced those of global competitors, such as Japan and Western Europe. For example, the level of production in the United States was twice as high as that in Europe and quadruple that in Japan. The level of research and development carried out by U.S. corporations was also well ahead of overseas firms. For these reasons, the United States was perceived as setting a global standard for other nations to emulate.

The power of these large U.S. corporations was largely mirrored by the autonomy of their top managers.[33] This autonomy could be characterized as "largely unchecked," as most such managers had the authority to make whatever decisions they thought necessary. Because of the relative lack of global competition and shareholder input during the 1950s and 1960s, there were few formal governance procedures to restrain management's actions. However, this laxity permitted management to focus not just on profit margins but also on a wide variety of discretionary activities, including charitable giving. Thus, it is interesting to note that although top managers' actions were rarely questioned or scrutinized, these managers did use their company's resources to address broader concerns than self-interest. Although the general public was sometimes suspicious of the power held by top managers in large corporations, it also recognized the gains it received from these corporations, such as better products, more choices, good employee salaries, and other such benefits. During this period, many corporations put money into their communities. Although these firms had high executive pay, organizational inefficiencies, high overhead costs, and various other problems, they were quick to share their gains. Employees in the lower echelons of these large corporations received substantially higher wages and better benefits than the national average. This practice has continued into the present; for example, what major automobile manufacturers pay their workers is 50 percent above the national average and 40 percent above the manufacturing national average.[34]

During the 1950s and 1960s, these companies provided other benefits that are often overlooked. Their contributions to charities, the arts, culture, and other community activities were often quite generous. They spent considerable sums of money on research that was more beneficial to the industry or to society than to the companies' own profitability. For example, the lack of competition meant that companies had the profits to invest in higher-quality products for consumer and industrial use. Although the government passed laws that required companies to take actions to protect the natural environment, make products safer, and promote equity and diversity in the workplace, many companies voluntarily adopted responsible practices and did not constantly fight government regulations and taxes. These corporations once provided many of the services that are now provided by the government in the United States. For example, during this period, the U.S. government spent less than the government of any other industrialized nation on such things as pensions and health benefits, as these were provided by companies rather than by the government.[35] In the 1960s and 1970s, however, the business landscape changed.

Economic turmoil during the 1970s and 1980s almost eliminated the old corporations. Venerable firms that had dominated the economy in the 1950s and 1960s became extinct or ineffective as a result of bankruptcies, takeovers, or other threats, including high energy prices and an influx of foreign competitors. The stability experienced by the U.S. firms of mid-century dissolved. During the 1960s and 1970s, the *Fortune* 500 had a relatively low turnover of about 4 percent. By 1990, however, one-third of the companies in the *Fortune* 500 of 1980 had disappeared, primarily as a result of takeovers and bankruptcies. The threats and instability led companies to protect themselves from business cycles by becoming more focused on their core competencies and reducing their product diversity. To combat takeovers, many companies adopted flatter organizational hierarchies. Flatter organizations meant workforce reduction but also entailed increasing empowerment of lower-level employees.

Thus, the 1980s and 1990s brought a new focus on profitability and economies of scale. Efficiency and productivity became the primary objectives of business. This fostered a wave of downsizing and restructuring that left some people and communities without financial security. Before 1970, large corporations employed about one of every five Americans, but by the 1990s, they employed only one in ten. The familial relationship between employee and employer disappeared, and along with it went employee loyalty and company promises of lifetime employment. Companies slashed their payrolls to reduce costs, and employees changed jobs more often. Workforce reductions and "job hopping" were almost unheard of in the 1960s but had become commonplace two decades later. These trends made temporary employment and contract work the fastest-growing forms of employment throughout the 1990s.[36]

Along with these changes, top managers were stripped of their former freedom. Competition heated up, and both consumers and stockholders grew more demanding. The increased competition led business managers to worry more and more about the bottom line and about protecting the company. Escalating use of the Internet provided unprecedented access to information about corporate decisions and conduct and fostered communication among once unconnected groups, furthering consumer awareness and shareholder activism. Consumer demands put more pressure on companies and their employees. The education and activism of stockholders had top management fearing for their jobs. Throughout the last two decades of the twentieth century, legislators and regulators initiated more and more regulatory requirements every year. These factors resulted in difficult trade-offs for management.

The benefits of the corporations of old were largely forgotten in the 1980s, but concern for corporate responsibilities was renewed in the 1990s. Partly as a result of business scandals and Wall Street excesses in the 1980s, many industries and companies decided to pursue and expect more responsible and respectable business practices. Many of these practices focused on creating value for stakeholders through more effective processes and decreased the narrow and sole emphasis on corporate profitability. At the same time, consumers and employees became less interested in making money for its own sake and turned toward intrinsic rewards and a more holistic approach to life and work.[37] This resulted in increased interest in the development of human and intellectual capital; the installation of corporate ethics programs; the development of programs to promote employee volunteerism in the community, strategic philanthropy efforts, and trust in the workplace; and the initiation of a more open dialog between companies and their stakeholders.

Despite major advances in the 1990s, the sheer number of corporate scandals at the beginning of the twenty-first century prompted a new era of social responsibility. The downfall of Enron, WorldCom, and other corporate stalwarts caused regulators, former employees, investors, nongovernmental organizations, and ordinary citizens to question the role and integrity of big business and the underlying economic system. Federal legislators passed the Sarbanes-Oxley Act to overhaul securities laws and governance structures. The new Public Company Accounting Oversight Board was implemented to regulate the accounting and auditing profession. Harvey Pitt, the Securities and Exchange Commission chair, resigned after a series of gaffes reduced his ability to lead in turbulent times. America's home-decorating guru, Martha Stewart, was indicted on charges related to the sale of ImClone stock. The ImClone CEO, Sam Waksal, lost his job amid insider trading and securities fraud charges and began serving a seven-year sentence in mid-2003. Newspapers, business magazines, and news websites devoted entire sections—often labeled as Corporate Scandal, Year of the Apology, or Year of the Scandal—to the trials and tribulations of executives, their companies and auditors, and stock analysts.

Near the end of the first decade of the twenty-first century, the global economy slowed in the wake of numerous financial scandals and widespread corporate losses. Amidst growing resentment over executive pay, Wall Street maneuverings, Ponzi schemes, and government bailouts of failing firms, *The Economist* opined, "Another tough question will be what to do about those costly corporate-citizenship commitments that big firms have made in recent years. These commitments—such as Coca-Cola's investments in water projects in developing countries—have lately been justified as a core part of long-term profit-maximising strategy. The coming year will test whether they really believe that."[38] Table 1.3 lists some of the "lessons learned" from the economic debacle of 2008 and 2009.

Mark Lilla, a professor at the University of Chicago, notes that perceptions of business and society often represent the confluence of the ideas of two decades, the 1960s and 1980s. From the 1960s, we gained a stronger interest in social issues and in how all parts of society can help prevent these issues from arising and resolve them when they do. The economic upheaval and excess of the 1980s alerted many people to the influence that companies have on society when the desire to make money profoundly dominates their activities.[39] The economic growth and gains of the 1990s brought sharp reminders of the 1980s, involving both exorbitant executive salaries and exorbitant executive personal wealth, which eventually took their toll on markets and companies.[40] Events of the past and the scandalous start to the twenty-first century brought calls for a stronger balance between the global market economy and social responsibility, social justice, and cohesion. This is evident on a global scale as special-interest groups, companies, human rights activists, and governments strive to balance worldwide economic growth and spending with social, environmental, technological, and cultural issues.

Table 1.3 Seven Lessons of the Financial Crisis

1. *Transparency.* Companies that presented clear, accurate balance sheets and stayed away from special purpose vehicles or off-balance-sheet risk kept their financial reputations intact. In troubled financial times, questions about a company's financial condition or balance sheet create a level of uncertainty that can destroy confidence in any financial firm.
2. *A long-term perspective.* Serving the long-term interests of customers and policyholders has been the best defense against short-term economic disruption. Firms that didn't yield to the pressure of Wall Street— or the pressure to grow at any price—typically didn't expose themselves to more significant levels of risk and performed much better.
3. *Liquidity.* Many companies that relied on the credit markets for short-term funding ran into major difficulties. When the credit markets froze and capital became unavailable, rating agencies became concerned, often resulting in a downgrade, and these companies became even weaker. Companies that maintained liquidity didn't have to put themselves at the mercy of the credit markets.
4. *Limited use of derivatives.* Companies that tried to use derivatives to generate profits or bet on economic outcomes paid a heavy price in 2008. Those that used derivatives as a tool to manage risk effectively protected their balance sheets.
5. *Absence of ratings triggers.* Ratings triggers can cause significant repayment obligations when a company is downgraded, creating further financial stress at the worst possible time. Companies that do not include ratings triggers in agreements avoid having a capital call which magnifies their financial problems.
6. *Minimal counter-party exposure.* The financial crisis showed us that even the biggest, best-known firms can fail. Companies with well-managed counter-party exposure avoided the risk of being dragged into the failure or financial difficulties of a business partner.
7. *Diversification.* Companies without concentrated investment exposure to a particular asset class or type of security were better positioned when the market dropped.

Source: Robert L. Senkler, Securian Financial Group, "Seven Lessons the Financial Crisis Taught Us," http://www.securian.com/pdf/7Lessons.pdf, accessed May 10, 2009.

GLOBAL NATURE OF SOCIAL RESPONSIBILITY

Although many forces have shaped the debate on social responsibility, the increasing globalization of business has made it an international concern. For example, as people around the world celebrated the year 2000, there was also a growing backlash against big business, particularly multinational corporations. A wide variety of protests were held around the globe, but their common theme was criticism of the increasing power and scope of business. The corporate scandals fortified this criticism and awoke even the staunchest of business advocates. Questions of corruption, environmental protection, fair wages, safe working conditions, and the income gap between rich and poor were posed. Many critics and protesters believe that global business involves exploitation of the working poor, destruction of the planet, and a rise in inequality.[41] Ruy Teixeira, a pollster from the Century Foundation, says, "There's a widespread sense of unfairness and distrust today, where people think companies are not quite playing by the rules." *Business Week* weighed in with a cover story entitled

"Too Much Corporate Power?"[42] A Gallup poll showed that Americans were highly distrustful of executives in large businesses. Thirty-eight percent felt that big business had become a threat to the U.S. future, and nearly 80 percent believed that executives would take improper actions to benefit themselves.[43] More recent polls indicate that trust is rebounding in certain countries, but companies are still vulnerable to the ramifications of distrust.[44] In an environment where consumers distrust business, greater regulation and lower brand loyalty are likely results. We discuss more of the relationship between social responsibility and business outcomes later in this chapter.

The globalization of business is fodder for many critics, who believe the movement is detrimental because it destroys the unique cultural elements of individual countries, concentrates power within developed nations

"Although many forces have shaped the debate on social responsibility, the increasing globalization of business has made it an international concern."

and their corporations, abuses natural resources, and takes advantage of people in developing countries. Multinational corporations are perhaps most subject to criticism because of their size and scope. More than half of the world's top 100 economies are not national economies at all; they are corporations like Wal-Mart and Royal Dutch Shell. For example, General Motor's revenues are roughly the size of the combined revenues of Hungary, Ireland, and New Zealand. Table 1.4 lists the top fifty economies in the world, which includes a combination of countries and companies. Because of the economic and political power they potentially wield, the actions of large, multinational companies are under scrutiny by many stakeholders. For example, a victims' advocate group charged that Unocal, a large U.S.-based oil and gas exploration and production firm, knew that the government of Myanmar forced peasants to help build a pipeline for the company. Peasants who resisted the military government were tortured or killed. Unocal has denied knowing of the oppression but faced charges under a 1789 U.S. law called the Alien Tort Claims Act. The case was eventually settled for an undisclosed amount.[45] Most allegations by anti-globalization protestors are not this extreme, but the issues are still of consequence. For example, the pharmaceutical industry has long been criticized for excessive pricing, interference with clinical evaluations, some disregard for developing nations, and aggressive promotional practices. Critics have called on governments, as well as public health organizations, to influence the industry in changing some of its practices.[46]

Advocates of the global economy counter these allegations by pointing to increases in overall economic growth, new jobs, new and more effective products, and other positive effects of global business. Although these differences of opinion provide fuel for debate and discussion, the global economy probably, in the words of author John Dalla Costa, "holds much greater potential than its critics

Table 1.4 Top Fifty Economies in the World

	Country/Corporation	GDP/sales ($mil)		Country/Corporation	GDP/sales ($mil)
1	United States	8,708,870.0	26	*Exxon Mobil*	163,881.0
2	Japan	4,395,083.0	27	*Ford Motor*	162,558.0
3	Germany	2,081,202.0	28	*Daimler Chrysler*	159,985.7
4	France	1,410,262.0	29	Poland	154,146.0
5	United Kingdom	1,373,612.0	30	Norway	145,449.0
6	Italy	1,149,958.0	31	Indonesia	140,964.0
7	China	1,149,814.0	32	South Africa	131,127.0
8	Brazil	760,345.0	33	Saudi Arabia	128,892.0
9	Canada	612,049.0	34	Finland	126,130.0
10	Spain	562,245.0	35	Greece	123,934.0
11	Mexico	474,951.0	36	Thailand	123,887.0
12	India	459,765.0	37	*Mitsui*	118,555.2
13	Korea, Rep.	406,940.0	38	*Mitsubishi*	117,765.6
14	Australia	389,691.0	39	*Toyota Motor*	115,670.9
15	Netherlands	384,766.0	40	*General Electric*	111,630.0
16	Russian Federation	375,345.0	41	*Itochu*	109,068.9
17	Argentina	281,942.0	42	Portugal	107,716.0
18	Switzerland	260,299.0	43	*Royal Dutch/Shell*	105,366.0
19	Belgium	245,706.0	44	Venezuela	103,918.0
20	Sweden	226,388.0	45	Iran, Islamic rep.	101,073.0
21	Austria	208,949.0	46	Israel	99,068.0
22	Turkey	188,374.0	47	*Sumitomo*	95,701.6
23	*General Motors*	176,558.0	48	*Nippon Tel & Tel*	93,591.7
24	Denmark	174,363.0	49	Egypt, Arab Republic	92,413.0
25	*Wal-Mart*	166,809.0	50	*Marubeni*	91,807.4

Source: Corporate Watch, "Top 200: The Rise of Corporate Global Power," http://www.corpwatch.org/downloads/top200.pdf, accessed May 2, 2009.

think, and much more disruption than its advocates admit. By definition, a global economy is as big as it can get. This means that the scale of both the opportunity and the consequences are at an apex."[47] In responding to this powerful situation, companies around the world are increasingly implementing programs and practices that strive to achieve a balance between economic responsibilities and other social responsibilities. The Nestlé Company, a global foods manufacturer and marketer, published the Nestlé Corporate Business Principles in 1998 and revised them in 2002 and 2004. These principles serve as a management tool for decision making at Nestlé and have been translated into over forty languages. The updated principles are consistent with the United Nations' Global Compact, an accord that covers environmental standards, human rights, and labor conditions.[48] We explore the global context of social responsibility more fully in Chapter 12.

In most developed countries, social responsibility involves stakeholder accountability and the economic, legal, ethical, and philanthropic dimensions discussed earlier in the chapter. However, a key question for implementing social responsibility on a global scale is: "Who decides on these responsibilities?" Many executives and managers face the challenge of doing business in diverse countries while attempting to maintain their employers' corporate culture and satisfy their expectations. Some companies have adopted an approach in which broad corporate standards can be adapted at a local level. For example, a corporate goal of demonstrating environmental leadership could be met in a number of different ways depending on local conditions and needs. The Compaq Computer Corporation, which merged with Hewlett-Packard in 2002, implemented its goal of environmental responsibility in different ways depending on the needs in various regions of the world. In North America, Compaq focused on recycling and reducing waste. In Latin America, corporate resources were devoted to wastewater treatment and cleanup of contaminated soil. Efforts in the firm's Asia-Pacific division included the distribution of "green kits" to educate managers, employees, and other stakeholders about Compaq's commitment to environmental leadership.[49]

Global social responsibility also involves the confluence of government, business, trade associations, and other groups. For example, countries that belong to the Asia-Pacific Economic Cooperation (APEC) are responsible for half the world's annual production and trade volume. As APEC works to reduce trade barriers and tariffs, it has also developed meaningful projects in the areas of sustainable development, clean technologies, workplace safety, management of human resources, and the health of the marine environment. This powerful trade group has demonstrated that economic, social, and ethical concerns can be tackled simultaneously.[50] Like APEC, other trade groups are also exploring ways to enhance economic productivity within the context of legal, ethical, and philanthropic responsibilities.

Another trend involves business leaders becoming "cosmopolitan citizens" by simultaneously harnessing their leadership skills, worldwide business connections, access to funds, and beliefs about human and social rights. Bill Gates, the founder of Microsoft, is no longer active day-to-day in the company, as he and his wife spearhead the Bill and Melinda Gates Foundation to tackle AIDS, poverty, malaria, and the need for educational resources. Patrick Cescau of Unilever is leading the British food giant to establish sustainable and responsible business processes in developing countries. Celso Grecco, a former advertising executive in Brazil, founded the Social and Environmental Stock Exchange to meet the needs of investors and donors for transparency as they consider nonprofit needs and opportunities. Donors find and fund nonprofits through a website, which also includes extensive reporting and accountability for each nonprofit's effectiveness and efficiency. These business leaders are acting as agents to ensure the economic promises of globalization are met with true concern for social and environmental considerations. In many cases, such efforts supplant those historically associated with government responsibility and programs.[51]

In sum, progressive global businesses and executives recognize the "shared bottom line" that results from the partnership among business, communities, government, customers, and the natural environment. In the Millennium Poll, a survey of more than 25,000 citizens in twenty-three countries, 66 percent of the respondents indicated that they want companies to go beyond their traditional role of making a profit, paying taxes, and providing jobs. More than half the respondents said that they believe their national government and companies should focus more on social and environmental goals than on economic goals in the first decade of the new millennium.[52] This survey reiterates our philosophy that business is accountable to a variety of stakeholders and has a number of responsibilities. Thus, our concept of social responsibility is applicable to businesses around the world, although adaptations of implementation and other details on the local level are definitely required. In companies around the world, there is also the recognition of the relationship between strategic social responsibility and benefits to society and organizational performance.

BENEFITS OF SOCIAL RESPONSIBILITY

The importance of social responsibility initiatives in enhancing stakeholder relationships, improving performance, and creating other benefits has been debated from many different perspectives.[53] Many business managers view such programs as costly activities that provide rewards only to society at the expense of the bottom line. Another view holds that some costs of social responsibility cannot be recovered through improved performance. Although it is true that some aspects of social responsibility may not accrue directly to the bottom line, we believe that organizations benefit both directly and indirectly over the long run from these activities. Moreover, ample research evidence demonstrates that there are many rewards for companies that implement such programs.

Some of the specific rewards include increased efficiency in daily operations, greater employee commitment, higher product quality, improved decision making, increased customer loyalty, and improved financial performance. In short, companies that establish a reputation for trust, fairness, and integrity develop a valuable resource that fosters success, which then translates to greater financial performance (see Figure 1.7). This section provides evidence that resources invested in social responsibility programs reap positive outcomes for organizations and stakeholders.

Figure 1.7 The Role of Social Responsibility in Performance

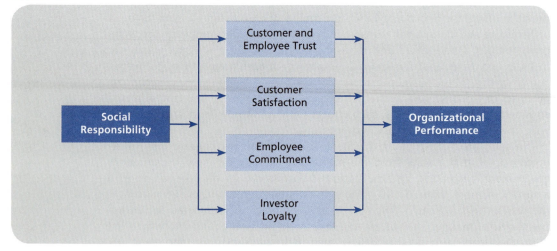

Trust

Trust is the glue that holds organizations together and allows them to focus on efficiency, productivity, and profits. According to Stephen R. Covey, author of *The 7 Habits of Highly Effective People,* "Trust lies at the very core of effective human interactions. Compelling trust is the highest form of human motivation. It brings out the very best in people, but it takes time and patience, and it doesn't preclude the necessity to train and develop people so their competency can rise to that level of trust." When trust is low, organizations decay and relationships deteriorate, resulting in infighting, playing politics within the organization, and general inefficiency. Employee commitment to the organization declines, product quality suffers, employee turnover skyrockets, and customers turn to more trustworthy competitors.[54]

"Trust is the glue that holds organizations together and allows them to focus on efficiency, productivity, and profits."

In a trusting work environment, however, employees can reasonably expect to be treated with respect and consideration by both their peers and their superiors. They are also more willing to rely and act on the decisions and actions of their coworkers. Thus, trusting relationships between managers and their subordinates and between peers contribute to greater decision-making efficiencies. Research by the Ethics Resource Center indicates that this trust is pivotal for supporting an ethical climate. Employees of an organization with a strong ethical culture are much more likely to report misconduct but are much less likely to observe misconduct than employees in firms with a weak ethical culture.[55] Figure 1.8 provides a model of ten key factors that affect how employees develop trust or distrust in the workplace. Three factors relate to the employee as the decision maker; the remaining seven factors reflect the specific work situation that the employee experiences and evaluates.

Trust is also essential for a company to maintain positive long-term relationships with customers. A study by Cone-Roper reported that three of four consumers say they avoid or refuse to buy from certain businesses. Poor service was the number one reason cited for refusing to buy, but business conduct was the second reason that consumers gave for avoiding specific companies.[56] For example, after the *Exxon Valdez* oil spill in 1989, certain groups and individual citizens aggressively boycotted Exxon because of its response to the environmental disaster.

Customer Satisfaction

The prevailing business philosophy about customer relationships is that a company should strive to market products that satisfy customers' needs through a coordinated effort that also allows the company to achieve its own objectives. It is well accepted that customer satisfaction is one of the most important factors for business success. Although companies must continue to develop and adapt

Figure 1.8 To Trust or Not to Trust?

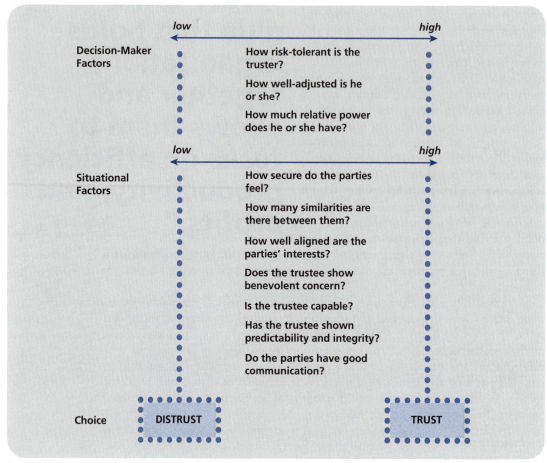

Source: Robert F. Hurley, "The Decision to Trust," *Harvard Business Review* 84 (September 2006): 55-62.

products to keep pace with consumers' changing desires, it is also crucial to develop long-term relationships with customers. Relationships built on mutual respect and cooperation facilitate the repeat purchases that are essential for success. By focusing on customer satisfaction, a business can continually strengthen its customers' trust in the company, and as their confidence grows, this in turn increases the firm's understanding of their requirements.

In a Cone-Roper national survey of consumer attitudes, 81 percent of consumers indicated they would be likely to switch to brands associated with a good cause if price and quality were equal. These results were up 11 percent from the same study in 1997 and show that consumers take for granted that they can buy high-quality products at low prices; therefore, companies need to stand out as doing something—something that demonstrates their commitment to society. The survey also indicated that consumers believed companies should continue supporting causes, even during an economic downturn.[57] A study by Harris Interactive Inc. and the Reputation Institute reported that one-quarter of the respondents had boycotted a firm's products or lobbied others to do so when they did not agree with the firm's policies or activities.[58] Another way of looking at these results is that irresponsible behavior could trigger disloyalty and refusals to buy, whereas good social responsibility initiatives could draw customers to a company's products. For example, many firms use cause-related marketing programs to donate part of a product's sales revenue to a charity that is meaningful to the product's target market. Among the best-known cause-related marketing programs is Avon's "pink ribbon," which we discuss in Chapter 10.

Employee Commitment

Employee commitment stems from employees who believe their future is tied to that of the organization and are willing to make personal sacrifices for the organization.[59] Hershey Foods is an example of a business that historically drew substantial benefits from its long-lasting commitment to social responsibility. Every year, Hershey employees receive a booklet entitled *Key Corporate Policies,* which describes the values—fairness, integrity, honesty, respect—at the heart of the company's way of doing business. Employees are asked to sign the booklet and are made aware of procedures for reporting concerns about proper conduct or policies in the workplace. These efforts help employees understand the importance of developing and maintaining respectful relationships with both colleagues and customers. Because they support the idea that customers should receive full value for their money, employees are also committed to delivering the highest quality standards possible. Today, Hershey claims about 43 percent of the U.S. chocolate market.[60]

When companies fail to provide value for their employees, loyalty and commitment suffer. A survey by Walker Information Global Network found low levels of employee loyalty and commitment worldwide. The study, which surveyed thousands of employees in thirty-two countries, found that only one in three workers is "truly loyal" to the organization for which he or she works.[61] Employees spend many of their waking hours at work; thus, an organization's commitment to goodwill and respect of its employees usually results in increased employee loyalty and support of the company's objectives.

Investor Loyalty

Investors look at a corporation's bottom line for profits or the potential for increased stock prices. To be successful, relationships with stockholders and other investors must rest on dependability, trust, and commitment. But investors also look for potential cracks or flaws in a company's performance. Companies perceived by their employees as having a high degree of honesty and integrity had an average three-year total return to shareholders of 101 percent, whereas companies perceived as having a low degree of honesty and integrity had a three-year total return to shareholders of just 69 percent.[62] When the Securities and Exchange Commission investigated Sunbeam for improprieties in accounting procedures, the company's stock plummeted from a high of $54 to almost worthless. The negative publicity associated with the alleged misconduct had an enormous impact on investors' confidence in Sunbeam—a previously trusted and respected U.S. brand.[63]

Many shareholders are also concerned about the reputation of companies in which they invest. Investors have even been known to avoid buying the stock of firms they view as irresponsible. For example, fifteen mutual fund managers announced a boycott of Mitsubishi stock after the Japanese firm refused to cancel a plan to build a factory on a Mexican lagoon that is also a major breeding site for gray whales.[64] Many socially responsible mutual funds and asset management firms are available to help concerned investors purchase stock in responsible companies. These investors recognize that corporate responsibility is the foundation for efficiency, productivity, and profits. On the other hand, investors know that fines or negative publicity can decrease a company's stock price, customer loyalty, and long-term viability. Consequently, many chief executives spend a great deal of time communicating with investors about their firms' reputations and financial performance and trying to attract them to their stock.

The issue of drawing and retaining investors is a critical one for CEOs, as roughly 50 percent of investors sell their stock in companies within one year, and the average household replaces 80 percent of its common stock portfolio each year.[65] This focus on short-term gains subjects corporate managers to tremendous pressure to boost short-term earnings, often at the expense of long-term strategic plans. The resulting pressure for short-term gains deprives corporations of stable capital and forces decision makers into a "quarterly" mentality. Conversely, those shareholders willing to hold onto their investments are more willing to sacrifice short-term gains for long-term income. Attracting these long-term investors shields companies from the vagaries of the stock market and gives them flexibility and stability in long-term strategic planning. In the aftermath of the recent business scandals, however, trust and confidence in financial audits and published financial statements were severely shaken. Membership in grassroots investment clubs declined, retail stock investments declined, and investors called for increased transparency in company operations and reports.[66] Gaining investors' trust and confidence is vital for sustaining a firm's financial stability.

The Bottom Line: Profits

Social responsibility is positively associated with return on investment, return on assets, and sales growth.[67] A company cannot continuously be socially responsible and nurture and develop an ethical organizational culture unless it has achieved financial performance in terms of profits. Businesses with greater resources—regardless of their staff size—have the ability to promote their social responsibility along with serving their customers, valuing their employees, and establishing trust with the public.

Many studies have identified a positive relationship between social responsibility and financial performance.[68] For example, a survey of the 500 largest public corporations in the United States found that those that commit to responsible behavior and emphasize compliance with codes of conduct show better financial performance.[69] A managerial focus on stakeholder interests can affect financial performance, although the relationships between stakeholders and financial performance vary and are very complex.[70] A meta-analysis

of twenty-five years of research identified thirty-three studies (63 percent)
demonstrating a positive relationship
between corporate social performance
and corporate financial performance,
five studies (about 10 percent) indicating a negative relationship, and
fourteen studies (27 percent) yielding
an inconclusive result or no relationship.[71] Research on the effects of legal
infractions suggests that the negative
effect of misconduct does not appear
until the third year following a conviction, with multiple convictions being
more harmful than a single one.[72]

"Many studies have identified a positive relationship between social responsibility and financial performance."

In summary, a company with strong efforts and results in social responsibility is generally not penalized by market forces, including the intention of
consumers to purchase the firm's products. Social responsibility efforts and
performance serve as a reputational lever that managers may use to influence stakeholders. A high-performing company may also receive endorsements
from governmental officials or other influential groups that are more believ-
able than company messages. A company with a strong social responsibility
orientation often becomes quite proactive in managing and changing conditions that yield economic benefits, including avoiding litigation and increased
regulation. Finally, corporate social performance and corporate financial performance are positively correlated. These findings subjugate the belief that
social responsibility is just a "cost factor" for business and has no real benefits
to the firm.[73]

National Economy

An often-asked question is whether business conduct has any bearing on a
nation's overall economic performance. Many economists have wondered why
some market-based economies are productive and provide a high standard of
living for their citizens, whereas other market-based economies lack the kinds
of social institutions that foster productivity and economic growth. Perhaps a
society's economic problems can be explained by a lack of social responsibility.
Trust stems from principles of morality and serves as an important "lubricant
of the social system."[74] Many descriptions of market economies fail to take into
account the role of such institutions as family, education, and social systems in
explaining standards of living and economic success. Perhaps some countries do a
better job of developing economically and socially because of the social structure
of their economic relationships.

Social institutions, particularly those that promote trust, are important for
the economic well-being of a society.[75] Society has become economically successful over time "because of the underlying institutional framework persistently
reinforcing incentives for organizations to engage in productive activity."[76] In
some developing countries, opportunities for political and economic development

have been stifled by activities that promote monopolies, graft, and corruption and by restrictions on opportunities to advance individual, as well as collective, well-being. Author L. E. Harrison offers four fundamental factors that promote economic well-being: "(1) The degree of identification with others in a society—the radius of trust, or the sense of community; (2) the rigor of the ethical system; (3) the way authority is exercised within the society; and (4) attitudes about work, innovation, saving, and profit."[77]

Countries with strong trust-based institutions foster a productivity-enhancing environment because they have ethical systems in place that reduce transaction costs and make competitive processes more efficient and effective. In market-based systems with a great degree of trust, such as Japan, Great Britain, Canada, the United States, and Sweden, highly successful enterprises can develop through a spirit of cooperation and the ease in conducting business.[78]

Superior financial performance at the firm level within a society is measured as profits, earnings per share, return on investment, and capital appreciation. Businesses must achieve a certain level of financial performance to survive and reinvest in the various institutions in society that provide support. On the other hand, at the institutional or societal level, a key factor distinguishing societies with high standards of living is trust-promoting institutions. The challenge is to articulate the process by which institutions that support social responsibility can contribute to firm-level superior financial performance.[79]

"A key factor distinguishing societies with high standards of living is trust-promoting institutions."

A comparison of countries that have high levels of corruption and underdeveloped social institutions with countries that have low levels of corruption reveals differences in the economic well-being of the country's citizens. Transparency International, an organization discussed earlier, publishes an annual report on global corruption that emphasizes the effects of corruption on the business and social sectors. This annual review recently focused on corruption in health-care systems and discovered five key types of corruption, which are listed in Table 1.5. Since health care is managed through a system of both public expenditures and private investment, the industry is especially interesting to examine. Transparency International concluded, "Corruption in the health sector deprives those most in need of essential medical care and helps spawn drug-resistant strains of deadly diseases." The organization recognizes that health care is largely affected by a country's economic well-being and social institutions that support ethics and responsibility. Countries with better access to quality health care are more likely to be economically and socially stable. As stated several times in this chapter, conducting business in an ethical and responsible manner generates trust and leads to relationships that promote higher productivity and a positive cycle of effects.[80]

Table 1.5 Forms of Corruption in Private and Public Health-Care Systems

- *Embezzlement and theft* from the health budget or user-fee revenue. This can occur at central or local government level or at the point of allocation to a particular health authority or health center. Medicines and medical supplies or equipment may be stolen for personal use, use in private practice, or resale.

- *Corruption in procurement.* Engaging in collusion, bribes, and kickbacks in procurement results in overpayment for goods and contracted services, or in failure to enforce contractual standards for quality. In addition, hospital spending may include large investments in building construction and purchase of expensive technologies, areas of procurement that are particularly vulnerable to corruption.

- *Corruption in payment systems.* Corrupt practices include waiving fees or falsifying insurance documents for particular patients or using hospital budgets to benefit particular favored individuals; illegally billing insurance companies, government, or patients for services that are not covered or services not actually provided, in order to maximize revenue; falsification of invoice records, receipt books, or utilization records, or creation of "ghost" patients.

- *Corruption in the pharmaceutical supply chain.* Products can be diverted or stolen at various points in the distribution system; officials may demand "fees" for approving products or facilities for clearing customs procedures or for setting prices; violations of industry marketing code practices may distort medical professionals' prescribing practices; demands for favors may be placed on suppliers as a condition for prescribing medicines; and counterfeit or other substandard medicines may be allowed to circulate.

- *Corruption at the point of health service delivery* can take many forms: extorting or accepting under-the-table payments for services that are supposed to be provided free of charge; soliciting payments in exchange for special privileges or treatment; and extorting or accepting bribes to influence hiring decisions and decisions on licensing, accreditation, or certification.

Source: Transparency International, "Global Corruption Report 2006," http://www.transparency.org/publications/gcr/gcr_2006, accessed May 2, 2009.

FRAMEWORK FOR STUDYING SOCIAL RESPONSIBILITY

The framework we developed for this text is designed to help you understand how businesses fulfill social expectations. Figure 1.9 illustrates the concept that social responsibility is a process. It begins with the social responsibility philosophy, includes the four levels of social responsibilities, involves many types of stakeholders, and ultimately results in both short- and long-term performance benefits. As we discussed earlier, social responsibility must have the support of top management—both in words and in deeds—before it can become an organizational reality. Like many organizations, Cummins Engine Company has faced a number of challenges over the past several decades. Cummins, founded in 1919 and based in Columbus, Indiana, is currently the world leader in the design and manufacture of diesel engines. Cummins was Columbus's largest employer for many years, and the firm provided many benefits to the community, including job opportunities and economic growth.

Throughout its first sixty years of business, Cummins also performed well for its shareholders. The company enjoyed increased profits for forty-three consecutive years, until 1979. Cummins suffered during the 1980s, however, and it had

Figure 1.9 Social Responsibility Model

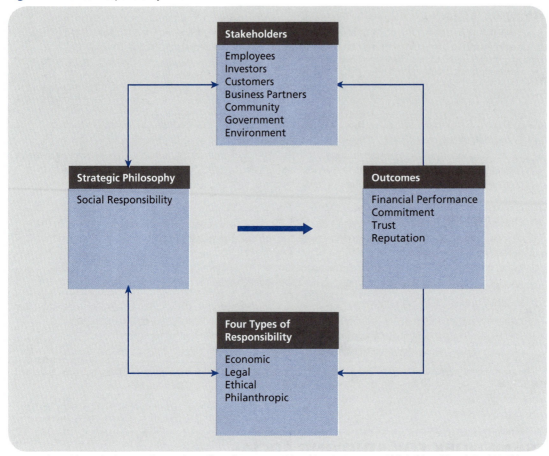

Source: Adapted from Charles J. Fombrun, "Three Pillars of Corporate Citizenship," in *Corporate Global Citizenship,* ed. Noel M. Tichy, Andrew R. McGill, and Lynda St. Clair (San Francisco: New Lexington Press, 1997), pp. 27–42.

to fend off the threat of hostile takeovers. Its stock price plummeted and stock owners demanded short-run profits at the expense of the company's long-term goals. The founding family repelled one takeover attempt with a large infusion of capital and thwarted another attempt by expanding the firm's shareholder-rights program. Despite its financial woes, Cummins remained focused on research and development, managed to produce a more environmentally friendly diesel engine, and even engaged in limited charitable giving. These actions were consistent with the personality and beliefs of Henry Schacht, Cummins's CEO for more than twenty years, who believed that the company should not aim solely at profit but rather should develop a balanced set of values.

Although Schacht's beliefs provided a strong foundation, Cummins did not always achieve its social and economic goals. In 1983, for the first time ever, the company was forced to lay off some employees. Later in the decade, the company closed plants and laid off even more people. To reverse these trends, Schacht adopted a new business plan that included cooperation with unions, former employees, and other firms to spur economic development. Expansion into Japan, India, and China soon followed.

Throughout this difficult period, Cummins still managed to donate to charities, participate in civic activities, and invest in employee programs and innovative benefits. For example, Cummins is one of several companies implementing steps to reduce workloads and improve work/life balance, which we discuss in Chapter 7. By the end of the twentieth century, Cummins was back on track financially, with sales topping $6.6 billion, up 6 percent from the prior year. Sales in mid-2000s nearly reached $10 billion. Cummins's drive to build positive relationships with its employees, its customers, and its community led *Business Ethics* to rank the firm on the magazine's list of the "100 Best Corporate Citizens. By the global recession of 2009, Cummins was facing revenue shortfalls and employee layoffs, but still received the highest possible rating for its corporate governance practices from GovernanceMetrics International (GMI)."[81]

Once the social responsibility philosophy is accepted, the four aspects of corporate social responsibility are defined and implemented through programs that incorporate stakeholder input and feedback. Cummins, like other companies, is aware of the potential costs associated with addressing social responsibility issues and stakeholder requirements. When social responsibility programs are put into action, they have both immediate and delayed outcomes.

Figure 1.10 depicts how the chapters of this book fit into our framework. This framework begins with a look at the importance of working with stakeholders to achieve social responsibility objectives. The framework also includes an examination of the influence on business decisions and actions of the legal, regulatory, and political environment; business ethics; and corporate governance. The remaining chapters of the book explore the responsibilities associated with specific stakeholders and issues that confront business decision makers today, including the process of implementing a social responsibility audit.

Strategic Management of Stakeholder Relationships

Social responsibility is grounded in effective and mutually beneficial relationships with customers, employees, investors, competitors, government, the community, and others who have a stake in the company. Increasingly, companies are recognizing that these constituents both affect and are affected by their actions. For this reason, many companies attempt to address the concerns of stakeholder groups, recognizing that failure to do so can have serious

> **"Many companies attempt to address the concerns of stakeholder groups, recognizing that failure to do so can have serious long-term consequences."**

Figure 1.10 An Overview of This Book

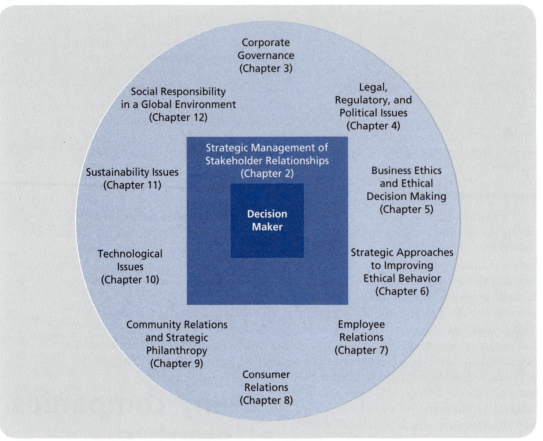

long-term consequences. For example, the Connecticut Better Business Bureau revoked the membership of Priceline.com after the Internet company failed to address complaints related to misrepresentation of products, billing problems, and refunds.[82] Chapter 2 examines the types of stakeholders and their attributes, how stakeholders become influential, and the processes for integrating and managing stakeholders' influence on a firm. It also examines the impact of corporate reputation and crisis situations on stakeholder relationships.

Corporate Governance

Because both daily and strategic decisions affect a variety of stakeholders, companies must maintain a governance structure to ensure proper control of their actions and assign responsibility for those actions. In Chapter 3, we define corporate governance and discuss its role in achieving strategic social responsibility. Key governance issues addressed include the rights of shareholders, the accountability of top management for corporate actions, executive compensation, and strategic-level processes for ensuring that economic, legal, ethical, and philanthropic responsibilities are satisfied.

Legal, Regulatory, and Political Issues

In Chapter 4, we explore the complex relationship between business and government. Every business must be aware of and abide by the laws and regulations that dictate acceptable business conduct. This chapter also examines how business can influence government by participating in the public policy process. A strategic approach for legal compliance is also provided.

Business Ethics and Strategic Approaches to Improving Ethical Behavior

Because individual values are a component of organizational conduct, these findings raise concerns about the ethics of future business leaders. Chapters 5 and 6 are devoted to exploring the role of ethics in business decision making. These chapters explore business responsibilities that go beyond the conduct that is legally prescribed. We also examine the factors that influence ethical decision making and consider how companies can apply this understanding to increase their ethical conduct.

Employee Relations

In today's business environment, most organizations want to build long-term relationships with a variety of stakeholders, but particularly with employees—the focus of Chapter 7. Employees today want fair treatment, excellent compensation and benefits, and assistance in balancing work and family obligations. Raytheon developed a computer program called SilentRunner that can detect patterns of data activity that may reflect employee fraud, insider trading, espionage, or other unauthorized activity.[83] Critics, however, question whether the use of such software contributes to an environment of trust and commitment. Research has shown that committed and satisfied employees are more productive, serve customers better, and are less likely to leave their employers. These benefits are important to successful business performance, but organizations must be proactive in their human resources programs if they are to receive them.

© David Brabyn/CORBIS

Pitney Bowes offers on- site health clinics, where employees get personalized service from nurse practitioners

Consumer Relations

Chapter 8 explores companies' relationships with consumers. This constituency is part of a firm's primary stakeholder group, and there are a number of economic, legal, ethical, and philanthropic responsibilities that companies must address. Chapter 8 therefore considers the obligations that companies have toward their customers, including health and safety issues, honesty in marketing, consumer rights, and related responsibilities.

Community and Philanthropy

Chapter 9 examines community relations and strategic philanthropy, the synergistic use of organizational core competencies and resources to address key stakeholders' interests and to achieve both organizational and social benefits. Whereas traditional benevolent philanthropy involves donating a percentage of sales to social causes, a strategic approach aligns employees and organizational resources and expertise with the needs and concerns of stakeholders, especially the community. Strategic philanthropy involves both financial and nonfinancial contributions (employee time, goods and services, technology and equipment, and facilities) to stakeholders and reaps benefits for the community and company.

Technological Issues

Thanks to the Internet and other technological advances, we can communicate faster than ever before, find information on just about anything, and live longer, healthier lives. However, not all of the changes that occur as a result of new technologies are positive. Chapter 10 explores a wide range of technological issues. For example, because shopping via the Internet does not require a signature to verify transactions, online credit-card fraud is significantly greater than fraud through mail-order catalogs and traditional storefront retailers. A major identity theft ring in New York affected thousands of people. Members of the theft ring illegally obtained the credit records of consumers and then sold them to criminals for about $60 per record. The criminals used the credit records to obtain loans, drain bank accounts, and perform other fraudulent activities.[84]

Sustainability Issues

In Chapter 11, we dedicate an entire chapter to issues of sustainability, including the interdependent nature of economic development, social development, and environmental impact. Sustainability has become a watchword in business and community circles and this chapter explores the ways in which companies develop goals, implement programs, and contribute to sustainability concerns. The Dow Jones Sustainability Stoxx Index (DJSSI) makes an annual assessment of companies' economic, environmental, and social performance, based on more than fifty general and industry-specific criteria. One employment services company, The Randstad Group, scored near the top on the social dimension and scored above average on the economic indicators. The DJSSI includes 167 companies from 13 European countries and is used by investors who prefer to make financial investments in companies engaged in socially responsible and sustainable practices.[85]

Global Social Responsibility

Finally, in order for many businesses to remain competitive, they must continually evolve to reach global markets and anticipate emerging world trends. Chapter 12 delves into the complex and intriguing nature of social responsibility in a global economy. Building on key concepts discussed throughout the book, we

The Marine Stewardship Council Today, many consumers are using sustainability criteria when making routine purchases, including the seafood they eat in restaurants or cook at home. The Marine Stewardship Council (MSC) has offices around the world and is a key player in transforming the supply chain for seafood so that consumers, restaurant owners, and grocery store purchasing agents can choose seafood harvested in an environmentally responsible manner.

The MSC is an international organization that works with the seafood industry at all stages of the supply chain. The council has developed the world's leading environmental certification for wild-capture fisheries, along with a detailed seafood traceability system. The standards they have set for sustainable fishing and seafood traceability have sought to increase the availability of certified sustainable seafood. The MSC offers fisheries around the world a way to be recognized and rewarded for good management by certifying their products with the MSC blue eco label to make them stand out from the others. The MSC has joined forces with some of the world's leading retailers, restaurants, and seafood businesses to help them meet customer expectations by increasing their sustainable seafood offering.

According to the United Nations Food and Agriculture Organization, overfishing tripled in the last thirty years and half of the world's fish stocks are overfished or depleted of the stock. The MSC's unique "Chain of Custody" certification requires every company along the supply chain to keep the certified seafood separate from other products. This process makes it clear which seafood can be purchased and consumed without fear of depleting stock. More than 1,500 retail packaged products sold in thirty-seven countries bear the MSC logo and the numbers are growing.

The Dakota Forth Bridge was the first Scottish restaurant to receive certification from the MSC. Bamboo Sushi in Portland, Oregon, which opened in late November of 2008, was the first independent restaurant in the United States to become certified for MSC Chain of Custody. These are two examples of the many restaurants who are aiming for better sustainability standards for seafood today. Pret A Manger is an up-market chain of 178 sandwich shops mostly in southern United Kingdom. Nearly all of the shops have their own kitchen to prepare food, but decisions about products are made by a central office to ensure consistent supply and use of MSC-labeled products.

Ultimately, the demand for sustainable seafood derives from consumers who are wary of what they eat and where it comes from. As a rule, consumers should try to avoid young, undersized fish, as catching these can exacerbate pressure on stocks. Healthy fish stocks are a vital part of the marine ecosystem, and provide protein and livelihoods for billions of people. According to *The Good Fish Guide,* fish that are fine to consume include the Alaska or Walleye Pollock, Flounder, Oysters (farmed Native and Pacific), Tilapia (farmed), and Mahi Mahi. The guide recommends staying away from the Cod (except from Iceland), Atlantic Salmon (wild caught), Chilean Sea Bass, Grouper, and Tiger Shrimp (except organic). Overfishing is widely acknowledged as a significant and growing threat to marine biodiversity and sustainability. Consumers, retailers, fisheries, and other partners in the supply chain are key to ensuring the livelihood and availability of seafood for future generations.

Sources: Duncan Clark and Richie Unterberger, *A Rough Guide to Shopping with a Conscience* (New York: Rough Guides Ltd, 2007) pp. 126–129; "The Front Burner," *Washington Restaurant Association Magazine*, August 2008, pp. 6–7; Marine Conservational Society, http://www.fishonline.org, accessed May 10, 2009; The Marine Stewardship Council, http://www.msc.org, accessed May 10, 2009.

NASA

examine the forces that make overseas business plans and activities of paramount concern to host countries, local and national governments, nongovernmental organizations, and other members of society. The chapter covers a wide range of challenges and opportunities, such as outsourcing, environmental protection, living wages, indigenous culture, labor standards, and trade restrictions.

The Social Audit

Without reliable measurements of the achievement of social responsibility goals, a company has no concrete way to verify the importance of these objectives, link them to organizational performance, justify expenditures on them to stockholders and investors, or address any stakeholder concerns involving them. The Appendix describes an auditing and assurance procedure that can be used to measure and improve the social responsibility effort. Such an audit is important for demonstrating commitment and ensuring the continuous improvement of the social responsibility effort.

We hope this framework provides you with a way of understanding the range of concepts, ideas, and practices that are involved in an effective social responsibility initiative. So that you can learn more about the practices of specific companies, a number of cases are provided at the end of the book. In addition, every chapter includes an opening vignette and other examples that shed more light on how social responsibility works in today's businesses. Every chapter also includes a real-life scenario entitled "What Would You Do?," a contemporary debate issue, and another exercise to help you apply concepts and examine your own decision-making process. As you will soon see, the concept of social responsibility is both exciting and controversial; it is in a constant state of development—just like all important business concepts and practices.

A recent survey of thought leaders in the area of social responsibility found that a majority believes social responsibility has made steady progress into conventional business thinking. Much like the social responsibility continuum introduced in this chapter, the thought leaders described several stages of commitment to corporate social responsibility. These stages range from light, where companies are concerned about responding to complaints, to deep, where companies are founded on a business model of improving social or environmental circumstances. Many companies fall somewhere in between, with a focus on complying with new standards and surviving in a climate of increasing social responsibility expectations.[86] We encourage you to draw on current news events and your own experiences to understand social responsibility and the challenges and opportunities it poses for your career, profession, role as a consumer, leadership approach, and the business world.

SUMMARY

The term *social responsibility* came into widespread use during the last several decades, but there remains some confusion over the term's exact meaning. This text defines social responsibility as the adoption by a business of a strategic focus for fulfilling the economic, legal, ethical, and philanthropic responsibilities expected of it by its stakeholders.

All types of businesses can implement social responsibility initiatives to further their relationships with their customers, their employees, and the community at large. Although the efforts of large corporations usually receive the most attention, the actions of small businesses may have a greater impact on local communities.

The definition of social responsibility involves the extent to which a firm embraces the social responsibility philosophy and follows through with the implementation of initiatives. Social responsibility must be fully valued and championed by top managers and given the same planning time, priority, and management attention as is given to any other company initiative.

Many people believe that businesses should accept and abide by four types of responsibility: economic, legal, ethical, and philanthropic. Companies have a responsibility to be economically viable so that they can provide a return on investment for their owners, create jobs for the community, and contribute goods and services to the economy. They are also expected to obey laws and regulations that specify what is responsible business conduct. Business ethics refers to the principles and standards that guide behavior in the world of business. Philanthropic activities promote human welfare or goodwill. These responsibilities can be viewed holistically, with all four related and integrated into a comprehensive approach. Social responsibility can also be expressed as a continuum.

Because customers, employees, investors and shareholders, suppliers, governments, communities, and others have a stake in or claim on some aspect of a company's products, operations, markets, industry, and outcomes, they are known as stakeholders. Adopting a stakeholder orientation is part of the social responsibility philosophy.

The influence of business has led many people to conclude that corporations should benefit their employees, their customers, their business partners, and their community as well as their shareholders. However, these responsibilities and expectations have changed over time. After World War II, many large U.S. firms dominated the global economy. Their power was largely mirrored by the autonomy of their top managers. Because of the relative lack of global competition and stockholder input during the 1950s and 1960s, there were few formal governance procedures to restrain management's actions. The stability experienced by mid-century firms dissolved in the economic turmoil of the 1970s and 1980s, leading companies to focus more on their core competencies and reduce their product diversity. The 1980s and 1990s brought a new focus on efficiency and productivity, which fostered a wave of downsizing and restructuring. Concern for corporate responsibilities was renewed in the 1990s. In the 1990s and beyond, the balance between the global market economy and an interest in social justice and cohesion best characterizes the intent and need for social responsibility. Despite major advances in the 1990s, the sheer number of corporate scandals at the beginning of the twenty-first century prompted a new era of social responsibility.

The increasing globalization of business has made social responsibility an international concern. In most developed countries, social responsibility involves economic, legal, ethical, and philanthropic responsibilities to a variety of stakeholders. Global social responsibility also involves responsibilities to a confluence of governments, businesses, trade associations, and other groups. Progressive global businesses recognize the "shared bottom line" that results from the partnership among businesses, communities, governments, and other stakeholders.

The importance of social responsibility initiatives in enhancing stakeholder relationships, improving performance, and creating other benefits has been debated from many different perspectives. Many business managers view such programs as costly activities that provide rewards only to society at the expense of the bottom line. Others hold that some costs of social responsibility cannot be recovered through improved performance. Although it is true that some aspects of social responsibility may not accrue directly to the bottom line, we believe that organizations benefit indirectly over the long run from these activities. Moreover, ample research and anecdotal evidence demonstrate that there are many rewards for companies that implement such programs.

The process of social responsibility begins with the social responsibility philosophy, includes the four responsibilities, involves many types of stakeholders, and ultimately results in both short- and long-term performance benefits. Once the social responsibility philosophy is accepted, the four types of responsibility are defined and implemented through programs that incorporate stakeholder input and feedback.

RESPONSIBLE BUSINESS DEBATE

How to Regulate Global Business

ISSUE: Are less formal systems and agreements likely to be more successful than formal legal and regulatory systems?

A key lesson learned from recent business scandals is that responsible, transparent, and ethical leadership is needed in order for companies to develop and maintain a long-term commitment to social responsibility for the benefit of multiple stakeholders. This is especially true of multinational corporations (MNCs) because of the power and influence these businesses and their executives represent. MNCs operate in multiple environments and contexts where laws, rules, expectations, and mores are divergent. In addition, the enforcement and monitoring mechanisms to oversee these expectations range from the barely existent to well-resourced government agencies.

The failure to have a global legal and regulatory scheme has resulted in environmental disasters, child labor, financial fraud, antitrust violations, tainted food products, and other problems. For example, Mattel paid a $12 million settlement to thirty-nine U.S. states for shipping Chinese-made toys containing unsafe amounts of lead. The country's largest toy maker also agreed to new standards for lead content in its toys. To save on manufacturing costs, many U.S. companies make products where wages are lower and regulatory standards often differ.

Despite the new coverage of corporate wrongdoing and questionable decision making, many firms are making the commitment to social responsibility through self-regulation. More than 5,000 companies in 135 countries are signatories to the United Nation's (UN) Global Compact, signaling their agreement to ten principles on human rights, anticorruption, environmental issues, and labor. The Global Reporting Initiative (GRI) provides a framework for companies developing social responsibility reports that discuss key standards, are comparable to peers, and capture performance over time. The new ISO 26000 standards will assist in voluntary organizational self-analysis, media review, investor due diligence, and other reviews of social responsibility efforts.

There Are Two Sides to Every Issue:

1. Defend the need for a legal and regulatory system that would oversee international and multinational business operations. How would the system be developed? How would the system enact its responsibility for enforcing legal and regulatory standards?

2. Defend the efficacy of assurance systems and agreements, such as the UN Global Compact and ISO 26000 standards. Why are these less formal systems and agreements likely to be more successful than a formal legal and regulatory system?

KEY TERMS

social responsibility (p. 7)

stakeholders (p. 16)

DISCUSSION QUESTIONS

1. Define social responsibility. How does this view of the role of business differ from your previous perceptions? How is it consistent with your attitudes and beliefs about business?

2. If a company is named to one of the "best in social responsibility" lists, what positive effects can it potentially reap? What are the possible costs or negative outcomes that may be associated with being named to one of these lists?

3. What historical trends have affected the social responsibilities of business? How have recent scandals affected the business climate, including any changes in responsibilities and expectations?

4. How would you respond to the statement that this chapter presents only the positive side of the argument that social responsibility results in improved organizational performance?

5. On the basis of the social responsibility model presented in this chapter, describe the philosophy, responsibilities, and stakeholders that make up a company's approach to social responsibility. What are the short- and long-term outcomes of this effort?

6. Consider the role that various business disciplines, including marketing, finance, accounting, and human resources, have in social responsibility. What specific views and philosophies do these different disciplines bring to the implementation of social responsibility?

EXPERIENTIAL EXERCISE

Evaluate *Fortune* magazine's annual list of the most admired companies found on the magazine's website (http://www.fortune.com). These companies as a group have superior financial performance compared to other firms. Go to each company's website and try to assess its management commitment to the welfare of stakeholders. If any of the companies have experienced legal or ethical misconduct, explain how this may affect specific stakeholders. Rank the companies on the basis of the information available and your opinion on their fulfillment of social responsibility.

WHAT WOULD YOU DO?

Jamie Ramos looked out her window at the early morning sky and gazed at the small crowd below. The words and pictures on their posters were pretty tame this time, she thought. The last protest group used pictures of tarred lungs, corpses, and other graphic photos to show the effects of smoking on a person's internal organs. Their words were also hateful, so much so that employees at the Unified Tobacco headquarters were afraid to walk in and out of the main building. Those who normally took smoking breaks on the back patio decided to skip the break and eat something instead at the company-subsidized cafeteria. By midday, Unified hired extra security to escort employees in and out of the building and to ensure that protestors followed the state guideline of staying at least fifteen feet from the company's entrance. The media picked up on the story—and the photos—and it caused quite a stir in the national press.

At least this protest group seemed fairly reasonable. Late yesterday, a state court provided a reduced judgment to the family of a lifelong smoker, now deceased. This meant that Unified was going to owe millions less than originally expected. The length and stress of the lawsuit had taken its toll, especially on top management, although all employees were certainly affected. After two years of being battered in the media, learning of a huge settlement, and then continuing on with the appeals process, emotions were wearing thin with the continued criticism.

Jamie wondered what this day would bring. As the manager of community relations, her job was to represent Unified in the community, manage the employee volunteer program, create a quarterly newsletter, serve as a liaison to the company's philanthropic foundation, develop solid relationships, and serve on various boards related to social welfare and community needs. The company's foundation donated nearly $1.5 million a year to charities and causes. Over one-quarter of its employees volunteered ten hours a month in their communities.

Jamie reported to a vice president and was pleased with the career progress she had made since graduating from college eight years earlier. Although some of her friends wondered out loud how she could work for a tobacco company, Jamie was steadfast in her belief that even a tobacco firm could contribute something meaningful to society. She had the chance to effect some of those contributions in her community relations role.

Jamie's phone rang and she took a call from her vice president. The VP indicated that, although the protestors seemed relatively calm this time, he was not comfortable with their presence. Several employees had taped signs in office windows telling the protestors to "Go away." Other VPs had dropped by his office to discuss the protest and thought that the responsibility for handling these issues fell to his group. He went on to say that he needed Jamie's help, and the assistance of a few others, in formulating a plan to (1) deal with the protest today and (2) strengthen the strategy for communicating the company's message and goodwill in the future. Their meeting would begin in one hour, so Jamie had some time to sketch out her recommendations on both issues. What would you do?

Strategic Management of Stakeholder Relationships

Chapter Objectives

- To define stakeholders and understand their importance

- To distinguish between primary and secondary stakeholders

- To discuss the global nature of stakeholder relationships

- To consider the impact of reputation and crisis situations on social responsibility performance

- To examine the development of stakeholder relationships

- To explore how stakeholder relationships are integral to social responsibility

Chapter Outline

Stakeholders Defined

Stakeholder Issues and Interaction

Performance with Stakeholders

Development of Stakeholder Relationships

Implementing a Stakeholder Perspective in Social Responsibility

Link Between Stakeholder Relationships and Social Responsibility

© Tom Tomczyk

Stakeholders in the Fight Against Childhood Obesity

America's children are growing not in height or intellectual capacity but in weight. Advertising of fast food, highly processed, corn syrup laced foods is at the heart of the controversy. While TV advertising of food and restaurants has dropped 34 percent from 1977 to 2004, the use of the Internet, promotions, school advertising and vending machines, sponsored sports stadiums, and licensing are on the rise. United States senators recently sponsored the Improved Nutrition and Physical Activity Act to curb obesity and increase nutrition and exercise programs. Regulators, government, parents, and our society in general are concerned with the health of our children.

Studies conducted by the Kaiser Family Foundation have found that the average child sees around 40,000 advertisements per year on television; most of these encourage children to consume candy, cereal, fast food, and soft drinks. The Institute of Medicine released a report in that compiled 123 research studies over the course of thirty years—there is "strong evidence" in the report that advertising is linked with obesity in young children. What seems to be particularly problematic is the use of popular licensed children's cartoon characters (e.g., SpongeBob SquarePants and Scooby Doo) to advertise these unhealthy foods. Critics believe food manufacturers are not being socially responsible by encouraging children to eat food that is detrimental to their health. Some companies are choosing to do something about this problem.

Kraft Foods began limiting its use of cartoon characters in a promise to promote better nutritional standards for children younger than twelve. Coca-Cola, Pepsi, Hershey, and General Mills also agreed to stop advertising products that don't meet nutritional guidelines to kids. Cadbury voluntarily reduced the use of LeBron James as the Bubblicious spokesperson in advertising targeting children. In addition to advertising changes, Kraft introduced a line of 100-percent whole grain crackers and Fig Newtons, toasted chips, and 100-calorie snack packs. McDonald's responded to stakeholders' health concerns by eliminating Super Size menu options, introducing salads and healthier snacks, and attractively repackaging milk. In similar fashion, Burger King began offering a children's meal featuring apple sticks and low-fat caramel dipping sauce. These companies' actions demonstrate sensitivity and concern for consumer health and stakeholder interests.[1]

As this example illustrates, most organizations have a number of constituents, who in turn have other stakeholders to consider. In this case, the food industry and its member companies are facing the complex task of balancing government, parent, children, and corporate concerns. These stakeholders are increasingly expressing opinions that have an effect on the industry's time, operations, member relationships, and products. Today, many organizations are learning to anticipate such issues and to address them in their plans and actions long before they become the subject of media stories or negative attention.

In this chapter, we examine the concept of stakeholders and explore why these groups are important for today's businesses. First, we define stakeholders and examine primary, secondary, and global stakeholders. Then, we examine the concept of a stakeholder orientation to enhance social responsibility. Next, we consider the impact of corporate reputation and crisis situations on stakeholder relationships. Finally, we examine the development of stakeholder relationships implementing a stakeholder perspective and the link between stakeholder relationships and social responsibility.

STAKEHOLDERS DEFINED

In Chapter 1, we defined stakeholders as those people and groups to whom an organization is responsible—including customers, investors and shareholders, employees, suppliers, governments, communities, and many others—because they have a "stake" or claim in some aspect of a company's products, operations, markets, industry, or outcomes. Not only are these groups influenced by businesses, but they also have the ability to affect businesses.

Responsibility issues, conflicts, and successes revolve around stakeholder relationships. Building effective relationships is considered one of the more important practices of business today. The stakeholder framework is recognized as a management theory that attempts to balance stakeholder interests. Issues related to indivisible resources and unequal levels of stakeholder salience constrain managers' efforts to balance stakeholder interests.[2] A business exists because of relationships among employees, customers, shareholders or investors, suppliers, and managers that develop strategies to attain success. In addition, an organization usually has a governing authority, often called a *board of directors*, that provides oversight

© AP Photo/Paul Sakuma

Apple Inc. takes care to interact with its primary stakeholders, especially customers

and direction to make sure the organization stays focused on objectives in an ethical, legal, and socially responsible manner. When misconduct is discovered in organizations, it is often found that there has been knowing cooperation or compliance that has facilitated the acceptance and perpetuation of the unethical conduct.[3] Therefore, relationships are associated not only with organizational success but also with organizational failure to assume responsibility.

> **"Building effective relationships is considered one of the more important practices of business today."**

The historical assumption that the foremost objective of business is profit maximization led to the belief that business is accountable primarily to investors and others involved in the market and economic aspects of an organization. Because shareholders and other investors provide the financial foundation for business and expect something in return, managers and executives naturally strive to maintain positive relationships with them.[4]

In the latter half of the twentieth century, perceptions of business accountability evolved toward an expanded model of the role and responsibilities of business in society. The expansion included questions about the normative role of business: "What is the appropriate role for business to play in society?" and "Should profit be the sole objective of business?"[5] Many businesspeople and scholars have questioned the role of social responsibility in business. Legal and economic responsibilities are generally accepted as the most important determinants of performance: "If this is well done," say classical theorists, "profits are maximized more or less continuously and firms carry out their major responsibilities to society."[6] Some economists believe that if companies address economic and legal issues, they are satisfying the demands of society, and that trying to anticipate and meet additional needs would be almost impossible. Milton Friedman has been quoted as saying that "the basic mission of business [is] thus to produce goods and services at a profit, and in doing this, business [is] making its maximum contribution to society and, in fact, being socially responsible."[7] Even with the business ethics scandals of the twenty-first century, Friedman suggests that, although individuals guilty of wrongdoing should be held accountable, the market is a better deterrent than new laws and regulations that discourage firms from wrongdoing.[8] Thus, Friedman would diminish the role of stakeholders such as the government and employees in requiring that businesses demonstrate responsible and ethical behavior.

This Darwinian form of capitalism has unfortunately been exported to many less developed and developing countries and is associated with a Wild West economy where anything goes in business. Friedman's capitalism is a far cry from Adam Smith's, one of the founders of capitalism. Smith created the concept of the invisible hand and spoke about self-interest; however, he went on to explain that this common good is associated with psychological motives and that each individual has to produce for the common good, "with values such as Propriety, Prudence, Reason, Sentiment and promoting the happiness of mankind."[9] These values could be associated with the needs and concerns of stakeholders.

In the twenty-first century, is Friedman's form of capitalism being replaced by Smith's original concept of capitalism (or what is now called enlightened capitalism), a notion of capitalism that reemphasizes stakeholder concerns and issues? This shift may be occurring faster in developed countries than in those still being developed. Theodore Levitt, a renowned business professor, once wrote that, although profits are required for business just like eating is required for living, profit is not the purpose of business any more than eating is the purpose of life.[10] Norman Bowie, a well-known philosopher, extended Levitt's sentiment by noting that focusing on profit alone can create an unfavorable paradox that causes a firm to fail to achieve its objectives. Bowie contends that when a business also cares about the well-being of stakeholders, it earns trust and cooperation that ultimately reduce costs and increase productivity.[11]

These perspectives take into account both market and nonmarket constituencies that may interact with a business and have some effect on the firm's policies and strategy.[12] Market constituencies are those who are directly involved with and affected by the business purpose, including investors, employees, customers, and other business partners. Nonmarket groups include the general community, media, government, special-interest groups, and others who are not always directly tied to issues of profitability and performance.

"Much evidence exists that social responsibility is associated with increased profits."

Much evidence exists that social responsibility is associated with increased profits. For example, one survey indicates that three of four consumers refused to buy from certain businesses, and a business's poor conduct was an important reason to avoid a business.[13] An important academic study found that there is a direct relationship between social responsibility and profitability. The study also found that social responsibility contributes to employee commitment and customer loyalty—vital concerns of any firm trying to increase profits.[14]

STAKEHOLDER ISSUES AND INTERACTION

Stakeholders provide resources that are more or less critical to a firm's long-term success. These resources may be both tangible and intangible. Shareholders, for example, supply capital; suppliers offer material resources or intangible knowledge; employees and managers grant expertise, leadership, and commitment; customers generate revenue and provide loyalty and positive word-of-mouth promotion; local communities provide infrastructure;

and the media transmits positive corporate images. When individual stakeholders share similar expectations about desirable business conduct, they may choose to establish or join formal communities that are dedicated to better defining and advocating these values and expectations. Stakeholders' ability to withdraw—or to threaten to withdraw—these needed resources gives them power over businesses.[15]

New reforms to improve corporate accountability and transparency also suggest that other stakeholders—including banks, law firms, and public accounting firms—can play a major role in fostering responsible decision making.[16] Stakeholders apply their values and standards to many diverse issues, such as working conditions, consumer rights, environmental conservation, product safety, and proper information disclosure, issues that may or may not directly affect an individual stakeholder's own welfare. We can assess the level of social responsibility an organization bears by scrutinizing its effects on the issues of concern to its stakeholders. Table 2.1 provides examples of common stakeholder issues along with indicators of businesses' impacts on these issues.[17]

> **"We can assess the level of social responsibility an organization bears by scrutinizing its effects on the issues of concern to its stakeholders."**

Identifying Stakeholders

We can identify two different types of stakeholders. **Primary stakeholders** are those whose continued association is absolutely necessary for a firm's survival; these include employees, customers, investors, and shareholders, as well as the governments and communities that provide necessary infrastructure. For example, many large companies diluted pensions of salaried employees and cut medical benefits to retired employees who were primary stakeholders. Figure 2.1 shows the national trend of firms with over 200 employees to offer fewer health benefits for retirees, dropping from a high of around 66 percent in 1988 to around 31 percent twenty years later.

Secondary stakeholders do not typically engage in transactions with a company and thus are not essential for its survival; these include the media, trade associations, and special-interest groups. The American Association of Retired People (AARP), a special-interest group, works to support the rights of retirees in areas such as health-care benefits. Both primary and secondary stakeholders embrace specific values and standards that dictate what constitutes acceptable or unacceptable corporate behaviors. It is important for managers to recognize that primary groups may present more day-to-day concerns, but secondary groups cannot be ignored or given less consideration in the ethical decision-making process.

primary stakeholders
those whose continued association is absolutely necessary for a firm's survival; these include employees, customers, investors, and shareholders, as well as the governments and communities that provide necessary infrastructure

secondary stakeholders
those who do not typically engage in transactions with a company and thus are not essential for its survival; these include the media, trade associations, and special-interest groups

Table 2.1 Examples of Stakeholder Issues and Associated Measures of Corporate Impacts

Stakeholder Groups and Issues	Potential Indicators of Corporate Impact on These Issues
Employees	
1. Compensation and benefits	1. Ratio of lowest wage to chief executive officer wage
2. Training and development	2. Changes in average training dollars spent per year per employee
3. Employee diversity	3. Percentages of employees from different genders and races, especially in leadership roles
4. Occupational health and safety	4. Standard injury rates and absentee rates
5. Communications with management	5. Availability of open-door policies or ombudsmen management
Customers	
1. Product safety and quality	1. Number of product recalls over time
2. Management of customers	2. Number of customer complaints and availability of complaint procedures to answer them
3. Services to customers with disabilities	3. Availability and nature of measures taken to ensure services to customers with disabilities
Investors	
1. Transparency of shareholder	1. Availability of procedures to inform shareholders about corporate activities
2. Shareholder rights	2. Frequency and type of litigation involving violations of shareholder rights
Suppliers	
1. Encouraging suppliers in developing countries	1. Prices offered to suppliers in developing and developed countries in comparison to other suppliers
2. Encouraging minority suppliers	2. Percentage of minority suppliers
Community	
1. Public health and safety	1. Availability of emergency response plan protection
2. Conservation of energy and materials	2. Data on reduction of waste produced and materials compared to industry
3. Donations and support of local organizations	3. Annual employee time spent in community service organizations
Environmental Groups	
1. Minimizing the use of energy	1. Amount of electricity purchased; percentage of "green" electricity
2. Minimizing emissions and waste	2. Type, amount, and designation of waste generated
3. Minimizing adverse environmental effect of products	3. Percentage of reclaimed product weight reused, recycled, or remanufactured

Figure 2.1 Declining Retiree Health Benefits (1988–2008)

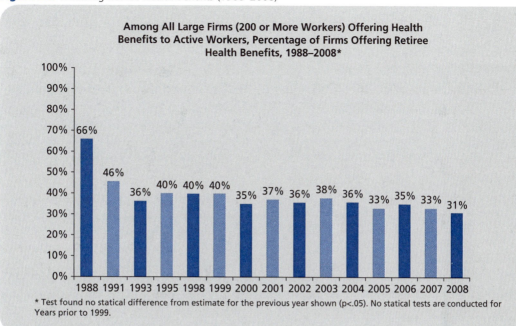

Among All Large Firms (200 or More Workers) Offering Health Benefits to Active Workers, Percentage of Firms Offering Retiree Health Benefits, 1988–2008*

* Test found no statical difference from estimate for the previous year shown (p<.05). No statical tests are conducted for Years prior to 1999.

Source: Kaiser Family Foundation, http://www.kff.org/insurance/7672/sections/ehbs07-11-1.cfm, accessed May 10, 2009.

Figure 2.2 offers a conceptualization of the relationship between businesses and stakeholders. In this **stakeholder interaction model**, there are two-way relationships between the firm and a host of stakeholders. In addition to the fundamental input of investors, employees, and suppliers, this approach recognizes other stakeholders and explicitly acknowledges the dialog that exists between a firm's internal and external environments.

A Stakeholder Orientation

The degree to which a firm understands and addresses stakeholder demands can be referred to as a **stakeholder orientation**. This orientation comprises three sets of activities: (1) the organization-wide generation of data about stakeholder groups and assessment of the firm's effects on these groups, (2) the distribution of this information throughout the firm, and (3) the organization's responsiveness as a whole to this intelligence.[18]

Generating data about stakeholders begins with identifying the stakeholders that are relevant to the firm. Relevant stakeholder communities should be analyzed on the basis of the power each enjoys as well as by the ties between them. Next, the firm should characterize the concerns about the business's conduct that each relevant stakeholder group shares. This information can be derived from formal research, including surveys, focus groups, Internet searches, or press reviews. For example, Ford Motor Company obtains input on social and environmental responsibility issues from company representatives, suppliers, customers, and community leaders. Shell has an online discussion forum where website visitors

stakeholder interaction model a conceptualization of the relationship between businesses and stakeholders in which there are two-way relationships between the firm and a host of stakeholders

stakeholder orientation the degree to which a firm understands and addresses stakeholder demands

Fate of Dealers in the Automotive Industry As Chrysler headed into bankruptcy and General Motors (GM) tried to fend off economic failure, media outlets carried stories about significant ramifications to the companies' employees and suppliers, especially the impact on certain manufacturing communities. One primary stakeholder was left out of early discussions—the dealers that ensure people in large cities and small towns alike have access to Chrysler and GM products. When both car firms announced the decision to drop certain dealers from their retail networks, economic reverberations were felt on a variety of stakeholders, in a number of communities, across the United States (U.S.). Although Chrysler and GM are typically categorized as part of the automotive industry, they are pivotal to financial markets, consumer confidence, and the economic prospects of the nation.

State franchise laws make it arduous and expensive for automotive manufacturers to force dealers out of business, but franchise contracts can be annulled in bankruptcy court. That was exactly the strategy utilized by Chrysler, as it told 789 of its 3,200 dealers that their contracts would be voided under corporate bankruptcy protection. Although GM was not officially bankrupt at the time, the company informed 1,100 dealerships that it would discontinue sales to them by October 2010. Among them were 450 dealerships for Saturns, Saabs, and Hummers, all brands that GM planned to sell or eliminate.

President Obama established the Auto Task Force to review plans by GM and Chrysler to restructure, modernize, and become more competitive. On March 30, 2009, the task force issued its findings, including the need for the automotive manufacturers to reduce dealer operations. The National Automobile Dealers Association (NADA) said the affected GM dealerships employed about 63,000 salespeople, mechanics, and other personnel. The Chrysler closings affected 40,000 employees at Jeep, Dodge, and Chrysler dealerships. Ultimately, the NADA estimated that over 150,000 dealer employees would be affected. In a position paper on dealer closures, the association laid out five major concerns and financial effects on laid-off employees, dealer owners, local communities and governments, and other stakeholders by contagion:

1. The Auto Task Force is unnecessarily putting nearly 150,000 employees out of work.
2. Forced dealer closings will hurt communities.
3. Fewer dealers will mean state and local governments will lose millions of dollars in auto sales tax revenue.
4. Fewer dealers will mean reduced competition and convenience for consumers.
5. Cutting dealers at this time will do nothing to make GM or Chrysler more viable.

Sources: National Automobile Dealers Association, "NADA Opposes Unnecessary, Forced Dealership Closures," www.nada.org, accessed May 17, 2009; "Remarks by the President on the American Automotive Industry," http://www.whitehouse.gov/the_press_office/Remarks-by-the-President-on-the-American-Automotive-Industry-3/30/09/, accessed May 17, 2009; Sharon Terlop, "GM to Close 1100 Dealerships," wsj.com, May 16, 2009.

are invited to express their opinions on the company's activities and their implications. This information can also be generated informally by employees and managers as they carry out their daily activities. For example, purchasing managers know about suppliers' demands, public relations executives about the media,

Figure 2.2 Stakeholder Model for Implementing Social Responsibilities

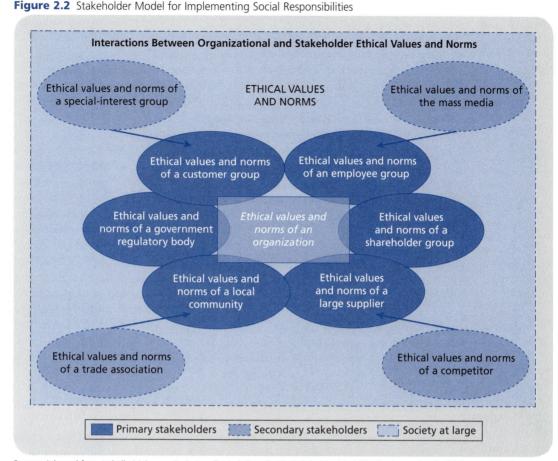

Source: Adapted from Isabelle Maignan, O. C. Ferrell, Linda Ferrell, "A Stakeholder Model for Implementing Social Responsibility in Marketing," *European Journal of Marketing* 39 (September/October 2005): 956–977. Used with permission.

legal counselors about the regulatory environment, financial executives about investors, sales representatives about customers, and human resources advisors about employees. Finally, the company should evaluate its impact on the issues that are important to the various stakeholders it has identified.[19] To develop effective stakeholder dialogs, management needs to appreciate how others perceive the risks of a specific decision. A multiple stakeholder perspective must take into account communication content and transparency when communicating with specific stakeholders.[20]

Given the variety of the employees involved in the generation of information about stakeholders, it is essential that this intelligence be circulated throughout the firm. This requires that the firm facilitate the communication of information about the nature of relevant stakeholder communities, stakeholder issues, and the current impact of the firm on these issues to all members of the organization. The dissemination of stakeholder intelligence can be organized formally through activities such as newsletters and internal information forums.[21]

A stakeholder orientation is not complete unless it includes activities that actually address stakeholder issues. For example, The Gap reported that although it is improving factory inspections, it is still struggling to wipe out deep-seated problems such as discrimination and excessive overtime. Gap revoked approval of seventy factories that violated its code of vendor conduct. Gap also realized that it sometimes contributes to problems by making unreasonable demands on factories; therefore, it is becoming stricter about its own deadlines to ensure that dumping rush jobs on factories does not occur.[22] The responsiveness of the organization as a whole to stakeholder intelligence consists of the initiatives the firm adopts to ensure that it abides by or exceeds stakeholder expectations and has a positive impact on stakeholder issues. Such activities are likely to be specific to a particular stakeholder group (e.g., family-friendly work schedules) or to a particular stakeholder issue (e.g., pollution-reduction programs). These responsiveness processes typically involve the participation of the concerned stakeholder groups. Kraft, for example, includes special-interest groups and university representatives in its programs to become sensitized to present and future ethical issues.

A stakeholder orientation can be viewed as a continuum in that firms are likely to adopt the concept to varying degrees. To gauge a given firm's stakeholder orientation, it is necessary to evaluate the extent to which the firm adopts behaviors that typify both the generation and dissemination of stakeholder intelligence and responsiveness to it. A given organization may generate and disseminate more intelligence about certain stakeholder communities than about others and, as a result, may respond to that intelligence differently.[23]

Stakeholder Attributes[24]

Traditionally, companies have had an easier time understanding the issues stakeholders raise than their attributes and the tactics they use to affect organizational decision making. It is therefore necessary to understand both the content (specific issues) and process (actions, tactics) of each stakeholder relationship. For example, animal rights activists sometimes use an unreasonable process to communicate the content of their beliefs. Although they are controversial, animal rights issues do have solid support from a number of citizens. One mechanism for understanding stakeholders and their potential salience to a firm involves assessing three stakeholder attributes: power, legitimacy, and urgency. This assessment provides one analytical tool to help managers uncover the motivations and needs of stakeholders and how they relate to the company and its interests. In addition, stakeholder actions may also sensitize the firm to issues and viewpoints not previously considered.[25]

"Power, legitimacy, and urgency are not constant, meaning stakeholder attributes can change over time and context."

Power, legitimacy, and urgency are not constant, meaning stakeholder attributes can change over time and context. For example, there was a very strong "Buy American" sentiment in the United States in the 1980s, a time when Japanese manufacturers were making steady market share gains. Today, there is less consumer activism or retailer strategy on activism toward this nationalistic buying criterion. Thus, although these stakeholders may still have a legitimate claim for buying from U.S. firms, they are neither using their power nor creating a sense of urgency regarding this issue today. It seems that nationalism, as it relates to retail purchasing, is no longer a key buying criterion. The U.S. economy has been strong, so products from other countries have not been seen as threatening. In polls after September 11, 30 percent of Americans said they preferred to buy American-made goods, but over 40 percent said they pay little attention to a good's origin.[26]

Power A stakeholder has power to the extent that it can gain access to coercive, utilitarian, or symbolic means to impose or communicate its views to an organization.[27] *Coercive power* involves the use of physical force, violence, or some type of restraint. *Utilitarian power* involves financial or material control, such as boycotts that affect a company's bottom line. Finally, *symbolic power* relies on the use of symbols that connote social acceptance, prestige, or some other attribute. Symbolism contained in letter-writing campaigns, advertising messages, and websites can be used to generate awareness and enthusiasm for more responsible business actions. In fact, the Internet has conferred tremendous power on stakeholder groups in recent years. A number of "hate sites" have been placed on the Internet by disgruntled stakeholders, especially customers and former employees, to share concerns about certain corporate behaviors. Richard B. Freeman, a Harvard labor economist, says, "With the Internet, information flows instantly, so even if we don't have more people concerned about companies, those who are can do more about it."[28] Symbolic power is the least threatening of the three types.

Utilitarian measures, including boycotts and lawsuits, are also fairly prevalent, although they often come about after symbolic strategies fail to yield the desired response. For example, the U.S. government, an important stakeholder for most firms, recently banned the importation of goods made by children under the age of fifteen through indentured or forced labor.[29] This action came about after the media and activist groups exposed widespread abuses in the apparel industry. This law carries financial—utilitarian—repercussions for firms that purchase products manufactured under unacceptable labor conditions.

Finally, some stakeholders use coercive power to communicate their message. During a rally to protest McDonald's as a symbol of global capitalism, worker exploitation, and environmental insensitivity, a handful of protesters stormed a McDonald's restaurant in London, eventually tearing down the hamburger chain's famous "golden arches." A company spokesperson said that although the company abhors violence and destruction, it planned to reopen the damaged restaurant and start a dialog with activists to counter false allegations and accusations. The spokesperson emphasized the local, not global, nature of McDonald's in the United Kingdom, where the company employs 70,000 people and has over 1,200 restaurants.[30]

Legitimacy The second stakeholder attribute is legitimacy, which is the perception or belief that a stakeholder's actions are proper, desirable, or appropriate

power
the extent to which a stakeholder can gain access to coercive, utilitarian, or symbolic means to impose or communicate its views to the organization; power may be coercive, utilitarian, or symbolic

legitimacy
the perception or belief that a stakeholder's actions are proper, desirable, or appropriate within a given context

within a given context.[31] This definition suggests that stakeholder actions are considered legitimate when claims are judged to be reasonable by other stakeholders and by society in general. Legitimacy is gained through the stakeholder's ability and willingness to explore the issue from a variety of perspectives and then to communicate in an effective and respectful manner on the desire for change. Thus, extremist views are less likely to be considered legitimate because these groups often use covert and inflammatory measures that overshadow the issues and create animosity. For example, extreme groups have destroyed property, threatened customers, and committed other acts of violence that ultimately discredit their legitimacy.[32] McDonald's remained open to stakeholder dialog after the London restaurant was destroyed, although other companies might have shunned further communication with the protesters, citing their irrational and dangerous behavior. McDonald's also faced criticism for its unhealthy food, which was linked to obesity; in the UK, the health lobby claimed McDonald's food was bad for consumers. McDonald's took the claims to heart and decided to change their image. They intensified efforts to include healthy options on their menus. One issue arose concerning their Chicken Caesar salad, which had more fat and calories than McDonald's world-famous hamburger. However, management listened to consumers and, within three months, introduced a new low-fat dressing option. McDonald's has recovered well from its negative publicity and, by listening to its customers, has been able to change not only its image, through makeovers of its restaurants and sponsorship deals with Justin Timberlake and Destiny's Child, but also its focus. In the UK, McDonald's launched an "It's What I Eat and What I Do" initiative to increase activity among young children and try to counteract the obesity epidemic.[33] Although an issue, such as environmental sensitivity, may be legitimate, it is difficult for the claim to be evaluated independently of the way the stakeholder group communicates on it.

Urgency Stakeholders exercise greater pressures on managers and organizations when they stress the urgency of their claims. Urgency is based on two characteristics: time sensitivity and the importance of the claim to the stakeholder. Time sensitivity usually heightens the stakeholder's effort and may compress an organization's ability to research and react to a claim. For example, protesters in Thailand formed a human chain around a hotel hosting the Asian Development Bank's annual meeting. The protest was aimed at increasing the bank's efforts to revitalize the regional economy and create more economic equity for the working poor. The protest was timed to occur during the bank's annual meeting, when officials would be developing new policies. Although bank officials did not formally meet with the protesters, the Asian Development Bank committed monies and projects to reduce poverty and other socioeconomic ills.[34]

In another example, labor and human rights are widely recognized as critical issues because they are fundamental to the well-being of people around the world. These rights have become a focal point for college student associations that criticized Nike, the world's leading shoe company, for its failure to improve the working conditions of employees of suppliers and in not making information available to interested stakeholders. Nike experienced a public backlash from its use of offshore subcontractors to manufacture its shoes and clothing. When Nike claimed no responsibility for the subcontractors' poor working conditions

urgency
the time sensitivity and the importance of the claim to the stakeholder

and extremely low wages, some consumers demanded greater accountability and responsibility by engaging in boycotts, letter-writing campaigns, public-service announcements, and so forth. Nike ultimately responded to the growing negative publicity by changing its practices and becoming a model company in managing offshore manufacturing.

Overall, stakeholders are considered more important to an organization when their issues are legitimate, their claims are urgent, and they can make use of their power on the organization. These attributes assist the firm and employees in determining the relative importance of specific stakeholders and making resource allocations for developing and managing the stakeholder relationship.

PERFORMANCE WITH STAKEHOLDERS

Managing stakeholder relationships effectively requires careful attention to a firm's reputation and the effective handling of crisis situations. Motorola, a large telecommunications company, was not aware that one of its European distributors sold Motorola semiconductor chips to a manufacturer of landmine component parts. When Motorola, the recipient of numerous social responsibility accolades, learned of the situation, it investigated, stopped selling to the distributor, and created better oversight for its distribution channels. In the process, Motorola was mindful of potential effects on its reputation with stakeholders. In a similar turn, De Beers, the world's largest diamond producer, announced it would stop buying diamonds from Angola, after a group of European organizations launched a campaign to alert the public to the fact that an Angolan rebel group, Unita, funded wars and casualties through diamond sales.[35]

Reputation Management

There are short- and long-term outcomes associated with positive stakeholder relationships. One of the most significant of these is a positive reputation. Because a company's reputation has the power to attract or repel stakeholders, it can be either an asset or a liability in developing and implementing strategic plans and social responsibility initiatives.[36] Reputations take a long time to build or change, and it is far more important to monitor reputation than many companies believe. Whereas a strong reputation may take years to build, it can be destroyed seemingly overnight if a company does not handle crisis situations to the satisfaction of the various stakeholders involved.

Corporate reputation, image, and brands are more important than ever and are among the most critical aspects of sustaining

"Reputations take a long time to build or change, and it is far more important to monitor reputation than many companies believe."

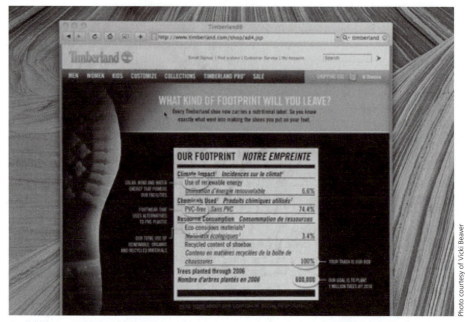

Socially responsible companies communicate with stakeholders in a variety of ways, like Timberland's use of its corporate website

relationships with constituents, including investors, customers, financial analysts, media, and government watchdogs. It takes companies decades to build a great reputation, yet just one slip can cost a company dearly. Although an organization does not control its reputation in a direct sense, its actions, choices, behaviors, and consequences do influence the reputation that exists in perceptions of stakeholders. Companies such as Exxon Mobil, Citgo, Halliburton, Chrysler, AIG, and General Motors received low ratings from the public in a corporate reputation survey for what the public perceived as the "heartless" spike in prices at the pump, irresponsible management, bankruptcy, and record executive salaries and bonuses. In the same survey, despite corporate-governance reforms and a growing commitment to ethics and social responsibility, the overall reputation of American corporations continued to slip. In 2009, 88 percent of respondents rated American businesses' reputation as "not good" or "terrible" compared to 68 percent in 2004.[37]

Reputation management is the process of building and sustaining a company's good name and generating positive feedback from stakeholders. A company's reputation is affected by every contact with a stakeholder.[38] Various trends may affect how companies manage their reputations. These trends include market factors, such as increased consumer knowledge and community access to information, and workplace factors, including technological advances, closer vendor relationships, and more inquisitive employees. These factors make companies more cautious about their actions because increased scrutiny in this area requires more attention from management. A company needs to understand these factors and how to properly address them to achieve a strong reputation. These factors have also helped companies recognize a link between reputation and competitive advantage. If these trends are dealt with wisely and if internal and external communication

reputation management
the process of building and sustaining a company's good name and generating positive feedback from stakeholders

strategies are used effectively, a firm can position itself positively in stakeholders' minds and thus create a competitive advantage. Intangible factors related to reputation can account for as much as 50 percent of a firm's market valuation.[39]

The importance of corporate reputation has created a need for accurate reputation measures. As indicated in Table 2.2, business publications, research firms,

Table 2.2 Reputation Measures

Reputation List	Conducted By	Groups Surveyed	Primary Purpose
100 Best Companies to Work for in America	Robert Lebering & Milton Moskowitz and Hewitt Associates	*Fortune* companies' employees and top managers	Publication
100 Best Corporate Citizens	*Business Ethics* magazine, KLD Research & Analytics, Sandra Waddock and Samuel Graves, and Boston College	Drawn from 650 firms used in the socially screened Domini Index: the S&P 500, plus 150 other firms selected for industry balance and social excellence	Publication
America's Most Admired Companies	*Fortune* magazine and Clark, Martire & Bartolomeo	Company officers, directors, and analysts of *Fortune* 500 companies	Publication
Best and Worst: Social Responsibility	*Fortune* magazine and Clark, Martire & Bartolomeo	Company officers, directors, and analysts of *Fortune* 500 companies	Publication
Corporate Branding Index	Corporate Branding LLC	Vice president–level executives and above in the top 20 percent of U.S. businesses	Customized for clients
Corporate Reputation Index	Delahaye Medialink	Print and broadcast media	Sold as syndicated research
Global Reputation Pulse	Reputation Institute	Consumers familiar with each company	Publication
Maximizing Corporate Reputation	Burston-Marsteller	CEOs, executives, board members, financial community, government officials, business media, and consumers	Customized for clients
Reputation Quotient	Reputation Institute and Harris Interactive	General public	Customized for clients
World's Most-Respected Companies	Pricewaterhouse Coopers	CEOs from 75 countries	Publication

Sources: Prema Nakra, "Corporate Reputation Management: 'CRM' with a Strategic Twist," *Public Relations Quarterly* 45 (Summer 2000): 35; Reputation Institute, "2009 Global Reputation Pulse," http://www.reputationinstitute.com/advisory-services/global-pulse, accessed May 3, 2009; Steven L. Wartick, "Measuring Corporate Reputation: Definition and Data," *Business & Society* 41 (2002): 371–392.

consultants, and public relations agencies have established a foothold in the new field of reputation management through research and lists of "the most reputable" firms. However, some questions have arisen as to who can best determine corporate reputation. For example, some measures survey only chief executives, whereas others also elicit perceptions from the general public. Although executives may be biased toward a firm's financial performance, the general public may lack experience or data on which to evaluate a company's reputation. Regardless of how it is measured, reputation is the result of a process involving an organization and various constituents.[40]

The process of reputation management involves four components that work together: organizational identity, image, performance, and ultimately, reputation.[41] Organizational identity refers to how an organization wants to be viewed by its stakeholders, whereas organizational image is how stakeholders interpret the various aspects of a company to form an overall impression of it. Organizational performance involves the actual interaction between the company and its stakeholders. The interaction of organizational image and performance results in organizational reputation, the collective view of all stakeholders after their image of the firm is shaped through interactions with the company.

To build and manage a good reputation, these four areas must be aligned. Companies must manage identity and culture by pinpointing those standards and responsibilities that will allow them to achieve their objectives, work with stakeholders effectively, and continuously monitor and change for effectiveness.[42] The top corporate citizens selected for the *Business Ethics* 100 Best Corporate Citizens list provide recognition and publicity for outstanding performance using corporate responsibility criteria. Green Mountain Coffee ranked number two in

Table 2.3 Top 20 Corporate Citizens

1. Green Mountain Coffee Roasters, Inc.	11. Salesforce.com, Inc.
2. Advanced Micro Devices, Inc.	12. Applied Materials, Inc.
3. NIKE, Inc.	13. Texas Instruments Incorporated
4. Motorola, Inc.	14. Herman Miller, Inc.
5. Intel Corporation	15. Rockwell Collins
6. International Business Machines Corporation	16. Interface, Inc.
7. Agilent Technologies, Inc.	17. Steelcase, Inc.
8. Timberland Company (The)	18. Dell Inc.
9. Starbucks Corporation	19. Cisco Systems, Inc.
10. General Mills Incorporated	20. Lam Research Corporation

Source: "Business Ethics 100 Best Corporate Citizens 2007," *Business Ethics*, http://www.business-ethics.com/node/75, accessed May 3, 2009.

2005 and number one in 2007 as shown in Table 2.3. Green Mountain Coffee roasts high-quality Arabica coffees and offers over 100 coffee selections, including single-origins, estates, certified organics, Fair Trade Certified™, proprietary blends, and flavored coffees. They carefully select their coffee beans and then *appropriately roast* the coffees to maximize their taste and flavor differences. Green Mountain Coffee Roasters has consistently appeared on *Forbes Magazine* 200 Best Small Companies in America. It has been on the list for six years, and in 2004, it ranked sixty-eight compared to its 2003 position of seventy. In 2005, it ranked 126. It also placed number one on *Business Ethics* magazine's 100 Best Corporate Citizens in 2006, up from its 2005 position of second. There is openness in all aspects of communication that allows employees to have regular access to all levels of the organization, including CEO Bob Stiller. This encourages passion and commitment so that employees get to the crux of issues rather than play politics. The company uses technology such as voicemail or e-mail to inform the group of decisions and allows individual employees to voice their opinions and ideas. In this way, they have achieved a culture of involving people in ideas and issues to come up with better solutions together rather than allowing just one individual to come up with solutions that might not necessarily be the best. The empowerment of employees means that the company may seem chaotic at times. However, the communication across channels, in what is sometimes termed a "constellation of communication," ensures that the collaborative nature of getting things done spreads the word across the company and anyone can express their ideas and opinions. Although employees are encouraged to share their views in many meetings, the information is shared by following an agenda, which ensures that efficient decision making occurs seamlessly across the company.[43]

Thus, all these elements must be continually implemented to ensure that the company's reputation is maximized through community relations. However, most firms will, at one time or another, experience crisis situations that threaten or harm this reputation. How a company reacts, responds, and learns from the situation is indicative of its commitment and implementation of social responsibility.

Reputation management is becoming a key consideration for corporations around the world. A recent study delved into the reasons that German firms invest resources into building, maintaining, and strengthening their reputations. Roughly two-thirds of the respondents felt that reputation management was of "very high" or "high" importance to their companies. Firms operating in the food and services industries attached the most importance to reputation, whereas those in the automotive, retail, and manufacturing sectors indicated the least importance.

Table 2.4 lists a number of reputation objectives, with the percentage of respondents who believed the objective was of high importance to the organization. Developing a positive image and improving relationships with employees and customers were key considerations for the majority of companies. Other stakeholders, such as investors, suppliers, and the media, were seen as less relevant to reputation objectives and strategies. Only 15 percent of the respondents indicated that reputation management was helpful with improving supplier relations; just over 20 percent believed the same for improving investor relations.

Table 2.4 Reputation Objectives of German Companies

Reputation Objectives	Percent Indicating Very Important
Development of a positive image	76.3
Heightening of customer satisfaction and loyalty	72.5
Improvement of customer relationships	66.4
Increase of corporate identity	60.3
Acquiring new customers	57.3
Heightening of employee motivation	56.5
Heightening of employee satisfaction	53.4
Increase in profits	48.4
Simplification of launching products on the market	37.2
Positive support by media	35.1
Improvement of corporate public image	31.3
Improvement of investor relations	25.8
Lowering the cost of capital	23.8
Improvement of investor relations	21.0
Improvement of supplier relations	15.3
Easier high-potential recruiting	13.7

Source: K. P. Wiedmann and H. Buxel, "Corporate Reputation Management in Germany: Results of an Empirical Study," *Corporate Reputation Review* 8, no. 2 (2005): 145–163.

"**Organizational crises are far-reaching events that can have dramatic effects on both the organization and its stakeholders.**"

Nearly 50 percent of the companies, however, believed that reputation objectives were very important to increasing profits.

Crisis Management[44]

Organizational crises are far-reaching events that can have dramatic effects on both the organization and its stakeholders. Along with the industrialization of society, companies and their products have become ever more complex and therefore more susceptible to crisis. As a result, disasters and crisis situations are increasingly common events from which few organizations are exempt. For example, the size and geographic diversity of IBM's workforce and operations required the firm to develop a worldwide network of crisis management personnel. This group is trained to implement the company's crisis management team model in the event of natural disaster, product recall, major lawsuit, violence, or other misfortune. IBM put its plan into motion on September 11, 2001, and was able to restore core services within three days, lend its extra office space to house displaced customers and noncustomers, assist employees and communities affected by the tragedy, and use its technology and call centers to aid government agencies.[45]

An *ethical misconduct disaster* (EMD) can be an unexpected organizational crisis that results from employee misconduct, illegal activities such as fraud, or unethical decisions that significantly disrupt operations and threaten or are perceived to threaten the firm's continuity of operations. An EMD can even be more devastating than natural disasters such as a hurricane or technology disruptions.[46]

As organizations plan for natural disasters and insure against traditional risks, so too should they prepare for ethical crises. An EMD can be managed by organizational initiatives to recognize, avoid, discover, answer, and recover from the misconduct. The potential damage of an ethical disaster can affect both business and society. The costs of an EMD from both a financial and reputation perspective can be assessed, as well as the need for planning to avoid an EMD. The role of leadership in preventing a crisis relates to a contingency plan to develop effective crisis management programs.

The risks facing organizations today are significant, and the reputational damage caused can be far greater for companies that find themselves unprepared. The key is to recognize that the risks associated with misconduct are real and that, if insufficient controls are in place, the company can suddenly find itself the subject of an EMD. Although it is hard to predict an ethical disaster, companies can and must prepare for one.

According to HealthSouth, they have spent "approximately $440 million in, among other things, stabilizing [their] operations, reconstructing [their] accounting records, producing restated and other financial statements, restructuring the Company finances and restoring HealthSouth's credibility—all responses to the crises created as a direct result of the fraud perpetrated while Richard Scrushy was CEO and Chairman." The result was "a cumulative net reduction in shareholders' equity of $3.9 billion."[47] In addition, the company agreed to pay "$100 million to settle a lawsuit claiming violations of federal securities laws" and "$325 million plus interest as part of a global settlement regarding certain alleged inappropriate Medicare billing practices."

Although HealthSouth Corporation's CEO Richard Scrushy was acquitted of participating in a $27 billion accounting fraud, many of his executives plea-bargained deals with the government for more lenient sentences.[48] In 2006, Scrushy was found guilty of paying a half million dollars in bribes to a former Alabama governor in exchange for a seat on a state health-care board. Moreover, the resulting damage to the firm's reputation was a disaster, and their only means of distancing themselves from their former leader was to provide the following comment on the company's website:

As HealthSouth continues its unprecedented recovery from a massive fraud that occurred during the tenure of Richard Scrushy as CEO and Chairman, it is astonishing that he would have the audacity and shamelessness to comment on the current operations or the dedication of our approximately 40,000 employees. As we have stated in the past, Scrushy will not be offered any position within the Company by this management team or this Board of Directors. Under no circumstances would we reach out to Scrushy, who by his own defense has claimed a complete lack of knowledge as to the financial workings of the Company during his tenure as CEO and Chairman, despite his claims of possessing valuable expertise.[49]

Of course, not every unethical decision relates to accounting fraud. Many often begin as a marketing effort, and only in retrospect is it revealed to be unethical. And clearly not every decision becomes a crisis. When Blockbuster introduced its "The End of Late Fees" policy and promotion, a lawsuit brought by the New Jersey attorney general's office over possible deceptive pricing did not seem to dampen Blockbuster's reputation and stakeholder confidence. The attorney general's office was concerned that some consumers did not understand that they would have to pay the cost of the videocassette or DVD if they failed to return movies to Blockbuster within a stated period of time.[50]

crisis management
the process of handling a high-impact event characterized by ambiguity and the need for swift action

It is critical for companies to manage crises effectively because research suggests that these events are a leading cause of organizational mortality. What follows are some key issues to consider in **crisis management,** the process of handling a high-impact event characterized by ambiguity and the need for swift action. In most cases, the crisis situation will not be handled in a completely effective or ineffective manner. Thus, a crisis usually leads to both success and failure outcomes for a business and its stakeholders and provides information for making improvements to future crisis management and social responsibility efforts.[51]

"The nature of crises requires a firm's leadership to communicate in an often stressful, emotional, uncertain, and demanding context."

Organizational crises are characterized by a threat to a company's high-priority goals, surprise to its membership, and stakeholder demands for a short response time. The nature of crises requires a firm's leadership to communicate in an often stressful, emotional, uncertain, and demanding context. Crises are very difficult on a company's stakeholders as well. For this reason, the firm's stakeholders, especially its employees, shareholders, customers, government regulators, competitors, creditors, and the media, will closely scrutinize communication after a crisis. Hence, a crisis has widespread implications not only for the organization but also for each group affected by the crisis.

To better understand how crises develop and move toward resolution, some researchers use a medical analogy. Using the analogy,

Figure 2.3 Crisis Management Process

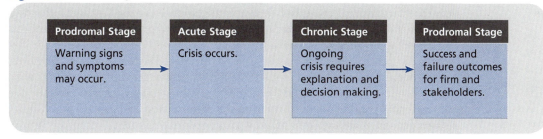

Prodromal Stage	Acute Stage	Chronic Stage	Prodromal Stage
Warning signs and symptoms may occur.	Crisis occurs.	Ongoing crisis requires explanation and decision making.	Success and failure outcomes for firm and stakeholders.

the organization proceeds through chronological stages similar to a person with an illness. The prodromal stage is a precrisis period during which warning signs may exist. Next is the acute stage, in which the actual crisis occurs. During the third (or chronic) stage, the business is required to sufficiently explain its actions to move to the final stage, crisis resolution. Figure 2.3 illustrates these stages. Although the stages are conceptually distinct, some crises happen so quickly and without warning that the organization may move from the prodromal to acute stage within minutes. Many organizations faced this situation after Hurricane Katrina crashed into New Orleans and the Mississippi Gulf Coast, disrupting all business and social activity for years.

One of the fundamental difficulties that a company faces is how to communicate effectively to stakeholders during and after a disaster. Once a crisis strikes, the firm's stakeholders need a quick response in the midst of the duress and confusion. They need information about how the company plans to resolve the crisis as well as what each constituent can do to mitigate its own negative effects. If a company is slow to respond, stakeholders may feel that the company does not care about their needs or is not concerned or remorseful, if the company is at fault, about the crisis. Furthermore, a delayed response may in fact increase the suffering of particular stakeholder groups. For instance, some stakeholders may take on considerable debt due to medical expenses as a result of the crisis. Therefore, a rapid response to stakeholders is central to any crisis resolution strategy so that these groups can plan their recovery.

Ironically, crisis events are often so chaotic that a company's leadership may not be certain of the cause of the situation before the media and other relevant groups demand a statement. Thus, it is not surprising for organizations to begin their crisis response with some degree of ambiguity in their statements. In fact, some crisis theorists advise companies to avoid too much detail in their initial response due to the embarrassment that results from changing positions later in the crisis when more information is available. Still, stakeholder groups want and, as a matter of safety in some cases, need access to whatever information the firm can share. Although tensions between the public's needs and the organization's fear of litigation can hamper an organization's willingness to communicate, the demand for information in such situations is unyielding.

Not only should the firm's leadership make a public statement quickly, but it is also necessary for the organization to communicate about specific issues to stakeholder groups. First, leadership should express concern and/or remorse for the event. Second, the organization should delineate guidelines regarding how it intends to address the crisis so that stakeholders can be confident that the situation will not escalate or recur. Finally, the company should provide explicit criteria to stakeholders regarding how each group will be compensated for any negative effects it experiences as a result of the crisis. Many companies, however, overlook these three essential conditions of crisis management. More often, they focus on minimizing harm to the organization's image, denying responsibility for the crisis, and shifting blame away from the organization and toward other stakeholder groups. Although this may be an appropriate strategy when the firm is not actually responsible, too often companies choose this course of action under the stress of the crisis when they are responsible or partially responsible for the crisis without expressing sufficient remorse for their involvement or concern for their stakeholders.

The varying communication needs and levels of concern of stakeholders during and after a crisis often hamper effective communication. The firm's leadership should try to communicate as much accurate information to these groups as possible to minimize their uncertainty. When a firm fails to do so, its credibility, legitimacy, and reputation in the eyes of stakeholders often suffer. Adding to the complexity of communication challenges, the needs of various stakeholder groups may conflict. For instance, the needs of customers who become ill as a result of a contaminated product and their desire to have medical bills paid may be at odds with the company's ability to bolster its stock price to satisfy shareholders. Some stakeholders will obviously have more opportunities than others to voice their concerns after a crisis. Victims and the general public rarely have an opportunity to meet with the organization's leadership after a crisis. Conversely, the organization's stockholders and employees will likely have a greater opportunity to express their views about the crisis and therefore may have their ideas accepted by management. Some researchers suggest that, due to this ability to communicate directly with leadership, internal stakeholder needs often take precedence over those of external stakeholders. Organizations have a responsibility to manage the competing interests of stakeholders to ensure that all stakeholder groups are treated fairly in the aftermath of a crisis. Responsible companies try to balance the needs of their stakeholders rather than favoring some groups over others. The Walt Disney Corporation experienced a potential crisis of public concern after an elderly woman died riding the Magic Kingdom's Pirates of the Caribbean and a four-year-old died after riding the EPCOT Resort's Mission: Space as well as a series of other incidents.[52] Since Disney is not directly regulated by the state of Florida, it released a written statement to the press and various stakeholders stating that its own engineers deemed the rides safe. At a very small cost, Disney's invitation to state inspectors to inspect its rides sent a message that the company was going beyond the minimum (legal) requirement in its response to recover ground in the perception crisis over ride safety.[53] Organizations that fail to accomplish this communication function risk alienating stakeholder groups and intensifying the negative media attention toward the company. For many reasons, including effective crisis management, organizations need to understand and pursue solid and mutually beneficial relationships with stakeholders.

DEVELOPMENT OF STAKEHOLDER RELATIONSHIPS

Relationships of any type, whether they involve family, friends, coworkers, or companies, are founded on principles of trust, commitment, and communication. They also are associated with a certain degree of time, interaction, and shared expectations. For instance, we do not normally speak of "having a relationship" with someone we have just met. We even differentiate between casual acquaintances, work colleagues, and close friends.

In business, the concept of relationships has gained much acceptance. Instead of just pursuing one-time transactions, companies are now searching for ways to develop long-term and collaborative relationships with their customers and business partners.[54] Many companies focus on relationships with suppliers, buyers, employees, and others directly involved in economic exchange. These relationships involve investments of several types. Some investments are tangible, such as buildings, equipment, new tools, and other elements dedicated to a particular relationship. For example, Hormel Foods implemented an Internet-based procurement system that allowed its suppliers to view the firm's production schedules and revise their own business operations accordingly.[55] Other investments are less tangible, such as the time, effort, trust, and commitment required to develop a relationship. Although Hormel's suppliers need the electronic infrastructure and employee knowledge to use the new procurement process, these suppliers must also trust that their relationship with Hormel is solid and will be worth these investments. Some suppliers may have concerns that their investment in Hormel's system may not be transferable to other business opportunities and partnerships. They may also have concerns about information privacy.

Whereas tangible investments are often customized for a specific business relationship, intangible efforts have a more lucid and permeable quality. Although social responsibility involves tangible activities and other communication signals, the key to good stakeholder relationships resides in trust, communication quality, and mutual respect. As a company strives to develop a dialog and a solid relationship with one stakeholder, investments and lessons learned through the process should add value to other stakeholder relationships. For example, Starbucks provides excellent benefits, including health care for part-time employees, and supports fair trade or a fair income for farmers growing its coffee.

> "Instead of just pursuing one-time transactions, companies are now searching for ways to develop long-term and collaborative relationships with their customers and business partners."

social capital
an asset that resides in relationships and is characterized by mutual goals and trust

These efforts result in **social capital**, an asset that resides in relationships and is characterized by mutual goals and trust.[56] Like financial and intellectual capital, social capital facilitates and smoothes internal and external transactions and processes. For example, social capital among companies in the chemical industry led to the development of Responsible Care, a progressive and voluntary program of environmental, health, and safety (EHS) standards. Several high-profile accidents had eroded chemical companies' social capital with their communities, the government, and other stakeholder groups. The Chemical Manufacturers Association implemented the program to promote stronger EHS performance and to "improve the legislative, regulatory, market, and public interest climate for the industry." Thus, Responsible Care was aimed at advancing internal company operations as well as various stakeholder relationships. The industry continues to update and refine the initiative.[57] Unlike financial and intellectual capital, however, social capital is not tangible or the obvious property of one organization. In this same regard, social responsibility is not compartmentalized or reserved for a few issues or stakeholders but should have the companywide strategic focus discussed in Chapter 1.

© AP Photo/Battle Creek Enquirer, John Grap

Two non-governmental organizations, Greenpeace and the Michigan Resistance Against Genetic Engineering, protest the use of genetically engineered foods outside of Kellogg's corporate headquarters

IMPLEMENTING A STAKEHOLDER PERSPECTIVE IN SOCIAL RESPONSIBILITY[58]

An organization that develops effective corporate governance and understands the importance of business ethics and social responsibility in achieving success should develop some processes for managing these important concerns. Although many different approaches exist, we provide some steps that have been found effective to utilize the stakeholder framework in managing responsibility and business ethics. The steps include: (1) assessing the corporate culture, (2) identifying stakeholder groups, (3) identifying stakeholder issues, (4) assessing the organization's commitment to social responsibility, (5) identifying resources and determining urgency, and (6) gaining stakeholder feedback. The importance of these steps is to include feedback from relevant stakeholders in formulating organizational strategy and implementation.

Step 1: Assessing the Corporate Culture

To enhance organizational fit, a social responsibility program must align with the corporate culture of the organization. The purpose of this first step is to identify the organizational mission, values, and norms that are likely to have implications for social responsibility. In particular, relevant existing values and norms are those that specify the stakeholder groups and stakeholder issues that are deemed most important by the organization. Very often, relevant organizational values and norms can be found in corporate documents such as the mission statement, annual reports, sales brochures, or websites. For example, Green Mountain Coffee is a pioneer in helping struggling coffee growers by paying them fair trade prices. The company also offers microloans to coffee-growing families to underwrite business ventures that diversify agricultural economies. It has been on the *Business Ethics* 100 Best Corporate Citizens since 2003 and climbed to the number one position in 2006.[59]

Step 2: Identifying Stakeholder Groups

In managing this stage, it is important to recognize stakeholder needs, wants, and desires. Many important issues gain visibility because key constituencies such as consumer groups, regulators, or the media express an interest. When agreement, collaboration, or even confrontations exist on an issue, there is a need for a decision-making process. A model of collaboration to overcome the adversarial approaches to problem solving has been suggested. Managers can identify relevant stakeholders that may be affected by or may influence the development of organizational policy.

Stakeholders have some level of power over a business because they are in the position to withhold, or at least threaten to withhold, organizational resources. Stakeholders have most power when their own survival is not really affected by the success of the organization and when they have access to vital organizational resources. For example, most consumers of shoes do not have a specific need to buy Nike shoes. Therefore, if they decide to boycott Nike, they have to endure only minor inconveniences. Nevertheless, their loyalty to Nike is vital to the continued success of the sport apparel giant. The proper assessment of the power held by a given stakeholder community also requires an evaluation of the extent to which that community can collaborate with others to pressure the firm.

Step 3: Identifying Stakeholder Issues

Together, steps 1 and 2 lead to the identification of the stakeholders who are both the most powerful and legitimate. The level of power and legitimacy determines the degree of urgency in addressing their needs. Step 3 consists then in understanding the nature of the main issues of concern to these stakeholders. Conditions for collaboration exist when problems are so complex that multiple stakeholders are required to resolve the issue and the weaknesses of adversarial approaches are understood.

For example, obesity in children is becoming an issue across groups and stakeholders. In the current Congress, there are fifty-five bills introduced that contain the word *obesity,* which is approaching the number containing *gun.*[60] According to a recent survey of readers in *The Wall Street Journal,* most people (60 percent) believed that consumers should bear the main burden of health-care costs. Only 28 percent believed the government should bear the burden, and a small 13 percent believed employers should foot the bill for rising costs associated with obesity and other problems.[61]

Step 4: Assessing the Organization's Commitment to Social Responsibility

Steps 1 through 3 consist of generating information about social responsibility among a variety of influencers in and around the organization. Step 4 brings these three first stages together to arrive at an understanding of social responsibility that specifically matches the organization of interest. This general definition will then be used to evaluate current practices and to select concrete social responsibility initiatives. Firms such as Starbucks have selected activities that address stakeholder concerns. Starbucks has formalized its initiatives in official documents such as annual reports, web pages, and company brochures. They have a website devoted to social responsibility. Starbucks is concerned with the environment and integrates policies and programs throughout all aspects of operations to minimize their environmental impact. They also have many community building programs that help them be good neighbors and contribute positively to the communities where their partners and customers live, work, and play.[62]

Step 5: Identifying Resources and Determining Urgency

The prioritization of stakeholders and issues along with the assessment of past performance provides for allocating resources. Two main criteria can be considered. First, the levels of financial and organizational investments required by different actions should be determined. A second criterion when prioritizing social responsibility challenges is urgency. When the challenge under consideration is viewed as significant and when stakeholder pressures on the issue could be expected, then the challenge can be treated as urgent. For example, Wal-Mart has been the focus of legislation in Maryland that forced the retailer to pay more for its employee health care. The legislation requires employers with more than 10,000 workers to spend at least 8 percent of their payroll on employee health care.[63] The legislation is now being considered by twenty-two other states. Wal-Mart recently offered to improve health-care benefits for its employees as a direct result of the pressure.[64]

Step 6: Gaining Stakeholder Feedback

Stakeholder feedback can be generated through a variety of means. First, stakeholders' general assessment of the firm and its practices can be obtained through satisfaction or reputation surveys. Second, to gauge stakeholders' perceptions of the firm's contributions to specific issues, stakeholder-generated media such as blogs, websites, podcasts, and newsletters can be assessed. Third, more formal research may be conducted using focus groups, observation, and surveys. Websites can be both positive and negative; for example, www.wakeupwalmart. com launched by the United Food and Commercial Workers union has over 115,000 members, and another group called Wal-Mart Watch is also gaining members. Both groups have articles and stories about the retail giant on their websites that do not flatter Wal-Mart. The pressure has forced the retail giant to listen to its consumers and change its ways. To counter the claims by these groups, Wal-Mart launched its own site, www.walmartfacts.com, to tell its side of the story.

In the process of developing stakeholder relationships, most strategies are focused on increasing the trust that a stakeholder has in a particular company. Of course, there is not a "one size fits all" approach for building and sustaining

Table 2.5 The Truth About Stakeholder Trust

Conventional Wisdom	Reality
To increase stakeholder trust, companies need to make their operations more transparent.	Transparency actually can diminish trust depending on what is disclosed. Transparency with respect to executive compensation, for example, might easily decrease trust if it reveals no apparent link between pay and performance.
Integrity is crucial for building trust.	Integrity is important, but stakeholders who engage with the company on a regular basis (many employees and customers, for example) must also feel that the organization cares about their personal well-being. Even well-meaning, ethical organizations can destroy trust if they are perceived as being fair but callous.
To engender trust, businesses must continually display competency in what they do.	Nobody trusts the incompetent, but people don't all demand the same kind of know-how. Employees and investors look most for managerial competence, whereas customers and suppliers are more concerned about technical proficiency.
When trust is compromised, a company should act quickly to remedy the situation with the stakeholder group that's been affected.	Managers first need to determine who all the relevant stakeholder groups are. Only then can they deploy a balanced approach to managing trust that takes into account the various concerns and interests of the different parties. Otherwise, an organization might find itself exacerbating one problem even as it solves another.
The desire to identify with the values of an organization is an important factor in building trust only for employees, regular customers, and others who have a close relationship with the company.	Identification (or value congruence) is important for all stakeholders. That is, not only employees and customers, but also suppliers, investors, and stakeholders of all types are interested in associating with organizations that they can identify with—and that they perceive match their values.

Source: Michael Pirson and Deepak Malhotra, "Unconventional Insights for Managing Stakeholder Trust," *Sloan Management Review* 49 (Summer 2008): 42–50.

trusting relationships with stakeholders. As we discussed earlier in the chapter, not all stakeholders engage with a company with the same level of intensity or locus of control, whether internal or external. For example, employees are highly engaged internal stakeholders while suppliers may be considered low-intensity external stakeholders. Depending on the specific issues at hand, historical interactions, relationships intensity, and other factors, managers must understand the relative importance of transparency, competence, benevolence, integrity, values, and other factors. [65] Table 2.5 explores both conventional wisdom and emerging insights on these factors.

LINK BETWEEN STAKEHOLDER RELATIONSHIPS AND SOCIAL RESPONSIBILITY

You may be wondering what motivations companies have for pursuing stakeholder relationships. As the previous section indicates, a great deal of time, effort, and commitment goes into the process of developing and implementing a stakeholder perspective. Some companies have been accused of "window dressing," or publicizing their stakeholder efforts without having a true commitment behind them. For example, The Body Shop, which has received much positive attention for its social responsibility efforts, has also been accused of selectively communicating information and hiding less favorable company issues.[66] Its latest values report communicates strongly held values that go to the core of the organization and permeate all of its practices. Previously, The Body Shop crafted reports for specific stakeholder groups, and The Body Shop was criticized in 2005 for returning to an all-in-one format no longer crafted for specific stakeholder groups.[67] As was discussed in Chapter 1, social responsibility is a relational approach and involves the views and stakes of a number of groups. Stakeholders are engaged in the relationships that both challenge and support a company's efforts. Thus, without a solid understanding of stakeholders and their interests, a firm may miss important trends and changes in its environment and not achieve strategic social responsibility.

Rather than holding all companies to one standard, our approach to evaluating performance and effectiveness resides in the specific expectations and actual results that develop between each organization and its stakeholders. Max Clarkson, an influential contributor to our understanding of stakeholders, sums up this view:

> *Performance is what counts. Performance can be measured and evaluated. Whether a corporation and its management are motivated by enlightened self-interest, common sense or high standards of ethical behavior cannot be determined by empirical methodologies available today. These are not questions that can be answered by economists, sociologists, psychologists, or any other kind of social scientist. They are interesting questions, but they are not relevant when it comes to evaluating a company's performance in managing its relationships with its stakeholder groups.*[68]

Table 2.6 The Reactive-Defensive-Accommodative-Proactive Scale

Rating	Strategy	Performance	Example
Reactive	Deny responsibility	Doing less than required	Exxon's refusal to continue oil spill clean-up after a certain date
Defensive	Admit responsibility, but fight it	Doing the least that is required	Valero Energy's claim that it meets federal regulations, and therefore community complaints are not legitimate
Accommodative	Accept responsibility	Doing all that is required	General Motors promise of job security if productivity gains were realized
Proactive	Anticipate responsibility	Doing more than is required	Xerox's sharing of product blueprints with suppliers and taking suggestions before production

Source: Max B. E. Clarkson, "A Stakeholder Framework for Analyzing and Evaluating Corporate Social Performance," *Academy of Management Review* 20 (January 1995): 92–117; I. M. Jawahar and Gary McLaughlin, "Toward a Descriptive Stakeholder Theory: An Organizational Life Cycle Approach," *Academy of Management Review* 26 (July 2001): 397–414.

Although critics and some researchers may seek answers and evidence as to the motivations of business for social responsibility, we are interested in what companies are actually doing that is positive, negative, or neutral for their stakeholders and their stakeholders' interests. The Reactive-Defensive-Accommodative-Proactive Scale (see Table 2.6) provides a method for assessing a company's strategy and performance with each stakeholder. This scale is based on a continuum of strategy options and performance outcomes with respect to stakeholders.[69] This evaluation can take place as stakeholder issues arise or are identified. Therefore, it is possible for one company to be rated at several different levels because of varying performance and transitions over time. For example, a poorly handled crisis situation may provide feedback for continuous improvement that creates more satisfactory performance in the future. Or a company may demonstrate a proactive stance toward employees yet be defensive with consumer activists.

The reactive approach involves denying responsibility and doing less than is required. This approach can be characterized as "fighting it all the way."[70] A firm that fails to

"Today, many organizations are giving money and other resources to community organizations as a way of demonstrating social responsibility."

THE STEALTH CORPORATE JET

"It has all the comfort of a regular jet, but it's invisible to shareholders."

Courtesy of CartoonStock.com

invest in safety and health measures for employees is denying its responsibilities. An organization with a defensive strategy acknowledges reluctantly and partially the responsibility issues that may be raised by its stakeholders. A firm in this category fulfills basic legal obligations and demonstrates the minimal responsibility discussed in Chapter 1. With an accommodative strategy, a company attempts to satisfy stakeholder demands by doing all that is required and may be seen as progressive because it is obviously open to this expanded model of business relationships.[71] Today, many organizations are giving money and other resources to community orga-

nizations as a way of demonstrating social responsibility. Finally, the proactive approach not only accepts but also anticipates stakeholder interests. In this case, a company sincerely aligns legitimate stakeholder views with its responsibilities and will do more than is required to meet them.[72] Hoechst, a German life sciences company now part of Aventis, gradually assumed the proactive orientation with the communities in which it operates. The initiation of a community discussion group led to information sharing and trust building and helped transform Hoechst into a society-driven company.[73]

The Reactive-Defensive-Accommodative-Proactive Scale is useful because it evaluates real practice and allows an organization to see its strengths and weaknesses within each stakeholder relationship. SABMiller, the second largest brewer in the world, uses a risk assessment program to understand the stakeholders and issues that may pose a potential risk to its reputation. These risks are prioritized, planned for, monitored, and, if necessary, responded to if SABMiller cannot predict, preempt, or avoid the concern.[74] Results from a stakeholder assessment like the one at SABMiller should be included in the **social audit**, which assesses and reports a firm's performance in adopting a strategic focus for fulfilling the economic, legal, ethical, and philanthropic social responsibilities expected of it by its stakeholders. This book's appendix takes an extensive look at this audit. Because stakeholders are so important to the concept of social responsibility, as well as to business success, Chapters 3 through 10 are devoted to exploring significant stakeholder relationships and issues.

social audit
the process of assessing and reporting a firm's performance in adopting a strategic focus for fulfilling the economic, legal, ethical, and philanthropic social responsibilities expected of it by its stakeholders

SUMMARY

Stakeholders refer to those people and groups who have a "stake" in some aspect of a company's products, operations, markets, industry, or outcomes. The relationship between organizations and their stakeholders is a two-way street.

The historical assumption that the key objective of business is profit maximization led to the belief that business is accountable primarily to investors and others involved in the market and economic aspects of the organization. In the latter half of the twentieth century, perceptions of business accountability evolved to include both market constituencies that are directly involved with and affected by the business purpose (e.g., investors, employees, customers, and other business partners) and nonmarket constituencies that are not always directly tied to issues of profitability and performance (e.g., the general community, media, government, and special-interest groups).

In the stakeholder model, relationships, investors, employees, and suppliers provide inputs for a company to benefit stakeholders. This approach assumes a relatively mechanistic, simplistic, and nonstakeholder view of business. The stakeholder model assumes a two-way relationship between the firm and a host of stakeholders. This approach recognizes additional stakeholders and acknowledges the two-way dialog and effects that exist with a firm's internal and external environment.

Primary stakeholders are fundamental to a company's operations and survival and include shareholders and investors, employees, customers, suppliers, and public stakeholders, such as government and the community. Secondary stakeholders influence and/or are affected by the company but are neither engaged in transactions with the firm nor essential for its survival.

As more firms conduct business overseas, they encounter the complexity of stakeholder issues and relationships in tandem with other business operations and decisions. Although general awareness of the concept of stakeholders is relatively high around the world, the importance of stakeholders varies from country to country.

A stakeholder has power to the extent that it can gain access to coercive, utilitarian, or symbolic means to impose or communicate its views to the organization. Such power may be coercive, utilitarian, or symbolic. Legitimacy is the perception or belief that a stakeholder's actions are proper, desirable, or appropriate within a given context. Stakeholders exercise greater pressures on managers and organizations when they stress the urgency of their claims. These attributes can change over time and context.

The degree to which a firm understands and addresses stakeholder demands can be referred to as a stakeholder orientation. This orientation comprises three sets of activities: (1) the organization-wide generation of data about stakeholder groups and assessment of the firm's effects on these groups, (2) the distribution of this information throughout the firm, and (3) the organization's responsiveness as a whole to this intelligence.

Reputation management is the process of building and sustaining a company's good name and generating positive feedback from stakeholders. The process of reputation management involves the interaction of organizational identity (how the firm wants to be viewed), organizational image (how stakeholders initially perceive the firm), organizational performance (actual interaction between the company and stakeholders), and organizational reputation (the collective view of stakeholders after interactions with the company). Stakeholders will reassess their views of the company on the basis of how the company has actually performed.

Crisis management is the process of handling a high-impact event characterized by ambiguity and the need for swift action. Some researchers describe an
organization's progress through a prodromal, or precrisis, stage to the acute stage,
chronic stage, and finally, crisis resolution. Stakeholders need a quick response
with information about how the company plans to resolve the crisis, as well as
what they can do to mitigate negative effects to themselves. It is also necessary
to communicate specific issues to stakeholder groups, including remorse for the
event, guidelines as to how the organization is going to address the crisis, and criteria regarding how stakeholder groups will be compensated for negative effects.

Companies are searching for ways to develop long-term, collaborative relationships with their stakeholders. These relationships involve both tangible and
intangible investments. Investments and lessons learned through the process of
developing a dialog and relationship with one stakeholder should add value to
other stakeholder relationships. These efforts result in social capital, an asset
that resides in relationships and is characterized by mutual goals and trust.

The first step in developing stakeholder relationships is to acknowledge
and actively monitor the concerns of all legitimate stakeholders. A firm should
adopt processes and modes of behavior that are sensitive to the concerns and
capabilities of each stakeholder. Information should be communicated consistently across all stakeholders. A firm should be willing to acknowledge
and openly address potential conflicts. Investments in education, training,
and information will improve employees' understanding of and relationships
with stakeholders. Relationships with stakeholders need to be periodically
assessed through both formal and informal means. Sharing feedback with
stakeholders helps establish the two-way dialog that characterizes the stakeholder model.

An organization that develops effective corporate governance and understands the importance of business ethics and social responsibility in achieving
success should develop some processes for managing these important concerns.
Although there are many different approaches, we provide some steps that have
been found effective to utilize the stakeholder framework in managing responsibility and business ethics. The steps include (1) assessing the corporate culture,
(2) identifying stakeholder groups, (3) identifying stakeholder issues, (4) assessing
the organization's commitment to social responsibility, (5) identifying resources
and determining urgency, and (6) gaining stakeholder feedback. The importance
of these steps is to include feedback from relevant stakeholders in formulating
organizational strategy and implementation.

The Reactive-Defensive-Accommodative-Proactive Scale provides a method
for assessing a company's strategy and performance with one stakeholder. The
reactive approach involves denying responsibility and doing less than is required.
The defensive approach acknowledges only reluctantly and partially the responsibility issues that may be raised by the firm's stakeholders. The accommodative
strategy attempts to satisfy stakeholder demands. The proactive approach accepts
and anticipates stakeholder interests. Results from this stakeholder assessment
should be included in the social audit, which assesses and reports a firm's performance in fulfilling the economic, legal, ethical, and philanthropic social
responsibilities expected of it by its stakeholders.

RESPONSIBLE BUSINESS DEBATE

Prioritizing Stakeholder Concerns

ISSUE: A stakeholder or shareholder orientation—whose company is it?

For decades, the question of "Whose company is it?" has permeated discussions of the role of business in society. Famously, some economists have long argued for the primacy of profit, noting that without economic stability and prospects for growth, a firm cannot continue to pay employees, buy from suppliers, pay taxes, and meet other economic and legal expectations. Adam Smith made this point succinctly, "It is not from the benevolence of the butcher, the brewer, or the baker that we expect our dinner, but from their regard to their own interest." In the United States and United Kingdom, the belief is that shareholders are the owners of firms and managers have a fiduciary responsibility to act in the interests of shareholders. The shareholder orientation is dominant in most business and investment communities, although this mindset is shifting.

In other countries, a stakeholder, not shareholder, orientation is the norm. Several European countries operate under a system of "co-determination," where both employees and shareholders in large companies hold seats on the oversight board and are required to consider multiple interests in decision making. In Denmark, employees in firms with more than thirty-five workers elect one-third of the firm's board

members, with a minimum of two. In Sweden, companies with more than twenty-five employees have two labor representatives appointed to the board. In large German corporations, employees and shareholders hold an equal number of seats. Finally, in Japan, executives can be liable for managerial negligence, but do not have fiduciary duties to shareholders and are expected to meet an array of stakeholder expectations.

There Are Two Sides to Every Issue:

1. Defend the belief that companies exist first and foremost for the benefit of shareholders and investors. For what reasons should the maximization of shareholder value be the accepted corporate paradigm?

2. Defend the belief that companies, in addition to shareholders and investors, have equally important stakeholders, such as employees, customers, and suppliers. What about responsibilities to the community, society, and the natural environment?

Sources: "Whose Company Is It? New Insights into the Debate over Shareholders vs. Stakeholders," http://knowledge.wharton.upenn.edu/article.cfm?articleid=1826, accessed May 17, 2009; Tibor R. Machan, "Stakeholder vs. Shareholder Theory of the Ethics of Corporate Management," *International Journal of Economics and Business Research* 1 (2009): 12–20.

KEY TERMS

primary stakeholders (p. 51)
secondary stakeholders (p. 51)
stakeholder interaction model (p. 53)
stakeholder orientation (p. 53)
power (p. 57)
legitimacy (p. 58)

urgency (p. 58)
reputation management (p. 60)
crisis management (p. 66)
social capital (p. 69)
social audit (p. 76)

DISCUSSION QUESTIONS

1. Define *stakeholder* in your own terms. Compare your definition with the definition used in this chapter.

2. What is the difference between primary and secondary stakeholders? Why is it important for companies to make this distinction?

3. How do legitimacy, urgency, and power attributes positively and negatively affect a stakeholder's ability to develop relationships with organizations?

4. What is reputation management? Explain why companies are concerned about their reputation and its effects on stakeholders. What are the four elements of reputation management? Why is it important to manage these elements?

5. Define *crisis management*. What should a company facing a crisis do to satisfy its stakeholders and protect its reputation?

6. Describe the process of developing stakeholder relationships. What parts of the process seem most important? What parts seem most difficult?

7. How can a stakeholder orientation be implemented to improve social responsibility?

8. What are the differences between the reactive, defensive, accommodative, and proactive approaches to stakeholder relationships?

EXPERIENTIAL EXERCISE

Choose two companies in different industries and visit their respective websites. Peruse these sites for information that is directed at three company stakeholders: employees, customers, and the media. For example, a company that places its annual reports online may be appealing primarily to the interests of investors. Make a list of the types of information that are on the site and indicate how the information might be used and perceived by these three stakeholder groups. What differences and similarities did you find between the two companies?

WHAT WOULD YOU DO?

Literally hundreds of buildings dotted the ground below and the thousands of cars on highways looked like ants on a mission. The jet airliner made its way to the Bangkok International Airport and eased into the humid afternoon. The group of four passed through customs control and looked for the limousine provided by Suvar Corporation, their Thai liaison in this new business venture. Representing Global Amusements were the vice president of corporate development, director of Asian operations, vice president of global relations, and director of governmental relations for Southeast Asia.

Global Amusements, headquartered in London, was considering the development of a Thai cultural amusement center on the island of Phuket. Phuket is a tourist destination known for its stunning beaches, fine resorts, and famous

Thai hospitality. Both Global Amusements and Suvar Corporation believed Phuket was a great candidate for a new project. The amusement center would focus on the history of Thailand and include a variety of live performances, rides, exhibits, and restaurants. Domestic and international travelers who visited Phuket would be the primary target market.

Global Amusements had been in business for nearly twenty years and currently used a joint venture approach in establishing new properties. Suvar was its Thai partner, and the two firms had been successful two years ago in developing a water amusement park outside Bangkok. Phuket could hold much promise, but there were likely to be concerns about the potential destruction of its beauty and the exploitation of this well-preserved island and cultural reserve.

Following a day to adjust to the time zone and refine the strategy for the visit, the next three days would be spent in Bangkok, meeting with various company and governmental officials who had a stake in the proposed amusement facility. After a short flight to Phuket, the group would be the guest of the Southern Office of the Tourism Authority of Thailand for nearly a week. This part of the trip would involve visits to possible sites as well as meetings with island government officials and local interest groups.

After arriving at the hotel, the four employees of Global Amusement agreed to meet later that evening to discuss their strategy for the visit. One of their main concerns was the development of an effective stakeholder analysis. Each member of the group was asked to bring a list of primary and secondary stakeholders and indicate the various concerns or "stakes" that each might have with the proposed project. What would you do?

Corporate Governance

Chapter Objectives

- To define corporate governance

- To describe the history and practice of corporate governance

- To examine key issues to consider in designing corporate governance systems

- To describe the application of corporate governance principles around the world

- To provide information on the future of corporate governance

Chapter Outline

Corporate Governance Defined

History of Corporate Governance

Corporate Governance and Social Responsibility

Issues in Corporate Governance Systems

Corporate Governance Around the World

Future of Corporate Governance

© Tom Tomczyk

Fannie Mae and Freddie Mac: Poor Decisions Contributed to Crisis

Fannie Mae and Freddie Mac will go down in history as major players in the mortgage crisis. Fannie Mae is a stockholder-owned corporation created to purchase and securitize mortgages so funds are available to institutions that lend money to homebuyers. Freddie Mac buys and sells mortgages and resells them as mortgage-backed securities. This increases the money available for mortgage lending and home purchases. Both companies were encouraged by President Clinton and Congress to buy loans from banks that made higher-interest mortgage loans to low-income families (known as subprime loans). Yet with a lack of proper oversight, the companies mismanaged the situation and the government had to intervene during the 2008 mortgage crisis.

Before 2008, Fannie Mae and Freddie Mac guaranteed about half of the $12 trillion in the mortgage market. Yet with the economy in decline homeowners increasingly could not afford the mortgage payments on their houses. The shares of Fannie and Freddie plummeted as more houses were foreclosed on and fewer people were in the market to buy.

As early as 1999, the *New York Times* predicted that giving out subprime loans could cause trouble during an economic downturn, requiring government intervention. Yet the companies appeared to ignore these warnings. They donated large amounts to lawmakers sitting on committees that regulated their industry; and as late as 2007, the government passed new rules saying that Fannie Mae and Freddie Mac could buy $200 billion more in subprime loans. The prophetic warnings of critics came true during the next economic downturn, forcing the companies to regret their poor decisions.

However, Fannie Mae's situation went beyond bad decision making. The company was also under investigation for accounting errors. Civil charges had already been filed against Fannie Mae's CEO, CFO, and the former controller, who allegedly manipulated earnings to increase their bonuses.

Similarly, in 2003 Freddie Mac announced that it had underreported earnings by over $5 billion, which was the largest corporate restatement in financial history. Three years later, it was forced to pay $3.8 million after it was revealed the company had been making illegal campaign contributions between 2000 and 2003.

In 2008, James Lockhart of the Federal Housing Finance Agency (FHFA) announced that Fannie Mae and Freddie Mac would be put into a conservatorship of the FHFA, using funds from the U.S. Treasury, as part of the government efforts to stem the hemorrhaging in the mortgage industry. CEOs Daniel Mudd and Ryan Syron were investigated for allegedly lying to investors about earnings, portraying Fannie Mae and Freddie Mac as being more stable than they were. Bad decisions and managerial misconduct clearly contributed to these companies' downfall and to the financial crisis of 2008–2009.[1]

Business decisions today are increasingly placed under a microscope by stakeholders and the media, especially those made by high-level personnel in publicly held corporations. Stakeholders are demanding greater transparency in business, meaning that company motives and actions must be clear, open for discussion, and subject to scrutiny. Although some organizations have operated fairly independently in the past, recent scandals and the associated focus on the role of business in society have highlighted a need for systems that take into account the goals and expectations of various stakeholders. To respond to these pressures, businesses must effectively implement policies that provide strategic guidance on appropriate courses of action. This focus is part of corporate governance, the system of checks and balances that ensures that organizations are fulfilling the goals of social responsibility.

Governance procedures and policies are typically discussed in the context of publicly traded firms, especially as they relate to corporations' responsibilities to investors.[2] However, the trend is toward discussing governance within many industry sectors, including nonprofits, small businesses, and family-owned enterprises. We believe governance deserves broader consideration because there is evidence of a link between good governance and strong social responsibility. Corporate governance and accountability are key drivers of change for business in the twenty-first century. It is abundantly clear, to experts and nonexperts alike, that corporate governance is in need of immediate attention by a wide range of firms and stakeholders. The corporate scandals at firms such as AIG, Countrywide Financial, and Lehman Brothers represented a fundamental breakdown in basic principles of the capitalist system. Investors and other stakeholders must be able to trust management while boards of directors oversee managerial decisions.

Late 2008 and 2009 marked the beginning of a crisis of confidence in global business, particularly in the financial industry. Some of the nation's oldest and most respected financial institutions teetered on the brink of failure and were either bailed out or acquired by other firms. The 2008–2009 global recession was caused in part by a failure of the financial industry to take appropriate responsibility for its decision to utilize risky and complex financial instruments. Loopholes in regulation and the failures of regulators were exploited. Corporate cultures were built on rewards for taking risks rather than rewards for creating value for stakeholders. The governance systems at many of these companies did not take into account the risks or how to provide adequate oversight to prevent misconduct. In some cases, managers looked for loopholes in the laws or in unregulated areas such as derivatives. Ethical decisions were based more on what is legal rather than what was the right thing to do.

Unfortunately, most stakeholders, including the public, regulators, and the mass media, do not always understand the nature of the financial risks taken on by banks and other institutions to generate profits. The intangible nature of financial products makes it difficult to understand complex financial transactions. Problems in the subprime mortgage market, which deals with giving higher-rate mortgages to people who do not qualify for regular credit, sounded the alarm in the most recent economic downturn.

In this chapter, we define corporate governance and integrate the concept with the other elements of social responsibility. Then, we examine the corporate governance framework used in this book. Next, we trace the evolution of corporate governance and provide information on the status of corporate governance systems in several countries. We look at the history of corporate governance and the relationship of corporate governance to social responsibility. We also examine primary issues that should be considered in the development and improvement of corporate governance systems, including the roles of boards of directors, shareholders and investors, internal control and risk management, and executive compensation. Finally, we consider the future of corporate governance and indicate how strong governance is tied to corporate performance and economic growth. Our approach in this chapter is to demonstrate that corporate governance is a fundamental aspect of social responsibility.

CORPORATE GOVERNANCE DEFINED

In a general sense, the term *governance* relates to the exercise of oversight, control, and authority. For example, most institutions, governments, and businesses are organized so that oversight, control, and authority are clearly delineated. These organizations usually have an owner, president, chief executive officer (CEO), or board of directors that serves as the ultimate authority on decisions and actions. Nonprofit organizations, such as homeowners associations, have a president and board of directors to make decisions in the interest of a community of homeowners. A clear delineation of power and accountability helps stakeholders understand why and how the organization chooses and achieves its goals. This delineation also demonstrates who bears the ultimate risk for organizational decisions. Sarbanes-Oxley and the Federal Sentencing Guidelines put responsibility on top officers and the board of directors.

Although many companies have adopted decentralized decision making, empowerment, team projects, and less hierarchical structures, governance remains a required mechanism for ensuring continued growth, change, and accountability to regulatory authorities. Even if a company has adopted a consensus approach for its operations, there has to be authority for delegating tasks, making tough and controversial decisions, and balancing power throughout the organization. Governance also provides oversight to uncover and address mistakes, risks, and misconduct. Consider the failure of boards at Enron, AIG, and Tyco to address risks and provide internal controls to prevent misconduct.

We define **corporate governance** as the formal system of oversight, accountability, and control for organizational decisions and resources. Oversight relates to a system of checks and balances that limit employees' and managers' opportunities to deviate from policies and codes of conduct. Accountability relates to how well the content of workplace decisions is aligned with a firm's stated strategic direction. Control involves the process of auditing and improving organizational decisions and actions. The philosophy that is embraced by a board or firm regarding oversight, accountability, and control directly affects how corporate governance works.

corporate governance
the formal system of oversight, accountability, and control for organizational decisions and resources

"The philosophy that is embraced by a board or firm regarding oversight, accountability, and control directly affects how corporate governance works."

Corporate Governance Framework

The majority of businesses and many courses taught in colleges of business operate under the belief that the purpose of business is to maximize profits for shareholders. In 1919, the Michigan Supreme Court in the case of *Dodge v. Ford Motor Co.*[3] ruled that a business exists for the profit of shareholders, and the board of directors should focus on that objective. On the other hand, the stakeholder model places the board of directors in the central position to balance the interests and conflicts of the various constituencies. External control of the corporation includes government regulation, but also includes key stakeholders such as employees, consumers, and communities, who exert pressures for responsible conduct. Many of the obligations to balance stakeholder interest have been institutionalized in legislation that provides incentives for responsible conduct. The Federal Sentencing Guidelines for Organizations (FSGO) provides incentives for developing an ethical culture and efforts to prevent misconduct. At the heart of the FSGO is the carrot-and-stick approach: By taking preventive action against misconduct, a company may avoid onerous penalties should a violation occur. Sarbanes-Oxley legislation holds top officers and the board of directors legally responsible for accurate financial reporting.

Today, the failure to balance stakeholder interests can result in a failure to maximize shareholders' wealth. General Motors and Chrysler failed to understand customer needs, employee reactions to downsizing, and government regulatory issues. This resulted in both companies failing to achieve shareholder goals. Most firms are moving more toward a balanced stakeholder model, as they see that this approach will sustain the relationships necessary for long-run success.

Both directors and officers of corporations are fiduciaries for the shareholders. Fiduciaries are persons placed in positions of trust who use due care and loyalty in acting on behalf of the best interests of the organization. There is a duty of care, also called a *duty of diligence,* to make informed and prudent decisions.[4] Directors have an obligation to avoid ethical misconduct in their role and to provide leadership in decisions to prevent ethical misconduct in the organization. Directors are not held responsible for negative outcomes if they are informed and diligent in their decision making. Ford's directors can be held responsible for the accuracy of financial reporting, however. Manufacturing cars that lose market share is a serious concern, although it is not a legal issue. This means directors have an obligation to request information and research, use accountants and attorneys, and obtain the services of consultants in matters where they need assistance or advice.

The duty of loyalty means that all decisions should be in the interests of the corporation and its stakeholders. Conflicts of interest exist when a director uses the position to obtain personal gain, usually at the expense of the organization. For example, before the Sarbanes-Oxley Act, directors could give themselves and officers interest-free loans. Scandals at Tyco, Kmart, and WorldCom were all associated with officers receiving personal loans that damaged the corporation. More recently, Texas financier Allen Stanford was also accused of using his banks to give himself over $1.6 million in personal loans.[5] Officer compensation packages challenge directors, especially those on the board and not independent. Directors have an opportunity to vote for others' compensation in return for their own increased compensation. Opportunities to know about the investments, business ventures, and stock market information create issues that could violate the duty of loyalty. Insider trading of a firm's stock is illegal and and violations can result in serious punishment. Former Countrywide Financial CEO Angelo Mozilo was accused of insider trading after emails came to light that showed that he was aware of the riskiness of subprime mortgages granted by his company, even as he was publicly extolling Countrywide's high standards.[6]

The ethical and legal obligations of directors and officers interface with their fiduciary relationships to the company. Ethical values should guide decisions and buffer the possibility of illegal conduct. With increased pressure on directors to provide oversight for organizational ethics, there is a trend toward director training to increase their competence in ethics program development as well as other areas, such as accounting.

Corporate governance establishes fundamental systems and processes for oversight, accountability, and control. This requires investigating, disciplining, and planning for recovery and continuous improvement. Effective corporate governance creates compliance and values so that employees feel that integrity is at the core of competitiveness.[7] Even if a company has adopted a consensus approach to decision making, there should be oversight and authority for delegating tasks, making difficult and sometimes controversial decisions, balancing power throughout the firm, and maintaining social responsibility. Governance also provides mechanisms for identifying risks and planning for recovery when mistakes or problems occur.

The development of stakeholder orientation should interface with the corporation's governance structure. Corporate governance is also part of a firm's corporate culture that establishes the integrity of all relationships. A governance system that does not provide checks and balances creates opportunities for top managers to put their own self-interests before those of important stakeholders. Luxury retailer Saks Inc. voted to hold annual board member elections, as opposed to every three years, and that directors must receive a majority of votes to win. The change is part of an effort to improve accountability at the company, which, along with many other retailers, suffered a serious decline in share prices over the course of 2008 and 2009.[8]

Concerns about the need for greater corporate governance are not limited to the United States. Reforms in governance structures and issues are occurring all over the world.[9] In many nations, companies are being pressured to implement

© Lee Jae-Won/Reuters/Landov

Samsung Vice-Chairman and CEO maintains a commitment to corporate governance

stronger corporate governance mechanisms by international investors; by the process of becoming privatized after years of unaccountability as state companies; or by the desire to imitate successful governance movements in the United States, Japan, and the European Union.[10] As the business world becomes more global, standardization of governance becomes important in order for multinational and international companies to maintain standards and a level of control.

Table 3.1 lists examples of major corporate governance issues. These issues normally involve strategic-level decisions and actions taken by boards of directors, business owners, top executives, and other managers with high levels of authority and accountability. Although these people have often been relatively free from scrutiny, changes in technology, consumer activism, government attention, recent ethical scandals, and other factors have brought new attention to such issues as transparency, executive pay, risk and control, resource accountability, strategic direction, stockholder rights, and other decisions made for the organization.

Table 3.1 Corporate Governance Issues

Shareholder rights
Executive compensation
Composition and structure of the board of directors
Auditing and control
Risk management
CEO selection and termination decisions
Integrity of financial reporting
Stakeholder participation and input into decisions
Compliance with corporate governance reform
Role of the CEO in board decisions
Organizational ethics programs

HISTORY OF CORPORATE GOVERNANCE

In the United States, a discussion of corporate governance draws on many parallels with the goals and values held by the U.S. Founding Fathers.[11] As we mentioned earlier in the chapter, governance involves a system of checks and balances, a concept associated with the distribution of power within the executive, judiciary, and legislative branches of the U.S. government. The

"Reforms in governance structures and issues are occurring all over the world."

U.S. Constitution and other documents have a strong focus on accountability, individual rights, and the representation of broad interests in decision making and resource allocation.

In the late 1800s and early 1900s, corporations were headed by such familiar names as Carnegie, DuPont, and Rockefeller. These "captains of industry" had ownership investment and managerial control over their businesses. Thus, there was less reason to talk about corporate governance because the owner of the firm was the same individual who made strategic decisions about the business. The owner primarily bore the consequences—positive or negative—of decisions. During the twentieth century, however, an increasing number of public companies and investors brought about a shift in the separation of ownership and control. By the 1930s, corporate ownership was dispersed across a large number of individuals. This raised new questions about control and accountability for organizational resources and decisions.

One of the first known anecdotes that helped shape our current understanding of accountability and control in business occurred in the 1930s. In 1932, Lewis Gilbert, a stockholder in New York's Consolidated Gas Company, found his questions repeatedly ignored at the firm's annual shareholders' meeting. Gilbert and his brother took the problem to the federal government and pushed for reform, which led the creation of the U.S. Securities and Exchange Commission (SEC), which requires corporations to allow shareholder resolutions to be brought to a vote of all stockholders. Because of the Gilbert brothers' activism, the SEC formalized the process by which executives and boards of directors respond to the concerns and questions of investors.[12]

Since the mid-1900s, the approach to corporate governance has involved a legal discussion of principals and agents to the business relationship. Essentially, owners are "principals" who hire "agents," the executives, to run the business. A key goal of businesses is to align the interests of principals and agents so that organizational value and viability are maintained. Achieving this balance has been difficult, as evidenced by these business terms coined by media—*junk bonds, empire building, golden parachute,* and *merger madness*—all of which have negative connotations. In these cases, the long-term value and competitive stance of organizations were traded for short-term financial gains or rewards. The results of this short-term view included workforce reduction, closed manufacturing plants, struggling communities, and a generally negative perception of corporate leadership. In our philosophy of social responsibility, these long-term effects should be considered alongside decisions designed to generate short-run gains in financial performance.

The Sarbanes-Oxley Act provided the most significant piece of corporate governance reform since the 1930s. Under these rules, both CEOs and CFOs are required to certify that their quarterly and annual reports accurately reflect performance and comply with requirements of the SEC. Among other changes, the act also required more independence of boards of directors, protected whistle-blowers, and established a Public Company Accounting Oversight Board. The New York Stock Exchange (NYSE) and NASDAQ also overhauled the governance standards required for listed firms. Business ethics, director qualifications, unique concerns of foreign firms, loans to officers and directors, internal auditing, and many other issues were part of the NYSE and NASDAQ reforms.[13]

The 2008–2009 Financial Meltdown

The U.S. financial system collapsed in late 2008. The cause was pervasive use of instruments like credit default swaps, risky debt like subprime lending, and corruption in major corporations. The government was forced to step in and bail out many financial companies. Later on, because of the weak financial system and reduced consumption, the government also had to step in to help major automotive companies GM and Chrysler. The U.S. government is now a majority shareholder in GM, an unprecedented move. Not since the Great Depression and President Franklin Delano Roosevelt has the United States seen such widespread government intervention and regulation—something that most deem necessary, but is nevertheless worrisome to free market capitalists. The basic assumptions of capitalism are under debate as countries around the world work to stabilize markets and question those that have managed the money of individual corporations and nonprofits. The financial crisis caused many to question government institutions that provide oversight and regulation. As changes are made, there is a need to address issues related to law, ethics, and the required level of compliance necessary for government and business to serve the public interest.

Financial Crisis and Corporate Governance Reforms

In response to the financial crisis and recession, President Obama very quickly began to work on legislation that would reform corporate governance and provide additional oversight. The federal government has become a "reluctant shareholder" to a degree not seen since the 1930s in the likes of General Motors and AIG, among others, as the giant corportions seek to regain financial liquidity and competitiveness. Previously loosely regulated areas such as hedge funds and brokers are facing new laws that will constrain their behavior. For example, President Obama's regulatory policy requires brokers to put their clients' interests ahead of their own.[14] For firms that received government rescue funds under TARP, the government became a shareholder and helped to select new members of the board of directors. AIG, for example, was one of the largest insurance companies in the world. It suffered a liquidity crisis and received over $180 billion from the government in exchange for stock warrants that gave 80-percent ownership to the U.S. Federal Reserve Bank. Most of the nation's top banks suddenly became partners with the federal government, and the government became involved in corporate governance. All firms that received TARP bailout money must pay back that money before they can return to full control of their firms.

The lack of effective control and accountability mechanisms prompted a strong interest in corporate governance. Beyond the legal issues associated with governance, there has also been interest in the board's role in social responsibility and stakeholder engagement. Table 3.2 provides *Fortune*'s assessment of the best and worst companies for social responsibility. The board of directors should provide leadership for social responsibility initiatives. The ten worst firms should examine their corporate governance, board of directors' leadership, and the cause of their low rating. It is apparent that some boards have been assuming greater responsibility for strategic decisions and have decided to focus on building more effective social responsibility, as indicated by the ten best companies in Table 3.2.

> **"The board of directors should provide leadership for social responsibility initiatives."**

Table 3.2 *Fortune*'s Best and Worst Companies for Social Responsibility

Best Companies	Worst Companies
Anheuser-Busch	Circuit City Stores
Marriot International	Family Dollar Stores
Integrys Energy Group	Dillards
Walt Disney	Sears Holdings
Herman Miller	Tribune
Edison	Hon Hai Precision Industry
Starbucks	Fiat
Steelcase	Pemex
Union Pacific	Surgutneftegas
Fortune Brands	Huawei Technologies

Source: "America's Most Admired Companies 2009: The Best and Worst Companies for Social Responsibility," *Fortune*, March 16, 2009, http://money.cnn.com/magazines/fortune/mostadmired/2009/best_worst/best4.html, accessed June 26, 2009.

CORPORATE GOVERNANCE AND SOCIAL RESPONSIBILITY

Corporate social responsibility can be a difficult concept to define. While there is broad agreement among professionals, academics, and policy makers that being socially responsible does pay, corporate social responsibility always involves trade-offs, and most businesses have yet to formulate an idea of what social responsibility really entails for their organization.[15] Interpreted narrowly, a company can consider itself socially responsible if it generates returns for shareholders and provides jobs for employees (called the *shareholder* model). A broad definition of social responsibility interprets the corporation as a vehicle for stakeholders and for public policy (called the *stakeholder* model). A company that takes the latter view would be more concerned with the public good as well as with profitability and shareholder return. Because most firms have so many potential stakeholders, a key to developing a socially responsible agenda involves determining which of these groups are most important for your business. Social responsibility should seek to help a firm's principle stakeholders. For example, a line of high-end organic soaps might seek to source its ingredients from sustainable sources, avoid products that have been tested on animals, and to hire workers at living wages.

To understand the role of corporate governance in business today, it is also important to consider how it relates to fundamental beliefs about the purpose of business organizations. Some people believe that as long as a company is maximizing shareholder wealth and profitability, it is fulfilling its core responsibility. Although this must be accomplished in accordance with legal and ethical standards, the primary focus is on the economic dimension of social responsibility. Thus, this belief places the philanthropic dimension beyond the scope of business. Other people, however, take the view that a business is an important member, or citizen, of society and must assume broad responsibilities. This view assumes that business performance is reflexive, meaning it both affects and is influenced by internal and external factors. In this case, performance is often considered from a financial, social, and ethical perspective. From these assumptions, we can derive two major conceptualizations of corporate governance: the shareholder model and the stakeholder model.

shareholder model of corporate governance
model that bases management decisions toward what is in the best interests of investors; founded in classic economic precepts, including the maximization of wealth for investors and owners

The **shareholder model of corporate governance** is founded in classic economic precepts, including the maximization of wealth for investors and owners. For publicly traded firms, corporate governance focuses on developing and improving the formal system of performance accountability between top management and the firms' shareholders.[16] Thus, the shareholder orientation should drive management decisions toward what is in the best interests of investors. Underlying these decisions is a classic agency problem, where ownership (i.e., investors) and control (i.e., managers) are separate. Managers act as agents for investors and their primary goal is to generate value for shareholders. However, investors and managers are distinct parties with unique insights, goals, and values with respect to the business. Managers, for example, may have motivations beyond shareholder value, such as market share, personal compensation, or attachment to particular products and projects. Because of these potential differences, corporate governance mechanisms are needed to ensure an alignment between investor and management interests.

For example, a former Qwest Communications International Inc. chief financial officer, Robin Szeliga, pleaded guilty to one count of insider trading. She was accused of improperly selling 10,000 shares of Qwest stock, earning a net profit of $125,000, when she knew that some business units would fail to meet revenue targets. Szeliga, former CEO Joseph Nacchio, and five other former executives were accused of orchestrating a financial fraud that forced Qwest Communications to restate billions of dollars in revenue. The SEC sought repayment and civil penalties from all of the accused.[17] After being convicted of nineteen counts of insider trading, Joseph Nacchio was finally ordered to prison to serve a six-year sentence. Szeliga pleaded guilty to one count of insider trading and testified against Nacchio in exchange for a sentence of six months' home detention, two years' probation, and a $250,000 fine.[18] Because of these potential differences, corporate governance mechanisms are needed to align investor and management interests. The shareholder model has been criticized for its somewhat singular purpose and focus because there are other ways of "investing" in a business. Suppliers, creditors, customers, employees, business partners, the community, and others also invest their resources in the success of the firm.

In the **stakeholder model of corporate governance**, the purpose of business is conceived in a broader fashion. Although a company has a responsibility for economic success and viability, it must also answer to other parties, including employees, suppliers, government agencies, communities, and groups with which it interacts. This model presumes a collaborative and relational approach to business and its constituents. Because management time and resources are limited, a key decision within the stakeholder model is to determine which stakeholders are primary. Once primary groups have been identified, appropriate corporate governance mechanisms are implemented to promote the development of long-term relationships.[19] As we discussed in Chapter 2, primary stakeholders include stockholders, suppliers, customers, employees, the government, and the community. Governance systems that consider stakeholder welfare in tandem with corporate needs and interests characterize this approach. After years of bad publicity regarding environmental damage and its poor treatment of workers, Wal-Mart appears to have realized the importance of corporate social responsibility to a company's bottom line. Over 92 percent of Wal-Mart associates now have health insurance, and Wal-Mart has been working hard to improve diversity as well. In 2008 alone, Wal-Mart received thirty-seven separate awards and distinctions for its diversity efforts. The company has taken strides toward being more sustainable as well—by doing everything from introducing low-emissions vehicles to its shipping fleet and installing solar panels on store rooftops. Wal-Mart has even stated a goal to be zero-waste.[20]

Although these two approaches seem to represent ends of a continuum, the reality is that the shareholder model is often a precursor to the stakeholder model. Many businesses have evolved into the stakeholder model as a result of government initiatives, consumer activism, industry activity, and other external forces. In the aftermath of corporate scandals it became clear how the economic accountability of corporations could not be detached from other responsibilities and stakeholder concerns. Although this trend began with large, publicly held firms,

stakeholder model of corporate governance model that sees management as having a responsibility to its stakeholders in addition to its responsibility for economic success; based on a collaborative and relational approach to business and its constituents

"Many businesses have evolved into the stakeholder model as a result of government initiatives, consumer activism, industry activity, and other external forces."

WalMart addresses concerns over the cost and availability of health care by offering basic health services at select stores

© Julie Steenuysen/Landov

its aftereffects are being felt in many types of organizations and industries. Public hospitals, for example, have experienced a transition to the more holistic approach to corporate governance. Although public hospitals serve as a "safety net" for local governments' ability to provide health care, some experts object to the influence of government officials on these hospitals' boards of directors and operations. A new model of governance has emerged that calls for fewer government controls, more management autonomy and accountability, formal CEO and board evaluation systems, and more effective community involvement.[21]

The shareholder model focuses on a primary stakeholder—the investor—whereas the stakeholder model incorporates a broader philosophy toward internal and external constituents. According to the World Bank, a development institution whose goal is to reduce poverty by promoting sustainable economic growth around the world, corporate governance is defined by both internal (i.e., long-term value and efficient operations) and external (i.e., public policy and economic development) factors.[22] We are concerned with the broader conceptualization of corporate governance in this chapter.

In the social responsibility model that we propose, governance is the organizing dimension for keeping a firm focused on continuous improvement, accountability, and engagement with stakeholders. Although financial return, or economic viability, is an important measure of success for all firms, the legal dimension of social responsibility is also a compulsory consideration. The ethical and philanthropic dimensions, however, have not been traditionally mandated through regulation or contracts. This represents a critical divide in our social responsibility model and associated governance goals and systems because there are some critics who challenge the use of

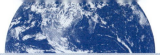
Bank of America Stakeholders Support Sustainability

Along with many other U.S. banks, Bank of America faced a difficult financial situation in 2008–2009. In the midst of a global banking crisis, BofA was faced with the choice of either possible failing or of accepting a $20 billion government rescue—the bank chose the latter option. Because of the bank's poor performance and highly controversial acquisitions of the failing financial institutions Merrill Lynch and Countrywide Financial, shareholders were concerned about the quality of decision making at BofA. A scandal had also emerged regarding $3.6 billion in bonuses paid to Merrill executives after the bank had failed and had been acquired by BofA. Many viewed it as wrong that executives of a failing bank would be rewarded, and approved a proposal to split the positions of chair of the board and CEO. They also called for an overhaul of the board by replacing six directors.

However, all of the negative press obscured the environmentally friendly choices the bank has made. BofA has long focused on energy efficiency, reducing emissions, and limiting waste, in addition to addressing concerns over its financial performance, a stance shareholders

NASA

support, even in the wake of its financial meltdown-related troubles. The company offers customers eco-friendly products and services such as the Brighter Planet™ Visa® and online banking to reduce paper waste. BofA is active in communities promoting energy efficiency and environmental responsibility. The company committed $20 billion over ten years to aid businesses addressing global climate change, to create loans for companies developing renewable energy, and to create new jobs. BofA won California's 2008 Governor's Environmental and Economic Leadership Award (GEELA) for its focus on melding environmental stewardship with long-term company management. BofA won this award because of its involvement in solar school initiatives, the creation of Clean Renewable Energy Bonds, and the preservation of redwood forests.

Although BofA admits that its focus on protecting the environment is for profit and economic growth, it also acknowledges it is the responsible stance to take. BofA intends to maintain its sustainability efforts no matter what the economic climate. In fact, BofA has performed so well that Citigroup even told its clients to invest in BofA stock, as it is the strongest performing bank.[24]

organizational resources for concerns beyond financial performance and legalities. This view was summarized in an editorial in *National Journal*, a nonpartisan magazine on politics and government: "Corporations are not governments. In the everyday course of their business, they are not accountable to society or to the citizenry at large. . . . Corporations are bound by the law, and by the rules of what you might call ordinary decency. Beyond this, however, they have no duty to pursue the collective goals of society."[23] This type of philosophy, long associated with the shareholder model of corporate governance, prevailed throughout the twentieth century. However, as the consequences of neglecting the stakeholder model of corporate social responsibility have become clearer, fewer parties adhere to such a narrow view anymore.

ISSUES IN CORPORATE GOVERNANCE SYSTEMS

Organizations that strive to develop effective corporate governance systems consider a number of internal and external issues. In this section, we look at four areas that need to be addressed in the design and improvement of governance mechanisms. We begin with boards of directors, which have the ultimate responsibility for ensuring a governance focus. Then, we discuss the role of shareholders and investors, internal control and risk management, and executive compensation within the governance system. These issues affect most organizations, although individual businesses may face unique factors that create additional governance questions. For example, a company operating in several countries will need to resolve issues related to international governance policy.

Boards of Directors

Members of a company's board of directors assume responsibility for the firm's resources and legal and ethical compliance. The board appoints top executive officers and is responsible for providing oversight of their performance. This is also true of a university's board of trustees, and there are similar arrangements in the nonprofit sector. In each of these cases, board members have a fiduciary duty, which was discussed earlier in this chapter. These responsibilities include acting in the best interests of those they serve. Thus, board membership is not designed as a vehicle for personal financial gain; rather, it provides the intangible benefit of ensuring the success of the organization and the stakeholders affected and involved in the fiduciary arrangement.

For public corporations, boards of directors hold the ultimate responsibility for their firms' ethical culture and legal compliance. This governing authority is held responsible by the 2004 and 2007 amendments to the Federal Sentencing Guidelines for creating an ethical culture that provides leadership, values, and compliance. The members of a company's board of directors assume legal responsibility for the firm's resources and decisions, and they appoint its top executive officers. In an effort to revamp the company after the 2008–2009 financial crisis, Citigroup appointed new directors to its board. This overhauled board now includes financial experts from government, the banking industry, and academia—all in an effort to increase transparency and accountability.[25]

The traditional approach to directorship assumed that board members managed the corporation's business. Research and practical observation have shown that boards of directors rarely, if ever, perform the management function.[26] Because boards meet usually four to six times a year, there is no way that time allocation would allow for effective management. In small nonprofit organizations, the board may manage most resources and decisions. The complexity of large organizations requires full attention on a daily basis. Today, boards of directors are concerned primarily with monitoring the decisions made by managers on behalf of the company. This includes choosing top executives, assessing their performance, helping to set strategic direction, evaluating company performance, developing CEO succession plans, communicating with stakeholders, maintaining legal and ethical practices, ensuring that control and accountability mechanisms are in place, and evaluating the board's own performance. In sum, board members assume the ultimate authority for organizational effectiveness and subsequent performance.

Independence Just as social responsibility objectives require more of employees and executives, boards of directors are also experiencing increasing accountability and disclosure mandates. The desire for independence is one reason that a few firms have chosen to split the powerful roles of chair of the board and CEO. Although the practice is common in the United Kingdom and activists have called for this move for years, the idea is newer to U.S. and Canadian firms. Chubb Corporation, Midas, Pathmark Stores, Toronto Dominion Bank, and Closure Medical are companies that have made the transition. In addition to independence concerns, it is unlikely that one person can devote the time and energy it takes to be effective in both roles. The National Association of Corporate Directors is in favor of splitting the roles, whereas other experts suggest that a "presiding" chair take over most of the chair's and CEO's duties with respect to the board. Finally, opponents believe the new rules and practices emerging from governance reform may negate the role-split debate by improving other aspects of the board's membership and impact.[27]

Traditionally, board members were retired company executives or friends of current executives, but the trend since the corporate scandals associated with Enron, WorldCom, and more recently Countrywide Financial and AIG has been toward "outside directors," who have valuable expertise yet little vested interest in the firm before assuming the director role. Thus, directors today are more likely chosen for their competence, motivation, and ability to bring enlightened and diverse perspectives to strategic discussions. Outside directors are thought to bring more independence to the monitoring function because they are not bound by past allegiances, friendships, a current role in the company, or some other matter that may create a conflict of interest. However, independent directors who sit on a board for a long time may eventually lose some of the outsider perspective. While they are more likely to be impartial, independent directors are not always guaranteed to avoid conflict of interest issues. For example, the Indian IT business Satyam Computer Services has independent directors on its board. The chair of Satyam, Ramalinga Raju, admitted to committing massive financial fraud and inflating earnings and assets by billions of dollars for years. Although independent directors served on the board, they are also under investigation for being complicit in the crime.[28] Directors have to avoid "group think" and be competent enough to understand risks. They must also be willing to ask for information relevant to avoiding organizational misconduct.

Quality Finding board members who have some expertise in the firm's industry or who have served as chief executives at similar-sized organizations is a good strategy for improving the board's overall quality. Directors with competence and experiences that reflect some of the firm's core issues should bring valuable insights to bear on discussions and decisions. Directors without direct industry or comparable executive experience may bring expertise on important issues, such as auditing, executive compensation, succession planning, and risk management, to improve decision making.

Board members must understand the company's strategy and operations; this suggests that members should limit the number of boards on which they serve. Directors need time to read reports, attend board and committee meetings, and participate in continuing education that promotes strong understanding and quality guidance. For example, directors on the board's audit committee may need to be educated on new accounting and auditing standards. Experts recommend that fully employed board members sit on no more than four boards, whereas retired members should limit their memberships to seven boards. Directors should be able to attend at least 75 percent of the meetings. Thus, many of the factors that promote board quality are within the control of directors.[29]

Performance An effective board of directors can serve as a type of insurance against the business cycle and the natural highs and lows of the economy. A company with a strong board free from conflicts of interest and with clearly stated corporate governance rules will be more likely to weather a storm if something bad does happen.[30] As federal regulations increase and the latitude afforded boards of directors shrinks, boards are going to be faced with greater responsibility and transparency.

Board independence, along with board quality, stock ownership, and corporate performance, is often used to assess the quality of corporate boards of directors. Many CEOs have lost their jobs because the board of directors is concerned about performance, ethics, and social responsibility. The main reason for this is the boards' fear of losing their personal assets. This fear comes from lawsuits by shareholders who sued the directors of financial firms over their roles in the collapse on Wall Street. Both settlements called for the directors to pay large sums from their own pockets.[31] These events make it clear that board members are accountable for oversight.

Just as improved ethical decision making requires more of employees and executives, so too are boards of directors feeling greater demands for ethics and transparency. Directors today are increasingly chosen for their expertise, competence, and ability to bring diverse perspectives to strategic discussions. Outside directors are also thought to bring more independence to the monitoring function because they are not bound by past allegiances, friendships, a current role in the company, or some other issue that may create a conflict of interest. The chair of the board audit committee must be an outside independent director with financial expertise.

Many of the corporate scandals uncovered in recent years might have been prevented if each of the companies' boards of directors had been better qualified, more knowledgeable, and less biased. The U.S. Treasury Secretary, Timothy Geithner, is trying to change how the government goes about overseeing risk-taking in financial markets. He is pushing for stricter rules on financial management and controls on hedge funds and money-market mutual funds. He believes that the United States needs greater openness and transparency, greater oversight and enforcement, as well as clearer, more commonsense language in the financial system.[32] Board members are being asked to understand changes in regulations and participate in providing better oversight on risk-taking in their firms.

Rules promulgated by the Sarbanes-Oxley Act and various stock exchanges now require a majority of independent directors on the board; regular meetings between nonmanagement board members; audit, compensation, governance, and nominating committees either fully made up of or with a majority of independent directors; and a financial expert on the audit committee. The governance area will continue to evolve as corporate scandals are resolved and the government and companies begin to implement and test new policies and practices. Regardless of the size and type of business for which boards are responsible, a system of governance is needed to ensure effective control and accountability. As a corporation grows, matures, enters international markets, and takes other strategic directions, it is likely that the board of directors will evolve to meet its new demands. Sir Adrian Cadbury, former president of the Centre for Board Effectiveness at the Henley Business School in Reading, England, and an architect of corporate governance changes around the world, has outlined responsibilities of strong boards:

- Boards are responsible for developing company purpose statements that cover a range of aims and stakeholder concerns.
- Annual reports and other documents need to include more nonfinancial information.
- Boards are required to define their role and implement self-assessment processes better.
- Selection of board members will become increasingly formalized, with less emphasis on personal networks and word of mouth.
- Boards need to work effectively as teams.
- Serving on boards will require more time and commitment than in the past.[33]

These trends are consistent with our previous discussion of social responsibility. In all facets of organizational life, greater demands are being placed on business decisions and people. Many of these expectations emanate from those who provide substantial resources in the organization—namely, shareholders and other investors.

> "Regardless of the size and type of business for which boards are responsible, a system of governance is needed to ensure effective control and accountability."

Shareholders and Investors

Because they have allocated scarce resources to the organization, shareholders and investors expect to grow and reap rewards from their investments. This type of financial exchange represents a formal contractual arrangement and provides

WalMart announces plans to buy back $15 billion in stock at their annual shareholders meeting in Bentonville, Arkansas

the capital necessary to fund all types of organizational initiatives, such as new product development and facilities construction. A shareholder is concerned with his or her ownership investment in publicly traded firms, whereas *investor* is a more general term for any individual or organization that provides capital to a firm. Investments include financial, human, and intellectual capital.

Shareholder Activism Shareholders, including large institutional ones, have become more active in articulating their positions with respect to company strategy and executive decision making. *Activism* is a broad term that can encompass engaging in dialog with management, attending annual meetings, submitting shareholder resolutions, bringing lawsuits, and other mechanisms designed to communicate shareholder interests to the corporation. Table 3.3 lists characteristics of effective shareholder activism campaigns.

Shareholder resolutions are nonbinding, yet important, statements about shareholder concerns. A shareholder that meets certain guidelines may bring one resolution per year to a proxy vote of all shareholders at a corporation's annual meeting. Recent resolutions brought forward relate to auditor independence, executive compensation, independent directors, environmental impact, human rights, and other social responsibility issues. In some cases, the company will modify its policies or practices before the resolution is ever brought to a vote. In other situations, a resolution will receive less than a majority vote, but the media attention, educational value, and other stakeholder effects will cause a firm to reconsider, if not change, its original position to meet the resolution's proposal. The accounting scandals prompted many resolutions about executive compensation among shareholders who believe that improper compensation structures are often a precursor

Table 3.3 Characteristics of a Successful Shareholder Activism Campaign

Alliances with social movements or public interest groups, where shareholder concerns and activity mesh with and play a part in a larger, multifaceted campaign
Grass-roots pressure, such as letter writings or phone-ins to public investors to generate support for the resolution
Communications: media outreach, public and shareholder education, etc.
High-level negotiations with senior decision makers
Support and active involvement from large institutional investors
A climate that makes it difficult for the company not to make the "right decision." For example, if you have a plainly compelling financial argument, you have a better chance of getting company management and other shareholders on board with your proposal.
Persistence. Shareholders don't go away. They own the company and have a right to be heard. Often shareholder activists stick with issues for years.

Source: "Characteristics of a Successful Shareholder Activism Campaign," Friends of the Earth, http://www.foe.org/international/shareholder/characteristics.html, accessed April 25, 2006. Courtesy Friends of the Earth © 2006.

to accounting mismanagement.[34] The resolution process is regulated by the SEC in the United States and by complementary offices in other countries; some claim this is more favorable to the corporation than to shareholders.

Although labor and public pension fund activities have waged hundreds of proxy battles in recent years, they rarely have much effect on the target companies. Now shareholder activists are attacking the process by which directors themselves are elected. After poor performance during the 2008 financial crisis on Wall Street, Bank of America shareholders voted to oust six board members. The move got rid of entrenched directors with possible conflicts of interest and replaced them with qualified financial experts.[35] Although shareholders and investors want their resources used efficiently and effectively, they are increasingly willing to take a stand to encourage companies to change for reasons beyond financial return.

Social Investing Many investors assume the stakeholder model of corporate governance, which carries into a strategy of social investing, "the integration of social and ethical criteria into the investment decision-making process."[36] Roughly three-quarters of U.S. investors take social responsibility issues into account when choosing investment opportunities. Twelve percent indicate they are willing to take a lower rate of return if the company is a strong performer in the social responsibility area.[37] Most social investors do not have to worry about a poor return on their investments. Socially conscious firms are strong performers for many of the reasons we discussed in Chapter 1. There remains a large gap between the recognition that social responsibility is important and the actual implementation of social responsibility programs in firms. While nearly three-quarters of top executives identify corporate social responsibility as something that must be a business priority, only 39 percent include social responsibility in their business planning, and an even smaller number (29 percent) have written CSR policies in place.[38]

"There remains a large gap between the recognition that social responsibility is important and the actual implementation of social responsibility programs in firms."

While social investing has traditionally been conducted through managed mutual funds, like those with Domini Social Investments, TIAA-CREF, Vanguard, and Calvert Group, some individual investors are using Web-based research to venture on their own. Websites such as FOLIOfn, SocialFunds.com, Morningstar, Inc., and others provide information and services to help the socially conscious investor in decision making.[39] Thus, there are a number of opportunities for individuals to demonstrate an active strategy with respect to investing and social responsibility. Whereas a passive investor is mainly concerned with buying and selling stock and receiving dividends, social investors are taking a variety of stakeholder issues into account when making investment decisions. A social investor takes the social responsibility of "ownership" seriously because a firm in which he or she invests implements plans and strategies on behalf of its owners. It could be argued that the dishonest actions of a firm were carried out on behalf of shareholders; thus, an investor in the firm would also be responsible. Conversely, it could be argued that a firm implementing a strong social responsibility strategy and agenda is doing so on behalf of its owners.[40] Shareholder activism is the strategy for ensuring that owners' perspectives on social responsibility are included on the corporate agenda.

Although social investing has received strong media attention over the last few years, the idea has a long history. For example, the Quakers, a religious group, applied social investment criteria in the seventeenth century when they refused to invest in, patronize, or partner with any business involved in the slave trade or military concerns.[41] Investors today use similar screening criteria in determining where to place their funds and resources. On the whole, investments tied to environmental causes and to community advocacy have grown rapidly in the 2000s. Many people, for example, now look at the types of investments included in mutual funds when deciding where to put their money; and institutional investors and money managers are including criteria (e.g., related to the crisis in Darfur) into their portfolio management as a way to signal an interest in humanitarian causes, and therefore the greater good.[42] Despite its subjective nature, professionally managed social investments total more than $2.71 trillion in the United States—an increase of 324 percent since 1995.[43] This means that about 11 percent of all money under professional investment in the United States is used for socially responsible investing. Not only do these social investments help individuals and institutions meet their social responsibility goals, but they also provide strong financial returns.

Shareholder activism and social investing are especially prevalent in the United States and United Kingdom, two countries that score relatively high on various corporate governance indexes. Several other European countries are also experiencing increasing rates of activism and social investing. Most activism and investing take place on an organizational level through mutual funds and other institutional arrangements, but some individual investors have affected company strategy and policy. Robert Monks, a leading corporate governance activist, once described Warren Buffett, the legendary investor from Omaha, Nebraska, as "epitomizing the kind of monitoring shareholder whose involvement enhances the value of the whole enterprise." Warren Buffett and his company Berkshire Hathaway command significant respect from investors because of their track record of financial returns and the integrity of their organizations. Buffett says, "I want employees to ask themselves whether they are willing to have any contemplated act appear the next day on the front page of their local paper—to be read by their spouses, children and friends—with the reporting done by an informed and critical reporter." The high level of accountability and trust Buffett places in his employees translates into investor trust and confidence.[44] Although few investors have Buffett's financial clout and respect, he serves as a role model by paying attention to the control and accountability mechanisms of the companies in which he invests.

Investor Confidence Shareholders and other investors must have assurance that their money is being placed in the care of capable and trustworthy organizations. These primary stakeholders are expecting a solid return for their investment, but as illustrated earlier, they have additional concerns about social responsibility. When these fundamental expectations are not met, the confidence that investors and shareholders have in corporations, market analysts, investment houses, stockbrokers, mutual fund managers, financial planners, and other economic players and institutions can be severely tested. In Chapter 1, we discussed the importance of investor trust and loyalty to organizational and societal performance. Part of this trust relates to the perceived efficacy of corporate governance. Figures 3.1 and 3.2 demonstrate the extent to which strong governance is now considered an investment criterion and reason for a premium price.

Bankruptcies and financial misconduct in the early 2000s shook investor confidence. The same thing happened during the subprime mortgage crisis, Wall Street financial sector crash, and recession of 2008–2009. People felt that they could no longer trust large financial firms and banks, which added to the financial tailspin. CEOs, whom many stakeholders felt should be blamed for their firms' losses, were accused of misconduct. People such as Bernard Madoff, who ran the world's largest Ponzi scheme, were given harsh jail sentences. Madoff was sentenced to 150 years for his crimes. Nevertheless, people's retirement and investment accounts dwindled. The federal government took quick action to stop the fiscal hemorrhaging, pumping nearly $1 trillion into the nation's banks. The collapses in the United States were echoed in other markets around the world. People around the world began to question their nations' regulatory systems and whether businesses truly had their stakeholders' best interests in mind. Essentially, stakeholders were calling for boards of directors and others with access to financial records and the power to demand accountability to tighten the control and risk environment in companies today

Figure 3.1 Corporate Governance Challenges Related to the Global Financial Crisis

- Improve public confidence and trust in the financial soundness of the organization

- Communicate the complexity of financial products and the risk to the organization and consumers

- Develop a position on financial regulation to protect all participants in the financial system

- Develop improved transparency in financial decisions for all stakeholders

- Demonstrate participation of shareholders in all corporate governance discussions

- Maintain ethics and compliance oversight to address key areas of risk

Figure 3.2 Percentage of Investors Who Say They are Willing to Pay a Premium for a Well-Governed Company

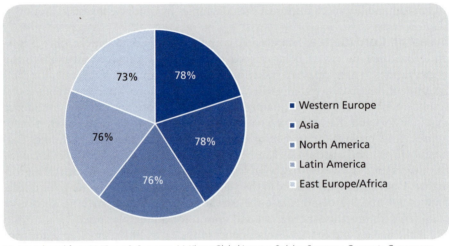

Source: Adapted from McKinsey & Company. *McKinsey Global Investor Opinion Survey on Corporate Governance.* Copyright © 2002 by McKinsey & Company.

Internal Control and Risk Management

Controls and a strong risk management system are fundamental to effective operations, as they allow for comparisons between the actual performance and the planned performance and goals of the organization. Controls are used to safeguard corporate assets and resources, protect the reliability of organizational information, and ensure compliance with regulations, laws, and contracts. Risk management is the process used to anticipate and shield the organization from unnecessary or overwhelming circumstances, while ensuring that executive leadership is taking the appropriate steps to move the organization and its strategy forward.

Internal and External Audits Auditing, both internal and external, is the linchpin between risk and controls and corporate governance. Boards of directors must ensure that the internal auditing function of the company is provided with adequate funding, up-to-date technology, unrestricted access, independence, and authority to carry out its audit plan. To ensure these characteristics, the internal audit executive should report to the board's audit committee and, in most cases, the chief executive officer.45

The external auditor should be chosen by the board and must clearly identify its client as the board, not the company's chief financial officer. Under Sarbanes-Oxley, the board audit committee should be directly responsible for the selection, payment, and supervision of the company's external auditor. The act also prohibits an external auditing firm from performing some non-audit work for the same public company, including bookkeeping, human resources, actuarial services, valuation services, legal services, and investment banking. However, even with regulations in place many auditors failed to properly do their jobs in years leading up to the 2008–2009 recession. For example, trustees of New Century Financial Corporation sued its auditor, KPMG, for "reckless and grossly negligent audits" that hid the company's financial problems and sped its collapse. New Century was one of the early casualties of the subprime mortgage crisis, but was once one of the country's largest mortgage lenders to those with poor credit histories. After it disclosed accounting errors not discovered by KPMG, the company collapsed.[46] Part of the problem relates to the sheer size and complexity of organizations, but these factors do not negate the tremendous responsibility that external auditors assume.

Control Systems The area of internal control covers a wide range of company decisions and actions, not just the accuracy of financial statements and accounting records. Controls also foster understanding when discrepancies exist between corporate expectations and stakeholder interests and issues. Internal controls effectively limit employee or management opportunism or the use of corporate assets for individualistic or nonstrategic purposes. Controls also ensure the board of directors has access to timely and quality information that can be used to determine strategic options and effectiveness. For these reasons, the board of directors should have ultimate oversight for the integrity of the internal control system.47 Although board members do not develop or administer the control system, they are responsible for ensuring that an effective system exists. The need for internal controls is rarely disputed, but implementation can vary. As Figure 3.3 shows, the CEO or chair appears to be the key decision maker relating to public and political debates that have an impact on shareholder value. Thus, internal control represents a set of tasks and resource commitments that require high-level attention.

Although most large corporations have designed internal controls, smaller companies and nonprofit organizations are less likely to have invested in a complete system. For example, a small computer shop in Columbus, Ohio, lost thousands of dollars due to embezzlement by the accounts receivable clerk. Because of the clerk's position and role in the company, she was able to post

Figure 3.3 Leadership is the Key to Shareholder Value: Who takes the lead in large companies when managing sociopolitical issues?

Chief Executive Officer or Chair	56%
Public or Corporate Affairs Department	14%
Other Executive Members of the Board	10%
Core Business Divisions	5%
Department of Corporate Social Responsibility	5%
Human Relations Department	2%
Strategy Department	1%

Source: The McKinsey Global Survey of Business Executives: Business and Society. *The McKinsey Quarterly*, The Online Journal of McKinsey & Co., January 2006.

credit card payments due her employer to her own account and later withdraw the income. Although she faced felony theft charges, her previous employer admitted feeling ashamed and did not want his business associated with a story on employee theft.[48] Such crime is common in small businesses because they often lack effective internal controls. Simple, yet proven, control mechanisms that can be used in all types of organizations are listed in Table 3.4. These techniques are not always costly, and they conform to best practices in the prevention of ethical and legal problems that threaten the efficacy of governance mechanisms.

The 2004 and 2007 amendments to the Federal Sentencing Guidelines for Organizations make it clear that a corporation's governing authority must be well informed about its control systems with respect to implementation and effectiveness. This places the responsibility squarely on the shoulders of the firm's leadership, usually the board of directors. The board must ensure that there is a high-ranking officer accountable for the day-to-day operational responsibility of the control systems. The board must also provide for adequate authority, resources, and access to the board or an appropriate subcommittee of the board. The guidelines further call for confidential mechanisms whereby the organization's employees and agents may report or seek guidance about potential or actual misconduct without fear of retaliation. Finally, the board is required to oversee the discovery of risks and to design, implement, and modify approaches to deal with those risks. Thus, the board of directors is clearly accountable for discovering risks associated with a firm's specific industry and assessing the firm's ethics program to ensure that it is capable of uncovering misconduct.[49]

Risk Management A strong internal control system should alert decision makers to possible problems, or risks, that may threaten business operations, including worker safety, company solvency, vendor relationships, proprietary

Table 3.4 Internal Control Mechanisms for Small Businesses and Nonprofits

Develop and disseminate a code of conduct that explicitly addresses ethical and legal issues in the workplace.
Rotate and segregate job functions to reduce the opportunity for opportunism (e.g., the person reconciling bank statements does not make deposits or pay invoices).
Screen employment applicants thoroughly, especially those who would assume much responsibility if hired.
Watch new employees especially carefully until they have gained knowledge and your trust.
Require all employees to take at least one week of vacation on an annual basis.
Limit access to valuable inventory and financial records. Use technology to track inventory, costs, human resources, finances, and other valuable business processes.
Implement unannounced inspections, spot checks, or "tests" of departments, systems, and outcomes.
Keep keys and pass codes secure and limit their duplication and distribution.
Insist that operating statements are produced on at least a monthly basis.
Ask questions about confusing financial statements and other records.

Sources: *Curtailing Crime: Inside and Out,* Crime Prevention Series, U.S. Small Business Administration, http://www.sba.gov/library/pubs/cp-2.doc, accessed May 9, 2006; "Protecting Against Employee Fraud," *Business First–Western New York,* June 14, 1999, p. 31; Kathy Hoke, "Eyes Wide Open," *Business First–Columbus,* August 27, 1999, pp. 27–28.

information, environmental impact, and other concerns. As we discussed in Chapter 2, having a strong crisis management plan is part of the process for managing risk. The term *risk management* is normally used in a narrow sense to indicate responsibilities associated with insurance, liability, financial decisions, and related issues. Kraft General Foods, for example, has a risk management policy for understanding how prices of commodities, such as coffee, sugar, wheat, and cocoa, will affect its relationships throughout the supply chain.[50]

Most corporate leaders' greatest fear is discovering serious misconduct or illegal activity somewhere in their organization. The fear is that a public discovery can immediately be used by critics in the mass media, competitors, and skeptical stakeholders to undermine a firm's reputation. Corporate leaders worry that something will be uncovered outside their control that will jeopardize their careers and their organizations. Fear is a paralyzing emotion. Of course, maybe even executives like Bernie Madoff, Alan Stanford,

"The board of directors is clearly accountable for discovering risks associated with a firm's specific industry and assessing the firm's ethics program to ensure that it is capable of uncovering misconduct."

and Angelo Mozilo experienced fear as they participated in misconduct. The former chair of Satyam Computer Services, Ramalinga Raju, said it was a terrifying experience to watch a small act of fudging some numbers snowball out of control. He compared knowingly engaging in misconduct for years to "riding a tiger, not knowing how to get off without being eaten."[51] These leaders were the captains of their respective ships, and they made a conscious decision to steer their firms into treacherous waters with a high probability of striking an iceberg.[52]

Corporate leaders do fear the possibility of reputation harm, financial loss, or a regulatory event that could potentially end their careers and even threaten their personal lives through fines or prison sentences. Indeed, the whole concept of risk management involves recognizing the possibility of a misfortune that could jeopardize or even destroy the corporation.[53] Organizations face significant risks and threats from financial misconduct. There is a need to identify potential risks that relate to misconduct that could devastate the organization. If risks and misconduct are discovered and disclosed, they are more likely to be resolved before they become front-page news.

Risk is always present within organizations, so executives must develop processes for remedying or managing its effects. A board of directors will expect the top management team to have risk management skills and plans in place. There are at least three ways to consider how risk poses either a potentially negative or positive concern for organizations.[54] First, risk can be categorized as a hazard. In this view, risk management is focused on minimizing negative situations, such as fraud, injury, or financial loss. Second, risk may be considered an uncertainty that needs to be hedged through quantitative plans and models. This type of risk is best associated with the term *risk management,* which is used in financial and business literature. Third, risk also creates the opportunity for innovation and entrepreneurship. Just as management can be criticized for taking too much risk, it can also be subject to concerns about not taking enough risk. All three types of risk are implicitly covered by our definition of corporate governance because there are risks for both control (i.e., preventing fraud and ensuring accuracy of financial statements) and accountability (i.e., innovation to develop new products and markets). For example, the Internet and electronic commerce capabilities have introduced new risks of all types for organizations. Privacy, as we discuss in Chapter 10, is a major concern for many stakeholders and has created the need for policies and certification procedures. A board of directors may ensure that the company has established privacy policies that are not only effective but also can be properly monitored and improved as new technology risks and opportunities emerge in the business environment.[55]

Financial Misconduct

The failure to understand and manage ethical risks played a significant role in the financial crisis and recession of 2008–2009. While there is a difference between bad business decisions and business misconduct, there is also a thin line between the ethics of using only financial incentives to gauge performance and the use of holistic measures that include ethics, transparency, and responsibility to stakeholders. From CEOs to traders and brokers, lucrative financial incentives existed for performance in the financial industry.

Ethics issues emerged early in the arena of subprime lending, with loan officers receiving commissions on securing loans from borrowers with no consequences if the borrower defaulted on the loan. Some appraisers provided inflated home values in order to increase the loan amount. In other instances consumers were asked to falsify their incomes to make the loan more attractive to the lending institution. The opportunity for misconduct was widespread. Top managers, boards of directors, and even CEOs were complacent about the wrongdoings as long as profits were good. Congress and President Clinton encouraged Fannie Mae and Freddie Mac to support home ownership among low-income people by giving out home mortgages. Throughout the early 2000s, in an economy with rapidly increasing home values, the culture of unethical behavior was not apparent to most people. When home values started to decline and individuals were "upside down" on their loans (owing more that the equity of the home), the failures and unethical behavior of lending and borrowing institutions became more obvious.

Derivatives, a financial trading instrument, can pose high amounts of risk for small or inexperienced investors. Because derivatives offer the possibility of large rewards, they offer an attraction to individual investors. But the basic premise of derivatives is to transfer risk among parties based on their willingness to assume additional risk, or hedge against it. Warren Buffett, a well known investor, has stated that he regards derivatives as "financial weapons of mass destruction." Derivatives have been used to leverage the debt in an economy, sometimes to a massive degree. When something unexpected happens, an economy will find it very difficult to pay its debts, thus causing a recession or even depression. This is why corporate governance systems must have contingency plans for unexpected events.

Because derivatives are so complex, Wall Street turned to mathematicians and physicists to create models and computer programs that could analyze these exotic instruments. It has become apparent that the use of derivatives such as credit default swaps became so profitable that traders and managers lost sight of anything but their incentives for selling these instruments. In other words, financial institutions sold what could be called defective products because the true risk of these financial instruments was not understood or disclosed to the customer. In some cases these defective products were given to traders to sell without any due diligence from the company as to the level of risk. Better corporate

© AP Photo/Louis Lanzano

External investigations and audits by the Securities and Exchange Commission failed to uncover Bernard Madoff's massive pyramid scheme and investor fraud

governance of financial divisions dealing in risky instruments, combined with compensation packages that do not encourage excessive risk-taking, may help to minimize the widespread problems experienced in the financial industry before the 2008 meltdown.

In hindsight, the enormous risks taken by traders and companies seem to be unwise and unfair to stakeholders. An ethical issue relates to the level of transparency that exists in using complex financial instruments to create profits. Irresponsible derivatives trading with limited regulatory oversight gave traders almost unlimited opportunities to manipulate the use of derivatives. In many financial institutions, there is no doubt that a number of key decision makers not only pushed the limits of legitimate risk-taking, but also engaged in manipulation and, in some cases, fraud to deceive shareholders by lying about the company's true financial condition. The federal government has worked to increase government regulation of the financial industry, but it is also clear that internal corporate governance is important in reducing misconduct as well. Additionally, the amount and types of compensation offered to employees should minimize the temptations to take risks, not encourage risk-taking.

> **"The federal government has worked to increase government regulation of the financial industry, but it is also clear that internal corporate governance is important in reducing misconduct as well."**

Executive Compensation

Executive compensation has been a topic rife with controversy in the aftermath of the 2008–2009 recession. While major companies had to turn to the government for help to stay afloat, and while regular people lost their life savings, top executives continued to receive incredibly high bonuses. Top executives at Merrill Lynch were awarded $3.6 billion in bonuses shortly before its merger with Bank of America in 2008. A combined $121 million went to four top executives. This was done in spite of the fact that Merrill Lynch had to be rescued by the government to save it from bankruptcy. Two ethics issues are at play: first, paying out the bonuses at all; and second, rushing their distribution in order to complete the job before Bank of America's takeover. Risk management in the financial industry is a key concern, including paying bonuses to executives who have failed in their duties. Regulatory agencies and Congress were not proactive in investigating early cases of financial misconduct and the systemic issues that led to the crisis. The legal and regulatory systems were more focused on individual misconduct rather than systemic ethical failures. AIG received a great deal of criticism after it paid out $165 million in bonuses to executives, even after the company received $180 billion in bailout money. Many feel that large executive bonuses point to a pervasive culture of greed and a sense of entitlement that has caused many of the problems on Wall Street in recent years.[56]

Executive compensation is such an important topic that many boards spend more time deciding how much to compensate top executives than they do ensuring the integrity of the company's financial reporting systems. How executives are compensated for their leadership, organizational service, and performance has become a controversial topic. Because of the large government bailouts of 2008 and 2009, many people are enraged because they feel that the government is sponsoring corporate excess with taxpayer money. Even many boards of directors—which are responsible for setting executive pay—feel that the United States has a problem in that executive pay is not in line with performance or demonstration of stewardship to the company.[57] According to the AFL–CIO, average executive pay is $10.4 million, which is 344 times the pay of the average U.S. worker. Executive bonuses alone are an average of $336,248. Added to this is the fact that companies have received nearly a billion dollars in government bailout money, money which comes from taxpayers.[58]

An increasing number of corporate boards are imposing performance targets on the stock and stock options they include in their CEOs' pay package. The SEC proposed that companies disclose how they compensate lower-ranking employees, as well as top executives. This was part of a review of executive pay policies that addresses the belief that many financial corporations have historically taken on too much risk. The SEC believes that compensation may be linked to excessive risk-taking.[59] Another issue is whether performance-linked compensation encourages executives to focus on short-term performance at the expense of long-term growth.[60] Shareholders today, however, may be growing more concerned about transparency than short-term performance and executive compensation.

Some people argue that because executives assume so much risk on behalf of the company, they deserve the rewards that follow from strong company performance. In addition, many executives' personal and professional lives meld to the point that they are "on call" twenty-four hours a day. Because not everyone has the skill, experience, and desire to become an executive, with the accompanying pressure and responsibility, market forces dictate a high level of compensation. When the pool of qualified individuals is limited, many corporate board members feel that offering large compensation packages is the only way to attract and retain top executives and so ensure that their firms are not left without strong leadership. In an era when top executives are increasingly willing to "jump ship" to other firms that offer higher pay, potentially lucrative stock options, bonuses, and other benefits, such thinking is not without merit.[61]

Executive compensation is a difficult but important issue for boards of directors and other stakeholders to consider because it receives much attention in the media, sparks shareholder concern, and is hotly debated in discussions of corporate governance. One area for board members to consider is the extent to which executive compensation is linked to company performance. Plans that base compensation on the achievement of several performance goals, including profits and revenues, are intended to align the interests of owners with management.

Table 3.5 Chief Executive Officer Compensation

Company	Executive	Pay ($ millions)
Oracle	Lawrence J. Ellison	$556.98
Occidental Petroleum	Ray R. Irani	$222.64
Hess	John B. Hess	$154.58
Ultra Petroleum	Michael D. Watford	$116.93
EOG Resources	Mark Papa	$90.47
WR Berkley	William R. Berkley	$87.48
Burlington Santa Fe	Matthew K. Rose	$68.62
Allegheny Energy	Paul J. Evanson	$67.26
Monsanto	Hugh Grant	$64.6
Deere & Co.	Robert W. Lane	$61.3

Source: "Special Report: CEO Compensation," *Forbes*, April 22, 2009, http://www.forbes.com/lists/2009/12/best-boss-09_CEO-Compensation_Rank.html, accessed June 26, 2009.

Table 3.5 shows the top CEO compensations at some of the world's largest companies. While still hundreds of times higher than what the average worker makes, overall CEOs did take paycuts for two years in a row in 2007 and 2008—only the second time in U.S. history when that happened. This downward shift may show a slight change in how executives are compensated, or it may represent that firms are listening to stakeholder protests regarding pay. However, those making the most money brought in more than their counterparts did in previous years.

CORPORATE GOVERNANCE AROUND THE WORLD

Increased globalization, enhanced electronic communications, economic agreements and zones, and the reduction of trade barriers have created opportunities for firms around the world to conduct business with both international consumers and industrial partners. These factors are propelling the need for greater homogenization in corporate governance principles. Standard & Poor's has a service called Corporate Governance Scores, which analyzes four macro-forces that affect the general governance climate of a country, including legal infrastructure, regulation, information infrastructure, and market infrastructure. On the basis of these factors, a country can be categorized as having strong, moderate, or weak support for effective governance practices at the company level. Institutional investors are very interested in this measure, as it helps determine possible risk.[62] As financial, human, and intellectual capital crosses borders, a number of business, social, and cultural concerns arise. Institutional investors in companies based in emerging markets claim to be willing to pay more for shares in companies that are well governed. Global shareholders also would like companies in their countries to disclose more financial data, to adopt CEO pay plans that reward only strong performance, and to use independent boards with no ties to management.

In response to this business climate, the Organisation for Economic Co-operation and Development (OECD), a forum for governments to discuss, develop, and enhance economic and social policy, issued a set of principles intended to serve as a global model for corporate governance.[63] After years of discussion and debate among institutional investors, business executives, government representatives, trade unions, and nongovernmental organizations, thirty OECD member governments signaled their agreement with the principles by signing a declaration to integrate them within their countries' economic systems and institutions. The purpose of the OECD Corporate Governance Principles (see Table 3.6) is to formulate minimum standards of fairness, transparency, accountability, disclosure, and responsibility for business practice. The principles focus on the board of directors, which the OECD says should recognize the impact of governance on the firm's competitiveness. In addition, the OECD charges boards, executives, and corporations with maximizing shareholder value while responding to the demands and expectations of their key stakeholders.

Table 3.6 OECD Principles of Corporate Governance

Principle	Explanation
1. Ensuring the basis for an effective corporate governance framework	The corporate governance framework should promote transparent and efficient markets, be consistent with the rule of law, and clearly articulate the division of responsibilities among different supervisory, regulatory, and enforcement authorities.
2. The rights of shareholders and key ownership functions	The corporate governance framework should protect and facilitate the exercise of shareholders' rights.
3. The equitable treatment of shareholders	The corporate governance framework should ensure the equitable treatment of all shareholders, including minority and foreign shareholders. All shareholders should have the opportunity to obtain effective redress for violation of their rights.
4. The role of stakeholders in corporate governance	The corporate governance framework should recognize the rights of stakeholders as established by law and encourage active cooperation between corporations and stakeholders in creating wealth, jobs, and the sustainability of financially sound enterprises.
5. Disclosure and transparency	The corporate governance framework should ensure that timely and accurate disclosure is made on all material matters regarding the corporation, including the financial situation, performance, ownership, and governance of the company.
6. The responsibilities of the board	The corporate governance framework should ensure the strategic guidance of the company, the effective monitoring of management by the board, and the board's accountability to the company and the shareholders

Source: "OECD Principles for Corporate Governance," Organisation for Economic Co-operation and Development, http://www.oecd.org/document/49/0,2340,en_2649_201185_31530865_1_1_1_1,00.html, accessed June 26, 2009.

The OECD Corporate Governance Principles cover many specific best practices, including (1) ensuring the basis for an effective corporate governance framework; (2) rights of shareholders to vote and influence corporate strategy; (3) greater numbers of skilled, independent members on boards of directors; (4) fewer techniques to protect failing management and strategy; (5) wider use of international accounting standards; and (6) better disclosure of executive pay and remuneration. Although member governments of the OECD are expected to uphold the governance principles, there is some room for cultural adaptation.

Best practices may vary slightly from country to country because of unique factors such as market structure, government control, role of banks and lending institutions, labor unions, and other economic, legal, and historical factors. Both industry groups and government regulators moved quickly in the United Kingdom after the Enron crisis was revealed. Because some British bankers were indicted in the scandal, corporate governance concerns increased in that country. Several British reforms resulted, including annual shareowners' votes on board compensation policies and greater supervision of investment analysts and the accounting profession.

Corporate governance, or lack of it, was one of the reasons for the financial crisis that occurred in Southeast Asia in the late 1990s. For example, the government structure of some Asian countries created greater opportunities for corruption and nepotism. Banks were encouraged to extend credit to companies favored by the government. In many cases, these companies were in the export business, which created an imbalance in financing for other types of businesses. The concentration of business power within a few families and tycoons reduced overall competitiveness and transparency. Many of these businesses were more focused on size and expanded operations than profitability. Foreign investors recognized the weakening economies and pulled their money out of investments. An extreme example of growth at all costs was the country of Iceland. In a country with few resources, it became one of the fastest-growing nations in the world during the 2000s because of heavy involvement in the financial sector. In fact, the entire country nearly went bankrupt in the fallout of the failure of the global financial markets in 2008–2009, and the nation's leading banks were nationalized. Iceland's governments and corporations failed to install reasonable checks and balances until the entire country was hugely overleveraged.[64]

FUTURE OF CORPORATE GOVERNANCE

As the issues discussed in the previous section demonstrate, corporate governance is primarily focused on strategic-level concerns for accountability and control. Although many discussions of corporate governance still revolve around responsibility in investor-owned companies, good governance is fundamental to effective performance in all types of organizations. As you have gleaned from history and government classes, a system of checks and balances is important for ensuring a focus on multiple perspectives and constituencies; proper distribution of resources, power, and decision authority; and the responsibility for making changes and setting direction.

To pursue social responsibility successfully, organizations must consider issues of control and accountability. As we learned earlier, the concept of corporate governance is in transition from the shareholder model to one that considers broader stakeholder concerns and inputs to financial performance. A number of market and environmental forces, such as the OECD and shareholder activism, have created pressures in this direction. This evolution is consistent with our view of social responsibility. Although some critics deride this expanded focus, a number of external and internal forces are driving business toward the stakeholder orientation and the formalization of governance mechanisms. One concern centers on the cost of governance. However, the failure of the financial sector, the subprime mortgage crisis, and the recession in 2008 and 2009 have taught us that not instilling good governance can be immensely more costly. For example, companies like Nike and Wal-Mart, which have had problems in the past and have implemented strong ethics and compliance systems, survived comparatively well during the more recent recession. However, many of the largest firms on Wall Street, which were overleveraged and did not have strong ethics and compliance programs in place, either failed or had to be bailed out in order not to fail.[65]

Most businesspeople and academicians agree that the benefits of a strong approach to corporate governance outweigh its costs. However, the positive return on governance goes beyond organizational performance to benefit the industrial competitiveness of entire nations, something we discussed in Chapter 1. For example, corrupt organizations often fail to develop competitiveness on a global scale and can leave behind financial ruin, thus negating the overall economic growth of the entire region or nation. At the same time, corrupt governments usually have difficulty sustaining and supporting the types of organizations that can succeed in global markets. Thus, a lack of good governance can lead to insular and selfish motives because there is no effective system of checks and balances. In today's interactive and interdependent business environment, most organizations are learning the benefits of a more cooperative approach to commerce. It is possible for a company to retain its competitive nature while seeking a "win-win" solution for all parties to the exchange.[66] Further, as nations with large economies embrace responsible governance principles, it becomes even more difficult for nations and organizations that do not abide by such principles to compete in these lucrative and rich markets. There is a contagion effect toward corporate governance among members of the global economy, much like peer pressure influences the actions and decisions of individuals. Portugal is a good example of this effect.

Because governance is concerned with the decisions made by boards of directors and executives, it has the potential for far-reaching positive—and negative—effects. A recent study by the OECD found that stronger financial performance is the result of several governance factors and practices, including (1) large institutional shareholders that are active monitors of company decisions and boards; (2) owner-controlled firms; (3) fewer mergers, especially between firms with disparate corporate values and business lines; and (4) shareholders', not board of directors', decisions on executive remuneration.[67]

"The positive return on governance goes beyond organizational performance to benefit the industrial competitiveness of entire nations."

The authors of the study note that these practices may not hold true for strong performance in all countries and economic systems. However, they also point out that a consensus view is emerging, with fewer differences among OECD countries than among all other nations. Similarities in organizational-level accountability and control should lead to smoother operations between different companies and countries, thereby bolstering competitiveness on many levels.

The future of corporate governance is directly linked to the future of social responsibility. Because governance is the control and accountability process for achieving social responsibility, it is important to consider who should be involved in the future. First and most obviously, business leaders and managers will need to embrace governance as an essential part of effective performance. Some of the elements of corporate governance, particularly executive pay, board composition, and shareholder rights, are likely to stir debate for many years. However, business leaders must recognize the forces that have brought governance to the forefront as a precondition of management responsibility. Thus, they may need to accept the "creative tension" that exists among managers, owners, and other primary stakeholders as the preferable route to mutual success.[68]

Second, governments have a key role to play in corporate governance. National competitiveness depends on the strength of various institutions, with primacy on the effective performance of business and capital markets. Strong corporate governance is essential to this performance, and thus, governments will need to be actively engaged in affording both protection and accountability for corporate power and decisions. Just like the corporate crises in the United States, the Asian economic crisis discussed earlier prompted companies and governments around the world to consider tighter governance procedures. Finally, other stakeholders may become more willing to use governance mechanisms to influence corporate strategy or decision making. Investors—whether shareholders, employees, or business partners—have a stake in decisions and should be willing to take steps to align various interests for long-term benefits. Many investors and stakeholders are willing to exert great influence on underperforming companies.

Until recently, governance was one area in the business literature that had not received the same level of attention as other issues, such as environmental impact, diversity, and sexual harassment. Over the next few years, however, corporate governance will emerge as the operational centerpiece to the social responsibility effort. The future will require that business leaders have a different set of skills and attitudes, including the ability to balance multiple interests, handle ambiguity, manage complex systems and networks, create trust among stakeholders, and improve processes so leadership is pervasive throughout the organization.[69]

In the past, the primary emphasis of governance systems and theory was on the conflict of interests between management and investors.[70] Governance today holds people at the highest organizational levels accountable and responsible to a broad and diverse set of stakeholders. Although top managers and boards of directors have always assumed responsibility, their actions are now subject to greater accountability and transparency. A *Wall Street Journal* writer put the shift succinctly, indicating, "Boards of directors have been put on notice." A key issue going forward will be the board's ability to align corporate decisions with various stakeholder interests.[71] Robert Monks, the activist money manager and leader on corporate governance issues, wrote that effective corporate governance requires understanding that the "indispensable link between the corporate constituents is the creation of a credible structure (with incentives and disincentives) that enables people with overlapping but not entirely congruent interests to have a sufficient level of confidence in each other and the viability of the enterprise as a whole."[72] We will take a closer look at some of these constituents and their concerns in the next few chapters.

SUMMARY

To respond to stakeholder pressures that companies be more accountable for organizational decisions and policies, organizations must implement policies that provide strategic guidance on appropriate courses of action. Such policies are often known as corporate governance, the formal system of accountability and control for organizational decisions and resources. Accountability relates to how well the content of workplace decisions is aligned with the firm's stated strategic direction, whereas control involves the process of auditing and improving organizational decisions and actions.

Both directors and officers of corporations are fiduciaries for the shareholders. Fiduciaries are persons placed in positions of trust who use due care and loyalty in acting on behalf of the best interests of the organization. There is a duty of care, also called a duty of diligence, to make informed and prudent decisions. Directors have a duty to avoid ethical misconduct in their director role and to provide leadership in decisions to prevent ethical misconduct in the organization. Directors are not held responsible for negative outcomes if they are informed and diligent in their decision making. The duty of loyalty means that all decisions should be in the interests of the corporation and its stakeholders. Conflicts of interest exist when a director uses the position to obtain personal gain, usually at the expense of the organization.

There are two major conceptualizations of corporate governance. The shareholder model of corporate governance focuses on developing and improving the formal system of performance accountability between top management and the firm's shareholders. The stakeholder model of corporate governance views the purpose of business in a broader fashion in which the organization not only has a responsibility for economic success and viability but also must answer to other stakeholders. The shareholder model focuses on a primary stakeholder—the investor—whereas the stakeholder model incorporates a broader philosophy that focuses on internal and external constituents.

Governance is the organizing dimension for keeping a firm focused on continuous improvement, accountability, and engagement with stakeholders. Although financial return, or economic viability, is an important measure of success for all firms, the legal dimension of social responsibility is also a compulsory consideration. The ethical and philanthropic dimensions, however, have not been traditionally mandated through regulation or contracts. This represents a critical divide in our social responsibility model and associated governance goals and systems because there are some critics who challenge the use of organizational resources for concerns beyond financial performance and legalities.

In the late 1800s and early 1900s, corporate governance was not a major issue because company owners made strategic decisions about their businesses. By the

1930s, ownership was dispersed across many individuals, raising questions about control and accountability. In response to shareholder activism, the Securities and Exchange Commission required corporations to allow shareholder resolutions to be brought to a vote of all shareholders. Since the mid-1900s, the approach to corporate governance has involved a legal discussion of principals (owners) and agents (managers) in the business relationship. The lack of effective control and accountability mechanisms in years past has prompted a current trend toward boards of directors playing a greater role in strategy formulation than they did in the early 1990s. Members of a company's board of directors assume legal responsibility and a fiduciary duty for organizational resources and decisions. Boards today are concerned primarily with monitoring the decisions made by managers on behalf of the company. The trend today is toward boards composed of outside directors who have little vested interest in the firm. Shareholder activism is helping to propel this trend, as they seek better representation from boards that are less likely to have conflicts of interest.

Shareholders have become more active in articulating their positions with respect to company strategy and executive decision making. Many investors assume the stakeholder model of corporate governance, which implies a strategy of integrating social and ethical criteria into the investment decision-making process. Although most activism and investing take place on an organizational level through mutual funds and other institutional arrangements, some individual investors have affected company strategy and policy.

Another significant governance issue is internal control and risk management. Controls allow for comparisons between actual performance and the planned performance and goals of the organization. They are used to safeguard corporate assets and resources, protect the reliability of organizational information, and ensure compliance with regulations, laws, and contracts. Controls foster understanding when discrepancies exist between corporate expectations and stakeholder interests and issues. A strong internal control system should alert decision makers to possible problems or risks that may threaten business operations. Risk can be categorized as (1) a hazard, in which case risk management focuses on minimizing negative situations, such as fraud, injury, or financial loss; (2) an uncertainty that needs to be hedged through quantitative plans and models; or (3) an opportunity for innovation and entrepreneurship.

How executives are compensated for their leadership, service, and performance is another governance issue. Many people believe the ratio between the highest-paid executives and median employee wages in the company should be reasonable. Others argue that because executives assume so much risk on behalf of the organization, they deserve the rewards that follow from strong company performance. One area for board members to consider is the extent to which executive compensation is linked to company performance.

The financial meltdown on Wall Street, the subprime mortgage crisis, and the recession of 2008–2009 have all shown stakeholders and regulators that the system still carries a lot of risk. This is in spite of actions taken after the events of the early 2000s involving companies like Enron and Worldcom. Increased government regulation of industries is not sufficient to ensure good corporate governance and reasonable risk-taking. Companies must take actions to implement ethics and compliance programs, to strengthen the accountability of their boards, and to align employee incentives with stakeholder interests. Better corporate governance across industries will not be attained without internal controls and risk management working in tandem with external government laws.

The Organisation for Economic Co-operation and Development has issued a set of principles from which to formulate minimum standards of fairness, transparency, accountability, disclosure, and responsibility for business practice. These principles help guide companies around the world and are part of the convergence that is occurring with respect to corporate governance.

Most businesspeople and academicians agree that the benefits of a strong approach to corporate governance outweigh its costs. Because governance is concerned with the decisions taken by boards of directors and executives, it has the potential for far-reaching positive, and negative, effects. The future of corporate governance is directly linked to the future of social responsibility. Business leaders and managers will need to embrace governance as an essential part of effective performance. Governments also have a role to play in corporate governance. National competitiveness depends on the strength of various institutions, with primacy on the effective performance of business and capital markets. Other stakeholders may become more willing to use governance mechanisms to affect corporate strategy or decision making.

RESPONSIBLE BUSINESS DEBATE

Vasella Steers Novartis Away from the Pack

ISSUE: Are pharmaceutical profits more important than curing disease?

Most businesses have a CEO and board of directors that operate under the conviction that their purpose is to maximize profits for the shareholders. They are trusted to make decisions that will grow the company and increase profits, without failing to conduct due diligence. No matter what the social interests of a company are, profits must be the most important consideration. Without earning profits, a company will not be successful in the long run and likely will not survive long enough to pursue stakeholder interests.

Novartis is a pharmaceutical company that is trying to responsibly grow profits while also maintaining a balanced stakeholder model. CEO Dan Vasella is a former doctor who knows the pharmaceutical industry from the manufacturer and the consumer side. Because of his medical background, Vasella holds the belief that Novartis's core stakeholders are the patients who use the company's drugs, not the shareholders who demand high returns.

While competitors focus on so-called "blockbuster" drugs, like those for depression or impotence, that hold the potential for enormous profits, Vasella wants Novartis to focus on curable diseases that may not hold as much profit potential. For example, employees at Novartis are pushing Vasella to spend hundreds of millions on an Alzheimer's vaccine. Although an Alzheimer's drug could net the company billions in profits, the disease is so complex that a cure is not yet within reach.

Vasella, on the other hand, wants to focus on targeted diseases, such as the inflammatory disease Muckle-Wells syndrome that affects a few thousand people worldwide. The genetics behind this disease are better understood and a cure is reasonably within reach—only a drug has never been developed because most pharmaceutical companies do not think it is profitable enough. Vasella, however, thinks it is a worthwhile disease on which to spend research and development (R&D) money because Novartis could cure a devastating disease, and he hopes that what the company learns from developing the drug could be applied to other similar diseases such as type 2 diabetes and arthritis. While not all shareholders understand his approach, Vasella has the support of the board and nine senior executives who make up what is called the Innovation Board. While Novartis is definitely taking a different approach to pharmaceutical development, Vasella's ideas have the potential to distinguish Novartis from the pack. Only time will tell if this stakeholder model maximizes profits for shareholders.

There Are Two Sides to Every Issue:

1. The Novartis stakeholder model will maximize profits in the long run.

2. Competitors that focus on an alternative financial return model (that emphasizes blockbuster drugs over curing more obscure diseases) will maximize profits in the long run.

Sources: Karry Capell, "Novartis: Radically Remaking Its Drug Business," *BusinessWeek*, June 22, 2009, pp. 30–35; "Comprehensive Compliance Program," Novartis Diagnostics, http://www.novartisdiagnostics.com/ethics/compliance.shtml, accessed July 10, 2009; "Lifesaving Research Rewarded," Novartis Newsroom, http://www.novartis.com/newsroom/news/2009-05-20_european-inventor.shtml, accessed July 10, 2009.

KEY TERMS

corporate governance (p. 85)
shareholder model of corporate governance (p. 92)

stakeholder model of corporate governance (p. 93)

DISCUSSION QUESTIONS

1. What is corporate governance? Why is corporate governance an important concern for companies that are pursuing the social responsibility approach? How does it improve or change the nature of executive and managerial decision making?

2. Compare the shareholder and stakeholder models of corporate governance. Which one seems to predominate today? What implications does this have for businesses in today's complex environment?

3. What role does executive compensation play in risk-taking and accountability? Why do some people partially blame compensation for the failures of the subprime mortgage and financial industries in 2008–2009?

4. What is the role of the board of directors in corporate governance? What responsibilities does the board have?

5. What role do shareholders and other investors play in corporate governance? How can investors effect change?

6. Why are internal control and risk management important in corporate governance? Describe three approaches organizations may take to managing risk.

7. Why is the issue of executive compensation controversial? Are today's corporate executives worth the compensation packages they receive?

8. In what ways are corporate governance practices becoming standardized around the world? What differences exist?

9. As corporate governance becomes a more important aspect of social responsibility, what new skills and characteristics will managers and executives need? Consider how pressures for governance require managers and executives to relate and interact with stakeholders in new ways.

EXPERIENTIAL EXERCISE

Visit the website of the Organisation for Economic Co-operation and Development (http://www.oecd.org). Examine the origins of the organization and its unique role in the global economy. After visiting the site, answer the following questions:

1. What are the primary reasons that OECD exists?

2. How would you describe OECD's current areas of concern and focus?

3. What role do you think OECD will play in the future with respect to corporate governance and related issues?

WHAT WOULD YOU DO?

The statewide news carried a story about Core-Tex that evening. There were rumors swirling that one of the largest manufacturers in the state was facing serious questions about its social responsibility. A former accountant for Core-Tex, whose identity was not revealed, made allegations about aggressive accounting methods and practices that overstated company earnings. He said he left Core-Tex after his supervisor and colleagues did not take his concerns seriously. The former accountant hinted that the company's relationship with its external auditor was quite close, since Core-Tex's new CFO had once been on the external auditing team. Core-Tex had recently laid off 270 employees—a move that was not unexpected in these turbulent financial times. However, the layoff hit some parts of the site's community pretty hard. Finally, inspectors from the state environmental protection agency had just issued a series of citations to Core-Tex for improper disposal and high emissions at one of its larger manufacturing plants. A television station had run an exposé on the environmental citations a week ago.

CEO Kelly Buscio clicked off the television set and thought about the company's next steps. Core-Tex's attorney had cautioned the executive group earlier that week about communicating too much with the media and other constituents. The firm's vice president for marketing countered the attorney by insisting that Core-Tex needed to stay ahead of the rumors and assumptions that were being made about the company. The vice president of marketing said that suppliers and business partners were starting to question Core-Tex's financial viability. The vice president of information technology and the vice president of operations were undecided on the proper next steps. The vice president of manufacturing had not been at the meeting. Buscio rubbed her eyes and wondered what tomorrow could bring.

To her surprise, the newspapers were pretty gentle on Core-Tex the next day. There had been a major oil spill, the retirement of a *Fortune* 500 CEO, and a major league baseball championship game the night before, so the reporters were focused on those stories. The company's stock price, which averaged around $11.15, was down $0.35 by midmorning. Her VP of marketing suggested that employees needed to hear from the CEO and be reassured about Core-Tex's strong future. Her first call after lunch came from a member of the firm's board of directors. The director asked Buscio what the board could do to help the situation.

What would you do?

Legal, Regulatory, and Political Issues

Chapter Objectives

- To understand the rationale for government regulation of business

- To examine the key legislation that structures the legal environment for business

- To analyze the role of regulatory agencies in the enforcement of public policy

- To compare the costs and benefits of regulation

- To examine how business participates in and influences public policy

- To describe the government's approach for legal and ethical compliance

Chapter Outline

Government's Influence on Business

Business's Influence on Government and Politics

The Government's Strategic Approach for Legal and Ethical Compliance

Bear Stearns: Deceit and Derivatives Cause Destruction

Bear Stearns was an American institution that survived the Great Depression, but it met its ruin in 2008. Bear Stearns was the fifth largest investment bank and was one of the early institutions to fall during the financial crisis. Many see it as having kicked off the string of subsequent business failures and bailouts. While not as large and esteemed as Goldman Sachs or Morgan Stanley, it was among a group of large, trusted institutions that many people had previously thought were too big to fail.

Two things caused the doom of this eighty-five-year-old company: subprime mortgages and derivatives. Like many financial institutions, Bear Stearns, a global investment bank and securities brokerage firm, invested heavily in subprime mortgages. However, Bear Stearns misrepresented information to achieve its success. The company had inaccurately reported client information on some loan applications to make them appear less risky.

After securing the loans, Bear Stearns sold the debt to other institutions in the form of a financial instrument known as a derivative. In other words, Bear Stearns agreed to insure the debt that it sold to other companies. The derivatives were supposed to be backed by cash flows from the loans. This allowed Bear Stearns to move the risk onto investors. In November 2007, Bear Stearns had $13.4 trillion in derivatives. There was just one problem. When the economic downturn hit, the cash flows from the loans dried up and the bank could not make good on its promise to "bail out" investors.

After the firm fell, top executives made claims that they did not understand how risky the securities were in which they were investing. While this may be true to a certain extent, comments like this set off a rally of public outcry asking for justice. Stakeholders were rightfully enraged that top financial executives were gambling investors' money without disclosing or even knowing the risks involved.

The situation was made worse by the misconduct of executives Ralph Cioffi and Matthew Tannin. As the company's hedge funds were failing, the executives deceived investors by portraying the funds as great investments. A month later, the funds collapsed, losing $1.6 billion in investor assets. Although the U.S. government attempted to save Bear Stearns, the damage was irrevocable. JP Morgan purchased the firm for $10 a share, a far cry from its previous fifty-two-week high of $133.20 per share. Cioffi and Tannin were arrested, but this does little to recover the billions in investor assets they helped lose.[1]

The government has the power through laws and regulations to structure how businesses and individuals achieve their goals. The purpose of regulating firms is to create a fair competitive environment for businesses, consumers, and society. All stakeholders need to demonstrate a commitment to social responsibility through compliance with relevant laws and proactive consideration of social needs. The law is one of the most important business subjects in terms of its effect on organizational practices and activities. Thus, compliance with the law is an important foundation of social responsibility. Because the law is based on principles, norms, and values found within society, the law is the foundation of responsible decision making.

This chapter explores the complex relationship between business and government. First, we discuss some of the laws that structure the environment for the regulation of business. Major legislation relating to competition and regulatory agencies is reviewed to provide an overview of the regulatory environment. We also consider how businesses can participate in the public policy process through lobbying, political contributions, and political action committees. Finally, we offer a framework for a strategic approach to managing the legal and regulatory environment.

GOVERNMENT'S INFLUENCE ON BUSINESS

The government has a profound influence on business. Most Western countries have a history of elected representatives working through democratic institutions to provide the structure for the regulation of business conduct. For example, one of the differences that have long characterized the two major parties of the U.S. political system involves the government's role with respect to business. In general terms, the Republican Party tends to favor smaller central government with less regulation of business, while the Democratic Party is more open to government oversight, federal aid program, and sometimes higher taxes. From the start, President Obama worried some businesspeople, as he has promised more oversight of many different areas of the economy. For example, he has promised to be tough on antitrust violations and has followed through by reversing a Bush-era policy that made it more difficult for the government to pursue antitrust violations. The Bush administration brought a historically low number of antitrust cases to trial, a tactic that the Obama administration reversed.[2]

President Obama has brought U.S. policy regarding antitrust cases more in line with Europe's model, which marks a return to a historic norm after eight years of Bush's noninterventionism.[3] Third-party and independent candidates typically focus on specific business issues or proclaim their distance from the two major political parties. However, the power and freedom of big business have resulted in conflicts among private businesses, government, private-interest groups, and even individuals as businesses try to influence policy makers.

In the United States, the role that society delegates to government is to provide laws that are logically deduced from the Constitution and the Bill of Rights and to enforce these laws through the judicial system. Individuals and businesses, therefore, live under a rule of law that protects society and supports an acceptable quality of life. Ideally, by controlling the limitation of force by some parties, the overall welfare and freedom of all participants in the social system will be protected.

The provision of a court system to settle disputes and punish criminals, both organizational and individual, provides for justice and order in society. Both Intel and Microsoft have been hit with enormous fines for alleged antitrust activity in Europe, where the companies have been accused of engaging in behavior that prevents smaller companies from competing. The European Commission fined Intel a record-setting $1.45 billion after it was found guilty of taking anticompetitive measures against smaller competitor Advanced Micro Devices. Competitors in Europe have accused Microsoft of contractual tying because the company has been preloading its own Internet Explorer as part of the Windows operating system. Due to pressures from the Commission, Microsoft has agreed that it will now release a new version of Windows without a browser.[4] The European Union is famous for being tough on companies suspected of antitrust cases, igniting the ire of many multinational corporations that feel as if they are being punished for being successful. Being aware of antitrust laws is important for all large corporations around the world, no matter what the country, because judicial systems can punish businesses that fail to comply with laws and regulatory requirements.

The legal system is not always accepted in some countries as insurance that business will be conducted in a legitimate way. For example, after generations of being known for its top-secret bank accounts, Swiss banks were ordered by the U.S. Internal Revenue Service to disclose information about some of their clients because of concerns over illegal activities. In many places around the world, the business climate has become less tolerant of illegal and immoral actions, and countries like Switzerland, Liechtenstein, and Luxembourg now are being pressured to share information on potential tax dodgers with government agencies like the IRS. One bank alone, UBS, may harbor the secret bank accounts of 52,000 American tax dodgers.[5] The Swiss government ordered UBS not to divulge the U.S. clients' information on the grounds that it violated Swiss privacy laws.[6] This case illustrates the complexity of complying with international business laws.

While many businesses may object to regulations aimed at maintaining ethical cultures and preserving stakeholder welfare, businesses' very existence is based on laws permitting their creation, organization, and dissolution. From a social perspective, it is significant that a corporation has the same legal status as a "person" who can sue, be sued, and be held liable for debts. Laws may protect managers and stockholders from being personally liable for a company's debts, but individuals as well as organizations are still responsible for their conduct. Because corporations have a perpetual life, larger companies like ExxonMobil, Ford, and Sony take on an organizational culture, including social responsibility values, that extends beyond a specific time period, management team, or geographical region. Organizational culture plays an important role in the ability of corporations to outlive individual executives—it sets the tone for the business and allows for continuity even during times of leadership turnover.

Most, generally smaller, companies are owned by individual proprietors or operated as partnerships. However, large incorporated firms like those just mentioned often receive more attention because of their size, visibility, and impact on so many aspects of the economy and society. In a pluralistic society, diverse stakeholder groups such as business, labor, consumers, environmentalists, privacy advocates, and others attempt to influence public officials who legislate, interpret laws, and regulate business. The public interest is served though open participation and debate that result in effective public policy. Because no system of government is perfect, legal and regulatory systems are constantly evolving and changing in response to changes in the business environment and social institutions. For example, increasing use of the Internet for information and business created a need for legislation and regulations to protect the owners of creative materials from unauthorized use and consumers from fraud and invasions of privacy. The line between acceptable and illegal activity on the Internet is increasingly difficult to discern and is often determined by judges and juries.

> **"The public interest is served though open participation and debate that result in effective public policy."**

In response, the Better Business Bureau (BBB) offers an Online Accredited Business certification to 55,020 retailers, which certifies their high ethical standards and safety for online shoppers. The BBB lists the companies on its website and directs consumers to approved businesses' websites.[7] More than a million times a month, web users click on the BBB*OnLine* seals to check a firm's credibility and high standards.[8]

Companies that adopt a strategic approach to the legal and regulatory system develop proactive organizational values and compliance programs that identify areas of risks and include formal communication, training, and continuous improvement of responses to the legal and regulatory environment.

In the next section, we take a closer look at why and how the government affects businesses through laws and regulation, the costs and benefits of regulation, and how regulation may affect companies doing business in foreign countries.

The Rationale for Regulation

The United States was established as a capitalist system, but the prevailing capitalistic theory has changed over time. Adam Smith published his critical economic ideas in *The Theory of Moral Sentiments* and *Inquiry into the Nature and Causes of the Wealth of Nations,* which are still considered important today. Smith observed the supply and demand, contractual efficiency, and division of labor of various companies within England. Smith's writings formed the basis of modern economics. Smith's idea of *laissez-faire,* or "the invisible hand," is critical to capitalism in that it assumes the market, through its own inherent mechanisms, will keep commerce in equilibrium.

A second form of capitalism gained support at the beginning of the Great Depression. During the 1930s John Maynard Keynes argued that the state could stimulate economic growth and improve stability in the private sector—through, for example, controlling interest rates, taxation, and public projects.[9]

Keynes argued that government policies could be used to increase aggregate demand, thus increasing economic activity and reducing unemployment and deflation. He argued that the solution to depression was to stimulate the economy through some combination of a reduction in interest rates or government investment in infrastructure. President Franklin D. Roosevelt employed Keynesian economic theories to pull the United States out of the Great Depression, as President Obama is now trying to do with the 2008–2009 economic recession.

The third and most recent form of capitalism was developed by Milton Friedman, and represented a swing to the right on the political spectrum. Friedman had lived through the Great Depression but rejected the Keynesian conclusion that the market sometimes needs some intervention in order to function most efficiently. Friedman instead believed in deregulation because he thought that the system could reach equilibrium without government intervention.[10] Friedman's ideas were the guiding principles for government policy making in the United States, and increasingly throughout the world, starting in the second half of the twentieth century, especially during the presidencies of Presidents Ronald Reagan, George H. W. Bush, and George W. Bush.

Although the view of which form of capitalism is best has changed over time, the federal and state governments in the United States have always stepped in to enact legislation and create regulations to address particular issues and restrict the behavior of business in accordance with society's wishes. Many of the issues used to justify business regulation can be categorized as economic or social.

Economic and Competitive Reasons for Regulation A great number of regulations have been passed by legislatures over the last 100 years in an effort "to level the playing field" on which businesses operate. When the United States became an independent nation in the eighteenth century, the business environment consisted of many small farms, manufacturers, and cottage industries operating on a primarily local scale. With the increasing industrialization of the United States after the Civil War, "captains of industry" like John D. Rockefeller (oil), Andrew Carnegie (railroads and steel), Andrew Mellon (aluminum), and J. P. Morgan (banking) began to consolidate their business holdings into large national trusts. **Trusts** are organizations generally established to gain control of a product market or industry by eliminating competition. Such organizations are often considered detrimental because, without serious competition, they can potentially charge higher prices and provide lower-quality products to consumers. Thus, as these firms grew in size and power, public distrust of them likewise grew because of often-legitimate concerns about unfair competition. This suspicion and the public's desire to require these increasingly powerful companies to act responsibly spurred the first antitrust legislation. If trusts are successful in eliminating competition, a monopoly can result.

trust
an organization established to gain control of a product market or industry by eliminating competition

A **monopoly** occurs when just one business provides a good or service in a given market. Utility companies that supply electricity, natural gas, water, or cable television are examples of monopolies. The government tolerates these monopolies because the cost of supplying the good or providing the service is so great that few companies would be willing to invest in new markets without some protection from competition. Monopolies may also be allowed by patent laws that grant the developer of a new technology a period of time (usually seventeen years) during which no other firm can use the same technology without the patent holder's consent. Patent protections are permitted to encourage businesses to engage in riskier research and development by allowing them time to recoup their research, development, and production expenses and to earn a reasonable profit.

Because trusts and monopolies lack serious competition, there are concerns that they may either exploit their market dominance to restrict their output and raise prices or lower quality to gain greater profits. This concern is the primary rationalization for their regulation by the government. Public utilities, for example, are regulated by state public utility commissions and, where they involve interstate commerce, are subject to federal regulation as well. In recent years, some of these industries have been deregulated with the idea that greater competition will police the behavior of individual firms. However, in areas like utilities it is difficult to develop perfect competition because of the large sunk costs required. Oftentimes deregulation has led to increased costs to stakeholders. For example, Maryland deregulated the state's residential energy market in the late 1990s, and when rate caps came off in 2004 residences were hit with skyrocketing utilities costs. The problem has been market prices—when petroleum costs are high, so are the costs to generate energy. In a deregulated privatized market, these costs are passed on to consumers. The governor has tried numerous tactics to relieve the burden, including a one-time handout, but stakeholders remain concerned.[11]

Related to the issue of regulation of trusts and monopolies is society's desire to restrict destructive or unfair competition. What is considered unfair varies with the standard practice of the industry, the impact of specific conduct, and the individual case. When one company dominates a particular industry, it may engage in destructive competition or employ anticompetitive tactics. For example, it may slash prices in an effort to drive competitors out of the market and then raise prices later. It may conspire with other competitors to set, or "fix," prices so that each firm can ensure a certain level of profit. Other examples of unfair competitive trade practices are stealing trade secrets or obtaining other confidential information from a competitor's employees, trademark and copyright infringement, false advertising, and deceptive selling methods such as "bait and switch" and false representation of products.

Regulation is also intended to protect consumers from unethical business practices. Seniors, for instance, are a highly vulnerable demographic and are often the victims of business scams. New laws have taken aim at financial scams on seniors, such as free-lunch seminars. The state of Arkansas has taken the forefront on this issue, conducting police sweeps of suspected scams, increasing fines, and amending laws to impose increased penalties for those who prey on the elderly. Older people are the most vulnerable group when it comes to financial scams, as they rely on their savings for retirement security.[12]

monopoly
the situation where one business provides a good or service in a given market

Social Reasons for Regulation

Regulation may also occur when marketing activities result in undesirable consequences for society. Many manufacturing processes, for example, create air, water, or land pollution. Such consequences create uncounted "costs" in the form of contamination of natural resources, illness, and so on that neither the manufacturer nor the consumer "pays" for directly, although consumers end up paying for these costs nevertheless. Because few companies are willing to shoulder these costs voluntarily, regulation is necessary to ensure that all firms within an industry do their part to minimize

Regulations can result from marketing activities that cause negative effects on stakeholders and society

damages and pay their fair share. Likewise, regulations have proven necessary to protect resources, both natural (e.g., forests, fishing grounds, and other habitats) and social (e.g., historical and architecturally or archeologically significant structures). We will take a closer look at some of these environmental protection regulations and related issues in Chapter 11, which covers sustainability.

Other regulations have come about in response to social demands for equality in the workplace, especially after the 1960s. Such laws and regulations require that companies ignore race, ethnicity, gender, religion, and disabilities in favor of qualifications that more accurately reflect an individual's capacity for performing a particular job. Likewise, deaths and injuries because of employer negligence resulted in regulations designed to ensure that people can enjoy a safe working environment. The airline industry has become a prime example of tough economic times resulting in overworked, undertrained employees. Many pilots receive low compensation, poor health benefits, and are forced to work long hours—all factors that may have played a part in a tragic crash in Buffalo, New York, that killed all forty-nine passengers and one person on the ground. Even Captain Sully Sullenberger who safely landed a plane on the Hudson River after colliding with some geese confessed that his pay had been cut 40 percent from its high. Because the industry cannot pay for the best and the brightest, significant factors like experience and skill have become less important when hiring new pilots. Many airlines simply hire the best they can afford.[13]

Still other regulations have resulted from special-interest group crusades for safer products. For example, Ralph Nader's *Unsafe at Any Speed,* published in 1965, criticized the automobile industry as a whole, and General Motors specifically, for putting profit and style ahead of lives and safety. Nader's consumer protection organization, popularly known as Nader's Raiders, successfully campaigned for legislation that required automakers to provide safety belts, padded dashboards, stronger door latches, head restraints, shatterproof windshields, and collapsible steering columns in automobiles. As we will see in Chapter 8, consumer activists also helped secure passage of several other consumer protection laws, such as the Wholesome Meat Act of 1967, the Clean Water Act of 1972, and the Toxic Substance Act of 1976.

Issues arising from the increasing use of the Internet have led to demands for new laws protecting consumers and business. It is estimated that spam levels (unwanted emails) are up 156 percent since 2008. Google Message Security has been recording historically high spam levels, with an average of 194 spam messages blocked per user per day.[14] With an increase in spam comes an increase in viruses and malware programs. Although spam-blocking technology exists, spammers are increasingly finding ways to bypass these programs to reach their targets. For this reason, Internet access services in the past have pressed for tougher federal legislation in a quest to stop illicit commercial email. However, legislators often have difficulty with finding a way to block deceptive spammers without violating their First Amendment rights. Yet stiffer penalties are being enforced for well-known spammers, as evidenced by the conviction of the "Spam King" Sanford Wallace. Sanford Wallace and his partner, whose company sent up to 30 million junk emails per day in the 1990s, was accused by MySpace of sending over 730,000 deceitful spam messages to MySpace members. The pair now owe MySpace approximately $230 million in damages.[15]

As we shall see in Chapter 10, the technology associated with the Internet has generated a number of issues related to privacy, fraud, and copyrights. For instance, creators of copyrighted works such as movies, books, and music are calling for new laws and regulations to safeguard their ownership of these works. In response to these concerns, Congress enacted the Digital Millennium Copyright Act in 1998, which extended existing copyright laws to better protect "digital" recordings of music, movies, and the like. Many other countries have implemented similar measures. However, copyright violations continue to plague many global industries, which to some critics calls into question the effectiveness of legal action. A team of security specialists recommends technological, not legal, solutions as most effective in the fight against piracy and copyright infringement.[16]

Concerns about the collection and use of personal information, especially regarding children, resulted in the passage of the Children's Online Privacy Protection Act of 2000 (COPPA). The Federal Trade Commission (FTC) enforces the act by levying fines against noncomplying website operators. For example, the FTC imposed the largest COPPA penalty to date on Sony BMG. Sony agreed to pay $1 million to the FTC for collecting and disclosing information on thousands of children under age thirteen without parental consent.[17]

Internet safety among children is a major topic of concern. Research has shown that

> **"The technology associated with the Internet has generated a number of issues related to privacy, fraud, and copyrights."**

Table 4.1 Consumer Risk in Auctions

Type of risk	In-person auction	Online auction
Price information risk	High	Low
Time risk	Low	High
Vendor risk	Low	High
Security risk	Low	High
Privacy risk	Low	High
Performance risk	Low	High

Source: Dylan Cameron and Alison Galloway, "Consumer Motivations and Concerns in Online Auctions: An Exploratory Study," *International Journal of Consumer Studies* 29 (May 2005): 181–192.

filtering and age verification are not effective in making the Internet safer—businesses, regulators, and parents are all trying to find answers in how to protect children from dangers ranging from online predators to pornography.[18]

With good reason, consumers are worried about becoming victims of online fraud. According to the Internet Crime Complaint Center (IC3), online fraud contributes to the loss of nearly $300 million a year, with costs escalating every year.[19] Online auction fraud makes up a large percentage of Internet crime. In 2008, one in every four Internet scams reported to the IC3 involved online auction scams.[20] Table 4.1 describes the types of risk that consumers encounter in both in-person and online auctions. It is clear that online auctions present significantly greater risk than in-person transactions, which is linked to the degree of protection that consumers demand or require from the government.

Laws and Regulations

As a result of business abuses and social demands for reform, the federal government began to pass legislation to regulate business conduct in the late nineteenth century. In this section, we will look at a few of the most significant of these laws. Table 4.2 summarizes many more laws that affect business operations.

Sherman Antitrust Act The Sherman Antitrust Act, passed in 1890, is the principal tool employed by the federal government to prevent businesses from restraining trade and monopolizing markets. Congress passed the law, almost unanimously, in response to public demands to curtail the growing power and abuses of trusts in the late nineteenth century. The law outlaws "every contract, combination in the form of trust or otherwise, or conspiracy, in restraint of trade or commerce."[21] It also makes a violation of the law a felony crime, punishable by a fine of up to $10 million for corporate violators and $350,000 and/or three years in prison for individual offenders.[22]

Table 4.2 Major Federal Legislation

Act (Date Enacted)	Purpose
Sherman Antitrust Act (1890)	Prohibits contracts, combinations, or conspiracies to restrain trade; establishes as a misdemeanor monopolizing or attempting to monopolize
Clayton Act (1914)	Prohibits specific practices such as price discrimination, exclusive dealer arrangements, and stock acquisitions in which the effect may notably lessen competition or tend to create a monopoly
Federal Trade Commission Act (1914)	Created the Federal Trade Commission (FTC); gives the FTC investigatory powers to be used in preventing unfair methods of competition
Robinson-Patman Act (1936)	Prohibits price discrimination that lessens competition among wholesalers or retailers; prohibits producers from giving disproportionate services of facilities to large buyers
Wheeler-Lea Act (1938)	Prohibits unfair and deceptive acts and practices regardless of whether competition is injured; places advertising of foods and drugs under the jurisdiction of the FTC
Lanham Act (1946)	Provides protections and regulation of brand names, brand marks, trade names, and trademarks
Celler-Kefauver Act (1950)	Prohibits any corporation engaged in commerce from acquiring the whole or any part of the stock or other share of the capital assets of another corporation when the effect substantially lessens competition or tends to create a monopoly
Fair Packaging and Labeling Act (1966)	Makes illegal the unfair or deceptive packaging or labeling of consumer products
Magnuson-Moss Warranty (FTC) Act (1975)	Provides for minimum disclosure standards for written consumer product warranties; defines minimum consent standards for written warranties; allows the FTC to prescribe interpretive rules in policy statements regarding unfair or deceptive practices
Consumer Goods Pricing Act (1975)	Prohibits the use of price maintenance agreements among manufacturers and resellers in interstate commerce
Antitrust Improvements Act (1976)	Requires large corporations to inform federal regulators of prospective mergers or acquisitions so that they can be studied for any possible violations of the law
Trademark Counterfeiting Act (1988)	Provides civil and criminal penalties against those who deal in counterfeit consumer goods or any counterfeit goods that can threaten health or safety
Trademark Law Revision Act (1988)	Amends the Lanham Act to allow brands not yet introduced to be protected through registration with the Patent and Trademark Office
Nutrition Labeling and Education Act (1990)	Prohibits exaggerated health claims and requires all processed foods to contain labels with nutritional information
Telephone Consumer Protection Act (1991)	Establishes procedures to avoid unwanted telephone solicitations; prohibits marketers from using an automated telephone dialing system or an artificial or prerecorded voice to certain telephone lines

Table 4.2 Major Federal Legislation (*continued*)

Act (Date Enacted)	Purpose
Federal Trademark Dilution Act (1995)	Provides trademark owners the right to protect trademarks and requires relinquishment of names that match or parallel existing trademarks
Digital Millennium Copyright Act (1998)	Refined copyright laws to protect digital versions of copyrighted materials, including music and movies
Children's Online Privacy Act (2000)	Regulates the collection of personally identifiable information (name, address, email address, hobbies, interests, or information collected through cookies) online from children under age thirteen
Sarbanes-Oxley Act (2002)	Requires corporations to take responsibility to provide principles-based ethical leadership and holds CEOs and CFOs personally accountable for the credibility and accuracy of their company's financial statements
Emergency Economic Stabilization Act (2008)	Responded to the subprime mortgage crisis by creating the Troubled Assets Recovery Program (TARP), a program that authorized the U.S. Treasury to spend up to $700 billion to purchase troubled assets like mortgage-backed securities
Housing and Economic Recovery Act (2008)	A program lasting until 2011 that offers government insurance to lenders who volunteer to reduce their mortgages by at least 90 percent of the market's current value

Sources: "What Is the Troubled Asset Relief Program," *About.com: US Politics,* http://uspolitics.about.com/od/20072008/a/2008_TARP. htm, accessed July 3, 2009; "Housing and Economic Recovery Act of 2008 FAQ," *U.S. Department of Housing and Urban Development*, August 5, 2008, http://www.hud.gov/news/recoveryactfaq.cfm, accessed July 3, 2009.

The Sherman Antitrust Act applies to all firms operating in interstate commerce as well as to U.S. firms engaged in foreign commerce. The law has been used to break up some of the most powerful companies in the United States, including the Standard Oil Company (1911), the American Tobacco Company (1911), and AT&T (1984). There was also an attempt to break up Microsoft. In the Microsoft case, a U.S. district court judge ruled that the software giant inhibited competition by using unlawful tactics to protect its Windows monopoly in computer operating systems and by illegally expanding its dominance into the market for Internet Web-browsing software. In ordering that the company be split into two independent firms, Judge Thomas Penfield Jackson said that Microsoft had placed "an oppressive thumb on the scale of competitive fortune" by targeting competitors that threatened its Windows software monopoly. However, the ruling to break up Microsoft was appealed, and the order by Judge Jackson was overturned. The Supreme Court refused to hear an appeal by Microsoft that other aspects of its conviction should be overturned. Microsoft agreed to adhere to a consent decree, where it would comply with stricter remedies to prevent noncompetitive business practices through 2010. The Sherman Act remains the primary source of antitrust law in the United States, although it has been supplemented by several amendments and additional legislation.

Clayton Antitrust Act Because the provisions of the Sherman Antitrust Act were vague, the courts have interpreted the law in different ways. To rectify this situation, Congress enacted the Clayton Antitrust Act in 1914 to limit mergers and acquisitions that have the potential to stifle competition.[23] The Clayton Act also specifically prohibits price discrimination, tying agreements (when a supplier furnishes a product to a buyer with the stipulation that the buyer must purchase other products as well), exclusive agreements (when a supplier forbids an intermediary to carry products of competing manufacturers), and the acquisition of stock in another corporation where the effect may be to substantially lessen competition or tend to create a monopoly. In addition, the Clayton Act prohibits members of one company's board of directors from holding seats on the boards of competing corporations. The law also exempts farm corporations and labor organizations from antitrust laws.

Federal Trade Commission Act In the same year the Clayton Act was passed, Congress also enacted the Federal Trade Commission Act to further strengthen the antitrust provisions of the Sherman Act. Unlike the Clayton Act, which prohibits specific practices, the Federal Trade Commission Act more broadly prohibits unfair methods of competition. More significantly, this law created the Federal Trade Commission (FTC) to protect consumers and businesses from unfair competition. Of all the federal regulatory agencies, the FTC has the greatest influence on business activities.

When the FTC receives a complaint about a business or finds reason to believe that a company is engaging in illegal conduct, it issues a formal complaint stating that the firm is in violation of the law. If the company continues the unlawful practice, the FTC can issue a cease-and-desist order, which requires the offender to stop the specified behavior. For example, Stanley Works, a maker of tools and equipment, was ordered to cease advertising practices that the FTC deemed as misleading with respect to the origin of its products. Stanley was accused of misrepresenting the foreign origin of some of its products. Several years later, the FTC relaunched its probe of Stanley Works and found that the company was not fully compliant with the cease-and-desist order. At this point, Stanley agreed to pay a $205,000 civil penalty for failing to provide accurate country-of-origin information on product labels.[24]

Thus, although a firm can appeal to the federal courts to have the order rescinded, the FTC can seek civil penalties in court, up to a maximum penalty of $10,000 a day for each infraction, if a cease-and-desist order is ignored. The commission can also require businesses to air corrective advertising to counter previous ads the commission considers misleading. For example, the maker of Doan's pills was required by the FTC to run corrective advertising to counter its unproven claim that its product is more effective than other pain relievers at alleviating back pain.[25]

In addition, the FTC helps to resolve disputes and makes rulings on business decisions,

> **"In response to the 2008–2009 financial crisis, administrative leaders have proposed sweeping reforms to increase consumer protection."**

especially in emerging areas such as Internet privacy. For example, the commission approved a settlement that would permit the bankrupt Internet retailer Toysmart. com to sell its customer list as long as the buyer of the list agrees to abide by Toysmart's privacy guarantees.[26] In this case, the FTC helped to reinforce corporate guarantees of consumer privacy on the Internet.

Proposed Financial Reforms In response to the 2008–2009 financial crisis, administrative leaders have proposed sweeping reforms to increase consumer protection. This proposed legislation would be a step away from the deregulation practices of the last several decades, instead giving government a freer hand in regulating the financial industry. The Obama administration proposes giving the Federal Reserve more power over the financial industry and establishing a new Consumer Financial Protection Agency that would help to regulate banks and other financial institutions. More specifically, the agency would monitor financial instruments like subprime mortgages and other high-risk lending practices. Part of the problems leading up to the financial crisis included inaction on the part of federal regulators to protect consumers from fraud and predatory lending practices, lack of responsibility on the part of mortgage brokers taking large risks, conflicts of interest among credit rating industries, and complex financial instruments that investors did not understand.

To prevent these problems from leading to future financial crises, the current administration proposes legislation that would include the following reforms among others: removing some of the FTC's powers and other regulators and creating a Consumer Financial Protection Agency; creating a Financial Services Oversight Council to identify and address key risks to the financial industry; establishing a new National Bank Supervisor to oversee federally chartered lenders; requiring loan bundlers to retain a percentage of what they sell (a proposal also being considered by the EU); new powers for the Securities and Exchange Commission to monitor credit rating industries for objectivity; and requiring complex financial instruments to be traded on a regulated exchange.

The administration believes major changes in the regulatory system are needed. Republicans and other industry groups are against such extensive regulation, fearing that the government would assume too much control over the financial industry and threaten the free market system. Instead, they call for better regulation over more regulation, including holding current regulators and financial institutions more accountable for their actions. Whatever the outcome, one thing is generally agreed upon: reforms of the financial industry are needed to prevent future financial crises.[27]

© Zhang Yan/Xinhua/Landov

U.S. Treasury Secretary Timothy Geithner shares his vision for reshaping financial regulation with the Senate Banking Committee

Enforcement of the Laws Because violations of the Sherman Antitrust Act are felony crimes, the Antitrust Division of the U.S. Department of Justice enforces the act. The FTC enforces antitrust regulations of a civil, rather than criminal, nature. There are many additional federal regulatory agencies (see Table 4.3) that oversee the enforcement of other laws and regulations. Most states also have regulatory agencies that make and enforce laws for individuals and businesses. In recent years, cooperation among state attorneys general, regulatory agencies, and the federal government has increased, particularly in efforts related to the control of drugs, organized crime, and pollution.

The 2008–2009 financial meltdown revealed the need for better enforcement of the financial industry. Institutions took advantage of loopholes in the regulation system to make quick profits. For example, some adjustable mortgage rates offered low "teaser" rates that did not even cover the monthly interest on loans. This ended up increasing the principal balances on mortgages, resulting in debt that many consumers could not pay off. Unethical actions such as these led to the financial crisis. However, since these institutions were not as carefully monitored as other institutions, such as banks, regulators did not catch them until it was too late.[28] Part of the plan is to create a single bank regulator to oversee financial standards, and to establish the Consumer Financial Protection Agency to standardize options for consumer loans. New enforcement aims to require brokers to display a greater fiduciary duty to their clients, requiring them to put their clients' interests above their own and eliminating any conflicts of interest. This could cause them to offer products that are less costly and more tax-efficient for consumers over encouraging products that would benefit their companies at consumers' expense.[29]

In addition to enforcing stricter regulations for financial institutions, the Obama administration also wants to take steps to protect consumers. The Obama administration will encourage consumers to manage credit cards, savings, and mortgages more carefully; provide cardholders with warnings about how long it will take to pay off their debt if they only pay the minimum on their credit cards each month; and possibly prevent certain credit card issuers from offering credit cards to people under the age of twenty-one. Other proposed laws are more controversial. For instance, one plan includes a proposal requiring employers that do not offer retirement savings accounts to automatically enroll workers into individual retirement accounts. Employers would pay for this by taking deposits from employees' paychecks. Another plan proposes sending tax refunds directly into taxpayers' savings accounts instead of sending taxpayers checks in the mail. Although consumers could choose to opt out of these new approaches, opponents have said these proposed changes would create a more authoritarian government and leave room for governmental errors.[30]

In addition to enforcement by state and federal authorities, lawsuits by private citizens, competitors, and special-interest groups are used to enforce legal and regulatory policy. Through private civil actions, an individual or organization can file a lawsuit related to issues such as antitrust, price fixing, or unfair advertising. An organization can even ask for assistance from a federal agency to address a concern. For example, American Express gained the assistance of the Department of Justice's Antitrust Division in accusing Visa and MasterCard

Table 4.3 Federal Regulatory Agencies

Agency (Date Established)	Major Areas Of Responsibility
Food and Drug Administration (1906)	Enforces laws and regulations to prevent distribution of adulterated or misbranded foods, drugs, medical devices, cosmetics, veterinary products, and potentially hazardous consumer products
Federal Reserve Board (1913)	Regulates banking institutions; protects the credit rights of consumers; maintains the stability of the financial system; conducts the nation's monetary policy; and serves as the nation's central bank
Federal Trade Commission (1914)	Enforces laws and guidelines regarding business practices; takes action to stop false and deceptive advertising and labeling
Federal Deposit Insurance Corporation (1933)	Insures deposits in banks and thrift institutions for at least $250,000; identifies and monitors risks related to deposit insurance funds; and limits the economic effects when banks or thrift institutions fail
Federal Communications Commission (1934)	Regulates communication by wire, radio, and television in interstate and foreign commerce
Securities and Exchange Commission (1934)	Regulates the offering and trading of securities, including stocks and bonds
National Labor Relations Board (1935)	Enforces the National Labor Relations Act; investigates and rectifies unfair labor practices by employers and unions
Equal Employment Opportunity Commission (1970)	Promotes equal opportunity in employment through administrative and judicial enforcement of civil rights laws and through education and technical assistance
Environmental Protection Agency (1970)	Develops and enforces environmental protection standards and conducts research into the adverse effects of pollution
Occupational Safety and Health Administration (1971)	Enforces the Occupational Safety and Health Act and other workplace health and safety laws and regulations; makes surprise inspections of facilities to ensure safe workplaces
Consumer Product Safety Commission (1972)	Ensures compliance with the Consumer Product Safety Act; protects the public from unreasonable risk of injury from any consumer product not covered by other regulatory agencies
Commodity Futures Trading Commission (1974)	Regulates commodity futures and options markets; protects market users from fraud and abusive trading practices
Federal Housing Finance Industry (2008)	Combined the agencies of the Office of the Federal Housing Enterprise Oversight, the Federal Housing Finance Board, and the GSE mission office of the Department of Housing and Urban Development to oversee the country's secondary mortgage markets including Fannie Mae, Freddie Mac, and the Federal Home Loan Banks.

of antitrust violations.[31] Visa eventually agreed to settle the antitrust lawsuit by settling with American Express for $2.25 billion.[32]

In 2009, antitrust regulators also began investigating Google's intentions to scan millions of books and book titles into an online database. Recently, the company settled a copyright lawsuit with book publishers for $125 million. This settlement could allow Google to make millions of out-of-print books available online. Antitrust regulators are concerned that allowing one company to have rights to millions of books would give it too much power in the marketplace.[33]

Global Regulation

The twentieth century brought a number of regional trade agreements that decreased the barriers to international trade. NAFTA and the EU are two of these agreements that were formed with the intention of enhancing regional competitiveness and decreasing inequalities. The North American Free Trade Agreement (NAFTA), which eliminates virtually all tariffs on goods produced and traded between the United States, Canada, and Mexico, makes it easier for businesses of each country to invest in the other member countries. The agreement also provides some coordination of legal standards governing business transactions among the three countries. NAFTA promotes cooperation among various regulatory agencies to encourage effective law enforcement in the free trade area. Within the framework of NAFTA, the United States and Canada have developed many agreements to enforce each other's antitrust laws. The agreement provides for cooperation in investigations, including requests for information and the opportunity to visit the territory of the other nation in the course of conducting investigations.

The European Union (EU) was established in 1958 to promote free trade among its members and now includes twenty-seven European nations, with more expected to be admitted in coming years.[34] To facilitate trade among its members, the EU standardized business laws and trade barriers, to eliminate customs checks among its members, and introduced the Euro as a standard currency. Moreover, the Commission of the European Communities has entered into an agreement with the United States, similar to NAFTA, regarding joint antitrust laws. The European Union is in favor of tighter financial-market regulation in the wake of the financial crisis. Among the proposals is one by the European Commission establishing new regulatory bodies to oversee the bloc's financial industries. EU countries like France and Germany support such legislation, but the United Kingdom and some eastern European countries oppose a European financial body that would monitor individual financial firms in different countries. Some are concerned that were such a financial body to fail it could doom the entire EU. The UK does not want individual taxpayers to bear the brunt of a bank failure from another country.[35]

A company that engages in commerce beyond its own country's borders must contend with the potentially complex relationship among the laws of its own nation, international laws, and the laws of the nation in which it will be trading, as well as various trade restrictions imposed on international trade. International business activities are affected to varying degrees by each nation's laws, regulatory agencies, courts, the political environment, and special-interest groups. The European Union, for example, has been tough on large businesses, leaving some critics in the

United States to call the EU anticompetitive and anti-innovative. After the 2008–2009 financial crisis, which hit the EU hard, the European Commission has taken a tough stance on risk takers in the financial industry. These standards could place U.S. financial firms at a disadvantage, critics allege, preventing them from selling securities on the European market because of the differences in national legislation. A plan proposed by the European Parliament forces financial firms to maintain a 5 percent stake in asset-backed securities. Financial companies outside the European Union that have agencies to monitor major insurance industries may be exempt from the new rules, but U.S. insurers fear that the United States does not qualify. If not, U.S. firms could be penalized.[36]

These examples demonstrate how companies can experience major barriers when doing business in foreign countries. In addition to stricter regulations, countries can also establish import barriers, including tariffs, quotas, minimum price levels, and port-of-entry taxes that affect the importation of products. Other laws govern product quality and safety, distribution methods, and sales and advertising practices.

Although there is considerable variation and focus among different nations' laws, many countries have laws that are quite similar to those in the United States. Indeed, the Sherman Act has been copied throughout the world as the basis for regulating fair competition. Antitrust issues, such as price fixing and market allocation, have become a major area of international cooperation in the regulation of business.[37] Table 4.4 provides a list of situations and signs that antitrust may become a concern.

Table 4.4 Signs of Possible Antitrust Violation

• any evidence that two or more competing sellers of similar products have agreed to price their products a certain way, to sell only a certain amount of their product, or to sell only in certain areas or to certain customers
• large price changes involving more than one seller of very similar products of different brands, particularly if the price changes are of an equal amount and occur at about the same time
• suspicious statements from a seller suggesting that only one firm can sell to a particular customer or type of customer
• fewer competitors than normal submit bids on a project
• competitors submit identical bids
• the same company repeatedly has been the low bidder on contracts for a certain product or service or in a particular area
• bidders seem to win bids on a fixed rotation
• there is an unusual and unexplainable large dollar difference between the winning bid and all other bids
• the same bidder bids substantially higher on some bids than on others, and there is no logical cost reason to explain the difference

Source: U.S. Department of Justice, "Antitrust Enforcement and the Consumer," http://www.usdoj.gov/atr/public/div_stats/211491.pdf, accessed July 4, 2009.

Costs and Benefits of Regulation

Costs of Regulation Regulation results in numerous costs for businesses, consumers, and society at large. Although many experts have attempted to quantify these costs, it is quite difficult to find an accurate measurement tool. To generate such measurements, economists often classify regulations as economic (applicable to specific industries or businesses) or social (broad regulations pertaining to health, safety, and the environment). One yardstick for the direct costs of regulation is the administrative spending patterns of federal regulatory agencies. The 2009 estimated cost of regulatory activities was over $51 billion, which was up from $48 billion on 2008, $39.5 billion in 2005, and around $3 billion in 1960. Many people in the business world and beyond are concerned about the upward trajectory of regulatory costs. Another way to measure the direct cost of regulation is to look at the staffing levels of federal regulatory agencies. The expenditures and staffing of state and local regulatory agencies also generate direct costs to society. Federal regulatory agency jobs have been on the rise in recent years, to 263,989 full-time jobs in 2009.[38]

Still another way to approach the measurement of the costs of regulation is to consider the burden that businesses incur in complying with regulations. Various federal regulations, for example, may require companies to change their manufacturing processes or facilities (e.g., smokestack "scrubbers" to clean air and wheelchair ramps to make facilities accessible to customers and employees with disabilities). Companies also must keep records to document their compliance and to obtain permits to implement plans that fall under the scope of specific regulatory agencies. Again, state regulatory agencies often add costs to this burden. Regulated firms may also spend large amounts of money and other resources to prevent additional legislation and to appear responsible. Of course, businesses generally pass these regulatory costs on to their consumers in the form of higher prices, a cost that some label a "hidden tax" of government. Additionally, some businesses contend that the financial and time costs of complying with regulations stifle their ability to develop new products and make investments in facilities and equipment. Moreover, society must pay for the cost of staffing and operating regulatory agencies, and these costs may be reflected in federal income taxes. Table 4.5 describes the primary drivers to the cost of regulation, including those associated with administering, enforcing, and complying with the regulation.

Table 4. 5 Cost of Regulation

Type of Cost	Description
Administration and enforcement	Expenditures by government to develop and administer regulatory requirements, including the salaries of government workers, hiring inspectors, purchasing office supplies, and other overhead expenses
Compliance	Expenditures by organizations, both private and public, to meet regulatory requirements, such as hiring personnel, training employees, and monitoring compliance

Benefits of Regulation

Despite business complaints about the costs of regulation, it provides many benefits to business, consumers, and society as a whole. These benefits include greater equality in the workplace, safer workplaces, resources for disadvantaged members of society, safer products, more information about and greater choices among products, cleaner air and water, and the preservation of wildlife habitats to ensure that future generations can enjoy their beauty and diversity.

Companies that fail to respond to consumer desires or that employ inefficient processes are often forced out of the marketplace by more efficient and effective firms. Truly competitive markets also spur companies to invest in researching and developing product innovations as well as new, more efficient methods of production. These innovations benefit consumers through lower prices and improved goods and services. For example, companies such as Apple, IBM, and Dell Computer continue to engineer smaller, faster, and more powerful computers that help individuals and businesses to be more productive.

Regulatory Reform Many businesses and individuals believe that the costs of regulation outweigh its benefits. They argue that removing regulation will allow Adam Smith's "invisible hand of competition" to more effectively and efficiently dictate business conduct. Some people desire complete **deregulation,** or removal of all regulatory authority. Proponents of deregulation believe that less government intervention allows business markets to work more effectively. For example, many businesses want their industries deregulated to decrease their costs of doing business. Many industries have been deregulated to a certain extent since the 1980s, including trucking, airlines, telecommunications (long-distance telephone and cable television), and more recently, electric utilities. In many cases, this deregulation has resulted in lower prices for consumers as well as in greater product choice.

However, the onset of the 2008–2009 crisis has slowed the call for deregulation. After the economy plummeted, the United States and other countries around the world saw the need for greater regulation, particularly of the financial industry, and began to reverse the deregulatory trend of the previous two or three decades. Although the economic crisis stemmed from a variety of factors, many perceived that much of it stemmed from lack of appropriate governmental oversight and a dearth of ethical leadership in businesses. However, governments' reactions have many fearing that governments will assume too much control. There has always been considerable debate on the relative merits and costs of regulation, and these new changes resulting from the worst financial crisis since the Great Depression are not likely to lessen this controversy.

Self-Regulation Many companies attempt to regulate themselves in an effort to demonstrate social responsibility, to signal responsibility to stakeholders, and to preclude further regulation by federal or state government. Often these firms choose to join trade associations that have self-regulatory programs, many of which were established as a preventative measure to stop or delay the development of laws and regulations that would restrict the associations' business practices. Some trade associations establish codes of conduct by which their members must

deregulation
removal of all regulatory authority

"Many companies attempt to regulate themselves in an effort to demonstrate social responsibility, to signal responsibility to stakeholders, and to preclude further regulation by federal or state government."

abide or risk discipline or expulsion from the association.

Perhaps the best-known self-regulatory association is the Better Business Bureau (BBB), an organization supported by member businesses around the country. Founded in 1912, today there are more than 125 bureaus in the United States and Canada. The bureaus currently oversee more than 3 million local and national businesses and charities and resolve problems for millions of consumers and businesses each year.[39] Each bureau also works to champion good business practices within a community, although it usually does not have strong tools for enforcing its business conduct rules. When a company violates what the BBB believes to be good business practices, the bureau warns consumers through local newspapers or broadcast media.

If the offending organization is a member of the BBB, it may be expelled from the local bureau. For example, the membership of Priceline.com was revoked by a Connecticut Better Business Bureau after the online retailer failed to address numerous complaints related to misrepresentation of products, failure to provide promised refunds, and failure to correct billing problems.[40]

Self-regulatory programs like the Better Business Bureau have a number of advantages over government regulation. Establishment and implementation of such programs are usually less costly, and their guidelines or codes of conduct are generally more practical and realistic. Furthermore, effective self-regulatory programs reduce the need to expand government bureaucracy. However, self-regulation also has several limitations. Nonmember firms are under no obligation to abide by a trade association's industry guidelines or codes. Moreover, most associations lack the tools or authority to enforce their guidelines. Finally, these guidelines are often less strict than the regulations established by government agencies.

BUSINESS'S INFLUENCE ON GOVERNMENT AND POLITICS

Although the government has a profound effect on business activities, especially through its regulatory actions, business has an equal influence on government, and that influence has grown in recent years as multinationals grow in size and resources. Managing this relationship with government officials while navigating the dynamic world of politics is a major challenge for firms, both large and small. In our pluralistic society, many participants are involved in the political process, and the economic stakes are high. Because government is a stakeholder of business (and vice versa), businesses and government can work together as both legitimately participate in the political process. For example, the SAFE-BioPharma Association was established by a group of international biopharmaceutical companies and is working with the FDA to create a secure means of conducting business and transferring information electronically for the pharmaceutical industry. The goal of the association is to transform the biopharmaceutical and health-care industries to a completely electronic business environment by 2012. The SAFE-BioPharma Association has worked to develop pilot programs for using digital signatures in the hopes of attaining a fully electronic environment.[41]

Obviously, many people believe that businesses should not be allowed to influence government because of their size, resources, and vested interests. Business participation can either be direct or indirect, positive or negative for society's interest depending not only on the outcome but also on the perspective of various stakeholders.

Figure 4.1 describes four approaches to the relationship between social responsibility and political involvement by companies. Firms with a high level of social responsibility and political involvement are considered corporate activists because they take political actions that may be seen as positive or negative by stakeholder groups. For example, Shell was accused of being anti-activist after the company refused to intervene with the Nigerian government on the execution of the nine leaders of MOSOP, Movement for the Survival of the Ogoni People. Although Shell wrote to government officials asking for human treatment of the MOSOP leaders, the company maintained a policy against involvement in domestic politics.

Figure 4.1 Social Responsibility and Political Involvement

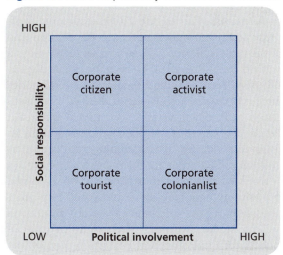

Source: Daniel Malan, "Corporate Citizens, Colonialists, Tourists or Activists? Ethical Challenges Facing South African Corporations in Africa," *Journal of Corporate Citizenship* 18 (Summer 2005): 49–60.

On the other hand, firms that are relatively weak in terms of social responsibility and political involvement may be called corporate tourists. This label implies that, much like tourists, these companies are relatively uninvolved on a social or political level and are able to exit with ease and a low level of consequence.

Good corporate citizens strive for strategic social responsibility but are not overly involved in the political climate of an area or country. In this regard, corporate citizens are focused on the four levels of social responsibility without resorting to aggressive activity in the political and governmental arena. This type of company would consider the needs of primary and secondary stakeholders without granting special privilege or resources to political stakeholders. Finally, firms with low levels of social responsibility but high levels of political interest are considered corporate colonialists. These companies are typically focused on obtaining competitive and economic power, even if it is detrimental to the local culture, environment, economy, or other social element. One example is the British South Africa Company, which was formed with the consent of the British government. The company had its own police force and flew a flag with the motto, "Justice, Commerce, Freedom." The company's founder, Cecil John Rhodes, stated that "Africa awaits us still, and it is our duty to seize every opportunity of acquiring more territory and we should keep this one idea steadily before our eyes. . . ."[42] Before we look at specific tactics businesses use to influence government policy, it is useful to briefly examine the current political environment to understand how business influence has grown.

The Contemporary Political Environment

Beginning in the 1960s, a significant "antiestablishment" public that was growing more hostile to business mounted protests to effect reform. Their increasingly vocal efforts spurred a fifteen-year wave of legislation and regulation to address a number of issues of the day, including product safety, employment discrimination, human rights, energy shortages, environmental degradation, and scandals related to bribery and payoffs. During the Republican-dominated 1980s, the pendulum swung back in favor of business. During the 1990s, economic prosperity driven by technological advances encouraged both the Republican and Democratic Parties to encourage the self-regulation of business while protecting competition and the natural environment. President George W. Bush continued these policies through 2008, with continued self-regulation of industries and the rolling back of environmental laws that businesses deemed detrimental. However, 2009 and the election of President Barack Obama has marked a change back toward more regulation. The onset of the financial crisis created an even greater need for stricter legislation under the Obama administration, such as the Troubled Assets Recovery Program (TARP) that authorized the U.S. Treasury to purchase up to $700 billion of troubled assets like mortgage-backed securities. It has also resulted in support for entirely new regulation and regulatory agencies like President Obama's proposal for a new Consumer Financial Protection Agency. These new regulations will have wide-sweeping effects over the financial industry. Other organizations such as the Environmental Protection Agency and the Food and Drug Administration also began to regulate with the aim of protecting stakeholders with renewed vigor beginning in 2009.

Such changes in the political environment over the last fifty years shaped the political environment in which businesses operate and created new avenues for businesses to participate in the political process. Among the most significant factors shaping the political environment were changes in Congress and the rise of special-interest groups. As the current administration seeks to revive and increase oversight of the finance industry, more companies will hire lobbyists to campaign on behalf of their interests in Washington.

Changes in Congress Among the calls for social reform in the 1960s were pressures for changes within the legislative process of the U.S. Congress itself. Bowing to this pressure, Congress enacted an amendment to the Legislative Reorganization Act in 1970, which ushered in a new era of change for the political process. This legislation significantly revamped the procedures of congressional committees, most notably stripping committee chairpersons of much of their power, equalizing committee and chair assignments, and requiring committees to record and publish all roll-call votes taken in committee. By opening up the committee process to public scrutiny and reducing the power of senior members and committee leaders, the act reduced the level of secrecy surrounding the legislative process and effectively brought an end to an era of autonomous committee chairs and senior members.[43]

Another significant change occurred in 1974 when Congress amended the Federal Election Campaign Act to limit contributions from individuals, political parties, and special-interest groups organized to get specific candidates elected or policies enacted.[44] Around the same time, many states began to shift their electoral process from the traditional party caucus to primary elections, further eroding the influence of the party in the political process. These changes ultimately had the effect of reducing the importance of political parties by decreasing members' dependence on their parties. Many candidates for elected offices began to turn to special-interest groups to raise enough funds to mount serious campaigns and reelection bids.

In 2002, Congress passed the Bipartisan Campaign Reform Act (BRCA), sponsored by Senators John McCain and Russell Feingold. This new act limited the amount of contributions parties could donate to political campaigns and it implemented rules for how corporate and labor treasury funds could be used in federal elections. The act also forbade national party committees from raising or spending unregulated funds. Though the act outraged certain legislators, who appealed to the Supreme Court over its constitutionality, the Supreme Court upheld the act.[45]

Rise of Special-Interest Groups The success of activists' efforts in the 1960s and 1970s marked the rise of special-interest groups. The movements to promote African-American and women's rights and to protest the Vietnam War and environmental degradation evolved into well-organized groups working to educate the public about significant social issues and to crusade for legislation and regulation of business conduct they deemed irresponsible. These progressive groups were soon joined on Capitol Hill by more conservative groups working to further their agendas on issues such as business deregulation, restriction of abortion and gun control, and promotion of prayer in schools. Businesses joined in by forming industry and trade associations. These increasingly powerful special-interest groups now focused on getting candidates elected who could further their own political agendas. Common Cause, for example, is a nonprofit, nonpartisan organization working to fight corrupt government and special interests backed by large sums of money. Since 1970, Common Cause, with more than 200,000 members, has campaigned for greater openness and accountability in government. Some of its self-proclaimed "victories" include reform of presidential campaign finances, tax systems, congressional ethics, open meeting standards, and disclosure requirements for lobbyists. Table 4.6 lists the dates and subject matter of Common Cause's major accomplishments over the past three decades.

Table 4.6 Accomplishments of Common Cause

1971: Helped pass the Twenty-Sixth Amendment, giving eighteen-year-olds the right to vote
1974: Led efforts to pass presidential public financing, contribution limits, and disclosure requirements
1974–1975: Helped pass Freedom of Information Act (FOIA) and open meetings laws at federal, state, and local levels
1978: Led effort to pass the historic Ethics in Government Act of 1978, requiring financial disclosure for government officials and restricting the "revolving door" between business and government
1982: Worked to pass extension of the Voting Rights Act
1989: Successfully lobbied for passage of the Ethics in Government Act
1990: Worked to help pass the Americans with Disabilities Act, guaranteeing civil rights for the disabled
1995: Lobbied for limits on gifts in the House and Senate and for passage of the Lobby Reform Act, providing disclosure of lobbyists' activity and spending
2000: Successfully worked for legislation to unmask and require disclosure of "527" political groups
2001: Lobbied successfully with a coalition for the Help America Vote Act, which provided funding to states for improvement of the nation's system of voting
2002: Led successful multiyear campaign to enact the Bipartisan Campaign Reform Act, banning soft money in federal campaigns; in 2003, in a landmark decision, the U.S. Supreme Court upheld the law
2004: Launched major voter mobilization and election monitoring programs for the presidential election
2005: Won the fight against efforts to cut federal funding for the Corporation for Public Broadcasting, and gathered 150,000 petition signatures calling for the resignation of CPB Chair Ken Tomlinson for partisan and unethical behavior
2005–2006: Led the charge against disgraced Majority Leader Tom DeLay, and fought for major ethics reform
2007: Fought successfully for passage of the Honest Leadership and Open Government Act of 2007, making major improvements in ethics and lobby laws and rules

Source: Common Cause, "History and Accomplishments," http://www.commoncause.org/site/pp.asp?c=dkLNK1MQIwG&b=4860205, accessed July 5, 2009.

Corporate Approaches to Influencing Government

Although some businesses view regulatory and legal forces as beyond their control and simply react to conditions arising from those forces, other firms actively seek to influence the political process to achieve their goals. In some cases, companies publicly protest the actions of legislative bodies. More often, companies work for the election of political candidates who regard them positively. Lobbying, political action committees, and campaign contributions are some of the tools businesses employ to influence the political process.

"Lobbying, political action committees, and campaign contributions are some of the tools businesses employ to influence the political process."

Lobbying Among the most powerful tactics business can employ to participate in public policy decisions is direct representation through full-time staff who communicate with elected officials. **Lobbying** is the process of working to persuade public and/or government officials to favor a particular position in decision making. Organizations may lobby officials either directly or by combining their efforts with other organizations.

Many companies concerned about the threat of legislation or regulation that may negatively affect their operations employ lobbyists to communicate their concerns to officials on their behalf. Microsoft, for example, had a Washington office with a staff of fourteen lobbyists and spent $4.6 million to persuade federal officials that breaking up the company for antitrust violations would harm the computer industry and U.S. economy.[46] The company's efforts were successful. However, its lobbyists wield less power internationally and therefore have not been as helpful in fighting its antitrust allegations in the EU.

The financial industry has long employed lobbyists to push for increased deregulation so that it can pursue riskier and more profitable avenues, but under a Democratically-controlled congress, financial industry lobbyists will be working harder than usual. The current administration plans to change compensation practices among bank employees. In the past few years, bank officials have often been awarded for the quantity of business they do, rather than the quality, which encouraged employees to engage in riskier business practices to increase their compensation packages. The administration wants to change bank compensation packages to award a "best practices" pay structure and limit the amount of bonuses top bank officials can receive. Additionally, new Treasury laws would also force banks to better inform borrowers about the costs of certain loans, create greater supervision of bank practices, and even establish a capital surcharge for certain banks. Banks are expected to fight these potential financial reforms through discreet lobbying and industry groups.[47]

Companies may attempt to influence the legislative or regulatory process more indirectly through trade associations and umbrella organizations that represent

lobbying
the process of working to persuade public and/or government officials to favor a particular position in decision making

Organizations such as the Pet Food Initiative attempt to protect consumers and in this case testify before a Senate subcommittee on recent pet food recalls

collective business interests of many firms. Virtually every industry has one or more trade associations that represent the interests of their members to federal officials and provide public education and other services for their members. Examples of such trade associations include the National Association of Home Builders, the Tobacco Institute, the American Book-sellers Association, and the Pet Food Institute. Additionally, there are often state trade associations, such as the Hawaii Coffee Association and the Michigan Beer and Wine Wholesalers Association, which work on state- and regional-level issues. Umbrella organizations such as the National Federation of Independent Businesses and the U.S. Chamber of Commerce also help promote business interests to government officials. The U.S. Chamber of Commerce takes positions on many political, regulatory, and economic questions. With more than 200,000 member companies, its goal is to promote its members' views of the ideal free enterprise marketplace.

The cozy relationship between corporations and the government has been a growing concern for years, and was a topic of serious discussion after the 2008–2009 financial industry meltdown. For example, more than one-quarter of the forty-eight members of the House Energy and Commerce Committee own stock in energy, oil, and natural gas companies. Some citizens are concerned that these investments could create a conflict of interest among legislators, as they are at the forefront of climate-change legislation. However, House and Senate ethics do not forbid Congress from having a stake in companies unless they pass a law that would benefit only their own interests.[48]

Political Action Committees Companies can also influence the political process through political action committees. **Political action committees (PACs)** are organizations that solicit donations from individuals and then contribute these funds to candidates running for political office. Companies are barred by federal law from donating directly to candidates for federal offices or to political action committees, and individuals are limited to relatively small donations. However, companies can organize PACs to which their executives, employees, and stockholders can make significant donations as individuals. PACs operate independently of business and are usually incorporated. Labor unions and other special-interest groups, such as teachers and medical doctors, can also establish PACs to promote their goals.

The Federal Election Committee has rules to restrict PAC donations to $5,000 per candidate for each election. However, many PACs exploit loopholes

political action committees (PACs)
organizations that solicit donations from individuals and then contribute these funds to candidates running for political office

in these regulations by donating so-called soft money to political parties that do not support a specific candidate for federal office. Under current rules, these contributors can make unlimited donations to political parties for general activities. Even though President Obama refused contributions from PACs during his presidential campaign, a USA Today analysis revealed that 175 members of Congress received at least half of their campaign funds from PACs that year. This amounted to a record $416 million on the federal election. The PAC of the National Association of Realtors alone contributed $4.8 million to the election.[49]

Campaign Contributions Although federal laws restrict direct corporate contributions to election campaigns, corporate money may be channeled into candidates' campaign coffers as corporate executives' or stockholders' personal contributions. Such donations can violate the spirit of corporate campaign laws. A sizable contribution to a candidate may carry with it an implied understanding that the elected official will perform some favor, such as voting in accordance with the contributor's desire on a particular law. Occasionally, some businesses find it so important to ensure favorable treatment that they make illegal corporate contributions to campaign funds. For example, Californian Gladwin Gill admitted to making illegal corporate campaign contributions. He convinced numerous employees and friends to give him funds for campaign contributions, which he put under their names. In exchange, he paid them out-of-pocket or from corporate funds. In total, Gill made approximately $67,000 in illegal contributions to political campaigns between 2003 and 2005.[50]

Although laws limit corporate contributions to specific candidates, it is acceptable for businesses and other organizations to make donations to political parties. Table 4.7 lists selected industry sectors and their contributions to political parties.

Table 4.7 Political Contributions by Industry Sector

Industry Sector	To Democrats	To Republicans
Lobbyists	$19,953,419	$15,131,715
Lawyers and law firms	$180,116,431	$54,624,091
Health professionals	$50,342,919	$45,187,330
Insurance	$20,992,420	$25,681,947
Pharmaceuticals	$14,514,128	$14,604,667
Education	$46,835,701	$10,089,965
Commercial banks	$17,724,944	$19,316,312

Source: Center for Responsive Politics, "Industry Profiles," http://www.opensecrets.org/industries/index.php, accessed July 5, 2009.

Gatekeepers Provide Oversight for Accountability in the Financial Industry

Gatekeepers are types of "watchdogs" that make sure that certain organizations are behaving ethically toward stakeholders. Dr. John Coffee from Columbia University calls them "intermediaries who provide verification and certification of services to investors." They are especially important in the financial industry. Financial gatekeepers include accountants, who are expected to disclose accurate financial information about companies. Unfortunately, some accountants, like the accounting firm Arthur Andersen, have failed to do so. Arthur Andersen was focused more on company growth than it was on accurate financial reporting. Thus, it looked the other way when faced with questionable accounting practices at Enron. Its negligence eventually led to its destruction. This emphasizes that gatekeepers must exhibit high ethical standards since they are in such an important position of financial trust.

Gatekeepers like Standard & Poor's assess the risks of companies and then express it through a lettering system. "AAA" is the highest rating, whereas "C" means it is a bad investment. In light of the financial crisis, investors must have confidence in financial-rating systems if they are to invest during this troubled time. Regulatory agencies like the Federal Deposit Insurance Corporation (FDIC) and the Securities and Exchange Commission (SEC) also act as gatekeepers. The FDIC guarantees the safety of checking and savings deposits in the bank. The SEC enforces securities laws and oversees financial markets. Both have received recent criticism. As a gatekeeper of banks, the FDIC did not discourage them from engaging in risky subprime mortgages. Additionally, the SEC had received tips that investor Bernie Madoff was operating an illegal scam since 1999, yet they did nothing. The scam lost investors an estimated $65 billion.

The mistakes of financial gatekeepers in this past decade demonstrate all the more need for efficient gatekeepers in this area. Gatekeepers are what cement the trust between stakeholders and financial organizations. However, critics have accused these risk assessors of giving good ratings to mortgage-backed debt, the debt which helped lead to the financial crisis. When homeowner defaults arose, the risk assessors were slow to lower their ratings. An investigation revealed that conflicts of interest may exist with these risk assessors, as some of their funds come from the very firms they rate. The Securities and Exchange Commission (SEC) found that risk assessors had been putting profits over quality when determining ratings for mortgage-backed securities. This scandal has led the SEC to reevaluate how risk assessors are regulated and consider changing the pay structure to eliminate this conflict of interest.[51]

THE GOVERNMENT'S APPROACH FOR LEGAL AND ETHICAL COMPLIANCE

Thus far, we have seen that, although legal and regulatory forces have a strong influence on business operations, businesses can also affect these forces through the political process. In addition, socially responsible firms strive to comply with society's wishes for responsible conduct through legal and ethical behavior. Indeed, the most effective way for businesses to manage the legal and regulatory environment is to establish values and policies that communicate and reward appropriate conduct. Most employees will try to comply with an organization's leadership and directions for responsible conduct. Therefore, top management must develop and implement a highly visible strategy for effective compliance. This means that top managers must take responsibility and be accountable for assessing legal risks and developing corporate programs that promote acceptable conduct.

"Top managers must take responsibility and be accountable for assessing legal risks and developing corporate programs that promote acceptable conduct."

Federal Sentencing Guidelines for Organizations

More and more companies are establishing organizational compliance programs to ensure that they operate legally and responsibly, as well as to generate a competitive advantage based on a reputation for responsible citizenship. There are also strong legal incentives to establish such programs. The U.S. Sentencing Commission established the **Federal Sentencing Guidelines for Organizations (FSGO)** in 1991 not only to streamline the sentencing and punishment for organizational crimes but also to hold companies, as well as their employees, responsible for misconduct. Previously, the law punished only those employees responsible for an offense, not the company. Under the FSGO, if a court determines that a company's organizational culture rewarded or otherwise created opportunities that encouraged wrongdoing, the firm may be subject to stiff penalties in the event that one of its employees breaks the law. The guidelines apply to all felonies and Class A misdemeanors committed by employees in association with their work.

The assumption underlying the FSGO is that good, socially responsible organizations maintain compliance systems and internal governance controls that deter misconduct by their employees. Thus, the guidelines focus on crime prevention and detection by mitigating penalties for firms that have implemented such compliance programs in the event that one of their employees commits a crime. To avoid or limit fines and other penalties as a result of wrongdoing by an employee, the employer must be able to demonstrate that it has implemented a reasonable program for deterring and preventing unlawful behavior.

The U.S. Sentencing Commission has delineated seven steps that companies must implement to demonstrate the existence of an effective compliance effort and thereby avoid penalties in the event of an employee's wrongdoing. These steps, which are listed in Table 4.8, are based on the commission's determination to emphasize compliance programs and to provide guidance for both organizations and courts regarding program effectiveness. The steps help companies

Federal Sentencing Guidelines for Organizations (FSGO) established in 1991 to streamline the sentencing and punishment for organizational crimes and to hold companies, as well as their employees, responsible for misconduct

Table 4.8 Seven Steps to Effective Compliance and Ethics Programs

1. Establish codes of conduct (identify key risk areas).
2. Appoint or hire high-level compliance manager (ethics officer).
3. Take care in delegating authority (background checks on employees).
4. Institute a training program and communication system (ethics training).
5. Monitor and audit for misconduct (reporting mechanisms).
6. Enforce and discipline (management implementation of policy).
7. Revise program as needed (feedback and action).

Source: Adapted from Nick Ciancio, "The Seven Pillars of an Effective Ethics and Compliance Program," Health Care Compliance Association, http://www.globalcompliance.com/pdf/the-seven-pillars-of-an-effective-ethics-and-compliance-program.pdf, accessed July 7, 2009.

understand what is required of a compliance and ethics program that is capable of reducing employees' opportunities to engage in misconduct.

To cultivate an effective ethics and compliance program, an organization should first develop a code of conduct that communicates the standards it expects of its employees and identifies key risk areas for the firm. Next, oversight of the program should be assigned to high-ranking personnel in the organization (e.g., an ethics officer, a vice president of human resources, or a general counsel) who are recognized as individuals who abide by the legal and ethical standards of the industry. Authority should never be delegated to anyone with a known propensity to engage in misconduct. An effective compliance program also requires a meaningful communications system, often in the form of ethics training, to disseminate the company's standards and procedures. This system should provide for mechanisms, such as anonymous toll-free phone lines or company ombudsmen, through which employees can report wrongdoing without fear of retaliation. Monitoring and auditing systems designed to detect misconduct are also crucial ingredients for an effective compliance program. If a company does detect criminal behavior or other wrongdoing by an employee, it must take immediate, appropriate, and fair disciplinary action toward all individuals both directly and indirectly responsible for the offense. Finally, if a company discovers that a crime has occurred, it must take steps to prevent similar offenses in the future. This usually involves modifications to the compliance program, additional employee training, and communications about specific types of conduct. In 2007 and 2008, more responsibility was placed on the board and top management to create an ethical organizational culture. This clearly places the responsibility for ethics and compliance on top leadership.[52]

A Supreme Court decision held that the sentences for violations of law were not mandatory but should serve only as recommendations for judges to use in their decisions. Some legal and business experts believe that this decision might weaken the implementation of the FSGO, but most sentences have been in the same range as before the Supreme Court decision. The guidelines remain an important consideration in developing an effective ethics and compliance program.

Table 4.9 Institutionalization of Ethics Through the U.S. Sentencing Guidelines for Organizations

1991	*Law:* U.S. Sentencing Guidelines for Organizations created means for federal prosecutions of organizations. These guidelines provide for just punishment, adequate deterrence, and incentives for organizations to prevent, detect, and report misconduct. Organizations need to have an effective ethics and compliance program to receive incentives in the case of misconduct.
2004	*Amendments:* The definition of an effective ethics program now includes the development of an ethical organizational culture. Executives and board members must assume the responsibility of identifying areas of risk, provide ethics training, create reporting mechanisms, and designate an individual to oversee ethics programs.
2007–2008	*Additional definition of a compliance and ethics program:* Firms should focus on due diligence to detect and prevent misconduct and to promote an organizational culture that encourages ethical conduct. More details are provided encouraging the assessment of risk and appropriate steps to design, implement, and modify ethics programs and training to include all employees, top management, and the board or governing authority. These modifications continue to reinforce the importance of an ethical culture in preventing misconduct.

The most recent amendments to the FSGO extend the ethics training of individuals to members of the board or governing authority, high-level personnel, employees, and the organizations' agents, as illustrated by Table 4.9. This applies not only to oversight, but to mandatory training at all levels of the organization. Merely distributing a code of ethics does not meet the training requirements. The 2007 and 2008 amendments now require most governmental contractors to provide ethics and compliance training. As new FSGO amendments are implemented, more explicit responsibility is being placed on organizations to improve and expand ethics and compliance provisions to include all employees and board members.

A strong program acts as a buffer to keep employees from committing crimes and to protect a company's reputation should wrongdoing occur despite its best efforts. If a firm can demonstrate that is has truly made an effort to communicate to its employees about their legal and ethical responsibilities, the public's response to any wrongdoing may be reduced along with any corporate punishment the courts mete out for the offense. It is important to point out, however, that executives who focus on strict legal compliance are missing part of the picture when it comes to social responsibility. By developing a work environment that supports and expects ethical decision making, management can avoid the perilous situation where employees ask, "Is this legal?" Strong corporate values and ethical standards, which are consistent with and more restrictive than legal standards, should minimize the missteps that are likely to occur in a compliance-driven firm. An effective program must feature ethics and values as the driving force, as we shall see in the next few chapters.

Sarbanes-Oxley Act

During probes into financial reporting fraud at many of the world's largest companies, investigators learned that hundreds of public corporations were not reporting their financial results accurately. Accounting firms, lawyers, top corporate officers, and boards of directors had developed a culture of deception to attempt to gain investor approval and competitive advantage. The downfall of many of these companies resulted in huge losses to thousands of investors, and employees even lost much of their savings from 401k accounts. The **Sarbanes-Oxley Act (SOX)** was enacted to restore stakeholder confidence and provide a new standard of ethical behavior for U.S. businesses in the wake of Enron and WorldCom in the early 2000s.

The act had almost unanimous support by Congress, government regulatory agencies, and the general public. When President Bush signed the act, he emphasized the need for the standards it provides, especially for top management and boards of directors responsible for company oversight. Table 4.10 details the requirements of the act.

The section of SOX that has caused the most concern for companies has been compliance with section 404. Section 404 comprises three central issues: it requires that (1) management create reliable internal financial controls; (2) management attest to the reliability of those controls and the accuracy of financial statements that result from those controls; and (3) an independent auditor further attests to the statements made by management. Because the cost of compliance

Sarbanes-Oxley Act (SOX)
legislation to protect investors by improving the accuracy and reliability of corporate disclosures

Table 4.10 Major Provisions of the Sarbanes-Oxley Act

1.	Requires the establishment of an Independent Accounting Oversight Board in charge of regulations administered by the Securities and Exchange Commission
2.	Requires CEOs and CFOs to certify that their companies' financial statements are true and without misleading statements
3.	Requires that corporate board of directors' audit committees consist of independent members with no material interests in the company
4.	Prohibits corporations from making or offering loans to officers and board members
5.	Requires codes of ethics for senior financial officers; codes must be registered with the SEC
6.	Prohibits accounting firms from providing both auditing and consulting services to the same client
7.	Requires company attorneys to report wrongdoing to top managers and, if necessary, to the board of directors; if managers and directors fail to respond to reports of wrongdoing, the attorney should stop representing the company
8.	Mandates "whistle-blower protection" for persons who disclose wrongdoing to authorities
9.	Requires financial securities analysts to certify that their recommendations are based on objective reports
10.	Requires mutual fund managers to disclose how they vote shareholder proxies, giving investors information about how their shares influence decisions
11.	Establishes a ten-year penalty for mail/wire fraud
12.	Prohibits the two senior auditors from working on a corporation's account for more than five years; other auditors are prohibited from working on an account for more than seven years; in other words, accounting firms must rotate individual auditors from one account to another from time to time

is so high for many companies, some publicly traded companies have even considered de-listing themselves from the U.S. Stock Exchange.

Many company boards failed to provide the necessary oversight of the financial decisions of top officers and executives. This trend of fraud by top company officials contributed to the severity of the 2008–2009 financial crisis. Many top executives were charged with behaving in unethical and illegal ways. For example, the Securities and Exchange Commission (SEC) filed civil fraud and insider trading charges against Countrywide Financial CEO Angelo Mozilo, who was charged with misleading investors about the credit risks Countrywide was taking.[53] The Federal Bureau of Investigation (FBI) also investigated Fannie Mae, Freddie Mac, Lehman Brothers, and American International Group (AIG) for corporate fraud, either for misrepresenting their company's financial well-being or providing extensive compensation packages to company executives when the companies were in the midst of a financial meltdown.[54]

To address fraudulent occurrences such as these, SOX required the creation of the Public Company Accounting Oversight Board, which is supposed to provide oversight of the accounting firms that audit public companies and set standards and rules for the auditors in these firms. The board has investigatory and disciplinary power over accounting firm auditors and securities analysts who issue reports about companies. Specific duties include: (1) registration of public accounting firms; (2) establishment of auditing, quality control, ethics, independence, and other standards relating to preparation of audit reports; (3) inspection of accounting firms; (4) investigations, disciplinary proceedings, and imposition of sanctions; and (5) enforcement of compliance with accounting rules of the board, professionals standards, and securities laws relating to the preparation and issuance of audit reports and obligations and liabilities of accountants.

SOX requires corporations to take more responsibility and to provide principles-based ethical leadership. Enhanced financial disclosures are required, including certification by top officers that audit reports are complete and that nothing material has been withheld from auditors. For example, registered public accounting firms are now required to identify all material correcting adjustments to reflect accurate financial statements. Also, all material off-balance sheet transactions and other relationships with unconsolidated entities that affect current or future financial conditions of a public company must be disclosed in each annual and quarterly financial report. In addition, public companies must also report "on a rapid and current basis" material changes in the financial condition or operations.

SOX sought to hold CEOs and CFOs personally accountable for the credibility and accuracy of their company's financial statements—although the 2008–2009 financial meltdown revealed that even this legislation has loopholes. To prevent future misconduct like that displayed by accounting firm Arthur Andersen, Title VIII of the Sarbanes–Oxley Act, Corporate and Criminal Fraud Accountability, increased the punishment for company fraud. Under the new law, the knowing destruction or creation of documents that "impede, obstruct or influence" any existing or contemplated federal investigation is now a felony. The White Collar Crime Penalty Enhancements Act of 2002 increased the maximum penalty for mail and wire fraud from five to ten years in prison. It also makes record tampering or otherwise impeding with any official preceding a crime. If necessary, the SEC could freeze extraordinary payments to directors, officers, partners, controlling persons, and agents of employees.

Other provisions of the act include whistle-blower protection and changes in the attorney-client relationship so that attorneys are now required to report wrongdoing to top managers or to the board of directors. Employees of public companies and accounting firms, in general, are also accountable to report unethical behavior. SOX intends to motivate employees through whistle-blower protection that would prohibit the employer from taking certain actions against employees who lawfully disclose private employer information to, among others, parties in a judicial proceeding involving a fraud claim. Whistle-blowers are also granted a remedy of special damages and attorneys' fees. This protection is designed to encourage whistle-blowers to come forward when detecting business misconduct, as much of the fraud that eludes audits or other controls may be detected by employees. According to a 2008 report published by the Association of Certified Fraud Examiners, data compiled on 959 cases of occupational fraud between 2006 and 2008 revealed that 46 percent of the cases were detected by tipsters such as employees or vendors.[55] Actions of retaliation that harm informants, including interference with the lawful employment or livelihood of any person, shall result in fines and/or imprisonment for ten years. Table 4.11 lists the benefits of the act.

There are some concerns with SOX, however. Although a law may help prevent misconduct, it will not stop executives who are determined to lie, steal, manipulate, or deceive for personal gain. We saw this in 2008 and 2009 when the crumbling of Wall Street and the housing market revealed widespread misconduct among executives of major firms. The law requires that accountants and executives do the right thing, but a deep commitment by top company leadership is necessary to create an ethical corporate culture. In addition to these concerns,

Table 4.11 Benefits of Sarbanes-Oxley

1. Greater accountability by top management and board of directors to employees, communities, and society. The goals of the business will be to provide stakeholders with a return on their investment, rather than providing a vehicle for management to reap excessive compensation and other benefits.
2. Renewed investor confidence providing managers and brokers with the information they need to make solid investment decisions, which will ultimately lead to a more stable and solid growth rate for investors.
3. Clear explanations by CEOs of why their compensation package is in the best interest of the company. It will also eliminate certain traditional senior management perks, including company loans, and require disclosures about stock trades, thus making executives more like other investors.
4. Greater protection of employee retirement plans. Employees can develop greater trust that they will not lose savings tied to such plans.
5. Improved information from stock analysts and rating agencies.
6. Greater penalties and accountability of senior managers, auditors, and board members. The penalties now outweigh the rewards of purposeful manipulation and deception.

the implementation of SOX can take a great deal of organizational time and resources.

The national cost of compliance of the Sarbanes–Oxley Act is estimated at $1 million per $1.7 billion in revenues.[56] These costs come from internal costs, external costs, and auditor fees. Whereas very large corporations may be able to hire staff and make other arrangements for implementation, small and medium-sized organizations may have fewer resources at their disposal. Finally, publicly traded multinational companies with operations in the United States must implement SOX in addition to the regulatory requirements of other countries. Since there is no global standard on these responsibilities and accountability mechanisms, this implementation is costly and complicated for such firms.[57] After years of complaints from firms, in spring 2009 the Supreme Court agreed to hear arguments over the constitutionality of Sarbanes-Oxley, which has gained new critics as it failed to detect wrongdoing that led to the subprime mortgage crisis and the meltdown on Wall Street in 2008–2009.[58]

> **"A deep commitment by top company leadership is necessary to create an ethical corporate culture."**

SUMMARY

In a pluralistic society, many diverse stakeholder groups attempt to influence the public officials who legislate, interpret laws, and regulate business. Companies that adopt a strategic approach to the legal and regulatory system develop proactive organizational values and compliance programs that identify areas of risks and include formal communication, training, and continuous improvement of responses to the legal and regulatory environment.

Economic reasons for regulation often relate to efforts to level the playing field on which businesses operate. These efforts include regulating trusts, which are generally established to gain control of a product market or industry by eliminating competition and eliminating monopolies, which occur when just one business provides a good or service in a given market. Another rationale for regulation is society's desire to restrict destructive or unfair competition. Social reasons for regulation address imperfections in the market that result in undesirable consequences and the protection of natural and social resources. Other regulations are created in response to social demands for safety and equality in the workplace, safer products, and privacy issues.

The Sherman Antitrust Act is the principal tool used to prevent businesses from restraining trade and monopolizing markets. The Clayton Antitrust Act limits mergers and acquisitions that could stifle competition and prohibits specific activities that could substantially lessen competition or tend to create a monopoly. The Federal Trade Commission Act prohibits unfair methods of competition and created the Federal Trade Commission (FTC). Legal and regulatory policy is also enforced through lawsuits by private citizens, competitors, and special-interest groups.

A company that engages in commerce beyond its own country must contend with the complex relationship among the laws of its own nation, international laws, and the laws of the nation in which it will be trading. There is considerable variation and focus among different nations' laws, but many countries' antitrust laws are quite similar to those of the United States.

Regulation creates numerous costs for businesses, consumers, and society at large. Some measures of these costs include administrative spending patterns, staffing levels of federal regulatory agencies, and costs businesses incur in complying with regulations. The cost of regulation is passed on to consumers in the form of higher prices and may stifle product innovation and investments in new facilities and equipment. Regulation also provides many benefits, including greater equality in the workplace, safer workplaces, resources for disadvantaged members of society, safer products, more information about and greater choices among products, cleaner air and water, and the preservation of wildlife habitats. Antitrust laws and regulations strengthen competition and spur companies to invest in research and development. Many businesses and individuals believe that the costs of regulation outweigh its benefits. Some people desire complete deregulation, or removal of regulatory authority.

Because government is a stakeholder of business (and vice versa), businesses and government can work together as both legitimately participate in the political process. Business participation can be a positive or negative force in society's interest, depending not only on the outcome but also on the perspective of various stakeholders.

Changes over the last fifty years have shaped the political environment in which businesses operate. Among the most significant of these changes were amendments to the Legislative Reorganization Act and the Federal Election Campaign Act, which had the effect of reducing the importance of political parties. Many candidates for elected offices turned to increasingly powerful special-interest groups to raise funds to campaign for elected office.

Some organizations view regulatory and legal forces as beyond their control and simply react to conditions arising from those forces; other firms seek to influence the political process to achieve their goals. One way they can do so is through lobbying, the process of working to persuade public and/or government officials to favor a particular position in decision making. Companies can also influence the political process through political action committees, which are organizations that solicit donations from individuals and then contribute these funds to candidates running for political office. Corporate funds may also be channeled into candidates' campaign coffers as corporate executives' or stockholders' personal contributions, although such donations can violate the spirit of corporate campaign laws. Although laws limit corporate contributions to specific candidates, it is acceptable for businesses and other organizations to make donations to political parties.

More companies are establishing organizational compliance programs to ensure that they operate legally and responsibly as well as to generate a competitive advantage based on a reputation for good citizenship. Under the Federal

Sentencing Guidelines for Organizations (FSGO), a company that wants to avoid or limit fines and other penalties as a result of an employee's crime must be able to demonstrate that it has implemented a reasonable program for deterring and preventing misconduct. To implement an effective compliance program, an organization should develop a code of conduct that communicates expected standards, assign oversight of the program to high-ranking personnel who abide by legal and ethical standards, communicate standards through training and other mechanisms, monitor and audit to detect wrongdoing, punish individuals responsible for misconduct, and take steps to continuously improve the program. A strong compliance program acts as a buffer to keep employees from committing crimes and to protect a company's reputation should wrongdoing occur despite its best efforts.

Enacted after many corporate financial fraud scandals, the Sarbanes-Oxley Act created the Public Company Accounting Oversight Board to provide oversight and set standards for the accounting firms that audit public companies. The board has investigatory and disciplinary power over accounting firm auditors and securities analysts. The act requires corporations to take responsibility to provide principles-based ethical leadership and holds CEOs and CFOs personally accountable for the credibility and accuracy of their company's financial statements. Ideally, the act will provide for a new standard of ethical behavior for U.S. business, especially for top management and boards of directors responsible for company oversight.

However, the 2008–2009 recession, collapse of the subprime mortgage market, and troubles on Wall Street all pointed to systemic flaws and gaps in the regulatory system. SOX was not able to prevent major financial mishaps that were so large and widespread as to make Enron look benign in comparison. The current administration has a lot of continued work to do to ensure that businesses behave ethically and that stakeholders are protected.

RESPONSIBLE BUSINESS DEBATE

Mark to Market Accounting

ISSUE: Should mark to market accounting in the financial industry stay or go?

One of the problems banks faced in the 2008–2009 financial crisis was an accounting rule called mark to market. This form of accounting was developed to value exchanges on the future market. It requires companies to mark their assets to the market price that existed on that day. Using mark to market in this context makes sense because futures traders buy assets at a fixed future price. When markets are working correctly and there is active trading in the market for financial assets, this rule makes good sense.

However, mark to market accounting has been used in more questionable ways in recent decades and it has been linked with a number of high-profile corporate collapses, including Enron. Enron misused mark to market by tabulating anticipated future profits as real, thereby driving up the company's appearance of profitability. Mark to market works just fine under normal market conditions when trading is steady and assets have agreed-upon market prices. It can be difficult to use this method, however, to value complex or intangible assets, such as those often found in the financial industry. In this case, mark to market accounting becomes an easy way to commit accounting fraud.

Mark to market also does not work well when trading stops on a good because a market price cannot be determined. When a market dries up, as the mortgage-backed securities market did in late 2008, no active trading occurs and prices do not exist. How do accountants value something that does not have a listed price that day? That was the problem the banks faced in late 2008. Banks had mortgages and other assets and debts that were technically marketable, but investors perceived that there was a high level of risk involved and did not want to invest. Many feared that investors would not make their mortgage payments, and that investors would end up losing money. Because of this fear, there were no buyers for banks' debt. If the banks marked their assets to zero or 20 cents on the dollar, they would be grossly undervaluing these instruments. Unfortunately, banks were forced to write down assets based on the mark to market rule, and wrote off billions of dollars of losses that some argue were not warranted.

To help each of the problems on Wall Street, Congress put pressure on the Securities and Exchange Commission and Federal Accounting Standards Board to relax the mark to market rules. Finally in April of 2009, the rule was relaxed to allow banks and other financial institutions to use discounted cash flow models to value these types of assets. These models allow banks more flexibility in their accounting so that they do not have to mark down valuations as much in times of crisis. Time will tell whether the relaxation of the rule was a good thing.

There Are Two Sides to Every Issue:

1. Defend keeping the mark to market accounting rule. When is this rule useful and why should the government allow the financial industry to continue to use it?

2. Defend doing away with mark to market accounting in the financial industry. Is the potential for committing fraud too high with mark to market accounting?

KEY TERMS

trust (p. 127)
monopoly (p. 128)
deregulation (p. 141)
lobbying (p. 147)

political action committees (PACs) (p. 148)
Federal Sentencing Guidelines for
    Organizations (FSGO) (p. 151)
Sarbanes-Oxley Act (SOX) (p. 154)

DISCUSSION QUESTIONS

1. Discuss the existence of both cooperation and conflict between government and businesses concerning the regulation of business.

2. What is the rationale for government to regulate the activities of businesses? How is our economic and social existence shaped by government regulations?

3. What was the historical background that encouraged the government to enact legislation such as the Sherman Antitrust Act and the Clayton Act? Do these same conditions exist today?

4. What is the role and function of the Federal Trade Commission in the regulation of business? How does the FTC engage in

proactive activities to avoid government regulation?

5. How do global regulations influence U.S. businesses operating internationally? What are the major obstacles to global regulation?

6. Compare the costs and benefits of regulation. In your opinion, do the benefits outweigh the costs or do the costs outweigh the benefits? What are the advantages and disadvantages of deregulation?

7. Name three tools that businesses can employ to influence government and public policy.

Evaluate the strengths and weaknesses of each of these approaches.

8. How do political action committees influence society, and what is their appropriate role in a democratic society?

9. Why should an organization implement the Federal Sentencing Guidelines for Organizations (FSGO) as a strategic approach for legal compliance?

10. What is the significance of Sarbanes-Oxley to business operations in the United States?

EXPERIENTIAL EXERCISE

Visit the website of the Federal Trade Commission (FTC) (http://www.ftc.gov/). What is the FTC's current mission? What are the primary areas for which the FTC is responsible?

Review the last two months of press releases from the FTC. On the basis of these releases, what appear to be major issues of concern at this time?

WHAT WOULD YOU DO?

The election of a new governor brings many changes to any state capital, including the shuffling of a variety of appointed positions. In most cases, political appointees have contributed a great deal to the governor's election bid and have expertise in a specific area related to the appointed post. Joe Barritz was in that position when he became assistant agricultural commissioner in January 2003. He was instrumental in getting the governor elected, especially through his fundraising efforts. Joe's family owned thousands of acres in the state and had been farming and ranching since the 1930s. Joe earned a bachelor's degree in agricultural economics and policy and a law degree from one of the state's top institutions. He worked as an attorney in the state's capital city for over eighteen years and represented a range of clients, most

of whom were involved in agriculture. Thus, he had many characteristics that made him a strong candidate for assistant commissioner.

After about six months on the job, Joe had lunch with a couple of friends he had known for many years. During that June lunch, they had a casual conversation about the fact that Joe never did have a true "celebration" after being named assistant agricultural commissioner. His friends decided to talk with others about the possibility of holding that celebration in a few months. Before long, eight of Joe's friends were busy planning to hold a reception in his honor on October 5. Two of these friends were currently employed as lobbyists. One represented the beef industry association, and the other worked for the cotton industry council. They asked Joe if they could hold the celebration at his lake home in the capital city. Joe talked with the commission's ethics officer about the party and learned that these types of parties, between close friends, were common for newly appointed and elected officials. The ethics officer told Joe that the reception and location were fine, but only if his lobbyist friends paid for the reception with personal funds. The state's ethics rules did not allow a standing government official to take any type of gift, including corporate dollars, that might influence his or her decision making. Joe communicated this information to his friends.

During the next few months, Joe was involved in a number of issues that could potentially help or harm agriculture-based industries. Various reports and policy statements within the Agricultural Commission were being used to tailor state legislation and regulatory proposals. The beef and cotton councils were actively supporting a proposal that would provide tax breaks to farmers and ranchers. Staff on the Agricultural Commission were mixed on the proposal, but Joe was expected to deliver a report to a legislative committee on the commission's preferences. His presentation was scheduled for October 17.

On October 5, nearly sixty of Joe's friends gathered at the catered reception to reminisce and congratulate him on his achievements. Most were good friends and acquaintances, so the mood and conversation were relatively light that evening. A college football game between two big rivals drew most people to the big-screen TV. By midnight, the guests were gone. Back at the office the following week, Joe began working on his presentation for the legislative committee. Through a series of economic analyses, long meetings, and electronic discussions, he decided to support the tax benefits for farmers and ranchers. News reports carried information from his presentation.

It was not long before some reporters made a "connection" between the reception in Joe's honor and his stand on the tax breaks for agriculture industries. An investigation quickly ensued, including reports that the beef and cotton industry associations had not only been present but also financially supported the reception on October 5. The small company used to plan and cater the party indicated that checks from the cotton industry council and beef industry association were used to cover some of the expenses. A relationship between the "gift" of the reception and Joe's presentation to the legislative committee would be a breach of his oath of office and state ethics rules. If you were Joe, what would you do?

CHAPTER 5

Business Ethics and Ethical Decision Making

Chapter Objectives

- To define and describe the importance of business ethics

- To understand the diverse and complex nature of existing and emerging ethical issues

- To discuss the individual factors that influence ethical or unethical decisions

- To explore the effect of organizational relationships on ethical decision making

- To evaluate the role of opportunity in ethical or unethical decisions

Chapter Outline

The Nature of Business Ethics

Foundations of Business Ethics

Ethical Issues in Business

Understanding the Ethical Decision-Making Process

© Tom Tomczyk

Cereal Companies Revamp in Response to Sugary Cereal Criticisms

Cereal has long been thought of as a healthy breakfast. Yet in terms of sugar, parents might as well feed their children a cookie to start their day. Some sugary cereals are as much as 50 percent sugar. Honey Smacks, for example, contains 15 grams of sugar per serving, which is 3 grams more than is found in a glazed donut. In spite of their poor nutritional profiles, it is often the sweetest cereals that are targeted toward children. Many parents are upset that they have unwittingly fed their children food that is so blatantly unhealthy, which has led to lawsuits against cereal industries. In order to deal with the backlash and to gain a competitive advantage, companies like Kellogg's have worked to reposition themselves as healthy breakfast choices.

Cereal companies began specifically marketing to children in the 1950s, the same decade in which sugar became a common additive to cereal. As one might imagine, kids gravitated toward these sugary sweets. Cereal company marketers also introduced cartoon characters to get kids interested in their brands. Tony the Tiger and Trix Rabbit became beloved child icons. Eventually, cereal companies began placing free toys into cereal boxes. These marketing ploys worked; children craved these fun cereals, making sugary cereals a popular item on the breakfast table for decades. In the 1970s, concerned parents began worrying about the health hazards of the cereal their children were eating. In 1983, a lawsuit was filed against the General Foods Corporation claiming that certain cereal advertisements were deceptive, leading children to believe that by eating certain cereals, they could become stronger, happier, or even gain magical powers. The court ruled in favor of the plaintiffs.

In 2007, a lawsuit was filed against Nickelodeon and Kellogg's for using cartoon characters from movies and TV shows on cereal boxes to attract children. Cereal companies stopped co-branding, but the parents were not appeased. Sugary cereals were still as popular as ever among children. In response, Kellogg's took a proactive stance to address parental concerns. It stopped advertising cereals that did not meet the Institute of Medicine and World Health Organization's health guidelines for cereal. No longer will you find a Kellogg's cereal being advertised that contains over 12 grams of sugar or 200 calories per serving. It also created guidelines advising consumers to eat sugary cereals in moderation.

Additionally, cereals like Special K and the Koshi brand have become popular as people have started preferring healthier cereals, although these cereals will never hold the same cache with children as Lucky Charms or Fruity Pebbles. Many major cereal companies are going further to respond to criticism by listing health benefits prominently on cereal labels. Even companies promoting sugary cereals are trying to appeal to the health-conscious customer with claims that they contain essential vitamins and minerals. A few brands, such as Frosted Flakes, have even introduced reduced sugar versions of their more popular kids' cereals. As long as stakeholders remained concerned, traditional cereal companies will keep working to revamp their images to keep up with the public's changing health preferences.[1]

Key business ethics concerns relate to questions about whether various stakeholders consider specific business practices acceptable. The global financial crisis took a toll on consumer trust of financial services companies. A study by Lightspeed Research and Cohn & Wolfe of 650 U.S. consumers revealed that 66 percent of respondents did not feel that the financial services industry would help them to regain the wealth that they lost during the recession. Words used to describe this industry included: *greedy, impersonal, opportunistic,* and *distant.* Table 5.1 summarizes the survey results.[2]

By its very nature, the field of business ethics is controversial, and no universally accepted approach has emerged for resolving its questions. Nonetheless, most businesses are establishing initiatives that include the development and implementation of ethics programs designed to deter conduct that some stakeholders might consider objectionable. Lockheed Martin, a technology, aerospace manufacturing, and global security company that employs 146,000 people worldwide, has a comprehensive ethics program. It believes that companies should go above doing merely what is legal to doing what is right. To help achieve this goal, Lockheed has a President and Vice President of Ethics and Business Conduct and publishes a manual explaining the program as well as what employees should do if they see an ethics violation occurring. Lockheed even publishes an Ethics Directory that contains contact information for Ethics Officers who are responsible for covering each company within Lockheed, as well as a helpline.[3]

The definition of social responsibility that appears in Chapter 1 incorporates society's expectations and includes four levels of concern: economic, legal, ethical, and philanthropic. Because ethics is becoming an increasingly important

Table 5.1 American Distrust of the Financial Services Industry

Negative Responses Related to the Industry	%
Greedy	32
Impersonal	32
Opportunistic	26
Distant from me	22
Positive Responses Related to the Industry	%
Trustworthy	13
Honest	10
Ethical	5
Transparent	3
Sympathetic	3

Source: "New US Consumer Survey Shows High Distrusts of Financial Services Companies," *Business Wire,* January 20, 2009, http://findarticles.com/p/articles/mi_m0EIN/is_2009_Jan_20/ai_n31202849/, accessed May 27, 2009.

issue in business today, this chapter and Chapter 6 are devoted to exploring this dimension of social responsibility. First, we define business ethics, examine its importance from an organizational perspective, and review its foundations. Next, we define ethical issues in business to help understand areas of risk. We then look at the individual, organizational, and opportunity factors that influence ethical decision making in the workplace.

THE NATURE OF BUSINESS ETHICS

Business decisions can be both acceptable and beneficial to society. It is necessary to examine business ethics to understand decisions made in the context of an organizational culture. The term *ethics* relates to choices and judgments about acceptable standards of conduct that guide the behavior of individuals and groups. These standards require both organizations and individuals to accept responsibility for their actions and to comply with established principles and values. Without a shared view of which values and norms are appropriate and acceptable, companies may fail to balance their desires for profits against the wishes and needs of society.

"Most businesses are establishing initiatives that include the development and implementation of ethics programs designed to deter conduct that some stakeholders might consider objectionable."

Maintaining this balance often demands compromises or trade-offs. Ethical conduct results in shareholder loyalty and can contribute to success that supports even broader social causes and concerns. Former Wal-Mart CEO Lee Scott has stated: "As businesses, we have a responsibility to society. We also have an extraordinary opportunity. Let me be clear about this point, there is no conflict between delivering value to shareholders and helping solve bigger societal problems. In fact, they can build upon each other when developed, aligned, and executed right."[4] Society has developed rules—both legal and implied—to guide companies in their efforts to earn profits through means that do not bring harm to individuals or to society at large.

Business ethics comprises the principles and standards that guide the behavior of individuals and groups in the world of business. Most definitions of business ethics relate to rules, standards, and moral principles regarding what is right or wrong in specific situations. *Principles* are specific and pervasive boundaries for behavior that are universal and absolute. Principles often become the basis for rules. Some examples of principles include freedom of speech, principles of justice, and equal rights to civil liberties. *Values* are used to develop norms that are socially enforced. Integrity, accountability, and trust

business ethics
the principles and standards that guide the behavior of individuals and groups in the world of business

are examples of values. Investors, employees, customers, interest groups, the legal system, and the community often determine whether a specific action is right or wrong, ethical or unethical. Although these groups are not necessarily "right," their judgments influence society's acceptance or rejection of a business and its activities.

Managers, employees, consumers, industry associations, government regulators, business partners, and special-interest groups all contribute to these conventions, and they may change over time. The most basic of these standards have been codified as laws and regulations to encourage companies to conform to society's expectations of business conduct. As we said in Chapter 4, public concerns about accounting fraud and conflicts of interest in the securities industry led to the passage of the Sarbanes-Oxley Act to restore the public's trust in the stock market.

It is vital to recognize that business ethics goes beyond legal issues. Ethical business decisions foster trust in business relationships, and as we discussed in Chapter 1, trust is a key factor in improving productivity and achieving success in most organizations. When companies deviate from the prevailing standards of industry and society, the result is customer dissatisfaction, lack of trust, and lawsuits. A survey by Harris Interactive shows that corporate reputation is at its lowest point in the past decade of their annual "Reputation Quotient" polls. Eighty-eight percent rated the reputation of corporate America today as "not good" or "terrible." Among the least admired companies: AIG, Halliburton, General Motors, Chrysler, Washington Mutual, Citigroup, Merrill Lynch, ExxonMobil, and Ford Motor Company. There remain companies that are admired by respondents; they include: Johnson & Johnson, Google, Sony, Coca-Cola, Kraft Foods, Amazon.com, Microsoft, General Mills, 3M, and Toyota Motor. The economic lapses associated with the recession have damaged the "emotional appeal" of many companies that is often the strongest driver of reputation.[5]

Largely in response to this crisis, business decisions and activities have come under greater scrutiny by many different constituents, including consumers, employees, investors, government regulators, and special-interest groups. Additionally, new legislation and regulations designed to encourage higher ethical standards in business have been put in place.

Some businesspeople choose to behave ethically because of enlightened self-interest or the expectation that "ethics pays." They want to act responsibly and assume that the public and customers will reward the company for its ethical actions. For example, Caraco Pharmaceutical Laboratories, a generic drug manufacturer, voluntarily recalled all tablets of its Digoxin drug used by patients with heart failure and abnormal heart rhythms. The drug was recalled because of variation in sizing that could impact the actual dosage received by a patient. The recall was designed to protect those who were using the drug, and the company had to carefully assess the product and the potential harm it could cause in its inconsistent form. Significant medical expertise and testing resulted in the ultimate recall.[6]

FOUNDATIONS OF BUSINESS ETHICS

Because all individuals and groups within a company may not have embraced the same set of values, there is always the possibility of ethical conflict. Most ethical issues in an organizational context are addressed openly whenever a policy, code, or rule is questioned. Even then, it may be hard to distinguish between the ethical issue and the legal means used to resolve it. Because it is difficult to draw a boundary between legal and ethical issues, all questionable issues need an organizational mechanism for resolution.

The legal ramifications of some issues and situations may be obvious, but questionable decisions and actions more often result in disputes that must be resolved through some type of negotiation or even litigation. After HealthSouth Corporation was investigated for allegedly inflating earnings by $2.5 billion, eleven former employees, including all of the firm's former chief financial officers, pleaded guilty to fraud charges.[7] HealthSouth agreed to issue stocks and warrants valued at $215 million, and the company insurers agreed to pay $230 million cash.[8] Richard M. Scrushy, founder and former CEO, was acquitted of criminal charges in a jury trial in Alabama. However, four months later, he was indicted by a federal grand jury, along with former Alabama governor Don Siegelman, to whom Scrushy was accused of funneling over $500,000 in exchange for a seat on the state hospital regulatory board. Scrushy and Siegelman were found guilty of 30 counts of money laundering, racketeering, bribery, and obstruction of justice, among other things. Scrushy pleaded not guilty on all charges, but was found guilty and ordered to jail in Texas in 2006. His sentence was 6 years and 10 months in prison, $267,000 in restitution to Alabama for legal fees, 3 years' probation, and an additional fine of $150,000. Scrushy also must personally pay for his time in jail and perform 500 hours of community service. In 2009, Scrushy was transferred to an Alabama jail in order to be present to testify in a civil trial brought by HealthSouth

© AP Photo/Richard Drew

Organizations should establish formal ethics and compliance programs to better address ethical issues when they arise

shareholders. Scrushy was found guilty of perpetrating HealthSouth's fraud and was ordered to pay $2.87 billion.[9] Such highly publicized cases strengthen the perception that ethical standards in business need to be raised.

When ethical disputes wind up in court, the costs and distractions associated with litigation can be devastating to a business. In addition to the compensatory or nominal damages actually incurred, punitive damages may be imposed on a company that is judged to have acted improperly to punish the firm and to send an intimidating message to others. The legal system, therefore, provides a formal venue for businesspeople to resolve ethical as well as legal disputes; in fact, many of the examples we cite in this chapter had to be resolved through the courts. To avoid the costs of litigation, companies should develop systems to monitor complaints, suggestions, and other feedback from stakeholders. In many cases, issues can be negotiated or resolved without legal intervention. Strategic responsibility entails systems for listening to, understanding, and effectively managing stakeholder concerns.[10]

A high level of personal morality may not be sufficient to prevent an individual from violating the law in an organizational context in which even experienced attorneys debate the exact meaning of the law. Because it is impossible to train all the members of an organization as lawyers, the identification of ethical issues and the implementation of standards of conduct that incorporate both legal and ethical concerns are the best approach to preventing crime and avoiding civil litigation. Codifying ethical standards into meaningful policies that spell out what is and is not acceptable gives businesspeople an opportunity to reduce the probability of behavior that could create legal problems. Without proper ethical training and guidance, it is impossible for the average business manager to understand the exact boundaries for illegal behavior in the areas of product safety, price fixing, fraud, export-import violations, copyright violations, and so on. For example, many Chinese manufacturers and companies that use Chinese suppliers have been under attack in recent years over concern for product safety. From lead-tainted toys at Mattel, melamine-tainted dairy products, and potentially deadly generic drugs (a highly lucrative $75-billion-a-year business that employs more than 5 million Chinese people), China has faced serious allegations and criticisms over its lack of oversight and concern for consumer welfare.[11]

Although the values of honesty, respect, and trust are often assumed to be self-evident and universally accepted, business decisions

> **"Codifying ethical standards into meaningful policies that spell out what is and is not acceptable gives businesspeople an opportunity to reduce the probability of behavior that could create legal problems."**

involve complex and detailed discussions in which correctness may not be so clear-cut. Both employees and managers need experience within their specific industry to understand how to operate in gray areas or to handle close calls in evolving areas. Warren Buffett and his company Berkshire Hathaway command significant respect from investors because of their track record of financial returns and the integrity of their organizations. Buffett says, "I want employees to ask themselves whether they are willing to have any contemplated act appear the next day on the front page of their local paper—to be read by their spouses, children and friends—with the reporting done by an informed and critical reporter." The high level of accountability and trust Buffett places in his employees translates into investor trust and confidence.[12]

Many people who have limited business experience suddenly find themselves required to make decisions about product quality, advertising, pricing, sales techniques, hiring practices, privacy, and pollution control. For example, how do advertisers know when they are making misleading statements in advertising versus "puffery"? Bayer is "the world's best aspirin," Hush Puppies, "the earth's most comfortable shoes," and Firestone (before recalling 6.5 million tires) promised "quality you can trust."[13] The personal values learned through non-work socialization from family, religion, and school may not provide specific guidelines for these complex business decisions. In other words, a person's experiences and decisions at home, in school, and in the community may be quite different from the experiences and the decisions he or she has to make at work. Moreover, the interests and values of individual employees may differ from those of the company in which they work, from industry standards, and from society in general. When personal values are inconsistent with the configuration of values held by the work group, ethical conflict may ensue. It is important that a shared vision of acceptable behavior develop from an organizational perspective to cultivate consistent and reliable relationships with all concerned stakeholders. A shared vision of ethics that is part of an organization's culture can be questioned, analyzed, and modified as new issues develop. However, business ethics should relate to work environment decisions and should not control or influence personal ethical issues.

ETHICAL ISSUES IN BUSINESS

Classification of Ethical Issues

An **ethical issue** is a problem, situation, or opportunity requiring an individual, group, or organization to choose among several actions that must be evaluated as right or wrong, ethical or unethical. Surveys can render a useful overview of the many unsettled ethical issues in business. A constructive next step toward identifying and resolving ethical issues is to classify the issues relevant to most business organizations. In this section, we examine ethical issues related to abusive behavior, lying, conflict of interest, fraud, and discrimination. There are also issues related to business decisions that harm consumers, such as products that cause obesity, or that encourage socially unacceptable behavior in children, such as the consumption of alcohol. Ethical issues related to information technology are addressed in Chapter 10.

ethical issue
a problem, situation, or opportunity requiring an individual, group, or organization to choose among several actions that must be evaluated as right or wrong, ethical or unethical

Stanford Financial, a Mini-Madoff, or Innocent Investor? Recently, it seems that Ponzi schemes are being uncovered everywhere. One alleged Ponzi scheme was committed by R. Allen Stanford and Stanford Financial, who have been accused of operating a $7 billion Ponzi scheme. Stanford is from Texas, but it was a bank on the island of Antigua that was the focus of investigation. By now you should be familiar with Ponzi, or pyramid, schemes, which occur when funds from new investors are used to pay off older investors. What may appear to be a lucrative investment is a scam that pays off only as long as new investors join. Once money stops pouring in, the Ponzi scheme collapses, often with disastrous results.

Authorities have accused Stanford and other executives of creating fraudulent certificates of deposit (CDs). Those investing in Stanford's Antigua bank were promised 9.87 percent compounded annual interest, about six percentage points higher than the U.S. average CD rates at the time. For years many people, including employees and investors, were unclear how Stanford Financial CDs generated such high returns. After inquiring, they were told the information was proprietary and could not be disclosed. Starting in 2003, some people became wary and began to accuse Stanford of running a Ponzi scheme. Stanford was charged with 21 counts of conspiracy, fraud, bribery, and obstruction of justice, but pleaded not guilty to all charges.

Stanford employees were given high incentives to sell as many CDs as possible, perhaps encouraging them to not ask questions about the investment's high returns. At the time, the IRS was already investigating Stanford for failing to pay $226.6 million in back taxes. Finally in 2008, Stanford's scheme came to the light of authorities and investigations subsequently ensued. As in the Bernie Madoff case, this begs the question: Why did the Securities and Exchange Commission not spot the Ponzi scheme earlier? The SEC did not file a civil lawsuit against Stanford until 2009, and by then significant damage had been done. Less than 50 percent of the money from the CDs is recoverable, since most of the money never existed in the first place. This case has added fuel to the fire of those calling for a serious revamping of regulatory bodies' monitoring systems.[14]

Although not all-inclusive or mutually exclusive, these classifications provide an overview of some major ethical issues that business decision makers face. Just because an unsettled situation or activity is an ethical issue does not mean the behavior is necessarily unethical. An ethical issue is simply a situation, a problem, or even an opportunity that requires thought, discussion, or investigation to determine the moral impact of the decision. And because the business world is dynamic, new ethical issues are emerging all the time. Table 5.2 defines specific ethical issues identified by employees in the National Business Ethics Survey (NBES). Three types of misconduct make up 30 percent of the ethical problems within organizations. Putting one's own interests ahead of the organization, abusive behavior, and lying to employees are all personal in nature. Misreporting hours worked, safety violations, and provision of low-quality goods and services are the top three issues that directly relate to the firm's agenda.

Table 5.2 Specific Types of Observed Misconduct

P denotes Personal Lapses, M denotes Misconduct that furthers the company's agenda.

		2007	2005	Change
P	Putting own interests ahead of organization's interests	22%	18%	+4%
P	Abusive behavior	21%	21%	0%
P	Lying to employees	20%	19%	+1%
M	Misreporting hours worked	17%	16%	+1%
P	Internet abuse	16%	13%	+3%
M	Safety violations	15%	16%	−1%
P	Lying to stakeholders	14%	19%	−5%
P	Discrimination	13%	12%	+1%
P	Stealing	11%	11%	0%
P	Sexual harassment	10%	9%	+1%
M	Provision of low-quality goods and services	10%	8%	+2%
P	Improper hiring practices	10%	NA	—
M	Environmental violations	7%	NA	—
M	Misuse of confidential organization information	6%	7%	−1%
M	Alteration of documents	5%	5%	0%
M	Alteration of financial records	5%	5%	0%
M	Bribes	4%	3%	+1%
M	Using competitors' inside information	4%	4%	0%

Source: From *2007 National Business Ethics Survey: An Inside View of Private Sector Ethics,* Copyright © 2007, Ethics Resource Center (ERC). Used with permission of the ERC, 1747 Pennsylvania Ave., N.W., Suite 400, Washington, DC, www.ethics.org.

Table 5.2 compares the percentage of employees who observed specific types of misconduct over the past two National Business Ethics Surveys. Employees could select more than one form of misconduct; therefore, each type of misconduct represents the percentage of employees who saw that particular act. Although Table 5.2 documents many types of ethical issues that exist in organizations, due to the almost infinite number of ways that misconduct can occur, it is impossible in this chapter to list every conceivable ethical issue. Any type of manipulation, deceit, or even just the absence of transparency in decision making can create harm to others.

Abusive or Intimidating Behavior

Abusive or intimidating behavior is one of the most common ethical problems for employees, but what does it mean to be abusive or intimidating? The concepts can mean anything from physical threats, false accusations, annoying a coworker, profanity, insults, yelling, harshness, and ignoring someone to being unreasonable; and the meaning of these words can differ by person. It is important to understand that each term falls along a continuum. For example, what one person may define as yelling might be another's definition of normal speech. Civility in our society has been a concern, and the workplace is no exception. The productivity level of many organizations has been damaged by the time spent unraveling abusive relationships.

Abusive behavior is difficult to assess and manage because of diversity in culture and lifestyles. What does it mean to speak profanely? Is profanity only related to specific words or other such terms that are common in today's business world? If you are using words that are normal in your language but others consider profanity, have you just insulted, abused, or disrespected them?

Within the concept of abusive behavior, intent should be a consideration. If the employee was trying to convey a compliment when the comment was considered abusive, then it was probably a mistake. The way a word is said (voice inflection) can be important. In addition, the fact that we now live in a multicultural environment, doing business and working with many different cultural groups, highlights the depth of the ethical and legal issues that may arise. There are problems of word meanings by age and within cultures. For example, an expression such as "Did you guys hook up last night?" can have various meanings, including some that could be considered offensive in a work environment.

> **"The fact that we now live in a multicultural environment, doing business and working with many different cultural groups, highlights the depth of the ethical and legal issues that may arise."**

These are only a few helpful points to remember in avoiding abusive or intimidating ethical issues in business today. Each company has formal and informal ways of interaction. Every company has different standards for this issue, and not all of them are ethical. It takes time within a firm to understand where the acceptable and unacceptable line is, and that the line can change at any time. Do not assume that communication used with close friends will fit into the work environment.

Bullying is associated with a hostile workplace when someone (or a group) considered a target is threatened, harassed, belittled, verbally abused, or overly criticized. Although bullying may create what some call a hostile environment, this term is generally associated with sexual harassment. Although sexual harassment has legal recourse, bullying has little legal recourse at this time. Bullying can cause psychological damage that can result in health-endangering consequences to the target. As Table 5.3 indicates, bullying can use a mix of verbal, nonverbal, and manipulative threatening

Table 5.3 Actions Associated with Bullies

1. Spreading rumors to damage others.
2. Blocking others' communication in the workplace.
3. Flaunting status or authority to take advantage of others.
4. Discrediting others' ideas and opinions.
5. Using e-mails to demean others.
6. Failing to communicate or return communication.
7. Insulting, yelling, and shouting.
8. Using terminology to discriminate by gender, race, or age.
9. Using eye or body language to hurt others or their reputation.
10. Taking credit for others' work or ideas.

Source: © O. C. Ferrell 2010.

expressions to damage workplace productivity. One may wonder why workers tolerate such activities, but the problem is that 81 percent of workplace bullies are supervisors. A top officer at Boeing cited an employee survey indicating 26 percent had observed abusive or intimidating behavior by management.[15]

The concept of *bullying* in the workplace is now considered a legal issue. Some 37 percent of employees surveyed said that they have been bullied in the workplace and that 72 percent of the perpetrators were employers. Some suggest that employers take the following steps to minimize workplace bullying:

- They should have policies in place that make it clear that bullying behaviors will not be tolerated.

- The employee handbook should emphasize that workers must treat each other with respect.

Employers should encourage employees who feel bullied to report the conduct, and should handle such complaints in much the same way as discriminatory harassment complaints are handled.[16]

Bullying can also occur between companies that are in intense competition. Even respected companies such as Intel have been accused of monopolistic bullying. A competitor, Advanced Micro Devices (AMD), claimed in a lawsuit that thirty-eight companies, including Dell and Sony, were strong-arming customers into buying Intel chips rather than those marketed by AMD. The AMD lawsuit seeks billions of dollars and will take years to litigate. In many cases, the alleged misconduct can not only have monetary and legal implications but also can threaten reputation, investor confidence, and customer loyalty. A front-cover *Forbes* headline stated "Intel to AMD: Drop Dead." An example of the intense competition and Intel's ability to use its large size won it the high-profile Apple account, displacing IBM and Freescale. AMD said it had no opportunity to bid because Intel offered to deploy 600 Indian engineers to help Apple software run more smoothly on Intel chips. Intel's actions have landed it in trouble in the European Union as well, where courts found the company guilty of antitrust violations and anticompetitive behavior regarding competitor Advanced Micro Devices (AMD). AMD alleged that Intel was preventing the company from being competitive through such practices as paying computer makers rebates for using Intel chips and selling chips at below costs. The EU courts sided with AMD and Intel was fined a record $1.45 billion, which it continues to fight in courts. The EU is notoriously hard on antitrust cases. Microsoft too has been found guilty and has racked up $2 billion in fines over multiple years in the EU.[17]

Lying

To be honest is to tell the truth to the best of your ability; lying relates to distorting the truth. There are three major types of lies. The first includes joking without malice, and the so-called white lie that is told in order to avoid hurting someone's feelings. The second type of lie is lying by commission, or creating a perception or belief by words that intentionally deceive the receiver of the message. Examples include lying about being at work, on expense reports, or when carrying out work assignments. Commission also entails intentionally creating "noise" within the communication that knowingly confuses or deceives the receiver. Noise can be defined as technical explanations that the communicator knows the receiver does not understand. It can be the intentional use of communication forms that make it difficult for the receiver to hear the true message. Using legal terms or terms relating to unfamiliar processes and systems to explain what was done in a work situation facilitates this type of lie. Lying by commission also can involve using complex forms, procedures, contracts, or words that are spelled the same but have different meanings, or refuting the truth with a false statement.[18]

The third type of lie, lying by omission, involves intentionally not informing the receiver of material facts. A classic example for decades was the tobacco manufacturers that did not allow negative research results to appear on cigarettes and cigars. The drug Vioxx is being questioned because the manufacturer allegedly did not inform consumers as to the degree and occurrence of side effects, one of which is death. When lying damages others, it can be the focus of a lawsuit. You should be able to understand when a lie becomes unethical in business based on the context and intent to distort the truth. A lie becomes illegal if it is determined by the judgment of courts to damage others. Some businesspersons may believe that one must lie a little or that the occasional lie is sanctioned by the organization. The question you need to ask is whether lies are distorting openness, transparency, and other values that are associated with ethical behavior.[19]

Conflict of Interest

conflict of interest
the situation of an individual who must choose whether to advance his or her own interests, those of his or her organization, or those of some other group

A **conflict of interest** exists when an individual must choose whether to advance his or her own interests, those of his or her organization, or those of some other group. The medical industry has been faced with many accusations of conflicts of interest with doctors and medical schools regarding payments. For example, Harvard Medical School received an "F" grade on its conflict of interest policies from the American Medical Student Association. One professor alone was forced to disclose 47 company affiliations from which he was receiving money.[20] To address the problem, a government panel has called for full disclosure of all payments made to doctors, researchers, and universities. The fear is that financial donations from medical and pharmaceutical companies could sway the outcomes of researchers' findings and what is taught in classrooms.[21] To avoid conflicts of interest, employees must be able to separate their private interests from their business dealings.

Organizations, too, must avoid potential conflicts of interest in providing goods or services. Democratic lawmakers and private companies found themselves the subject of a federal ethics investigation after it was discovered that the lawmakers may have attended events in the Caribbean sponsored by Citigroup, AT&T Corp., Pfizer Inc., and Verizon Communications. The ethical issue at question is whether lobbyists helped to sponsor the lawmakers' attendance of the conferences and whether the lawmakers properly disclosed which organizations were hosting the events. Lawmakers from both parties must be careful not to create the appearance that corporations are influencing their decisions.[22]

In many developed countries, it is generally recognized that employees should not accept bribes, personal payments, gifts, or special favors from people who hope to influence the outcome of a decision. However, as discussed later in this text, bribery is an accepted way of doing business in many countries. The U.S. Department of Justice cracked down on cases of bribery involving hundreds of companies. Under these investigations, Halliburton Company agreed to pay nearly $600 million after bribing officials in Nigeria in order to win oil contracts.[23] Bribes also have been associated with the downfall of many managers, legislators, and government officials. When a government official accepts a bribe, it is usually from a business that seeks some favor, perhaps a chance to influence legislation that affects it. Giving bribes to legislators or public officials, then, is a business ethics issue.

Fraud

When an individual engages in deceptive practices to advance his or her own interests over those of the organization or some other group, charges of illegal fraud may result. In general, **fraud** is any false communication that deceives, manipulates, or conceals facts to create a false impression when others are damaged or denied a benefit. It is considered a crime, and convictions may result in fines, imprisonment, or both. Fraud costs U.S. organizations hundreds of billions of dollars a year, although exactly how much is unclear given that no single agency exists to track fraud statistics in the United States. Among the most common fraudulent activities employees report about their coworkers are stealing office supplies or shoplifting, claiming to have worked extra hours, and stealing money or products.[24] Table 5.4 indicates what fraud examiners view as the biggest risks to companies. In recent years, accounting fraud has become a major ethical issue, but as we will see, fraud can relate to marketing and consumer issues as well. Online frauds are also a large concern and have grown as Internet use has expanded.[25]

fraud
any false communication that deceives, manipulates, or conceals facts to create a false impression and damage others

Accounting Fraud The field of accounting has changed dramatically over the last decade. The profession used to have a club-type mentality: Those who became certified public accountants (CPAs) were not concerned about competition. Now CPAs advertise their skills or short-term results in an environment in which

Table 5.4 Greatest Fraud Risks for Companies

Conflicts of interest	56%
Fraudulent financial statements	57%
Billing schemes	22%
Expense and reimbursement schemes	41%
Bribery/economic extortions	35%

Source: "The 2007 Oversight Systems Report on Corporate Fraud," Ethics World, http://www.ethicsworld.org/ethicsandemployees/PDF%20links/Oversight_2007_Fraud_Survey.pdf, accessed March 12, 2009.

competition has increased and overall billable hours have significantly decreased because of technological innovations. Pressures on accountants include time, reduced fees, client requests for altered opinions concerning financial conditions or for lower tax payments, and increased competition. Because of such pressures and the ethical predicaments they spawn, some accounting firms have had problems.

Accounting firms have a responsibility to report a true and accurate picture of the financial condition of the companies for which they work. Failure to do so may result in charges and fines for both the accounting firm and the employing company. For example, trustees of New Century Financial Corporation sued its auditor, KPMG, for "reckless and grossly negligent audits" that hid the company's financial problems and sped its collapse. New Century was one of the early casualties of the subprime mortgage crisis, but was once one of the country's largest mortgage lenders to those with poor credit histories. After it disclosed accounting errors not discovered by KPMG, the company collapsed.[26]

Other issues that accountants face daily involve complex rules and regulations that must be followed, data overload, contingent fees, and commissions. An accountant's life is filled with rules and data that have to be interpreted correctly. As a result, accountants must abide by a strict code of ethics, which defines their responsibilities to their clients and the public interest. The code also discusses the concepts of integrity, objectivity, independence, and due care. Finally, the code delineates an accountant's scope and the nature of services that ethically should be provided. In this last portion of the code, contingent fees and commissions are indirectly addressed.

Despite the standards provided by the code, the accounting industry has been the source of numerous fraud investigations in recent years. As a result of the negative publicity surrounding the allegations of accounting fraud at a number of companies, many firms were forced to take a second look at their financial documents. More than a few chose to restate their earnings to avoid being drawn into the scandal.[27] For example, WellCare Health Plans, Inc., was forced to restate over three years of its earnings following a Florida Medicare fraud investigation that also led to changes in management and a loss of profits.[28] Danny Pang, a financier from California, allegedly fraudulently earned $83 million in inflated fees and loans from his investment firm before federal regulators seized it, accusing him of international fraud. The SEC accused Pang of "outright theft" and running a Ponzi scheme, mostly out of Taiwan.[29]

Congress passed the Sarbanes-Oxley Act in 2002 to address many of the issues that could create conflicts of interest for accounting firms auditing public corporations. The law generally prohibits accounting firms from providing both auditing and consulting services to the same firm. Additionally, the law specifies that corporate boards of directors must include outside directors with financial knowledge on the company's audit committee.

Marketing Fraud *Marketing fraud*—the intentional misrepresentation or deceit during the process of creating, distributing, promoting and pricing products—is another business area that generates potential ethical issues. False or misleading marketing communications can destroy customers' trust in a company. Lying, a major ethical issue involving communications, is potentially a significant problem. In both external and internal communications, it causes ethical predicaments because it destroys trust. Misleading marketing can also cost consumers hard-earned money. A U.S. district court passed judgment on Ira Rubin and his company Global Marketing Group. Rubin allegedly debited millions of dollars from U.S. consumers' bank accounts on behalf of many telemarketing scams dating back to 2003. The judgment involved a halt on all payment processing associated with the case.[30]

False or deceptive advertising is a key issue in marketing communications. One set of laws that is common to many countries are laws concerning deceptive advertising—that is, advertisements that are not clearly labeled as advertisements. For example, in the United States, Section 5 of the Federal Trade Commission (FTC) Act addresses deceptive advertising. Abuses in advertising can range from exaggerated claims and concealed facts to outright lying, although improper categorization of advertising claims is the critical point. Courts place false or misleading advertisements into three categories: puffery, implied falsity, and literal falsity.

Puffery can be defined as exaggerated advertising, blustering, and boasting upon which no reasonable buyer would rely and is not actionable under the Lanham Act. For example, in a Lanham Act suit between two shaving products companies, the defendant advertised that the moisturizing strip on its shaving razor was "six times smoother" than its competitors' strips, while showing a man rubbing his hand down his face. The court rejected the defendant's argument that "six times smoother" implied that only the moisturizing strip on the razor's head was smoother. Instead, the court found that the "six times smoother" advertising claim implied that the consumer would receive a smoother shave from the defendant's razor as a whole, a claim that was false.[31]

Implied falsity means that the message has a tendency to mislead, confuse, or deceive the public. The advertising claims that use implied falsity are those that are literally true but imply another message that is false. In most cases, this can be done only through a time-consuming and expensive consumer survey, whose results are often inconclusive.[32]

The characterization of an advertising claim as *literally false* can be divided into two subcategories: *tests prove* (*establishment claims*), in which the advertisement cites a study or test that establishes the claim; and *bald assertions* (*nonestablishment claims*), in which the advertisement makes a claim that cannot be substantiated, as when a commercial states that a certain product is superior to any other on the market. For example, the FTC filed formal complaints against Stock Value 1 Inc. and Comstar Communications Inc. for making unsubstantiated claims that their radiation-protection patches block the electromagnetic energy emitted by cellular telephones. The FTC's complaint charged that the companies "made false statements that their products had been scientifically 'proven' and tested," when in fact that was not the case.[33]

Another form of advertising abuse involves making ambiguous statements in which the words are so weak or general that the viewer, reader, or listener must infer the advertiser's intended message. These "weasel words" are inherently vague and enable the advertiser to deny any intent to deceive. The verb *help* is a good example (as in expressions such as "helps prevent," "helps fight," "helps make you feel").[34] Consumers may view such advertisements as unethical because they fail to communicate all the information needed to make a good purchasing decision or because they deceive the consumer outright.

Labeling issues are even murkier. For example, Netgear Inc. agreed to settle a class-action suit that claimed it exaggerated the data-transfer speeds of its wireless equipment. As part of the settlement, the company must pay $700,000 in legal fees, give a 15 percent discount to members of the class action, donate $25,000 of products to charity, and include disclaimers about the data-transfer speed of its products.[35]

Advertising and direct sales communication can also mislead by concealing the facts within the message. For instance, a salesperson anxious to sell a medical insurance policy might list a large number of illnesses covered by the policy but fail to mention that it does not cover some commonly covered illnesses. Indeed, the fastest-growing area of fraudulent activity is in direct marketing, which employs the telephone and impersonal media to communicate information to customers, who then purchase products via mail, telephone, or the Internet.

Consumer Fraud Consumer fraud occurs when consumers attempt to deceive businesses for their own gain. The FTC estimates that more than 25 million consumers have engaged in consumer fraud.[36] Shoplifting, for example, accounts for nearly 32 percent of the losses of the 118 largest U.S. retail chains, although this figure is still far outweighed by the nearly 49 percent of losses perpetrated by store employees, according to the National Retail Security Survey. Together with vendor fraud and administrative error, these losses cost U.S. retailers more than $31 billion annually.[37]

Consumers engage in many other forms of fraud against businesses, including price-tag switching, item switching, lying to obtain age-related and other discounts, and taking advantage of generous return policies by returning used items, especially clothing that has been worn (with the price tags still attached). Such behavior by consumers affects retail stores as well as other consumers who, for example, may unwittingly purchase new clothing that has actually been worn.[38]

consumer fraud
consumers attempt to deceive businesses for their own gain

Consumer fraud involves intentional deception to derive an unfair economic advantage by an individual or group over an organization. Examples of fraudulent activities include shoplifting, collusion or duplicity, and guile. Collusion typically involves an employee who assists the consumer in fraud. For example, a cashier may not ring up all merchandise or may give an unwarranted discount.

Duplicity may involve a consumer staging an accident in a grocery store and then seeking damages against the store for its lack of attention to safety. A consumer may purchase, wear, and then return an item of clothing for a full refund. In other situations, the consumer may ask for a refund by claiming a defect. Although some of these acts warrant legal prosecution, they can be very difficult to prove, and many companies are reluctant to accuse patrons of a crime when there is no way to verify it. Businesses that operate with the "customer is always right" philosophy have found that some consumers will take advantage of this promise and have therefore modified return policies to curb unfair use.

Discrimination

Another important ethics issue in business today is discrimination. Once dominated by white men, the U.S. workforce today includes significantly more women, African Americans, Hispanics, and other minorities, as well as workers with disabilities and older workers. Experts project that within the next fifty years, Hispanics will represent 24 percent of the population, while African Americans and Asians/Pacific Islanders will make up 15 percent and 9 percent, respectively.[39] These groups have traditionally faced discrimination and higher unemployment rates and have been denied opportunities to assume leadership roles in corporate America.

Discrimination remains a significant ethical issue in business despite nearly forty years of legislation to outlaw it. The most significant piece of legislation is Title VII of the Civil Rights Act of 1964, which prohibits employment discrimination on the basis of race, national origin, color, religion, and gender. This law is fundamental to employees' rights to join and advance in an organization according to merit rather than one of the characteristics just mentioned. As a result of racial discrimination class-action settlements, some companies, such as Coca-Cola, have been required to establish an independent task force to monitor and modify company practices to combat racial discrimination.

Additional laws passed in the 1970s, 1980s, and 1990s were designed to prohibit discrimination related to pregnancy, disabilities, age, and other factors. The Americans with Disabilities Act, for example, prohibits companies from discriminating on the basis of physical or mental disability in all employment practices and requires them to make facilities accessible to and usable by persons with disabilities. The Age Discrimination in Employment Act specifically outlaws hiring practices that discriminate against people between the ages of forty-nine and sixty-nine, and it also bans policies that require employees to retire before the age of seventy. Despite this legislation, charges of age discrimination persist in

© AP Photo/Steve Simoneau

While most organizations have made strides to reduce instances of discrimination, it remains an important legal issue in the workplace

the workplace. Currently, about half of the U.S. workforce is forty or older. This is a large segment of the workplace, and naturally age discrimination suits are prevalent. In a 5–4 split ruling, the U.S. Supreme Court ruled to make it more difficult for workers to claim age discrimination in lawsuits. Now employees must be able to prove that their employers terminated them for age-related reasons. Because this is a difficult thing to prove for certain, the ruling signaled a major coup for employers. The ruling was part of a case brought to trial by Jack Gross, who at fifty-four was demoted from a director position by his employer, the FBL Financial Group.[40] Given that nearly 20 percent of the nation's workers will be fifty-five years old or over by 2015, many companies need to change their approach toward older workers.[41]

To help build workforces that reflect their customer base, many companies have initiated **affirmative action programs**, which involve efforts to recruit, hire, train, and promote qualified individuals from groups that have traditionally been discriminated against on the basis of race, gender, or other characteristics. Such initiatives may be imposed on an employer by federal law, on federal government contractors, and on subcontractors as part of a settlement agreement with a state or federal agency, or by a court order.[42] Many companies voluntarily implement affirmative action plans to build a more diverse workforce.[43] For example, a Chicago real estate developer launched the Female Employment Initiative, an outreach program designed to create opportunities for women in the construction industry through training programs, counseling and information services, and referral listings to help employers identify available women workers.[44]

Although many people believe that affirmative action requires the use of quotas to govern employment decisions, it is important to note that two decades of Supreme Court rulings have made it clear that affirmative action does *not* require or permit quotas, reverse discrimination, or favorable treatment of unqualified women or minorities. To ensure that affirmative action programs are fair, the Supreme Court has established a number of standards to guide their implementation: (1) there must be a strong reason for developing an affirmative action program, (2) affirmative action programs must apply only to qualified candidates, and (3) affirmative action programs must be limited and temporary and therefore cannot include "rigid and inflexible quotas."[45]

The Equal Employment Opportunity Commission (EEOC) monitors compliance with Title VII, with a mission to "promote equal opportunity in employment through administrative and judicial enforcement of the federal civil rights laws and through education and technical assistance."[46] Sexual harassment is a form of sex discrimination that violates Title VII of the Civil Rights Act of 1964. To understand the magnitude of this volatile issue, in one year the EEOC received 13,136 charges of sexual harassment; men filed more than 15 percent of these. In another recent year, the EEOC resolved 13,786 sexual harassment charges and recovered $37.1 million in penalties.[47] **Sexual harassment** can be defined as any repeated, unwanted behavior of a sexual nature perpetrated upon one individual by another. It may be verbal, visual, written, or physical and can occur between people of different genders or those of the same sex. "Workplace display of sexually explicit material—photos, magazines, or posters—may constitute a hostile work environment harassment, even though

affirmative action programs
programs that involve efforts to recruit, hire, train, and promote qualified individuals from groups that have traditionally been discriminated against on the basis of race, gender, or other characteristics

sexual harassment
any repeated, unwanted behavior of a sexual nature perpetrated upon one individual by another

the private possession, reading, and consensual sharing of such materials is protected under the Constitution."[48]

Even the United Nations (U.N.), an organization whose mission is to protect human rights globally, has dealt with a series of sexual harassment cases. Many U.N. employees who have made or faced accusations claim that the system is poorly equipped to handle complaints, resulting in unfair, slow, and arbitrary rulings. For example, one employee who claimed she was harassed for years in Gaza saw her superior cleared by one of his colleagues.[49]

According to the EEOC, an employer may not fire, harass, or otherwise "retaliate" against an individual for filing a charge of discrimination, participating in a discrimination proceeding, or otherwise opposing discrimination. The Americans with Disabilities Act also protects individuals from coercion, intimidation, threat, harassment, or interference in the exercise of their own rights or their encouragement of someone else's exercise of rights granted by the act.[50] Legal specialists say employers can take steps to minimize retaliation complaints through beefed-up training, investigations, and follow-up efforts.

Information Technology

The final category of ethical issues relates to technology and the numerous advances made in the Internet and other forms of electronic communications in the last few years. As the number of people who use the Internet increases, the areas of concern related to its use increase as well. Some issues that must be addressed by businesses include monitoring employee use of available technology, consumer privacy, site development and online marketing, and legal protection of intellectual properties, such as music, books, and movies. The issue of technology and intellectual property has become an ever more important one, as more and more information is stored in a digital format and as more people begin to use the Internet. Some believe that the Internet should be an open and egalitarian format, while others think that incentives to innovate will be stifled if people do not pay for access to material.[51]

> "The issue of technology and intellectual property has become an ever more important one, as more and more information is stored in a digital format and as more people begin to use the Internet."

Recognizing an Ethical Issue

Although we have described a number of relationships and situations that may generate ethical issues, it can be difficult to recognize specific ethical issues in practice. Failure to acknowledge ethical issues is a great danger in any organization, particularly if business is treated as a game in which ordinary rules of fairness do not apply. Sometimes,

Figure 5.1 Personal Misconduct in the Workplace Is Increasing

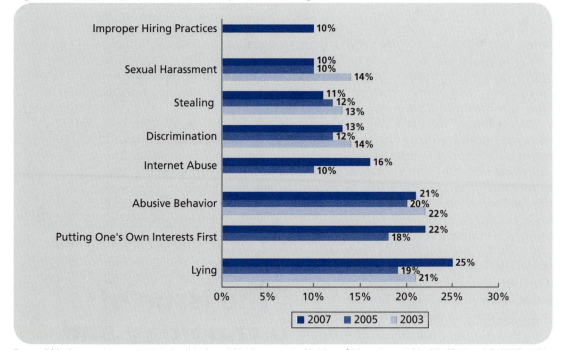

Source: Ethics Resource Center, *2007 National Business Ethics Survey: An Inside View of Private Sector Ethics* (Washington, DC: 2007), p. 29. Reprinted with permission.

people who take this view do things that are not only unethical but also illegal to maximize their own position or boost the profits or goals of the organization.

Figure 5.1 identifies the frequency of misconduct observed by employees in the most recent Ethics Resource Center Survey. While the number of corporate ethics programs countrywide is on the rise, over half (56 percent) of the national sample of employees observed some type of misconduct. Figure 5.1 shows that personal misconduct at work has been on the rise, although instances of organizational misconduct have gone down slightly. This figure shows how important it is to have a comprehensive ethics and compliance program in place to assess risk and to reduce instances of personal misconduct. These data provide evidence that misconduct is widespread and a significant issue in business.

However, just because an unsettled situation or activity is an ethical issue does not mean the behavior is necessarily unethical. An ethical issue is simply a situation, a problem, or even an opportunity that requires thought, discussion, or investigation to determine the moral impact of the decision. Because the business world is dynamic, new ethical issues are emerging all the time.

One way to determine whether a specific behavior or situation has an ethical component is to ask other individuals in the business how they feel about it and whether they approve. Another way is to determine whether the organization has adopted specific policies on the activity. An activity approved of by most members of an organization, if it is also customary in the industry, is probably ethical. An issue, activity, or situation that can withstand open discussion between many stakeholders, both inside and outside the organization, and survive untarnished probably does not pose ethical problems. For instance, when engineers and designers at Ford Motor Co. discussed what type of gas-tank protection should be used in its Pinto automobile, they reached consensus within the organization, but they did not take into account the interests of various external stakeholders, such as the public's desire for maximum safety. Consequently, even though they might have believed the issue had no ethical dimension, Ford erred in not opening up the issue to public scrutiny. (As it turned out, the type of gas-tank protection in the Pinto resulted in several fires and deaths when the cars were involved in rear-end collisions.)

UNDERSTANDING THE ETHICAL DECISION-MAKING PROCESS

To grasp the significance of ethics in business decision making, it is important to understand how ethical decisions are made within the context of an organization. Understanding the ethical decision-making process can help individuals and businesses design strategies to deter misconduct. Our descriptive approach to understanding ethical decision making does not prescribe what to do but, rather, provides a framework for managing ethical behavior in the workplace. Figure 5.2 depicts this framework, which shows how individual factors, organizational relationships, and opportunity interact to determine ethical decisions in business.

Individual Factors

Individuals make ethical choices on the basis of their own concepts of right or wrong, and they act accordingly in their daily lives. Studies suggest that individual ethics are reaching a new low. A Junior Achievement/Deloitte survey of teens showed that 71 percent feel prepared to make ethical decisions in the workplace. However, of those surveyed, 38 percent feel it is sometimes necessary to lie, cheat,

Figure 5.2 Factors That Influence the Ethical Decision-Making Process

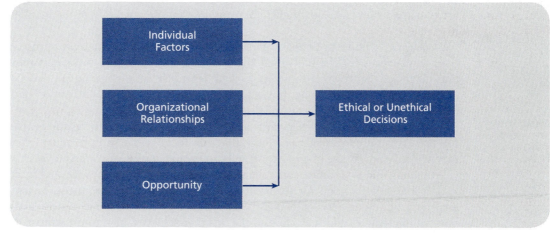

plagiarize, or engage in violence to succeed. One-fourth think cheating on a test is acceptable and most can justify it saying that their desire to succeed is grounds for the behavior.[52] According to another poll by Deloitte and Touche of teenagers aged thirteen to eighteen years old, when asked if people who practice good business ethics are more successful than those who don't, 69 percent of teenagers agreed.[53] On the other hand, another survey indicated that many students do not define copying answers from another student's paper or downloading music or content for classroom work as cheating.[54]

If today's students are tomorrow's leaders, there is likely to be a correlation between acceptable behavior today and tomorrow, adding to the argument that the leaders of today must be prepared for the ethical risks associated with this downward trend. Significant factors that affect the ethical decision-making process include an individual's personal moral philosophy, stage of moral development, motivation, and other personal factors such as gender, age, and experience.

Moral Philosophy Many people have justified difficult decisions by citing the golden rule ("Do unto others as you would have them do unto you") or some other principle. Such principles, or rules, which individuals apply in deciding what is right or wrong, are often referred to as **moral philosophies.** It is important to understand the distinction between moral philosophies and business ethics. A moral philosophy is a person's principles and values that define what is moral or immoral. Moral philosophies are person-specific, whereas business ethics is based on decisions in groups or those made when carrying out tasks to meet business objectives. In the context of business, ethics refers to what the group, firm, or strategic business unit (SBU) defines as right or wrong actions pertaining to its business operations and the objective of profits, earnings per share, or some other financial measure of success as defined by the group. Socialization by family members, social groups, religion, and formal education teach moral philosophies. Most moral philosophies can be classified as consequentialism, ethical formalism, or justice.

Consequentialism is a class of moral philosophy that considers a decision right or acceptable if it accomplishes a desired result such as pleasure, knowledge, career growth, the realization of self-interest, or utility. Egoism and utilitarianism are two important consequentialist philosophies that often guide decision making in business.

Egoism is a philosophy that defines right or acceptable conduct in terms of the consequences for the individual. Egoists believe they should make decisions that maximize their own self-interest, which, depending on the individual, may be defined as physical well-being, power, pleasure, fame, a satisfying career, a good family life, wealth, and so forth. In a decision-making situation, the egoist will probably choose the alternative that most benefits his or her self-interest. Many people feel that egoists are inherently unethical, that they focus on the short term, and that they will take advantage of any opportunity to exploit consumers or employees.

Utilitarianism is another consequentialist philosophy that is concerned with seeking the greatest good for the greatest number of people. Using a cost-benefit analysis, a utilitarian decision maker calculates the utility of the consequences of all possible alternatives and then chooses the one that achieves the greatest utility.

moral philosophies
principles, or rules, that individuals apply in deciding what is right or wrong

consequentialism
a class of moral philosophy that considers a decision right or acceptable if it accomplishes a desired result such as pleasure, knowledge, career growth, the realization of self-interest, or utility

egoism
a philosophy that defines right or acceptable conduct in terms of the consequences for the individual

utilitarianism
a consequentialist philosophy that is concerned with seeking the greatest good for the greatest number of people

In contrast with consequentialism, **ethical formalism** is a class of moral philosophy that focuses on the rights of individuals and on the intentions associated with a particular behavior rather than on its consequences. Ethical formalists regard certain behaviors as inherently right, and their determination of rightness focuses on the individual actor, not on society. Thus, these perspectives are sometimes referred to as nonconsequentialism and the ethics of respect for persons.

Contemporary ethical formalism has been greatly influenced by the German philosopher Immanuel Kant, who developed the so-called categorical imperative: "Act as if the maxim of thy action were to become by thy will a universal law of nature."[55] Unlike utilitarians, ethical formalists contend that there are some things that people should not do, even to maximize utility. For example, an ethical formalist would consider it unacceptable to allow a coal mine to continue to operate if some workers became ill and died of black lung disease. A utilitarian, however, might consider some disease or death an acceptable consequence of a decision that resulted in large-scale employment and economic prosperity.

Justice theory is a class of moral philosophy that relates to evaluations of fairness, or the disposition to deal with perceived injustices of others. Justice demands fair treatment and due reward in accordance with ethical or legal standards. In business, this requires that the rules an individual uses to determine justice be based on the perceived rights of individuals and on the intentions associated with a business interaction. Justice, therefore, is more likely to be based on nonconsequentialist moral philosophies than on consequentialist philosophies. Justice primarily addresses the issue of what individuals feel they are due based on their rights and performance in the workplace.

> **"There is no one 'correct' moral philosophy to apply in resolving ethical and legal issues in the workplace."**

For example, the U.S. Equal Employment Opportunity Commission exists to help employees who suspect the injustice of discrimination in the workplace.

Three types of justice can be used to assess fairness in different situations. *Distributive justice* evaluates the outcomes or results of a business relationship. For example, if an employee feels that she is paid less than her coworkers for the same work, she has concerns about distributive justice. *Procedural justice* assesses the processes and activities employed to produce an outcome or results. Procedural justice concerns about compensation would relate to the perception that salary and benefit decisions were consistent and fair to all categories of employees. Procedural justice is associated with group cohesiveness and helping behaviors.[56] *Interactional justice* evaluates the communication processes used in the business relationship. Being untruthful about the reasons for missing work is an example of an interactional justice issue.[57]

It is important to recognize that there is no one "correct" moral philosophy to apply in resolving ethical and legal issues in the workplace. It is also important to acknowledge that each philosophy presents an ideal perspective and that most people seem to adapt a number of moral philosophies as they interpret the

ethical formalism
a class of moral philosophy that focuses on the rights of individuals and on the intentions associated with a particular behavior rather than on its consequences

justice theory
a class of moral philosophy that relates to evaluations of fairness, or the disposition to deal with perceived injustices of others

context of different decision-making situations. Each philosophy could result in a different decision in a situation requiring an ethical judgment. And depending on the situation, people may even change their value structure or moral philosophy when making decisions.[58]

Strong evidence shows that individuals use different moral philosophies depending on whether they are making a personal decision outside the work environment or making a work-related decision on the job.[59] Two possible reasons may explain this. First, in the business arena, some goals and pressures for success differ from the goals and pressures in a person's life outside of work. As a result, an employee might view a specific action as "good" in the business sector but "unacceptable" in the non-work environment. It is often suggested that business managers are morally different from other people. In a way, this is correct in that business has one variable that is absent from other situations: the profit motive. The weights on the various factors that make up a person's moral philosophy are shifted in a business (profit) situation. The statement "it's not personal, it's just business" demonstrates the conflict businesspeople can have when their personal values do not align with utilitarian or profit-oriented decisions. The reality is that if firms do not make a profit, they will fail. This should not be construed to be a justification for seeking excessive profits or executive pay, issues which stakeholders are now questioning.

The second reason people change moral philosophies could be the corporate culture where they work. When a child enters school, for example, he or she learns certain rules such as raising your hand to speak or asking permission to use the restroom. So it is with a new employee. Rules, personalities, and historical precedence exert pressure on the employee to conform to the new firm's culture. As this occurs, the individual's moral philosophy may change to be compatible with the work environment. The employee may alter some or all of the values within his or her moral philosophy as he or she shifts into the firm's different moral philosophy. There are many examples of people known for their goodness at home or in their communities making unethical decisions in the workplace.

Stage of Moral Development[60] One reason that different people make different decisions when confronted with similar ethical situations may be that they are in different stages of moral development. Psychologist Lawrence Kohlberg proposed that people progress through stages in their development of moral reasoning or, as he called it, cognitive moral development.[61] He believes that people progress through the following six stages:

1. The stage of punishment and obedience. An individual in this stage of development defines right as literal obedience to rules and authority and responds to rules in terms of the physical power of those who determine such rules. Individuals in this stage do not associate right and wrong with any higher order or moral philosophy but instead with a person who has power. For example, a plant supervisor may choose to go along with a superior's order to release untreated wastewater into a nearby stream, even though she knows it would be illegal, because she fears the superior's power to fire her if she does not comply.

2. The stage of individual instrumental purpose and exchange. A person in this stage defines right as that which serves his or her own needs. In this stage, people evaluate behavior on the basis of its fairness to themselves rather than solely on the basis of specific rules or authority figures. For example, a corporate buyer may choose to accept an expensive gift from a salesperson, despite the presence of a company rule prohibiting the acceptance of gifts, because the gift is something he needs or wants. This stage is sometimes labeled the stage of reciprocity because, from a practical standpoint, ethical decisions are based on "you-scratch-my-back-and-I'll-scratch-yours" agreements instead of on principles such as loyalty or justice.

3. The stage of mutual interpersonal expectation, relationships, and conformity. An individual in this stage emphasizes others over himself or herself. Although these individuals still derive motivation from obedience to rules, they also consider the well-being of others. For example, a production manager might choose to obey an order from upper management to speed up an assembly line because she believes this action will generate more profit for the company and thereby preserve her employees' jobs.

4. The stage of social justice and conscience maintenance. A person in this stage determines what is right by considering duty to society as well as to other specific people. Duty, respect for authority, and maintaining social order become fundamental goals in decision making. For example, Jeffrey Wigand, a former executive at Brown & Williamson Tobacco Corporation, believed that the company was hiding from the public the truth that cigarettes are addictive and dangerous. He chose to "blow the whistle" by testifying against his former employer after he was fired.[62] Wigand's story was later dramatized in the movie *The Insider*.

5. The stage of prior rights, social contract, or utility. In this stage, an individual is concerned with upholding the basic rights, values, and legal contracts of society. Such individuals feel a sense of obligation or "social contract" to other groups and recognize that legal and moral points of view may conflict in some instances. To minimize conflict, persons in this stage base decisions on a rational calculation of overall utilities. For example, a business owner may choose to establish an organizational compliance program because it will serve as a buffer to prevent legal problems and to protect the company's good name.

6. The stage of universal ethical principles. A person in this stage believes that right is determined by universal ethical principles that everyone should follow. Such individuals believe that there are inalienable rights that are universal in nature and consequence. Justice and equality are examples of such universal rights. Thus, a businessperson in this stage may be more concerned with social ethical issues and rely less on the company for direction in situations with an ethical component.[63] For example, a marketing manager may argue for the termination of a toy that has resulted in injury and death because she believes the product threatens the universal value of right to life.

Most ethical decisions in the workplace are made jointly or by groups, not by individuals

Because there is some spillover effect among these stages, cognitive moral development can be viewed as a continuum. Kohlberg's theory suggests that people may change their moral beliefs and behavior as they gain education and experience in resolving conflicts, and this helps accelerate their progress along the moral development continuum. Kohlberg's model also suggests that there are universal values by which people in the highest level of moral development abide. These rights are considered valid not because of a particular society's laws or customs but because they rest on the premise of universality. Many organizations and researchers have attempted to identify a set of global or universal ethical standards that all individuals should follow regardless of where they live or work.

Organizational Relationships

Although individuals can and do make ethical decisions, they do not operate in a vacuum.[64] Ethical choices in business are most often made jointly in committees and work groups or in conversations with coworkers. Moreover, people learn to settle ethical issues not only from their individual backgrounds but also from others with whom they associate in the business environment. The outcome of this learning process depends on the strength of each individual's personal values, opportunity for unethical behavior, and exposure to others who behave ethically or unethically. Consequently, the culture of the organization, as well as superiors, peers, and subordinates, can have a significant impact on the ethical decision-making process.

"The culture of the organization, as well as superiors, peers, and subordinates, can have a significant impact on the ethical decision-making process."

Organizational Culture Organizational, or corporate, culture can be defined as a set of values, norms, and artifacts shared by members or employees of an organization. It answers questions such as "What is important?" "How do we treat each other?" and "How do we do things around here?" Culture may be conveyed formally in employee handbooks, codes of conduct, memos, and ceremonies, but it is

also expressed informally through dress codes, extracurricular activities, and anecdotes. A firm's culture gives its members meaning and offers direction as to how to behave and deal with problems within the organization. The corporate culture at American Express, for example, includes numerous anecdotes about employees who have gone beyond the call of duty to help customers out of difficult situations. This strong tradition of customer service might encourage an American Express employee to take extra steps to help a customer who encounters a problem while traveling overseas.

On the other hand, an organization's culture can also encourage employees to make decisions that others may judge as unethical or socially irresponsible. Most misconduct comes from employees trying to attain the performance objectives of the firm. Derivatives used in financial markets to transfer risk, for example, have been so complex, difficult to value, poorly regulated, and widely used that they have brought down companies. They also contributed a great deal to the severity of the 2008–2009 financial crisis, bringing the financial system to its knees. To make ethical decisions when using derivatives, one requires a great deal of transparency, financial expertise and competence, and responsibility.[65] Because of their complexity, derivatives provide openings for manipulation and misconduct. When a corporation uses certain compensation systems, employees striving for financial success may be inadvertently rewarded for their sales of dangerous derivatives.

Whereas a firm's overall culture establishes ideals that guide a wide range of behaviors for members of the organization, its **ethical climate** focuses specifically on issues of right and wrong. We think of ethical climate as the part of a corporate culture that relates to an organization's expectations about appropriate conduct. To some extent, ethical climate is the character component of an organization. Corporate policies and codes, the conduct of top managers, the values and moral philosophies of coworkers, and opportunity for misconduct all contribute to a firm's ethical climate. When top managers strive to establish an ethical climate based on responsibility and citizenship, they set the tone for ethical decisions.

Such is the case at the White Dog Café in Philadelphia. Owner Judy Wicks grew her business from a coffee and muffin take-out joint in the first floor of her home to a 200-seat restaurant and store that grossed $5 million annually, all while being socially and environmentally responsible. Wicks paid a living wage to all restaurant employees, even the dishwashers; however, most employees at the White Dog Café made well above this amount. The restaurant used 100 percent wind-powered electricity, and 10 to 20 percent of the profits were donated to the affiliated nonprofit, White Dog Café Foundation, which works to build a more socially just and environmentally sustainable local economy in the greater Philadelphia region, and other nonprofits. When Wicks decided to sell the business, she built a social contract into the franchise agreement so that all new restaurants must adhere to the original's principles, including buying local whenever possible and using renewable energy. Wicks says she used "good food to lure innocent consumers into social activism."[66] Thus, the White Dog Café management has established an ethical climate that promotes responsible conduct.

organizational, or corporate, culture
a set of values, norms, and artifacts shared by members or employees of an organization

ethical climate
part of a corporate culture that relates to an organization's expectations about appropriate conduct that focuses specifically on issues of right and wrong

Ethical climate also determines whether an individual perceives an issue as having an ethical component. Recognizing ethical issues and generating alternatives to address them are manifestations of ethical climate.

Significant Others **Significant others** include superiors, peers, and subordinates in the organization who influence the ethical decision-making process. Although people outside the firm, such as family members and friends, also influence decision makers, organizational structure and culture operate through significant others to influence ethical decisions. The Ethics Resource Center's National Business Ethics Survey (NBES) found that more than two out of every five employees surveyed did not report what they saw.[67] Reporting misconduct is most likely to come from upper levels of management compared to lower-level supervisors and nonmanagement employees. Employees in lower-level positions have more of a tendency not to understand misconduct or to be complacent about the misconduct they observe. Figure 5.3 shows employees' preferred channels for reporting misconduct. While other options like ethics officers and ethics hotlines exist, the vast majority of employees surveyed prefer to report to supervisors and other higher management.

Most experts agree that the chief executive officer establishes the ethical tone for the entire firm. Lower-level managers obtain their cues from top managers, and they in turn impose some of their personal values on the company. This interaction between corporate culture and executive leadership helps determine the ethical value system of the firm. However, obedience to authority can also explain why many people resolve workplace issues by following the directives of a superior. An employee may feel obligated to carry out the orders of a superior even if those orders conflict with the employee's values of right and wrong. If that decision is later judged to have been wrong, the employee may justify it

significant others
superiors, peers, and subordinates in the organization who influence the ethical decision-making process

Figure 5.3 Preferred Reporting Methods

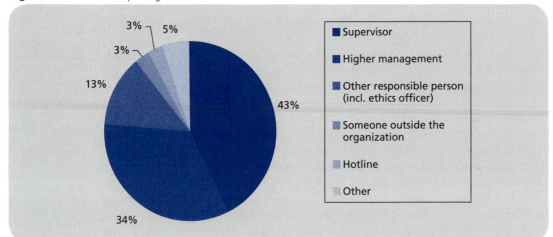

Source: Ethics Resource Center, *2007 National Business Ethics Survey: An Inside View of Private Sector Ethics* (Washington, DC: Ethics Resource Center, 2007), p. 17.

by saying, "I was only carrying out orders" or "My boss told me to do it this way."

Coworkers' influence on ethical decision making depends on the person's exposure to unethical behavior in making ethical decisions. The more a person is exposed to unethical activity by others in the organization, the more likely it is that he or she will behave unethically, especially in ethically "gray" areas. Thus, a decision maker who associates with others who act unethically is more likely to behave unethically as well. Within work groups, employees may be subject to the phenomenon of "groupthink," or going along with group decisions even when those decisions run counter to their own values. They may rationalize such a decision with "safety in numbers" when everyone else appears to back a particular decision. Most business-people take their cues or learn from coworkers how to solve problems—including ethical dilemmas.[68] "We evaluate other people based upon their behavior; we evaluate ourselves based upon our intentions."[69] Close friends at work exert the most influence on ethical decisions that relate to roles associated with a particular job.

"The interaction between corporate culture and executive leadership helps determine the ethical value system of the firm."

Superiors and coworkers can create organizational pressure, which plays a key role in creating ethical issues. Concealing evidence of defects that could result in a recall is not uncommon in Japanese culture, which views product recalls as a source of great humiliation. In such a culture, pressure from superiors and coworkers to remain silent may be enormous.

Nearly all businesspeople face difficult issues where solutions are not obvious or where organizational objectives and personal ethical values may conflict. For example, a salesperson for a Web-based retailer may be asked by a superior to lie to a customer over the telephone about a late product shipment. In one survey, 47 percent of human resources managers said they had felt pressured by other employees or managers to compromise their firm's standards of business conduct to attain business objectives.[70] A study by the Ethics Resource Center found that more than a third of employees who fail to report misconduct do so because they fear retaliation.[71]

Opportunity

Together, organizational culture and the influence of coworkers may foster conditions that either hinder or permit misconduct. **Opportunity** is a set of conditions that limits barriers or provides rewards. When these conditions provide rewards—be it financial gain, recognition, promotion, or simply the good feeling from a job well done—the opportunity for unethical conduct may be encouraged or discouraged. For example, a company policy that fails to specify the punishment for employees who violate the rules provides an opportunity for unethical behavior because

opportunity
a set of conditions that limits barriers or provides rewards

it allows individuals to engage in such behavior without fear of consequences. Thus, company policies, processes, and other factors may create opportunities to act unethically. Advancing technology associated with the Internet is challenging companies working to limit opportunities to engage in unethical and illegal behavior. Individual factors as well as organizational relationships may influence whether an individual becomes opportunistic and takes advantage of situations in an unethical or even illegal manner.

Opportunity usually relates to employees' immediate job context—where they work, with whom they work, and the nature of the work. This context includes the motivational "carrots and sticks," or rewards and punishments, that superiors can use to influence employee behavior. Rewards, or positive reinforcers, include pay raises, bonuses, and public recognition, whereas reprimands, pay penalties, demotions, and even firings act as negative reinforcers. For example, a manager who decides to sell customers' personal data may be confident that such behavior is an easy way to boost revenue because other companies sell customer account information. Even if this activity violates the employee's personal value system, it may be viewed as acceptable within the organization's culture. This manager may be motivated by opportunities to increase company revenue and his or her performance standing within the organization. A survey by Vault.com indicates that 67 percent of employees take office supplies for personal use. As Figure 5.4 shows, many employees pilfer office supply rooms for matters unrelated to the job. It is possible that the opportunity is provided, and in some cases, there are no concerns if employees take pens, Post-Its, envelopes, notepads, and paper. Respondents to the Vault survey indicate that 25 percent feel that no one cares if they take office supplies, 34 percent never got caught, and 1 percent got caught.[72] One concern is that if there is no policy against this practice, employees will not learn where to draw the line and will get into the habit of taking even more expensive items for personal use.

Figure 5.4 Items Employees Pilfer in the Workplace

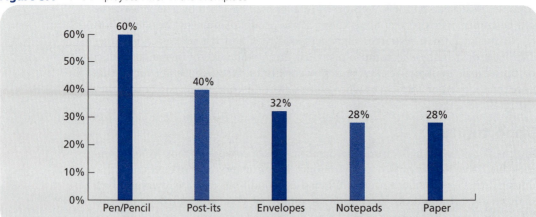

Source: "Top Items Employees Pilfer." Most popular items employees take from office supply rooms for matters unrelated to the job. Vault's office survey of 1,152 respondents. In *USA Today*, Snapshots, March 29, 2006, p. B1.

Often, opportunity can arise from someone whose job is to create opportunity for others. Barbara Toffler, an ethics consultant and professor, learned firsthand how difficult it can be to follow one's own moral compass when she worked as a consultant at Arthur Andersen creating ethics programs for Andersen clients (the firm itself had no internal ethics program). After charging a client $1 million for developing an ethics program that should have cost $500,000, the praise Toffler earned from Andersen "was the only day in four years that I felt truly valued by Arthur Andersen." Despite her expertise, she learned that "unethical or illegal behavior happens when decent people are put under the unbearable pressure to do their jobs and meet ambitious goals without the resources to get the job done right."[73]

General Electric has taken steps to place itself at the head of the ethical pack. Its "healthymagination" campaign is designed to bolster its faltering health business, which has struggled as fewer hospitals and health-care centers purchase its medical imaging and diagnostic machines. The new strategy aims to develop 100 products by 2015 and is focusing on reducing costs and increasing quality by 15 percent. These moves should make health products and services more afford-able and accessible to customers.[74]

If an employee takes advantage of an opportunity to act unethically and is rewarded or suffers no penalty, he or she may repeat such acts as other opportu-nities arise. Mark Walsh, former head of Lehman Brothers, pushed his managing directors to take excessive risks and possibly to misrepresent the value of the corporation's real estate holdings. Managing directors received larger bonuses on riskier deals, creating an incentive to engage in risky activities. The real estate and finance crises in 2008 and 2009 caused the collapse of Lehman, with Walsh and seventeen former executives accused of defrauding New Jersey pension funds, among many other allegations.[75] When company managers get away with unethical conduct, their behavior is reinforced and a culture of manipulation and misconduct can develop. Indeed, opportunity to engage in unethical conduct is often a better predictor of unethical activities than personal values.[76]

In addition to rewards and the absence of punishment, other elements in the business environment tend to create opportunities. Professional codes of conduct and ethics-related corporate policies also influence opportunity by prescribing what behaviors are acceptable. Compliance programs are necessary to provide internal controls to prevent situations. The larger the rewards and the milder the punishment for unethical behavior, the greater is the probability that unethical behavior will be practiced.

SUMMARY

Business ethics comprises principles and standards that guide individual and work group behavior in the world of business. Stakeholders determine these conventions, and they may change over time. The most basic of these standards have been codified as laws and regulations. Business ethics goes beyond legal issues.

Because individuals and groups within a company may not have embraced the same set of values, ethical conflict may occur. Questionable decisions and actions may result in disputes that must be resolved through some type of negotiation or even litigation. Codifying ethical standards into meaningful policies that spell out what is and is not acceptable gives businesspeople an opportunity to reduce the possibility of behavior that could create legal problems. Business decisions involve complex and detailed discussions in which correctness may not be clear-cut. It is important that a shared vision of acceptable behavior develop from an organizational perspective to create consistent and reliable relationships with all concerned stakeholders.

Understanding the ethical decision-making process can help individuals and businesses design strategies to prevent misconduct. Three of the important components of ethical decision making are individual factors, organizational relationships, and opportunity.

Significant individual factors that affect the ethical decision-making process include personal moral philosophy, stage of moral development, motivation, and other personal factors such as gender, age, and experience. Moral philosophies are the principles or rules that individuals apply in deciding what is right or wrong. Most moral philosophies can be classified as consequentialism, ethical formalism, or justice. Consequentialist philosophies consider a decision to be right or acceptable if it accomplishes a desired result such as pleasure, knowledge, career growth, the realization of self-interest, or utility. Consequentialism may be further classified as egoism and utilitarianism. Ethical formalism focuses on the rights of individuals and on the intentions associated with a particular behavior rather than on its consequences. Justice theory relates to evaluations of fairness, or the disposition to deal with perceived injustices of others. Kohlberg proposed that people progress through six stages in their cognitive moral development.

The culture of the organization, as well as superiors, peers, and subordinates, can have a significant impact on the ethical decision-making process. Organizational, or corporate, culture can be defined as a set of values, beliefs, goals, norms, and rituals shared by members or employees of an organization. Whereas a firm's overall culture establishes ideals that guide a wide range of behaviors for members of the organization, its ethical climate focuses specifically on issues of right and wrong. Significant others include superiors, peers, and subordinates in the organization who influence the ethical decision-making process. Interaction between corporate culture and executive leadership helps determine the ethical value system of the firm, but obedience to authority can also explain why many people resolve workplace issues by following the directives of a superior. The more exposed a person is to unethical activity in the organization, the more likely it is that he or she will behave unethically. Superiors and coworkers can create organizational pressure, which plays a key role in creating ethical issues.

Opportunity is a set of conditions that limit barriers or provide rewards. Individuals who take advantage of an opportunity to act unethically and escape punishment or gain rewards may repeat such acts when circumstances favor them.

RESPONSIBLE BUSINESS DEBATE

Zicam Takes Advantage of Regulatory Loophole

ISSUE: Are companies obliged to disclose potentially damning evidence about their products?

Being truthful about the products one's company sells is an important ethical issue. Withholding information because it makes a product look less desirable, less safe, or less valuable is called omission lying. For example, omission lying occurred when tobacco companies possessed information for decades on the health consequences of smoking yet did nothing to inform consumers.

The Food and Drug Administration (FDA) is a consumer regulatory agency charged with protecting consumers from dangerous food and drug products. While one would hope that companies take responsibility and inform consumers when they have information concerning the safety of their products, history has shown that companies sometimes prize profits over consumer welfare.

In 2009 the FDA issued a warning concerning the homeopathic cold remedy Zicam because studies had shown that the main ingredient, zinc, can cause permanent loss of taste and smell. At the time of the warning, Zicam's manufacturer, Matrixx Initiatives Inc., had information that a minimum of 130 people had reported losing their sense of smell, some of them permanently. Studies dating back 70 years have shown that zinc can be toxic in large doses, yet the company was not required to disclose this information until 2007 when the FDA changed its rules because Zicam is classified as a homeopathic remedy. The FDA under the new administration has taken its task of protecting stakeholder welfare seriously, and moved to speak up about Zicam.

After the FDA issued its warning, Matrixx responded by claiming that its products are safe. However, this is not the first time the company has suffered from this allegation. In 2006, Matrixx settled 300 lawsuits brought by consumers who alleged that Zicam had destroyed their senses of smell. The FDA asserts that zinc can be toxic when absorbed through mucous membranes like those in the nose. Additionally, the FDA claims that Zicam products have not been effective in their purported purpose—to reduce the duration and severity of colds. To respond to the FDA's demands, Zicam stopped shipping nasal sprays and swabs and promised to reimburse consumers who requested a refund. Over-the-counter drug products like Zicam do not require FDA approval before going on the market.

There Are Two Sides to Every Issue:

1. The FDA should require preapproval of all over-the-counter drug products, including those deemed natural or homeopathic.
2. Drug companies should have to report side effects and should not be required to get preapproval.

Source: Jonathan D. Rockoff, "Matrixx Receives SEC Inquiry," *Wall Street Journal*, June 24, 2009, http://online. wsj.com/article/SB124579292298543745.html, accessed June 9, 2009; "Matrixx Initiatives Confirms Voluntary Recall of Zicam Cold Remedy Nasal Gel, Zicam Cold Remedy Nasal Swabs," PR Newswire, June 24, 2009, http://news. prnewswire.com/ViewContent.aspx?ACCT=109&STORY=/ www/story/06-24-2009/0005049392&EDATE=, accessed July 10, 2009.

KEY TERMS

business ethics (p. 177)
ethical issue (p. 181)
conflict of interest (p. 186)
fraud (p. 187)
consumer fraud (p. 190)
affirmative action programs (p. 191)
sexual harassment (p. 191)
moral philosophies (p. 196)
consequentialism (p. 196)

egoism (p. 196)
utilitarianism (p. 196)
ethical formalism (p. 197)
justice theory (p. 197)
organizational, or corporate,
  culture (p. 200)
ethical climate (p. 201)
significant others (p. 202)
opportunity (p. 203)

DISCUSSION QUESTIONS

1. Why is business ethics a strategic consideration in organizational decisions?

2. How do individual, organizational, and opportunity factors interact to influence ethical or unethical decisions?

3. How do moral philosophies influence the individual factor in organizational ethical decision making?

4. How can ethical formalism be used in organizational ethics programs and still respect diversity and the right for individual values?

5. What are the potential benefits of an emphasis on procedural justice?

6. How can knowledge of Kohlberg's stages of moral development be useful in developing an organizational ethics program?

7. How do organizations create an ethical climate?

8. Why are we seeing more evidence of widespread ethical dilemmas within organizations?

EXPERIENTIAL EXERCISE

Visit http://www.bbb.org, the home page for the Better Business Bureau. Locate the International Marketplace Ethics award criteria. Find recent winners of the award and summarize what they did to achieve this recognition. Describe the role of the BBB in supporting self-regulatory activities and business ethics.

WHAT WOULD YOU DO?

On Sunday, Armando went to work to pick up a report he needed to review before an early Monday meeting. While at work, he noticed a colleague's light on and went over to her cubicle for a short visit. Monica was one of the newest systems designers on the department's staff. She was hired six weeks ago to assist with a series of human resources (HR) projects for the company. Before joining the firm, she worked as an independent consultant to organizations trying to upgrade their human resources systems that track payroll, benefits, compliance, and other issues. Monica was very well qualified, detail oriented, and hard working. She was the only female on the systems staff.

In his brief conversation with Monica, Armando felt that he was not getting the full story of her reason for being at work on a Sunday. After all, the systems team completed the first HR systems proposal on Thursday and was prepared to present its report and recommendations on Monday. Monica said she was "working on a few parts" of the project but did not get more specific. Her face turned red when Armando joked, "With the beautiful sunshine outside, only someone hoping to earn a little extra money would be at work today."

Armando and another coworker, David, presented the systems team's report to the HR staff on Monday. HR was generally pleased with the recommendations but wanted a number of specifications changes. This was normal and the systems designers were prepared for the changes. Everyone on the team met that afternoon and Tuesday morning to develop a plan for revamping the HR system. By Tuesday afternoon, each member was working on his or her part of the project again.

On Friday afternoon, David went up and down the hall, encouraging everyone to go to happy hour at the pub down the street. About ten people, including Monica and Armando, went to the pub. The conversation was mainly about work and the new HR project. On several occasions, Monica offered ideas about other systems and companies with which she was familiar. Most of the systems designers listened, but a few were quick to question her suggestions. Armando assumed her suggestions were the result of work with previous clients. Over the weekend, however, Armando began to wonder whether Monica was talking about current clients. He remembered their conversation on Sunday and decided to look into the matter.

On Monday, Armando asked Monica directly whether she still had clients. Monica said yes and that she was finishing up on projects with two of them. She went on to say that she worked late hours and on the weekends and was not skimping on her company responsibilities. Armando agreed that she was a good colleague but was not comfortable with her use of company resources on personal, moneymaking projects. He was also concerned that the team's intellectual capital was being used. What would you do?

Strategic Approaches to Improving Ethical Behavior

Chapter Objectives

- To provide an overview of the need for an organizational ethics program

- To consider crucial keys to development of an effective ethics program

- To examine effective implementation of an ethics program

Chapter Outline

The Need for Organizational Ethics Programs

Codes of Conduct

Ethics Officers

Ethics Training and Communication

Establishing Systems to Monitor and Enforce Ethical Standards

Continuous Improvement of the Ethics Program

Implementing Organizational Ethics Programs

© Tom Tomczyk

Is Greenwashing the Newest Ethical Issue?

As concerns about the environment grow among consumers and stakeholder groups, more companies are trying to portray themselves in an eco-friendly light. This is causing a new ethical issue called *greenwashing,* which occurs when companies market products as environmentally friendly when they are actually not. It is a way for companies to appeal to green consumers while avoiding the costs of developing truly "green" products and services.

Businesses accused of greenwashing can be exposed as misguiding the public and face the possibility of negative publicity and decreased sales revenue. In the United States, firms that label or advertise products as organic or environmentally friendly are supposed to abide by the Federal Trade Commission's "Green Guides" or risk fines, reimbursement to consumers, and negative publicity. The FTC says that with a small budget mainly focused on identity theft, credit fraud, and monopolies, it is difficult to track greenwashing. European governments are cracking down on greenwashing. British Gas was censured when it claimed that its energy was "carbon zero," which led consumers to believe that the company was emissions free when it was not. Norway went even further and banned all green claims in car advertising after concerns about greenwashing in the auto industry.

While greenwashing legislation in the United States is limited, firms should still worry about the accuracy of environmental claims. A survey by Terra Choice Environmental found that 10.4 percent of magazine advertising in this country made environmental claims. If greenwashing occurs in ads such as these, then various stakeholders, including the press and interest groups, usually work to publicize untruthful claims.

One U.S. company, Pottery Barn, was accused of greenwashing in marketing its Eco Chic line. In reality only a few bedding collections are 100 percent organic, and most only contain 5 percent organic cotton. Much of its furniture is made of medium-density fiberboard, which contributes negatively to indoor air pollution. The greenest part of the Eco Chic line may be their outdoorsy design patterns.

To avoid being duped by greenwashing, ask the right questions. When buying green, investigate what materials are used in the products and how the company obtained those materials. Always look for evidence to back up claims about a green product. Also, remember that claims do not have to be false to be misleading. A product claiming to be CFC-free is telling the truth but is irrelevant since CFCs are banned by law. With greenwashing incidents increasing, consumers must be willing to go the extra mile to verify that the products they buy are truly eco-friendly.[1]

A strategic approach to ethical decisions will contribute to both business and society. This chapter provides a framework that is consistent with research, best practices, and regulatory requirements. Many companies have not implemented effective business ethics programs, but they should because ethics and compliance programs create good systems to manage organizational misconduct. Our framework for developing effective ethics programs is consistent with the ethical decision-making process described in Chapter 5. In addition, the strategic approach to an ethics program presented here is consistent with the Federal Sentencing Guidelines for Organizations and the Sarbanes-Oxley Act described in Chapter 3. These legislative reforms require managers to assume responsibility and ensure that ethical standards are implemented properly on a daily basis. Ethics programs include not only the need for top executive leadership but also responsibility by boards of directors for corporate governance.

Unethical and illegal business conduct occurs, even in organizations that have ethics programs. For example, although Enron had a code of ethics and was a member of the Better Business Bureau, the company was devastated by unethical activities and corporate scandal. Many business leaders believe that personal moral development and character are all that is needed for corporate responsibility. There are those who feel that ethics initiatives should arise inherently from a company's culture and that hiring good employees will limit unethical behavior within the organization. Many executives and board members do not understand how organizational ethical decisions are made and how to develop an ethical corporate culture. Customized ethics programs may help many organizations provide guidance for employees from diverse backgrounds to gain an understanding of acceptable behavior within the organization. Many ethical issues in business are complex and include considerations that require organizational agreement regarding appropriate action. Top executives and boards of directors must provide the leadership, a system to resolve these issues, and support for an ethical corporate culture.

"Top executives and boards of directors must provide the leadership, a system to resolve ethical issues, and support for an ethical corporate culture."

In this chapter, we provide an overview of why businesses need to develop an organizational ethics program. Next, we consider the factors that are crucial for the development of such a program: a code of conduct, an ethics officer and appropriate delegation of authority, effective ethics training, a system to monitor and support ethical compliance, and continual efforts to improve the ethics program. Finally, we discuss implementation of an organizational ethics program, including the roles of leadership and corporate culture.

THE NEED FOR ORGANIZATIONAL ETHICS PROGRAMS

Usually, an organization is held accountable for the conduct of its employees. Companies must assess their ethical risks and develop values and compliance systems to avoid legal and ethical mistakes that could damage the organization. The Federal Sentencing Guidelines for Organizations holds corporations responsible for conduct engaged in as an entity. Some corporate outcomes cannot be tied to one individual or even a group, and misconduct can result from a collective pattern of decisions supported by a corporate culture. Therefore, corporations can be held accountable, fined, and even receive the death penalty when they are operating in a manner inconsistent with major legal requirements. Organizations are sensitive to avoid infringing on employees' personal freedoms and ethical beliefs. In cases where an individual's personal beliefs and activities are inconsistent with company policies on ethics, conflict may develop. If the individual feels that ethical systems in the organization are deficient or directed in an inappropriate manner, some type of open conflict resolution may be needed to deal with the differences.

Understanding the factors that influence how individuals make decisions to resolve ethical issues, as discussed in Chapter 5, can help companies encourage ethical behavior and discourage undesirable conduct. Fostering ethical decisions within an organization requires eliminating unethical behavior and improving the firm's ethical standards. Some people are "bad apples" who will always do things in their own self-interest regardless of organizational goals or accepted standards of conduct. For example, major league baseball players know the use of steroids is prohibited yet some players use them anyway in order to gain an edge. Random drug tests are conducted to determine such abuses. Yankee superstar Alex Rodriguez tested positive for steroid use in 2003, when playing for the Texas Rangers, along with 103 other major league baseball players who also tested positive for the anabolic steroids, Primobolan, and testerone.[2] At the time, there were no penalties for such drug use, but today they are

© Ap Photo/Daniel Hulshizer

Johnson & Johnson maintains an excellent ethics program and commitment to integrity in the workplace

on the Major League Baseball list of banned substances with definite penalties for use. Eliminating bad apples through screening techniques and enforcement of the firm's ethical standards can help improve the firm's overall ethical conduct.

Organizations can foster unethical corporate cultures not because individuals within them are bad, but because the pressures to succeed create opportunities that reward unethical decisions. In the case of an unethical corporate culture, the organization must redesign its ethical standards to conform to industry and stakeholder standards of acceptable behavior. Most businesses attempt to improve ethical decision making by establishing and implementing a strategic approach to improving organizational ethics. Companies such as Texas Instruments, Starbucks, Levi's, and Johnson & Johnson take a strategic approach to organizational ethics but monitor their programs on a continuous basis and make improvements when problems occur.

To be socially responsible and promote legal and ethical conduct, an organization should develop an organizational ethics program by establishing, communicating, and monitoring ethical values and legal requirements that characterize the organization's history, culture, industry, and operating environment. Without such programs and uniform standards and policies of conduct, it is difficult for employees to determine what behaviors are acceptable within a company. As discussed in Chapter 5, in the absence of such programs and standards, employees generally will make decisions based on their observations of how their coworkers and managers behave. A strong ethics program includes a written code of conduct, an ethics officer to oversee the program, care in the delegation of authority, formal ethics training, auditing, monitoring, enforcement, and revision of program standards. Without a strong customized program, problems are much more likely to arise. Figure 6.1 outlines what employees questioned in a recent survey identified as the causes of organizational misconduct.

"A strong ethics program includes a written code of conduct, an ethics officer to oversee the program, care in the delegation of authority, formal ethics training, auditing, monitoring, enforcement, and revision of program standards."

The corporate ethics crises in the United States have destroyed trust in top management and significantly lowered the public's trust of business. A survey by Golin/Harris International revealed five top recommendations to CEOs for rebuilding trust and confidence in American firms. These are: make customers the top priority; assume personal responsibility and accountability; communicate openly and frequently with customers; handle crises

Figure 6.1 Root Causes of Misconduct

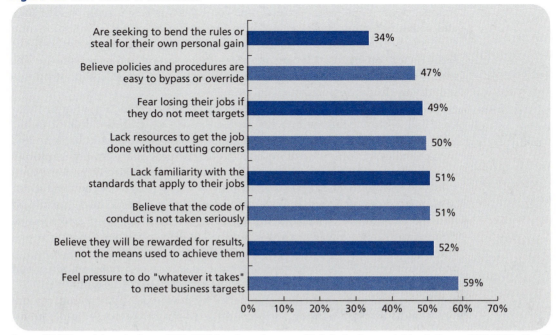

Source: KPMG Forensic Integrity Survey: 2008–2009, http://www.kpmg.com/SiteCollectionDocuments/Integrity-Survey—2008–2009.pdf, p. 6.

more honestly; and stick to the code of business ethics no matter what.[3] This is a recurring theme among primary stakeholders. Consumers are looking for clear, creative, and constructive leadership from CEOs that demonstrates trust is a priority. Survey respondents were asked to make recommendations they considered essential or important to establishing and maintaining trust.

No universal standards exist that can be applied to organizational ethics programs everywhere, but most companies develop codes, values, or policies for guidance about business behavior. The majority of companies that have been in ethical or legal trouble usually have stated ethics codes and programs. Often, the problem is that top management, as well as the overall corporate culture, has not integrated these codes, values, and standards into daily decision making. For example, Merrill Lynch CEO John Thain spent over $1.2 million to decorate his Manhattan office at a time when the company was facing record losses. Thain also worked to provide large bonuses to company employees before its acquisition by Bank of America, shortly after which Thain resigned from Merrill Lynch. Thain's questionable actions stood in contrast to companies like Citigroup that began systemwide cutbacks in the face of declining income by eliminating such luxuries as BlackBerrys and color copies.[4] If a company's leadership fails to provide the vision and support needed for ethical conduct, then an ethics program will not be effective. Ethics is not something to be delegated to lower-level employees while top managers break the rules.

No matter what their specific goals, ethics programs are developed as organizational control systems, the aim of which is to create predictability in employee behavior. There are two types of control systems. A compliance orientation creates order by requiring that employees identify with and commit to specific required conduct. It uses legal terms, statutes, and contracts that teach employees the rules and penalties for noncompliance. The other type of system is a values orientation, which strives to develop shared values. Although penalties are attached, the focus is more on an abstract core of ideals such as respect and responsibility. The goal is to create an environment where employees are compelled and willing to support an ethical organizational culture.

Almost half of employees in the KPMG Forensic Ethics Survey stated that they had observed misconduct that could cause "a significant loss of public trust if discovered." The number has risen to 60 percent in the banking and finance industry.[5] The goal of an effective ethics program is to get employees to report wrongdoing when they become aware. Research into compliance- and values-based approaches reveals that both types of programs can interact or work toward the same end, but a values orientation can better help explain and influence employees. Values-based programs increase employees' awareness of ethics at work, their integrity, their willingness to deliver bad news to supervisors, and the perception that better decisions are made. Compliance-based programs are linked to employees' awareness of ethical issues at work and their perception that decision making is better because of the expectations of its employees.

To meet the public's escalating demands for ethical decision making, companies need to develop plans and structures for addressing ethical considerations. Some directions for the improvement of ethics have been mandated through regulations, but companies must be willing to have in place a values and ethics implementation system that exceeds the minimum regulatory requirements. According to a study by the Open Compliance and Ethics Group (OCEG), among companies with an ethics program in place for ten years or more, none have experienced "reputational damage" in the last five years—"a testament to the important impact these programs can have over time." In addition, companies that have experienced reputational damage in the past are much further along compared to their peers in establishing ethics and compliance programs.[6]

CODES OF CONDUCT

Because people come from diverse family, educational, and business backgrounds, it cannot be assumed that they know how to behave appropriately when they enter a new organization or job. Most companies begin the process of establishing organizational ethics programs by developing **codes of conduct** (also called codes of ethics), which are formal statements that describe what an organization expects of its employees. Figure 6.2 indicates that many elements of ethics and compliance programs (such as codes and training) focus on the negative by telling people what should be avoided, versus what should be done.

codes of conduct formal statements that describe what an organization expects of its employees

A code of ethics has to reflect the board of directors' and senior management's desire for organizational compliance with the values, mission, rules, and policies that support an ethical climate. Development of a code of ethics should involve the board of directors, president, and senior managers who will be implementing the code. Legal staff should be called on to ensure that the code has

Figure 6.2

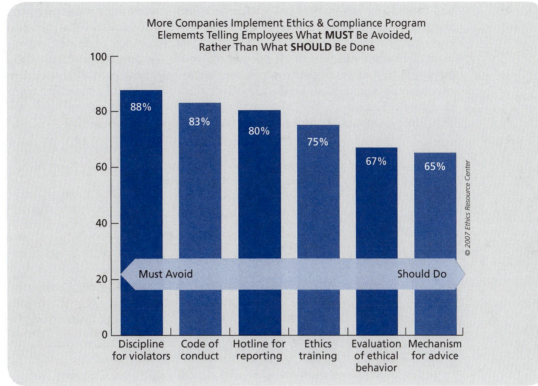

Source: Ethics Resource Center, *2007 National Business Ethics Survey: An Inside Look of Private Sector Ethics* (Washington, DC: Ethics Resource Center), p. 19.

Table 6.1 Developing and Implementing a Code of Ethics

1. Consider areas of risk and state values as well as conduct necessary to comply with laws and regulations. Values are an important buffer in preventing serious misconduct.
2. Identify values that specifically address current ethical issues.
3. Consider values that link the organization to a stakeholder orientation. Attempt to find overlaps in organizational and stakeholder values.
4. Make the code understandable by providing examples that reflect values.
5. Communicate the code frequently and in language that employees can understand.
6. Revise the code every year with input from organizational members and stakeholders.

correctly assessed key areas of risk and that potential legal problems are buffered by standards in the code. A code of ethics that does not address specific high-risk activities within the scope of daily operations is inadequate for maintaining standards that can prevent misconduct. Table 6.1 shows considerations in developing and implementing a code of ethics.

A large multinational firm, Texas Instruments (TI), manufactures computers, calculators, and other high-technology products. Its code of ethics resembles that of many other organizations. The code addresses issues relating to policies and procedures; government laws and regulations; relationships with customers, suppliers, and competitors; acceptance of gifts, travel, and entertainment; political contributions; expense reporting; business payments; conflicts of interest; investment in TI stock; handling of proprietary information and trade secrets; use of TI employees and assets to perform personal work; relationships with government officials and agencies; and enforcement of the code. The TI code emphasizes that ethical behavior is critical to maintaining long-term success and that each individual is responsible for upholding the integrity of the company:

> *We achieve business excellence by encouraging and expecting the creative involvement of every employee, listening to our customers, and continuously improving our processes, products, and services.*
>
> *One of the most important documents in establishing a company's culture is a statement of its mission, principles, and values. At TI, that document is titled "The TI Commitment" and is part of our Ethics Booklet. The first stated business principle is to "perform with unquestionable ethics and integrity."*

Since it is important that two-way expectations be established early in any relationship, The TI Commitment contains a statement of company values, what the company expects from an employee, and what the employee can expect from TI:

> *TIers expect the highest levels of performance and integrity from ourselves and each other. We will create an environment where people are valued as individuals and team members and treated with respect, dignity, and fairness. We strive to create opportunities for TIers to develop and reach full development and to achieve our professional and personal goals.*[7]

To ensure that its employees understand the nature of business ethics and the ethical standards they are expected to follow, TI also provides the "ethics quick test" to help employees when they have doubts about the ethics of specific situations and behaviors:

> Is the action legal?
>
> Does it comply with our values?
>
> If you do it, will you feel bad?
>
> How will it look in the newspaper?
>
> If you know it's wrong, don't do it!
>
> If you're not sure, ask.
>
> Keep asking until you get an answer.[8]

Texas Instruments explicitly states what it expects of its employees and what behaviors are unacceptable. By enforcing the codes wholeheartedly, TI has taken logical steps to safeguard its excellent reputation for ethical and responsible behavior. When such standards of behavior are not made explicit, employees sometimes base ethical decisions on their observations of the behavior of peers and management. The use of rewards and punishments to enforce codes and policies controls the opportunity to behave unethically and increases employees' acceptance of ethical standards.

As we stated, codes of conduct may address a variety of situations, from internal operations to sales presentations and financial disclosure practices. As seen in Figure 6.3, Netflix offers its key stakeholders a comprehensive code of conduct. Research has found that corporate codes of ethics often have five to seven core values or principles, in addition to more detailed descriptions and examples of appropriate conduct.[9] The six values that have been suggested as desirable to appearing in the codes of ethics include: (1) trustworthiness, (2) respect, (3) responsibility, (4) fairness, (5) caring, and (6) citizenship. These values will not be effective without distribution, training, and the support of top management in making the values a part of the corporate culture. Employees need specific examples of how the values can be implemented.

Codes of conduct will not resolve every ethical issue encountered in daily operations, but they help employees and managers deal with ethical dilemmas by prescribing or limiting specific actions. Many companies have a

"Codes of conduct will not resolve every ethical issue encountered in daily operations, but they help employees and managers deal with ethical dilemmas by prescribing or limiting specific actions."

Figure 6.3 Netflix: Code of Ethics

The Board of Directors of Netflix, Inc. (the "Company") has adopted this Code of Ethics (this "Code") for its directors, officers and other employees (individually, "Netflix Party" and collectively, "Netflix Parties"). As used herein, the principal executive officer, principal financial officer, principal accounting officer or controller, or persons performing similar functions are sometimes also referred to as the "Senior Financial Officers." This Code has been reasonably designed to deter wrongdoing and to promote: Honest and ethical conduct, including the ethical handling of actual or apparent conflicts of interest between personal and professional relationships; Full, fair, accurate, timely, and understandable disclosure in reports and documents that a registrant files with, or submits to, the Securities and Exchange Commission and in other public communications made by the Company; Compliance with applicable governmental laws, rules and regulations; The prompt internal reporting to an appropriate person or persons identified in this Code of violations of this Code; and Accountability for adherence to this Code.

I. HONEST AND ETHICAL CONDUCT
Netflix Parties are expected to act and perform their duties ethically and honestly and with the utmost integrity. Honest conduct is considered to be conduct that is free from fraud or deception. Ethical conduct is considered to be conduct conforming to accepted professional standards of conduct. Ethical

(continued)

Figure 6.3 Netflix: Code of Ethics (*continued*)

conduct includes the ethical handling of actual or apparent conflicts of interest between personal and professional relationships as discussed in below.

II. CONFLICTS OF INTEREST

A conflict of interest exists where the interests or benefits of one person or entity conflict or appear to conflict with the interests or benefits of the Company. While it is not possible to describe every situation in which a conflict of interest may arise, Netflix Parties must never use or attempt to use their position with the Company to obtain improper personal benefits. Any Netflix Party who is aware of a conflict of interest, or is concerned that a conflict might develop, is required to discuss the matter with a higher level of management or the General Counsel promptly. Senior Financial Officers may, in addition to speaking with the General Counsel, also discuss the matter with the Audit Committee.

III. DISCLOSURE

Senior Financial Officers are responsible for ensuring that the disclosure in the Company's periodic reports is full, fair, accurate, timely and understandable. In doing so, Senior Financial Officers shall take such action as is reasonably appropriate to (i) establish and comply with disclosure controls and procedures and accounting and financial controls that are designed to ensure that material information relating to the Company is made known to them; (ii) confirm that the Company's periodic reports comply with the requirements of Section 13(a) or 15(d) of the Securities Exchange Act of 1934; and (iii) ensure that information contained in the Company's periodic reports fairly presents in all material respects the financial condition and results of operations of the Company. Senior Financial Officers will not knowingly (i) make, or permit or direct another to make, materially false or misleading entries in the Company's, or any of its subsidiary's, financial statements or records; (ii) fail to correct materially false and misleading financial statements or records; (iii) sign, or permit another to sign, a document containing materially false and misleading information; or (iv) falsely respond, or fail to respond, to specific inquiries of the Company's independent auditor or outside legal counsel.

IV. COMPLIANCE

It is the Company's policy to comply with all applicable laws, rules and regulations. It is the personal responsibility of each Netflix Party to adhere to the standards and restrictions imposed by those laws, rules and regulations, and in particular, those relating to accounting and auditing matters. Any Netflix Party who is unsure whether a situation violates any applicable law, rule, regulation or Company policy should discuss the situation with the General Counsel.

V. INTERNAL REPORTING

Netflix Parties shall take all appropriate action to stop any known misconduct by fellow Netflix Parties that violate this Code. To this end, Netflix Parties shall report any known or suspected misconduct to the General Counsel or, in the case of misconduct by a Senior Financial Officer, also to the Chair of the Company's Audit Committee. In addition, Netflix Parties are encouraged to use the Company's confidential internal reporting system to report breaches of this Code. Information concerning the Company's confidential internal reporting system can be located on the Company's Intranet. The Company will not retaliate or allow retaliation for reports made in good faith.

VI. ACCOUNTABILITY

Any violation of this Code may result in disciplinary action, including termination, and if warranted, legal proceedings. This Code is a statement of certain fundamental principles, policies and procedures

(continued)

Figure 6.3 Netflix: Code of Ethics

that govern the Netflix Parties in the conduct of the Company's business. It is not intended to and does not create any rights in any employee, customer, supplier, competitor, shareholder or any other person or entity. The General Counsel and/or the Audit Committee will investigate violations and appropriate action will be taken in the event of any violation of this Code.

VII. WAIVERS AND AMENDMENTS OF THE CODE
The Company is committed to continuously reviewing and updating our policies and procedures. Therefore, this Code is subject to modification. Any amendment or waiver of any provision of this Code must be approved in writing by the Company's Board of Directors and promptly disclosed pursuant to applicable laws and regulations. Any waiver or modification of the Code by a Senior Financial Officer will be promptly disclosed to stockholders if and as required by law or the rules of the stock exchange or over the counter trading system on which Netflix's stock is traded or quoted.

Source: Netflix Code of Ethics, http://files.shareholder.com/downloads/NFLX/678367447x0x17642/ccfbe9a7-f0a5-4c16-a3a4-9471252b4144/73.pdf, accessed July 9, 2009.

code of ethics, but is it communicated effectively? According to the Ethics Resource Center, when looking at the effectiveness of an overall ethics and compliance program, only 25 percent of employees viewed their ethics and compliance program as being well implemented.[10] A code that is placed on a website or in a training manual is useless if it is not reinforced on a daily basis. By communicating to employees both what is expected of them and what punishments they face if they violate the rules, codes of conduct curtail opportunities for unethical behavior and thereby improve ethical decision making. Wells Fargo Bank offers a comprehensive code of conduct that specifies: "If you violate any provision of the Code or fail to cooperate fully with any inquiries or investigations, you will be subject to corrective action, which may include termination of your employment."[11] Codes of conduct do not have to be so detailed that they take into account every situation, but they should provide guidelines and principles that are capable of helping employees achieve organizational ethical objectives and address risks in an accepted manner.

ethics officer usually a high-ranking person known to respect legal and ethical standards who is responsible for assessing the needs and risks addressed in an organizational ethics program.

ETHICS OFFICERS

Organizational ethics programs also must have oversight by a high-ranking person known to respect and understand legal and ethical standards. This person is often referred to as an **ethics officer**. Corporate wrongdoings and scandal-grabbing headlines have a profound negative impact on public trust. To ensure compliance with state and federal regulations, many corporations are now appointing chief compliance officers and ethics and business conduct professionals to develop and oversee corporate compliance programs.

Consistent enforcement and necessary disciplinary action are essential to a functional ethical compliance program. The ethics or compliance officer is usually responsible for companywide disciplinary systems, implementing all disciplinary actions the company takes for violations of its ethical standards. Many companies are including ethical compliance in employee performance appraisals. During performance appraisals, employees may be asked to sign an acknowledgment that they have read the company's current guidelines on its ethical policies. The company must also promptly investigate any known or suspected misconduct. The appropriate company official, often the ethics officer, needs to make a recommendation to senior management on how to deal with a particular ethical infraction.

The Ethics and Compliance Officer Association (ECOA) has over 1,350 members. They are frontline managers of ethics programs in over 30 industries and 600 organizations.[12] In addition to U.S.–based organizations, members are based in Belgium, Canada, Germany, Great Britain, Greece, Hong Kong, India, Japan, the Netherlands, and Switzerland.[13] Ethics and compliance officers are in the front lines of managing ethics programs and now have the attention of top managers and boards of directors.[14] The ethics officer position has existed for decades, but its importance increased tremendously when the Federal Sentencing Guidelines for Organizations (FSGO) was passed in 1991. The guidelines gave companies that faced federal charges for misconduct the incentive of fine reductions up to 95 percent if they had an effective comprehensive ethics program in place. The financial reporting requirements of the Sarbanes-Oxley Act put more pressure on ethics officers to monitor financial reporting, as well as reporting of sales and inventory movements, to prevent fraud in reporting revenue and profits. In most firms, ethics officers do not report directly to the board of directors, but this is changing rapidly.

Building an ethics program and hiring an ethics officer to avoid fines will not be effective alone. Only with the involvement of top management and the board can an ethics officer earn the trust and cooperation of all key decision makers. Ethics officers are responsible for knowing about thousands of pages of regulations as well as communicating and reinforcing values that build an ethical corporate culture.

ETHICS TRAINING AND COMMUNICATION

Instituting a training program and a system to communicate with and educate employees about the firm's ethical standards is a major step in developing an effective ethics program. Such training can educate employees about the firm's policies and expectations, relevant laws and regulations, and general social standards. Training programs can make employees aware of available resources, support systems, and designated personnel who can assist them with ethical and legal advice. Training also can help empower employees to ask tough questions and make ethical decisions.

Ethics officers provide the oversight and management of most ethics training. Although training and communication should reinforce values

Ethics officers meet with company employees on a regular basis to provide ethics training as well as code and policy updates

© Fancy/Alamy

and provide learning opportunities about rules, it is only one part of an effective ethics program. The employee's capacity to exercise judgments that result in ethical decisions must be reinforced and developed. Ethics training that is done only because it is required or because ethics involvement is considered something that other companies do will not be effective. Ethics training must be customized to the specific nature of the employees in the organization and risk areas they face.

If ethical performance is not a part of regular performance appraisals, the message employees will interpret is that ethics is not an important component of decision making. For ethics training to make a difference, employees must understand why it is conducted, how it fits into the organization, and what is their own role in its implementation.

Top corporate executives must communicate with managers at the operations level (e.g., in production, sales, and finance) and enforce overall ethical standards within the organization. Table 6.2 lists the factors crucial to successful ethics training. It is most important to help employees identify ethical issues and give them the means to address and resolve such issues in ambiguous situations. In addition, employees must be offered direction on seeking assistance from managers or other designated personnel in resolving ethical problems. An effective ethics program can reduce criminal, civil, and administrative consequences, including fines, penalties, judgments, debarment from government contracts, and court control of the organization. An ineffective ethics program

"For ethics training to make a difference, employees must understand why it is conducted, how it fits into the organization, and what is their own role in its implementation."

Table 6.2 Factors Crucial to Ethics Training

1. Identify the key ethical risk areas.
2. Relate ethical decisions to the organization's values and culture.
3. Communicate company codes, policies, and procedures regarding ethical business conduct.
4. Provide leadership training to model desired behavior.
5. Provide directions for internal questions and reporting mechanisms.
6. Engage in regular training events using a variety of educational tools.
7. Establish manuals, websites, and other communication to reinforce ethics training.
8. Evaluate and use feedback to improve training.

Source: © O. C Ferrell 2009.

that results in many unethical acts may cause negative publicity and a decrease in organizational financial performance. An ethical disaster can be more damaging to a company than a natural disaster.

Companies can implement ethical principles in their organizations through training programs. Discussions conducted in ethical training programs sometimes break down into personal opinions about what should or should not be done in particular situations. To be successful, business ethics programs need to educate employees about formal ethical frameworks and models for analyzing business ethics issues. Then employees are able to base ethical decisions on their knowledge of choices rather than on emotions.

Training and communication initiatives should reflect the unique characteristics of an organization: its size, culture, values, management style, and employee base. It is important for the ethics program to differentiate between personal and organizational ethics. If ethics training is to be effective, it must start with a foundation, a code of ethics, an ethical concerns procedure, line and staff involvements, and executive priorities on ethics that are communicated to employees. Managers from every department must be involved in the development of an ethics training program.

Most experts on training agree that one of the most effective methods of ethics training is involvement in resolving ethical dilemmas that relate to actual situations employees may experience while performing their jobs. For example, Lockheed Martin developed a training game called *Gray Matters*. This training device is available on your textbook website and includes dilemmas that can be resolved by teams. Each member of the team can offer his or her perspective and understand the ramifications of the decision for coworkers and the organization. Figure 6.4 gives an example of the type of issues covered in the game.

A relatively new training device is the behavioral simulation or role-play exercise in which participants are given a short hypothetical ethical issue situation to review. The participants are assigned roles within the hypothetical organization and are provided with varying levels of information about the issue. They then must interact to provide recommended courses of action representing short-term, midrange, and long-term considerations. The simulation recreates the complexities of organizational relationships and of having to address a situation without complete information. Learning objectives of the simulation exercise include (1) increased awareness by participants of the ethical, legal, and social dimensions of business decision making; (2) development of analytical skills for resolving ethical issues; and (3) exposure to the complexity of ethical decision making in organizations. According to recent research, "the simulation not only instructs on the importance of ethics but on the processes for managing ethical concerns and conflict."[15]

A growing number of small businesses deliver "learning-management" systems software and content to train and certify employees on a variety of topics. In addition to streamlined training, the systems provide real-time records of instruction that increasingly are the first line of defense for companies facing litigation or questions about whether they are accountable for an employee's actions. The e-learning market is growing very rapidly both in education and business. For multinational companies, the computerized training elements of such systems

Figure 6.4 Gray Matters

MINI-CASE

For several months now, one of your colleagues has been slacking off, and you are getting stuck doing the work. You think this is unfair. What do you do?

POTENTIAL ANSWERS

A. Recognize this as an opportunity for you to demonstrate how capable you are.
B. Go to your supervisor and complain about this unfair workload.
C. Discuss the problem with your colleague in an attempt to solve the problem without involving others.
D. Discuss the problem with the human resources department.

MINI-CASE

Your coworker is copying company-purchased software and taking it home. You know a certain program costs $400, and you have been saving for a while to buy it. What do you do?

POTENTIAL ANSWERS

A. You figure you can copy it too since nothing had ever happened to your coworker.
B. You tell your coworker he can't legally do this.
C. You report the matter to the ethics office.
D. You mention this to your boss.

MINI-CASE

You are aware that a fellow employee uses drugs on the job. Another friend encourages you to confront the person instead of informing the supervisor. What do you do?

POTENTIAL ANSWERS

A. You speak to the alleged user and encourage him to get help.
B. You elect to tell your supervisor that you suspect an employee is using drugs on the job.
C. You confront the alleged user and tell him to quit using drugs or you'll "turn him in."
D. You report the matter to employee assistance.

Source: Sammet, Jr., George, *Gray Matters: The Ethics Game.* Mr. Sammet published the game while serving as Vice President of Ethics for Martin Marietta. © 1992. Reprinted with permission.

provide consistency of content and delivery to all locations and allow for customization of languages and to cultures.

Some of the goals of an ethics training program might be to improve employee understanding of ethical issues and the ability to identify them, to inform employees of related procedures and rules, and to identify the contact person who could help in resolving ethical problems. In keeping with these goals, the purpose of Boeing's Code of Ethics and Business Conduct program is to:

- Communicate the Boeing Values and standards of ethical business conduct to employees
- Inform employees of company policies and procedures regarding ethical business conduct

- Establish company-wide processes to assist employees in obtaining guidance and resolving questions regarding compliance with the company's standards of conduct and the Boeing Values

- Establish company-wide criteria for ethics education and awareness programs.[16]

Boeing also asks employees to take ethics refresher training each year. On the company's "Ethics Challenge" web page, employees (as well as the general public) can select from a variety of ethical dilemma scenarios, discuss them with their peers, and select from several potential answers. After clicking the answer they think is most ethically correct, employees get feedback: the company's own opinion of the correct response and its rationale for it.

Ethical decision making is influenced by organizational culture, by coworkers and supervisors, and by the opportunity to engage in unethical behavior. All three types of influence can be affected by ethics training. Full awareness of the philosophy of management, rules, and procedures can strengthen both the organizational culture and the ethical stance of peers and supervisors. Such awareness also arms employees against opportunities for unethical behavior and reduces the likelihood of misconduct. Thus, the existence and enforcement of company rules and procedures limit unethical practices in the organization. The key goal of ethics training is to make employees aware of the risks associated with their jobs, industry, stakeholders; provide an understanding of the culture and expectations within the organization; create accountability for individual actions; and to inform employees of not only the behavior that is unacceptable, but also the behavior that is acceptable and supported in the organization.

ESTABLISHING SYSTEMS TO MONITOR AND ENFORCE ETHICAL STANDARDS

Ethical compliance involves comparing employee ethical performance with the organization's ethical standards. Ethical compliance can be measured through employee observation, internal audits, surveys, reporting systems, and investigations. An effective ethics program uses a variety of resources to effectively monitor ethical conduct. Sometimes, external auditing and review of company activities are helpful in developing benchmarks of compliance.

Systems to Monitor and Enforce Ethical Standards

Many companies set up ethics assistance lines, also known as "hotlines," to provide support and give employees the opportunity to ask questions or report concerns. The most effective ethics hotlines operate on an anonymous basis and are supported 24 hours a day, 365 days a year. Approximately 50 percent of hotline calls occur at night or on the weekends, when employees are not at work. Many times troubling ethical issues can cause employees to lose sleep or ponder conduct during free time.[17]

About half of the issues raised on helplines relate to human resources and complaints such as coworker abuse, failure of management to intervene in such abuse, and inappropriate language. Ethical issues have ranged from an employee who used the corporation to advance a personal business to human resource–related issues such as sexual harassment.[18]

Organizations need avenues through which employees and managers can report suspected cases of unethical conduct. Critical comments, dilemmas, and advice can be handled at a central contact point where the most appropriate person can deal with a specific case. A helpline or desk is characterized by ease of accessibility and simple procedures, and it serves as a safety net that facilitates monitoring and reporting. Companies such as Global Compliance provide automated case management systems that collect, categorize, and provide alerts to the appropriate manager for dealing with ethics issues in the organization. Companies are increasingly using case management services and software to track employees and issues throughout their entire organization. These programs provide reports of employee concerns, complaints, or observations of misconduct. Systems such as these allow the company to track investigations, analysis, resolutions, documentation, emerging/declining issues, and the time required for resolution. Overall, the process assists in preventing lawsuits and increasing awareness of how and where to make ethics program improvements.

> **"Organizations need avenues through which employees and managers can report suspected cases of unethical conduct."**

Observation and Feedback

To determine whether a person is performing his or her job adequately and ethically, observation might focus on how the person handles an ethically charged situation. For example, many businesses use role-playing in the training of salespeople and managers. Ethical issues can be introduced into the discussion, and the results can be videotaped so that both the participant and the superior can evaluate the results of the ethical dilemma.

Questionnaires that survey employees' ethical perceptions of their company, their superiors, their coworkers, and themselves, as well as ratings of ethical or unethical practices within the firm and industry, can serve as benchmarks in an ongoing assessment of ethical performance. Then, if unethical behavior is perceived to increase, management will have a better understanding of what types of unethical practices may be occurring and why. A change in the ethics training within the company may be necessary.

Appropriate action involves rewarding employees who comply with company policies and standards and punishing those who do not. When employees comply with organizational standards, their efforts may be acknowledged and rewarded through public recognition, bonuses, raises, or some other means. Conversely, when employees deviate from organizational standards, they may be reprimanded, transferred, docked, suspended, or even fired.

Figure 6.5 Propensity to Report Misconduct

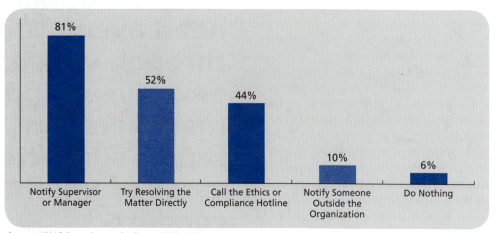

Source: KPMG Forensic Integrity Survey 2008–2009, KPMG LLP, p. 8.

Figure 6.5 shows employee propensity to report misconduct. As was discussed in Chapter 5, employees much prefer to deal with ethical issues through their supervisor or manager over using other reporting methods.

Whistle-Blowing

Interpersonal conflict ensues when employees think they know the right course of action in a situation, yet their work group or company promotes or requires a different, unethical decision. In such cases, employees may choose to follow their own values and refuse to participate in the unethical or illegal conduct. If they conclude that they cannot discuss what they are doing or what should be done with their coworkers or immediate supervisors, these employees may go outside the organization to publicize and correct the unethical situation. **Whistle-blowing** means exposing an employer's wrongdoing to outsiders, such as the media or government regulatory agencies.

Whistle-blowers have provided pivotal evidence documenting corporate malfeasance at a number of companies. Harry Markopolos, a financial fraud examiner, warned the Securities and Exchange Commission repeatedly that Bernie Madoff was running a massive investment fraud. Markopolos started following Madoff after a supervisor asked him to try and analyze how Madoff was experiencing such high returns from his investment strategy. Quickly he determined that the numbers were fraudulent and set about notifying authorities. At one point he even began to fear for his life because he believed that Madoff clients included drug dealers and mobsters. As a whistle-blower who uncovered the largest financial fraud in history (an estimated $65 billion), Markopolos testified before Congress stating that the regulatory system was flawed and regulators possessed inadequate "financial literacy" to catch fraud and criminal activity. In addition, Markopolos stated that many SEC, as well as other financial regulatory, employees eventually end up working on Wall Street. This creates a conflict of interest, not wanting to uncover potential wrongdoing among potential employers.[20]

whistle-blowing
exposing an employer's wrongdoing to outsiders, such as the media or government regulatory agencies

From Oilman to Pickens Plan

The Pickens Plan made headlines across the country as a way to wean the United States off carbon fuels. The mastermind behind this plan, billionaire T. Boone Pickens, has undergone a dramatic transformation from oilman to wind farm advocate. Pickens has such faith in his plan that he invested nearly $60 million on a media campaign. Pickens owes his wealth to oil. He formed the Mesa Petroleum Company, which became the largest independently owned oil company. Pickens then formed the BP Management Hedge Fund, which is invested in energy stock and commodities.

Pickens's most recent endeavor is the Pickens Plan, which aims to reduce U.S. oil dependency using a three-pronged approach. First, Pickens plans to install thousands of wind turbines. Second, Pickens wants the government to upgrade electric transmission lines so that wind farms can connect to the power grid. Third, Pickens wants more cars to use natural gas. If all cars switched to natural gas, Pickens estimates the United States could reduce foreign oil dependency by 38 percent. Wind power could supply 20 percent of the country's electricity, but upgrading power grids would cost approximately $185 billion.

While the Pickens Plan has widespread support, the 2008–2009 recession threw up some roadblocks. Pickens was forced to shelve his plan to build the world's largest wind farm in the Texas Panhandle because of tight credit markets and electrical grid limitations. Pickens sees this decision as merely a setback.

While many believe the Pickens Plan is worth supporting, some do question his motives. As the majority shareholder in Clean Energy Fuels, Pickens invests heavily in wind energy. Some question whether Pickens is truly an advocate for green energy, or just promoting his economic interests. Pickens maintains that he is a businessperson first, but that he has put so much of his own money into this project because it will benefit society. Whatever his motives, the Pickens Plan could affect how the United States powers the country, potentially placing Pickens as the major innovator behind a new energy source for America.[19]

NASA

Historically, the fortunes of whistle-blowers have not been positive: Most are labeled traitors, and many lose their jobs. A study of 300 whistle-blowers by researchers at the University of Pennsylvania found that 69 percent lost their jobs or were forced to retire after exposing their companies' misdeeds.[21] Ted Beatty, for example, worked for Houston-based Dynegy. After he was passed over for promotion, he began collecting information on Dynegy's complex energy trades. When Beatty gave the information to the Securities and Exchange Commission, an investment fund, and the media, it led to the resignation of the firm's top officers. Beatty did not benefit financially from blowing the whistle on Dynegy. In fact, he has been unable to find another job, has had his home broken into, and has received numerous threats.[22]

Although most whistle-blowers do not receive positive recognition for pointing out corporate misconduct, some have turned to the courts and obtained substantial settlements. Because of the risk involved in being a whistle-blower,

Table 6.3 Questions to Ask Before Engaging in External Whistle-Blowing

1. Have I exhausted internal anonymous reporting opportunities within the organization?
2. Have I examined company polices and codes that outline acceptable behavior and violations of standards?
3. Is this a personal issue that should be resolved through other means?
4. Can I manage the stress that may evolve from exposing potential wrongdoing in the organization?
5. Can I deal with the consequences of resolving an ethical or legal conflict within the organization?

Source: © O. C. Ferrell 2009.

Table 6.3 provides a checklist of questions an employee should ask before blowing the whistle.

Fearful about retaliation, a large number of employees do not report organizational wrongdoing that they witness. In fact, many are concerned that reporting misconduct will not make a difference. One out of every eight employees surveyed who reported misconduct experienced some type of retaliation in response to their action.[23]

CONTINUOUS IMPROVEMENT OF THE ETHICS PROGRAM

Improving the system that encourages employees to make more ethical decisions is not very different from implementing other types of business strategies. Implementation means putting strategies into action. Implementation of ethical compliance programs involves the design of activities to achieve organizational objectives using available resources and given existing constraints. Implementation translates a plan for action into operational terms and establishes a means by which organizational ethical performance will be monitored, controlled, and improved.

A firm's ability to plan and implement ethical business standards depends in part on the organization's structuring resources and activities to achieve its ethical objectives in an effective and efficient manner. Some U.S. companies are setting up computer systems that encourage whistle-blowing. With more than 5,500 employees, Marvin Windows (one of the world's largest custom manufacturers of wood windows and doors) is concerned about employees feeling comfortable reporting violations of safety conditions, bad management, fraud, or theft. This company's system is anonymous and allows for reporting in native country languages. The system is used to alert management to potential problems in the organization and facilitate an investigation.[24] Systems such as these help alleviate employee concerns when reporting observed misconduct. In one study, 45 percent of whistle-blowing cases were reported by employees who maintained their anonymity.[25]

A firm's values statement (see Table 6.4) is its foundation. It guides the company in all of its actions. People's attitudes and behavior must be guided by a shared commitment to the business instead of by obedience to traditional managerial authority. Encouraging diversity of perspectives, disagreement, and the empowerment of people within the organization helps to align the company's leadership with its employees.

If a company determines that its performance has not been satisfactory in ethical terms, the company's management may want to reorganize the way certain kinds of ethical decisions are made. For example, a decentralized organization may need to centralize key decisions, if only for a time, so that top-level managers can ensure that the decisions are ethical. Centralization may reduce the opportunity for lower-level managers and employees to make unethical decisions. Top management can then focus on improving the corporate culture and infusing more ethical values throughout the organization by providing rewards for positive behavior and sanctions for negative behavior.

Table 6.4 Proctor & Gamble's Values

Integrity	Leadership	Ownership
• We always try to do the right thing. • We are honest and straightforward with each other. • We operate within the letter and spirit of the law. • We uphold the values and principles of P&G in every action and decision. • We are data-based and intellectually honest in advocating proposals, including recognizing risks.	• We are all leaders in our area of responsibility, with a deep commitment to delivering leadership results. • We have a clear vision of where we are going. • We focus our resources to achieve leadership objectives and strategies. • We develop the capability to deliver our strategies and eliminate organizational barriers.	• We accept personal accountability to meet our business needs, improve our systems and help others improve their effectiveness. • We all act like owners, treating the Company's assets as our own and behaving with the Company's long-term success in mind.

Passion For Winning	Trust	
• We are determined to be the best at doing what matters most. • We have a healthy dissatisfaction with the status quo. • We have a compelling desire to improve and to win in the marketplace.	• We respect our P&G colleagues, customers and consumers, and treat them as we want to be treated. • We have confidence in each other's capabilities and intentions. • We believe that people work best when there is a foundation of trust.	

Source: "Purpose, Values, and Princples," P&G, http://www.pg.com/company/who_we_are/ppv.shtml, accessed July 13, 2009.

Dell Computer is an example of a centralized organization, possibly because of its focus on manufacturing processes. In other companies, decentralization of important decisions may be a better way to attack ethical problems so that lower-level managers, familiar with the forces of the local business environment and local culture and values, can make more decisions. Coca-Cola is a more decentralized company due to its use of independent distributors and unique localized cultures. Whether the ethics function is centralized or decentralized, the key need is to delegate authority in such a way that the organization can achieve ethical performance.

IMPLEMENTING ORGANIZATIONAL ETHICS PROGRAMS

There is increasing support that it is good business for an organization to be ethical and that ethical cultures emerge from strong leadership. Many agree that the character and success of the most admired companies emanate from their leader. Leadership expert John Kotter noted that leaders must do four things. First they should create a common goal or vision for the company. They also need to get "buy-in" or support from significant partners. Third, great leaders are great motivators and know how to use the resources available to them. The last character is the spirit of great leaders who enjoy their jobs and approach them with an almost contagious tenacity, passion, and commitment.[26]

If a company is to maintain ethical behavior, top management must model its policies and standards. Maintaining an ethical culture can be difficult if top management does not support such behavior. In an effort to keep earnings high and boost stock prices, many firms have given into the temptation to falsify revenue reports. Top executives in these firms encouraged the behavior because they held stock options—and could receive bonus packages—tied to the company's performance. Thus, higher reported revenues meant larger executive payoffs.

A KPMG Forensic Integrity Survey (Figure 6.6) asked employees whether their chief executive officer (CEO) and other senior executives exhibited characteristics attributable to personal integrity and ethical leadership. Nearly two-thirds of employees believed that their leaders served as positive role models for their organizations. However, 51 percent suggested a lack of confidence (based on "unsure" and "disagree" responses) that their CEOs knew about behaviors further down in the organization. Nearly half (46 percent) indicated a lack of confidence that their leaders would be approachable if employees had ethics concerns. Seventy percent agreed that their CEOs would respond appropriately to matters brought to their attention. Overall, nearly two-thirds of employees agreed their leaders set the right tone at the top, leaving one-third unsure or in disagreement.

Along with strong ethical leadership, a strong corporate culture in support of ethical behavior can also play a key role in guiding employee behavior. While most firms have at least part of a comprehensive ethics and compliance program in place, only 38 percent of companies have all elements in place according to

Figure 6.6 Perceived Tone and Culture; Tone at the Top; and Perceptions of CEOs and Other Senior Executives

Source: "Forensic Integrity Survey 2008–2009," KPMG, http://uskpmg.com/RutUS_prod/Documents/8/IntegritySurvey08_09.pdf, p.13.

the National Business Ethics Survey.[27] In the following sections, we discuss the roles of leadership and culture in shaping organizational ethics. The "tone at the top" is often cited as a determining factor in creating a high-integrity organization.

The Role of Leadership

Leadership influences many aspects of organizational behavior, including employees' acceptance of and adherence to organizational norms and values. Leadership that focuses on building strong organizational values among employees creates agreement on norms of conduct. Leaders in highly visible positions in the organization play a key role in transmitting values and diffusing values, norms, and codes of ethics. Two dominant styles are transactional and transformational leadership. Transactional leadership attempts to create employee satisfaction through negotiating for levels of performance or "bartering" for desired behaviors. Transformational leaders, in contrast, try

"Leadership influences many aspects of organizational behavior, including employees' acceptance of and adherence to organizational norms and values."

© AP Photo/Paul White

Billionaire investor Warren Buffett understands the importance of managing business risks in growing and developing successful companies

to raise the level of commitment of employees and create greater trust and motivation.[28] Transformational leaders attempt to promote activities and behavior through a shared vision and common learning experiences. Both transformational and transactional leaders can positively influence the organizational climate.

Transformational Leadership

Transformational leaders communicate a sense of mission, stimulate new ways of thinking, and enhance as well as generate new learning experiences. Transformational leadership considers the employees' needs and aspirations in conjunction with organizational needs. Therefore, transformational leaders have a stronger influence on coworker support and the building of an ethical culture than transactional leaders. Transformational leaders also build a commitment and respect for values that provide agreement on how to deal with ethical issues. Transformational ethical leadership is best suited for higher levels of ethical commitment among employees and strong stakeholder support for an ethical climate.

Transactional Leadership Transactional leadership focuses on making certain that the required conduct and procedures are implemented. The "barter" aspects of negotiation to achieve the desired outcomes result in a dynamic relationship between leaders and employees where reactions, conflicts, and crises influence the relationship more than ethical concerns. Transactional leaders produce employees who achieve a negotiated level of required ethical performance or compliance. As long as employees and leaders find the exchange mutually rewarding, the compliance relationship is likely to be successful. However, transactional leadership is best suited to quickly changing ethical climates or reacting to ethical problems or issues. Michael Capellas used transactional leadership to change WorldCom's—renamed MCI—culture and ethical conduct when he took over as CEO and chair after an accounting scandal forced the company into bankruptcy proceedings. Capellas sought to restore WorldCom's credibility in the marketplace by bringing in a new board of directors, creating a corporate ethics office, enhancing the code of ethics, and launching new employee financial reporting and ethics training initiatives.[29]

Leaders Influence Corporate Culture

Organizational leaders use their power and influence to shape corporate culture. Power refers to the influence that leaders and managers have over the behavior and decisions of subordinates. An individual has power over others when his or her presence causes them to behave differently. Exerting power is one way to influence the ethical decision-making framework we described in Chapter 5 (especially significant others and opportunity).

The status and power of leaders are directly related to the amount of pressure they can exert on employees to conform to their expectations. A superior in a position of authority can put strong pressure on employees to comply, even when their personal ethical values conflict with the superior's wishes. For example, a manager might say to a subordinate, "I want the confidential data about our competitor's sales on my desk by Monday morning, and I don't care how you get it." A subordinate who values his or her job or who does not realize the ethical questions involved may feel pressure to do something unethical to obtain the data.

There are five power bases from which one person may influence another: (1) reward power, (2) coercive power, (3) legitimate power, (4) expert power, and (5) referent power.[30] These five bases of power can be used to motivate individuals either ethically or unethically.

Reward Power Reward power refers to a person's ability to influence the behavior of others by offering them something desirable. Typical rewards might be money, status, or promotion. Consider, for example, a retail salesperson who has two watches (a Timex and a Casio) for sale. Let us assume that the Timex is of higher quality than the Casio but is priced about the same. In the absence of any form of reward power, the salesperson would logically attempt to sell the Timex watch. However, if Casio gave him an extra 10 percent commission, he would probably focus his efforts on selling the Casio watch. This "carrot dangling" and incentives have been shown to be very effective in getting people to change their behavior in the long run. In the short run, however, it is not as effective as coercive power.

Coercive Power Coercive power is essentially the opposite of reward power. Instead of rewarding a person for doing something, coercive power penalizes actions or behavior. As an example, suppose a valuable client asks an industrial salesperson for a bribe and insinuates that he will take his business elsewhere if his demands are not met. Although the salesperson believes bribery is unethical, her boss has told her that she must keep the client happy or lose her chance at promotion. The boss is imposing a negative sanction if certain actions are not performed. Every year, 20 percent of Enron's workforce was asked to leave because they were ranked as "needs improvement" or other issues were noted. Employees not wanting to fall into the bottom 20 percent engaged in corruption or exhibited complacency toward corruption.[31]

Coercive power relies on fear to change behavior. For this reason, it has been found to be more effective in changing behavior in the short run than in the long run. Coercion is often employed in situations where there is an extreme imbalance in power. However, people who are continually subjected to coercion may seek a counterbalance by aligning themselves with other more powerful persons or simply by leaving the organization. In firms that use coercive power, relationships usually break down in the long run. Power is an ethical issue not only for individuals but also for work groups that establish policy for large corporations.

"The company is doing much better since we outsourced our ethics division to tribal warlords."

Courtesy of CartoonStock.com

Legitimate Power Legitimate power stems from the belief that a certain person has the right to exert influence and that certain others have an obligation to accept it. The titles and positions of authority that organizations bestow on individuals appeal to this traditional view of power. Many people readily acquiesce to those who wield legitimate power, sometimes committing acts that are contrary to their beliefs and values. Betty Vinson, an accountant at WorldCom, objected to her supervisor's requests to produce improper accounting entries in an effort to conceal WorldCom's deteriorating financial condition. She finally gave in to their requests, however, after being told that this was the only way to save the company. She and other WorldCom accountants eventually pleaded guilty to conspiracy and fraud charges. She was sentenced to five months in prison and five months of house arrest.[32]

Such staunch loyalty to authority figures can also be seen in corporations that have strong charismatic leaders and centralized structures. In business, if a superior tells an employee to increase sales "no matter what it takes" and that employee has a strong affiliation to legitimate power, the employee may try anything to fulfill that order.

Expert Power Expert power is derived from a person's knowledge (or the perception that the person possesses knowledge). Expert power usually stems from a superior's credibility with subordinates. Credibility, and thus expert power, is positively related to the number of years a person has worked in a firm or industry, the person's education, or the honors he or she has received for performance. Expert power can also be conferred on a person by others who perceive him or her as an expert on a specific topic. A relatively low-level secretary may have expert power because he or she knows specific details about how the business operates and can even make suggestions on how to inflate revenue through expense reimbursements.

Expert power may cause ethical problems when it is used to manipulate others or to gain an unfair advantage. Physicians, lawyers, or consultants can take unfair advantage of unknowing clients, for example. Accounting firms may gain extra income by ignoring concerns about the accuracy of financial data they are provided in an audit.

Referent Power Referent power may exist when one person perceives that his or her goals or objectives are similar to another's. The second person may attempt to influence the first to take actions that will lead both to achieve their objectives. Because they share the same objectives, the person influenced by the other will perceive the other's use of referent power as beneficial. For this power relationship to be effective, however, some sort of empathy must exist between the individuals. Identification with others helps to boost the decision maker's confidence when making a decision, thus increasing his or her referent power.

Consider the following situation: Lisa Jones, a manager in the accounting department of a manufacturing firm, has asked Michael Wong, a salesperson, to speed up the delivery of sales contracts, which usually take about one month to process after a deal is reached. Michael protests that he is not to blame for the slow process. Rather than threaten to slow delivery of Michael's commission checks (coercive power), Lisa makes use of referent power. She invites Michael to lunch, and they discuss some of their work concerns, including the problem of slow-moving documentation. They agree that if document processing cannot be sped up, both will be hurt. Lisa then suggests that Michael start faxing contracts instead of mailing them. He agrees to give it a try, and within several weeks, the contracts are moving faster. Lisa's job is made easier, and Michael gets his commission checks a little sooner.

The five bases of power are not mutually exclusive. People typically use several power bases to effect change in others. Although power in itself is neither ethical nor unethical, its use can raise ethical issues. Sometimes, a leader uses power to manipulate a situation or a person's values in a way that creates a conflict with the person's value structure. For example, a manager who forces an employee to choose between staying home with his sick child and keeping his job is using coercive power, which creates a direct conflict with the employee's values.

The Role of an Ethical Corporate Culture

Top management provides a plan for the corporate culture. If executives and CEOs do not explicitly address these issues, a culture may emerge where unethical behavior is sanctioned and rewarded. To be most successful, ethical standards and expected behaviors should be integrated throughout every organizational process from hiring, training, compensating, and rewarding to firing. Many employees who view unethical conduct do not report it because they fear inaction, they are afraid they will not remain anonymous, or they believe their organization is not concerned about the activity. Frank Navran, a consultant to the Ethics Resource Center, has identified seven steps to changing the ethical culture of an organization (see Table 6.5).

Organizational ethical culture is important to employees. A fair, open, and trusting organizational climate supports an ethical culture and can be attributed to lower turnover and higher employee satisfaction. Southwest Airlines has a very strong organizational culture that has remained consistent from the days of its key founder Herb Kelleher. All Southwest employees have heard the stories of Kelleher donning a dress and feather boa and joining baggage handlers on Southwest flights. He ran an awards ceremony that, to employees, was on par with the Academy Awards. Kelleher strove to treat employees like family. Today, Southwest continues that legacy and culture. Over 1,300 Southwest employees are married couples. This family-friendly environment has

Table 6.5 Steps for Changing the Ethical Culture of an Organization

1. State position, philosophy, or belief.
2. Create formal organizational systems.
3. Communicate expectations through informal (leadership) systems.
4. Reinforce policy through measurements and rewards.
5. Implement communications and education strategies.
6. Use response to critical events to underscore commitment.
7. Avoid perception of hidden agendas.

Source: Ethics Resource Center, http://www.ethics.org/resources/articles-organizational-ethics.asp?aid=864, accessed July 10, 2009.

encouraged multiple generations of families to work for the carrier. In one case, fifteen members of the same Chicago family work for the airline. Pilots willingly support the "Adopt a Pilot" program that allows students in classrooms countrywide to adopt a Southwest pilot for a 4-week educational and mentoring program. Pilots attend classes, and e-mail and send postcards to students from a variety of destinations. Southwest's culture means it consistently ranks among the best companies to work for and allows it to attract some of the best talent in the industry.[33]

"A fair, open, and trusting organizational climate supports an ethical culture and can be attributed to lower turnover and higher employee satisfaction."

Some leaders assume that hiring or promoting good, ethical managers will automatically produce an ethical organizational climate. This ignores the fact that an individual may have limited opportunity to enforce his or her own personal ethics on management systems and informal decision making that occurs in the organization. The greatest influence on employee behavior is that of peers and coworkers.[34] Many times, workers do not know what constitutes specific ethical violations such as price fixing, deceptive advertising, consumer fraud, and copyright violations. The more ethical the culture of the organization is perceived to be, the less likely it is that unethical decision making will occur. Over time, an organization's failure to monitor or manage its culture may foster questionable behavior. FedEx maintains a strong ethical culture and has woven its values and expectations throughout the company. FedEx's open-door policy specifies that employees may bring up any work issue or problem with any manager in the organization.[35]

Variation in Employee Conduct

Although the corporation is required to take responsibility for conducting its business ethically, a substantial amount of research indicates that there are significant differences in the values and philosophies that influence how the individuals that comprise corporations make ethical decisions.[36] In other words, because people are culturally diverse and have different values, they interpret situations differently and will vary in the ethical decisions they make on the same ethical issue.

Table 6.6 shows that approximately 10 percent of employees take advantage of situations to further their own personal interests. These individuals are more likely to manipulate, cheat, or be self-serving when the benefits gained from doing so are greater than the penalties for the misconduct. Such employees may choose to take office supplies from work for personal use if the only penalty they may suffer if caught is paying for the supplies. The lower the risk of being caught, the higher the likelihood that that advantage-taking 10 percent will engage in unethical activities.

Another 40 percent of workers go along with the work group on most matters. These employees are most concerned about the social implications of their actions and want to fit into the organization. Although they have their own personal opinions, they are easily influenced by what people around them are doing. These individuals may know that using office supplies for personal use is improper, yet they view it as acceptable because their coworkers do so. These employees rationalize their action by saying that the use of office

"Because people are culturally diverse and have different values, they interpret situations differently and will vary in the ethical decisions they make on the same ethical issue."

Table 6.6 Variation in Employee Conduct

10 Percent	40 Percent	40 Percent	10 Percent
Follow their own values and beliefs; believe that their values are superior to those of others in the company	Always try to follow company policies	Go along with the work group	Take advantage of situations if the penalty is less than the benefit, or the risk of being caught is low

These percentages are based on a number of studies in the popular press and data gathered by the authors. The percentages are not exact and represent a general typology that may vary by organization. The 10 percent that will take advantage is adapted from John Fraedrich and O. C. Ferrell, "Cognitive Consistency of Marketing Managers in Ethical Situations," *Journal of the Academy of Marketing Science* 20 (Summer 1992): 243–252.

Copyright © 2009 O. C. Ferrell.

supplies is one of the benefits of working at their particular business, and it must be acceptable because the company does not enforce a policy precluding the behavior. Coupled with this philosophy is the belief that no one will get into trouble for doing what everybody else is doing, for there is safety in numbers.

About 40 percent of a company's employees, as shown in Table 6.6, always try to follow company policies and rules. These workers not only have a strong grasp of their corporate culture's definition of acceptable behavior, but they also attempt to comply with codes of ethics, ethics training, and other communications about appropriate conduct. If the company has a policy that prohibits taking office supplies from work, these employees probably would observe it. However, they likely would not speak out about the 40 percent who choose to go along with the work group, for these employees prefer to focus on their jobs and steer clear of any organizational misconduct. If the company fails to communicate standards of appropriate behavior, members of this group will devise their own.

The final 10 percent of employees try to maintain formal ethical standards that focus on rights, duties, and rules. They embrace values that assert certain inalienable rights and actions, which they perceive to be always ethically correct. In general, members of this group believe that their values are right and superior to the values of others in the company, or even to the company's value system, when an ethical conflict arises. These individuals have a tendency to report the misconduct of others or to speak out when they view activities within the company as unethical. Consequently, members of this group would probably report colleagues who take office supplies.

The significance of this variation in the way individuals behave ethically is simply this: Employees use different approaches when making ethical decisions. Because of the probability that a large percentage of any work group will either take advantage of a situation or at least go along with the work group, it is vital that companies provide communication and control mechanisms to maintain an ethical culture. Companies that fail to monitor activities and enforce ethics policies provide a low-risk environment for employees who are inclined to take advantage of situations to accomplish their personal, and sometimes unethical, objectives.

Good business practice and concern for the law require organizations to recognize this variation in employees' desire to be ethical. The percentages in Table 6.6 are only estimates, and the actual percentages of each type of employee may vary widely across organizations based on individuals and corporate culture. The specific percentages are less important than the fact that research has identified these variations as existing within most organizations. Organizations should focus particular attention on managers who oversee the day-to-day operations of employees within the company. They should also provide training and communication to ensure that the business operates ethically; that it does not become the victim of fraud or theft; and that employees, customers, and other stakeholders are not abused through the misconduct of people who have a pattern of unethical behavior.

As we have seen throughout this book, many examples can be cited of employees and managers who have no concern for ethical conduct but are nonetheless hired and placed in positions of trust. Some corporations continue to support executives who ignore environmental concerns, poor working conditions, or defective products or who engage in accounting fraud. Executives who can get results, regardless of the

Table 6.7 Worst CEOs in Managing Organizational Risks

1. Dick Fuld—Lehman Brothers
   - CEO who oversaw the largest bankruptcy in U.S. history with $613 billion in outstanding debts

2. Angelo Mozilo—Countrywide
   - CEO who oversaw the manipulation of loans and was key in creating the "subprime crisis" through "liar loans," which manipulated consumer and home data to generate business

3. Ken Lay—Enron
   - CEO who oversaw a massive accounting fraud and watched the stock value of the company he had created fall 99.7% in 2001

4. Jimmy Cayne—Bear Stearns
   - CEO who oversaw the demise of his company and ultimate sale to JPMorgan; Cayne's personal stock holding fell from $993 million to less than $200 million

5. Bernie Ebbers—WorldCom
   - CEO who oversaw $11 billion in accounting fraud and is now serving 25 years in prison

Source: "20 Worst CEOs," *Portfolio Magazine,* April 22, 2009, http://www.portfolio.com/executives/2009/04/22/20-Worst-CEOs, accessed July 1, 2009.

consequences, are often admired and lauded, especially in the business press. When their unethical or even illegal actions become public knowledge, however, they risk more than the loss of their positions. Table 6.7 lists the top five worst CEOs for managing organizational risks. These men represent some of the most high-profile corporate failures of the past few decades, and most of them paid for their misconduct with public vilification, fines, and jail time. Such large corporate failures may have been prevented with a more cautious approach to risk taking, more support for ethics from the top, and stronger ethics and compliance programs.

Reducing unethical behavior is a business goal no different from increasing profits. If progress is not being made toward creating and maintaining an ethical culture, the company needs to determine why and take corrective action, either by enforcing current standards more strictly or by setting higher standards. If the code of ethics is aggressively enforced and becomes part of the corporate culture, it can be effective in improving ethical behavior within the organization. If the code is merely window-dressing and not genuinely part of the corporate culture, it will accomplish very little.

SUMMARY

A strategic approach to ethical decisions will contribute to both business and society. To be socially responsible and promote legal and ethical conduct, an organization should develop an organizational ethics program by establishing, communicating, and monitoring ethical values and legal requirements that characterize its history, culture, industry, and operating environment. Most companies begin the process of establishing an organizational ethics program by developing a code of conduct, a formal statement that describes what the organization expects of its employees. A code should reflect senior management's desire for organizational compliance with values, rules, and policies that support an ethical climate. Codes of conduct help employees and managers address ethical dilemmas by prescribing or limiting specific activities.

Organizational ethics programs must have oversight by high-ranking persons known to respect legal and ethical standards. Often referred to as ethics officers, these persons are responsible for assessing the needs and risks to be addressed in an organization-wide ethics program, developing and distributing a code of conduct, conducting training programs for employees, establishing and maintaining a confidential service to answer questions about ethical issues, making sure the company is in compliance with government regulations, monitoring and auditing ethical conduct, taking action on possible violations of the organization's code, and reviewing and updating the code. Instituting a training program and a system to communicate with and educate employees about the firm's ethical standards is a major step in developing an effective ethics program.

Ethical compliance involves comparing employee ethical performance with the organization's ethical standards. Ethical compliance can be measured through employee observation, internal audits, reporting systems, and investigations. An internal system for reporting misconduct is especially useful. Employees who conclude that they cannot discuss current or potential unethical activities with coworkers or superiors and go outside the organization for help are known as whistle-blowers.

Consistent enforcement and necessary disciplinary action are essential to a functional ethical compliance program. Continuous improvement of the ethics program is necessary. Ethical leadership and a strong corporate culture in support of ethical behavior are necessary to implement an effective organizational ethics program.

RESPONSIBLE BUSINESS DEBATE

Enron: The Capitalist Manifesto?

ISSUE: Was it greed, corporate culture, or something else that caused the downfall of Enron?

"Greed is good," said Gordon Gekko in the movie Wall Street—a mindset that permeated the financial firms of Wall Street for decades. If this phrase is the capitalist manifesto, Enron is the archetype of this philosophy. The company marked both the height and the beginning of the end of that kind of corporate mentality.

Ken Lay, former CEO of Enron, has become the ultimate symbol of unethical conduct. He was the key executive involved in a massive fraud that destroyed thousands of jobs, thousands of employees' savings accounts, and billions in shareholder value. Lay was put on trial and found guilty of "consciously avoiding knowing about wrongdoing" at Enron. Yet even after his conviction, Lay maintained that "with 30,000 employees in 30 countries and 200 executives at the vice president level," the corruption had existed without his knowledge. Most experts believe that ethical corporate cultures are a top-down phenomenon, and after the fall of Enron, most people felt Lay had to be held responsible.

Enron whistle-blower Sherron Watkins asserted that Lay was indeed some distance from the fraud, and that Jeff Skilling, also CEO for a short time, was the one who had created a strong culture of greed where bad behavior was rewarded as long as it delivered profits for the company. Aggressive business practices included finding loopholes in regulation, extreme pressure to perform, periodic firing of the lowest-performing employees, paying huge salaries and bonuses to those who did perform well (regardless of what ethical corners they may have cut), and paying large amounts of money to lawyers, bankers, accountants, and other so-called gatekeepers. A culture of greed evolved where everyone took risks and expected a big reward. And yet, until his death, Ken Lay claimed the firm had strong values of respect, integrity, communication, and excellence, including a detailed code of ethics.

How could these two corporate cultures—the greedy one created by Skilling and the ethical one Lay believed Enron had—exist in the same company? In the end, Lay stated that internal controls were not effective and that he believed the frauds of Andy Fastow, the former CFO, were what brought down the company. Sherron Watkins, although she was a key whistle-blower,

did not blame Lay. She thought that Jeff Skilling's charismatic and intimidating leadership had been the central problem. Watkins believes that if Skilling had been out of the picture, the fraud would not have happened. The Enron disaster created more regulatory legislation and incited an ongoing debate about the nature of capitalism and what is an effective business ethics program.

There Are Two Sides to Every Issue:

1. Ethical misconduct was caused by the corporate culture at Enron.
2. Ethical misconduct at Enron was caused by Ken Lay's and Jeff Skilling's leadership.

Sources: Gerard Beenen and Jonathan Pinto, "Resisting Organizational Level Corruption: An Interview with Sherron Watkins," *Academy of Management Learning and Education* 8, no.2 (June 2009): 275–289; O. C. Ferrell and Linda Ferrell, "Conversations with Ken Lay," June 2006; Fareed Zakaria, "Greed Is Good (to a Point)," *Newsweek*, June 22, 2009, p. 41.

KEY TERMS

codes of conduct (p. 206)
ethics officer (p. 211)
whistle-blowing (p. 218)

DISCUSSION QUESTIONS

1. How can an organization be socially responsible and promote legal and ethical conduct?

2. What are the elements that should be included in a strong ethics program?

3. What is a code of conduct and how can a code be communicated effectively to employees?

4. How and why are a training program and a communications system important in developing an effective ethics program?

5. What does ethical compliance involve and how can it be measured?

6. What role does leadership play in influencing organizational behavior?

7. Compare transformational leadership and transactional leadership.

EXPERIENTIAL EXERCISE

Visit the website of the Ethics and Compliance Officer Association (http://www.theecoa.org). What is the association's current mission and membership composition? Review the website to determine the issues and concerns that comprise the ECOA's most recent programs, publications, and research. What trends do you find? What topics seem most important to ethics officers today?

WHAT WOULD YOU DO?

Robert Rubine flipped through his messages and wondered which call he should return first. It was only 3:30 P.M., but he felt as though he had been through a week's worth of decisions and worries. Mondays were normally busy, but this one was anything but normal. Robert's employer, Medic-All, is in the business of selling a wide array of medical supplies and equipment. The company's products range from relatively inexpensive items, like bandages, gloves, and syringes, to more costly items, such as microscopes, incubators, and examination tables. Although the product line is broad, it represents the "basics" required in most health-care settings. Medic-All utilizes an inside sales force to market its products to private hospitals, elder-care facilities, government health-care institutions, and other similar organizations. The company employs 275 people and is considered a small business under government rules.

The inside sales force has the authority to negotiate on price, which works well in the highly competitive market of medical supplies and equipment. The salespeople are compensated primarily on a commission basis. The sales force and other employees receive legal training annually. All employees are required to sign Medic-All's code of ethics each year and attend an ethics training session. Despite the importance of the inside sales force, Medic-All has experienced a good deal of turnover in its sales management team. A new lead manager was hired about four months ago. Robert oversees the sales division in his role as vice president of marketing and operations.

Late Friday afternoon last week, Robert received word that two employees in the company's headquarters were selling products to the government at a higher price than they were selling them to other organizations. Both employees have been on the job for over two years and seem to be good performers. A few of their sales colleagues have complained to the lead sales manager about the high quarterly commissions that the two employees recently received. They insinuated that these commissions were earned unfairly by charging government-run hospitals high prices. A cursory review of their accounts showed that, in many instances, the government is paying more than other organizations. Under procurement rules, the government is supposed to pay a fair price, one that other cost-conscious customers would pay. When asked about the situation, the two employees said that the price offered was based on volume, so the pricing always varied from customer to customer.

Robert took the information to his boss, the company president. The president and Robert discussed how these employees received legal and ethics training, signed the company code of ethics, and should have been knowledgeable about rules related to government procurement. The president said that these two salespeople sounded liked "rogue employees," who committed acts without management approval to increase their commissions. Robert and the president discussed many issues and scenarios, such as how to deal with the two salespeople, whether to continue the investigation and inform the government, strategies for preventing the problem in the future, how to protect the firm's good name, whether the company could face suspension from lucrative government business, and others. What would you do?

Employee Relations

Chapter Objectives

- To discuss employees as stakeholders

- To examine the economic, legal, ethical, and philanthropic responsibilities related to employees

- To describe an employer of choice and the employer of choice's relationship to social responsibility

Chapter Outline

Employee Stakeholders

Responsibilities to Employees

Strategic Implementation of Responsibilities to Employees

© Tom Tomczyk

Shell's Commitment to Employees and Community

Although large oil and energy companies are often the target of criticism, Royal Dutch Shell has invested many resources into its social responsibility initiatives. Environmental issues are at the forefront of the company's agenda, but Shell collaborates and innovates with stakeholders on a range of other issues. Companies like Shell have to meet the expectations of a variety of stakeholders and are in a constant state of maintaining relationships, communicating, and making decisions that affect one, several, or all stakeholder groups. At any point in time, it is possible for a company to have varying levels of success with these groups because of historical issues, current conditions, and other transitions taking place. Thus, Shell could be in early stages of trust with environmental rights groups, but is considered quite proactive with investors.

Shell has ventures in more than 100 countries and operates on the basis of eight business principles that define specific expectations in the company's code of business conduct. These principles were first established in 1976 and have been revised several times, with the latest revision in 2005. These principles are related to key business processes, outcomes, and stakeholders and include: (1) communication and engagement, (2) compliance, (3) business integrity, (4) local communities, (5) political activities, (6) economic responsibilities, (7) fair competition, and (8) health, safety, security, and environmental management. For example, even in the midst of shutting down industrial operations in one Norwegian city, Shell recently proved its solid commitment to employees and communities.

When Shell decided to close an oil refinery in Sola, Norway, the company engaged various groups in the decision-making process. Shell provided job assistance and worked with area employers and organizations to find new positions for employees. Shell also created a dialog with the local government and other constituencies, who had a voice in how the plant closing was implemented. Based on these conversations, the community was able to benefit from the refinery closing. Laboratory equipment was donated to local schools. The refinery's boiling system was installed in a retirement community. To date, over 98 percent of the refinery plant and materials have been recycled or used for another purpose. The city does not have an abandoned and dilapidated area; instead, new businesses occupy the land where the refinery once stood.

Shell recognizes that, far beyond the economic impact, business affects communities and local infrastructure in many other ways. Health, safety, local culture, natural resources, security, and secondary economic effects are part of Shell's stakeholder assessment for strategic social responsibility. Even when faced with the difficult task of workforce reduction, the company is committed to engaging stakeholders so that various interests and needs are considered from a long-term perspective.[1]

This vignette illustrates the extent to which some firms consider the needs, wants, and characteristics of employees and other stakeholders in designing various business processes and practices. Although it is widely understood that employees are of great importance, beliefs about the extent and types of responsibilities that organizations should assume toward employees are likely to vary. For example, some managers are primarily concerned with economic and legal responsibilities, whereas proponents of the stakeholder interaction model would advocate for a broader perspective. As this chapter will show, a delicate balance of power, responsibility, and accountability resides in the relationships a company develops with its employees.

Because employee stakeholders are so important to the success of any company, this chapter is devoted to the employer-employee relationship. We explore the many issues related to the social responsibilities employers have to their employees, including the employee-employer contract, workforce reduction, wages and benefits, labor unions, health and safety, equal opportunity, sexual harassment, whistle-blowing, diversity, and work-life balance. Along the way, we discuss a number of significant laws that affect companies' human resources programs. Finally, we look at the concept of "employer of choice" and what it takes to earn that reputation and distinction.

EMPLOYEE STAKEHOLDERS

Think for a minute about the first job or volunteer position you held. What information were you given about the organization's strategic direction? How were you managed and treated by supervisors? Did you feel empowered to make decisions? How much training did you receive? The answers to these questions may reveal the types of responsibilities that employers have toward employees. If you worked in a restaurant, for example, training should have covered safety, cleanliness, and other health issues mandated by law. If you volunteered at a hospital, you may have learned about the ethical and economic considerations in providing health care for the uninsured or poor and the philanthropic efforts used to support the hospital financially. Although such issues may have seemed subtle or even unimportant at the time, they are related to the responsibilities that employees, government, and other stakeholders expect of employing organizations.

RESPONSIBILITIES TO EMPLOYEES

In her book *The Working Life: The Promise and Betrayal of Modern Work*, business professor Joanne B. Ciulla writes about the different types of work, the history of work, the value of work to a person's self-concept, the relationship between work and freedom, and, as the title implies, the rewards and pitfalls that exist in the employee-employer relationship. Ciulla contends that two common phrases—"Get a job!" and "Get a life!"—are antithetical in today's society, meaning they seem diametrically opposed goals or values.[2]

For the ancient Greeks, work was seen as the gods' way of punishing humans. Centuries later, Benedictine monks, who built farms, church abbeys, and villages, were considered the lowest order of monks because they labored. By the eighteenth century, the Protestant work ethic had emerged to imply that work was a method for discovering and creating a person.[3] Today, psychologists, families, and friends lament how work has become the primary source of many individuals' fulfillment, status, and happiness.

Like the complicated history of work, the responsibilities, obligations, and expectations between employees and employers are fraught with challenges and debates. In this section, we review the four levels of corporate social responsibilities as they relate to employees. Although we focus primarily on the responsibilities of employers to employees, we also acknowledge the role that employees have in achieving strategic social responsibility.

Economic Issues

Perhaps no story in recent memory underscores the economic realm of employment more vividly than the saga of Malden Mills Industries. In 1995, 750,000 square feet of factory and office space at Malden Mills burned to the ground. It was just a few weeks before the winter holidays, and in addition, workers were injured. In an unusual move, CEO Aaron Feuerstein paid end-of-year bonuses and employees' full wages and benefits while the buildings were reconstructed. Human resource managers set up a temporary job training center, collected Christmas gifts for employees' children, and worked with community agencies to support employees and their families.[4] Even after injured employees filed a workers' compensation claim against Malden Mills, Feuerstein said, "The welfare of our employees has always been and continues to be a priority of Malden Mills."[5] When economic factors forced Malden Mills through several employee layoffs in the late 1990s, employees were offered jobs at another plant and received career transition assistance. Essentially, Feuerstein believes in an unwritten contract that considers the economic prospects of both employer and employees.

Several years later, Malden Mills filed for bankruptcy protection, part of which was blamed on losses from the fire. Lenders provided funding for the company to continue operations and develop a reorganization strategy to emerge from bankruptcy. The company emerged from bankruptcy, but the plan took the CEO's responsibility from Feuerstein and placed it with lenders and creditors. By 2007, however, the company went bankrupt again and decided to liquidate. That year Malden Mills' assets were sold to Chrysalis Capital Partners, and the company name was changed to Polartec, LLC. Polartec started as the original synthetic fleece developed by Malden, and today the company offers 300 different fabrics designed to keep people warm, dry, and comfortable during outdoor activities. While Feuerstein is long-removed from the company, his original product invention and commitment to social responsibility exists at Polartec today.[6]

Employee-Employer Contract As we discussed in Chapter 1, the recent history of social responsibility has brought many changes to bear on stakeholder relationships. One of the more dramatic shifts has been in the "contract" and mutual understanding that exist between employee and employer. At the beginning of the twenty-first century, many companies had to learn and accept new rules for recruiting, retaining, and compensating employees. For example, although

After a fire destroyed Malden Mills Industries, the owner publicly assured employees their wages and benefits would be extended for at least 30 days

employers held the position of power for many years, the new century brought record employment rates and the tightest job market in years. Huge salaries, signing bonuses, multiple offers, and flexible, not seniority-based, compensation plans became commonplace throughout the late 1990s. The economic downturn, the attacks of September 11, 2001, and a series of business scandals in the early 2000s brought a decline in lucrative employment opportunities and forced many firms to implement layoffs and other cost-cutting measures. Pay raises, health-care benefits, mental health coverage, retirement funding, paid maternity leave, and other benefits were reduced or costs were shifted to employees.[7]

Regardless of salary, perks, and specific position, a **psychological contract** exists between an employee and employer. This contract is largely unwritten and includes the beliefs, perceptions, expectations, and obligations that make up the agreement between individuals and the organizations that employ them.[8] Details of the contract develop through communications, via interactions with managers and coworkers, and through perceptions of the corporate culture. These interactions are especially important for new employees, who are trying to make sense of their new roles.[9] This contract, though informal, has a signifi-cant influence on the way employees act. When promises and expectations are not met, a psychological contract breach occurs, and employees may become less loyal, less trusting, inattentive to work, or otherwise dissatisfied with their employment situation.[10] On the other hand, when employers present informa-tion in a credible, competent, and trustworthy manner, employees are more likely to be supportive of and committed to the organization. Therefore, there are two groups that contribute to the development, maintenance, and evolution

psychological contract
the beliefs, perceptions, expectations, and obligations that make up the agreement between individuals and the organizations that employ them

Table 7.1 Examples of Employee Contributions and Employer Promises to the Psychological Contract

Employee Contributions
In- and extra-role behavior:
Cooperate well with your colleagues
Work fast and efficiently
Flexibility:
Volunteer to do tasks that are strictly no part of your job if necessary
Ethical behavior:
Protect confidential information about the company
Use the organization's properties honestly
Follow policies and norms of the organization
Loyalty:
Remain with the organization for at least some years
Employability:
Take personal initiative to attend additional training courses
Employer Promises
Career development:
Opportunities for promotion
Opportunities for career development within the organization
Job content:
A job in which you can make decisions yourself
Opportunities to use your skills and capacities
Social atmosphere:
A good atmosphere at work
Positive relationships between colleagues
Financial rewards:
Financial rewards for exceptional performance
An attractive pay and benefits package
Work-life balance:
Opportunities for flexible working hours depending on your personal needs

Source: Ans DeVos, Dirk Buyens, and Rene Schalk, "Psychological Contract Development During Organizational Socialization: Adaptation to Reality and the Role of Reciprocity," *Journal of Organizational Behavior* 24 (August 2003): 537–559.

of the psychological contract at work—employees and employers. Table 7.1 provides an overview of the dimensions that characterize each group's role in creating the psychological contract.

An employee's perception of how well employer promises are kept provides for an ongoing psychological assessment of the employment relationship, including whether or not the employee will choose to leave the organization. The promises, or inducements, made by the organization are valuable to nearly all employees, but a recent study of more than 5,000 employees indicates this rank order for their importance to employees: (1) social atmosphere, (2) career development opportunities, (3) job content, (4) work-life balance, and (5) financial rewards. This same sample ranked the organizational fulfillment of these promises as: (1) job content, (2) social atmosphere, (3) work-life balance, (4) career development opportunities, and (5) financial rewards. Based on these results, it is clear that career development opportunities deserve more attention from managers to strengthen the psychological contract and provide incentives for employee retention.

Organizations that are able to implement the key promises so that employees view them as fulfilled reap rewards in terms of increased employee loyalty and decreased intentions to leave and/or search for a new employer.[11] Strong employee commitment is then revealed through their positive interactions with key stakeholders, especially customers, and ultimately has a positive influence on organizational success, as we discussed in Chapter 1.[12]

Just as in other stakeholder relationships, expectations in the employment psychological contract are subject to a variety of influences. This section discusses how the contract has ebbed and flowed over the last 100 years. As an overview, Table 7.2 profiles ten characteristics that have evolved over the past few decades in employees' psychological contract with employers.

Until the early 1900s, the relationship between employer and employee was best characterized as a master-servant relationship.[13] In this view, there was a natural imbalance in power that meant employment was viewed as a privilege that included few rights and many obligations. Employees were expected to work for the best interests of the organization, even at the expense of personal and family welfare. At this time, most psychologists and management scholars believed that good leadership required aggressive and domineering behavior.[14] Images from Upton Sinclair's novel *The Jungle*, which we discuss briefly in the next chapter, characterized the extreme negative effects of this employment contract.[15]

In the 1920s and 1930s, employees assumed a relationship with an employer that was more balanced in terms of power, responsibilities, and obligations. This shift meant that employees and employers were coequals, and in legal terms,

Table 7.2 Changes in Employees' Psychological Contract with Employers

Characteristic	Old	New
Attachment to employer	Long term	Near term
Readiness to change jobs	Not interested	Not looking, but will listen
Priorities on the job	Company and its goals	Personal life and career
Devotion to employer goals	Follows orders	Usually buys in
Effort on the job	100 percent	110 percent
Motto	Semper fidelis ("Always faithful")	Carpe diem ("Seize the day")
Professional future	Training	Learning & development
Employee focus	Internal	Customers & stakeholders
Information sharing	Closed	Open
Type of work	Functional	Project-based

Source: Tim B. Baker, "The New Employee-Employer Relationship Model," *Organization Development Journal 27* (Spring 2009): 27–36; Neil Conway and Rob B. Briner, *Understanding Psychological Contracts at Work* (London: Oxford University Press, 2006).

employees had many more rights than under the master-servant model.[16] Much of the employment law in the United States was enacted in the 1930s, when legislators passed laws related to child labor, wages, working hours, and labor unions.[17] Throughout the twentieth century, the employee-employer contract evolved along the coequals model, although social critics began to question the influence large companies had on employees.

In the 1950s, political commentator and sociologist C. Wright Mills criticized white-collar work as draining on employees' time, energy, and even personalities. He also believed that individuals with business power were apt to keep employees happy in an attempt to ward off the development of stronger labor unions and unfavorable government regulations.[18] A few years later, the classic book *The Organization Man*

by William H. Whyte was published. This book examined the social nature of work, including the inherent conflict between belonging and contributing to a group on the job while maintaining a sense of independence and identity.[19]

Organizational researchers and managers in the 1960s began to question authoritarian behavior and consider participatory management styles that assumed employees were motivated and eager to assume responsibility for work. A study by the U.S. Department of Health, Education, and Welfare in the early 1970s confirmed that employees wanted interesting work and a chance to demonstrate their skills. The report also recommended job redesign and managerial approaches that increased participation, freedom, and democracy at work.[20]

By the 1980s, a family analogy was being used to describe the workplace. This implied strong attention to employee welfare and prompted the focus on business ethics that we explored in previous chapters. At the same time, corporate mission statements touted the importance of customers and employees, and a best-selling book by distinguished professor Thomas J. Peters and business consultant Robert H. Waterman Jr., *In Search of Excellence*, profiled companies with strong corporate cultures that inspired employees toward better work, products, and customer satisfaction.[21] The total quality management (TQM) movement increased empowerment and teamwork on the job throughout the 1990s and led the charge toward workplaces simultaneously devoted to employee achievement at work and home.[22]

Although there were many positive initiatives for employees in the 1990s, the confluence of economic progress with demands for global competitiveness convinced many executives of the need for cost cutting. For individuals accustomed to messages about the importance of employees to organizational success, workforce reduction

Table 7.3 Top Ten Financial Losses—Fortune 500 Companies

Company	Loss
American International Group (AIG)	$99.3 billion
Fannie Mae	$58.7 billion
Freddie Mac	$50.1 billion
General Motors	$30.9 billion
Citigroup	$27.7 billion
Merrill Lynch	$27.6 billion
ConocoPhillips	$17 billion
Ford Motor	$14.7 billion
Time Warner	$13.4 billion
CBS	$11.7 billion

Source: "The Fortune 500's Biggest Losers, "*Fortune,* http://money.cnn.com/galleries/2009/fortune/0904/gallery.f500_biggestlosers.
fortune/index.html, accessed August 17, 2009.

was both unexpected and traumatic. These experiences effectively ended the loyalty- and commitment-based contract that employees had developed with employers. A study of young employees showed that their greatest psychological need in the workplace is security but that they viewed many employers as "terminators."[23]

By the time Barack Obama became president of the United States in 2009, his administration was facing an economy in terrible condition. Table 7.3 lists the top ten financial collapses of 2008, which contributed to the negative repercussions throughout the global economy. By mid-2009, more than eight million employees had been laid off and recessionary effects loomed large. The Conference Board, which publishes the Employment Trend Index (ETI) monthly, announced the index was declining faster than at any other time in the 35-year history of the ETI. Eight indicators contribute to the index, including, among others, claims for unemployment insurance, number of part-time workers due to economic reasons, consumer confidence, industrial production, and manufacturing and trade sales.

Workforce Reduction[24] At different points in a company's history, there are likely to be factors that beg the question, "How can we decrease our overall costs?" In a highly competitive business environment, where new companies, customers, and products emerge and disappear every day, there is a continuous push for greater organizational efficiency and effectiveness. This pressure often leads to difficult decisions, including ones that require careful balance and consideration for the short-run survival and long-term vision of the company. This situation can create the need for **workforce reduction**, the process of eliminating employment positions. This process places considerable pressure on top management, causes speculation and tension among employees, and raises public ire about the role of business in society.[25]

Companies can use several strategies to reduce overall costs and expenditures. For example, organizations may choose to reduce the number of employees,

workforce reduction
the process of eliminating employment positions

simplify products and processes, decrease quality and promises in service delivery, or develop some other mechanism for eliminating resources or nonperforming assets. Managers may find it difficult to communicate about cost reductions, as this message carries both emotional and social risk. Employees may wonder, "What value do I bring to the company?" and "Does anyone really care about my years of service?" Customers may inquire, "Can we expect the same level of service and product quality?" Governments and the community may ask, "Is this really necessary? How will it affect our economy?" For all of these questions, company leadership must have a clear answer. This response should be based on a thorough analysis of costs within the organizational system and how any changes are likely to affect business processes and outcomes. In 2005, IBM announced it would cut its American and European workforces by 13,000. This would appear to be a reduction, but the company is actually adding 14,000 workers in India. Many companies have already outsourced certain positions to places outside the United States and Europe, where labor is much cheaper and cost savings can be realized.

In the last two decades, many firms chose to adopt the strategy that also creates the most anxiety and criticism—the reduction of the workforce. Throughout the 1990s, the numbers were staggering, as Sears eliminated 50,000 jobs and Kodak terminated nearly 17,000 people. Economic decline and financial scandals in the first decade of the twenty-first century also created a wave of layoffs. In early 2009, General Motors (GM) announced intentions to cut 18,000 hourly jobs in the United States and approximately 47,000 salaried and hourly jobs worldwide by the end of 2009. In the previous three years, GM had already laid off 60,000 hourly employees. These actions effectively signaled the "end of the old contract" that employees had with employers.[26]

This strategy, sometimes called *downsizing* or *rightsizing,* usually entails employee layoffs and terminations. In other cases, a company freezes new hiring, hopes for natural workforce attrition, offers incentives for early retirement, or encourages job sharing among existing employees. Table 7.4 provides information on the different tactics that may be used to effect downsizing in the workplace. The reality is that some employees will lose their current positions one way or another. Thus, although workforce reduction may be the strategy chosen to control and reduce costs, it may have profound implications for the welfare of employees, their families, and the economic prospects of a geographical region and other constituents as well as for the corporation itself.

As with other aspects of business, it is difficult to separate financial considerations for

"Downsizing makes the private relationship between employee and employer a public issue that affects many stakeholders and subsequently draws heavy criticism."

Table 7.4 Three Downsizing Tactics

Tactic	Characteristics	Examples
Workforce reduction	Aimed at headcount reduction Short-term implementation Fosters transition and transformation	Attrition Transfer and outplacement Retirement incentives Buyout packages Layoffs
Organization redesign	Aimed at organization change Moderate-term implementation Fosters transition and transformation	Eliminates functions Merges units Eliminates layers Eliminates products and services Redesigns tasks
Systemic redesign	Aimed at culture change Long-term implementation Fosters transformation	Change responsibility Involves all constituents Fosters continuous improvement and innovation Simplification Downsizing: a way of life

Source: Thomas G. Cummings and Christopher G. Worley, *Organization Development and Change* (Cincinnati, OH: South-Western Cengage Learning, 2009).

costs from other obligations and expectations that develop between a company and its stakeholders. Depending on a firm's resource base and current financial situation, the psychological contract that exists between an employer and employee is likely to be broken through layoffs, and the social contract between employers, communities, and other groups may also be threatened. Downsizing makes the private relationship between employee and employer a public issue that affects many stakeholders and subsequently draws heavy criticism.[27] Fundamentally, top managers must recognize the many different types of "costs" that occur through workforce reduction. These include costs associated with future talent and leadership, company morale, perceptions on Wall Street, and rehiring needs.[28]

The impact of the workforce reduction process depends on a host of factors, including corporate culture, long-term plans, and creative calculations on both quantitative and qualitative aspects of the workplace. Because few human resource directors and other managers have extensive experience in restructuring the workforce, there are several issues to consider before embarking on the process.[29] First, a comprehensive plan must be developed that takes into account the financial implications and qualitative and emotional toll of the reduction strategy. This plan may include a systematic analysis of workflow so that management understands how tasks are currently completed and how they will be completed after restructuring. Second, the organization should commit to assisting employees who must make a career transition as a result of the reduction process. To make the transition productive for employees, this assistance should begin as soon as management is aware of possible reductions. Through the Worker Adjustment and Retraining Notification Act (WARN), U.S. employers are required to give at least sixty days' advance notice if a layoff will affect 500 or more employees or more than one-third of the workforce.[30] Offering career assistance is beneficial over the long term, as it demonstrates a firm's commitment to social responsibility.

External factors also play a role in how quickly employees find new work and affect perceptions of a firm's decision to downsize. When the Opryland Hotel in Nashville, Tennessee, laid off 160 employees, other hotels in the area quickly hired them. With the unemployment rate in Nashville below 2.7 percent at the time, the other hotels appreciated the service training and competence of the former Opryland employees.[31] Thus, the Opryland Hotel probably did not suffer the types of reputation problems that other firms may have experienced in less favorable labor markets. Individuals who are reemployed quickly, whether through company efforts or market circumstances, experience fewer negative economic and emotional repercussions. In addition, employees who are kept well informed of the downsizing decision process are more likely to retain positive attitudes toward the company, even if they experience job loss.[32]

Companies must be willing to accept the consequences of terminating employees. Although workforce reduction can improve a firm's financial performance, especially in the short run, there are costs to consider, including the loss of intellectual capital.[33] The years of knowledge, skills, relationships, and commitment that employees develop cannot be easily replaced or substituted, and the loss of one employee can cost a firm between $50,000 and $100,000.[34] Skandia Assurance and Financial Services, based in Stockholm, Sweden, is one of a few firms to measure and report its intellectual capital to investors, a move that illuminates an intangible asset for better decision making. Skandia has been recognized by *Fortune* magazine as one of ten great companies in Europe.[35] While workforce reduction lowers costs, it often results in lost intellectual capital, strained customer relationships, negative media attention, and other issues that drain company resources.

© Gu Xinrong/Xinhua/Landov

While the U.S. flag flew proudly at its headquarters, General Motors' executives announced plans to eliminate brands and reduce its workforce and dealer network

Employees who retain their jobs may suffer guilt, depression, or stress as a result of the reduction in workforce. Thus, a long-term understanding of the qualitative and quantitative costs and benefits should guide downsizing decisions.[36]

Although workforce reduction is a corporate decision, it is also important to recognize the potential role of employees in these decisions. Whereas hiring and job growth reached a frantic pace by the late 1990s, a wave of downsizings in the early 1990s and 2000s meant that some individuals had embraced the reality of having little job security. Instead of becoming cynical or angry, employees evidently have reversed roles and began asking, "What is this company doing for me?" and "Am I getting what I need from my employer?" Employees of all types began taking more responsibility for career growth, demanding balance in work and personal responsibilities, and seeking opportunities in upstart firms and emerging industries. Thus, although workforce reduction has negative effects, it has also shifted the psychological contract and power between employee and employer. The following suggestions examine how individuals can potentially mitigate the onset and effects of downsizing.

First, all employees should understand how their skills and competencies affect business performance. Not recognizing and improving this relationship makes it more difficult to prove their worth to managers faced with workforce reduction decisions. Second, employees should strive for cost-cutting and conservation strategies regardless of the employer's current financial condition. This is a workforce's first line of defense against layoffs—assisting the organization in reducing its costs before drastic measures are necessary. Third, today's work environment requires that most employees fulfill diverse and varying roles. For example, manufacturing managers must understand the whole product development and introduction process, ranging from engineering to marketing and distribution activities. Thus, another way of ensuring worth to the company, and to potential employers, is through an employee's ability to navigate different customer environments and organizational systems. It is now necessary to "cross-train," show flexibility, and learn the entire business, even if a company does not offer a formal program for gaining this type of experience and exposure. Although this advice may not prevent workforce reduction, it does empower employees against some of its harmful effects.

"Employment law is a very complex and evolving area."

employment at will
a common-law doctrine that allows either the employer or the employee to terminate the relationship at any time as long as it does not violate an employment contract

Through laws and regulations, the government has also created a system for ensuring that employees are treated properly on the job. The next section covers the myriad of laws that all employers and employees should consider in daily and strategic decisions.

Legal Issues

Employment law is a very complex and evolving area. Most large companies and organizations employ human resource managers and legal specialists who are trained in the detail and implementation of specific statutes related to employee hiring, compensation, benefits, safety, and other areas. Smaller organizations often

Table 7.5 Major Employment Laws

Act (Date Enacted)	Purpose
National Labor Relations Act (1935)	Established the rights of employees to engage in collective bargaining and to strike.
Fair Labor Standards Act (1938)	Established minimum wage and overtime pay standards, recordkeeping, and child labor standards for most private and public employers.
Equal Pay Act (1963)	Protects women and men who perform substantially equal work in the same establishment from gender-based wage discrimination.
Civil Rights Act, Title VII (1964)	Prohibits employment discrimination on the basis of race, national origin, color, religion, and gender.
Age Discrimination in Employment Act (1967)	Protects individuals age forty or older from age-based discrimination.
Occupational Safety and Health Act (1970)	Ensures safe and healthy working conditions for all employees by providing specific standards that employers must meet.
Employee Retirement Income Security Act (1974)	Sets uniform minimum standards to assure that employee benefit plans are established and maintained in a fair and financially sound manner.
Americans with Disabilities Act (1990)	Prohibits discrimination on the basis of physical or mental disability in all employment practices and requires employers to make reasonable accommodation to make facilities accessible to and usable by persons with disabilities.
Family and Medical Leave Act (1993)	Requires certain employers to provide up to twelve weeks of unpaid, job-protected leave to eligible employees for certain family and medical reasons.
Uniformed Services Employment and Reemployment Rights Act (1994)	The pre-service employer must reemploy service members returning from a period of service in the uniformed services if those service members meet five criteria.

Sources: Gillian Flynn, "Looking Back on 100 Years of Employment Law," *Workforce 78* (November 1999): 74–77; Roger LeRoy Miller and Gaylord A. Jentz, *Business Law Today* (Cincinnati, OH: Cengage South-Western, 2009); U.S. Department of Labor, *Employment Law Guide*, http://www.dol.gov/compliance/guide/index.htm, accessed August 17, 2009.

send human resource managers to workshops and conferences to keep abreast of legal imperatives in the workplace. Table 7.5 lists the major federal laws that cover employer responsibilities with respect to wages, labor unions, benefits, health and safety, equal opportunity, and other areas. Until the early 1900s, employment was primarily governed by the concept of **employment at will**, a common-law doctrine that allows either the employer or the employee to terminate the relationship at any time as long as it does not violate an employment contract. Today, many states still use the employment-at-will philosophy, but laws and statutes may limit total discretion in this regard.[37] The following discussion highlights employment laws and their fundamental contribution to social responsibility.[38]

Wages and Benefits After the Great Depression, the U.S. Congress enacted a number of laws to protect employee rights and extend employer responsibilities. The Fair Labor Standards Act (FLSA) of 1938 prescribed minimum wage and overtime pay, recordkeeping, and child labor standards for most private and public employers. The minimum wage is set by the federal government and is periodically revised, although states have the option to adopt a higher standard. For example, the federal minimum wage was raised from $4.45 per hour to $5.15 per hour in September 1997. The majority of states abide by the federal standard, although Alaska, California, Oregon, Vermont, Washington, and several others have adopted a higher minimum wage. Most employees who work more than forty hours per week are entitled to overtime pay in the amount of one and a half times their regular pay. There are exemptions to the overtime pay provisions for four classes of employees: executives, outside salespeople, administrators, and professionals.[39]

The FLSA also affected child labor, including the provision that individuals under the age of fourteen are allowed to do only certain types of work, such as delivering newspapers and working in their parents' businesses. Children under age sixteen are often required to get a work permit, and their work hours are restricted so that they can attend school. Persons between the ages of sixteen and eighteen are not restricted in terms of number of work hours, but they cannot be employed in hazardous or dangerous positions. Although passage of the FLSA was necessary to eliminate abusive child labor practices, its restrictions became somewhat problematic during the booming economy of the late 1990s, when unemployment rates were extremely low in the United States. Some business owners may have even considered lobbying for relaxed standards in very restrictive states so that they could hire more teens. In addition, general FLSA restrictions have created problems in implementing job-sharing and flextime arrangements with employees who are paid on an hourly basis.[40]

Two other pieces of legislation relate to employer responsibilities for benefits and job security. The Employee Retirement Income Security Act (ERISA) of 1974 set uniform minimum standards to assure that employee benefit plans are established and maintained in a fair and financially sound manner. ERISA does not require companies to establish retirement pension plans; instead, it developed standards for the administration of plans that management chooses to offer employees. A key provision relates to **vesting**, the legal right to pension plan benefits. In general, contributions an employee makes to the plan are vested immediately, whereas company contributions are vested after five years of employment. ERISA is a very complicated aspect of employer responsibilities because it involves tax law, financial investments, and plan participants and beneficiaries.[41]

The Family and Medical Leave Act (FMLA) of 1993 requires certain employers to provide up to twelve weeks of unpaid, job-protected leave to eligible employees for certain family and medical reasons. However, if the employee is paid in the top 10 percent of the entire workforce, the employer does not have to reinstate him or her in the same or comparable position.[42] Typical reasons for this type of leave include the birth or adoption of a child, personal illness, or the serious health condition of a close relative. The FMLA applies to employers with fifty or more employees, which means that its provisions do not cover a large number of U.S. employees. In addition, employees must have worked at least one

vesting
the legal right
to pension plan
benefitst

year for the firm and at least twenty-five hours per week during the past year before the FMLA is required.

Labor Unions In one of the earliest pieces of employment legislation, the National Labor Relations Act (NLRA) of 1935 legitimized the rights of employees to engage in collective bargaining and to strike. This law was originally passed to protect employee rights, but subsequent legislation gave more rights to employers and restricted the power of unions. Before the NLRA, many companies attempted to prohibit their employees from creating or joining labor organizations. Employees who were members of unions were often discriminated against in terms of hiring and retention decisions. This act sought to eliminate the perceived imbalance of power between employers and employees. Through unions, employees gained a collective bargaining mechanism that enabled greater power on several fronts, including wages and safety.[43] For example, after a weeks-long strike against Verizon Communications, members of the Communications Workers of America (CWA) and International Brotherhood of Electrical Workers (IBEW) negotiated a deal that gave workers of the telecommunications firm a 12 percent pay raise (over three years), a cap on overtime hours, and other provisions, including the elimination of the threat of layoffs for the period of the labor contract. Verizon also upgraded its website for delivering information and services to its employees.[44]

Health and Safety In 1970, the Occupational Safety and Health Act (OSHA) sought to ensure safe and healthy working conditions for all employees by providing specific standards that employers must meet. This act led to the development of the Occupational Safety and Health Administration, also known as OSHA, the agency that oversees the regulations intended to make U.S. workplaces the safest in the world. In its more than thirty-five years of existence, OSHA has made great strides to improve and maintain the health and safety of employees. For example, since the 1970s, the workplace death rate in the United States has been reduced by 50 percent, and the agency's initiatives in cotton dust and lead standards have reduced disease in several industries. The agency continues to innovate and uses feedback systems for improving its services and standards. For example, OSHA recently translated a variety of its documents into Spanish and posted them to a prominent place on its website. OSHA officials were concerned about Spanish-speaking workers' understanding of the agency and their rights in the workplace.[45]

OSHA has the authority to enter and make inspections of most employers. Because of its far-reaching power and unwarranted inspections made in the 1970s, the agency's relationship with business has not always been positive. For example, OSHA recently proposed rules to increase employer responsibility for ergonomics, the design, arrangement, and use of equipment to maximize productivity and minimize fatigue and physical discomfort. Without proper attention to ergonomics, employees may suffer injuries and long-term health issues as a result of work motion and tasks. Many business and industry associations have opposed the proposal, citing enormous costs and unsubstantiated claims. A federal ergonomics rule was established under the Clinton presidency but was repealed by President George W. Bush. However, the issue continues to be raised

ergonomics
the design, arrangement, and use of equipment to maximize productivity and minimize fatigue and physical discomfort

on the regulatory agenda. OSHA is currently focusing its ergonomics efforts on one industry at a time, while individual states, such as Alaska, Washington, and California, are forging ahead with their own ergonomics rules.[46]

Despite differences between this federal agency and some states and companies on a number of regulations, most employers are required to display the poster shown in Figure 7.1 or one required by their state safety and health agency. The John Deere Company has become a leader in workplace ergonomics. At its Waterloo Works facility in Iowa, employees are helping create safer and more ergonomic workplaces. Workstations are tested in three dimensions before actually being built, and the facility was awarded the 2008 Millionaires Safety Award from the American Foundry Society for more than seven consecutive years of safe working conditions.[47]

Figure 7.1 Job Safety and Health Protection Poster

Source: "New OSHA Workplace Poster," Occupational Safety and Health Administration, http://www.osha.gov/Publications/osha3165low-res.pdf, accessed August 17, 2009.

An emerging issue in the area of health and safety is the increasing rate of violence in the workplace. According to OSHA, 1.5 million workers are assaulted and nearly 1,000 are murdered in the workplace every year.[48] A recent survey of *Fortune* 1000 companies indicates that workplace violence is one of the most important security issues they face, costs $36 billion annually, and results in three deaths daily and thousands of injuries each year. The third leading cause of all occupational fatalities is homicide.[49] Surveys in the insurance industry show that nearly 25 percent of insurance employees have been threatened, harassed, or attacked in job-related circumstances.[50]

The state of California's Occupational Safety and Health Agency has identified three types of workplace violence: (1) crimes committed by strangers and intruders in the workplace; (2) acts committed by nonemployees, such as customers, patients, students, and clients, who have regular and routine contact with employees; and (3) violence committed by coworkers.[51] Taxi drivers and clerks working late-night shifts at convenience stores are often subject to the first type of violence. Airline attendants are increasingly experiencing the second category of workplace violence when passengers become unruly, drunk, or otherwise violent while in flight. Airline employees across the United States, Australia, and Switzerland staged a campaign to combat "air rage," the uncivil and dangerous acts of passengers that not only are punishable by large fines but also can threaten the safety of everyone aboard the aircraft. The groups asked government officials to toughen penalties and control of air rage perpetrators. The terrorist attacks on the World Trade Center and the Pentagon further highlighted workplace risks and violence, including the steps that many organizations are taking to protect employees and other stakeholders. Some organizations with employees who travel frequently have hired training firms to educate employees on aircraft evacuation, air rage, how to respond to hijackers, and other safety measures.[52]

Finally, disagreements and stress in the workplace may escalate into employee-on-employee violence. For example, a Xerox Corporation warehouse employee opened fire during a team meeting at a facility in Honolulu, killing seven coworkers. The employee, Bryan Uyesugi, was eventually convicted of murder and sentenced to life in prison without parole for the shooting, which Xerox officials described as the "worst tragedy" in the company's history. The Hawaii Occupational Safety and Health Division later cited Xerox for failing to enforce workplace-violence policies that might have prevented the deaths.[53] In many of these cases, the perpetrator has been recently reprimanded, dismissed, or received other negative feedback that prompted the violent attack.

Although workplace crimes reflect general problems in society, employers have a responsibility to assess risks and provide security, training, and safeguards to protect employees and other stakeholders from such acts. Experts estimate that 50 percent of all companies have no workplace-violence prevention program, whereas 40 percent have a program "in name only."[54] Companies often purchase insurance policies to cover the costs of workplace violence, including business interruption, psychological counseling, informant rewards, and medical claims related to injuries. One expert suggests that all organizations publish and communicate an antiviolence policy and make employees and managers aware of antecedents to workplace violence.[55]

Equal Opportunity Title VII of the Civil Rights Act of 1964 prohibits employment discrimination on the basis of race, national origin, color, religion, and gender. This law is fundamental to employees' rights to join and advance in an organization according to merit rather than one of the characteristics just mentioned. For example, employers are not permitted to categorize jobs as only for men or women unless there is a reason gender is fundamental to the tasks and responsibilities. Additional laws passed in the 1970s, 1980s, and 1990s were also designed to prohibit discrimination related to pregnancy, disabilities, age, and other factors. For example, the Americans with Disabilities Act prohibits companies from discriminating on the basis of physical or mental disability in all employment practices and requires them to make facilities accessible to and usable by persons with disabilities. The Pregnancy Discrimination Act, now thirty years old, was created to help protect the rights of mothers and mothers-to-be in the workplace. The act has been modified many times since its inception. From 1992 to 2007, the number of pregnancy discrimination complaints filed with the Equal Employment Opportunity Commission (EEOC) increased by 65 percent.[56] Figure 7.2 depicts the number of complaints and resolutions on pregnancy discrimination cases from 1997 through 2008.

These legal imperatives require that companies formalize employment practices to ensure that no discrimination is occurring. Thus, managers must be fully aware of the types of practices that constitute discrimination and work to ensure that hiring, promotion, annual evaluation, and other procedures are fair and based on merit. The spread of HIV and AIDS has prompted multinational firms

Figure 7.2 Growth in Filings and Resolutions of Pregnancy Discrimination Act Complaints to the EEOC

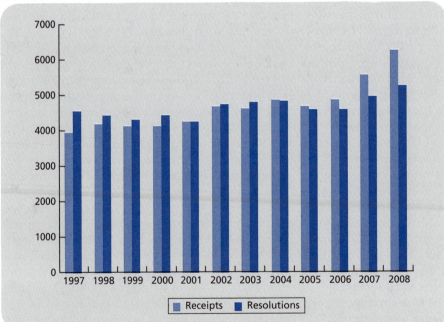

Source: Equal Employment Opportunity Commission, "Pregnancy Discrimination Charges," http://www.eeoc.gov/stats/pregnanc.html, accessed August 17, 2009.

with operations in Africa to distribute educational literature and launch prevention programs. Some companies work with internal and external stakeholders and even fund medical facilities that help prevent the disease and treat HIV/AIDS patients. Another component to their initiatives involves education on fair treatment of employees with the disease. Recently, multinational companies in Mexico produced a written commitment to eliminate the stigma and discrimination often surrounding HIV/AIDS in the workplace.[57]

To ensure that they build balanced workforces, many companies have initiated affirmative action programs, which involve efforts to recruit, hire, train, and promote qualified individuals from groups that have traditionally been discriminated against on the basis of race, sex, or other characteristics. Safeway, a chain of supermarkets, established a program to expand opportunities for women in middle- and upper-level management after settling a sex-discrimination lawsuit.[58] However, many companies voluntarily implement affirmative action plans to build a more diverse workforce.[59] A key goal of these programs is to reduce any bias that may exist in hiring, evaluating, and promoting employees. A special type of discrimination, sexual harassment, is also prohibited through Title VII.

> "Managers must be fully aware of the types of practices that constitute discrimination and work to ensure that hiring, promotion, annual evaluation, and other procedures are fair and based on merit."

Sexual Harassment The flood of women into the workplace during the last half of the twentieth century brought new challenges and opportunities for organizations. Although harassment has probably always existed in the workplace, the presence of both genders in roughly equal numbers changed norms of behavior. When men dominated the workplace, photos of partially nude women or sexually suggestive materials may have been posted on walls or in lockers. Today, such materials could be viewed as illegal if they contribute to a work environment that is intimidating, offensive, or otherwise interferes with an employee's work performance.

The U.S. government indicates the nature of this illegal activity: Unwelcome sexual advances, requests for sexual favors, and other verbal or physical conduct of a sexual nature constitutes **sexual harassment** when submission to or rejection of this conduct explicitly or implicitly affects an individual's employment, unreasonably interferes with an individual's work performance, or creates an intimidating, hostile, or offensive work environment.[60]

Prior to 1986, sexual harassment was not a specific violation of federal law in the United States. In *Meritor Savings Bank v. Vinson*, the U.S. Supreme Court ruled that sexual harassment creates a "hostile environment" that violates Title

sexual harassment unwelcome sexual advances, requests for sexual favors, and other verbal or physical conduct of a sexual nature when submission to or rejection of this conduct explicitly or implicitly affects an individual's employment, unreasonably interferes with an individual's work performance, or creates an intimidating, hostile, or offensive work environment

VII of the Civil Rights Act, even in the absence of economic harm or demand for sexual favors in exchange for promotions, raises, or related work incentives.[61] In other countries, sexual harassment in the workplace is considered an illegal act, although the specific conditions may vary by legal and social culture. In Mexico, the law protects employees only if their jobs are jeopardized on the basis of the exchange of sexual favors or relations. Employees of Mexican public entities, such as government offices, will be fired if found guilty of the offending behavior.[62] In the European Union (EU), sexual harassment legislation focuses on the liability that employers carry when they fail to promote a workplace culture free of harassment and other forms of discrimination. The EU recently strengthened its rules on sexual harassment, including definitions of direct and indirect harassment, the removal of an upper limit on victim compensation, and the requirement that businesses develop and make "equality reports" available to employees.[63]

There are two general categories of sexual harassment: quid pro quo and hostile work environment.[64] **Quid pro quo sexual harassment** is a type of sexual extortion, where there is a proposed or explicit exchange of job benefits for sexual favors. For example, telling an employee, "You will be fired if you do not have sex with me," is a direct form of sexual harassment. Usually, the person making such a statement is in a position of authority over the harassed employee, and thus, the threat of job loss is real. One incident of quid pro quo harassment may create a justifiable legal claim.

Hostile work environment sexual harassment is less direct than quid pro quo harassment and can involve epithets, slurs, negative stereotyping, intimidating acts, and graphic materials that show hostility toward an individual or group, and other types of conduct that affect the employment situation. For example, an e-mail message containing sexually explicit jokes that is broadcast to employees could be viewed as contributing to a hostile work environment. Some hostile work environment harassment is nonsexual, meaning the harassing conduct is based on gender without explicit reference to sexual acts. For example, in *Campbell v. Kansas State University* (1991), the courts found repeated remarks about women "being intellectually inferior to men" to be part of a hostile environment. Unlike quid pro quo cases, one incident may not justify a legal claim. Instead, the courts will examine a range of acts and circumstances to determine if the work environment was intolerable and the victim's job performance was impaired.[65]

From a social responsibility perspective, a key issue in both types of sexual harassment is the employing organization's knowledge and tolerance for these types of behaviors. A number of court cases have shed more light on the issues that constitute sexual harassment and organizations' responsibility in this regard.

In *Harris v. Forklift Systems* (1993), Teresa Harris claimed that her boss at Forklift Systems made suggestive sexual remarks, asked her to retrieve coins from his pants pocket, and joked that they should go to a motel to "negotiate her raise." Courts at the state level threw out her case because she did not suffer major psychological injury. The U.S. Supreme Court overturned these decisions and ruled that employers can be forced to pay damages even if the worker suffered no proven psychological harm. This case brought about the "reasonable person" standard in evaluating what conduct constitutes sexual harassment.

quid pro quo sexual harassment a type of sexual extortion, where there is a proposed or explicit exchange of job benefits for sexual favors

hostile work environment sexual harassment conduct that shows hostility toward an individual or group in a work environment; it can involve epithets, slurs, negative stereotyping, intimidating acts, and graphic materials; less direct than quid pro quo harassment

From this case, juries now evaluate the alleged conduct with respect to commonly held beliefs and expectations.[66]

Several global firms have been embroiled in sexual harassment suits. For example, Ford Motor Company settled a class-action lawsuit for $7.75 million in the late 1990s, the fourth-largest sexual harassment settlement in the Equal Employment Opportunity Commission's history, after more than 500 female employees claimed they were groped and sexually harassed at two different Ford plants. The settlement also required that the company spend an additional $10 million on sensitivity training programs.[67] Mitsubishi Motors agreed in 1998 to pay $34 million in a settlement with 350 women who made serious allegations of harassment and brought lawsuits against the company. Their allegations of sexual harassment included the distribution of lewd videos and photos, inappropriate conversations and jokes, and general tolerance by management for these actions and overtones. As part of the settlement, the company also agreed to periodic monitoring by a three-member panel and to implement an effective sexual harassment policy.[68]

United States Supreme Court decisions on sexual harassment cases indicate that (1) employers are liable for the acts of supervisors; (2) employers are liable for sexual harassment by supervisors that culminates in a tangible employment action (loss of job, demotion, etc.); (3) employers are liable for a hostile environment created by a supervisor but may escape liability if they demonstrate that they exercised reasonable care to prevent and promptly correct any sexually harassing behavior and that the plaintiff employee unreasonably failed to take advantage of any preventive or corrective measures offered by the employer; and (4) claims of hostile environment sexual harassment must be severe and pervasive to be viewed as actionable by the courts.[69]

Much like the underlying philosophy of the Federal Sentencing Guidelines for Organizations that we discussed in earlier chapters, these decisions require top managers in organizations to take the detection and prevention of sexual harassment seriously. To this end, many firms have implemented programs on sexual harassment. To satisfy current legal standards and set a higher standard for social responsibility, employees, supervisors, and other close business partners should be educated on the company's zero-tolerance policy against harassment. Employees must be educated on the policy prohibiting harassment, including the types of behaviors that constitute harassment, how offenders will be punished, and what employees should do if they experience harassment. Just like an organizational compliance program, employees must be assured of confidentiality and no retaliation for reporting harassment. Training on sexual harassment should be balanced in terms of legal definitions and practical tips and tools.

Although employees need to be aware of the legal issues and ramifications, they also may need assistance in learning to recognize and avoid behaviors that may constitute quid pro quo harassment, create a hostile environment, or appear to be retaliatory in nature. In fact, retaliation claims have more than doubled since the early 1990s, prompting many companies to incorporate this element into sexual harassment training. Finally, employees should be aware that same-sex conduct may also constitute sexual harassment.[70] Table 7.6 lists facts about

Table 7.6 Sexual Harassment in the Workplace

Facts
Sexual harassment is a form of sex discrimination that violates Title VII of the Civil Rights Act of 1964.
Unwelcome sexual advances, requests for sexual favors, and other verbal or physical conduct of a sexual nature constitute sexual harassment when submission to or rejection of this conduct explicitly or implicitly affects an individual's employment, unreasonably interferes with an individual's work performance, or creates an intimidating, hostile, or offensive work environment.
Sexual harassment can occur in a variety of circumstances including but not limited to the following: • The victim as well as the harasser may be a woman or a man. The victim does not have to be of the opposite sex. • The harasser can be the victim's supervisor, an agent of the employer, a supervisor in another area, a coworker, or a nonemployee. • The victim does not have to be the person harassed but could be anyone affected by the offensive conduct. • Unlawful sexual harassment may occur without economic injury to or discharge of the victim. • The harasser's conduct must be unwelcome.
It is helpful for the victim to inform the harasser directly that the conduct is unwelcome and must stop. The victim should use any employer complaint mechanism or grievance system available. When investigating allegations of sexual harassment, the Equal Employment Opportunity Commission looks at the whole record: the circumstances, such as the nature of the sexual advances, and the context in which the alleged incidents occurred. A determination of the allegations is made from the facts on a case-by-case basis.

Source: "Facts About Sexual Harassment," U.S. Equal Employment Opportunity Commission, www.eeoc.gov/facts/fs-sex.html, accessed August 17, 2009.

sexual harassment that should be used in company communication and training on this workplace issue.

Whistle-Blowing[71] An employee who reports individual or company wrongdoing to either internal or external sources is considered a whistle-blower.[72] Whistle-blowers usually focus on issues or behaviors that need corrective action, although managers and other employees may not appreciate reports that expose company weaknesses, raise embarrassing questions, or otherwise detract from organizational tasks. Although not all whistle-blowing activity leads to an extreme reaction, whistle-blowers have been retaliated against, demoted, fired, and even worse as a result of their actions. For example, Jacob F. Horton, senior vice president at Gulf Power, was on his way to talk with company officials about alleged thefts, payoffs, and cover-ups at the utility when he died in a plane crash in 1989. Allegations that his death was related to whistle-blowing still linger.[73]

Partly as a result of business and industry scandals in the 1980s, most large corporations have formal organizational ethics and compliance programs, including toll-free phone lines and other anonymous means for employees to ask questions, gain clarification, or report suspicious behavior. These programs are designed to facilitate internal whistle-blowing, as they engender a more ethical organizational culture and provide mechanisms for monitoring and supporting appropriate behavior. Thus, an effective ethics and legal compliance program should provide employees and other stakeholders with opportunities to make possible transgressions known (e.g., ethics hotline, open-door policy, and strong ethical climate).

The federal government and most state governments in the United States have enacted measures to protect whistle-blowers from retaliation. For example, the Whistleblower Protection Act of 1986 shields federal employees from retaliatory behavior. The Sarbanes-Oxley Act provides solid protection to whistle-blowers and strong penalties for those who retaliate against them. Other legislation actually rewards whistle-blowers for revealing illegal behavior. Under the False Claims Act of 1986, an individual who reports fraud perpetrated against the federal government may receive between 15 and 25 percent of the proceeds if a suit is brought against the perpetrator.

Ethical Issues

Laws are imperative for social responsibility. The ethical climate of the workplace, however, is more subjective and dependent on top management leadership and corporate culture. In this section, we examine several trends in employment practices that have not fully reached the legal realm. Company initiatives in these areas indicate a corporate philosophy or culture that respects and promotes certain ethical values.

Training and Development As discussed in the business ethics chapters, organizational culture and the associated values, beliefs, and norms operate on many levels and affect a number of workplace practices. Some organizations value employees as individuals, not just "cogs in a wheel." Firms with this ethical stance fund initiatives to develop employees' skills, knowledge, and other personal characteristics. Although this development is linked to business strategy and aids the employer, it also demonstrates a commitment to the future of the employee and his or her interests. The Cracker Barrel restaurant chain offers Spanish-speaking employees a program to help them learn English. The interactive kit utilizes a laptop and microphone. Employees complete the six-level program at home.[74]

Professionals also appreciate and respect a training and development focus from their employers. For example, the Los Angeles–based law firm of Latham & Watkins launched a series of initiatives, including "Latham & Watkins University," for first- and fourth-year associates. This training program covers legal updates, professional skill development, and information on career management and planning. Other law firms have upgraded their development opportunities, including mentoring programs, sabbaticals, and feedback sessions

> "There is a link between investments in employees and the amount of commitment, job satisfaction, and productivity demonstrated by them."

for commenting on firm policies and procedures.[75] These firms are finding many benefits of employee training and development, including stronger employee recruitment and retention outcomes.

Indeed, there is a link between investments in employees and the amount of commitment, job satisfaction, and productivity demonstrated by them. Happier employees tend to stay with their employers and to better serve coworkers, customers, and other constituents, which has a direct bearing on the quality of relationships and financial prospects of a firm. Leadership training is also critical, as the main reason employees leave a company is because of poor or unskilled leadership, not salary, benefits, or related factors. In exit interviews, departing employees often mention their desire for more meaningful feedback and steady communication with managers.[76]

Employees recognize when a company is diligently investing in programs that not only improve operations but also increase empowerment and provide new opportunities to gain knowledge and grow professionally. Through formal training and development classes, workers get a better sense of where they fit and how they contribute to the overall organization. This understanding empowers them to become more responsive, accurate, and confident in workplace decisions. Training also increases conflict resolution skills, accountability, and responsibility, a situation most employees prefer to micromanaging or "hand-holding." All these effects contribute to the financial and cultural health of an organization.[77] Thus, a commitment to training enables a firm to enhance its organizational capacity to fulfill stakeholder expectations.

Training and development activities require resources and the commitment of all managers to be successful. For example, a departmental manager must be supportive of an employee using part of the workday to attend a training session on a new software package. At the same time, the organization must pay for the training, regardless of whether it uses inside or outside trainers and develops in-house materials or purchases them from educational providers. A study by the American Society for Training and Development indicates that, on average, employers in developed countries spend about $630 per employee on training every year. Survey respondents in Latin America reported spending the least per employee ($311), whereas their Middle Eastern counterparts reported the highest rate per employee ($783). Companies in all regions indicated they were training more employees than ever before, with an average of 76.7 percent of employees being trained in a given year. Australia and New Zealand had the highest figures, with over 90 percent of all employees receiving training in those surveyed companies.

Despite the differences in training expenditures, the types of training programs and workplace practices in effect in all countries are remarkably similar. Managerial skills, supervisory strategies, information technology skills, occupational safety and compliance, and customer relations are the primary topics of training programs everywhere.[78] Another area that has received much attention in the United States but less focus in other countries involves the diverse nature of today's workforce.

workplace diversity
initiatives focused on recruiting and retaining a diverse workforce as a business imperative

Diversity Whereas Title VII of the Civil Rights Act grants legal protection to different types of employees, initiatives in **workplace diversity** focus on recruiting and retaining a diverse workforce as a business imperative.[79] With diversity programs, companies assume an ethical obligation to employ and empower individuals regardless of age, gender, ethnicity, physical or mental ability, or other characteristics. These firms go beyond compliance with government guidelines to develop cultures that respect and embrace the unique skills, backgrounds, and contributions of all types of people. Thus, legal statutes focus on removing discrimination, whereas diversity represents a leadership approach for cultivating and appreciating employee talent.[80] Firms with an effective diversity effort link their diversity mission statement with the corporate strategic plan, implement plans to recruit and retain a diverse talent pool, support community programs of diverse groups, hold management accountable for various types of diversity performance, and have tangible outcomes of the diversity strategy. Each firm must tailor its diversity initiative to meet unique employee, market, and industry conditions.[81]

Many firms embrace employee diversity to deal with supplier and customer diversity. Their assumption is that to effectively design, market, and support products for different target groups, a company must employ individuals who reflect its customers' characteristics.[82] Organizations and industries with a population-wide customer base may use national demographics for assessing their diversity effort. For example, the Newspaper Association of America implemented a minority recruitment and diversity strategy to help the industry better align staff demographics to community demographics. A study in the newspaper industry found that although racial and ethnic minorities make up nearly 30 percent of the U.S. population, fewer than 12 percent of all news reporters fall into that category. This finding prompted the National Association of Black Journalists to call for greater attention to diversity in the newsroom. Several years later, the Scripps Howard Foundation, associated with the Cincinnati media conglomerate, funded a media school at Hampton University, a historically African American school in Virginia.[83]

After the 2000 U.S. census data were released, some companies began to reconsider marketing strategy, including the link between employee and customer characteristics. For example, census data revealed sharp growth in the Hispanic population and, for some firms, prompted hiring of Hispanic employees and consultants. Frito-Lay introduced Guacamole Chips after its diverse product team tapped into the ideas and perspectives of the company's Latino/Hispanic Advisory Board and Hispanic Employee Network.[84]

As we discussed in Chapter 1, there are opportunities to link social responsibility objectives with business performance, and many firms are learning the benefits of employing individuals with different backgrounds and perspectives. For example, at New York Life, diversity is treated like all other business goals. The company employs a chief diversity officer to create accountability and inclusion strategies with employees, suppliers, community members, and other stakeholders.[85] Even small businesses are discovering these advantages. Global Products, Inc. makes a point of hiring mentally challenged workers, especially those who have suffered head injuries. The company has established a flexible workplace that designs jobs around workers' abilities instead of trying to fit the person into a job description. By partnering with the Center for Head Injury Services, Global Products has been richly rewarded with loyal, creative, hardworking employees

"This is the first time in history that the workforce has been composed of so many generations at one time."

who stay for years and enhance the company's culture of social responsibility.[86] Verizon, a global provider of wireless communication services, is also committed to including people with disabilities into the workplace. The company was recently named Private-Sector Employer of the Year by *CAREERS and the disABLED* magazine, a publication that provides career advice for people with disabilities. In addition, Verizon's outreach manager at the Verizon Center for Customers with Disabilities received the magazine's employee of the year award for his use of Verizon's technology to enable customers while creating employment opportunities.[87]

Conflicting views and voices of different generations abound in the workplace, and this is the first time in history that the workforce has been composed of so many generations at one time. Generations have worked together in the past, but these groups were usually divided by organizational stratification. Many workplaces now include members of multiple generations sitting side by side and working shoulder to shoulder. The result may be greater dissension among the age groups than when they were stratified by the organizational hierarchy. Because employees serve an important role in the social responsibility framework, managers need to be aware of generational differences and their potential effects on teamwork, conflict, and other workplace behaviors. Table 7.7 lists the four generations in today's workplace as well as their key characteristics.

Veterans tend to bring stability and loyalty to the workplace. Although veterans are very hardworking and detail oriented, they are often uncomfortable with conflict and ambiguity and reluctant to buck the system. The baby boomers are service oriented, good team players, and want to please. However, they are also known for being self-centered, overly sensitive to feedback, and not budget minded. People in Generation X are adaptable, technologically literate, independent, and not intimidated by authority. However, their liabilities include impatience, cynicism, and inexperience. The latest generation to enter

Table 7.7 Profiles of Generations at Work

Generation Name	Birth Years	Key Characteristics
Veterans	1922–1943	Hardworking, detail-oriented, uncomfortable with conflict
Baby boomers	1943–1960	Service-oriented, good team players, sensitive to feedback
Generation X	1960–1980	Adaptable, independent, impatient
Millennials (Generation Y)	After 1980	Optimistic, technologically and financially savvy, need supervision, multitaskers

Source: Ron Zemke, Claire Raines, and Bob Filipczak, *Generations at Work: Managing the Clash of Veterans, Boomers, Xers, and Nexters in Your Workplace* (New York: AMACOM, 2000).

the workforce, the Nexters or the Millennials, is technologically savvy. They also bring the assets of collective action, optimism, multitasking ability, and tenacity to the workplace. However, they bring the liabilities of inexperience, especially with difficult people issues, and a need for supervision and structure.

Although generational issues existed in the workforce in the 1920s and the 1960s, there are some new twists today. The older generations no longer have all the money and power. Times of anxiety and uncertainty can aggravate differences and generational conflict, and these conflicts need to be handled correctly when they occur. Understanding the different generations and how they see things is a crucial part of handling this conflict. The authors of *Generations at Work: Managing the Clash of Veterans, Boomers, Xers, and Nexters in Your Workplace* developed the ACORN acronym to describe five principles that managers can use to deal with generational issues. **A**ccommodating employee differences entails treating employees as customers and giving them the best service that the company can give. **C**reating workplace choices as to what and how employees work can allow for change and satisfaction. **O**perating from a sophisticated management style requires that management be direct but tactful. **R**especting competence and initiative assumes the best from the different generations and responds accordingly. **N**ourishing retention means keeping the best employees. When combined with effective communication efforts, the ACORN principles can help managers mend generational conflicts for the benefit of everyone in the company.[88]

Although workplace diversity reaps benefits for both employees and employers, it also brings challenges that must be addressed. For example, diverse employees may have more difficulty communicating and working with each other. Although differences can breed innovation and creativity, they can also create an atmosphere of distrust, dissatisfaction, or lack of cooperation.[89] Many companies found a way to turn fear and confusion over the September 11, 2001, terrorist strikes into an opportunity for discussing diversity and creating stronger bonds among employees of different ethnicities, religions, beliefs, and experiences related to the strikes. Other firms engage employees in community service projects and similar initiatives that promote teamwork and cohesion and help to minimize any negative effects of diversity.

Finally, the diversity message will not be taken seriously unless top management and organizational systems fully support a diverse workforce. After Home Depot settled a gender-discrimination lawsuit, it developed an automated hiring and promotion computer program. Although the Job Preference Program (JPP) was originally intended as insurance against discrimination, the system opens all jobs and applicants to the companywide network, eliminates unqualified applications, and enables managers to learn employee aspirations and skills in a more effective manner. JPP has also brought positive change to the number of female and minority managers within Home Depot.[90] In contrast to this success story, some employees of companies with diversity training programs have viewed such training as intended to blame or change white men only. Other training has focused on the reasons diversity should be important, not the actual changes in attitudes, work styles, expectations, and business processes that are needed for diversity to work.[91]

DuPont employees appreciate the variety of work-life programs available at the company's diverse locations, including the Chamber Works plant in New Jersey

Work-Life Balance A recent in-depth study focused on two women and their career and family progression over sixteen years. Both women had great work achievements in their twenties and later decided to marry, have children, and devote more time to family than career. From this study and many others, the authors note the inherent trade-offs between work and family life. They conclude that most working women are typically forced to make tough trade-offs among career goals, child rearing, household management, and economic realities. These are difficult decisions for everyone, thus giving rise to potential stress and conflict at home and work.[92]

Just as increasing numbers of women in the workplace have changed the norms of behavior at work and prompted attention to sexual harassment, they have also brought challenges in work-life balance. This balance is not just an issue for women, as men also have multiple roles that can create the same types of stress and conflict.[93] The work-life balance may take another form, such as people who are torn between work and home on a regular basis. Employees who think about work (or actually work) when at home, and vice versa, are ultimately struggling with multiple responsibilities.[94]

Because employees have roles within and outside the organization, there is increasing corporate focus on the types of support that employees have in balancing these obligations. Deloitte & Touche (now part of Deloitte Touche Tohmatsu), an international professional services firm, recently came to grips with issues of work-life balance when it discovered the alarming rate at which women were leaving the firm. In the early 1990s, only four of the fifty employees being considered for partner status were women, despite the company's heavy recruitment of women from business schools. A closer examination of the company's turnover rate also illuminated the gender issue, although many executives assumed the women had left to have and raise children. The company convened the Initiative for the Retention and Advancement of Women task force and soon uncovered cultural beliefs and practices that needed modification. The task force found that younger employees—both male and female—wanted a balanced life, were willing to forgo some pay for more time with family and less stress, and had similar career goals. Thus, Deloitte & Touche set out to change its culture and operating practices so that all employees were given similar opportunities and to ensure that concerns and issues were open for discussion. A major initiative included reduced travel schedules and flexible work arrangements to benefit both male and female employees of the firm.

According to a recent survey, issues related to telecommuting, flexible scheduling, and assistance with child care and elder care are almost equally important to male and female employees. Whereas men rarely utilized these benefits in the past, this is no longer the case. Many midlevel executives, both male and female, are part of dual-earner couples "sandwiched" between raising children and caring for aging parents.[95]

Such **work-life programs** assist employees in balancing work responsibilities with personal and family responsibilities. A central feature of these programs is flexibility so that employees of all types are able to achieve their own definition of balance. For example, a single parent may want child care and consistent work hours, whereas another employee may need assistance in finding elder care for a parent with Alzheimer's disease. A working mother may need access to "just-in-time" care when a child is sick or school is out of session. Employees of all types appreciate flextime arrangements, which allow them to work forty hours per week on a schedule they develop within a range of hours specified by the company. Other employees work some hours at home or in a location more conducive to their personal obligations. DuPont, for example, has been recognized by *Working Mother* magazine for its exceptional flexibility to support work-life balance. At nearly all of its eighty-five locations, DuPont's employees enjoy compressed scheduling, telecommuting, job sharing, and other arrangements. More than half of DuPont's 28,000 employees use a flextime arrangement. The company has installed data lines to support employee telecommuting, which benefits nearly one-third of its workforce.[96] Work-life balance not only enhances employee productivity, but it is also an imperative to attracting and maintaining a healthy workforce.

> **"Managers must become sensitive to cues that employees need to create a stronger work-life balance."**

More than 65 million Americans suffer from symptoms of stress at work, including headaches, sleeplessness, and other physical ailments. To remedy these concerns, Americans spend more than $370 million per year on stress-reducing products, services, and strategies. Compared to Japanese workers, however, the U.S. figures are moderate. A study by the Japanese government found that nearly 60 percent of Japanese employees feel fairly fatigued from work, whereas less than 30 percent of U.S. workers feel the same way. Nearly 10,000 Japanese men die every year as a result of job-related stressors, physical problems, and associated psychological ramifications. The Japanese Ministry of Health, Labour and Welfare recently proposed legislation that would require companies to encourage employees to take breaks for holidays and vacations.[97]

Managers must become sensitive to cues that employees need to create a stronger work-life balance. Frustration, anger, moodiness, a myopic focus, and physiological symptoms are often present when an employee needs to take vacation, work fewer hours, utilize flexible scheduling, or simply reduce his or her workload. One manager of a telecommunications firm in California returned to the workplace around 11:30 P.M. every night to send people home. Otherwise, she knew many of them would sleep on the floor in the office. Not only do some

work-life programs programs to assist employees in balancing work responsibilities with personal and family responsibilities

employees work too many hours, but they may largely ignore nutrition and fitness, friendships, community involvement, and other aspects of work-life balance.[98]

There is no generic work-life program. Instead, companies need to consider their employee base and the types of support their employees are likely to need and appreciate. For the employees of SAS Institute, the world's largest private software company, the workplace resembles a modern-day utopia. Although the North Carolina company competes with Silicon Valley firms, its workplace bears little resemblance to the demanding atmosphere that often characterizes high-tech companies. James Goodnight, SAS's founder, believes that dinnertime should be spent with family and friends, not in the office. Most employees leave by 5:00 P.M., and others participate in flextime or job-sharing arrangements. Other perks, such as on-site day care and a health center staffed with dentists and physicians, also contribute to the company's high ranking on *Fortune* magazine's annual list of the 100 Best Companies to Work For. The company has also been named to *Working Mother* magazine's 100 Best Companies for Working Mothers.[99]

Successful work-life programs, like that developed by the SAS Institute, are an extension of the diversity philosophy so that employees are respected as individuals in the process of contributing to company goals. Thus, connecting employees' personal needs, lives, and goals to strategic business issues can be fruitful for both parties. This perspective is in contrast to the "employee goals versus business goals" trade-off mentality that has been pervasive. IBM implemented a work-life strategy over two decades ago and periodically conducts employee surveys to see if changes or additions are needed.[100]

A study by jobtrack.com found that nearly 50 percent of all applicants consider work-life balance the most important consideration in identifying potential employers and considering job offers.[101] For this reason, companies have become quite innovative in their approach to work-life balance. Management consulting firm Booz Allen Hamilton, for example, provides up to $5,000 per child in adoption benefits and also covers up to four in vitro fertilization attempts.[102] Texas Instruments holds summer camps for employees' children at its Dallas headquarters and two other locations. For a reasonable fee, each child is involved in supervised and educational field trips, arts and crafts, sports, community projects, and other fun activities, which eases parents' worries about dependable child care and aids in children's personal development.[103] Such efforts demonstrate the company's willingness to accommodate employee needs and responsibilities beyond the workplace.

Philanthropic Issues

In Chapter 9, we examine the philanthropic efforts of companies and the important role that employees play in the process of selecting and implementing projects that contribute time, resources, and human activity to worthy causes. In social responsibility, philanthropic responsibilities are primarily directed outside the organization, so they are not directly focused on employees. However, employees benefit from participating in volunteerism and other philanthropic projects. A recent study by the Points of Light Foundation asked corporate executives about the effect of employee volunteerism on organizational competitiveness and success. The surveyed executives reported that this aspect of philanthropy increases employee productivity and builds teamwork skills. In a tight job market, employees may even view philanthropic activity, such as volunteer opportunities, as an important criterion in evaluating potential employers.[104]

Many employers help organize employees to participate in walkathons, marathons, bikeathons, and similar events. The executive vice president of FedEx Kinkos, now FedEx Office, Ken May, says, "The esprit de corps it builds is incredible." While employees exercise and feel a part of the "team," charitable organizations also benefit financially, as these types of events raise over $1 billion annually.[105] Thus, the benefits of corporate philanthropy in the community reflect back positively on the organization.

There are many strategies for demonstrating community involvement and care. McDonald's launched a series of websites intended to serve both employment needs and community relations goals. On a state-by-state basis, the venerable fast-food chain set up sites, such as www.McWisconsin.com and www.McMinnesota.com, to aid both corporate and local franchisees' ability to hire new employees, educate consumers, deliver promotional materials, and reach other business goals. McDonald's released its first corporate responsibility report in 2004 and continues to release a report every year. These reports include a section on the ways in which the company and its franchises positively affect local communities. A recent report stated "For McDonald's, giving back comes in many shapes and sizes. . . . Whatever shape it takes, the intent remains the same—to make a positive difference in the lives of our customers and the communities where we operate."[106]

STRATEGIC IMPLEMENTATION OF RESPONSIBILITIES TO EMPLOYEES

As this chapter has demonstrated, responsibilities toward employees are varied and complex. Legal issues alone require full-time attention from lawyers and human resource specialists. These issues are also emotional because corporate decisions have ramifications on families and communities as well as on employees. In light of this complexity, many companies have chosen to embrace these obligations to benefit both employee and organizational goals. This philosophy stands in stark contrast to the master-servant model popular more than 100 years ago. Today, companies are using distinctive programs and initiatives to set themselves apart and to become known as desirable employers.

Low unemployment levels in the late 1990s, along with diversity, work-life balance, outsourcing, and generational differences, prompted companies to use marketing strategy and business insight normally applied to customer development in the employee recruitment and retention realm. Even in a time of economic downturn, employers will need to be mindful of keeping top talent and maintaining employee satisfaction. For example, Small Dog Electronics, a small Vermont retailer, offers a rather unusual perk to satisfy and retain its fourteen employees: dog insurance. The firm allows employees to bring their dogs to work and picks up 80 percent of veterinarians' bills, minus a deductible. Along with this perk, Small Dog focuses on multiple stakeholders and was recently awarded a Better Business Bureau Local Torch Award for Excellence for its ethical company practices. T3, an integrated marketing agency, also has a pet-friendly workplace and other types of progressive policies. "T3 and Under" is the name of the agency's family-friendly work program. At this firm based in Austin, Texas, employees bring their babies to work, which relieves the stress of finding trustworthy and reliable daycare for infants. The program also enables employees to return to work more quickly after a child is born. By its tenth anniversary, 46 babies, 30 mothers, and 10 fathers had gone through the T3 and Under program. As these examples illustrate, a company's policies may differentiate its work environment and create a unique organizational culture that employees prefer over those of other employers.[107]

An **employer of choice** is an organization of any size in any industry that is able to attract, optimize, and retain the best employee talent over the long term. ENSR, a European environmental consulting firm, created a cross-functional and geographically diverse committee to provide guidance for maintaining and strengthening the company's positive culture. The committee focuses on ways in which ENSR's top management can ensure that integrity, respect, open communications, flexibility, and balance are the key values and defining qualities of every ENSR career. Essentially, ENSR is taking great strides to recruit and retain a talented workforce.[108]

Advertising, websites, and other company communications often use the term *employer of choice* to describe and market the organization to current and potential employees. These messages center on the various practices that companies have implemented to create employee satisfaction. Firms with this distinction value the human component of business, not just financial considerations, ensure that employees are engaged in meaningful work, and stimulate the intellectual curiosity of employees. These businesses have strong training practices, delegate authority, and recognize the link between employee morale, customer satisfaction, and other performance measures.[109] Thus, becoming an employer of choice is an important manifestation of strategic social responsibility.

"Potential employees may look for signs that social responsibility is a top concern."

Potential employees may look for signs that social responsibility is a top concern. For example, recent college graduates often evaluate a potential employer's socially responsible and ethical behavior when deciding on a career path. Table 7.8 shows the percentage of college graduates who indicated they were not willing to work for a company that committed certain actions. The table provides results from college graduates in both 1982 and 2008 and demonstrates the trend toward individuals avoiding potential employers with known ethical problems.

Despite the negative effects that certain actions may have on perceptions of a company's social responsibility, there are strategies and programs that demonstrate a proactive approach to employee relations. One traditional way to strengthen trust is through employee stock ownership plans (ESOPs), which provide the opportunity both to contribute to and gain from organizational success. Such programs confer not only ownership but also opportunities for employees

employer of choice an organization of any size in any industry that is able to attract, optimize, and retain the best employee talent over the long term

Home Versus Work

While people around the world have taken steps to reduce their environmental impact at home, a key concern for many companies is whether employees are taking similar actions in the workplace. Results from a recent Gallup Environmental Poll indicate that 55 percent of Americans have made minor lifestyle changes to help protect the environment. Approximately 30 percent of Americans say that they have made major changes in terms of their living and shopping habits out of concern for the environment. However, these personal changes have not fully transitioned into the office.

A recent survey found that while at home, 94 percent of those people surveyed switch off lights and 85 percent switch off their home PC when not in use. But when asked about these actions in the workplace, few people stated that these green practices are carried out in the office. One reason for this "green divide" is that employees can't see the impact their actions have on their workplace, making them feel disconnected from effects of their green efforts. Such split attitudes between work and home can perhaps be explained by the fact that just under half of all those surveyed believed their employer only pays lip service to environmental issues, or is simply not interested in them at all.

This belief is supported by the research which found that three quarters of employers provide bins and facilities for recycling paper, but don't use recycled materials themselves. While staff usually has access to double-sided printing and copying machines, less than a quarter have been offered training in using the equipment. When employees were questioned about the environmental impact of their own organizations, 49 percent of staff believed their company wastes too much electricity and should put programs in place to help save resources and promote sustainability in the work place.

Companies that have successfully transitioned these efforts have found that a green workplace results in more productivity and increased employee engagement, and also reinforces a more socially responsible workplace. The challenge to successfully establishing a green-friendly environment is balancing leadership guidance with ownership and customization at the local level. In order to engage employees on environmental issues, Yahoo launched a "Green Screen," an interactive display that monitors live energy use at the company's Sunnyvale headquarters. It's located in Yahoo's cafeteria for employees to see, touch, and follow along with real-time updates on energy use at the campus. The Green Screen gives users the ability to see, for example, how many pounds of carbon have been emitted per person on the Sunnyvale campus. Employees will also be able to see energy consumption across buildings and compare trends viewed over time. In addition, Yahoo provides green tips on commute options and where to shop for green products.

Sources: Gallup Environmental Poll, April 18, 2008; "Gallup's Pulse of Democracy, The Environment," http://www.gallup.com/poll/1615/Environment.aspx?version=print, accessed May 17, 2009; Logicalis Group, "Switched On, Turned Off? Environmental Attitudes at Home and Work," Survey 2007, http://www.logicalis.com/news/2007-01-15.asp; "Deliotte Offers How-To on Taking 'Green' to Work," Sustainable Life Media, http://www.sustainablelifemedia.com, October 29, 2008; "Yahoo's Launches 'Green Screen' Energy-Use Monitor," Environmental Leader, March 3, 2008.

NASA

Table 7.8 Graduating Student Survey: Not Willing to Work for Certain Employers

Employer Action	2008 Graduates	1982 Graduates
1. Producing a harmful product	59%	42%
2. Paying women or minorities less	46%	28%
3. Using lie detector for theft	40%	45%
4. Paying off foreign officials	22%	18%
5. Restricting foreign competition	9%	4%

Sources: "Ethics as Recruiting Tool," *Journal of Accountancy 207* (January 2009): 21; *Moving On: Student Approaches and Attitudes Toward the Job Market for the College Class of 2008*, National Association of Colleges and Employers, www.naceweb.org, accessed March 18, 2009; Edwin L. Koc, "The Oldest Young Generation—A Report from the 2008 'NACE Graduating Student Survey,'" *NACE Journal 68* (May 2008): 23–28.

to participate in management planning, which fosters an environment that many organizations believe increases profits.

Several studies of companies with ESOPs cast a positive light on these plans. ESOPs appear to increase sales by about 2.3 to 2.4 percent over what would have been expected without an ESOP. ESOP companies were also found to pay better benefits, higher wages, and provide nearly twice the retirement income for employees than their non-ESOP counterparts. Under these plans, employees must take on an ownership perspective, work as a team in an environment that forges trust, and provide excellent interactions and service to customers. Some of the 10,000 "employee-owned" firms include Lowe's, Acadian Ambulance, Publix Supermarkets, Procter & Gamble, Hallmark Cards, and Ferrellgas. Of *Fortune* magazine's 100 Best Companies to Work For (2009), nearly 15 percent are employee-owned.

Results from the Employee Ownership Foundation's 17th Annual ESOP Economic Performance Survey indicate that the decision to become an employee-owned company enhances company performance and provides higher wealth accumulation for employee owners. Nearly 93 percent of those surveyed indicated that creating an ESOP was "a good business decision that has helped the company." ESOPs are associated with stronger employee loyalty and lower employee turnover rates.[110] Despite the advantages of ESOPs, experts also warn that some plans are potentially risky for employees, as in the case of Enron.[111] Just like any other company initiative, management must take responsibility for managing an ESOP well.

Becoming an employer of choice has many benefits, including an enhanced ability to hire and retain the best people, who in turn offer strong commitment to the company mission and its stakeholders. The expectations of such businesses are very high because employee stakeholders often have specific criteria in mind when assessing the attractiveness of a particular employer. Some people may be focused on specific environmental issues, whereas others may be searching for a company that markets healthy and helpful products.

Although top managers must decide on how the firm will achieve strategic social responsibility with employees, Table 7.9 provides guidance on eight key principles that are typically exhibited and managed by employers of choice. Most companies have long understood the importance of attracting and keeping

Table 7.9 Key Principles of Employers of Choice

Principle	Explanation
1. Company image	Employees prefer to work in a company with a good reputation that is respected by various stakeholders.
2. Organizational culture	Employees want the company culture to reflect strong values, high standards, and a sense of community.
3. Respected leadership	Employees expect ethical and visible leaders who can successfully navigate the company into the future.
4. Caring of people	Employees seek a company that demonstrates commitment to managing quality of life and work-life balance issues.
5. Growth and opportunity	Employees are motivated by personal and professional growth opportunities, including company training programs.
6. Meaningful work	Employees strive to be actively engaged, involved, and must see value in their work contributions.
7. Compensation and benefits	Employees want equitable pay but also examine the total compensation package, including broad benefits.
8. Making a difference	Employees want to work for companies that have a social conscience.

Sources: Barbara J. Bowen, "Being an Employer of Choice Has Bottom-Line Benefits," *CMA Management 82* (November 2008): 14–15; "Main Page," Employer of Choice.net, http://www.employerofchoice.net/, accessed August 17, 2009; Roger E. Herman and Joyce L. Gioia, *How to Become an Employer of Choice* (Winchester, VA: Oakhill Press, 2000).

customers through strong branding efforts, but many are newer to the idea and implementation of similar strategies to create an employer brand.[112]

Finally, the global dimensions of today's workplace shape an organization's ability to effectively work with employee stakeholders and to become an employer of choice. Firms with offices and sites around the world must deal with a complexity of norms and expectations, all of which can affect their reputations at home.

For example, when Nike was first accused of dealing with suppliers that used child labor in the mid-1990s, the company claimed that it was not in the business of manufacturing shoes and that it could therefore not be blamed for the practices of Asian manufacturers. Following media criticism, Nike publicized a report claiming that the employees of its Indonesian and Vietnamese suppliers were living quite well. The veracity of this report was tarnished by contradictory evidence produced by activists. Next, Nike started introducing workers' rights and environmental guidelines for its suppliers. Yet some company representatives explained that any additional social responsibility initiative would damage the competitive position of the firm. In the late 1990s, Nike designed a suppliers' auditing process that invited student representatives along with other activists to visit manufacturing plants and provide recommendations for better practice. Before the company's shift, many media reports discussed Nike's manufacturing practices, and it is likely that some consumers and potential employees turned their attention away from Nike. Nike actually settled the legal case that rose all the way to the Supreme Court. Nike agreed to pay $1.5 million to the Fair Labor Association to help fund worker development programs. In this case, Nike's relationships with its manufacturing suppliers and their employees affected its ability to achieve strategic social responsibility.[113]

SUMMARY

Throughout history, people's perceptions of work and employment have evolved from a necessary evil to a source of fulfillment. The relationship between employer and employee involves responsibilities, obligations, and expectations as well as challenges.

On an economic level, many believe there is an unwritten, informal psychological contract that includes the beliefs, perceptions, expectations, and obligations that make up the agreement between individuals and their employers. This contract has evolved from a primarily master-servant relationship, in which employers held the power, to one in which employees assume a more balanced relationship with employers. Workforce reduction, the process of eliminating employment positions, breaches the psychological contract that exists between an employer and employee and threatens the social contract among employers, communities, and other groups. Although workforce reduction lowers costs, it often results in lost intellectual capital, strained customer relationships, negative media attention, and other issues that drain company resources.

Employment law is a complex and ever-evolving area. In the past, employment was primarily governed by employment at will, a common-law doctrine that allows either the employer or employee to terminate the relationship at any time as long as it does not violate an employment contract. Many laws have been enacted to regulate business conduct with regard to wages and benefits, labor unions, health and safety, equal employment opportunity, sexual harassment, and whistle-blowing. Title VII of the Civil Rights Act, which prohibits employment discrimination on the basis of race, national origin, color, religion, and gender, is fundamental to employees' rights to join and advance in an organization according to merit. Sexual harassment is defined as unwelcome sexual advances, requests for sexual favors, and other verbal or physical conduct of a sexual nature when submission to or rejection of this conduct explicitly or implicitly affects an individual's employment, unreasonably interferes with an individual's work performance, or creates an intimidating, hostile, or offensive work environment. Sexual harassment may take the form of either quid pro quo harassment or hostile work environment harassment. An employee who reports individual or corporate wrongdoing to either internal or external sources is considered a whistle-blower.

Although legal compliance is imperative for social responsibility, the ethical climate of the workplace is more subjective and dependent on top management support and corporate culture. Companies with a strong ethical stance fund initiatives to develop employees' skills, knowledge, and other personal characteristics. With diversity programs, companies assume an ethical obligation to employ and empower individuals regardless of age, gender, physical and mental ability, and other characteristics. Work-life programs assist employees in balancing work responsibilities with personal and family responsibilities.

Employees may play an important role in a firm's philanthropic efforts. Employees benefit from such initiatives through participation in volunteerism and other projects.

In light of the complexity of and emotions involved with responsibilities toward employees, many companies have chosen to embrace these obligations to benefit both employee and organizational goals. An employer of choice is an organization of any size in any industry that is able to attract, optimize, and retain the best employee talent over the long term. One traditional way to strengthen trust is through ESOPs, which provide the opportunity both to contribute to and gain from organizational success. Finally, the global dimensions of today's workplace shape an organization's ability to effectively work with employee stakeholders and to become an employer of choice.

RESPONSIBLE BUSINESS DEBATE

Employing Undocumented Immigrant Workers

ISSUE: Immigration and Employment

One spring morning, U.S. Immigration and Customs Enforcement (ICE) agents raided the offices of IFCO Systems. Seven executives were arrested and many employees were handed deportation orders. The executives were charged with conspiracy to transport, harbor, and encourage illegal aliens to reside in the United States for commercial advantage and private financial gain. The federal government alleges that IFCO was able to produce record profits because it heavily utilized an illegal workforce. The company claims that many of these workers produced fraudulent or altered documentation when they were hired. The government insists that illegal aliens were a fundamental part of IFCO's business plan and that working conditions were unsafe. With the IFCO incident, top government officials declared a heightened enforcement strategy against companies that violate immigration law.

IFCO is not alone. Wal-Mart stores agreed to pay $11 million to settle allegations that the company knowingly contracted with cleaning services that employed illegal immigrants. The charges also pointed to the mistreatment of the workers, including long working hours and few breaks. The case came to light when these employees filed a civil suit against Wal-Mart, demanding to be paid for overtime they allegedly worked for the contractor.

Because of these cases and others like them, a national debate was forged on the topic of immigration and employment. Business owners often claim that undocumented workers will take jobs that U.S. citizens refuse to consider and, therefore, are adding positively to business and the economy. Employee rights advocates question whether these workers are taking jobs away from U.S. citizens and whether they are paid fairly and treated well. Relatives of illegal aliens do not understand the reasoning behind the law, as they are often supported by lucrative wages sent to them from the United States.

There Are Two Sides to Every Issue:

1. Defend the belief of some employers that hiring undocumented foreign workers is in the best interests of the potential employees, their families, employers, and the economy. What are the benefits and risks to this approach?

2. Defend the government's right to restrict who works in a particular nation. What would happen if the government created a path to legal status for many of the nation's unauthorized immigrants?

Sources: Nicole Gaouette, "What Was Behind the Big Raid," *Los Angeles Times*, April 22, 2006, p. A1; Abigil Goldman, "Wal-Mart Looks to Polish Image, but Detractors Gear Up, Too," *Los Angeles Times*, April 19, 2006, p. C1; Armando Villafranca, "Raided Company Says Hirers Duped by Fake ID Papers," *Houston Chronicle*, April 22, 2006, p. 1.

KEY TERMS

psychological contract (p. 240)
workforce reduction (p. 244)
employment at will (p. 248)
vesting (p. 250)
ergonomics (p. 251)
sexual harassment (p. 255)

quid pro quo sexual harassment (p. 256)
hostile work environment sexual harassment
   (p. 256)
workplace diversity (p. 260)
work-life programs (p. 264)
employer of choice (p. 266)

DISCUSSION QUESTIONS

1. Review Table 7.1, which illustrates changes in employees' psychological contract with employers. Create additional columns to indicate the positive and negative effects associated with the "old" and "new" contract characteristics. For example, what is positive and negative about the belief that employees should follow orders? What is positive and negative about giving 110 percent effort on the job?

2. What is workforce reduction? How does it affect employees, consumers, and the local community? What steps should a company take to address these effects?

3. What responsibilities do companies have with respect to workplace violence? Using the three categories of violence presented in the chapter, describe the responsibilities and actions that you believe are necessary for an organization to demonstrate social responsibility in this area.

4. Describe the differences between workplace diversity and equal employment opportunity. How do these differences affect managerial responsibilities and the development of social responsibility programs?

5. Why it is important to understand the profiles of different generations at work? How can managers use the ACORN principles to develop a strong sense of community and solidarity among all employee groups?

6. Why are organizations developing work-life programs? What trends have contributed to these programs?

7. What is an employer of choice? Describe how a firm could use traditional marketing concepts and strategies to appeal to current and potential employees.

8. Review the best practices in Table 7.9 for becoming an employer of choice. What are some potential drawbacks to each practice? Rank the seven practices in terms of their importance to you.

EXPERIENTIAL EXERCISE

Develop a list of five criteria that describe your employer of choice. Then, visit the websites of three companies in which you have some employment interest. Peruse each firm's website to find evidence on how it fulfills your criteria. On the basis of this evidence, develop a chart to show how well each firm meets your description of and criteria for your employer of choice. Finally, provide three recommendations on how these companies could better communicate their commitment and employer of choice criteria to employees.

WHAT WOULD YOU DO?

Dawn Burke, director of employee relations, glanced at her online calendar and remembered her appointment at 3:00 P.M. today. She quickly found the file labeled "McCullen and Aranda" and started preparing for the meeting. She recalled that this was essentially an employee-supervisor case, where the employee had been unwilling or unable to meet the supervisor's requests. The employee claimed that the supervisor was too demanding and impatient. Their conflict had escalated to the point that both were unhappy and uncomfortable in the work environment. Other employees had noticed, and overheard, some of the conflict.

In her role, Dawn was responsible for many programs, including a new mediation initiative to resolve workplace conflict. The program was designed to help employees develop stronger communication and conflict resolution skills. In this case, the program was also providing an intermediary step between informal and formal discipline. Today, she was meeting with both parties to discuss mediation guidelines, a time line, their goal, and their general points of conflict.

John McCullen, fifty-one, a buyer in the facilities department, and Terry Aranda, the director of facilities procurement, arrived separately. John had been with the company for thirty-two years and had started his career with the company right out of high school. Terry, thirty-one, was hired from another firm to oversee the procurement area a year ago and recently graduated from a prestigious MBA program. Dawn started the meeting by reviewing the mediation guidelines and time line. She reminded John and Terry that their goal was to develop a workable and agreeable solution to the current situation. Dawn then asked for each party to explain his or her position on the conflict.

John began, "Ms. Aranda is a very smart lady. She seems to know the buying and procurement area, but she knows less about the company and its history. I am not sure she has taken the time to learn our ways and values. Ms. Aranda is impatient with our use of the new software and computer system. Some of us don't have college degrees, and we haven't been using computers since we were young. I started working at this company about the time she was born, and I am not sure that her management style is good for our department. Everything was going pretty well until we starting changing our systems."

Terry commented, "John is a valuable member of the department, as he knows everyone at this company. I appreciate his knowledge and loyalty. On the other hand, he has not completed several tasks in a timely manner, nor has he asked for an extension. I feel that I must check up on his schedule and proof all of his work. John has attended several training classes, and I asked that he use an electronic calendar so that projects are completed on time. He continues to ignore my advice and deadlines. We've had several conversations, but John's work has not substantially improved. We have many goals to achieve in the department, and I need everyone's best work in order to make that happen."

Dawn thanked them for their candor and told them she would meet with them next week to start the mediation process. As she contemplated what each had said, she remembered an article that discussed how people born in different generations often have contrasting perceptions about work. Dawn started to jot a few notes about the next steps in resolving their conflict. What would you do?

CHAPTER 8

Consumer Relations

Chapter Objectives

- To describe customers as stakeholders

- To investigate consumer protection laws

- To examine six consumer rights

- To discuss the implementation of responsibilities to consumers

Chapter Outline

Consumer Stakeholders

Responsibilities to Consumers

Strategic Implementation of Responsibilities to Consumers

© Tom Tomczyk

Banco Azteca: Banking for All Consumers

Banco Azteca, Mexico's first bank aimed at the country's middle and working class, opened its doors in late 2002. For a security guard and father of four, Humberto Vidal, Banco Azteca is a welcome sight. He received a personal loan of $350 and commented, "Now I have a place where I can go if I need support." Before the bank opened, most Mexican consumers had little access to credit unless they chose to pay exorbitant interest rates. Banco Azteca targets the 73 million people in Mexico who live in households with combined incomes of $250 to $1,300 a month, a market long neglected by Mexico's traditional banking system. Company executives speak of a greater mission than just profit: improving the personal financial situation of millions of Mexican citizens.

Many of the bank's 1,500 branches are located inside the retail stores of Elektra, Salinas & Rocha, and Bodega de Ramates, all owned by Grupo Elektra S.A. de C.V., Latin America's leading specialty retailer and consumer finance company. The retail stores had been providing credit for the poor for decades, so the creation of the bank was a natural progression. Mexican consumers had faith and trust in Grupo Elektra as they tried out its new mechanism, Banco Azteca, to access credit.

In its first few months of operation, Banco Azteca opened nearly 250,000 savings accounts. One customer, Stephanie Diaz, started a savings account with only $5 but planned to have her employer deposit her paycheck with Banco Azteca, some of which would go into the savings account. Consumers who work in the informal business sector, such as taxi drivers, street merchants, and electricians, now have access to loans. Small business owners and would-be entrepreneurs also benefit from Banco Azteca.

In addition to savings accounts and personal loans, Banco Azteca offers car loans, mortgage loans, installment plans, debit cards, and other services. The company is fervent in its belief that low and middle income is not necessarily synonymous with loan defaults and high risk, as long as the right control mechanisms are in place. Banco Azteca's success has lead to more ventures, including locations in Panama, Guatemala, Honduras, and Peru and new operations in Brazil. The bank's business model and focus on the ordinary consumer are consistent with its vision: *Our vision is to develop plain financial products and services to improve the lives of our clients.*"[1]

This vignette illustrates that organizations with profit objectives, operations expertise, customer insights, and related competencies can also be focused on implementing social responsibility and satisfying stakeholder groups. From a social responsibility perspective, the key challenge is how an organization assesses its stakeholders' needs, integrates them with company strategy, reconciles differences between stakeholders' needs, strives for better relationships with stakeholders, achieves mutual understandings with them, and finds solutions for problems. In this chapter, we explore relationships with consumers and the expectations of the economic, legal, ethical, and philanthropic responsibilities that must be addressed by business.

CONSUMER STAKEHOLDERS

For the past twenty years, "green marketing," the promotion of more environmentally friendly products, has become a much-discussed strategy in the package goods industry. Both Energizer and Rayovac, for example, marketed environmentally friendly batteries throughout the 1990s. Today, those products have disappeared from most store shelves, replaced by the alkaline batteries needed to run electronic devices that have become so common for both children and adults. Also in the 1990s, Procter & Gamble (P&G), the venerable manufacturer of soap, paper goods, and other household products, feared that increasing environmental consciousness among consumers would lead to a resurgence in the use of cloth diapers, which would have had a negative effect on its disposable diaper business. P&G launched a marketing campaign touting the benefits of disposables, including the fact that their use does not require hot water for laundering or fuel for diaper service trucks. P&G also initiated a pilot project for composting disposable diapers. Today, the debate over cloth versus disposables has largely faded, and the P&G marketing campaign has disappeared.

The dawn of the twenty-first century brought many new products, including disposable tableware, food containers that can be used repeatedly or thrown away, and electrostatic mops with cloths that are disposed of after one use. Although these product introductions suggest a decline in environmental consciousness among consumers, other initiatives counter this assumption. Whole Foods Markets, a grocery chain that specializes in organic and environmentally friendly items, reports $689 sales per square

> **"Although the future of different marketing strategies can be debated, the real test of effectiveness lies in the expectations, attitudes, and ultimate buying patterns of consumers."**

foot versus the $400 sales per square foot earned by most supermarkets. With nearly 300 stores in North America and the United Kingdom, the company is the world's largest retailer of natural and organic goods and underwrote a thirteen-part PBS special, "Chefs A'Field," to expose consumers to sustainable practices, from the field to the table. Today, the company utilizes a myriad of approaches to reinforce its green philosophy, including blogs, store projects, loans for local producers, selling organic foods, and the use of biodiesel for its trucks.[2]

Indeed, environmental and related social initiatives have become a global phenomenon. One goal of the annual International Buy Nothing Day, sponsored by consumer associations around the world, is to encourage consumers to consider the environmental consequences of their buying habits. The event's organizers remind consumers that the richest 20 percent of people consume 80 percent of the world's resources.[3]

Although the future of different marketing strategies can be debated, the real test of effectiveness lies in the expectations, attitudes, and ultimate buying patterns of consumers. The preceding examples illustrate that there is no true consensus around issues such as environmental responsibility, and companies therefore face complex decisions about how to respond to them. This is true for all types of expectations, including the ones we explore in this chapter. In the sections that follow, we examine the economic, legal, ethical, and philanthropic responsibilities that businesses have to **consumers**, those individuals who purchase, use, and dispose of products for themselves and their homes.

RESPONSIBILITIES TO CONSUMERS

Consumers International, a London-based nonprofit federation of more than 230 consumer organizations and government agencies in 113 countries, is dedicated to protecting and promoting consumers' interests and rights and implementing campaigns and research programs to aid governments, businesses, and nonprofit groups in decision making.[4] The federation sponsors an annual World Consumer Rights Day every March 15 to further solidarity among the global consumer movement by promoting consumer rights, demanding the protection of these rights, and protesting abuses and injustices. Each observance has a particular theme—a pressing issue that is likely to affect a majority of consumers around the world. Issues over the last few years have included unhealthy food for children, access to electricity, genetically modified foods, the safety and affordability of water, the natural environment, the promotion of pharmaceutical drugs, and consumer representation in government decision making. Another recent project evaluated the credibility and integrity of information found on the Internet. Consumers International worked with researchers in thirteen consumer organizations around the world and concluded that most consumers have difficulty evaluating the credibility of information sources on the Web.[5]

Consumer International's many efforts have led to the development of the Consumer Charter for Global Business, which offers guidance on a variety of business practices, including product standards, marketing, service guarantees, information and labeling, consumer complaint procedures, and competitive

consumers
individuals who purchase, use, and dispose of products for themselves and their homes

Figure 8.1 Consumer Charter for Global Business

Intent of This Charter

This Charter was prepared by Consumers International, the international federation of consumer organisations. It is based on the eight consumer rights: the right to basic needs, safety, information, choice, a fair hearing, redress, consumer education, and a healthy environment. The Charter sets out best business practice in areas of interest to consumers such as ethical standards, competition, product standards, marketing, labelling, disclosure of information, and consumer redress. It draws on the experience of consumer organisations and is modelled on existing international codes of practice. The aim of the Charter is to develop corporate practice in light of consumer concerns. The accompanying Charter Assessment Form translates the Charter's principles into practical goals for business. The Form helps assess the company's progress in attaining the standards set by the Charter. The Charter's provisions can also be the basis for national and international regulation of business practices. They provide a focus for consumer education campaigns and highlight how different corporate activities can affect consumer rights.

Source: Consumers International, www.consumersinternational.org, accessed August 17, 2009.

tactics. At a minimum, the charter compels companies to consider their economic relationship with consumers through all stages of the production, distribution, and marketing process; to obey all relevant laws; and to establish clear ethical standards for business practice.[6] Figure 8.1 provides the preamble to the charter, which covers three of the four responsibilities we have discussed throughout this book.

> **"Consumers are primary stakeholders because their awareness, purchase, use, and repurchase of products are vital to a company's existence."**

Economic Issues

As discussed Chapter 2, consumers are primary stakeholders because their awareness, purchase, use, and repurchase of products are vital to a company's existence. Fundamentally, therefore, consumers and businesses are connected by an economic relationship. This relationship begins with an exchange, usually of a good or service for money, which often leads to deeper attachments or affiliation. A well-known advertising campaign slogan, "You are what you drive," typifies the close relationship that some consumers develop with the products they purchase. Other consumers may choose to shun particular brands or opt for the environmentally sensitive products described earlier. In all of these cases, however, consumers expect the products they purchase to perform as guaranteed by their sellers. Thus, a firm's economic responsibilities include following through on promises made in the exchange process.

Although this responsibility seems basic today, business practices have not always been directed in this way. In the early part of the 1900s, the caveat "Let the buyer beware" typified the power that business—not consumers—wielded in most exchange relationships.[7] In less developed parts of the world, this phrase often accurately describes the consumer marketplace. For example, despite recent government regulation, investors in Bangladesh are wary of company prospectuses and other financial documents used to make sound investment decisions. Experts believe that this lack of investor confidence is the primary reason Bangladesh securities markets have not flourished and remain in an embryonic state.[8]

Fulfillment of economic responsibilities depends on interactions with the consumer. However, there are situations in which the consumer does not act as a fair participant in the exchange.[9] **Consumer fraud** involves intentional deception to derive an unfair economic advantage over an organization. Examples of fraudulent activities include shoplifting, collusion or duplicity, and guile. Collusion typically involves an employee who assists the consumer in fraud. For example, a cashier may not scan all merchandise or may give an unwarranted discount. Duplicity may involve a consumer staging an accident in a grocery store and then seeking damages against the store for its lack of attention to safety. A consumer may purchase, wear, and then return an item of clothing for a full refund. In other situations, the consumer may ask for a refund by claiming a defect that either is nonexistent or was caused by consumer misuse.[10]

Although some of these acts warrant legal prosecution, they can be very difficult to prove, and many companies are reluctant to accuse patrons of a crime when there is no way of verifying it. Businesses that operate with the "customer is always right" philosophy have found that some consumers will take advantage of this promise and have therefore modified return policies to curb unfair use. However, some people persist in illegitimate complaining. Table 8.1 describes six motivations that consumers may have when committing this type of behavior.

consumer fraud intentional deception to derive an unfair economic advantage over an organization

Table 8.1 Motivations for Illegitimate Consumer Complaints

Motivationation	Description
Freeloaders	Consumer attempts to obtain free goods or services by making a fraudulent complaint
Fraudulent Return	Consumer buys product and knows that he or she will attempt to return it for a refund
Fault Transferors	Consumer avoids fault by making fraudulent claims and trying to shift responsibility to company
Solitary Ego Gains	While alone, consumer voices illegitimate complaints to enhance his or her feelings of self-worth and ego
Peer-Induced Esteem Seekers	If there is an audience, consumer perceives there to be benefits of voicing fraudulent complaints
Disruptive Gains	Consumer expresses insincere complaints solely to cause disruption (e.g., get employee into trouble)

Source: Kate L. Reynolds and Lloyd C. Harris, "When Service Failure Is Not Service Failure: An Exploration of the Forms and Motives of 'Illegitimate' Customer Complaining," *Journal of Services Marketing* 19 (August 2005): 321–335.

Because of the vague nature of some types of consumer fraud, its full finan-cial toll is somewhat difficult to tally. However, rough estimates indicate that inventory shrinkage costs U.S. businesses more than $40 billion per year, with half of the shrinkage perpetrated by employees. While shrinkage is most often considered in the context of brick-and-mortar establishments, companies in many industries have problems with fraud and related issues that raise costs and lower profitability. Table 8.2 lists five tools that assist online merchants in detecting and deterring fraud. These merchants have developed a number of strategies, includ-ing customer follow-up, credit card verification, address verification, and even statistical techniques to stay ahead of sophisticated criminals. The information was published by the Merchant Risk Council, a trade association representing 7,500 businesses, law enforcement agencies, financial institutions, and other orga-nizations committed to establishing best practices in cyberfraud prevention.[11]

Many consumers, of course, do not engage in such activities. However, there are cases when buyers and sellers disagree on whether or how well companies have satisfied their economic responsibilities. Thus, a consumer may believe that a product is not worth the price paid, perhaps because he or she believes the product's benefits have been exaggerated by the seller. For example, although some marketers claim that their creams, pills, special massages, and other

Table 8.2 Online Fraud Prevention Tools

1. Real-Time Credit Card Authorization

   Obtaining a real-time authorization will ensure that the credit card has not been reported as lost or stolen and that it is a valid card number. However, an authorization does not tell you if the person using the card is authorized to use the card.

2. Address Verification Systems (U.S. Only)

   An address verification system (also called AVS) is a system that runs during the credit card authorization process. AVS will match the billing address provided by the customer with the billing address on file for that credit card.

3. Card Verification Codes

   Card verification codes (known as CVV2 for Visa, CVVC for MasterCard, and CID for American Express) are a fairly new way of verifying that a credit card is valid. The code does not get printed on any receipts.

4. Rule-Based Detection

   With rule-based detection software, merchants define a set of criteria that each transaction must meet. Often called a "negative file," this set of rules can be based on past experiences, price limits, names, addresses, and the knowledge of human experts, such as risk analysts.

5. Predictive Statistical Models

   Predictive statistical model software analyzes data from millions of online sales to extract the profile of fraudulent transactions. Each transaction then receives a risk score based on a number of attributes.

Source: "Five Tools You Can Use to Prevent Online Fraud," Merchant Risk Council, https://www.merchantriskcouncil.org/, accessed July 7, 2009.

Super Capitalism While companies were suffering great losses during the financial turmoil of the late 2000s, they were also highly scrutinized for a lack of ethics and values. The melee prompted one looming question from the pages of *Supercapitalism: The Transformation of Business, Democracy and Everyday Life.* How do we reconcile democratic values with a global economy? This book, written by former U.S. Secretary of Labor Robert B. Reich, explores the relationship between citizenship and consumerism. As citizens, people have ideals. As consumers, people have needs and wants.

The most compelling example of the consumer-citizen paradox is Wal-Mart. On the one hand, Wal-Mart offers extremely low prices and employs more than two million people in its stores and warehouses. On the other, the company is known for its aggressive approach with suppliers to cut costs and employee wages are relatively low. Communities are often torn by the "big box" store that carries new products and creates jobs, yet causes traffic congestion and jeopardizes the future prospects of local pharmacies, grocery stores, and other retailers. While thousands of consumers shop Wal-Mart for everyday low prices, as citizens they regret the demise of Main Street and small business.

This paradox plays out in other arenas, too. Consider the consumer purchase of "must have" running shoes, while the citizen wonders if child labor or low-wage labor is part of the manufacturing supply chain. A consumer may appreciate the opportunity to purchase once highly valued stock at low prices, but the citizen loathes the nightly news stories of corporate lay-offs. Reich argues that the best solution is for citizens to ensure that economic rules and laws better reflect our democratic ideals. He states, "Capitalism's role is to enlarge the economic pie. How the slices are divided and whether they are applied to private goods like personal computers or public goods like clean air is up to society to decide. This is the role we assign to democracy."

Sources: Edward H. Baker, "Paradox of Capitalism," http://www.strategy-business.com/li/leadingideas/li00112, *strategy+business,* accessed July 2, 2009; Linda Kulman, "Robert Reich Issues a Warning in *Supercapitalism,*" http://www.npr.org/templates/story/story.php?storyId=14848767, accessed July 7, 2009; Robert B. Reich, *Supercapitalism: The Transformation of Business, Democracy and Everyday Life* (New York: Knopf, 2007).

techniques can reduce or even eliminate cellulite, most medical experts and dermatologists believe that only exercise and weight loss can reduce the appearance of this undesirable condition. Products for reducing cellulite remain on the market, but many consumers have returned these products and complained about the lack of results. In the United Kingdom, a number of cosmetic companies have been reprimanded by the Advertising Standards Authority for making misleading claims in advertising and packaging.[12]

If a consumer believes that a firm has not fulfilled its basic economic responsibilities, he or she may ask for a refund, tell others about the bad experiences, discontinue patronage, post a complaint to a website, contact a consumer agency, and even seek legal redress. Many consumer and government agencies keep track of consumer complaints. For example, district attorneys in California recently reported the top five consumer scams being investigated by their offices. Problems related to identity theft, Internet fraud, unreasonable interest rates, bogus charities, and unlicensed professionals posing as licensed professionals topped the list.[13] To protect consumers and provide businesses with guidance, a number of laws and regulations have been enacted to ensure that economic responsibility is met in accordance with institutionalized standards.

Legal Issues

As we discussed in an earlier chapter, legal issues with respect to consumers in the United States primarily fall under the domain of the Federal Trade Commission (FTC), which enforces federal antitrust and consumer protection laws. Within this agency, the Bureau of Consumer Protection works to protect consumers against unfair, deceptive, and fraudulent practices. The bureau is further organized into eight divisions, including those focused on marketing practices, privacy and identity protection, advertising practices, and international consumer protection.[14] For example, consumer complaints about problems with credit counseling agencies prompted the FTC to investigate. Under a recent settlement, Lighthouse Credit Foundation Inc. and its codefendants will pay more than $2.4 million in consumer redress. They are prohibited from making deceptive claims about credit counseling or debt management services. Consumers did not receive individualized credit counseling or the significantly lower interest rates promised by Lighthouse and several other firms.[15] In this case, the companies' inability to honor the economic exchange agreement resulted in legal action and continuing oversight on behalf of consumers. To aid consumers who are facing economic distress, the FTC publishes a guide entitled, "Fiscal Fitness: Choosing a Credit Counselor."

In addition to the FTC, several other federal agencies regulate specific goods, services, or business practices to protect consumers. The Food and Drug Administration, for example, enforces laws and regulations enacted to prevent distribution of adulterated or misbranded foods, drugs, medical devices, cosmetics, veterinary products, and potentially hazardous consumer products. The Consumer Product Safety Commission enforces laws and regulations designed to protect the public from unreasonable risk of injury from consumer products. Many states also have regulatory agencies that enforce laws and regulations regarding business practices within their states. Most federal agencies and states have consumer affairs or information offices to help consumers. The Federal Communications Commission's Consumer Affairs and Outreach Division educates consumers on issues related to cable and satellite service, telecommunications, wireless technology, and other areas under the FCC's domain.[16] In Iowa, the attorney general's Consumer Protection Division publishes brochures to assist consumers in complaining effectively, buying a new or used car, recognizing scams, and avoiding identity theft.[17]

In this section, we focus on U.S. laws related to exchanges and relationships with consumers. Table 8.3 summarizes some of the laws that are likely to affect a wide range of companies and consumers. State and local laws can be more

Table 8.3 Major Consumer Laws

ACT (Date Enacted)	Purpose
Pure Food and Drug Act (1906)	Established the Food and Drug Administration; outlaws the adulteration or mislabeling of food and drug products sold in interstate commerce.
Cigarette Labeling and Advertising Act (1965)	Requires manufacturers to add to package labels warning about the possible health hazards associated with smoking cigarettes.
Fair Packaging and Labeling Act (1966)	Outlaws unfair or deceptive packaging or labeling of consumer products.
Truth in Lending Act (1968)	Requires creditors to disclose in writing all finance charges and related aspects of credit transactions.
Child Protection and Toy Safety Act (1969)	Requires childproof devices and special labeling.
Fair Credit Reporting Act (1970)	Promotes accuracy, fairness, and privacy of credit information; gives consumers the right to see their personal credit reports and to dispute any inaccurate information therein.
Consumer Product Safety Act (1972)	Established the Consumer Product Safety Commission to regulate potentially hazardous consumer products.
Odometer Act (1972)	Provides protections for consumers against odometer fraud in used-car sales.
Equal Credit Opportunity Act (1974)	Outlaws denial of credit on the basis of race, color, religion, national origin, sex, marital status, age, or receipt of public assistance and requires creditors to provide applicants, on request, with the reasons for credit denial.
Magnuson-Moss Warranty (FTC) Act (1975)	Establishes rules for consumer product warranties, including minimum content and disclosure standards; allows the FTC to prescribe interpretive rules in policy statements regarding unfair or deceptive practices.
Consumer Goods Pricing Act (1975)	Prohibits the use of price maintenance agreements among manufacturers and resellers in interstate commerce.
Fair Debt Collection Practices Act (1977)	Prohibits third-party debt collectors from engaging in deceptive or abusive conduct when collecting consumer debts incurred for personal, family, or household purposes.
Toy Safety Act (1984)	Authorizes the Consumer Product Safety Commission to recall products in tended for use by children when they present substantial risk of injury.
Nutrition Labeling and Education Act (1990)	Prohibits exaggerated health claims and requires all processed foods to contain standardized labels with nutritional information.

(continued)

Table 8.3 (continued)

ACT (Date Enacted)	Purpose
Telephone Consumer Protection Act (1991)	Establishes procedures to avoid unwanted telephone solicitations; prohibits marketers from using automated telephone dialing systems or an artificial or prerecorded voice to certain telephone lines.
Home Ownership and Equity Protection Act (1994)	Requires home equity lenders to disclose to borrowers in writing the payment amounts, the consequences of default, and the borrowers' right to cancel the loan within a certain time period.
Telemarketing and Consumer Fraud and Abuse Prevention Act (1994)	Authorizes the FTC to establish regulations for telemarketing, including prohibiting deceptive, coercive, or privacy-invading telemarketing practices; restricting the time during which unsolicited telephone calls may be made to consumers; and requiring telemarketers to disclose the nature of the call at the beginning of an unsolicited sales call.
Identity Theft Assumption and Deterrence Act (1998)	Makes the FTC a central clearinghouse for identity theft complaints and requires the FTC to log and acknowledge such complaints, provide victims with relevant information, and refer their complaints to appropriate entities (e.g., the major national consumer reporting agencies and other law enforcement agencies).
Children's Online Privacy Protection Act (1998)	Protects children's privacy by giving parents the tools to control what information is collected from their children online.
Do-Not-Call Registry Act (2003)	Allows the FTC to implement and enforce a do-not-call registry.
Fair and Accurate Credit Transactions Act (2003)	Amends the Fair Credit Reporting Act (FCRA), gives consumers the right to one free credit report a year from the credit reporting agencies, adds provisions designed to prevent and mitigate identity theft, and grants consumers additional rights with respect to how information is used.
Bankruptcy Abuse Prevention and Consumer Protection Act (2005)	Amends the Truth in Lending Act including requiring certain creditors to disclose on the front of billing statements a minimum monthly payment warning for consumers and a toll-free telephone number, established and maintained by the Commission, for consumers seeking information on the time required to repay specific credit balances.

Sources: "Statutes Relating to Consumer Protection Mission," Federal Trade Commission, www.ftc.gov/ogc/stat3.htm, accessed August 17, 2009.

stringent than federal statutes, so it is important that businesses fully investigate the laws applicable to all markets in which they operate. In Texas, for example, the Deceptive Trade Practices Act prohibits a business from selling anything to a consumer that he or she does not need or cannot afford.[18]

Health and Safety One of the first consumer protection laws in the United States came about in response to public outrage over a novel. In The Jungle,

Upton Sinclair exposed atrocities, including unsanitary conditions and inhumane labor practices, by the meat-packing industry in Chicago at the turn of the twentieth century. Appalled by the unwholesome practices described in the book, the public demanded reform. Congress responded by passing the Pure Food and Drug Act in 1906, just six months after The Jungle was published.[19] In addition to prohibiting the adulteration and mislabeling of food and drug products, the new law also established one of the nation's first federal regulatory agencies, the Food and Drug Administration.

"Most federal agencies and states have consumer affairs or information offices to help consumers."

Since the passage of the Pure Food and Drug Act, public health and safety have been major targets of federal and state regulation. For example, the Consumer Product Safety Act established the Consumer Product Safety Commission (CPSC), and the Flammable Fabrics Act set standards for the flammability of clothing, children's sleepwear, carpets and rugs, and mattresses. The Standard Mattress Co. paid $460,000 to settle charges that it violated the Flammable Fabrics Act by manufacturing and selling futons that failed to meet flammability standards. Despite its agreement with the CPSC, the company denied that it violated any consumer product safety laws.[20] Other laws attempt to protect children from harm, including the Child Protection and Toy Safety Act and the Children's Online Privacy Protection Act.

Credit and Ownership Abuses and inequities associated with loans and credit have resulted in the passage of laws designed to protect consumers' rights and public interests. The most significant of these laws prohibits discrimination in the extension of credit, requires creditors to disclose all finance charges and related aspects of credit transactions, gives consumers the right to dispute and correct inaccurate information on their credit reports, and regulates the activities of debt collectors. For example, the Home Ownership and Equity Protection Act requires home equity lenders to disclose, in writing, the borrower's rights, payment amounts, and the consequences of defaulting on the loan. Together, the U.S. Department of Justice and Department of Housing and Urban Development (HUD) enforce laws that ensure equal access to sale and rental housing. Every April, the government sponsors Fair Housing Month to educate property owners, agents, and consumers on rights with respect to housing. After Hurricane Katrina wreaked havoc on Louisiana, Alabama, and Mississippi, HUD located temporary and permanent housing for many displaced citizens. HUD also developed a campaign to encourage fairness and equity in housing during this difficult time.[21]

While home ownership is often considered part of the American Dream, specific business practices in the banking and finance industry have been questioned. The alarming number of mortgage foreclosures in the late 2000s arose from a combustible situation involving risky lending practices, subprime mortgage disasters, and a general economic downturn. Lenders such as Freddie Mac, Fannie

Mae, IndyMac, and Countrywide played a key role in the meltdown, including top executives misleading investors about the riskiness of their loan strategies. Many Americans assumed high-interest-rate loans or bought a house they could not really afford and, eventually, could no longer make mortgage payments.

In some cases, these consumers were victim of predatory practices. So-called predatory mortgage loans usually have one of the following four characteristics. First, the bank charges more in fees and interest than is needed to cover the additional risk associated with poor credit. Second, the bank traps individuals into loans and, possibly, increased debt. Third, the bank does not consider the individual's ability to pay the loan back. Fourth, the bank violates the law by targeting minorities and the poor. Financial institutions in other countries have also been accused of similar practices. For example, one Irish bank allegedly required African immigrants to take HIV/AIDS tests to qualify for home loan packages. However, Irish nationals were not asked to take the medical tests. Whereas many financial institutions are now providing credit for traditionally underserved markets, equitable access to affordable credit is not always clearly available.[22]

Marketing, Advertising, and Packaging Legal issues in marketing often relate to sales and advertising communications and information about product content and safety. Abuses in promotion can range from exaggerated claims, concealed facts, and deception to outright lying. Such misleading information creates ethical issues because the communicated messages do not include all the information consumers need to make sound purchasing decisions.

In the last few years, thousands of homeowners in the U.S. lost their homes due to mortgage foreclosure

© Ap Photo/Reed Saxon

Publishers Clearing House recently settled charges brought by twenty-six states and the District of Columbia that it used deceptive sweepstakes promotions to get consumers to buy magazines. The settlement required the company to pay $34 million to the states to give refunds to customers, especially the elderly, who bought magazines under the belief that such purchases would boost their chances of winning the oft-touted million-dollar sweepstakes. Although Publishers Clearing House did not admit to any wrongdoing, it agreed to stop using the phrase "You are a winner," unless adequately balanced with statements specifying the conditions necessary to win, and to clearly indicate the odds of winning in sweepstakes promotions. In the same year, United States Sales Corporation and Time Inc. agreed to similar settlements over allegations of deceptive sweepstakes promotions with forty-eight states and the District of Columbia. An academic review of sweepstakes letters and promotions concluded that, rather than being merely "junk mail," these efforts were actually quite skillful and elegant. Researchers concluded that the language used in letters and other materials did an excellent job of establishing rapport, building excitement, and persuading readers to take action.[23]

Although a certain amount of exaggeration and hyperbole is tolerated, deceptive claims or claims that cannot be substantiated are likely to invite legal action from the FTC. For example, the FTC levied a $3 million fine against the marketers of Blue Stuff pain relievers for marketing campaigns that used unsupported claims. The FTC also sued Body Solutions over ads that declared consumers could eat pizza, tacos, and other fatty foods and burn away the fat while sleeping. Cases such as these prompted the FTC to develop a list of phrases that should alert both consumers and marketers to unsubstantiated or false claims about weight loss products (see Figure 8.2).[24]

Since the Federal Trade Commission Act of 1914 outlawed all deceptive and unfair trade practices, additional legislation has further delineated which activities are permissible and which are illegal. For example, the Telemarketing and Consumer Fraud and Abuse Prevention Act requires telemarketers to disclose the nature of the call at the beginning of an unsolicited sales call and restricts the times during which such calls may be made to consumers.

Another legal issue in marketing has to do with the promotion of products that involve health or safety. Numerous laws regulate the promotion of alcohol and tobacco products, including the Public Health Cigarette Smoking Act (1970) and the Cigarette Labeling and Advertising Act (1965). The Eighteenth Amendment to the U.S. Constitution prohibited the manufacture and sale of alcoholic beverages in 1919; the prohibition was repealed in 1933 by the Twenty-first Amendment. However, this amendment gave states the power to regulate the transportation of alcoholic beverages across state lines. Today, each state has unique regulations, some of which require the use of wholesalers and retailers to limit direct sales of alcoholic beverages to final consumers in other states. In this case, a law aimed at protecting consumers by promoting temperance in alcohol consumption now affects wine sellers' ability to implement e-commerce and subsequent interstate sales. Currently, roughly nineteen states prohibit the

Figure 8.2 Red Flags: Bogus Weight Loss Claims

- Cause weight loss of two pounds or more a week for a month or more without dieting or exercise
- Cause substantial weight loss no matter what or how much the consumer eats
- Cause permanent weight loss (even when the consumer stops using product)
- Block the absorption of fat or calories to enable consumers to lose substantial weight
- Safely enable consumers to lose more than three pounds per week for more than four weeks
- Cause substantial weight loss for all users
- Cause substantial weight loss by wearing it on the body or rubbing it into the skin

Source: Federal Trade Commission, "Bogus Weight Loss Claims," http://www.ftc.gov/bcp/edu/microsites/redflag/falseclaims.html, accessed August 17, 2009.

interstate sale of wine, nineteen states allow interstate sales on a limited basis, and twelve states provide for reciprocal transactions only (e.g., between the states of Colorado and New Mexico).[25]

Sales and Warranties Another area of law that affects business relationships with consumers has to do with warranties. Many consumers consider the warranty behind a product when making a purchase decision, especially for expensive durable goods such as automobiles and appliances. One of the most significant laws affecting warranties is the Magnuson-Moss Warranty (FTC) Act of 1975, which established rules for consumer product warranties, including minimum content and standards for disclosure. All fifty states have enacted "lemon laws" to ensure that automobile sales are accompanied by appropriate warranties and remedies for defects that impair the safety, use, or value of the vehicle. Courts have recently ruled that consumers who lease instead of purchase automobiles are also entitled to warranty protection under Magnuson-Moss.[26]

Product Liability One area of law that has a profound effect on business and its relations with consumers is **product liability**, which refers to a business's legal responsibility for the performance of its products. This responsibility, which has evolved through both legislation and court interpretation (common law), may include a legal obligation to provide financial compensation to a consumer who has been harmed by a defective product. To receive compensation, a consumer who files suit in the United States must prove that the product was defective, that the defect caused an injury, and that the defect made the product unreasonably dangerous. Under the concept of *strict liability,* an injured consumer can apply this legal responsibility to any firm in the supply chain of a defective product, including contractors, suppliers of component parts, wholesalers, and retailers.

> **"Companies with operations in other countries must understand the various forms of product liability law that exist."**

Companies with operations in other countries must understand the various forms of product liability law that exist. For example, South Korea recently passed a new law making it easier for consumers to win product liability cases. In response to the law, many South Korean firms developed product liability teams for assessing risk and safety issues, reviewing insurance coverage, and educating employees on the importance of product safety. Product recalls jumped 50 percent in the first year after the law was enacted. In addition, the market for business insurance has grown substantially.[27]

Because the law typically holds businesses liable for their products' performance, many companies choose to recall potentially harmful products; such recalls may be required by legal or regulatory authorities as well. Warner-Lambert, for example, was asked by the Food and Drug Administration to recall Rezulin, a diabetes drug, after thirty-five cases of liver damage occurred in patients using the

product liability
a business's legal responsibility for the performance of its products

drug during its first year on the market. Roche Diagnostics recalled certain models of its ACCU-CHECK diabetes monitors after the company discovered the potential for electronic malfunction and improper readings.[28]

Product liability lawsuits have increased dramatically in recent years, and many suits have resulted in huge damage awards to injured consumers or their families. In a much-publicized case, a jury awarded a McDonald's customer $2.9 million after she was scalded when she spilled hot McDonald's coffee on her lap. Although that award was eventually reduced on appeal, McDonald's and other fast-food restaurants now display warning signs that their coffee is hot to eliminate both further injury and liability. Because of multimillion-dollar judgments like that against McDonald's, companies sometimes pass on the costs of damage awards to their customers in the form of higher prices. Most companies have taken steps to minimize their liability, and some firms—such as pharmaceutical firms making serum for the DPT (diphtheria-pertussis-tetanus) vaccine and manufacturers of small planes—

MARKETING DEPT

"IF WE INCREASE THE PRICE BY FIFTEEN PER CENT WE'LL BE ABLE TO GIVE BIGGER DISCOUNTS."

Courtesy of CartoonStock.com

have stopped making products or withdrawn completely from problematic markets because of the high risk of expensive liability lawsuits.

Although some states have limited damage awards and legislative reform is often on the agenda, the issue of product liability remains politically sensitive. Recently, several product liability lawsuits against TASER International have been dismissed. The firm manufactures and markets the TASER technology, which is used by law enforcement officials as an alternative to other types of physical force. Plaintiffs have claimed that the electroshock devices cause injury or death.[29]

International Issues Concerns about protecting consumers' legal rights are not limited to the United States. Most developed nations have laws and offices devoted to this goal. For example, the Chinese government recently enacted tougher safety standards for automobiles, bringing Chinese expectations in line with safety standards in the United States and Europe.[30] In the European Union (EU), the health and consumer protection directorate general oversees efforts to increase consumer confidence in the unified market. Its initiatives center on health, safety, economic, and public-health interests. One recently passed EU directive establishes minimum levels of consumer protection in member states. For example, EU consumers now have a legal guarantee of two years on all consumer goods. If they find a defective product, they may choose repair or replacement or, in special circumstances, ask for a price reduction or rescind the contract altogether.[31]

In Japan, unlike in the United States, product liability lawsuits are much less common. In the early 1990s, Chikara Minami filed one of the first such lawsuits against Japanese automaker Mitsubishi. Minami's suit alleged a defect in the Mitsubishi Pajero. Although the court sided with the automaker in that case, ten years later Mitsubishi was accused of deliberately covering up consumer complaints. Despite this revelation and an enhanced product liability law in 1995, consumer rights are often subverted to preserve the power and structure of big business in Japan.[32]

Much like Japan, China's consumer rights movement is relatively new and resulted from economic policy changes away from isolationism and central economic planning. The China Consumers' Association was established in 1984 and has helped create consumer expectations and company responses that are starting to resemble those found in Western economies. Despite this action, however, there have been numerous consumer scares surrounding products manufactured in China and other countries. Table 8.4 discloses a number of cases involving food products, medicine, and toys.[33]

As we have discussed in this section, many laws influence business practices with respect to consumers all over the world. Every year, new laws are enacted, and existing rules are modified in response to the changing business environment, including the incidence of consumer product scares. For example, the EU recently

TABLE 8.4 A Decade of Consumer Product Scares

Year	Product Scare
2003	Nearly 700 people were sickened by Mexican-grown scallions that caused a hepatitis A outbreak in Pennsylvania.
2006	The bacteria *E. coli* was found in packets of spinach sold by more than two dozen brands in the United States.
2007	Over 40 million Chinese-made toys were recalled after they were found to be coated with poisonous lead paint.
2007	U.S.-based ConAgra Foods recalled all peanut butter after more than 600 people got sick from salmonella bacteria.
2007	An antifreeze chemical was found in "ShiR Fresh" toothpaste made in China.
2008	A contaminant was found in the Chinese-made heparin, a blood thinner, and was eventually linked to dozens of deaths; resulted in the execution of China's former head of the State Food and Drug Administration.
2008	Maple Leaf Foods of Canada recalled nearly 200 packaged meat products after at least 17 deaths from deadly bacteria.
2008	52,000 Chinese schoolchildren were sickened by milk tainted with an industrial chemical, melamine.

Source: "How Tainted Goods Have Spread Death or Sickness," *Business Week,* http://images.businessweek.com/ss/08/09/0924_tainted_products/index.htm, accessed July 6, 2009.

implemented new accountability standards for the chemical industry, which manufactures and provides ingredients for an array of consumer products. Under the new guidelines, approximately 30,000 chemicals will be registered, evaluated, and approved for use by an EU agency. A key focus of the agency will be the effects of chemicals on human and environmental health.[34] Although companies must monitor and obey all laws and regulations, they also need to keep abreast of the ethical obligations and standards that exist in the marketplace.

Ethical Issues

In 1962, President John F. Kennedy proclaimed a Consumer Bill of Rights that includes the rights to choose, to safety, to be informed, and to be heard. Kennedy also established the Consumer Advisory Council to integrate consumer concerns into government regulations and processes. These four rights established a philosophical basis on which state and local consumer protection rules were later developed.[35] Around the same time, Ralph Nader's investigations of auto safety and his publication of *Unsafe at Any Speed* in 1965 alerted citizens to the dangers of a common consumer product. Nader's activism and Kennedy's speech provided support for **consumerism**, the movement to protect consumers from an imbalance of power on the side of business and to maximize consumer welfare in the marketplace.[36] When Nader ran for the U.S. presidency in 2000, his platform included many of the same concerns about consumers and business that were being discussed thirty-five years earlier.[37] As we have pointed out, the consumer movement is a global phenomenon, as highlighted by the World Consumer Rights Day celebrated every year.

consumerism
the movement to protect consumers from an imbalance of power on the side of business and to maximize consumer welfare in the marketplace

Over the last four decades, consumerism has affected public policy through a variety of mechanisms. Early efforts were aimed primarily at advocating for legislation and regulation, whereas more recent efforts have shifted to education and protection programs directed at consumers.[38] The Consumers Union (CU), for example, works with regional and federal legislators and international groups to protect consumer interests, sponsors conferences and research projects, tests consumer products, and evaluates consumer services, and publishes the results in its information products, including *Consumer Reports* magazine, http://www.ConsumerReports.org, http://www.ConsumerReportsHealth.org, and http://www.ConsumersUnion.org. An issue of Journal of Public Policy & Marketing details business practices that the CU deems unfair to consumers, including predatory lending, the poor value of some life insurance products, and advertisements aimed at vulnerable people, like children.[39] The Internet and electronic communication have also created new vehicles for consumer advocacy, education, and protection. Visitors to www.consumerreports.org and consumersunion.org as well as to the National Consumers League website at http://www.nclnet.org/ or www.consumerworld.org find publications

© Vicki Beaver

The Consumers Union conducts tests on a wide range of consumer products and communicates its findings and recommendations in Consumer Reports magazine

on many consumer issues, research and campaign reports, product reviews, retailer rankings, updates on legal matters, ways to track used-car histories, and many other types of services. Thus, consumer groups and information services have shifted the balance of power between consumer and business because consumers are able to compare prices, read independent rankings, communicate with other buyers, and in general, have greater knowledge about products, companies, and competitors.[40]

Despite the opportunities to exert more power, some researchers question whether most consumers take the time and energy to do so. For example, although the Internet provides a great deal of information and choices, access to the Internet partly depends on educational level and income. In addition, the volume of information available online may actually make it more difficult to analyze and assimilate. Even with these issues, the Consumers Union has developed a legion of e-activists, who e-mail legislators and regulators through CU-sponsored websites. In its first eighteen months of existence, nearly 1 million messages were sent through these websites, which are organized by state and legislative agenda. Because of this consumer action, cell phone companies in California, Georgia, and Washington State must get permission before listing subscribers' cell phone numbers in a directory. Several states, including Missouri and Virginia, are now required to provide public information on infection rates at hospitals. The CU provides a number of consumer advocacy tools on its website, including recommendations for writing letters to government agencies and corporations (see Figure 8.3).[41]

"Although consumer rights were first formalized through a presidential speech and subsequent affirmations, they have not yet reached the legal domain of social responsibility."

All U.S. presidents since Kennedy have confirmed the four basic consumer rights and added new ones in response to changing business conditions. President William J. Clinton, for example, appointed a commission to study the changing health-care environment and its implications for consumer rights. The result was the proposal of a Patient's Bill of Rights and Responsibilities to ensure rights to confidentiality of patient information, to participate in health-care decisions, to access to emergency services, and for other needs.[42] During the same period, a Financial Consumer's Bill of Rights Act was proposed in the U.S. House of Representatives to curb high bank fees, automated teller machine surcharges, and other practices that have angered consumers.[43]

Although consumer rights were first formalized through a presidential speech and subsequent affirmations, they have not yet fully reached the legal domain of social responsibility. Some specific elements of these rights have been mandated through law, but the relatively broad nature of the rights means they must be interpreted and implemented on a company-by-company basis. Table 8.5 lists

Figure 8.3 Consumers Union's Guidelines for Letters

General Guidelines for Letters

Thank you for your interest in writing a letter! The letter you write can influence actions taken by government and corporations.

The sample letter included in each CU action alert is designed so that it can be changed. We encourage you to personalize the message you send. Adding your own personal experience makes letters more effective.

Below are some suggested guidelines to make sure your letter is as effective as possible.

Style and Format

- Be brief.
- Be specific.
- Ask for a response.
- Thank the recipient for his/her attention and cooperation.

Substance

- Identify yourself (and your organization, if applicable).
- If you're writing to a legislator, member of Congress, or Senator, let them know if you're from their home district/state.
- If you're writing to a company, let them know if you are a customer.
- Be polite and show respect, and give reasons for the requested action.
- Try to put the issue in terms of your own personal experience.
- Avoid technical jargon. Put the argument in layman's terms.
- Do not make threats. He/she is far more likely to do what you want if you build a responsible and credible relationship.
- Do not use profanity or language that slanders or disrespects others. You will only hurt your case.

Source: Consumers Union, "General Guidelines for Letters," http://www.ConsumersUnion.org/Letter_Guidelines, accessed 10/14/2009.

TABLE 8.5 Basic Consumer Rights

Right	General Issues
To choose	Access to a variety of products at competitive and reasonable prices
To safety	Protection of health, safety, and financial well-being in the marketplace
To be informed	Opportunity to have accurate and adequate information on which to base decisions and protection from misleading or deceptive information
To be heard	Consideration given to consumer interests in government processes
To redress	Opportunity to express dissatisfaction and to have the complaint resolved effectively
To privacy	Protection of consumer information and its use

Source: Adapted from E. Thomas Garman, *Consumer Economic Issues in America* (Stamford, CT: Thomson Learning, 2005).

six consumer rights that have become part of the ethical expectations of business. Although these rights are not necessarily provided by all organizations, our social responsibility philosophy requires their attention and implementation.

Right to Choose The right to choose implies that, to the extent possible, consumers have the opportunity to select from a variety of products at competitive prices. This right is based on the philosophy of the competitive nature of markets, which should lead to high-quality products at reasonable prices. Antitrust activities that reduce competition may jeopardize this right. This right has been called into question with respect to safety in some parts of the United States. Domino's Pizza, for example, was accused of discriminating against African-American customers through a delivery policy that seemed to be based on a neighborhood's racial composition rather than the legitimate threat of danger to drivers delivering in those neighborhoods. In effect, consumers in these neighborhoods were denied access to pizza delivery service. Although no lawsuit was filed, Domino's worked with the U.S. Department of Justice to revise the delivery policy to narrowly define delivery limitations on the basis of real safety threats and to reevaluate the status of excluded areas on a yearly basis.[44]

Right to Safety The right to safety means that businesses have an obligation not to knowingly market a product that could harm consumers. Some consumer advocates believe that this right means that the manufacture and sale of firearms should be outlawed in the United States. Although organizations like the National Rifle Association have vehemently opposed this view, questions about gun safety, especially around children, have prompted a number of state laws to regulate the manufacture and sale of guns. For example, Massachusetts recently required that all guns sold in that state meet stringent standards and carry internal identification numbers. Maryland requires that all guns be equipped with trigger locks.[45]

The right to safety also implies that all products should be safe for their intended use, include instructions for proper and safe use, and have been sufficiently tested to ensure reliability. Companies must take great care in designing warning messages about products with potentially dangerous or unsafe effects. These messages should take into account consumers' ability to understand and respond to the information. Warnings should be relevant and meaningful to every potential user of the product. Some warnings use symbols or pictures to communicate.

Companies that fail to honor the right to safety risk expensive product liability lawsuits. In 1998, the five largest tobacco manufacturers in the United States reached a landmark $246 billion settlement with the attorneys general of forty-six states. The master settlement agreement (MSA) required the companies to give billions of dollars to the state governments every year to help relieve the burden that smoking-related illnesses put on state health-care systems and to fund campaigns designed to discourage smoking, especially among children. Under the settlement, the companies agreed to stop using cartoon characters, like R. J. Reynolds's Joe Camel. The MSA barred companies from a number of traditional marketing strategies, such as using billboards or direct-mail advertising or passing out samples at shopping malls to tout their products. To help pay for the costs of the settlement, the companies raised prices. Thus, the settlement was designed to force the tobacco firms to bear more of the costs of illnesses caused by their product and to make them act more responsibly. Although corporate executives point to declining teen smoking rates as evidence of their responsibility, many antismoking activists believe that the responsible thing to do is to stop selling a product that causes illness and death.[46]

Right to Be Informed Consumers also have the right to be informed. Any information, whether communicated in written or verbal format, should be accurate, adequate, and free of deception so that consumers can make a sound decision. This general assertion has also led to specific legislation, such as the Nutrition Labeling and Education Act of 1990, which requires certain nutrition facts on food labels and limits the use of terms such as *low fat*. This right can be associated with safety issues if consumers do not have sufficient information to purchase or use a product effectively. For example, a woman in New York leveled a $50 million lawsuit against Robert's American Gourmet Food, Inc., for mislabeling its snack products and causing her "weight gain . . . mental anguish, outrage and indignation." The snacks, branded Pirate's Booty, Veggie Booty, and Fruity Booty, were sold in packages that claimed to have 120 calories

© Susan Van Etten

Robert's American Gourmet Food, Inc. claimed the Pirate's Booty snack had 2.5 grams of fat, while independent tests found the snack contained 8.5 grams of fat

and 2.5 grams of fat. When independently tested, however, the Good Housekeeping Institute published numbers that came as a shock to many dieters; the snack actually contained 147 calories and 8.5 grams of fat. Bags that claimed to have 1 ounce of product actually had 1.25 ounces of the product. Robert's recalled the snacks prior to the *Good Housekeeping* magazine report and blamed new manufacturing equipment on the mislabeling and fat content problem. The snack, once so popular that it made the pages of *Vanity Fair*, reminded consumers that "if something tastes too good to be true, it probably is too good to be true."[47]

In an age of rapid technological advances and globalization, the degree of complexity in product marketing is another concern related to consumers' right to information. This complexity may relate to the ways in which product features and benefits are discussed in advertising, how effective salespeople are in answering consumer questions, the expertise needed to operate or use the product, and the ease of returning or exchanging the product. To help consumers make decisions based on adequate and timely information, some organizations sponsor consumer education programs. For example, pharmaceutical companies and health maintenance organizations sponsor free seminars, health screenings, websites, and other programs to educate consumers about their health and treatment options.

The proliferation of websites devoted to consumer health information prompted the American Accreditation Healthcare Commission to develop a Health Web Site Accreditation program. The program's "seal of approval" should let consumers know that the website's content is trustworthy and reliable.[48] In Russia, consumer advocacy organizations have established a telephone hotline to educate consumers about their rights and to advise them when they encounter poor-quality products marketed as leading consumer brands. According to the hotline director, Yelena Poluektova, "Although there has been a law on consumer rights since 1992 it turns out very many people have no knowledge of their rights."[49]

Right to Be Heard The right to be heard relates to opportunities for consumers to communicate or voice their concerns in the public policy process. This also implies that governments have the responsibility to listen and take consumer issues into account. One mechanism for fulfilling this responsibility is through the FTC and state consumer affairs offices. Another vehicle includes congressional hearings held to educate elected officials about specific issues of concern to consumers. At the same time, consumers are expected to be full participants in the process, meaning they must be informed and willing to take action against wrongs in the marketplace.

Right to Seek Redress In addition to the rights described by Kennedy, consumers also have the right to express dissatisfaction and seek restitution from a business when a good or service does not meet their expectations. However, consumers need to be educated in the process for seeking redress and to recognize that the first course of action in such cases should be with the seller. At the same time, companies need to have explicit and formal processes for dealing with customer dissatisfaction.

Although some product problems lead to third-party intervention or legal recourse, the majority of issues should be resolvable between the consumer and the business. One third party that consumers may consult in such cases is the Better Business Bureau (BBB), which promotes self-regulation of business. To gain and maintain membership, a firm must agree to abide by the ethical standards established by the BBB. This organization collects complaints on businesses and makes this information, along with other reports, available for consumer decision making. The BBB also operates the dispute resolution division to assist in out-of-court settlements between consumers and businesses. For example, this division has a program, BBB Auto Line, to handle disputes between consumers and twenty-five automobile manufacturers.[50] This self-regulatory approach not only provides differentiation in the market but also can stave off new laws and regulations.

Right to Privacy The advent of new information technology and the Internet has prompted increasing concerns about consumer privacy. This right relates to consumers' awareness of how personal data are collected and used, and it places a burden on firms to protect this information. How information is used can create concerns for consumers. Although some e-commerce firms have joined together to develop privacy standards for the Internet, many websites do not meet the FTC's criteria for fair information practices, including notice, choice, access, and security.[51] We will take a closer look at the debate surrounding privacy rights in Chapter 10.

A firm's ability to address the six consumer rights that have become part of the ethical expectations of business can serve as a competitive advantage. CMC Properties, a recent recipient of the National Torch Award for Marketplace Ethics given by the Better Business Bureau, is highly regarded for the ethical approach to consumers of its real estate and property management services. Instead of viewing its business as "bricks and mortar," the company is focused on "bodies and souls." As the company's mission states, CMC strives to simplify the lives of its customers.[52] Another example is in the highly competitive market for air travel. Many airlines have developed a strong focus on customer service and satisfaction. Together with the air transport association, several airlines launched the airline customer service commitment to demonstrate an industry focus on alleviating passenger frustrations and complaints. Southwest Airlines established a lengthy Customer Service Commitment that details the airline's practices before, during, and after a customer flight (see Figure 8.4).[53]

> **"A firm's ability to address the six consumer rights that have become part of the ethical expectations of business can serve as a competitive advantage."**

When consumers believe a firm is operating outside ethical or legal standards, they may be motivated to take some type of action. As we discussed earlier, there are a number of strategies consumers can employ to communicate their dissatisfaction, such as complaining or discontinuing the exchange relationship. For example, some people believe Wal-Mart's presence has contributed to the demise of locally owned pharmacies and variety stores in

Figure 8.4 Southwest Airlines' Customer Service Commitment

Our Customer Service Commitment Section	Page Number
Airport Operations and Scheduled Service	1
Irregular Operations	2
Fares, Reservations, and Ticketing	5
Reservations	7
Overbooking	9
Tickets and Refunds	10
Southwest Airlines' All-Jet, All-Boeing Fleet	11
Baggage	12
Customers with Special Needs	15
Frequent Flyer Program	19
Commitment with Codeshare Airlines	20
How to Contact Southwest Airlines	21

Source: Southwest Airlines, "Customer Service Commitment," http://www.southwest.com/about_swa/customer_service_commitment/csc.pdf, accessed July 7, 2009.

many small towns. The chain's buying power ensures lower prices and wider product variety for consumers but also makes it difficult for smaller retailers to compete. Other consumers and community leaders worry about the traffic congestion and urban sprawl that accompany new retail sites. Some Wal-Mart critics have taken their discontent with the retailer to the Internet. Disgruntled customers and others share complaints about the retail chain, provide updates about legal action, and promote campaigns against the retailer on http://www.wakeupwalmart.com/. Another website, http://www.walmartsurvivor.com, details court rulings against Wal-Mart and lists attorneys who have been successful in opposing the retail giant.[54]

Stakeholders may use the three types of power—symbolic, utilitarian, and coercive—discussed in Chapter 2 to create organizational awareness on an important issue. For example, some Chinese consumers feel that Japanese people believe they are racially superior to the Chinese. This sentiment stems from Japan's occupation of China in the 1940s. More recently, Toshiba has been accused of racism for not compensating Chinese users of potentially faulty Toshiba laptop computers. This perceived slight, along with feelings of nationalism, have prompted Chinese consumers to dismiss Toshiba and other Japanese manufacturers. Chinese retailers have pulled Japanese products off their shelves as well.[55] These consumers are engaging in another form of consumer action, a **boycott**, by abstaining from using, purchasing, or dealing with an organization. The World Jewish Congress encouraged its members to boycott the insurance company Transamerica after its parent company, Aegon NV, refused to join the international commission on Holocaust-era insurance claims. The commission was established to resolve insurance claims that resulted from the Holocaust and World War II.[56]

Other boycotts, while of corporate interest, may not be based on traditional social responsibility issues. For example, fans of the James Bond movies initially boycotted a new production that starred a young and inexperienced Bond. The movie's director explained, "He's just got his 007 stripes when he gets into the story so he's got some rough edges on him to begin with and hopefully, by the end of it, he'll become the 007 we all know and love." Fans created a website, where the prequel was denounced and derided for several reasons, including the replacement of Pierce Brosnan with a much younger and relatively unknown actor named Daniel Craig. Craig was said to be less attractive, less experienced, and less suited to the role. The website urged fans to write Sony Pictures, get friends involved, and take other actions to ensure a successful boycott of the film. Since that time, Craig has starred several times as 007 and is continuing a solid big-screen career.[57]

Philanthropic Issues

Although relationships with consumers are fundamentally grounded in economic exchanges, the previous sections demonstrate that additional levels of expectations exist. A national survey by Cone/Roper reported that 70 percent of consumers would be likely to switch to brands associated with a good cause, as long as price and quality were equal. These results suggest that today's consumers take for granted that they can obtain high-quality products at reasonable prices, so businesses need to do something to differentiate themselves from the competition.[58] More firms are therefore investigating ways to link their philanthropic efforts

boycott consumer action of abstaining from using, purchasing, or dealing with an organization

with consumer interests. Eastman Kodak, for example, has funded environmental literacy programs of the World Wildlife Fund. These programs not only link between the company's possible effects and its interest in the natural environment but also provide a service to its customers and other stakeholders.[59]

From a strategic perspective, a firm's ability to link consumer interests to philanthropy should lead to stronger economic relationships. As we shall see in Chapter 9, philanthropic responsibilities to consumers usually entail broader benefits, including those that affect the community. For example, large pharmaceutical and health insurance firms provided financial support to the Foundation for Accountability (FACCT), a nonprofit organization that assists health-care consumers in making better decisions. FACCT initiated an online system for patients to evaluate their physician on several quality indicators. Although FACCT ceased its operations recently, the Markle Foundation continues to host the nonprofit's legacy documents and white papers. The foundation partners with other organizations to improve the role of technology in addressing critical public health needs.[60]

Companies will have more successful philanthropic efforts when the cause is a good fit with the firm's product category, industry, customer concerns, and/or location. This alignment is an important contributor to the long-term relationships that often develop between specific companies and cause-related organizations. Many firms involved in medicine and pharmaceuticals will contribute to causes that improve access to proper health care and medication, provide stronger patient support and outcomes, decrease accidents and injuries, and respond to emergency or critical needs of a community. Figure 8.5 describes the philanthropic contribution levels of nine health-care–related firms, all of which rank in the top 50 corporate foundations in terms of annual giving. These companies have established corporate foundations with large endowments, which means that annual contributions are relatively unaffected by corporate profitability and the economic cycle. Nonprofits prefer consistent donations rather than wide variance from year to year.

Figure 8.5 Putting Money Where Their Mouths Are

Corporate Foundation	Annual Giving ($)
Sanofi-Aventis Patient Assistance Foundation	177,414,396
Johnson & Johnson Family of Companies Contribution Fund	58,734,462
The Pfizer Foundation, Inc.	45,837,661
The Merck Company Foundation	44,085,873
Blue Shield of California Foundation	31,461,056
Eli Lilly and Company Foundation	28,902,259
Abbott Fund	26,821,486
The Medtronic Foundation	23,392,823
The Bristol-Myers Squibb Foundation, Inc.	22,987,066

Source: Foundation Center, "50 Largest Corporate Foundations by Total Giving," http://foundationcenter.org/findfunders/topfunders/top50giving.html, accessed August 20, 2009.

STRATEGIC IMPLEMENTATION OF RESPONSIBILITIES TO CONSUMERS

As this chapter has demonstrated, social responsibility entails relationships with a variety of stakeholders—including consumers—and many firms are finding creative ways to meet these responsibilities. Just as in other aspects of social responsibility, these relationships must be managed, nurtured, and continuously assessed. Resources devoted to this effort may include programs for educating and listening to consumers, surveys to discover strengths and weaknesses in stakeholder relationships, hiring consumer affairs professionals, the development of a community relations office, and other initiatives. Business in the Community, a coalition of companies in the United Kingdom, developed nine marketplace responsibility principles to guide its members and other businesses in dealing with consumers and the supply chain. Figure 8.6 lists these principles, along with eight best practices for effectively putting them into action.

Understanding consumer and stakeholder issues can be especially complex in the global environment. For example, a group of 150 Nigerian women led a peaceful protest that shut down most of ChevronTexaco's Nigerian oil operations for a week. These women, who live in the Niger Delta, are among the poorest in Nigeria, although they live on oil-rich land. The women demanded that ChevronTexaco hire their sons and provide electricity in their villages.

Figure 8.6 Business in the Community Marketplace Responsibility

The Marketplace Responsibility Principles:

- Respect your customers
- Support vulnerable customers
- Seek potential customers within excluded groups
- Manage the impact of product or service
- Actively discourage product misuse
- Actively manage responsibility in your supply chain
- Treat suppliers as partners
- Work with the rule makers
- Have consistent standards

Best Practice for Marketplace Responsibility:

- Be consistent
- Anticipate trends
- Aim to deliver quality results
- Put it at the heart of business strategy
- Part of the culture
- Encourage and motivate responsible behavior
- Mainstream not niche
- Share best practice within the business

Source: Business in the Community, http://www.bitc.org.uk/marketplace/marketplace_responsibility_principles/index.html, accessed August 17, 2009.

The company viewed the women's complaints as unjustified and pointed to its local employment rates and contributions to development projects in the area. Because the government had failed to develop good roads, schools, and utility systems in the area, these activists turned to a multinational corporation for some resolution.[61]

The utility industry represents an interesting case study in its resource investments and relationships with both consumers and the community. There is much public interest in issues related to utility prices, environmental impact, plant closures, plant location, and more. Larger utilities hold "town hall" meetings and other sessions to obtain stakeholder views and feedback. Kansas City Power & Light (KCPL), for example, held an open house that attracted more than 1,000 people. Employees of KCPL served as babysitters while parents learned more about electric and magnetic fields and other emerging topics. The Municipal Utilities staff of the City of Redding (California) held a similar meeting to explain and gain feedback on a proposed rate increase. Such open houses not only address the information needs of customers but also exemplify a strong stakeholder orientation.[62] Both KCPL and the City of Redding understand the importance of integrating all stakeholders in social responsibility efforts, including employees, as we explored in Chapter 7, and the general community, which we examine in Chapter 9.

> **"Social responsibility entails relationships with a variety of stakeholders—including consumers—and many firms are finding creative ways to meet these responsibilities."**

SUMMARY

Companies face complex decisions about how to respond to the expectations, attitudes, and buying patterns of consumers, those individuals who purchase, use, and dispose of products for personal and household use. Consumers are primary stakeholders because their awareness, purchase, use, and repurchase of products are vital to a company's existence.

Consumers and businesses are fundamentally connected by an economic relationship. Economic responsibilities include following through on promises made in the exchange process. Consumer fraud involves intentional deception to derive an unfair economic advantage over an organization. If consumers believe that a firm has not fulfilled its economic responsibility, they may ask for a refund, tell others about the bad experience, discontinue their patronage, contact a consumer agency, or seek legal redress.

In the United States, legal issues with respect to consumers fall under the jurisdiction of the Federal Trade Commission (FTC), which enforces federal anti-trust and consumer protection laws. Other federal and state agencies regulate specific goods, services, or business practices. Among the issues that may have been addressed through specific state or federal laws and regulations are consumer health and safety, credit and ownership, marketing and advertising, sales and warranties, and product liability. Product liability refers to a business's legal responsibility for the performance of its products. Concerns about protecting consumers' legal rights are not limited to the United States.

Ethical issues related to consumers include the Consumer Bill of Rights enumerated by President Kennedy. Consumerism refers to the movement to protect consumers from an imbalance of power with business and to maximize consumer welfare in the marketplace. Some specific elements of consumer rights have been mandated by law, but the relatively broad nature of the rights means they must be interpreted and implemented on a company-by-company basis. Consumer rights have evolved to include the right to choose, the right to safety, the right to be informed, the right to be heard, the right to seek redress, and the right to privacy. When consumers believe a firm is operating outside ethical or legal standards, they may be motivated to take action, including boycotting—abstaining from using, purchasing, or dealing with an organization.

More firms are investigating ways to link their philanthropic efforts with consumer interests. From a strategic perspective, a firm's ability to link consumer interests to philanthropy should lead to stronger economic relationships.

Many companies are finding creative ways to satisfy their responsibilities to consumers. Much like employee relationships, these responsibilities must be managed, nurtured, and continuously assessed. Resources devoted to this effort may include programs for educating and listening to consumers, surveys to discover strengths and weaknesses in stakeholder relationships, hiring consumer affairs professionals, working with industry groups, and the development of other initiatives that engage consumers.

RESPONSIBLE BUSINESS DEBATE

Who Is Responsible for Healthy Weight?

ISSUE: Consumer Versus Government Responsibility

Each year, the Trust for America's Health publishes a ranking of American states. This ranking, unlike some others, is not one in which a governor hopes his or her state will be at the top of the list. For Mississippi, Alabama, West Virginia, and Tennessee, the list is a sobering reminder that adult obesity is a statewide concern. These four states have adult obesity rates over 30 percent and also have high rates of childhood obesity. Childhood obesity rates have more than tripled since 1980; adult obesity rates have doubled.

The Trust for America's Health points to both positive outcomes and continuing negative factors surrounding the high rates of obesity:

- The current economic crisis could exacerbate the obesity epidemic. Food prices, particularly for more nutritious foods, are expected to rise. At the same time, safety-net programs are increasingly overextended as the numbers of unemployed, uninsured, and underinsured continue to grow.
- Nineteen states now have nutritional standards for school lunches, breakfasts, and snacks that are stricter than current USDA requirements.
- Twenty states have passed requirements for body mass index (BMI) screenings of children and adolescents or have passed legislation requiring other forms of weight-related assessments in schools.
- As the baby boomer generation ages, obesity-related costs to Medicare and Medicaid are likely to grow significantly because of the large number of people in this population and its high rate of obesity.

There Are Two Sides to Every Issue:

1. Individuals are solely responsible for what they eat and whether they exercise. There is no mechanism that the government or any other group can use to change the way people buy, prepare, and consume food or to encourage people to exercise more. It is up to individuals to make better choices for themselves and their children.

2. The government and other groups have influence on the availability and price of healthy food choices and accessibility to safe and healthy places to exercise. Schools should provide quality meals and require more physical activity. Companies should encourage wellness programs for employees.

Source: Trust for America's Health, "New Report Finds Obesity Epidemic Increases, Mississippi Weighs in as Heaviest State: Experts Recommend Addressing Obesity through Health Reform, National Strategy," http://healthyamericans.org/newsroom/releases/?releaseid=182, accessed July 10, 2009.

KEY TERMS

consumers (p. 279)
consumer fraud (p. 281)
product liability (p. 290)

consumerism (p. 293)
boycott (p. 300)

DISCUSSION QUESTIONS

1. List and describe the consumer rights that have become social expectations of business. Why have some of these rights been formalized through legislation? Should these rights be considered ethical standards?

2. Review Southwest Airline's plan for customer service. Create a chart to link each

of the twelve points to a specific economic, legal, ethical, or philanthropic responsibility that the airline has to its customers.

3. What is the purpose of a boycott? Describe the characteristics of companies and consumers that are likely to be involved in a boycott situation. What circumstances

would cause you to consider participating in a boycott?

4. How can companies strive for successful relationships with consumers, including meeting their economic, legal, ethical, and philanthropic expectations?

5. How will consumer rights and activism change over the next decade? Will the movement strengthen or decline? Why?

EXPERIENTIAL EXERCISE

Visit the website of Consumers International (http://www.consumersinternational.org/). What is the purpose of this website? Select any element of the "Key Issues" section and read the information provided by CI on that issue.

How useful is this information to you? With what information do you agree and/or disagree? How could a business manager use this site to understand and improve a company's relationship and reputation with consumers?

WHAT WOULD YOU DO?

Justin Thompson was excited. He really enjoyed his job at the Kingston's department store downtown. This location housed Kingston's first store and still had many of its original features. As he rode the subway into the city center, Justin thought about the money he would earn this summer and the great car he hoped to buy before school started. He was lucky to have secured this type of job, since many of his friends were working early or late hours at fast-food chains or out in the summer heat. The management team at Kingston's had initiated a program with his high school counselors, hoping to attract top high school seniors into retail management throughout their college career and beyond. Justin was a strong student from a single-parent background, and his counselor was highly complimentary of his work ethic and prospects for professional employment.

Justin's first week was consumed with various training sessions. There were eight students in the special high school program.

They watched a company video that discussed Kingston's history, ethics policy, current operations, and customer service philosophy. They met with staff from Human Resources to fill out paperwork. They learned how to scan merchandise and operate the computer software and cash register. They toured the store's three levels and visited with each department manager. Justin was especially excited about working in the electronics department, but he was assigned to men's clothing.

Justin worked alongside several employees during the first few weeks on the store floor. He watched the experienced employees approach customers, help them, and ring up the sale. He noticed that some employees took personal telephone calls and that others did not clean up the dressing rooms or restock items very quickly. On slower days, he eventually worked alone in the department. Several times when he came to work in the afternoon, he had to clean up the mess left behind by the morning shift. When he spoke to various colleagues about it in the break room, they told him it was best to keep quiet. After all, he was a high school student earning money for a car, not a "real employee" with kids to feed and bills to pay. Justin assumed that retail work was much like team projects in school—not everyone pulled their weight but it was hard to be the tattletale.

One Saturday morning was extremely busy, as Kingston's was running a big sale. People were swarming to the sales racks, and Justin was amazed at how fast the time was passing. In the late afternoon, several friends of one of his coworkers dropped by the men's section. Before long, their hands were filled with merchandise. The crowd was starting to wane, so Justin took a few minutes to clean up the dressing room. When he came out of the dressing room, his coworker was ringing up the friends' merchandise. Justin saw two ties go into the bag, but only one was scanned into the system. He saw an extra discount provided on an expensive shirt. Justin was shocked to see that not every item was scanned and that improper discounts were applied, and his mind was racing. Should he stop his coworker? Should he "take a break" and get security? Was there another alternative? What would you do?

Community Relations and Strategic Philanthropy

Chapter Objectives

- To describe the community as a stakeholder

- To discuss the community relations function

- To distinguish between strategic philanthropy and cause-related marketing

- To identify the benefits of strategic philanthropy

- To explain the key factors in implementing strategic philanthropy

Chapter Outline

Winners On and Off the Field: Kansas City Chiefs

The Kansas City Chiefs were founded in 1960 by Lamar Hunt. The Chiefs are known as a one-of-a-kind professional sports franchise. Administrative employees, players, coaches, and other staff give back to the community that provides so much support and enthusiasm for the team.

The Chiefs' organization is what it is today because of Hunt and Carl Peterson, who served as the franchise's top executive from 1998 to 2009. The Chiefs were the first professional sports franchise to contractually obligate players to attend charitable events. Today, many sports teams have similar agreements with players. Since the early days of the Chiefs, Hunt has taken players to school functions, fundraising events, parades, and Rotary Club meetings. Many players have started nonprofits through the Greater Kansas City Community Foundation. Since 1998, over $20 million have been raised for charitable organizations through the Chiefs. Annually, the franchise gives away 2,000 autographed items, most of which are used in auctions to benefit community groups.

An example of the Chiefs' widespread fundraising efforts occurred after September 11, 2001, when the Chiefs faced off against the New York Giants. Hunt announced that the team would match the total donations collected from fans at the game. At the end of the game, a total of $225,000 had been raised by fans. The Chiefs kept the promise, and $450,000 was donated to charities of the NYPD, FDNY, and the Port Authority. As another example, each holiday season the Chiefs collect toys and monetary donations at the Arrowhead Stadium for the annual Toys for Tots drive. In 2008 the Chiefs collected more than 1,200 toys and $11,000 for the drive.

Through these efforts, and a deep commitment to social responsibility, the Chiefs have become winners both on and off the field. New recruits quickly learn that they should be dedicated to their roles on the field and in the community. Other franchise owners come to Kansas City to observe the Chiefs' operations and learn best practices in community relations. The organization is a role model for community and philanthropic success in the world of professional sports.[1]

The Kansas City Chiefs, like most organizations with operational expertise and other core competencies, can also focus on implementing social responsibility and satisfying stakeholder groups. From a social responsibility perspective, the key challenge is how an organization assesses its stakeholders' needs, integrates them with company strategy, reconciles differences between stakeholders' needs, strives for better relationships with stakeholders, achieves mutual understandings with them, and finds solutions for problems.

In this chapter, we explore community stakeholders and how organizations deal with stakeholder needs through philanthropic initiatives. We examine the relationship with communities and the economic, legal, ethical, and philanthropic responsibilities that must be addressed by business. We define strategic philanthropy and integrate this concept with other elements of social responsibility. Next, we trace the evolution of corporate philanthropy and distinguish the concept from cause-related marketing. We also provide examples of best practices of addressing stakeholders' interests that meet our definition of strategic philanthropy. From there, we consider the benefits of investing in strategic philanthropy to satisfy both stakeholders and corporate objectives. Finally, we examine the process of implementing strategic philanthropy in business. Our approach in this chapter is to demonstrate how companies can link strategic philanthropy with economic, legal, and ethical concerns for the benefit of all stakeholders.

COMMUNITY STAKEHOLDERS

The concept of *community* has many varying characteristics that make it a challenge to define. The community does not always receive the same level of acceptance as other stakeholders. Some people even wonder how a company determines who is in the community. Is a community defined by city or county boundaries? What if the firm operates in multiple locations? Or is a community prescribed by the interactions a firm has with various constituents who do not fit neatly into other stakeholder categories?

For a small restaurant in a large city, the owner may define the community as the immediate neighborhood where most patrons live. The restaurant may demonstrate social responsibility by hiring people from the neighborhood, participating in the neighborhood crime watch program, donating food to the elementary school's annual parent-teacher meetings, or sponsoring a neighborhood Little League team. For example, Merlino's Steak House in North Conway, New Hampshire, sponsors an annual golf tournament that benefits the Center for Hope, an organization that provides transportation for local individuals with disabilities. Merlino's has raised more than $1 million for local charities with tournament proceeds.[2] For a corporation with facilities in North and South America, Europe, and Africa, the community may be viewed as virtually the entire world. To focus its social responsibility efforts, the multinational corporation might employ a community relations officer in each facility who reports to and coordinates with the company's head office.

Under our social responsibility philosophy, the term *community* should be viewed from a global perspective, beyond the immediate town, city, or state where a business is located. Thus, we define community as those members of society who are aware of, concerned with, or in some way affected by the operations and output of an organization. With information technology, high-speed travel, and the emergence of global business interests, the community as a constituency can be quite geographically, culturally, and attitudinally diverse. Issues that could become important include pollution of the environment, land use, economic advantages to the region, and discrimination within the community, as well as exploitation of workers or consumers.

From a positive perspective, an organization can significantly improve the quality of life through employment opportunities, economic development, and financial contributions for educational, health, artistic, and recreational activities. Through such efforts, a firm may become a neighbor of choice, an organization that builds and sustains trust with the community.[3] To become a neighbor of choice, a company should strive for positive and sustainable relationships with key individuals, groups, and organizations; demonstrate sensitivity to community concerns and issues; and design and implement programs that improve the quality of community life while promoting the company's long-term business strategies and goals.[4]

Home Depot's Neighbor of Choice program involves the following considerations: partnering with cities and towns, reflecting the community in hiring associates, creating jobs and opportunities for other businesses, purchasing locally to keep dollars in the community, valuing volunteerism, generating local tax revenue, and offering home solutions in your neighborhood.[5] As a part of its Neighbor of Choice program, FedEx, headquartered in Memphis, Tennessee, serves as a major corporate sponsor of the National Civil Rights Museum in Memphis. This museum exists to help the public understand the lessons of the Civil Rights Movement and its impact and influence on the human rights movement worldwide. The museum is a key component in the company's diversity training, and FedEx has helped fund the Exploring the Legacy project, which expanded the museum's exhibit space by almost 13,000 square feet.[6]

Similar to other areas of life, the relationship between a business and the community should be symbiotic. A business may support educational opportunities in the community because the owners feel it is the right thing to do, but it also helps develop the human resources and consumer skills necessary to operate the business. Customers and employees are also community members who benefit from contributions supporting recreational activities, environmental initiatives, safety, and education. Many firms rely on universities and community colleges to provide support for ongoing education of their employees. Sykes Enterprises, for example, often locates its customer call and support centers in towns where the local community college is willing to develop courses that educate employees in the skills and aptitude needed to effectively operate a call center.

To build and support these initiatives, companies may invest in community relations, the organizational function dedicated to building and maintaining relationships and trust with the community. In the past, most businesses have not viewed community relations as strategically important or associated them with the firm's ultimate performance. Although the community relations department interacted with the community and often doled out large sums of money

community those members of society who are aware of, concerned with, or in some way affected by the operations and output of an organization

neighbor of choice an organization that builds and sustains trust with the community

community relations the organizational function dedicated to building and maintaining relationships and trust with the community

"Community relations activities have achieved greater prominence and responsibility within most companies, especially due to the rise of stakeholder power and global business interests."

to charities, it essentially served as a buffer between the organization and its immediate community.

Today, community relations activities have achieved greater prominence and responsibility within most companies, especially due to the rise of stakeholder power and global business interests. The function has gained strategic importance through linking to overall business goals, professionalizing its staff and their knowledge of business and community issues, assessing its performance in quantitative and qualitative terms, and recognizing the breadth of stakeholders to which the organization is accountable.[7]

Community relations also assist in short-term and crisis situations, such as disaster relief. Cisco was honored with an Excellence Award on Corporate Philanthropy Day by the Committee to Encourage Corporate Philanthropy for employees donating over 200,000 hours of community service in seven months. Cisco offers an innovative program to encourage employees to volunteer their time, including post–Hurricane Katrina rebuilding and a global Leadership Fellows Program, which allows employees to work full time for nonprofits for up to one year (at no cost to the nonprofit).[8] Progressive companies manage community relations with partnership in mind. They seek out community partners for a range of interests and activities—philanthropy, volunteerism, quality educational system and qualified workforce, appropriate roads and infrastructure, quality housing, and other community assets.

Over the past two decades, corporate support for philanthropy has been steadily growing. According to Giving USA Foundation, corporate giving totaled $12.65 billion for 2006 and reached $14.50 billion in 2008. However, the economic downturn of late 2008 and 2009 brought fears to nonprofit organizations and other groups accustomed to corporate largesse. General Electric announced that it would steer its philanthropy toward those areas most affected by the economic crisis, such as food and shelter services. CSX Corporation planned to reduce its giving to arts and cultural projects by at least 25 percent to be more strategic about its efforts.

Table 9.1 provides findings from a study of 108 of the largest U.S. corporations, focusing on how the poor economy would affect their giving. Even before the economic downturn, corporate giving was becoming more effective and strategic. Companies are working to align their stakeholder interests and develop partnerships that are more closely aligned to business goals, community interests, and sustainable activities.[9]

In a diverse society, however, there is no general agreement as to what constitutes the ideal model of business responsibility to the community. Businesses

Table 9.1 How the Economy Affects Corporate Relations in Communities

- Of the 96 companies that provided predictions about how much they would donate in cash and products in 2009, 51 said the amount would stay roughly the same as in 2008, 15 expected it to decline, and 5 said it would grow.

- Of the 72 companies that laid off workers last year, 33 said they had laid off workers or eliminated positions in their corporate-giving departments. For example, Caterpillar, the industrial and farm equipment company in Peoria, IL, which cut 20,000 jobs this year, laid off one person from its foundation's staff of six.

- Businesses awarded a median of 1 percent of their 2007 pretax profits to charity in 2008. This represented a decline from the previous year, when they donated 1.4 percent of their profits.

- Ten companies have reduced or cut their employee matching-gift program. Northrop Grumman, the aerospace and defense company, decreased the maximum it would match from $5,000 to $1,000. The move allows the grant maker to do more for its primary philanthropic interest, which is math and science education.

- Companies continue to step up efforts to encourage employees to volunteer. For example, Eli Lilly and Company started a new program in November in which employees were paired with 46 Teach for America participants. The Lilly program, which is the first of its kind, will help the new teachers get acclimated to working in Indianapolis, where the pharmaceutical company's headquarters is located.

- Companies are shifting priorities. Johnson and Johnson plans to keep its level of giving steady to causes that reflect its business expertise: children, education, and global health. But to find the money to do so, it is not paying for charity galas and other fundraising events that it has historically supported.

- With America facing an economic crisis often compared with the Great Depression, 33 companies are shifting philanthropic money to provide food, shelter, and clothing to unemployed Americans and others experiencing hardship.

- Total combined giving by 50 big companies that provided data for the past five years has increased by 4 percent, adjusted for inflation.

Source: Noelle Barton and Ian Wilhelm, "Businesses Buckle Up," *Chronicle of Philanthropy*, July 2, 2009, p. 7.

are likely to experience conflicts among stakeholders about what constitutes a real commitment to the community. Therefore, the community relations function should cooperate with various internal and external constituents to develop community mission statements, assess opportunities, and identify priorities for the types of contributions the business will make to the community. Table 9.2 provides several examples of company missions and programs with respect to community involvement. As you can see, these missions are specific to the needs of the people and areas in which the companies operate and are usually aligned with the competencies of the organizations involved and their employees.

Community mission statements are likely to change as needs are met and new issues emerge. For example, when Delphi Automotive opened a manufacturing site in Mexico, it worked with the Mexican government to build subsidized housing for Delphi employees. The project helped more than 2,000 employees find better housing and was extended to serve nonemployees through a partnership with

Table 9.2 Community Mission Statements

Organization	Community Mission
Aetna, Inc.	Aetna Employees Reaching Out (AERO), Aetna's employee volunteering and giving program, integrates community involvement and business. When employees get involved in communities to teach underprivileged children dental hygiene, serve on hospital governance boards, and conduct other caring acts, they help Aetna to "build trusting, value-added relationships" with constituents, "anticipate the future" in health care, and invigorate other values expressed in The Aetna Way—Aetna's business approach.
Capital One	At Capital One, we have always believed that as business leaders we have a unique opportunity to create value in the communities where we live and work. One of the most impactful ways Capital One serves the community is through the volunteer efforts of its thousands of talented associates. In the past year, Capital One associates volunteered more than 70,000 hours in the community, teaching financial literacy in schools, building homes, mentoring at-risk youth, and providing valuable pro bono and leadership guidance to local nonprofit organizations to expand their reach deeper into the community.
Cisco Systems, Inc.	Cisco's corporate giving and citizenship programs build stakeholder trust and loyalty that have a powerful impact on the global community. Cisco's community investment programs are designed to help build stronger and more productive communities by providing resources to nonprofit organizations that address critical needs in the community. Cisco employees volunteer their time and technical expertise to develop strategies that help nonprofits maximize their reach and effectiveness.
Eli Lilly and Company	Lilly's commitment to corporate responsibility is not new—it's a fundamental part of the corporate culture. Through its Lilly Hands and Hearts Employee Volunteer Program, employees have committed to building healthier communities where they live and work, looking beyond operations to address significant societal challenges. In 2008, 35,000 Lilly employees worldwide logged more than 155,000 volunteer hours. Lilly and its employees are creating communities that are healthier in the traditional sense—as well as cleaner, more vibrant and prosperous, and with citizens who are better educated.
Pinnacol Assurance	Pinnacol's community involvement program, Pinnacol in Action, is an integral part of the company's culture. Employees receive paid time off to participate in volunteer activities such as youth mentoring and education, human services programs, community beautification and promoting health awareness. In 2008, Pinnacol employees volunteered 5,121 hours and, with the company's 100 percent match, pledged $68,000 to the local United Way.
Salesforce.com	Salesforce.com established the Salesforce.com Foundation soon after the company was founded in 1999 to ensure that community service was a central part of the corporate culture. To formalize this vision, salesforce.com implemented "1/1/1 Model" to harness the power of salesforce.com's people, resources, and technology through 1% Time, 1% Equity, and 1% Product to improve its communities, inspire youth to be more successful, support the world during times of extreme need, and promote compassionate capitalism.
The Washington Trust Company (Westerly, RI)	Washington Trust's service to the community, through both its employee volunteerism and charitable contributions, unites its employees, customers, and community by spreading a sense of social responsibility and goodwill among them. This creates a positive response that reflects the importance of Washington Trust's employee-selected core values—quality, integrity, and community.

Source: "Awards for Excellence in Workplace Volunteer Programs," Points of Light Foundation, http://www.pointsoflight.org/about/mediacenter/releases/2005/08-05a.cfm, accessed May 18, 2009; "Five Companies Recognized for Workplace Volunteer Programs with 2009 Corporate Engagement Award of Excellence," Points of Light Foundation, http://www.pointsoflight.org/current-news/points-light-institute-honors-corporate-americas-renewed-call-service, accessed July 11, 2009.

Habitat for Humanity.[10] This effort addressed a basic need in life, and now that it has largely been met, Delphi has added investments in other community areas, including education and health care. Delphi's employees still participate in Habit for Humanity, but may also choose to "Adopt a Child for Christmas," support Mexican cultural events, and take payroll deductions to support local charities.

Thus, as stakeholder needs and concerns change, organizations need to adapt their community relations efforts. To determine key areas that require support and to refine the mission statement, a company should periodically conduct a community needs assessment like the one presented in Table 9.3.[11]

"As stakeholder needs and concerns change, organizations need to adapt their community relations efforts."

Table 9.3 Community Needs Assessment

For each of the questions in the survey, circle the number that corresponds to your assessment:

Community Issues	Exceptional	Adequate	Inadequate	Don't know
Parks	3	2	1	0
Culinary water system	3	2	1	0
Street maintenance	3	2	1	0
Garbage collection	3	2	1	0
Snow removal	3	2	1	0
Fire protection	3	2	1	0
Police protection	3	2	1	0
Ambulance service	3	2	1	0
Building inspection	3	2	1	0
Animal control	3	2	1	0
Other code enforcement (weeds, junk cars, etc.)	3	2	1	0
Arts	3	2	1	0
Street lighting	3	2	1	0

Other issues that can be evaluated: grocery stores, pharmacies, clothing stores, fast-food restaurants, entertainment, hardware/lumber stores, auto services, banking/financial services, affordable housing, business offices, warehouses, convenience stores, community colleges, and higher-education satellite campuses.

Source: "Community Needs Assessment Survey Guide," Utah State University Extension, http://extension.usu.edu/files/uploads/surveyguide.pdf, accessed June 1, 2009.

RESPONSIBILITIES TO THE COMMUNITY

It is important for a company to view community stakeholders in a trusting manner, recognizing the potential mutual benefit to each party. In a networked world, much about a company can be learned with a few clicks of a mouse. Activists and disgruntled individuals have used websites to publicize the questionable activities of some companies. McDonald's Corporation, like Wal-Mart, has been the target of numerous "hate" websites that broadcast concerns about the company's products, pricing strategies, and marketing to children. Because of the visibility of business activities and the desire for strategic social responsibility, successful companies strive to build long-term mutually beneficial relationships with relevant communities.

Achieving these relationships may involve some trial and error. Table 9.4 illustrates some of the common mistakes organizations make in planning for and implementing community responsibilities. In contrast, Eli Lilly Pharmaceuticals, headquartered in Indianapolis, Indiana, is a strong supporter of the Indianapolis Symphony Orchestra. In return, the orchestra stages private concerts for Eli Lilly employees. Dell Computer has a similar relationship with the Round Rock Express, a minor league (Texas League) baseball team. A community focus can

Table 9.4 Ten Common Myths and Mistakes About Community Relations

1. *We won't need consent or support from our local government officials or local community.* Many organizations have learned the importance of community relations the hard way when they have tried to clean up sites; get permits; and site, expand, and operate facilities. It is difficult to put a dollar value on community relations until negative relations threaten or jeopardize a company's goals or operations. Organizations often do not allocate sufficient resources to community relations until it is too late. Unresolved conflicts that result from inadequate communication or poor relations can have ugly and expensive ramifications for companies, including injunctions from localities, permit denials, delays in projects, negative press, cease-and-desist orders, lawsuits, new legislation, and so on. Community relations are much more rewarding and well received than crisis management.

2. *We will be stirring up trouble if we talk to the community.* Many project managers are afraid to talk with the community because they are afraid that they will make things worse by stirring up issues that might not already exist. It generally works the opposite. In fact, community members are usually flattered and disarmed (and maybe a tad suspicious) when organizations care enough to talk with them. If you have never initiated dialog before, you can expect the first few times to be contentious, as negative comments, complaints, and fears are expressed. But if you are committed to establishing and maintaining good relations, you have the opportunity to turn those negative comments into positive ones, or at least neutral and balanced ones, as long as your organization's plans are solid. Proactive community relations efforts are very rewarding and can actually make your job much easier in the future. You can even establish yourself as a leader in the community.

3. *We can improve relations with one-way communications efforts (without interaction with interested parties).* If your company or facility is experiencing negative press or strained relations with the community, controlled one-way communication is not the answer. Human nature causes us to want to play it close to the chest. Productive (and perhaps facilitated) interaction is necessary to allow both parties to work through and resolve the issues. Many conflicts are caused by a lack of information, misinformation, different interpretations, stereotypes, repetitive negative behavior, and a perception of different interests. Many of these conflicts can only be resolved through improved, effective communication and joint problem solving, which can only occur through interaction and dialog.

4. *The community cannot add anything meaningful to this process because it is too technically complex.* The authors have been consistently amazed at the level of contribution communities have made to a number of very complex projects with which we have been involved. When given the opportunity and sufficient time to review technical information, it is amazing how much local residents can grasp and contribute to projects. Local involvement and buy-in on engineering projects may even reduce the liability of technical decisions in the future.

5. *Community leaders will request the most unreasonable or costly solutions.* We usually approach issues based on the way we define them. As a community relations firm, we often find that the way our clients define community relations issues and the way the community defines them are quite different. We can't truly know how people will react until we talk with them. We often find that community leaders are sympathetic to companies and facilities in terms of the cost associated with regulatory compliances and environmental cleanup and are much more practical (e.g., when it comes to cleanup levels) than one might imagine.

6. *We shouldn't talk to the community until we have all the answers.* Actually, you gain more credibility by being open enough to allow the community to be involved throughout the process. There is a comfort in knowing all the layers, steps, models, assumptions, and coordination that organizations are undertaking to develop and implement cleanup and other engineering projects. The more the community knows about this effort, the more credible the information will be.

7. *Consulting with elected officials is enough community relations.* The old-fashioned public affairs approach focused on covering your bases with the media and with elected officials. The truth is that elected officials and the media usually tend to their constituents when issues stir up. Your efforts are better spent on improving relations with the local community. This is not to suggest that you shouldn't have relations with the local media and elected officials, but be careful of relying too heavily (or exclusively) on them when an issue escalates.

8. *If our relations are currently strained, we will make relations worse by communicating with the community now.* The first step is to find out why relations are strained (which may require an independent reliable source to uncover). If your intentions are sound and mutually beneficial in some way, how can communication make relations worse? How can relationships get better if you don't communicate?

9. *It will be easier to implement our project without community relations.* Reactive communication efforts resulting from unexpected community concern or media interest always seem to cause more upheaval, require more time and money, and are more disruptive to our clients than planned communication efforts.

10. *We need to do a better job communicating the technical issues.* Don't underestimate the value of the trust and credibility factors that are less technically based: caring and empathy, commitment, openness, and honesty. Messages that communicate these are much more powerful in relations building than technical knowledge.

Source: "10 Common Myths About Community Relations," Chaloux Environmental Communications, Inc., http://www.ce-com.com/10myths.htm, accessed July 11, 2009.

be integrated with concerns for employees and consumers. Chapter 1 provided evidence that satisfied customers and employees are correlated with improved organizational performance.

Economic Issues

From an economic perspective, business is absolutely vital to a community. Companies play a major role in community economic development by bringing jobs to the community and allowing employees to support themselves and their families. These companies also buy supplies, raw materials, utilities, advertising services, and other goods and services from area firms; this in turn produces more economic

"Some companies are dedicated to finding local or regional business partners in an effort to enhance their economic responsibility."

effects. In communities with few employers, an organization that expands in or moves to the area can reduce some of the burden on community services and other subsidized support. Even in large cities with many employers, some companies choose to address social problems that tax the community. In countries with developing economies, a business or industry can also provide many benefits. A new company brings not only jobs but also new technology, related businesses, improvements to infrastructure, and other positive factors. Conversely, the "McDonaldization" of developing countries is a common criticism regarding the effects of U.S. businesses on other parts of the world. For example, although Coca-Cola has been criticized for selling sugared water and exploiting consumers in developing countries, the firm's market expansion strategy often involves creating a network of distributors that improves both employment and entrepreneurship opportunities in a given area.[12]

Interactions with suppliers and other vendors also stimulate the economy. Some companies are even dedicated to finding local or regional business partners in an effort to enhance their economic responsibility. For example, BP feels its most valuable contribution to local economies is to encourage enterprise through job creation, the use of local suppliers, sharing business skills, and the promotion of investment in the economy.[13] Furthermore, there is often a contagion effect when one business moves into an area: By virtue of its prestige or business relationships, such a move can signal to other firms that the area is a viable and attractive place for others to locate. There are parts of the United States that are highly concentrated with automotive manufacturing, financial services, or technology. Local chambers of commerce and economic development organizations often entice new firms to a region because of the positive reputation and economic contagion it brings. Finally, business contributions to local health, education, and recreation projects not only benefit local residents and employees but also may bring additional revenue into the community from tourism and other businesses that appreciate the region's quality of life. FedEx, for example, hosts the FedEx St. Jude Classic PGA golf tournament. The tournament has raised more than $21 million for St. Jude's Children's Hospital and has generated significant tourism for the city of Memphis.[14]

© Nikki Boertman/Reuters/CORBIS

Professional golfer Phil Mickelson tips his hat to applause while playing in the St. Jude Classic golf tournament, a significant fundraiser for the St. Jude Children's Research Hospital

Just as a business brings positive economic effects by expanding in or relocating to an area, it can also cause financial repercussions when it exits a particular market or geographical location. Thus, workforce reduction, or downsizing—a topic discussed in Chapter 7—is a key issue with respect to economic responsibility. The impact of layoffs due to plant closings and corporate restructuring often extends well beyond the financial well-being of affected employees. Laid-off employees typically limit their spending to basic necessities while they look for new employment, and many may ultimately leave the area altogether. Even employees who retain their jobs in such a downsizing may suffer from poor morale, distrust, guilt, and continued anxiety over their own job security, further stifling spending in a community.

Because companies have such a profound impact on the economic viability of the communities in which they operate, firms that value social responsibility consider both the short- and long-term effects on the community of changes in their workforce. Today, many companies that must reduce their workforce—regardless of the reasons—strive to give both employees and the community advance notice and offer placement services to help the community absorb employees who lose their jobs. For example, when Ford Motor Company announced layoffs in St. Paul, Minnesota, they noted that laid-off employees would receive unemployment benefits and additional benefits that would bring them close to their normal wages. Minnesota Governor Tim Pawlenty worked on strategies with Ford to keep the plant open, knowing the potential economic impact of losing 1,770 workers. Eventually, Ford agreed to keep the plant, which manufactures Ford Ranger trucks, open to employ 1,000. Some laid-off workers would be placed on Ford's "GEN pool," which continues to pay out most of their wages and benefits. GEN stands for Guaranteed Employment Number and is part of the UAW contract. Other workers, however, were temporarily laid off with no compensation and benefits.[15] Depending on economic circumstances and business profitability, companies may choose to offer extra compensation commensurate with an employee's length of employment that gives laid-off employees a financial cushion while they find new work. However, the realities of economic turmoil mean that many employees receive little compensation.

Legal Issues

To conduct business, a company must be granted a "license to operate." For many firms, a series of legal and regulatory matters must be resolved before the first employee is hired or the first customer is served. If you open a restaurant, for example, most states require a business license and sales tax number. These documents require basic information, such as business type, ownership structure, owner information, number of expected employees, and other data.

On a fundamental level, society has the ability to dictate what types of organizations are allowed to operate. In exchange for the license to operate, organizations are expected to uphold all legal obligations and standards. We have discussed many of these laws throughout this book, although individual cities, counties, and municipalities will have additional laws and regulations that firms must obey. For example, five fishing companies were charged with dumping squid parts and wastewater that contaminated a suburban Los Angeles harbor, killing sharks, sting rays, and other sea life. These fishing companies violated city ordinances and state water and fish and game regulations.[16]

Other communities have concerns about whether and how businesses fit into existing communities, especially those threatened by urban sprawl and small towns working to preserve a traditional way of life. Some states, cities, and counties have enacted legislation that limits the square footage of stores in an effort to deter "big-box stores," such as Wal-Mart and Home Depot, unless local voters specifically approve their being allowed to build. In most cases, these communities have called for such legislation to combat the noise and traffic congestion that may be associated with such stores, to protect neighborhoods, and to preserve the viability of local small businesses.[17] Thus, although living wages and store location may be ethical issues for business, some local governments have chosen to move them into the legal realm.

Ethical Issues

As more companies view themselves as responsible to the community, they will contemplate their role and the impact of their decisions on communities from an ethical perspective. Consider Clyde Oatis, who renovated an abandoned rice mill in Houston's Fifth Ward to house a business that addresses both environmental and economic issues in the low-income neighborhood. Oatis's U.S. Custom Feed processes food waste once destined for landfills into nutritious food pellets customized for the needs of different species of animals. The company employs and pays a living wage to workers in an area that desperately needs the jobs. Says Oatis, "You've got to have some social responsibility. . . . I think I should do my part."[18]

Business leaders are increasingly recognizing the significance of the role their firms play in the community and the need for their leadership in tackling community problems. Bill Daniels was an extremely successful entrepreneur having founded Cablevision. The Daniels Fund is having a significant impact on business ethics education and other social concerns in the states of Wyoming, Colorado, New Mexico, and Utah. The Daniels Fund donated over $3.5 million to the University of Wyoming to support a statewide business ethics initiative impacting students at the University of Wyoming and throughout the community college system.[19]

These examples demonstrate that the ethical dimension of community responsibility can be multifaceted. This dimension and related programs are not legally mandated but emanate from the particular philosophy of a company and its top managers. For example, since many cities have not mandated a living wage, Clyde Oatis's actions in Houston are based on an ethical obligation that he feels to employees and the community. A company can demonstrate its ethical commitment to the community in many ways. As Bill Daniels's commitment to business ethics illustrates, a common extension of "doing the right thing" ethically is for companies and individuals to begin to allocate funds to assist communities and others in need.

Philanthropic Issues

The community relations function has always been associated with philanthropy, as one of the main historical roles of community relations was to provide gifts, grants, and other resources to worthy causes. Today, that thinking has shifted. Although businesses have the potential to help solve social issues, the success of a business can be enhanced from the publicity generated by and through stakeholder acceptance of community activities. For example, Colorado-based New

Belgium Brewing Company donates $1 for every barrel of beer brewed the prior year to charities within the markets it serves. The brewery tries to divide the funds among states in proportion to interests and needs, considering environmental, social, drug and alcohol awareness, and cultural issues. Donation decisions are made by the firm's philanthropy committee, which is a volunteer group of diverse employees and one or two of the owners; employees are encouraged to bring philanthropy suggestions to the committee.[20] However, New Belgium belongs to an industry that some members of society believe contributes to social problems. Thus, regardless of the positive contributions such a firm makes to the community, some members will always have a negative view of the business.

One of the most significant ways that organizations are exercising their philanthropic responsibilities is through volunteer programs. **Volunteerism** in the workplace, when employees spend company-supported time in support of social causes, has been increasing among companies of all sizes. In 2007, 60.8 million Americans spent over 8 billion hours supporting formal volunteer activities. The four main activities that volunteers perform are fundraising, collecting and distributing food, helping with general labor needs, and tutoring or teaching. These activities are performed for a variety of organizations, with religious, education, and social service agencies topping the list.[21] Figure 9.1 shows the states, large cities, and mid-sized cities with the highest rates of volunteerism.

volunteerism when employees spend company-supported time in support of social causes

Figure 9.1 States and Cities with Highest Volunteerism

Top States:

1	Utah	43.9%
2	Nebraska	39.8%
3	Minnesota	39.7%
4	Alaska	38.6%
5	Montana	38.0%

Top Large Cities:

1	Minneapolis–St. Paul	Minnesota	39.3%
2	Salt Lake City	Utah	37.2%
3	Portland	Oregon	35.6%
4	Seattle	Washington	35.5%
5	Austin	Texas	35.3%

Top Mid-Sized Cities:

1	Provo	Utah	63.8%
2	Iowa City	Iowa	45.1%
3	Madison	Wisconsin	42.3%
4	Ogden	Utah	41.0%
5	Greenville	South Carolina	41.0%

Source: Corporation for National and Community Service, "How We Volunteer in the U.S.," http://www. volunteeringinamerica. gov/national.cfm, accessed July 11, 2009.

People who volunteer feel more connected to other people and society, and ultimately have lower mortality rates, greater functional ability, and lower rates of depression later in life than those who do not volunteer. When volunteering is a result of employment, benefits of volunteering accrue to both the individual, in terms of greater motivation, enjoyment, and satisfaction, and to the organization through employee retention and productivity increases.[22] Communities benefit from the application of new skills and initiatives toward problems, better relations with business, a greater supply of volunteers, assistance to stretch limited resources, and social and economic regeneration.[23] Philanthropic issues are just another dimension of voluntary social responsibility and relate to business's contributions to stakeholders.

At the Toyota manufacturing site in Kentucky, for example, the Volunteers in Place (VIP) program offers incentives to encourage employees to volunteer at least thirty hours per year. The top volunteers win recognition and additional cash contributions to the charity of their choice. A spokesperson for Toyota Motor Manufacturing states, "Employee morale, productivity, and turnover have all improved since the VIP program was implemented."[24] Vanderbilt University's Owen Graduate School of Management is targeting 100 percent volunteerism among its business students, faculty, and staff. The 100 percent Owen Club has raised money for disaster relief and supported Habitat for Humanity, Boys and Girls Clubs of Middle Tennessee, and numerous other causes.[25] Finally, the European Union (EU) declared 2011 as the "European Year of Volunteering," budgeting €15 million, or approximately $20 million, for the promotion of volunteerism across member states. Efforts include joint cooperation by EU institutions, national governments, local authorities, voluntary organizations, the business sector, and the media.[26]

> **"People who volunteer feel more connected to other people and society, and ultimately have lower mortality rates, greater functional ability, and lower rates of depression later in life than those who do not volunteer."**

There are several considerations in deciding how to structure a volunteer program. Attention must be paid to employee values and beliefs; therefore, political or religious organizations should be supported on the basis of individual employee initiative and interest. Warner Brothers, the motion picture company, allows its employees to select from a menu outlining volunteer opportunities. One very successful program for the Turner television division of Time Warner Communications is the division's annual Turner Volunteer Day, which takes place in Turner communities across the world. Now in its tenth year, employees enjoy a day of service and volunteerism at the local charity or cause of their choice.[27] Another issue is what to do when some employees do not wish to volunteer. If the company is not paying for the employees' time to volunteer and volunteering is not a condition of employment or an aspect of the job description, it may be difficult to convince a certain percentage of the workforce to participate. If the organization is paying for one day a month, for example, to allow the employee exposure to volunteerism, then individual compliance is usually expected.

CORPORATE PHILANTHROPY

Philanthropy, which involves any acts of benevolence and goodwill (e.g., making gifts to charities, volunteering for community projects, and taking action to benefit others), provides four major benefits to society. First, it improves the quality of life and helps make communities places where people want to do business, raise families, and enjoy life. Thus, improving the quality of life in a community makes it easier to attract and retain employees and customers. Second, philanthropy reduces government involvement by providing assistance to stakeholders. Third, philanthropy develops employee leadership skills. Many firms, for example, use campaigns by the United Way and other community service organizations as leadership- and skill-building exercises for their employees. Finally, philanthropy helps create an ethical culture and the values that can act as a buffer to organizational misconduct.[28]

In the United States, charitable giving has remained fairly consistent at 1.9 percent of gross domestic product annually. Natural disasters such as hurricanes, floods, and earthquakes can divert giving from traditional causes, with 80 percent of nonprofits surveyed indicating their contributions were flat or down from 2005.[29] Figure 9.2 provides a brief history of the evolution of corporate giving.

The most common way that businesses demonstrate philanthropy is through donations to local and national charitable organizations. Corporations gave more than $14 billion to environmental, educational, and social causes in 2008. Individual giving, which is always the largest component of charitable contributions, was an estimated $229.28 billion, or 75 percent of the total, in 2008. Figure 9.3 displays the sources of charitable giving. Individuals made 75 percent of these donations, with corporations contributing 5 percent. Figure 9.4 displays the major recipients of the $307.65 billion in philanthropic donations made in 2008. Religious organizations received 35 percent of all contributions, with educational causes collecting 13 percent of the funds.[30]

In a general sense, philanthropy involves any acts of benevolence and goodwill, such as making gifts to charities, volunteering for community projects, and taking action to benefit others. For example, your parents may have spent time on nonwork projects that directly benefited the community or a special population. Perhaps you have participated in similar activities through work,

philanthropy
involves any acts of benevolence and goodwill, such as making gifts to charities, volunteering for community projects, and taking action to benefit others

Figure 9.2 Brief History of Corporate Giving

1600–1850	Early American and British corporations are most often granted charters by the government to serve the public through some defined task, such as building a bridge or a road. They have clearly defined restrictions on their time and goals and, because their existence was granted by the people, they have a corresponding responsibility to their community.
1889	Carnegie's "Gospel of Wealth" is published as two separate essays for the *North American Review.* It stresses that industry is good for society, but that those made wealthy by these companies have a responsibility to give back to the communities where they made their money. While the essays do not encourage corporate giving, they recognize that the corporation owes its prosperity to the consumers and is responsible to pay back this debt.
1935	The Revenue Act allows businesses to deduct up to 5% of their profits as charitable gifts.
1953	A Supreme Court decision not to rule on the case *Smith v. Barlow* ensures that corporations can make gifts, even if their generosity does not provide a direct benefit to the business.
1981	A provision in the Economic Recovery Tax Act makes in-kind donations more beneficial to corporations.
1986	The corporate income tax rate is decreased from 46% to 34%, thereby reducing the tax benefits of corporate philanthropy.
2001	Corporations give more than $660 million after the attacks of September 11.
2005	Corporations give more than $344 million after the Indian Ocean Tsunami and another $936 million after Hurricane Katrina.

Source: Giving USA Foundation, "Giving USA Spotlight," Issue 2, 2008, p. 6.

school groups, or associations. Have you ever served Thanksgiving dinner at a homeless shelter? Have you ever raised money for a neighborhood school? Have you ever joined a social club that volunteered member services to local charities?

Most religious organizations, educational institutions, and arts programs rely heavily on philanthropic donations from both individuals and organizations. Philanthropy is a major driver of the nonprofit sector of the economy, as these organizations rely on the time, money, and talents of both individuals and organizations to operate and fund their programs. Consider the Moscow Center for Prison Reform (MCPR) in Moscow. The museum and public center, built in honor of the Nobel peace prize winner and human rights activist Andrei Sakharov, recently faced a severe financial crisis because Russia lacks a culture of

Figure 9.3 Sources of Charitable Giving ($ in billions)

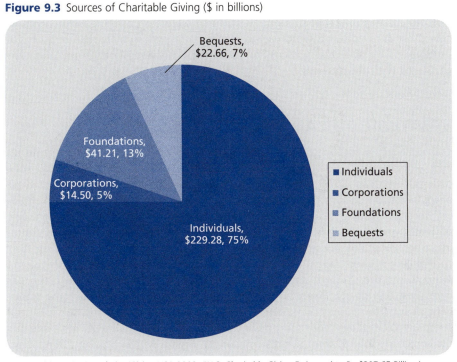

Source: Giving USA Foundation/Giving USA 2009, "U.S. Charitable Giving Estimated to Be $307.65 Billion in 2008," http://www.givingusa.org/press_releases/gusa/GivingReaches300billion.pdf, accessed July 12, 2009.

Figure 9.4 Recipients of Charitable Giving ($ in billions)

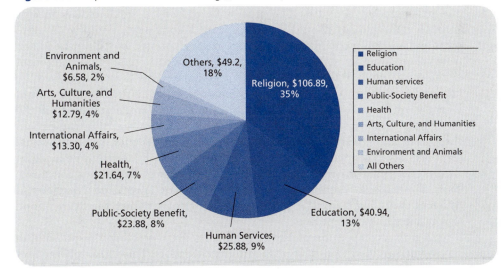

Source: Giving USA Foundation/Giving USA 2009, "U.S. Charitable Giving Estimated to Be $307.65 Billion in 2008," http://www.givingusa.org/press_releases/gusa/GivingReaches300billion.pdf, accessed July 12, 2009.

corporate philanthropy and the associated funding of nongovernment museums. The museum's political bent, along with Russian laws prohibiting tax benefits on charitable donations, caused museum managers to look outside their country for funding. As a result, the Moscow office of the U.S.-based Ford Foundation has partnered with the museum.[31]

STRATEGIC PHILANTHROPY DEFINED

Our concept of corporate philanthropy extends beyond financial contributions and explicitly links company missions, organizational competencies, and various stakeholders. Thus, we define **strategic philanthropy** as the synergistic use of an organization's core competencies and resources to address key stakeholders' interests and to achieve both organizational and social benefits. Strategic philanthropy goes well beyond the traditional benevolent philanthropy of donating a percentage of sales to social causes by involving employees (utilizing their core skills), organizational resources and expertise (equipment, knowledge, and money), and the ability to link employees, customers, suppliers, and social needs with these key assets. Strategic philanthropy involves both financial and nonfinancial contributions to stakeholders (employee time, goods and services, and company technology and equipment as well as facilities), but it also benefits the company. John Damonti, president of the Bristol-Myers Squibb Foundation, reflected, "When you align your contributions with your business focus, you then can draw on the greater wealth of the corporation's people, information, and resources."[32]

Organizations are best suited to deal with social or stakeholder issues in areas with which they have some experience, knowledge, or expertise. From a business perspective, companies want to refine their intellectual capital, reinforce their core competencies, and develop synergies between business and philanthropic activities. The process of addressing stakeholder concerns through philanthropy should be strategic to a company's ongoing development and improvement. For example, American Express, a global financial and travel company, contributed funds and know-how to initiate the development of the Academy of Travel and Tourism in Hungary. This project benefited the Hungarian economy, tested the entrepreneurial spirit and skills of American Express employees, and reinforced the company's understanding of the Hungarian market.[33] Some critics would argue that this was not true philanthropy because American Express received business benefits. However, social responsibility takes place on many levels and effective philanthropy depends on the synergy between stakeholder needs and business competencies and goals. Thus, the fact that each partner to the Academy of Travel and Tourism had different goals and earned unique benefits does not diminish the overall good that resulted from the project.

As global competition escalates, companies are increasingly responsible to stakeholders in justifying their philanthropic endeavors. This ultimately requires greater planning and alignment of philanthropic efforts with overall strategic goals. Table 9.5 provides additional examples of philanthropic activities.

strategic philanthropy the synergistic use of an organization's core competencies and resources to address key stakeholders' interests and to achieve both organizational and social benefits

Table 9.5 Examples of Corporate Philanthropy

- After British Petroleum (now BP) was criticized by Greenpeace for its environmental practices, the company created a $1 billion business and many new jobs in solar power, a renewable and nonpolluting source of energy.

- The Target Corporation regularly donates 5 percent of its pretax income to charities, whereas employees both select and volunteer in many of these community-based organizations.

- Altria spent over $1 billion in the past decade to combat domestic abuse, feed the ill and elderly, and respond to natural disasters.

- Customers of Hanna Andersson, a manufacturer of high-quality children's clothes, can return worn clothing for credit toward their next purchase, with the used clothing donated to needy children.

- Boeing Company donated $15 million to the National Air and Space Museum. Since the museum opened in 1976, Boeing has been deeply involved in the aircraft collection and restoration of artifacts.

- Businesspeople from the toy industry in Brazil created the Abrinq Foundation for Children's Rights, which is dedicated to promoting the rights of children and youth at risk in Brazil.

- Seafirst Bank's partnership with Indian Nations in the state of Washington resulted in education programs for Native Americans in financial management and tribal economic development and helped Seafirst employees better understand cultural issues related to business relationships and development.

- More than 6,000 companies sponsor matching-gift programs, where an employee's personal donation to an educational institution is matched by the employer.

Sources: Peggy Dulany and David Winder, "The Status of and Trends in Private Philanthropy in the Southern Hemisphere," Synergos Institute, http://www.synergos.org/globalphilanthropy/02/philanthropyinsouthernhemisphere.htm, accessed January 28, 2003; Reynold Levy, *Give and Take: A Candid Account of Corporate Philanthropy* (Boston: Harvard Business School Press, 1999); "Better to Give and to Receive," *Hemispheres* (January 1997); Luba Krekhovetsky, "Charity Begins with Homes," *Canadian Business* (December 30, 2002): 91–93; Glen Peters, *Waltzing with the Raptors: A Practical Roadmap to Protecting Your Company's Reputation* (New York: John Wiley, 1999); Ann Svendsen, *The Stakeholder Strategy* (San Francisco: Berrett-Koehler, 1998); Nanette Byrnes, "Smarter Corporate Giving," *Business Week Online*, November 28, 2005, http://www.businessweek.com/print/magazine/content/05_48/b39616707.htm, accessed May 11, 2006; Jacqueline Trescott, "Boeing Donates $15 Million to Expand Smithsonian Aviation Annex at Dulles," *Washington Post*, April 11, 2006, p. C01.

STRATEGIC PHILANTHROPY AND SOCIAL RESPONSIBILITY

It is important to place strategic philanthropy in the context of organizational responsibilities at the economic, legal, ethical, and philanthropic levels. Most companies understand the need to be economically successful for the benefit of all stakeholders and to comply with the laws required within our society and others in which they do business. Additionally, through the establishment of core values

"Strategic social responsibility can reduce the cost of business transactions, establish trust among stakeholders, improve teamwork, and preserve the social capital necessary for an infrastructure for doing business."

and ethical cultures, most firms are recognizing the many benefits of good ethics. As we saw in Chapter 1, evidence is accumulating that there is a positive relationship between social responsibility and performance, especially with regard to customer satisfaction, investor loyalty, and employee commitment. Strategic social responsibility can reduce the cost of business transactions, establish trust among stakeholders, improve teamwork, and preserve the social capital necessary for an infrastructure for doing business. In sum, these efforts improve the context and environment for corporate operations and performance.[34]

When Noah's Bagels began expanding beyond its original Berkeley, California, location in the late 1980s, the company focused not only on opening new retail stores but also on helping surrounding neighborhoods. Noah's sought to be a positive, dynamic force in its local communities because it "recognizes the importance of giving the community more than just exhilarated taste buds." Thus, the company began to link its philanthropic efforts directly with the core operations and skills required to run the business. For example, Noah's donates bagels and other foods to fight community hunger. The company also gives employees paid time off to work on service projects that benefit surrounding neighborhoods. Store managers can choose a local charity and apply for matching funds from corporate headquarters. Customers are encouraged to comment on the company's bagels, coffee, and community affairs. All of these efforts directly link Noah's philanthropy to issues that positively affect, and reflect, its operations and marketing. Because the company carefully chooses projects and charities that are aligned with its core competencies, Noah's Bagels is taking a strategic approach to its philanthropy.[35]

Many companies consider philanthropy only after they have met their financial, legal, and ethical obligations. As companies strive for social responsibility, their ability to meet each obligation lays the foundation for success with other responsibilities. In addition, there is synergy in corporate efforts directed at the four levels of responsibility. As one of the most voluntary dimensions of social responsibility, philanthropy has not always been linked to profits or business ethics. In fact, the traditional approach to philanthropy disconnects giving from business performance and its impact on stakeholders. Before the evolution of strategic philanthropy, most corporate gift programs separated the company from the organizations, causes, and individuals that its donations most benefited.[36]

Research has begun to highlight organizations' formalization of philanthropic activities and their efforts to integrate philanthropic goals with other business strategies and implementation. United States companies are adopting a more businesslike approach to philanthropy and experiencing a better image, increased employee loyalty, and improved customer ties.[37] Philanthropy involves using organizational resources, and specific methods are used to measure its impact on key stakeholders. In this case, philanthropy is an investment from which a company can gain some type of value.

The traditional approach to corporate philanthropy is characterized by donations and related activities that are not purposefully aligned with the strategic goals and resources of the firm. For instance, employees may be encouraged to volunteer in the community but receive little direction on where or how to spend their time. Employees of Fuji Bank of Japan, for example, may apply for leaves of absence to take part in volunteer opportunities.[38] After the September 11, 2001, terrorist attacks, companies and employees became quite creative in their philanthropic efforts. One result was "leave-based donation programs," which allow employees to donate the value of accumulated vacation and sick- and personal-leave days to a nonprofit cause. The U.S. Treasury Department approved the idea and clarified regulations to benefit employees, companies, and nonprofits.[39] Indeed, there are numerous examples of companies supporting community involvement. Although these actions are noble, they are not always considered in tandem with organizational goals and strengths.

In some cases, corporate contributions may be made to nonprofit organizations in which top managers have a personal interest. When Unilever acquired Ben and Jerry's Homemade, they agreed to support the following causes and initiatives that are extremely important to founders Ben Cohen and Jerry Greenfield. Unilever agreed to maintain the Vermont employment and manufacture base, pay workers a livable wage with complete benefits, buy milk from Vermont dairy farmers who do not use bovine growth hormones, contribute over $1.1 million annually to the Ben and Jerry's Foundation, open more Partner Shops owned by nonprofit organizations providing employment opportunities for disadvantaged persons, and maintain relationships with alternate suppliers.[40] Finally, many companies will match employees' personal gifts to educational institutions. Although gift-matching programs instill employee pride and assist education, they are rarely linked to company operations and competencies.[41] In the traditional approach to corporate philanthropy, then, companies have good intentions, but there is no solid integration with organizational resources and objectives.

In the social responsibility model that we propose, philanthropy is only one focal point for a corporate vision that includes both the welfare of the firm and benefits to stakeholders. This requires support from top management as well as a strategic planning structure that incorporates stakeholder concerns and benefits. Corporate giving, volunteer efforts, and other contributions should be considered and aligned not only with corporate strategy but also with financial, legal, and ethical obligations. The shift from traditional benevolent philanthropy to strategic philanthropy has come about as companies struggled in the 1990s and 2000s to redefine their missions, alliances, and scope, while becoming increasingly accountable to stakeholders and society.

Strategic Philanthropy Versus Cause-Related Marketing

The first attempts by organizations to coordinate organizational goals with philanthropic giving emerged with cause-related marketing in the early 1980s. Whereas strategic philanthropy links corporate resources and knowledge to address broader social, customer, employee, and supplier problems and needs, **cause-related marketing** ties an organization's product(s) directly to a social concern through a marketing program. Table 9.6 compares cause-related marketing and strategic philanthropy.

With cause-related marketing, a percentage of a product's sales is usually donated to a cause appealing to the relevant target market. The Avon Breast Cancer Crusade, for example, generates proceeds for the breast cancer cause through several fundraising efforts, including the sale of special "pink ribbon" products by Avon independent sales representatives nationwide (see Figure 9.5). Gifts are awarded by the Avon Products Foundation, Inc., a nonprofit 501(c)(3) accredited public charity, to support six vital areas of the breast cancer cause with a focus on medically underserved women, biomedical research, clinical care, financial assistance and support services, educational seminars and advocacy training, and early detection and awareness programs nationwide. Both the cause and Avon Crusade "pink ribbon" products appeal to Avon's primary target market, women. Between 1992 and 2008, the Avon Breast Cancer Crusade generated more than $585 million net in total funds raised worldwide to fund access to care and finding a cure for breast cancer.[42]

cause-related marketing business strategy that ties an organization's product(s) directly to a social concern through a marketing program

Table 9.6 Strategic Philanthropy Contrasted with Cause-Related Marketing

	Strategic Philanthropy	Cause-Related Marketing
Focus	Organizational	Product or product line
Goals	Improvement of organizational competence or tying organizational competence to social need or charitable cause; builds brand equity	Increase of product sales
Time frame	Ongoing	Traditionally of limited duration
Organizational members involved	Potentially all organizational employees	Marketing department and related personnel
Cost	Moderate—alignment with organizational strategies and mission	Minimal—alliance development and promotion expenditures

Figure 9.5 The Avon Breast Cancer Crusade

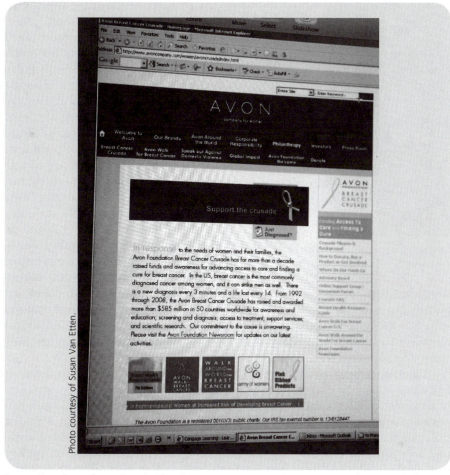

Photo courtesy of Susan Van Etten.

Source: "Avon Breast Cancer Crusade," http://www.avoncompany.com/women/avoncrusade/, accessed July 12, 2009.

American Express was the first company to use cause-related marketing widely, when it began advertising in 1983 that it would give a percentage of credit card charges to the Statue of Liberty and Ellis Island Restoration Fund.[43] As is the case with Avon, American Express companies generally prefer to support causes that are of interest to their target markets. In a single year, organizations paid more than $500 million for the rights to support various social programs, ultimately raising roughly $2.5 billion for these causes.[44] Thus, a key feature of cause-related marketing is the promise of donations to a particular social cause based on customer sales or involvement. Whereas strategic philanthropy is tied to the entire organization, cause-related marketing is linked to a specific product and marketing program. The program may involve in-store promotions, messages on packages and labels, and other marketing communications.[45]

Although cause-related marketing has its roots in the United States, the marketing tool is gaining widespread usage in other parts of the world. A study by

For every pair of shoes the company sells, Toms donates a pair of shoes to a child living in poverty

PR NewsFoto/Tom's Shoes

Saatchi & Saatchi found that about 40 percent of European senior marketers were aligning their cause-related marketing budgets with brand communication programs. For example, the New Covent Garden Soup Co. recently partnered with a homeless charity in Great Britain. During the Christmas season, portions of sales of New Covent Garden's pea and ham soup were donated to help renovate the charity's kitchens. Tesco, a large European grocery chain, also joined the cause by donating funds based on every soup carton sold in the six-week holiday season.[46] Business in the Community, a nonprofit group in the United Kingdom, sponsors annual awards for British firms that demonstrate excellence in cause-related marketing. Walkers, a manufacturer of cookies and biscuits, is a recent winner due to its distribution of more than 2.3 million books to schools in the United Kingdom. Bettys and Taylors of Harrogate Yorkshire Tea also received an award for its cause-related marketing program to plant trees and slow forest degradation in regions where it sources its teas and commodities.[47]

Cause-related marketing activities have real potential to affect buying patterns. For cause-related marketing to be successful, consumers must have awareness of and affinity for the cause, the brand and cause must be associated and perceived as a good fit, and consumers should be able to transfer feelings toward the cause to their brand perceptions and purchase intentions. Studies have found that a majority of consumers said that, given equal price and product quality, they would be more likely to buy the product associated with a charitable cause. Eighty percent of customers say they have more positive perceptions of firms that support causes about which they personally care. These surveys have also noted that most marketing directors felt that cause-related marketing would increase in importance over the coming years.[48] Through cause-related marketing, companies first become aware that supporting social causes, such as environmental awareness, health and human services, education, and the arts, can support business goals and help bolster a firm's reputation, especially those with an ethically neutral image. However, firms that are perceived as unethical may be suspected of ulterior motives in developing cause-related campaigns.[49]

One of the main weaknesses with cause-related marketing is that some consumers cannot link specific philanthropic efforts with companies.[50] Consumers may have difficulty recalling exact philanthropic relationships because many cause-related marketing campaigns have tended to be of short duration and have not always had a direct correlation to the sponsoring firm's core business. Because strategic philanthropy is more pervasive and relates to company attributes and skills, such alliances should have greater stakeholder recognition, appreciation, and long-term value.

STAKEHOLDERS IN STRATEGIC PHILANTHROPY

Although more businesses are moving toward adopting a strategic philanthropy model, others are still focusing only on the needs of individual stakeholders. Although these efforts are important and commendable, companies may not be realizing the full benefits for themselves and their stakeholders. For example, the implementation of cause-related marketing efforts may not reinforce employee skills and competencies. Instead, such campaigns usually focus on generating product sales and donations to a specific cause. Volunteer programs may benefit the community and employee morale, but the value of this service could be greatly enhanced through synergies between current and future job-related aptitude and nonprofit needs.

In this section, we offer examples of organizations that have effectively collaborated with various stakeholders in the pursuit of mutual benefits. Their efforts serve as examples of best practices in implementing and managing strategic philanthropy by engaging, not just managing, stakeholder relationships.[51] The following strategic philanthropic efforts demonstrate a dual concern for meeting stakeholder needs while strengthening organizational competencies.

By providing a free networking curriculum to schools, Cisco contributes to education and also ensures an ongoing supply of skilled maintenance people who can service Cisco equipment. In addition, in consideration of varied stakeholder interests, Cisco believes such involvement boosts brand equity with customers, investors, and the community in general.[52] Sony's philanthropic efforts reflect the diverse interests of their key businesses and focus on several distinct areas and stakeholder interests: arts education, arts and culture, health and human services, civic and community outreach, education, and volunteerism. Each operating company has its own philanthropic priorities and unique resources, from product donations to recordings and screenings that benefit a multitude of causes. Sony Corporation of America is a strong supporter of arts and culture, and education and volunteerism are key components of Sony Electronics' philanthropic efforts.[53]

Employees

A key to organizational success is the ability of organizations to attract, socialize, and retain competent and qualified employees. Through strategic philanthropy initiatives, companies have the opportunity to increase employee commitment, motivation, and skill refinement. For example, United Airlines Foundation supports and encourages volunteerism among its 63,000 employees. Every holiday season for years, United employees in communities around the world have hosted Fantasy Flights—magical flights that take disadvantaged or seriously ill children on a trip to Santa's workshop at the North Pole. Clowns, magicians, and elves entertain the children in specially decorated gate areas. The children also receive goodies and presents to take home for the holidays. Many local companies and charitable organizations join in these festivities. United Airlines' strengths include the ability to allow employees to link the company's competencies to social causes of interest.[54]

BE&K, an international construction and engineering firm headquartered in Birmingham, Alabama, has mobilized its retirees for supporting special community service projects. Because these retirees have years of experience in the construction business, they are particularly suited for philanthropic efforts that involve renovation, design, and related skills. For example, one retired employee heads a YWCA effort to renovate housing for disabled and low-income women.[55] BE&K has also extended its employee safety and drug abuse programs into the philanthropic realm. These programs were originally designed to assist employees, reduce accidents, and help the business perform more effectively. After taking this experience and program to others in the industry and beyond, the company received the FBI Director's Community Leadership Award for outstanding contributions to the community in the prevention of drug abuse.[56]

Customers

As industries become increasingly competitive, companies are seeking ways to differentiate themselves in customers' minds. Home Depot, for example, has been progressive in the way it approaches philanthropy. The company has aligned its expertise and resources to address community needs. Its relationship with Habitat for Humanity gives employees a chance to improve their skills and bring direct knowledge back into the workplace to benefit customers. It also enhances Home Depot's image of expertise as the do-it-yourself center. Home Depot has invested $57 million to support rebuilding efforts throughout the Gulf region as a result of numerous natural disasters. Combining capital construction with philanthropic support, this investment will create jobs, drive economic activity, and support local community efforts to rebuild homes.[57]

Bankers Trust Private Bank, part of German-headquartered Deutsche Bank AG, introduced its Wealth with Responsibility program to assist wealthy families in planning for philanthropy. In addition to financial experts, the bank employs consultants and advisors who help families set goals, invest for future wealth, and provide funds to charities and other groups. Thus, the bank is providing services that not only benefit wealthy clients but also direct assets into philanthropic directions to benefit society. The program targets clients around the world, with a focus on Europeans who are just beginning to become interested in philanthropy.[58]

The Verizon Reads program is multifaceted to affect the largest number of stakeholders. With an estimated 40 million U.S. citizens classified as illiterate, Verizon feels it can influence customers' quality of life with broad-based initiatives, most of which are chronicled on www.verizonreads.net. Employees are encouraged to volunteer in education-related programs and to take part in initiatives that will strengthen their own literacy and technology use.[59] Target is another firm that contributes significant resources to education, including direct donations of $170 million to schools as well as fundraising and scholarship programs to assist teachers and students. Through the retailer's Take Charge of Education program, customers using a Target Guest Card can designate a specific school to which Target donates 1 percent of that customer's total purchases. This program is designed to make customers feel that their purchases are benefiting their community while increasing the use of Target Guest Cards.[60]

Business Partners

More companies are using philanthropic goals and social concerns as a measure of with whom they would like to do business. Companies are increasingly requiring social audits and the adoption of industry codes of ethics on the part of their business partners. The Freeplay Group, based in South Africa, is an example of a company founded on the principle of "making money and making a difference." The company's first product was wind-up radios that were originally intended for use in poor nations where electricity and batteries are scarce. For example, these radios have been used to transmit elementary school lessons in South Africa and election results in Ghana. The radios now sell in many countries at retailers such as Sharper Image, Radio Shack, and Harrod's. Rotary International and other community organizations are using the radios to implement programs that benefit society and communities. Freeplay's investors include the General Electric Pension Trust and Liberty Life, a South African insurance firm. These investors and customers have chosen Freeplay for its solid business plan founded on broader social goals. Freeplay continues to innovate and now offers a range of products, including lanterns, flashlights, radios, and other consumer products that "make energy available to everybody all of the time."[61]

BJC HealthCare works with other area health-care systems to make health insurance available to St. Louis, Missouri, residents who cannot afford it, including the Care Partners and ConnectCare programs. Care Partners offers twenty-four-hour emergency care and primary-care facilities to anyone in need, whether they are insured or not. ConnectCare was launched by city officials and community leaders with the same goal of providing health services to all citizens. BJC has won praise for its ability to work with insurers, other systems, and the public in supporting health insurance initiatives with the collective goal of improving people's lives. These collaborative ventures allocate the costs of caring for indigent and uninsured patients across the community, a strategy that benefits all hospitals and care providers representing suppliers and business partners' best interests.[62]

> **"Society expects businesses to be socially responsible and to contribute to the well-being of the communities in which they operate."**

Community and Society

Society expects businesses to be socially responsible and to contribute to the well-

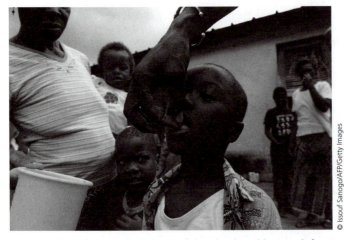

A nurse administers Ivermectin, a medicine developed by Merck for treating river blindness, to a young child in Africa

being of the communities in which they operate. The Coca-Cola Company takes a strategic view of its role in society by linking its company resources and operating practices to stakeholder issues. Although it acknowledges the profusion of problems in today's world, Coca-Cola has chosen to focus its energies and resources on environmental issues where the company has an impact and relevant expertise. Water quality, water conservation, and waste reduction are therefore key considerations in its packaging and operational decisions.[63]

Coca-Cola has also contributed funds and expertise around the world to support collaborations that respond to these environmental concerns. These projects involve bottlers, employees, suppliers, regulators, customers, and other corporations interested in building strategies for environmental excellence.

Merck developed a drug to combat river blindness, a disease afflicting more than 18 million people worldwide. Merck's expertise as a pharmaceutical laboratory allowed it to develop Mectizan to treat river blindness, and its humanitarian orientation led it to donate the drug to nearly 25 million people at risk in ten African countries. Jimmy Carter, former U.S. president and cofounder of the Carter Center notes, "I think Merck has set a standard of the highest possible quality. [The MECTIZAN Donation Program has] been one of the most remarkable and exciting and inspiring partnerships that I have ever witnessed."[64] The benefits of the decision to develop and donate the drug to heavily afflicted areas demonstrates Merck's understanding of strategic philanthropy and the positive effects on society, as well as on employees, investors, and even customers.

LensCrafters is a key member of One Sight, a family of charitable programs dedicated to improving vision for people in need. Employees and doctors of LensCrafters participate by hand-delivering eye care and eye wear to people in local and global locations. Not wanting the firm's motives questioned, the CEO directed employees not to seek publicity. He states, "I do not want anyone thinking the company is doing this for any reason other than it's the right thing to do." Employees can engage in other philanthropy, but this effort makes more sense because it leverages LensCrafters' eye-care provision skills and competencies.[65]

Finally, groups of companies and industry associations are also working to extend the philanthropic efforts of their member companies. For example, the American Apparel and Footwear Association assists manufacturers in donating surplus apparel to the needy, homeless, and disaster victims.[66] By working with their trade association, apparel manufacturers have been able to benefit from strategic philanthropy.

Global Social Entrepreneurs Many companies worldwide have become increasingly concerned with the society and communities in which they operate. This new breed of business is concerned about bettering the lives of the surrounding community while providing a profitable good or service at the same time. This new type of business is called *social entrepreneurship.* Leaders in organizations from the United States to Egypt are becoming social entrepreneurs.

Social entrepreneurs typically follow a four-stage process. In the first stage of envisioning, a clear need, gap, and opportunity are identified. The second stage is engaging in the opportunity and doing something about it. Enabling something to happen is the third stage. The final stage is enacting and leading the project to completion.

The Institute of OneWorld Health, based in San Francisco, has been a leader in social entrepreneurship. OneWorld's focus is on creating medicines to cure diseases that affect Third World countries. The nonprofit organization is currently working on creating a cure for VL. VL is known as the black fever and is carried by sand flies. Over 1.5 million people are infected with the black fever worldwide. It is estimated that 200,000 people die of VL annually, and about 500,000 new cases are discovered each year. The black fever has a devastating effect in Third World countries.

The efforts of OneWorld have not gone unnoticed. The institute has received a $10 million grant from the Bill and Melinda Gates Foundation to help continue its fight against diseases. The Institute of OneWorld also received the 2005 Skoll Award for Social Entrepreneurship. The award comes with a $615,000 donation over the next few years. The Skoll Foundation awards funds to several organizations yearly that are leaders in social entrepreneurship.

The nonprofit status offers many advantages to OneWorld. Most of its funding comes from the government or philanthropic organizations. Biotech companies have gained a channel for intellectual property that might normally have gone unused because of lack of profit potential. Many members of the scientific community have donated time and effort to help fight disease in Third World countries.

Social entrepreneurs are present all over the world. Take, for example, Sekem, located just north of Cairo, Egypt. Sekem was founded in 1977 by Dr. Ibrahim Abouleish. Since 1977, the organization has grown from one person to several business firms. Sekem produces several organic products on its farms. The company focuses on these long-term objectives:

- We endeavor to build our economic, social and cultural activities so that they invigorate each other.
- We wish to build a long-term, trusting and fair relationship with our partners.
- We nurture the development of all co-workers by facilitating the possibility to learn through their work, to commit themselves to their task and to practice agriculture.
- We intend to restore the earth through implementing and developing biodynamic agriculture.
- We want to provide various products and services of the highest standards to meet the needs of the consumer.
- We educate and train children and youth according to contemporary human sciences.
- We provide Primary Health Care and therapy using holistic medicine.
- We strive through our research to meet the questions of all aspects of life for the present age.

(Continued)

Sekem developed an alternative method for using pesticides to protect cotton crops. This new system led to a ban on crop dusting in Egypt. In 2003, Sekem received the Right Livelihood Award. The award is given by the Swedish Parliament for advancing social and cultural developments. This award is known as the "Alternative Nobel Prize." The award recipient also receives $230,000 to help further social responsibility.

Sekem has also opened a school for holistic education. The profits earned by Sekem have helped fund medical centers and education for both children and adults. They are committed to helping the community break away from the poverty that has taken control of their lives. Sekem is continually expanding operations to help the community achieve a higher quality of life.

Sources: Anonymous, "Two Awards for the Institute of OneWorld Health," *Appropriate Technology* (June 2005): 26; Christian Seelos and Johanna Mair, "Social Entrepreneurship," *Business Horizons* 48, no. 3 (May–June 2005): 241–246; http://www. sekem.com/objectives.html; http://www.skollfoundation.org/aboutsocialentrepreneurship/index.asp; John L. Thompson, "The World of the Social Entrepreneur," *International Journal of Public Sector Management* 15 (2002): 412–432.

Natural Environment As we will see in Chapter 11, environmental causes have become increasingly important to stakeholders in recent years. Environmental abuses have damaged company and industry reputations and resulted in lost sales. 3M is one company that has been very aggressive in implementing environmentally friendly processes and procedures throughout its operations. This commitment extends to employees, as the company provides van transportation to work for employees within a fifteen-mile radius of the corporate office. If a van has only a few riders, each rider pays a minimal monthly fee to help offset some of the costs of the program. If the number of employees using the program increases to a specified level, 3M drops the monthly fee. The van-pooling initiative has minimized pollution levels.[67] 3M is able to coordinate its commitment to various stakeholders, including employees, customers, the natural environment, and the community. For this reason, 3M has been selected for inclusion in the Dow Jones Sustainability Index as a "gold class" leader.[68] The company also scores very highly on *Fortune* magazine's annual Most Admired Companies list.

BENEFITS OF STRATEGIC PHILANTHROPY

To pursue strategic philanthropy successfully, organizations must weigh both the costs and benefits associated with planning and implementing it as a corporate priority. Companies that assume a strategic approach to philanthropy are using an investment model with respect to their charitable acts and donations. In other words, these firms are not just writing checks; they are investing in solutions to stakeholder problems and corporate needs. Such an investment requires the commitment of company time, money, and human talent to succeed. Companies often need to hire staff to manage projects, communicate goals and opportunities throughout the firm, develop long-term priorities and programs, handle requests for funds, and represent the firm on other aspects of philanthropy. In addition, philanthropy consumes the time and energy of all types of employees within the organization. Thus, strategic philanthropy involves real corporate costs that must be justified and managed.

Most scholars and practitioners agree that the benefits of strategic philanthropy ultimately outweigh its costs. The positive return on strategic philanthropy is closely aligned with benefits obtained from strong social responsibility. First, in the United States, businesses can declare up to 10 percent of pretax profits as tax-deductible contributions. Most firms do not take full advantage of this benefit, as 10 percent is viewed as a very generous contribution level.

"Strategic philanthropy involves real corporate costs that must be justified and managed."

In fact, corporate giving has averaged just over 1 percent of pretax profits in the last several decades. Second, companies with a strategic approach to philanthropy experience rewards in the workplace. Employees involved in volunteer projects and related ventures not only have the opportunity to refine their professional skills, but they also develop a stronger sense of loyalty and commitment to their employer. A national survey of employees demonstrated that corporate philanthropy is an important driver in employee relations. Those who perceive their employer as strong in philanthropy were four times as likely to be very loyal as those who believed their employer was less philanthropic. Employees in firms with favorable ratings on philanthropy are also more likely to recommend the company and its products to others and have intentions to stay with the employer. Positive impressions of the executives' role in corporate philanthropy also influenced employees' affirmative attitudes toward their employer.[69] Results such as these lead to improved productivity, enhanced employee recruitment practices, and reduced employee turnover, each contributing to the overall effectiveness and efficiency of the company.

As a third benefit, companies should experience enhanced customer loyalty as a result of their strategic philanthropy. By choosing projects and causes with links to its core business, a firm can create synergies with its core competencies and customers. For example, Rosie O'Donnell used her celebrity status and television talk show to establish the For All Kids Foundation to support the social and cultural development of disadvantaged children. The foundation has been funded by a number of creative projects, including *Kids Are Punny,* a compilation of riddles, puns, and drawings sent by kids to the *Rosie O'Donnell Show.* Warner Books, the publisher, agreed to contribute its net profits to the foundation. Warner-Lambert, the manufacturer of Listerine Antiseptic mouthwash, donated $500,000 for kisses ($1,000 a kiss) Rosie received from guests on her show. In addition to grants from corporations, the foundation is also funded through celebrity charity auctions on eBay.[70] To the benefit of Warner Brothers studio and production, these creative projects not only support hundreds of children's causes and charities but also earned the show critical praise and customer loyalty. Because a majority of Rosie O'Donnell's viewers were women with children, her For All Kids Foundation was a natural and strategic vehicle.

Finally, strategic philanthropy should improve a company's overall reputation in the community and ease government and community relations. Research indicates a strong negative relationship between illegal activity and reputation, whereas firms that contribute to charitable causes enjoy enhanced reputations. Moreover, companies that contribute to social causes, especially to problems that arise as a result of their actions, may be able to improve their reputations after committing a crime.[71]

If a business is engaged in a strategic approach to contributions, volunteerism, and related activities, a clear purpose is to enhance and benefit the community. By properly implementing and communicating these achievements, the company will "do well by doing good." Essentially, community members and others use cues from a strategic philanthropy initiative, along with other social responsibility programs, to form a lasting impression—or reputation—of the firm. These benefits, together with others discussed in this section, are consistent with research conducted on European firms. Figure 9.6 highlights the perceived benefits of corporate philanthropy to companies located in France, Germany, and the United Kingdom. The table suggests that companies in these countries believe that their charitable activities generally have a positive effect on goodwill, public relations, community relations, employee motivation, and customer loyalty.[72]

Figure 9.6 Benefits of Socially Responsible Corporate Philanthropy

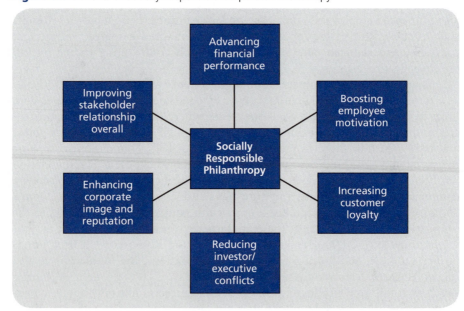

Source: Adapted from *Insight Business* published by USC's Center for Management Communication www. marshallinsight.com © copyright 2006 by USC Marshall School of Business. All Rights Reserved.

IMPLEMENTATION OF STRATEGIC PHILANTHROPY

Attaining the benefits of strategic philanthropy depends on the integration of corporate competencies, business stakeholders, and social responsibility objectives to be fully effective. However, fruitfully implementing a strategic philanthropy approach is not simple and requires organizational resources and strategic attention. In this section, we examine some of the key factors associated with implementing strategic philanthropy.

Although some organizations and leaders see beyond economic concerns, other firms are far less progressive and collaborative in nature. To the extent that corporate leaders and others advocate for strategic philanthropy, planning and evaluation practices must be developed just as with any other business process. Almost all effective actions taken by a company are well-thought-out business plans. However, although most large organizations have solid plans for philanthropy and other community involvement, these activities typically do not receive the same attention that other business forays garner. A study by the American Productivity and Quality Center found that many organizations are not yet taking a systematic or comprehensive approach in evaluating the impact of philanthropy on the business and other stakeholders.[73]

Top Management Support

The implementation of strategic philanthropy is impossible without the endorsement and support of the chief executive officer and other members of top management. Although most executives care about their communities and social issues, there may be debate or confusion over how their firms should meet stakeholder concerns and social responsibility. When Al Dunlap became CEO of Sunbeam, for example, he eliminated the company's annual giving program of $1 million. He was very clear that he felt Sunbeam's primary responsibility was to shareholders, noting that the company was giving to society by making money for shareholders.[74] Bernie Ebbers, former CEO of WorldCom, engaged in a much more minor cost-cutting tactic by eliminating free coffee for his employees. In contrast, Robert Allen, chair of the board for AT&T, observed that although some corporations are solely motivated by financial returns, he is confident that "the men and women who guide AT&T firmly believe that our business has the responsibility to contribute to the long-term well-being of the society."[75]

Top managers often have unique concerns with respect to strategic philanthropy. For example, chief executive officers may worry about having to defend the company's commitment to charity. Some investors may see these contributions as damaging to their portfolios. A related concern involves the resources required to manage a philanthropy effort. Top managers must be well versed in the performance benefits of social responsibility that we discussed in Chapter 1. Additionally, some executives may believe that less philanthropic-minded competitors have a profit advantage. If these competitors have any advantage at all, it is probably just a short-term situation. The tax benefits and other gains that philanthropy provides should prevail over the long run.[76] In today's environment, there are many positive incentives and reasons that strategic philanthropy and social responsibility make good business sense.

Planning and Evaluating Strategic Philanthropy

As with any initiative, strategic philanthropy must prove its relevance and importance. For philanthropy and other stakeholder collaborations to be fully diffused and accepted within the business community, a performance benefit must be evident. In addition, philanthropy should be treated as a corporate program that deserves the same professionalism and resources as other strategic initiatives. Thus, the process for planning and evaluating strategic philanthropy is integral to its success.

To make the best decisions when dealing with stakeholder concerns and issues, there should be a defensible, workable strategy to ensure that every donation is wisely spent. Author Curt Weeden, CEO of the Contributions Academy, has developed a multistep process for ensuring effective planning and implementation of strategic philanthropy:

1. **Research.** If a company has too little or inaccurate information, it will suffer when making philanthropic decisions. Research should cover the internal organization and programs, organizations, sponsorship options, and events that might intersect with the interests and competencies of the corporation.

2. **Organize and Design.** The information collected by research should be classified into relevant categories. For example, funding opportunities can be categorized according to the level of need and alignment with organizational competencies. The process of organizing and designing is probably the most crucial step in which management should be thoroughly involved.

3. **Engage.** This step consists of engaging management early on so as to ease the approval process in the future. Top managers need to be co-owners of the corporate philanthropy plan. They will have interest in seeing the plan receive authorization, and they will enrich the program by sharing their ideas and thoughts.

4. **Spend.** Deciding what resources and dollars should be spent and where is a very important task. A skilled manager who has spent some time with the philanthropy program should preferably handle this. If the previous steps were handled appropriately, this step should go rather smoothly.[77]

Evaluating corporate philanthropy should begin with a clear understanding of how these efforts are linked to the company's vision, mission, and resources. As our definition suggests, philanthropy can only be strategic if it is fully aligned with the values, core competencies, and long-term plans of an organization. Thus, the development of philanthropic programs should be part of the strategic planning process.

Assuming that key stakeholders have been identified, organizations need to conduct research to understand stakeholder expectations and their willingness to collaborate for mutual benefit. Although many companies have invested time and resources to understand the needs of employees, customers, and investors, fewer have examined other stakeholders or the potential for aligning stakeholders and company resources for philanthropic reasons. Philanthropic efforts should be evaluated for their effects on and benefits to various constituents.[78]

Although philanthropists have always been concerned with results, the aftermath of September 11 brought not only widespread contributions but also a heightened sensitivity to accountability. For example, the American Red Cross suffered intense scrutiny after its leaders initially decided to set aside a portion of donations received in response to the terrorist strikes. The rationale for setting aside $200 million was that a long-term program on terrorism response needed to be developed and funded. Other funds were earmarked for expansion, maintenance, and other purposes not directly related to September 11. Many donors rejected this plan, and the Red Cross reversed its decision. There were also outright scams after the attacks, including people who claimed loved ones were killed in the World Trade Center to collect money, entrepreneurs who sold patriotic items supposedly for charitable reasons, and fake charities for police and fire personnel. A survey in late 2002 indicated that 42 percent of Americans have less confidence in charities than they did before the September 11 attacks.

Major philanthropists are stepping up their expectations for accountability, widespread impact, strategic thinking, global implications, and results. A recent report by the The Panel on the Nonprofit Sector discusses four major areas that all nonprofit organizations need to address in order to demonstrate solid governance and ethical practices. Table 9.7 lists these areas, along with

Table 9.7 Principles for Sound Practice for Charities and Foundations

1. Legal Compliance and Public Disclosure

A charitable organization should have a formally adopted, written code of ethics with which all of its directors or trustees, staff, and volunteers are familiar and to which they adhere.

A charitable organization should establish and implement policies and procedures that enable individuals to come forward with information on illegal practices or violations of organizational policies. This "whistleblower" policy should specify that the organization will not retaliate against, and will protect the confidentially of, individuals who make good-faith reports.

A charitable organization should establish and implement policies and procedures to protect and preserve the organization's important documents and business records.

A charitable organization should make information about its operations, including its governance, finances, programs, and activities, widely available to the public.

2. Effective Governance

A charitable organization must have a governing body that is responsible for reviewing and approving the organization's mission and strategic direction, annual budget and key financial transactions, compensation practices and policies, and fiscal and governance policies.

The board of a charitable organization should establish its own size and structure and review these periodically. The board should have enough members to allow for full deliberation and diversity of thinking on governance and other organizational matters.

The board of a charitable organization should include members with the diverse background (including, but not limited to, ethnic, racial, and gender perspectives), experience, and organizational and financial skills necessary to advance the organization's mission.

A substantial majority of the board of a public charity, usually meaning at least two-thirds of the members, should be independent. Independent members should not: (1) be compensated by the organization as employees or independent contractors; (2) have their compensation determined by individuals who are compensated by the organization; (3) receive, directly or indirectly, material financial benefits from the organization except as a member of the charitable class served by the organization; or (4) be related to anyone described above (as a spouse, sibling, parent, or child) or reside with any person so described.

(continued)

Table 9.7 (continued)

The board should establish an effective, systematic process for educating and communicating with board members to ensure that they are aware of their legal and ethical responsibilities, are knowledgeable about the programs and activities of the organization, and can carry out their oversight functions effectively.

Board members are generally expected to serve without compensation, other than reimbursement for expenses incurred to fulfill their board duties. A charitable organization that provides compensation to its board members should use appropriate comparability data to determine the amount to be paid, document the decision and provide full disclosure to anyone, upon request, of the amount and rationale for the compensation.

3. Strong Financial Oversight

A charitable organization must keep complete, current, and accurate financial records. Its board should receive and review timely reports of the organization's financial activities and should have a qualified, independent financial expert audit or review these statements annually in a manner appropriate to the organization's size and scale of operations.

The board of a charitable organization must institute policies and procedures to ensure that the organization (and, if applicable, its subsidiaries) manages and invests its funds responsibly, in accordance with all legal requirements. The full board should review and approve the organization's annual budget and should monitor actual performance against the budget.

A charitable organization should spend a significant percentage of its annual budget on programs that pursue its mission.

A charitable organization should establish clear, written policies for paying or reimbursing expenses incurred by anyone conducting business or traveling on behalf of the organization, including types of expenses that can be paid for or reimbursed and the documentation required. Such policies should require that travel on behalf of the organization is to be undertaken in a cost-effective manner.

4. Responsible Fundraising

Solicitation materials and other communications addressed to donors and the public must clearly identify the organization and be accurate and truthful.

Contributions must be used for purposes consistent with the donor's intent, whether as described in the relevant solicitation materials or as specifically directed by the donor.

A charitable organization should provide appropriate training and supervision of the people soliciting funds on its behalf to ensure that they understand their responsibilities and applicable federal, state, and local laws, and do not employ techniques that are coercive, intimidating, or intended to harass potential donors.

A charitable organization should not compensate internal or external fundraisers based on a commission or a percentage of the amount raised.

A charitable organization should respect the privacy of individual donors and, except where disclosure is required by law, should not sell or otherwise make available the names and contact information of its donors without providing them an opportunity at least once a year to opt out of the use of their names.

Source: Panel on the Nonprofit Sector, "Principles for Good Governance and Ethical Practice: A Guide for Charities and Foundations," http://www.nonprofitpanel.org/Report/principles/Principles_Executive_Summary.pdf, accessed July 12, 2009.

Figure 9.7 A Donor Bill of Rights

Philanthropy is based on voluntary action for the common good. It is a tradition of giving and sharing that is primary to the quality of life. To assure that philanthropy merits the respect and trust of the general public and that donors and prospective donors can have full confidence in the not-for-profit organizations and causes they are asked to support, we declare that all donors have these rights:

1. To be informed of the organization's mission, of the way the organization intends to use donated resources, and of its capacity to use donations effectively for their intended purposes
2. To be informed of the identity of those serving on the organization's governing board and to expect the board to exercise prudent judgment in its stewardship responsibilities
3. To have access to the organization's most recent financial statements
4. To be assured their gifts will be used for the purposes for which they were given
5. To receive appropriate acknowledgment and recognition
6. To be assured that information about their donations is handled with respect and with confidentiality to the extent provided by law
7. To expect that all relationships with individuals representing organizations of interest to the donor will be professional in nature
8. To be informed whether those seeking donations are volunteers, employees of the organization, or hired solicitors
9. To have the opportunity for their names to be deleted from mailing lists that an organization may intend to share
10. To feel free to ask questions when making a donation and to receive prompt, truthful, and forthright answers

The text of this statement in its entirety was developed by the American Association of Fundraising Counsel (AAFRC), Association for Healthcare Philanthropy (AHP), Council for Advancement and Support of Education (CASE), the Association of Fundraising Professionals (AFP), and the Giving Institute.

Source: Association of Fundraising Professionals, "A Donor Bill of Rights," http://www.afpnet.org/ka/ka-3.cfm?content_item_id=9988, accessed July 12, 2009. The Donor Bill of Rights was created by the Association of Fundraising Professionals (AFP), the Association for Healthcare Philanthropy (AHP), the Council for Advancement and Support of Education (CASE), and the Giving Institute: Leading Consultants to Non-Profits. It has been endorsed by numerous organizations.

specific recommendations on how charitable organizations can go about preserving the soundness and integrity of the nonprofit community.[79] Figure 9.7 lists ten guidelines that potential donors should use in evaluating and choosing organizations with which to partner or provide funding. Both types of input are important to individuals and companies in the process of deciding where to donate time and money.

Methods to evaluate strategic philanthropy should include an assessment of how these initiatives are communicated to stakeholders. Vancouver City Savings and Credit Union of Canada (VanCity) initiated the process of increasing its social accountability to its various stakeholders when its executives and board of directors recognized that VanCity's

> **"Philanthropy is based on voluntary action for the common good. It is a tradition of giving and sharing that is primary to the quality of life."**

level of disclosure, not necessarily its social responsibility, was below that of many other financial institutions in Canada. By increasing its disclosure and reporting, VanCity improved awareness of its commitment to social responsibility and ultimately refined its corporate strategy to meet other stakeholder concerns.[80] Such reporting mechanisms not only improve stakeholder knowledge but also lead to improvements and refinements. Although critics may deride organizations for communicating their philanthropic efforts, the strategic philanthropy model is dependent on feedback and learning to create greater value for the organization and its stakeholders, as we shall see in the next chapter.

SUMMARY

More firms are investigating ways to link their philanthropic efforts with consumer interests. From a strategic perspective, a firm's ability to link consumer interests to philanthropy should lead to stronger economic relationships. Community relations are the organizational functions dedicated to building and maintaining relationships and trust with the community. To determine the key areas that require support and to refine the mission statement, a company should periodically conduct a community needs assessment.

Companies play a major role in community economic development by bringing jobs to the community, interacting with other businesses, and making contributions to local health, education, and recreation projects that benefit residents and employees. When a company leaves an area, financial repercussions may be devastating. Because they have such a profound impact on the economic viability of their communities, firms that value social responsibility consider both the short- and long-term effects of changes in their workforce on the community.

For many firms, a series of legal and regulatory matters must be resolved before launching a business. On a basic level, society has the ability to dictate what types of organizations are allowed to operate. As more companies view themselves as responsible to the community, they consider their role and the impact of their decisions on communities from an ethical perspective.

The success of a business can be enhanced by the publicity generated from and through stakeholder acceptance of community activities. One way that organizations are exercising their philanthropic responsibilities is through volunteerism, the donation of employee time by companies in support of social causes. In structuring volunteer programs, attention must be paid to employee values and beliefs.

Many companies are finding creative ways to satisfy their responsibilities to consumers and the community. These relationships must be managed, nurtured, and continuously assessed. Resources devoted to this effort may include programs for educating and listening to consumers, surveys to discover strengths and weaknesses in stakeholder relationships, hiring consumer affairs professionals, the development of a community relations office, and other initiatives.

Generally, philanthropy involves any acts of benevolence and goodwill. Strategic philanthropy is defined as the synergistic use of organizational core competencies and resources to address key stakeholders' interests and to achieve organizational and social benefits. Strategic philanthropy involves both financial and nonfinancial contributions to stakeholders, but it also benefits the company. As such, strategic philanthropy is part of a broader philosophy that recognizes how social responsibility can help an organization improve its overall performance. Research suggests that companies that adopt a more businesslike approach to philanthropy will experience a better image, increased employee loyalty, and improved customer ties.

Corporate giving, volunteer efforts, and other philanthropic activities should be considered and aligned with corporate strategy and financial, legal, and ethical obligations. The concept of strategic philanthropy has evolved since the middle of the twentieth century, when contributions were prohibited by law, to emerge as a management practice to support social responsibility in the 1990s. Whereas strategic philanthropy links corporate resources and knowledge to address broader social, customer, employee, and supplier problems and needs, cause-related marketing ties an organization's product(s) directly to a social concern. By linking products with charities and social causes, organizations acknowledge the opportunity to align philanthropy to economic goals and to recognize stakeholder interests in organizational benevolence.

Many organizations have skillfully used their resources and core competencies to address the needs of employees, customers, business partners, the community and society, and the natural environment. To pursue strategic philanthropy successfully, organizations must weigh the costs and benefits associated with planning and implementing it as a corporate priority. The benefits of strategic philanthropy are closely aligned with benefits obtained from social responsibility. Businesses that engage in strategic philanthropy often gain a tax advantage. Research suggests that they may also enjoy improved productivity, stronger employee commitment and morale, reduced turnover, and greater customer loyalty and satisfaction. In the future, many companies will devote more resources to understand how strategic philanthropy can be developed and integrated to support their core competencies.

The implementation of strategic philanthropy is impossible without the support of top management. To integrate strategic philanthropy into the organization successfully, the efforts must fit with the company's mission, values, and resources. Organizations must also understand stakeholder expectations and the propensity to support such activities for mutual benefit. This process relies on the feedback of stakeholders in improving and learning how to better integrate the strategic philanthropy objectives with other organizational goals. Finally, companies will need to evaluate philanthropic efforts and assess how these results should be communicated to stakeholders.

RESPONSIBLE BUSINESS DEBATE

The Influence of Business on Society

ISSUE: Does business owe anything to society?

For decades, there have been two clear and opposing responses when answering the question, "What is the role of business in society?" One camp argues that the business of business is business, and therefore, there ought to be little consideration beyond profit and shareholder return. The other group focuses on the prospects for social responsibility and for business to play a critical and positive role in society.

Beyond the theoretical question, however, emerges the reality of the funds, time, and ideas that business contributes to a host of charitable, social, and quasi-governmental platforms. Implied in these activities is that business has a role to play beyond its own industry, products, and employees. Clearly, if society expects business to make these contributions, then there ought to be consideration to the level and type of influence that business will have on society over the long term.

There Are Two Sides to Every Issue:
1. Big business is already too influential on our daily lives. If society relinquishes its decision authority and power to businesspeople, then there are likely to be negative effects. Business is about making a profit and business ideas probably won't work for confronting societal issues. It is also not clear how much business can be trusted.

2. There are many social problems today and there is no way that the government can effectively solve them without a great deal of outside support. Businesses have the financial resources and human talent that can be effectively applied to community needs and problems. Social issues are fundamental, not tangential, to business interests.

KEY TERMS

community (p. 311)
neighbor of choice (p. 311)
community relations (p. 311)
volunteerism (p. 321)

philanthropy (p. 323)
strategic philanthropy (p. 326)
cause-related marketing (p. 330)

DISCUSSION QUESTIONS

1. What are some of the issues you might include in a defense of strategic philanthropy to company stockholders?

2. Describe your personal experiences with philanthropy. In what types of activities have you participated? Which companies that you do business with have a philanthropic focus? How did this focus influence your decision to buy from those companies?

3. How have changes in the business environment contributed to the growing trend of strategic philanthropy?

4. Compare and contrast cause-related marketing with strategic philanthropy. What are the unique benefits of each approach?

5. What role does top management play in developing and implementing a strategic philanthropy approach?

6. Describe the four-stage process for planning and implementing strategic philanthropy.

EXPERIENTIAL EXERCISE

Choose one major corporation and investigate how closely its philanthropic efforts are strategically aligned with its core competencies. Visit the company's website, read its annual reports, and use other sources to justify your conclusions.

Develop a chart or table to depict how the company's core competencies are linked to various philanthropic projects and stakeholder groups. Finally, provide an analysis of how these efforts have affected the company's performance.

WHAT WOULD YOU DO?

As a new vice president of corporate philanthropy, Jack Birke is looking forward to the great initiatives and partnerships the company can create through his office. During his eighteen-year career, Jack has worked for several large nonprofit organizations and has earned an excellent reputation for his ability to raise funds, develop advisory boards, and, in general, work well with the business community. About a year ago, Jack decided to investigate other opportunities within the fundraising industry and started looking at companies that were formalizing their philanthropy efforts. He was hired as vice president less than a month ago, and is now in the process of developing an office structure, getting to know the organization, and creating a strategic plan.

His charge over the next year is to develop a stronger reputation for philanthropy and social responsibility with the company's stakeholders, including employees, customers, and the community. An executive assistant, director of volunteerism, and director of community relations are already on board, and Jack is looking for additional staff.

The position and office are new to the company, and Jack has already heard dissent from other employees, who openly question how important philanthropy is to the business. After all, the economy is slowing, and it seems that customers are more concerned about price and value than any "touchy feely" program. About half of the company's employees work on the manufacturing line, and the other half is employed in administrative or professional positions. Both groups seem to be equally suspicious of Jack and his office.

The company developed an employee volunteer program two years ago, but it was never very successful. A program to gather food, gifts, and money to support needy families at Christmas, however, has drawn strong support. The firm has had fairly good relationships in the community, but these have been primarily the top executives' connections through the chamber of commerce, industry associations, nonprofit boards, and so forth. In sum, while Jack has the support of top management, many employees are unsure about philanthropy and its importance to the company.

Jack is starting to think about short-term policies and long-term strategy for "marketing" his office and goals to the rest of the organization. What would you do?

Technology Issues

Chapter Objectives

- To examine the nature and characteristics of technology

- To explore the economic impact of technology

- To examine technology's influence on society

- To provide a framework for the strategic management of technology issues

Chapter Outline

The Nature of Technology

Technology's Influence on the Economy

Technology's Influence on Society

Strategic Implementation of Responsibility for Technology

© Tom Tomczyk

Protecting the Olympic Brand

As Beijing prepared for the 2008 Olympics, questions about the Chinese government's stance on piracy and trademark violations were being asked. It is common to find phony Adidas, Mickey Mouse, Diesel, and Nike merchandise across China, but there were precautions taken on official Olympic merchandise. Although shop owners in the counterfeit center of Xu Chao are accustomed to selling Western knock-offs, they were clearly aware that the penalties for selling fake Olympic items would be quite steep. Much like the Chinese government protects high-end brands such as Burberry, Chanel, and Prada, it also took steps to protect the Olympic brand. In 2002, the government passed a national law to defend the intellectual property rights associated with Olympic symbols. An executive of the Beijing Olympiad Committee noted, "We have no fixed assets. So the Olympic logo is the most valuable thing we own."

Official manufacturers were given very strict orders to keep the Olympic merchandise in the formal supply chain. Unlike other supply chains, the route of products from manufacturer to retailers was highly controlled for the Olympic merchandise. The channel was kept necessarily tight, so the products did not become diffused and distributed into unapproved retail stores. In addition, manufacturing output was carefully monitored so that no black market merchandise appeared. The Olympic merchandise carried innovative and sophisticated tags, including ones with holograms, watermarks, bar codes, and serial numbers. There were only twenty-four official retail stores allowed to carry Beijing commemorative items.

China is not the first country to guard its Olympic brand; Australia passed a similar law before the 2000 Sydney games. By the time the Olympics started there, however, the city was flooded with counterfeit items. Beijing officials expressed the hope that the nationalistic pride of Chinese citizens would make them less inclined to manufacture, buy, or sell fake Olympic merchandise because the honor of the 2008 games belonged to the whole country.

Although the Chinese government made great strides, police found counterfeit Olympics gold medals, torches, and memorabilia coins in several provinces. In total, China's State Intellectual Property Office prosecuted 1,700 cases for the illegal use of the Olympic symbol and 5,800 cases of copyright infringement. For a country steeped in counterfeit products, outsiders hoped the enforcement signaled a new era. Tian Lipu, director of the State Intellectual Property Office, proudly declared, "China launched harsh strikes on all kinds of illegalities and crimes of IPR infringement last year with a focus on fighting piracy and maintaining market order."[1]

In this chapter, we explore the nature of technology and its positive and negative effects on society. Technology's influence on the economy is very powerful, especially with regard to growth, employment, and working environments. This influence on society includes issues related to the Internet, privacy, intellectual property, health, and the general quality of life. The strategic direction for technology depends on government as well as on business's ability to plan, implement, and audit the influence of technology on society.

THE NATURE OF TECHNOLOGY

Technology relates to the application of knowledge, including the processes and applications to solve problems, perform tasks, and create new methods to obtain desired outcomes. It includes intellectual knowledge as well as the physical systems devised to achieve business and personal objectives.

The evolution of civilization is tied to developments in technology. Through technological advances, humans have moved from a hunter-gatherer existence to a stable agricultural economy to the Industrial Revolution. Today, our economy is based more on information technology and services than on manufacturing. This technology is changing the way we take vacations, have dinner, do homework, track criminals, know where we are, and maintain friendships. Technology has made it possible to go to work or attend meetings without leaving the house. Our new economy is based on these dynamic technological changes in our society.

Characteristics of Technology

Some of the characteristics of technology include the dynamics, reach, and self-sustaining nature of technological progress. The *dynamics* of technology relate to the constant change that often challenges the structure of social institutions. The automobile, airplane, and personal computer all created major changes and influenced government, the family, social relationships, education, the military, and leisure. These changes can happen so fast that they require significant adjustments in the political, religious, and economic structures of society.

Some societies have difficulty adjusting to this rate of change to the point that they even attempt to legislate against new technologies to isolate themselves. In the past, China tried to isolate its citizens from innovations such as the Internet and social trends that result from the application of new technology to music, movies, and other carriers of culture. But even China responded to the new Internet technology by issuing online advertising licenses in a country where advertising has not been widely accepted, allowing the Internet to be used for market research purposes, and permitting the establishment of over 100,000 cybercafés. Since then, Internet use in China has grown, with the number of people logging on regularly totaling more than 220 million users. Today, China ranks number one in the world. However, the government utilizes a number of strategies for reminding Chinese citizens and monitoring their behavior when they are surfing on the Internet, including the use of "cybercops" who are able to have real-time, online discussions with Internet users.[2]

The future dynamics of technology are challenging many traditional products, including books. E Ink and Xerox, for example, have developed thin paper

technology
the application of knowledge, including the processes and applications to solve problems, perform tasks, and create new methods to obtain desired outcomes

and plastic films that can function as screens with digital ink. Users of the technology are still able to turn the pages as with a traditional book or newspaper, but the pages can be reloaded with a new article or best-seller through wireless transmission. Ultimately, Amazon.com introduced the Kindle in 2007, a hardware device that utilizes E Ink and allows the user to download and read books and other materials.[3] As this example demonstrates, new models in contrast to traditional ways of receiving information are accelerating change in every aspect of life. In

© Photographer's Choice/Getty Images

Companies take advantage of technology to hold business meetings, especially when not all participants are able to physically attend

many cases, a new technology may become obsolete very shortly after its introduction. Thus, the dynamic characteristic of technology keeps challenging society to adjust.

Reach relates to the broad nature of technology as it moves through society. For instance, every community in both developed and developing countries has been influenced by cellular and wireless telephones. The ability to make a call from almost any location has many positive effects, but negative side effects include increases in traffic accidents and noise pollution as well as fears about potential health risks. Through telecommunications, businesses, families, and governments have been linked from far distances. Satellites allow instant visual and voice electronic connections almost anywhere in the world. These technologies have reduced the need for in-person meetings via business travel, as shown in Figure 10.1. Web conferencing and video conferencing are becoming more popular alternatives, although it may be difficult for technology to fully replace the nature of face-to-face encounters. Even though collaboration technology continues to grow in lieu of business travel, companies recognize that some occasions demand the face-to-face interaction, such as meeting a new client for the first time, dealing with certain cultures, and discussing significant financial and legal transactions.

The *self-sustaining nature* of technology relates to the fact that technology acts as a catalyst to spur even faster development. As innovations are introduced, they stimulate the need for more technology to facilitate further development. For example, the Internet has created the need for broadband transmission of electric signals through phone lines (DSL), satellites, and cable. Broadband allows connections to the Internet to be fifty times faster than through a traditional telephone modem, allows users to download large files, and creates the opportunity for a rich multimedia experience. As broadband continues to reach more businesses and households, other technologies will have to advance to keep up with the ability to access so much data quickly.[4] In the future, it could be possible to have broadband transmission to computers through electric lines. This means that users could have a broadband connection anywhere that a computer can be plugged in.

FIGURE 10.1 Technology and Business Travel: Percentage of Business Meetings Held in Various Formats

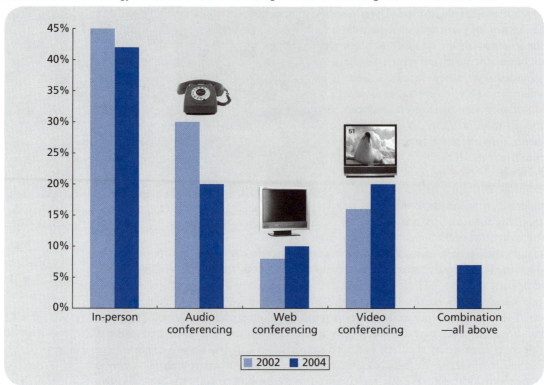

Source: Wainhouse Research, "Usage Trends of Collaboration Technology by Business Travelers 2004," www.ivci.com/pdf/conferencingAndBusinessTravelSurvey.2004.pdf, accessed August 2, 2009.

The invention of the personal computer (PC) resulted in changes in personal financial management related to banking, insurance, taxes, and stock trading. Technology starts a change process that creates new opportunities for new technologies in every industry segment or personal life experience that it touches. At some point, there is even a multiplier effect that causes an even greater demand for more change to improve performance. In the marketing sense, technology is not really fulfilling a new need; it is simply filling an old need more efficiently and effectively.

"Civilizations must harness and adapt to changes in technology to maintain a desired quality of life."

Effects of Technology

Civilizations must harness and adapt to changes in technology to maintain a desired quality of life. The cell phone, for example, has dramatically altered communication patterns, particularly in developing countries where there are few telephone lines. Innovations can also change entire industries. Companies like IBM are creating supercomputers that will be

2 million times more powerful than today's PCs. The computers are revolutionizing financial markets, as stock exchanges are now able to handle very large orders electronically, perform complex trading strategies, and manage many more transactions each day.[5] Such examples illustrate how technology can provide new methods to accomplish tasks that were once thought impossible. These advancements create new processes, new products, and economic progress—and ultimately have profound effects on society.

The global economy experienced the greatest acceleration of technological advancement that ever occurred, propelling increased productivity, output, corporate profits, and stock prices over the last decade.[6] Among the positive contributions of these advances were reductions in the number of worker hours required to generate the nation's output. At the same time, the economic conditions that accompanied this period of technical innovation resulted in increased job opportunities. But in the early 2000s, with the fall of the dot-coms and the integrity meltdown of major U.S. corporations, the economy had taken a downturn, along with the falling stock market. Many information technology firms expanded too rapidly and misreported revenue and earnings to hold onto stock prices and please executives and investors. The result was incidences of massive accounting fraud that damaged confidence and the economy. Earlier chapters dealt with many of these cases and their effect on social responsibility expectations. The traditional work environment has changed because telecommunications (e.g., e-mail and video conferencing) reduce the need for face-to-face interaction. Through online shopping, the Internet can also reduce the need for trips to a shopping center and has increased the amount of business done by UPS and FedEx. In addition, the ease and number of business-to-business transactions have expanded.

However, there are concerns that dramatic shifts in the acceleration and innovations derived from technology may be spurring imbalances not only in the economy but also in our social existence. The flow of technology into developing countries can serve as a method to jump-start economic development. On the other hand, a failure to share technology or provide methods to disseminate technology could cause a major divide in the quality of life. It is in the best interest of the United States to be supportive of technology development throughout the world. Limited resources in underdeveloped countries and the lack of a technology infrastructure will lead to many social, political, and economic problems in the future. In addition, trade with the United States would be affected by these problems.

In the United States, the federal government implemented plans to spend $50 million to subsidize computers and Internet access for 300,000 low-income households across the nation. Although this initiative was somewhat controversial, proponents argued it had the potential to raise the standard of living for low-income families much as the Rural Electrification Administration (REA) did in the 1930s, after President Franklin Delano Roosevelt established it to extend electrical power and telephone services to remote communities and rural areas.[7] Some companies are also trying to help bridge the technology gap that exists between those who can afford technology and those who are on the other side of the so-called digital divide. Gateway, Inc., in partnership with the Hispanic Association of Colleges and Universities (HACU), provides discounted pricing and rebate programs on computers to colleges and universities affiliated with

HACU. Gateway also works with these universities to provide paid internships and other career opportunities to encourage Hispanic employment in the technology sector.[8] Gateway is an example of a corporate attempt to keep the positive effects of the reach of technology available to all segments of society.

Although information technology can improve the quality of life for society, there are concerns about the negative consequences of the reduction of privacy and the emergence of cybercrime. At some point, abrupt adjustment could occur from changes in our economy, and members of society could become unhappy about changes in their lifestyles or the role of business and government in their lives. Public advocacy organizations are helping by participating in charting the future of computer networks to integrate these technological innovations into the way we live.[9] Timothy Berners-Lee, the crafter of the Internet, has a new futuristic scenario. The Semantic Web, a sequel to the World Wide Web, offers controlled access to U.S. health-care data, plus databases charting the location and status of rivers, underground water, and forests and local vegetation, along with economic data on local industries and what they produce—all marked up in special vocabularies that would allow scientists to run global queries across the Web, fishing randomly for correlations that might exist between, for example, where sick people live, work, and play, such as a polluted stream or industrial dump. He is trying to create a tool that might replace our aging Web browsers, letting us display data by color codes, by geographical maps, or by types of sources searched.[10]

TECHNOLOGY'S INFLUENCE ON THE ECONOMY

Technological advancements have had a profound impact on economic growth and employment, but they raise concerns as well.

Economic Growth and Employment

Over the past fifty years, technology has been a major factor in the economic growth of the United States. Investments in educational technologies, increased support for basic government research, and continued commitment to the mission of research and development (R&D) in both the public and private sectors have become major drivers of economic growth. Through deficit reduction, lower interest rates, tax credits, and liberalization of export controls, the government established the economic infrastructure for using technology to drive economic development. The expansion of industry-led technology partnerships among corporations, governments, and nonprofit organizations has also been a key component of growth. Table 10.1 shows the industries that have received strong federal support for research and development.

Investments in research and development are among the highest-return investments a nation can make. A report by the Council of Economic Advisors notes that over the past fifty years, technological innovation has been responsible for half or more of the nation's growth in productivity.[11] For example, the ability to access information in real time through the electronic data interface among retailers, wholesalers, and manufacturers has reduced delivery lead times as well

TABLE 10.1 Industries with Strong Federal Support for Research and Development

Industry	Payoff
Computers and communications	Defense-related research and development to provide for communications in the event of war led to what has become the Internet.
Semiconductors	The U.S. semiconductor industry developed as a direct result of federal R&D investments and procurement activities.
Biotechnology	Federally funded discoveries in biology, food science, agriculture, genetics, and drugs provided a base on which the private sector could build and expand a world-class industry.
Aerospace	The federal government traditionally has funded the lion's share of aerospace R&D, and this support has made U.S. aerospace companies the world's most advanced.
Environmental technologies	The federal government provides nearly $2 billion a year in support of R&D related to environmental technologies.
Energy efficiency	Many of the products sold and installed by this industry are the product of partnerships between the federal government and private industry.
Lasers	Refined though government, industry, and university research, lasers are now one of the most powerful, versatile, and pervasive technologies in our lives.
Magnetic resonance imaging	Nuclear physicists and chemists worked out the fundamental technique of using radio beams and magnetic fields to analyze the chemical structure of biomedical and other materials.

Source: "Technology and Economic Growth: Producing Real Results for the American People," The White House, http://clinton3.nara.gov/WH/EOP/OSTP/html/techgrow.html, accessed August 3, 2009.

as the hours required to produce and deliver products. Likewise, product design times and costs have declined because computer modeling has minimized the need for architectural drafters and some engineers required for building projects. Medical diagnoses have become faster, more thorough, and more accurate thanks to access to information and records over the Internet, hastening treatment and eliminating unnecessary procedures.[12]

The relationship between businesses and consumers already is being changed by the expanding opportunities for e-commerce, the sharing of business information, maintaining business relationships, and conducting business transactions by means of telecommunications networks. Business-to-business (B2B) e-commerce involving companies buying from and selling to each other online is the fastest-growing segment of e-commerce. It has facilitated supply chain management as more companies outsource purchasing over the Internet.[13]

More and more people are turning to the Internet to purchase computers and related peripherals, software, books, music, and even furniture; consumers are increasingly using the Internet to book travel reservations, transact banking business, and trade securities. The forces unleashed by the Internet are particularly important in business-to-business relationships, where the improved quantity, reliability, and timeliness of information have reduced uncertainties. This is the case in companies such as General Motors, IBM, and Procter & Gamble, which are learning to consolidate and rationalize their supply chains using the Internet.[14] Consider the Covisint alliance among Ford, General Motors, DaimlerChrysler, Renault, Nissan, Oracle, and Commerce One, which makes parts from suppliers available through a competitive online auction, reducing months of negotiations to a single day. The goal of the alliance, started in 1999, was to reduce the time it takes to bring a new vehicle to market from fifty-four months to eighteen. Covisint has expanded beyond its automotive manufacturing roots into health care, financial services, and other industries.[15] In many cases, companies are moving toward making most of their purchases online.[16] The downturn in the economy hasn't stopped the momentum of the Contract Division of office supplies retailer Staples Inc., the company's main business-to-business arm. The unit had annual sales of $1 billion and managed double-digit quarterly growth for more than three years; it is the second largest e-tailer behind Amazon.com.[17]

Science and technology are powerful drivers of economic growth and improvements in the quality of life in the United States. Advances in technology have created not only millions of new jobs but also better health and longer lives, new opportunities, and enrichment of our lives in ways we could not have imagined half a century ago. Public and private investment in R&D means more jobs and improved living standards. Americans hold millions of jobs in industries that have grown as a result of innovations in technology. These include biotechnology, computers, communications, software, aerospace, and semiconductors; even retailing, wholesaling, and other commercial institutions have been transformed by technology. Average pay for workers in these high-technology industries is about 60 percent higher than the average wage for all U.S. workers.

Economic Concerns About the Use of Technology

Despite the staggering economic growth fostered by technological advancements, there are economic downsides to technology. Small businesses in particular may have difficulty taking advantage of the opportunities surrounding the Internet and other information technology (IT). The ability to purchase other types of technology may affect the nature of competition and the success of various types of businesses. For example, a recent study examined the effectiveness of IT in small businesses and found that nearly 25 percent of respondents believed IT operations were failing. Another 37 percent reported that their IT operations were passable, but barely. However, over 66 percent of the survey group reported that IT, including electronic commerce, is fundamental to business success. Because of tough economic times, small businesses may have to cancel, modify, or delay IT projects; decrease IT budgets; and reduce staffing and training levels. Experts recommend several solutions to IT problems in small business:

1. Focus on core competencies while seeking to explore outsourcing options.

2. Take advantage of free software and other offerings.

3. Explore the benefits of "cloud computing" where applications are utilized and maintained on a subscription basis.

4. Consider IT infrastructure alternatives to capital expenditures through hosted hardware, software, and services.[18]

As mentioned earlier, a key concern today with advancing technology is the digital divide that occurs when certain groups have limited access to the latest technology, especially high-speed Internet services at home, and therefore derive fewer benefits from it. The divide, however, is grounded in a much more basic concern: Who can afford to purchase a home computer and the access services? While the early debate on this issue centered on the gap between rich and poor populations, it is now framed as the gap between those who are information rich and information poor. Also part of the debate is access issues for certain populations, such as persons with disabilities and people who are barely literate, whether the latest technology is available mainly in affluent neighborhoods, and accommodations for senior citizens.[19]

There are several ways to address these problems that are the inevitable consequences of accelerating change in the technology drivers of the new economy. One way is to examine the outcomes associated with the attempts to use technology. For example, the small town of Glasgow, Kentucky, thanks to the foresight of local leaders, was hard-wired for high-speed Internet access years before the technology was available in many larger urban areas. Community leaders thought the technology would not only benefit citizens but also lead to a high-tech boom for the town of 14,000. The city exploits the high-speed wiring to control traffic lights, share computerized maps to coordinate utility repairs, and monitor electric meters, and a number of businesses have incorporated Internet access into their business strategies. Many other small communities installed similar high-speed links in preparation

> **"A key concern today with advancing technology is the digital divide that occurs when certain groups have limited access to the latest technology, especially high-speed Internet services at home, and therefore derive fewer benefits from it."**

Many consumers are comfortable with online shopping and use credit cards to facilitate retail transactions

© Monkey Business Images/Shutterstock

for the future.[20] Another way to address the negative consequences of accelerating new technology is to assess problems related to its impact on competition. Restraining competition, domestic or international, to suppress competitive turmoil is a major concern of governments. Allowing anticompetitive practices, price fixing, or other unfair methods of competition would be counterproductive to rising standards of living.[21]

TECHNOLOGY'S INFLUENCE ON SOCIETY

Information and telecommunications technology minimizes the borders between countries, businesses, and people and allows people to overcome the physical limitations of time and space. Technological advances also enable people to acquire customized goods and services that cost less and are of higher quality than ever imagined.[22] For example, parents can give their children robotic pets and dolls, which often cost less than $50, that can be programmed to respond to their child's voice.[23] Airline passengers can purchase tickets online and print out boarding passes on their home or office printers so that they can go straight to their plane on arrival at the airport after clearing security.[24] Cartographers and geologists can create custom maps—even in three dimensions—that may help experts manage water supplies, find oil, and pinpoint future earthquakes.[25]

In this section, we explore four broad issues related to technology and its impact on society, including the Internet, privacy, intellectual property, and health and biotechnology. Although there are many other pressing issues related to technology, these seem to be the most widely debated at this time. Given the rapid advance of technology, there will probably be more issues by the time you read this book.

The Internet

The Internet, the global information system that links many computer networks together, has profoundly altered the way people communicate, learn, do business, and find entertainment. Although many people believe the Internet began in the early 1990s, its origins can be traced to the late 1950s (see Table 10.2). Over

Table 10.2 History of the Internet

Year	Event	Significance
1836	Telegraph	The telegraph revolutionized human (tele)communications with Morse Code, a series of dots and dashes used to communicate between humans.
1858–1866	Transatlantic cable	Transatlantic cable allowed direct instantaneous communication across the Atlantic Ocean.
1876	Telephone	The telephone created voice communication, and telephone exchanges provide the backbone of Internet connections today.
1957	USSR launched *Sputnik*	*Sputnik* was the first artificial Earth satellite and the start of global communications.
1962–1968	Packet switching	The Internet relies on packet-switching networks that split data into tiny packets that may take different routes to a destination.

1971	Beginning of the Internet	People communicate over the Internet with a program to send messages across a distributed network.
1973	Global networking became a reality	Ethernet outlined—this is how local networks are basically connected today, and gateways define how large networks (maybe of different architecture) can be connected together.
1991	World Wide Web with text-based, menu-driven interface to access Internet resources	User-friendly interface to World Wide Web established.
1992	Multimedia changed the face of the Internet	The term *surfing the Internet* was coined.
1993	World Wide Web revolution begins	Mosaic, a user-friendly Graphical Front End to the World Wide Web, made the Web more accessible and evolved into Netscape.
1995	Internet service providers advanced	Online dial-up systems (CompuServe, America Online, and Prodigy) began to provide Internet access.
2000	Broadband emerged	Provides fast access to multimedia and large text files.
2002	Wireless expanded	Devices for wireless linkage to the Internet grew rapidly.
2004	Broadband expanded	Media companies started selling music and video online. E-commerce continued to escalate.
2004	Social networking began	At Harvard University, Mark Zuckerberg launched Facebook, which now has over 200 million users.
2006	Social networking transformed	Twitter was created. Unlike lengthy blog posts, Twitter messages are limited to 140 characters.
2008	Google turned 10	The company that began with a search engine also dominates online advertising and has a leading presence in online mapping, webmail, and online document collaboration.
2008	Mobile Internet took off	In the United States, there are 95 million mobile Internet subscribers and 40 million active users. U.S. mobile penetration is 15.6%, compared to 12.9% in the UK.
2009	The ultimate tweet	Actor Ashton Kutcher became the first person on Twitter to have a million people subscribing to his "tweets."

Source: Adapted from "A Short History of the Internet," http://www.sean.co.uk/a/science/history_of_the_internet.shtm, accessed August 7, 2009.

five decades, the network evolved from a system for government and university researchers into an information and entertainment tool used by millions around the globe. With the development of the World Wide Web, which organizes the information on the Internet into interconnected "pages" of text, graphics, audio, and video, use of the Internet exploded in the 1990s.

Today, nearly half a billion people around the world utilize the Internet. In the United States alone, about 155 million Americans access the Internet at home, with some citizens accessing the Internet only at work. Internet use by consumers in other countries, especially Japan (49 million users), the United Kingdom (29 million), Germany (36 million), Brazil (25 million), and France (31 million), has escalated rapidly.

Table 10.3 shows the recent pattern of active Internet usage in households.[26] To keep up with the growing demand for new e-mail and website addresses, the Internet Corporation for Assigned Names and Numbers has added eight new domain name suffixes to allow for the creation of millions of new addresses. In addition to .com (companies), .edu (schools and universities), .gov (government agencies and offices), .mil (military use), .net (networks), and hundreds of country codes, computer users may see addresses followed by .zero (air-transport industry), .biz (businesses), .coop (nonprofit cooperatives), .info (unrestricted), .museum (museums), .name (personal names), .travel (travel and tourism industry) and .pro (professionals such as doctors and accountants).[27]

The interactive nature of the Internet has created tremendous opportunities for businesses to forge relationships with consumers and business customers, target markets more precisely, and even reach previously inaccessible markets. The Internet also facilitates supply chain management, allowing companies to network with manufacturers, wholesalers, retailers, suppliers, and outsource firms to serve customers more efficiently.[28] Despite the growing importance and popularity of the Internet, fraud has become a major issue for businesses and consumers. Because shopping via the Internet does not require a signature to verify transactions, credit card fraud online is more than three and a half times

Table 10.3 Active Home Use of the Internet

Worldwide Active Internet Home Users, May 2009				
Country	**April 2009**	**May 2009**	**Growth (%)**	**Difference**
Australia	10,929,536	11,237,351	2.82	307,815
Brazil	25,460,307	25,566,439	0.42	106,132
France	29,457,939	31,099,132	5.57	1,641,193
Germany	36,158,816	36,706,500	1.51	544,684
Italy	17,662,655	17,769,768	0.61	107,113
Japan	48,567,721	49,711,242	2.35	1,143,520
Spain	19,375,214	19,826,831	2.33	451,617
Switzerland	3,721,585	3,765,629	1.18	44,044
U.K.	29,063,326	29,048,332	−0.05	−14,994
U.S.	154,525,974	156,557,641	1.31	2,031,667

Source: Nielsen Online, 2009.

greater than credit card fraud through mail-order catalogs and almost nine times greater than for traditional storefront retailers.[29] Some businesses are attempting to fight fraud by embracing two new credit card protection systems: Visa's Verified by Visa and MasterCard's Universal Cardholder Authentication Field (UCAF) standard and Secure Payment Application (SPA).[30]

Consumers are also increasingly worried about becoming victims of fraud online. For example, complaints about fraud in online auctions have risen dramatically over the last decade.[31] A survey conducted by Harris Interactive found that 31 percent of Americans who go online, or approximately 35 million people, participate in online auctions. However, the survey found that online auctions made up 78 percent of Internet fraud complaints, with an average loss of $326 per victim. Still, a majority of respondents who have participated as bidders said they are somewhat or very confident that as the winning bidder in an online auction, they will get what they pay for from a seller.[32] The online auction site eBay has more than 16 million regular customers exchanging $14 million every day. The company received 10,700 fraud complaints in one year. Among the complaints were accusations of "shill bidding," which involves sellers bidding on their own items to heighten interest, and competitive bidding. Another problem has been sellers not delivering promised items after receiving the buyers' funds. The formula for fraud is enhanced by anonymity, quick access, low overhead, satellite access, and little regulation.[33]

> "Despite the growing importance and popularity of the Internet, fraud has become a major issue for businesses and consumers."

Corporations are buying industrial-strength IT gear via online auctions. Todd Lutwak, director of San Jose–based eBay Inc.'s Technology Marketplace, says that in fiscal year 2001, $1.8 billion worth of equipment was sold in that division (which includes consumer electronics and computers in addition to enterprise IT equipment). eBay has auction offerings in used business equipment that are complemented by both financial and inspection services. Customers interested in purchasing used farm tractors, printing presses, forklifts, trailers, and other capital equipment are assured of fair pricing and quality through eBay's Business Equipment Purchase Protection program.[34]

Despite such programs in the business-to-business market, complaints about online auctions have made them one of the Federal Trade Commission's top ten "dot cons" (see Figure 10.2). Similarly, the U.S. Federal Bureau of Investigation (FBI) reports that one in four complaints for e-commerce deals with online auctions, with most complaints for the nondelivery of auction items (32.9 percent), and fraudulent or misleading auction items (25.5 percent). Consumers, government agencies, and merchants alike are exploring options, including regulation, to protect the security of online transactions.[35]

FIGURE 10.2 The Top Ten "Dot Cons"

1. Internet Auctions

The Bait: Shop in a "virtual marketplace" that offers a huge selection of products at great deals.

The Catch: After sending their money, consumers say they've received an item that is less valuable than promised or, worse yet, nothing at all.

The Safety Net: When bidding through an Internet auction, particularly for a valuable item, check out the seller and insist on paying with a credit card or using an escrow service.

2. Internet Access Services

The Bait: Free money, simply for cashing a check.

The Catch: Consumers say they've been "trapped" into long-term contracts for Internet access or another Web service, with big penalties for cancellation or early termination.

The Safety Net: If a check arrives at your home or business, read both sides carefully and look inside the envelope to find the conditions you're agreeing to if you cash the check. Read your telephone bill carefully for unexpected or unauthorized charges.

3. Credit Card Fraud

The Bait: Surf the Internet and view adult images online for free, just for sharing your credit card number to prove you're over eighteen.

The Catch: Consumers say that fraudulent promoters have used their credit card numbers to run up charges on their cards.

The Safety Net: Share credit card information only when buying from a company you trust. Dispute unauthorized charges on your credit card bill by complaining to the bank that issued the card. Federal law limits your liability to $50 in charges if your card is misused.

4. International Modem Dialing

The Bait: Get free access to adult material and pornography by downloading a "viewer" or "dialer" computer program.

The Catch: Consumers complain about exorbitant long-distance charges on their telephone bill. Through the program, their modem is disconnected, and then reconnected to the Internet through an international long-distance number.

The Safety Net: Don't download any program to access a so-called free service without reading all the disclosures carefully for cost information. Just as important, read your telephone bill carefully and challenge any charges you didn't authorize or don't understand.

5. Web Cramming

The Bait: Get a free custom-designed website for a thirty-day trial period, with no obligation to continue.

The Catch: Consumers say they've been charged on their telephone bills or received a separate invoice, even if they never accepted the offer or agreed to continue the service after the trial period.

The Safety Net: Review your telephone bills and challenge any charges you don't recognize.

6. Multilevel Marketing Plans/Pyramids

The Bait: Make money through the products and services you sell as well as those sold by the people you recruit into the program.

The Catch: Consumers say that they've bought into plans and programs, but their customers are other distributors, not the general public. Some multilevel marketing programs are actually illegal pyramid schemes. When products or services are sold only to distributors like you, there's no way to make money.

The Safety Net: Avoid plans that require you to recruit distributors, buy expensive inventory, or commit to a minimum sales volume.

7. Travel and Vacation

The Bait: Get a luxurious trip with lots of "extras" at a bargain-basement price.

The Catch: Consumers say some companies deliver lower-quality accommodations and services than they've advertised or no trip at all. Others have been hit with hidden charges or additional requirements after they've paid.

The Safety Net: Get references on any travel company you're planning to do business with. Then, get details of the trip in writing, including the cancellation policy, before signing on.

8. Business Opportunities

The Bait: Be your own boss and earn big bucks.

The Catch: Taken in by promises about potential earnings, many consumers have invested in a "biz op" that turned out to be a "biz flop." There was no evidence to back up the earnings claims.

The Safety Net: Talk to other people who started businesses through the same company, get all the promises in writing, and study the proposed contract carefully before signing. Get an attorney or an accountant to take a look at it, too.

9. Investments

The Bait: Make an initial investment in a day trading system or service and you'll quickly realize huge returns.

The Catch: Big profits always mean big risk. Consumers have lost money to programs that claim to be able to predict the market with 100 percent accuracy.

The Safety Net: Check out the promoter with state and federal securities and commodities regulators, and talk to other people who invested through the program to find out what level of risk you're assuming.

10. Health-Care Products/Services

The Bait: Items not sold through traditional suppliers are "proven" to cure serious and even fatal health problems.

The Catch: Claims for "miracle" products and treatments convince consumers that their health problems can be cured. But people with serious illnesses who put their hopes in these offers might delay getting the health care they need.

The Safety Net: Consult a health-care professional before buying any "cure-all" that claims to treat a wide range of ailments or offers quick cures and easy solutions to serious illnesses.

Source: "Facts for Consumers: Dot Cons," Federal Trade Commission, http://www.ftc.gov/bcp/edu/pubs/consumer/tech/tec09.shtm, accessed August 2, 2009.

Privacy

The extraordinary growth of the Internet has generated issues related to privacy. Businesses have long tracked consumers' shopping habits with little controversy. However, observing the contents of a consumer's shopping cart or the process a consumer goes through when choosing a box of cereal generally involves the collection of aggregate data rather than specific personally identifying data. And although some consumers' use of credit cards, shopping cards, and coupons involves giving up a certain degree of anonymity in the shopping process, consumers could still choose to remain anonymous by paying cash.

Shopping on the Internet, however, allows businesses to track consumers on a far more personal level, from their online purchases to the websites they favor.[36] Respondents surveyed in a *Consumer Reports* study indicated they are generally skeptical about websites but have learned to trust certain websites by repeated visits, interactions, and positive experiences. Over 85 percent of these consumers believe that the most important factor in evaluating websites is whether their personal information will be kept safe, confidential, and private. Of this same group, 81 percent indicate that being able to trust the information on the website is also very important.[37]

> **"Current technology has made it possible to amass vast quantities of personal information, often without consumers' knowledge."**

Indeed, current technology has made it possible to amass vast quantities of personal information, often without consumers' knowledge. The Internet allows for the collection, sharing, and selling of this information to interested third parties. The website peoplesearch.com, for example, permits anyone to do asset verification checks and criminal background checks on any individual for a fee of $39 to $125. Another website, UsSearch.com, supplies background information, including property ownership, civil judgments, driver's license, physical description, and summary of assets, on any individual in its database for $39.95 and up.[38]

Because of the ease of access to personal information, unauthorized use of this information sometimes occurs.[39] Spam has reached an epidemic level, affecting hundreds of millions of e-mail users worldwide, impairing productivity, and sapping network resources. Estimates now indicate that about 80 percent of e-mail consists of spam. A number of spam-blocking software packages are available to revitalize productivity and to stop unwanted e-mails, but those behind the e-mail barrages are quick to find new methods for escaping detection.[40]

Information can be collected on the Internet with or without a person's knowledge. Many websites follow users' tracks through their site by storing a "cookie," or identifying string of text, on their computers. These cookies permit website operators to track how often a user visits the site, what he or she looks at while there, and in what sequence. Cookies also allow website visitors to customize services, such as virtual shopping carts, as well as the particular content they see when they log on to a web page. However, if website operators can exploit cookies to link visitors' interests to their names and addresses, that information also can be sold to advertisers and other parties without visitors' consent or even knowledge. The potential for misuse has left many consumers rather uncomfortable with this technology.[41]

Identity theft is one of the fastest-growing crimes in the nation, hitting nearly 8.3 million people a year. The most common types of theft include the misuse of credit card information, misuse of savings or banking account information, and the use of personal information to open unauthorized credit card accounts. Recently, federal authorities broke up one of the biggest identity-theft cases in U.S. history and charged three men with stealing credit information via the Internet from more than 30,000 people, draining bank accounts, and ruining credit ratings.[42]

A growing number of Internet websites require visitors to register and provide information about themselves to access some or all of the site's content. How this information will be used is generating concern. For example, 75 percent of users of health-related websites worry that the information they supply when they register for access to the site or respond to surveys may be sold to third parties without their permission.[43] Some people are concerned that personal information about their health may be sold to insurance companies which may deny them coverage on the basis of that information. Although many health-oriented and other websites post privacy policies that specify whether and how they will use any personal information they gather, some consumers still worry that such policies are just "lip service." Amazon.com received complaints through the Federal Trade Commission (FTC) after it modified its privacy policy, which allows it to disclose personal information to third parties and to sell customer information in the event it goes out of business or sells assets.[44]

Privacy issues remain at the forefront of the FTC's investigative and enforcement activities. CVS Caremark, the largest pharmacy chain and provider in the United States, settled charges that it failed to adequately protect the financial and medical information of both employees and customers. The FTC investigated allegations that employees were disposing of sensitive documents in dumpsters, including old prescription bottles, physician's orders, employment applications, computer order forms for customers, and other documents that included social security numbers, drivers' license numbers, payroll data, medical diagnoses, and a host of other private matters. In releasing its findings, the FTC stated: "CVS Caremark did not dispose securely of personal information, did not adequately train employees, did not use reasonable measures to assess compliance with its policies and procedures for disposing of personal information, and did not employ a reasonable process for discovering and remedying risks to personal information."[45]

Privacy issues related to children are generating even more debate, as well as laws to protect children's interests. Concerns about protecting children's privacy were highlighted in a recent study by the Annenberg Public Policy Center, which reported that two-thirds of children ages ten to seventeen would divulge their

ETHICAL RESPONSIBILITIES IN FINANCE

Consumer Privacy in the Financial Industry For decades, the financial services industry sought to repeal the Glass-Steagall Act, legislation enacted in 1933 to formalize the separation between banking and securities. The act followed the Great Depression, when it came to light that conflicts of interest and fraud were prevalent in institutions offering both banking and securities services. Key provisions were intended to stabilize the integrity of the banking system, prevent self-dealing and other abuses, and limit stock market speculation. Repeated industry calls for a review, along with the advancement of technology and new markets, prompted the U.S. Congress to revisit the legislation and its applicability in today's economic environment. The resulting bill, known as the Financial Modernization Act, or the Gramm-Leach-Bliley Act, repealed many provisions of Glass-Steagall and allowed commercial banks, securities firms, insurance companies, and investment banks to consolidate. One of the first mergers occurred between Citicorp and Travelers Group. As a result, the Citibank, Primerica, Smith Barney, and Travelers insurance brands were united under one corporate roof.

The act also implemented new privacy rules to govern the collection, storage, and disclosure of customers' personal financial information. While financial institutions now have opportunities for integration, they are also faced with mandatory guidelines overseen by eight federal agencies and the states. Thus, the political pressure that institutions applied for changes to the Glass-Steagall Act resulted in more regulation of security and privacy practices. Now, all financial firms—banks, mortgage brokers, "payday" lenders, insurance companies, securities firms, wire transfer companies, travel agencies linked to financial institutions, credit counselors, tax preparation firms, and many others—are required to implement policies and training on three core issues:

1. *Financial privacy rule:* Requires financial institutions to provide each consumer with a privacy notice when the consumer relationship is established. Afterward, consumers must be notified on an annual basis about how the information is collected, where the information is shared, how the information is used, and how the information is protected. Companies must also notify consumers that they have the right to opt out of unaffiliated parties receiving their information.

2. *Safeguards rule:* Requires financial institutions to develop, implement, maintain, and monitor safeguards to protect the integrity and security of consumer information. The security plan should include clear management responsibility, risk management processes, testing procedures, and regular opportunities for revision.

3. *Pretexting protection:* Requires financial institutions to implement security and safeguard measures against pretexting, which occurs when an individual or company tries to obtain a consumer's personal financial information under false pretenses. Institutions must have written plans, training protocols, and testing procedures to guard against the fraudulent collection of consumer financial information.

Sources: Federal Deposit Insurance Corporation, "Safe Internet Banking," http://www.fdic.gov/bank/individual/online/protect.html, accessed August 8, 2009; Federal Trade Commission, *Protecting Personal Information: A Guide for Business*, http://www.ftc.gov/infosecurity/, accessed August 9, 2009; Federal Trade Commission, "Financial Institutions and Consumer Information: Complying with Safeguards," http://www.ftc.gov/bcp/edu/pubs/business/idtheft/bus54.shtm, accessed August 9, 2009; Federal Trade Commission, "The Gramm-Leach-Bliley Act," http://www.ftc.gov/privacy/privacyinitiatives/glbact.html, accessed August 8, 2009.

favorite online stores to receive a free gift, whereas more than half would reveal their parents' favorite stores, and another quarter would disclose details about their parents' activities on the weekend. The study also found that many children would share information about the family car and the amount of their allowance. It should be noted that this survey was conducted before the U.S. Children's Online Privacy Protection Act (COPPA) went into effect. That law prohibits websites and Internet providers from seeking personal information from children under age thirteen without parental consent.[46] Recent Census Bureau statistics bear out the increasing use of computers and the Internet among children. That's provoking a lot of worries and assorted attempts to tame the Internet. The government has waded in with the Children's Internet Protection Act, which requires schools that receive federal funds to block access to inappropriate content.[47] Table 10.4 provides recommendations for improving child safety on the Internet, courtesy of Microsoft.

Some measure of protection for personal privacy is already provided by the U.S. Constitution as well as Supreme Court rulings and federal laws (see Table 10.5). The U.S. Federal Trade Commission (FTC) also regulates and enforces privacy standards and monitors websites to ensure compliance. A recent

Table 10.4 Ten Ideas to Improve Child Safety on the Internet

1.	Encourage your kids to share their Internet experiences with you.
2.	Teach your kids to trust their instincts.
3.	If your kids visit chat rooms or use instant messaging (IM) programs, online video games, or other activities on the Internet that require a login name to identify themselves, help them choose that name and make sure it doesn't reveal any personal information about them.
4.	Insist that your kids never give out your address, phone number, or other personal information, including where they go to school or where they like to play.
5.	Teach your kids that the difference between right and wrong is the same on the Internet as it is in real life.
6.	Show your kids how to respect others online. Make sure they know that rules for good behavior don't change just because they're on a computer.
7.	Insist that your kids respect the property of others online. Explain that making illegal copies of other people's work—music, video games, and other programs—is just like stealing it from a store.
8.	Tell your kids that they should never meet online friends in person. Explain that online friends may not be who they say they are.
9.	Teach your kids that not everything they read or see online is true.
10.	Control your children's online activity with advanced Internet software. Parental controls can help you filter out harmful content, monitor the sites your child visits, and find out what they do there.

Source: Microsoft Corporation, "10 Things You Can Teach Kids to Improve Their Web Safety," http://www.microsoft.com/athome/security/children/kidsonlinetips.mspx, accessed August 2, 2009.

TABLE 10.5 Privacy Laws

Act (Date Enacted)	Purpose
Privacy Act (1974)	Requires federal agencies to adopt minimum standards for collecting and processing personal information; limits the disclosure of such records to other public or private parties; requires agencies to make records on individuals available to them on request, subject to certain conditions.
Right to Financial Privacy Act (1978)	Protects the rights of financial institution customers to keep their financial records private and free from unjust government investigation.
Computer Security Act (1987)	Brought greater confidentiality and integrity to the regulation of information in the public realm by assigning responsibility for the standardization of communication protocols, data structures, and interfaces in telecommunications and computer systems to the National Institute of Standards and Technology (NIST), which also announced security and privacy guidelines for federal computer systems.
Computer Matching and Privacy Protection Act (1988)	Amended the Privacy Act by adding provisions regulating the use of computer matching, the computerized comparison of individual information for purposes of determining eligibility for federal benefits programs.
Video Privacy Protection Act (1988)	Specifies the circumstances under which a business that rents or sells videos can disclose personally identifiable information about a consumer or reveal an individual's video rental or sales records.
Telephone Consumer Protection Act (1991)	Regulates the activities of telemarketers by limiting the hours during which they can solicit residential subscribers, outlawing the use of artificial or prerecorded voice messages to residences without prior consent, prohibiting unsolicited advertisements by telephone facsimile machines, and requiring telemarketers to maintain a "do-not-call list" of any consumers who request not to receive further solicitation.
Driver Privacy Protection Act (1993)	Restricts the circumstances under which state departments of motor vehicles may disclose personal information about any individual obtained by the department in connection with a motor vehicle record.
Fair Credit Reporting Act (amended in 1997)	Promotes accuracy, fairness, and privacy of information in the files of consumer reporting agencies (e.g., credit bureaus); grants consumers the right to see their personal credit reports, to find out who has requested access to their reports, to dispute any inaccurate information with the consumer reporting agency, and to have inaccurate information corrected or deleted.

Children's Online Privacy Protection Act (2000)	Regulates the online collection of personally identifiable information (name, address, e-mail address, hobbies, interests, or information collected through cookies) from children under age thirteen by specifying what a website operator must include in a privacy policy, when and how to seek consent from a parent, and what responsibilities an operator has to protect children's privacy and safety online.

Sources: "Privacy Act of 1974," U.S. Bureau of Reclamation, http://www.usbr.gov/foia/privacy.html, accessed August 2, 2009; Federal Deposit Insurance Corporation, "Financial Institutions Regulatory and Interest Rates Control Act of 1978," http://www.fdic.gov/regulations/laws/rules/6500-2550.html, accessed August 2, 2009; E. Maria Grace, "Privacy vs. Convenience: The Benefits and Drawbacks of Tax System Modernization," *Federal Communications Law Journal* 47 (December 1994), www.law.indiana.edu/fclj/pubs/v47/no2/grace.html, accessed August 2, 2009; "Sec. 2710. Wrongful Disclosure of Video Tape Rental or Sale Records," Legal Information Institute, www4.law.cornell.edu/uscode/18/2710.text.html, accessed August 2, 2009; "Comments Sought in Important FCC Proceeding Impacting Non-Profit Organizations and Other Entities That Make Unsolicited Telephone Calls," Arent Fox, PLLC, http://www.arentfox.com/publications/index.cfm?fa=legalUpdateDisp&content_id=834%20class=, accessed August 2, 2009; "Sec. 2721. Prohibition on Release and Use of Certain Personal Information from State Motor Vehicle Records," Legal Information Institute, www4.law.cornell.edu/uscode/18/2721.text.html, accessed August 2, 2009; "A Summary of Your Rights Under the Fair Credit Reporting Act," Federal Trade Commission, http://www.ftc.gov/bcp/edu/pubs/consumer/credit/cre35.pdf, accessed August 2, 2009; "How to Comply with the Children's Online Privacy Protection Rule According to the Federal Trade Commission," COPPA, http://www.coppa.org/comply.htm, accessed August 2, 2009.

study commissioned by the FTC reported that 98 percent of the 100 top websites collect at least one type of personal information, and 93 percent have posted at least one type of disclosure (privacy policy notice or the site practices).[48] In the 2009 Online Customer Respect Study of top telecommunications firms, Verizon was ranked best in class for the second successive year for overall customer service and led in both Online Help (providing customers with setup and problem resolution) and Account Management (allowing customers to self-manage bills and services online). The Customer Respect Index (CRI) includes five subindexes: Content, Navigation, Search, Trust, and Dialog, which converge on important issues of privacy and information protection.[49]

International Initiatives on Privacy Privacy concerns are not limited to the United States. The European Union (EU) has made great strides in protecting the privacy of its citizens. The 1998 European Union Directive on Data Protection specifically requires companies that want to collect personal information to explain how the information will be used and to obtain the individual's permission. Companies must make customer data files available on request, just as U.S. credit-reporting firms must grant customers access to their personal credit histories. The law also bars website operators from selling e-mail addresses and using cookies to track visitors' movements and preferences without first obtaining permission. Because of this legislation, no company may deliver personal information about EU citizens to countries whose privacy laws do not meet EU standards.[50] Some European countries have taken further steps to protect their citizens. Italy, for example, established an Italian Data Protection Commission to enforce its stringent privacy laws. Such agencies highlight the differences in how Europeans and Americans approach the online privacy issue.[51]

In Canada, private industry has taken the lead in creating and developing privacy policies through the Direct Marketing Association of Canada (DMAC). The DMAC's policies resulted in the proposal of legislation to protect personal privacy. The Personal Information Protection and Electronic Documents Act, which went into effect on January 1, 2001, established a right of personal privacy for information collected by Canadian businesses and organizations. The new law instituted rules governing the collection, use, and disclosure of personal information in the private sector. The law also works in conjunction with other legislation that protects personal information collected by federal and/or provincial governments. The Canadian Standards Association (CSA) was also instrumental in bringing about privacy protection guidelines in Canada. The CSA Model Code for the Protection of Personal Information requires organizations to protect personal information and to allow individuals access to their own personal information, allowing for correction if necessary.[52]

In Japan, the Ministry of International Trade and Industry established the Electronic Network Consortium (ENC) to resolve issues associated with the Internet. The ENC (which comprises ninety-two corporate members, fifty-one local community organizations, and fifteen special members) has prepared guidelines for protecting personal data gathered by Japanese online service providers. These guidelines require websites to obtain an individual's consent before collecting personal data or using or transferring such data to a third party. The guidelines also call for organizations to appoint managers who understand the ENC guidelines to oversee the collection and use of personal data and to utilize privacy information management systems such as the Platform for Privacy Protection (P3P).[53] P3P is a set of standards under development by the World Wide Web Consortium that would permit websites to translate their privacy statements and standards into a uniform format that Web-browsing software could access to supply users with relevant information about a particular firm's policies. Website visitors could then decide what information, if any, they are willing to share with websites.[54]

Protection of citizens' privacy on the Internet is not a major public concern in Russia. Few Russian websites have a privacy policy or disclosure statements explaining how collected information will be used. International companies conducting business in Russia or managing Russian subsidiaries often maintain online privacy information for their U.S. and European customers but not for Russian customers.[55] The country is not currently looking to tighten its information privacy laws. Corporate databases as well as comprehensive files on customers of retail product and service providers are readily available across Russia. It is a common practice in Russia to sell databases.[56] Until recently, Russian law gave authorities the right to monitor private e-mail. However, Nail Murzakhanov, the founder of a small Internet service provider in Volgograd, challenged this right when he refused to purchase the equipment that would have permitted Russian security agencies to eavesdrop on his customers' e-mail. Murzakhanov stood firm in his belief that complying with the law would jeopardize his guarantee of privacy to his customers, even after the Ministry of Communications threatened to revoke his license to operate. Eventually, the Ministry of Communications dropped all charges against Murzakhanov's company, setting a precedent for other Internet service providers who wish to protect their customers' privacy.[57]

Privacy Officers and Certification

Businesses are beginning to recognize that the only way to circumvent further government regulation with respect to privacy is to develop systems and policies to protect consumers' interests. In addition to creating and posting policies regarding the gathering and use of personal information, more companies—including American Express, AT&T, Citigroup, and Prudential Insurance—employ chief privacy officers (CPOs). The International Association of Privacy Professionals (IAPP) started in 2000 as a result of this movement. IAPP is responsible for developing and launching the first broad-based credentialing program in information privacy, the Certified Information Privacy Professional

> **"Businesses are beginning to recognize that the only way to circumvent further government regulation with respect to privacy is to develop systems and policies to protect consumers' interests."**

(CIPP). Recent laws requiring companies to protect consumer privacy will create 30,000 jobs. Most health-care–related businesses must appoint a privacy official to safeguard patient data. About 20 percent of the new jobs will be for executives, where privacy officers typically earn between $100,000 and $350,000 a year and report either to a company's general counsel or its chief operating officer.[58] High-level executives are typically given broad powers to establish policies to protect consumer privacy and, in so doing, to protect their companies from negative publicity and legal scrutiny.

Figure 10.3 lists the major provisions of the FTC's Fair Information Practices, which can be used as a starting point in developing a corporate privacy policy and determining key issues for a privacy offer to monitor.

Several nonprofit organizations have also stepped in to help companies develop privacy policies. Among the best known are TRUSTe and the BBB*OnLine*. TRUSTe is a nonprofit organization devoted to promoting global trust in Internet technology by providing a standardized, third-party oversight program that addresses the privacy concerns of consumers, website operators, and government regulators. Companies that agree to abide by TRUSTe's privacy standards may display a "trustmark" on their websites. These firms must disclose their personal information collection and privacy policies in a straightforward privacy statement. TRUSTe is supported by a network of corporate, industry, and nonprofit sponsors, including the Electronic Frontier Foundation, CommerceNet, America Online, Compaq, Ernst & Young, Excite, IBM, MatchLogic, Microsoft, Netcom,

Figure 10.3 Fair Information Practices

The Fair Information Practices

- **Notice.** Web sites should provide full disclosure of what personal information is collected and how it is used.
- **Choice.** Consumers at a Web site should be given choice about how their personal information is used.
- **Access.** Once consumers have disclosed personal information, they should have access to it.
- **Security.** Personal information disclosed to Web sites should be secured to ensure the information stays private.
- **Redress.** Consumers should have a way to resolve problems that may arise regarding sites, use, and disclosure of their personal information.

Source: Federal Trade Commission, "Fair Information Practice Principles," http://www.ftc.gov/reports/privacy3/fairinfo.htm, accessed August 2, 2009.

and Netscape.[59] For example, eBay's website is TRUSTe certified, which means that its online privacy practices fulfill TRUSTe's requirements. The online auction company's privacy policy promises that eBay will not share any personal information gathered from customers with any third parties and specifies how it will use the information it obtains. TRUSTe maintains the largest privacy seal program with more than 1,500 websites certified throughout the world. The organization is very active in educating and encouraging companies to improve privacy, security, and related aspects of business. Table 10.6 describes a real-life case scenario, along with an explanation of how TRUSTe's security guidelines could be applied to improve the situation.[60]

The mission of BBB*OnLine* is to promote trust and confidence in the Internet by encouraging ethical business practices. The BBB*OnLine* program provides verification, monitoring and review, consumer dispute resolution, a compliance seal, enforcement mechanisms, and an educational component. It is managed by the Council of Better Business Bureaus, an organization with considerable experience in conducting self-regulation and dispute-resolution programs, and it employs guidelines and requirements outlined by the Federal Trade Commission and the U.S. Department of Commerce.[61] More than 40,000 websites have qualified to display the BBB*OnLine* trustmarks, which demonstrates an organization's commitment to protecting consumer privacy in the online marketplace and certifies that an organization has qualified for the Department of Commerce/EU Safe Harbor allowing for the transfer of customer data between the United States and the European Union. Together with PlanetFeedback.com, whose 400,000 registered users make it one of the largest online consumer feedback services, the BBB created consumer feedback solutions for several top companies, including Procter & Gamble, Nokia, and others. This venture assisted companies in meeting whistle-blower provisions of recent corporate reform legislation.[62]

TABLE 10.6 Applying TRUSTe Guidelines to a Case Study

Case Study	How the TRUSTe Guidelines Would Help
(1) Company ABC maintains a database containing customers' names, addresses, and account numbers. The database is unencrypted, but is only accessible by employees using the proper usernames and passwords. Some employees have access to laptops for their jobs. ABC has a security policy requiring all laptops to be locked in employee cabinets while not in use. However, ABC does not enforce this aspect of the policy.	(1) The Security Guidelines suggest that all companies establish an employee awareness and training program. If all employees undergo basic initial and refresher security training, they are more likely to remember company policies and abide by them.
(2) One night, Employee 1 left a laptop on his desk. Even though the building was locked, somehow a thief broke in and stole the laptop. A disgruntled former Employee 2 was contacted by the thief and was convinced to sell her old username and password.	(2) If ABC had implemented an incident investigation and notification procedure, it is more likely that security personnel could have changed the passwords as soon as the theft was discovered and the thief would not have been able to access the database on that laptop.
(3) The former Employee 2's username and password worked for both the laptop and the database. The thief was able to use the laptop to get access to the network and the database. Thousands of customers were impacted.	(3) Assigning access privileges based on a need to know might have prevented this breach. Additionally, forcing password expiration would have prevented access to the network and the database. If the company had terminated inactive accounts or the accounts of terminated employees, access would have likewise been prevented. If the company had abided by the guidelines, the information would have been encrypted and the impact of the breach would have been less severe.
(4) Because it had never considered what it should do in the event of a breach, ABC had a significant delay before it could assemble a list of affected customers and notify them of the incident. Major media picked up the story and portrayed the company as unprepared and sloppy in their response.	(4) Motion detectors, micro-switches, or pressure pads, used to indicate when doors are opened and rooms entered, may have been useful to alert security personnel and prevent the theft in the first place. Another option would be closed-circuit cameras. Having an incident response and breach notification plan would have helped the company respond more quickly and avoid bad publicity.

Source: TRUSTe, "Security Guidelines Examples," http://www.truste.org/docs/Security_Guidelines_Examples.doc, accessed August 2, 2009.

Intellectual Property

In addition to protecting personal privacy, Internet users and others are concerned about protecting their rights to property they create, including songs, movies, books, and software. Such **intellectual property** consists of the ideas and creative materials developed to solve problems, carry out applications, educate, and entertain others. It is the result, or end product, of the creative process.

Intellectual property (IP) is generally protected by patents and copyrights. However, technological advancements are increasingly challenging the ownership of such property. For example, the FTC sued to block Internet retailer Toysmart. com from selling the names, addresses, billing information, family profiles, and buying habits of customers who have visited its website. The company, which filed for bankruptcy, had posted a privacy policy specifying that it would not share

intellectual property
the ideas and creative materials developed to solve problems, carry out applications, educate, and entertain others; the end product of the creative process

such information with third parties and had once been certified by TRUSTe. The FTC's suit opens the door for litigation against other failing Internet companies that attempt to sell their only significant assets—their databases, which often contain both customer contact information and intellectual insights on buying behavior gleaned through sophisticated technologies.[63]

Intellectual property losses in the United States total more than $11 billion a year in lost revenue from the illegal copying of computer programs, movies, compact discs, and books. IP losses also relate to stolen business plans, customer-related information, basic research reports, manufacturing process plans, product specifications, and many other proprietary documents. IP and other intangible assets typically represent about 75 percent of a company's value and source of revenue creation. Some experts estimate that companies lose over $59 billion in proprietary information and intellectual property each year through a variety of channels. Most cases involve one of the following scenarios:

1. *Inadvertent actions by current or former employees,* such as oral seminar presentations, discussions at an exhibit booth, and electronically misdirected fax and/or e-mail.

2. *Deliberate actions by current or former employees,* such as unauthorized physical access to information and deliberate disclosure to unauthorized parties.

3. *Deliberate actions by individuals/entities in trusted relationships other than employee relationships,* such as the exploitation of vendor-client relationships, subcontractor knowledge, joint ventures, and other relationships.

4. *Deliberate actions or activities by outsiders—those without a trusted relationship,* such as data mining of open-source data and public information and the practice of hiring away employees and placing them in a position where they must use trade secrets from a former employer.[64]

This issue has become a global concern because of disparities in enforcement of laws throughout the world. For example, according to the trade association International Intellectual Property Alliance, more than half of the business software used in Israel is pirated, costing U.S. companies roughly $170 million in one year.[65] The Business Software Alliance says business software producers, including alliance members, such as Microsoft Corporation, Adobe Systems Inc., and Apple Computer Inc., are losing $34 billion a year to piracy worldwide. The price of software lost to piracy ranges from $40 for desktop utilities to $13,000 for computer-aided design programs. According to trade group officials, roughly 35 percent of all commercial software is pirated. Illegal use of software downloaded from the Internet is a growing concern for the trade group.

Another major concern is software piracy rates, which are finally starting to decline slightly.[66] Russia and China are the two worst countries in terms of piracy violations. It is predicted that the trade-related aspects of intellectual property rights disputes will make countries more accountable for adhering to copyright standards.[67] Cisco Systems Inc. filed a lawsuit against Chinese network equipment maker Huawei Technologies and its subsidiaries, claiming unlawful

Photo courtesy of Susan Van Etten

Microsoft Corporation utilizes its website to educate stakeholders about software piracy

copying of its intellectual property. Cisco claims that Huawei copied extensively from Cisco's copyrighted technical documentation and portions of the Cisco IOS source code and included the technology in its operating system.[68]

Microsoft has been particularly aggressive in battling software piracy. The company has initiated legal action against 7,500 Internet listings in thirty-three countries for products it says are pirated. The company's efforts to stamp out piracy have been facilitated by software that searches the Internet for offers to sell counterfeit or illegally copied software.[69] Microsoft is working to transform the economics of the software business, allowing cheaper, more innovative software to be available for legitimate, paying customers.[70] Microsoft has even opened up a howtotell.com website for people to consult when loading software onto their computers. The website helps educate customers on how to tell if their software is genuine. Microsoft is also employing an Office Registration Wizard that authorizes purchasers of its software to load the programs onto only one desktop and one portable computer. If a purchaser attempts to register the software on more than two computers, the program will abort.[71] Can you think of another industry that would tolerate 40 percent of its products being stolen?

Table 10.7 provides a list of ways in which electronic documents may be stolen, misplaced, or passed along to unauthorized parties. Electronic document security is concerned with digital leakage, the undesired distribution of confidential information stored in electronic form. The distribution may be unintentional or malicious.

United States copyright laws protect original works in text form, pictures, movies, computer software, musical multimedia, and audiovisual work. Owners of copyrights have the right to reproduce, derive from, distribute, and publicly

Table 10.7 Threats to Electronic Document Security

Type of Loss	How Loss Occurs
Employee theft	Employee with legitimate access to confidential documents passes information to competitors, journalists, or government agencies.
Accidental distribution	E-mail allows documents to be transmitted anywhere in the world within seconds. A careless employee can send documents to the wrong parties with virtually no paper trail to follow.
Hackers	Companies make a significant investment in firewalls and other security software and systems. Even so, determined hackers can still cause security breaches.
No perceived value	An employee may pass on information that he or she considers valueless, not realizing the continued sensitivity of the information.
Change in trust	An employee who is planning to leave the firm may take sensitive documents to a new job with a competitor.
Lost devices	There are countless stories of notebook PCs and storage devices (floppy disks, flash drives, and zip disks) that were stolen or mislaid in hotels or airports.

Source: Edward H. Freeman, "Document Theft: Appropriate Responses," *EDPACS* 32 (November 2004): 1–7.

display and perform the copyrighted works. Copyright infringement is the unauthorized execution of the rights reserved by a copyright holder. Congress passed the Digital Millennium Copyright Act (DMCA) in 1998 to protect copyrighted materials on the Internet and to limit the liability of online service providers (OSPs). The DMCA provides a "safe harbor" provision that limits judgments that can be levied against OSPs for copyright infringement by their customers. To limit their liability, service providers must pay a nominal fee and comply with the act's reporting requirements.[72] In a lawsuit brought by Ticketmaster against Tickets.com under the DMCA, a judge ruled that Tickets.com could legally place a hypertext link to Ticketmaster on its website. Although Ticketmaster claimed that the link infringed its copyrights, Tickets.com contended that it placed the Ticketmaster and other similar hot links on its website so that its customers could access those sites to obtain tickets not available through Tickets.com. Because the link automatically directed potential customers to Ticketmaster's actual website, the court ruled no copyright violation occurred.[73] Table 10.8 provides additional facts about copyrights.

The Internet has created other copyright issues for some organizations that have found that the Web addresses (URLs) of other online firms either match or are very similar to their own trademarks. In some cases, "cybersquatters" have deliberately registered Web addresses that match or relate to other firms' trademarks and then have attempted to sell the registration to the trademark owners. A number of companies, including Taco Bell, MTC, and KFC, have paid thousands of dollars to gain control of names that match or parallel company trademarks.[74]

Registering a domain name is currently done on the honor system; a registrant simply fills out an online form to automatically reserve a domain name. Thus, the process is ideal for cybersquatters or other scammers looking to

Table 10.8 Facts About Copyrights

• A copyright notice is not necessary to protect private and original work created after April 1, 1989.
• Granting work to the public domain relinquishes all of the copyright holder's rights.
• The "fair use" exemption to copyright law allows for commentary, parody, news reporting, as well as research and education without seeking the copyright holder's permission, but giving acknowledgment is appropriate.
• Legal defense of a copyright is not necessary for maintaining the copyright—unlike trademarks, which may be damaged if not defended.
• Derivative works, based on another copyrighted work, come under the control of the original copyright holder. A notable exception is parody—making fun of an original work.
• Most copyright litigation is civil rather than criminal in nature, but criminal litigation is possible with more than ten copies of an original work and a valuation of over $2,500 (representing a commercial copyright violation).

Source: Brad Templeton, "10 Big Myths About Copyrights Explained," Brad Templeton's homepage, www.templetons.com/brad/copymyths.html, accessed August 2, 2009.

defraud businesses and consumers. The Federal Trademark Dilution Act of 1995 was enacted to help companies resolve this conflict. The law gives trademark owners the right to protect their trademarks, prevents the use of trademark-protected entities by others, and requires cybersquatters to relinquish trademarked names.[75]

The Internet Corporation for Assigned Names and Numbers (ICANN), a nonprofit organization charged with overseeing basic technical matters related to addressing on the Internet, has had success, including the introduction of a competitive domain registrar and registration market, the Uniform Dispute Resolution Policy (UDRP), and the creation of eight new top-level domains.[76] Many trademark holders immediately turn to the Internet Corporation for Assigned Names and Numbers' Uniform Dispute Resolution Policy as a vehicle for combating cybersquatters. However, remedies available in federal court under the Anti-Cybersquatting Consumer Production Act may better protect the rights of trademark holders. All ICANN-authorized registrars of domain names in the .com, .net, and .org top-level domains must agree to abide by the UDRP. Under the terms of the UDRP, a domain name will be transferred between parties only by agreement between them or by order of a court of competent jurisdiction or a UDRP-authorized dispute resolution provider.[77]

Since ICANN is overseen by the U.S. Department of Commerce, leaders in other countries have begun to question whether the United States has too much control of the Internet. Under the philosophy that the Internet is above the domain of any one government, these leaders pose several concerns. First, ICANN controls the master root file that provides users with access to the Internet. Some countries have threatened to develop a competing master root file, which would create parallel Internets. China has already developed a competing file and is encouraging other countries to join its effort. Second, ICANN has the power to affect selective parts of the Internet. For example, ICANN recently delayed adoption

"The debate over governance of the Internet is related to a number of significant issues, including intellectual property, privacy, security, and other top-level concerns of the public and government."

of a new .xxx top-level domain (TLD) for adult content because of pressure from U.S. government agencies. Third, because ICANN is a private corporation performing a significant public service, critics point to a lack of transparency and effectiveness in its operations and decisions. Finally, some leaders worry that ICANN will serve as a social and cultural gatekeeper, since all new TLD names and other requests must be approved by ICANN. The debate over governance of the Internet is related to a number of significant issues, including intellectual property, privacy, security, and other top-level concerns of the public and government.[78]

Health and Biotechnology

The advance of life-supporting technologies has raised a number of medical and health issues related to technology. **Bioethics** refers to the study of ethical issues in the fields of medical treatment and research, including medicine, nursing, law, philosophy, and theology, though today medical ethics is also recognized as a separate discipline.[79] All of these fields have been influenced by rapid changes in technology that require new approaches to solving issues. New genetic technologies promise to give medical ethics an even greater role in social decision making. For example, the Human Genome Project, a fifteen-year, $3 billion federally funded program to decode the entire human genetic map, identified a number of genes that may contribute to particular diseases or traits.

Because so many of our resources are spent on health care, the role of the private sector in determining the quality of health care is an important consideration to society. The pharmaceutical industry, for example, has been sharply criticized by politicians, health-care organizations, and consumers because of escalating drug costs. Investigators from federal and state agencies have threatened legal action over allegations that Medicare and Medicaid overpaid for drugs by $1 billion or more a year.[80] Pfizer Inc. agreed to pay $49 million to settle a whistle-blower case that lawyers predict will be followed by others. The case involved claims that Pfizer had bilked the federal government out of millions when selling Lipitor, an anticholesterol drug. This case, in essence, signifies a new niche of cases against the drug industry that falls under the federal False Claims Act. Under federal law, it is illegal for a drug company to pay a doctor or an organization, such as an HMO, as an inducement for that company to give a drug preferred status.[81]

On the other hand, pharmaceutical companies claim that the development of new lifesaving drugs and tests requires huge expenditures in research and

bioethics
the study of ethical issues in the fields of medical treatment and research, including medicine, nursing, law, philosophy, and theology, though today medical ethics is also recognized as a separate discipline

Figure 10.4 Research and Development Expenditures in Health

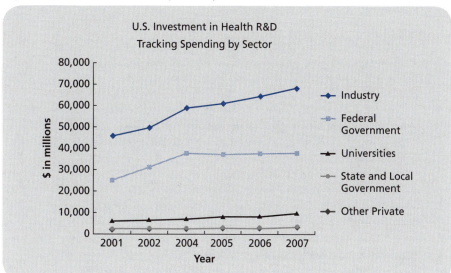

U.S. Investment in Health R&D
Tracking Spending by Sector

Source: Research!America, "2007 Investment in U.S. Health Research," http://www.researchamerica.org/uploads/healthdollar07.pdf, accessed August 2, 2009.

development. Figure 10.4 provides evidence that large amounts of money are spent in this process and others in the health-care field. The pharmaceutical industry is among the most profitable U.S. industries and spends nearly $14 billion a year in marketing, including drug samples provided to doctors, advertising in medical journals, and other strategies. The visibility of pharmaceutical advertising and promotion prompted Pharmaceutical Research & Manufacturers of America, an industry association, to develop its Guiding Principles on Direct-to-Consumer (DTC) Advertising. The voluntary guidelines are designed to ensure that DTC advertising is accurate, accessible, and useful. Figure 10.5 shows the preamble that accompanies the association's booklet on the fifteen guiding principles.[82]

Biotechnology The biotechnology industry emerged nearly forty years ago when Stanley Cohen and Herbert Boyer published a new recombinant DNA technique, a method of making proteins, such as human insulin, in cultured cells under controlled manufacturing conditions. Boyer went on to co-found Genentech, which today is biotechnology's largest company by market capitalization. From these insights, other scientists set out to map the human genome, a fifteen-year project to discover all of the estimated 20,000–25,000 human genes and make them accessible for further biological study. The ability to map the human genome has spurred over 200 new vaccines and medicines and many more are being tested in product trials. These innovations are changing the way that cancer, diabetes, AIDS, arthritis, and multiple sclerosis are treated.

Biotech innovations in other fields, such as manufacturing, have led to cleaner processes that produce less waste and use less energy and water. Most laundry detergents marketed in the United States contain biotechnology-based enzymes that combine better with bleach, are biodegradable, and reduce the need for hot

Figure 10.5 Preamble to PhRMA Guiding Principles for Direct-to-Consumer Advertisements

Preamble

Given the progress that continues to be made in society's battle against disease, patients are seeking more information about medical problems and potential treatments so they can better understand their health care options and communicate effectively with their physicians. An important benefit of direct-to-consumer (DTC) advertising is that it fosters an informed conversation about health, disease, and treatments between patients and their health care practitioners.

A strong empirical record demonstrates that DTC communications about prescription medicines serve the public health by:

- Increasing awareness about diseases;
- Educating patients about treatment options;
- Motivating patients to contact their physicians and engage in a dialogue about health concerns;
- Increasing the likelihood that patients will receive appropriate care for conditions that are frequently under-diagnosed and under-treated; and
- Encouraging compliance with prescription drug treatment regimens.

Source: Pharmaceutical Research & Manufacturers of America, "PhRMA Guiding Principles: Direct-to-Consumer Advertisements About Prescription Medicines," http://www.phrma.org/files/DTCGuidingprinciples.pdf, accessed August 2, 2009.

> **"The government and the private sector often partner with academic researchers and nonprofit institutes to develop new technologies in health and biotechnology."**

water. Law enforcement officials use DNA finger printing, a biotech process, to catch criminals, increase conviction rates, and perform stronger investigations and forensic science.[83] There are over 1,500 biotechnology companies in the United States with a market capitalization of nearly $400 billion. Biotech employees earn strong wages, estimated at nearly $75,000 per year, which is $29,000 above the average private sector annual compensation. Finally, the top five firms invest approximately $170,000 per year per employee in research and development activities.[84] Not surprisingly, more than 500,000 patents have been applied for on genes or gene sequences worldwide according to the activist group GeneWatch UK.[85]

The government and the private sector often partner with academic researchers and nonprofit institutes to develop new technologies in health and biotechnology. Research ranges from mapping the human genetic code to finding drugs that cure cancer to genetically modifying food products.

Many of these collaborative efforts to improve health involve scientists, funded globally by a variety of sources. For example, the Avon Foundation granted nearly $30 million through the Avon Kiss Goodbye to Breast Cancer Crusade, which supports virtually every facet of the cause by funding five critical areas: breast cancer biomedical research, clinical care, support services, education, and early detection programs.[86] National Institutes of Health scientists created great excitement when they reported that embryonic stem cells had been coaxed to form pancreatic cells that make insulin, a potential treatment for diabetes. But a new study suggests that the cells didn't really make insulin and instead just absorbed it from the culture medium they were grown in and later released it.[87] Using cell-engineering techniques, scientists may have found a way to generate unlimited supplies of brain cells for transplanting into patients with Parkinson's disease. These examples illustrate technology advances that could result in commercially viable products that save and/or prolong life.

Cloning, the replication of organisms that are genetically identical to their parent, has become a highly controversial topic in biotechnology and bioethics. Human cloning has raised unanswered questions about the future of human reproduction. Since Scottish scientists first cloned Dolly the sheep, scientists have also successfully cloned mice, cows, pigs, goats, and cats but with mixed reports about the health of the cloned progeny. While cloning humans would appear to be the final step of scientific reproduction, indisputable proof of the first human clone will actually serve as a starting point for many years of research. Like in vitro fertilization, human clones will need to grow up before scientists know the effects that this process will have on a person's physical, mental, and emotional states.[88] Cloning has the potential to revolutionize the treatment of diseases and conditions such as Parkinson's disease and cancer. Cloning technology might also allow doctors to create replacement organs, thereby lengthening human lives. Some scientists believe that cloning could be used to re-create extinct or endangered species in a last-ditch conservation effort. The ability to create and modify life processes is often generated through business and government collaborative research; the results of such research may contribute to life-altering products of tomorrow.

Despite the potential of this technology, many people have negative views about cloning. Some contend that it is unethical to "meddle with nature," whereas others believe that cloning is wrong because every time it is used to treat a patient, a cloned human embryo is destroyed, one that might otherwise have been capable of life.[89] The cloning of a miniature pig, named Goldie, lacking both copies of a gene involved in immediate immune rejection, has brought the prospect of transplanting pig organs into people a little closer. The small pig's organs are similar in size to those of humans, and the missing genes make the organs less likely to be rejected. But although Goldie's creation may have solved the problem of immediate transplant rejection, there is a slower rejection in which the transplant is attacked by the recipient's white blood cells.[90]

Some people argue that cloning of human beings should be banned, and several bills have been introduced in Congress and various state legislatures to do just that. Additionally, nineteen European nations have signed an agreement prohibiting the genetic replication of humans. Harvesting stem cells from surplus in vitro fertilization (IVF) embryos was given the go-ahead by the Australian Senate by a vote of nearly two to one in favor of a bill legalizing the procedure. The new Australian law lies between those in the United Kingdom and the United States. In the United Kingdom, the law already allows researchers to harvest stem cells from surplus IVF embryos and to conduct therapeutic cloning. But in the United States, federally funded researchers cannot pursue therapeutic cloning or harvest stem cells from discarded embryos, although private companies can.[91]

Genetic research holds the promise to revolutionize how many diseases are diagnosed and treated. However, consumer advocates have urged the World Trade Organization (WTO) to place limits on gene patents, which they claim are tantamount to "ownership of life." Patents dealing with human DNA have increased dramatically in the last decade as researchers have identified more genes that play a role in a number of diseases. The WTO rules governing patents on intellectual property currently permit patents to be owned for twenty years and allow patent holders to prevent other firms from profiting from a particular technology during that period. But some consumer groups, including Ralph Nader's Public Citizen, fear that these patents have the potential to permit a company to "corner the market" on the diagnosis and treatment of specific diseases for years. These groups worry that such long-term protection could prohibit other companies from developing alternative tests and treatments that might result in improved care at lower prices.[92] The fact that genes are both material molecules and informational systems helps explain the difficulty that the patent system is going to continue to have.[93]

A final concern with genetics is the increasing availability of direct-to-consumer testing kits. With these kits, consumers can proactively manage their health, including gaining access to knowledge about predispositions to cancer, diseases, and illnesses. Most specialists agree that the results of such tests are best delivered in a professional medical setting, not via the Internet or mail. For example, through a mail-order kit, a consumer could receive a positive finding on a DNA-based prostate cancer screening test. The consumer may have cancerous growths that can be removed, cancer that has spread, or neither because the test is a false positive. Medical advice is warranted at this point because the consumer has no way of determining the appropriate course of action.[94]

Genetically Modified Foods As many as 800 million people around the world don't have enough to eat. Increasing food production to satisfy the growing demand for food without increasing land use will require farmers to achieve significant increases in productivity. Genetically modified (GM) foods offer a way to quickly improve crop characteristics such as yield, pest resistance, or herbicide tolerance, often to a degree not possible with traditional methods. Further, GM crops can be manipulated to produce completely artificial substances, from the precursors of plastics to consumable vaccines.[95] Also discussed in Chapter 11, genetically modified, or transgenic, crops are created when scientists introduce a gene from one organism to another. Scientists believe that genetically engineered crops could raise overall crop production in developing countries by as much as

25 percent.[96] According to a report by seven independent academies from both developed and developing countries, to combat world hunger, developed countries must boost funding for research into genetically modified crops, and poor farmers must be protected from corporate control of the technology.[97]

The European public calls GM products "Frankenfood" for fear it could pose a health threat or create an environmental disaster where genes jump from GM crops to wild plants and reduce biodiversity or create superweeds. For four years, Europe has held up new approvals of U.S. exports of Frankenfood. The European Parliament voted to require extensive labeling and traceability of food containing genetically modified organisms, even if no remnants of genetic modification are detectable. With European public confidence in food safety badly shaken by foot-and-mouth and mad-cow disease, no new GM products have been authorized for use in Europe since 1998. European Union officials admit this is likely illegal under WTO rules and hurts largely U.S. farm exporters. In an effort to restart the approval process by addressing public concerns over consumer choice and environmental protection, the EU proposed burdensome new rules for biotech food and animal feed labeling and for "farm-to-fork" traceability measures on products.[98]

Table 10.9 lists some examples of genetically modified foods. Genetic modification has raised numerous health, ethical, and environmental questions.

Many people do not realize that some of the foods they eat were made from genetically engineered crops. Consumer groups are increasingly concerned that these foods could be unhealthy and/or harmful to the environment. Concerns

Table 10.9 Genetically Modified Foods

Product	Genetic Modification	Purpose
Tomatoes, peas, peppers, tropical fruit, broccoli, raspberries, melons	Controlled ripening	Allows shipping of vine-ripened tomatoes; improves shelf life, quality
Tomatoes, potatoes, corn, lettuce, coffee, cabbage family, apples	Insect resistance	Reduces insecticide use
Peppers, tomatoes, cucumbers	Fungal resistance	Reduces fungicide use
Potatoes, tomatoes, cantaloupe, squash, cucumbers, corn, oilseed rape (canola), soybeans, grapes	Viral resistance	Reduces diseases caused by plant viruses and, because insects carry viruses, reduces use of insecticides
Soybeans, tomatoes, corn, oilseed rape (canola), wheat	Herbicide tolerance	Improves weed control
Corn, sunflowers, soybeans, and other plants	Improved nutrition	Increases amount of essential amino acids, vitamins, or other nutrients in the host plants
Oilseed rape (canola), peanuts	Heat stability	Improves the processing quality; permits new food uses for healthier oils

Source: Food Marketing Institute, "Bioengineered Food and You," http://www.fmi.org/consumer/biotech/biotechnology.pdf, accessed August 2, 2009. Courtesy of Food Marketing Institute.

about the safety of genetically altered crops have led to a backlash in Europe and, more recently, in the United States and Japan. For example, Campbell Soup, the first firm to license a genetically modified food—the FlavSavr tomato, which was engineered for a longer shelf life—was the target of a massive letter-writing campaign by consumers worried about the lack of safety testing and labels on foods containing gene-altered crops.[99] The power of genetic modification techniques raises the possibility of human health, environmental, and economic problems, including unanticipated allergic responses to novel substances in foods, the spread of pest resistance or herbicide tolerance to wild plants, inadvertent toxicity to benign wildlife, and increasing control of agriculture by biotechnology corporations.[100] Many consumers are boycotting products made from genetically modified materials.

Several countries have opposed trade in GM foods through the World Trade Organization, and Japan has asked U.S. corn producers not to include genetically modified corn in animal feed exported to Japan. The European Parliament has called for all GM foods to be labeled.[101] Insects and birds transport seeds from one field to the next, allowing cross-pollination geneticists never intended. Unlike chemical or nuclear contamination, gene pollution can never be cleaned up.

Table 10.10 demonstrates the millions of hectares that are being used to cultivate GM crops in various countries. There has been solid growth of GM crops since 1998.[102]

A number of companies have responded to public concerns about genetically modified food products by limiting or avoiding their use altogether. Archer Daniels Midland, the largest buyer of genetically modified crops in the United States, asked farmers and grain merchants to segregate GM crops from traditionally grown plants. Large agribusiness purchasers of farm crops are paying less per bushel for genetically altered products.[103] Gerber and Heinz both announced that they will not permit genetically engineered corn or soybeans in their baby-food products. Corn growers in the United States say they are losing $300 million annually because their GM crops are largely barred—along with many other modified products—from the European market.[104]

Ethical questions about the use of some types of genetically modified products have also been raised. For example, Monsanto and other companies are developing so-called terminator technology to create plants that are genetically engineered to produce sterile seeds. Dr. Jane Rissler, a scientist with the Union of Concerned Scientists, says, "The fact that terminator technology will work to the disadvantage of the subsistence farmer who depends on harvesting seeds for the next year's crops illustrates the intent of the companies, which is to get the maximum return on their investment." Other plants in development will require spraying with chemicals supplied by the seed companies to produce desired traits, such as resistance to certain pests or disease. Farmers say the issue isn't the technology itself but, rather, who controls the technology—in most cases, the multinational seed companies. In response to global concerns about this issue, Monsanto announced that it would halt commercial development of the terminator technology, although it plans to continue researching it.[105]

Defenders of biotechnology say consumer fears about genetically modified foods have not been substantiated by research.[106] As the U.S. agriculture industry is

Table 10.10 Commercial Cultivation of Genetically Modified Crops (in millions of hectares)

Rank	Country	Area (million hectares)	Biotech Crops
1*	USA*	62.5	Soybean, maize, cotton, canola, squash, papaya, alfalfa, sugarbeet
2*	Argentina*	21.0	Soybean, maize, cotton
3*	Brazil*	15.8	Soybean, maize, cotton
4*	India*	7.6	Cotton
5*	Canada*	7.6	Canola, maize, soybean, sugarbeet
6*	China*	3.8	Cotton, tomato, poplar, petunia, papaya, sweet pepper
7*	Paraguay*	2.7	Soybean
8*	South Africa*	1.8	Maize, soybean, cotton
9*	Uruguay*	0.7	Soybean, maize
10*	Bolivia*	0.6	Soybean
11*	Philippines*	0.4	Maize
12*	Australia*	0.2	Cotton, canola, carnation
13*	Mexico*	0.1	Cotton, soybean
14*	Spain*	0.1	Maize
15	Chile	< 0.1	Maize, soybean, canola
16	Colombia	< 0.1	Cotton, carnation
17	Honduras	< 0.1	Maize
18	Burkina Faso	< 0.1	Cotton
19	Czech Republic	< 0.1	Maize
20	Romania	< 0.1	Maize
21	Portugal	< 0.1	Maize
22	Germany	< 0.1	Maize
23	Poland	< 0.1	Maize
24	Slovakia	< 0.1	Maize
25	Egypt	< 0.1	Maize

*14 biotech mega-countries growing 50,000 hectares, or more, of biotech corps

Source: ISAAA Brief No. 39—2008, Global Status of Commercialized Biotech/GM Crops: 2008, ISAAA Briefs, http://www.isaaa.org/resources/publications/briefs/default.asp, accessed August 4, 2009.

eager to point out, the technology has been a big success: It has reduced the amount of pesticides farmers have had to spray on their cornfields, with happy consequences for the environment and human health. United States health regulators have not been able to find anything wrong with eating Bt (*Bacillus thuringiensis*) corn. It is now found in roughly two-thirds of all corn products on U.S. store shelves.[107]

STRATEGIC IMPLEMENTATION OF RESPONSIBILITY FOR TECHNOLOGY

To accrue the maximum benefits from the technologies driving the new economy, many parties within society have important roles to play. While the media and public continue to debate the issues associated with technology, the government must take steps to provide support for continued technological advancements and establish regulations, as needed, to ensure that the benefits of technology apply to as many people as possible while minimizing any potential for harm, especially to competition, the environment, and human welfare. Various stakeholders, including employees, customers, and special-interest groups, as well as the general public, can influence the use and control of technology through the public policy process. Businesses also have a significant role to play in supporting technology. New technologies are developed, refined, and introduced to the market through the research and development and marketing activities of business. Businesses that aspire to be socially responsible must monitor the impact of technology and harness it for the good of all.

> **"Businesses that aspire to be socially responsible must monitor the impact of technology and harness it for the good of all."**

The Role of Government

With an economy that is increasingly driven by technology, the government must maintain the basic infrastructure and support for technology in our society. The Department of Defense, for example, explores ways that technology can improve the quality of life. The government also serves as a watchdog to ensure that technology benefits society, not criminals. However, as the pace of technology continues to escalate, law enforcement agencies ranging from the FBI to local police forces are struggling to recruit and retain officers and prosecutors who are knowledgeable about the latest technology and the ways criminals can exploit it. The nation currently has only a few hundred high-caliber forensic computer experts, but many of these officers are being lured to technology firms and private security outfits by salaries more than twice their government paychecks. Only a handful of police and sheriffs' departments across the country have enough money to support squads of high-tech investigators, and many top detectives leap to the corporate realm anyway.[108]

Computer crimes currently share sentencing guidelines with larceny, embezzlement, and theft, where the most significant sentencing factor is the amount of financial loss inflicted, and additional points are awarded for using false ID or ripping off more than ten victims. But in a congressional session that heard much talk about "cyberterrorism," lawmakers became convinced that computer outlaws have more in common with al Qaeda than common thieves. The U.S. Supreme Court's Federal Sentencing Guidelines set the range of sentences a court can choose from in a given case on the basis of a point system that sets a starting value for a particular crime and then adds or subtracts points for specific aggravating or mitigating circumstances.[109]

In addition to cybercriminals, many commercial users of the Internet are implementing new technologies in ways that our existing legal system could not have conceived of when our laws were framed. Hollywood film studios, for example, are concerned that new technology will allow computer users to copy and trade entire videos on the Internet, much like they traded music recordings via Napster and other peer-to-peer file-sharing services. The recording and movie industry saw the threat of this technology when Shawn Fanning, the creator of the peer-to-peer file-swapping service, was a child.

Indeed, the road to the controversial Digital Millennium Copyright Act (DMCA) probably began in 1975, when Sony Corporation introduced the Betamax VCR. That was the start of a long series of court battles and legislative fights over electronic duplication of copyrighted material. But it wasn't until PCs were in wide use that Congress acted in a broad way to extend copyright protections to the digital domain. President Clinton signed the DMCA in October 1998. Five years later, copyright holders are using the DMCA to successfully fight Napster-like services and protect their anticopying technology. But the law has many critics and challengers who say it impinges on the right of consumers to copy content and creates a predicament for scientists conducting certain kinds of security research.[110]

Both the Napster and RIAA (Recording Industry Association of America) lawsuits illustrate a significant difference of opinion in the interpretation of existing laws when exploiting the evolving multimedia potential of the Internet. Although the government's strategy thus far has been not to interfere with the commercial use of technology, disputes and differing interpretations of current laws increasingly bring technology into the domain of the legal system. New laws related to breakthrough technologies that change the nature of competition are constantly being considered. Usually, the issues of privacy, ownership of intellectual property, health and safety, environmental impact, competition, and consumer welfare are the legislative platforms for changing the legal and regulatory system.

The Role of Business

Business, like government, is involved in both reactive and proactive attempts to market and make effective use of technology. Reactive concerns relate to issues that have legal and/or ethical implications as well as issues of productivity, customer welfare, or other stakeholder concerns. One example of a reactive response to the consequences of new technologies relates to employee access to and use of the

World Wide Web. Websense is the worldwide leader of employee Internet management (EIM) solutions. Websense Enterprise software enables businesses to manage how their employees use the Internet, improving productivity, conserving network bandwidth and storage costs, and mitigating legal liability. Founded in 1994, Websense serves more than 18,100 worldwide customers, ranging in size from 100-person firms to global corporations. Clients include Blue Bell Creameries, Harvey Nichols department store, Carnival Cruise Lines, and the City of Cincinnati.[111]

At any given time, about 20 percent of employee PCs are surfing nonbusiness-related sites, such as ESPN.com or sexually oriented websites. This includes both staff and executives, such as the CIO, chief technology officer, and even the CEO.[112] Many large firms have suffered public embarrassment, legal bills, compensation claims, and clean-up costs when employees seek inappropriate material online, send e-mails to people they shouldn't, accidentally circulate confidential information outside a business, or spread a computer virus. The Department of Trade and Industry security survey conducted in the United Kingdom revealed that 62 percent of businesses have suffered a security breach of some type, a figure that has climbed in every survey.[113]

Some companies are purchasing software that assists employees in managing the Internet time they spend on personal activities. Kozy Shack Enterprises, the manufacturer of ready-to-eat pudding, allows employees one hour per day to shop, browse, chat, and complete other personal tasks. Harvey Nichols, a high-end retailer in London, uses similar software to ensure that employees do not have access to pornography, gambling, and other inappropriate sites. A majority of large U.S. companies are monitoring employee communications, including telephone calls, e-mail, and Internet connections.[114] The courts have ruled that because communications occurring on company-provided equipment are not private under current law, such monitoring is legal.[115] However, established high-tech companies like Microsoft and Oracle, and many technology startups, often choose not to monitor or limit employees' Web usage or e-mail. Managers at these companies believe they cannot be innovators with technology while strictly monitoring employee use of and time on the Web.[116]

Concerns about undesirable employee use of telecommunications equipment represent reactions to changes in information technology that affect the workplace. Even though companies may be legally within their right to monitor and control the use of certain websites by employees, such control raises strategic issues related to trust and the type of long-run relationships that firms want to have with their employees.

On the other hand, a strategic, proactive approach to technology will consider its impact on social responsibility. Proactive management of technology requires developing a plan for utilizing resources to take advantage of competitive opportunities. For example, there is great demand for high-speed Internet connections, including cable modems, DSL, and other broadband connections, because computing speed and power have moved beyond current bandwidth capacity. Many telecommunications firms are racing to install and market the infrastructure for broadband connections to satisfy this demand. In a few years, however, new technologies, probably wireless connections, will more than likely provide even greater connection speeds, and the opportunity for new companies to provide broadband service will vanish.

With competition increasing, companies are spending more time and resources to establish technology-based competitive advantages. The strategic approach to technology requires an overall mission, strategy, and coordination of all functional activities, including a concern for social responsibility, to have an effective program. To promote the responsible use of technology, a firm's policies, rules, and standards must be integrated into its corporate culture. Reducing undesirable behavior in this area is a goal that is no different from the goals of reducing costs, increasing profits, or improving quality that are aggressively enforced and integrated into the corporate culture in order to be effective in improving appropriate behavior within the organization.

Top managers must consider the social consequences of technology in the strategic planning process. When all stakeholders are involved in the process, everyone can better understand the need for and requirements of responsible development and use of technology. There will always be conflicts in making the right choices, but through participation in decision making, the best solutions can be found. Individual participants in this process should not abdicate their personal responsibility as concerned members of society. Organizations that are concerned about the consequences of their decisions create an environment for different opinions on important issues. As Richard Purcell, Microsoft's first chief privacy officer, once said, "No matter what legislation is enacted, it is the responsibility of the leaders in the online industry to provide and implement technologies that help consumers feel safer and more comfortable online."[117]

Strategic Technology Assessment

To calculate the effects of new technologies, companies can employ a procedure known as **technology assessment** to foresee the effects new products and processes will have on their firm's operation, on other business organizations, and on society in general. This assessment is a tool that managers can use to evaluate their firm's performance and to chart strategic courses of action to respond to new technologies. With information obtained through a technology assessment or audit, managers can estimate whether the benefits of adopting a specific technology outweigh costs to the firm and to society at large. The assessment process can also help companies ensure compliance with government regulations related to technology. Remember that one of the four components of social responsibility is legal compliance. Because technology is evolving so rapidly, even attorneys are struggling to keep up with the legal implications of these advances. Social institutions, including religion, education, the law, and business, have to respond to changing technology by adapting or developing new approaches to address the evolving issues. A strategic technology assessment or audit can help organizations understand these issues and develop appropriate and responsible responses to them (see Table 10.11).[118]

If the assessment process indicates that the company has not been effective at utilizing technologies or is using them in a way that raises questions, changes may be necessary. Companies may need to consider setting higher standards, improving reporting processes, and improving communication of standards and training programs, as well as participating in aboveboard discussions with other organizations. If performance has not been satisfactory, management may want to reorganize the way certain kinds of decisions are made. Table 10.11 contains some issues to

technology assessment a procedure that companies can use to foresee the effects new products and processes will have on their operation, on other business organizations, and on society in general

Table 10.11 Strategic Technology Assessment Issues

Yes	No	Checklist
O	O	Are top managers in your organization aware of the federal, state, and local laws related to technology decisions?
O	O	Does your organization have an effective system for monitoring changes in the federal, state, and local laws related to technology?
O	O	Is there an individual, committee, or department in your organization responsible for overseeing government technology issues?
O	O	Does your organization do checks on technology brought into the organization by employees?
O	O	Are there communications and training programs in your organization to create an effective culture to protect employees and organizational interests related to technology?
O	O	Does your organization have monitoring and auditing systems to determine the impact of technology on key stakeholders?
O	O	Does your organization have a method for reporting concerns about the use or impact of technology?
O	O	Is there a system to determine ethical risks and appropriate ethical conduct to deal with technology issues?
O	O	Do top managers in your organization understand the ramifications of using technology to communicate with employees and customers?
O	O	Is there an individual or department in your organization responsible for maintaining compliance standards to protect the organization in the areas of privacy and intellectual property?

assess for proactive and reactive technology responsibility issues. Some social concerns might relate to a technology's impact on the environment, employee health and working conditions, consumer safety, and community values.

Finally, the organization should focus on the positive aspects of technology to determine how it can be used to improve the work environment, its products, and the general welfare of society. Technology can be used to reduce pollution, encourage recycling, and save energy. Also, information can be made available to customers to help them maximize the benefits of products. Technology has been and will continue to be a major force that can improve society.

SUMMARY

Technology relates to the application of knowledge, including the processes and applications to solve problems, perform tasks, and create new methods to obtain desired outcomes. The dynamics of technology relate to the constant change that requires significant adjustments in the political, religious, and economic structures of society. Reach relates to the far-reaching nature of technology as it moves through society. The self-sustaining nature of technology relates to the fact that technology acts as a catalyst to spur even faster development. Civilizations must harness and adapt to changes in technology to maintain a desired quality of life. Although technological advances have improved our quality of life, they have also raised ethical, legal, and social concerns.

Advances in technology have created millions of new jobs, better health and longer lives, new opportunities, and the enrichment of lives. Without greater access to the latest technology, however, economic development could suffer in underserved areas. The ability to purchase technology may affect the nature of competition and business success. Information and telecommunications technology minimizes borders, allows people to overcome the physical limitations of time and space, and enables people to acquire customized goods and services that cost less and are of higher quality.

The Internet, a global information system that links many computer networks together, has altered the way people communicate, learn, do business, and find entertainment. The growth of the Internet has generated issues never before encountered and that social institutions, including the legal system, have been slow to address.

Because current technology has made it possible to collect, share, and sell vast quantities of personal information, often without consumers' knowledge, privacy has become a major concern associated with technology. Many websites follow users' tracks through their site by storing a cookie, or identifying string of text, on the users' computers. What companies do with the information about consumers they collect through cookies and other technologies is generating concern. Privacy issues related to children are generating even more debate and laws to protect children's interests. Identity theft occurs when criminals obtain personal information that allows them to impersonate someone else to use that individual's credit to obtain financial accounts and to make purchases. Some measure of protection of personal privacy is provided by the U.S. Constitution, as well as by Supreme Court rulings and federal laws. Europe and other regions of the world are also addressing privacy concerns. In addition to creating and posting policies regarding the gathering and use of personal information, more companies are beginning to hire chief privacy officers.

Intellectual property consists of the ideas and creative materials developed to solve problems, carry out applications, educate, and entertain others. Copyright infringement is the unauthorized execution of the rights reserved by a copyright holder. Technological advancements are challenging the ownership of intellectual property. Other issues relate to "cybersquatters" who deliberately register Web addresses that match or relate to other firms' trademarks and then attempt to sell the registration to the trademark owners.

Bioethics refers to the study of ethical issues in the fields of medical treatment and research, including medicine, nursing, law, philosophy, and theology. Genetic research, including cloning, may revolutionize how diseases are diagnosed and treated. Genetically modified crops are created when scientists introduce a gene from one organism to another. However, these technologies are controversial because some people believe they are immoral, unsafe, or harmful to the environment.

To accrue the maximum benefits from the technology driving the new economy, many parties within society have important roles to play. With an economy that is increasingly driven by technology, the government must maintain the basic infrastructure and support for technology in our society. The government also serves as a watchdog to ensure that technology benefits society, not criminals.

Business is involved in both reactive and proactive attempts to make effective use of technology. Reactive concerns relate to issues that have legal or ethical implications as well as to productivity, customer welfare, or other stakeholder issues. Proactive management of technology requires developing a plan for utilizing resources to take advantage of competitive opportunities. The strategic approach to technology requires an overall mission, strategy, and coordination of all functional activities, including a concern for social responsibility, to produce an effective program. To calculate the effects of new technologies, companies can employ a procedure known as technology assessment to foresee the effects of new products and processes on their firm's operation, on other business organizations, and on society in general.

RESPONSIBLE BUSINESS DEBATE

Is Technology Healthy for Society?

ISSUE: What are the benefits and drawbacks of technology to social interaction?

While technology has brought advancements, conveniences, and efficiencies to our lives, some critics wonder if the benefits outweigh the costs, especially those that are transforming the ways we communicate, connect with other people, solve problems, and generally interact as human beings. In other words, are we are losing the relationships that have made the United States a great place to live and work?

In 1831, Alexis de Tocqueville visited the United States on behalf of the French government. He set out to study the prison system, but ended up writing a grand treatise, *Democracy in America*. In his book, de Tocqueville noted how Americans were dedicated to social cohesion, equality, common purpose, and concern for both individuals and the community. Years later, writers on the topic of social capital, mentioned in Chapter 2, drew from de Tocqueville's work to describe the American approach to community service, active neighborhood associations, and other types of civic engagement. Recent studies, however, indicate civic engagement is declining. Is technology part of the problem?

Consider these daily occurrences: Students do not talk to classmates after class, as they are quick to begin texting people they already know. People on the subway rarely acknowledge the riders they see every day, because they are busy checking their personal digital assistants (PDAs) and getting a jumpstart on the day. Co-workers send each other e-mails, rather than walk thirty steps to the next office for a brief conversation. Finally, handwriting is so passé that a handwritten envelope will be opened much sooner than any other piece of mail.

There Are Two Sides to Every Issue:

1. Defend the changes that technology has brought to society's communication patterns, such as the expediency of e-mail and texting, reduced costs, and access to people around the world.

2. Defend the need for society to rely less on technology and more on traditional communication patterns, such as face-to-face meetings, verbal conversations, and handwritten correspondence.

KEY TERMS

technology (p. 352)
intellectual property (p. 375)

bioethics (p. 380)
technology assessment (p. 391)

DISCUSSION QUESTIONS

1. Define technology and describe three characteristics that can be used to assess it.

2. What effect has technology had on the U.S. and global economies? Have these effects been positive or negative?

3. Many people believe that the government should regulate business with respect to privacy online, but companies say self-regulation is more appropriate. Which approach would benefit consumers most? Business?

4. What is intellectual property? How can owners of intellectual property protect their rights?

5. What is bioethics? What are some of the consequences of biomedical research?

6. Should genetically modified foods be labeled as "genetically modified"? Why or why not?

7. How can a strategic technology assessment help a company?

EXPERIENTIAL EXERCISE

Visit three websites that are designed primarily for children or that focus on products of interest to children under age thirteen. For example, visit the websites for new movies, games, action figures, candy, cereal, or beverages. While visiting these sites, put yourself in the role and mindset of a child. What types of language and persuasion are used? Is there a privacy statement on the site that can be understood by children? Are there any parts of the site that might be offensive or worrisome to parents? Provide a brief evaluation of how well these sites attend to the provisions of the Children's Online Privacy Protection Act.

WHAT WOULD YOU DO?

James Kitling thought about his conversation with Ira Romero earlier that day. He was not really surprised that the human resources (HR) department was concerned about the time employees were spending on personal issues during the workday. Several departments were known for their rather loose management approach. Internet access for personal tasks, like shopping, using Instant Messaging services, and answering nonwork e-mails, had been a concern for several months. Recent news reports had indicated that more than 50 percent of large companies now filter or monitor e-mail. Companies are also monitoring Web browsing, file downloads, chat room use, and group postings. A survey published in the media reported that workers spend an average of eight hours a week looking at nonwork Internet sites.

As the director of information technology, James was very dedicated to the effective use of technology to enhance business productivity. Although he was knowledgeable about technology, James was equally attuned to the ways in which technology can be abused in a work setting. He knew that some employees were probably using too much Internet time on personal tasks.

On the other hand, his company mainly employed professionals, administrative staff, and customer service personnel. All 310 employees were expected to use the computer a great deal throughout the day. At present, the company had a skeleton code of ethics and policy on the use of company resources, including the Internet.

A couple of managers and now HR had spoken with James about the prospects of monitoring employee computer and Internet use. Ira's inquiry about the software, however, was a bit more serious. An employee had recently been formally reprimanded for downloading and printing nonwork documents from the Internet. These documents were designed to help the employee's spouse in a new business venture. Although the employee did most of the searching and downloading during lunch, the supervisor felt this was an improper use of company resources. Other employees had been informally spoken with about their use of the Internet for personal matters. Ira believed this was a growing problem that definitely affected productivity. He had read the news reports and believed that monitoring software was becoming a necessary tool in today's workplace.

So far, James had been hesitant to purchase and implement one of these systems. The employee Internet management software was somewhat expensive, running approximately $25 per computer. He felt that the software could cause employee trust to sharply decline, resulting in even greater problems than currently existed. After all, employees engage in some personal tasks during work hours, including making telephone calls home, getting coffee, chatting with co-workers, going to the doctor, and so forth. James wondered if the Internet was that much different from these other personal activities. He recalled a discussion in a management class in his MBA program, where they learned that employees in the early 1900s were only allowed to use the telephone to call the police. Thus, the telephone was once thought of as a great distracter, much like the Internet today.

Ira and a few other managers were pretty firm in their beliefs about the Internet monitoring system. James was still not convinced that it was the best route to curbing the problem. In his role, however, he was expected to provide leadership in developing a solution. What would you do?

Sustainability Issues

Chapter Objectives

- To define the nature of sustainability as it relates to social responsibility

- To explore a variety of environmental issues faced by business and society

- To examine the impact of environmental policy and regulations

- To discuss a strategic approach to respond to environmental issues

Chapter Outline

Global Environmental Issues

Environmental Policy and Regulation

Alternative Energy

Business Response to Sustainability Issues

Strategic Implementation of Environmental Responsibility

Green Initiatives Get Boost from Slow Economy

Contrary to what you might think, the latest recession might have helped the environment. The recession caused the greenhouse gas emissions growth rate to reduce by half in 2008—which means emissions only increased by just over 1 percent that year. Industries like steel, which have traditionally been antagonistic to the environmental movement, are joining forces with environmentalists in an attempt to curb foreign competition. The closing of factories around the globe, while bad for unemployment rates, is slowing CO_2 emissions. European factory closings reduced CO_2 emissions by an estimated 100 million tons. Polluting factories failed at a rapid rate during the recession because they are less likely to be bailed out by governments. China, for instance, is less likely to provide aid to major polluters.

However, environmental movements will face many complications once the recession ends. Although governments around the world recognize the importance of green initiatives, job creation is more important in helping economies recover. The Russian Baikal Pulp and Paper Mill in central eastern Siberia laid off 2,300 workers, for example. All of these people needed new jobs, and lived in a place with few employment options. This scenario played out in manufacturing sectors around the world. The challenge governments will face in upcoming years is to bolster the "green-collar" job sector and to find cleaner ways to manufacture goods. In response to this concern, Baikal, for example, has transitioned to the hotels and travel industry in an attempt to create jobs while keeping the polluting factory closed. The town is located on a lake near mountains and ski resorts—making tourism a reasonable option. Similar to the United States, the Chinese government also offered stimulus money to help the economy. Part of the package was earmarked for green projects to improve energy efficiency.

Even those who are sworn enemies are uniting. United States steelmakers and environmentalists are banding together to fight pollution and dumping. Dumping occurs when a country sells a product at cheaper prices in foreign countries than it does in the home country to reduce foreign competition. Steel is one product commonly "dumped" in the United States. Currently foreign steel makes up 20 to 25 percent of U.S. consumption but could go even higher during the recession. Unfortunately, the amount of pollution foreign steel emits is much greater than domestic steel. Chinese steel, it is believed, creates a carbon footprint three times the amount American steel companies create. Therefore, environmentalists and U.S. steelmakers find themselves unexpected allies in an endeavor to impose a pollution equalization tax on foreign steel. The tax would deter foreign importation of steel and hopefully decrease pollution in the process. Hence, because of a mixture of recession woes, protectionism, and pollution concerns, we may soon see more green initiatives throughout the world.[1]

As concerns over global warming, erratic weather patterns, and diminished quality of life continue to rise, public and business support for environmental causes has increased a great deal since the first Earth Day was held in 1970. Most Americans claim that they have made at least minor changes in their lifestyles, like switching to energy-efficient light bulbs or recycling, to help the environment, according to a Gallup poll, with 39 percent of them saying they have helped the environment by recycling and 17 percent by driving less.[2] Many businesses have adopted environmental policies in their operations, and fifty-three Fortune 500 corporations purchase over 6 billion kilowatt hours (kWH) of green power each year.[3]

In this chapter, we explore the concept of sustainability in the context of social responsibility in today's complex business environment. First, we define sustainability and explore some of the significant environmental issues that businesses and society face. Next, we consider the impact of government environmental policy and regulation on business and examine how some companies are going beyond the scope of these laws to address environmental issues and act in an environmentally responsible manner. Finally, we highlight a strategic approach to environmental issues, including risk management and strategic audits.

GLOBAL ENVIRONMENTAL ISSUES

Most people probably associate the term *environment* with nature, including wildlife, trees, oceans, rivers, mountains, and prairies. Until the twentieth century, people generally thought of the environment solely in terms of how these resources could be harnessed to satisfy their needs for food, shelter, transportation, and recreation. As Earth's population swelled throughout the twentieth century, however, humans began to use more and more of these resources and, with technological advancements, to do so with ever greater efficiency. Although these conditions have resulted in a much-improved standard of living, they come with a cost. Plant and animal species, along with wildlife habitats, are disappearing at an accelerated rate; water use has become a critical issue in many parts of the globe, including the United States; and pollution has rendered the atmosphere of some cities a gloomy haze. How to deal with these issues has become a major concern for business and society in the twenty-first century.

sustainability
the potential for long-term well-being of the natural environment, including all biological entities, as well as the interaction among nature and individuals, organizations, and business strategies

Although the scope of the word *sustainability* is broad—including plants, animals, human beings, oceans and other waterways, land, and the atmosphere—in this book, we discuss the term from a strategic business perspective. Thus, we define **sustainability** as the potential for long-term well-being of the natural environment, including all biological entities, as well as the interaction among nature and individuals, organizations, and business strategies. Sustainability includes the assessment and improvement of business strategies, economic sectors, work practices, technologies, and lifestyles while maintaining the natural environment. In recent years, business has played a significant role in adapting, using, and maintaining the quality of sustainability.

The protection of air, water, land, biodiversity, and renewable natural resources emerged as a major issue in the twentieth century in the face of increasing evidence that pollution, uncontrolled use of natural resources, and population growth were putting increasing pressure on the long-term sustainability of these resources. As the environmental movement sounded the alarm over these issues, governments around the globe responded with environmental protection laws during the 1970s. In recent years, companies have been increasingly incorporating these issues into their overall business strategies. Most of these issues have been the focus of concerned citizens as well as government and corporate efforts. Some nonprofit organizations have stepped forward to provide leadership in gaining the cooperation of diverse groups in responsible environmental activities. For example, the Coalition for Environmentally Responsible Economies (CERES), a union of businesses, consumer groups, environmentalists, and other stakeholders, has established a set of goals for environmental performance.

In the following section, we examine some of the most significant environmental issues facing business and society today, including air pollution, acid rain, global warming, water pollution and water quantity, land pollution, waste management, deforestation, urban sprawl, biodiversity, and genetically modified foods.

Atmospheric Issues

Among the most far-reaching and controversial environmental issues are those that relate to the air we breathe. These include air pollution, acid rain, and global warming.

Air Pollution Air pollution typically arises from three different sources: stationary sources such as factories and power plants; mobile sources such as cars, trucks, planes, and trains; and natural sources such as windblown dust and volcanic eruptions.[4] These sources discharge gases, as well as particulates, that can be carried long distances by surface winds or linger on the surface for days if there is a lack of winds or geographical conditions permit. Linfen City in Shanxi Province, China, has the dirtiest air in the world, largely because of large coal-burning power plants in the region. In fact, China's heavy emphasis on manufacturing gives it the dubious honor of hosting sixteen of the top twenty cities with the poorest air quality in the world.[5] Such conditions can cause markedly shorter life spans, along with chronic respiratory problems (e.g., asthma, bronchitis, and allergies) in humans and animals, especially in the elderly and the very young. Some of the chemicals associated with air pollution may contribute to birth defects, cancer, and brain, nerve, and respiratory system damage. Air pollution can also harm plants, animals, and

© AP Photo/Kike Calvo

Global initiatives seek to limit pollution such as that being emitted by this paper factory in Zaragora, Spain

water bodies. Haze caused by air pollution can reduce visibility, interfering with aviation, driving, and recreation.[6]

Acid Rain In addition to the health risks posed by air pollution, when nitrous oxides and sulfur dioxides emitted from manufacturing facilities react with air and rain, the result is acid rain. This phenomenon has contributed to the deaths of many valuable forests and lakes in North America as well as in Europe. Acid rain can also corrode paint and deteriorate stone, leaving automobiles, buildings, and cultural resources such as architecture and outside art vulnerable unless they are protected from its effects.[7] The United States alone emits around 9 million tons of sulfur dioxide emissions and 3.3 million tons of nitrogen oxide into the atmosphere each year. Cleaning up emissions from factories and cars is one way to help reduce acid rain.

Global Warming When carbon dioxide and other gases collect in Earth's atmosphere, they trap the sun's heat like a greenhouse and prevent Earth's surface from cooling. Without this process, the planet would become too cold to sustain life. However, during the twentieth century, the burning of fossil fuels—gasoline, natural gas, oil, and coal—accelerated dramatically, increasing the concentration of "greenhouse" gases like carbon dioxide and methane in Earth's atmosphere. Chlorofluorocarbons—from refrigerants, coolants, and aerosol cans—also harm Earth's ozone layer, which filters out the sun's harmful ultraviolet light. World carbon dioxide emissions are currently around 30 billion metric tons and are expected to rise to 40.4 billion metric tons by 2030.[8] The United States and China are by far the two largest greenhouse gas emitters in the world.[9] In the future, developing nations like China and India are going to make up an increasing percentage of overall emissions, as they are most likely to use coal, which is the dirtiest of all fossil fuels in terms of emissions.

Figure 11.1 shows emissions outputs by OECD (Organisation for Economic Co-operation and Development) countries (mostly developed regions like the United States, Canada, and Europe) and non-OECD countries (which comprise the developing world). As you can see, developing nations such as China and India will produce most new emissions in the future.

To cut greenhouse gas emissions, the Obama administration favors congressional action. Obama announced stricter standards for new cars, with plans to cut the amount of greenhouse gases emitted from new cars by 25 percent. Proposed legislation aims to reduce U.S. greenhouse gas emissions 17 percent from 2005 levels by 2020 and 83 percent by 2050.[10]

Most scientists believe that concentrations of greenhouse gases like methane and carbon dioxide in the atmosphere are accelerating a warming of the planet. Accumulations of greenhouse gases have increased dramatically in the past century. The year 1998 was the hottest year on record. The second hottest year on record was 2005, and 2003 was recorded as the third hottest around the world. In 2003, Europe was hotter than it had been in 500 years. 2008 tied with 2001 for the eighth warmest year on record, and 2009 was in the top ten as well—showing a definite prolonged trend toward warmer temperatures and more extreme weather patterns.[11] The accumulation of gases appears to have increased average temperatures by more than 1°F over the last century.

Figure 11.1 World Energy-Related Carbon Dioxide Emissions, 2006–2030

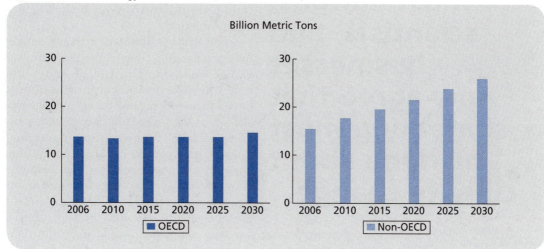

Sources: Energy Information Administration (EIA), *International Energy Annual 2006* (June–December 2008), http://www.eia.doe.gov/iea; EIA, *World Energy Projections Plus* (2009).

Although 1°F doesn't sound like much of a change, it is sufficient to increase the rate of polar ice sheet melting, which is occurring at unprecedented rates. 2008 and 2009 both marked record years for severity of summer ice cap melting. Climate change has caused such dramatic melting of glaciers along the Italian/Swiss border in the Alps that mapmakers were forced to redraw the border between the two countries to follow the new glacial boundaries.[12] Climate change has also affected weather in this region—making Switzerland to the north more prone to flooding and Italy to the south more drought-ridden.

As the polar icecaps melt, scientists fear that rising sea levels will flood many coastal areas and even submerge low-lying island nations. With less snow and ice cover to reflect the sun's rays, Earth absorbs even more of the sun's heat, accelerating the warming process. Some scientists also think that global warming may alter long-term weather patterns, causing drought in some parts of the world while bringing floods to others—something that many believe we are already witnessing in the form of extreme weather patterns. For example, the 2004, 2005, 2007, and 2008 hurricane seasons were all categorized as above normal in the United States, which some researchers link to the effects of global warming.[13]

The concept of global warming has been controversial amongst some groups, especially in the United States. Critics of global warming argue that apparent temperature increases are part of a natural cycle of temperature variation that the planet has experienced over millions of years. Some people even like the sound of global warming, as it brings to mind warmer temperatures and longer growing seasons. Many companies and organizations have also maligned the theory because reducing emissions and tightening environmental laws means greater expenses at the outset. Nevertheless, most nations, scientists, and businesses now agree that something must be done about climate change. Failure to

"Most nations, scientists, and businesses now agree that something must be done about climate change."

act and to become more efficient now may end up costing companies far more money in the long run.

The **Kyoto Protocol** is a treaty among industrialized nations aimed at slowing global warming. The United States has not ratified the treaty and therefore is not bound to it—many hope that this stance will change, as the United States is the most polluting nation on the planet. Since its creation in 1997, the Kyoto Protocol has been highly unpopular amongst polluting multinational corporations such as Texaco. Signing the treaty would require slashing its level of greenhouse gas emissions by 6 percent of 1990 levels. United States leaders fear that compliance would jeopardize U.S. businesses and the economy.[14] The treaty went into effect in 2005 and by 2006, the number of signatory nations topped 150. Because major countries like the United States, Canada, and Australia have all failed to ratify the treaty, some experts suggest that global leaders are moving away from the Kyoto Protocol toward environmental solutions based on scientific evidence and market factors. The United States, under President Bush, created its own carbon emissions reduction initiative called the Global Climate Change Initiative (see Table 11.1), which laid out some limited emissions-reductions strategies but was not as stringent as the Kyoto Protocol would have been.

Many U.S. businesses are responding to stakeholder pressure and are committing to self-regulatory standards with respect to global warming and related areas, even in the absence of strict federal mandates. States like California have also fought hard to gain the right to issue their own environmental legislation. After losing a battle with the Bush administration over controlling California state emissions, the new U.S. Environmental Protection Agency (EPA) in the Obama administration has granted California the right to impose tough emissions standards on cars and trucks. California had wanted to re-implement the toughest reading of the Clean Air Act legislation in forty years. This change in ruling opened the door for thirteen other states to pass similar emissions legislation and demonstrated a willingness on the part of the EPA to let states decide how strict they want to be on polluters.[15] A host of energy-efficient designations now exist to help consumers make more environmentally friendly choices. For example, Energy Star, a joint program between the EPA and the U.S. Department of Energy, has helped Americans and businesses reduce greenhouse gas emissions equal to those given off by 29 million cars—all while saving them $19 billion on utility bills.[16]

Other countries are also creating self-regulatory programs. Japan, China, India, and South Korea formed the Asia-Pacific Partnership on Clean Development and Climate, which includes voluntary standards and a focus on creating technologies that reduce emissions without harming the economy. PricewaterhouseCoopers, a global consulting firm, provided services and advice for companies on how

Kyoto Protocol
a treaty among industrialized nations to slow global warming

Table 11.1 Elements of the U.S. Global Climate Change Initiative

- Enhancement of the 1605(b) Voluntary Reporting of Greenhouse Gases Program

- Significantly expanded funding for basic scientific research and advanced technology development

- Tax incentives, such as credits for renewable energy, cogeneration, and new technology

- Challenges for business to undertake voluntary initiatives and commit to greenhouse gas intensity goals, such as through recent agreements with the semiconductor and aluminum industries

- Transportation programs, including technology research and development and fuel economy standards

- Carbon sequestration programs, which include increased funding for U.S. Department of Agriculture conservation programs under the Farm Bill

- Investments in climate observation systems in developing countries

- Funding for "debt-for-nature" forest conservation programs

- Use of economic incentives to encourage developing countries to participate in climate change initiatives

- Expanding technology transfer and capacity building in the developing world

- Joint research with Japan, Italy, and Central America

Source: Energy Information Administration, U.S. Department of Energy, "Voluntary Reporting of Greenhouse Gases—Summary," http://www.eia.doe.gov/oiaf/1605/vrrpt/summary/special_topic.html, accessed July 14, 2009.

to improve energy efficiency, environmental performance, and their images in advance of the United Nations' Copenhagen Climate Change Conference that occurred in late 2009.[17] The time leading up to and the aftermath of the conference were important times for businesses to clean up their acts and prove that they are ready to make changes to ensure long-term stakeholder well-being. PricewaterhouseCoopers emphasizes stakeholder management and communication for all companies seeking to improve their images and become greener.

Figure 11.2 depicts the process of embedding a climate change strategy into a utility company. Many aspects of the process would be similar in other industries.

Cap-and-Trade Program Many worldwide governments believe that self-regulatory programs aimed to reduce greenhouse gas emissions are not enough, and government intervention is needed. Cap-and-trade programs have been the answer in the European Union (EU), and will likely be part of the solution for the United States as well. A **cap-and-trade** program sets carbon emissions limits (caps) for businesses, countries, or individuals. Companies are given a certain amount of carbon they are allowed to emit, and to legally emit anything beyond the limit a company must purchase carbon credits from another company that did not pollute as much. The EU, which has been at the forefront of emissions

cap-and-trade a program that sets carbon emissions limits (caps) for businesses, countries, or individuals

Figure 11.2 Climate Change Strategy

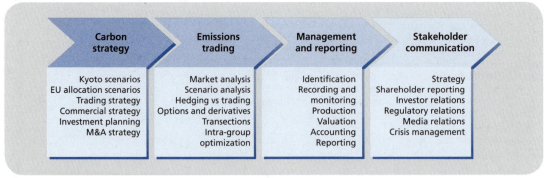

Carbon strategy	Emissions trading	Management and reporting	Stakeholder communication
Kyoto scenarios	Market analysis	Identification	Strategy
EU allocation scenarios	Scenario analysis	Recording and monitoring	Shareholder reporting
Trading strategy	Hedging vs trading		Investor relations
Commercial strategy	Options and derivatives	Production	Regulatory relations
Investment planning	Transections	Valuation	Media relations
M&A strategy	Intra-group optimization	Accounting Reporting	Crisis management

Source: PricewaterhouseCoopers, *Responding to a Changing Environment: Applying Emissions Trading Strategy to Industrial Companies,* *2005.* Copyright PricewaterhouseCoopers LLP. Reprinted with permission.

reductions, mandated and implemented a cap-and-trade program on carbon emissions known as the European Union Emission Trading Scheme.

When the EU signed the Kyoto Protocol in 1995, it committed to collectively reduce its greenhouse gas emissions by 8 percent. The EU does this by issuing a fixed number of permits to businesses and other parties that limits the amount of emissions their companies can give off. A carbon emissions cap can strain many businesses, especially manufacturing companies, which emit large amounts of carbon in the process of operating. Opponents of this scheme argue that a single cap puts certain companies at a financial disadvantage, as they can only reduce their carbon footprint by so much before they begin sacrificing productivity. To solve this problem, a cap-and-trade system allows for businesses to sell the carbon permits they do not use. In other words, companies that do not release as much carbon emissions can sell their permits to companies that do. Companies that pollute less are therefore rewarded with extra income, while companies that produce more are allowed to continue working. In order to give companies time to adapt more efficient technologies, governments impose progressively smaller caps over the years.[18]

The cap-and-trade program gained popularity among American legislators as well, who included the system in President Obama's first major environmental bill. This could be a major step toward combating the increase of greenhouse gas emissions. Yet there are some problems with the cap-and-trade system that must be addressed. First, the cost of complying with a cap could be passed onto consumers. For example, farmers who rely heavily on inexpensive coal-burning power plants might suffer profit losses that would result in higher prices for consumers.[19] Critics of the cap-and-trade system, like Danish business professor Bjorn Lomborg, believe a cap-and-trade system generates negligible reductions, and that far more drastic measures are needed. Lomborg believes that businesses will not change their ways because of a lack of viable energy alternatives. Lomborg proposes that governments should instead invest as much as .05 percent of gross domestic product on clean-energy research and impose a $7 tax per ton of carbon dioxide, instead of emissions caps.[20] This leads up to a final problem: Would a cap-and-trade system actually convince companies to reduce pollution? In order to be effective, the amount of carbon emissions allowed by the cap would have to be reduced over time.

Although some businesses bemoan the advent of stricter environmental legislation in the United States and abroad, some banks are actually looking forward to the change. In the battered financial sector, many are already looking ahead to the highly profitable market of carbon trading. Financial analysts anticipate that new environmental rules will be in place by 2013, and that carbon trading will be a $1 trillion market by 2020. Financial firms may be able to enter the business of trading carbon credits, much like they trade other commodities now. Other banks, such as Citigroup, have set up advisory services to companies looking at how to prepare for the new energy economy.[21]

Forward-looking businesses do not have to wait for legislation to be passed to reduce their carbon footprint. Many companies have created "best practices" programs which utilize cleaner energy over dirty forms of energy like gasoline or coal. More efficient building codes are another way businesses have reduced their carbon use, which can be used to cut energy consumption by as much as 75 percent according to some estimates.[22] However, most companies have a long way to go. According to research by Access Accounting, only 39 percent of companies actively monitor their carbon emissions; a business needs to know the size of its carbon footprint before it can effectively reduce emissions and other environmental pollutants.[23] Wal-Mart has actively monitored its carbon output and has set ambitious goals, such as eventually becoming net zero when it comes to emissions.

Water Issues

Even more than oil, water is emerging as the most important and contested resource of the twenty-first century. Nothing is more important to human survival, yet fresh water is being polluted and consumed at an unprecedented rate. In order to remain viable, all businesses must think about water conservation, purification, and allocation.

Water Pollution Water pollution results from the dumping of sewage and toxic chemicals from manufacturing into rivers and oceans; from oil and gasoline spills; and from the burial of trash and industrial waste in the ground where it can contaminate underground water supplies. Fertilizers and pesticides used in farming and grounds maintenance also drain into water supplies with each rainfall. These chemicals are harmful to all life that depends on oceans and streams. Fertilizers upset algae balances in rivers causing fish to die. Mercury contaminates the oceans and therefore human food supplies. Overuse of water can lead to shortages; and deforestation and climate change are contributing to desertification of sections of China and even the United States. Additionally, more than 1.2 billion people currently do not have access to clean water, which causes 80 percent of infectious diseases.[24]

During the Bush administration years, more than half of all lakes, rivers, streams, and drinking water sources lost government protections against pollution and development. From the passage of the Clean Water Act in 1972 to 2001, the United States made significant strides to clean up and protect water sources.

However, the water preservation movement lost federal backing in the early 2000s. According to the EPA, more than one-third of the United States' lakes and a quarter of its rivers are contaminated with pollutants. The Great Lakes, for example, has forty-three areas of concern where water quality has been seriously degraded and some types of fish are unsafe to eat.[25] Water pollution problems are especially notable in heavily industrialized areas.

While the United States has one of the safest drinking water supplies in the world, pollution remains a problem. It is estimated that 1.6 million deaths per year in the United States stem from unclean water and poor sanitation.[26] Pollutants can come from a wide variety of sources in today's industrialized world, and many of them have unknown side effects on people and wildlife. An ongoing Associated Press investigation found a wide range of antibiotics and pharmaceuticals in the drinking supplies of at least 46 million Americans.[27] Pharmaceutical companies have released the drugs into the water supply, but consumers who take the drugs are the largest contributor to the problem. Pharmaceuticals have also been found in water sources in Europe, Asia, and Australia. Although concentrations of these antibiotics have been small, scientists worry about the long-term health effects they could have upon humans. Chlorine does not always kill these antibiotics; in fact, some evidence shows the presence of chlorine could make antibiotics more toxic. Fish and frogs are also highly susceptible to living in and near water tainted with drugs—it could affect them in as-yet unknown ways. Agricultural operations, including animal-feeding, pesticide use, and plowing, are also a major source of pollution in the nation's lakes and rivers.

The Audubon Society believes that many industries—agribusiness, logging, and power plants—that are also major polluters have excessively strong political lobbying power and can resist regulation efforts to reduce contamination in water supplies. A 2006 Supreme Court decision made it more challenging to deduce which bodies of water would qualify for the Clean Water Act—endangering over half of the nation's water supplies.[28] The decision has made it easier for companies to dump toxic waste from strip mining in the Smoky Mountains to gold mining in Alaska directly into lakes and streams without being required to clean up the damage.

While environmental groups in the United States criticize U.S. water policy, special interests make it even more difficult to regulate water pollution in other parts of the world. Tougher regulations are needed globally to address pollution from activities such as dumping wastes into the ocean, large animal-feeding operations, logging sites, public roads, parking lots, and industrial waste created by production operations.

Water Quantity In addition to concerns about the quality of water, some parts of the globe are increasingly worried about its quantity. There has been a sixfold increase in water use worldwide since 1990, and as a result, one-fifth of the world's population now has no access to safe drinking water. Since 1960, irrigation has jumped by 60 percent, with 70 percent of the world's total water consumption now going to agriculture.[29] This has had serious consequences for the global water supply. Not only is water needed for drinking, but reduced water availability will lead to lower food crops and will affect businesses as well. Coca-Cola, for example, met with hostility in many areas of India over concerns that its beverage production would draw excessively on already-strained water tables.[30]

It is estimated that by 2030, almost half of the world's population will live in areas with major water stress. After several of the hottest years on record and below-average precipitation across most of the nation, water fears have hit home. As much as 31 percent of the United States experienced a drought during June of 2008, according to the National Climatic Data Center. These conditions put added pressure on facility managers to conserve water. The nation's supply of accessible fresh water is decreasing drastically, in no small part because of consumption rates. The average American household uses more than 100,000 gallons of water a year—a rate that most experts believe is not sustainable beyond the short term.[31] Companies and individuals can do many small things to slow down water consumption rates. For example, switching to low-flow toilets could save as much as 640 billion gallons of water.[32]

Around the world, growing populations and increased industrialization have outpaced nature's ability to replenish surface and underground water sources, especially during periods of drought. This is hitting the American West especially hard. 2002 was the driest year and 2007 was the second driest for the Southwest. The Colorado River, which supplies water for 30 million people, fell to one-quarter its long-term average in 2002. Because weather patterns in the south are changing, with less rainfall and hotter summers, trees and forests are being destroyed by drought and fire at an increased rate.[33] Most climate models predict that the U.S. Southwest will not pull out of the current drought cycle for hundreds of years, and that climate change will accelerate the drying. The changing landscape also affects water availability, which has already led to intense political and legal wrangling in a number of states. Water usage and rights has been a contentious issue for millennia. The American humorist and sage Mark Twain has been attributed as saying, "Whiskey is for drinking, water is for fighting over."

Land Issues

Land Pollution Land pollution results from the dumping of residential and industrial wastes, strip mining, and poor forest conservation. Such pollution causes health problems in humans, jeopardizes wildlife habitats, causes erosion, alters watercourses (leading to flooding), and can eventually poison groundwater supplies. China has been at the epicenter of a

© Reuters/Landov

With over 10% of China's farmland contaminated, wildlife and crop production are threatened

"In order to reduce pollution around the planet, businesses are all going to have to be aware of and accept responsibility for the problem of pollution."

debate over pollution. The country's rapid development as manufacturer to the world has exposed hundreds of millions of people to the ill effects of pollution, as well as poisoning waterways, wiping out wildlife, and converting once healthy land into barren deserts. The United Nations Human Development Report singles out China for its failure to curb pollution.[34] However, Chinese spokespeople insist that they are not wholly to blame. They believe that it is the system that should be blamed—they do, after all, mainly produce goods to be sold in other countries. In order to reduce pollution around the planet, businesses are all going to have to be aware of and accept responsibility for the problem of pollution.

Waste Management Another aspect of the land pollution problem is the issue of how to dispose of waste in an environmentally responsible manner. American consumers are by far the world's biggest wasters. They contribute an average of 222 million tons of waste annually, which strains declining landfill space. The United States has up to 40,000 abandoned landfills, which are often left untreated and are filled with plastics and other materials that can take 1,000 years to break down. Landfills are also thought to be the biggest producers of methane gas, which is twenty times more powerful than carbon dioxide in terms of atmospheric heating. However, some companies have learned to convert that gas into power. Europe, for example, has more than 8,000 biogas plants that convert methane from farm waste and trash into electricity.[35]

Another concern is the disposal of electronic waste (e-waste) into landfills. It is estimated that Americans dump between 300 and 400 million electronic products a year. As these items deteriorate in landfills, officials worry that they could release harmful toxins into the air and water. Increasingly, electronics firms are being pressured to take back used electronics for recycling. Many large chains such as Best-Buy offer e-recycling, as do companies such as Dell. Most perceive this as the environmentally responsible thing to do. Washington State even passed a law requiring electronics manufacturers to accept old electronics and to fund recycling programs. New York City passed a city ordinance that requires that electronics companies go door-to-door to pick up old devices for recycling. Many stakeholders, including environmental groups and some politicians, believe that companies that produce the goods should be responsible for their proper disposal and recycling. Companies, on the other hand, argue that this practice is excessively expensive and that smaller companies might even be forced out of business because of this type of legislation.[36]

Deforestation Although rainforests help to absorb 2 billion metric tons of carbon dioxide annually, for many people and businesses rainforest land seems more profitable when stripped of trees. Because of this, rainforests are being destroyed at a rate of nearly 5,000 square miles a year. The reasons for deforestation are varied. Because of the boom in biofuels, Southeast Asia and the Pacific regions have been cutting down trees to make room for palm oil plantations. Brazil has long cut down the Amazon for farming or for raising sugarcane. A competitive global economy drives the need for money in economically challenged tropical countries.

In the short term, logging and converting forestlands to other uses seems the profitable thing to do. However, a study conducted by an international team from *Science* has shown that the profits from deforestation are very short lived. While initially the profit can create a boom of prosperity, it is only sustainable by moving and cutting down more trees. Rainforest soil is of very poor quality and can become very difficult to cultivate within a short time after the trees are removed.[37] The Kyoto Protocol does not include protections of forests, but it was an important item on the agenda at the 2009 U.N. Climate Summit in Copenhagen.

Companies are now adopting designations like that granted by the Forest Stewardship Council (FSC), a nonprofit organization comprised of loggers, environmentalists, and sociologists. The FSC seeks to coordinate forest management around the world and to develop a uniform set of standards. Being FSC-certified can help companies indicate to consumers and stakeholders that they are committed to preserving forest resources, that they are responsible companies, and that they take a long-term view of environmental management. There is ample evidence based on cases in places as diverse as Pennsylvania and Guatemala that FSC-certification leads to higher timber sales and slower rates of deforestation.[38]

Table 11.2 lists some facts about the harmful effects of global deforestation.

Table 11.2 Facts About Global Deforestation

• Almost 20 percent of all global CO_2 emissions are caused by deforestation.
• People who are cutting down trees (i.e., illegal loggers in Borneo, soy growers in Brazil, subsistence farmers in Laos) together send as much carbon into the atmosphere as do all the activities of the entire United States (factories, vehicles, buildings, farming, power plants, etc.).
• Every four hours the world loses tropical forests equivalent in size to the island of Manhattan.
• By conserving just *one* acre of threatened tropical forest, the yearly emissions of 40 cars, trucks, and SUVs can be offset.
• Burning and clearing forests costs the global economy 2 trillion dollars per year, as valued through lost fresh water, food, timber, and carbon reduction.

Source: Adapted from Alan Grey, "Tropical Deforestation and Global Warming Linkage," *News Blaze,* June 25, 2009, http://newsblaze.com/story/20090625101021zzzz.nb/topstory.html, accessed July 14, 2009.

Urban Sprawl While the global recession of 2008–2009 helped to slow some urban sprawl in the United States and elsewhere, it remains a significant problem. Urban sprawl began in the United States with the post–World War II building boom that transformed the nation from primarily low-density communities designed to accommodate one-car households, bicyclists, and pedestrians to large-scale suburban developments at the edges of established towns and cities. Downtowns and inner cities deteriorated as strip and shopping malls, office parks, corporate campuses, and residential developments sprang up on what was once forest, prairie, or farm and ranch land.

As the places where people live, work, and shop grew farther apart, people began spending more time in automobiles, driving ever greater distances. Urban sprawl not only has consumed wildlife habitat, wetlands, and farmland, but it also has contributed to land, water, and especially air pollution. Lack of urban planning means that these places grow without reason, contributing to uneven development of services. In an age of erratic gas prices, traffic congestion, and obesity, it has become increasingly expensive in terms of dollars and health to live in sprawling cities.

Some urban areas are fighting to limit sprawl. Portland, Oregon, for example, has established an Urban Growth Boundary to restrict growth and preserve open space and rural land around the city. In Texas, the city of Austin implemented a Smart Growth initiative that directs development away from environmentally sensitive areas. The California legislature also passed a bill that limits urban sprawl through better transportation and more efficient land use.

Adding to the appeal of returning to cities is a movement to increase urban parks. Rather than allowing loggers to profit from forests, more and more cities are buying forested land to convert to park space. In fact, more than 3,000 cities in 43 states own more than 4.5 million acres of forested parkland. Many studies have shown that peoples' health improves with exposure to green space.[39]

People are beginning to realize that living near where they work is more convenient, cheaper, and better for their health. Stemming urban sprawl also preserves natural spaces outside cities. Although the concept of people living closer together and driving less may scare some car and oil companies, many businesses can benefit from urban renewal movements that are limiting sprawl.

Biodiversity

Deforestation, pollution, development, and urban sprawl have put increasing pressure on wildlife, plants, and their habitats. Many plants and animals have become extinct, and thousands more are threatened. In the Florida Everglades, for example, channeling, damming, and diverting water for urban and agricultural uses have dramatically altered the sensitive ecosystem by destroying 50 percent of its wetlands in just fifty years. As a result, fifteen of the Everglades' native resident species, including the manatee and the panther, are endangered.[40]

The world's tropical forests, which cover just 6 percent of Earth's land surface, account for more than half of the planet's biological species. The importance of these ecosystems is highlighted by the fact that 25 percent of the world's prescription drugs are extracted from plants growing primarily in tropical rainforests. Seventy percent of the 3,000 plants identified as sources of cancer-fighting drugs come from tropical forests, and scientists suspect that many more tropical plants may have pharmaceutical benefits. Unfortunately, countless beneficial plants and animals have already been eradicated because of deforestation, pollution, and development. One-quarter of the world's mammal species, one-third of amphibian species, and one-eighth of bird species are currently endangered and risk going extinct without proper care. However, it is impossible to know how many plant and animal species are actually threatened or extinct, given that many of them remain undiscovered.[41]

Many ecologists and other experts fear that overutilization of natural resources, so that human activities cause harm to ecosystems, will cause catastrophic imbalance to the environment. Because each biological species plays a unique role in its ecosystem and is part of a complex chain of events, the loss of any one of them may threaten the entire ecosystem. Pollinators, for example, play a significant role in that they help fruits and vegetables to grow by spreading pollen from plant to plant. Increasing development and widespread use of pesticides have reduced the populations of bees, insects, and bats that help plants reproduce. Populations of domestic honeybees, the primary pollinators of food-producing plants, have declined by one-third, whereas many wild honeybees have become virtually extinct in many places around the world. Declines in pollinating species not only threaten the success of their relevant ecosystems but also may harm long-term global food production because one-third of all food products require pollinators to reproduce.[42]

"People and businesses must use resources more carefully in order to maintain a livable world for many generations to come."

People and businesses must use resources more carefully in order to maintain a livable world for many generations to come. Peet's Coffee, for example, produces Rainforest Alliance–certified coffee that not only tastes good, but also is organic and produces in such a way that forests are not harmed. The growers at Finca Santa Isabel in Guatemala were happy to go organic because the costs of chemical fertilizers are high.[43] Sometimes it takes some innovation, but oftentimes what is better for the environment ends up being better for the business in the long run.

Genetically Modified Organisms

Depending on who you ask, genetically modified (GM) foods are either going to save impoverished areas from starvation and revolutionize agriculture, or they will destroy biodiversity and make us all sick. **Genetically modified organisms (GMOs)** are created through manipulating plant and animal genes so as to produce a desired effect like resistance to pests and viruses, drought resistance, or high crop yield. This process generally involves transferring genes from one organism to another in a way that would never occur naturally to create a new life form that has unique traits. Companies like Monsanto and DuPont develop genetically

genetically modified organisms (GMOs) created through manipulating plant and animal genes so as to produce a desired effect like resistance to pests and viruses, drought resistance, or high crop yield

modified corn, soybeans, potatoes, canola oil seeds, and cotton plants that they claim are more pest and insecticide resistant, sometimes require fewer chemicals to produce, and may even have higher yields.

Many people fear that these unnatural genes will have negative effects on nature, somewhat like how invader species of plants and animals can wipe out native ones, or that GM produce may have negative effects on humans. Even so, a lot of interest in GM products remains. In poor countries where malnutrition is a problem, the idea of higher yields is very appealing, even if the seed itself is more expensive. Over 282 million acres worldwide are devoted to genetically modified crops. Their use has increased corn crop yields in some parts of the world from 70 bushels an acre in 1970 to 150 bushels an acre. The long-term impact of this genetic tinkering is not known. A study sponsored by the National Academy of Sciences reported that the GM varieties developed so far do not pose allergy problems. However, the report called for further research to determine how to prevent GM crops from killing beneficial and harmless insects, such as the monarch butterfly, and how to deter herbicide-resistant genes from spreading into weeds.[44]

Today, as much as 75 percent of all processed food contains GMO ingredients—and the United States does not require labeling. Regardless of the health effects of GMO foods, many consumers demand to know what is in their food, and the idea of unknowingly ingesting GMO products bothers them. The large natural food chain Whole Foods has adopted a system of labels for processed foods so that consumers can know whether or not they are purchasing GMO foods.[45] All of these concerns have prompted consumers around the world, particularly in Europe and Japan, to boycott products made from GM crops. Thirty countries—including all of the EU, Australia, and Japan—have even imposed bans or restrictions on GMO products.

Another example of the backlash against GMOs is in the dairy industry. Many large dairy producers use hormones, called recombinant bovine growth hormones, or rBGH, to increase milk production in cows. Many cows get sick from the hormones and are also given antibiotics. Even in America, where government bans are not in place and GM food is more accepted, many Americans refuse to buy milk that has come from cows given these drugs because it is perceived as less healthful. Wal-Mart stopped carrying rBGH milk after strong consumer backlash.[46] The mega-chain's decision followed similar pledges from Starbucks and the Kroger and Safeway grocery store chains. Some people feel that the age of rBGH milk effectively ended after even Wal-Mart customers refused to purchase it.

GM foods may be controversial, but some researchers and scientists see the technology as a valuable way to develop drugs in the future. The U.S. Food and Drug Administration approved the first GMO drug, ATryn, created to treat people who suffer from the blood-clotting condition antithrombin deficiency. The drug comes from goats that were genetically engineered to produce human antithrombin in their milk. The companies creating the drug assure the public that the goats' milk and/or meat will not be available for human consumption and that they do not cause adverse effects on the environment, although that is surely going to be a debate issue for a long time to come.[47]

As with GM plants, the problem with the genetic engineering of animals and animal products is that the long-run effects are unknown. Large numbers of genetically altered animals could upset the balance in relationships among various species with undetermined effects, such as upsets in the ability to reproduce or to fight diseases and pests. Additionally, if genetically modified plant seeds are carried by wind or pollinators to areas with native plants, it is possible that genetic contamination could take place among native plants, thus reducing biological diversity. Further research is needed to address public concerns about the safety and long-term environmental effects of these technologies.

ENVIRONMENTAL POLICY AND REGULATION

The United States, like most other nations, has passed numerous laws and established regulatory agencies to address environmental issues. Most of these efforts have focused on the activities of businesses, government agencies, and other organizations that use natural resources in providing goods and services.

Environmental Protection Agency

The most influential regulatory agency that deals with environmental issues and enforces environmental legislation in the United States is the **Environmental Protection Agency (EPA)**. The EPA's founding in 1970 was the culmination of a decade of growing protests over the deterioration of environmental quality. This movement reached a significant climax with the publication of Rachel Carson's *Silent Spring,* an attack on the indiscriminate use of pesticides, which rallied scientists, activists, and citizens from around the country to crusade to protect the environment from abuses of the time.

"The most influential regulatory agency that deals with environmental issues and enforces environmental legislation in the United States is the Environmental Protection Agency (EPA)."

Twenty million Americans joined together on April 22, 1970, for the first Earth Day, a nationwide demonstration for environmental reforms. President Richard Nixon responded to these events by establishing the EPA as an independent agency to establish and enforce environmental protection standards, conduct environmental research, provide assistance in fighting pollution, and assist in developing and recommending new policies for environmental protection. The agency is also charged with ensuring that

- All Americans are protected from significant risks to their health and to the environment in which they live and work.
- National efforts to manage environmental risk are based on the best scientific information available.

Environmental Protection Agency (EPA) the most influential regulatory agency that deals with environmental issues and enforces environmental legislation in the United States

- Federal laws protecting human health and the environment are enforced fairly and effectively.

- Environmental protection is an integral consideration in U.S. policies concerning natural resources, human health, economic growth, energy, transportation, agriculture, industry, and international trade, and these factors are considered in establishing environmental policy.

- All parts of society have access to accurate information sufficient to participate effectively in managing human health and environmental risks.

- Environmental protection contributes to diverse, sustainable, and economically productive communities and ecosystems.

- The United States plays a leadership role in working with other nations to protect the environment.[48]

With these charges, the EPA has become a powerful regulatory force in the United States. The EPA under the Bush administration relaxed many regulations, especially those affecting the oil and gas industries and large agriculture. Under the current administration, the EPA is seeking to increase reductions in greenhouse gases, as well as improve sustainable agriculture technologies and reduce contamination in water sources.[49]

To fulfill its primary mission to protect human health and sustainability into the twenty-second century, the EPA established ten long-term strategic goals to define its planning, budgeting, analysis, and accountability processes (see Table 11.3). To determine these goals, the agency solicited and evaluated significant stakeholder

Table 11.3 Goals of the Environmental Protection Agency

Goal	Long-Term Outcome
1	Clean air
2	Clean and safe water
3	Safe food
4	Preventing pollution and reducing risk in communities, homes, workplaces, and ecosystems
5	Better waste management, restoration of contaminated waste sites, and emergency response
6	Reduction of global and cross-border environmental risks
7	Quality environmental information
8	Sound science, improved understanding of environmental risk, and greater innovation to address environmental problems
9	A credible deterrent to pollution and greater compliance with the law
10	Effective management

Source: "Strategic Plan," Office of the Chief Financial Officer, Environmental Protection Agency, www.epa.gov/ocfo/plan/plan.htm, accessed July 15, 2009.

input on priority areas related to human health and environmental protection activities. Thus, these goals reflect public priorities as voiced by Congress in the form of statutes and regulations designed to achieve clean air and water, proper waste management, and other important concerns.[50]

To achieve these goals and carry out its public mission, the EPA is empowered to file civil charges against companies that violate the law. For years, many companies involved in the mining and extraction industries were not forced to pay for cleanup of environmental damage. However, the EPA under the current administration has taken steps to ensure that in the future companies, not taxpayers and other stakeholders, are financially responsible for environmental damage.[51]

Environmental Legislation

A significant number of laws have been passed to address both general and specific environmental issues, including public health, threatened species, toxic substances, clean air and water, and natural resources. Table 11.4 summarizes some significant laws related to environmental protection.

Table 11.4 Major Environmental Laws

ACT (Date Enacted)	Purpose
National Environmental Policy Act (1969)	Established national environmental policy, set goals, and provided a means for implementing the policy; promotes efforts to prevent damage to the biosphere and to stimulate human health and welfare; established a Council on Environmental Quality.
Occupational Safety and Health Act (1970)	Ensures worker and workplace safety by requiring employers to provide a place of employment free from health and safety hazards.
Clean Air Act (1970)	Regulates emissions from natural, stationary, and mobile sources; authorized the EPA to establish National Ambient Air Quality Standards (NAAQS) to protect public health and the environment.
Federal Insecticide, Fungicide, and Rodenticide Act (1972)	Provides for federal control of pesticide distribution, sale, and use; requires users to register when purchasing pesticides.
Endangered Species Act (1973)	Established a conservation program for threatened and endangered plants and animals and their habitats; prohibits the import, export, interstate, and foreign commerce or any action that results in a "taking" of a listed species or that adversely affects habitat.
Safe Drinking Water Act (1974)	Protects the quality of drinking water in the United States; authorized the EPA to establish water purity standards and required public water systems to comply with health-related standards.
Toxic Substances Control Act (1976)	Empowered the EPA to track industrial chemicals currently produced or imported into the United States; authorized the EPA to require reporting or testing of chemicals and to ban the manufacture and import of chemicals that pose an unreasonable risk.
Resource Conservation Recovery Act (1976)	Empowered the EPA to control the generation, transportation, treatment, storage, and disposal of hazardous waste.

(continued)

Table 11.4 (continued)

Clean Water Act (1977)	Authorized the EPA to set effluent standards on an industry-wide basis and to continue to set water quality standards for all contaminants in surface waters; made it unlawful for any person to discharge any pollutant from a point source into navigable waters without a permit.
Comprehensive Environmental Response, Compensation, and Liability Act (1980)	Established prohibitions and requirements concerning closed and abandoned hazardous waste sites; authorized a tax on the chemical and petroleum industries to establish a "superfund" to provide for cleanup when no responsible party could be identified.
Superfund Amendments Reauthorization Act (1986)	Amended the Comprehensive Environmental Response, Compensation, and Liability Act to increase the size of the superfund; required superfund actions to consider the standards and requirements found in other state and federal environmental laws and regulations; provided new enforcement authorities and tools.
Emergency Planning and Community Right-to-Know Act (1986)	Enacted to help local communities protect public health and safety and the environment from chemical hazards; requires each state to appoint a State Emergency Response Commission (SERC) and to establish Emergency Planning Districts.
Oil Pollution Act (1990)	Requires oil storage facilities and vessels to submit plans detailing how they will respond to large spills; requires the development of area contingency plans to prepare and plan for responses to oil spills on a regional scale.
Pollution Prevention Act (1990)	Promotes pollution reduction through cost-effective changes in production, operation, and use of raw materials and practices that increase efficiency and conserve natural resources, such as recycling, source reduction, and sustainable agriculture.
Food Quality Protection Act (1996)	Amended the Federal Insecticide, Fungicide, and Rodenticide Act and the Federal Food, Drug, and Cosmetic Act to change the way the EPA regulates pesticides; applies a new safety standard—reasonable certainty of no harm—to all pesticides used on foods.
Beaches Environmental Assessment and Coastal Health Act (2000)	Amended the Clean Water Act to include provisions decreasing the risks of illness due to using the nation's recreational waters.
Energy Policy Act (2005)	Addresses the way energy is produced in the United States in terms of energy efficiency, renewable energy, oil and gas, coal, Tribal energy, nuclear matters and security, vehicles and motor fuels, hydrogen, electricity, energy tax incentives, hydropower and geothermal energy, and climate change technology.
American Clean Energy Act (2009)	Seeks to create clean energy jobs; more energy independence; reduce greenhouse gas emissions; and lay the groundwork for a clean energy economy.

Sources: "Major Environmental Laws," Environmental Protection Agency, http://www.epa.gov/epahome/laws.htm, accessed June 20, 2006; "Summary of the Energy Policy Act," Environmental Protection Agency, http://www.epa.gov/lawsregs/laws/epa.html, accessed June 22, 2009; "Beaches Environmental Assessment and Coastal Health Act," Environmental Protection Agency, http://www.epa.gov/EPA-WATER/2009/January/Day-23/w1397.htm, accessed June 22, 2009; "H.R. 254 (American Clean Energy Act)," http://energycommerce.house.gov/Press_111/20090515/hr2454.pdf, accessed July 14, 2009.

Clean Air Act The Clean Air Act, passed in 1970, is a comprehensive federal law that regulates atmospheric emissions from a variety of sources.[52] Among its most significant provisions is the requirement that the Environmental Protection Agency establish national air quality standards as well as standards for significant new pollution sources and for all facilities emitting hazardous substances. These maximum pollutant standards, called National Ambient Air Quality Standards (NAAQS), were mandated for every state to protect public health and the environment. The states were further directed to develop state implementation plans (SIPs) pertinent to the industries in each state. The law also mandated reduced auto emission levels, which most states did not meet within the deadline. The Clean Air Act was amended in 1977 to set new dates for attainment of the NAAQS. The Clean Air Act was revised again as the Clean Air Act Amendments of 1990 to address lingering problems and issues that were not acknowledged in the original law, such as acid rain, ground-level ozone, stratospheric ozone depletion, and air toxins.

Endangered Species Act The Endangered Species Act of 1973 established a program to protect threatened and endangered species as well as the habitats in which they live.[53] An endangered species is one that is in danger of extinction, whereas a threatened species is one that may become endangered without protection. The U.S. Fish and Wildlife Service of the Department of the Interior maintains the list of endangered and threatened species, which currently includes 1,010 endangered species (600 are plants) and 308 threatened species (146 are plants).[54] The Endangered Species Act prohibits any action that results in harm to or death of a listed species or that adversely affects an endangered species habitat. It also makes the import, export, and interstate and foreign commerce of listed species illegal. Protected species may include birds, insects, fish, reptiles, mammals, crustaceans, flowers, grasses, cacti, and trees.

The Endangered Species Act has been a highly controversial environmental law. In some cases, threatened or endangered species that are deemed a nuisance by ranchers and farmers, for example, have been harmed or killed by landowners seeking to avoid the hassle or expense of complying with the law. Concerns about the restrictions and costs associated with the law are not entirely unfounded. Consider the case of Brandt Child, who purchased 500 acres in Utah with the intention of building a campground and golf course. However, the U.S. Fish and Wildlife Service ordered Child not to use the land because 200,000 federally protected Kanab ambersnails, a critically endangered breed of snail, inhabited three lakes on the premises. The snails only inhabit two known locations, one of which was the property purchased by Child. The federal government not only refused to compensate Child for his loss of the use of the property, but it also threatened to fine him $50,000 per snail if geese that wandered onto the property had eaten any of the snails (the geese were later found to be snail free).[55] However, when President Clinton designated the Grand Staircase/Escalante National Monument, Child was able to turn his land into an RV park. Although furor over the Endangered Species Act has died down, many people and businesses still butt heads with the EPA from time to time.

Toxic Substances Control Act Congress passed the Toxic Substances Control Act in 1976 to empower the Environmental Protection Agency with the ability to track the 75,000 industrial chemicals currently produced or imported into the United States. The agency repeatedly screens these chemicals and can require reporting or testing of those that may pose an environmental or human health hazard. It can also ban the manufacture and import of chemicals that pose an unreasonable risk. The EPA has the ability to track the thousands of new chemicals developed by industry each year with either unknown or dangerous characteristics. It then can control these chemicals as necessary to protect human health and the environment.[56]

Clean Water Act In 1977, Congress amended the federal Water Pollution Control Act of 1972 as the Clean Water Act. This law granted the EPA the authority to establish effluent standards on an industry basis and continued the earlier law's requirements to set water quality limits for all contaminants in surface waters. The Clean Water Act makes it illegal for anyone to discharge any pollutant from a point source into navigable waters without a permit.[57] A five-year-long investigation found that ships owned by Royal Caribbean Cruises Ltd. used secret bypass pipes to dump oil and hazardous materials overboard, often at night. Government officials accused the company of dumping to save the expense of properly disposing of the waste. At the time, the company was also promoting itself as environmentally friendly. Royal Caribbean eventually paid $27 million in fines and spent up to $90,000 per ship to install new water treatment systems. The company also placed environmental officers on board each vessel.[58]

Pollution Prevention Act The Pollution Prevention Act of 1990 focused industry, government, and public attention on reducing pollution through cost-effective changes in production, operation, and raw materials use. Practices include recycling, source reduction, sustainable agriculture, and other practices that increase efficiency in the use of energy, water, or other natural resources and protect resources through conservation.[59]

Food Quality Protection Act In 1996, the Food Quality Protection Act amended the Federal Insecticide, Fungicide, and Rodenticide Act and the Federal Food, Drug, and Cosmetic Act to fundamentally change the way the EPA regulates pesticides. The law included a new safety standard—reasonable certainty of no harm—that must be applied to all pesticides used on foods.[60] The legislation establishes a more consistent, science-based regulatory environment and mandates a single health-based standard for all pesticides in all foods. The law also provides special protections for infants and children, expedites approval of safer pesticides, provides incentives for the development and maintenance of effective crop protection tools for farmers, and requires periodic reevaluation of pesticide registrations and tolerances to ensure that they are up-to-date and based on good science.

Energy Policy Act Signed into law in 2005, the Energy Policy Act aimed to focus the nation's priorities on alternative forms of energy in the hopes of lessening U.S. dependence on foreign oil. The bill gives tax breaks and loan guarantees to alternative energy companies like nuclear power plants and wind energy and also requires utilities to comply with federal reliability standards for the electricity grid. Additionally, the bill gives tax benefits to consumers who purchase hybrid gasoline-electric cars and for taking other energy-saving measures. The bill also extends daylight savings time by one month to save energy.[61]

ALTERNATIVE ENERGY

With ongoing plans to reduce global carbon emissions, countries and companies alike are looking toward alternative energy sources. Traditional fossil fuels are problematic because of their emissions, but also because stores have been greatly depleted. Foreign fossil fuels are often imported from politically and economically unstable regions, often making it unsafe to conduct business there. The United States spent a high of $700 billion on foreign oil in 2007.[62] With global warming concerns and rising gas prices, the U.S. government has begun to recognize the need to look toward alternative forms of energy as a source of fuel and electricity. There have been many different ideas as to which form of alternative energy would best suit the United States' energy needs. These sources include wind power, solar power, nuclear power, biofuels, electric cars, and hydro and geothermal power.

Wind Power

The Great Plains of the United States is one of the greatest sources of wind energy in the world, and many people believe that harnessing this energy will go a long way toward providing for the United States' energy needs in the future, possibly up to 20 percent of total energy needs. Proponents like oil tycoon T. Boone Pickens have invested a lot of money and faith into getting the industry off the ground. However, a number of roadblocks are standing between taking abundant wind and turning it into affordable energy. Restructuring the nation's power grids to efficiently transmit wind, solar, and other forms of renewable energy will take a lot of money. T. Boone Pickens' plan, known as the Pickens' Plan, would require around $200 billion alone to hook up his planned wind farms to the national grid. Widespread adoption

"With ongoing plans to reduce global carbon emissions, countries and companies alike are looking toward alternative energy sources, including wind power, solar power, nuclear power, biofuels, electric cars, and hydro and geothermal power."

With the Rocky Mountains in the background, the Ponnequin Wind Farm, near Carr, CO, generates significant electricity

of wind power has been slowed by the high cost of the turbines as well as limitations on an outdated national power grid. The technology is more expensive and less efficient than fossil fuels currently, but advances are being made all the time. Many people believe that the United States will be a wind power hot spot in the future, and more Americans than ever are supporting the movement. The United States has surpassed Germany as the largest producer of wind power.

Wind energy has long been popular in other countries such as The Netherlands and Denmark, and is becoming a lucrative business for many companies. A Danish company called Vestas Wind Systems is the world's largest producer of wind turbines and has a 28 percent market share in the wind energy industry. It has even expanded production to the United States in order to take advantage of the growing interest in wind energy.[63]

Mexico also has goals to become one of the top twelve producers of wind power. Mexico's Isthmus of Tehuantepec, in southern Mexico, is a great wind corridor that the Mexican government believes could produce 2,500 megawatts of power. Yet this ambitious goal is not without opposition. The building of enough wind turbines would require large parcels of farmland currently owned by impoverished Mexican farmers. The project is rife with potential conflict, with some supporting the plans and others opposing it. Corruption is also an omnipresent problem in Mexico and many farmers in the area fear wind companies seeking to use their land have cheated them. Conversely, other Mexican farmers say they have benefited from the business the wind energy companies are bringing.[64]

Geothermal Power

Another form of renewable energy is geothermal power. Geothermal energy comes from the natural heat inside the Earth, which is extracted by drilling into steam beds. Though startup costs are high to build geothermal plants, geothermal energy is a relatively clean energy source. The drilling is not pollution free, but its carbon dioxide emissions are one-sixth those produced by efficient natural gas power plants. Occasionally, the extraction of fluids from the ground can cause the land to subside, but careful environmental measures should reduce this impact. Geothermal plants also use a lot less water than coal power plants, and unlike wind or solar energy, geothermal power can provide a steady flow of electricity every day of the year.

Despite these advantages, geothermal energy extraction is expensive and only supplied 0.4 percent of the world's global production as of 2007. It provides one-third of 1 percent of the energy utilized in the United States. Part of the problem may be that geothermal drilling sites are not readily available everywhere; certain factors, like the permeability of rock, must be taken into account. Lipscomb University in Nashville, Tennessee, utilizes a geothermal heating and cooling system in its Ezell Center that saves the university $70,000 annually on heating and cooling.

The advantages of geothermal power have caught the eye of numerous scientists, prompting more research into its viability as an alternative source of energy.[65] A study by a New York University Stern School professor, Melissa Schilling, found that geothermal energy is the most efficient of the major renewable energy sources, that it is improving the fastest, and that it generates a higher return on investment than other forms.[66] Wind energy came in second in terms of fastest-improving technology. Schilling believes that geothermal energy could become cheaper than fossil fuels with as little as $3.3 billion extra spending on research and development. Schilling also believes that both wind and geothermal energy initiatives have been underfunded by the government, given their high potential.

Solar Power

Solar power uses the light and heat from the sun to generate electricity. This 100 percent renewable, passive energy source can be converted into electricity through the use of either photovoltaic cells (solar cells) on homes and other structures or solar power plants. The major disadvantages of solar power are that the technology remains expensive and inefficient compared to traditional fossil fuel–generated energy, and that the infrastructure for mass production of solar panels is not in place in many locations. Even cloudy days are not necessarily a problem as the UV rays needed to generate power filter through clouds. Germany, a country not exactly known for its abundant sunshine, is number one in the world for solar power implementation.

Given the strong sunshine in places like the U.S. Southwest and California, solar power has gained a lot of support in the United States. A report from the U.S. Department of Energy states that solar energy usage is at a new high, having increased by 17 percent between 2007 and 2008 alone.[67] Solar energy is becoming an increasingly viable alternative for businesses to cut their pollution and emissions. For instance, many California Wal-Mart facilities, with their huge flat roofs perfect for solar panels, now use solar power to generate the electricity of some stores. This move has doubled the mega-chain's usage of solar power in the state, to 32 million kilowatt hours per year.[68]

Other companies, like British Petroleum (BP), are recognizing that investing in solar power can realize benefits in terms of both profits and reputation. Predominantly an oil company with a number of ethical lapses in its past, BP partnered with Wal-Mart stores in California to install its solar panels in order to demonstrate the company's dedication to cleaner forms of energy. BP has also built the two largest solar power plants in the world in Spain. Additionally, the company has built solar-powered pumps in its Moxa Gas field in Wyoming, which was formerly powered by the gas being pumped.[69] Even the Middle East and North Africa, regions previously known for oil production, are looking into turning their powerful sunshine into profits. For example, Saudi Aramco Oil Company teamed up with Japanese Showa Shell Sekiyu KK to form a solar power business in Saudi Arabia.[70] Twelve European firms, including giants Deutsche Bank and Siemens, have teamed up on a project that will feed solar power from the Sahara to Europe. Although the project is rife with complications involving international harvesting and transportation of energy, as well as sky-high expenses, Europe has long been at the forefront of renewable energy implementation.[71] Everywhere you look, the move to harvest the sun's power is growing.

Nuclear Power

Countries throughout Europe have managed to greatly reduce their emissions through the implementation of nuclear power plants, yet this form of power remains controversial. Because of the danger associated with nuclear meltdowns and radioactive waste disposal, nuclear power has earned a bad reputation in the United States. On the one hand, nuclear power is pollution-free and cost-competitive. Uranium is abundant enough that generating even 60 times more energy than what is produced today would not be a problem. On the other hand, critics are concerned with the safety of nuclear power plants and the disposal of waste. As the production of nuclear power gives off radiation, the safety of workers and the transport of nuclear waste are prime concerns. The Chernobyl accident in the Ukraine in 1986 is the most well-known incident. In this disaster, the nuclear reactor malfunctioned, resulting in the deaths of thirty people from radiation and hundreds more experiencing negative health effects to this day. The malfunction resulted from faulty engineering. Since then, nuclear reactor safety has been significantly improved, yet the potential dangers of nuclear power are still major issues.[72] Some are also concerned that nuclear power plants could be targets for terrorist attacks.

Currently, nuclear energy generates 16 percent of the world's electricity, with more than thirty countries using nuclear energy to generate up to three-fourths of their supplies. The United States has more than 100 nuclear reactors that supply nearly 20 percent of its electricity, and more nuclear reactors will undoubtedly be built in the near future as the country seeks solutions to its energy problems.[73]

Biofuels

Biofuels are fuels derived from organic materials like corn, sugarcane, vegetable oil, and even trash. While ethanol made from sugarcane has been widely used in Brazil for decades, the idea of biofuels is relatively new in the United States. This idea has become especially popular with those who want to reduce their car's carbon output or who are concerned with the nation's addiction to foreign oil. Automobile makers have begun to create flex fuel and hybrid vehicles that can run on biofuels or gasoline. General Motor's Chevrolet Volt is an electric car with a backup motor for distances over 40 miles. When it uses gasoline, the Volt is designed to run on E85, a blend of 85 percent ethanol (a type of alcohol that can be used as a biofuel) and 15 percent gasoline.[74]

Legal mandates to incorporate biofuels have been passed in some countries. In 1976, for example, the Brazilian government made it a requirement to blend gasoline with ethanol. As a result, Brazil currently is the largest exporter of bioethanol. Part of the reason why biofuels have not been as popular in the United States has to do with the source of the fuel. While Brazil uses sugarcane, which is readily convertible to fuel because of its high sugar content, the United States relies on corn, which is highly energy intensive to produce. Biofuels are also controversial because they currently use food crops—widespread adoption of biofuels could lead to food shortages. The biofuel infrastructure in the United States also lags behind that in Brazil. It would not be feasible for a U.S. consumer to purchase a car that would run only on ethanol, as not every gas station currently offers ethanol pumps. Biofuel production in other countries like the Philippines has been criticized because it has contributed to rapid deforestation of ecologically sensitive areas—companies in a rush to create profits from the popularity of biofuels have installed plantations on former jungle land, for example.

Researchers have been hard at work developing new technologies that could produce biofuels without deforestation of land or engendering food supplies. Cellulosic ethanol would be made from nonedible plants like grasses, sugarcane waste, algae, and wood waste. Although firms like the Verenium Corporation are still in the early stages of researching the use and production of cellulosic ethanol, it is believed that it might some day be an important fuel alternative as it does not endanger the food supply and grasses are easily grown in areas like the Great Plains.[75]

Hydropower

Throughout history, people have used water as a power source and a means of transportation. From the water-powered mills of centuries past to modern hydroelectric dams, water is a powerful renewable energy source. Although in the United States, hydroelectric power only provides 7 percent of total output, hydroelectric provides 19 percent of total electricity production worldwide, making it the largest form of renewable energy.

As with all other forms of energy production, hydropower has benefits and downsides. One of the major downsides is the destruction of wildlife habitats, and sometimes even human habitations, when valleys are flooded using dams. Hydroelectricity also disrupts the lifecycles of aquatic life. Damming the Columbia River between Washington and Oregon states decimated the region's salmon industry, for example. Benefits of hydroelectric energy include little pollution and inexpensive maintenance costs, once the infrastructure is in place.[76] The world's largest hydropower facility, the Three Gorges Dam in China, is a major breakthrough in hydroelectricity and has resulted in reducing greenhouse gases in a country plagued with pollution problems. At the same time, the Three Gorges Dam is causing major changes in the river, placing already endangered river wildlife at risk. Although hydroelectricity offers many benefits, hydroelectric facilities should be built to minimize negative environmental impacts.

BUSINESS RESPONSE TO SUSTAINABILITY ISSUES

Partly in response to federal legislation and partly due to stakeholder concerns, businesses are applying creative, technological, and business resources to respond to environmental issues. Many businesses have adopted a triple-bottom-line approach. With this strategy, businesses take into consideration social and environmental performance in addition to economic performance. Many firms are learning that being environmentally friendly and sustainable has numerous benefits—including increased goodwill from stakeholders and even money savings from being more efficient and less wasteful. Many companies even have a vice president of environmental affairs, including Staples, Disney, and Hyatt Hotels & Resorts. This position is designed to help companies achieve their business goals in an environmentally responsible manner. Businesses like Wal-Mart and IBM have also developed environmental scorecards for their suppliers.[77] Corporate efforts to respond to environmental issues focus on green marketing, recycling, emissions reductions, and socially responsible buying.

Yet despite the importance of the environment, companies are in business to make a profit. Economic performance is still a necessary bottom line for most businesses. This begs the question: Is going green cost-effective for companies?

> "Studies suggest that improving a company's environmental performance can increase revenues and reduce costs."

Studies suggest that improving a company's environmental performance can in fact increase revenues and reduce costs. Figure 11.3 suggests mechanisms through which this can occur.

As shown in Figure 11.3, better environmental performance can increase revenue in three ways: through better access to certain markets, differentiation of products, and the sale of pollution-control technology. A firm's innovation in sustainability can be based on applying existing knowledge and technology or creating a completely new approach. Studies have revealed that 12 percent of the nation's population claims to regularly buy green products, with another 68 percent claiming to buy green products occasionally.[78] Improving a firm's reputation for environmental stewardship may help companies capture this growing market niche. Since even large companies like Wal-Mart are requiring their suppliers to be more environmentally friendly, improving a supply chain's environmental performance may be key to attracting more business from the retail industry. Wal-Mart is even going so far as to require suppliers to provide labels that report the environmental impact of their products. Shoppers will see these labels alongside the price tag in Wal-Mart stores, which should go a long way toward helping consumers make "greener" choices.[79] Going green may also help firms to differentiate their products from competitors. Whole Foods, a natural foods retailer, has made being environmentally friendly part of its image from the start. Finally, going green has opened

Figure 11.3 Positive Links Between Environmental and Economic Performance

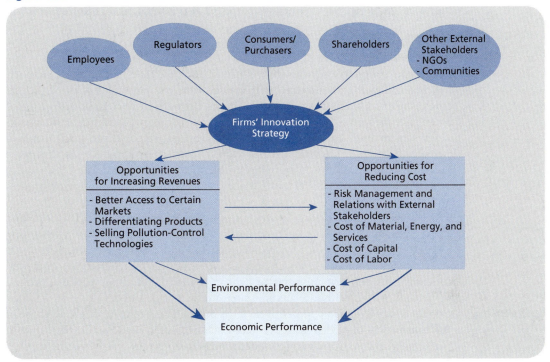

Source: Stefan Ambec and Paul Lanoie, "Does It Pay to Be Green? A Systematic Overview," *Academy of Management Perspectives* 22, no. 4 (November 2008): 47.

up a whole new industry referred to as the eco-industry, where some firms have actually discovered pollution-control technology and are now able to sell this technology to other firms.

Better environmental performance can also reduce costs by improving risk management and stakeholder relationships, reducing the amount of materials and energy used, and reducing capital and labor costs. Improved environmental standards should help prevent some major environmental disasters in the future. For those disasters that cannot be avoided, firms can at least show that they applied due diligence with their environmental performance, which may reduce companies' culpability in the public's eye. Companies can also decrease the costs of compliance with governmental regulations and reduce fines if they become more energy efficient.

Today's greener firms may also find that they have better access to capital. Banks often have environmental experts evaluate the environmental performance of potential borrowers to determine whether to grant bank loans. They have begun to recognize poor environmental management as an increased liability. Finally, labor surveys have shown that even workers care about the environmental impact of the firms for which they work. In fact, a survey of MBAs revealed that 97 percent were willing to give up an average of 14 percent of income to work for companies with a good reputation for social responsibility, something that many students have learned to prize over money in the wake of the financial meltdowns on Wall Street. Clearly, company environmental performance is ceasing to be simply an environmental matter; it also influences the bottom line.[80]

Green Marketing

Green marketing is a strategic process involving stakeholder assessment to create meaningful long-term relationships with customers, while maintaining, supporting, and enhancing the natural environment. One company that is known for its commitment to being green is New Belgium Brewery in Fort Collins, Colorado. From its conception, New Belgium has been a company committed to sustainability. Its facilities use natural lighting and evaporative coolers to save on energy costs, and the buildings themselves were constructed of pine trees that were killed by invasive beetles (a growing problem in the Rockies). The brewery has been wind powered for over a decade and uses waste from the brewing process to produce on-site methane gas for energy as well. New Belgium produces an organic beer, and undoubtedly will introduce more in the future. The company encourages its employees to bike to work, and actively engages in benchmarking and setting ambitious goals for reducing energy and waste even further.[81]

Even some real estate developers are attempting to integrate environmental concerns into new communities to protect the land. Buildings produce around 40 percent of all greenhouse gas emissions in the world, and developers are realizing that a way to gain a competitive edge is through being green. The University of Wisconsin, School of Business, even hosts a Sustainable Real Estate Development Conference. As environmental mandates on emissions and waste become stricter, an important way for real estate developers to cut costs and increase compliance will be by utilizing green technology and materials as much as possible.

Many products are certified as "green" by environmental organizations such as Green Seal and carry a special logo identifying them as such. In Europe, companies can voluntarily apply for an Eco-Label (see Figure 11.4) to indicate that their product is less harmful to the environment than competing products based on scientifically determined criteria. The European Union supports the Eco-Label program, which has been utilized in product categories as diverse as refrigerators,

green marketing a strategic process involving stakeholder assessment to create meaningful long-term relationships with customers, while maintaining, supporting, and enhancing the natural environment

Figure 11.4 The European Eco-Label (German)

Source: "European Union Eco-Label Logo," *Europa,* European Union, http://ec.europa.eu/environment/ecolabel/, accessed August 20, 2009.

mattresses, vacuum cleaners, footwear, and televisions. Certification does not include food and medicine.[82] Home Depot is one of the nation's largest carriers of Forest Stewardship Council–certified wood, which means the lumber was harvested from sustainable forests using environmentally friendly methods, and the company gives preferential treatment to suppliers who are FSC-certified.[83]

However, a study by Consumers International suggests that consumers are being confused and even misled by green marketing claims. As you read in Chapter 6, this is called **greenwashing**. Greenwashing involves misleading a consumer into thinking that a product or service is more environmentally friendly than it is. It can range from making environmental claims that are required by law and are therefore irrelevant (e.g., CFC-free) to puffery, or exaggerating environmental claims, to fraud.

Researchers compared claims on products sold in ten countries, including the United States, to labeling guidelines established by the International Organization for Standardization (ISO), which prohibit vague and misleading claims as well as unverifiable ones such as "environmentally friendly" and "nonpolluting." The study found that many products' claims are too vague or misleading to meet ISO standards. Further studies performed by the environmental marketing firm Terrachoice confirmed this finding.[84] For example, some products will be labeled as "chemical-free" when, in fact, everything contains chemicals, including plants and animals. Among the products with the highest number of misleading or unverifiable claims were laundry detergents, household cleaners, and paints. Anna Fielder, the director of Consumers International, contends the study shows that although many useful claims are made about the environmental responsibility of products, there is still a long way to go to ensure that shoppers are adequately informed about the environmental impact of the products they buy.[85]

Although the demand for legal and practical solutions to environmental issues is widespread, the environmental movement includes many diverse groups whose values and goals often conflict. There is growing agreement among environmentalists and businesses, however, that companies should work to protect and preserve sustainability by implementing a number of goals. First, companies should strive to eliminate waste. Because pollution and waste usually stem from inefficiency, the issue should not be what to do with waste but, rather, how to make things more efficiently so that no waste is produced.

Second, companies should rethink the concept of a product. Products can be classified as consumables, which are eaten or biodegradable; durable goods, such as cars, televisions, computers, and refrigerators; and unsalables, including such undesirable by-products as radioactive materials, heavy metals, and toxins. The design of durable goods should utilize a closed loop system of manufacture and use, and a return to the manufacturing process that allows products and resources to be disassembled and recycled and minimizes the disposal of unsalables. Third, the price of products should reflect their true costs, including the costs of replenishing natural resources that are utilized or damaged during the production process.

Finally, businesses should seek ways to make their commitment to the environment profitable.[86] For example, Sharon de Cloet founded Caeran, a manufacturer of environmentally responsible cleaning and personal care products because she was a frustrated consumer. Her son was highly sensitive to allergens so she developed her own cleaning products. Today, Caeran manufactures

greenwashing
involves misleading a consumer into thinking that a product or service is more environmentally friendly than it is

products in 24 product categories and utilizes a 150-person sales team. Each product label details the ingredients, which are fully explained in the company catalog. Customers receive only two mailings a year, including a newsletter that focuses on environmental issues and new products. De Cloet is a mentor to other entrepreneurs and uses her business success to better the community and support environmental causes.[87]

Recycling Initiatives

Many organizations engage in **recycling,** the reprocessing of materials, especially steel, aluminum, paper, glass, rubber, and some plastics, for reuse. In fact, recycling is one of the country's greatest sustainability success stories. Fifty-seven percent of all paper used in the United States is now recycled.[88] More than 50 percent of all products sold in stores are packed in recycled paperboard.

Paper is not the only thing that is recyclable, however. New Belgium Brewery engages in a type of recycling by using waste from beer production to generate methane gas that powers its facilities. Gills, the largest onion processor in the country, uses onion waste to make 600 kilowatts of electricity and cattle feed. Starbucks makes coffee grounds available free to those who wish to use them for compost to add nutrition to their gardens.

More than 2,000 organizations are part of a group called WasteWise, which aims to reduce municipal solid waste and industrial waste.[89] Groups like this help companies save money through reducing waste, receive positive publicity, and track how they reduce waste over time.

Companies and even local and regional governments are finding ways to recycle water to avoid discharging chemicals into rivers and streams and to preserve diminishing water supplies. While many companies such as Coca-Cola have taken steps to reduce water use, even geographic regions have had to heed the call to recycle water. After decades of siphoning water from surrounding regions, the city of Dallas, Texas, has had to answer for its lust for water. Many conservationists see city-dwellers' love of green lawns and golf courses in a drought-prone region as simply wasteful and irresponsible. Part of the plan to address this thirst for water is the installation of more and larger water recycling facilities.[90]

STRATEGIC IMPLEMENTATION OF ENVIRONMENTAL RESPONSIBILITY

Businesses have responded to the opportunities and threats created by environmental issues with varying levels of commitment. Some companies, like New Belgium Brewing, consider sustainability a core component of the business. Other companies engage in greenwashing and do not actively seek to be more sustainable at all.

As Figure 11.5 indicates, a low-commitment business attempts to avoid dealing with environmental issues and hopes that nothing bad will happen or that no one will find out about an environmental accident or abuse. Such firms may

recycling the reprocessing of materials, especially steel, aluminum, paper, glass, rubber, and some plastics, for reuse

Vestas Wind Power Brings Danish Wind Technology to the United States

With the United States now surpassing Germany as the largest producer of wind power, one Danish company is setting its sights on America's wind. Vestas Wind Systems is the world's largest producer of wind turbines and is looking to gain a foothold in the American wind farm market.

Vestas is coming into the United States at a time when American wind power has been gaining in popularity as an alternative form of energy, and many initiatives are being pursued that promote wind power as a means of electricity. The Pickens Plan, supported by oil executive T. Boone Pickens, proposes the construction of wind generation facilities that could produce 20 percent of America's electricity.

Additionally, Congress has discussed levying a tax on carbon emissions, which has caused some utilities to avoid building coal plants in favor of wind energy facilities. Congressional Democrats are also backing legislation requiring that 25 percent of the country's electric generation come from renewables like wind by 2025. It looks like the demand for wind power will continue to increase.

Vestas, which has a 28 percent market share in the wind energy industry, is ready to meet that demand. As of last year, the company had built 725 turbines in the United States, which accounted for 22 percent of Vestas's revenue. The company has built a blade factory in the prairie town of Windsor and two manufacturing facilities in Brighton, Colorado. Vestas chief executive Ditlev Engel is optimistic about his company's prospects in the United States.[91]

NASA

Figure 11.5 Strategic Approaches to Environmental Issues

Low Commitment	Medium Commitment	High Commitment
Deals only with existing problems	Attempts to comply with environmental laws	Has strategic programs to address environmental issues
Makes only limited plans for anticipated problems	Deals with issues that could cause public relations problems	Views environment as an opportunity to advance the business strategy
Fails to consider stakeholder environmental issues	Views environmental issues from a tactical, not a strategic, perspective	Consults with stakeholders about their environmental concerns
Operates without concern for long-term environmental impact	Views environment as more of a threat than an opportunity	Conducts an environmental audit to assess performance and adopts international standards

"Proactive firms develop strategic management programs that view the environment as an opportunity for advancing organizational interests."

try to protect themselves against lawsuits. Multinational oil company Chevron faces $27 billion in damages and fines in a lawsuit that pits the corporation against vulnerable Amazonian indigenous groups. The government of Ecuador alleges that many thousands of people have been harmed by improperly treated oil drilling pits that Chevron abandoned decades ago. Many of these pits are still open today and leach chemicals into the air and into water supplies, harming people and animals. The company claims that it was the government's responsibility to clean up the drilling sites, while the government alleges that Chevron acted irresponsibly and must pay for the needed cleanup, as well as compensate people who were harmed.[92]

Other firms are more proactive in anticipating risks and environmental issues. Such firms develop strategic management programs that view the environment as an opportunity for advancing organizational interests. These companies respond to stakeholder interests, assess risks, and develop a comprehensive environmental strategy. Home Depot, for example, has established a set of environmental principles that include selling responsibly marketed products, eliminating unnecessary packaging, recycling and encouraging the use of products with recycled content, and conserving natural resources by using them wisely. The company also makes contributions to many environmental organizations.

Stakeholder Assessment

Stakeholder analysis, as discussed in Chapter 2, is an important part of a high-commitment approach to environmental issues. This process requires acknowledging and actively monitoring the environmental concerns of all legitimate stakeholders. Thus, a company must have a process in place for identifying and prioritizing the many claims and stakes on its business and for dealing with trade-offs related to the impact on different stakeholders. Although no company can satisfy every claim, all risk-related claims should be evaluated before a firm decides to take action on or ignore a particular issue. To make accurate assumptions about stakeholder interests, managers need to conduct research, assess risks, and communicate with stakeholders about their respective concerns.

Based on an understanding of its stakeholders, Herman Miller, an ergonomic furniture maker, has implemented a comprehensive strategy to protect the environment. The firm's environmental responsibility initiatives encompass every element of its product supply chain, from the acquisition of raw materials, through production and design, to the end user who ultimately purchases its furniture. Herman Miller is committed to designing and manufacturing environmentally friendly furniture that has minimal impact on the environment. The strategy begins with an analysis of the "life cycle" of raw materials and finished goods to identify opportunities to reduce, reuse, and recycle. Miller's environmental initiatives not only have supported its founder's and managers' own personal beliefs of environmental stewardship and self-actualization but also have proven effective in reducing costs, building shareholder value, and earning stakeholder respect. The company has received multiple WasteWise awards from the EPA, has been recognized as one of the Top 20 Sustainable Stocks worth investing in by Sustainable Business, and has received the Recycling Design Award from the Institute of Scrap Recycling Industries, Inc.[93]

However, not all stakeholders are equal. Specific regulations and legal requirements govern some aspects of stakeholder relationships, such as air and water quality. A business cannot knowingly harm the water quality of other stakeholders in order to generate a profit. Additionally, some special-interest groups take extreme positions that, if adopted, would undermine the economic base of many other stakeholders (e.g., fishing rights, logging, and hunting).

Regardless of the final decision a company makes with regard to particular environmental issues, information should be communicated consistently across all stakeholders. This is especially important when a company faces a crisis or negative publicity about a decision. Another aspect of strong relationships is the willingness to acknowledge and openly address potential conflicts. Some degree of negotiation and conciliation will be necessary to align a company's decisions and strategies with stakeholder interests.

Risk Analysis

The next step in a high-commitment response to environmental concerns is assessing risk. Through industry and government research, an organization can usually identify environmental issues that relate to manufacturing, marketing, and consumption and use patterns associated with its products. Through risk analysis, it is possible to assess the environmental risks associated with business decisions. The real difficulty is measuring the costs and benefits of environmental decisions, especially in the eyes of interested stakeholders. Research studies often conflict, which only adds to the confusion and controversy over sustainability.

Debate surrounding environmental issues will force corporate decision makers to weigh the evidence and take some risks in final decisions. The important point for high-commitment organizations is to continue to evaluate the latest information and to maintain communication with all stakeholders. For example, if all of the millions sport utility vehicles (SUVs) on U.S. roads today were replaced with fuel-efficient electric-powered cars and trucks, there would be a tremendous reduction of greenhouse gas emissions. However, the cooperation and commitment needed to gain the support of government, manufacturers, consumers, and other stakeholders to accomplish this would be almost impossible to achieve. Although SUVs may harm the environment, many of their owners prefer them for reasons like they provide greater protection in an accident.

The issue of environmental responsibility versus safety in SUVs illustrates that many environmental decisions involve trade-offs for various stakeholders' risks. Through risk management, it is possible to quantify these trade-offs in determining whether to accept or reject environmentally related activities and programs.

Usually, the key decision is between the amount of investment required to reduce the risk of damage and the amount of risk acceptable in stakeholder relationships. A company should assess these relationships on an ongoing basis.

Both formal and informal methods are needed to get feedback from stakeholders. For example, the employees of a firm can use formal methods such as exit interviews, an open-door policy, and toll-free telephone hotlines. Conversations between employees can provide informal feedback. But it is ultimately the responsibility of the business to make the best decision possible after processing all available research and information. Then, if it is later discovered that a mistake has been made, change is still possible through open disclosure and thoughtful reasoning. A high-commitment organization incorporates new information and insights into the strategic planning process.

The Strategic Environmental Audit

Organizations that are highly committed to environmental responsibility may conduct an audit of their efforts and report the results to all interested stakeholders. Table 11.5 provides a starting point for examining environmental sensitivity.

Table 11.5 Strategic Sustainability Audit

Yes	No	Checklist
O	O	Does the organization show a high commitment to a strategic environmental policy?
O	O	Do employees know the environmental compliance policies of the organization?
O	O	Do suppliers and customers recognize the organization's stand on environmental issues?
O	O	Are managers familiar with the environmental strategies of other organizations in the industry?
O	O	Has the organization compared its environmental initiatives with those of other firms?
O	O	Is the company aware of the best practices in environmental management regardless of industry?
O	O	Has the organization developed measurable performance standards for environmental compliance?
O	O	Does the firm reconcile the need for consistent responsible values with the needs of various stakeholders?
O	O	Do the organization's philanthropic efforts consider environmental issues?
O	O	Does the organization comply with all laws and regulations that relate to environmental impact?

Such organizations may also wish to use globally accepted standards, such as ISO 14000, as benchmarks in a strategic environmental audit. The International Organization for Standardization developed **ISO 14000** as a comprehensive set of environmental standards that encourage a cleaner, safer, and healthier world. There is currently considerable variation among the environmental laws and regulations of nations and regions, making it difficult for high-commitment organizations to find acceptable solutions on a global scale. The goal of the ISO 14000 standards is to promote a common approach to environmental management and to help companies attain and measure improvements in environmental performance.

Companies that choose to abide by the ISO standards must review their environmental management systems periodically and identify all aspects of their operations that could impact the environment.[94] Those companies that choose to do so receive a certificate to indicate their compliance. Ford was the first automaker to require all suppliers and manufacturing facilities to be ISO 14000 certified. The initiative was designed to reduce Ford's environmental impact and save millions in business expenses.[95]

Other performance benchmarks available for use in environmental audits come from nonprofit organizations such as CERES, which has also developed standards for reporting information about environmental performance to interested stakeholders. The Green Globe program, which can be traced back to the 1992 United Nations Rio de Janiero Earth Summit, also offers environmental auditing and benchmarking services along with worldwide environmental certification for businesses. Originally established to promote sustainable tourism and travel, Green Globe's worldwide network currently extends across fifty countries.[96]

> **"Social responsibility entails responding to stakeholder concerns about the environment, and many firms are finding creative ways to address environmental challenges."**

As this chapter has demonstrated, social responsibility entails responding to stakeholder concerns about the environment, and many firms are finding creative ways to address environmental challenges. Although many of the companies mentioned in this chapter have chosen to implement strategic environmental initiatives to capitalize on opportunities and achieve greater efficiency and cost savings, most also believe that responding to stakeholders' concerns about environmental issues will both improve relationships with stakeholders and make the world a better place.

ISO 14000 a comprehensive set of environmental standards that encourage a cleaner, safer, and healthier world

SUMMARY

Although the scope of sustainability is quite broad, we define it as the potential for long-term well-being of the natural environment, including all biological entities, as well as the interaction among nature and individuals, organizations, and business strategies. Sustainability includes the assessment and improvement of business strategies, economic sectors, work practices, technologies, and lifestyles while maintaining the natural environment.

A major part of achieving sustainability is reducing sources of pollution. Air pollution arises from stationary sources such as factories and power plants; mobile sources such as cars, trucks, planes, and trains; and natural sources such as windblown dust and volcanic eruptions. Acid rain results when nitrous oxides and sulfur dioxides emitted from manufacturing facilities react with air and rain. Scientists believe that increasing concentrations of greenhouse gases in the atmosphere are warming the planet, although this theory is still controversial. The Kyoto Protocol is a treaty among industrialized nations to slow global warming. However, major polluters such as the United States and China are not signatories of the Kyoto Protocol. Another possible solution is a cap-and-trade program, which places a limit (cap) on carbon emissions, but allows businesses to purchase carbon permits from other companies.

Water pollution results from the dumping of raw sewage and toxic chemicals into rivers and oceans, from oil and gasoline spills, from the burial of industrial waste in the ground where it can reach underground water supplies, and from the runoff of fertilizers and pesticides used in farming and grounds maintenance. The amount of clean water available is also a concern and the topic of political disputes.

Land pollution results from the dumping of residential and industrial waste, strip mining, and poor forest conservation. How to dispose of waste in an environmentally responsible manner is an important issue. Deforestation to make way for agriculture and development threatens animal and plant species, as well as humans. Urban sprawl, the result of changing human development patterns, consumes wildlife habitat, wetlands, and farmland.

Deforestation, pollution, and urban sprawl threaten wildlife, plants, and their habitats and have caused many species to become endangered or even extinct. Biodiversity is threatened by all these activities, and should be an important topic of consideration for organizations and businesses. Scientists do not as yet fully understand rainforests and other biologically diverse environments, but we do know that they still hold many important discoveries. Pharmaceuticals and other products have been derived from plants and animals discovered in these wildernesses, and it is good business strategy to want to protect them.

Genetically modified organisms (GMOs) are created through manipulating plant and animal genes so as to produce a desired effect like resistance to pests and viruses, drought resistance, or high crop yield. Many farmers now plant GMO corn, soybeans, potatoes, canola oil seeds, and cotton plants that are more pest and insecticide resistant, require fewer chemicals to produce, and have higher yields. The long-term consequences of these scientific innovations are unknown. Some fear that because these GMOs are not naturally occurring, they could harm biodiversity or cause health problems in humans. Even so, a lot of interest in GM products remains as a way to solve problems such as world hunger, drought, and pest invasions. Today, as much as 75 percent of all processed food contains GMO ingredients—and the United States does not require labeling. GMOs also hold potential for developing new life-saving drugs and other products.

The U.S. Environmental Protection Agency (EPA) is an independent regulatory agency that establishes and enforces environmental protection standards, conducts environmental research, provides assistance in fighting pollution, and assists in developing and recommending new policies for environmental protection.

To reduce greenhouse gas emissions and dependence on fossil fuels, many countries and businesses are investigating in alternative forms of renewable energy. Wind power utilizes large turbines to convert wind into electricity. It has long been popular in windy regions such as northern Europe, and is catching on in places like the United States and Mexico. Geothermal power harnesses the heat trapped inside the earth to generate power. While not feasible everywhere, it is an attractive option because energy is available all of the time, unlike with wind or solar power. Wind and geothermal energy, while expensive to set up initially, are the sources of renewable energy improving the most rapidly and are the most likely to become affordable soon. Geothermal energy is currently the best form of renewable energy in which to invest. Solar power can also be converted to electricity, and businesses like British Petroleum are using solar energy to reduce fossil fuel use at some of its facilities. Sunny places like the American Southwest, Spain, and even the Sahara are the sites of intensive solar power research.

Nuclear power is another possible, albeit controversial in the United States, alternative energy source. Countries in Europe and Asia continue to use nuclear power a great deal, but concerns remain over possible meltdowns and how to dispose of the waste. Biofuels have gained in popularity as a way to reduce the consumption of gasoline. Brazil has a highly successful sugarcane ethanol program that has allowed the country to reduce its gasoline consumption. However, adopting corn ethanol in the United States has been more problematic as it involves using a key food source and production is less efficient than when using sugarcane. Hydropower is the most common alternative fuel used in the world, but is expensive to initially set up and can have detrimental effects on river systems and surrounding areas.

Businesses are applying creative, technological, and business resources to respond to environmental issues. Some firms have a vice president of environmental affairs position, to help them achieve their business goals in an environmentally responsible manner. Green marketing is a strategic process involving stakeholder assessment to create meaningful long-term relationships with customers, while maintaining, supporting, and enhancing the natural environment. Although green marketing has become more popular, companies must be careful not to engage in greenwashing, which involves misleading a consumer into thinking that a product or service is more environmentally friendly than it is. Greenwashing can range from making environmental claims that are required by law and are therefore irrelevant (e.g., CFC-free) to puffery, or exaggerating environmental claims, to fraud.

There is growing agreement among environmentalists and businesses that companies should work to protect and preserve sustainability by implementing a number of goals: (1) eliminate the concept of waste, (2) rethink the concept of a product, (3) make the price of products reflect their true costs, and (4) seek ways to make business's commitment to the environment profitable. Many organizations engage in recycling, the reprocessing of materials—especially steel, aluminum, paper, glass, rubber, and some plastics—for reuse. To combat air pollution and the threat of global warming, many companies are striving for greater efficiency, waste reduction, and the reduction of greenhouse-gas emissions. Becoming more efficient can result in substantial cost savings for companies as well. Companies should perceive waste and pollution as evidence of inefficiencies and strive to reduce them as much as possible. Socially responsible buying initiatives are another way that companies incorporate environmental responsibility into their business strategies.

Businesses have responded to the opportunities and threats created by environmental issues with varying levels of commitment. A high-commitment business develops strategic management programs, which view the environment as an opportunity for advancing organizational interests. Stakeholder analysis requires a process for identifying and prioritizing the many claims and stakes on its business and for dealing with trade-offs related to the impact on different stakeholders. Risk analysis tries to assess the environmental risks and trade-offs associated with business decisions. Organizations that are highly committed to environmental responsibility may conduct an audit of their efforts and report the results to all interested stakeholders. Such organizations may use globally accepted standards, such as ISO 14000, as benchmarks in a strategic environmental audit.

RESPONSIBLE BUSINESS DEBATE

Are Consumers Being Greenwashed?

ISSUE: Is it acceptable for companies to exaggerate environmental claims in order to sell products, or is this practice deceiving consumers?

Environmentally friendly products are more popular than ever. In the United States, consumers spend $25 billion a year on products that are dubbed "natural" or "organic." Being perceived as "green" can help many firms create a competitive advantage, as it is a quality increasingly valued by consumers. However, greenwashing has also become a problem as more companies seek to jump on the eco-friendly bandwagon. Greenwashing involves misleading a consumer into thinking that a product or service is more environmentally friendly than it is. It can range from making environmental claims that are required by law and are therefore irrelevant (e.g., CFC-free) to puffery, or exaggerating environmental claims, to fraud. Firms need to be careful when using words like *green, sustainable,* or *environmentally friendly* so as not to mislead consumers and face potential litigation.

The FTC can take firms to court that ignore "green guides" and seek fines to reimburse consumers. However, most companies do not face legal repercussions from their claims. Between 1992 and 2000 the FTC filed about two complaints a year, but none of them went to court. Since then, the FTC has taken legal action against three companies, all of which were announced on June 9, 2009, the day of a congressional hearing about environmental marketing.

The current administration has taken a tougher stand on environmental issues, and as greenwashing becomes more prevalent, it is likely that legal action will increase. A survey in twelve large retail stores found 1,700 different products with green claims. In addition, a recent survey found that 10.4 percent of advertisements in six national magazines made environmental claims. Since one-third of consumers rely exclusively on labels to decide if a product is environmentally friendly, it is important that labels tell the truth. Some organizations have taken on the challenge of developing a certification system to help consumers make informed decisions when buying supposedly green products. For example, the Carbon Trust offers a certification that validates claims about reducing carbon output. However, certification organizations are not always trustworthy either. Some of them charge a fee and do not hold products to rigorous standards. For the time being, the best way for consumers to be informed about eco-friendly products is to do some research before going shopping.

There Are Two Sides to Every Issue:

1. Government regulation will be necessary to force companies to remain truthful in their green claims.

2. Private green certification programs are the best method for consumers to evaluate and compare claims.

Sources: Traci Watson, "Eco-Friendly Claims Go Unchecked," *USA Today*, June 22, 2009, p. A1; Linda Ferrell and O. C. Ferrell, *Ethical Business* (London: Dorling Kindersley Limited, 2009), pp. 38–39.

KEY TERMS

sustainability (p. 400)
Kyoto Protocol (p. 404)
cap-and-trade (p 405)
genetically modified organisms
   (GMOs) (p 413)
Environmental Protection Agency
   (EPA) (p 415)

green marketing (p. 428)
greenwashing (p. 429)
recycling (p. 430)
ISO 14000 (p. 435)

DISCUSSION QUESTIONS

1. Define sustainability in the context of social responsibility. How does adopting this concept affect the way businesses operate?

2. How does cap-and-trade work? Do you think this is a good idea for helping the United States to reduce its greenhouse gas emissions?

3. Discuss renewable energy initiatives such as wind, solar, and geothermal. Which do you think are most feasible and most important for businesses to focus on?

4. Think of instances of greenwashing that you have encountered. What is the harm of greenwashing?

5. What is the role of the EPA in U.S. environmental policy? What impact does this agency have on businesses?

6. What federal laws seem to have the greatest impact on business efforts to be environmentally responsible?

7. What role do stakeholders play in a strategic approach to environmental issues? How can businesses satisfy the interests of diverse stakeholders?

8. What is environmental risk analysis? Why is it important for an environmentally conscious company?

9. What is ISO 14000? What is its potential impact on key stakeholders, community, businesses, and global organizations concerned about environmental issues?

10. How can businesses become more sustainable? What are the advantages and disadvantages of striving to become more sustainable?

EXPERIENTIAL EXERCISE

Visit the website of the U.S. EPA (http://www.epa.gov/newsroom/). What topics and issues fall under the authority of the EPA? Peruse the agency's most recent news releases. What themes, issues, regulations, and other areas is the EPA most concerned with today? How can this site be useful to consumers and businesses?

WHAT WOULD YOU DO?

The Sustainability Committee's first meeting was scheduled for Thursday afternoon. Although it was only Tuesday, several people had already dropped by committee members' offices to express their opinions and concerns about the company's new focus on sustainability. Some colleagues had trouble with the broad definition of sustainability—"to balance the economic, environmental, and social needs of today's world while planning for future generations." Others worried the sustainability project was just another passing fad. A small group of colleagues believed the company should be most concerned with performance and should forget about trying to become a leader in the social responsibility movement. In general, however, most employees were either supportive or neutral on the initiative.

As the committee's meeting started, the committee chair reminded the group that the company's CEO was very committed to sustainability for several reasons. First, the company was engaged in product development and manufacturing processes that had environmental effects. Second, most companies in the industry were starting initiatives on sustainable development. Third, recent scandals had negatively affected public opinion about business in general. Finally, the company was exploring markets in Europe where environmental activism and rules are often more stringent. With these reasons in mind, the committee set out to develop plans for the next year.

For an hour, the committee discussed the general scope of sustainability in the company. They agreed that sustainability was concerned with increasing positive results while reducing negative effects on a variety of stakeholders. They also agreed that sustainability focused on the "triple bottom line" of financial, social, and environmental performance. For example, a company dedicated to sustainability could design and build a new facility that used alternative energy sources, minimized impact on environmentally sensitive surrounding areas, and encouraged recycling and composting. Another firm might implement its sustainability objectives by requiring suppliers to meet certain standards for environmental impact, business ethics, economic efficiency, community involvement, and others.

After this discussion, the committee made a list of current and potential projects that were likely to be affected by the company's new sustainability focus. These projects included

Energy consumption	Philanthropy
Manufacturing emissions and waste	Product development
Employee diversity	Technology
Community relations	Supplier selection
Corporate governance	Employee health and safety
Regulations and compliance	Volunteerism

After much discussion, the committee agreed that each member would take one of these twelve projects and prepare a brief report on its link to the environmental component of sustainability. This report should review the ways environmental issues can be discussed, changed, improved, or implemented within that area to demonstrate a commitment to sustainability. What would you do?

Social Responsibility in a Global Environment

Chapter Objectives

- To define cultural intelligence and its importance

- To discuss the global nature of stakeholder relationships

- To examine the importance of national competitiveness

- To describe the role of business in global development

- To explore global standards for social responsibility reporting

Chapter Outline

Cultural Intelligence

Global Stakeholders

National Competitiveness

Global Development

Global Reporting Initiative

© Toni Tomczyk

Poverty Reduction Through Partnerships

The United Nations (UN) is a supraregional organization of nearly two hundred nations and states from all parts of the world. The organization is involved in hundreds of projects and established a set of goals, entitled the Millennium Development Goals, in the early twenty-first century. The first goal is to halve the number of people on earth whose income is less than $1 U.S. per day. Roughly one billion people fall into this category.

To respond to this goal, nongovernment organizations (NGOs) and business groups have worked together in assessing the problems and providing solutions. Oxfam and Unilever collaborated on a research project to (1) investigate the impact of business on the lives of poor people and (2) explore potential links between international business and poverty reduction. Unilever is a global corporation that operates in the food, home-care, and personal-care categories. The company has many well-known brands, including Dove, Lipton, Knorr, Surf, and Vaseline.

Oxfam International is a leading NGO, comprised of twelve organizations and more than 3,000 partners, who are working together on the fight against poverty, suffering, and injustice. Examples of its projects include improving the production of rice in Laos, curbing violence against women in Guatemala, investigating poor labor conditions in Asia, providing emergency food relief in Niger, and teaching farmers in Georgia, once part of the Soviet Union, to grow tropical fruits.

Together, Oxfam and Unilever examined ways in which Unilever's employment, products, and value chain affect the poorest people of Indonesia. Specifically, they were looking for win-win scenarios that linked Unilever's economic development clout with sustainable poverty reduction. Ultimately, this information can be used to assist other companies in understanding how value chains create employment and income, both directly and indirectly. The insights and outcomes from this study include:

1. Cleaning up the Brantas River, so Unilever had clean water for its manufacturing facilities and local residents could begin new businesses using the clean water source.
2. Participating in value chains does not automatically guarantee improvements in the lives of people living in poverty.
3. Employing workers who are closely and more formally linked with Unilever's operations provides greater benefit to the employees and their families.
4. Contracting out employment may reduce a company's ability to monitor the situation and result in gaps between corporate policy and practice.
5. Learning that, in addition to business, other social institutions and resources are needed to create a long-term reduction in poverty.[1]

The expanding global marketplace requires that executives and managers develop the ability to conduct business effectively and socially responsibly in different regions of the world. As the Unilever example illustrates, there are also unique opportunities to successfully apply business resources and interests to solve societal problems.

In this chapter, we elaborate on key topics and concepts discussed in Chapters 1 through 11 by examining the unique nature of issues in the global environment and trends around the world. We discuss the importance of cultural intelligence, delve into the complexities of working with stakeholders, provide emerging trends with primary stakeholders, examine the role of national competitiveness in social responsibility, and point to global standards of social reporting.

CULTURAL INTELLIGENCE

cultural intelligence
the ability to interpret and adapt successfully to different national, organizational, and professional cultures

The movement of people across cities and continents means that ideas, values, traditions, languages, and customs have also migrated. While managers in different parts of the world may have unique and even contrasting perspectives, they also identify with a number of similar problems and opportunities, such as employee turnover, new business development, environmental protocols, and product innovation plans. Therefore, any culturally diverse work group will have a set of common experiences and another set of differences that must be recognized and managed.

Managers who demonstrate cultural intelligence are more effective when conducting business in different countries

The potential for the group to achieve positive outcomes is largely based on each member's level of cultural intelligence. **Cultural intelligence** is the ability to interpret and adapt successfully to different national, organizational, and professional cultures.[2] There are three components to the development and use of cultural intelligence (CQ):

1. *Cognitive*—Knowledge of economic, legal, ethical, and social systems prevalent in different cultures and subcultures

2. *Motivational*—Intrinsic desire to learn about different cultures and subcultures and the confidence to function effectively in situations where differences are present

3. *Behavioral*—Ability to use appropriate verbal and nonverbal actions when interacting with people from different cultures and subcultures[3]

Cultural intelligence is desired of all employees, but is mandatory for those who work in different countries, manage diverse groups, and, in general, have responsibilities that require the ability to interpret unfamiliar gestures, behaviors, and situations. These employees must be comfortable suspending immediate judgment and practice "thinking, then acting." For example, when an American businesswoman made multiple presentations to potential partners in Bangkok, Thailand, she was surprised there were so many side discussions while she presented. Since she did not speak Thai, she did not know the content of their discussions and wondered if they were bored, disinterested, or even disrespectful. She decided to relax, continue, and accept the chatter. It occurred to her that these side discussions were likely a cultural norm, or perhaps, simply the act of translating key points to a colleague who had less familiarity with English. In this example, the businesswoman demonstrated strong cultural intelligence and, in so doing, ensured that her company established a strong market presence in Thailand and Southeast Asia. If she had shown anger or frustration, the potential partners might have decided to take their business elsewhere.

Figure 12.1 provides a short self-assessment activity to determine your own CQ.

The effective practice of cultural intelligence requires a manager to parcel out what actions are true of all people, those that are unique to a particular group or culture, or whether the action lies somewhere along this continuum.[4] A person with high CQ will be skilled at recognizing how one individual or group is influenced by national, professional, and organizational cultures. For example, there are multiple layers of cultural effects to manage when an Irish manufacturing process expert from a consulting firm works with a Croatian engineer for a government agency. The Irish expert would have to interpret and act according to Croatia's national culture, laws and governmental system, the agency's role and scope, the engineering profession's code of ethics, and the engineer's personality and values. Therefore, to achieve social responsibility in a global context, CQ is integral. Cognitively, employees are obliged to learn the rules, values, and standards of different cultures. This entails studying the history, law, symbols, customs, and related facets of a new culture. Motivationally, they should be willing and confident enough to adapt to these standards, but also strong enough to resist adapting when a legal, ethical, or other social responsibility expectation is in jeopardy. Finally, employees must develop a keen capacity to mirror gestures, words, and other behaviors that demonstrate they have "entered the world" of their cultural counterparts.[5]

> **"A person with high cultural intelligence (CQ) will be skilled at recognizing how one individual or group is influenced by national, professional, and organizational cultures."**

It is important to remember that even one country is not entirely homogeneous. The extent to which a country has experienced immigration, supported and encouraged diversity, and realized the "melting pot" effect determines the internal homogeneity or heterogeneity of the country. For example, Japan, Norway, Saudi Arabia, and Poland are relatively homogeneous when compared to India, Australia,

Figure 12.1 Self-Assessment of CQ

Quick CQ Self-Assessment Tool

Think about your cultural intelligence in each of the following areas.
　　　Select the answer (1–5) that BEST describes you as you really are.
　　　　　1 - None of the description fits me.
　　　　　2 - Only some of this fit me.
　　　　　3 - Half of the description fits me.
　　　　　4 - Most of the description fits me.
　　　　　5 - The statements describe me perfectly.

CQ-Strategy　　　　　　　　　　　　　1　　2　　3　　4　　5

I plan carefully before I meet with someone who is from a different cultural background. After one of these experiences, I reflect carefully and try to make sense of the interaction.

CQ-Knowledge　　　　　　　　　　　　1　　2　　3　　4　　5

I generally understand other cultures and cultural values. I know about the basic ways in which cultures are similar and the ways they are different.

CQ-Motivation　　　　　　　　　　　　1　　2　　3　　4　　5

I am very interested in other cultures, and I enjoy meeting people who have different cultural backgrounds. I am confident that I can live in different cultures and that I can adapt to different parts of the world

CQ-Behavior　　　　　　　　　　　　　1　　2　　3　　4　　5

I modify my behavior to make others more comfortable when I interact with people who are from different cultural backgrounds. I change the way I speak and act when I am in cross-cultural setting. I mimic others to make sure that I follow local conventions so that my speech patterns and body language are not offensive.

Interpreting Your Quick CQ Self-Assessment Responses

Sum your answers to the four questions in the Quick CQ Assessment Tool. Your score can range from 4 to 20.

4–7 points You see yourself as low in cultural intelligence. A CQ personal development plan could help you to become more capable of functioning effectively in culturally diverse situations.

8–16 points You see yourself as moderate in cultural intelligence. A CQ personal development plan could help you to enhance your capabilities in areas where you see yourself as less capable of functioning effectively in culturally diverse situations.

17–20 points You see yourself as high in cultural intelligence. A CQ personal development plan could help you to build on your impressive CQ strengths and become even more capable of functioning effectively in culturally diverse situations.

Source: Cultural Intelligence Center, "Self-Assessment of Your CQ," http://www.culturalq.com/selfassess.html, accessed August 15, 2009.

Britain, the United States, and Canada. The world's 200 countries contain 5,000 different ethnic groups. Approximately two-thirds of all countries have at least one minority group that comprises 10 percent of the total population and, therefore, represents a distinct subculture.[6] In more heterogeneous countries, astute managers will need to recognize and respond to subcultures. This, of course, requires a higher commitment to the cognitive, motivational, and behavioral aspects of CQ amidst an array of stakeholder interests and influences.

GLOBAL STAKEHOLDERS

In Chapter 1, we defined stakeholders as those people and groups to whom an organization is responsible—including customers, investors and shareholders, employees, suppliers, governments, communities, and many others—because they have a "stake" or claim in some aspect of a company's products, operations, markets, industry, or outcomes. These groups not only are influenced by businesses, but they also have the ability to affect businesses. Table 12.1 describes stakeholder issues that are likely to be present when planning and conducting

Table 12.1 Examples of Stakeholder Issues in a Global Environment

Stakeholder Groups	Potential Issues
Employees	Wages and benefits relative to home country standards
	Attitudes toward employees from different genders and ethnicities, especially in executive positions
	Existence of collective bargaining efforts
	Laws and regulations for employee rights, health, and safety
	Norms of employee volunteering
	Availability and comfort with open-door policies and other management practices
Customers	Laws and regulations on product safety and liability
	Presence and power of consumer rights groups
	Respect for the product needs of subcultures and minority groups
	Attitudes and accommodations for customers with disabilities
Shareholders	Laws and regulations regarding ownership and corporate governance
	Stability and governance of stock exchanges
	Willingness and ability to participate in shareholder meetings
Suppliers	Ethical and social considerations in the supply chain
	Prices offered to suppliers in developed countries and developing countries in comparison to other suppliers
	Availability and attitudes toward minority suppliers
Community	Norms of community relations and dialogue
	Expectations of community service and/or philanthropy
	Rights of indigenous people
	Availability and quality of infrastructure (roads, utilities, schools, etc.)

(continued)

Table 12.1 (continued)

Environmental Groups	Environmental law and regulations
	Availabilty of "green" electricity, recycled materials, and other environmentally friendly inputs
	Environmental expectations relative to those in home country
	Use of natural resources to achieve business goals

business outside of the home country. Note that these issues include economic, legal, ethical, and philanthropic considerations of other cultures and countries.

From an economic perspective, differences in the development of countries can easily pose new challenges with stakeholders. As more companies have moved manufacturing and customer services operations to less-developed nations, critics opine about job loss in the home country and the pay and working conditions in the new operation. While overseas outsourcing adds another layer of complexity for management, economic considerations for cost-cutting typically trump social and political concerns. Some firms report 50 percent savings on salary costs and note the eagerness and productivity of workers, meaning that the salary dollar goes even further in less-developed nations.[7]

Clearly, the legal and regulatory environment varies from country to country. Managers will need to understand the written code as well as the nuances to implementation and enforcement. One of the most widely discussed stakeholder issues in the global economy is the extent to which "facilitating payments" or bribery is a common and expected practice. Since the passage of the Foreign Corrupt Practices Act during the Watergate-era, United States–based multinational corporations have claimed the law severely reduces their ability to compete in the global marketplace. Energy companies are under investigation for making payments to Nigerian customs officials. One automotive manufacturer is fighting claims that it paid government officials in Eastern Europe, Asia, and Africa in order to win lucrative contracts. The number of bribery cases filed by civil and criminal investigators has more than doubled in the United States over the past five years. This resurgence is supported by new efforts in the European Union and Japan to prosecute bribery cases.[8]

Beyond the complexities of the law lay the ethical standards of stakeholders around the world. As discussed in earlier chapters, several factors influence the ethical decision-making process, with top management setting the tone and expectations for all employees and, increasingly, suppliers and business partners. For companies with operations in several countries, the code of conduct originating from the home office may not provide sufficient guidance. The United Parcel Service (UPS) published its first ethics code for domestic employees in 1996 but soon realized an international version was needed. Instead of imposing the American version, the company established advisory panels in different regions and conducted thirty-five focus groups around the world. Using the domestic code as a starting point, UPS ultimately produced twenty-eight codes of conduct for its overseas operations. The codes incorporated cultural differences that did not override key corporate values. For example, UPS employees in France knew that a policy prohibiting alcohol consumption would not work; in France, it is customary to have a glass of wine at lunch. When language experts started to translate antitrust law into other languages, it translated as "against trust" and needed to be revised. Executives at UPS acknowledge the tremendous resources expended on the process, but are confident the culturally intelligent approach is most effective.[9]

Finally, the philanthropic expectations of stakeholder are also subject to wide variation. While the United States is steeped in a culture of business philanthropy and employee volunteerism, this is not true around the world. In Latin America, for example, the roots of philanthropy extend to the Catholic Church, which provided education, health care, and social services. Later, wealthy families provided funds to "secular societies of social benefit" that implemented welfare and social projects. Corporate interest in philanthropy is more recent, but has grown significantly as a way for business to become socially engaged. The Inter-American Development Bank hosts an annual conference for Latin American business leaders to learn more about social responsibility and philanthropy. Attendance has tripled over the past eight years and outgrowths include increases in corporate social investing, social reporting activities, and membership associations for philanthropy executives.[10]

Shareholder Relations and Corporate Governance

While the prospect for global agreement on economic, legal, ethical, and philanthropic standards for business may seem far-fetched, existing efforts hold great promise. In whatever form it takes, a successful initiative must begin and end with the role of corporate governance and shareholder power in corporate decision making. First and foremost, the board of directors must be committed to a system of oversight, accountability, and control that incorporates a social responsibility perspective. Without this commitment, checks and balances are not in place to limit opportunism and self-interests, advocate for stakeholder rights, or ensure that a firm's corporate culture establishes integrity in all relationships. As discussed in Chapter 3, corporate governance reflects fundamental beliefs about the purpose of business organizations—ranging from maximizing shareholder value to a more collaborative and relational approach with multiple stakeholders.

The movement to write and implement widely accepted codes of conduct is several decades old and was foreshadowed by social activists who derided apartheid in South Africa and urged companies to withdraw their investments and business interests from the country. Led by Reverend Leon Sullivan, who sat on the board of General Motors, interested citizens and other groups developed requirements any company should demand for its employees and workplace conditions. These standards covered nonsegregation, equal, and fair compensation, programs to move minorities into management ranks, and other measures that clearly conflicted with South African law permitting racial segregation and unequal rights. Eventually, the Sullivan Principles were adopted by over one hundred companies in the United States and included their withdrawal of existing operations and investments from South Africa.[11]

Since the Sullivan Principles, several groups have developed codes of conduct or similar documents in an effort to build multicultural agreement on acceptable corporate governance and business practices. Perhaps the most successful initiative resulted in the Caux Round Table Principles for Business found in Table 12.2.

Table 12.2 Caux Round Table Principles for Business

PRINCIPLE 1 – RESPECT STAKEHOLDERS BEYOND SHAREHOLDERS
• A responsible business acknowledges its duty to contribute value to society through the wealth and employment it creates and the products and services it provides to consumers.
• A responsible business maintains its economic health and viability not just for shareholders, but also for other stakeholders.
• A responsible business respects the interests of, and acts with honesty and fairness towards, its customers, employees, suppliers, competitors, and the broader community.
PRINCIPLE 2 – CONTRIBUTE TO ECONOMIC, SOCIAL, AND ENVIRONMENTAL DEVELOPMENT
• A responsible business recognizes that business cannot sustainably prosper in societies that are failing or lacking in economic development.
• A responsible business therefore contributes to the economic, social, and environmental development of the communities in which it operates, in order to sustain its essential "operating" capital – financial, social, environmental, and all forms of goodwill.
• A responsible business enhances society through effective and prudent use of resources, free and fair competition, and innovation in technology and business practices.
PRINCIPLE 3 – RESPECT THE LETTER AND THE SPIRIT OF THE LAW
• A responsible business recognizes that some business behaviors, although legal, can nevertheless have adverse consequences for stakeholders.
• A responsible business therefore adheres to the spirit and intent behind the law, as well as the letter of the law, which requires conduct that goes beyond minimum legal obligations.
• A responsible business always operates with candor, truthfulness, and transparency, and keeps its promises.
PRINCIPLE 4 – RESPECT RULES AND CONVENTIONS
• A responsible business respects the local cultures and traditions in the communities in which it operates, consistent with fundamental principles of fairness and equality.
• A responsible business, everywhere it operates, respects all applicable national and international laws, regulations and conventions, while trading fairly and competitively.
PRINCIPLE 5 – SUPPORT RESPONSIBLE GLOBALIZATION
• A responsible business, as a participant in the global marketplace, supports open and fair multilateral trade.
• A responsible business supports reform of domestic rules and regulations where they unreasonably hinder global commerce.
PRINCIPLE 6 – RESPECT THE ENVIRONMENT
• A responsible business protects and, where possible, improves the environment, and avoids wasteful use of resources.
• A responsible business ensures that its operations comply with best environmental management practices consistent with meeting the needs of today without compromising the needs of future generations.
PRINCIPLE 7 – AVOID ILLICIT ACTIVITIES
• A responsible business does not participate in, or condone, corrupt practices, bribery, money laundering, or other illicit activities.
• A responsible business does not participate in or facilitate transactions linked to or supporting terrorist activities, drug trafficking, or any other illicit activity.
• A responsible business actively supports the reduction and prevention of all such illegal and illicit activities.

Source: Caux Round Table, "Principles for Business," http://www.cauxroundtable.org/, accessed August 15, 2009.

The round table consists of business leaders from all regions of the world who have a strong desire and interest in promoting socially responsible capitalism. The group was founded in 1986 by Frederick Phillips, former president of Phillips Electronics, and Olivier Giscard d'Estaing, former vice-chair of INSEAD, a preeminent business school. Although the original intent was to reduce trade tensions, the round table quickly turned to global corporate responsibility and established its principles. Today, the group's governing board includes executives from multinational corporations, such as CEMEX (Mexico), Microsoft Corporation (United States), Central Nippon Expressway Company (Japan), Banyan Tree Holdings (Singapore), Blanco GmbH & Company (Germany), and Westpac Banking (Australia).[12]

In addition to this fundamental guidance, the Caux Round Table publishes periodic opinions on a range of social responsibility issues, including executive compensation, environmental protection, corruption, Wall Street, and recovery from economic crisis. For example, Table 12.3 enumerates the round table's plan for restoring trust in the global financial system. The seven recommendations are explicit on enhancing the role and expectations of the board of directors, integrating stakeholders into company policy, implementing risk assessment across social responsibility issues, and ensuring that executive pay is linked to long-term corporate performance. We discussed similar concerns in Chapter 3, reflecting the ongoing dialogue about improving and streamlining corporate governance in a global economy.

Table 12.3 The Caux Round Table's Seven Point Reform Plan to Restore Trust in Business and in the Global Financial System

1. Require board directors to consider interests beyond shareholders, which may affect the company's success, by codifying the principle of *"enlightened shareholder value"* in company law.
2. Require minimum standards of corporate governance knowledge and expertise for corporate board directors.
3. Require corporate boards to have a dedicated board committee responsible for risk oversight across the full spectrum of risks—financial, governance, social, environmental.
4. Regulate executive remuneration structures to ensure that they are consistent with prudent risk management, align with long-term wealth creation, and do not reward poor performance.
5. Implement stronger and globally coordinated financial and banking regulatory reforms to prevent systemic risk build-up or market manipulation.
6. Regulate all financial market instruments and investment activities that materially impact on financial system stability and on superannuation and pension system viability.
7. Reform and adequately resource the IMF and other multilateral institutions to ensure they are effective forces for economic and social justice globally.

Source: Caux Round Table, "Seven Point Reform Plan to Restore Trust in Business and in the Global Financial System," press release March 30, 2009, http://www.cauxroundtable.org/newsmaster.cfm?&menuid=99&action=view&retrieveid=11, accessed August 15, 2009.

"Meeting the economic, legal, ethical, and philanthropic expectations of employee stakeholders in different countries is clearly complex."

Employee Relations

A critical consideration for companies conducting business around the world is how to manage differences that exist in employment standards and expectations. Modern corporations recognize the importance of tapping into global markets and talent pools in order to remain competitive. Even in the best cases, building a workforce, especially a dedicated, engaged, and satisfied one, takes strategic planning and daily oversight by management. Executing this process in a new culture or across cultures takes more than merely transferring the policies and practices from the home country and home office. Meeting the economic, legal, ethical, and philanthropic expectations of employee stakeholders in different countries is clearly complex. For example, Table 12.4 outlines ten key differences between employment law in Canada and the United States. Even in culturally similar nations, there are important variances to learn and consider.

Longitudinal research has affirmed what many global managers already know: Employee attitudes and perceptions about work vary from country to country. As discussed in Chapter 7, employees typically value high ethical standards and volunteer activities, and they become more loyal and satisfied with their employer when these are present. Thus, understanding the variations in employee attitudes and perceptions is integral to the successful implementation of social responsibility programs. For example, workers in France value a work-life balance more than any other national group. Japanese employees are often pleased with incentive compensation but lament relatively low base pay. Australians want a manager who acts as a coach, and Chinese employees yearn for more training opportunities.

In its annual survey, Mercer, an international research firm, has identified the factors most important for **employee engagement,** the psychological state in which employees feel a vested interest in the company's success and are motivated to perform at levels that exceed job requirements. Figure 12.2 depicts the results of Mercer's annual study of employees in Brazil, China, the United Kingdom, and the United States. While national differences are clear, Mercer has also identified four global drivers of employee engagement. Employees in different parts of the world are fairly consistent in noting the importance of (1) the work itself, including opportunities for development; (2) confidence and trust in leadership; (3) recognition and rewards; and (4) organizational communication. This information is valuable to managers, as it improves the cognitive nature of cultural intelligence and provides direction on motivational and behavioral competencies that should be impactful across nations. In addition, understanding the

employee engagement
the psychological state in which employees feel a vested interest in the company's success and are motivated to perform at levels that exceed job requirements

Table 12.4 Differences in Employment Law: United States and Canada

Legal Issue	Canada	United States
Termination of Employment	Employers must give statutory notice of termination or pay in lieu.	Employment is "at will" and notice of termination is by company policy.
Severance	Severance plans or policies are uncommon and do not override statutory rights.	Most severance plans require the severed employee to execute a release of claims before receiving the severance pay.
Employment Litigation	Litigation against employers is generally settled quickly and easily, with predictable damage awards.	Litigation against employers is typically written as a claim of human rights discrimination; litigation is costly and unpredictable.
Consideration for Employment Changes	Material and adverse changes to the terms and conditions of employment can only be made on reasonable notice.	Absent a written agreement or statutory rights (minimum wage, overtime pay), employment terms may be modified without prior notice.
Restrictive Covenants	Courts enforce noncompetition clauses if they are reasonable and do not unduly limit the ability to gain new employment.	Courts enforce noncompetition agreements that are reasonable, especially for protecting the trade secrets or proprietary rights of an employer.
Compensation Disclosure	Canadian law was patterned after U.S. law on the disclosure of executive compensation for "Named Executive Officers."	Public companies must fully disclose the compensation of executives and boards members in plain English, including the objectives and implementation of executive compensation programs.
Options	The usual tax treatment of a stock option is that the difference between exercise price and fair market value is taxed to the employee at effective capital gains rates when the underlying share is disposed.	United States has similar tax treatment for incentive stock options.
Restricted Stock	Grants of restricted stock are taxed to employees at the time of grant.	Grants of restricted stock are taxed to employees at the time the restrictions end.
Changes to Post-Retirement Benefits	Very difficult to reduce post-retirement benefits without notice and almost impossible to reduce benefits for existing retirees.	There is more flexibility in making changes to post-retirement benefits.
Human Rights	Discrimination in employment is prohibited on specified grounds such as color, gender, ethnic origin, religion/creed, age, and in some states sexual orientation.	Discrimination in employment is also prohibited on the same grounds; preemployment drug screening more prevalent.

Source: Christina Medland, "Ten Key Differences in Canadian and U.S. Employment Law," *TLOMA Today*, April 2008, www.tloma.com, accessed August 14, 2009.

Figure 12.2 Employee Engagement Factors in Four Countries

United States
1. Confident can achieve career objectives
2. Sense of personal accomplishment
3. Confident organization will be successful
4. Quality is a high priority
5. Opportunity for growth/development
6. Information/assistance to manage career
7. Flexibility to provide good customer service

United Kingdom
1. Sense of personal accomplishment
2. Confidence in senior management
3. Opportunities for training
4. Paid fairly, given performance
5. Good reputation for customer service
6. Regular feedback on performance
7. Comparable benefits to industry
8. Cooperation between groups

China
1. Sense of personal accomplishment
2. Paid fairly, given performance
3. Comparable benefits to industry
4. Confidence in senior management
5. IT systems support business needs
6. Opportunities for training
7. Regular feedback on performance

Brazil
1. Sense of personal accomplishment
2. Confidence in senior management
3. Opportunities for training
4. Paid fairly, given performance
5. Good reputation for customer service
6. Comparable benefits to industry

Source: Mercer, *Engaging Employees to Drive Global Business Success*, 2007, http://www.mercer.com/whatsworking, accessed August 14, 2009.

four drivers enables human resource (HR) professionals to inculcate consistency across some HR policies in a multinational firm.[13]

As discussed earlier in this chapter, cultural intelligence (CQ) is an integral part of employees' ability to manage and succeed in a global economy. In the context of business ethics, CQ is especially critical. Applying the legal requirements of the host or home country to the problem may be a starting point. However, as we have noted, legal standards are not sufficient for a firm dedicated to ethical business practices. Some industries operate under a set of values or principles, which may also serve a purpose in the international arena. For example, the tourism industry has established a global code of ethics that enumerates the industry's obligation to build respect between societies, assist in sustainable development, maintain cultural heritage, treat employees well, and promote individual fulfillment.[14] In other cases, guidance from a broad set of guidelines, such as the Caux Round Table Principles for Business, can be utilized. However, broad principles are often less useful in day-to-day situations.

The ethical decision-making framework discussed in Chapter 5 is fully effective in the global environment, but cultural differences introduce new complexities to the process. For this reason, companies know that training rubrics are pivotal to an employee's ability to assess an ethical issue and determine the most appropriate decision and action. Figure 12.3 describes a heuristic model for employees in multinational enterprises, as it explicitly incorporates questions about differences in law, customs, values, and other cultural phenomena. The heuristic approach is designed to take the decision maker through a straightforward method of solving a particular problem. In practice, there will be information lacking, unknown

Figure 12.3 Heuristic Model of Ethical Decision Making

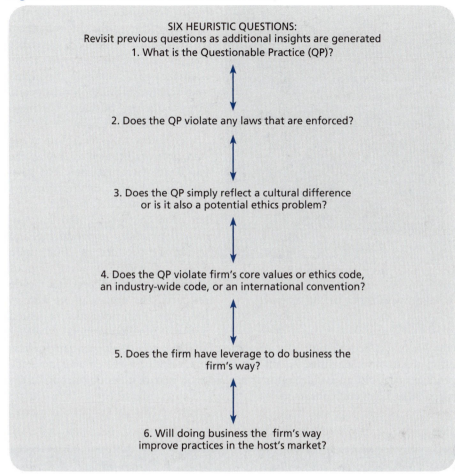

SIX HEURISTIC QUESTIONS:
Revisit previous questions as additional insights are generated
1. What is the Questionable Practice (QP)?

2. Does the QP violate any laws that are enforced?

3. Does the QP simply reflect a cultural difference
or is it also a potential ethics problem?

4. Does the QP violate firm's core values or ethics code,
an industry-wide code, or an international convention?

5. Does the firm have leverage to do business the
firm's way?

6. Will doing business the firm's way
improve practices in the host's market?

Source: J. Brooke Hamilton, Stephen B. Knouse, and Vanessa Hill, "Google in China: A Manager-Friendly Heuristic Model for Resolving Cross-Cultural Ethical Conflicts," *Journal of Business Ethics* 86, no. 2 (2009): 143–157.

variables, and perhaps, a continuous loop throughout the six questions until the employee is confident in the ethical action to be taken.[15]

Consumer Relations

International trade leaves some members of the economy, whether independent or corporate, marginalized and vulnerable to economic exploitation. From some consumer perspectives, conventional trade interferes with the ability of many people, particularly those in poor nations, to secure basic, sustainable livelihoods and have the opportunity to develop further. By contrast, **fair trade** is a trading partnership based on dialogue, transparency, and respect that seeks greater equity in international trade and contributes to sustainable development. Fair trade benefits those

fair trade a trading partnership based on dialogue, transparency, and respect that seeks greater equity in international trade and contributes to sustainable development

Consumers are increasingly interested in purchasing fair trade certified products

Source: TransFair USA, http://www.transfairusa.org/, accessed August 13, 2009.

who have limited opportunities to begin with and are further stunted by market forces that identify them as negligible. Table 12.5 describes the five principles of fair trade organizations, including the rights and responsibilities of producers, intermediaries, business partners, resellers, and consumers.

Products that meet fair trade standards are licensed to display the Fair Trade Certified label. The label signifies fair trade certification and stands for a producer's adherence to fair economic, social, and environmental practices in producing and selling the product. In 2008, there were nearly nine hundred organizations that produced fair trade products. The organizations were in fifty-eight countries and represented almost 1.5 million farmers and workers. When adjusted for economic effects on families and dependents, fair trade is estimated to have benefitted 7.5 million people. Over the past few years, fair trade product sales grew an average of forty percent each year, representing strong acceptance by retailers and consumers.[16]

Table 12.5 Charter of Fair Trade Principles

Principle	Description
1. Market access for marginalized producers	Fair Trade helps producers realize the social benefits of traditional forms of production. It enables buyers to trade with producers who would otherwise be excluded from the markets. It helps shorten trade chains so that producers receive more from the final selling price of their goods than is the norm in conventional trade via multiple intermediaries.
2. Sustainable and equitable trading relationships	The economic basis of transactions within Fair Trade relationships takes account of all costs of production, both direct and indirect. Fair Trade buyers offer trading terms that enable producers and workers to maintain a sustainable livelihood. Prices and payment terms are determined by assessment of economic, social, and environmental factors rather than just reference to current market conditions. The commitment to long-term trading partnerships found in Fair Trade enables both sides to cooperate through information sharing and planning.
3. Capacity building and empowerment	Fair Trade relationships assist producer organizations to understand more about market conditions and trends and to develop knowledge, skills, and resources to exert more control and influence over their lives.

4. Consumer awareness raising and advocacy	Fair Trade relationships provide the basis for connecting producers with consumers and for informing consumers of the need for social justice and the opportunities for change. Consumer support enables Fair Trade Organizations to be advocates and campaigners for wider reform of international trading rules and to achieve the ultimate goal of a just and equitable global trading system.
5. Fair trade as a "social contract"	Fair Trade transactions exist within an implicit "social contract" in which buyers agree to do more than is expected by the conventional market. In return, producers use the benefits of Fair Trade to improve their social and economic conditions, especially among the most disadvantaged members of the organization. Fair Trade is not charity but a partnership for change and development through trade.

Source: Fairtrade Labelling Organizations International, "A Charter of Fair Trade Principles," January 2009, http://www.fairtrade.net/fileadmin/user_upload/content/2009/about_us/documents/Fair_Trade_Charter.pdf, accessed August 13, 2009.

As fair trade statistics reveal, consumers are increasingly concerned with the origins of products they purchase, including the working conditions, ethical standards, and related social responsibility practices of manufacturers. For example, child labor and substandard working conditions have historically marked the reputation of football manufacturers. In an effort to minimize these costs, the International Fairtrade Labelling Organizations International certified footballs in 2002 and has since awarded its certification to five producers. Footballs and other sports balls were among the first non-food products to be certified. In the United States, Fair Trade Sports, Inc., distributes Fair Trade Sports Balls that are produced by adults working in safe and healthy manufacturing conditions.

Rice farming appears all over the world and is responsible for billions of jobs, making it important in the social well-being of numerous communities. The pesticides and chemicals used in rice farming initially increase production but eventually work to reduce production and negatively affect workers' health. A decline in global rice prices can find farmers in extremely difficult situations. Often when prices fall, farmers must apply for loans with high interest rates or lose their livelihoods. Areas particularly dense with rice farms are reported to have high suicide rates and incidents of children being sold for sex. Fair trade rice seeks to improve these conditions by providing

"Consumers are increasingly concerned with the origins of products they purchase, including the working conditions, ethical standards, and related social responsibility practices of manufacturers."

Table 12.6 Sellers of Fair Trade Certified Products

Ben & Jerry's Scoop Shops	Seattle's Best Coffee	Safeway
Bruegger's	Starbucks Coffee	Sam's Club
Caribou Coffee	Tully's Coffee	Target
Dunkin' Donuts	Costco	Trader Joe's
Einstein Bagels	Fred Meyer	Wal-Mart
Noah's Bagels	Giant	Wegman's
Peet's Coffee and Tea	Kroger	Whole Foods Market

Source: TransFair USA, www.transfairusa.org/content/WhereToBuy, accessed August 13, 2009.

stability in the market, seeking organic methods, and regulating of the use of chemicals in production.[17]

Finally, GlobeScan recently completed a study that indicates many consumers are committed to sustainable development through fair trade. The majority of Americans believe that companies working with poor countries should provide fair pay, safe work environments, and community development contributions. The Fair Trade Certified label positively affects 81 percent of American consumers, and just over half of those surveyed would pay more for fair trade certified products. The study, along with other reports, suggests the durability of fair trade certified products during times of economic downturn. Even in the wake of a global recession, attitudes remain favorable for fair trade products and retailers are pleased to stock their shelves for interested consumers (see Table 12.6).[18]

NATIONAL COMPETITIVENESS

Chapter 1 described the link between social responsibility and national economies. The reflexive nature of the global economy means that the success of a particular company is a function of many factors, including the extent to which the firm's home country is comprised of trust-based institutions. Some nations have well-developed systems for ensuring economic, legal, and ethical standards in business activities. In other cases, corporations are interested in a particular market, but know that fundamental institutions and standards are sorely underdeveloped and negatively affect market potential.

responsible competitiveness involves the positive effects of socially responsible business practices on a nation's economic success

The Responsible Competitiveness Index (RCI), published by AccountAbility, contextualizes competitiveness within a sustainable development paradigm and measures a country's ability to achieve economic growth through responsible business practices. Therefore, **responsible competitiveness** involves the positive effects of socially responsible business practices on a nation's economic success. The RCI is guided by the notion that "Securing responsible and successful business practices can only be achieved through the combined effects of engaged businesses, smart public policy, and a vibrant civil society."

In *The State of Responsible Competitiveness* reports, sustainable development and other social responsibility practices are understood as opportunities on which organizations may capitalize to increase the stability of their future economic growth. Data for the report is provided by credible, disinterested sources such as the World Bank Institute and Transparency International. The RCI identifies twenty-one indicators, which are measured using hard data and subjective findings of survey results. Figure 12.4 describes the indicators for each of the three drivers of responsible competitiveness:

Figure 12.4 Drivers of Responsible Competitiveness

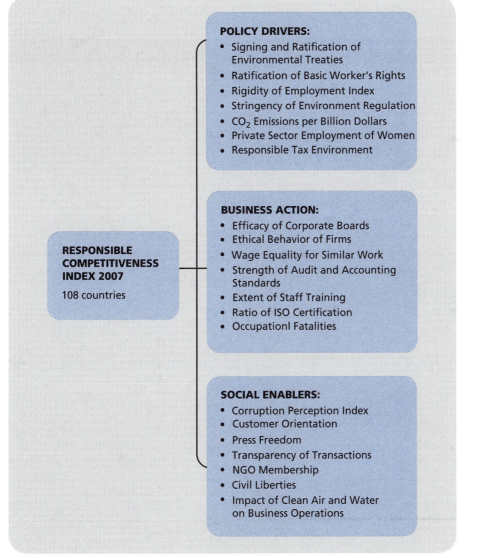

Source: AccountAbility, "The State of Responsible Competitiveness 2007," http://www.accountability21.net/uploadedFiles/publications/The_State_of_Responsible_Competitiveness.pdf, accessed August 8, 2009.

1. Policy drivers indicate the degree to which public policy and "soft power" entice organizations to utilize responsible practices.

2. Business action indicates the degree to which responsible practices, codes, and management systems are utilized.

3. Social enablers indicate the conduciveness of the socio-political environment to government and organization collaboration reshaping markets.[19]

Based on the RCI, countries may be categorized at four stages of development with respect to policy drivers, business action, and social enablers. Table 12.7

Table 12.7 Selected Countries in Responsible Competitiveness Index (RCI) Clusters: Starters, Compliers, Asserters, and Innovators

Starters	Compliers	Asserters	Innovators
Angola	Argentina	Chile	Australia
Bangladesh	Brazil	Costa Rica	Austria
Bolivia	Bulgaria	Czech Republic	Belgium
Cambodia	Colombia	Estonia	Canada
Chad	Croatia	Greece	Denmark
China	Egypt	Hungary	Finland
Ecuador	Georgia	Israel	France
Ethiopia	Honduras	Italy	Germany
Kenya	India	Jamaica	Hong Kong, China
Madagascar	Indonesia	Korea, Rep.	Iceland
Malawi	Jordan	Kuwait	Ireland
Mongolia	Mexico	Lithuania	Japan
Morocco	Nicaragua	Malaysia	Netherlands
Nepal	Panama	Portugal	New Zealand
Nigeria	Peru	Slovenia	Norway
Pakistan	Philippines	South Africa	Singapore
Russian Federation	Poland	Spain	Sweden
Uganda	Romania	Taiwan, China	Switzerland
Ukraine	Turkey	Thailand	United Kingdom
Zambia	Venezuela, RB	United Arab Emirates	United States

Source: AccountAbility, "The State of Responsible Competitiveness, 2007," http://www.accountability21.net/uploadedFiles/publications/ The%20State%20of%20Responsible%20Competitiveness.pdf, accessed August 8, 2009.

classifies countries as either starters, compliers, asserters, or innovators. In general, more developed nations score higher on the RCI, especially those in Europe. Thirteen of the top twenty countries are European, with Sweden receiving the highest rating for integrating responsible business practices into its national economy. Other Nordic countries, including Denmark and Norway, score in the top six. The emerging economies of Chile, Republic of Korea, and Malaysia actually score better on the RCI than a number of states that have recently joined the European Union, such as Poland, Romania, and Bulgaria. Uganda and Zambia have responsible competitiveness indexes that belie their relatively low level of economic development. Conversely, countries with similar levels of development, including Bangladesh, Cambodia, and Morocco, score relatively low on the RCI. Overall, the RCI provides conclusions that mirror our discussions in Chapter 1—social responsibility reinforces the economic competitiveness of countries.[20]

GLOBAL DEVELOPMENT

While companies certainly benefit from national competitiveness, businesses are increasing efforts to enhance the infrastructure, human rights, and educational systems of particular countries, states, and cities. According to Amartya Sen, winner of the Nobel Prize in Economics, political, social, and economic freedoms are fundamental to national competitiveness and development. Without widespread trust and the effective operations of different institutions, a given society will not be able to enhance and enrich the lives of its people. Sen refers to the contagion effect of freedom; political freedoms, such as free speech and elections, lead to economic security. Social freedoms in terms of education and health care also lead to stronger economic participation. Finally, economic security frees people to participate in social and political activities.[21] Multinational corporations are increasingly interested in mechanisms for promoting freedom and development.

Development refers to improvement in the economic, environmental, educational, and health conditions of a country. Common issues in development include poverty, health-care quality, access to education, voting rights, water quality, governance and rule of law, domestic finance systems, and climate change. A major goal of the United Nations (U.N.) is to realize improvements in the development of countries around the world. While these improvements may be grounded in ethical reasons, they are also critical to the stability of the global economy. Essentially, the U.N. is working from the philosophy that "a rising tide lifts all boats." In other words, it is in the world's best interest to tackle problems that limit the capacity of some people to live healthy and prosperous lives. The U.N.'s Millennium Development Goals, which are designed to meet these challenges, include: (1) eradicate extreme poverty and hunger; (2) achieve universal primary education; (3) eliminate gender disparity in primary and secondary education; (4) reduce child mortality; (5) improve maternal health; (6) combat HIV/AIDS, malaria, and other diseases; (7) ensure environmental sustainability; and (8) develop a global partnership for development.

development
refers to improvement in the economic, environmental, educational, and health conditions of a country

Table 12.8 provides more information on these issues, including targets the U.N. is striving to meet by 2015.

At the World Summit for Sustainable Development in 2002, Kofi Annan, seventh Secretary-General of the U.N., declared, "The Summit represents a major leap forward in the development of partnerships with the U.N., governments,

Table 12.8 United Nations' Millennium Development Goals

Goal 1: Eradicate Extreme Hunger and Poverty
Target 1.A: Halve, between 1990 and 2015, the proportion of people whose income is less than one dollar a day
Target 1.B: Achieve full and productive employment and decent work for all, including women and young people
Target 1.C: Halve, between 1990 and 2015, the proportion of people who suffer from hunger
Goal 2: Achieve Universal Primary Education
Target 2.A: Ensure that, by 2015, children everywhere, boys and girls alike, will be able to complete a full course of primary schooling
Goal 3: Promote Gender Equality and Empower Women
Target 3.A: Eliminate gender disparity in primary and secondary education, preferably by 2005, and in all levels of education no later than 2015
Goal 4: Reduce Child Mortality
Target 4.A: Reduce by two-thirds, between 1990 and 2015, the under-five mortality rate
Goal 5: Improve Maternal Health
Target 5.A: Reduce by three quarters, between 1990 and 2015, the maternal mortality ratio
Goal 6: Combat HIV/AIDS, Malaria, and Other Diseases
Target 6.A: Have halted by 2015 and begun to reverse the spread of HIV/AIDS
Target 6.B: Achieve, by 2010, universal access to treatment for HIV/AIDS for all those who need it
Target 6.C: Have halted by 2015 and begun to reverse the incidence of malaria and other major diseases
Goal 7: Ensure Environmental Sustainability
Target 7.A: Integrate the principles of sustainable development into country policies and programs and reverse the loss of environmental resources
Target 7.B: Reduce biodiversity loss, achieving, by 2010, a significant reduction in the rate of loss
Target 7.C: Halve, by 2015, the proportion of people without sustainable access to safe drinking water and basic sanitation
Target 7.D: By 2020, to have achieved a significant improvement in the lives of at least 100 million slum dwellers

Goal 8:	Develop a Global Partnership for Development
	Target 8.A: Develop further an open, rule-based, predictable, nondiscriminatory trading and financial system
	Target 8.B: Address the special needs of the least developed countries
	Target 8.C: Address the special needs of landlocked developing countries and small island developing states
	Target 8.D: Deal comprehensively with the debt problems of developing countries through national and international measures in order to make debt sustainable in the long term
	Target 8.E: In cooperation with pharmaceutical companies, provide access to affordable essential drugs in developing countries
	Target 8.F: In cooperation with the private sector, make available the benefits of new technologies, especially information and communications

Source: United Nations, "Millennium Development Goals," http://www.un.org/millenniumgoals/, accessed August 16, 2009.

business and civil society coming together to increase the pool of resources to tackle global problems on a global scale."[22] The U.N.'s Global Compact, a set of ten universally accepted principles in the areas of human rights, labor, environment, and anticorruption, was the key driver behind Annan's proclamation. The Global Compact was first introduced in 2000, and today approximately 3,000 companies have officially declared their commitment to these principles. Figure 12.5 replicates the "corporate commitment" to the Global Compact, including the five expectations of membership. Corporate signatories attest to their willingness to integrate the ten principles into everyday business practices,

Figure 12.5 Corporate Commitment to the Global Compact

The Corporate Commitment

The UN Global Compact is a leadership initiative, requiring a commitment signed by the company's chief executive, and, where applicable, endorsed by the highest-level governance body of the organization. In the context of this commitment, any company joining the initiative is expected to:

- Make the UN Global Compact and its principles an integral part of business strategy, day-to-day operations, and organizational culture;

- Incorporate the UN Global Compact and its principles in the decision-making processes of the highest-level governance body (i.e., board);

- Engage in partnerships to advance broader development objectives (such as the Millennium Development Goals);

- Integrate in its annual report (or in a similar public document, such as a sustainability report) a description of the ways is which it implements the principles and supports broader development objectives (also known as the Communication on Progress); and

- Advance the UN Global Compact and the case for responsible business practices through advocacy and active outreach to peers, partners, clients, consumers, and the public at large.

Source: United Nations, "Global Compact: Corporate Citizenship in the World Economy," http://www.unglobalcompact.org/docs/news_events/8.1/GC_brochure_FINAL.pdf, accessed August 16, 2009.

publish examples of its commitment and projects on an annual basis, and commit to a stronger alignment between the objectives of the international community and those of the business world.[23]

Although the U.N. has been most progressive in gaining corporate support for global development and popularizing business partnerships, corporations have aligned themselves with nonbusiness organizations to advance development for a number of years.[24] For example, a company may be interested in building an offshore call center yet realizes roadways and utilities need to be improved in the area. In another situation, a firm may know a natural resource is abundant in a developing country, yet realizes the people and government of the country do not have the economic and educational resources to market it worldwide. In both cases, the company may choose to invest resources by partnering with the local government, nonprofit agencies, and other nongovernmental organizations (NGOs). Critics muse that while this approach certainly has a social component, the business case for profit-making is the overriding concern. An extensive review of the outcomes of development partnerships between large oil companies and local governments in the Nigerian Delta region revealed (1) the linkage between improvement in social infrastructures and economic growth is nonexistent, (2) because these communities have long been neglected, it is almost impossible for business investments to make significant gains, and (3) business-driven investment in social infrastructure has been unevenly distributed and failed to prioritize community needs.[25] Conversely, there are examples of highly successful partnerships.

"Many diverse types of partnerships for development exist; businesses may join with government, multilateral bodies, nongovernmental organizations, local community organizations, charity groups, industry coalitions, or others."

Many diverse types of partnerships for development exist. While the partnership consists of at least one public entity and one private entity, the specific kinds of public and private entities involved vary to include a wide range of social and economic players. Businesses may join with government, multilateral bodies, NGOs, local community organizations, charity groups, industry coalitions, or others. However, each partnership must confront two elements: the level of social control via stakeholder influence they maintain, and the challenges they pose to conventional business management and goals. In light of these two points, partnerships for development may be categorized into four types: conventional business partnerships, corporate social responsibility partnerships, corporate accountability partnerships, and social economy partnerships. Table 12.9 provides a brief description of the four types.

Table 12.9 Four Types of Partnerships for Development

Conventional business partnerships are found in infrastructure sectors and their main focus is on increasing efficiency in the delivery of a certain product or service. Consumers receive the benefits of increased efficiency. Government monitors efficiency gains and ensures access and affordability for vulnerable members of society. Partners benefit from revenue generated. Social responsibility is rarely a consideration. Example: privatization of public utilities.
Corporate social responsibility partnerships provide resources and enhance economic opportunities of partners in a win-win fashion. Agreements are voluntary, business-friendly, and often based on core values and social responsibility. These are also present after fall-out from a scandal. Example: microcredit lending to promote small business development.
Corporate accountability partnerships typically focus on developing rules and transparency around key social issues. They establish a set of requirements and framework for accountability, and utilize third-party review. Example: Fair Labor Association accountability standards and process.
Social economy partnerships are based on a core social mission, not just profit. They provide different types of support, especially to fledging start-ups. Partners benefit from relationships they develop with other social economy partners. Example: Fair trade.

Source: Ananya Mukherjee Reed and Darryl Reed, "Partnerships for Development: Four Models of Business Involvement," *Journal of Business Ethics* 90, supplement 1 (May 2009): 3–37.

Conventional Business Partnerships

Conventional business partnerships (CBPs) for development may seem unlikely. However, in the case of some public services, such as utilities, conventional business partnerships for development do emerge. The goal of conventional business partnerships for development is to promote efficiency in markets where competition does not exist. This assumes that, by nature, states are inefficient and that a business organization provides the best solution. In these partnerships, the role of business is to increase efficiency, while the role of government is to make sure that the benefits of increased efficiency are delivered to consumers. Government also monitors access to and affordability of the public service. CBPs do not have to prove a specific effort toward social responsibility but are commonly recognized and supported by the United Nations, World Bank, and other supraregional organizations. Specifically, these organizations have sought privatization through conventional business partnerships.

Privatization occurs when public operations are sold to private entities. Public-private partnerships count as partial privatization. Full privatization further reduces the public element of the equation. Social services often attract privatization interest, particularly those in developing nations since privatization provides a point of entry into new markets for investors. But long-standing public provision of goods and services carries deeply imbedded interests in keeping the goods and services public.[26]

The World Bank began advocating the privatization of public utilities in the early 1990s, and eventually this became a requirement for some countries seeking substantial loans. While there have been successes, water privatization efforts in Bolivia provide a stark reminder that CBPs may be fraught with difficulty. In 2005, protesters in El Alto, Bolivia, demanded that control of water be taken back from Suez, a French water company affiliated with the World

privatization
occurs when public operations are sold to private entities

Bank who had taken over water service in 1997. In the span of three days, the president of Bolivia met the public's demand and canceled the deal. Only five years earlier, Bolivian citizens protested in Cochabamba against the control of water by the Bechtel Corporation. That protest was much more dramatic and violent, with the government declaring martial law. At this time, however, the reluctance to cancel the foreign control of water service was due to financial and political pressure. To cancel the deal would have made foreign investors hesitant to pursue investment opportunities in Bolivia. But Bolivian citizens were not hesitant to voice their grievances. Bolivians never came to the decision to privatize water. Like other poor nations, Bolivia was forced to privatize in order to receive much-needed aid from the World Bank. While many citizens did not agree with the principle of privatizing water service, their outrage came from the practical results that followed the change in service. Theoretically, privatization would bring investment and successful management to services traditionally run with little efficiency and much corruption. When implemented, however, investment translated to unaffordable, market-rate pricing and successful management translated to indifference to poor social conditions either introduced or exacerbated by privatization.[27] The World Bank eventually softened its position by becoming open to other options besides privatization, but the idea that poor governments need to increase their reliance on private agents for political and economic risks remains.

Corporate Social Responsibility Partnerships

Corporate social responsibility partnerships (CSRPs) are voluntary and business centered, where potential benefits alone compel individual businesses to enter into these partnerships. The success of CSRPs rests in the motivation causing corporate engagement. Such motivation may be philosophical or ethical, though it may be that pragmatic concerns are the major sources of motivation. For example, CSRPs provide resources for social initiatives such as job training and entrepreneurial development that contribute to a citizen's livelihood. While these initiatives benefit members of society, they also provide for a stronger workforce and economic contagion. Micro-credit programs are part of a CSRP's activity in resource provision, with the largest such partnership being the Global Microcredit Summit, a nonprofit organization dedicated to improving access to credit and financial self-sufficiency for the poorest people in the world.[28]

The micro-credit area of development activity began in Bangladesh. The initiative produced remarkable success, so much so that the prominent figures of the endeavor, Grameen Bank and founder Muhammad Yunus, received the Nobel Peace Prize in 2006. Micro-credit works toward moving large populations out of poverty through financial assistance. In late 1970s Bangladesh, Muhammad Yunus began efforts to make loans for unlikely candidates a possibility. His efforts included the establishment of Grameen Bank. In 2002, micro-credit in Bangladesh was made even more widely available through the World Bank's Financial Services for the Poorest. Grameen Bank remains an influential model for micro-credit institutions and partnerships all over the world. While micro-credit allows borrowers, the overwhelming majority of whom are women, to take action that directly improves their income, indirect improvements in quality of life follow. Borrowers have access to better housing, food, sanitation, and education and are better able to take advantage of the improved options.[29]

Corporate Accountability Partnerships

The final two categories of partnerships for development take a distrust of corporate social responsibility models as a starting point for defining their framework. Corporate accountability partnerships (CAPs) spring from the idea that corporate social responsibility partnerships are neither accountable nor effective and are only really interested in public relations. As the name implies, corporate accountability partnerships focus on accountability and the setting of requirements and standards based on what society expects.

For CAPs to be successful, they must gain and direct public support, maximize the limited resources they tend to have, plan for the long-term, and convince public institutions of the necessity and importance of enforcing socially demanded standards. CAPs use legal and social means ranging from policy and certification initiatives to protests and activism. Certification CAPs focus mainly on labor rights and the environment and try to achieve answerability, enforcement, and universality. CAPs seek to achieve corporate recognition of standards deemed appropriate by society and utilize third-party audits and checks on the partnership.

A widely known certification CAP is the Fair Labor Association (FLA), which was organized after numerous media reports decrying child labor, poor working conditions, and low wages. Today, the FLA works to end sweatshop conditions for factory workers and organizes universities, social groups, and socially responsible organizations to protect workers' rights and insist on better working conditions all over the globe. The Russell Corporation is an example of a corporation being held accountable by the FLA. Russell was investigated for its decision to close Jerzees de Honduras, a large manufacturing facility. The company gave business reasons for the closure, but there were persistent allegations that Russell was closing the plant because of organized labor. In January of 2009, the FLA released a report on the closure of Jerzees de Honduras. The FLA report was based on information gathered by three independent investigators and concluded that "inappropriate and unacceptable actions were taken that raise serious questions about Russell Corporation's adherence to freedom of association and the protection of workers' rights." While the report acknowledged that the plant closure was primarily a business decision, the FLA asked for nine remedial steps to be taken by Russell. A few months later, the FLA completed its follow-up report and determined that a detailed

© Morel/EFE/CORBIS

Ela Bhatt, the founder of the Self-Employed Women's Association (SEWA), has won numerous awards for her efforts to end poverty among working women in India

remediation plan was still required. Russell participated in the development of the new remediation plan and agreed to comply.[30]

Social Economy Partnerships

Social economy partnerships (SEPs) pursue alternatives to conventional corporations and profit maximization. SEPs have a distinctly social purpose, use democratic governance, and cooperate with other social economy partnerships. Social economy organizations include nonprofits, community economic-development corporations, cooperatives, and cooperative development organizations.

The SEP philosophy emphasizes cooperation and assistance rather than traditional business logic. One function of these partnerships, to provide resources and support, appears most vividly in informal sectors of the urban poor. In these cases, SEPs bring people together for recycling and street vending, work that many other citizens will not perform. Entrepreneurship is viewed collectively and the group stays connected to social and political movements. SEPs in the informal sectors of the urban poor provide economic profits as well as social benefits that are usually reserved for those with full-time jobs in the formal sector.

> **"Cooperatives are organizations that seek a variety of benefits by approaching economics and entrepreneurship in social terms."**

As another example, the Self Employed Women's Association (SEWA) is a trade union in India for poor, self-employed women. These women compose the majority of the labor force, but are part of the unorganized sector and not provided with the regular salaries and benefits. The SEWA organizes cooperative arrangements to help women find regular employment, increase their incomes, become literate, access better health care, obtain child care, and increase their financial assets. Through various cooperatives, women obtain insurance, get assistance in marketing their goods worldwide, participate in leadership training, and access significant loans and banking products. Without SEWA and its extended partnerships, these women would be destined for a life of poverty.[31]

Development Efforts of Countries

The four models of business involvement in development allow almost any firm the opportunity to engage in partnerships that improve health, education, economic, and other prospects for people around the world. In addition to corporate efforts, individual countries are also engaged in development efforts. The Center for Global Development produces a Commitment to Development Index (CDI) that ranks twenty-two developed nations by their contributions to and support of development in poorer, developing countries. While these contributions are the "right thing to do" and usually reflect national ideals and values, there are also benefits to global security and economic health. Countries included in the

Cooperative Banking

Profit, investors, and distant corporate offices are not the ruling terms of the cooperative, or co-op. Instead of profit, which they often generate, cooperatives are organizations that seek a variety of benefits by approaching economics and entrepreneurship in social terms. Instead of investors, the co-op is developed by members who have one vote a piece in governance matters. The integration of business and social interests is made easier by the democratic governance of the co-op.

Equality in voting also means accountability and transparency are requisite. A co-op may have individual people as members or it may have small business and organization members. While cooperatives can be surprisingly successful financially, the traditional dynamics that motivate and relate owners, consumers, and workers are altered. Employer and employee are no longer binary. Wage-labor is not a satisfactory work life.

The cooperative began to emerge in the beginning of the nineteenth century in Europe. First, owners of a cotton mill in Scotland came together in order to extend the distribution of profits to employees. A few years later, a group of English textile workers called the Rochdale Pioneers established a cooperative in 1844. This cooperative joined together weavers and other artisans who were facing poverty, yet decided they should pool their meager resources to open a store selling food they could no longer afford. They opened their store with a small number of items, but quickly expanded their product range. Before long, the Rochdale Pioneers offered one of the best selections of food and household items in the area and was fully meeting its objective: *to form arrangements for the pecuniary benefit and the improvement of the social and domestic conditions of its members.* The concept spread to a variety of industries and countries.

Rabobank is a group of Dutch banks that has its origins in two rural cooperative banks founded in 1898. In 1972, the two banks merged to form Rabobank. Rabobank is now owned by more than 150 local banks and identified as one of the safest cooperative banks in the world. Rabobank's growth was made possible through the retention of its profits. It is owned and controlled by its members and works for its members. Rabobank has always had a commitment to corporate social responsibility and implements social responsibility in its lending practices. Accordingly, in making credit decisions, Rabobank assesses a company's strategy and track record for handling sensitive issues that call for corporate social responsibility. Rabobank views companies that lack social responsibility as a credit risk and also a risk to the co-op's reputation.

Issues for Rabobank Corporate Social Responsibility Assessment
Corruption
Poor working conditions
Exploitation of employees or benefitting from such exploitation (direct or indirect)
Inadmissible child labor
Discrimination
Environmental pollution
Depletion of scarce natural resources
Cruelty against animals
Violation of rights of indigenous peoples
Products and services involving health or safety risks for consumers

Sources: Kevin M. Blakely, "At Rabobank, It's All About the Customer," *The RMA Journal*, 91, no. 10 (July/August 2000): 36–43, accessed via ProQuest Database; Riccardo Lottie, Peter Mensing, and Davide Valenti, "A Cooperative Solution," *strategy+business* 43 (Summer 2006); Rabobank, "Lending Procedures," http://www.rabobank.com/content/about_us/corporate_social_responsibility/lending_procedures/, accessed August 13, 2009; David Thompson, "Cooperative Principles: Then and Now," http://www.cooperativegrocer.coop/articles/index.php?id=158, accessed August 17, 2009.

NASA

index are assessed based on governmental policy efforts in areas including aid, trade, investment, migration, the environment, security, and technology. Policy efforts are used as indicators partly to control for the varying sizes of economies among the countries ranked. The CDI 2008 ranks countries as follows: The Netherlands, Sweden, Norway, Denmark, Ireland, the United Kingdom, Finland, Australia, Austria, New Zealand, Canada, Spain, Germany, Portugal, Belgium, France, the United States, Switzerland, Greece, Italy, Japan, and South Korea. For the CDI, policies of rich countries, particularly the coherence of those policies, are important to development. The CDI also provides evidence that development involves more than monetary aid and that partnerships can provide greater benefits than individual partners can produce alone.[32]

GLOBAL REPORTING INITIATIVE

Regardless of the social responsibility activities a company pursues, it must also consider the best mechanisms for communicating its values and plans, highlighting successes, and gaining feedback for the future. In some cases, a firm may be a signatory to a set of standards, member of a particular association, or otherwise obligated to formally assess and document social responsibility outcomes. As stated earlier, companies that commit to the Global Compact are required to present an annual account of how they implement the ten principles and support the U.N.'s development goals. This document, entitled the Communication on Progress, may be part of the company's annual report, sustainability report, or some other social reporting mechanism.

"Regardless of the social responsibility activities a company pursues, it must also consider the best mechanisms for communicating its values and plans, highlighting successes, and gaining feedback for the future."

The Global Reporting Initiative (GRI) provides a framework for businesses and other organizations to assess their performance across an array of social responsibility indicators. Some firms use this as a self–audit, but others choose to formally share the audit results with stakeholders. One of the greatest benefits of the GRI is that it makes comparisons possible because it uses a globally applicable and well-vetted framework.

Established through collaboration between several nongovernmental organizations in 1997, the GRI emphasizes consensus and continuous improvement in developing and maintaining the GRI Sustainability Reporting Framework, which seeks to provide transparency and accountability in sustainability reporting akin to that found in financial reporting. Diverse representatives contribute business, civil, academic, labor, and other professional perspectives in deciding which areas of sustainability are to be included in the framework and the appropriate measures to be used for determining performance in those areas. The framework is in perpetual draft form, with innovation in technologies and shifts in cultural attitudes accommodated by the GRI's continuous improvement approach. The third edition, or generation, of the GRI Guidelines was published in 2006.

Courtesy of CartoonStock.com

"You drive a Japanese car, drink French wine, eat Chinese food, own an American computer, buy Canadian lumber and vacation in Mexico. How can you be AGAINST free trade?!"

The GRI Sustainability Reporting Framework includes three categories of core indicators: economic, environmental, and social performance. The economic category examines an organization's interaction with the economic system in which it operates. The economic impact of the organization on stakeholders at large is measured by economic performance, market presence, and indirect economic impact indicators. While the indicators are defined separately, overlap exists.

The environmental category covers an organization's energy use, both direct use by the organization itself and indirect use by those who provide service to the organization, and pollution. The category assumes a link between energy consumption and emissions that contribute to climate change, and thus emphasizes efficient energy use and an increasing reliance on renewable energy sources over fossil fuel.

The society category examines the organization as it functions in relation to market structures and social institutions. Measures include the impact on local communities, bribery and corruption, and public policy making. The social category of core indicators is further divided into labor practice, human rights, product responsibility, and society. Quantitative or qualitative performance indicators are used to evaluate different aspects of each category.

Table 12.10 provides a sample of indicators for each category of the GRI framework. The human rights indicators consider the operation of an organization as it provides for basic human rights. Measures in this category observe incidents regarding human rights and provisions made for human rights in an organization's internal and external business relationships. The labor practices category is an extension of the human rights category that focuses specifically on the environment and practices to which workers are subject. Measures for this category examine workforce demographics, communications between the organization and its employees, and opportunities extended to workers for personal development. Finally, the product responsibility category focuses on the products of an organization as they affect

Table 12.10 Examples of GRI Performance Indicators

Category	Performance Indicators
Economic	Direct economic value generated and distributed, including revenues, operating costs, employee compensation, donations, retained earnings, and payments to capital providers and governments.
	Procedures for local hiring and proportion of senior management hired from the local community at significant locations of operation.
	Development and impact of infrastructure investments and services provided primarily for public benefit through commercial, in-kind, or pro bono engagement.
Human Rights	Percentage of significant suppliers and contractors that have undergone screening on human rights and actions taken.
	Total number of incidents of discrimination and actions taken.
	Operations identified in which the right to exercise freedom of association and collective bargaining may be at significant risk, and actions taken to support these rights.
	Operations identified as having significant risk for incidents of child labor, and measures taken to contribute to the elimination of child labor.
	Operations identified as having significant risk for incidents of forced or compulsory labor, and measures taken to contribute to the elimination of forced or compulsory labor.
	Percentage of security personnel trained in the organization's policies or procedures concerning aspects of human rights that are relevant to operations.
	Total number of incidents of violations involving rights of indigenous people and actions taken.
Labor Practices	Benefits provided to full-time employees that are not provided to temporary or part-time employees, by major operations.
	Percentage of employees covered by collective bargaining agreements.
	Rates of injury, occupational diseases, lost days, and absenteeism, and total number of work-related fatalities by region.
	Percentage of employees receiving regular performance and career development reviews.
	Composition of governance bodies and breakdown of employees per category according to gender, age group, minority group membership, and other indicators of diversity.
Environment	Percentage of materials used that are recycled input materials.
	Initiatives to provide energy-efficient or renewable energy-based products and services, and reductions in energy requirements as a result of these initiatives.
	Percentage and total volume of water recycled and reused.
	Description of significant impacts of activities, products, and services on biodiversity in protected areas and areas of high biodiversity value outside protected areas.
	Initiatives to reduce greenhouse gas emissions and reductions achieved.
	Percentage of products sold and their packaging materials that are reclaimed by category.

	Monetary value of significant fines and total number of nonmonetary sanctions for noncompliance with environmental laws and regulations.
	Significant environmental impacts of transporting products and other goods and materials used for the organization's operations, and transporting members of the workforce.
	Total environmental protection expenditures and investments by type.
Product Responsibility	Total number of incidents of noncompliance with regulations and voluntary codes concerning health and safety impacts of products and services, by type of outcomes.
	Practices related to customer satisfaction, including results of surveys measuring customer satisfaction.
	Total number of incidents of noncompliance with regulations and voluntary codes concerning marketing communications, including advertising, promotions, and sponsorship, by type of outcomes.
	Total number of substantiated complaints regarding breaches of customer privacy and losses of customer data.
	Monetary value of significant fines for noncompliance with laws and regulations concerning the provision and use of products and services.
Society	Nature, scope, and effectiveness of any programs and practices that assess and manage the impacts of operations on communities, including entering, operating, and exiting.
	Actions taken in response to incidents of corruption.
	Public policy positions and participation in public policy development and lobbying.
	Total number of legal actions for anticompetitive behavior, antitrust, and monopoly practices and their outcomes.
	Monetary value of significant fines and total number of nonmonetary sanctions for noncompliance with laws and regulations.

Source: GRI, "G3 Indicator Protocols," http://www.globalreporting.org/ReportingFramework/ReportingFrameworkDownloads/, accessed August 8, 2009.

consumers. Measures consider safety, product information, and privacy rights of customers. Indicators appear in pairs with one addressing the relevant processes of the organization and the second addressing the compliance of the organization.

In the first decade of the twenty-first century, thousands of reports were delivered to the GRI, with each company offering a self-rating in terms of how well it adhered to guidelines and indicator protocols in the previous year. MTR, a Hong Kong-based railways corporation, was recognized for its outstanding adherence to GRI standards in its ninth annual sustainability report. Several components of the MTR 2008 report illustrated the company's social responsibility efforts, including a timeline of its activities and a self-assessment of the firm's annual progress on meeting social responsibility, sustainability, and stakeholder goals. MTR's "maturity matrix" is shown in Figure 12.6. Each item in the matrix is scored from 1 (lowest) to 4 (highest), which means that by 2008, MTR was demonstrating excellent progress on its vision for strategic social responsibility.

Figure 12.6 MTR's Maturity Matrix

Maturity Matrix
Performance under BS 8900:2006 Guidance for Managing Sustainable Development

Principles	Practices	2004	2005	2006	2007	2008
Inclusivity	Stakeholder engagement	3	3.5	3.6	3.7	3.5
Integrity	Key drivers	3	3.5	3.5	3.6	3.6
	Leadership, vision, and governance	3.5	4	4	4	4
	Managing risk	3.2	3.5	3.6	3.8	3.8
Stewardship	Sustainability development culture	3.4	3.5	3.5	3.5	3.2
	Building capability	3	3	3.2	3	3.3
	Key management issues	3	3.5	3.5	3.6	3.6
	Environmental assessment	3.5	3.8	3.8	6.8	4
Transparency	Review	3.5	3.8	4	4	4
	Reporting	3.5	3.8	6.8	4	3.8

Source: MTR Corporation, "2008 Sustainability Report: Engagement," http://www.mtr.com.hk/eng/sustainability/2008rpt/
MTRSustainabilityReport2008.pdf, accessed August 9, 2009.

GRI has also noted the exemplary effort of Banarra, an Australian-based firm providing consulting and assurance services in the area of sustainability. The company centers its advice on results obtained from a proprietary assessment protocol, named the Banarra Assurance Methodology (BAM), which utilizes survey instruments and more traditional audit tools. In keeping with its consulting approach, Banarra recently solicited employee feedback on the quality of its management practices. More than 300 organizations across Australia participated in the survey, so it was useful for comparative purposes. The results were discussed in Banarra's most recent report to the GRI and are located in Figure 12.7. It is important to note that in keeping with the true spirit of self-assessment, Banarra reported results that reflected both strengths and weaknesses in management practices. For example, employees were very pleased with management's ethical standards, social and environmental responsibility, and innovation. In contrast, employees noted areas for improvement, including role clarity, well-being, and competitive position.

SUMMARY

In this chapter, we discussed a variety of social responsibility issues and stakeholders from a global perspective. The expanding global marketplace requires that executives and managers develop the ability to conduct business effectively and socially responsibly in different regions of the world. The movement of people across cities and continents means that ideas, values, traditions, languages, and customs have also migrated and that global employees need many

Figure 12.7 Results of Employee Survey at Banarra

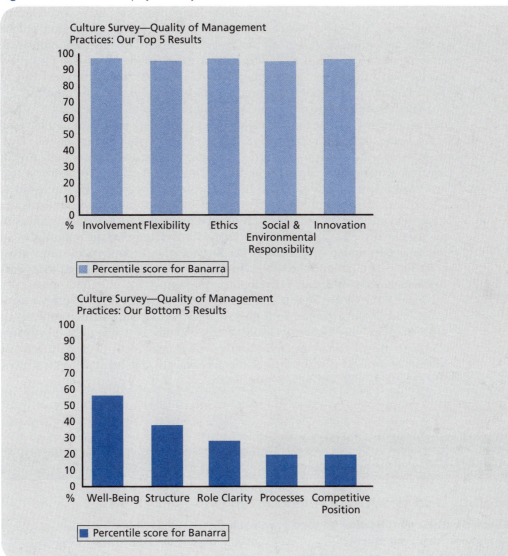

Source: Banarra Corporation, "The Banarra Sustainability Report," http://www.banarra.com/pdfs/Banarra%20Sustainability%20Report%20 2007.pdf, accessed August 9, 2009.

skills. Cultural intelligence is the ability to interpret and adapt successfully to different national, organizational, and professional cultures. The development and use of cultural intelligence involves three components: cognitive, motivational, and behavioral. Cultural intelligence is desired of all employees, but is mandatory for those who work in different countries, manage diverse groups, and have responsibilities that require them to interpret unfamiliar behaviors and situations.

Cultural intelligence is critical for dealing effectively with stakeholders, including customers, investors and shareholders, employees, suppliers, governments, communities, and others. Stakeholders in other countries and cultures bring unique insights and attitudes to bear on the business relationship, including differences in economic, legal, ethical, and philanthropic expectations. We delved into a few trends related to stakeholders in the global economy, including the Caux Round Table Principles for Business, fair trade, employee engagement, and others.

The reflexive nature of the global economy means that the success of a particular company is a function of many factors, including the extent to which the firm's home country is comprised of trust-based institutions. Some nations have well-developed systems for ensuring economic, legal, and ethical standards in business activities. We explored the concept of responsible competitiveness and its effects on a national economy. In other cases, corporations are interested in a particular market, but know that fundamental institutions and standards are sorely underdeveloped and negatively affect market potential. The four models of business involvement in development allow almost any firm the opportunity to engage in partnerships that improve health, education, economic, and other prospects for people around the world. In addition to corporate efforts, individual countries are also engaged in development efforts.

Finally, the Global Reporting Initiative (GRI) provides a framework for businesses and other organizations to assess their performance across an array of social responsibility indicators. Some firms use this as a self-audit, but others choose to formally share the audit results with stakeholders. One of the greatest benefits of the GRI is that it makes comparisons possible because it uses a globally applicable and well-vetted framework.

RESPONSIBLE BUSINESS DEBATE

Technology and the Africa Rice Center

ISSUE: Should genetic modification be used to further economic development?

In Africa, the rice industry is represented by the Africa Rice Center, formerly known as West Africa Rice Development Association (WARDA). The mission of the center is to contribute to poverty alleviation and food security in Africa through research, development, and partnership activities aimed at increasing the productivity and profitability of the rice sector in ways that ensure the sustainability of the farming environment. The association started in 1970 and now boasts twenty-two African nations as members and partners, along with many international organizations, including the United Nations, European Commission, and the World Health Organization.

In carrying out its mission, the center recognizes three key barriers: (1) low productivity and sustainability of rice, (2) poor quality of the marketed product, and (3) unfavorable market and policy environment. To overcome these issues, the center has established a strategic plan, including the use of research and development protocols to bridge genetic diversity and produce new variations of rice and disease-resistant crops. The center's current technologies allow for the introduction of NERICA (New Rice for Africa) rice varieties.

NERICA was created by crossing *O. glaberrima* and *O. sativa*, two species of rice that demonstrate different strengths and weaknesses when grown in Africa. Rice farmers had long hoped to combine the best traits of the two species, but efforts had been fruitless. In the early 1990s, WARDA breeders turned to biotechnology in an attempt to overcome the infertility problem. Because the different species do not naturally interbreed, a technique called embryo-rescue was used to ensure that crosses between the two varieties would survive and grow to maturity. By 2000, more than 20,000 farmers were growing NERICA varieties in Africa.

To many, NERICA is central to solving Africa's severe poverty and nutrition problems. To others, NERICA is the latest attempt by government and business to promote a solution that is not fully tested. Critics claim that NERICA requires more fertilizer and care and fails to adapt well to the soil and techniques that small farmers have used for generations. While proponents tout the modern revolution in rice, others are waiting for the empirical evidence that NERICA is good for development.

There Are Two Sides to Every Issue:

1. Defend the belief that NERICA is an appropriate use of biotechnology and genetic modification. What are the benefits of these techniques?
2. Defend the belief that scientists should not be using genetic modification to create new species of any food, including NERICA. What are the risks associated with these techniques?

Sources: Africa Rice Center, "About Us," http://www.warda.org/warda/aboutus.asp, accessed August 17, 2009; "Nerica: Another Trap for Small Farmers in Africa," http://www.grain.org/briefings/?id=215, accessed August 15, 2009; West Africa Rice Development Association, "NERICA: Rice for Life," http://www.warda.cgiar.org/publications/NERICA8.pdf, accessed August 16, 2009.

KEY TERMS

cultural intelligence (p. 444)
employee engagement (p. 452)
fair trade (p. 455)

responsible competitiveness (p. 458)
development (p. 461)
privatization (p. 465)

DISCUSSION QUESTIONS

1. Define *cultural intelligence* in your own terms. Compare your definition with the definition used in this chapter.

2. How are stakeholder relationships in a global context different from those in a domestic context? In what ways are they alike?

3. What is the likelihood that corporate leaders can agree on a global set of social responsibility standards? What evidence do you have?

4. How can organizations create stronger engagement with employees? What would be the effects on social responsibility? How would social responsibility affect engagement?

5. Define *fair trade* in your own terms. In what ways should consumers consider fair trade issues when making purchases and investments?

6. What is *national competitiveness*? Describe the ways in which the three drivers of the Responsibility Competitiveness Index (RCI) affect business and vice versa.

7. Review the Millennium Development Goals in Table 12.8. In what ways are these goals and issues related to a successful global economy? What benefits and/or challenges do they present to multinational corporations?

8. Review the Global Reporting Initiative performance indicators in Table 12.10. How would a company measure its progress in these areas? Propose both quantitative and qualitative measures.

EXPERIENTIAL EXERCISE

Choose two multinational companies, each based in a different home country, and visit their respective websites. Peruse these sites for information that is directed at three company stakeholders: employees, customers, and the community. Make a list of the types of information that are on the site and indicate how the information might be used and perceived by these three stakeholder groups. What differences and similarities did you find between the two companies? How are the differences attributable to cultural nuances?

WHAT WOULD YOU DO?

Jaime and Catherine looked at each other. Each was thinking, "How do we do this?" Neither offered any immediate suggestions. Both were mid-level executives with a multinational corporation that manufactured clothing, handbags, and accessories in developing countries, including Guatemala and Honduras. The company is a member of the Fair Labor Association and takes pride in its commitment to a safe, healthy, and equitable work environment for all employees. Jaime, a native of Mexico, had professional experience in Peru, Chile, and Mexico. Catherine, a native of the United States, spoke fluent Spanish and was being groomed to take international assignments. Two weeks ago, the Vice President of Latin American Operations called Jaime and Catherine, asking them to take on an internal consulting project.

The vice president was concerned about rumors surrounding the company's largest manufacturing site in Honduras. This site employs more than 1,000 people, the majority of whom work in low-skilled manufacturing roles. Although no employee has come forward, or used the firm's ethics hotline, the site's regional manager (RM) has been concerned about management practices and workplace conditions. Each time the RM visited the site, he sensed that he was not experiencing the daily "reality" of the manufacturing site. So far, he has had little proof but has decided to share his concerns with other executives. Specifically, he has been worried about (1) possible intimidation of union members and leaders, (2) discriminatory management tactics, and (3) forced overtime that is not properly compensated.

Two weeks later, Jaime and Catherine arrive at the site, tasked with determining whether management practices and workplace conditions are compatible with corporate standards and FLA principles. First, they need to develop a plan for gathering information from employees, including those who are either scared of retaliation or generally mistrusting of corporate management. What would you do?

Monsanto Attempts to Balance Stakeholder Interests

Think Monsanto, and you probably do not think about small farms. Rather, the phrase *genetically modified* likely comes to mind. The Monsanto Company is the world's largest seed company, with sales of over $8.6 billion. It specializes in biotechnology, or the genetic manipulation of organisms. Monsanto scientists have spent the last few decades modifying crops, often by inserting new genes or adapting existing genes within plant seeds, to better meet certain aims such as higher yield or insect resistance. Monsanto produces plants that can survive weeks of drought, ward off weeds, and kill invasive insects. Monsanto's genetically modified (GM) seeds have increased the quantity and availability of crops, helping farmers worldwide increase food production and revenues.

Today, 90 percent of the world's GM seeds are sold by Monsanto or by companies that use Monsanto genes. Monsanto also holds 70–100 percent market share on certain crops. Yet Monsanto has met with its share of criticism from sources as diverse as governments, farmers, activists, and advocacy groups. Monsanto supporters say it is creating solutions to world hunger by generating higher crop yields and hardier plants. Critics accuse the multinational giant of trying to take over the world's food supply, and destroying biodiversity. Since biotechnology is relatively new, they also express concerns about the possibility of negative health and environmental effects from biotech food. However, such criticisms have not deterred Monsanto from becoming one of the world's most successful companies.

The following analysis first looks at the history of Monsanto as it progressed from a chemical company to an organization focused on biotechnology, and then examines Monsanto's current focus on developing genetically modified seeds, including stakeholder concerns regarding the safety and environmental effects of these seeds. The controversy surrounding the drug Posilac is also examined. Next, some ethical concerns, including organizational misconduct and patent issues, are discussed. The analysis also looks at some of Monsanto's corporate responsibility initiatives. It concludes by examining the challenges and opportunities Monsanto may face in the future.

HISTORY: FROM CHEMICALS TO FOOD

The original Monsanto was very different from the current company. It was started by John F. Queeny in 1901 in St. Louis and was named after his wife, Olga Monsanto Queeny. The company started making artificial food additives. Its first product was the artificial sweetener saccharine, which it sold to Coca-Cola. Monsanto followed by selling Coca-Cola caffeine extract and vanillin, an artificial vanilla flavoring. At the start of WWI, company leaders realized the growth opportunities in the industrial chemicals industry and renamed the company The Monsanto Chemical Company. The company began specializing in plastics,

Jennifer Sawayda, under the direction of O.C. Ferrell and Jennifer Jackson, prepared this case for classroom discussion, rather than to illustrate either effective or ineffective handling of an administrative, ethical, or legal decision by management. All sources used for this case were obtained through publicly available material.

its own agricultural chemicals, and synthetic rubbers.

Due to its expanding product lines, Monsanto was renamed again the Monsanto Company in 1964. By this time, Monsanto was producing such diverse products as petroleum, fibers, and packaging. A couple years later, Monsanto created its first Roundup herbicide, a successful product that would propel the company even more into the public's consciousness.

However, during the 1970s, Monsanto hit a major legal snare. The company had produced a chemical known as Agent Orange that was used during the Vietnam War to quickly deforest the thick Vietnamese jungles. Agent Orange contained dioxin, a chemical that caused a legal nightmare for Monsanto. Dioxin was found to be extremely carcinogenic, and in 1979, a lawsuit was filed against Monsanto on behalf of hundreds of veterans who claimed they were harmed by the chemical. Monsanto and several other manufacturers agreed to settle for $180 million. The repercussions of dioxin would continue to plague the company for decades.

In 1981, Monsanto leaders determined that biotechnology would be the company's new strategic focus. The quest for biotechnology was on, and in 1994 Monsanto introduced the first biotechnology product to win regulatory approval. Soon the company was selling soybean, cotton, and canola seeds that were engineered to be tolerant to Monsanto's Roundup Ready herbicide. Many other herbicides killed the good plants as well as the bad ones. Roundup Ready seeds allowed farmers to use the herbicide to eliminate weeds while sparing the crop.

In 1997, Monsanto spun off its chemical business as Solutia, and in 2000 the company entered into a merger and changed its name to the Pharmacia Corporation. Two years later, a new Monsanto, focused entirely on agriculture, broke off from Pharmacia, and the companies became two separate legal entities. The company before 2000 is often referred to as "old Monsanto," while today's company is known as "new Monsanto."

The emergence of new Monsanto was tainted by some disturbing news about the company's conduct. It was revealed that Monsanto had been covering up decades of environmental pollution. For nearly forty years, the Monsanto Company had released toxic waste into a creek in an Alabama town called Anniston. It had also disposed of polychlorinated biphenyls (PCBs), a highly toxic chemical, in open-pit landfills in the area. The results were catastrophic. Fish from the creek were deformed, and the population had elevated PCB levels that astounded environmental health experts. A paper trail showed that Monsanto leaders had known about the pollution since the 1960s, but had not stopped production. Once the cover-up was discovered, thousands of plaintiffs from the city filed a lawsuit against the company. In 2003, Monsanto and Solutia agreed to pay a settlement of $700 million to more than 20,000 Anniston residents. However, no amount of money will give people back their health or the health of their environment.

When current CEO Hugh Grant took over in 2003, scandals and stakeholder uncertainty over Monsanto's GM products had tarnished the company's reputation. The price of Monsanto's stock had fallen by almost 50 percent, down to $8 a share. The company had lost $1.7 billion the previous year. Grant knew the company was fragile; yet through a strategic focus on GM foods, the company has recovered and is now prospering.

In spite of their controversial nature, GM foods have become popular both in developed and developing countries. Monsanto became so successful with its GM seeds that it acquired Seminis, Inc., a leader in the fruit and vegetable seed industry. The acquisition transformed Monsanto into a global leader in the seed industry. Today, Monsanto employs nearly 20,000 people in 160 countries. It has been recognized as the top employer in Argentina, Mexico, India, and, for eight times in a row, Brazil.

THE SEEDS OF CHANGE: MONSANTO'S EMPHASIS ON BIOTECHNOLOGY

While the original Monsanto made a name for itself through the manufacturing of chemicals, new Monsanto took quite a different turn. It switched its emphasis from chemicals to food. Today's Monsanto owes its $8.6 billion in sales to biotechnology, specifically to its sales of genetically modified (GM) plant seeds. These seeds have revolutionized the agriculture industry.

Throughout history, weeds, insects, and drought have been the bane of the farmer's existence. In the past century, herbicides and pesticides were invented to ward off pests. Yet applying these chemicals to an entire crop was both costly and time-consuming. Then Monsanto scientists, through their work in biotechnology, were able to implant seeds with genes that make the plants themselves kill bugs. They also created seeds containing the herbicide Roundup Ready, an herbicide that kills weeds but spares the crops.

The broad introduction of these GM seeds in the 1990s unleashed a stream of criticism. Monsanto was nicknamed "Mutanto," and GM produce was called "Frankenfood." Critics believed that influencing the gene pools of plants we eat could result in negative health consequences, a fear that remains to this day. Others worried about the health effects on beneficial insects and plants. Could pollinating GM plants have an effect on nearby insects and non-GM plants? CEO Hugh Grant decided to curtail the tide of criticism by focusing biotechnology on products that would not be directly placed on the dinner plate, but instead on seeds that produce goods like animal feed and corn syrup. In this way, Grant was able to reduce some of the opposition. Today, the company invests largely in four crops: corn, cotton, soybeans, and canola.

Thus far, the dire predictions of critics have not occurred. Monsanto owes approximately 60 percent of its revenue to its work in GM seeds, and today, more than half of U.S. crops, including most soybeans and 70 percent of corn, are genetically modified. Approximately 282 million acres worldwide are now devoted to biotech crops, and the fastest growth is in developing countries. However, critics are wary that long-term effects still might be discovered.

Farmers who purchase GM seeds can now grow more crops on less land and with less left to chance. GM crops have saved farmers billions by preventing loss and increasing crop yields. For example, in 1970 the average corn harvest yielded approximately 70 bushels an acre. With the introduction of biotech crops, the average corn harvest has increased to roughly 150 bushels an acre. Monsanto predicts even higher yields in the future, possibly up to 300 bushels an acre by 2030. "As agricultural productivity increases, farmers are able to produce more food, feed, fuel, and fiber on the same amount of land, helping to ensure that agriculture can meet humanity's needs in the future," said Monsanto CEO Hugh Grant concerning Monsanto technology.

As a result of higher yields, the revenues of farmers in developing countries have increased dramatically. According to company statistics, the cotton yield of Indian farmers rose by 50 percent, doubling their income in one year. Additionally, the company claims that its insect-protected corn has raised the income level in the Philippines to above poverty level. Critics argue that these numbers are inflated; they say the cost of GM seeds is dramatically higher than that of traditional seeds, and therefore they actually reduce farmers' take-home profits.

Monsanto's GM seeds have not been accepted everywhere. Attempts to introduce them into Europe have been met with extreme consumer backlash. Consumers have gone so far as to destroy fields of GM crops and arrange sit-ins. Greenpeace has fought Monsanto for years, especially in the company's efforts to promote GM crops in developing countries.

This animosity toward Monsanto's products is generated by two main concerns: worries about the safety of GM food, and concerns about the environmental effects.

Concerns About the Safety of GM Food

Of great concern for many stakeholders are the moral and safety implications of GM food. Many skeptics see biotech crops as unnatural, with the Monsanto scientist essentially "playing God" by controlling what goes into the seed. Also, because GM crops are relatively new, critics maintain that the health implications of biotech food may not be known for years to come.

They also contend that effective standards have not been created to determine the safety of biotech crops. Some geneticists believe the splicing of these genes into seeds could create small changes that might negatively impact the health of humans and animals that eat them. Also, even though the FDA has declared biotech crops safe, critics say they have not been around long enough to gauge their long-term effects.

One major health concern is the allergenicity of GM products. Critics fear that a lack of appropriate regulation could allow allergens to creep into the products. Another concern is toxicity, particularly considering that many Monsanto seeds are equipped with a gene to allow them to produce their own Roundup Ready herbicide. Could ingesting this herbicide, even in small amounts, cause detrimental effects on consumers? Some stakeholders say yes, and point to statistics on glyphosate, Roundup's chief ingredient, for support. According to an ecology center fact sheet, glyphosate exposure is the third most commonly reported illness among California agriculture workers, and glyphosate residues can last for a year. Yet the EPA lists glyphosate as having a low skin and oral toxicity, and a study from the New York Medical College states that Roundup does not create a health risk for humans.

Despite consumer concerns, the FDA has proclaimed that GM food is safe to consume. As a result, it also has determined that Americans do not need to know when they are consuming GM products. Thus, this information is not placed on labels in the United States, although other countries, most notably Great Britain and the European Union, do require GM food products to state this fact in their labeling.

Bovine Growth Hormone Concerns

Monsanto has also come under scrutiny for its synthetic hormone Posilac, the brand name of a Monsanto drug that contains recombinant bovine growth hormone (rBST). This hormone is a supplement to the naturally occurring hormone BST in cows. Posilac causes cows to produce more milk, a boon to dairy farmers but a cause of concern to many stakeholders who fear that Posilac may cause health problems in cows and in the humans who drink their milk. After numerous tests, the FDA has found that milk from Posilac-treated cows is no different in terms of safety than milk from rBST-free cows. Yet these assurances have done little to alleviate stakeholder fears, especially since some studies maintain that rBST increases health problems in cows.

Public outcry from concerned consumers has become so loud that many grocery stores and restaurants have stopped purchasing rBST-treated milk. Starbucks, Kroger, Ben & Jerry's, and even Wal-Mart have responded to consumer demand by only using or selling rBST-free milk, which has put a damper on Monsanto's Posilac profits.

In the past few years, certain groups, including Monsanto, have fought back against the popularity of rBST-free milk. They maintain that consumers are being misled by implications that rBST-free milk is safer than rBST-treated milk. The grassroots organization AFACT, short for American Farmers for the Advancement and Conservation of Technology, has pressured the government to pass laws forbidding the use of labels that state that milk is free of rBST. Their efforts have been met with some support from legislators. In 2006, Pennsylvania senator and agriculture secretary Dennis Wolff tried to ban milk that was labeled as rBST-free, but stakeholder outrage prevented the law from being enforced. Instead, tighter restrictions on labels have been initiated. All rBST-free milk must now contain the following FDA claim: "No significant difference has been shown between milk derived from rBST-treated and non-rBST-treated cows."

Although Monsanto denies influencing AFACT in any way, many have accused the company of secretly governing the organization. Lori Hoag, spokeswoman for the dairy unit of Monsanto, admitted that the company did provide funds to AFACT, but says that the company has nothing to do with the governing decisions AFACT makes. In fact, on its website, Monsanto stresses that it has no problem with milk labels listed as rBST-free as long as the label contains the claim of the FDA. However, critics are still accusing Monsanto of being behind AFACT in what they say is an attempt to curtail the unpopularity of Posilac.

Concerns About Environmental Effects of Monsanto Products

Studies have supported the premise that Roundup herbicide, which is used in conjunction with the hearty GMO seeds called Roundup Ready, can be harmful to birds, insects, and particularly amphibians. Such studies have revealed that small concentrations of Roundup may be deadly to tadpoles, which is a major concern, as frog and toad species are rapidly disappearing around the globe. A test using Roundup, performed by University of Pittsburgh assistant professor of biological sciences Rick Relyea and his doctoral students, killed 71 percent of tadpoles in outdoor tanks at one-third the maximum concentrations found in nature. Relyea also maintains that soil does not lessen the herbicide's negative effects. Roundup was never approved for water use; however, Relyea and others fear

that water runoff may carry Roundup into water sources.

Another concern with GM seeds in general is the threat of environmental contamination. Bumblebees, insects, and wind can carry a crop's seeds to other areas, sometimes to fields containing non-GM crops. These seeds and pollens might then mix in with the farmer's crops. In the past, organic farmers have complained that genetically modified seeds from nearby farms have "contaminated" their crops. This environmental contamination could pose a serious threat. Some scientists fear that GM seeds that are spread to native plants may cause those plants to adopt the GM trait, thus creating new genetic variations of those plants that could negatively influence (through genetic advantages) the surrounding ecosystem. Andrew Kimbrell, director of the Centre for Technology Assessment in Washington, predicts that "biological pollution will be the environmental nightmare of the twenty-first century."

Monsanto has not been silent on these issues and has acted to address some of these concerns. The company maintains that the environmental impact of everything it creates has been studied by the EPA and approved. Monsanto officials claim that glyphosate in Roundup Ready does not usually end up in ground water, and cites a study which revealed that less than 1 percent of glyphosate contaminates ground water through runoff. The company also claims that when it does contaminate ground water, it is soluble and will not have much effect on aquatic species. This conflicts with Relyea's study, leaving stakeholders unsure about what to believe.

Crop Resistance to Pesticides and Herbicides Another environmental problem that has emerged is the possibility of weed and insect resistance to the herbicides and pesticides on Monsanto crops. Critics fear that continual use of the chemicals could result in "super weeds" and "super bugs," much like overuse of antibiotics in humans has resulted in drug-resistant bacteria. The company's Roundup Ready line, in particular, has come under attack. Monsanto points out, and rightly so, that Roundup herbicide has been used for thirty years, largely without resistance issues. However, GMO plants labeled Roundup Ready are genetically engineered to withstand large doses of the herbicide Roundup. As Roundup is being used more frequently and exclusively because of the Roundup Ready plants' tolerance, even weeds have started developing a resistance to this popular herbicide. As early as 2003, significant numbers of Roundup resistant weeds had been found in the United States and Australia.

To combat "super bugs," the government requires farmers using Monsanto's GMO products to create "refuges," in which they plant 20 percent of their fields with a non-genetically modified crop. The theory is that this allows nonresistant bugs to mate with those that are resistant, preventing a new race of super bugs. To prevent resistance to the Roundup herbicide, farmers are supposed to vary herbicide use and practice crop rotations. However, since Roundup is so easy to use, particularly in conjunction with Roundup Ready seeds, many farmers do not take the time to institute these preventative measures. When they do rotate their crops, some will rotate one Roundup Ready crop with another type of Roundup Ready crop, which does little to solve the problem. This is of particular concern in Latin America, Africa, and Asia where farmers may not be as informed of the risks of herbicide and pesticide overuse.

Monsanto has taken action to deter weed herbicide resistance. In 2009, the company agreed to offer rebates, up to $12/acre, to farmers in thirteen states who use combinations of herbicides on their crops. Monsanto is offering rebates on six of the products, only one of which is a Monsanto product. The company is taking a proactive stance to show that it cares about preventing resistance; however, this does little to stem what might become a global problem.

DEALING WITH ORGANIZATIONAL ETHICAL ISSUES

In addition to concerns over the safety of GM seeds and environmental issues, Monsanto has had to deal with concerns about organizational conduct. Organizations face significant risks from strategies and also from employees striving for high performance standards. Such pressure sometimes encourages employees to engage in illegal or unethical conduct. All firms have these concerns, and in the case of Monsanto, bribes and patents have resulted in legal, ethical, and reputational consequences.

Bribery Issues

Bribery presents a dilemma to multinational corporations because different countries have different perspectives on it. While it is illegal in the United States, other countries allow it. Monsanto faced such a problem with Indonesia, and its actions resulted in the company being fined a large sum.

In 2002, a senior manager at Monsanto instructed an Indonesian consulting firm to pay a bribe of $50,000 to a high-level official in the country's environment ministry. The bribe apparently was for the company to disguise an invoice, which showed that Monsanto was facing opposition from farmers and activists in regard to the introduction of GM cotton in Indonesia.

It was later revealed that such bribery was not an isolated event; the company had paid off many officials between 1997 and 2002. Monsanto first became aware of the problem after discovering some irregularities at their Indonesian subsidiary in 2001. As a result, the company launched an internal investigation and reported the bribery to the U.S. Department of Justice and the Securities and Exchange Commission (SEC).

Monsanto accepted full responsibility for its employees' behavior and agreed to pay $1 million to the Department of Justice and

$500,000 to the SEC. It also agreed to three years of close monitoring of its activities by American authorities. The incident showed that although Monsanto has not been immune to scandals, it has been willing to work with authorities to correct them.

Patent Issues

Like most businesses, Monsanto wants to patent its products. A problem arises, however, when it comes to patenting seeds. As bioengineered creations of the Monsanto Company, Monsanto's seeds are protected under patent law. Under the terms of the patent, farmers using Monsanto seeds are not allowed to harvest seeds from the plants for use in upcoming seasons. Instead, they must purchase new Monsanto seeds each season. By issuing new seeds each year, Monsanto ensures it will secure a profit as well as maintain control over its property.

Unfortunately, this is a new concept for most farmers. Throughout agricultural history, farmers have collected and saved seeds from previous harvests to plant the following year's crops. Critics argue that requiring farmers to suddenly purchase new seeds year after year puts an undue financial burden on them and allows Monsanto too much power. However, the law protects Monsanto's right to have exclusive control over its creations, and farmers must abide by these laws. When they are found guilty of using Monsanto seeds from previous seasons, either deliberately or out of ignorance, they are often fined.

Since it is fairly easy for farmers to violate the patent, Monsanto has found it necessary to employ investigators from law firms to investigate suspected violations. The resulting investigations are a source of contention between Monsanto and accused farmers. According to Monsanto, investigators approach the farmers suspected of patent infringement and ask them some questions. The investigators must practice transparency with the farmers and tell them why they are there and who they represent. If after the initial interview is completed, suspicions still exist, the investigators may pull the farmer's records (after assuring the farmer they will do so in a respectful manner). Sometimes they bring in a sampling team, with the farmer's permission, to test the farmer's fields. If found guilty, the farmer often has to pay Monsanto. According to Monsanto, in the past ten years, it has only filed suit against farmers 120 times, and only eight of these suits have proceeded to trial. Each time the ruling was in Monsanto's favor.

Some farmers, on the other hand, tell a different story about Monsanto and its seed investigators, calling the investigators the "seed police" and even referring to them with such harsh words as "Gestapo" or "mafia." One controversial suit was a case involving storeowner Gary Rinehart from Missouri. As Rinehart relates it, a Monsanto seed investigator entered his store and accused him of saving seeds from previous seasons. The investigator then threatened him with a suit if he did not settle. The company filed suit but eventually found it had the wrong man. Monsanto dropped the suit against him but never apologized. Rinehart also claims the investigators were inspecting other farmers in the area. Other complaints against investigators include similar acts of intimidation, with some farmers even going so far as to accuse investigators of following them and secretly videotaping them.

Such accusations are disturbing, but Monsanto has countered them with its own stories. It claims that Rinehart refused to cooperate and became irate, finally throwing the investigators out of his store. Monsanto filed suit, but eventually found that it was Rinehart's nephew who was transporting the saved seed. The company dropped the suit against Rinehart, and the nephew eventually agreed to settle. According to their website, the nephew still has not paid the settlement.

In order to prevent so many instances of patent infringement, some have suggested that Monsanto make use of GURT, or gene use restriction technology. This technology would let Monsanto create "sterile" seeds. Dubbed by stakeholders as "Terminator seeds," these seeds have several risks and have spurred much controversy among the public, including a concern that these sterile seeds might somehow get transported to other plants, which could create sterile plants that would reduce genetic diversity. In 1999, Monsanto pledged not to commercialize sterile seed technology in food crops. The company has promised that it will only do so in the future after consulting with experts, stakeholders, and relevant NGOs.

CORPORATE RESPONSIBILITY AT MONSANTO

It is a common expectation today for multinational companies to take actions to advance the interests and well-being of the people in the countries in which they do business. Monsanto is no exception. The company has given millions of dollars in programs to help improve the communities in developing countries. In fact, *Corporate Responsibility Magazine* ranked Monsanto number 20 on its 100 Best Corporate Citizens list of 2009, a jump from number 88 the previous year.

In addition, as an agricultural company, Monsanto must address the grim reality facing the world in the future: The world's population is increasing at a fast rate, and the amount of available land and water for agriculture is decreasing. Some experts believe that our planet will have to produce more food in the next 50 years to feed the world's population than it has grown in the past 10,000 years, requiring us to double our food output. As a multinational corporation dedicated to agriculture, Monsanto is expected to address these problems. In fiscal year 2008, the company expended $980 million for researching new farmer tools. The company has also developed a three-tiered commitment policy: (1) produce more yield in crops, (2) conserve

more resources, and (3) improve the lives of farmers. The company hopes to achieve these goals by taking some initiatives in sustainable agriculture.

Sustainable Agriculture

Agriculture intersects the toughest challenges we all face on the planet. Together, we must meet the needs for increased food, fiber and energy while protecting the environment. In short, the world needs to produce more and conserve smarter.

This quote by Monsanto CEO Hugh Grant demonstrates the challenges agriculture is facing today, along with Monsanto's goals to meet these challenges head-on. For instance, Monsanto is quick to point out that its biotech products added more than 100 million tons to worldwide agriculture production between 1996 and 2006, which they estimate has increased farmer's incomes by $33.8 billion. Monsanto has also created partnerships between nonprofit organizations across the world to enrich the lives of farmers in developing countries. Two regions on which Monsanto is focusing are India and Africa.

The need for better agriculture is apparent in India, where the population is estimated to hit 1.3 billion by 2017. Biotech crops have helped to improve the size of yields in India, allowing some biotech farmers to increase their yields by 50 percent. Monsanto estimates that cotton farmers in India using biotech crops earn approximately $176 more in revenues per acre than their non-biotech contemporaries. In February 2009, Monsanto announced that it would launch Project SHARE, a sustainable yield initiative done in conjunction with the nonprofit Indian Society of Agribusiness, to try and improve the lives of 10,000 cotton farmers in 1,100 villages.

In Africa, Monsanto has helped many farmers prosper and thrive through difficult periods. For example, in 2007 the government of Malawi provided farmers with vouchers worth about $3 each, which farmers could exchange for Monsanto seeds. Some of the farmers using these seeds saw their crop yields increase from a few bags to hundreds. Monsanto has also provided help to Project Malawi, a program to improve food security and health care to thousands of Malawians. Monsanto has provided the program with hybrid maize seed and has sent experts from the company to provide training for farmers in how to use the seed. Additionally, the large seed company has agreed to donate 240 tons of hybrid corn seed through 2010 to villages in Malawi, Tanzania, and Kenya. The goal of Monsanto is to improve farmers' lives in a way that will help them become self-sufficient.

Not all view Monsanto's presence in Africa as an outreach in corporate responsibility. Some see it as another way for Monsanto to improve the bottom line. Critics see the company as trying to take control of African agriculture and destroy African agricultural practices that have lasted for thousands of years. Yet, despite this criticism, there is no denying that Monsanto has positively affected African farmers' lives, along with increasing the company's profits for its shareholders. As CEO Hugh Grant writes, "This initiative isn't simply altruistic; we see it as a unique business proposition that rewards farmers and shareowners."

Charitable Giving

In 1964, the Monsanto Company established the Monsanto Fund. Much of the Monsanto Fund's contributions fund the company's projects in Africa. In 2006, the Fund awarded a $15 million gift to the Donald Danforth Plant Science Center, which will help to support crop research in Africa. Other projects of the Fund include the "Healthy Children, Healthy Future" program, which seeks to reduce diseases in Brazilian children through education on good health and basic hygiene, and the funding of the Monsanto Insectarium at the St. Louis Zoo.

The Monsanto Company also supports youth programs. In the first decade of the twenty-first century, the company donated nearly $1.5 million in scholarships to students who want to pursue agriculture-related degrees. The company also supports Future Farmers of America, the 4-H program, and the program Farm Safety 4 Just Kids, a program which helps teach rural children about safety while working on farms.

THE FUTURE OF MONSANTO

Monsanto faces some challenges that it needs to address, including lingering concerns over the safety and the environmental impact of its products. The company needs to enforce its code of ethics effectively to avoid organizational misconduct (like bribery) in the future. Monsanto also may be facing increased competition from other companies. The seed company Pioneer Hi-Bred International Inc. is using pricing strategies and seed sampling to attract price-conscious customers. Additionally, lower grain prices may convince farmers to switch from Monsanto to less expensive brands.

Yet, despite the onslaught of criticism from Monsanto detractors and the challenge of increased competition from other companies, Monsanto has numerous opportunities to thrive in the future. The company is currently working on new innovations that could increase its competitive edge as well as provide enormous benefits to farmers worldwide. In 2009, the company announced that it had finished regulatory submissions for the planet's first biotech drought-tolerant corn. This corn could be a major boon to farmers in areas where drought is prevalent. Monsanto is also working with the African Agriculture Technology Foundation to bring drought-resistant technology to Africa (without having them pay royalties).

Although Monsanto has made ethical errors in the past, it is trying to portray itself as a socially responsible company dedicated to improving agriculture. As noted, the company still has some problems. The predictions from Monsanto critics about biotech food have not yet come true, but that has not totally eradicated the fears of stakeholders. With the increasing popularity of organic food and staunch criticism from opponents, Monsanto will need to continue working with stakeholders to promote its technological innovations and to eliminate fears concerning its industry.

QUESTIONS

1. Does Monsanto maintain an ethical culture that can effectively respond to various stakeholders?

2. Compare the benefits of growing GMO seeds for crops with the potential negative consequences of using them.

3. How should Monsanto manage the potential harm to plant and animal life from using products such as Roundup?

SOURCES

"Agriculture Scholarships," Monsanto, http://www.monsanto.com/responsibility/youth/scholarship.asp, accessed April 1, 2009.

"Backgrounder: Glyphosate and Environmental Fate Studies," Monsanto, 2005, http://www.monsanto.com/content/products/productivity/roundup/gly_efate_bkg.pdf, accessed April 1, 2009.

Barlett, Donald L., and James B. Steele, "Monsanto's Harvest of Fear," May 5, 2008, Vanity Fair, http://www.vanityfair.com/politics/features/2008/05/monsanto200805, accessed August 25, 2009

"Biotech Cotton Improving Lives of Farmers, Villages in India." Monsanto, http://www.monsanto.com/responsibility/sustainable-ag/biotech_cotton_india.asp, accessed March 31, 2009.

"Corporate Profile," Monsanto, http://www.monsanto.com/investors/corporate_profile.asp, accessed March 15, 2009.

Environmental Protection Agency, "R.E.D. Facts," September 1993, http://www.epa.gov/oppsrrd1/REDs/factsheets/0178fact.pdf, accessed April 1, 2009.

Etter, Lauren, and Rebecca Townsend, "Monsanto's Profits Shoot Higher," January 8, 2009.

Etter, Lauren, and Rebecca Townsend, "Monsanto: Winning the Ground War," BusinessWeek, pp. 35–41.

"Even Small Doses of Popular Weed Killer Fatal to Frogs, Scientist Finds," ScienceDaily, August 5, 2005, http://www.sciencedaily.com/releases/2005/08/050804053212.htm, accessed March 24, 2009.

"Farm Safety 4 Just Kids," Monsanto, http://www.monsanto.com/responsibility/youth/fs4jk.asp, accessed April 1, 2009.

"Follow-Up to Monsanto Lawsuits," Monsanto, http://www.monsanto.com/monsanto_today/for_the_record/monsanto_farmer_lawsuits_followup.asp, accessed March 30, 2009.

Gibson, Ellen, "Monsanto," BusinessWeek, December 22, 2008, p. 51.

"GMOs Under a Microscope," Science & Technology in Congress, October 1999, http://www.aaas.org/spp/cstc/pne/pubs/stc/bulletin/articles/10-99/GMOs.htm, accessed March 25, 2009.

"Great Place to Work," Monsanto, http://www.monsanto.com/careers/culture/great_place.asp, accessed April 2009.

"Growing Hope in Africa," Monsanto, http://www.monsanto.com/responsibility/our_pledge/stronger_society/growing_self_sufficiency.asp, accessed March 31, 2009.

Grunwald, Michael, "Monsanto Hid Decades of Pollution," Washington Post, January 1, 2002, p. A1.

"Healthy Children, Healthy Future Project—Brazil," Monsanto Fund, http://www.monsantofund.org/asp/pop_ups/BRAZIL_HealthyChildren_Project.asp, accessed April 1, 2009.

"Is Monsanto Going to Develop or Sell 'Terminator' Seeds?," Monsanto, http://www.monsanto.com/monsanto_today/for_the_record/monsanto_terminator_seeds.asp, accessed March 28, 2009.

Martin, Andrew, "Fighting on a Battlefield the Size of a Milk Label," New York Times, March 9, 2008, http://www.nytimes.com/2008/03/09/business/09feed.html?ex=1362805200&en=56197f6ee92b4643&ei=5124&partner=permalink&exprod=permalink, accessed March 2, 1999.

"Milk Labeling—Is Monsanto Opposed to Truth in Labeling?," Monsanto, http://www.monsanto.com/monsanto_today/for_the_record/rbst_milk_labeling.asp, accessed March 2, 2009.

"Monsanto & NGO ISAP Launch Project Share—Sustainable Yield Initiative to Improve Farmer Lives," Monsanto, http://monsanto.mediaroom.com/index.php?s=43&item=693, accessed March 31, 2009.

"Monsanto Company—Company Profile, Information, Business Description, History, Background Information on Monsanto Company," http://www.referenceforbusiness.com/history2/92/Monsanto-Company.html, accessed March 20, 2009.

"Monsanto Completes Regulatory Submissions in U.S. and Canada for World's First Biotech Drought-Tolerant Corn Product," Monsanto, March 9, 2009, http://monsanto.mediaroom.com/index.php?s=43&item=695, accessed April 1, 2009.

"Monsanto Expanding Residual Herbicide Rebates," Delta Farm Press, January 12, 2009, http://deltafarmpress.com/cotton/herbicide-rebates-0112/, accessed March 2, 2009.

"Monsanto Fined $1.5M for Bribery," BBC News, January 7, 2005, http://news.bbc.co.uk/2/hi/business/4153635.stm, accessed March 15, 2009.

"Monsanto Fund," Monsanto Fund, http://www.monsantofund.org/asp/About_the_Fund/Main_Menu.asp, accessed April 1, 2009.

"Monsanto Mania: The Seed of Profits," iStockAnalyst, http://www.istockanalyst.com/article/viewarticle.aspx?articleid=1235584&zoneid=Home, accessed April 12, 2009.

Oxborrow, Claire, Becky Price, and Peter Riley, "Breaking Free," Ecologist 38, no. 9 (November 2008): 35–36.

"Phinizy Swamp Nature Park," Monsanto Fund, http://www.
    monsantofund.org/asp/Priorities/pop_ups/science.asp, accessed
    April 1, 2009.

Pollack, Andrew, "So What's the Problem with Roundup?"
    Ecology Center, January 14, 2003, http://www.ecologycenter.
    org/factsheets/roundup.html, accessed March 25, 2009.

Pollan, Michael, "Playing God in the Garden," *New York Times
    Magazine,* October 25, 1998, http://www.michaelpollan.com/
    article.php?id=73.

"Produce More," Monsanto, http://www.monsanto.com/
    responsibility/sustainable-ag/produce_more.asp, accessed
    April 1, 2009.

"Report on Animal Welfare Aspects of the Use of Bovine
    Sematotrophin," Report of the Scientific Committee on Animal
    Health and Animal Welfare, March 10, 1999, http://ec.europa.
    eu/food/fs/sc/scah/out21_en.pdf, accessed August 25, 2009.

"Seed Police?," Monsanto, http://www.monsanto.com/
    seedpatentprotection/monsanto_seed_police.asp, accessed
    March 30, 2009.

"$700 Million Settlement in Alabama PCB Lawsuit," *New
    York Times,* August 21, 2001, http://www.nytimes.
    com/2003/08/21/business/700-million-settlement-in-alabama-
    pcb-lawsuit.html, accessed March 15, 2009.

Weintraub, Arlene, "The Outcry over 'Terminator' Genes
    in Food," *BusinessWeek,* July 14, 2003, http://www.
    businessweek.com/magazine/content/03_28/b3841091.htm,
    accessed March 25, 2009.

"Widely Used Crop Herbicide Is Losing Weed Resistance,"
    New York Times, January 14, 2003, http://www.nytimes.
    com/2003/01/14/business/widely-used-crop-herbicide-is-
    losing-weed-resistance.html, accessed August 25, 2009.

Williams, G. M., R. Kroes, and I. C. Monro, "Safety Evaluation
    and Risk Assessment of the Herbicide Roundup and Its
    Active Ingredient, Glyphosate, for Humans," NCBI, April
    2000, http://www.ncbi.nlm.nih.gov/pubmed/10854122,
    accessed April 1, 2009.

Wal-Mart: The Future Is Sustainability

Wal-Mart Stores, Inc., is an icon of American business. From small-town business to multinational, from hugely controversial to a leader in renewable energy, Wal-Mart has long been a lightning rod for news and criticism. With 2008 sales of over $405.6 billion and more than two million employees worldwide, the world's largest public corporation must carefully manage many different stakeholder relationships. It is a challenge that has sparked significant debate.

Although Wal-Mart reportedly can save the average family $3,200 annually, the company has historically received plenty of criticism regarding its treatment of employees, suppliers, and economic impacts on communities. Feminists, activists, and labor union leaders have all voiced their beliefs that Wal-Mart has engaged in misconduct in order to provide low prices. However, Wal-Mart has been turning over a new leaf. New emphases on diversity, charitable giving, and sustainability have contributed to Wal-Mart's revitalized image.

The story of Wal-Mart and its low prices includes both positive and negative impacts on society. Positively, Wal-Mart reportedly saves consumers over $287 billion annually, equating to about $950 per person. On the flip side, research shows that communities can be negatively impacted by Wal-Mart's arrival in their areas.

This analysis attempts to show both sides of the controversy. It begins by briefly examining the growth of Wal-Mart, and then discusses Wal-Mart's various relationships with its stakeholders, including competitors, suppliers, and employees. Some of the ethical issues concerning these stakeholders include accusations of discrimination, illegal immigration issues, and leadership misconduct as demonstrated by Wal-Mart former vice chair Thomas Coughlin. Yet, in an effort to show Wal-Mart's attempts to position itself as a socially responsible company, this case also examines Wal-Mart's sustainability plans, its ethical initiatives, and former CEO Lee Scott's impressive leadership qualities. The analysis concludes by highlighting Wal-Mart's strategy during the most recent recession and recovery.

HISTORY: THE GROWTH OF WAL-MART

The story of Wal-Mart began in 1962, when founder Sam Walton opened the first Wal-Mart Discount Store in Rogers, Arkansas. Although it had a slow start due to lack of funds, Wal-Mart grew at an accelerated rate during the next forty years. The company grew from a small chain to more than 7,000 facilities in thirteen countries. In 2008 Wal-Mart opened its 3,000th international store. Only Exxon Mobil had more revenue than Wal-Mart did in 2008. The company now serves more than 176 million customers per year.

Much of the success that Wal-Mart has experienced can be attributed to its founder. A

This case was prepared by O.C. Ferrell, with the editorial assistance of Jennifer Jackson and Jennifer Sawayda. Melanie Drever, Lisa Heldt, Tabitha Payton, and Rob Boostrom made significant contributions to previous editions of this case, which was prepared for classroom discussion, rather than to illustrate either effective or ineffective handling of an administrative, ethical, or legal decision by management. All sources used for this case were obtained through publicly available material and the Wal-Mart website.

shrewd businessman, Walton believed in customer satisfaction and hard work. He convinced many of his associates to abide by the "ten-foot rule," where employees pledged that whenever they got within ten feet of a customer, they would look the customer in the eye, greet him or her, and ask if he or she needed help with anything. Walton's famous mantra, known as the "sundown rule," was: "Why put off until tomorrow what you can do today?" Due to this staunch work ethic and dedication to customer care, Wal-Mart claimed early on that a formal ethics program was unnecessary because the company had Mr. Sam's ethics to follow.

In 2002 Wal-Mart officially became the largest grocery chain, topping the Fortune 500 (a position it held seven times between 2002 and 2009). The company also has become known for its efforts toward sustainability growth. Former Wal-Mart CEO Lee Scott was even ranked seventh in the Ethisphere list of 100 top contributors to business ethics, based on his support of sustainability. Additionally, *Fortune* named Wal-Mart the "most admired company in America" in 2003 and 2004. Although it has slipped since then, it remained high on the list in 2009, when it was ranked eleventh most admired.

EFFECTS ON COMPETITOR STAKEHOLDERS

Possibly the greatest complaint against Wal-Mart is that it puts other companies out of business. With its low prices, Wal-Mart makes it harder for local stores to compete. Wal-Mart is often accused of being responsible for the downward pressure on wages and benefits in towns in which the company is located. Some businesses have tried to file lawsuits against Wal-Mart with mixed success, claiming that the company uses predatory pricing to put competing stores out of business. Wal-Mart counters by defending its pricing, asserting that its purpose is to provide quality, low-cost products to the average consumer. Yet,

although Wal-Mart has saved consumers millions of dollars and is a popular shopping spot for many, there is no denying that many competing stores go out of business once Wal-Mart comes to town.

In order to compete against the retail giant, other stores must reduce wages. Studies have shown that overall payroll wages, including Wal-Mart wages, are reduced by 5 percent after Wal-Mart enters a new market. As a result, some activist groups and citizens have refused to allow Wal-Mart to take up residence in their towns.

RELATIONSHIPS WITH SUPPLIER STAKEHOLDERS

Wal-Mart focuses on keeping costs low to achieve its "everyday low prices" (EDLPs) by streamlining its company. Well-known for operational excellence in its ability to handle, move, and track merchandise, Wal-Mart expects its suppliers to continually improve their systems as well. Wal-Mart often works closely with suppliers to cut prices in order to save the consumer money. For instance, Wal-Mart typically works with suppliers to reduce costs of packaging and shipping, which lessens costs for consumers. In 2006, Wal-Mart launched a plan to reduce packaging by 5 percent, an initiative reflecting Wal-Mart's desire to improve sustainability.

In 2008, Wal-Mart introduced its "Global Responsible Sourcing Initiative," which contains the following policies and requirements that will be included in new supplier agreements:

- "Manufacturers' facilities must certify compliance with laws and regulations where they operate as well as rigorous social and environmental standards, set by government agencies, beginning with suppliers in China in January 2009 and for all other Wal-Mart suppliers in 2011."

- "By 2012, suppliers must work with Wal-Mart to make a 20 percent improvement in the energy efficiency inside the top 200 factories in China that Wal-Mart directly sources from."

- "Suppliers must create a plan to eliminate, by 2012, defective merchandise reaching the Wal-Mart supply chain."
- "And by 2012, all suppliers Wal-Mart buys from must source 95 percent of their production from factories that receive the highest ratings on environmental and social practices."

If achieved, these goals will increase the sustainability of Wal-Mart suppliers significantly.

Some critics, however, believe that pressures to achieve these standards will shift more of a cost burden onto suppliers. Since Wal-Mart is specifically targeting its largest supplier network in China, many believe these lofty goals will be hard to implement in the allotted time period and will be hard to enforce and track due to the intricate maze of suppliers in China and other countries. When suppliers do not meet its demands, Wal-Mart ceases to carry the supplier's product or, often, will find another supplier for the product at the desired price.

Wal-Mart's power centers around its size and the volume of products needed. Many companies depend on Wal-Mart for the bulk of their business. Examples are Clorox, which does 23 percent of its business with Wal-Mart, Revlon (22 percent), and Kellogg's (12 percent). This type of relationship allows Wal-Mart to influence terms with its vendors. Indeed, there are benefits to suppliers; as they become more efficient and streamlined for Wal-Mart, they help their other customers as well. Numerous companies believe that supplying Wal-Mart has been the best thing for their businesses. However, many have found the amount of power that Wal-Mart wields to be disconcerting.

The constant drive by Wal-Mart for lower prices can have a negative effect on suppliers. Many have been forced to move production from the United States to less expensive locations in Asia. Wal-Mart imports around $20 billion in products from China and encourages its suppliers to move production there in order to lower costs. China's annual exports amount to $583 billion, and Wal-Mart ranks as China's eighth-largest trading partner. Companies such as Master Lock, Fruit of the Loom, and Levi's, as well as many other Wal-Mart suppliers, have moved production overseas at the expense of U.S. jobs.

This was not founder Sam Walton's original intention. In the 1980s, after learning that his stores were putting other American companies out of business, founder Sam Walton started his "Buy American" campaign in which much of Wal-Mart's merchandise would come from American stores. However, the quest to maintain low prices has pushed many Wal-Mart suppliers overseas, and some experts now estimate that as much as 80 percent of Wal-Mart's global suppliers are stationed in China.

ETHICAL ISSUES INVOLVING EMPLOYEE STAKEHOLDERS

Employee Benefits

Much of the Wal-Mart controversy over the years has focused on the way the company treats its employees, or "associates" as Wal-Mart refers to them. Although Wal-Mart is the largest retail employer in the world, it also has been highly criticized for its low wages and benefits. Wal-Mart has been accused of failing to provide health insurance to more than 60 percent of its employees. Many part-timers are not eligible, although efforts have been made to increase the coverage of part-time workers. In a Wal-Mart memo sent to the board of directors by Susan Chambers, Wal-Mart's executive vice-president for benefits, Chambers encouraged the hiring of more part-time workers while also encouraging the hiring of "healthier, more productive employees." After this bad publicity, Wal-Mart's stock decreased 27 percent between 2000 and 2005.

Because of the deluge of bad press, Wal-Mart has taken action to improve relations with its employee stakeholders. In 2006, Wal-Mart raised pay tied to performance in about one-third of its stores. The company also improved its health benefits package for 2008 by offering lower deductibles and implementing a generic prescription plan estimated to save employees $25 million. A Wal-Mart spokesperson claims that more than 90 percent of employees are currently insured and that the company is taking steps to increase that number.

Wal-Mart's Stance on Unions

Some critics believe that workers' benefits could be improved if workers could become unionized. However, unions have been discouraged since Wal-Mart's foundation. Sam Walton believed that unions were a divisive force and might render the company uncompetitive. Wal-Mart maintains that it is not against unions in general, but that it sees no need for unions to come between workers and managers. The company says that it supports an "open-door policy" in which associates can bring problems to managers without having to resort to third parties. Wal-Mart associates have voted against unions in the past.

Although the company officially states that it is not opposed to unions, Wal-Mart often seems to fight against them. Critics claim that when the word *union* surfaces at a Wal-Mart location, the top dogs in Bentonville are called in to instantly thwart union movement. In 2000, seven of ten Wal-Mart butchers in Jacksonville, Texas, voted to join the United Food Workers Union. Wal-Mart responded by announcing it would only sell precut meat in its Supercenters, getting rid of its meat-cutting department. Although Wal-Mart offers justifiable claims for actions such as this, many see the company as aggressively working to prevent unionization in its stores.

However, Wal-Mart's stance against unions has not always held up in foreign countries. In China, Wal-Mart faced a similar decision regarding unions. To grow in China, it appeared necessary to accept a union. Poor working conditions and low wages were generating social unrest and the government was attempting to craft a new set of labor laws giving employees greater protection and giving the All-China Federation of Trade Unions (ACFTU) more power. In 2004, the Chinese Labor Federation pushed Wal-Mart to allow the formation of unions. As a result, Wal-Mart technically allowed this, but critics claim that Wal-Mart made it increasingly difficult for the workers to form new unions. In 2006, employees announced the first formation of a Wal-Mart union, and within a week, four more branches had announced their formations of unions. Wal-Mart initially reacted to these announcements by stating it would not renew the contracts of unionized workers. However, the pressure mounted, and later that year Wal-Mart signed a memorandum with the ACFTU allowing unions in stores. Chinese Wal-Marts are now some of the few worldwide Wal-Marts that have unionized workers.

Workplace Conditions and Discrimination

Despite accusations of low employee benefits and a strong stance against unions, Wal-Mart remains the largest nongovernment employer in the United States, Mexico, and Canada. It provides jobs to millions of people and has been a mainstay of *Fortune*'s "Most Admired Companies" list since the start of the twenty-first century. However, in December 2005, Wal-Mart was ordered to pay $172 million to more than 100,000 California employees in a class-action lawsuit claiming that Wal-Mart routinely denied meal breaks. The California employees also alleged that they were denied rest breaks and that Wal-Mart managers deliberately altered time cards to prevent overtime. Similar accusations began to pop up in other states as well. Wal-Mart denied the allegations and filed an appeal in 2007. In 2008, Wal-Mart agreed to pay up to $640 million to settle sixty-three such lawsuits.

Wal-Mart also has received accusations of discrimination from its female employees. Although women account for more than two-thirds of all Wal-Mart employees, they make up less than 10 percent of store management. Wal-Mart insists it trains and promotes women fairly, but in 2001 an internal study showed that the company paid female store managers less than males in the same positions. In 2004, a federal judge in San Francisco granted class-action status to a sex-discrimination lawsuit against Wal-Mart involving 1.6 million current and former female Wal-Mart employees. The plaintiffs claimed that Wal-Mart discriminated against them in regard to promotions, pay, training, and job assignments. Wal-Mart argued against the class-action suit, claiming that promotions were made on an individual basis by each store. So far, the company has not been able to appeal the case.

Yet, interestingly enough, Wal-Mart also has received recognition for its good treatment of female workers. Between 2007 and 2009, the National Association for Female Executives recognized the company three years in a row as a "Top Company for Executive Women." It makes one wonder if Wal-Mart truly is trying to turn over a new leaf in how it treats its female employees.

Illegal Immigrants

In October 2003, a series of raids by U.S. Immigration and Customs Enforcement officials revealed that 250 illegal immigrants were working on cleaning crews at 61 Wal-Mart stores in 21 states. Several Wal-Mart contractors had hired the undocumented workers from Mexico, Eastern Europe, and other countries. In March 2005, this investigation ended in a landmark $11 million civil settlement. According to a *Wall Street Journal* article, three top Wal-Mart executives knew the company's cleaning contractors used illegal immigrants yet did nothing to stop the practice. The immigrants worked as many as seven days a week for less than minimum wage.

Wal-Mart answered these charges with an unusual response. It admitted that it knew about the illegal immigrants because it had been cooperating with the federal government for three years prior to the raids. Wal-Mart officials also remarked that the reason why they did not end ties with the contractors was because the federal government asked them not to do so. Additionally, Wal-Mart pointed to a prior lawsuit against Wal-Mart by the Immigration and Naturalization Service (INS) because the company required immigrants to show more verification than required by law. "Accordingly, our company was very hesitant to ask for more assurances about the status of our contractors' employees," stated Wal-Mart spokeswoman Mona Williams.

Sweatshop Workers

Wal-Mart has taken measures to show that it is against sweatshop labor. In 2003, it hired an anti-sweatshop expert to expand its global inspection program. The following year, Wal-Mart teamed up with the nonprofit Business for Social Responsibility to reinforce its global monitoring programs.

However, in December 2007, Wal-Mart fell prey to criticism after Senator Byron Dorgan accused the company of selling Christmas decorations made in Chinese sweatshops. The information came from a National Labor Committee study indicating that workers as young as 12 were working 15-hour days for as little as 26 cents an hour. In response, Wal-Mart stated that it was investigating the allegations and emphasized its code against such practices.

ETHICAL LEADERSHIP ISSUES

Aside from Sam Walton, many other distinguished people have been associated with Wal-Mart. One of them is Hillary Clinton, who served on Wal-Mart's board six years before her husband took the presidency. Another is former board vice chair Thomas Coughlin, although Coughlin achieved his fame for the corporate scandal he caused.

In March 2005, Coughlin was forced to resign from the board of directors for stealing as much as $500,000 from Wal-Mart in the form of bogus expenses, reimbursements, and the unauthorized use of gift cards. Coughlin, a protégé and hunting buddy of Sam Walton, was a legend at Wal-Mart. He often spent time on the road with Sam Walton expanding SAM's CLUB locations. At one time he was the second highest-ranking Wal-Mart executive and was a candidate for CEO.

In January 2006, Coughlin agreed to plead guilty to federal wire-fraud and tax-evasion charges. Although he took home millions of dollars in compensation, Coughlin secretly had been using Wal-Mart funds to pay for a range of his personal expenses, including hunting vacations, a $2,590 dog enclosure at his home, and a pair of handmade alligator boots. Coughlin's deceit was discovered when he asked a subordinate to approve $2,000 in expense payments without receipts.

Wal-Mart rescinded Coughlin's retirement agreement worth more than $10 million; and for his crimes, he was sentenced to 27 months of home confinement, $440,000 in fines, and 1,500 hours of community service. Wal-Mart spokesperson Mona Williams said the experience was "embarrassing and painful. Someone we expected to operate with the highest integrity let us down in a very public way." The case created concerns about leadership, corporate governance, and the ethical culture of Wal-Mart.

PROBLEMS WITH ENVIRONMENTAL STAKEHOLDERS

Like many large corporations, Wal-Mart has been targeted as a violator of safe environmental practices. The Environmental Protection Agency (EPA) has cited Wal-Mart for violating storm water regulations and air quality restrictions. In 2005, Wal-Mart received a grand jury subpoena from the U.S. Attorney's Office in Los Angeles, California, seeking documents and information relating to the company's receipt, transportation, handling, identification, recycling, treatment, storage, and disposal of certain merchandise constituting hazardous material or hazardous waste.

However, probably the greatest environmental concern associated with Wal-Mart has been urban sprawl. The construction of a Wal-Mart can stress a city's infrastructure of roads, parking, and traffic flow. There have been concerns about the number of acres of city green space devoured by Wal-Mart construction (Wal-Mart Supercenters occupy about twenty to thirty acres of land). Another issue is the number of abandoned stores (between 350 and 400 annually), deserted when the company outgrows locations. Currently, over 26 million square feet of empty Wal-Mart space exists— enough to fill 534 football fields. Allegedly, Wal-Mart goes out of its way to prevent other retail companies from buying its abandoned stores, contributing to the empty spaces.

Sustainability 360

Wal-Mart has attempted to address its environmental stakeholders by becoming a "greener" company. Some of the company goals include the following:

- Reducing greenhouse gases at existing store, club, and distribution center bases around the world by 20 percent by 2012

- Designing new prototypes to be 25 to 30 percent more efficient by the end of 2009

- Developing and implementing innovative energy-efficient technology into existing and new stores

- Reducing the amount of packaging in the supply chain by 5 percent by 2013 (which the company has promoted through annual packaging expos)

Currently Wal-Mart is working on four main green areas: waste improvement and recycling, natural resources, energy, and social/community impact. Wal-Mart's long-term goals are to be supplied 100 percent by renewable energy, create zero waste, and carry products that sustain the environment and its resources.

Sustainability Leadership

Wal-Mart has already taken strides to obtain its sustainability objectives. It has opened two environmentally friendly stores in McKinney, Texas, and Aurora, Colorado—locations chosen for their different weather and climate considerations. The stores get electricity from solar panels and wind turbines. The company hopes these experiments will provide examples of the ways building owners, scientists, engineers, architects, contractors, and landscape designers can work together to create stores designed to save energy, conserve natural resources, and reduce pollution. According to Wal-Mart vice president Kim Saylors-Laster, this is one step in Wal-Mart's plan of being supplied by 100 percent renewable energy. Wal-Mart intends to take information gained at these stores and apply it to new stores.

To reduce energy consumption, Wal-Mart facilities are conserving energy in two major ways. First, most new stores include a "daylighting" feature enabling stores to dim or turn off lights as daylight increases and enters through skylights, thereby reducing the demand for electricity during peak hours. Second, Wal-Mart manages energy consumption by centrally controlling the heating and cooling of U.S. Wal-Mart stores.

Wal-Mart is also attempting to reduce fossil fuel use and to sell more "green" products. Throughout 2009 Wal-Mart tested new technologies, including two types of hybrid trucks and two alternatively fueled heavy-duty trucks, in order to achieve its goals of creating a more environmentally friendly trucking fleet. Wal-Mart is proud to point out that between 2005 and 2008 the company increased its fleet efficiency by 25 percent through its use of new technologies, routes, and loading procedures. Wal-Mart's new goal is to double its fleet efficiency by 2015.

Additionally, Wal-Mart has announced a goal to reduce phosphates, a water pollutant that encourages the growth of oxygen-depleting algae and can kill fish and other wildlife, in laundry and dish detergents by 70 percent by 2011. The company hopes to use its worldwide influence to make a global difference in sustainability initiatives. "Our reach around the world puts us in a unique position to drive sustainable change across national boundaries and into the global supply chain," said Craig Herkert, Wal-Mart President and CEO of the Americas.

Wal-Mart is also trying to get its associates personally involved with sustainability. Approximately 500,000 Wal-Mart associates throughout the United States have participated in the Personal Sustainability Project (PSP), a voluntary program encouraged by former CEO Lee Scott. Associates at Wal-Mart stores would select sustainability goals and make commitments to monitor their progress for several weeks. The PSP counts successes, such as recycling over 3 million pounds of plastic, and encouraging people to winterize their homes and switch to low-energy fluorescent light bulbs, but also includes health goals. Healthier employees are better for the environment, for the health-care system, and for the business. Participants have lost a collective 184,000 pounds and 20,000 have quit smoking. The PSP has also been launched in Brazil, Canada, and Japan.

To measure how its eco-friendly products are faring with consumers, Wal-Mart launched the Wal-Mart Sustainability Live Better Index in 2007. This index allows Wal-Mart to track, on a state-by-state basis, consumers' demand for low-cost products, health and welfare products, and green products. In the sustainability category, consumers can track adoption rates at Wal-Mart in the following categories: compact florescent light bulbs, organic milk, extended-life paper products, organic baby food, organic cleaning products, and organic coffee. Wal-Mart believes that consumers can "make a conscious decision to purchase them for their environmentally friendly and cost-saving benefits versus conventional versions." So far results have been good, with a 66 percent increase in average adoption rates.

Even during the 2008–2009 economic recession, Wal-Mart tried to portray itself as a firm that cares about green initiatives. It continued to partner with other large companies to promote green jobs. In 2009, Wal-Mart announced its intention to contribute $5.7 million in grants to the U.S. Conference of Mayors and Veterans Green Jobs to support the creation of green jobs in the United States. Wal-Mart expects the money to be used to train the workforce in the growing sector of the green industry. The company believes it is making a profitable investment, as 10 percent of job growth in the United States is expected to be in the "green-collar" sector by 2032. With this investment, Wal-Mart hopes to encourage mayors to promote jobs in their cities' green industries and provide veterans with training in green skills. It is clear that Wal-Mart is trying to improve its relationship with environmental activists and stakeholders.

Savings: Is Going Green Cost-Effective?

Wal-Mart's green initiatives have secured it the goodwill of many environmentally conscious consumers, but does going green save the company costs in other ways? So far Wal-Mart's initiatives have racked up the following savings:

- $25 million/year in savings from auxiliary power systems on trucks to run the air conditioning when trucks are stopped. The store further plans to double the fuel efficiency of its new heavy-duty trucks by 2015.
- $7 million/year in savings from replacing all incandescent bulbs in store display ceiling fans with compact fluorescent bulbs.

WHAT IS WAL-MART DOING TO IMPROVE ETHICS AND SOCIAL RESPONSIBILITY?

Although it has received much criticism in the past years, Wal-Mart has been working to improve its ethical reputation along with its reputation for sustainability and corporate governance. In 2004, Wal-Mart formed the Global Ethics Office and released a revised Global Statement of Ethics. The intent of the Global Ethics Office is to spread an ethical corporate culture among its global stakeholders. The Global Ethics Office provides guidance on ethical decision making based on the Global Statement of Ethics and an ethics helpline. The helpline is an anonymous and confidential way for associates to contact the company regarding ethical issues. Additionally, Wal-Mart has an Ethical Standards Team that consists of 200 associates. The intent of the team is to monitor the compliance of supplier factories with the company's "Standards for Suppliers" and local laws.

In 2005, Wal-Mart introduced a full-page newspaper ad that promoted the company's concern with ethics and its stakeholders. Its newspaper ad was a direct letter from Wal-Mart CEO Lee Scott. The ad stated that it was time for the public to read the "unfiltered truth" about Wal-Mart and time for it to stand up on behalf of a workforce that included 1.2 million Americans. Scott called for Congress to increase the minimum wage and noted that Wal-Mart had increased spending on employee health insurance.

Wal-Mart also has contributed significantly to disaster management projects. The company donated millions to relief efforts for Hurricane Katrina, $300,000 to support flood relief efforts in Southern Brazil, and $3 million for earthquake relief in China. Wal-Mart attempts to help its associates who are caught in disasters, allocating $2 million in grants for associates whose homes have been damaged and creating a toll-free number for associates who need help.

Despite its efforts, Wal-Mart's reputation was significantly tarnished again with the Coughlin scandal. It was therefore eager to reestablish its credibility with stakeholders. It found its solution in the person of Lee Scott, CEO of Wal-Mart from January 2002 to January 2009. Lee Scott was recognized as a leader in investing in clean energy. Due to him, many California facilities are now powered by solar energy, and the energy needs of 15 percent of Texas stores can now be met with wind power. Scott's leadership had such a positive effect on the company that he was given one of the top spots in the 100 Most Influential People in Business Ethics in 2008. Wal-Mart has taken great strides to portray itself as an ethically responsible business with good leadership.

The company's reputation for low prices helped Wal-Mart to remain a healthy business even during the 2008–2009 recession. Wal-Mart claims a commitment to improving the standard of living for customers worldwide, and has backed that claim with large charitable donations, amounting to $423 million globally in fiscal year 2009. Its key retailing strategy is offering a broad assortment of merchandise and services at everyday low prices (EDLP) while fostering a culture claiming to reward and embrace mutual respect, integrity, and diversity. Wal-Mart has always targeted lower-income customers, a strategy that paid dividends during the 2008–2009 recession. While many companies struggled to re-brand themselves as affordable, Wal-Mart had an early advantage. Wal-Mart is known for excellent market orientation—focusing on consumers, defeating competitors, and increasing shareholder value.

WAL-MART'S RESPONSE TO THE FINANCIAL CRISIS

Interestingly enough, the financial meltdown of 2008–2009 may have enhanced Wal-Mart's reputation. Unlike many stores, Wal-Mart's sales increased by 2 percent in 2008 as shoppers sought good deals. An influx of new shoppers forced Wal-Mart to create better crowd-control measures in its New York stores after an employee was trampled to death and others were injured on Black Friday 2008 by a mob of shoppers. Although refusing to admit any wrongdoing in the incident, Wal-Mart agreed to have its crowd-control measures approved by safety consultants (in addition to providing $400,000 to victims of the incident). Wal-Mart is also donating $1.5 million to a Nassau County social service program.

In addition to creating better safety measures, Wal-Mart has launched new initiatives targeting families facing financial dilemmas. For example, the company formed the Wal-Mart MoneyCard, a reloadable Visa debit card to help lower-income consumers who do not use traditional checking accounts. Because of the economic crisis, Wal-Mart has decreased the fees for this card; consumers can now purchase it for $3, rather than the $9 it cost originally. The card has no overdraft fees, and the fees for maintenance and reloading are low. With this move, Wal-Mart hopes to save consumers $500 million in money service fees each year.

The Wal-Mart Foundation has partnered with United Way and One Economy Corporation to provide free filing and tax services for low-income consumers. The Wal-Mart Foundation is donating a $3.6 million grant to this endeavor in an attempt to demonstrate social responsibility while increasing the popularity of its stores.

THE FUTURE OF WAL-MART

Wal-Mart can be viewed through two very different lenses. Some think that the company represents all that is wrong with America, and others love it. In response to criticism and in an attempt to initiate goodwill with consumers, the company has continued to improve stakeholder relationships and made efforts to exhibit itself as an ethically responsible company. Although it has faced controversy regarding competition, suppliers, employees, and workplace discrimination, it has increasingly demonstrated concern for its stakeholders.

Wal-Mart's endeavors that have sparked consumer attention deal with sustainability initiatives and social responsibility. Its goals to decrease its waste and carbon emissions extend to all facets of its operations, including suppliers. Though some consider these objectives to be unrealistic, the effort demonstrates Wal-Mart's desire (whether through genuine concern for the environment or for its own bottom-line profits) to become a more sustainable company.

Similarly, Wal-Mart's creation of an ethics and compliance program shows it has come a long way since its beginning when formal ethics programs were deemed unnecessary. Likewise, its initiatives to help families during the recession helped to reinforce its image as a caring company. Both critics and supporters of Wal-Mart alike are waiting to see whether Wal-Mart's efforts will position the company as a large retail company dedicated to social responsibility.

QUESTIONS

1. Do you think Wal-Mart is doing enough to become more sustainable?

2. What are the problems that Wal-Mart has faced, and what has the company done to address them?

3. Why has Wal-Mart tended to improve performance when other retail outlets have been suffering financially?

SOURCES

Associated Press, "Ex-Wal-Mart Vice Chairman Pleads Guilty in Fraud Case," *Wall Street Journal,* January 31, 2006, www.online.wsj.com.

Bandler, James, "Former No. 2 at Wal-Mart Set to Plead Guilty," *Wall Street Journal,* January 7, 2006, p. A1.

Bandler, James, and Ann Zimmerman, "A Wal-Mart Legend's Trail of Deceit," *Wall Street Journal,* April 8, 2005, p. A10.

Barbaro, Michael, "Image Effort by Wal-Mart Takes a Turn," *New York Times,* May 12, 2006, pp. C1, C4.

Barbaro, Michael, "Return to Low-Price Basics Pays Off Well for Wal-Mart," Wal-MartStores.com, January 12, 2009, http://www6.lexisnexis.com/publisher/EndUser?Action=UserDisplay FullDocument&orgId=2708&topicId=100019774&docId=l:728129992, accessed February 20, 2009.

"Buy Blue: Wal-Mart," http://www.buyblue.org/node/2137/view/summary, accessed January 10, 2006.

Chan, Anita, "Made in China: Wal-Mart Unions," *Yale Global Online,* October 12, 2006, http://yaleglobal.yale.edu/display.article?id=8283, accessed February 21, 2009.

Coleman-Lochner, Lauren, "Independent Look at Wal-Mart Shows Both Good and Bad. With Savings and Jobs Come Falling Wages and Rising Medicaid Costs," *San Antonio Express-News,* November 5, 2005, p. 4D.

Connolly, Ceci, "At Wal-Mart, a Health-Care Turnaround," *Washington Post,* February 13, 2009, http://www.washingtonpost.com/wp-dyn/content/article/2009/02/12/AR2009021204096_pf.html, accessed February 21, 2009.

"Ethical Sourcing," Wal-Mart, http://walmartstores.com/Sustainability/7785.aspx, accessed May 12, 2009.

Etter, Lauren, "Gauging the Wal-Mart Effect," *Wall Street Journal,* December 3–4, 2005, p. A9.

"Event Highlights the Wal-Mart Health Care Crisis: New Study Declares Wal-Mart in Critical Condition," November 16, 2005, http://Wal-Martwatch.com, accessed January 18, 2006.

Fishman, Charles, "The Wal-Mart You Don't Know; Why Low Prices Have a High Cost," *Fast Company,* December 2003, pp. 68–80.

Fong, Mei, and Ann Zimmerman, "China's Union Push Leaves Wal-Mart with Hard Choice," *Wall Street Journal,* May 13–14, 2006, pp. A1, A6.

"Global Ethics Office," Wal-Mart, https://www.walmartethics.com/, accessed December 13, 2008.

"Global Insight Releases New Study on the Impact of Wal-Mart on the U.S. Economy," http://www.globalinsight.com/MultiClientStudy/MultiClientStudyDetail2438.htm, accessed January 23, 2005.

Gold, Russell, and Ann Zimmerman, "Papers Suggest Wal-Mart Knew of Illegal Workers," *Wall Street Journal,* November 5, 2005, p. A3.

Grant, Lorrie, "Wal-Mart Faces a New Class Action," *USA Today,* September 14, 2005, p. 63.

Heldt, Lisa, and Tabitha Peyton, "Wal-Mart's Green Marketing Strategy," April 27, 2009.

"Is Wal-Mart Really a 'Green' Company?" Wal-Mart Watch, http://walmartwatch.com/img/blog/environmental_fact_sheet.pdf, accessed December 13, 2008.

"Judah Schiller on Sustainability: Make It Personal," Sustainable Brands 09, http://www.sustainablelifemedia.com/people/innovators/strategy/judah_schiller_on_sustainability_make_it_personal, accessed February 23, 2009.

Kabel, Marcus, "Wal-Mart at War: Retailer Faces Bruised Image, Makes Fixes," *Marketing News,* January 15, 2006, p. 25.

"Live Better Index," Wal-Mart, Inc., http://www.livebetterindex.com/, accessed August 27, 2009.

McGinn, Daniel, "Wal-Mart Hits the Wall," *Newsweek,* November 14, 2005, pp. 44–46.

Morrison, Kimberly, "Coughlin's Sentence Will Stand: U.S. Attorney Will Not Appeal," March 28, 2008, http://www.nwaonline.net/articles/2008/03/29/news/032908wzcoughlinappeal.txt, accessed February 21, 2009.

"Most Admired Companies," *Fortune,* http://money.cnn.com/magazines/fortune/mostadmired/2009/snapshots/2255.html, accessed August 27, 2009.

Much, Marilyn, "Wal-Mart Holds Up in Sharp Recession, Beating EPS Views; Rare Winner: Shares Up 4%; Middle Class Now Willing to Shop at Discount King for Low Prices on Basics," Wal-MartStores.com, http://www6.lexisnexis. com/publisher/EndUser?Action=UserDisplayFullDocument &orgId=2708&topicId=100019774&docId=l:928281151, accessed February 20, 2009.

Norman, Al, "The Case Against Wal-Mart," Raphel Marketing, 2004.

Olsson, Karen, "Up Against Wal-Mart," www.MotherJones. com, March/April 2003, http://www.motherjones.com/news/ feature/2003/03/ma_276_01.html, accessed January 10, 2006.

"100 Most Influential People in Business Ethics 2008," Ethisphere, December 31, 2009, http://ethisphere.com/100-most-influential-people-in-business-ethics-2008/#6, accessed February 20, 2009.

"Personal Sustainability Project Fact-Sheet," Wal-Mart, Inc., http://walmartstores.com/FactsNews/ FactSheets/#Sustainability, accessed August 27, 2009.

PR Newswire, "Wal-Mart Foundation Donates $5.7 Million to Support the Creation of Green Jobs in U.S.," CNBC, http://www.cnbc.com/id/28993728/site/14081545, accessed February 20, 2009.

Quinn, Steve, "Wal-Mart Green with Energy," Fort Collins Coloradoan, July 24, 2005, pp. E1–E2.

Sebok, Anthony J., "Wal-Mart Wants to Declassify Lawsuit," CNN.com, August 11, 2004, http://www.cnn.com/2004/ LAW/08/11/sebok.walmart.suit/index.html, accessed December 13, 2008.

Shine, Tom, and Z. Byron Wolf, "Report Cites Holiday Abuse in Chinese Factory," ABC News, December 12, 2007, http://abcnews.go.com/Business/HolidayTheme/ story?id=3989096&page=1, accessed December 13, 2008.

"Sustainability Progress to Date 2007–2008," Wal-Mart, http://walmartfacts.com/reports/2006/sustainability/ associatesPersonal.html, accessed February 23, 2009.

"Top Companies: The 2009 List," National Association for Female Executives, http://www.nafe.com/ web?service=vpage/3847, accessed August 27, 2009.

"2009 Fortune 500," Fortune, http://money.cnn.com/magazines/ fortune/fortune500/2009/snapshots/2255.html, accessed August 27, 2009.

Wailgum, Thomas, "Wal-Mart's Green Strategy: Supply Chain Makeover Targets Chinese Manufacturers," CIO, http://www.cio.com/article/456625/Wal_Mart_s_Green_ Strategy_Supply_Chain_Makeover_Targets_Chinese_ Manufacturers?page=1, accessed May 13, 2009.

"Wal-Mart Americas Aim to Reduce Detergent Phosphates 70%," Wal-MartStore.com, January 26, 2009, http:// walmartstores.com/FactsNews/NewsRoom/8938.aspx, accessed February 20, 2009.

"Wal-Mart Annual Report 2008," Wall-MartStores.com, http:// walmartstores.com/sites/AnnualReport/2008/, accessed February 21, 2009.

"Wal-Mart Concedes China Can Make Unions," China Daily, November 23, 2004, http://www.chinadaily.com.cn/english/ doc/2004-11/23/content_394129.htm, accessed February 21, 2009.

"Wal-Mart Foundation Teams Up with United Way and One Economy to Provide Free Tax Preparation and Filing Services," Wal-MartStores.com, February 10, 2009, http:// walmartstores.com/FactsNews/NewsRoom/8962.aspx, accessed February 20, 2009.

"Wal-Mart Steps Up Efforts to Help Americans Manage Their Finances with $3 Rollback Price on Key Money Service," Wal-MartStores.com, February 8, 2009, http:// walmartstores.com/FactsNews/NewsRoom/8982.aspx, accessed February 20, 2009.

"Wal-Mart Stores, Inc.," United States Security and Exchange Commission, January 31, 2008, http://msnmoney.brand. edgar-online.com/EFX_dll/EDGARpro.dll?FetchFilingHTM L1?ID=5835838&SessionID=5RgcWZDBP11rCl9, accessed February 21, 2009.

"Wal-Mart Stores, Inc. Recognized as Top Company for Executive Women by the National Association for Female Executives," Wal-Mart, April 3, 2007, http:// walmartstores.com/FactsNews/NewsRoom/6374.aspx, accessed May 12, 2009.

"Wal-Mart Tests New Hybrid Trucks, Alternative Fuels," Wal-MartStores.com, http://walmartstores.com/FactsNews/ NewsRoom/8949.aspx, accessed February 20, 2009.

"Wal-Mart Will Pay $640M to Settle Wage Lawsuits," Newser, December 23, 2008, http://www.newser.com/story/46142/ wal-mart-will-pay-640m-to-settle-wage-lawsuits.html?utm_ source=ssp&utm_medium=cpc&utm_campaign=story, accessed May 12, 2009.

Zimmerman, Anne, "Federal Officials Asked to Probe Wal-Mart Firing," Wake-Up Wal-Mart, April 28, 2005, http://www. wakeupwalmart.com/news/20050428-wsj.html, accessed February 21, 2009.

Zimmerman, Anne, "Labor Pains: After Huge Raid on Illegals, Wal-Mart Fires Back at U.S.," Wall Street Journal, December 19, 2003, p. A1.

The American Red Cross

The American Red Cross (ARC) is an independent organization, supported by public financial donations and volunteerism. Its mission is to "provide relief to victims of disasters and help people prevent, prepare for and respond to emergencies." The ARC responds to more than 70,000 disasters annually. However, the ways in which it handled 9/11 in 2001 and Hurricane Katrina in 2005 were widely criticized as being inadequate and poorly managed. The ARC has had to address allegations of fraud, bribery, and even theft on the part of volunteers and employees working for the organization. The ARC also has faced a number of internal challenges due to high turnover, as well as charges of overcompensation and possible corruption among its board of directors and upper management.

A BRIEF HISTORY

Clara Barton initially founded the ARC in 1881. She was inspired by the work of the International Red Cross while on a trip to Europe during the Franco-Prussian War of 1870–1871. Barton brought the model back to the United States, and subsequently led the organization through its first domestic and international relief missions, including assisting the U.S. military during the Spanish-American War in 1898. The ARC is one of a handful of organizations chartered by the U.S. government, receiving its first federal charter in 1900.

As a member of the International Federation of Red Cross and Red Crescent Societies, the ARC joins more than 175 other national societies in bringing aid to victims of disasters throughout the world. The ARC follows the seven fundamental bylaws to which all Red Cross societies must conform: humanity, impartiality, neutrality, independence, voluntary service, unity, and universality.

ORGANIZATIONAL STRUCTURE

Today the American Red Cross consists of roughly half a million volunteers and 35,000 employees. For many years the ARC has had a fifty-member, all-volunteer board of governors. The president of the United States is the honorary chair of the Red Cross and appoints eight governors, including the chair of the board. The chair nominates and the board elects the president of the ARC, who is responsible for carrying into effect the policies and programs of the board. This arrangement is undergoing changes that will be discussed later in the case.

The ARC is made up of more than 700 local chapters across the country. These chapters receive funding from the national Red Cross. Directors of local chapters are authorized to run day-to-day operations. Representatives of the local chapters nominate members of the local boards of governors. In recent history,

This case was prepared by Michelle Watkins and John-Paul Schilling under the direction of O.C. Ferrell and the development of Jennifer Jackson. This case was prepared for classroom discussion, rather than to illustrate either effective or ineffective handling of an administrative, ethical, or legal decision by management. All sources used for this case were obtained through publicly available material.

members of the local boards of directors have clashed with top national management.

ORGANIZATIONAL AND LEADERSHIP UPHEAVAL

Trouble at the Top: Executive Turnover

The first decade of the twenty-first century saw a high rate of turnover in the boardroom at the Red Cross. Since Elizabeth Dole's resignation as chair in 1999, the ARC has had seven different permanent or acting heads. President Bernadine Healy (1999–2001) was forced to resign following mismanagement of the response to the September 11 attacks. Similarly, president and chief executive officer Marsha J. Evans (2002–2005) was ousted after the ARC's botched handling of Hurricane Katrina, though the official reason for her departure was communication problems with the board. Mark W. Everson was president and CEO for the brief period between May 29 and November 27, 2007. He was forced to resign after an inappropriate sexual relationship with a subordinate came to light.

This frequent executive turnover has significantly weakened the organization's ability to carry out its federal mandate. Some blame the oversized board of directors. "The board seems to think it is a hiring and firing agency, and does not see its role as building a strong Red Cross," said Paul C. Light, a professor of public service at New York University. "The constant change in leadership is debilitating and does nothing to address the real problem, which is years and years of underinvestment in telecommunications, technology and other infrastructure to help the organization with its mission." In the cases of both Healy and Everson, the board spent a considerable amount of time and money conducting a search for the "right person," nearly two years and eighteen months, respectively.

The agency's reputation has been further tarnished by the ARC's history of awarding large severance packages for ousted executives, no matter how short the term served. Bernadine Healy received $1.9 million in salary and severance pay upon her departure in late 2001. Marsha Evans received a total of $780,000 in 2005; this comprised eighteen months' severance pay and a $36,495 unpaid bonus. Speaking of the damage to the organization, Diana Aviv, president and chief executive of the Independent Sector, a nonprofit trade association, said, "The tragedy of this is that the American Red Cross is probably the best-known nonprofit organization in this country. When the stories about it are more about governance and management and less about how it saves lives, it's sad and not just for the Red Cross."

Leadership troubles have extended into the local chapters as well, indicating systemic problems. In a story on the ARC, CBS News cited a laundry list of misconduct: "the fundraiser in Louisiana caught padding her own bank account with donations; the manager in Pennsylvania who embezzled to support her crack cocaine habit; and the executive in Maryland who forged signatures on purchase orders meant for disaster victims." One of the biggest charity frauds in history occurred at the ARC's Hudson County chapter in New Jersey. Chief executive Joseph Lecowitch and bookkeeper Catalina Escoto stole well over $1 million in Red Cross funds, squandering it on gambling and gifts to themselves. Escoto also gave herself at least $75,000 in bonuses. Even after Congress mandated changes meant to do away with such problems, in 2007 an executive in Orange County pleaded guilty to federal charges that she embezzled at least $110,000 of the organization's money.

The systemic problems at the American Red Cross have continued, with the nonprofit running about a $200 million deficit and eliminating 1,000 jobs in 2008 alone. Management turmoil and a slow economy combined to dampen fundraising, and the new CEO, Gail McGovern, split the organization's number-two executive position into three separate president-level positions. McGovern filled two of these positions with former AT&T executives with whom she had worked. The ARC was forced to ask for a $150 million appropriation, along with funding to help victims of wildfires, tornados, and floods.

Organizational Changes at the Top

In 2006 Congress took action to try to improve the ARC's effectiveness and efficiency after the scandals of September 11, Hurricane Katrina, and the myriad problems at local chapters when Senator Charles E. Grassley filed legislation to overhaul the organization. Grassley's legislation also forced the organization to become more transparent. In 2006 the ARC disclosed thousands of pages of documents that had not previously been available to the public. This marked the first time in almost sixty years that Congress had moved to amend the organization's charter. The legislation sought to assuage the difficulties in the board by cutting its numbers by more than half, to twenty members by the year 2012. It also restructured the role of the president of the United States in making board appointments. In the past, the president appointed the chair and eight board members, typically cabinet secretaries who rarely attended meetings. Under the legislation, the board nominates a chair for approval and appointment by the president. All other presidential appointments to the board were abolished. An independent ombudsman position was created to take charge of annually reporting to Congress as well as assisting whistle-blowers should agency misconduct be reported.

The American Red Cross Code of Business Ethics and Conduct was updated in January 2007. All employees and volunteers are required to read and sign the two-page document. The ARC offers a twenty-four-hour, confidential, anonymous hotline, the "Concern Connection Line," that provides American Red Cross staff, volunteers, and members of the public a way to report concerns or ask questions regarding potentially illegal, unsafe, or unethical conduct.

The ARC also published an eight-page "Ethics Rules and Policies," which outlines how business funds, property, and time may be allocated, as well as addressing conflicts of interest, recordkeeping, and addressing media inquiries. By far the longest section of this document is the page addressing writings by employees and volunteers about September 11, 2001, which details a policy for "creating, marketing and selling books and other literary works relating to the events of September 11, 2001."

The word *ethics* does not appear a single time in the main promotional document the ARC provides to governmental agencies. *Compliance* appears only in reference to the ARC's requirements related to the collection of blood donations. No mention is made of employee or volunteer ethics training in any official ARC documents available at its website, making it clear that this is not a high priority for the organization.

In light of the scandals that have plagued the ARC, stakeholders must be assured repeatedly of the genuine efforts the organization is making to institutionalize ethical best practices. It may be the ARC believes that because its mission is to respond to and assist people in need, organizational ethics will automatically occur. Perhaps the assumption is that all employees will be ethical without direction or training.

SEPTEMBER 11, 2001

Slow Response

After the September 11 attacks on New York City's World Trade Center, the ARC was widely criticized for its response. The criticisms began the very day of the incident, as the Pentagon called the office of Red Cross President Bernadine Healy at noon to ask, "Where the hell are you guys? Where is the Red Cross?" The Virginia-based command center known as the Disaster Operations Center (DOC) had, for more than a day afterward, failed to activate the specialized teams normally sent out after a plane crash or similar disaster. The trouble did not stop there. In the days and weeks following the attacks, the ARC was continually criticized for its management of the financial donations from thousands of Americans.

Monetary Donation Mismanagement

After September 11, monetary donations poured in at an unprecedented rate. Healy set up a separate fund, the "Liberty Fund," for donations earmarked for victims. By the end of October, the fund had received $543 million in pledges. It had, however, distributed less than one third of those funds to 9/11 relief efforts. The ARC announced that more than half would be spent to increase the organization's ability to prepare for and respond to future catastrophes instead.

Angry outcries prompted a U.S. congressional hearing in November 2001. Healy attempted to defend the use of the money, saying it was clear to donors that not all gifts would go directly to immediate relief efforts. To this Representative Billy Tauzin replied, "It was specially funded for this event, for September 11, and we're also being told parenthetically, 'by the way, we're going to give two thirds of it away to other important Red Cross needs.'" The ethical issue of asking for funds for 9/11 relief efforts, and then appropriating those funds for other purposes, created an explosive debate. At the time of the hearing, Healy had already been forced to resign as ARC president. The ARC subsequently announced that all Liberty Funds monies would go to September 11 victims and their families.

HURRICANE KATRINA

ARC and FEMA Miscommunication

During August and September of 2005, the American Red Cross responded to the disastrous effects of Hurricanes Katrina and Rita, the largest national emergencies in the history of the organization. Katrina hit New Orleans on August 23 as a category 3 storm, making it the sixth strongest hurricane ever recorded in the Atlantic. It was also the costliest hurricane in history. Hurricane Rita hit the coast of Louisiana and Texas only a month later and was an even larger category 3 storm. The ARC raised more than $2 billion in private donations to fund massive relief efforts for both these disasters.

Yet again, following this outpouring of charitable giving, the American public was left largely unsatisfied by the inadequate and untimely relief efforts depicted in the media. These subpar emergency responses were the outcome of a host of fraudulent, questionable, and inefficient decisions made by the ARC, as well as its federal, state, and local disaster relief counterparts. As a result of these faulty responses, and at the request of various congressional committees, the Government Accountability Office (GAO) wrote a report detailing the inadequacies of the ARC and the Federal Emergency Management Agency (FEMA).

The GAO found that the National Response Plan written by the Department of Homeland Security (DHS) in December 2004 was not properly followed and that coordination between the ARC and FEMA was not satisfactory. The DHS plan depicted the ARC as the primary agency responsible for coordinating federal mass care assistance in support of state and local governments and other voluntary organizations in charge of meeting needs such as shelter, food, and emergency first aid. During their disaster relief efforts, FEMA and ARC officials disagreed about their roles and responsibilities and failed to communicate appropriate points of contact for each agency. Additionally, ARC staff was criticized for rotating support positions every two to three weeks. This made it difficult for ARC staff to maintain working relationships with counterparts or to gain expertise in their job functions. Lastly, FEMA failed to implement a comprehensive system to track requests for assistance received from the ARC. One of the ARC's main objectives is properly categorizing and responding to requests for specific goods or necessary services by state and local governments as well as other voluntary organizations.

Mismanagement of Funds and Volunteers

Along with the failures in communication between FEMA and the ARC, there have been numerous accusations about the improper management of donated funds and of volunteers following Hurricanes Katrina and Rita. A *New York Times* article summarizes these actions as follows: "The accusations include the improper diversion of relief supplies, failure to follow Red Cross procedures in tracking and distributing supplies, and use of felons as volunteers in the disaster area in violation of Red Cross rules."

Numerous Katrina volunteers reported the disappearance of rented cars, electricity generators, and even some 3,000 air mattresses. During the relief efforts, the ARC had more than 235,000 volunteers working in the hurricane disaster areas, more than five times the previous peak of 40,000 volunteers for other relief efforts. It was reported that several of these volunteers had arrest warrants or other felony charges in their backgrounds. The ARC has a screening process that normally would detect potential volunteers with criminal backgrounds, but during Katrina, the organization was so overwhelmed with people seeking to volunteer that it dropped its usual standards.

Other volunteers complained of unauthorized possession and use of Red Cross computer equipment by staff and volunteers. This equipment was equipped with software to add donated money to debit cards for immediate use by hurricane victims and could easily be misused by unscrupulous volunteers. Other incidents included an ARC call center employee writing money orders in the names of various relief victims and fraudulently cashing them herself.

The ARC launched an investigation into claims that, as an organization, it had virtually no cost controls, little oversight of inventory, and no mechanism for basic background checks on volunteers that were given substantial responsibilities. These examples of mismanagement of charitable funds and volunteers pose questions regarding the ARC's ability to prevent fraud and protect resources amid the chaos of major national disasters.

Encouragement of Corporate Partnerships

Another story that emerged from relief efforts for Hurricane Katrina victims regards the ARC's acceptance and choice of corporate partnerships. During the national emergency situation, many corporations were eager to help. Corporate donations not only help victims, but they also cast companies in a good light as the companies demonstrate their compassion and concern for stakeholders. As a nonprofit organization, and the lead agency in charge of various aspects of the disaster relief, the ARC had a duty to scrutinize the corporate donations. Examples of corporate partnerships during the Katrina disaster relief efforts included Coca-Cola donating water, Anheuser Busch canning and delivering water in Anheuser Busch cans, Master Card and J.P. Morgan issuing ATM cards with access to ARC-donated funds for relief victims, and the Southwest Drycleaners Association (SDA) donations of funds that were intended to help the SDA portray themselves as a compassionate and community-involved industry.

In a national emergency, these corporate partnerships help to provide access to resources that otherwise may not be available. The ARC deserves praise for incorporating the generosity of private corporations effectively into its overall disaster relief strategy. However, it should be noted that in the future a more active approach to monitoring private firms' donations would benefit the transparency and overall goals of keeping the ARC apolitical and independent from large businesses. The danger of large corporate donations is that they could make the ARC appear to be in collusion with or biased toward certain corporations. As a nonprofit organization, the ARC should always take steps to ensure impartiality. A greater level of transparency would allow the ARC to assure regular citizens that their charitable donations will not be affected or misused, regardless of corporate involvement. The ARC must be especially careful with whom it is willing to partner during times of national disaster so as not to appear to be using a disaster as a means to promote corporate products.

An article published in the *Harvard Business Review* states that entities such as the ARC would benefit from greater cooperation and partnerships with private businesses. "It's a good thing when companies pitch in after natural or other calamities. It would be a far better thing if they partnered with aid agencies to make plans before disaster struck." As an example, the authors use the agreement for a partnership between Abbott Laboratories and the ARC to supply blood-screening equipment to prove their point that preplanned private partnerships with aid agencies could expedite relief efforts to disaster victims. Through this agreement, Abbott Laboratories will donate a variety of pharmaceutical products ranging from antibiotics to baby food.

Donation Acceptance and Insufficient Capacity

The last point worth mentioning in this analysis of the ARC's donation management involves the organization's capacity to electronically accept donations. The ARC's website has become the main source for receiving individual charitable donations. After September 11, 2001, the organization had to expand its Web-based infrastructure to accommodate additional web traffic. After the tsunami in Southeast Asia, the ARC found itself once again overwhelmed with Internet traffic to donate money. Internet technology staff was forced to offload some of the expansion capabilities work to contractors in the technology processing industry.

The magnitude of donations for Hurricane Katrina victims was unprecedented in the ARC's history. Internet donors immediately overwhelmed the ARC website's capacity. More than fifty Internet technology staff members worked around-the-clock to expand capacity sixfold. The ARC once again outsourced some of the workload to Akamai Technologies, Inc.

There is a lesson to be learned from these continued action-and-reaction scenarios regarding online donation acceptance capacity. The lesson is that the ARC would benefit greatly from a plan outlining how to deal with the next crisis of insufficient capacity. Dave Clark, the chief technology officer at the ARC, believes that it would be a good idea to install a collaboration system. This would consist of a plan to effectively partner with various Internet technology firms to alleviate long-term problems regarding online capacity needs, as well as to deter the ARC from dealing with each disaster on a case-by-case basis, thus better serving the increasingly large online donor community.

MARKETING CHALLENGES AT THE RED CROSS

After much bad press, the ARC faces many challenges in marketing itself as a prominent, ethical, and transparent nonprofit organization. The ARC must effectively reduce perceived risk associated with giving to it, and must carefully choose partnerships with private corporations that will continue to encourage blood donations. The organization also must overcome any frivolous lawsuits that might damage its reputation. Lastly, the ARC must focus on marketing the positive impacts the organization has on society, including the vital role it plays in disaster relief. These marketing efforts will ideally translate into increased positive exposure and enhanced support for the organization.

Perceived Risks of Charitable Giving

Unfortunately for the ARC, many donors have been irritated by the numerous reports of fraudulent use of donations. Donors now associate a degree of uncertainty with giving to the ARC, as they question whether the funds will be used properly. The ARC has increased competition for funding as well. The number of nonprofit organizations searching for donor funds has increased dramatically in the past twenty years. In 1987 there were 422,000 nonprofit organizations in the United States; by 2005 the number had nearly doubled to 800,000. This growth obviously increases competition for charitable donations, especially in tough economic times. In order to maintain a strong donor base and continue to increase the monetary amount of donations, the ARC must increase transparency to assure donors that their money is being used responsibly.

Partnerships and the Red Cross Symbol

In 2004 the ARC joined in a unique marketing partnership with the independent film studio Lionsgate to co-market the release of a horror film entitled *Saw IV* while promoting blood collection services. The *Saw* "Give Till It Hurts" blood drive was a key element of the marketing campaign for the fourth installment of the most successful horror franchise of all time. Due in large part to promotions like the *Saw* blood drive in 2004, filmgoers' blood donations increased from 4,200 pints to 41,000 pints by 2007. In 2008, the *Saw* franchise again held a nationwide blood drive to draw attention to the release of *Saw V*. Marketing efforts such as these benefit both the film producers and the ARC by adding to the ARC's main goal of increasing blood supplies while also promoting the film. Many marketers

believe that this sort of age-specific marketing strategy, accompanied by word-of-mouth advertising, is the best way to reach a new pool of potential volunteers.

Lastly, the ARC benefits from brand recognition in the form of its internationally recognized Red Cross symbol, although this symbol also has generated controversy in the form of a lawsuit filed by Johnson & Johnson Company regarding licensing the Red Cross icon for use on commercial products. In 1887, Johnson & Johnson began using a red cross symbol on its surgical packages and registered the trademark for commercial use with the U.S. Patent Office in 1906. The ARC, on the other hand, cites its federal charter from the year 1900 as the adoption date for its emblem, and further points out that the image was developed in Switzerland in 1863 by the International Committee of the Red Cross, where the group decided that "volunteer nurses braving battlefields shall wear in all countries, as a uniform distinctive sign, a white armlet with a red cross."

In total, the ARC has sold first aid kits, preparedness kits, and related products that have generated over $2 million in revenue. Johnson & Johnson believed that the ARC was benefiting from consumers confusing the ARC packages for those of Johnson & Johnson, which has very similar packaging. The lawsuit was resolved in 2008, with both parties dismissing their suits and countersuits.

Focusing on Positive International Effects

From a marketing perspective, the greatest strength the ARC possesses is its ability to focus on the positive doings of its sister international organizations. The International Federation of Red Cross and Red Crescent Societies (IFRC) wrote a report discussing discrimination against women, the elderly, and the disabled in disasters. The IFRC concluded in this report that these situations, as well as sexual violence, can be prevented with an improvement in disaster-preparedness programs. This conclusion states that with stronger support by charitable organizations, such harsh discriminations can be reduced or eliminated in the future.

Even in incidents where the International Committee of the Red Cross (ICRC) is forced to evacuate a country, such as the case of Myanmar in 2006, the ARC has gained publicity from write-ups on the international association. An article in *The Economist,* for example, summarized Myanmar's decision regarding removal of the ICRC: "Last year the organization paid individual visits to more than 3,000 prisoners in 55 places. It has also been providing aid—foods, medicines, help with sanitation, and so on—to villages on the border." The article went on to state that "the ICRC announced that the ruling junta last month ordered it to close its five field offices in the country." Thus, even in negative circumstances, the positive coverage on the ICRC has benefitted the overall marketability of the ARC.

ETHICAL RISKS AND CHALLENGES

The American Red Cross faces many ethical risks and challenges. Some are common challenges for any organization of its size, such as executive compensation, preventing and handling employee misconduct, and considering all stakeholders in its operating model. Other risks are unique to the Red Cross, such as transparent and accurate representation of the organization's need for, and use of, monetary donations, volunteer time, and blood donations. Also, the ARC has the ethical challenges of maintaining effective and efficient operations to respond to disasters and transparently reporting the organization's accomplishments, failures, and opportunities for improvement in disaster response activities.

The executive turnover experienced by the ARC has brought to light the compensation awarded top executives. Bernadine Healy was given $1.9 million in salary and severance pay when she left in 2001. Marsha Evans was given $780,000 when she left in 2005. Much time and money was also spent in the search for and training of these top executives.

Employee misconduct also has been an issue, from the discrimination in disbursing relief after disasters to employee embezzlement. Such misconduct has occurred from New Orleans to Maryland and New Jersey, indicating a systemic problem. Addressing stakeholder needs, particularly those of the ARC's thousands of donors, is an ongoing challenge. Donors have a multitude of choices among nonprofits to support with their money and their time. They need open, honest, and transparent communication about how their resources are allocated and why such decisions are made. Issues like misrepresenting the use of the "Liberty Fund" collected after September 11 must be prevented if the ARC wishes to continue to be relevant.

The ARC must also address the specific ethical risks with its disaster response duties. Clear and efficient communications with federal and local government agencies is a challenge, as shown by the breakdown of communications in the aftermath of Hurricane Katrina. The ARC must develop strategic plans to better accomplish disaster response goals. These plans must include how to respond to organizational missteps and failures. Transparent, honest reporting of the ARC's goals, accomplishments, opportunities for improvement, and mistakes would go a long way to restoring the country's trust in the organization.

CONCLUSION

In short, the American Red Cross has a stakeholder obligation to fulfill its charter's expectations and deliver these promises effectively and efficiently. Charitable donations fund the nonprofit's operations and volunteers comprise 95 percent of its workers. The ARC staff and volunteers need to be well managed by capable directors and executives within ARC. Improvements to the ARC as an organization must begin with executive leadership and flow downward to every level of the group. Congressional oversight and interaction with federal, state, and local organizations must continue to be reviewed and modified to suit current needs.

Disaster relief cooperation in the form of partnering with private corporations to provide efficient and effective responses to victims of disasters should be continued. Joint marketing practices between the ARC and private businesses should also continue, as long unethical interactions or associations do not compromise the mission of the ARC. Close monitoring must be carried out by the many stakeholders of the ARC, including donors, staff, volunteers, and society in general.

QUESTIONS

1. Explain the possible problems in the ethical culture of the Red Cross that created the issues discussed in this case.

2. Name some of the problems the ARC has encountered with handling donation money.

3. What are some of the reasons for the ARC's ethical dilemmas, and how can the organization guarantee that these problems will not recur in the future?

4. What effect does organizational structure and compensation have on ethical behavior among chief executives at ARC?

SOURCES

"About Us," ARC, http://www.redcross.org/aboutus, accessed November 27, 2008.

American Red Cross, "Ethics Rules and Policies," http://www.redcross.org/www-files/Documents/Governance/file_cont5874_lang0_2226.pdf, pp. 7–8.

Archibold, Randal C., "California: Ex-Executive at Red Cross Pleads Guilty," *New York Times,* May 26, 2007, http://www.nytimes.com/2007/05/26/us/26brfs-EXEXECUTIVEA_BRF.html?_r=1, accessed December 22, 2008.

Attkisson, Sharyl, "Disaster Strikes in Red Cross Backyard," CBS Evening News, July 29, 2002, http://www.cbsnews.com/stories/2002/07/29/eveningnews/main516700.shtml, accessed April 21, 2008.

"The Battle Stations of the Cross," *Modern Healthcare* (August 20, 2007): 36.

Breitkopf, David, "Stored-Value Cards for Katrina Victims," *American Banker* 170, no. 173 (2005): 20.

"Caveat, Donor," *Searcher* 15, no. 2 (2007): 14.

"Discrimination in Disasters," *Time,* December 31, 2007, p. 31; "Red Cross Does Not Mark the Spot," *The Economist* (December 2, 2006): 47.

Dreazen, Yochi, "More Katrina Woes: Incidents of Fraud at Red Cross Centers," *Wall Street Journal,* October 14, 2005, p. B1.

Hackl, Franz, and Gerald Josef Pruckner, "Demand and Supply of Emergency Help: An Economic Analysis of Red Cross Services," *Health Policy* 77, no. 3 (2006): 338.

"Johnson & Johnson and American Red Cross Announce Resolution to Lawsuit," *Fox Business Online,* June 17, 2008, http://www.foxbusiness.com/story/markets/industries/health-care/johnson--johnson-american-red-cross-announce-resolution-lawsuit, accessed December 22, 2008.

Mullman, Jeremy, "Shoe on the Other Foot for Marin Institute," *Advertising Age* 77, no. 20 (2006): 8.

Nobel, Carmen, "Donations Test Red Cross Staff," *Eweek* 22, no. 37 (2005): 23.

"Overview of Red Cross Services," American Red Cross, 2008, http://www.redcross.org/portal/site/en/menuitem.86f46a12f382290517a8f210b80f78a0/?vgnextoid=1aa644e75215b110VgnVCM10000089f0870aRCRD&vgnextfmt=default, p. 3.

"Red Crossing the Line," *Brandweek,* September 3, 2007, p. 38.

Salmon, Jacqueline L., "Red Cross Gave Ousted Executive $780,000 Deal," *Washington Post,* March 4, 2006, p. A9.

Sontag, Deborah, "What Brought Bernadine Healy Down?," *New York Times,* December 21, 2001, http://query.nytimes.com/gst/fullpage.html?res=9C02EEDC173EF930A15751C1A9679C8B63, accessed December 22, 2008.

Spector, Mike, "Red Cross CEO Shuffles Executive Ranks," *Wall Street Journal,* September 23, 2008, http://online.wsj.com/article/SB122220688507068655.html, accessed October 21, 2008.

Strom, Stephanie, "Bill Would Restructure Red Cross," *New York Times,* December 5, 2006, http://www.nytimes.com/2006/12/05/washington/05cross.html, accessed April 17, 2008.

Strom, Stephanie, "Firing Stirs New Debate Over Red Cross," *New York Times,* November 29, 2007, http://www.nytimes.com/2007/11/29/us/29cross.html?ref=us, accessed April 14, 2008.

Strom, Stephanie, "President of Red Cross Resigns; Board Woes, Not Katrina, Cited," *New York Times,* December 14, 2005, http://www.nytimes.com/2005/12/14/politics/14redcross.html, accessed December 22, 2008.

Strom, Stephanie, "Red Cross Sifting Internal Charges Over Katrina Aid," *New York Times,* March 24, 2006, p. A2.

Suarez, Ray, "Red Cross Woes," The NewsHour with Jim Lehrer, December 19, 2001.

Thomas, Anisya, and Lynn Fritz, "Disaster Relief, Inc.," *Harvard Business Review* 84, no. 11 (2006): 121.

U.S. Government Accountability Office, "Coordination Between FEMA and the Red Cross Should Be Improved for the 2006 Hurricane Season," Report to Congressional Committees: Hurricanes Katrina and Rita, June 2006, p. 2.

Countrywide Financial: The Subprime Meltdown

Not too long ago, Countrywide Financial seemed to have everything going for it. Co-founded in part by Angelo Mozilo in 1969, it had become the largest provider of home loans in the United States within a few decades. By the early 2000s, one in six U.S. loans originated with Countrywide. In 1993, loan transactions reached the $1 trillion mark. Additionally, it was the number-one provider of home loans to minorities in the United States and had lowered the barriers of home ownership for lower-income individuals. Countrywide also offered loan closing, capital market, insurance, and banking services to its clients. In the 1970s, Countrywide had diversified into the securities market as well.

In 1992, Countrywide created a program called "House America" that enabled more consumers to qualify for home loans, as well as to make smaller down payments. In 2003, the company proposed the "We House America" program with a goal to provide $1 trillion in home loans to low-income and minority borrowers by 2010.

At the time, Countrywide's reputation in the industry was stellar. *Fortune* magazine called it the "23,000% stock" because between 1982 and 2003, Countrywide delivered investors a 23,000 percent return, exceeding the returns of Washington Mutual, Wal-Mart, and Warren Buffett's Berkshire Hathaway. In 1999, the company serviced $216.5 billion in loans. By 2000 the continued increase in revenues was attributed, in part, to home equity and subprime loans. The annual report for that year states: "Fiscal 2000 shows a higher margin for home equity and sub-prime loans (which, due in part to their higher cost structure charge a higher price per dollar loaned)."

Subprime loans were a key factor to Countrywide's immense success and rapid growth. However, the company's reliance on what was originally intended to aid low-income individuals also ended up contributing to its downfall.

UNDERSTANDING SUBPRIME LOANS

To understand Countrywide's failure, one must first understand the concept of subprime lending. Simply put, subprime lending means lending to borrowers, generally people who would not qualify for traditional loans, at a rate higher than the prime rate (market rate), although how far above depends on factors like credit score, down payment, debt-to-income ratio, and payment delinquencies. Subprime lending is risky because clients are less likely to be able to pay back their loans.

Although subprime loans can be made for a variety of purposes, mortgages have gained the most news coverage. Subprime mortgages fall into three categories. First is the interest-only mortgage, through which borrowers pay only the loan's interest for a set period of time. The second type allows borrowers to pay monthly, but this often means that

This case was prepared by John Fraedrich, O.C. Ferrell, and Jennifer Jackson, with the editorial assistance of Jennifer Sawayda. This case was prepared for classroom discussion, rather than to illustrate either effective or ineffective handling of an administrative, ethical, or legal decision by management. All sources used for this case were obtained through publicly available material.

borrowers opt to pay an amount smaller than that needed to reduce the amount owed on the loan. Third, borrowers can find themselves with mortgages featuring a fixed interest rate for a period, converting to variable rates after a while.

Typically, subprime loans are offered to high-risk clients who do not qualify for conventional loans. The average borrower has a credit score of below 620 and is generally in the low-income bracket. However, a 2007 *Wall Street Journal* study revealed that from 2004 to 2006, the rate of middle- and upper-income subprime loan borrowers rose dramatically. During the early to mid 2000s, when real estate prices were booming and confidence levels were high, even clients who could have qualified for regular loans chose to take out subprime loans to finance their real estate speculations. As real estate prices peaked, more well-to-do investors turned to subprime mortgages to finance their expensive homes.

Although they have caused an immense amount of damage in the financial sector, in relation to the loan market as a whole, subprime loans comprise a relatively small part. In 2008, more than 6 million U.S. homeowners had subprime loans with a combined value of over $600 billion. In comparison, all other U.S. loans amounted to over $10 trillion. Although these loans make up only a small chunk of the overall loan market, many consider subprime loans to be a key contributor to the 2008 financial crisis.

One of the tools of the subprime loan is the adjustable rate mortgage (ARM) that allows borrowers to pay low introductory payments for three to five years, which would then be adjusted annually as the prime interest rate increases or decreases. Another type of ARM involves paying interest for a set number of years with balloon payments, meaning that people would make interest payments only for the life of the loan, and then would be expected to pay the entire principal at once upon maturity of the loan. These tools worked as long as the housing market remained on an upward trajectory, but when housing prices fell or interest rates increased, people discovered that they were unable to pay.

Many financial experts contributed to the problem by telling clients that in the future they would certainly have more income because of the increases in their property's value. They assured home buyers that even if their monthly payments increased, they would be able to afford them because the value of their homes would have increased so much. Even consumers with good credit looking to refinance were attracted to the attractive interest rates of these mortgages without fully recognizing the possible consequences.

THE SUBPRIME CRISIS

When first popularized, the financial tool of subprime loans was praised for lowering barriers to home ownership. The U.S. Department of Housing and Urban Development stated that the subprime loan was helping many minorities afford homes, and was therefore a good tool.

Although subprime lending became a major news topic only in the early part of the twenty-first century, the subprime concept began in the 1970s in Orange County, California. At this time, rural farmland was being converted into suburbs, and subprime loans were a way for people to buy homes even if their credit was poor. The typical subprime recipient would not have met normal lending standards. At that time, the subprime loans made sense as a means to fuel southern California's growth. Homes were appreciating rapidly, so if a family decided to buy a house and live there for three to five years, they could reasonably expect that home to sell for over 50 percent more than what they had paid. In addition, Congress passed the Equal Credit Opportunity Act in 1974 to help ensure that all consumers had an equal chance to receive a loan. Potential homeowners, in theory, would no longer be rejected based on sex, race, national origin, or any other factor considered discriminatory.

Contractors also wanted a part of the action. They began to build houses and "flip" them. Flipping is when the contractor builds homes without buyers on credit, and then takes the sale of the homes to the lending institution as collateral to obtain more credit to build more homes. Speculators also flipped existing homes by buying them on credit with no intention of keeping them, waiting until the value had increased, and selling them at a profit.

Industries that supplied homebuilders were profiting as well, and costs of materials increased with the high demand. Realtors were motivated to push sales through because of commissions they could earn (on average 6 percent of the sales price). Commissions were a significant part of many mortgage officers' compensation. Even real estate appraisers began to inflate the value of homes to ensure loans would go through. This was to become one of the chief accusations against Countrywide during the financial crisis.

But then something happened that no one had considered. The U.S. economy began to slow. People started working more and earning less money. Jobs started moving abroad, health insurance became more expensive, gas prices increased, and the baby boomers began to sell their homes to fund their retirement. In spite of this, builders kept on building, and the financial industry continued to lend to increasingly risky buyers. Homeowners found that they had less and less disposable income to make housing payments.

The result was a surplus of housing in which homeowners could no longer afford their homes. Banks began to foreclose on houses when the homeowners could not pay. As the demand for housing decreased, banks lost significant amounts of money. Many other industries, like the automobile industry and insurance companies, were also negatively affected as struggling citizens tried to cope with the economic downturn. With plummeting stock prices, the United States began

experiencing a financial crisis that had a rippling effect across the world. Economist Alan Greenspan said the crisis could be "the most wrenching since the end of the Second World War."

Late 2007 marked the tipping-point for the burgeoning mortgage crisis. Foreclosure rates skyrocketed, and borrowers and investors began to feel the full ramifications of taking the subprime risk. Mortgage defaults played a part in triggering a string of serious bank and financial institution failures as well. Investors began to abandon their mortgage-backed securities, causing huge institutions such as Morgan Stanley, Merrill Lynch, and Citigroup to lose large sums of money. Morgan Stanley, for example, lost over $265 billion internationally. Bear Stearns required government intervention to stay afloat. Analysts have attributed the banks' failings to poor intra-bank communication and a lack of effective risk management.

Although the chief financial officer (CFO) is supposed to be in charge of risk management, it appears that many institutions viewed the role as merely advisory. It was highly risky for these firms to downplay the importance of the CFO. Not only did many of these banks fail at risk management, but they also were in violation of the Sarbanes-Oxley Act—which requires that a company verify its ability to internally control its financial reporting. A CFO not directly in charge of a company's finances is signing off on something that he or she actually knows little about. The extent of the 2008–2009 financial crisis has made it clear to many that a massive overhaul of the financial industry's regulatory system is needed.

COUNTRYWIDE'S INVOLVEMENT IN THE SUBPRIME CRISIS

During the early 2000s, Countrywide reaped the benefits of subprime loans. In 2001, mortgages contributed to 28 percent of Countrywide's earnings, with subprime loans up to $280 million (the year before, subprime loans represented $86.9 million). In 2002, Countrywide's loan portfolio to minorities and low- to moderate-income borrower tracts had dramatically and rapidly increased. Countrywide had also increased its commissioned sales force by nearly 60 percent, to 3,484 salespeople in 2003, with the goal of increasing overall market share.

Some critics have argued that salespeople were given incentives to undertake riskier transactions in order to continue to grow the company at a rapid rate. One allegation against Countrywide is that, in order to increase its profit, it would even offer subprime loans to people who qualified for regular loans. Leading the day-to-day operations of the Consumer Markets Division was David Sambol, who would later be implicated in the scandal.

After years of fast growth and upbeat projections, Countrywide's 2007 annual report had a somber tone. The financial crisis had begun and the company was feeling its negative effects. A significant amount of the report focused on the details of accounting for its mortgage portfolio and default rates. In one year, Countrywide depreciated over $20 billion and absorbed over $1 billion in losses. By 2008, the company had accrued over $8 billion in subprime loans with a 7 percent delinquency rate. The industry average was 4.67 percent delinquency. That year foreclosures doubled, and the firm laid off 10 to 20 percent of its employees, or 10,000 to 20,000 people.

The company attempted to ease loan terms on more than 81,000 homeowners with a program called the Countrywide Comprehensive Home Preservation Program. The program allowed consumers to refinance or modify loans with an adjustable rate mortgage for a lower interest rate or switch to a fixed-rate mortgage. The president and chief operating officer, David Sambol, stated, "Countrywide believes that none of our subprime borrowers that have demonstrated the ability to make payments should lose their home to foreclosure solely as a result of a rate [increase]. This is yet another step in our continuing effort to identify and improve existing programs that assist our customers."

Countrywide also created special divisions to help borrowers, and actively informed its customers about their options. The company offered phone counseling teams, personalized resource mailings, and counselors within communities who could meet face-to-face. Countrywide appeared to be genuine in its attempts to help homeowners, but it was too little too late. By then questions and accusations had begun to develop against company leaders.

In 2008, Alphonso Jackson, Secretary of Housing and Urban Development (HUD), reported that more than 500,000 Countrywide consumers were in danger of facing foreclosure. The blame for this was focused primarily on subprime lending and adjustable rate mortgages. Countrywide Financial countered that there were other reasons for delinquencies and foreclosures. It maintained the main causes of delinquencies and foreclosures were unrelated to the company's investment decisions—issues like medical problems, divorce, and unemployment—not adjustable rate mortgages. It further claimed that less than 1 percent of its consumers had defaulted on account of adjustable rate mortgages. Still, consumers began to question whether Countrywide's risky lending played a role in the larger financial crisis.

ISSUES RELATED TO THE BANK OF AMERICA ACQUISITION

In 2008, Bank of America, one of the United States' top financial institutions with $683 billion in assets, offered to buy Countrywide Financial for $4 billion. The price tag was a substantial discount on what the company was actually worth. Bank of America paid approximately $8/share while shares were valued at $20/share earlier in the year. Kenneth D. Lewis, chair, president, and CEO of Bank of America, said at the time, "We are aware of the issues within the housing and mortgage industries. The transaction reflects those challenges. Mortgages will continue to be an important relationship product, and we now will have an opportunity to better serve our customers and to enhance future profitability."

At the time, Bank of America held $1.5 trillion in assets, which better equipped them to deal with the crisis. "Their balance sheet can take a shock much better than Countrywide," said CreditSights senior analyst David Hendler. "When you take the shocks at Countrywide, they have a big, busting consequence that's negative." Bart Narter, senior analyst at Celent, a Boston-based financial research and consulting firm, said, "There's still plenty of risk involved. He's brave to do it. But I think that it's very likely down the road to be profitable, maybe not immediately, but long-term."

However, there may have been other reasons why Countrywide allowed Bank of America to acquire it. It may be that Countrywide thought Bank of America was better able to handle the ethical investigations concerning Countrywide taken on by the government. Among other issues, Countrywide was coming under increased scrutiny for giving out so-called *liar loans*. Liar loans are mortgages that require no proof of the borrower's income or assets. These loans allowed consumers to purchase homes while having few or no assets. With the additional burden of the financial crisis, many homeowners with liar loans could not pay their mortgages, nor were they able to refinance their homes because housing prices plummeted. Some were forced into foreclosure, generating substantial losses for mortgage companies and the economy. One economic website estimated that the true cost of liar loans totaled over $100 billion in losses.

Countrywide Financial was one of the top providers of liar loans. These loans allowed the industry to profit, at least for a little while, because people with liar loans were riskier clients, and therefore had to pay higher fees and interest rates to the mortgage company. Many accuse Countrywide of negligence, of giving out highly risky loans to people who could

not afford them for the sake of quick profits. Others accuse the company of even more unethical dealings. Some homeowners who are now struggling under liar loans are accusing Countrywide of *predatory lending*, saying the company misled them.

Although some homeowners may have been truly misled into liar loans, an estimated 90 percent of liar loan applicants knowingly overstated their income, with three out of five overstating it by at least 50 percent. This rampant dishonesty, critics charge, could not have occurred without the mortgage company's awareness. It has sparked new investigations into whether Countrywide *aided* borrowers in falsifying information. Hence, some attest that Countrywide's buyout by Bank of America may have been more than just an economic choice. Instead, it could have been a way to prepare for the onslaught of criticism that would arise against Countrywide.

In March 2008, Bank of America decided to retain David Sambol, Executive Managing Director of Business Segment Operations at Countrywide, as well as to pay him a hefty compensation package. Sambol received a bachelor's degree in Business Administration and Accounting from California State University, Northridge, in 1982. Prior to joining Countrywide in 1985, Sambol served as a certified public accountant with the accounting firm of Ernst & Whinney. After getting hired at Countrywide, his unit led all revenue-generating functions of the company. He was instrumental in Countrywide's mortgage division expanding to become the most comprehensive in the industry.

In March 2008, Bank of America agreed to set up a $20 million retention account for Sambol, payable in equal installments on the first and second anniversaries of the merger, plus $8 million in restricted stock. Sambol's retention package also included the use of a company car or car allowance, country club dues, and financial consulting services through the end of 2009. He was also to continue to have access to a company airplane for business and personal travel.

Much of the public was outraged that Sambol would receive such high compensation after taking part in Countrywide's questionable business dealings. The outcry over Countrywide Financial and other companies that had participated in the subprime mortgage market was so great that the U.S. Congress held a series of hearings to investigate dealings in the subprime market. Senator Charles E. Schumer, D–NY, chair of Congress' Joint Economic Committee, asked Bank of America to reconsider the decision to put Sambol in charge of home lending. "There seem to be two economic realities operating in our country today," said Representative Henry A. Waxman, D–CA, the committee chair. "Most Americans live in a world where economic security is precarious and there are real economic consequences for failure. But our nation's top executives seem to live by a different set of rules. The question before the committee was: when companies fail to perform, should they still give millions of dollars to their senior executives?" After the hearings, Bank of America announced that Barbara Desoer, Bank of America's chief technology and operations officer, would replace Sambol. Sambol would continue to receive some, though not all, of his perks.

THE ROLE OF COUNTRYWIDE'S CEO ANGELO MOZILO

Angelo Mozilo is being investigated by the SEC for potential fraud, although Mozilo maintains his innocence. Particularly, the SEC is concerned about the sale of company stock options that netted Mozilo over $400 million between 2002 and 2008. Mozilo has always maintained his innocence. In a 2007 *Business Week* interview, Mozilo was asked about allegations that he profited over $100 million on stock sales in the previous year. Mozilo asserted, "I have not sold any stock, to my recollection, in 10 years. Everything I've sold was options. The selling is because [when the options] expire, I no longer have the benefit of what I have built and what this team has built for the last 40 years. Up until this debacle, I created $25 billion in value for shareholders. There have been very few—only about 11 stocks—that have performed better over the last 25 years than Countrywide. I could have sold all of those shares at 40 bucks a share and didn't because I want to be aligned with the shareholders."

The public did not seem to believe Mozilo's defense, especially after he received a $100 million severance package when Countrywide was sold to Bank of America. In 2007–2008, Mozilo was named as a defendant in many lawsuits. The plaintiffs included:

- International Brotherhood of Electrical Workers Local 98 Pension Fund
- Norfolk County Retirement System
- Arkansas Teacher Retirement System
- Fire & Police Pension Association of Colorado
- Public Employees' Retirement System of Mississippi
- Argent Classic Convertible Arbitrage Fund
- New Jersey Carpenters' Pension Fund
- New York City Employees' Retirement System

One lawsuit alleged misconduct and disregard of fiduciary duties, including a lack of good faith and lack of oversight of Countrywide's lending practices. The lawsuit also accused Countrywide of improper financial reporting and lack of internal controls, alleging that Mozilo was paid $10 million more than was disclosed. Additionally, the company claimed that Countrywide's officers and directors unlawfully sold over $848 million of stock between 2004 and 2008 at inflated prices using insider information.

Mozilo's pay also drew heavy scrutiny from members of Congress. Federal securities regulators and congressional investigators found that easy bonus targets and other underhanded methods helped him inflate his pay. In the hearings about executive pay, Congressman Elijah E. Cummings of Maryland said, "We've got golden parachutes drifting off to the golf course and have people I see every day who are losing their homes and wondering where their kids will do their homework." He then asked Mozilo about an e-mail message he sent demanding that the taxes due on his wife's travel on the corporate jet be covered by the company. "It sounds out of whack today because it is out of whack, but in 2006 the company was going great," said Mozilo. "In today's world I would never write that memo." He also apologized for another e-mail message in which he complained about his compensation. "It was an emotional time," he said. But in the same hearings, Mozilo also reminded the audience that Countrywide's stock price had appreciated over 23,000 percent from 1982 to 2007. Shareholders did approve Mozilo's performance-based bonuses and he exercised the options as he prepared for retirement. "In short, as our company did well, I did well," he said.

BANK OF AMERICA PLANS A RECOVERY

In July 2008, Bank of America bought Countrywide without Sambol or Mozilo. Since 2001, Bank of America has been focused on profit, not growth. However, it might be a while before Bank of America profits from the acquisition of Countrywide. According to the Securities and Exchange Commission, Bank of America has taken on $16.6 billion in Countrywide's debts. Exiting the subprime lending market is part of Bank of America's long-term plan. The company liquidated $26.3 billion of its subprime real estate portfolio in 2008–2009 and has managed its existing $9.7 billion portfolio over its remaining term.

Bank of America clearly understood that by buying Countrywide, it inherited a volatile earning stream that had become unattractive from a risk-reward standpoint. Kenneth Lewis, CEO of Bank of America said at the time, "We are committed to achieving consistent, above-average shareholder returns and these actions are aimed at achieving that mission." Bank of America plans to replace Countrywide's brand with its own.

In addition to managing Countrywide's debt, Bank of America must also handle the stream of lawsuits being filed against the company. Many of these lawsuits claim that the company duped homeowners with predatory loan practices. Countrywide has agreed to provide $8 billion in loan and foreclosure relief to more than 397,000 homeowners. It also has agreed to adjust the terms of ARMs according to borrowers' income. Bank of America's Barbara Doeser, who replaced David Sambol, said the company is committed to helping homeowners and is cutting interest rates to as low as 2.5 percent.

Countrywide is facing additional investigations for other alleged cases of misconduct. In March 2008, the FBI started an investigation to find out whether Countrywide misrepresented its financial information. Additionally, the FBI is investigating Countrywide's VIP program that, according to an insider, provided special mortgage deals to certain high-up officials, known as "Friends of Angelo's." These deals included discount rates and fees not offered to ordinary Countrywide customers. Those implicated in these dealings include Democratic senators Chris Dodd and Kent Conrad, two former cabinet members, and two CEOs from Fannie Mae. These officials have denied that they knew they were getting special discounts. Prosecutors are looking into whether these discounts constituted improper gifts and whether they qualified as illegal on Countrywide's part.

Despite these proceedings, Bank of America Barbara Doeser remains optimistic about the future. Like so many others, Bank of America suffered massive losses as 2008 came to a close, with a drop in net income of 95 percent in the fourth quarter. Yet Doeser has cited some improvements. She said, "But last quarter, the first quarter that Countrywide and Bank of America operated as one company, we made 250,000 first mortgages, worth $51 billion of principal, plus $6 billion of home-equity loans." The company is predicting that home prices will stabilize by late 2009.

CONCLUSION

Countrywide was not the only cause of the financial crisis. Numerous Wall Street companies are being investigated for unethical practices related to this scandal. (This list includes the Bank of America, which has been investigated for potential breaches of fiduciary duty concerning employee retirement funds.) However, Countrywide's unethical behavior was a key contributor to the problems with the economy in 2008–2009. Many consider it to be one of the central villains in this crisis. They allege that Countrywide knowingly engaged in risky loans, offering subprime loans even to those who qualified for regular loans, in order to profit from the higher rates. In the process, it may have helped to falsify lender information, allowing those with no assets to obtain loans. The consequence was a surplus of housing, plummeting housing prices, and a slew of foreclosures, all of which placed the economy in a precarious state. The result is that the United States has lost global credibility as an economic superpower of the free world.

The Countrywide scandal has brought up other issues, including that of executive compensation. Should executives receive hefty compensation packages and severance pay when their companies flounder? Should they be called into account for not exercising due care? Many people think so, as evidenced by the enormous public outrage facing those like David Sambol and Angelo Mozilo. It is clear that Countrywide has failed the majority of its stakeholders. Ethical misconduct and high-risk

business practices helped to create the disaster at Countrywide. It remains to be seen whether its acquisition by the Bank of America will be enough to salvage its reputation and to save the business that was once Countrywide Financial.

QUESTIONS

1. Are subprime loans an unethical financial instrument, or are they ethical but misused in a way that created ethical issues?

2. Discuss the ethical issues that caused the downfall of Countrywide Financial.

3. How should Bank of America deal with potential ethical and legal misconduct discovered at Countrywide?

SOURCES

"Bank of America Assumes $16.6B in Countrywide Debt," *Dayton Business Journal*, November 10, 2008, http://www.bizjournals.com/dayton/stories/2008/11/10/daily7.html, accessed November 14, 2008.

Bartiromo, Maria, "Countrywide Feels the Heat," *BusinessWeek*, August 29, 2007, http://www.businessweek.com/bwdaily/dnflash/content/aug2007/db20070829_117563.htm?chan=search, accessed March 16, 2008.

Caputo, Angela, "Countrywide Accord Paves Way for More Loan Remodifications," *Progress Illinois*, November 12, 2008, http://progressillinois.com/2008/11/12/loan-modification-plan.

Countrywide Financial, http://about.countrywide.com, accessed September 1, 2009.

"Countrywide Moves to Ease Mortgage Misery," *BusinessWeek*, October 23, 2007, www.businessweek.com/investor/content/oct2007/pi20071023_454573.htm, accessed March 16, 2008.

Colvin, Geoff, "Signs of Life from the Mortgage Frontline," *Forbes*, November 13, 2008, http://money.cnn.com/2008/11/12/magazines/fortune/colvin_desoer.fortune/?postversion=2008111311, accessed November 14, 2008.

Equal Credit Opportunity Act, Federal Trade Commission, http://www.ftc.gov/bcp/edu/pubs/consumer/credit/cre15.shtm, accessed September 1, 2009.

Farzad, Roben, "In Search of a Subprime Villain," *BusinessWeek*, January 24, 2008, http://www.businessweek.com/magazine/content/08_05/b4069077193810.htm?chan=search, accessed March 16, 2008.

Gimein, Mark, "Inside the Liar's Loan: How the Mortgage Industry Nurtured Deceit," *Slate*, April 24, 2008, http://www.slate.com/id/2189576/, accessed November 14, 2008.

Greenspan, Alan, "We Will Never Have a Perfect Model of Risk," *Financial Times*, March 16, 2008, http://www.ft.com/cms/s/edbdbcf6-f360-11dc-b6bc-0000779fd2ac,Authorised=false.html?_i_location=http%3A%2F%2Fwww.

ft.com%2Fcms%2Fs%2F0%2Fedbdbcf6-f360-11dc-b6bc-0000779fd2ac.html%3Fnclick_check%3D1&_i_referer=http%3A%2F%2Fsearch.yahoo.com%2Fsearch%3Fp%3Dthe%2Bmost%2Bwrenching%2Bsince%2Bthe%2Bend%2Bof%2Bthe%2Bsecond%2Bworld%2Bwar%252C%2BAlan%2BGreenspan%26fr%3Dyfp-t-501%26toggle%3D1%26cop%3Dmss%26ei%3DUTF-8&nclick_check=1, accessed November 15, 2008.

Gutierrez, Carl, "Countrywide's New Bad News," *Forbes*, March 10, 2008, http://www.forbes.com/markets/2008/03/10/countrywide-fbi-mortgage-markets-equity-cx_cg_0310markets26.html, accessed September 1, 2009.

"Judge Rules Mozilo and Countrywide Execs Must Face Multi-Million Dollar Federal Lawsuit," *New York Times*, May 22, 2008, http://www.nytimes.com/2008/03/07/business/07cnd-pay.html?_r=1&oref=slogin, accessed September 1, 2009.

"Kansas, 11 Other States Reach Agreement with Countrywide Financial Corporation," *Kansas City Info Zine,* November 14, 2008, http://www.infozine.com/news/stories/op/storiesView/sid/31858/, accessed September 1, 2009.

"'Liar Loans' Threaten to Prolong Mortgage Mess," MSNBC, August 18, 2008, http://www.msnbc.msn.com/id/26270434/, accessed November 14, 2008.

Marco, Meg, "Subprime Meltdown: Inside the Countrywide Subprime Lending Frenzy," *The Consumerist*, August 27, 2008, http://consumerist.com/consumer/subprime-meltdown/inside-the-countrywide-subprime-lending-frenzy-293902.php, accessed November 13, 2008.

Mortgage Industry Statistics, LenderRATEMATCH, freeratesearch.com/en/newsroom/mortgage_statistics/, accessed April 1, 2008.

Moyer, Liz, "A Subprime Solution," *Forbes*, December 6, 2007, http://www.forbes.com/wallstreet/2007/12/05/subprime-paulson-bush-biz-wall-cx_lm_1206subprime.html, accessed March 25, 2008.

Myers, Lisa, and Amna Nawaz, "Feds Probe Countrywide's 'VIP' Program," NBC News, October 30, 2008, http://deepbackground.msnbc.msn.com/archive/2008/10/30/1613877.aspx, accessed November 14, 2008.

Reckard, Scott, "Countrywide Head Ousted by Bank of America," *Los Angeles Times,* May 29, 2008, http://www2.tbo.com/content/2008/may/29/bz-countrywide-head-ousted-by-bank-of-america/?news-money, accessed June 2008.

Subprime Lending, United States Department of Housing and Urban Development, http://www.hud.gov/offices/fheo/lending/subprime.cfm, accessed March 16, 2008.

Wartzman, Rick, "The Countrywide Conundrum," *BusinessWeek*, November 9, 2007, http://www.businessweek.com/managing/content/nov2007/ca2007119_693870.htm?chan=search, accessed March 16, 2008.

Coping with Financial and Ethical Risks at American International Group (AIG)

When American International Group (AIG) collapsed in September 2008 and was subsequently saved by a government bailout, it became one of the most controversial players in the 2008–2009 financial crises. The corporate culture at AIG had been involved in a high-stakes risk-taking scheme supported by managers and employees that appeared entirely focused on short-term financial rewards. Out of a firm of 116,000 employees, one unit with around 500 employees, AIG Financial Products, was chiefly to blame. Current CEO Ed Liddy, who was summoned by former Treasury Secretary Hank Paulson, estimates that only twenty to thirty people were directly involved in bringing down the company.

The AIG Financial Products unit specialized in derivatives and other complex financial contracts that were tied to subprime mortgages or commodities. While its dealings were risky, the unit generated billions of dollars of profits for AIG. Nevertheless, during his long tenure as CEO of AIG, Maurice "Hank" Greenberg had been open about his suspicions of the AIG Financial Products unit. However, after Greenberg resigned as chief executive of AIG in 2005, the Financial Products unit became even more speculative in its activities.

Immediately before its collapse, AIG had exposure to $64 billion in potential subprime mortgage losses. The perfect storm formed with the subprime mortgage crisis and a sudden sharp downturn in the value of residential real estate in 2008. Since much of the speculation in the Financial Products unit was tied to derivatives, even small movements in the value of financial measurements could result in catastrophic losses.

In this case, we trace the history of AIG as it evolved into one of the largest and most respected insurance companies in the world, and the more recent events that led to its demise. AIG had a market value of close to $200 billion in 2007, and by 2009 this amount had fallen to a mere $3.5 billion. Only a government rescue of what has amounted to $180 billion in loans, investments, guarantees, and financial injections prevented AIG from facing total bankruptcy in late 2008.

Saving AIG was not meant as a reward, however. The government rescued the company not to keep it from bankruptcy, but to prevent the bankruptcies of many other global financial institutions that depended on AIG as counterparty on collateralized debt obligations. If AIG had been allowed to fail, it is possible that the financial meltdown that occurred in 2008–2009 would have been worse.

This case first examines the events leading up to the 2008 meltdown, including the philosophy of top management and the corporate culture that set the stage for AIG's demise. Then it reviews the events that occurred in 2008, including ethical issues related to transparency and failed internal controls. Finally, the analysis looks at the role of the government and its decision to bail out AIG, taking 79.9 percent ownership in a company that

O.C. Ferrell and John Fraedrich prepared this case with the assistance of Jennifer Jackson. This case was prepared for classroom discussion, rather than to illustrate either effective or ineffective handling of an administrative, ethical, or legal decision by management. All sources used for this case were obtained through publicly available material.

grossly mishandled its responsibility to its stakeholders.

AIG'S HISTORY

The saga of American International Group (AIG) began in 1919 with the U.S.-born Cornelius Vander Starr, who founded a company in Shanghai representing American insurance companies selling fire and marine coverage in Asia. Starr's success in Shanghai quickly led to expansion across Asia, and to the United States in 1926. While AIG began as a representative of American insurance companies abroad, in the United States it provided insurance risk coverage to insurance companies as a way to disperse liabilities. Reinsurers such as AIG were created to remove some of the risk associated with large disasters. Because of AIG and others, insurance companies could grow faster than ever before.

Insurance companies are educated risk takers. When insurance companies feel they have too much risk, they go to their reinsurance companies, such as AIG, to take out insurance so that if something catastrophic happens, they can still pay their clients. AIG utilizes models to determine how much insurance it can sell to insurers and still pay out. To put it simply, AIG charges insurance companies a premium in order to allow them to spread their risk so that they can sell insurance policies and grow more rapidly.

In 1968, Maurice "Hank" Greenberg, a native New Yorker and experienced insurance executive who had been with AIG for many years, took over as CEO. AIG grew exponentially during his tenure. By the end of the 1980s, the company had become the largest underwriter of commercial and industrial coverage in the United States and the leading international insurance organization.

AIG continued to expand throughout the 1990s, led by its return to China as the first foreign insurance organization granted a license by the Chinese authorities to operate a wholly-owned insurance business in Shanghai. AIG later expanded to Guangzhou, Shenzhen, Beijing, and Vietnam. In 2001 AIG established two joint ventures in general insurance and life insurance in India with the Tata Group, the leading Indian industrial conglomerate. New AIG subsidiary companies followed the fall of the Soviet Union into Eastern Europe, with general and life insurance companies formed in Russia, Poland, Hungary, and the Czech Republic, among other emerging markets.

In 2001 AIG purchased American General Corporation, a top U.S. life insurer. This acquisition made AIG a leader in the U.S. life insurance industry and consumer lending. Today, the four principal business areas of AIG are: General Insurance, Life Insurance and Retirement Services, Financial Services, and Asset Management. For the individual consumer, business, financial professional, or insurance professional, AIG provides: Accident and Health Insurance, Auto Insurance, Life Insurance, Banking and Loans, Retirement Services, Travel Insurance, Additional Services, and Annuities. Immediately before its 2008 collapse, AIG had revenues exceeding $110 billion, with total assets of over $1 trillion, and 116,000 employees around the world.

AIG'S CULTURE

Maurice "Hank" Greenberg was the CEO of AIG for 38 years, and was therefore a key player in shaping the modern face and corporate culture of the company. Many considered Greenberg a genius in the insurance business, and arguably he was one of the most successful and influential executives in the business. But critics called him autocratic in his drive to expand the company into an international powerhouse.

During his career, Greenberg championed innovative products that insure almost any type of risk, including Internet identity theft and hijacking. At least four U.S. presidents sought Greenberg's advice on international affairs and financial markets. And Greenberg was always known for utilizing his contacts and influence to help advance the company. Over the years, Greenberg aggressively lobbied for laws and rulings favorable to AIG. He was very involved with international politics and helped the U.S. government to secure information and develop back-door channels for classified dealings. In return, AIG was given the benefit of the doubt when regulatory agencies came questioning the company's doings. When billions or trillions of dollars are involved, global corporations have powers equal to or greater than those of governments and regulatory agencies.

In spite of Greenberg's active networking, the early 2000s found AIG under investigation by the Securities and Exchange Commission for its "finite insurance" deals—contracts that covered specific amounts of losses rather than unexpected losses of indeterminate size—and what appeared to be loans (since premiums were structured to match policy payouts and eliminate risk) rather than genuine risk allocation vehicles. A federal inquiry later found information that Greenberg might have been personally involved in creating a bogus reinsurance transaction with General Re to fraudulently boost AIG's reserves. New York Attorney General Spitzer subpoenaed Greenberg, who treated the summons far more lightly than he should have. As rumors swirled, AIG's stock began to plummet, and the AIG board started to become concerned.

In 2005, Greenberg was forced out as CEO. Martin Sullivan succeeded him and held the CEO position for three years, followed by Robert Willumstad for three months. Willumstad was forced to step down in 2008 in the wake of the corporation's meltdown. The current CEO is Edward Liddy, the former CEO of The Allstate Corporation. The SEC leveled charges of fraud against Greenberg resulting from the circumstances surrounding his departure. In order to settle the charges that AIG manipulated financial statements in 2005, the company paid the SEC $1.6 billion in 2006, and Greenberg agreed to pay an additional $15 million in 2009.

WHAT HAPPENED AT AIG TO CAUSE ITS DEMISE?

AIG's troubles leading up to the 2008 bailout were, at the heart, caused by a kind of derivative called credit default swaps (CDSs). Credit default swaps are financial products that transfer the credit exposure (risk) of fixed-income products (bonds) between parties. The buyer of a credit swap receives credit protection, whereas the seller of the swap guarantees the creditworthiness of the product. By doing this, the risk of default is transferred from the holder of the fixed-income security to the seller of the swap. One single credit default swap can be valued at hundreds of millions of dollars.

As a reinsurer, AIG used CDSs as a kind of insurance policy on complex collateralized debt obligations (CDOs). The company issued the swaps and promised to pay these institutions, AIG's counterparties, if the debt securities defaulted. However, AIG did not have a large enough safety net to weather the subprime mortgage collapse. These insurance contracts became essentially worthless because many people could not pay back their subprime mortgages and AIG did not have the creditworthiness for the big collateral call.

The government took the drastic step to bail out the company, providing the funds to purchase the CDOs that were being held by banks, hedge funds, and other financial institutions, and in the process ended up with 79.9 percent ownership of AIG. The U.S. government is now the senior partner in a special-purpose entity that will receive interest and share liability in the ownership of these tainted investment instruments. The fear behind this move was that if AIG had been allowed to go bankrupt, many banks throughout the world would have gone bankrupt as well.

Although overall AIG had a diversified insurance business, one unit, AIG Financial Products, was the source of many of the company's woes. Formed more than twenty years ago to trade over-the-counter derivatives, its creation was timed perfectly to ride the derivatives market boom. By and large, Financial Products was run like a hedge fund out of London and Wilton, Connecticut. Hedge funds are a special type of fund available to a select range of investors. They seek to utilize a wide variety of investment tools to mitigate, or *hedge,* risk—oftentimes the term refers to funds that use short selling as a means of increasing investment returns. Short selling is betting that the stock price of a company will change during a specified period of time. When the stocks move the expected direction, the investor makes money.

AIG Financial Products specialized in derivatives that generated billions of dollars in profits over the years. Derivatives are financial contracts or instruments whose value is derived from something else such as commodities (corn, wheat, soybeans, etc.), stocks, bonds, and even home mortgages. Gains or losses from derivatives come from betting correctly on the movement of these values. The unit also dealt in mortgage securities, a sector that turned rancid with the collapse of the housing bubble. Former New York Attorney General Eliot Spitzer, a champion of financial sector reform, claimed that AIG Financial Products was "the black hole of AIG."

The AIG Financial Products unit was founded in 1987 by Howard Sosin. When Sosin joined AIG he was given an unusual deal: a 20 percent stake in the unit and 20 percent of its profits. While AIG can be described as a conservative global conglomerate selling insurance policies to businesses and individuals, the Financial Products unit was staffed by quantitative specialists with doctorates in finance and math who, it seems, were very willing to take risks. This unit thought it was above the insurance operations, and its employees conducted themselves like investment bankers.

In the late 1990s under the leadership of Joseph Cassano, AIG Financial Products ramped up its business of selling credit default swaps, which were at the heart of the 2008–2009 financial meltdown. AIG Financial Products expanded into writing swaps to cover debt that was backed by mortgages. The unit sold swaps to large institutional investors. These collateralized debt obligations were backed by mortgages, and the swaps issued by AIG backed some $440 billion worth of obligations. To put this in perspective, the entire market worth of AIG was around $200 billion at the time. AIG made millions selling collateralized debt obligations (CDOs) and was able to post modest margin requirements, which is the amount the company keeps as a deposit to protect against the risk of loan defaults or nonpayments. For example, to buy stock on margin, you must have at least 50 percent of the purchase price in your account. AIG was able to make these CDO deals with a very small fraction of actual money on hand. Unfortunately, some of these CDOs were attached to home mortgages.

In spite of the risk, the company involved itself in bad mortgage lending by financial institutions that did not have sufficient capital to cover the loans, which in turn had bought this type of insurance from AIG that created an unstable financial environment. The loans and the CDOs were often sold to people who could not repay their debt. CEO Greenberg became concerned about this unit's derivative dealings and asked a group to shadow its trades. Greenberg was uncomfortable with the results and thought the unit was taking too many risks. However, Greenberg left the company in 2005 because of regulators investigating AIG over its accounting practices.

AIG sold credit protection on CDOs by simply writing pieces of paper that stated that AIG would cover the losses in case these obligations went bad. AIG agreed to either take over the obligations or cover the losses on CDOs. While AIG made billions of dollars in profits and managers received millions of dollars in compensation for selling these so-called insurance policies, it turned out to be a high-risk house of cards. The tools, CDOs and CDSs, were used recklessly and failed to assess systemic risk of counterparties not measuring their own exposures and not paying their obligations. The Financial Products unit has been under ongoing investigations around the world, including by the United Kingdom's Serious Fraud Office.

Although they have gained notoriety now, before 2008 derivatives were not widely understood by the public, mass media, regulators, and many of the executives who were providing the oversight for their use. AIG could have taken another approach by buying mortgages or CDOs and then having some other party package them into a credit default swap as insurance, but since AIG was an insurer it simply wrote policies on CDOs, thus increasing revenues with the hope that only a few would default. Of course, AIG guessed wrong and became the epicenter of a financial nightmare that has caused many bank failures and a worldwide financial depression.

AIG Lacked Transparency

There is evidence that AIG knew of potential problems in valuing derivative contracts before the 2008–2009 financial meltdown occurred. Outside auditors raised concerns about being excluded from conversations on the evaluation of derivatives. But during this time period, AIG executives Cassano and Sullivan continued to reassure investors and auditors that AIG had accurately identified all areas of exposure to the U.S. residential housing market and stated their confidence in their evaluation methods. PricewaterhouseCoopers (PwC), AIG'S auditor, had a right to know about the models and about market indicators that indicated that the value of AIG swaps should be lowered. If prosecutors find evidence that investors and PwC were misled, it could be considered a criminal fraud.

The market indicators in question came in the form of demands for collateral by AIG trading partners. At a congressional hearing, Sullivan stated that he believed the evaluations to be accurate, based on the information he possessed at the time. This situation is similar to executives at Enron who claimed that they did not know that Enron utilized derivatives

and off-the-book balance sheet partnerships that caused its demise. Many Enron executives ended up being found guilty of crimes.

AIG Provided Incentives to Take Risks

What were the factors within the corporate culture of AIG that promoted speculative risk-taking? Part of the problem may have been AIG's incentives. The AIG culture was focused on a reward system that placed little responsibility on executives who made very poor decisions. Although they produced nearly $40 billion in losses in 2008, a number of managers were selected to receive large bonuses. AIG offered cash awards and other perks to thirty-eight executives and a retention program with payments from $92,500 to $4 million for employees earning salaries between $160,000 and $1 million.

After receiving more than $152 billion in federal rescue funds, AIG publicly claimed that it would eliminate some of these bonuses for senior executives while all the time planning to hand out cash awards that doubled or tripled the salaries of some. AIG asserted that these types of payments were necessary to keep top employees at AIG, even as control of the company was being handed over to the government. The ethical ramifications of the rewards doled out in the face of excessive risk-taking and possible misconduct has been highly criticized by most stakeholders.

The central reason AIG was bailed out at all was that the government was seeking to prevent the failure of some of the world's largest banks, thereby potentially causing a global financial catastrophe. AIG's actions reflect an ethical culture that neglects the most important stakeholders that support a business.

The demise of AIG's Financial Products unit, in part, resulted from excessive risk-taking by economists and financial scholars using computer models that failed to take into account real-world market risks. For example, Gary Gorton, a finance professor at the Yale School of Management, was a scholar whose work was cited in speeches by Federal Reserve Chairman Ben Bernanke. AIG paid him large consulting fees for developing computer models to gauge risk for more than $400 billion in complicated credit default swaps. Remember that a single swap can be valued at hundreds of millions of dollars. AIG relied on Gorton's models to determine which swap deals were low risk. Unfortunately, his models did not anticipate how market forces and contract terms could turn swaps into huge financial liabilities. It was not Gorton's failing, as AIG did not assign him to assess those threats, and therefore his models did not consider them. However, the failure to assess the risk of credit default swaps correctly caused the demise of AIG and pushed the federal government to rescue it and the U.S. banking system.

Like other major firms, AIG entered a very lucrative but perilous new market without truly understanding the sheer complexity of the financial products that it was selling. What the company learned too late is that computers and academic experts cannot determine all of the variables, forces, and weights that cause a high- or low-risk investment to go bad. The blame lies with business placing too much trust in models with faulty assumptions. Models cannot predict with absolute certainty what humans will do because humans are not always rational. Warren Buffett, chief executive of Berkshire Hathaway and a billionaire many times over, said, "All I can say is, beware of geeks … bearing formulas."

AIG ultimately owed Wall Street's biggest firms about $100 billion dollars for speculative trades turned bad; $64 billion of it was tied to losses on subprime mortgages. This debt is particularly challenging because the rescue package for AIG does not include provisions for them. Questions remain about how the insurer will cover these debts. The company allegedly placed billions of dollars at risk through speculation on the movements of various mortgage pools, and the bottom line is that there are no actual securities backing these speculative positions on which AIG is losing

money. The losses stem from market wagers that were essentially bets on the performance of bundles of derivatives linked to subprime residential mortgages.

The government rescue of AIG protected many of its policyholders and counterparties from immediate losses on traditional insurance contracts, but these speculative trades by AIG were not a part of the government risk rescue. AIG's activities indicate that managers and traders were focused on financial rewards for assembling high-risk contracts and that the Financial Products division was conducting itself like a gambler in a casino that irrationally expected all bets to pay off. AIG had lost its underlying mission, the importance of strong moral principles, and good compliance programs that respect stakeholders.

The controversies regarding AIG did not end with government ownership. In fact, the problems critics identified regarding the company's culture and reckless spending were put on full display a mere two months after receiving its bailout money. Top AIG executives were spotted holding a lavish conference at a posh Point Hilton Squaw Peak Resort in Phoenix for 150 financial planners and top AIG executives. The three-day event reportedly cost over $343,000. Representatives of the corporation defend the conference, stating that most of the costs were underwritten by sponsors—however, such an episode mere weeks after receiving its government bailout did not sit well with stakeholders. Many believe that it demonstrates how little remorse AIG has for the decisions leading up to the failure, and how little has changed since the company received government money.

AIG'S CRISIS AND BAILOUT

AIG's problems came to a boil in September 2008. Due to the many issues outlined earlier, AIG's stock was downgraded by the rating companies, which caused the stock to drop, causing a run on the reinsurer's liquid assets (cash on hand) that revealed its lack of liquidity. Simply put, AIG did not have the capital to repay investors asking for their money back.

The federal government came to the rescue—as stated earlier, not out of concern for AIG, but to prevent the string of bank failures that would surely follow an AIG bankruptcy. Over the course of a month, the government doled out over $152 billion of taxpayer money, creating a line of credit for the company and buying up AIG stock. This was a highly controversial decision, particularly since the government did not do the same thing for the other financial giant Lehman Brothers. In March 2009, the government made the controversial decision to dole out another $30 billion in capital to the failing institution. The decision was made even more contentious when it was revealed that $165 million of the bailout money went to bonuses of employees of the failed Financial Products unit.

While the government concluded that it could not get the money back, it did resolve to increase the oversight of new bailout funds. When questioned about the decision to repeatedly bail out AIG, Federal Reserve Chair Ben Bernanke told U.S. lawmakers that "AIG exploited a huge gap in the regulatory system. There was no oversight of the financial products division. This was a hedge fund, basically, that was attached to a large and stable insurance company." He stated that AIG was the single case out of the entire 2008–2009 financial crisis that made him the angriest. However, Bernanke went on to say, "We had no choice but to try to stabilize the system because of the implications that the failure would have had for the broad economic system."

Although the bailouts were massive, they did not cover all that AIG owed and the company has had to sell off numerous assets. Two-thirds of the company needed to be sold in a tough market for sellers, resulting in auctions of dozens of the company's units around the world. Many of these sales resulted in disappointing prices for AIG. For example, Munich Re, the world's biggest reinsurer, agreed to buy AIG Inc.'s Hartford unit for $742 million, about a third less than AIG paid for it eight years before. The company also has given more than 2,000 employees cash incentives to stop them from quitting, saying that the payments are necessary. "Anybody who wants to start an insurance company or beef up their position, they will come to our organization and pick people off," Edward Liddy, the current CEO, said in the interview. "If that happens, we can't maintain the businesses we want to keep and we won't be able to sell them for the kinds of values that we need."

Former CEO Greenberg maintains his innocence, and insists that the company's upper management was the root cause of the collapse after he left. "AIG had a unique culture when I was its CEO, particularly in comparison with the way many large public companies operate today," he said. "Neither I nor other members of my senior management team had employment contracts. I received no severance package in connection with my retirement, and I never sold a single share of AIG stock during the more than 35 years that I served as CEO." Greenberg continues to hold substantial stock in the company. At the end of 2008, he and his firm, Starr International, owned more than 268 million shares, or nearly 10 percent.

In a 2008 interview, Greenberg explained what he sees as the real cause of the financial collapse. He blames low interest rates and excessively easy credit for the reckless risk-taking and poor decisions made within the financial industry. He also cites excessive leveraging and mark-to-market accounting practices as contributing to the meltdown. Mark-to-market is assigning a value to a position held in a financial instrument based on the current market price for the instrument. For example, the final value of a financial contract (grain futures) that expires in nine months will not be known until it expires. If it is marked to market, for accounting purposes, it is assigned the value that it would have at the end of each day. Greenberg believes that all these factors grew out of control to the point where the entire system had nowhere to go but toward failure.

CONCLUSION

The question remains: Was a bailout really necessary? Some say yes, like Greenberg himself. "You have to have a bailout. But I would call it something else rather than a bailout. That implies the wrong thing. It is really also helping Main Street, not just Wall Street, because if the economy doesn't grow, jobs are going to be lost and we're going to go into a depression rather than a recession. The taxpayer is not going to take a hit long-term because the money involved will be repaid over a period of time."

Others are not so certain. Critics of the AIG and auto industry bailouts, for example, cite lack of accountability in how the funds are used. Many also oppose this level of government intervention in corporations because it seems to be rewarding companies that have blatantly ignored the needs and desires of their stakeholders in favor of enriching themselves in the short term. Even months after the bailout, AIG continued to lose massive amounts of money. The company managed to slow the rate of its losses to $4.35 billion in the first quarter of 2009, but the damage to the company's reputation over this matter has been massive, and some critics wonder if it will ever recover.

The company has also had a difficult time selling off its assets in order to repay its debts, as many of its potential buyers also have been working to recover from the 2008–2009 recession. Without a doubt, the failure of AIG was massive and, bailout or not, its effects have rippled across the globe.

QUESTIONS

1. Discuss the role that AIG's corporate culture played, if any, in its downfall.

2. Discuss the ethical conduct of AIG executives, and how a stronger ethics program

might help the company to strengthen the ethics of its corporate culture.

3. What could AIG have done differently to prevent its failure and subsequent bailout?

SOURCES

Anderson, Jenny, "A.I.G. Profit Is Reduced by $4 Billion," *New York Times*, June 1, 2005, http://query.nytimes.com/gst/fullpage.html?res=9C01E1D81F39F932A35755C0A9639C8B63, accessed December 10, 2008.

Anderson, Jenny, "Greenberg Fires Back at Directors," *New York Times*, August 5, 2005, http://query.nytimes.com/gst/fullpage.html?res=9A02E7DE163EF936A3575BC0A9639C8B63&sec=&spon=&pagewanted=2, accessed December 10, 2008.

Behan, Beverly, "Memo to the Board of AIG," *BusinessWeek*, November 16, 2008, http://www.businessweek.com/managing/content/nov2008/ca20081118_408443.htm, accessed December 22, 2008.

Browning, Lynnley, "A.I.G.'s House of Cards," *Portfolio*, September 29, 2008, http://www.portfolio.com/news-markets/top-5/2008/09/29/AIGs-Derivatives-Run-Amok?, accessed December 22, 2008.

Byrnes, Nanette, "The Unraveling of AIG," *BusinessWeek*, September 16, 2008, http://www.businessweek.com/bwdaily/dnflash/content/sep2008/db20080915_552271.htm, accessed December 22, 2008.

Desmond, Mauma, "AIG. CDOs. CDS. It's a Mess," *Forbes.com*, November 15, 2008, http://www.forbes.com/markets/2008/11/15/aig-credit-default-markets-equity-cx_md_1110markets24.html, accessed November 19, 2008.

Drucker, Jesse, "AIG's Tax Dispute with U.S. Has Twist of Irony," *Wall Street Journal*, November 14, 2008, p. C2.

Eichenwald, Kurt, and Jenny Anderson, "How a Titan of Insurance Ran Afoul of the Government," *New York Times*, April 4, 2005, http://www.nytimes.com/2005/04/04/business/04aig.html?scp=1&sq=%22how+a+titan+of+insurance%22&st=nyt, accessed January 7, 2009.

"The Great Untangling," *The Economist*, November 8, 2008, pp. 85–86.

Henry, David, Matthew Goldstein, and Carol Matlack, "How AIG's Credit Loophole Squeezed Europe's Banks," *BusinessWeek*, October 16, 2008, http://www.businessweek.com/magazine/content/08_43/b4105032835044.htm, accessed December 22, 2008.

Kroft, Steve, "Why AIG Stumbled, and Taxpayers Now Own It" CBS News, March 17, 2009, http://www.cbsnews.com/stories/2009/05/15/60minutes/main5016760_page2.shtml, accessed March 18, 2009.

Loomis, Carol J., "AIG: The Company That Came to Dinner," *Fortune*, January 19, 2009, pp. 70–78.

Mollenkamp, Carrick, Serena Ng, Liam Pleven, and Randall Smith, "Behind AIG's Fall, Risk Models Failed to Pass Real-World Test," *Wall Street Journal*, November 3, 2008, pp. A1, A16.

Morgenson, Gretchen, "A.I.G.: Whiter Shade of Enron," *New York Times*, April 3, 2005, http://www.nytimes.com/2005/04/03/business/yourmoney/03gret.

html?_r=1&scp=1&sq=%22whiter%20shade%20of%20enron%22&st=cse, accessed January 7, 2009.

Ng, Serena, Carrick Mollenkamp, and Michael Siconolfi, "AIG Faces $10 Billion in Losses on Trades," *Wall Street Journal*, December 10, 2008, pp. A1–A2.

Ng, Serena, and Liam Pleven, "Revised AIG Rescue Is Bank Boon," *Wall Street Journal,* November 12, 2008, pp. C1, C5.

O'Brian, Timothy L., "Guilty Plea Is Expected in A.I.G.-Related Case," *New York Times*, June 10, 2005, http://query.nytimes.com/gst/fullpage.html?res=9801E3DC1138F933A25755C0A9639C8B63&sec=&spon=&pagewanted=2, accessed December 10, 2008.

Pleven, Liam, and Amir Efrati, "Documents Show AIG Knew of Problems with Valuations," *Wall Street Journal,* October 11–12, 2008, pp. B1–B2.

Rosenthal, Justine A., "Maurice Greenberg on What's Next for Wall Street," *National Interest Online,* October 2, 2008, http://www.nationalinterest.org/Article.aspx?id=19970, accessed December 22, 2008.

Scherer, Ron, "A Top Insurance Company as the New Enron? An Accounting Probe at AIG Worries Wall Street, and Involves Some of America's Richest Men," *Christian Science Monitor,* April 1, 2005, http://www.csmonitor.com/2005/0401/p03s01-usju.html, accessed January 7, 2009.

Son, Hugh, "AIG Plans to Repay U.S. in 2009, Liddy Tells CNBC," *Bloomberg.com*, December 22, 2008, http://www.bloomberg.com/apps/news?pid=20601087&sid=aDXR6Ayuezx4&refer=home, accessed December 22, 2008.

Son, Hugh, "AIG Says More Managers Get Retention Payouts Topping $4 Million," *Bloomberg.com*, December 9, 2008, http://www.bloomberg.com/apps/news?pid=newsarchive&sid=aKIvmgvNl6zA, accessed December 10, 2008.

Sweet, Ken, "Bernanke Tells Congress He's 'Angry' About AIG," Fox Business, March 03, 2009, http://www.foxbusiness.com/story/markets/economy/bernanke-recovery-hinges-financial-turnaround/, accessed March 5, 2009.

Walsh, Mary Williams, "A.I.G. Cuts Losses Sharply to $4.35 Billion in First Quarter," *New York Times,* May 8, 2009, p. B5.

Walsh, Mary Williams, "Bigger Holes to Fill," *Wall Street Journal,* November 11, 2008, pp. B1, B5.

Weisman, Jonathan, Sudeep Reddy, and Liam Pleven, "Political Heat Sears AIG," *Wall Street Journal,* March 17, 2009, http://online.wsj.com/article/SB123721970101743003.html, accessed March 17, 2009.

Starbucks' Mission: Social Responsibility and Brand Strength

Starbucks was founded in 1971 by three partners in Seattle's renowned open-air Pike Place Market and was named after the first mate in Herman Melville's *Moby Dick*. Howard Schultz joined Starbucks in 1982 as director of retail operations and marketing. Returning from a trip to Milan, Italy, with its 1,500 coffee bars, Schultz recognized an opportunity to develop a similar retail coffee-bar culture in Seattle.

In 1985, the company tested the first downtown Seattle coffeehouse, served the first Starbucks Café Latté, and introduced its Christmas Blend. Since then, Starbucks has been expanding across the United States and around the world, now operating nearly 17,000 stores in 49 countries. Historically, Starbucks has grown at a rate of about three stores a day, although the company cut back on expansion during 2009 in response to the global economic recession. In fact, in 2009 Starbucks made the decision to close 600 underperforming stores in the United States and 61 in Australia. The company nevertheless serves 50 million customers a week and has net revenues of approximately $10.4 billion a year.

Starbucks purchases and roasts high-quality whole coffee beans and resells them, along with freshly brewed coffee, Italian-style espresso beverages, cold blended beverages, bottled water, complementary food items, coffee-related accessories and equipment, premium teas, and a line of CDs primarily through company-operated retail stores. It also sells coffee and tea products and licenses its trademark through other channels and through some of its partners. Additionally, Starbucks produces and sells bottled Frappuccino coffee drinks, Starbucks Doubleshot espresso drinks, and a line of super-premium ice creams.

Starbucks locates its walk-in stores in high-traffic, high-visibility locations. While Starbucks can be found in a few shopping malls, the company generally focuses on locations that provide convenient access for pedestrians and drivers. The stores are designed to provide an inviting coffee-bar environment that is an important part of the Starbucks product and experience. Because the company is flexible regarding size and format, it can locate stores in or near a variety of settings, including downtown and suburban retail centers, office buildings, and university campuses. It can also situate retail stores in select rural and off-highway locations to serve a broader array of customers outside major metropolitan markets and to further expand brand awareness. To provide a greater degree of access and convenience for non-pedestrian customers, the company has increased development of stores with drive-through lanes.

A common criticism of Starbucks has to do with the company's strategy for location and expansion. Its "clustering" strategy, placing a Starbucks literally on every corner in some cases, has forced many smaller coffee shops out of business. This strategy was so dominant for most of the 1990s and 2000s

Ben Siltman and Melanie Drever prepared the original draft of this case under the direction of Linda Ferrell. The current edition was updated and edited by Jennifer Jackson, with the help of Jennifer Sawayda. This case is for classroom discussion, rather than to illustrate either effective or ineffective handling of an administrative, ethical, or legal decision by management. All sources used for this case were obtained through publicly available material and the Starbucks website.

that Starbucks became the butt of jokes. Many people began to wonder whether we really need two Starbucks directly across the street from each other. The 2008–2009 recession brought a change in policy, however. Starbucks began to pull back on expansion and, as stated, closed hundreds of stores around the United States.

Although Starbucks is always developing new products, a few drinks have fallen flat. In 2006 Starbucks pulled Chantico, its "drinkable dessert," from the menu. Chantico was marketed to resemble the thick, sweet, hot chocolate drinks found in European cafés, but it was available without any variation in a 6-ounce size. The limitations proved fatal. Customers are accustomed to dictating not only the size of their drinks, but also how they want them.

Seeking to get away from the high-priced drinks and back to its essentials, Starbucks introduced the Pike Place Blend, a bold-flavored coffee that Starbucks hoped would bring the company back to its roots of distinctive, expertly blended coffee. In order to get the flavor perfect, Starbucks enlisted the input of 1,000 customers over 1,500 hours. To kick off the new choice, Starbucks held the largest nationwide coffee tasting in history. Any customer who visited a Starbucks store at noon Eastern Standard Time on April 8, 2008, received a free 8-ounce cup of Pike Place roast. To make the brew even more appealing, Starbucks joined forces with Conservation International to ensure that the beans were sustainably harvested.

One of Starbuck's endeavors to respond to the 2008–2009 global recession was to create a value meal, Starbucks style. Called Breakfast Pairings, customers can order oatmeal or coffee cake and a latte or a breakfast sandwich and a drip coffee for $3.95. The offerings have proven popular. Oatmeal has become one of the most popular food offerings at Starbucks, as people continue to focus on their health while cutting back on fancier food items.

Starbucks is also seeking to ride another recession-spawned trend. As people cut back on their expenditures, many are choosing to brew their own coffee rather than purchase more expensive coffee shop concoctions. To gain a foothold in the potentially lucrative instant coffee market, Starbucks introduced VIA instant coffee. VIA is different from competing instant coffees in that it is processed in such a way as to retain that distinctive Starbucks taste. VIA is also aiming for a more premium market, as it retails for around $1 per serving. Only time will tell if VIA can ultimately be deemed a success. However, Starbucks has already experienced some triumphs with its new product. For instance, VIA became the official brew aboard select JetBlue flights in the United Kingdom and Spain.

Starbucks executives believe that the experience customers have in their stores should be the same in any country. During the 2008–2009 recession, Starbucks refocused on the customer experience as one of the key competitive advantages of the Starbucks brand. To enhance the European coffee shop experience for which Starbucks is known, shops are replacing their old espresso machines with new high-tech ones, and some Starbucks are switching over to Clover Brand single-cup brewing machines so that each customer receives a freshly brewed cup of coffee made to his or her specifications.

Additionally, Starbucks tries to foster brand loyalty by increasing repeat business. One of the ways it has done this is through the Starbucks Card, a reloadable card that was introduced in 2001. It has exceeded $2 billion in total activations and reloads, and more than 100 million cards have been activated. The typical Starbucks customer visits Starbucks about eighteen times a month.

STARBUCKS CULTURE

In 1990, Starbucks' senior executive team created a mission statement that laid out the guiding principles behind the company. They hoped that the principles included in the mission statement would help their partners determine the appropriateness of later decisions and actions. As Starbucks CEO Orin Smith explained, "Those guidelines are part of our culture and we try to live by them every day." After drafting the mission statement, the executive team asked all Starbucks partners to review and comment on the document. Based on their feedback, the final statement put "people first and profits last." In fact, the number one guiding principle in Starbucks' mission statement was to "provide a great work environment and treat each other with respect and dignity."

Starbucks has done three things to keep the mission and guiding principles alive over the decades. First, it distributes the mission statement and comment cards for feedback during orientation to all new partners. Second, Starbucks continually relates decisions back to the guiding principle or principles that they support. And finally, the company has formed a "Mission Review" system so any partner can comment on a decision or action relative to its consistency with one of the six principles. This continual emphasis on the guiding principles and the underlying values has become the cornerstone of a very strong culture of predominately young and educated workers who are extremely proud to work for Starbucks. Their pride comes from working for a famous and successful company that tries to act in accordance with the values they share.

Starbucks founder and chair Howard Schultz has long been a public advocate for increased awareness of ethics in business. In a 2007 speech at Notre Dame, he spoke to an audience of students about the importance of balancing "profitability and social consciousness." Schultz is a true believer that ethical companies do better in the long run, something that has been borne out by research. Schultz also spoke about how his early childhood experiences shaped the kind of businessperson he became. As a child in a housing project in Brooklyn, New York, Schultz remembers seeing his father struggle after he was injured on the job. He received no health benefits or workers' compensation from his employers. Watching his father's travails showed Schultz how important something like health care is to the health and happiness of employees. Having grown up poor, Schultz is also committed to helping to improve the lives of the poor farmers from whom Starbucks buys its beans. Schultz has always maintained that, while it can be difficult to do the right thing at all times, it is better for a company to take some short-term losses than to lose sight of its core values in the long term.

Starbucks has been ranked on *Fortune*'s "100 Best Companies to Work For" list for nearly a decade; and in 2009, the company ranked 24th. The care the company shows its employees is a large part of what sets it apart. Starbucks offers most employees a comprehensive benefits package that includes stock option grants through *Bean Stock*, as well as health, medical, dental, and vision benefits. It also embraces diversity as an essential component of doing business. The company has more than 146,000 U.S. employees and nearly 71,000 outside the United States. Of these, around 31 percent are minorities, and 67 percent are women.

Another key part of the Starbucks image involves its commitment to ethics and sustainability. To address concerns related to these issues, Starbucks launched the Shared Planet website. Shared Planet has three main goals: to achieve ethical sourcing, environmental stewardship, and greater community involvement. The website is a means of keeping customers up-to-date on initiatives within the company. It describes how well Starbucks is faring on achieving its social responsibility goals, and it even provides a means for customers to learn about things like the nutrition data of Starbucks' offerings and other concerns related to Starbucks products.

Starbucks also actively partners with nonprofits around the globe. Currently, 5 percent of total coffee purchases are Fair

Trade Certified. Starbucks joined with Bono's Product RED in an effort to raise money for HIV and AIDs research. Starbucks makes $12.5 million in loans to poor farmers around the world, and plans to increase that number in the future. Conservation International joined with Starbucks in 1998 to promote sustainable agricultural practices, namely, shade-grown coffee, and to prevent deforestation in endangered regions around the globe. The results of the partnership proved to be positive for both the environment and farmers. For example, in Chiapas, Mexico, shade-grown coffee acreage (which reduces the need to cut down trees for coffee plantations) has increased well over 220 percent, while farmers receive a price premium above the market price. Since the beginning of the partnership Starbucks made loan guarantees that helped provide nearly $1 million in loans to farmers. This financial support enabled those farmers to nearly double their income.

Starbucks works with many other organizations as well, including The African Wildlife Foundation and Business for Social Responsibility. The company's efforts at transparency, the treatment of its workers, and its dozens of philanthropic commitments demonstrate how genuine Starbucks is in its mission to be an ethical and socially responsible company.

CORPORATE SOCIAL MISSION

Although Starbucks has supported responsible business practices virtually since its inception, as the company has grown so has the importance of defending its image. At the end of 1999, Starbucks created a Corporate Social Responsibility department, now known as the Global Responsibility Department. Global Responsibility releases an annual report in order to allow shareholders to keep track of its performance, which can be accessed through the Shared Planet website. Starbucks is concerned about the environment, its employees, suppliers, customers, and its communities.

Environment

In 1992, long before it became trendy to be "green," Starbucks developed an environmental mission statement to articulate more clearly the company's environmental priorities and goals. This initiative created the Environmental Starbucks Coffee Company Affairs team tasked with developing environmentally-responsible policies and minimizing the company's "footprint." Additionally, Starbucks was active in using environmental purchasing guidelines, reducing waste through recycling and energy conservation, and continually educating partners through the company's "Green Team" initiatives. Concerned stakeholders can now track the company's progress and setbacks through its Shared Planet website, which clearly outlines Starbuck's environmental goals and how the company is faring in living up to those goals.

Employees

Growing up poor with a father whose life was nearly ruined by an unsympathetic employer that did not offer health benefits, Howard Schultz has always considered the creation of a good work environment a top priority. "I watched what would happen to the plight of working class families when society and companies turned their back on the worker," Schultz said. "I wanted to build the kind of company my father never got to work for." The result is one of the best health-care programs in the coffee shop industry. All Starbucks employees who work more than twenty hours per week are entitled to receive health benefits (including health, medical, dental, and vision benefits) and to receive stock options, known as *Bean Stock*. Schultz's key to maintaining a strong business is by "creating an environment where everyone believes they're part of something larger than themselves but believes they also have a voice." Understanding how vital employees are, Shultz is the first to admit that his company centers on personal interactions. "We are not in the coffee business serving people, but in the people business serving coffee."

However, being a great employer does take its toll on the company. In 2005, Starbucks spent more on health insurance for its employees than on raw materials required to brew its coffee. The company has faced double-digit increases in insurance costs for multiple years running. Nonetheless, the Starbucks benefits package is a key reason why it has remarkably low employee turnover and high productivity.

Suppliers

Even though it is one of the largest coffee brands in the world, Starbucks maintains a good reputation for social responsibility and business ethics throughout the international community of coffee growers. It attempts to build positive relationships with small coffee suppliers, while also working with governments and nonprofits wherever it operates. Starbucks practices conservation as well as Starbucks Coffee and Farmer Equity pactices (C.A.F.E.), which is a set of socially responsible coffee buying guidelines that ensure preferential buying status for participants who receive high scores in best practices. Starbucks pays coffee farmers premium prices to help them make profits and support their families.

The company is also involved in social development programs, investing in programs to build schools, health clinics, and other projects that benefit coffee-growing communities. Starbucks collaborates directly with some of its growers through the Farmer Support Center, located in Costa Rica, which provides technical support and training to ensure high-quality coffee into the future. It also is a major purchaser of Fair Trade Certified, shade-grown, and certified organic beans, which further supports environmental and economic efforts.

In 1991, Starbucks began contributing to CARE, a worldwide relief and development foundation, as a way to give back to coffee-origin countries. By 1995, Starbucks was CARE's largest corporate donor. Starbucks' donations help with projects like clean-water systems, health and sanitation training, and literacy efforts. Starbucks continues its long-term relationship with CARE, making Pike Place Blend its first CARE-certified brew.

Customers

Starbucks continually works to please customers. Strengthening its brand and customer satisfaction is more important than ever as Starbucks seeks to regroup after the 2008–2009 recession forced the company to rethink its strategy. In addition to shutting down stores, Starbucks refocused the brand by upgrading its coffee-brewing machines, introducing new food and drink items for the budget-conscious consumer, and refocusing on its core product. While Starbucks had for years been looking for ways to branch out into music, movies, and other merchandise, 2009 found Starbucks thinking small for the first time. The company started to focus more on the quality of the coffee, the atmosphere of the coffee shops, and the overall Starbucks experience, rather than on continuing its rapid expansion of stores and products.

Enhancing the customer experience in its stores also became a high priority. As a way to encourage people to relax and spend time there, Starbucks offers wireless Internet access with T1 speeds in more than 4,300 coffee houses in U.S. and European stores. Additionally, Starbucks supports discussions in their coffee houses through "The Way I See It," a collection of thoughts, opinions, and expressions provided by notable figures that appear on Starbucks cups. Starbucks focuses most of its efforts on the customer, as a way to enhance their experience and to build loyalty.

Communities

Starbucks coffee shops have long sought to become the "instant gathering spot" wherever they locate, a "place that draws people together." To enhance the local, community-oriented feel of Starbucks shops, store managers are encouraged to donate to local causes. For example, one Seattle store donated more than

$500,000 to Zion Preparatory Academy, an African American school for inner-city youth. Howard Schultz believes that literacy has the power to improve lives and to give hope to underprivileged children. Schultz even used the advance and ongoing royalties from his book, *Pour Your Heart Into It,* to create the Starbucks Foundation, which provides "opportunity grants" to nonprofit literacy groups, sponsors young writers programs, and partners with Jumpstart, an organization helping children to prepare developmentally for school.

SUCCESS AND CHALLENGES

For decades, Starbucks has been revolutionizing our leisure time. Starbucks is not only the most prominent brand of high-end coffee in the world, but it is also one of the defining brands of our time. Is there anyone in the United States, or any part of the developed world for that matter, who has not heard of Starbucks?

Psychologist Joyce Brother says that "there is a sense of security when you go there." This sense is consistent across all Starbucks stores because the experience is remarkably consistent. In most large cities, it is impossible to go more than a few blocks without seeing the familiar mermaid logo.

For nearly two decades, Starbucks achieved amazing levels of growth, creating financial success for shareholders. Starbuck's reputation is built on product quality, stakeholder concern, and a balanced approach to all of its business activities. Of course, Starbucks does receive criticism for its ability to beat the competition, putting other coffee shops out of business, and creating a uniform retail culture in many cities. Yet Starbucks excels in its relationship with its employees and is a role model for the fast-food industry in employee benefits. In addition, in an age of shifts in supply chain power, Starbucks is as concerned about its suppliers and meeting their needs as it is about any other primary stakeholder.

In spite of Starbucks' strides at sustainability and maintaining high ethical standards,

being one of the best-known brands in the world and operating in forty-four countries places it at risk for criticism. In the past, Starbucks has garnered harsh criticism on issues such as fair-trade coffee, generically modified milk, Howard Shultz's alleged financial links to the Israeli government, and the accusations that the relentless growth is forcing locally run coffee shops out of business. To counter these criticisms in the early 2000s, Starbucks began offering Fair Trade certified coffee in 2002, a menu item that was quickly made permanent. However, Starbucks has been slow to increase the share of Fair Trade products it purchases. While some competitors have switched to 100 percent Fair Trade coffee, Starbucks still buys only around 5 percent Fair Trade. However, offerings like the Pike Place Roast may increase that percentage somewhat.

Yet, starting in late 2008, Starbucks' proportion of Fair Trade offerings suddenly became the least of the company's worries. A global recession caused the market to bottom out for expensive coffee drinks. The company has responded by paring down and focusing on its core product, which is coffee, along with offering the low-priced breakfast pairings, the VIA instant coffee, and more affordably priced tall coffees. In conjunction with rolling out these lower-priced options, while still attempting to hold onto its trademark high-end coffee shop feel, Starbucks has had to rethink its rapid expansion strategy. The company has slowed its global growth plans after sixteen years of expanding at a nonstop pace in order to refocus on strengthening its brand, satisfying customers, and building consumer loyalty. As stated, the new plan included closing hundreds of underperforming stores in the United States and Australia.

Starbucks, like many businesses, is focusing on its core strengths until it can be sure that the global economy is ready for it to expand again. The company is treating this slower time in its history as an opportunity to focus on such things as community involvement, outreach work, and on improving its overall image and offerings.

QUESTIONS

1. Why do you think Starbucks has been so concerned with social responsibility in its overall corporate strategy?

2. Is Starbucks unique in being able to provide a high level of benefits to its employees?

3. Do you think that Starbucks has grown rapidly because of its ethical and socially responsible activities or because it provides products and an environment that customers want?

SOURCES

"C.A.F.E. Practices (Coffee and Farmer Equity Practices)," Starbucks Coffee Company, http://www.starbucks.ca/en-ca/_Social+Responsibility/C.A.F.E.+Practices.htm, accessed May 7, 2009.

"Coca-Cola May Take on Starbucks," MSNBC.com, January 30, 2006, http://www.msnbc.msn.com/id/11101825/, accessed May 5, 2009.

"Health Care Takes Its Toll on Starbucks," MSNBC.com, September 14, 2005, http://www.msnbc.msn.com/id/9344634/, accessed May 5, 2009.

Horovitz, Bruce, "Starbucks Aims Beyond Lattes to Extend Brand to Films, Music and Books," USA Today, May 19, 2006, pp. A1, A2.

Horovitz, Bruce, "Starbucks Unveils Menu Deal to Halt Slide," USA Today, February 8, 2009, www.usatoday.com/money/industries/food2009-02-08-value-menu-starbucks_N.htm, accessed May 5, 2009.

Horovitz, Adam, David Jacobson, Mark Lasswell, and Owen Thomas, "101 Dumbest Moments in Business," Business 2.0, February 1, 2006, http://money.cnn.com/magazines/business2/101dumbest/full_list/page6.html, accessed May 5, 2009.

McClelland, Kate, "Starbucks Founder Speaks on Ethics," Notre Dame Observer, March 30, 2007, http://media.www.ndsmcobserver.com/media/storage/paper660/news/2007/03/30/News/Starbucks.Founder.Speaks.On.Ethics-2814792.shtml, accessed September 1, 2009.

"100 Best Companies to Work For," Fortune, http://money.cnn.com/magazines/fortune/bestcompanies/2009/full_list/, accessed April 1, 2009.

"100 Best Corporate Citizens," Business Ethics, http://www.business-ethics.com/node/75, accessed April 1, 2009.

"The Proof Is in the Cup: Starbucks Launched Historic New Pike Place Roast™," Starbucks.com, April 7, 2008, http://news.starbucks.com/article_display.cfm?article_id=51, accessed May 4, 2009.

"In Rare Flop, Starbucks Scraps Chocolate Drink," MSNBC.com, February 10, 2006, http://www.msnbc.msn.com/id/11274445/, accessed May 5, 2009.

"Shade Grown Coffee," Eartheasy.com, http://www.eartheasy.com/eat_shadegrown_coffee.htm, accessed May 7, 2009.

"Starbucks Company Fact Sheet," http://www.starbucks.com/aboutus/Company_Factsheet.pdf, accessed May 5, 2009.

"Starbucks VIA Ready Brew Launches on EasyJet Airline Across Selected Routes in United Kingdom and Spain," Starbucks.com, April 21, 2009, http://news.starbucks.com/article_display.cfm?article_id=209, accessed May 4, 2009.

"2008 Annual Report," Starbucks.com, http://media.corporate-ir.net/media_files/irol/99/99518/AR2008.pdf, accessed April 1, 2009.

The Fraud of the Century: The Case of Bernard Madoff

The fraud perpetrated by Bernard Madoff that was discovered in December 2008 was what is known as a Ponzi scheme. A Ponzi scheme works similarly to a pyramid scheme. Madoff took money from new investors to pay earnings for existing customers, without ever actually investing the money. In order to keep making payouts to older clients, Madoff had to continually attract new investors. The Ponzi scheme was named after Charles Ponzi, who in the early twentieth century saw a way to profit from international reply coupons. International reply coupons were a guarantee of return postage in response to an international letter. Charles Ponzi determined that he could make money by swapping out these coupons for more expensive postage stamps in countries where the stamps were of higher value. Ponzi convinced investors to provide him with capital to trade coupons for higher-priced postage stamps. His promise to investors who joined in his scheme was a 50 percent profit in a few days.

Touted as a financial wizard, Ponzi lived a fairly opulent life outside of Boston. He would often bring in as much as $250,000 a day. Part of Ponzi's success came from his personal charisma and ability to con even savvy investors. People trusted Ponzi because he created an image of power, trust, and responsibility—much like Bernard Madoff did nearly a century later. The largest problem with his scheme is that it did not work, much like Madoff's did not. In order to keep giving earlier investors their promised return, he had to continually draw new people into the scheme. In July of 1920, the *Boston Post* ran an article exposing the scheme, and soon after that regulators raided his offices and charged him with mail fraud, knowing that his fabricated investment reports were mailed to his clients. Most Ponzi schemes self-destruct fairly quickly as the ability to keep attracting new investors dwindles. Bernard Madoff's case was unusual because he was able to continue his fraud for many years.

BERNARD L. MADOFF INVESTMENT SECURITIES LLC: "ALL IN THE FAMILY"

Bernard Madoff was not merely a criminal. He was also a highly successful, legitimate businessperson. He started a legal, investment business in 1960 by buying and selling over-the-counter stocks that were not listed on the New York Stock Exchange (NYSE). These stocks were traded via the telephone with no automation. This meant that an in-the-know individual such as Madoff could profit from variations between different quotes. Basically, he served as a "wholesaler" between institutional investors. In the early days, working with investment firms such as A.G. Edwards, Charles Schwab, and others, Madoff made his money based on the variance between the offer price and sales price of stocks.

In the 1990s, Madoff Securities was trading up to 10 percent of the NASDAQ (National

Linda Ferrell developed this case with the editorial assistance of Jennifer Jackson and Jennifer Sawayda. This case was prepared for classroom discussion, rather than to illustrate either effective or ineffective handling of an administrative, ethical, or legal decision by management. All sources used for this case were obtained through publicly available material.

Association of Securities Dealers Automated Quotations) shares on certain days. Early success and competitive advantage came from Bernie working with his brother Peter (the first of several family members to join his firm), who after graduating from law school joined Madoff's company and developed superior technology for trading, buying, and selling at the best prices. Madoff controlled the funds in-house and made his money, in this division, from commissions on sales and profits. The profits were not based on fraud; however, there is evidence that Madoff occasionally injected funds from his illegal business into his legal one during times of low revenues.

As Madoff became more successful, he moved the company's headquarters from Wall Street to the famous "Lipstick Building" on Third Avenue built by famed architect Philip Johnson. Not unlike Enron's Ken Lay and his lobbying efforts to deregulate the energy and gas industry, Bernie also became more involved in lobbying for regulatory changes that would make it easier to trade electronically. Brother Peter took on more oversight of the firm's securities business. Bernie served as chair of the NASDAQ in 1990, 1991, and 1993. In addition, he held a seat on the government advisory board on stock market regulation, served on charitable boards, and started his own foundation, all of which added to his credibility. He developed respectability and trust as a highly knowledgeable investment specialist.

For years Madoff had been using his legitimate success and high visibility to start a second business managing money. He seemed trustworthy and promised consistent returns of 10 to 12 percent, attracting billions of dollars from hundreds of investors. Part of the appeal of investing with Bernie was the appeal of exclusivity. Madoff made every client feel like he or she was his only client. His inaccessibility and "invitation only" approach to new investors created an air of exclusivity and desire to be involved. Ruth Madoff, Bernie's wife, also worked at the firm for a time, and

often functioned as a friendly face of the companies. Madoff was frequently excessively focused on work and order, while Ruth was pretty, gregarious, and smart.

Bernie's niece and Peter's daughter, Shana Madoff, was a rules and compliance officer at Madoff's legitimate firm and worked under her father, who was head of compliance in the market-making arm (not the firm's money management business). Shana, who was not charged with any crimes, is married to Eric Swanson, a former Securities and Exchange Commission (SEC) compliance lawyer. Shana Madoff has a respected career and was honored by the Girl Scouts of America as a "woman of distinction."

Although also under investigation, neither of Madoff's sons, Mark and Andrew, has been charged with any wrongdoing. It was to them that Madoff confessed his crime, and they were responsible for turning in their father to the authorities. The two deny any knowledge of the fraud and did not speak to their father or mother for months after Bernie's arrest. The family emphasizes the separation of the legitimate, stock-trading business (run on the nineteenth floor) and the illegitimate, investment management business (run on the seventeenth floor) by Bernie Madoff.

In March 2009, when Bernard Madoff stated his guilt in court, he never indicated the involvement of any other company employees or family members. He stated in the allocution that "I want to emphasize today that while my investment advisory business—the vehicle of my wrongdoing—was part of Bernard L. Madoff Securities, the other businesses that my firm engaged in, proprietary trading and market making, were legitimate, profitable and successful in all respects. Those businesses were managed by my brother and two sons" (Madoff Plea Allocution, p. 2). Further investigation will determine the extent and level of external support that Madoff had in defrauding thousands. Madoff chose to hire inexperienced, sometimes uneducated individuals with no background in finance to work in his investment management business. Some speculate that he did this so as to surround himself with unknowing participants.

EXPLAINING THE GROWTH NUMBERS

Madoff staked his investment business on claims that he could consistently generate 10 to 12 percent returns for investors, no matter what the economic climate. Many of his clients were already wealthy and just looking for a stable and constant rate of return. To these people, his friends at the Palm Beach Country Club, for example, reliable constant returns managed by one of their own seemed like the perfect way to go. His stated investment strategy was to buy stocks, while also trading options on those stocks as a way to limit the potential losses. His market timing strategy was called the "split strike-conversion." With the large financial portfolio Madoff managed, many indicate at least one "red flag" would have been the fact that he would have had to make more trades than the market would physically allow just to meet his everyday financial goals. Shocking to all of his clients, Madoff confessed in his "Plea Allocution" statement that he never invested any of his client's funds. All of the money was deposited in banks, and Madoff simply moved money between Chase Manhattan Bank in New York and Madoff Securities International Ltd., a United Kingdom Corporation. During his confession, Madoff stated that his fraud began in the early 1990s.

To help continuously draw in new clients, Madoff developed relationships with intermediaries, also known as "feeders" to his investment fund. They were other investment managers who trusted Madoff to take care of their clients' money, and it does not appear that they were integrally involved in the fraud. Many of these feeders had themselves invested money with Madoff. One such middleperson,

Rene-Thierry Magon de la Villehuchet, committed suicide after losing his life savings to Madoff. These feeders profited by receiving fees and ensuring that Madoff had a stream of money flowing into his operation. Robert Jaffe operated as a middleperson for Madoff starting in 1989 when he became the manager of Boston-based Cohmad Securities, a firm co-owned by Madoff to attract investors. Jaffe was the son-in-law of one of Madoff's earliest investors and was a member of the Palm Beach Country Club. Jaffe earned a small commission whenever Madoff took on an investor introduced to him by Jaffe.

FINANCIAL SUPPORT NEAR THE END AND THE ARREST

Toward the end of Madoff's fraud, he was getting desperate for funds. As the economy collapsed in late 2008, more and more clients were requesting deposits back. In order to pay them and to not be exposed, Madoff needed more cash quickly. He resorted to soliciting, and sometimes subtlety threatening, clients for more deposits—making them feel guilty for not being better clients of such a distinguished investment firm.

A week and a half before Madoff admitted to his sons that he was operating a Ponzi scheme, 95-year-old Palm Beach philanthropist and entrepreneur Carl Shapiro gave Madoff $250 million. Shapiro lost that money, as well as $100 million in additional funds that had belonged to a charitable organization. Martin Rosenman, the president of a fuel company in New York, also provided an additional $10 million in deposits. Rosenman is suing Madoff for the money. He alleges that Madoff told him that his funds would be invested in a new fund, and was even sent a nineteen-page promotional piece in advance of the investment.

Of course, even these hundreds of millions in additional deposits would not be enough to cover Madoff's losses. Possibly because he knew that the act was up, he turned himself in to his sons. Madoff was arrested on December 11, accused of operating a $65 billion Ponzi scheme. The official charge is criminal securities fraud. Madoff declared to his sons that he had roughly $200–300 million left in the business and that he wanted to provide the money to employees before turning himself over to authorities. This was news to his sons; they thought the investment arm of the business held between $8 billion and $15 billion in assets. The SEC records showed that the firm had $17 billion in assets at the beginning of 2008.

THE INVESTIGATION AND CHARGES

Investigators in this case included the SEC, FBI, federal prosecutors from the U.S. attorney's office for the Southern District of New York, and the Financial Industry Regulatory Authority. Forensic accountants will try to pull together the trail of investments and spending to determine where the money went. There is a belief that multiple offshore funds were created by Madoff to shelter assets prior to the collapse of the firm. Madoff's business was not registered with the SEC until 2006, after an SEC investigation.

Bernard Madoff has been charged with criminal securities fraud, and investigators are now evaluating documents dating back to 2000. The charges did not come as a surprise to the SEC when Madoff was finally exposed, however; beginning in 1992, federal regulators had been investigating allegations of wrongdoing by Madoff. Table 1 provides a summary of the nature of these investigations.

It is believed that much of the money invested with Madoff went either to offset losses in his legal business or to fund the Madoff family's lavish lifestyle. There is growing evidence that although family members may not have known that Bernie was running a Ponzi scheme, they thought nothing of treating his businesses like their personal piggy

Table 1 Government and Regulatory Investigations of Bernard Madoff

Year	Nature of Investigation
1992	SEC—Madoff's name came up in a Florida accounting investigation.
1999	SEC reviewed Madoff's trading practices.
2001	SEC—Harry Markopolos, securities industry executive, raised questions regarding Madoff's returns.
2004	SEC reviewed allegations of improper trading practices.
2005	SEC interviewed Madoff and family but found no improper trading activities.
2005	Industry-based regulatory group found no improper trading activities.
2005	SEC met with Harry Markopolos, who claimed Madoff was operating the world's largest Ponzi scheme.
2006	An SEC enforcement investigation found misleading behavior, and Madoff registered as an investment advisor.
2007	Financial Industry Regulatory Authority investigated Madoff, but no regulatory action was taken.

Source: Associated Press, "The Many Fruitless Probes into Bernie Madoff," APNewswire, January 5, 2009, http://news.moneycentral.msn.com/provider/providerarticle.aspx?feed=AP&date=20090105&id=9486677, accessed January 5, 2009.

banks. Investigators may pursue Ruth Madoff and their two sons in order to recover some of the money owed to bilked investors.

INVESTORS IMPACTED

The very long list of Madoff clients is a who's who of organizations, nonprofits, successful entrepreneurs and businesspeople, as well as entertainers. The Fairfield Greenwich Group, one of Madoff's largest feeder funds, had around $7.5 billion, or more than half of its assets, invested in the firm. The Noel family, owners of Fairfield Greenwich, has been so disgraced by their association with the Madoffs that their membership to the Round Hill Country Club in Greenwich, Connecticut, was revoked. Tremont Group Holdings, owned by Oppenheimer, had $3.3 billion invested. Ezra Merkin, head of a GMAC-operated hedge fund, lost $1.8 billion to Madoff.

Several victims have shared information about their history and relationship with Bernie Madoff. Richard Sonking met with Madoff in the mid 1990s after his father, who had an account with Madoff, recommended the investment firm for its steady 8–14 percent returns. Sonking pulled together the minimum $100,000 required for investment at that time, feeling confident that he was joining a highly select group of investors. Sonking continued to place money in Madoff's hands as he accumulated greater wealth. As with all of Madoff's clients, he was happy with the constant returns and with the detailed statements that were mailed to him each month. Like everyone else, he never questioned why Madoff did not make online records available, and he did not question the secrecy to which Madoff swore his investors. Upon retiring in 2005, Sonking requested quarterly distributions from his account. As with most of Madoff's loyal investors, Sonking received no warnings of fraudulent activity until he heard the news of Madoff's arrest.

Loretta Weinberg, a New Jersey state senator, was a conservative investor who embraced her late husband's philosophy that you should live on half of what you make and save the rest. She had no investments with Madoff, but she did place money in the hands of Stanley Chais, a Los Angeles money manager who provided quarterly investment reports and a 10–14 percent annual return. It just so happened that Chais was a feeder with Madoff, funneling much of his clients' money Madoff's way. Until the Madoff scandal hit the press, Weinberg had not even heard of Madoff. As a 73-year-old state senator making $49,000/year, she is coming

to terms with what it means to lose her entire $1.3 million in life savings.

Joseph Gurwin is 88 years old and lives in Palm Beach. Like many in Palm Beach, he came to know Madoff and had become his friend through the local social and philanthropic community. Madoff had a tremendous reputation for secure and conservative financial management, and it was considered a huge honor among the elites in Palm Beach to be invested with Madoff. Gurwin's foundation (The J. Gurwin Foundation, Inc.), operating with around $28 million in assets, donated $1.2 million annually to Jewish health care, services, and programs for frail, elderly, or disabled younger adults. After investing heavily with Madoff, Gurwin's charitable foundation lost all of its assets when Madoff's Ponzi scheme crashed.

Law firms in Florida are representing clients who believed they were investing with Westport National Bank (a regulated banking institution in Connecticut), and not with Madoff, but who have received a letter from Westport National indicating that the bank had a custodial agreement with Madoff, giving full discretionary authority to Bernard L. Madoff Investment Securities. Madoff's sweep went far beyond his immediate circle.

RESTITUTION FOR INVESTORS

So far, close to 9,000 people have submitted claims for restitution in the Madoff case. Some are suing the SEC for not catching this fraud sooner. However, paying back all these investors will be a difficult task. Although Madoff's fraud is being billed as a $65 billion Ponzi scheme, Madoff never had anywhere near that amount of money. The figure of $65 billion is the total amount Madoff told people they had invested and earned with him. The actual amount may be well below $10 billion. Investigators have considered pursuing legal action against Madoff family members in order to pay all of these claims.

In reaction to all the ethical scandals being uncovered in the investment and finance industries, the SEC is considering a new proposal that would place investment advisors under more government scrutiny. The proposal would require that advisors like Madoff demonstrate evidence to an independent accountant that they actually have the funds they claim to have. Although Madoff was investigated by the SEC repeatedly over the years, and in spite of skeptics providing the SEC with strong evidence that Madoff was indeed running a Ponzi scheme, investigators never thought to verify whether Madoff actually had all the money he claimed to have. This proposal to increase regulatory oversight comes at a time when it has become clear how easy it is for investment professionals to misuse client funds and then send them false reports to cover up their misdeeds.

Investigators are also looking into potential misconduct on the part of some of Madoff's clients. According to investigations, Madoff feeder funds withdrew over $12 billion in 2008, with half of that money being withdrawn in the three months leading up to his arrest—a huge sum that probably led to Bernie's confession when he could no longer pull together cash to make payments. Under federal law, the trustee for the Madoff bankruptcy suit can sue to retrieve this money in what are called "clawback" suits. The argument is that $12 billion was essentially "stolen" from other investors who actually owned the money. Hence, to protect their assets from seizure, many who received payout funds from Madoff are transferring the money to irrevocable trusts, homes, annuities, or life insurance policies.

One of these cases seeks repayment of $5.1 billion from a prominent Madoff client and Palm Beach investor named Picower. Although Picower's charitable fund was one of the highest-profile victims of the Madoff downfall, investigators suspect some foul play. Part of the concern is that as a professional investor, Picower should have known that the profits he was getting from Madoff were too high. The accusations further state that Picower was getting payments from Madoff to help perpetuate the Ponzi scheme, which means Picower would have known about the scheme all along. This is only one of what will surely amount to dozens of lawsuits related to the attempt to recover and redistribute funds from Madoff clients. Undoubtedly this web will take years to untangle as investigators seek to learn who knew about Madoff's scheme and which ones are, therefore, guilty of being complicit.

As mentioned earlier, some investors are suing the SEC for negligence in its regulatory responsibility and not being able to identify the fraud. Such attempts represent the first time investors have sought restitution from a regulatory agency. Christopher Cox, SEC chair at the start of the fraud investigation, has indicated that the SEC examiners missed "red flags" in reviewing the Madoff firm. Allegations of wrongdoing started in the early 1990s, and Madoff confirms fraud dating back to that time. Repeated investigations and examinations by the SEC showed no investment fraud. Because many SEC employees have ended up working in the investment business on Wall Street, there has been speculation that an overall lack of objectivity clouded these investigations. Some suspect incompetence on the part of the SEC as well. In the wake of the Madoff fallout, it has become clear that some SEC investigators were sufficiently knowledgeable about the kinds of complex financial instruments used on Wall Street. Thus, they should have been knowledgeable enough to be able to detect the fraud.

Perhaps the greatest restitution for some investors came as Bernard Madoff was handcuffed and taken to prison after his twelve-minute-long confession of guilt in a Lower Manhattan courthouse. Some victims asked the judge for a trial to uncover more about this extensive fraud and to determine why the government regulatory system failed so many investors. Judge Chin indicated there would be no trial since Madoff pleaded guilty and there was an ongoing investigation at hand. Madoff was sentenced to 150 years in prison.

THE FUTURE OF CHARITABLE GIVING

Due to the widespread impact of the Madoff-related losses upon charities, nonprofits, and educational institutions, donor skepticism and withdrawal are not unexpected consequences. Some of the organizations affected included the Elie Wiesel Foundation for Humanity, Yeshiva University, and Wunderkinder Foundation (Steven Spielberg's fund). This wariness comes at a time when the global recession resulted in losses of around 30 percent for many foundations' endowments. The vast majority of nonprofits indicate that the economy had a negative impact on fundraising, even before the Madoff scandal was exposed. In the future, it is certain that charities and donors alike will approach the donation process with greater care. One way to evaluate responsible charities is to develop guidelines for giving, which would include knowing what materials are readily available to potential investors/donors from the organization, who is running the fund/charity, and who is auditing the fund/charity. Another guideline is to diversify the investment portfolio, which avoids putting all investments in one basket. This is exactly what many of Madoff's victims *did not do*, choosing instead to place all their assets into Madoff's company and losing their investments in the resulting scandal.

CONCLUSION

Bernard Madoff is accused of creating a Ponzi scheme that destroyed $65 billion in investments. Many people are trying to understand how so many experienced investors, including banks, insurance companies, and nonprofit foundations, lost billions of dollars to an individual who was able to deceive them as well as regulators. Investigators are trying to determine who helped Madoff carry off what some say could have been a 30-year scheme that caused the $65 billion in losses that have affected thousands of people around the world. Accountants, auditors, and regulators are supposed to be gatekeepers that protect the public interest. Investigators believe that Madoff had a trading strategy that failed, then after a while, he made few trades for many years and his operation consisted of taking money from new clients and paying it out to existing clients, a classic Ponzi scheme.

From an ethical perspective, this would be an example of white-collar crime. White-collar criminals create victims by establishing trust and respectability. As in this case, victims of white-collar crime are trusting clients who believe there are many checks and balances to certify that an operation is legitimate. Madoff is an example of the classic white-collar criminal. He was an educated and experienced individual in a position of power, trust, respectability, and responsibility who abused his trust for personal gains. From the inception of his investment business, he knew that he was operating a Ponzi scheme and defrauding his clients. In the end, he said he "knew this day would come."

An important question is how one individual could deceive so many intelligent people and authorities that certified his operation as legitimate. Madoff's accountants, family, and other employees will have to answer to authorities about their knowledge of the operations. For example, investigators have issued a subpoena for David Friehling, a New York accountant who audited Madoff's financial statements. Although only Madoff was originally charged with misconduct and was adamant that he acted alone, other participants will undoubtedly be discovered and charged. Madoff's right-hand man, Frank DiPascali, has admitted to knowing of individuals and firms complicit in Madoff's scheme who knowingly broke the law.

White-collar crime is unique in that it is often perpetrated by a rogue individual who knowingly steals, cheats, or manipulates in order to damage others. Often, the only way to prevent white-collar crime is to have internal controls and compliance standards that detect misconduct. Perhaps the most difficult white-collar crime and fraud to expose is that perpetrated by the top executive. We count on leadership within an organization to create, manage, and motivate an ethical organizational culture with all the checks and balances in place. In the Madoff case, there was the opportunity to deceive others without effective audits, transparency, or understanding of the true nature of his operations. As a result of this case, individual investors, institutions, and hopefully regulators will exert more diligence in demanding transparency and honesty from those who manage investments.

QUESTIONS

1. What are the ethical issues involved in the Madoff case?

2. Do you believe that Bernard Madoff worked alone, or do you think he had help in creating and sustaining his Ponzi scheme? Would this represent a conflict of interest?

3. What should be done to help ensure that Ponzi schemes like this one do not happen in the future?

SOURCES

Bandler, James, and Nicholas Varchaver with Doris Burke, "How Bernie Did It," *Fortune,* May 11, 2009, pp. 50–71.

Bernstein, Elizabeth, "After Madoff, Donors Grow Wary of Giving," *Wall Street Journal,* December 23, 2008, http://online.wsj.com/article/SB122999068109728409.html, accessed September 2, 2009.

Bryan-Low, Cassel, "Inside a Swiss Bank, Madoff Warnings," *Wall Street Journal,* January 14, 2009, p. 1A.

Catan, Thomas, Christopher Bjork, and Jose De Cordoba, "Giant Bank Probe Over Ties to Madoff," *Wall Street Journal,* January 13, 2009, http://online.wsj.com/article/SB123179728255974859.html, accessed September 2, 2009.

Efrati, Amir, "Q&A on the Madoff Case," *Wall Street Journal,* March 12, 2009, http://online.wsj.com/article/SB123005811322430633.html, accessed September 2, 2009.

Efrati, Amir, "Scope of Alleged Fraud Is Still Being Assessed," *Wall Street Journal,* December 18, 2008, http://online.wsj.com/article/SB122953110854314501.html, accessed September 2, 2009.

Efrati, Amir, and Chad Bray, "U.S.: Madoff Had $173 Million in Checks," *Wall Street Journal,* January 9, 2009, http://online.wsj.com/article/SB123143634250464871.html, accessed September 2, 2009.

Efrati, Amir, Aaron Luccchetti, and Tom Lauricella, "Probe Eyes Audit Files, Role of Aide to Madoff," *Wall Street Journal,* September 2, 2009, http://online.wsj.com/article/

SB122999256957528605.html, accessed December 23, 2008.

Frank, Robert, and Amir Efrati, "Madoff Tried to Stave Off Firm's Crash Before Arrest," *Wall Street Journal,* January 7, 2009, http://online.wsj.com/article/SB123129835145559987.html, accessed September 2, 2009.

Frank, Robert, and Tom Lauricella, "Madoff Created Air of Mystery," *Wall Street Journal,* December 20, 2008, http://online.wsj.com/article/SB122973208705022949.html, accessed September 2, 2009.

Goldfarb, Zachary, "Investment Advisors Would Face More Scrutiny Under SEC Proposal," *Washington Post,* May 15, 2009, http://www.washingtonpost.com/wp-dyn/content/article/2009/05/14/AR2009051403970.html?hpid=topnews, accessed September 2, 2009.

Hays, Tom, "Trustee: Nearly 9,000 Claims in Madoff Scam," *San Francisco Chronicle,* May 14, 2009, http://www.sfgate.com/cgi-bin/article.cgi?f=/n/a/2009/05/14/financial/f090030D98.DTL&feed=rss.business, accessed September 2, 2009.

Henriques, Diana B., and Zachery Kouwe, "Billions Withdrawn Before Madoff Arrest," *New York Times,* May 12, 2009, http://www.nytimes.com/2009/05/13/business/13madoff.html?_r=1&scp=1&sq=madoff%20%2412%20billion&st=cse, September 2, 2009.

Kim, Jane J., "As 'Clawback' Suits Loom, Some Investors Seek Cover," *Wall Street Journal,* March 12, 2009, p. C3.

Lucchetti, Aaron, "Victims Welcome Madoff Imprisonment," *Wall Street Journal,* March 13, 2009, http://online.wsj.com/article/SB123687992688609801.html, accessed September 2, 2009.

"Madoff's Victims," *Wall Street Journal,* March 6, 2009, http://s.wsj.net/public/resources/documents/st_madoff_victims_20081215.html, accessed September 2, 2009.

"Plea Allocution of Bernard L. Madoff," *Wall Street Journal,* March 12, 2009, http://online.wsj.com/public/resources/documents/20090315madoffall.pdf, accessed September 2, 2009.

Scannell, Kara, "Investor Who Lost Money in Alleged Scheme Seeks Relief from SEC," *Wall Street Journal,* December 23, 2008, http://online.wsj.com/article/SB122999646876429063.html, accessed September 2, 2009.

Shapiro, Adam, "Who Are 'The Others' Who Helped Madoff?" Fox News, August 12, 2009, http://www.foxbusiness.com/story/personal-finance/financial-planning/helped-madoff/, accessed September 8, 2009.

Stapleton, Christine, "Madoff Scandal Ripples Among Palm Beach County Foundations," *Palm Beach Post,* February 8, 2009, http://www.palmbeachpost.com/localnews/content/local_news/epaper/2009/02/08/a1b_foundations_0209.html, accessed September 2, 2009.

Strasburg, Jenny, "Madoff 'Feeders' Under Focus," *Wall Street Journal,* December 27–28, 2008, pp. A1, A8.

Strasburg, Jenny, "Mass Mutual Burned by Madoff," *Wall Street Journal,* December 22, 2008, p. C1.

Trex, Ethan, "Who Was Ponzi—What the Heck Was His Scheme?" CNN.com, December 23, 2008, http://www.cnn.com/2008/LIVING/wayoflife/12/23/mf.ponzi.scheme/index.html, accessed September 2, 2009.

"Victims of Scandal Reflect on Shocking Turnabout," *Wall Street Journal,* December 23, 2008, http://online.wsj.com/article/SB122972955226822819.html, accessed September 2, 2009.

Williamson, Elizabeth, "Shana Madoff's Ties to Uncle Probed," *Wall Street Journal,* December 22, 2008, http://online.wsj.com/article/SB122991035662025577.html, accessed September 2, 2009.

Appendix Selected Group of Madoff Investor Losses

Fairfield Greenwich Advisors	An investment management firm	$7,500,000,000
Tremont Group Holdings	Asset management firm	$3,300,000,000
Banco Santander	Spanish bank	$2,870,000,000
Bank Medici	Austrian bank	$2,100,000,000
Ascot Partners	A hedge fund founded by billionaire investor, philanthropist, and GMAC chief J. Ezra Merkin	$1,800,000,000
Fortis	Dutch bank	$1,350,000,000
HSBC	British bank	$1,000,000,000
Carl Shapiro	The founder and former chair of apparel company Kay Windsor, Inc., and his wife	$500,000,000
Fairfield, Conn.	Town pension fund	$42,000,000
Jewish Community Foundation of Los Angeles	The largest manager of charitable gift assets for Los Angeles Jewish philanthropists	$18,000,000
Korea Teachers Pension	A 10 trillion won Korean pension fund	$9,100,000
Fred Wilpon	Owner of the New York Mets	N/A
Steven Spielberg	The Spielberg charity—the Wunderkinder Foundation	N/A
Chais Family Foundation	A charity that gave to Jewish causes	N/A
Allianz Global Investors	The asset management unit of German insurer Allianz SE	N/A
UBS AG	Swiss bank	N/A
Yeshiva University	A New York–based private university	$14,500,000
Elie Wiesel Foundation for Humanity	The charitable foundation of Nobel laureate	$15,200,000
Leonard Feinstein	The co-founder of retailer Bed Bath & Beyond	N/A
Sen. Frank Lautenberg	The charitable foundation of the New Jersey senator's family	N/A
Norman Braman	Former owner of the Philadelphia Eagles	N/A
Jeffrey Katzenberg	The chief executive of DreamWorks Animation SKG Inc.	N/A
Gerald Breslauer	The Hollywood financial advisor to Steven Spielberg and Jeffrey Katzenberg	N/A

(continued)

Appendix Selected Group of Madoff Investor Losses (Continued)

Fairfield Greenwich Advisors	An investment management firm	$7,500,000,000
Royal Dutch Shell pension fund	Global energy and petrochemical company	N/A
New York Law School	Law school in New York City	$300,000
J. Gurwin Foundation	Charity	N/A
Fire and Police Pension Association of Colorado	Pension fund	N/A
International Olympic Committee	Olympic organizer	$4,800,000
Kevin Bacon and wife Kyra Sedgwick	Hollywood actors	N/A
Eric Roth	Hollywood screenwriter	N/A
Henry Kaufman	Individual investor, former Salomon Brothers chief economist	N/A
New York University	University	$24,000,000
Burt Ross	Former mayor of a town in New Jersey	$5,000,000
Gabriel Partners	Money-management firm run by GMAC Chair Ezra Merkin	N/A
Diocese of St. Thomas	Catholic church in the U.S. Virgin Islands	$2,000,000
Members of the Hillcrest Golf Club of St. Paul, Minn., and Oak Ridge Country Club in Hopkins, Minn.	Country clubs	N/A
Bard College	University in New York	$3,000,000
Martin Rosenman	New York City–based heating oil distributor	$10,000,000

Source: WSJ reporting; Associated Press; the companies and charities, wsj.net/public/resources/documents/st_madoff_victims_20081215.html, accessed January 9, 2009.

NIKE: Managing Ethical Missteps—Sweatshops to Leadership in Employment Practices

Phil Knight and his University of Oregon track coach Bill Bowerman founded Blue Ribbon Sports, later renamed Nike, in 1964. The idea, born as a result of a paper written by Knight during his Stanford MBA program, was to import athletic shoes from Japan into the U.S. market otherwise dominated by German competitors Puma and Adidas. The company initially operated as a distributor for a Japanese athletic shoe company, Onitsuka Tiger, but also developed its own brand of athletic footwear to promote in the American market. The company's relationship with Onitsuka Tiger ended in 1971, and the Nike brand was created in 1972 ("Nike" after the Greek goddess of victory). The company was renamed Nike in 1978, and has grown to be the largest worldwide seller of athletic goods, with approximately 19,000 retail accounts in the United States and about 160 countries around the world.

Nike's main popularity came from celebrity athlete sponsors. As the popularity of the Nike product grew, so did its product demands and the need to produce more apparel to meet the demands of customers. In contrast to its meteoric rise in the 1980s after going public, the late 1990s began a period composed of combating allegations about labor and human rights violations in Third World countries in which manufacturing had been subcontracted. Nike's response to this issue has been considered by critics to be more of a damage-control stunt than a sincere attempt at labor reform.

CRITICISMS OF NIKE'S MANUFACTURING PRACTICES

In order to remain competitive and keep manufacturing costs low, athletic footwear production has moved to areas of the world with low labor costs. Assembly of shoes (as well as low-cost apparel, footwear, radios, TVs, toys, sporting goods equipment, and consumer electronics) began shifting offshore in the 1960s: first to Japan, then to Korea and Taiwan, and starting in the 1980s to Southern China. By the mid 1980s, Taiwan and Korea supplied 45 percent of the world footwear exports, and the trend has continued for production to continually shift to lower-cost Asian nations.

Because of its history and experience with Japanese manufacturing and production, Nike was a pioneer in overseas manufacturing as a way to cut costs on sports gear manufacturing. When Japan became too expensive, Nike shifted its contracts to Vietnam, Indonesia, and China. Now, around 700 independent contract factories, most of which are in poor Asian nations, manufacture the majority of Nike's products. The working conditions for the workers in these factories have been a source of heated debate. Allegations of poor conditions, child labor, widespread harassment, and abuse have all been issues for the company. Because the Asian factories have further subcontracted out the work, it has become

This case was prepared by O.C. Ferrell and Jennifer Jackson, based on work by Lisa Kiscaden and Megan Long, the University of New Mexico. We appreciate the editorial assistance of Jennifer Sawayda on this edition of the case, and of Melanie Drever and Alexi Sherrill on the previous edition. This case was prepared for classroom discussion, rather than to illustrate either effective or ineffective handling of an administrative, ethical, or legal decision by management. All sources used for this case were obtained through publicly available material and the Nike website.

increasingly difficult for Nike to keep track of and regulate the working conditions and wages in these factories.

Sweatshop labor is not merely an issue for Nike. It permeates the public consciousness across all manufacturing. Perhaps the incident that brought sweatshop labor to the forefront of American consciousness was the Kathy Lee Gifford debacle in 1996 when the human rights group, the National Labor Committee, uncovered that Gifford's clothing line was made in Honduran sweatshops that used child labor.

Since the mid 1990s, Nike has faced a barrage of criticism from labor rights activists, the mainstream media, and others for human and labor rights violations in its factories. The accusations have included deficiencies in health and safety conditions, extremely low wages, and indiscriminate hiring and firing practices. While much of the firestorm has died down as Nike and other athletic wear manufacturers have sought to clean up their images, the media criticisms have damaged the company's reputation.

In Indonesia, where Korean suppliers owned a majority of Nike factories, reports by labor activists and other nongovernmental organizations revealed several cases of human rights abuses and labor violations. Through the use of the mass media, these conditions came to the attention of the general public, one of the prominent instances being that of Roberta Baskin's CBS report on the conditions in Nike's manufacturing facilities in Indonesia in 1993.

In 1996, *Life* magazine published an exposé article complete with photos of Pakistani children stitching soccer balls for Nike, Adidas AG, and other companies. The images of these children, working in factories instead of being in school, had a devastating impact on Nike's sales and corporate reputation. Customers who had previously held the American athletics brand in high regard began to develop a lower opinion of the company. Another well-publicized critique against Nike was Bob Herbert's op-ed article in the *New York Times* in 1996. This report led to further

public interest, accompanied by protests and demonstrations all over the United States. Several demonstrations occurred at "Nike Towns," the Nike retail mega stores.

Nike also experienced problems with factory conditions in Vietnam. This was especially serious since the discovery came as a result of a report commissioned by Nike as part of an audit by Ernst and Young of one of its factories. The private report was leaked to the press, resulting in the *New York Times* running it as a front-page article. The audit reported unacceptable levels of exposure to chemicals in the factory and documented cases of resulting employee health problems, as well as other infringements of the established code of conduct.

In response to the criticisms of the 1990s, Nike had to take rapid measures not only to redeem its reputation, but also to rectify problematic policies and lack of international oversight of its operations. Nike's new priorities changed to make certain that its factories were not taking advantage of its workers as well as to ensure that each worker has a safe work environment and competitive wage.

ENVIRONMENTAL PROBLEMS RELATED TO THE TEXTILE INDUSTRY

Because of the nature of the textile industry, Nike faces numerous challenges and potentially critical problems. Because of the processes involved in making the materials, the textile industry negatively impacts the environment wherever manufacturing is located. Problems generated by the textile industry in general, and Nike specifically, are increased water deficits; climate change; pollution of land, air, and waterways; and large fossil fuel and raw material consumption. In addition to these environmental hazards, today's electronic textile plants expend significant amounts of energy. All of these issues are exacerbated by Western cultures that have a consumption-based mentality that clothing is disposable and that one must buy each new season's "must-have" items.

In addition to environmental considerations are the physical work conditions for employees. The demand for cheap labor in manufacturing plants can lead to the increased prevalence of child labor and abusive practices, especially in developing countries such as Pakistan, Indonesia, Vietnam, and China, where workplaces are not as regulated as in the United States.

In her book, *No Logo*, published in 2002, Naomi Klein targets Nike regulation policies quite extensively, alleging that Nike abandons manufacturing sites in favor of cheaper ones as these countries work to develop better pay and employment rights. She refers back to the 1996 photo from *Life* magazine of Pakistani children as an example of the exploitation of child labor. Many critics have suggested that Nike should improve transparency measures in all of its factories, allow independent inspection to verify conditions, and make all audits public. Nike has complied to a limited extent. For example, audits of Nike generally have determined that Nike pays wages above the legal minimum. Critics are not satisfied, however, arguing that in most cases the wages still do not constitute a fair living wage.

NIKE RESPONDS TO THE CHALLENGES

Public protests against Nike have taken the forms of boycotts and picketing of Nike stores. Universities have even been known to cancel their deals with Nike to produce branded athletic goods. In 1998, Nike revenues and stock prices decreased by approximately 50 percent, leading to the laying off of 1,600 workers. Nike's first reaction to all of the bad press was to do damage control. Nike launched a large public relations campaign involving individual consumer retailers and large university contracts to combat the damaging allegations of child labor, inhospitable working conditions, and low or nonexistent wages. In an effort to directly address the concerns of student activists, Nike visited several college campuses, opening dialog with students and university administration about its manufacturing policies. Nike even invited teams of Dartmouth graduate students to tour the Indonesian and Vietnamese factories for three weeks at Nike's expense.

The company has spent considerable resources focusing on improving the labor standards in each of its factories. It must weigh the expense of labor in nations where product manufacturing is available. However, no matter where it chooses, as these factories subcontract out to the local workforce, it becomes increasingly difficult for Nike to regulate their working environment. Nike must take extra measures to ensure that the independent subcontractors used to supply the workforce in their factories do not engage in any illegal activities such as child labor, excessive work hours, hostile work environments, inappropriate payment, or other unethical actions.

Nike also has implemented a code of conduct for all of its suppliers, and has been working with the Global Alliance to help review its factories. In August 1996, Nike Corporation joined the Apparel Industry Partnership, a coalition of companies and labor and human rights groups assembled by the Clinton administration, to draft an industry-wide code of conduct.

Nike believes that sharing factory locations with independent third parties on a confidential basis enables them to monitor their supply chain properly. It states that disclosure of the factory names, plus details of audits of those factories, would be used by nongovernmental organizations (NGOs) simply to make further attacks rather than as part of a dialog to help the company to address and resolve those problems that exist. As for wage rates, Nike feels that establishing what constitutes a "fair" wage is by no means as easy as critics would have the public believe—and disparages the constant quoting of wage rates in U.S. dollar equivalents, when these are meaningless given the different costs of living in the countries concerned.

Nike has used many other tactics to repair its tarnished image. Like other athletics brands, Nike has used celebrity endorsers to support its products. Most famously, Michael Jordan was a Nike spokesperson for years, and Kobe Bryant and LeBron James have worked with Nike as well.

Since universities form a core segment of Nike's market, and repercussions were felt in this area with several canceled deals, letters detailing the acceptable conditions in the factories and stressing Nike's commitment to corporate responsibility were sent to universities around the country. Representatives from Nike also visited campuses and spoke to students, assuring them of Nike's intention toward responsible corporate citizenship. A key visit in this context was that of Mr. Knight to the campus of the University of North Carolina at Chapel Hill. Numerous press conferences were also held with college newspapers across the United States.

Nike is clearly distressed at how it has become a central focus in this controversy. The company requests that people look at Nike's competitors to see how many of them have taken the kind of measures that Nike has in the past decade.

Amid the stress of trying to control the negative impact of Nike's increasingly controversial reputation, Nike's public relations department also has faced legal repercussions for its attempts to control damaging allegations. When media criticism began to arise, Nike launched a reputation management campaign to defend its corporate reputation. Its campaign included writing op-ed pieces, letters to the university, and press releases to defend its reputation and to refute critics' claims. It also hired an independent review by Goodworks International, LLC, which subsequently determined that the claims against Nike were false.

Marc Kasky, a California activist, maintained that Nike's claims were misleading and deceptive to the public. He subsequently filed a lawsuit, claiming that Nike's actions should be classified as commercial speech that violated California's unfair competition and advertising laws. The legal controversy culminated in the California Supreme Court's decision in *Kasky v. Nike*. This case is important because the courts assumed that public relations communication may constitute "commercial speech" that can be interpreted as "false advertising," even if there was disagreement about whether Nike's specific defense-of-reputation campaign could be legitimately so designated. As commercial speech is afforded less protection under the First Amendment, Nike could thus become liable for any claims under its public relations campaign that could be construed as misleading the public. After the ruling, Nike settled the lawsuit at approximately $2 million.

NIKE'S CORPORATE SOCIAL RESPONSIBILITY

Despite the challenges Nike has faced in the past few decades, the company has come far. Indeed, Nike's corporate social responsibility (CSR) practices have been evolving since 1991. At first Nike's approach to CSR could be characterized as insufficient and generally lacking in any true forms of regulation and implementation throughout its global supply chain. Manufacturers in foreign locations were simply trying to comply with the minimal contract requirements, while at times overlooking fair labor practices in order to perform as low-cost suppliers. Nike's initial response to criticism was reputation management rather than wide-scale changes in its practices. However, as more and more issues have surfaced and been brought to the attention of not only the corporation but also its consumers, Nike has increased its efforts to be more ethical in its manufacturing practices and has become somewhat of an industry leader in certain areas.

Corporate responsibility can evolve through five stages:

1. Defensive: "It's not our fault."

2. Compliance: "We'll do only what we have to."

3. Managerial: "It's the business."

4. Strategic: "It gives us a competitive edge."

5. Civil: "We need to make sure everybody does it."

Nike could be classified as having evolved from the defensive stage, through the compliance stage, to the managerial stage. The company's initial CSR report in 2001 was intended to show how Nike had handled complaints by labor rights and student groups who wanted to see better conditions at contract factories worldwide. In its second report in 2005, the company disclosed the names and locations of factories that produced its sneakers, apparel, and other products—a first for the industry and an appeal to critics. This represented a genuine effort to invite critics to review its factories. By its third CSR report, Nike officials said they were moving away from using corporate responsibility as a crisis-management tool and were instead using it as an opportunity for innovation and growth.

Nike must now grow fully into the fourth and fifth CSR stages. The company must continue to develop its corporate responsibility strategies and increase enforcement of its policies in its factories to ensure its market share dominance in the footwear industry. With its new emphasis on corporate responsibility as an innovative tool, Nike is migrating into the notion that implementing further CSR initiatives will make the company an industry leader and thus give it a competitive edge in the footwear industry.

The following sections further discuss some of Nike's CSR practices. The areas covered include environmental sustainability, Nike's code of conduct, audit tools used to evaluate Nike contractor practices, factory transparency, Nike's corporate responsibility board, and philanthropy.

Environmental Sustainability

In 1990, Nike began development of the ReUse-A-Shoe Program to help reduce the company's environmental footprint and reduce the amount of shoes that end up in landfills. The purpose of the program was to find an environmentally-friendly way to dispose of worn-out shoes. The material made from the recycled shoes was coined "Nike Grind." In 1995, Reuse-A-Shoe began collecting old shoes in Nike retail stores. In 2002, Nike expanded Reuse-A-Shoe by partnering with the National Recycling Coalition, as well as beginning plans to go international with drop-off stations in Europe and Australia. Since the program was created, more than 1.5 million pairs of used shoes are collected for recycling each year. This is in addition to thousands of tons of manufacturing scrap material that is recycled. Nike has collected more than 21 million pairs of used athletic shoes since 1995.

Code of Conduct

Initially drafted in 1991, Nike's Code of Conduct was its first step toward improving working conditions in their factories. It is the foundation of Nike's corporate ethic. The company founded its code of conduct on the belief that Nike is comprised of many different kinds of people, and in order to reach the desired level of employer responsibility, it was necessary to appreciate individual diversity and become more dedicated to offering equal opportunity for each individual.

Nike designs, manufactures, and markets products for sports and fitness consumers. The company is striving to satisfy not only what is required by law, but also the expectations of what is necessary as a leader. Nike shares this goal with its business partners and contractors and requires them to embrace the same commitment to best practices and continuous improvement in four key areas: management practices, environmental responsibility, safety in the workplace, and promoting the overall well-being of all employees. Contractors are required to recognize the dignity of each employee, and the right to a workplace free of harassment, abuse, or corporal punishment. Decisions on hiring, salary, benefits, advancement, termination, and retirement must be based solely on the employee's ability to do the job, free from discrimination based on race, creed, gender, marital or maternity status, religious or political beliefs, age, or sexual orientation.

Audit Tools

In 1998, Nike developed three main auditing tools to help provide increasing transparency and insight into the manner in which Nike contract factories are evaluated for compliance with company standards. Management Audit Verification (MAV) combines audit and verification into one tool. It helps to identify issues related to work hours, wages and benefits, freedom of association, and grievance systems, as well as to follow up on these issues and to create an action plan to correct them according to local law and Nike's Code Leadership Standards. The Safety, Health, Attitude of Management, People and Environment (SHAPE) tool is an audit tool used quarterly by contract factories to determine their compliance with Nike's Code Leadership Standards. This tool involves inspections that help to improve work conditions, for example, by reducing workers' exposure to toxic solvents and glues. The Environment, Safety and Health (ESH) audit is an in-depth audit tool used by Nike compliance teams to determine compliance with Nike's Code Leadership Standards. In addition to its own auditing tools, external organizations such as NGOs frequently audit Nike as well.

Factory Transparency

In 2000, Nike became even more proactive by becoming the first company to respond to college requests to publicly disclose the names and locations of its contracted factories that produced licensed collegiate products. A contract factory making Nike products could be producing for as many as thirty different schools. By disclosing its supply chain, Nike believes it can be more successful at monitoring and making changes once issues have been uncovered not only in its own factories but on an industry-wide basis. The company hopes that by disclosing its own supply chain, it can encourage other companies to do the same. The company also feels that transparency should work as a motivator for contract factories. Those with high compliance rankings can be confident that business will come their way.

With multiple brands, and many universities represented, contract factories must decide which company's code(s) of conduct to follow. This is not an easy task, as standards for the varying corporate codes of conduct can contradict each other. Nike has attempted to make it easier for contract factories to comply with its code of conduct by guaranteeing that its code aligns with that of the Fair Labor Association. The company hopes that eventually a standardized code of conduct followed by all companies in the industry can be implemented, creating widespread compliance and better working conditions. Even as Nike has taken dramatic steps to increase its transparency and accountability, activists have continued putting pressure on the company to improve its standards and practices.

Nike also has implemented the Balanced Scorecard for its suppliers. The Balanced Scorecard is a lettered grading system used to better assess factory compliance with the code of conduct. Rather than simply assessing financial factors, the Balanced Scorecard also measures labor, health, and environmental standards of factories. This system gives the company a reliable method for rewarding high-performance, compliant factories. The card measures cost, delivery, and quality, all of which need to be addressed equally for the work in factories to flow smoothly. The Balanced Scorecard gives factories incentives to improve working conditions, and Nike rewards those that show improvement.

Corporate Responsibility Board

In 2001, Nike developed a Corporate Responsibility (CR) Board to review policies and activities and to make recommendations to the board of directors regarding labor and environmental practices, community affairs, charitable and foundation activities, diversity and equal opportunity, and environmental and sustainability initiatives. The Board is currently composed of ten members, eight of whom are independent directors. Nike's Vice President of Corporate Responsibility reports directly to the CEO of Nike Inc., who in turn is a member of the board of directors. Nearly 120 Nike employees work on CR issues as their primary function or have CR work as a significant portion of their workload.

Thanks to the efforts of the CR board and other Nike social responsibility initiatives, the workers in factories manufacturing Nike products are now aware of their rights, such as the right to minimum wages, and other entitlements, like food at subsidized rates. The workers also have access to basic education. Nearly all of Nike's factories offer education and training programs, and the remaining factories have similar programs in the pipeline.

Philanthropy

One of Nike's newest goals to increase its CSR is by building a social network "where innovations are shared, new funds are mobilized and human and social capital is exchanged in support of a global movement based on the power of sport to unleash human potential." Nike's goal is to encourage the use of sports as a means of empowering individuals and building skills such as leadership, conflict resolution, equity, and trauma relief. Nike partners with various individuals and groups that work directly with low-income youth, minorities, young women, and youth living in conflict situations around the world. Nike is building networks that include consumer activism, strong research evidence, and advocacy to shift policies and funding.

Because sports require access to safe spaces, good coaches, safe equipment, and education, Nike is forming partnerships in the areas of sports, youth, and education. Nike's

new philanthropy initiatives have resulted in $315 million in grants, product donations, and other support through 2011 to give underprivileged youth greater access to sport programs. Nike contributes an additional $100 million annually in cash and products to nonprofit partners around the world. While contributing to the global community, the company also strives to invest in its own local communities of Portland, Oregon; Memphis, Tennessee; Hilversum, Holland; Laakdal, Belgium; and other places around the world with corporate offices.

With a continued focus on corporate responsibility, Nike hopes to build and improve its relationships with consumers, to achieve a high-quality supply chain, and to create top-quality, innovative products. Although this evolution is a rocky one filled with lessons learned along the way, the benefits are being seen for employees all around the world, and for the company itself.

NEW CHALLENGES IN THE FUTURE

In 2006, Nike veteran Mark Parker, formerly co-president, took over as CEO and director. Parker has been with Nike for nearly thirty years, has been part of most of Nike's top innovative plans, and is recognized as a product visionary. *Ethisphere* magazine praised him for his leadership under which Nike shoes have become more eco-friendly and questionable suppliers have been fired.

As a result of its positive changes, Nike appeared in *Business Ethics* magazine's "100 Best Corporate Citizens" list for 2005–2007. *Business Ethics* magazine cited its reasons for listing Nike as the strength of Nike's commitment to community and environment. Nike was actually ranked number one in the magazine's environmental category due to its efforts to eliminate waste and toxic substances from production processes. Nike also has made *Fortune* magazine's "100 Best Companies to Work

For" list, coming in at number 100 in 2006, but rising to 82nd in 2008. *Fortune*'s 2009 list of "The World's Most Admired Companies" ranked Nike as the number one most-admired apparel company, and ranked it 23 for overall most-admired. Nike also was listed as number 26 in *CRO (Corporate Responsibility Officer)* magazine's "Best Corporate Citizens" in 2009.

The news has not all been good for Nike, however. In March 2008, one of Nike's contract factories in China was found to have underage workers, unpaid wages for employees, and to have falsified documents for worker permits. In response, Nike has detailed the efforts it has made to enforce compliance with its code of conduct and with Chinese law. China is Nike's largest single-sourcing country, with some 180 manufacturers and about 210,000 employees.

Also in 2008 Nike's contract factory in Malaysia reported that workers were living in substandard housing conditions and that their passports were being withheld and wages not paid in full. The spokesperson for the factory blamed local government labor policies and lack of enforcement as the reasons these labor abuses were being committed.

The fact is that Nike's current supply chain has major flaws in both contract negotiation and supplier oversight. Even though some experts herald Nike as a leader in CSR, its use of hundreds of international contractors make detection and enforcement of abuses incredibly difficult. While Nike has come a long way since the 1990s, its ethics and compliance system still has a lot of room for improvement. For example, Nike employs only one compliance staff member for every ten factories. Nike tries to perform two inspections per year per active factory, but in reality it inspects only about 25 percent of factories per year. Nike also contracts third parties to inspect roughly 5 percent of its factories per year.

Social and environmental responsibility involves not only doing the right thing. It can be good for a company's bottom line in a highly competitive industry. Being perceived as a company that goes farther than the minimum required on social issues can attract and retain customers. Nike's target audience has broadened from mainly male athletes to females and more fashion-oriented offerings as well. As Nike's target audience widens, being perceived as an ethical company will help attract and retain new customers.

One of Nike's innovative product approaches is the Stand-Off Distance Singlet—a tank top for long-distance runners that uses a high-tech fabric designed to keep runners cool. It is made of 75 percent recycled soda bottles and uses 43 percent less energy to produce than standard fabrics. The tank is ultrasonically welded at the seams, which eliminates sewing thread, and does not contain any artificial dyes or toxic substances. Nike plans to develop more innovative and sustainable products like the singlet in the future.

Where wages, conditions, and other worker rights such as unions are concerned, Nike continues to strive to raise the bar and improve operations. Nike has worked hard to implement new policies, ensuring that in countries where it operates, the factories are considered the fairest and safest working environments. Nike also has joined coalitions that help them achieve this goal, such as Global Alliance. The company's ultimate goal is that everybody will benefit from their association with Nike. Customers are buying into an ideal, not just the product. In addition to customers' concerns for value, many also demand to know about the labor issues surrounding the production of their purchases. Brand management, customer awareness, and loyalty are all directly linked, and therefore maintenance of the relationship among brand images, quality, and corporate ethics has to be consistent.

Nike itself admits that it has a long way to go in the area of corporate responsibility, including continuing to improve its monitoring systems. However, the company is being rewarded for its efforts toward improvement by both positive results and industry response.

QUESTIONS

1. Why did Nike fail to address corporate social responsibility earlier?

2. Evaluate Nike's response to societal and consumer concerns about its contract manufacturing.

3. What are the challenges facing Nike in the future?

SOURCES

Balfour, Frederick, "Acting Globally but Selling Locally: Chinese Athletic Wear Maker Li Ning Is Raising Its International Profile to Win Over Shoppers at Home," *BusinessWeek*, May 12, 2008, pp. 27–29.

"*Business Ethics* 100 Best Corporate Citizens 2007," *Business Ethics,* http://www.business-ethics.com/node/75, accessed September 3, 2009.

Casey, Nicholas, and Raphael Pura, "Nike Addresses Abuse Complaints at Malaysia Plant," *Wall Street Journal*, August 4, 2008, http://online.wsj.com/article/SB121779204898108093.html?mod=dist_smartbrief, accessed September 3, 2009.

"Citizen Nike," *Fortune,* http://money.cnn.com/2008/11/17/news/companies/levenson_nike.fortune/index.htm, accessed September 3, 2009.

Collins, E. L., L. M. Zoch, and C. S. McDonald, "A Crisis in Reputation Management: The Implications of *Kasky v. Nike*," presented at the meeting of the International Communication Association, May 27, 2004, New Orleans Sheraton, New Orleans, LA, http://www.allacademic.com/meta/p113246_index.html, accessed September 3, 2009.

"Corporate Social Responsibility in Emerging Markets: The Role of Multinational Corporations," Foreign Policy Centre, http://fpc.org.uk/fsblob/919.pdf, accessed September 3, 2009.

"Corporate Social Responsibility Profile—Nike," CSR Wire, http://www.csrwire.com/profile/1262.html, accessed September 3, 2009.

DeTienne, Kristen B., and Lee W. Lewis, "The Pragmatic and Ethical Barriers to Corporate Social Responsibility Disclosure: The Nike Case," *Journal of Business Ethics* 60, no. 4 (2005): 359–376.

Elsasser, John, "Watching Nike Sweat," *Public Relations Tactics* 6 (1998): 1–4.

"FY05–06 Corporate Responsibility Report, 2005–2006," Nike, http://www.nikebiz.com/responsibility/documents/Nike_FY05_06_CR_Report_C.pdf, accessed September 8, 2009.

"Innovate for a Better World," *Nike FY05–06 Corporate Responsibility Report, 2005–2006*, http://www.nikebiz.com/responsibility/documents/Nike_FY05_06_CR_Report_C.pdf, accessed September 3, 2009.

Klein, Naomi, *No Logo* (New York: Riemann Verlag, 2002).

Krentzman, Jackie, "The Force Behind the Nike Empire," *Stanford Magazine,* http://www.stanfordalumni.org/news/magazine/1997/janfeb/articles/knight.html, accessed September 3, 2009.

"Labors' Pains," PBS, April 14, 1997, http://www.pbs.org/newshour/bb/business/jan-june97/sweatshops_4-14.html, accessed September 3, 2009.

"The Long Case for Nike—'Just Do It'" Seeking Alpha, http://seekingalpha.com/article/23192-the-long-case-for-nike-just-do-it, accessed September 3, 2009.

"Mark Parker (President & CEO, Nike)," *Ethisphere*, December 11, 2008, http://ethisphere.com/mark-parker/, accessed September 3, 2009.

"Nike Answers Critics on Corporate Responsibility," B & T Marketing, http://www.bandt.com.au/news/25/0c00d225.asp, accessed September 3, 2009.

"NIKE Failed on Sweatshop Reform Promises," *Albion Monitor*, http://www.albionmonitor.com/0105b/copyright/nikereport.html, accessed September 3, 2009.

"Nike-Funded Study Claims Workers at Nike's Indonesian Factories Are Subject to Abuse and Harassment," *Ethics Newsline*, February 26, 2001, http://www.globalethics.org/newsline/2001/02/26/nike-funded-study-claims-workers-at-nikes-indonesian-factories-are-subject-to-abuse-and-harassment/, accessed September 3, 2009.

"Nike's Corporate Social Responsibility Efforts Falling Short?," The World Is Green, http://worldisgreen.com/2007/06/05/csr-and-business-startegy-with-nike/, accessed September 3, 2009.

"Nike's New CSR Report. They Just Did It—Again," Perspectives in Responsible Sourcing, http://cscc.typepad.com/responsiblesourcing/2007/06/nikes_new_csr_r.html, accessed September 3, 2009.

"Nike University: Hooked on Sweatshops," Jonathon Speaks, http://irregulartimes.com/nike.html, accessed September 3, 2009.

"Nike in Vietnam: The Tae Kwang Vina Factory," World Bank, http://siteresources.worldbank.org/INTEMPOWERMENT/Resources/14826_Nike-web.pdf, accessed April 11, 2009.

"100 Best Companies to Work For," CNNMoney.com, http://money.cnn.com/magazines/fortune/bestcompanies/2008/full_list/index.html, accessed September 3, 2009.

"100 Best Corporate Citizens 2009," Corporate Responsibility Officer, http://www.thecro.com/files/100BestGatefold.pdf, accessed September 3, 2009.

"Our Community Programs: Reuse-A-Shoe & Nike Grind," nikebiz.com, October 28, 2008, http://www.nikebiz.com/responsibility/community_programs/reuse_a_shoe.html, accessed September 3, 2009.

"Shoes Sought in Recycling Project," *Wicked Local Lexington*, April 29, 2008, http://www.wickedlocal.com/lexington/news/business/x883026486, accessed September 3, 2009.

"Social Responsibility: The Nike Story," Branding Strategy, http://www.brandingstrategyinsider.com/2008/07/social-responsi.html, accessed September 3, 2009.

"World's Most Admired Companies 2009: Apparel," *Fortune,* http://money.cnn.com/magazines/fortune/mostadmired/2009/industries/3.html, accessed September 3, 2009.

Zwolinski, Matt, "The Promise and Perils of Globalization: The Case of Nike," in *Social Issues in America: An Encyclopedia,* ed. James Ciment (Armonk, NY: M.E. Sharpe, 2006).

Banking Industry Meltdown: The Ethical and Financial Risks of Derivatives

The 2008–2009 global recession was caused in part by a failure of the financial industry to take appropriate responsibility for its decision to utilize risky and complex financial instruments. Corporate cultures were built on rewards for taking risks rather than rewards for creating value for stakeholders. Unfortunately, most stakeholders, including the public, regulators, and the mass media, do not always understand the nature of the financial risks taken on by banks and other institutions to generate profits.

Problems in the subprime mortgage markets sounded the alarm in the 2008–2009 economic downturn. Very simply, the subprime market was created by making loans to people who normally would not qualify based on their credit ratings. The debt from these loans was often repackaged and sold to other financial institutions in order to take it off lenders' books and reduce their exposure. When the real estate market became overheated, many people were no longer able to make the payments on their variable rate mortgages. When consumers began to default on payments, prices in the housing market dropped and the values of credit default swaps (the repackaged mortgage debt, also known as CDSs) lost significant value. The opposite was supposed to happen. CDSs were sold as a method of insuring against loss. These derivatives, investors were told, would act as an insurance policy to reduce the risk of loss. Unfortunately, losses in the financial industry were so widespread that even the derivative contracts that had been written to cover losses from unpaid subprime mortgages could not be covered by the financial institutions that had written these derivatives contracts. The financial industry and managers at all levels had become focused on the rewards for these transactions without concerns about how their actions could potentially damage others.

In addition to providing a simplified definition of what derivatives are, this case allows for a review of questionable, often unethical or illegal, conduct associated with a number of respected banks in the 2008–2009 financial crisis. First, we review the financial terminology associated with derivatives, as they were an integral part of the downfall of these financial institutions. Derivatives were, and still are, considered a legal and ethical financial instrument when used properly, but they inherently hold a lot of potential for mishandling. When misused, they provide a ripe opportunity for misconduct. To illustrate the types of misconduct that can result, this case employs a number of examples. First, we examine Barings Bank, which ceased to exist because of a rogue trader using derivatives. Next, we look at United Bank of Switzerland (UBS) and its huge losses from bad mortgages and derivatives. Bear Stearns, an investment bank that suffered its demise through derivatives abuse, is the third example. Finally, Lehman Brothers is an investment bank that was involved with high-risk derivatives that also led to its bankruptcy. At the conclusion of this case, we examine the

This case was prepared by John Fraedrich, O.C. Ferrell, and Jennifer Jackson, with the editorial assistance of Jennifer Sawayda, for classroom discussion, rather than to illustrate either effective or ineffective handling of an administrative, ethical, or legal decision by management. All sources used for this case were obtained through publicly available material.

risk of derivatives and potential ethical risks associated with the use of these instruments in the financial industry.

DERIVATIVES DEFINED

Derivatives are financial instruments with values that change relative to underlying variables, such as assets, events, or prices. In other words, the value of derivatives is based on the change in value of something else, called the *underlying* trade or exchange.

The main types of derivatives are futures, forwards, options, and swaps. A *futures* contract is an agreement to buy or sell a set quantity of something at a set rate at a predetermined point in the future. The date on which this exchange is scheduled to take place is called the delivery, or settlement, date. Futures contracts are often associated with buyers and sellers of commodities who are concerned about supply, demand, and changes in prices. They can be traded only on exchanges. Almost any commodity, such as oil, gold, corn, or soybeans, can have a futures contract defined for a specific trade.

Forwards are similar to futures, except they can be traded between two individuals. A forward contract is a commitment to trade a specified item at a specific price in the future. The forward contract takes whatever form to which the parties agree.

An *option* is a less binding form of derivative. It conveys the right, but not the obligation, to buy or sell a particular asset in the future. A *call option* gives the investor the right to buy at a set price on delivery day. A *put option* gives the investor the option to sell a good or financial instrument at a set price on the settlement date. It is a financial contract with what is called a *long position,* giving the owner the right but not the obligation to sell an amount at a preset price and maturity date.

Finally, *swaps* live up to their name. A swap can occur when two parties agree to exchange one stream of cash flows against another one. Swaps can be used to hedge risks such as changes in interest rates, or to speculate on the changing prices of commodities or currencies. Swaps can be difficult to understand, so here is an example. JP Morgan developed CDSs that bundled together as many as 300 different assets, including subprime loans. Credit default swaps were meant as a form of insurance. In other words, securities were bundled into one financial package, and companies such as JP Morgan were essentially paying insurance premiums to the investors who purchased them, who were now on the hook if payments of any of the securities included in the CDSs did not come through.

As mentioned before, the value of derivatives is based on different types of underlying values, including assets such as commodities, equities (stocks), bonds, interest rates, exchange rates, or indexes such as a stock market index, consumer price index (CPI), or even an index of weather conditions. For example, a farmer and a grain storage business enter into a futures contract to exchange cash for grain at some future point. Both parties have reduced a future risk. For the farmer it is the uncertainty of the future grain price, and for the grain storage business it is the availability of the grain at a predetermined price.

Some believe derivatives lead to market volatility because enormous amounts of money are controlled by relatively small amounts of margin or option premiums. The job of a derivatives trader is something like a bookie taking bets on how people will bet. *Arbitrage* is defined as attempting to profit by exploiting price differences of identical or similar financial instruments, on different markets, or in different forms. As a result, derivatives can suffer large losses or returns from small movements in the underlying asset's price. Investors are like gamblers in that they can bet for or against the price (going up or down) and can consequently lose or win large amounts.

BARINGS BANK

Barings Bank, which had been in operation in the United Kingdom for 233 years, ceased to exist in 1995 when a futures trader named Nick Leeson lost approximately $1.4 billion in company assets. The extinction was due, in part, to a large holding position in the Japanese futures market. Leeson, chief trader for Barings Futures in Singapore, accumulated a large number of opening positions on the Nikkei Index. He then generated losses in the first two months of 1995 when the Nikkei dropped more than 15 percent. To try and recover these losses, Leeson placed what is called a short "straddle" on the Singapore and Tokyo stock markets. He was betting that the stock market would not move significantly in the short term. This strategy is risky but can be profitable in stable markets. However, when the Kobe earthquake hit and sent the Japanese stock market plummeting, Leeson lost a lot of money. He did not, however, change his approach. In fact, Leeson tried to cover his losses through a series of other risky investments that, instead, only increased the losses. When he finally quit his job, Leeson sent a fax to his manager, stating "sincere apologies for the predicament that I have left you in." Barings was purchased by ING, a Dutch bank for £1 (approximately $1), which then sold it under the name Baring Asset Management (BAM) to MassMutual and Northern Trust in 2005.

Nick Leeson's life is a rags-to-riches tale. Son of a plasterer, he started his career in 1984 as a clerk with royal bank Coutts and later worked briefly for Morgan Stanley. He then got a position in operations at Barings, and later was transferred to Jakarta. Leeson worked in a back office solving clients' problems of wrongly denominated certificates and difficulties of delivery. Before long, Leeson was appointed manager of a new operation in the futures markets on the Singapore Monetary Exchange (SIMEX). Leeson had the authority to hire traders and staff and to sell six financial products, but his main business was doing inter-exchange arbitrage or "switching." Switching is betting on small differences between contracts by buying and selling futures simultaneously on two different stock exchanges. For example, if a contract was worth the equivalent of $3 in London and $2.75 in Singapore, Leeson would buy in Singapore and sell in London, making a 25-cent profit.

The key to Leeson's strategy in the 1980s was the knowledge that one stock market was slower in processing trades than the other. To hide any bad bets, Leeson created an error account (named 8888 for its auspiciousness in Chinese numerology) for his losses. Because no one could see the losses hidden by this account, Leeson was widely regarded as a brilliant trader. He had assured Barings that he was not trading with company money and that all the positions were perfectly hedged and virtually risk-free. Barings managers had little knowledge in trading and did not suspect Leeson of deception. Based on their trust, Barings put a billion dollars into Leeson's account and made no attempt to check his statements. All it took to bring down this house of cards was one earthquake.

When the Kobe earthquake hit in 1995, Leeson's luck finally ran out. He fled to Malaysia, Thailand, and then Germany, and was finally arrested for fraud in Frankfurt. He was extradited back to Singapore and sentenced to six-and-a-half years in Singapore's Changi prison where he was diagnosed with colon cancer and divorced by his wife. During that time, Leeson wrote *Rogue Trader: How I Brought Down Barings Bank and Shook the Financial World*, which was later made into a movie. He was released from prison in 1999. Since then he has become CEO of the Galway United Football Club. Although he has tried to atone for his actions, to many he is still considered to be the rogue trader who, through his misuse of derivatives, destroyed the United Kingdom's oldest bank.

UBS

United Bank of Switzerland (UBS) is a diversified global financial services company, headquartered in Switzerland. It is the world's largest manager of private wealth assets and the second-largest bank in Europe with overall invested assets of approximately $3.167 trillion.

In 2000, UBS acquired PaineWebber Group Inc. to become the world's largest wealth management firm for private clients. Three years later, all UBS business groups rebranded under the UBS name as the company began operating as one large firm. As a result of the rebranding, UBS took a $1 billion write-down for the loss of goodwill associated with the retirement of the PaineWebber brand. (Write-downs represent a reduction in an asset's book value.) UBS is no longer an acronym but is the company's brand name. Its logo of three keys stands for confidence, security, and discretion. UBS had offices in the world's financial centers in 50 countries, and employed approximately 82,000.

In the late 2000s, UBS came under scrutiny for questionable practices. In 2008, Internal Revenue Service investigators asked for the names of some 20,000 American clients suspected of hiding as much as $20 billion in assets to avoid at least $300 million in federal taxes on funds in offshore accounts. The issue is complicated because using offshore accounts is not illegal in the United States, but hiding income in undeclared accounts is. However, Switzerland does not consider tax evasion a crime, and using undeclared accounts is legal. In 2008, former UBS banker Bradley Birkenfeld and Liechtenstein banker Mario Staggl were indicted in Florida for helping an American property developer evade taxes by creating bogus trusts and corporations to hide the ownership and control of offshore assets. They also were accused of advising clients to destroy bank records and of helping them to file false tax returns. UBS had asked the bankers to sign papers saying that they, not the bank, would be responsible if they broke non-Swiss tax laws.

Indian authorities also are probing suspected violations of foreign exchange controls involving accounts held at UBS by two companies controlled by India's richest man. The accusations involve transactions that were allegedly arranged by unspecified parties by taking overdrafts on accounts held with UBS London.

However, tax evasion accusations are not the only problems UBS faces. Like other banks, it has suffered from the subprime crisis due to its heavy dependence on derivatives and mortgage-related securities. In fact, UBS has suffered more losses than any other lender in Europe. By the end of 2008, the bank had been forced to write-down over $46 billion in losses on bad mortgages and derivatives. The bank blamed weak risk controls and risky investment dealings for its loss.

In 2008, UBS appealed to the Swiss government, which doled out an aid package of approximately $59.2 billion to the ailing bank. In exchange, UBS agreed to forgo nearly $27.7 million in pay to the company's top three executives. From then on, the bank promised, bonuses would depend more on the bank's performance, a decision that came to the relief of those who had criticized what they saw as the bank's excessive pay for CEOs. Additionally, some CEOs who resigned promised to return some of the compensation they received. Time will tell whether these combined decisions will be able to resolve the bank's burgeoning problems.

BEAR STEARNS

Unlike many companies that existed before the Great Depression of 1929, Bear Stearns thrived through much of the twentieth century. Unfortunately, in the early twenty-first century, Bear Stearns encountered another severe economic crisis that it did not survive. JP Morgan acquired the company in March 2008 after Bear Stearns lost billions in the subprime crisis.

Bear Stearns was a global investment bank and a securities and brokerage firm. Located in New York City, it was founded as an equity trading-house in 1923 by Joseph Bear, Robert Stearns, and Harold Mayer. With an initial $500,000 in capital, the company thrived in the twenties and even in the post–stock market crash of the 1930s. In fact, the company did so well that while other banks were failing by the dozens, Bear Stearns was able to pay out bonuses. By 1933, the company employed seventy-five people and opened its first regional office in Chicago. About twenty years later, the company began operating international offices. Bear Stearns continued to grow and prosper, and in 1985 it formed a holding company known as Bear Stearns Companies, Inc. In 2002, while other firms were struggling, Bear Stearns was the only securities firm to report a first-quarter profit increase. It also began focusing more on the housing industry, which would spell out its doom a mere five years later.

In 2005, Bear Stearns was listed as *Fortune* magazine's "America's Most Admired Securities Firm" for the second time in three years. At the end of 2006, the company's total capital was $66.7 billion and its assets totaled $350.4 billion. The subprime crisis first hit Bear Stearns early in 2007. Previously, the bank had seen a fifty-two-week high of $133.20 per share. By late 2007, two Bear Stearns hedge funds had collapsed, the company's third-quarter profit had decreased by 61 percent, and it had written off $1.2 billion in mortgage securities. In 2008, the Federal Reserve attempted to bail out the company, but it could not save Bear Stearns. JP Morgan agreed to buy the company for a mere $2 per share, which was a decrease of $131 per share in about a year. After lawsuits and intense negotiations, JP Morgan raised the buying price to $10 per share.

What caused a long-standing institution like Bear Stearns to fall? Its investment in subprime loans was a significant factor, but derivatives could also be a major reason. Since its failure, information has come out that Bear Stearns widely misrepresented clients' information on loan applications in order to make them appear more desirable mortgage recipients. Once these risky subprime loans were given out, the company packaged and sold the debt as securities to other institutions. In this way, Bear Stearns managed to keep the risky subprime lending debt off its books and moved the onus to investors. Bear Stearns had derivatives amounting to $13.4 trillion at the end of 2007. These securities were backed by cash flow from the loans, but that only works when loan payments come in as they are supposed to.

Since its failure, the Bear Stearns scheme has been exposed as a risky "house of cards." Executives have been charged with misleading investors by concealing that hedge funds were failing as the mortgage market crumbled. Investors lost $1.6 billion in assets. Executives Ralph R. Cioffi and Matthew M. Tannin were arrested and face criminal charges. Yet this has done little to console investors or Bear Stearns' employees as they have watched the company's fall and acquisition by JP Morgan.

LEHMAN BROTHERS

Another firm that had been around for a long time, more than 150 years in this case, found that it could not survive the subprime mortgage crisis either. In 2008, Lehman Brothers, the fourth-largest investment bank in the United States, filed for chapter 11 bankruptcy.

Lehman Brothers was founded by Henry, Emanuel, and Mayer Lehman, German immigrants who migrated to America in the mid-nineteenth century. It opened its first store in Montgomery, Alabama, in 1850. As cotton was the cash crop of the South, the brothers often accepted payment in cotton and began acting as brokers for those who were buying and selling the crop. The brothers' business expanded quickly, and they opened an office in New York in 1858. Soon they had transformed from brokerage to merchant banking, and Lehman Brothers became a member of the New York Stock Exchange in 1887.

The company continued to thrive even through the stock market crash of 1929. It advised and financed several other businesses, including Halliburton, Digital Equipment, and Campbell Soup. The firm opened its first international office in Paris in 1960. After going public in 1994, Lehman Brothers joined the S&P 100 Index in 1998 and watched its stock rise to $100 per share by the early 2000s.

In 2007, the year the subprime crisis began, Lehman Brothers was ranked as number one in the "Most Admired Firms" list by *Fortune* magazine. CEO Richard Fuld was placed on the list of the world's thirty best CEOs. For its third quarter, Lehman Brothers possessed assets worth $275 billion.

Then the subprime mortgage crisis came to a head. By late 2008, the company's shares had lost 73 percent of their value. Even as the company asked for government aid, its executives continued to pocket millions of dollars in bonuses, an action that caused public outrage. The company filed for bankruptcy that year, with $613 billion in debt. Company shares rapidly fell 90 percent to 21 cents per share. The bank received some relief after Barclay PLC agreed to purchase much of Lehman Brothers for $1.75 billion. The purchase of Lehman Brothers was welcome news for some workers, as many of them thought they were going to lose their jobs. Yet this did little to help many shareholders, who had already seen their stocks reduced to nothing. Even CEO Fuld had lost $600 million between 2007 and 2008.

What caused such a well-established company like Lehman Brothers to go belly-up? Its dependence on subprime mortgages was the central factor. Additionally, some are accusing the firm of unethical behavior in its dealings with First Alliance Mortgage, a company accused of "predatory lending." Lehman Brothers helped bundle millions of dollars in mortgages into derivatives instruments for First Alliance and helped make them seem like appealing investment vehicles for Wall Street. When the loans defaulted, these investments contributed to the massive financial crisis.

Lehman Brothers had also acquired several credit default swaps (CDSs), a type of derivative contract. The company had acquired large amounts of subprime mortgage debt and other lower-rated assets when securitizing the underlying mortgages. Even though Lehman had closed its subprime mortgage division in 2007, it maintained much of its subprime mortgage liability through 2008, resulting in large losses from the collapse of the subprime market. Creditors of Lehman Brothers, AIG among them, had taken out CDSs to hedge against the case of a Lehman bankruptcy. The estimated amount of settling these swaps stands at $100 to $400 billion.

Additionally, many major money market funds had significant exposure to Lehman Brothers. Lehman's bankruptcy caused the investors in these money market accounts to lose millions. Undoubtedly, the fall of Lehman Brothers will have severe effects on businesses across the world for a long time, a negative legacy of this once great company.

ETHICAL ISSUES WITH DERIVATIVES

Derivatives (especially swaps) expose investors to counter-party risk. For example, if a business wants a fixed-interest loan but banks only offer variable rates, the business swaps payments with another business that wants a variable rate, creating a fixed rate for the first business. However, if the second business goes bankrupt, the first business loses its fixed rate and has to pay the variable rate. If interest rates increase to the point where the first business cannot pay back the loan, it causes a chain reaction of failures.

Derivatives also can pose high amounts of risk for small or inexperienced investors. Because derivatives offer the possibility of large rewards, they are attractive to individual investors. However, the basic premise of derivatives is to transfer risk among parties based on their willingness to assume additional risk, or hedge against it. Many small investors do not comprehend this until they lose. As a result, a chain reaction leading to a domestic or global economic crisis can occur.

Warren Buffett, a well-known investor, has stated that he regards derivatives as "financial weapons of mass destruction." Derivatives have been used to leverage the debt in an economy, sometimes to a massive degree. When something unexpected happens, an economy will find it very difficult to pay its debts, thus causing a recession or even depression. Marriner S. Eccles, U.S. Federal Reserve chair from 1934 to 1948, stated that an excessively high level of debt was one of the primary causes of the Great Depression.

Some experts believe derivatives have significant benefits as well. Although it is always the case with derivatives that someone loses while someone else gains, under normal circumstances, derivatives should not adversely affect the economic system because it is not a zero-sum game—derivatives theoretically allow for absolute economic growth. In other words, while one party gains in relation to the other, both gain relative to their previous positions. Former Federal Reserve Board chair Alan Greenspan commented in 2003 that he believed that derivatives softened the impact of the economic downturn at the beginning of the twenty-first century, and UBS believed that derivatives were part of its future.

However, derivatives have a checkered history. In the 1900s, derivatives trading and bucket shops were rampant. Bucket shops are small operators in options and securities that lure clients into transactions and then flee with the money, setting up shop elsewhere. In 1922 the federal government attempted to stop this practice with the Grain Futures Act, and in 1936 options on grain futures were temporarily banned in the United States as well as in other countries. In 1972 the Chicago Mercantile Exchange (the Merc) created the International Monetary Market, allowing trading in currency futures, representing the first futures contracts associated with nonphysical commodities. In 1975 the Merc introduced the Treasury bill futures contract that was based purely on interest rate futures. In 1977 and 1982, T–bond (Treasury) futures contracts, Eurodollar contracts, and stock index futures were created. The 1980s marked the beginning of swaps and other over-the-counter derivatives. Soon every large, and even some not-so-large, corporations were using derivatives to hedge a wide

variety of investment risks. Derivatives soon became too complex for the average person to understand, and Wall Street turned to mathematicians and physicists to create models and computer programs that could analyze these exotic instruments.

In the end, the ethical issues in using derivatives hinge on the managers and traders who use these highly complex and risky financial instruments. Derivatives are used in sales transactions where there is an opportunity of great financial rewards. However, managers and traders often do not take into account the level of risk for investors or other stakeholders. If the risk associated with a derivative is not communicated to the investor, this can result in deception or even fraud. It has become apparent that the use of derivatives such as credit default swaps became so profitable that traders and managers lost sight of anything but their incentives for selling these instruments. In other words, financial institutions were selling what could be called defective products because the true risk of these financial instruments was not understood by or disclosed to the customer. In some cases, these defective products were given to traders to sell without any due diligence from the company as to the level of risk.

CONCLUSION

While derivatives, including credit default swaps, were not the only cause of the failure of the banks discussed in this case, the use of these instruments by decision makers resulted in these banks taking enormous risks. In hindsight, these actions seem to be unwise and unfair to stakeholders. An ethical issue relates to the level of transparency that exists in using complex financial instruments to create profits for customers. If purchasers do not understand the potential risks and the possibility of the loss of their money, then a chance for deception exists. In the banks examined in this case, there is no doubt that a number of key decision makers not only pushed the limits of legitimate risk-taking, but also engaged in manipulation, and in some cases fraud, to deceive stakeholders.

At this point, it is doubtful whether banks have learned enough about the 2008–2009 financial crises to avoid future failures. Investors and shareholders need to start looking beyond short-term results and understand the value of long-term thinking. CEOs and boards of directors need to develop a transparent business model that balances risk with market opportunity. The ethical risks of lower-level managers using deception and manipulation to create profits, often through loopholes and unregulated areas of decision making, are high. Through ethical leadership and compliance programs, all these risks can be minimized.

QUESTIONS

1. What are the ethical risks associated with derivatives?

2. What is the difference between making a bad business decision associated with derivatives and engaging in unethical conduct using derivatives?

3. What kinds of investment decisions drove Barings Bank, UBS, Bear Stearns, and Lehman Brothers to financial disasters?

4. How can an ethical corporate culture with adequate internal controls, including ethics and compliance policies, prevent future disasters in financial companies?

SOURCES

Aldrick, Philip, "UBS Sub-Prime Warning Fails to Rattle Markets," *Telegraph.co.uk*, October 3, 2007, http://www.telegraph.co.uk/finance/markets/2816866/UBS-sub-prime-warning-fails-to-rattle-markets.html, accessed September 3, 2009.

Bart, Katharina, "UBS Joins the 'Bonus Chop' for Executives," *Wall Street Journal*, November 17, 2008, http://online.wsj.com/article/SB122693338045733273.html, accessed September 3, 2009.

Bhugaloo, Sam, "Commodities Trading: Nick Leeson, Internal Controls and the Collapse of Barings Bank," Trade Futures, Ltd., http://www.tradefutures.co.uk/Nick_Leeson_Barings_Bank.pdf, accessed September 3, 2009.

Browning, Lynnley, "Federal Prosecutors Declare European Banker a Fugitive," *New York Times*, May 23, 2008, http://www.nytimes.com/2008/05/23/business/worldbusiness/23bank.html?scp=1&sq=Federal+Prosecutors+Declare+European+Banker+a+Fugitive&st=nyt, accessed September 3, 2009.

Browning, Lynnley, "Wealthy Americans Under Scrutiny in UBS Case," *New York Times*, June 6, 2008, http://www.nytimes.com/2008/06/06/business/worldbusiness/06tax.html?scp=1&sq=Wealthy%20Americans%20Under%20Scrutiny%20in%20UBS%20Case&st=cse, accessed September 3, 2009.

Cane, Jeffrey, "A Pilot for UBS Foundering Ship," *Conde Nast Portfolio*, February 13, 2008, http://www.portfolio.com/news-markets/top-5/2008/02/13/A-Pilot-for-UBS-Foundering-Ship, accessed September 3, 2009.

Chua-Eoan, Howard, "The Top 25 Crimes of the Century: #18 The Collapse of Barings Bank, 1995," *Time*, November 18, 2007, http://www.time.com/time/2007/crimes/18.html, accessed September 3, 2009.

Dealbook Blog, "Could Bear Stearns Do Better?" *New York Times*, http://www.nytimes.com/2008/03/17/business/17dealbook-could-be21779.html?_r=1, accessed September 3, 2009.

"Down the Matterhorn: UBS Falls from Grace," *The Economist*, July 12, 2007, http://www.economist.com/finance/displaystory.cfm?story_id=E1_JQRPGNT, accessed September 3, 2009.

Downey, John, "BofA Asks $20M in Dispute vs. Ex-Employees," *Charlotte Business Journal*, July 22, 2002, http://www.bizjournals.com/charlotte/stories/2002/07/22/story7.html, accessed September 3, 2009.

Drennan, Lynn T., "Ethics, Governance, and Risk Management: Lessons from Mirror Group Newspapers and Barings Bank," *Journal of Business Ethics* 52, no. 3 (2004): 257–266.

Eisinger, Jesse, "The $58 Trillion Elephant in the Room," November 20, 2008, http://www.portfolio.com/views/columns/wall-street/2008/10/15/Credit-Derivatives-Role-in-Crash#page1, accessed September 3, 2009.

Gomstyn, Alice, "Bleeding Green: The Fall of Fuld," ABC News, October 6, 2008, http://abcnews.go.com/Business/Economy/Story?id=5951669&page=1, accessed September 3, 2009.

Gresko, Jessica, "Ex-UBS Banker Pleads Guilty in US Tax Evasion Case," *USA Today*, June 19, 2008, http://www.usatoday.com/money/economy/2008-06-19-992401281_x.htm?csp=34, accessed September 3, 2009.

Grynbaum, Michael, "Bear Stearns Profit Plunges 61% on Subprime Woes," *New York Times*, http://www.nytimes.com/2007/09/21/business/20cnd-wall.html?scp=1&sq=Bear%20Stearns%20Plunges%2061%%20on%20Subprime%20Woes&st=cse, accessed September 3, 2009.

Gwynne, S. C., "Total Risk: Nick Leeson and the Fall of Barings Bank," Book Review, *Washington Monthly*, January–February 1996, http://findarticles.com/p/articles/mi_m1316/is_/ai_17761531, accessed September 3, 2009.

Kennedy, Simon, Greg Morcroft, and Robert Schroeder, "Lehman Failure, AIG Struggle Drive Financials Lower," Market Watch, September 15, 2008, http://www.marketwatch.com/news/story/lehman-falls-80-firm-readies/story.aspx?guid={8E886D48-E3C7-4CE2-95F4-7099CE1A49DB}&dist=msr_2, accessed September 4, 2009.

Koenig, David, "Case Study: Nick Leeson and Barings Bank," Ductilibility, 2008, http://www.scribd.com/doc/16606536/Case-Study-Barings-Bank-and-Nick-Leeson, accessed September 4, 2009.

Landon, Thomas, Jr., "Prosecutors Build Bear Stearns Case on E-Mails," *New York Times,* June 20, 2008, http://www.nytimes.com/2008/06/20/business/20bear.html?_r=1&hp&oref=slogin, accessed September 4, 2009.

Landon, Thomas, Jr., and Eric Dash, "Seeking Fast Deal, JPMorgan Quintuples Bear Stearns Bid," *New York Times,* March 25, 2008, http://www.nytimes.com/2008/03/25/business/25bear.html?scp=1&sq=Seeking+Fast+Deal%2C+JPMorgan+Quintuples+Bear+Stearns+Bid&st=nyt, accessed September 4, 2009.

"Lehman's CDS Mess: Who's on the Hook?" Seeking Alpha, October 13, 2008, http://seekingalpha.com/article/99619-lehman-s-cds-mess-who-s-on-the-hook, accessed September 4, 2009.

Lengle, Kim, "A Warning Sign from Lehman," CBS News, October 20, 2008, http://www.cbsnews.com/stories/2008/10/20/cbsnews_investigates/main4535072.shtml, accessed September 4, 2009.

Mamudi, Sam, "Lehman Folds with Record $613 Billion Debt," Market Watch, September 15, 2008, http://www.marketwatch.com/news/story/lehman-folds-613-billion-debt/story.aspx?guid={2FE5AC05-597A-4E71-A2D5-9B9FCC290520}, accessed September 4, 2009.

"Nick Leeson Blames the Banks," SOX First, April 11, 2008, http://www.soxfirst.com/50226711/nick_leeson_blames_the_banks.php, accessed September 4, 2009.

Ross, Brian, "Lehman Had Long Relationship with Suspect Mortgage Brokers," ABC News, September 15, 2008, http://abcnews.go.com/Blotter/story?id=5807408&page=, accessed September 4, 2009.

Smith, Randall, Diya Gullapalli, and Jeffery McCracken, "Lehman, Workers Score Reprieve," *Wall Street Journal,* September 17, 2008, http://online.wsj.com/article/SB122156586985742907.html, accessed September 4, 2009.

The Coca-Cola Company Struggles with Ethical Crises

As one of the most valuable brand names worldwide, Coca-Cola has generally excelled as a business over its long history. However, in recent decades the company has had difficulties meeting its financial objectives and has been associated with a number of ethical crises. As a result, some investors have lost faith in the company. For example, Warren Buffet (board member and strong supporter of and investor in Coca-Cola) resigned from the board in 2006 after years of frustration over Coca-Cola's failure to overcome its challenges.

Since the 1990s, Coca-Cola has been accused of unethical behavior in a number of areas such as product safety, anti-competitiveness, racial discrimination, channel stuffing, distributor conflicts, intimidation of union workers, pollution, and depletion of natural resources. A number of these issues have been dealt with, some via private settlements and some via court battles, while others still besmirch the Coca-Cola name. Although its handling of different ethical situations has not always been lauded, Coca-Cola generally has responded by seeking to improve its detection and compliance systems. However, it remains to be seen whether the company can permanently rise above its ethical problems, learn from its mistakes, make necessary changes, avoid further problems, and still emerge as the leader among beverage companies.

HISTORY OF THE COCA-COLA COMPANY

Founded in 1886, the Coca-Cola Company is the world's largest beverage company. In addition to Coca-Cola and Diet Coke, it also sells other profitable brands including Powerade, Minute Maid, and Dasani water. To service global demand, the company has the world's largest distribution system, which reaches customers and businesses in nearly every country on the planet. Coca-Cola estimates that more than one billion servings of its products are consumed every day.

Until the mid-twentieth century, Coca-Cola focused on expanding market share within the United States. After World War II, however, the company began to recognize the opportunities in global sales. In the last part of the twentieth century, Coca-Cola extended this global push, taking advantage of international revenue opportunities and fierce soft drink competition, in an effort to dominate the global soft drink industry. By the late 1990s, Coca-Cola had gained more than 50 percent global market share in the soft drink industry, while PepsiCo, Coke's greatest rival, stood around 15 to 20 percent. Coca-Cola remains largely focused on carbonated and sugary beverages, while PepsiCo has diversified into snack foods and New Age drinks like waters,

This case was developed under the direction of Debbie Thorne, O.C. Ferrell, and Jennifer Jackson. Kevin Sample and Rob Boostrum helped draft previous editions of this case. Thanks also to Jennifer Sawayda and Alexi Sherrill for their editorial assistance. This case was prepared for classroom discussion, rather than to illustrate either effective or ineffective handling of an administrative, ethical, or legal decision by management. All sources used for this case were obtained through publicly available material and the Coca-Cola website.

teas, and fruit juices. While Pepsi has tended to focus more on American markets, the largest portion of Coca-Cola's sales have come from outside the United States. As the late Roberto Goizueta, former CEO of Coca-Cola, once said, "Coca-Cola used to be an American company with a large international business. Now we are a large international company with a sizable American business."

In spite of international recognition and a strong brand, Coca-Cola has run into numerous difficulties. The company's problems began in the mid-1990s at the executive level. In 1997, Doug Ivester became CEO. Ivester, heralded for his ability to handle the financial flows and details of the soft drink giant, had been groomed for the position by former CEO Roberto Goizueta. However, Ivester's tenure as CEO did not last. He was not well equipped to handle the tough competition from Pepsi combined with the many ethical disasters Coke faced throughout the 1990s. Some people even began to doubt "Big Red's" reputation and its future prospects. For a company with a history of successful marketing and strong financial performance, Ivester's departure in 1999 represented a high-profile aberration in a relatively strong 100-year record.

In 2000, Doug Daft, the company's former president and chief operating officer (COO), replaced Ivester as CEO. Daft's tenure too was rocky, and the company continued to have problems throughout the early 2000s. For example, the company was allegedly involved in racial discrimination, misrepresentations of market tests, manipulation of earnings, and the disruption of long-term contractual arrangements with distributors.

By 2004, Neville Isdell was called out of retirement to improve Coca-Cola's reputation; however, the company continued to face ethical crises. Problems aside, Coca-Cola's overall performance seemed to improve under CEO and Chair Isdell's tenure. In 2008, Isdell relinquished the roll of CEO to then president and COO Muhtar Kent. Isdell also decided to step down as chair of the board in order to return to retirement. In 2009, under Kent's leadership, Coca-Cola, along with companies around the globe, sought to re-strategize in order to cope with the 2008–2009 global recession.

PEPSICO: SERIOUS COMPETITION TO COKE'S SUPREMACY

Historically, Coca-Cola has been a success for more than 120 years. In contrast, PepsiCo (founded at roughly the same time) did not become a serious competitor until after World War II, when it came up with the idea to sell its product in larger portions for the same price as Coke. The "cola wars" picked up more speed by the mid 1960s and have not abated since. Today, the two American companies wage war primarily on international fronts. While the fight occasionally grows ugly, with accusations of anticompetitive behavior, generally the two companies remain civil. They may even appreciate the serious competition the other represents. Without fierce competition, neither company would be as successful.

However, PepsiCo has surged ahead of Coke. By early 2006 PepsiCo enjoyed a market value greater than Coca-Cola for the first time. Pepsi's strategy of focusing on snack foods and innovative approaches in the non-cola beverage market has helped the company gain market share and surpass Coca-Cola in overall performance. During the 2008–2009 recession, PepsiCo's diversification strategy continued to pay off. Many analysts now see greater long-term strength for PepsiCo. On the other hand, some investors fear for Coca-Cola's long-term prospects because of how much the company depends on international sales and the fluctuating values of the dollar. Combined with the global recession in 2009, these are liabilities that may hurt Coca-Cola's long-term profitability. Because PepsiCo does 60 percent of its business in North America, a strong dollar does not adversely affect the company as much as it does Coca-Cola. These factors may give PepsiCo more of an upper-hand over Coca-Cola in the future.

COCA-COLA'S REPUTATION

Coca-Cola remains one of the most-recognized brand names in the world today, worth an estimated $68.73 billion in 2009. The company has always demonstrated strong market orientation, making strategic decisions and taking action to attract, satisfy, and retain customers. During World War II, for example, then company president Robert Woodruff distributed Coke around the world to sell to members of the armed services for a nickel a bottle. This strategy gave soldiers an affordable taste of home, created lifelong loyal customers, and increased global brand recognition in one of the first steps to creating a truly global brand. The presence of Coca-Cola products in almost every corner of the globe today shows how successful the company's international marketing strategy has been. Savvy marketing and a reputation for quality have always been hallmarks of Coca-Cola and have helped to make the product ubiquitous.

However, in the 1990s and 2000s, poor decisions, mismanagement, and alleged misconduct cast a shadow over the company. In 2000, Coca-Cola failed to make the top ten of *Fortune*'s annual "America's Most Admired Companies" list for the first time in ten years, although it still ranked first in the beverage industry. By 2009 Coca-Cola was in twelfth place and had fallen to third in the beverage industry. Leadership issues, disappointing economic performance, and other upheavals likely affected its standing on the *Fortune* list. In 2001, the company disappeared from the top 100 in *Business Ethics* magazine's annual list of "100 Best Corporate Citizens." For a company that had been on both lists for years, this was disappointing but not unexpected, given its several ethical crises. In 2007, Coca-Cola was still absent from the *Business Ethics* "100 Best Corporate Citizens" list, but PepsiCo was number forty-two.

CRISIS SITUATIONS

The following sections document the alleged misconduct and questionable behavior that have affected Coca-Cola stakeholders and possibly the company's financial performance. In 1996, Coca-Cola traded just below $50 a share. In the first half of 2009, it ranged from $59 to $37, showing little growth over a dozen years and underperforming against both the S&P 500 and NASDAQ. This slow growth may be attributed to various internal problems associated with top management turnover and departure of key investors, as well as external problems that have led to a loss of reputation. The following incidents exemplify some of the key crises Coca-Cola has faced in the last several years.

Contamination Scare

Perhaps the most damaging of Coca-Cola's crises—and a situation dreaded by every company—began in June 1999 when about thirty Belgian children became ill after consuming Coke products. Although the company issued an isolated product recall, the problem escalated. The Belgian government eventually ordered the recall of all Coca-Cola products, which prompted officials in Luxembourg and the Netherlands to recall Coke products as well. Coca-Cola finally determined that the illnesses were the result of an improperly processed batch of carbon dioxide. Coca-Cola was slow to issue a response to the problem, taking several days to address the media. Initially, Coca-Cola had not wanted to overreact over what it at first judged to be a minor problem and did not immediately investigate the extent of the issue. The slow response time led to a public relations nightmare. France soon reported more than 100 people sick from bad Coke and temporarily banned all Coca-Cola products as well. Soon thereafter, a shipment of Bonaqua, a new Coca-Cola water product, arrived in Poland contaminated with mold. In each of these instances, the company's slow responses and failure to acknowledge the severity of the situation harmed its reputation and cast doubt on then CEO Ivester's ability to successfully lead.

The contamination crisis was exacerbated in December 1999 when Belgium ordered Coca-Cola to halt the "Restore" marketing campaign it had launched in order to regain consumer trust and sales in Belgium. A rival firm claimed the campaign strategy—which included free cases of the product, discounts to wholesalers and retailers, and extra promotion personnel—was unlawful. Under Belgium's strict antitrust laws, the claim was upheld; Coca-Cola abandoned the campaign to avoid further problems. This decision, following the previous crisis, further reduced Coca-Cola's market standing in Europe.

Competitive Issues

Questions concerning Coca-Cola's market dominance and government inquiries into its marketing tactics plagued the company throughout Europe. Because the European Union countries have strict antitrust laws, all firms must pay close attention to market share and position when considering joint ventures, mergers, and acquisitions. During the summer of 1999, when Coca-Cola began an aggressive expansion push in France, the French government responded by refusing Coca-Cola's bid to purchase Orangina, a French beverage company. French authorities also forced Coca-Cola to scale back its acquisition of Cadbury Schweppes, maker of Dr. Pepper.

Moreover, in late 1999 Italy successfully won a court case against Coca-Cola over anti-competitive prices, prompting the European

Commission to launch a full-scale probe into the company's competitive practices. In addition, PepsiCo and Virgin Cola accused Coca-Cola of using rebates and discounts to crowd their products off the shelves. Coca-Cola's strong-arm tactics were again found to be in violation of European laws, once again demonstrating the company's lack of awareness of European culture and laws.

Despite these legal tangles, Coca-Cola products, along with many other U.S. products, dominate foreign markets worldwide. The growing omnipresence of U.S. products, especially in highly competitive markets, makes corporate reputation, both perceived and actual, essential to building relationships with business partners, government officials, and other stakeholders.

Racial Discrimination Allegations

In 1999, Coca-Cola's reputation was dealt another blow when 1,500 African American employees sued for racial discrimination. The lawsuit, which eventually grew to include 2,000 current and former employees, accused the company of discriminating in areas of pay, promotion, and performance evaluation. Plaintiffs charged that the company grouped African American workers at the bottom of the pay scale and that they earned around $26,000 a year less than Caucasian employees in comparable jobs. The suit also alleged that top management had known about companywide discrimination since 1995 but had done nothing about it. In 1992, Coca-Cola had pledged to spend $1 billion on goods and services from minority vendors, an action designed to show the public that Coca-Cola did not discriminate, but the lawsuit from its own employees painted a different picture. Although Coca-Cola strongly denied the allegations, the lawsuit provoked unrest within the company. In response, Coca-Cola created a diversity council and the company paid $193 million to settle the racial discrimination lawsuit.

Inflated Earnings Related to Channel Stuffing

Coca-Cola was also accused of channel stuffing during the early 2000s. Channel stuffing is the practice of shipping extra, nonrequested inventory to wholesalers and retailers before the end of a quarter. A company counts the shipments as sales although the product often remains in warehouses or is later returned. Because the goods have been shipped, the company counts them as revenue at the end of the quarter. Channel stuffing creates the appearance of strong demand (or conceals declining demand), and results in inflated financial statement earnings and the subsequent misleading of investors.

In 2004, Coca-Cola was accused of sending extra concentrate to Japanese bottlers between 1997 and 1999 in an effort to inflate its profits. The company was already under investigation; in 2000, a former employee filed a lawsuit accusing the company of fraud and improper business practices. The company settled the allegations, but the Securities and Exchange Commission (SEC) did find that channel stuffing had occurred. Coca-Cola had pressured bottlers into buying additional concentrate in exchange for extended credit.

Trouble with Distributors

In early 2006, Coca-Cola once again faced problems—this time on its home front. Fifty-four of its U.S. bottlers filed lawsuits against Coke and the company's largest bottler Coca-Cola Enterprises (CCE). The suit sought to block Coke and CCE, both based in Atlanta, from expanding delivery of Powerade sports drinks directly to Wal-Mart warehouses instead of to individual stores. Bottlers alleged that the Powerade bottler contract did not permit warehouse delivery to large retailers. They claimed that Coke breached the agreement by committing to provide warehouse delivery of Powerade to Wal-Mart and by proposing to use CCE as its agent for delivery. The main problem was that Coke was attempting to step away from the century-old tradition of direct-store delivery (DSD), in which bottlers deposit drinks at individual stores, stock shelves, and build merchandising displays. Bottlers claimed that if Coke and CCE went forward, it would greatly diminish the value of their businesses.

In their defense, Coke and CCE asserted they were simply trying to accommodate a request from Wal-Mart for warehouse delivery (how PepsiCo distributes its Gatorade brand). CCE had also proposed making payments to other bottlers in return for taking over Powerade distribution in their territories. However, bottlers feared such an arrangement violated antitrust laws. An undisclosed agreement between the bottlers and Coca-Cola was reached in 2007. Reports suggest warehouse deliveries were considered acceptable in some situations, and guidelines were developed for assessing those situations.

When addressing problems faced by Coca-Cola, the media tends to focus primarily on its reputation rather than on its relations with bottlers, distributors, suppliers, and other partners. Without these strategic partnerships, Coca-Cola would not be where it is today. Such partnerships involve sharing in risks and rewards. Issues such as the contamination scare and racial discrimination allegations, especially when handled poorly, can reflect on business relationships beyond the key company's business. When the reputation of one company suffers, all those within the supply chain suffer in some way. This is especially true because Coca-Cola adopted an enterprise-resource system that linked Coca-Cola's once highly secret information to a host of partners. Thus, the company's less-than-stellar handling of ethical crises may have introduced lax integrity standards to its partnerships. The interdependence between Coca-Cola and its partners requires a diplomatic and considerate view of the business and its effects on various stakeholders. Therefore, these crises harmed Coke's partner companies, their stakeholders, and eventually their bottom lines.

International Problems Related to Unions

Between 2001 and 2004, a more sinister accusation against Coke surfaced in Colombia. Since 1989 eight union Coca-Cola workers had died there, 48 were forced into hiding, and 65 had received death threats. Many believe the deaths and threats were the results of intimidation against union workers employed at the Coca-Cola bottling plant in Colombia. The union, which alleged that Coke and its local bottler were complicit in the intimidation and the deaths, is seeking reparations for the families of the slain and displaced Colombian workers. However, Coke completely denies the allegations and notes that only one of the eight workers was killed on the bottling plant premises. Also, the company maintains that the other deaths were by-products of Colombia's four-decade-long civil war. In 2007, a group of hundreds of people made up of Teamsters, environmentalists, human rights proponents, and student activists gathered in New York City to protest against Coca-Cola in regard to the problems in Colombia, among other concerns.

Issues Regarding Water Usage and Pollution

Coca-Cola has also encountered trouble at its bottling plants in India, fielding accusations of both groundwater depletion and contamination. In 2003, the Centre for Science and Environment (CSE) tested soft drinks produced in India by Coca-Cola and other companies; findings indicated extreme levels of pesticides from using contaminated groundwater. Supported in 2004 by an Indian parliamentary committee, the first set of standards for pesticides in soft drinks was developed. Although Coca-Cola denied allegations, stating that its water is filtered and its final products are tested before being released, sales dropped temporarily by 15 percent.

In the Indian city of Varanasi, Coca-Cola was also accused of contaminating the groundwater with wastewater. Officials at the company admitted that the plant did have a wastewater issue but insisted that a new pipeline had been built to eliminate the problem. However, during the early 2000s, a number of tests were conducted regarding "sludge" produced at Coca-Cola's Indian plants. These tests, conducted by the Central Pollution Control Board of India and the British Broadcasting Corporation, came up with toxic results.

The company runs bottling plants in a handful of drought-plagued areas around India, and groups of officials blame the plants for a dramatic decline in available water. In 2004, local officials closed a Coca-Cola plant in Kerala; however, the closure was overturned by Kerala's court. Although the court agreed that Coca-Cola's presence contributed to water depletion, the company was not solely to blame. Farmers and local residents, forced to vie with Coca-Cola for water, have protested Coca-Cola's presence there and throughout India.

In 2005, students at the University of Michigan asked the university to cancel its contracts with Coca-Cola based on these issues in India. In response, the university requested that the Energy and Resources Institute out of New Delhi research the issue. Findings indicated that Coca-Cola's soda did not contain higher-than-normal levels of pesticides. However, the report did indicate that the company's bottling plants were stressing water resources and suggested that the company do a better job of considering a plant's location based on resources and future impact. Protests regarding Coca-Cola's impact on India have continued in areas around the globe for years.

Coca-Cola's Impact on Health

In 2008, Coca-Cola launched a "Motherhood and Myth-Busting" campaign in Australia, attempting to convince the public that a diet including soda was healthy for children. The Australian Competition and Consumer

Commission promptly took Coca-Cola to court after the Obesity Policy Coalition, the Parents' Jury, and the Australian Dental Association all filed complaints. As a result, in 2009 the company was forced to release new advertisements in a number of Australian newspapers correcting information such as the amount of caffeine found in Diet Coke. In response, Coca-Cola admits that it did not supply consumers with detailed information during its campaign. Also in 2008, the FDA declared the company had violated the Federal Food, Drug, and Cosmetic Act when naming the Coca-Cola Diet Plus beverage. Using "plus" in the name indicated an unsubstantiated nutritional claim. The next year, Coca-Cola was sued by the Center for Science in the Public Interest regarding misleading marketing that concerned the contents of its VitaminWater. Although the beverage is marketed as healthy, it contains a high quantity of sugar. However, attacks on Coca-Cola for the health impacts of its products are nothing new. The company has been under fire since the 1940s regarding its products' impacts on human health.

RECOVERY FROM ETHICAL CRISES

Arguments abound on both sides as to whether Coca-Cola has recovered from its ethical crises. The following information indicates that the company has addressed the majority of its issues; however, some believe Coca-Cola is still not doing enough.

Regarding the health scare, Belgian officials closed their investigation involving Coca-Cola and announced that no charges would be filed. A Belgian health report indicated that no toxic contamination had been found inside Coke bottles. The bottles did contain tiny traces of carbonyl sulfide, producing a rotten-egg smell, but to be toxic the amount of carbonyl sulfide would have to have been a thousand times higher. Officials also reported no structural problems within Coca-Cola's production plant and said that the company had cooperated fully throughout the investigation.

Coca-Cola has taken strides toward countering diversity protests. The racial discrimination lawsuit, along with the threat of a boycott by the National Association for the Advancement of Colored People (NAACP), led to this correction. When Coca-Cola settled the racial discrimination lawsuit, the agreement stipulated that Coke would donate $50 million to a foundation supporting programs in minority communities, hire an ombudsman reporting directly to the CEO to investigate complaints of discrimination and harassment, and set aside $36 million to form a seven-person task force with authority to oversee the company's employment practices. The task force, which includes business and civil rights experts, has unprecedented power to dictate company policy regarding hiring, compensating, and promoting women and minorities. Despite the unusual provision granting such power, then-CEO Daft defended his company's measures to increase diversity, saying, "We need to have outside people helping us. We would be foolish to cut ourselves off from the outside world." It is worth noting that, as of May 2009, the task force had not issued a report since 2006.

In response to the SEC's findings regarding channel stuffing, the company created an ethics and compliance office and is required to verify quarterly that it has not altered the terms of payment or extended special credit. Additionally, the company agreed to work to reduce the amount of concentrate held by international bottlers.

Coca-Cola has defended itself against allegations of violence in Colombia, and the Colombian court and the Colombian attorney general support the company. In 2004, the company was dismissed as a defendant in the 2001 lawsuit; the case was dismissed two years later due to insufficient evidence. An appeal has been filed. According to Coca-Cola's company website, it does everything it can to protect its employees and works to aid Colombian children and families.

Although Coca-Cola's issues in India did cause a temporary dip in sales and ongoing protests, the company insists that it has taken measures to ensure safety and quality. Coca-

Cola has partnered with local governments, NGOs, schools, and communities to establish 320 rainwater-harvesting facilities. The goal is to work toward renewing and returning all groundwater. In addition, as recommended by the University of Michigan study, the company is strengthening its plant requirements and working with local communities to ensure sustainability of local water resources. The company recently launched the Coca-Cola India Foundation for Sustainable Development and Inclusive Growth. In 2008, Coca-Cola received the Golden Peacock Global Award for corporate social responsibility in water conservation, management, and community development initiatives.

Responding to health issues related to Coca-Cola's products is more complex. The company itself cannot be held responsible for how many sugary or artificially sweetened beverages the public consumes. Ultimately, Coca-Cola's responsibility is to disclose honest, detailed information regarding its products so that consumers may make educated beverage choices. Coca-Cola does make an effort to encourage consumers to exercise and embrace a healthy lifestyle through nutritional education and physical activity programs and engages in ongoing discussions with government, NGO, and public health representatives regarding obesity and health.

SOCIAL RESPONSIBILITY FOCUS

Because Coca-Cola is so globally recognized, the industry in which it operates is so pervasive, and it has a strong history of market orientation, the company has developed a number of social responsibility initiatives to further enhance its business. These initiatives are guided by the company's core beliefs in marketplace, workplace, community, and environment. As stated in its Mission, Vision & Values statements, Coca-Cola wants to "Inspire Moments of Optimism" through brands and actions as well as to create value and to make a difference in the countries in which it does business. The company seeks to provide sustainable growth by providing a great place to work, inspiring employees to use innovation to provide a portfolio of brands meeting consumer needs worldwide.

At the same time, the company strives to be a responsible business. For instance, Coca-Cola has made local education and community improvement programs top priorities—some of which are implemented through various Coca-Cola foundations. For example, Coca-Cola is involved in Education On Wheels in Singapore. This program brings history to life through an interactive discovery adventure for kids, which also enhances communication skills as children discover new insights into life in Singapore.

Coca-Cola offers grants to various colleges and universities both nationally and internationally. In addition to grants, Coca-Cola provides scholarships to hundreds of colleges, including thirty tribal colleges belonging to the American Indian College Fund. Coca-Cola also has become involved with the Hispanic Scholarship Fund. Such initiatives help enhance the Coca-Cola name, and ultimately benefit shareholders. Through the Coca-Cola Scholars Foundation, 250 new Coca-Cola Scholars are named each year and brought to Atlanta for interviews. Fifty students are then designated National Scholars, receiving awards of $20,000 for college; the remaining 200 are designated Regional Scholars, receiving $4,000 awards.

Like many other companies, Coca-Cola is addressing the issues of recycling and climate change. In 2007, the company launched "Drink2Wear" clothing made from recycled plastic bottles. In 2008, the company added bags, loungewear, and hats to the recycled line. As of 2009, the company had reused more than five million PET bottles in this fashion. Also in 2007, Coca-Cola signed the UN Global Compact's "Caring for Climate: The Business Leadership Platform." In doing so, the company pledged to increase energy efficiency and reduce emissions. To this end, Coca-Cola has co-founded the Refrigerants, Naturally! Initiative—a food and beverage industry alliance aimed to address climate change through the promotion of HFC-free alternative refrigeration technologies. In 2009, the company opened the world's largest plastic bottle-to-bottle recycling plant in South Carolina. Also in 2009, Coca-Cola released the PlantBottle™. This new bottle, made from 30 percent plant-based material, is fully recyclable and reduces use of nonrenewable resources and carbon emissions. The bottles are in use in a limited capacity, and the company plans to expand.

Coca-Cola chair Neville Isdell received the 2008 Ethics Advocate Award issued by the Center for Ethics and Corporate Responsibility at Georgia State University. Isdell was chosen thanks to his efforts to promote and address corporate social responsibility and environmental sustainability while at Coca-Cola. He was also being thanked for encouraging corporate responsibility throughout the business community.

In addition, Coca-Cola recognizes its responsibilities on a global scale and takes action to uphold this responsibility. The company remains proactive on issues such as the HIV/AIDS epidemic in Africa. Coca-Cola has partnered with UNAIDS and other nongovernment organizations, putting into place important initiatives and programs to help combat the threat of HIV/AIDS. The company is also working to create new jobs throughout the developing world in an effort to help combat poverty. In 2007 Coca-Cola joined the World Wildlife Fund (WWF) and pledged to reduce the amount of water Coca-Cola uses, to improve the recycling of water at Coca-Cola plants, and to replenish natural water sources. Coca-Cola pledged $20 million dollars to the initiative; these resources will be used in part to protect seven of the world's most important freshwater river basins.

Because consumers generally respect Coca-Cola, trust its products, and have strong attachments through brand recognition and product loyalty, Coca-Cola's actions foster relationship marketing. Because of this,

problems at a firm like Coca-Cola can stir the emotions of many stakeholders.

CURRENT SITUATION AT COCA-COLA

In the early part of the twenty-first century, Coca-Cola's financial performance was positive, with the company maintaining a sound balance sheet. However, earnings across the soft drink industry have been on a slow decline because of decreased consumption, increased competition, and the 2008–2009 global recession. Nevertheless, Coca-Cola is confident of its long-term viability and remains strong in the belief that the company is well positioned to succeed regardless of the economic situation.

In order to remain a successful company long into the future, Coca-Cola must resolve conflicts and lawsuits associated with ethical crises. While Coca-Cola is trying to establish its reputation based on quality products and socially responsible activities, it has failed its numerous stakeholders on a number of occasions over the years. Can Coca-Cola's strong emphasis on social responsibility, especially philanthropic and environmental concerns, help the company maintain its reputation in the face of highly public ethical conflicts and crises?

CONCLUSION

For more than a decade, Coca-Cola has been fighting for its reputation against allegations of lack of health and safety of its products, unlawful competitive practices, racial discrimination and employee intimidation, channel stuffing, unfair distributor treatment, and the pollution and pillaging of natural resources. It is difficult to decipher all available information and come to a clear conclusion. Under Nevill Isdell and Muhtar Kent's leadership, Coca-Cola has rebounded and begun to take strides toward improving its image. The company is focusing more on environmental stewardship, for example. However, the company's critics say that Coca-Cola is not doing enough—that its efforts are merely window dressing to hide its corruption. Case in point: Although the company claims to have addressed all issues in India and claims to be making an effort to aid the country's population, the Internet is rich with real-time criticism of Coca-Cola's practices in that country. People worldwide are caught up in emotional reactions—both positive and negative—to this massive corporation.

Regardless of emotion, it is clear that Coca-Cola is not a perfect company and that it has been involved in its share of ethical misconduct. Shareholder reactions have altered many times over the company's history, but the company has retained a large loyal base. The company hopes that its current leadership is strong enough to move Coca-Cola past this focus on ethics and into a profitable start to the twenty-first century. Thus, the question is whether leadership is doing what it takes to burnish Coca-Cola's image and practice what it preaches.

QUESTIONS

1. What role does corporate reputation play within organizational performance and social responsibility? Develop a list of factors or characteristics that different stakeholders may use in assessing corporate reputation. Are these factors consistent across stakeholders? Why or why not?

2. Assume you have just become CEO at Coca-Cola. Outline the strategic steps you would take to remedy the concerns emanating from the company's board of directors, consumers, employees, and business partners; governments; and the media. What elements of social responsibility would you draw from in responding to these stakeholder issues?

3. What do you think of Coca-Cola's environmental initiatives? Are they just window dressing, or does the company seem to be sincere in its efforts?

SOURCES

"America's Most Reputable Companies," *Fortune*, April 29, 2009, http://www.forbes.com/2009/04/28/america-reputable-companies-leadership-reputation_table.html, accessed September 4, 2009.

Ames, Paul, "Case Closed on Coke Health Scare," Associated Press, April 22, 2000, HighBeam Research, http://www.highbeam.com/doc/1P1-26137611.html, accessed September 4, 2009.

"Another Coke Plant, More Pollution Dumping," *South Asian*, June 10, 2007, http://www.thesouthasian.org/archives/2007/another_coke_plant_more_pollut.html, accessed September 4, 2009.

Beucke, Dan, "Coke Promises a Probe in Colombia," *BusinessWeek*, February 6, 2006, p. 11.

Brooker, Katrina, "The Pepsi Machine," *Fortune,* February 6, 2006, pp. 68–72.

Burke, Kelly, "Coca-Cola Busted for Big Fat Rotten Lies," *Sydney Morning Herald,* April 2, 2009, http://www.smh.com.au/national/cocacola-busted-for-big-fat-rotten-lies-20090402-9kn6.html?page=1, accessed September 4, 2009.

Chase, Randall, "Judge Dismisses Shareholder Suit Against Coca-Cola," Associated Press via SignOnSanDiego.com, October 22, 2007, http://www.signonsandiego.com/news/business/20071022-1441-coca-cola-lawsuit.html, accessed September 8, 2009.

"Coca Cola Appears to Have Settled Lawsuit over Distribution to Retail Distribution Centers," *Supply Chain Digest*, February 14, 2007, http://www.scdigest.com/assets/newsViews/07-02-14-2.cfm?cid=896&ctype=content, accessed September 4, 2009.

Coca Cola Company, http://www.thecoca-colacompany.com, accessed May 16, 2009.

Doyle, T. C., "Channel Stuffing Rears Its Ugly Head," *VARBusiness*, May 6, 2003, http://www.crn.com/it channel/18823602;jsessionid=TC1LHY0F4LAXYQSNDLPSKHSCJUNN2JVN, accessed September 4, 2009.

Faier, James, "The Name Is the Game," Retail Traffic, http://retailtrafficmag.com/mag/retail_name_game/index.html, accessed September 4, 2009.

Foust, Dean, and Geri Smith, "'Killer Coke' or Innocent Abroad? Controversy over Anti-Union Violence in Colombia Has Colleges Banning Coca-Cola," *BusinessWeek*, January 23, 2006, pp. 46–48.

Glovin, David, and Duane D. Stanford, "PepsiCo Sues Coca-Cola over Powerade Advertisements (Update3)," Bloomberg.com, April 13, 2009, http://www.bloomberg.com/apps/news?pid=20601110&sid=aYXGQIH6Hisk, accessed September 4, 2009.

"Grand Jury to Investigate Coke on Channel Stuffing Allegations," *Atlanta Business Chronicle*, May 3, 2004, atlanta.bizjournals.com/atlanta/stories/2004/05/03/daily2.html, accessed September 4, 2009.

Kelly, Marjorie, "100 Best Corporate Citizens," *Business Ethics* (Spring 2007): 23–24.

"Neville Isdell, Chairman of The Coca-Cola Company, to Receive Ethics Advocate Award," J. Mack Robinson College of Business, Georgia State University, http://robinson.gsu.edu/news/08/isdell.html, accessed September 4, 2009.

Peer, Melinda, "In Downturn, Pepsi May Beat Coke," *Forbes*, February 19, 2009, http://www.forbes.com/2009/02/19/coca-cola-pepsico-markets-equity_dividend_outlook_49.html, accessed September 4, 2009.

Simons, Craig, "Report Examines Coke Water Use in India," Cox News Service, January 15, 2008, http://www.statesman.

com/business/content/shared/money/stories/2008/01/COKE_
INDIA15_1STLD_COX_F4362_1.html, accessed September
4, 2009.

Srivastava, Amit, "Reality Check for Coca-Cola's Public
Relations," India Resource Center, April 16, 2009, http://
www.indiaresource.org/campaigns/coke/2009/realitycheck.
html, accessed September 4, 2009.

"Teamsters Converge on Times Square to Protest Coke's
Anti-Worker Tactics; Teamsters Put Coke on Notice for
Possible Job Actions over Worker Abuses," *PR Wire*,
April 2, 2007, http://www.prnewswire.com/cgi-bin/
stories.pl?ACCT=104&STORY=/www/story/04-02-
2007/0004557941&EDATE=, accessed September 4,
2009.

Terhune, Chad, "Bottlers' Suit Challenges Coke Distribution
Plan," *Wall Street Journal*, February 18–19, 2006, p. A5.

Terhune, Chad, "A Suit by Coke Bottlers Exposes Cracks in a
Century-Old System," *Wall Street Journal*, March 13, 2006,
p. A1.

Waldman, Amy, "India Tries to Contain Tempest over
Soft Drink Safety," *New York Times*, August 23, 2003,
http://query.nytimes.com/gst/fullpage.html?res=9A04E6DC
1439F930A1575BC0A9659C8B63, accessed September 4,
2009.

"WWF and Coca-Cola Embark on Water Conservation
Initiative," June 5, 2007, http://www.ens-newswire.com/
ens/jun2007/2007-06-05-07.asp, accessed September 4,
2009.

Enron: Questionable Accounting Leads to Collapse

Once upon a time, there was a gleaming headquarters office tower in Houston, with a giant tilted "E" in front, slowly revolving in the Texas sun. Enron's "E" suggested to Chinese *feng shui* practitioner Meihwa Lin a model of instability, which was perhaps an omen of things to come. The Enron Corporation, which once ranked among the top *Fortune* 500 companies, collapsed in 2001 under a mountain of debt that had been concealed through a complex scheme of off-balance-sheet partnerships. Forced to declare bankruptcy, the energy firm laid off four thousand employees; thousands more lost their retirement savings, which had been invested in Enron stock. The company's shareholders lost tens of billions of dollars after the stock price plummeted. The scandal surrounding Enron's demise engendered a global loss of confidence in corporate integrity that continues to plague markets, and eventually it triggered tough new scrutiny of financial reporting practices. To understand what went wrong, we'll examine the history, culture, and major players in the Enron scandal.

ENRON'S HISTORY

The Enron Corporation was created out of the merger of two major gas pipeline companies in 1985. Through its subsidiaries and numerous affiliates, the company provided products and services related to natural gas, electricity, and communications for its wholesale and retail customers. Enron transported natural gas through pipelines to customers all over the United States. It generated, transmitted, and distributed electricity to the northwestern United States, and marketed natural gas, electricity, and other commodities globally. It was also involved in the development, construction, and operation of power plants, pipelines, and other energy-related projects all over the world, including the delivery and management of energy to retail customers in both the industrial and commercial business sectors.

Throughout the 1990s, Chair Ken Lay, chief executive officer (CEO) Jeffrey Skilling, and Chief Financial Officer (CFO) Andrew Fastow transformed Enron from an old-style electricity and gas company into a $150 billion energy company and Wall Street favorite that traded power contracts in the investment markets. From 1998 to 2000 alone, Enron's revenues grew from about $31 billion to more than $100 billion, making it the seventh-largest company of the *Fortune* 500. Enron's wholesale energy income represented about 93 percent of 2000 revenues, with another 4 percent derived from natural gas and electricity. The remaining 3 percent came from broadband services and exploration. However, a bankruptcy examiner later reported that although Enron claimed a net income of $979 million in that year, it really earned just $42 million. Moreover, the examiner found that despite Enron's claim of $3 billion in cash flow in 2000, the company actually had a cash flow of negative $154 million.

This case was developed under the direction of O.C. Ferrell with the assistance of Jennifer Jackson and Jennifer Sawayda, University of New Mexico. Neil Herndon, helped to draft the original version of this case. The author conducted personal interviews with Ken Lay in 2006. This case is for classroom discussion, rather than to illustrate either effective or ineffective handling of an administrative, ethical, or legal decision by management. All sources used for this case were obtained through publicly available material.

ENRON'S CORPORATE CULTURE

When describing the corporate culture of Enron, people like to use the word *arrogant,* perhaps justifiably. A large banner in the lobby at corporate headquarters proclaimed Enron "The World's Leading Company," and Enron executives blithely believed that competitors had no chance against it. Jeffrey Skilling even went so far as to tell utility executives at a conference that he was going to "eat their lunch." There was an overwhelming aura of pride, carrying with it the deep-seated belief that Enron's people could handle increasing risk without danger. The culture also was about a focus on how much money could be made for executives. For example, Enron's compensation plans seemed less concerned with generating profits for shareholders than with enriching officer wealth. Enron's corporate culture reportedly encouraged flouting, possibly even breaking, the rules.

Skilling appears to be the executive who created a system in which Enron's employees were rated every six months, with those ranked in the bottom 20 percent forced out. This "rank and yank" system helped create a fierce environment in which employees competed against rivals not only outside the company but also at the next desk. Delivering bad news could result in the "death" of the messenger, so problems in the trading operation, for example, were covered up rather than being communicated to management.

Enron Chair Ken Lay once said that he felt that one of the great successes at Enron was the creation of a corporate culture in which people could reach their full potential. He said that he wanted it to be a highly moral and ethical culture and that he tried to ensure that people did in fact honor the values of respect, integrity, and excellence. On his desk was an Enron paperweight with the slogan "Vision and Values." Despite these intentions, however, ethical behavior was not put into practice. Instead, integrity was pushed to the side at Enron, particularly by top managers. Some employees at the company believed that nearly anything could be turned into a financial product and, with the aid of complex statistical modeling, traded for profit. Short on assets and heavily reliant on intellectual capital, Enron's corporate culture rewarded innovation and punished employees deemed weak.

ENRON'S ACCOUNTING PROBLEMS

Enron's bankruptcy in 2001 was the largest in U.S. corporate history at the time. The bankruptcy filing came after a series of revelations that the giant energy trader had been using partnerships, called *special-purpose entities (SPEs),* to conceal losses. In a meeting with Enron's lawyers in August 2001, the company's then chief financial officer Andrew Fastow stated that Enron had established the SPEs to move assets and debt off its balance sheet and to increase cash flow by showing that funds were flowing through its books when it sold assets. Although these practices produced a very favorable financial picture, outside observers believed they constitutes fraudulent financial reporting because they did not accurately represent the company's true financial condition. Most of the SPEs were entities in name only, and Enron funded them with its own stock and maintained control over them. When one of these partnerships was unable to meet its obligations, Enron covered the debt with its own stock. This arrangement worked as long as Enron's stock price was high, but when the stock price fell, cash was needed to meet the shortfall.

After Enron restated its financial statements for fiscal year 2000 and the first nine months of 2001, its cash flow from operations was changed from a positive $127 million in 2000 to a negative $753 million in 2001. In 2001, with its stock price falling, Enron faced a critical cash shortage. In October 2001, after it was forced to cover some large shortfalls for its partnerships, Enron's stockholder equity fell by $1.2 billion. Already shaken by questions about lack of disclosure in Enron's financial statements and by reports that executives had profited personally from the partnership deals, investor confidence collapsed, taking Enron's stock price with it.

For a time, it appeared that Dynegy might save the day by providing $1.5 billion in cash, secured by Enron's premier pipeline Northern Natural Gas, and then purchasing Enron for about $10 billion. However, when Standard & Poor's downgraded Enron's debt below investment grade on November 28, 2001, some $4 billion in off-balance-sheet debt came due, and Enron didn't have the resources to pay. Dynegy terminated the deal. On December 2, 2001, Enron filed for bankruptcy. Enron now faces 22,000 claims totaling about $400 billion.

The Whistle-Blower

Assigned to work directly with Andrew Fastow in June 2001, Enron vice president Sherron Watkins, an eight-year Enron veteran, was given the task of finding some assets to sell off. With the high-tech bubble bursting and Enron's stock price slipping, Watkins was troubled to find unclear, off-the-books arrangements backed only by Enron's deflating stock. No one seemed to be able to explain to her what was going on. Knowing she faced difficult consequences if she confronted then CEO Jeffrey Skilling, she began looking for another job, planning to confront Skilling just as she left for a new position. Skilling, however, suddenly quit on August 14, saying he wanted to spend more time with his family. Chair Ken Lay stepped back in as CEO and began inviting employees to express their concerns and put them into a box for later collection. Watkins prepared an anonymous memo and placed it into the box. When CEO Lay held a companywide meeting shortly thereafter and did not mention her memo, however, she arranged a personal meeting with him.

On August 22, Watkins handed Lay a seven-page letter she had prepared outlining her concerns. She told him that Enron would "implode in a wave of accounting scandals" if nothing was done. Lay arranged to have Enron's law firm, Vinson & Elkins, look into the questionable deals, although Watkins advised against having a party investigate that might be compromised by its own involvement in Enron's scam. Near the end of September, Lay sold some $1.5 million of personal stock options, while telling Enron employees that the company had never been stronger. By the middle of October, Enron was reporting a third-quarter loss of $618 million and a $1.2 billion write-off tied to the partnerships about which Watkins had warned Lay.

For her trouble, Watkins had her computer hard drive confiscated and was moved from her plush executive office suite on the top floor of the Houston headquarters tower to a sparse office on a lower level. Her new metal desk was no longer filled with the high-level projects that had once taken her all over the world on Enron business. Instead, now a vice president in name only, she faced meaningless "make work" projects. In February 2002, she testified before Congress about Enron's partnerships and resigned from Enron in November of that year.

The Chief Financial Officer

Chief Financial Officer Andrew Fastow was indicted in 2002 by the U.S. Justice Department on ninety-eight federal counts for his alleged efforts to inflate Enron's profits. These charges included fraud, money laundering, conspiracy, and one count of obstruction of justice. Fastow originally faced up to 140 years in jail and millions of dollars in fines if convicted on all counts. Federal officials attempted to recover all of the money Fastow earned illegally, and seized some $37 million.

Federal prosecutors argue that Enron's case is not about exotic accounting practices but fraud and theft. They contend that Fastow was the brain behind the partnerships used to conceal some $1 billion in Enron debt and that this led directly to Enron's bankruptcy. The federal complaints allege that Fastow defrauded Enron and its shareholders through the off-balance-sheet partnerships that made Enron appear to be more profitable than it actually was. They also allege that Fastow made about $30 million both by using these partnerships to get kickbacks that were disguised as gifts from family members who invested in them and by taking income himself that should have gone to other entities.

Fastow denied any wrongdoing and maintained that he was hired to arrange the off-balance-sheet financing and that Enron's board of directors, chair, and CEO directed and praised his work. He also claimed that both lawyers and accountants reviewed his work and approved what was being done and that "at no time did he do anything he believed was a crime." Jeffrey Skilling, chief operating officer (COO) from 1997 to 2000 before becoming CEO, reportedly championed Fastow's rise at Enron and supported his efforts to keep up Enron's stock prices.

Fastow eventually pleaded guilty to two counts of conspiracy, admitting to orchestrating myriad schemes to hide Enron debt and inflate profits while enriching himself with millions. He surrendered nearly $30 million in cash and property, and agreed to serve up to ten years in prison once prosecutors no longer needed his cooperation. He was a key government witness against Lay and Skilling. His wife Lea Fastow, former assistant treasurer, quit Enron in 1997 and pleaded guilty to a felony tax crime, admitting to helping hide ill-gotten gains from her husband's schemes from the government. She later withdrew her plea, and then pleaded guilty to a newly filed misdemeanor tax crime. In 2005 she was released from a year-long prison sentence, and then had a year of supervised release.

In the end, Fastow received a lighter sentence than he otherwise might have because of his willingness to cooperate with investigators. In 2006, Fastow delivered an eight-and-one-half-day deposition in his role as plaintiff's witness. He helped to illuminate how Enron managed to get away with what it did, including detailing how many major banks were complicit in helping Enron manipulate its financials to help it look better to investors. In exchange for his deposition, Fastow's sentence was lowered to six years from ten for the fraud he perpetrated while COO at Enron.

The case against Fastow was largely based on information provided by Managing Director Michael Kopper, a key player in the establishment and operation of several of the off-balance-sheet partnerships and the first Enron executive to plead guilty to a crime. Kopper, a chief aide to Fastow, pleaded guilty to money laundering and wire fraud. He faced up to fifteen years in prison and agreed to surrender some $12 million he earned from his illegal dealings with the partnerships. However, Kopper only had to serve three years and one month of jail time because of the crucial role he played in providing prosecutors with information. After his high-powered days at Enron, Kopper got a job as a salaried grant writer for Legacy, a Houston-based clinic that provides services to those with HIV and other chronically ill patients.

Others charged in the Enron affair include Timothy Belden, Enron's former top energy trader, who pleaded guilty to one count of conspiring to commit wire fraud. He was sentenced to two years of court-supervised release and required to pay $2.1 million. Three British bankers, David Bermingham, Giles Darby, and Gary Mulgrew, were indicted in Houston on wire-fraud charges related to a deal at Enron. They were able to use secret investments to take $7.3 million in income that belonged to their employer, according to the Justice Department. The three, employed by the finance group Greenwich National Westminster Bank, were arrested in 2004 and extradited to America to face sentencing. They were sentenced to thirty-seven months in prison but were eventually sent back to Britain to serve out the remainder of their sentencing.

The Chief Executive Officer

Former CEO Jeffrey Skilling, generally perceived as Enron's mastermind, was the most difficult to prosecute. At the time of the trial, he was so sure he had committed no crime that he waived his right to self-incrimination and testified before Congress, saying, "I was not aware of any inappropriate financial arrangements." However, Jeffrey McMahon, who took over as Enron's president and COO in February 2002, told a congressional subcommittee that he had informed Skilling about the company's off-balance-sheet partnerships in 2000, when he was Enron's treasurer. McMahon said that Skilling had told him "he would remedy the situation."

Calling the Enron collapse a "run on the bank" and a "liquidity crisis," Skilling said that he did not understand how Enron went from where it was to bankruptcy so quickly. He also said that the off-balance-sheet partnerships were Fastow's creation. During the case, however, the judge dealt a blow to defendants Lay and Skilling when he told the jury that they could find the defendants guilty of consciously avoiding knowing about wrongdoing at the company. Many former Enron employees refused to testify because they were not guaranteed that their testimony would not be used against them at future trials to convict them. For this reason, many questions about the accounting fraud remained after the trial.

Skilling was found guilty and sentenced to twenty-four years in prison, which he has been serving in Colorado. Skilling maintains his innocence and has appealed his conviction. In 2008 a panel of judges sitting in New Orleans rejected his requests for overturning convictions of fraud, conspiracy, misrepresentation, and insider trading. However, the judges did grant Skilling one concession. The three-judge panel determined that the original judge had applied flawed sentencing guidelines in determining Skilling's sentence. Skilling will be resentenced, but the reduction in duration will likely be modest, probably fifteen to nineteen years in place of the original twenty-four. In the years since the trial, this concession constitutes the only part of the Enron case that has been overturned. The nineteen counts of criminal conviction still stand. In October 2009, the Supreme Court agreed to hear Skilling's appeal. The court will examine two issues:

whether Skilling lied to investors about the health of the company, and they will examine whether Skilling received a fair trial in Houston– where Enron was headquartered and where many people lost their jobs and savings in the wake of the collapse.

The Chair

Kenneth Lay became chair and CEO of the company that was to become Enron in 1986. A decade later, Lay promoted Jeffrey Skilling to president and chief operating officer, and then, as expected, Lay stepped down as CEO in 2001 to make way for Skilling. Lay remained as chair of the board. When Skilling resigned later that year, Lay resumed the role of CEO.

Lay, who held a doctorate in economics from the University of Houston, contended that he knew little of what was going on, even though he had participated in the board meetings that allowed the off-balance-sheet partnerships to be created. He said he believed the transactions were legal because attorneys and accountants approved them. Only months before the bankruptcy in 2001, he reassured employees and investors that all was well at Enron, based on strong wholesale sales and physical volume delivered through the marketing channel. He had already been informed that there were problems with some of the investments that could eventually cost Enron hundreds of millions of dollars. Although cash flow does not always follow sales, there was every reason to believe that Enron was still a company with strong potential. In 2002, on the advice of his attorney, Lay invoked his Fifth Amendment right not to answer questions that could be incriminating.

Ken Lay was expected to be charged with insider trading, and prosecutors investigated why Lay began selling about $80 million of his own stock beginning in late 2000, even while he encouraged employees to buy more shares of the company. It appears that Lay drew down his $4 million Enron credit line repeatedly and then repaid the company with Enron shares. These transactions, unlike usual stock sales, do not have to be reported to investors. Lay says that he sold the stock because of margin calls on loans he had secured with Enron stock and that he had no other source of liquidity.

Lay was convicted on nineteen counts of fraud, conspiracy, and insider trading. However, the verdict was thrown out in 2006 after Lay died of heart failure at his home in Colorado. The ruling protected some $43.5 million of Lay's estate that the prosecution had claimed Lay stole from Enron.

Vinson & Elkins

Enron was Houston law firm Vinson & Elkins' top client, accounting for about 7 percent of its $450 million revenue. Enron's general counsel and a number of members of Enron's legal department came from Vinson & Elkins. Vinson & Elkins seems to have dismissed Sherron Watkins's allegations of accounting fraud after making some inquiries, but this does not appear to leave it open to civil or criminal liability. Of greater concern are allegations that Vinson & Elkins helped structure some of Enron's special-purpose partnerships. Watkins, in her letter to CEO Ken Lay, indicated that the law firm had written opinion letters supporting the legality of the deals. In fact, Enron could not have done many of the transactions without such opinion letters. The firm did not admit liability, but agreed to pay $30 million to Enron to settle claims that Vinson & Elkins contributed to the firm's collapse.

Merrill Lynch

The brokerage and investment-banking firm Merrill Lynch, which was in the news for its high-profile collapse and subsequent acquisition by Bank of America in 2008, also faced scrutiny by federal prosecutors and the SEC for its role in Enron's 1999 sale of Nigerian barges. The sale allowed Enron to improperly record about $12 million in earnings and thereby meet its earnings goals at the end of 1999. Merrill Lynch allegedly bought the barges for $28 million, of which Enron financed $21 million. Fastow gave his word that Enron would buy Merrill Lynch's investment out in six months with a 15 percent guaranteed rate of return.

Merrill Lynch went ahead with the deal despite an internal Merrill Lynch document that suggested that the transaction might be construed as aiding and abetting Enron's fraudulent manipulation of its income statement. Merrill Lynch denies that the transaction was a sham and said that it never knowingly helped Enron to falsify its financial reports.

There are also allegations that Merrill Lynch replaced a research analyst after his coverage of Enron displeased Enron executives. Enron reportedly threatened to exclude Merrill Lynch from a coming $750 million stock offering in retaliation. The replacement analyst is reported to have then upgraded his report on Enron's stock rating. Merrill Lynch maintains that it did nothing improper in its Enron business dealings. However, the firm agreed to pay $80 million to settle SEC charges related to the questionable Nigerian barge deal.

Arthur Andersen LLP

In its role as Enron's auditor, Arthur Andersen was responsible for ensuring the accuracy of Enron's financial statements and internal bookkeeping. Potential investors used Andersen's reports to judge Enron's financial soundness and future potential before they decided whether to invest, and current investors used those reports to decide if their funds should remain invested there. These investors expected that Andersen's certifications of accuracy and application of proper accounting procedures would be independent and without any conflict of interest. If Andersen's reports were in error, investors could be seriously misled.

However, Andersen's independence was called into question. The accounting firm was a major business partner of Enron, with more than one hundred employees dedicated to its account, and it sold about $50 million a year in consulting services to Enron. Some Andersen executives even accepted jobs with the energy trader. In March 2002, Andersen was found guilty of obstruction of justice for destroying Enron-related auditing documents during an SEC investigation of Enron. As a result, Anderson has been barred from performing audits.

It is still not clear why Andersen auditors failed to ask Enron to better explain its complex partnerships before certifying Enron's financial statements. Some observers believe that the large consulting fees Enron paid Andersen unduly influenced the company's decisions. An Andersen spokesperson said that the firm looked hard at all available information from Enron at the time; but shortly after speaking to Enron CEO Ken Lay, Vice President Sherron Watkins took her concerns to an Andersen audit partner, who reportedly conveyed her questions to senior Andersen management responsible for the Enron account. It is not clear what action, if any, Andersen took.

THE FALLOUT

Enron's demise caused tens of billions of dollars of investor losses, triggered a collapse of electricity-trading markets, and ushered in an era of accounting scandals that precipitated a global loss of confidence in corporate integrity. Now companies must defend legitimate but complicated financing arrangements. Legislation like Sarbanes-Oxley, passed in the wake of Enron, has placed more restriction on companies. On a more personal level, four thousand former Enron employees had to struggle to find jobs, and many retirees lost their entire retirement portfolios. One senior Enron executive committed suicide.

In 2003 Enron announced its intention to restructure and pay off its creditors. It was estimated that most creditors would receive between 14.4 cents and 18.3 cents for each dollar they were owed—more than most expected. Under the plan, creditors would receive about two-thirds of the amount in cash and the rest in equity in three new companies, none of which would carry the tainted Enron name. The three companies were CrossCountry Energy Corporation, Prisma Energy International Inc., and Portland General Electric.

CrossCountry Energy Corporation would retain Enron's interests in three North American natural gas pipelines. In 2004, Enron announced an agreement to sell CrossCountry Energy to CCE Holdings LLC for $2.45 billion. The money was to be used for debt repayment, and represented a substantial increase over a previous offer. Similarly, Prisma Energy International Inc., which took over Enron's nineteen international power and pipeline holdings, was sold to Ashmore Energy International Limited. The proceeds from the sale were given out to creditors through cash distributions. The third company, Portland General Electric (PGE), Oregon's largest utility, emerged from bankruptcy as an independent company through a private stock offering to Enron creditors.

All remaining assets not related to Cross-Country, Prisma, or Portland General were liquidated. Although Enron emerged from Chapter 11 bankruptcy protection in 2004, the company was wound down once the recovery plan was carried out. That year all of Enron's outstanding common stock and preferred stocks were cancelled. Each record holder of Enron Corporation stock on the day it was cancelled was allocated an uncertified, nontransferable interest in one of two trusts that held new shares of the Enron Corporation.

The Enron Creditors Recovery Corporation was formed to help Enron creditors. It states that its mission is "to reorganize and liquidate the remaining operations and assets of Enron following one of the largest and most complex bankruptcies in U.S. history." In the very unlikely event that the value of Enron's assets would exceed the amount of its allowed claims, distributions were to be made to the holders of these trust interests in the same order of priority of the stock they previously held. According to the Enron Creditors Recovery Corporation, over $128 million was distributed to creditors, which brings the total amount of recovery to $21.549 billion.

In addition to trying to pay back its jilted shareholders, Enron also had to pay California for fraudulent activities it committed against the state's citizens. The company was investigated in California for allegedly colluding with at least two other power sellers in 2000 to obtain excess profits by submitting false information to the manager of California's electricity grid. In 2005, Enron agreed to pay California $47 million for taking advantage of California consumers during an energy shortage. This serves to prove further that Enron's corporate culture was inherently flawed, with the company promoting profits at the expense of stakeholders.

LEARNING FROM ENRON

Enron was clearly the biggest business scandal of its time. Officials swore that such a disaster would never occur again and passed legislation like the Sarbanes-Oxley Act to prevent future business fraud. Yet, did the business world truly learn its lesson from Enron's collapse? The answer would be a resounding no, as the 2008–2009 financial crisis attested. The crisis made the Enron scandal look small in comparison and was the worst financial disaster since the Great Depression. Like the Enron scandal, the financial crisis largely stemmed from corporate misconduct. Corporations rewarded performance at all costs, even when employees cut ethical corners to achieve high performance. In the mortgage market, companies like Countrywide rewarded their sales force for making risky subprime loans, going so far as to approve loans that they knew contained falsified information in order to make a quick profit. Other companies traded in risky financial instruments like credit default swaps (CDSs) when they knew that buyers did not have a clear understanding of the risks of such instruments. Although they promised to insure against default of these instruments, the companies did not have enough funds to cover the losses after the housing bubble burst.

The bankruptcy of Enron was nothing compared to how many companies and individuals were negatively affected by the financial crisis. The resulting crisis affected the entire world, bankrupting such established companies as Lehman Brothers and requiring government intervention in the amount of nearly $1 trillion

in TARP (Troubled Asset Referendum Program) funds to salvage numerous financial firms. The U.S. government put forth $180 billion to rescue American International Group Inc. (AIG), and both Fannie Mae and Freddie Mac were placed in conservatorship of the Federal Housing Finance Industry. Merrill Lynch, who faced scrutiny during the Enron scandal, could not survive the crisis and was forced to sell to Bank of America. The 150-year-old company Lehman Brothers, which had survived the Great Depression, was forced to file for bankruptcy with $613 billion in debt. The losses from the crisis total in the hundreds of billions and probably will not be known for years to come.

The misconduct of corporate officers like Ken Lay and Jeffrey Skilling has not disappeared in the ensuing years. Many of the failures during the financial crisis stemmed from the same types of crimes as those in the Enron debacle, and in many ways the scandals were a lot worse. Much like Ken Lay, Richard Fuld of Lehman Brothers has become the epitome of corruption in the eyes of the public. He was forced to testify before Congress as to why he received hundreds of millions of dollars in salary, bonuses, and stock options since 2000. He was also called to explain his part in the bankruptcy and was forced to defend himself against accusations that he misled stockholders, just days before the company filed for bankruptcy, into thinking that the company was doing well. Additionally, the crimes of Ken Lay and Jeffrey Skilling are overshadowed by the likes of Bernie Madoff, who operated a $65 billion Ponzi scheme that cheated many thousands out of their savings.

It is an unfortunate fact that the enormity of the Enron scandal did not hinder this misconduct. Despite legislation that was passed as a result of the Enron scandal, corporate corruption continued on a massive scale. Like Lay, many Wall Street CEOs attempted to portray their companies as doing well even as they were floundering. They relied on risky financial instruments and in some cases false financial reporting to make a quick profit and inflate earnings.

However, Enron does not have to be reduced to a mere page in a history book. Although it did not prevent future business misconduct, Enron still has lessons to teach us. Along with the business scandals of the financial crisis, Enron demonstrates that, first, regulatory bodies must be improved so as to better detect corporate misconduct. For instance, the Securities and Exchange Commission has not done its job in terms of detecting business fraud, even when warning signs were readily available. Second, the warnings of concerned employees and "whistle-blowers" like Sherron Watkins should be taken more seriously (employees had been informing lawmakers for years that Bernie Madoff was operating a Ponzi scheme but to no avail). Third, CEOs must have a better understanding of the financial instruments their companies are using, as well as a thorough knowledge of the inner workings of their companies (something that Ken Lay claimed he did not have). These conditions are crucial to preventing similar business fraud in the future.

CONCLUSION

Enron shows how an aggressive corporate culture that rewards high performance and gets rid of the "weak links" can backfire. Enron's culture encouraged fierce competition, not only among employees from rival firms, but also among Enron employees themselves. Such behavior creates a culture where loyalty and ethics are cast aside in exchange for high performance. The arrogant tactics of Jeffrey Skilling and the seeming ignorance of Lay as to what was going on in his company further contributed to an unhealthy corporate culture that encouraged cutting corners and falsifying information to inflate earnings.

The allegations surrounding Merrill Lynch and Arthur Andersen's involvement in the debacle demonstrate that rarely does any scandal of such magnitude involve only one company. Whether a company or regulatory body participates directly in a scandal or whether it refuses to act by looking the other way, such actions or inactions can result in further perpetuation of fraud. This was emphasized even more during the 2008–2009 financial crisis, where the misconduct of several major companies and the failure of monitoring efforts by regulatory bodies contributed to the worst financial crisis since the Great Depression. With the country in the midst of widespread corporate corruption, the story of Enron is once again at the forefront of people's minds.

The Enron scandal has become legendary. A mere four years after the scandal, in 2005, a movie was made about the collapse of Enron called "Enron: The Smartest Guys in the Room." To this day, Jeffrey Skilling continues to maintain his innocence, appealing his case as far as the Supreme Court. Enron's auditor, Arthur Andersen, faced some forty shareholder lawsuits claiming damages of more than $32 billion. In 2009 it agreed to pay $16 million to Enron creditors. Enron itself faced many civil actions, and a number of Enron executives faced federal investigations, criminal actions, and civil lawsuits. As for the giant tilted "E" logo so proudly displayed outside of corporate headquarters, it was auctioned off for $44,000.

QUESTIONS

1. How did the corporate culture of Enron contribute to its bankruptcy?

2. Did Enron's bankers, auditors, and attorneys contribute to Enron's demise? If so, what was their contribution?

3. What role did the chief financial officer play in creating the problems that led to Enron's financial problems?

SOURCES

Aldrick, Philip, "NatWest Three Return to UK," *Telegraph.co.uk*, November 7, 2008, http://www.telegraph.co.uk/news/worldnews/northamerica/usa/3394139/NatWest-Three-return-to-UK.html, accessed September 7, 2009.
Associated Press, "Merrill Lynch Settles an Enron Lawsuit," *New York Times,* July 7, 2006, http://www.nytimes.com/2006/07/07/business/07enron.html?scp=3&

sq=%22merrill%20lynch%22%20enron&st=cse, accessed September 7, 2009.

Associated Press, "2 Enron Traders Avoid Prison Sentences," *New York Times*, February 15, 2007, http://www.nytimes.com/2007/02/15/business/15enron.html?ex=1329195600&en=0f87e8ca83a557ed&ei=5090&partner=rssuserland&emc=rss, accessed September 7, 2009.

Barrionuevo, Alexei, "Fastow Gets His Moment in the Sun," November 10, 2006, http://www.nytimes.com/2006/11/10/business/10fastow.html, accessed September 7, 2009.

Barrionuevo, Alexei, Jonathan Weil, and John R. Wilke, "Enron's Fastow Charged with Fraud," *Wall Street Journal*, October 3, 2002, pp. A3–A4.

Berger, Eric, "Report Details Enron's Deception," *Houston Chronicle*, March 6, 2003, pp. 1B, 11B.

"British Bankers Indicted in Enron Case; Three Men Accused of Siphoning Off $7.3 Million Owed to Their Employer," HighBeam Research, *The Washington Post*, September 13, 2002, http://www.highbeam.com/doc/1P2-369257.html, accessed September 7, 2009.

Chen, Christine Y., "When Good Firms Get Bad Chi," *Fortune*, November 11, 2002, p. 56.

Eichenwald, Kurt, "Enron Founder, Awaiting Prison, Dies in Colorado," *New York Times*, July 6, 2006, http://www.nytimes.com/2006/07/06/business/06enron.html, accessed September 7, 2009.

Elkind, Peter, and Bethany McLean, "Feds Move Up Enron Food Chain," *Fortune*, December 30, 2002, pp. 43–44.

"Enron Announces Completed Sale of Prisma Energy International Inc," Enron Creditors Recovery Corp., September 7, 2006, http://www.enron.com/index.php?option=com_content&task=view&id=94&Itemid=34, accessed September 7, 2009.

"Enron Settles California Price-Gouging Claim," CBCNews.ca, July 15, 2005, http://www.cbc.ca/money/story/2005/07/15/enron-gouge050715.html, accessed September 7, 2009.

Enron website, http://www.enron.com/, accessed September 7, 2009.

"Ex-Enron CFO Fastow Indicted on 78 Counts," *Los Angeles Times*, November 1, 2002, http://www.msnbc.com/news/828217.asp, accessed September 7, 2009.

"FAQs," Enron Creditors Recovery Corp., http://www.enron.com/index.php?option=com_content&task=view&id=17&Itemid=27, accessed September 7, 2009.

Farrell, Greg, "Former Enron CFO Charged," *USA Today*, October 3, 2002, p. B1.

Farrell, Greg, Edward Iwata, and Thor Valdmanis, "Prosecutors Are Far from Finished," *USA Today*, October 3, 2002, pp. 1B–2B.

Felsenthal, Mark, and Lillia Zuill, "AIG Gets $150 Billion Government Bailout; Posts Huge Losses," Reuters, November 10, 2008, http://www.reuters.com/article/topNews/idUSTRE4A92FM20081110?feedType=RSS&feedName=topNews, accessed September 7, 2009.

Ferrell, O. C., "Ethics," *BizEd*, May/June 2002, pp. 43–45.

Ferrell, O. C. and Linda, *Examining Systemic Issues That Created Enron and the Latest Global Financial Industry Crisis* (2009), white paper.

Ferrell, O. C. and Linda, "Understanding the Importance of Business Ethics in the 2008–2009 Financial Crisis," in Ferrell, Fraedrich, Ferrell, *Business Ethics*, updated 7th ed. (Boston: Houghton Mifflin, 2009).

Fick, Jeffrey A., "Report: Merrill Replaced Enron Analyst," *USA Today*, July 30, 2002, p. B1.

"Finger-Pointing Starts as Congress Examines Enron's Fast Collapse," *Investor's Business Daily*, February 8, 2002, p. A1.

Fonda, Daren, "Enron: Picking over the Carcass," *Fortune*, December 30, 2002–January 6, 2003, p. 56.

France, Mike, "One Big Client, One Big Hassle," *BusinessWeek*, January 28, 2002, pp. 38–39.

Gruley, Bryan, and Rebecca Smith, "Keys to Success Left Kenneth Lay Open to Disaster," *Wall Street Journal*, April 26, 2002, pp. A1, A5.

Hamburger, Tom, "Enron CEO Declines to Testify at Hearing," *Wall Street Journal*, December 12, 2001, p. B2.

Kahn, Jeremy, "The Chief Freaked out Officer," *Fortune*, December 9, 2002, pp. 197–198, 202.

Kranhold, Kathryn, and Rebecca Smith, "Two Other Firms in Enron Scheme, Documents Say," *Wall Street Journal*, May 9, 2002, pp. C1, C12.

McLean, Bethany, "Why Enron Went Bust," *Fortune*, December 24, 2001, pp. 58, 60–62, 66, 68.

Morse, Jodie, and Amanda Bower, "The Party Crasher," *Fortune*, December 30, 2002–January 6, 2003, pp. 53–56.

Needles, Belverd E., Jr., and Marian Powers, "Accounting for Enron," *Houghton Mifflin's Guide to the Enron Crisis* (Boston: Houghton Mifflin, 2003), pp. 3–6.

Norris, Floyd, "Ruling Could Open Door to New Trial in Enron Case," *New York Times*, January 6, 2009, http://www.nytimes.com/2009/01/07/business/07enron.html?scp=3&sq=skilling&st=nyt, accessed September 7, 2009.

Ross, Brian, and Alice Gomstyn, "Lehman Brothers Boss Defends $484 Million in Salary, Bonus," ABC News, October 6, 2008, http://www.abcnews.go.com/Blotter/Story?id=5965360&page=1, accessed September 7, 2009.

Schulman, Miriam, "Enron: What Ever Happened to Going Down with the Ship?" Markkula Center for Applied Ethics, www.scu.edu/ethics/publications/ethicalperspectives/schulman0302.html, accessed September 7, 2009.

Sigismond, William, "The Enron Case from a Legal Perspective," *Houghton Mifflin's Guide to Enron*, pp. 11–13.

Smith, Rebecca, and Kathryn Kranhold, "Enron Knew Portfolio's Value," *Wall Street Journal*, May 6, 2002, pp. C1, C20.

Smith, Rebecca, and Mitchell Pacelle, "Enron Plans Return to Its Roots," *Wall Street Journal*, May 2, 2002, p. A1.

Sorkin, Andrew Ross, "Ex-Enron Chief Skilling Appeals to Supreme Court," DealBook Blog, *New York Times*, March 12, 2009, http://dealbook.blogs.nytimes.com/2009/05/12/former-enron-chief-skilling-appeals-to-supreme-court/?scp=1-b&sq=skilling&st=nyt, accessed September 7, 2009.

"Times Topics: Enron," *New York Times*, http://topics.nytimes.com/top/news/business/companies/enron/index.html?scp=1-spot&sq=Enron&st=cse, accessed September 7, 2009.

Ulick, Jake, "Enron: A Year Later," CNN/Money, December 2, 2002, http://money.cnn.com/2002/11/26/news/companies/enron_anniversary/index.htm, accessed September 7, 2009.

Weber, Joseph, "Can Andersen Survive?" *BusinessWeek*, January 28, 2002, pp. 39–40.

Weidlich, Thomas, "Arthur Andersen Settles Enron Suit for $16 Million," Bloomberg.com, April 28, 2009, http://www.bloomberg.com/apps/news?pid=20601072&sid=avopmnT7eWjs, accessed September 7, 2009.

Winthrop Corporation, "Epigraph," *Houghton Mifflin's Guide*, p. 1.

Zellner, Wendy, "A Hero—and a Smoking-Gun Letter," *Business Week*, January 28, 2002, pp. 34–35.

BP (Beyond Petroleum) Focuses on Sustainability

BP, formerly British Petroleum and the Anglo-Persian Oil Company, has experienced a lot of ups and downs over its hundred-year history—from nearly bankrupting its founder William D'Arcy to becoming one of the world's largest energy companies. BP has also experienced its fair share of controversies regarding business practices, environmental damage, and hazards to workers. It and all other large energy companies have come under fire for being responsible for the release of huge amounts of greenhouse gasses into the atmosphere. BP, however, has attempted to turn a page in its history book toward a more environmentally-friendly future. The company has invested in renewable energy and has thrown large amounts of support behind ethics and compliance initiatives, even writing an expansive code of conduct for its 92,000 employees.

This case provides an opportunity to observe the efforts of BP to improve its image and manage decisions related to ethics and social responsibility. Before delving into recent issues that BP has faced, a brief history of BP is given to provide some background. Although BP has sought to establish itself as an ethically responsible company, certain disasters resulting from company negligence are detailed in this analysis to show that it has often failed at this goal in the past. In recent years, BP has realized the need to become more environmentally-friendly, being the first oil company to recognize the presence of global warming and to launch initiatives into producing cleaner forms of energy.

In so doing, the company also hopes to educate others about how they can personally reduce their impact on the environment in the hopes of repositioning itself as an environmentally-responsible company.

THE 100-YEAR HISTORY OF BP

BP was founded more than a century ago by William D'Arcy, a wealthy British gentleman who had invested all his savings in the quest for oil in the Middle East. While experts and scientists had encouraged D'Arcy to pursue the venture, after more than six years of drilling, both his patience and finances were running low. Finally, in 1908, the drillers reached almost 1,200 feet and a fountain of oil spewed out. After long years filled with disappointment, pain, and despair, the Anglo-Persian Oil Company, what would become BP, was born. The company quickly opened trade on the stock market, and D'Arcy, who had lost nearly his entire net worth, became rich.

A naptha field in Iran, formerly known as Persia, located around 130 miles from the mouth of the Persian Gulf, was the first place where the Anglo-Persian Oil Company established a refinery. (Naptha refers to any sort of petroleum product. In this case, the Anglo-Persian Oil Company was pumping crude oil.) George Reynolds, D'Arcy's head manager for all the miners, quickly discovered that navigating this rugged land was not going to be

This case was developed under the direction of O.C. Ferrell and Jennifer Jackson, with the editorial assistance of Jennifer Sawayda, University of New Mexico. It was adapted from a case by Eve Sieber and Lameck Lukanga, University of New Mexico. This case is meant for classroom discussion, and is not meant to illustrate either effective or ineffective handling of an administrative, ethical, or legal decision by management. All sources used for this case were obtained through publicly available material.

such an easy task. Simply moving equipment to the site had been a monumental task that took months. To facilitate transportation of the oil, BP started building a pipeline through the area, and many of the necessary supplies had to be shipped from the United States. In a time before paved roads, everything had to be hauled through the sand using manpower and mules. Because of the difficult mountainous terrain, the pipeline project took over two years to complete. The huge scope of the undertaking drew workers seeking to help build the largest refinery in the world. They came from nearby Arab countries and from far away India and China. The medical director for the project would eventually found a hospital in Abadan, originally created to serve BP employees, that would go on to become one of the two most important medical centers in the entire region.

By 1914, BP was about to go bankrupt again. The company had a lot of oil but a shortage of people to sell the oil to. In 1914 the automobile had not become a mass-market product yet, and companies in the New World and Europe had first-mover advantages in the industrial oils market. An even worse problem was the strong smell of Persian oil, which eliminated it from the heating and kerosene lamp markets.

Winston Churchill, who was at the time British First Lord of the Admiralty, changed all that. He felt that the British navy, which was the envy of the world, needed a reliable and dedicated source of oil. Oil executives had been courting the navy for some years, but until Churchill, commanders had been reluctant to abandon coal. Churchill was adamant that only Anglo-Persian, because it was a British-owned company, could adequately protect British interests. Parliament overwhelmingly agreed, and soon was a major shareholder in the oil company. Thus began the debate over the repercussions of involving politics in the oil industry, a debate that only became louder throughout World War II, the Persian Gulf War, and the Iraq War.

The twentieth century saw enormous growth in the oil industry, along with massive power shifts in the Middle East. In 1969, Muammar al-Gaddafi led a coup in Libya, promptly demanding a tax increase on all oil exports. Gaddafi eventually nationalized BP's share of an oil operation in Libya. This move led other oil-rich countries in the Middle East, including Iran, Saudi Arabia, Abu Dhabi, and Qatar, to eventually nationalize. The effect on BP was massive—between 1975 and 1983, the oil production in the Middle East fell from 140 million to 500,000 barrels.

In order to survive, BP had to find new places to dig for oil. The Forties Field off the coast of Scotland, capable of producing 400,000 barrels of crude oil a day, and Prudhoe Bay in Alaska, where BP had tapped its largest oil field yet in 1969, were the two great hopes for BP's future at this time. However, transportation of the oil was again a problem. The remoteness of BP's best sites would challenge not only BP's engineering capabilities, but more importantly its commitment to the environment. The Forties Field pipeline would eventually become the largest deepwater pipeline ever constructed, a project that required special attention due to the harsh weather. The Trans-Alaska pipeline system would become the largest civil engineering project in North America, measuring nearly 746 miles long. The company performed extensive research to identify any potential environmental risks, making sure the pipeline included long above-water stretches to ensure that the warm oil transporting through it wouldn't melt the permafrost. BP also had to take steps to ensure that habitat disruption would be minimal. The company tried to assure concerned stakeholders that the environment was a serious matter to them, which they would address with an intense level of focus and commitment.

However, BP's actions have not always coincided with its words. The company's promises to act as a responsible environmental steward would be questioned as parts of BP shares were sold off, as competition in the energy industry began to stiffen, and as mergers started to occur.

QUESTIONS ABOUT BP's ETHICAL CONDUCT

As one probes below the surface of BP's public façade, one finds numerous instances of questionable behavior within this multinational oil company. These questionable deeds include fraud, environmental crimes, deaths, and the endangering of habitats.

In March 2005, a huge explosion occurred at a BP-owned oil refinery in Texas that killed 15 employees and injured another 170 people. The company was found guilty by the Southern District of Texas for a one-count felony for violating the Clean Air Act and was ordered to pay $50 million in criminal fines. The explosion was the result of a leak of hydrocarbon liquid and vapor, which then ignited. This specific unit had to be shut down for nearly a month in order to be repaired. BP admitted that it had ignored several procedures required by the Clean Air Act for ensuring mechanical integrity and a safe startup between 1999 until the explosion in 2005. The BP case was the first prosecution under a section of the Clean Air Act, which was created to help prevent injuries from such accidental leaks of explosive substances.

The company was also charged with violating the Clean Water Act when Alaskan oil pipelines leaked crude oil into the tundra and a frozen lake. The fines resulting from this infraction included $12 million in criminal fines, $4 million in payments to the National Fish and Wildlife Foundation, and $4 million in criminal restitution to the state of Alaska. The leaks occurred in March and August of 2006, after BP failed to respond to numerous red flags. One of these flags was the dangerous corrosion of the pipes that went unchecked for more than a decade before the Clean Water Act violation. A contract worker discovered the first pipeline leak in March of 2006. This leak resulted in more than 200,000 gallons of crude oil spilling onto the fragile tundra and a nearby frozen lake and was the largest spill to ever occur on the North Slope. A second 1,000-gallon leak occurred shortly after the first, in August 2006. Although it was small, the second leak led to the shutdown of oil production in the east side of Prudhoe Bay until BP could guarantee that the pipelines were fit for use.

Regular routine cleaning of the pipes is simple and would have prevented the 2006 oil leaks in Alaska. Nevertheless, in October 2007, BP recorded yet another spill near Prudhoe Bay. This time it was 2,000 gallons of toxic methanol, a deicing agent, that spilled onto the tundra and killed many plants and animals.

In the Northern District of Illinois, BP was charged with conspiring to violate the Commodity Exchange Act and also to commit mail fraud and wire fraud. The fraud involved purchasing more than the available supply of TET propane, and then selling it to other market participants at a price inflated well above market value. This sort of market manipulation is not tolerated in the United States, and BP was forced to pay large fines. The company had to pay $100 million in criminal penalties, $25 million to the U.S. Postal Inspection Consumer Fraud Fund, and a restitution of $53 million. Additionally, BP had to pay a civil penalty of $125 million to the Commodity Futures Trading Commission. Furthermore, four former employees were indicted in February 2004 for conspiring to manipulate the propane market at an artificially high price. The estimated loss to consumers who paid over market value exceeded $53 million dollars. The violation resulted in a 20-count indictment by a federal grand jury in Chicago.

The legal, environmental, and ethical transgressions on the part of BP demonstrate clearly that the company has a history of disregarding the well-being of stakeholders. "The actions against BP, along with the criminal charges against the four former BP traders, reflect our continued efforts to ensure that companies and individuals that do not follow the law will face consequences for their actions," said Assistant Attorney General Alice

S. Fisher of the Criminal Division. While purporting to be an ethical company, concerned with stakeholder well-being, BP's violations tell a different story.

BP REPAIRS ITS IMAGE

BP has begun to work to repair its tattered image. The twenty-first century found stakeholders more wary of companies, especially after decades of repeated violations and misconduct on the part of the oil industry. Oil leaks, toxic emissions, dead animals, refinery fires, wars in the Middle East, rising gas prices, pollution, and dwindling supplies all have combined to paint a very ugly picture of the oil industry as a whole. A central topic of the debate over the future of the world's energy supply focuses on global warming and greenhouse gas emissions.

One way BP worked to repair its damaged image was by changing its name from British Petroleum to simply BP, and increasing alternative energy offerings in its product mix. John Browne, BP group chief executive proclaimed, "we are all citizens of one world, and we must take shared responsibility for its future and for its sustainable development." BP was the first global energy firm to publicly announce its recognition of the problem of climate change. Browne has publicly discussed BP's involvement in finding new sources of energy, and has stated that he believes in balancing the needs of development and environmental protection. While its primary product is still petroleum, BP accepts that global warming is human-made, and it has begun to seek alternative revenue streams in wind farms and other lower-emissions energy sources. The company invests around $1.4 billion, or 5 percent of its total capital investment, in renewable energy like wind, solar power, and biofuels.

BP also has worked hard to overcome its negligent image by focusing renewed efforts on areas, such as Alaska, where the company has received a lot of bad press. Every winter when the Alaskan tundra is icy and frozen, a team of BP specialists heads for the remote areas of the Alaska North slope oilfields. The specialists' purpose is to excavate gravel from the pads on which drilling rigs once stood. They also remove drill cuttings and other waste left behind by the original exploration teams. Most of the excavated gravel can be reused immediately or treated on-site. The remainder of the gravel is either processed for future use or is ground down before it is injected back into the ground. The specialists aim to do as much as possible to return the sites to their original tundra state. This includes selective replanting and reseeding of the area. The specialists are guided by scientists and engineers from BP's remediation management team. They have already completed approximately 40 percent of a clean-up and restoration exercise agreed upon by BP and the state of Alaska. The Sag Delta 1 site on the Beaufort Sea Coast and the Kuparuk 24-12-12 site by the Kuparak River are two examples of the sixteen sites already sanitized. The specialists will return on a regular basis until their job is complete. The estimated cost of BP's future efforts will be close to $250,000,000. Even with all that effort, ultimately, the final restoration is best left to nature, with native tundra species soon returning to cover any remaining evidence of human presence.

BP WORKS TO IMPROVE SUSTAINABILITY

To adapt in a changing world, BP launched its Alternative Energy business in 2005. While still a small part of its overall company at $1.4 billion in investments, BP sees "going green" as an increasingly important part of its business, which it will expand as it becomes more profitable to do so.

Wind

BP has over 500 megawatts (MW) of installed capacity, with 432 MW in operation. Starting in 2008, BP began full-scale commercial operation in conjunction with wind farms across the country, including Cedar Creek in Colorado, a 274–wind turbine outfit. BP's installed wind capacity has the potential to supply power to 6 million homes.

Solar

In order to affordably expand its solar capacity, BP signed agreements with numerous solar panel producers in Asia. BP has installed only 4 MW of solar panels in the United States, those going to Wal-Mart stores in California. It does 70 percent of its solar business in Europe where demand is higher. BP also has developed two of the largest solar power plants in the world in Spain, projects that will supply energy to up to a million homes. BP also supports the Solar Cities concept, which has brought more access to solar power to seven cities across Australia.

As BP has continued its worldwide efforts to reduce greenhouse gas emissions, it has introduced a new solar-driven pump system at the Moxa Gas Field site in Wyoming. Two kinds of pumps are located at each of the 460 wells: One pumps methanol, while the other circulates heated glycol to prevent the freezing of equipment, which is a recurring problem in the harsh fields of Wyoming. BP has installed 230 solar-driven methanol pumps to help reduce the amount of natural gas needed to run the site. BP estimates that by using these new solar pumps, it has reduced Moxa's annual natural gas needs by over 48 million cubic feet, which amounts to around $200,000 in savings. The new pumps also create a safer work environment, as they reduce the risk of gas cloud related hazards for the employees. BP has plans to install 460 additional solar-driven glycol pumps. By replacing all of the pumps, BP has the potential to completely eliminate the use of natural gas at the Moxa site, making the pumping system virtually greenhouse gas free.

Biofuels

Biofuels have received a lot of negative press for their contributions to diminished food supplies and increasing food prices, and for causing deforestation in places like the Philippines and Brazil where it has become increasingly profitable to plant biofuel stock like sugar cane and palm. However, BP sees biofuels as a significant part of its energy portfolio for the next two decades, until better alternative energy sources are perfected.

BP became the single largest foreign stockholder in a Brazilian bioethanol company when it purchased a 50 percent stake in Tropical Energia S.A. The company's facility in Goias state, Brazil, has a capacity of 115 million gallons of sugarcane bioethanol. BP has also been working with Dupont to develop biobutanol, a biofuel with higher energy content than bioethanol.

BP's push in the alternative energy sector prompted the creation of a special purpose entity (SPE) with Verenium Corporation, a leader in the development of cellulosic ethanol, a fuel that is still in its infancy but that many hope can be the future of biofuels. Both partners hope to speed the development of cellulosic ethanol, and to one day make it commercially viable. Cellulosic ethanol is a renewable fuel produced from grasses and nonedible plant parts, such as sugarcane waste (called bagasse), rice straw, switchgrass, and wood chips. Although at this point it is much more difficult and energy-intensive to produce than corn or sugarcane ethanol, many believe that, as the technology improves, cellulosic ethanol will provide such benefits as greater per-acre yields and lower environmental impact, and it will not affect commodity or food prices, since it uses only waste products. If all goes as planned, BP's and Verenium's strategic partnership will help stimulate the development, production, and consumption of cellulosic ethanol over other types of liquid fuels.

Carbon Sequestration and Storage

Although it is a tremendously expensive undertaking, many experts believe that one of the best ways to control greenhouse gas emissions is through carbon sequestration and storage

(CCS). CCS involves capturing greenhouse gas emissions from smokestacks and other sources of the pollutant and pumping the gasses deep underground to empty oil or gas fields or aquifers. BP has been researching CCS since 2000, and opened the Salah Gas Field in Algeria for experimentation in 2004. BP captures and stores up to 1 million tons of carbon dioxide per year at Salah, which is equivalent to removing 250,000 cars from the road. BP hopes to do the same thing at Hydrogen Energy, its joint venture with Rio Tinto to develop low-carbon-emissions power plants for Abu Dhabi and California. While questions remain about the long-term effectiveness of CCS (no one knows for sure if the CO_2 stays underground, or whether it eventually leaks out), many energy companies such as BP see it as a promising technology.

Other Energy-Saving Measures

Beyond alternative energy sources, BP is also looking to save energy through better planning and implementation of its many operations around the world. The BP Zhuhai (BPZ) PTA plant is setting an example by using more efficient forms of energy. This development of more efficient, cleaner energy and the reduction of CO_2 emissions is an increasing priority in China. Many companies in China still use heavy oil and coal for fuel. For the past four years, BPZ has worked to set new standards and make a greater contribution in this area. A sequence of heat recovery projects has allowed the plant to optimize the use of steam as a way to reduce liquefied petroleum gas (LPG) consumption significantly. This has greatly saved energy and reduced emissions. Since 2005, BPZ has reduced its CO_2 emissions by 35 percent and has reduced the use of LPG by 48 percent. Additionally, by reducing fuel consumption, BPZ also has reduced the road safety and operational risks associated with delivery and unloading of LPG. BPZ is recognized locally and regionally for its promotion of environmental values. It has set an environmental standard for other companies to follow. The

company also is a prime example of how being green can be cost-efficient. It has achieved a net savings for BP worth approximately $7.6 million a year.

BP is also working in Algeria to help sustainability. The Algerian business unit of BP is striving to lessen groundwater and soil impacts from its operations. The company is doing this by incorporating liability prevention processes early in the process, even into the planning stages of operations. However, in a desert area, where sandstorms and other disastrous weather patterns are common, planning ahead and anticipating problems is not easy to do. The BP Algeria team, working in conjunction with the state oil company Sonatrach and Norway's Statoil, has established two primary environmental objectives: (1) to impact the environment as minimally as possible, and (2) to take actions swiftly to correct any potential liabilities from earlier operations. BP's Remediation Management Liability Prevention team supports the Algeria team and Sonatrach in identifying potential causes of soil and groundwater problems incurred at any point during BP's operations. Together, they have been able to identify problems by conducting a series of site visits, doing risk-analysis work, administering prevention assessment tool surveys, and identifying improvement opportunities in the area of operations. All parties involved have been able to synthesize their findings into a long-term plan for the management and prevention of environmental liabilities in Algeria.

BP REACHES STAKEHOLDERS WITH ITS SUSTAINABILITY PROGRAMS

In addition to its Alternative Energy program, BP also has implemented environmental awareness programs in Britain to help stakeholders understand the impacts of global warming and the importance of sustainability issues. BP is trying to help the environment by making people more aware of their carbon footprint. BP Educational

Service (BPES) initiated the distribution of the Carbon Footprint Toolkit. It is an award-winning program designed to help high school students understand the effects of climate change and their own carbon footprint. Developed in conjunction with teachers and BP's experts, the toolkit enables students to examine their school's carbon footprint and to help develop carbon reduction plans for their schools. The Carbon Footprint Toolkit was originally developed as a response to teachers' demands that came out of a series of "green" workshops that BP held. Available free of charge to all high school students and their teachers, the Carbon Footprint Toolkit has been a successful initiative for BP. Available only in Britain, the kit is available in 80 percent of all British high schools.

The toolkit received a prestigious award for e-learning at the International Visual Communications Association (IVCA) awards in 2007. Follow-up research on the tool has shown that the toolkit has greatly helped to increase the profile of BPES and also has raised the level of trust and recognition for BP's education initiatives. In addition, the proportion of teachers surveyed who judged their students to be environmentally aware increased from 62 percent to 89 percent after using BPES resources.

THE CODE OF CONDUCT

To help deal with BP's growing reputation for ethical misconduct, BP's Ethics and Compliance team organized the creation, publication, and distribution of a company code of conduct in 2005. The code was distributed to BP employees around the globe and is also publicly available online at the BP website. Given the multinational nature of the BP business, the code seeks to unite its diverse employees behind a set of universal standards of behavior. The cross-functional team that drafted the code of conduct faced many major challenges, like how to agree upon and communicate consistent standards for all BP employees regardless of location, culture, and language. They had to devise a plan to make the code a one-stop

reference and guide to individual behavior at BP. It would have to cover everything from health and safety to financial integrity. The code of conduct was the largest mass communications exercise ever attempted in BP.

Work began in 2004 with a large-scale benchmarking exercise. The ethics and compliance team, with the help of many external specialists, studied, in great detail, the codes of fifty-two other companies. Using the information collected from preliminary research, a team of senior regional, functional, and business segment leaders worked to develop the content of the BP code. A preliminary version of the code was tested in global workshops involving more than 450 BP employees from all levels of the company.

All BP employees must read the code. To facilitate understanding, it is translated into languages as diverse as Mandarin, German, Azeri, and Arabic. The company also holds awareness meetings to help employees understand the contents of the code. Perhaps the most important role of the code is that it put in writing, for the first time, BP's ethical and legal expectations. It gives clear guidelines for individuals covering five key areas: health, safety, security, and the environment; employees; business partners; government and communities; and company assets and financial integrity. The code is entitled "Our Commitment to Integrity," making the ethical intent of this document clear from the first page.

CONCLUSION

From the beginning, BP proved that it was able to overcome significant obstacles. It went from near bankruptcy to being one of the largest energy companies worldwide. BP has experienced a range of ethical issues, the most well-known stemming from the company's own negligence and misconduct. Yet, although BP has had a spotty past when it comes to integrity, the company has worked hard to overcome its negative image. It is not only investing in cleaner energy but also is trying to repair its image by reducing its environmental impact and cleaning up areas after it has used them. Some question whether BP's new socially responsible initiatives are a public relations ploy or a genuine attempt toward change. However, there is no question that BP's emphasis on environmental responsibility is having a positive impact to some extent.

From publishing a thorough code of conduct to investing in more renewable energy to being the first major oil company to admit that global warming is a threat to our future, BP has sought to establish itself at the forefront of ethical energy companies. The company realizes that being environmentally sustainable and ethically responsible not only is the right thing to do, but is also profitable. Good publicity and stakeholder goodwill can be powerful forces in helping companies maintain a competitive edge and thrive.

QUESTIONS

1. Based on the history of the company, why did BP get involved in so much questionable conduct?

2. Analyze BP's efforts to improve sustainability. Do you think they are sufficient, or does the company need to do more?

3. Do you believe the BP code of conduct and ethics initiatives will prevent future misconduct?

SOURCES

BP Sustainability Review, 2008, http://www.bp.com/liveassets/bp_internet/globalbp/STAGING/global_assets/e_s_assets/e_s_assets_2008/downloads/bp_sustainability_review_2008.pdf, accessed April 30, 2009.

"British Petroleum to Pay More than $370 Million in Environmental Crimes, Fraud Cases," PR Newswire, http://www.prnewswire.com/cgi-bin/stories.pl?ACCT=104&STORY=/www/story/10-25-2007/0004690834&EDATE=, accessed April 30, 2009.

Browne, John, "Breaking Ranks," Stanford Business, 1997, http://www.gsb.stanford.edu/community/bmag/sbsm0997/feature_ranks.html, accessed May 7, 2009.

Frey, Darcey, "How Green Is BP?" New York Times, December 8, 2002, http://www.nytimes.com/2002/12/08/magazine/08BP.html?scp=3&sq=how%20green%20is%20BP&st=cse, accessed April 30, 2009.

Gold, Russell, "BP Jumps into Next-Generation Biofuels with Plans to Build Florida Refinery," Wall Street Journal, February 19, 2009, p. B1, http://online.wsj.com/article/SB123500538913818241.html#, accessed April 30, 2009.

"The History of BP," BP International website, http://www.bp.com/sectiongenericarticle.do?categoryId=2010123&contentId=7027817, accessed April 30, 2009.

Judd, Amy, "British Petroleum Ordered to Pay $180 Million in Settlement Case," Now Public.com, February 19, 2009, http://www.nowpublic.com/environment/british-petroleum-ordered-pay-180-million-settlement-case, accessed March 18, 2009.

Kaskey, Jack, "BP, Dow Chemical Post Losses as Recession Cuts Demand," Bloomberg, February 3, 2009, http://www.bloomberg.com/apps/news?pid=20601102&sid=a2e75bA8i47k&refer=uk, accessed March 13, 2009.

Mouawad, Jad, "Oil Giants Loath to Follow Obama's Green Lead," New York Times, April 7, 2009, http://www.nytimes.com/2009/04/08/business/energy-environment/08greenoil.html?fta=y, accessed April 30, 2009.

Palast, Greg, "British Petroleum's 'Smart Pig,'" Greg Palast: Journalism and Film, August 9, 2006, http://www.gregpalast.com/british-petroleums-smart-pig/, accessed April 30, 2009.

Tyco International: Leadership Crisis

On September 12, 2002, national television showcased Tyco International's former chief executive officer (CEO) L. Dennis Kozlowski and former chief financial officer (CFO) Mark H. Swartz in handcuffs after being arrested and charged with misappropriating more than $170 million from the company. They were also accused of stealing more than $430 million through fraudulent sales of Tyco stock and concealing the information from shareholders. The two executives were charged with more than thirty counts of misconduct, including grand larceny, enterprise corruption, and falsifying business records. Another executive, former general counsel Mark A. Belnick, was charged with concealing $14 million in personal loans. Months after the initial arrests, charges and lawsuits were still being filed—making the Tyco scandal one of the most notorious of the early 2000s.

This case begins with a brief history of Tyco, followed by an explanation of Tyco CEO L. Dennis Kozlowki's rise to power. As Kozlowki rose to become the second-highest-paid CEO, some red flags pointed toward the impending disaster. Most notably, Kozlowski's aggressive approach to business, his lavish lifestyle, his clashes with the former, more conservative CEO, and his ousting of employees who were critical of his decisions all acted as indicators of Kozlowki's unethical behavior. This analysis also shows how a decentralized corporate structure can make it difficult, even for the board of directors, to effectively monitor

a firm's dealings and finances. Kozlowski's fall and the repercussions of his dirty dealings (financial penalties and jail time) are also detailed. Finally, an explanation of how Tyco survived the scandal is provided, along with safeguards the company has put into place to ensure that similar misconduct does not occur in the future.

TYCO'S HISTORY

Founded in 1960 by Arthur J. Rosenberg, Tyco began as an investment and holding company focused on solid-state science and energy conversion. It developed the first laser with a sustained beam for use in medical procedures. Rosenberg later shifted his focus to the commercial sector. In 1964, Tyco became a publicly traded company. It also began a series of rapid acquisitions—sixteen companies by 1968. The expansion continued through 1982, as the company sought to fill gaps in its development and distribution networks. Between 1973 and 1982, the firm grew from $34 million to $500 million in consolidated sales. In 1982, Tyco was reorganized into three business segments: Fire Protection, Electronics, and Packaging.

By 1986, Tyco had returned to a growth-through-acquisitions model and had restructured the company into four core segments: Electrical and Electronic Components, Healthcare and Specialty Products, Fire and Security Services, and Flow Control, which Tyco maintained through the 1990s. During this

This case was developed under the direction of John Fraedrich and Rob Boostrom. It was edited by Jennifer Jackson, Jennifer Sawayda, and Alexi Sherrill. This case is meant for classroom discussion, and is not meant to illustrate either effective or ineffective handling of an administrative, ethical, or legal decision by management. All sources used for this case were obtained through publicly available material.

© Tom Tomczyk

time, the company changed its name to Tyco International, in order to signal its global presence to the financial community. By the early 2000s, the firm had acquired more than thirty major companies, including well-known firms such as ADT, Raychem, and the CIT Group.

THE RISE OF DENNIS KOZLOWSKI

In 1975, armed with a degree in accounting, Dennis Kozlowski went to work for Tyco, following brief stints at SCM Corporation and Nashua Corporation. He soon found a friend and mentor in then CEO Joseph Gaziano. Kozlowski was impressed by Gaziano's lavish lifestyle—company jets, extravagant vacations, company cars, and country club memberships. However, Gaziano's reign ended abruptly in 1982 when he died of cancer. Gaziano was replaced by John F. Fort III, who differed sharply in management style. Where Gaziano had been extravagant, Fort was analytical and thrifty. His goal was to increase profits for shareholders and cut the extravagant spending characterizing Gaziano's tenure, and Wall Street responded positively to Tyco's new direction.

Kozlowski, who had thrived under Gaziano, was forced to adapt to the abrupt change in leadership. Adept at crunching numbers, Kozlowski focused on helping to achieve Fort's vision of putting shareholders first. He soon gained Fort's attention, and was promoted to president of Grinnell Fire Protection Systems Company, Tyco's largest division. At Grinnell, Kozlowski reduced overhead, eliminated 98 percent of paperwork, and revised compensation programs. Although he slashed managers' salaries, he also designed a bonus compensation package that gave them greater control over possible earnings. He publicly recognized both high and low achievers at a yearly banquet, giving awards to the best and calling attention to the lowest-producing units. Perhaps most importantly, Kozlowski systematically worked to acquire Grinnell's competitors. A *BusinessWeek* article described

him as a "corporate tough guy, respected and feared in roughly equal measure."

Over the next few years, Kozlowski continued to rise up Tyco's corporate ladder. He became the company's president and later CFO. However, his aggressive approach concerned Fort, who wanted to slow the rate of acquisitions in Kozlowski's division. Kozlowski's largest acquisition was Wormald International, a $360 million global fire-protection concern. Integrating Wormald proved problematic, and Fort was reportedly unhappy with such a large purchase. Fort and Kozlowski also disagreed over rapid changes made to Grinnell. Kozlowski responded by lobbying to convince Tyco's board of directors that problems with Wormald were a "bump in the road" and that the firm should continue its strategy of acquiring profitable companies that met guidelines. The board sided with Kozlowski. In 1992, Fort resigned as CEO and later as chair of the board, although he remained a member of Tyco's board of directors until 2003.

KOZLOWSKI'S TYCO EMPIRE

After Fort's departure, Dennis Kozlowski, then 46, found himself CEO of Tyco International. With a new lifestyle—parties and multiple homes in Boca Raton, Nantucket, Beaver Creek, and New York City—and an aggressive management style, he appeared to be following in the footsteps of his mentor, former CEO Joseph Gaziano.

Kozlowski knew Tyco from the bottom up, and stated that he was determined to make it the greatest company of the next century. Among other things, he recognized that one of Tyco's major shortcomings was its reliance on cyclical industries, which tend to be very sensitive to economic ups and downs. He resolved to expand Tyco into noncyclical industries through even more acquisitions, such as the Kendall Company, a manufacturer of medical supplies that had declared bankruptcy two years earlier. Kozlowski quickly revived the business and doubled Tyco's earnings.

Kendall became the core of Kozlowski's new Tyco Healthcare Group, which grew to become the second-largest producer of medical devices behind Johnson & Johnson. The board rewarded Kozlowski's performance by increasing his salary to $2.1 million and giving him shares of the company's stock.

In 1997, Kozlowski acquired ADT Security Services, a British-owned company located in Bermuda. By structuring the deal as a "reverse takeover," wherein a public company is acquired by a private company so as to avoid the lengthy process of going public, Tyco acquired a global presence as well as ADT's Bermuda registration. Tyco was then able to create a network of offshore subsidiaries to shelter its foreign earnings from U.S. taxation.

Kozlowski also restructured Tyco by hand-picking a few trusted individuals and placing them in key positions. One of these individuals was Mark Swartz, who was promoted from director of Mergers and Acquisitions to CFO. Swartz, who had a strong financial background as a former auditor for Deloitte & Touche and a reputation for being more approachable than Kozlowski, was aware of Kozlowski's business practices. Kozlowski also recruited Mark Belnick, a former litigator at Paul, Weiss, Rifkind, Garrison & Wharton, to become Tyco's general counsel.

By this time, Tyco's corporate governance system was comprised of Kozlowski and the firm's board of directors—including Joshua Berman, a vice president of Tyco; Mark Swartz, CFO; Lord Michael Ashcroft, a British dignitary who joined with the ADT merger; Richard S. Bodman, a venture capitalist; Stephen W. Foss, CEO of a textile concern; and Frank E. Walsh Jr., director of the board—among other high-profile members. The majority of members had served for ten years or more, and they were familiar with Kozlowski's management style. As directors, they were responsible for protecting Tyco's shareholders through disclosure of questionable situations or issues that might seem unethical or inappropriate. Despite this, after the arrests of Kozlowski and

Swartz, investigations uncovered the following troubling relationships among the board's members:

- Richard Bodman invested $5 million for Kozlowski in a private stock fund managed by Bodman.
- Frank E. Walsh, Jr. received $20 million for helping to arrange the acquisition of CIT Group without the other board members' knowledge.
- Walsh also held controlling interest in two firms that received more than $3.5 million for leasing an aircraft and providing pilot services to Tyco between 1996 and 2002.
- Stephen Foss received $751,101 for supplying a Cessna Citation aircraft and pilot services.
- Lord Michael Ashcroft used $2.5 million in Tyco funds to purchase a home.

With his handpicked board in place, Kozlowski opened a Manhattan office overlooking Central Park, although the move was not broadcast to the public. For appearances, the firm maintained its humble Exeter, New Hampshire, office at which Kozlowski preferred to be interviewed. According to *BusinessWeek* magazine, he boasted to a guest, "We don't believe in perks, not even executive parking spots." However, the unpublicized Manhattan office became the firm's unofficial headquarters, and Kozlowski furnished it with every imaginable luxury, using Tyco funds to purchase and decorate apartments for key executives and employees.

Meanwhile, Jeanne Terrile, an analyst from Merrill Lynch who had Tyco as a client, was not impressed with Kozlowski's activities and Tyco's performance. Her job at Merrill Lynch was to make recommendations to investors on whether to buy, hold, or sell specific stocks. After Terrile wrote a negative review of Tyco's rapid acquisitions and mergers and refused to upgrade Merrill's position on Tyco's stock, Kozlowski met with David Komansky, the CEO of Merrill Lynch. Although the subject of the meeting was never confirmed, shortly thereafter Terrile was replaced by Phua Young and Merrill's recommendation for Tyco was upgraded to "buy" from "accumulate." Merrill Lynch continued as one of Tyco's top underwriters as well as one of its primary advisers for mergers and acquisitions.

Between 1997 and 2001, Tyco's revenues climbed 48.7 percent annually and its pretax operating margins increased to 22.1 percent. The pace of mergers and acquisitions escalated, assisted by Mark Swartz, Tyco's CFO. In February 2002, Tyco announced that it had spent over $8 billion on more than seven hundred acquisitions in the last three years. Some of the merged companies were dissatisfied with the arrangement. Kozlowski forced acquired companies to scale back sharply, eliminating any segments that were not profitable. The toll on workers in these companies was enormous. Tyco shareholders and directors, however, were thrilled with the company's performance, increasing Kozlowski's salary from $8 million in 1997 to $170 million in 1999, making him the second-highest-paid CEO in the United States at the time.

Between 1997 and 2002, Kozlowski's charismatic leadership style combined with the firm's decentralized corporate structure meant that few people, including members of the board of directors, accurately understood the firm's activities and finances. Tyco was organized into four distinct divisions—fire protection (53 percent); valves, pipes, and other flow-control devices (23 percent); electrical and electronic components (13 percent); and packaging materials (11 percent)—and there was little interaction between them. Each division's president reported directly to Kozlowski, who in turn reported to the board.

Those who dared to suggest that there were red flags at Tyco were shot down, including Jeanne Terrile at Merrill Lynch and David W. Tice, a short seller who questioned whether Tyco's use of large reserves in connection with its acquisitions was obscuring its financial results. A nonpublic investigation by the Securities and Exchange Commission (SEC) resulted only in Tyco amending its earnings per share (up 2 cents per share for the last quarter of 1999, and down 2 cents for the first quarter of 2000).

THE FALL OF DENNIS KOZLOWSKI AND OTHERS

In early 2002, Kozlowski announced Tyco's split of its four divisions into independent, publicly traded companies: Security and Electronics, Healthcare, Fire Protection and Flow Control, and Financial Services. Kozlowski stated, "I am extremely proud of Tyco's performance. We have built a great portfolio of businesses and over the five years ended September 30, 2001, we have delivered earnings per share growth at a compounded annual rate of over 40 percent and industry-leading operating profit margins in each of our businesses. During this same period, we have increased annual free cash flow from $240 million in 1996 to $4.8 billion in fiscal 2001. Nonetheless, even with this performance, Tyco is trading at a 2002 P/E multiple of 12.0x, a discount of almost 50% to the S&P 500."

Soon after, everything began to crumble. The board of directors learned that Frank Walsh (one of its members) had received a $20 million commission for his part in securing and aiding the CIT merger, without the knowledge of the rest of the board. Walsh was fined and later resigned. Troubled by the notion that Kozlowski had made a major payment without informing them, board members launched an investigation into whether other board members had earned such commissions. The probe uncovered numerous expense abuses.

Also in 2002, the New York State Bank Department observed large sums of money moving in and out of Tyco's accounts. What made this unusual was that the funds were being transferred into Kozlowski's personal accounts. Authorities discovered that Kozlowski had sought to avoid around $1 million in New York state import taxes.

After purchasing around $14 million in rare artwork, Kozlowski had the invoices shipped to New Hampshire, although the paintings were actually destined for his apartment in Manhattan. To assist in perpetrating the fraud, Kozlowski instructed the shipping company to send empty boxes to New Hampshire along with the invoices. Kozlowski was caught in the act and ended up facing jail time and having to pay out over $100 million in restitutions and back taxes. Learning that he was about to be indicted for tax evasion, Kozlowski resigned as CEO on June 2, 2002. On June 3, he was arrested, but the scandal had barely begun.

In September of that year, Dennis Kozlowski and Mark Swartz, who also had resigned, were indicted on thirty-eight felony counts for allegedly stealing $170 million from Tyco and fraudulently selling an additional $430 million in stock options. Among other allegations, Kozlowski was accused of taking $242 million from a program intended to help Tyco employees buy company stock. Together with former legal counsel Mark Belnick, the three faced criminal charges and a civil complaint from the SEC. Kozlowski was also accused of granting $106 million to various employees through "loan forgiveness" and relocation programs. Swartz was also charged with falsifying documents in this loan program in the amount of $14 million. Kozlowski and Swartz were sentenced from eight and one-third years to twenty-five years in prison with the possibility of reducing the minimum by one-sixth due to good behavior and enrollment in prison programs. Belnick was charged with larceny and attempting to steer a federal investigation, as well as taking more than $26 million from Tyco. In 2006, he agreed to pay $100,000 in penalties to the SEC.

In addition, several former board members have been cited for conflict of interest. Frank Walsh pleaded guilty and agreed to repay $20 million plus an additional $2 million in court costs. Jerry Boggess, the president of Tyco Fire and Security Division,

was fired and accused of creating a number of "bookkeeping issues" negatively impacting earnings of shareholders. Richard Scalzo, the PriceWaterhouse auditor who signed off on Tyco's 2002 audit, was fired. Tyco's stock plunged from $60 per share in January 2002 to $18 per share in December 2002, and investors lost millions of dollars. Many of the firm's 260,000 employees were also shareholders and watched their savings dwindle. Tyco's retirees found that their savings and retirement plans, which were tied up in company shares, plummeted with the company's stock price.

In 2005, Kozlowski and Swartz both were found guilty on twenty-two of twenty-three counts of grand larceny, conspiracy, and falsifying business records and violating business law. The judge ordered both to pay $134 million to Tyco. Kozlowski was also ordered to pay a $70 million fine and Swartz a $35 million fine. Jail time for both appears to be a little less than seven years in a state facility. Both have appealed their sentences, but their sentences have so far been upheld.

REBUILDING AN EMPIRE

After Kozlowski's resignation, Edward Breen replaced him as CEO. The company filed suit against Dennis Kozlowski and Mark Swartz for more than $100 million. The SEC allows companies to sue insiders who profited by buying and selling company stock within a six-month period. Tyco stated, "To hold him accountable for his misconduct, we seek not only full payment for the funds he misappropriated but also punitive damages for the serious harm he did to Tyco and its shareholders."

Breen launched a review of the company's accounting and corporate governance practices to determine whether any other fraud had occurred. Although the probe uncovered no additional fraud, the firm announced that it would restate its 2002 financial results by $382.2 million. In a regulatory filing, Tyco's new management declared that the firm's previous management had "engaged in a pattern of aggressive accounting which, even when in accordance with Generally Accepted Accounting Principles, was intended to increase reported earnings above what they would have been if more conservative accounting had been employed." Although Tyco's investigations located no further fraud, over the next six months the company repeatedly restated its financial results and took accounting charges totaling more than $2 billion.

To restore investors' faith, Tyco's new management team reorganized the company and recovered some of the funds allegedly taken by Kozlowski. At its annual meeting, shareholders elected a new board of directors, voted to make future executive severance agreements subject to shareholder approval, and voted to require the board chair to be an independent person rather than a Tyco CEO.

In 2006, Breen announced Tyco's split into three entities: Tyco Healthcare ($10 billion, 40,000 employees), one of the world's leading diversified health-care companies; Tyco Electronics ($12 billion, 88,000 employees), the world's largest passive electronic components manufacturer; and a combination of Tyco Fire & Security and Engineered Products & Services (TFS/TEPS) ($18 billion, 118,000 employees), a global business with leading positions in residential and commercial security, fire protection, and industrial products and services. Tyco has survived doomsday predictions, bringing in over $40 billion in revenue before the split, and preserving employee jobs and pensions. Tyco has worked hard to overcome its negative image.

In 2002, Eric Pillmore was hired as Vice President of Corporate Governance. His job was to transform Tyco from a model of poor governance to an exemplary leader of corporate governance done right. Pillmore installed a corporate ethics program, replacing 90% of headquarters staff. During his five years at Tyco, he helped to implement a dramatic corporate culture turnaround. Today Tyco's ethics program stands as a role model for how one can clean up corporate misconduct.

Tyco's efforts to rebuild its image have met with some success. In 2008, Tyco International was named Corporate Citizen of the Year by Catholic Charities for the company's work in helping the homeless in Mercer County, New Jersey. Kozlowski and company, however, have not recovered as well. Kozlowski and Swartz continue to appeal their convictions, most recently to the U.S. Supreme Court, but so far their efforts have been rebuffed.

CONCLUSION

The Tyco scandal offers major lessons for the business world, particularly in areas of corporate conduct. Above all, the story of Dennis Kozlowski shows what happens when too much company power is put into the hands of an individual—it can lead to a decentralized corporate structure that makes it difficult to detect misconduct. Tyco's story also reveals the decreasing tolerance that today's government and investors have for misconduct in any form, as even members of Tyco's board of directors faced consequences for their unethical behavior.

Tyco's survival proves that some companies can survive major ethical scandals if they take the correct courses of action. In response to the scandal, Tyco took actions that went beyond the bare minimum of what was needed. Although an investigation did not uncover additional fraud, the company still restated its financial results by hundreds of millions of dollars. It took measures to restore shareholder confidence by reorganizing the company and implementing safeguards to ensure greater objectivity on the part of the board of directors. As a result of its quick actions, the company has recovered significantly and has been praised by the public.

While the fortunes of Tyco International seem to be on the rebound, former CEO Dennis Kozlowski's fate remains in the hands of the law. After his sentencing in 2005 to twenty-five years in jail for grand larceny, securities fraud, other crimes, and for stealing $137 million in unauthorized bonuses as well as selling $410 million in inflated stock, Kozlowski remains adamant about his innocence. In an interview with Morley Safer for *60 Minutes*, Kozlowski claimed that jealous jurors sentenced him out of spite, not because he had done anything wrong. Kozlowski to this day feels that he was wrongly sentenced and claims to have no regrets over his dishonest behavior.

On an ironic note, Kozlowski did have the foresight to recognize the impending subprime mortgage disaster that came to a head in 2008. Perhaps this just shows that it takes a criminal to know others.

QUESTIONS

1. What role did Tyco's corporate culture play in the scandal?

2. How did did Dennis Kozlowski have the opportunity to steal $137 million in unauthorized bonuses?

3. Why is Kozlowski, now a prisoner for a long time, unrepentant about his conduct as CEO of Tyco?

SOURCES

Bandler, James, and Jerry Guidera, "Tyco Ex-CEO's Party for Wife Cost $2.1 Million, but Had Elvis," *Wall Street Journal*, September 17, 2002, p. A1.

Bianco, Anthony, William Symonds, and Nanette Byrnes, "The Rise and Fall of Dennis Kozlowski," *BusinessWeek*, December 23, 2002, pp. 64–77.

Bray, Chad, "Ex-Execs Kozlowski, Swartz Appeal to US Supreme Court," *Wall Street Journal*, April 14, 2009, http://online.wsj.com/article/BT-CO-20090414-711331.html, accessed April 28, 2009.

Cohen, Laurie P., "Tyco Ex-Counsel Claims Auditors Knew of Loans," *Wall Street Journal*, October 22, 2002, http://online.wsj.com/article/SB103524176089398951.html?mod=googlewsj, accessed September 10, 2009.

Cohen, Laurie P., and John Hechinger, "Tyco Suits Say Clandestine Pacts Led to Payments," *Wall Street Journal*, June 18, 2002, pp. A3, A10.

Cohen, Laurie P., and Mark Maremont, "Tyco Ex-Director Faces Possible Criminal Charges," *Wall Street Journal*, September 9, 2002, pp. A3, A11.

Cohen, Laurie P., and Mark Maremont, "Tyco Relocations to Florida Are Probed," *Wall Street Journal*, June 10, 2002, pp. A3, A6.

"Corporate Scandals: Tyco, International," MSNBC, www.msnbc.com/news/corpscandal_front.asp?odm=C2ORB, accessed September 10, 2009.

"Former Counsel for Tyco to Settle S.E.C. Charges," Reuters, May 3, 2006, via http://www.nytimes.com/2006/05/03/business/03tyco.html?_r=1&adxnnl=1&oref=slogin&adxn nlx=1214041391-Z+lUjZjI6TaIADXDvRXb8w, accessed September 10, 2009.

Gaspaino, Charles, "Merrill Replaced Its Tyco Analyst After Meeting," *Wall Street Journal*, September 17, 2002, pp. C1, C13.

Guidera, Jerry, "Veteran Tyco Director Steps Down," *Wall Street Journal*, November 12, 2002, p. A8.

"History," Tyco International, http://tyco.com/wps/wcm/connect/tyco+who+we+are/Who+We+Are/History, accessed September 10, 2009.

Lavelle, Louis, "Rebuilding Trust in Tyco," *BusinessWeek*, November 25, 2002, pp. 94–96.

Lublin, Loann, and Jerry Guidera, "Tyco Board Criticized on Kozlowski," *Wall Street Journal*, June 7, 2002, p. A5.

Maremont, Mark, "Tyco May Report $1.2 Billion in Fresh Accounting Problems," *Wall Street Journal*, April 30, 2003, http://online.wsj.com/article/SB105166908562976400.html?mod=googlewsj, accessed September 10, 2009.

Maremont, Mark, "Tyco Seeks Hefty Repayments from Former Financial Officer," *Wall Street Journal*, October 7, 2002, p. A6.

Maremont, Mark, and John Hechinger, "Tyco's Ex-CEO Invested in Fund Run by Director," *Wall Street Journal*, October 23, 2002, http://online.wsj.com/article/SB1035329530787240111.html?mod=googlewsj, accessed October 19, 2009.

McCoy, Kevin, "Directors' Firms on Payroll at Tyco," *USA Today*, September 18, 2002, p. 1B.

McCoy, Kevin, "Investigators Scrutinize $20M Tyco Fee," *USA Today*, September 16, 2002, p. 1B.

McCoy, Kevin, "Tyco Acknowledges More Accounting Tricks," *USA Today*, December 31, 2002, p. 3B.

Panter, Gary, "The Big Kozlowski," *Fortune*, November 18, 2002, pp. 123–126.

"Prisoner Dennis Kozlowski: Still Unrepentant," *Sox First*, February 5, 2008, www.soxfirst.com/50226711/prisoner_dennis_kozlowski_still_unrepentant.php, accessed May 5, 2009.

White, Ben, "Ex-Tyco Officers Sentenced: Pair Get Up to 25 Years in Prison, Must Pay Almost $240 Million," *Washington Post*, September 20, 2005, p. D01.

Mattel Responds to Ethical Challenges

Mattel, Inc. is a world leader in the design, manufacture, and marketing of family products. Well-known for toy brands such as Barbie, Fisher-Price, Disney, Hot Wheels, Matchbox, Tyco, Cabbage Patch Kids, and board games such as Scrabble, the company boasts nearly $6 billion in annual revenue. Headquartered in El Segundo, California, with offices in thirty-six countries, Mattel markets its products in more than one hundred and fifty nations.

HISTORY OF MATTEL, INC.

It all started in a California garage workshop when Ruth and Elliot Handler and Matt Matson founded Mattel in 1945. The company started out making picture frames, but the founders soon recognized the profitability of the toy industry and switched their emphasis to toys. Mattel became a publicly owned company in 1960, with sales exceeding $100 million by 1965. Over the next forty years, Mattel went on to become the world's largest toy company in terms of revenue.

In spite of its overall success, Mattel has had its share of losses over its history. During the mid to late 1990s, Mattel lost millions to declining sales and bad business acquisitions. In January 1997, Jill Barad took over as Mattel's CEO. Barad's management style was characterized as strict and her tenure at the helm proved challenging for many employees. While Barad had been successful in building the Barbie brand to $2 billion by the end of

the twentieth century, growth slowed in the early twenty-first. Declining sales at outlets such as Toys "R" Us marked the start of some difficulties for the retailer; Barad accepted responsibility for these problems and resigned in 2000.

Robert Eckert replaced Barad as CEO. Aiming to turn things around, Eckert sold unprofitable units and cut hundreds of jobs. In 2000, under Eckert, Mattel was granted the highly sought-after licensing agreement for products related to the *Harry Potter* series of books and movies. The company continued to flourish and build its reputation, even earning the Corporate Responsibility Award from UNICEF in 2003. Mattel released its first Annual Corporate Responsibility Report the following year. By 2008 Mattel had fully realized a turnaround and was recognized as one of *Fortune* magazine's "100 Best Companies to Work For" and *Forbes* magazine's "100 Most Trustworthy U.S. Companies."

MATTEL'S CORE PRODUCTS

Barbie and American Girl

Among its many lines of popular toy products, Mattel is famous for owning top girls' brands. In 1959, Mattel introduced a product that would change its future forever: the Barbie doll. One of the founders, Ruth Handler, had noticed how her daughter loved playing with paper cutout dolls. She decided

This case was prepared by Debbie Thorne, John Fraedrich, O.C. Ferrell, and Jennifer Jackson, with the editorial assistance of Jennifer Sawayda. This case is meant for classroom discussion, and is not meant to illustrate either effective or ineffective handling of an administrative, ethical, or legal decision by management. All sources used for this case were obtained through publicly available material and the Mattel website.

to create a doll based on an adult rather than on a baby. Barbie took off to become one of Mattel's critical product lines and the number-one girls' brand in the world. Since her introduction, Mattel has sold more than 1 billion Barbie dolls in more than 150 countries. The Barbie line today includes dolls, accessories, Barbie software, and a broad assortment of licensed products such as books, apparel, food, home furnishings, home electronics, and movies.

To supplement the Barbie line, in 1998 Mattel acquired a popular younger type of doll. Mattel announced it would pay $700 million to Pleasant Company for its high-end American Girl collection. American Girl dolls are sold with books about their lives, which take place during important periods of U.S. history. The American Girl brand includes several book series, accessories, clothing for dolls and girls, and a magazine that ranks in the top ten American children's magazines.

Hot Wheels

Hot Wheels roared into the toy world in 1968. More than forty years later, the brand is hotter than ever and includes high-end collectibles, NASCAR (National Association for Stock Car Auto Racing) and Formula One models for adults, high-performance cars, track sets, and play sets for children of all ages. The brand is connected with racing circuits worldwide. More than 15 million boys aged five to fifteen are avid collectors, each owning forty-one cars on average. Two Hot Wheels cars are sold every second of every day. The brand began with cars designed to run on a track and has evolved into a "lifestyle" brand with licensed Hot Wheels shirts, caps, lunch boxes, backpacks, and more. Together, Hot Wheels and Barbie generate 45 percent of Mattel's revenue and 65 percent of its profits.

Cabbage Patch Kids

Since the introduction of mass-produced Cabbage Patch Kids in 1982, more than 90 million dolls have been sold worldwide. In 1994, Mattel took over selling these beloved dolls after purchasing production rights from Hasbro. In 1996, Mattel created a new line of Cabbage Patch doll, called Snacktime Kids, which was expected to meet with immense success. The Snacktime Kids had moving mouths that enabled children to "feed" them plastic snacks. However, the product backfired. The toy had no on/off switch and reports of children getting their fingers or hair caught in the dolls' mouths surfaced during the 1996 holiday season. Mattel voluntarily pulled the dolls from store shelves by January 1997, and offered consumers a cash refund of $40 on returned dolls. The U.S. Consumer Product Safety Commission applauded Mattel's handling of the Snacktime Kids situation. Mattel effectively managed a situation that could easily have created bad publicity or a crisis situation. Mattel stopped producing Cabbage Patch Kids in 2000.

MATTEL'S COMMITMENT TO ETHICS AND SOCIAL RESPONSIBILITY

Mattel's core products and business environment create many ethical issues. Because the company's products are designed primarily for children, the company must be sensitive to social concerns about children's rights. It must also be aware that the international environment often complicates business transactions. Different legal systems and cultural expectations about business can create ethical conflicts. Finally, the use of technology may present ethical dilemmas, especially regarding consumer privacy. Mattel has recognized these potential issues and taken steps to strengthen its commitment to business ethics. The company also purports to take a stand on social responsibility, encouraging its employees and consumers to do the same.

Privacy and Marketing Technology

One issue Mattel has tried to address repeatedly is that of privacy and online technology.

Advances in technology have created special marketing issues for Mattel. The company recognizes that, because it markets to children, it must communicate with parents regarding its corporate marketing strategy. Mattel has taken steps to inform both children and adults about its philosophy regarding Internet-based marketing tools, such as the Hot Wheels website. This website contains a lengthy online privacy policy, part of which reads:

> Mattel, Inc. and its family of companies ("Mattel") are committed to protecting your online privacy when visiting a website operated by us. We do not collect and keep any personal information online from you unless you volunteer it and you are 13 or older. We also do not collect and keep personal information online from children under the age of 13 without consent of a parent or legal guardian, except in limited circumstances authorized by law and described in this policy. (Mattel, Inc., Online Privacy Policy, http://www.hotwheels.com/policy.asp, accessed March 8, 2009)

By assuring parents that their children's privacy will be respected, Mattel demonstrates that it takes its responsibility of marketing to children seriously.

Expectations of Mattel's Business Partners

Mattel, Inc. is also making a serious commitment to business ethics in its dealings with other industries. In late 1997, the company completed its first full ethics audit of each of its manufacturing sites as well as the facilities of its primary contractors. The audit revealed that the company was not using any child labor or forced labor, a problem plaguing other overseas manufacturers. However, several contractors were found to be in violation of Mattel's safety and human rights standards and were asked to change their operations or risk losing Mattel's business. The company now conducts an independent monitoring council audit in manufacturing facilities every three years.

In an effort to continue its strong record on human rights and related ethical standards, Mattel instituted a code of conduct entitled Global Manufacturing Principles in 1997. One of these principles requires all Mattel-owned and contracted manufacturing facilities to favor business partners committed to ethical standards comparable with those of Mattel. Other principles relate to safety, wages, and adherence to local laws. Mattel's audits and subsequent code of conduct were designed as preventative, not punitive, measures. The company is dedicated to creating and encouraging responsible business practices throughout the world.

Mattel also claims to be committed to its workforce. As one company consultant noted, "Mattel is committed to improving the skill level of workers...[so that they] will experience increased opportunities and productivity." This statement reflects Mattel's concern for relationships between and with employees and business partners. The company's code is a signal to potential partners, customers, and other stakeholders that Mattel has made a commitment to fostering and upholding ethical values.

Legal and Ethical Business Practices

Mattel prefers to partner with businesses similarly committed to high ethical standards. At a minimum, partners must comply with the local and national laws of the countries in which they operate. In addition, all partners must respect the intellectual property of the company, and support Mattel in the protection of assets such as patents, trademarks, or copyrights. They are also responsible for product safety and quality, protecting the environment, customs, evaluation and monitoring, and compliance.

Mattel's business partners must have high standards for product safety and quality, adhering to practices that meet Mattel's safety and quality standards. In recent years, however, safety standards have been seriously violated, which will be discussed in more detail later. Also, because of the global nature of Mattel's business and its history of leadership in this area, the company insists that business partners strictly adhere to local and international customs laws. Partners must comply with all import and export regulations. To assist in compliance with standards, Mattel insists that all manufacturing facilities provide the following:

- Full access for on-site inspections by Mattel or parties designated by Mattel

- Full access to those records that will enable Mattel to determine compliance with its principles

- An annual statement of compliance with Mattel's Global Manufacturing Principles, signed by an officer of the manufacturer or manufacturing facility ("Mattel's Commitment to Ethics," *eBusiness Ethics*, http://www.e-businessethics.com/mattel9. htm, accessed May 8, 2009)

With the creation of the Mattel Independent Monitoring Council (MIMCO), Mattel became the first global consumer products company to apply such a system to facilities and core contractors worldwide. The company seeks to maintain an independent monitoring system that provides checks and balances to help ensure that standards are met.

If certain aspects of Mattel's manufacturing principles are not being met, Mattel will try to work with contractors to help them fix their problems. New partners will not be hired unless they meet Mattel's standards. If corrective action is advised but not taken, Mattel will terminate its relationship with the partner in question. Overall, Mattel is committed to both business success and ethical standards, and it recognizes that it is part of a continuous improvement process.

Mattel Children's Foundation

Mattel takes its social responsibilities very seriously. Through the Mattel Children's Foundation, established in 1978, the company promotes philanthropy and community involvement among its employees and makes charitable investments to better the lives of children in need. Funding priorities have included building a new Mattel Children's Hospital at the University of California, Los Angeles (UCLA), sustaining the Mattel Family Learning Program, and promoting giving among Mattel employees.

In November 1998, Mattel donated a multiyear, $25 million gift to the UCLA Children's Hospital. The gift was meant to support the existing hospital and provide for a new state-of-the-art facility. In honor of Mattel's donation, the hospital was renamed Mattel Children's Hospital at UCLA.

The Mattel Family Learning Program utilizes computer learning labs as a way to advance children's basic skills. Now numbering more than eighty throughout the United States, Hong Kong, Canada, and Mexico, the labs offer software and technology designed to help children with special needs or limited English proficiency.

Mattel employees are also encouraged to participate in a wide range of volunteer activities, including Team Mattel, a program that allows Mattel employees to partner with local Special Olympics programs. Employees serving on boards of local nonprofit organizations or helping with ongoing nonprofit programs are eligible to apply for volunteer grants supporting their organizations. Mattel employees contributing to higher education or to nonprofit organizations serving children in need are eligible to have their personal donations matched dollar for dollar up to $5,000 annually.

International Manufacturing Principles

As a U.S.-based multinational company owning and operating facilities and contracting worldwide, Mattel's Global Manufacturing Principles reflects the company's needs both to conduct manufacturing responsibly and to respect the cultural, ethical, and philosophical differences of the countries in which it operates. These principles set uniform standards across Mattel manufacturers and attempt to benefit both employees and consumers.

Mattel's principles cover issues such as wages, work hours, child labor, forced labor, discrimination, freedom of association, and working conditions. Workers must be paid at least minimum wage or a wage that meets local industry standards (whichever is greater). No one under the age of sixteen or the local age limit (whichever is higher) may be allowed to work for Mattel facilities. Mattel refuses to work with facilities that use forced or prison labor, or to use these types of labor itself. Additionally, Mattel does not tolerate discrimination. The company states that an individual should be hired and employed based on his or her ability—not on individual characteristics or beliefs. Mattel recognizes all employees' rights to choose to affiliate with organizations or associations without interference. Regarding working conditions, all Mattel facilities and its business partners must provide safe working environments for their employees.

OVERSEAS MANUFACTURING

Despite Mattel's best efforts, not all overseas manufacturers have faithfully adhered to its high standards. Mattel has come under scrutiny over its sale of unsafe products. In 2007, Mattel announced recalls of toys containing lead paint. The problem surfaced when a European retailer discovered lead paint on a toy. An estimated 10 million individual toys produced in China were affected. Mattel quickly stopped production at Lee Der, the company officially producing the recalled toys, after it was discovered that Lee Der had purchased lead-tainted paint to be used on the toys. Mattel blamed the fiasco on the manufacturers' desire to save money in the face of increasing prices. "In the last three or five years, you've seen labor prices more than double, raw material prices double or triple," CEO Eckert said in an interview, "and I think that there's a lot of pressure on

guys that are working at the margin to try to save money."

The situation began when Early Light Industrial Co., a subcontractor for Mattel owned by Hong Kong toy tycoon Choi Chee Ming, subcontracted the painting of parts of *Cars* toys to another China-based vendor. The vendor, named Hong Li Da, decided to source paint from a nonauthorized third-party supplier—a violation of Mattel's requirement to use paint supplied directly by Early Light. The products were found to contain "impermissible levels of lead."

When it was announced that another of Early Light's subcontractors, Lee Der Industrial Company, used the same lead paint found on *Cars* products, China immediately suspended the company's export license. Afterward, Mattel pinpointed three paint suppliers working for Lee Der—Dongxin, Zhongxin, and Mingdai. This paint was used by Lee Der to produce Mattel's line of Fisher-Price products. It is said that Lee Der purchased the paint from Mingdai due to an intimate friendship between the two company's owners. In the latter part of 2007, Zhang Shuhong, operator of Lee Der, hung himself after paying his 5,000 staff members.

That same year, Mattel was forced to recall several more toys because of powerful magnets in the toys that could come loose and pose a choking hazard for young children. If more than one magnet is swallowed, the magnets can attract each other inside the child's stomach, causing potentially fatal complications. Over 21 million Mattel toys were recalled in all, and parents filed several lawsuits claiming that these Mattel products harmed their children.

At first, Mattel blamed Chinese subcontractors for the huge toys recalls; but the company later accepted a portion of the blame for the trouble, while maintaining that Chinese manufacturers were largely at fault. The Chinese viewed the situation quite differently. As reported by the state-run Xinhua news agency, the spokesperson for China's state Administration of Quality Supervision and Inspection and Quarantine (AQSIQ) said, "Mattel should improve its product design and supervision over product quality. Chinese original equipment manufacturers were doing the job just as importers requested, and the toys conformed to the U.S. regulations and standards at the time of the production." Mattel also faced criticism from many of its consumers, who believed Mattel was denying culpability by placing much of the blame on China. Mattel was later awarded the 2007 "Bad Product" Award by Consumers International.

How did this crisis occur under the watch of a company praised for its ethics and high safety standards? Although Mattel had investigated its contractors, it did not audit the entire supply chain, including subcontractors. This oversight left room for these violations to occur. Mattel has moved to enforce a rule that subcontractors cannot hire suppliers two or three tiers down. In a statement, Mattel claimed to have spent more than 50,000 hours investigating its vendors and testing its toys. Mattel also has announced a three-point plan that aims to tighten Mattel's control of production, discover and prevent the unauthorized use of subcontractors, and test the products itself rather than depending on contractors.

THE CHINESE GOVERNMENT'S REACTION

Chinese officials eventually did admit the government's failure to properly protect the public. The Chinese government is now promising to tighten supervision of exported products, but effective supervision is challenging in such a large country that is so burdened with corruption. In 2008, the Chinese government launched a four-month-long nationwide product quality campaign, offering intensive training courses to domestic toy manufacturers to help them brush up on their knowledge of international product standards and safety awareness. As a result of the crackdown, the state AQSIQ announced that it had revoked the licenses of

more than 600 Chinese toy makers. Also in 2008, the State Administration for Commerce and Industry (SACI) released a report claiming that 87.5 percent of China's newly manufactured toys met quality requirements. Although this represents an improvement, the temptation to cut corners remains strong in a country that uses price, not quality, as its main competitive advantage. Where there is demand, some people will always try to turn a quick profit.

MATTEL VERSUS FORMER EMPLOYEE AND MGA

Since 2004, Mattel has been embroiled in a bitter intellectual property rights battle with former employee Carter Bryant and MGA Entertainment Inc. over rights to MGA's popular Bratz dolls. Carter Bryant, an on-again/off-again Mattel employee, designed the Bratz dolls and pitched them to MGA. A few months after the pitch, Bryant left Mattel to work at MGA, which began producing Bratz in 2001. In 2002, Mattel launched an investigation into whether Bryant had designed the Bratz dolls while employed with Mattel. After two years of investigation, Mattel sued Bryant. A year later MGA fired off a suit of its own, claiming that Mattel was creating Barbies with looks similar to those of Bratz in an effort to eliminate the competition. Mattel answered by expanding its own suit to include MGA and its CEO, Isaac Larian.

For decades, Barbie had reigned supreme on the doll market. However, Bratz dolls have given Barbie a run for her money. In 2005, four years after the brand's debut, Bratz sales were at $2 billion. At the same time, Barbie was suffering from declining sales. In 2008 Barbie's gross sales fell by 6 percent, although Bratz was not immune to sluggish sales either once consumers began to cut back on their spending during the 2008–2009 recession.

Much evidence appears to point toward Bryant having conceived of Bratz dolls while at Mattel. Four years after the initial suit was filed, Bryant settled with Mattel under an undisclosed set of terms. However, although some decisions were made, the battle between Mattel and MGA has continued. In July 2008, a jury deemed MGA and its CEO liable for what it termed "intentional interference" regarding Bryant's contract with Mattel. In August 2008, Mattel received damages in the range of $100 million. Although Mattel first requested damages of $1.8 billion, the company was pleased with the principle behind the victory.

In December 2008, Mattel appeared to win another victory when a California judge banned MGA from issuing or selling any more Bratz dolls. In the worst-case scenario, MGA will have to discontinue its line of Bratz dolls completely or hand Bratz over to Mattel. Some analysts, however, think this outcome is unlikely. Instead, they expect Mattel to work out a deal with MGA in which MGA can continue to sell Bratz dolls as long as Mattel shares in some of the profits. MGA plans to appeal the court ruling. Whatever the outcome, Mattel has managed to gain some control over Barbie's stiffest competition.

MATTEL LOOKS TOWARD THE FUTURE

Like all major companies, Mattel has weathered its share of storms. In recent years, the company has faced a series of difficult and potentially crippling challenges. During the wave of toy recalls, some analysts suggested that the company's reputation was battered beyond repair. Mattel, however, has refused to go quietly. Although the company admits to poorly handling recent affairs, it is attempting to rectify its mistakes and to prevent future mistakes as well. The company appears to be dedicated to shoring up its ethical defenses to protect both itself and its customers.

With the economic future of the United States uncertain, Mattel may be in for slow growth for some time to come. What is certain is Mattel's commitment to rebuilding its reputation as an ethical company. Mattel is hard at work restoring goodwill and faith in its brands, even as it continues to be plagued with residual distrust over the lead paint scandal. Reputations are hard won and easily lost, but Mattel appears to be steadfast in its commitment to corporate ethics and delivering quality products.

QUESTIONS

1. Do manufacturers of products for children have special obligations to consumers and society? If so, what are these responsibilities?

2. How effective has Mattel been at encouraging ethical and legal conduct by its manufacturers? What changes and additions would you make to the company's Global Manufacturing Principles?

3. To what extent was Mattel responsible for issues related to its production of toys in China? How might Mattel have avoided these issues?

SOURCES

"About Us: Philanthropy," Mattel, http://www.mattel.com/about-us/philanthropy/, accessed September 8, 2009.

American Girl, www.americangirl.com, accessed September 8, 2009.

Bannon, Lisa, and Carlta Vitzhum, "One-Toy-Fits-All: How Industry Learned to Love the Global Kid," *Wall Street Journal,* April 29, 2003, http://online.wsj.com/article/SB105156578439799000.html?mod=googlewsj, accessed September 10, 2009.

"Barbie," Mattel, http://www.mattel.com/our-toys/barbie.aspx, accessed September 7, 2009.

Barboza, David, "Scandal and Suicide in China: A Dark Side of Toys," Iht.Com, August 23, 2007, http://www.iht.com/articles/2007/08/23/business/23suicide.php?page=1, accessed September 8, 2009.

Barboza, David, and Louise Story, "Toymaking in China, Mattel's Way," *New York Times,* July 26, 2007, http://www.nytimes.com/2007/07/26/business/26toy.html?pagewanted-1&_r-3&hp, accessed September 8, 2009.

"Bratz Loses Battle of the Dolls," BBC News, December 5, 2008, http://news.bbc.co.uk/2/hi/business/7767270.stm, accessed September 8, 2009.

Casey, Nicholas, "Mattel to Get Up to $100 Million in Bratz Case," *Wall Street Journal,* August 27, 2008, http://online.wsj.com/article/SB121978263398273857-email.html, accessed September 8, 2009.

Casey, Nicholas, "Mattel Prevails Over MGA in Bratz-Doll Trial," *Wall Street Journal,* July 18, 2008, pp. B-18, B-19.

Chen, Shu-Ching, "A Blow to Hong Kong's Toy King," Forbes.com, August 15, 2007, http://www.forbes.com/2007/08/15/mattel-china-choi-face-markets-cx_jc_0815autofacescan01.html, accessed September 8, 2009.

"Children's Foundation," Mattel, http://www.mattel.com/about-us/philanthropy/childrenfoundation.aspx, accessed September 8, 2009.

Duryea, Bill, "Barbie-holics: They're Devoted to the Doll," *St. Petersburg Times,* August 7, 1998.

Hitti, Miranda, "9 Million Mattel Toys Recalled," WebMD, August 14, 2007, http://children.webmd.com/news/20070814/9_million_mattel_toys_recalled, accessed September 8, 2009.

"Independent Monitoring Council Completes Audits of Mattel Manufacturing Facilities in Indonesia, Malaysia and Thailand," Mattel, press release, November 15, 2002, http://investor.shareholder.com/mattel/releasedetail.cfm?ReleaseID=95295, accessed September 8, 2009.

"International Bad Product Awards 2007," Consumers International, http://www.consumersinternational.org/Shared_ASP_Files/UploadedFiles/527739D3-1D7B-47AF-B85C-6FD25779149B_InternationalBadProductsAwards-pressbriefing.pdf, accessed September 8, 2009.

"Investors and Media," Mattel, www.mattel.com/about_us/, accessed September 8, 2009.

Keating, Gina, "MGA 'Still Assessing' Impact of Bratz Ruling: CEO," Reuters, December 4, 2008, http://www.reuters.com/article/ousivMolt/idUSTRE4B405820081205, accessed September 8, 2009.

"Learning from Mattel," Tuck School of Business at Dartmouth, http://mba.tuck.dartmouth.edu/pdf/2002-1-0072.pdf, accessed September 8, 2009.

"Mattel Annual Report 2008," http://www.shareholder.com/mattel/downloads/2007AR.pdf, accessed September 8, 2009.

"Mattel Awarded $100M in Doll Lawsuit," *USA Today,* August 27, 2008, p. B-1.

"Mattel CEO Jill Barad and a Toyshop That Doesn't Forget to Play," *New York Times,* October 11, 1998.

"Mattel Children's Foundation Rewards Second Round of Domestic Grants to 34 Nonprofit Organizations," Mattel, December 7, 2005, http://investor.shareholder.com/mattel/releasedetail.cfm?ReleaseID=181309, accessed September 8, 2009.

"Mattel Continues to Lead the Toy Industry with Release of Its First Corporate Social Responsibility Report," October 12, 2004, http://www.shareholder.com/mattel/news/20041012-145079.cfm, accessed September 8, 2009.

"Mattel History," Mattel, http://www.mattel.com/about-us/history/default.aspx, accessed September 8, 2009.

Mattel, Hot Wheels website, www.hotwheels.com, accessed September 8, 2009.

"Mattel, Inc., Launches Global Code of Conduct Intended to Improve Workplace, Workers' Standard of Living," *Canada NewsWire,* November 21, 1997.

"Mattel, Inc., Online Privacy Policy," Mattel, www.hotwheels.com/policy.asp, accessed September 8, 2009.

"Mattel Magnetic Toy Set Recall: Company Has History of Ignoring Product Safety Disclosure Laws. Did It Do So Again?," *Parker Waichman Alonso LLP,* September 4, 2007, http://www.yourlawyer.com/articles/read/13072, accessed September 8, 2009.

"Mattel Recalls Batman™ and One Piece™ Magnetic Action Figure Sets," CPSC, August 14, 2007, http://service.mattel.com/us/recall/J1944CPSC.pdf, accessed September 8, 2009.

"Mattel to Sell Learning Company," Direct, October 2, 2000, http://directmag.com/news/marketing_mattel_sell_learning/, accessed September 8, 2009.

"Mattel and U.S. Consumer Product Safety Commission Announce Voluntary Refund Program for Cabbage Patch Kids Snacktime Kids Dolls," U.S. Consumer Product Safety Commission, Office of Information and Public Affairs, Release No. 97-055, January 6, 1997.

Matzer, Marla, "Deals on Hot Wheels," *Los Angeles Times,* July 22, 1998.

Olshin, Benjamin B., "China, Culture, and Product Recalls," S2R, August 20, 2007, http://www.s2r.biz/s2rpapers/papers-Chinese_Product.pdf, accessed September 8, 2009.

"Product Recalls," Mattel Consumer Relations Answer Center, http://service.mattel.com/us/recall.asp, accessed September 8, 2009.

Raisner, Jack A., "Using the 'Ethical Environment' Paradigm to Teach Business Ethics: The Case of the Maquiladoras," *Journal of Business Ethics,* 1997, http://www.springerlink.com/content/nv62636101163v07/fulltext.pdf, accessed May 10, 2008.

Sellers, Patricia, "The 50 Most Powerful Women in American Business," *Fortune,* October 12, 1998.

Spark, Laura S., "Chinese Product Scares Prompt US Fears," BBC News, July 10 2007, http://news.bbc.co.uk/2/hi/americas/6275758.stm, accessed September 8, 2009.

"Third Toy Recall by Mattel in Five Weeks," *Business Standard,* September 6, 2006, http://www.business-standard.com/india/storypage.php?autono=297057, accessed September 8, 2009.

"Toymaker Mattel Bans Child Labor," *Denver Post,* November 21, 1998.

"UCLA Children's Hospital Receives $25 Million Pledge from Mattel Inc.," November 12, 1998, http://investor.shareholder.com/mattel/releasedetail.cfm?ReleaseID=141937, accessed September 8, 2009.

"The United States Has Not Restricted Imports Under the China Safeguard," U.S. Government Accountability Office, September 2005, http://www.gao.gov/new.items/d051056.pdf, accessed September 8, 2009.

White, Michael, "Barbie Will Lose Some Curves When Mattel Modernizes Icon," *Detroit News,* November 18, 1997.

Home Depot Implements Stakeholder Orientation

When Bernie Marcus and Arthur Blank opened the first Home Depot store in Atlanta in 1979, they forever changed the hardware and home-improvement retailing industry. Marcus and Blank envisioned huge warehouse-style stores stocked with an extensive selection of products offered at the lowest prices. Today, do-it-your-selfers and building contractors can browse from among 40,000 different products for the home and yard, from kitchen and bathroom fixtures to carpeting, lumber, paint, tools, and plant and landscaping items. If a product is not provided in one of the stores, Home Depot offers 250,000 products that can be special-ordered. Some Home Depot stores are open twenty-four hours a day, but customers can also order products online and pick them up from their local Home Depot stores or have them delivered. Additionally, the company offers free home-improvement clinics to teach customers how to tackle everyday projects like tiling a bathroom. For those customers who prefer not to "do it yourself," most stores offer installation services. Well-trained employ-ees, recognizable by their orange aprons, are always on hand to help customers find just the right item or to demonstrate the proper use of a particular tool.

Currently, Home Depot employs more than 300,000 people and operates approxi-mately 2,238 Home Depot stores, mostly in North America and Mexico. It also operates four wholly owned subsidiaries: Apex Supply Company, Georgia Lighting, Maintenance Warehouse, and National Blinds and Wallpaper. The company is the largest home-improvement retailer in the world (although revenue dropped from $81 billion to $65 bil-lion annually during the 2008–2009 recession). Home Depot continues to do things on a grand scale, including putting its corporate muscle behind a tightly focused social responsibil-ity agenda. Every week, 22 million customers visit Home Depot, which means that conflicts associated with providing services in a retail environment are inevitable.

MANAGING CUSTOMER RELATIONSHIPS

Since its inception, Home Depot has been focused on close customer relationships. Part of the company's competitive advantage has always been superior service. In 2006, John Costello was the chief marketing officer or, as he states, chief customer officer. Costello consolidated marketing and merchandising functions to help consumers achieve their goals in home-improvement projects more effectively and efficiently.

According to Costello, "Above all else, a brand is a promise. It says here's what you can expect if you do business with us. Our mission is to empower our customers to achieve the home or condo of their dreams." When Costello arrived in 2002, Home Depot's reputation was faltering. His plan called for overhauling the Home Depot website as well as integrating

This case was developed under the direction of O.C. Ferrell with the editorial assistance of Jennifer Jackson and Jennifer Sawayda. Melanie Drever helped to draft the previous edition. This case was prepared for classroom discussion, rather than to illustrate either effective or ineffective handling of an administrative, ethical, or legal decision by management. All sources used for this case were obtained through publicly available material and the Home Depot website.

mass marketing and direct marketing with in-store experience. It was all integrated with the new Home Depot mantra: "You can do it. We can help." Teams of people from merchandising, marketing, visual merchandising, and operations attempted to provide the very best shopping experience at Home Depot. The philosophy was simple; Home Depot believed that customers should be able to read and understand why one ceiling fan is better than another, while associates (employees) should be able to offer installation and design advice.

In 2008, Frank Bifulco took over as new chief marketing officer and senior vice president. He took over at a tough time for Home Depot. Because of the 2008–2009 recession, consumers were spending less on their homes. As a result, Home Depot's new marketing strategy was to emphasize the store's everyday low prices, high product value, and quality energy-saving products. At the same time, the company cut back on special offers like discounts and promotions. According to Bifulco, the company's energy-saving devices are becoming popular as a way to offset fuel and heating costs, and the relationship between price and value is more important than ever. Home Depot's website is also receiving more traffic as fewer people drive to visit the store.

Despite Home Depot's proactive strategy to address customer issues, Home Depot has had to deal with negative publicity associated with customer-satisfaction measures published by outside sources. The University of Michigan's annual American Customer Satisfaction Index in 2006 showed Home Depot slipping to last place among major U.S. retailers. "This is not competitive and too low to be sustainable. It's very serious," wrote Claes Fornell, professor of business at the University of Michigan. Fornell believed that the drop in satisfaction was one reason why Home Depot's stock was stagnant.

On the other hand, Robert Nardelli, the Home Depot CEO during that time, said that the survey was a "sham." Nardelli pointed out that Fornell created his own ethical concerns when he shorted Home Depot stock before the survey came out (purchase options that would cause Fornell to profit from Home Depot's stock price decreasing). Fornell defended himself by saying that the trades were part of research into a correlation between companies' customer-satisfaction scores and stock price performance, but the University of Michigan banned the practice anyway, indicating concerns over ethical problems with the practice.

Some former managers at Home Depot blamed the service issues on a culture that focused on military principles for execution. Under Nardelli, some employees feared being terminated unless they followed directions to a tee. Harris Interactive's 2005 Reputation Quotient survey ranked Home Depot number twelve among major companies and said that customers appreciated Home Depot's quality services. However, two years later it had lowered to number twenty-seven. Nardelli was ousted and replaced by Frank Blake in January 2007. The start of 2008 seemed more auspicious for Home Depot in terms of reputation, as it was listed as number six on *Fortune's* Most Admired Companies (still trailing behind Lowe's), up from 13 in 2006. Home Depot also bounced back up on the American Customer Satisfaction Index. Although it still trails behind Lowe's, Home Depot ranked 70 percent in 2008 (versus 5 percent at its lowest point).

A good example of a socially responsible activity meant to connect with customers is Home Depot's program to teach children skills related to home improvements. Home Depot provides a program called the Kids Workshop. The workshops are free, with how-to clinics designed for children ages five through twelve, available on the first Saturday of each month between 9 A.M. and noon at all Home Depot stores. Children, accompanied by an adult, use their skills to create objects that can be used in and around their homes or communities. Useful projects that kids can create include toolboxes, fire trucks, and mail organizers, as well as more educational projects such as building a window birdhouse, bughouse, or Declaration of Independence frame. Since 1997, more than 17.5 million projects have been built at Kids Workshops and more than 1 million children built their first toolbox at Home Depot. An average of 75 children attend Kids Workshops, while many stores have 200 kids who attend regularly. Home Depot also offers workshops specially designed for women and for people who have recently bought a new home. These workshops are all free of charge and open to the public.

ENVIRONMENTAL INITIATIVES

Cofounders Marcus and Blank nurtured a corporate culture that emphasized social responsibility, especially with regard to the company's impact on the natural environment. Home Depot began its environmental program on the twentieth anniversary of Earth Day in 1990 by adopting a set of Environmental Principles (see Table 1). These principles have since been adopted by the National Retail Hardware Association and Home Center Institute, which represents more than 46,000 retail hardware stores and home centers.

Guided by these environmental principles, Home Depot has initiated a number of programs to minimize the firm's—and its customers'—impact on the environment. In 1991, the retailer began using store and office supplies, advertising, signs, and shopping bags made with recycled-material content. It also established a process for evaluating the environmental claims made by suppliers. The following year, the firm launched a program to recycle wallboard shipping packaging, which became the industry's first "reverse distribution" program. In addition, it opened the first drive-thru recycling center in Duluth, Georgia, in 1993. In 1994, Home Depot became the first home-improvement retailer to offer wood products from tropical and temperate forests certified as "well-managed" by the Scientific Certification System's Forest Conservation Program. The company also began to replace wooden shipping pallets with reusable "slip sheets" to minimize waste and energy use and to reduce pressure on hardwood resources used to make wood pallets.

In 1999, Home Depot announced that it would endorse independent, third-party forest certification and wood from certified forests.

Table 1 Home Depot's Environmental Principles

The Home Depot acknowledges the importance of conservation. The following principles are Home Depot's response:
- We are committed to improving the environment by selling products that are manufactured, packaged and labeled in a responsible manner, that take the environment into consideration and that provide greater value to our customers.
- We will support efforts to provide accurate, informative product labeling of environmental marketing claims.
- We will strive to eliminate unnecessary packaging.
- We will recycle and encourage the use of materials and products with recycled content.
- We will conserve natural resources by using energy and water wisely and seek further opportunities to improve the resource efficiency of our stores.
- We will comply with environmental laws and will maintain programs and procedures to ensure compliance.
- We are committed to minimizing the environmental health and safety risk for our associates and our customers.
- We will train our employees to enhance understanding of environmental issues and policies and to promote excellence in job performance and all environmental matters.
- We will encourage our customers to become environmentally conscious shoppers.

Source: "The Home Depot Environmental Principles," Home Depot, http://corporate.homedepot.com/wps/portal/Environmental_Principles, accessed May 13, 2009. Reprinted by permission from The Home Depot Headquarters, Homer TLC.

The company joined the Certified Forests Products Council, a nonprofit organization that promotes responsible forest product buying practices and the sale of wood from Certified Well-Managed Forests. Yet environmentalists believed that the company was only interested in appearing environmentally-friendly and was not actually committed to the cause. Therefore, they picketed outside of stores in protest of Home Depot's practice of continuing to sell products made from wood harvested from old growth forests. Led by the Rainforest Action Network, environmentalists have picketed Home Depot and other home center stores for years in an effort to stop the destruction of old growth forests, of which less than 20 percent still survive. Later that year, during Home Depot's twentieth anniversary celebration, Arthur Blank announced that Home Depot would stop selling products made from wood harvested in environmentally sensitive areas.

To be "certified" by the Forest Stewardship Council (FSC), a supplier's wood products must be tracked from the forest, through manufacturing and distribution, to the customer. Harvesting, manufacturing, and distribution practices must ensure a balance of social, economic, and environmental factors. Blank challenged competitors to follow Home Depot's lead, and within two years several had met that challenge, including Lowe's, the number-two home-improvement retailer; Wickes, a lumber company; and Andersen Corporation, a window manufacturer. By 2003, Home Depot reported that it had reduced its purchases of Indonesian lauan, a tropical rainforest hardwood used in door components, by 70 percent, and it continued to increase its purchases of certified sustainable wood products. In addition to sustainable wood products, Home Depot offers compact fluorescent light bulbs (CFLs) in its stores and has even introduced an in-store recycling program for CFL bulbs. Customers can drop off their used bulbs in stores, and Home Depot works with an environmental management company to recycle the bulbs safely and responsibly.

Home Depot made cash and in-kind donations exceeding $50 million in 2008 and awarded $15.5 million in grant monies to housing development organizations. In 2002 the company founded the Home Depot Foundation, which provides additional resources to assist nonprofits in the United States and Canada. The Foundation awards grants to eligible nonprofits three times per year and partners with innovative nonprofits across the country that are working to increase awareness and successfully demonstrate the connection between housing, the urban forest, and the overall health and economic success of their communities. The company has established a carpooling program for more than three thousand employees in the Atlanta area, and remains the only North American home-improvement retailer with full-time staff dedicated to environmental issues.

These efforts have yielded many rewards in addition to improved relations with environmental stakeholders. Home Depot's environmental programs have earned the company an A on the Council on Economic Priorities Corporate Report Card, a Vision of America Award from Keep America Beautiful, and, along with Scientific Certification Systems and Collin Pine, a President's Council for Sustainable Development Award. The company was voted number five in *Fortune* magazine's "America's Most Admired Specialty Retailer" in 2008 and also has been recognized by the U.S. Environmental Protection Agency with its Energy Star Award for Excellence.

Despite the fact that Home Depot has established better relations with some environmental activists, it has not placated all of them. In 2008, Home Depot came under controversy for doing business with two Chilean wood suppliers that supported the building of a dam in the Chilean region of Patagonia, a project that would cause irreparable harm to a fragile ecosystem. An environmental institution known as International Rivers demanded that Home Depot pull its contracts with the suppliers if they refused to abandon the dam project. However, Home Depot's environmental chief Ron Jarvis said that the two suppliers were obeying the 2003 agreement not to cut down endangered forests for tree farms. Since they were also not supplying Home Depot with wood products from native forests, Home Depot had no legitimate reason to cancel the contracts. Additionally, Jarvis maintained that the two Chilean suppliers were only minor players in the dam project and that the company's pull-out would not have much of an effect.

This raises the question of how much responsibility major companies have for the environment, particularly when the company itself is not directly doing harm. Is it fair for environmentalists to target companies simply because they are large? No matter how environmentally-friendly Home Depot attempts to portray itself, these are questions it will likely have to weigh constantly as it struggles to address its environmental stakeholders.

CORPORATE PHILANTHROPY

In addition to its environmental initiatives, Home Depot focuses corporate social responsibility efforts on disaster relief, affordable housing, and at-risk youth. In 2008 the company supported thousands of nonprofit organizations with over $50 million in contributions. The company also posts a Social Responsibility Report on its website, detailing its annual charitable contributions and the community programs in which it has become involved over the years.

Home Depot works with more than 350 affiliates of Habitat for Humanity, a nonprofit organization that constructs and repairs homes for qualified low-income families. In March 2008, Home Depot and Habitat for Humanity announced a five-year initiative to provide funding for creating at least 5,000 energy-efficient homes. The Home Depot Foundation will provide $30 million in support of this program. Home Depot also awards grants to housing projects throughout the nation. One of its grant programs, Affordable Housing Built Responsibly, was used to produce 12,223 homes in 2007.

Home Depot supports YouthBuildUSA, a nonprofit organization that provides training and skill development for young people. YouthBuildUSA gives students the opportunity to help rehabilitate housing for homeless and low-income families. Additionally, Home Depot supports other programs to help at-risk youth, such as Big Brothers/Big Sisters, KaBOOM!, and the National Center for Missing and Exploited Children. Home Depot believes that every child should have a safe and fun place to play. In 2007, Home Depot partnered with KaBOOM! to create 1,000 play spaces in only 1,000 days. Home Depot donated $25 million and 1 million volunteer hours in support of the program.

Home Depot has addressed the growing needs for relief from disasters such as hurricanes, tornadoes, and earthquakes. After the 9/11 terrorist attacks in 2001, the company set up three command centers with more than 200 associates to help coordinate relief supplies such as dust masks, gloves, batteries, and tools to victims and rescue workers. After Hurricanes Katrina, Rita, and Wilma, Home Depot, the Home Depot Foundation, their suppliers, and Home Depot's Homer Fund contributed $9.3 million in cash and materials to support recovery. Home Depot also donated $500,000 to support the tsunami relief efforts of the American Red Cross in Southeast Asia, and donated $300,000 to the American Red Cross for disaster relief for people who suffer from hurricanes. Separately, Home Depot's Homer Fund donated $500,000 to 650 associates who had suffered through Hurricane Gustav in 2008.

EMPLOYEE AND SUPPLIER RELATIONS

Home Depot encourages employees to become involved in the community through volunteer and civic activities. Home Depot, with more than 300,000 employees, provides about 2 million volunteer service hours each year.

In 2005, Home Depot took part in the Corporate Month of Service. With the aid of the nonprofit Hands On Network, more than 40,000 volunteers from the Home Depot were able to help their communities log over 320,000 hours for thirteen hundred neighborhood projects. Home Depot continued to participate in Corporate Months of Service for the next two years.

Home Depot also strives to apply social responsibility to its employment practices, with the goal of assembling a diverse workforce that reflects the population of the markets it serves. However, in 1997 the company settled a class-action lawsuit brought by female employees who claimed they were paid less than male employees, awarded fewer pay raises, and promoted less often. The $87.5 million settlement represented one of the largest settlements of a gender discrimination lawsuit in U.S. history at the time. In announcing the settlement, the company emphasized that it was not admitting to wrongdoing and defended its record, saying it "provides opportunities for all of its associates to develop successful professional careers and is proud of its strong track record of having successful women involved in all areas of the company."

Since the lawsuit, Home Depot has worked to show that it appreciates workforce diversity and seeks to give all its associates an equal chance to be employed and advance in its stores. In 2005, Home Depot formed partnerships with the ASPIRA Association, Inc., the Hispanic Association of Colleges and Universities, and the National Council of La Raza to recruit Hispanic candidates for part-time and full-time positions. Additionally, in 2005, Home Depot became a major member of the American Association of Retired Persons' (AARP) Featured Retirement Program, which helps connect employees 50 years or older with companies that value their experience.

Home Depot also has a strong diversity supplier program. As members of the Women's Business Enterprise National Council and the National Minority Suppliers Development Council, Home Depot has come into contact and done business with a diverse range of suppliers, including many minority- and women-owned businesses. In 2005, the company became a founding member of The Resource Institute, whose mission is to help small minority- and women-owned businesses by providing them with resources and training. Home Depot's supplier diversity program has won it numerous recognitions. It ranked number nineteen on Diversity Business Top 50 Corporate Supplier Diversity Programs in 2006 and won Georgia's Minority Supplier Development Council Corporation of the Year award in 2008.

HOME DEPOT'S RESPONSE TO THE RECESSION

Home Depot's emphasis on expansion changed drastically in light of the 2008–2009 recession. CEO Frank Blake decided to halt expansion and focus on improving existing stores. Blake saw the warning signs of the impending crisis and began halting expansion in early 2007, reducing new store openings from around two a week to five a year, an enormous change from the company's decade of aggressive expansion. In early 2009, he shut down Home Depot's EXPO stores, which largely catered to the wealthier class, estimating that they would lose millions each year. The recession took a significant toll on Home Depot. While its 2007 revenue was over $80 billion, its revenue in 2009 fell to around $65 billion.

Home Depot's reaction to the crisis was swift and decisive. As the crisis worsened in September 2008, Home Depot managers transferred all extra cash to Home Depot headquarters, cut capital spending, and suspended a stock buy-back program in order to avoid losses and prevent having to borrow from the country's lenders. For the first time, Home Depot does not have to borrow money, but is instead paying all its expenses from its own revenue. This is a fiscally conservative strategy aimed at stemming future losses and reducing risk, yet it limits Home Depot's ability to grow and adapt quickly. Home Depot may need to develop new strategies in the future if revenues continue to fall.

Experts predict that if too many companies choose to cut back, the recession may in fact be prolonged. Additionally, Home Depot's tactic may put it at a disadvantage to competitors who choose the opposite approach. Lowe's, for instance, is continuing to expand, taking advantage of the recession's low costs of land and labor. Such an approach is risky, but may prove profitable once the recession ends. Essentially, Lowe's expansion could have one of two consequences: (1) overexpansion at a bad time might result in losses, or (2) its aggressive approach might pay off and make it an even more formidable foe for Home Depot to contend with. It remains to be seen whether Home Depot's cutbacks will keep it ahead of the competition once the recession ends.

A STRATEGIC COMMITMENT TO SOCIAL RESPONSIBILITY

Home Depot has strived to secure a socially responsible reputation with stakeholders. Although it received low scores in the past on customer surveys and the American Customer Satisfaction Index, it has worked hard to boost those scores back up. It has addressed environmentalist concerns by creating new standards and environmental principles to govern its relationship with its suppliers. Despite Home Depot's success, however, it does face challenges in the future. Though it remains the world's largest home retailer, its main competitor Lowe's is picking up the pace, and the recession has created an uncertain future for Home Depot. Still, Home Depot's philanthropic endeavors and its promotion of its low product prices and high value continue to make it a popular shopping destination for customers.

Knowing that stakeholders, especially customers, feel good about a company that actively commits resources to environmental and social issues, company executives believe that social responsibility can and should be a strategic component of Home Depot's business operations. The company should remain committed to its focused strategy of philanthropy,

volunteerism, and environmental initiatives even during the recession. Customers' concerns over social responsibility and green products have not abated, at least in Home Depot's case. Home Depot's sales of green products are still going strong. Its commitment to social responsibility extends throughout the company, fueled by top-level support from the cofounders and reinforced by a corporate culture that places great value on playing a responsible role within the communities it serves.

QUESTIONS

1. On the basis of Home Depot's response to environmentalist issues, describe the attributes (power, legitimacy, urgency) of this stakeholder. Using the Reactive-Defensive-Accommodative-Proactive Scale in Chapter 2 (Table 2.6), assess the company's strategy and performance with environmental and employee stakeholders.

2. As a publicly traded corporation, how can Home Depot justify budgeting so much money for philanthropy? What areas other than the environment, disaster relief, affordable housing, and at-risk youth might be appropriate for strategic philanthropy by Home Depot?

3. Is Home Depot's recessionary strategy of eliminating debt and halting growth a wise one? What would you recommend to the CEO?

SOURCES

"America's Most Admired Companies," *Fortune,* http://money.cnn.com/magazines/fortune/mostadmired/2008/industries/11.html, accessed September 8, 2009.

"Building a Home, Building a Community," The Home Depot Foundation, http://www.homedepotfoundation.org/, accessed September 8, 2009.

Carlton, Jim, "How Home Depot and Activists Joined to Cut Logging Abuse," *Wall Street Journal,* September 26, 2000, p. A1.

"CFL Recycling Program," Home Depot, http://www6.homedepot.com/ecooptions/index.html?MAINSECTION=cflrecycling, accessed September 8, 2009.

"Corporate Financial Review," Home Depot, http://corporate. homedepot.com/en_US/Corporate/Public_Relations/Online_ Press_Kit/Docs/Corp_Financial_Overview.pdf, accessed September 8, 2009.

Daniels, Cora, "To Hire a Lumber Expert, Click Here," *Fortune*, April 3, 2000, pp. 267–270.

Demaster, Sarah, "Use Proper Lumber, Demand Protesters," BNet, April 5, 1999, http://findarticles.com/p/articles/ mi_m0VCW/is_7_25/ai_54373184/, accessed September 8, 2009.

"Fourth Quarter, 2008," The American Customer Satisfaction Index, February 17, 2009, http://www.theacsi.org/index. php?option=com_content&task=view&id=190&Itemid=199, accessed September 8, 2009.

Grimsley, Kirstin Downey, "Home Depot Settles Gender Bias Lawsuit," *Washington Post,* September 20, 1997, p. D1.

"Habitat for Humanity and the Home Depot Foundation Announce National Green Building Effort," Habitat for Humanity, March 20, 2008, http://www.habitat.org/ newsroom/2008archive/03_21_08_Home_Depot.aspx, accessed September 8, 2009.

HarrisInteractive, February 17–March 8, 2008, http://www. harrisinteractive.com/news/mediaaccess/2008/HI_BSC_ REPORT_AnnualRQ_USASummary07-08.pdf, accessed September 8, 2009.

Heher, Ashley M., "Home Depot Reports Loss of $54M, but Beats Estimates," *USA Today,* February 24, 2009, http:// www.usatoday.com/money/companies/earnings/2009-02-24- home-depot_N.htm, accessed September 8, 2009.

"Home Depot Announces Commitment to Stop Selling Old Growth Wood; Announcement Validates Two-Year Grassroots Environmental Campaign," *Common Dreams Newswire,* August 26, 1999, http://www.commondreams.org/ pressreleases/august99/082699c.htm, accessed September 8, 2009.

"The Home Depot to Celebrate 25th Anniversary with Month of Service," PR Newswire, http://www.prnewswire.com/ cgi-bin/stories.pl?ACCT=105&STORY=/www/story/09-23- 2004/0002257339, accessed September 8, 2009.

"Home Depot CEO Nardelli Quits," MSNBC, January 3, 2007, http://www.msnbc.msn.com/id/16451112/, accessed March September 8, 2009.

"The Home Depot Donates $300,000 to American Red Cross for Hurricane Relief and Preparation Efforts," Home Depot, September 2, 2008, http://www. homedepotfoundation.org/redcross08.pdf, accessed September 8, 2009.

"The Home Depot and The Environment," http://corporate. homedepot.com/wps/portal/Environmental_Principles, accessed September 8, 2009.

"The Home Depot Launches Environmental Wood Purchasing Policy," PR Newswire, August 26, 1999, http://www. prnewswire.com/cgi-bin/stories.pl?ACCT=104&STORY=/ www/story/08-26-1999/0001010227&EDATE=, accessed September 8, 2009.

"Home Depot Retools Timber Policy," *Memphis Business Journal,* January 2, 2003, www.bizjournals.com/memphis/ stories/2002/12/30/daily12.html, accessed September 8, 2009.

"Home Depot Vs. Lowe's," CNBC, August 26, 2008, http:// www.cnbc.com/id/26406040/?__source=aol/headline/quote/ text/&par=aol, accessed September 8, 2009.

Jackson, Susan, and Tim Smart, "Mom and Pop Fight Back," *BusinessWeek,* April 14, 1997, p. 46.

Jacobs, Karen, "Home Depot Pushes Low Prices, Energy Savings," Reuters, September 10, 2008, http://www.reuters. com/article/ousiv/idUSN1051947020080910, accessed September 8, 2009.

Lloyd, Mary Ellen, "Home Improvement Spending Remains Tight," *Wall Street Journal,* May 6, 2009, http://online. wsj.com/article/SB124162405957992133.html, accessed September 8, 2009.

McGregor, Jena, "Home Depot Sheds Units," *BusinessWeek,* January 26, 2009, http://www.businessweek.com/bwdaily/ dnflash/content/jan2009/db20090126_454995.htm, accessed September 8, 2009.

"Message from the Supplier Diversity Director," Home Depot, http://corporate.homedepot.com/wps/portal/SupplierDiversity, accessed September 8, 2009.

"Our History," Home Depot, http://corporate.homedepot. com/wps/portal/!ut/p/c1/04_SB8K8xLLM9 MSSzPy8xBz9CP0os3gDdwNHH0tD U1M3g1APR0N31xBjAwgAykfC5H1Mz N0MzDycDANMYdIGBHT7eeTnpuoX5EaUAwDOvP5h/ dl2/d1/L2dJQSEvUUt3QS9ZQnB3LzZfMEcwQUw5TD Q3RjA2SEIxUEY5MDAwMDAwMDA!/, accessed September 8, 2009.

"Our Mission and Outreach Efforts," Home Depot, http:// corporate.homedepot.com/wps/portal/!ut/p/c1/04_ SB8K8xLLM9MSSzPy8xBz9CP0os3gDdwNHH0sfE3M3 AzMPJ8MAfzcDKADKR2LKmxrD5fHr9vPIz03VL8iN KAcAC4X4Kg!!/dl2/d1/L2dJQSEvUUt3QS9ZQnB3Lz ZfMEcwQUw5TDQ3RjA2SEIxUFBGMDAwMDAwMDA!/, accessed September 8, 2009.

Pettit, Dixie, "Home Depot Volunteers Give Youth Club a Facelift," *Ramona Sentinel,* November 12, 2008, http://www. ramonasentinel.com/article.cfm?articleID=18278, accessed September 8, 2009.

PR Newswire, "The Home Depot Forms Unprecedented Partnership with Four Leading National Hispanic Organizations," Hispanic Business.com, February 15, 2005, http://www.hispanicbusiness.com/news/newsbyid. asp?idx=20997&page=1&cat=&more=, accessed September 8, 2009.

"Profiles in Leadership: 2008 ENERGY STAR Award Winners," Energy Star, http://www.energystar.gov/ia/partners/pt_ awards/2008_profiles_in_leadership.pdf, accessed September 8, 2009.

Ramos, Rachel Tobin, "Home Depot in Middle of Patagonian Dam Debate," International Rivers, May 18, 2008, http:// internationalrivers.org/en/node/2828, accessed September 8, 2009.

"Renovating Home Depot," *BusinessWeek,* March 6, 2006, http://www.businessweek.com/print/magazine/ content/06_10/b3974001.htm?chan=gl, accessed September 8, 2009.

Scelfo, Julie, "The Meltdown in Home Furnishings," *New York Times,* January 28, 2009, http://www.nytimes. com/2009/01/29/garden/29industry.html, accessed September 8, 2009.

"2008 Annual Report," Home Depot, http://www.homedepotar. com/, accessed September 8, 2009.

Uchitelle, Louis, "Home Depot Girds for Continued Weakness," *New York Times,* May 18, 2009, http://www.nytimes.

com/2009/05/19/business/19depot.html, accessed September 8, 2009.

"United We Can—Take on Challenges, Shape Careers and Improve Communities," Home Depot, https://careers. homedepot.com/cg/content.do?p=/united, accessed May 21, 2009.

"We Build Community: Team Depot," Home Depot, http:// corporate.homedepot.com/wps/portal/!ut/p/c1/04_ SB8K8xLLM9MSSzPy8xBz9CP0os3gDdwNHH0sfE3 M3AzMPJ8MALxcDKADKR2LKmxrD5fHr9vPIz03V L8iNKAcAbzcnOw!!/dl2/d1/L2dJQSEvU

Ut3QS9ZQnB3LzZfMEcwQUw5TDQ3RjA2S EIxUE1EMDAwMDAwMDA!/, accessed March 12, 2009.

"What We Do," The Home Depot Foundation, http://www. homedepotfoundation.org/what.html, accessed September 8, 2009.

"World's Most Admired Companies: Home Depot," *Fortune*, http://money.cnn.com/magazines/fortune/ globalmostadmired/2008/snapshots/2968.html, accessed September 8, 2009.

Zimmerman, Ann, "Home Depot Spanish Site Is Shuttered," *Wall Street Journal*, May 2, 2009, http://online.wsj.com/article/ SB124122625291179435.html, accessed September 8, 2009.

New Belgium Brewing: Ethical and Environmental Responsibility

Although most of the companies frequently cited as examples of ethical and socially responsible firms are large corporations, it is the social responsibility initiatives of small businesses that often have the greatest impact on local communities and neighborhoods. These businesses create jobs and provide goods and services for customers in smaller markets that larger corporations often are not interested in serving. Moreover, they also contribute money, resources, and volunteer time to local causes. Their owners often serve as community and neighborhood leaders, and many choose to apply their skills and some of the fruits of their success to tackling local problems and issues that benefit everyone in the community. Managers and employees become role models for ethical and socially responsible actions. One such small business is the New Belgium Brewing Company, Inc., based in Fort Collins, Colorado.

HISTORY OF THE NEW BELGIUM BREWING COMPANY

The idea for the New Belgium Brewing Company began with a bicycling trip through Belgium. Belgium is arguably the home of some of the world's finest ales, some of which have been brewed for centuries in that country's monasteries. As Jeff Lebesch, an American electrical engineer, cruised around that country on his fat-tired mountain bike, he wondered if he could produce such high-quality beers back home in Colorado. After acquiring the special strain of yeast used to brew Belgian-style ales, Lebesch returned home and began to experiment in his Colorado basement. When his beers earned thumbs up from friends, Lebesch decided to market them.

The New Belgium Brewing Company (NBB) opened for business in 1991 as a tiny basement operation in Lebesch's home in Fort Collins. Lebesch's wife, Kim Jordan, became the firm's marketing director. They named their first brew Fat Tire Amber Ale in honor of Lebesch's bike ride through Belgium. New Belgium beers quickly developed a small but devoted customer base, first in Fort Collins and then throughout Colorado. The brewery soon outgrew the couple's basement and moved into an old railroad depot before settling into its present custom-built facility in 1995. The brewery includes an automated brew house, two quality assurance labs, and numerous technological innovations for which New Belgium has become nationally recognized as a "paradigm of environmental efficiencies."

Today, New Belgium Brewing Company offers a variety of permanent and seasonal ales and pilsners. The company's standard line includes Sunshine Wheat, Blue Paddle, Abbey, Mothership Wit, 1554, Trippel, and the original Fat Tire Amber Ale, still the firm's best-seller. Some customers even refer to the company as the Fat Tire Brewery. The brewery also markets four types of specialty beers on a seasonal basis. Seasonal ales include

This case was developed under the direction of O.C. Ferrell and Jennifer Jackson. Jennifer Sawayda, Nikole Haiar, and Melanie Drever provided editorial assistance. We appreciate the input and assistance of Greg Owsley, New Belgium Brewing, in developing this case. This case was prepared for classroom discussion, rather than to illustrate either effective or ineffective handling of an administrative, ethical, or legal decision by management. All sources used for this case were obtained through publicly available material and the New Belgium website.

Frambozen, released at Thanksgiving, Skinny Dip, released during the summer, 2° for winter, and Mighty Arrow for spring. The firm has started a Lips of Faith program, where small batch brews like La Folie, Biere de Mars, and Abbey Grand Cru are created for internal celebrations or landmark events. In addition, New Belgium is working in collaboration (or collabeeration) with Elysian Brewing Company, in which each company will be able to use the other's brewhouses though they are still independent businesses. Through this, they hope to create better efficiency and experimentation along with taking collaborative strides in the future of American beer making. One collabeeration beer resulting from this partnership is Trippel IPA.

Until 2005, NBB's most effective form of advertising was customers' word of mouth. Indeed, before New Belgium beers were widely distributed throughout Colorado, one liquor store owner in Telluride is purported to have offered people gas money if they would stop by and pick up New Belgium beer on their way through Ft. Collins. Although New Belgium beers are distributed in less than half of the United States, the brewery receives numerous e-mails and phone calls every day inquiring when its beers will be available elsewhere.

Although still a small brewery when compared to companies like its in-state rival Coors, NBB has consistently experienced strong growth and has become the third-largest "craft" brewery in the nation with 2007 sales of $96 million. Sales for its Fat Time brand were up 39 percent in 2009 over the year before. This was the largest increase in sales for any craft brewer in the nation. It now has its own blog, MySpace, and Facebook pages. The plant is currently capable of producing

Figure 1 New Belgium's Distribution Territories

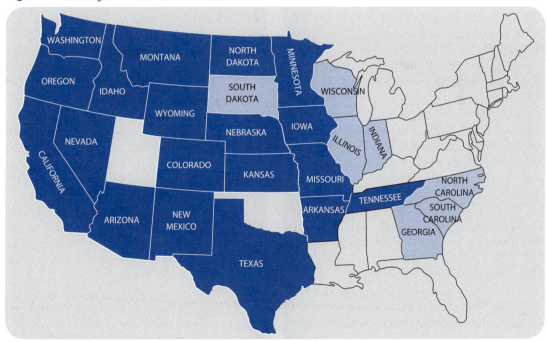

Source: Information obtained from http://www.newbelgium.com/faq.

700 bottles of beer a minute, and they are developing a capacity for canned beer of 50 to 60 per minute. In 2008, they were in twenty states from the Pacific coast to the Midwest and looking to release products in five more states in 2009 (see Figure 1). This growth has been driven by beer connoisseurs who appreciate the high quality of NBB's products as well as what the company stands for. When NBB began distribution in Minnesota, it was so popular that a liquor store had to open early and make other accommodations for the large number of customers. The store sold 400 cases of "Fat Tire" in the first hour it was open. The brewery is now the ninth largest of any kind in the country.

With expanding distribution, however, the brewery has recognized a need to increase its opportunities for reaching its far-flung customers. It consulted with Dr. Douglas Holt, an Oxford professor and cultural branding expert. After studying the young company, Holt, together with Marketing Director Greg Owsley, drafted a 70-page "manifesto" describing the brand's attributes, character, cultural relevancy, and promise. In particular, Holt identified in New Belgium an ethos of pursuing creative activities simply for the joy of doing them well and in harmony with the natural environment.

With the brand thus defined, New Belgium went in search of an advertising agency to help communicate that brand identity; it soon found Amalgamated, an equally young, independent New York advertising agency. Amalgamated created a $10 million advertising campaign for New Belgium that targets high-end beer drinkers, men ages 25 to 44, and highlights the brewery's image as being down-to-earth. The grainy ads focus on a man, Charles the Tinkerer, rebuilding a cruiser bike out of used parts and then riding it along pastoral country roads. Shot around Hotchkiss and Paonia, Colorado, the producers were going for a spontaneous, easygoing vibe. The product appears in just five seconds of each ad between the tag lines, "Follow Your Folly...Ours Is Beer." At first, New Belgium thought that "Folly" carried too much of a negative connotation, but department support encouraged the company to keep the line. With nostalgic music playing in the background, the ads have helped position the growing brand as whimsical, thoughtful, and reflective. In addition to the ad campaign, the company has maintained its strategy of promotion through event sponsorships.

NEW BELGIUM ETHICAL CULTURE

According to Greg Owsley, director of marketing for New Belgium Brewing, there is a fundamental focus on the ethical culture of the brand. Although consumers often regard the intentions of business with raised eyebrows, those in good standing—as opposed to those trading on hype—are eyed with iconic-like adoration. A new paradigm has emerged in which businesses that fully embrace citizenship in the communities they serve can forge enduring bonds with customers.

Meanwhile, these are precarious times for businesses that choose to ignore consumers who look at brands from an ethical perspective. More than ever before, what the brand says and what the company does must be synchronized. NBB believes that as the mandate for corporate social responsibility gains momentum beyond the courtroom to the far more powerful marketplace, any current and future manager of business must realize that business ethics are not so much about the installation of compliance codes and standards as they are about the spirit in which they are integrated. Thus, the modern-day brand steward—usually the most externally focused member of the business management team—must prepare to be the internal champion of the bottom-line necessity for ethical, values-driven company behavior.

At New Belgium, a synergy of brand and values occurred naturally as the firm's ethical culture (in the form of core values and beliefs) was in place long before NBB had a marketing department. Back in early 1991, New Belgium was just a home-brewed business plan of Jeff Lesbesch, an electrical engineer, and his social worker wife, Kim Jordan. Before they signed any business paperwork, the two took a hike into Rocky Mountain National Park. Armed with a pen and a notebook, they took their first stab at what the fledgling company's core purpose would be. If they were going forward with this venture, what were their aspirations beyond profitability? What was the real root cause of their dream? What they wrote down that spring day, give or take a little wordsmithing, are the core values and beliefs that you can read on the NBB website today.

More importantly, ask just about any New Belgium worker, and she or he can list for you many, if not all, of these shared values and can inform you about which are the most personally poignant. For NBB, branding strategies are as rooted in its company values as in other business practices.

NEW BELGIUM'S PURPOSE AND CORE BELIEFS

New Belgium's dedication to quality, the environment, and its employees and customers is expressed in its mission statement: "To operate a profitable brewery which makes our love and talent manifest." The company's stated core values and beliefs about its role as an environmentally concerned and socially responsible brewer include the following:

- Producing world-class beers
- Promoting beer culture and the responsible enjoyment of beer
- Continuous, innovative quality and efficiency improvements
- Transcending customers' expectations
- Environmental stewardship: minimizing resource consumption, maximizing energy efficiency, and recycling
- Kindling social, environmental, and cultural change as a business role model

- Cultivating potential: through learning, participative management, and the pursuit of opportunities
- Balancing the myriad needs of the company, staff, and their families
- Committing ourselves to authentic relationships, communications, and promises
- Having Fun

Employees believe that these statements help communicate to customers and other stakeholders what New Belgium, as a company, is about. These simple values developed nineteen years ago are just as meaningful to the company and its customers today as they were then, even though the company has experienced much growth.

EMPLOYEE CONCERNS

Recognizing employees' roles in the company's success, New Belgium provides many generous benefits for its 320 employees. In addition to the usual paid health and dental insurance and retirement plans, employees get a free lunch every other week as well as a free massage once a year, and they can bring their children and dogs to work. Employees who stay with the company for five years earn an all-expenses-paid trip to Belgium to "study beer culture." Perhaps most importantly, employees can also earn stock in the privately-held corporation, which grants them a vote in company decisions. Employees currently own about 32 percent of company stock. Open-book management also allows employees to see the financial costs and performance of the company.

New Belgium also wishes to get its employees involved not only in the company, but in sustainability efforts as well. To help their own sustainability efforts, employees are given a cruiser bike after one year's employment so they can ride to work instead of drive. The NBB sales force is provided with Toyota Prius hybrids. A recycling center on-site is provided for employees to recycle their old items.

Additionally, each summer New Belgium hosts the Tour de Fat, where employees can dress in costumes and lead locals on a bike tour. Other company perks include inexpensive yoga classes, free beer at quitting time, and a climbing wall. Due to its desire to create a pleasant worker atmosphere, New Belgium is considered to be the number-one place to work by *Outside Online*.

SUSTAINABILITY CONCERNS

New Belgium's marketing strategy involves linking the quality of its products, as well as its brand, with the company's philosophy toward affecting the planet. From leading-edge environmental gadgets and high-tech industry advancements to employee-ownership programs and a strong belief in giving back to the community, New Belgium demonstrates its desire to create a living, learning community.

NBB strives for cost-efficient, energy-saving alternatives for conducting its business and reducing its impact on the environment. In staying true to the company's core values and beliefs, the brewery's employee-owners unanimously agreed to invest in a wind turbine, making New Belgium the first fully wind-powered brewery in the United States. Since the switch from coal power, New Belgium has been able to reduce its CO_2 emissions by 1,800 metric tons per year. The company further reduces its energy use by employing a steam condenser that captures and reuses the hot water that boils the barley and hops in the production process to start the next brew. The steam is redirected to heat the floor tiles and de-ice the loading docks in cold weather. NBB also purchased a brew kettle, the second of its kind installed in the nation, which heats wort sheets instead of the whole kettle at once. This kettle heating method conserves energy more than standard kettles do. Another way that NBB conserves energy is by using "sun tubes," which provide natural daytime lighting throughout the brew house all year long. Finally, the brewery uses a complex system to capture its waste water and extract methane from it. This can contribute up to 15 percent of the brewery's power needs while reducing the strain on the local municipal water treatment facility.

New Belgium takes pride in reducing waste through recycling and creative reuse strategies. The company strives to recycle as many supplies as possible, including cardboard boxes, keg caps, office materials, and the amber glass used in bottling. The brewery stores spent barley and hop grains in an on-premise silo and invites local farmers to pick up the grains, free of charge, to feed their pigs. Going further down the road to producing products for the food chain, NBB is working with partners to take the same bacteria that create methane from NBB waste water and convert them into a harvestable, high-protein fish food. NBB even encourages its employees to reduce air pollution by using alternative transportation like the cruiser bikes the company provides for employees after a year of company employment.

New Belgium has been a long-time participant in green building techniques. With each expansion of the facility, it has incorporated new technologies and learned a few lessons along the way. In 2002, NBB agreed to participate in the U.S. Green Building Council's Leadership in Energy and Environment Design for Existing Buildings (LEED-EB) pilot program. From sun tubes and daylighting throughout the facility to reusing heat in the brew house, NBB continues to search for new ways to close loops and conserve resources.

Reduce, Reuse, Recycle—the three Rs of being an environmental steward—are taken seriously at NBB. The company's reuse program includes heat for the brewing process, cleaning chemicals, water, and much more. Recycling at New Belgium takes on many forms, from turning "waste" products into something new and useful (like spent grain to cattle feed), to supporting the recycling market in creative ways (like turning their keg caps into table surfaces). The company also buys recycled products whenever possible, from paper to office furniture. The graph in Figure 2 depicts New Belgium's 2008 recycling efforts.

To measure its efforts in the area of the first "R," reduction, New Belgium has created its own Life-cycle Assessment that helps the company to account for the energy flows of its products' lifecycles in order to see how much energy has been reduced. Its numerous reduction efforts, including everything from motion sensors on the lights throughout the building to induction fans that pull in cool winter air to chill the beer, offset New Belgium's energy needs and are the cornerstone to being environmentally efficient.

Finally, NBB has begun changing its product line-up to include an organic beer. This beer is really a microcosm of the company—it is a wit (white) beer, which is a traditional Belgian style of unfiltered wheat beer with orange and coriander flavors. This new organic beer coincides with New Belgium's environmental initiatives, as making it from organic ingredients poses less of a threat to the environment.

New Belgium has made significant achievements in the area of sustainability,

Figure 2 Recycling at New Belgium

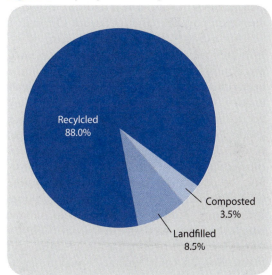

Source: Information obtained from http://www.newbelgium.com/blog/post/waste-not-want-not, accessed September 11, 2009.

particularly compared to other companies in the industry. For one, New Belgium uses only 4 gallons of water to make 1 gallon of beer, which is 20 percent less than most other companies in the industry. New Belgium was able to recycle 73 percent of its waste in 2007, and today 100 percent of its electricity comes from renewables. Despite these achievements, New Belgium has no intention of halting its sustainability efforts. It hopes to reduce the amount of water used to make beer by 10 percent through better production processes and to decrease its carbon footprint by 25 percent per barrel of its Fat Tire Beer by 2015.

SOCIAL CONCERNS

Beyond its use of environmental-friendly technologies and innovations, New Belgium Brewing Company strives to improve communities and enhance people's lives through corporate giving, event sponsorship, and philanthropic involvement.

Since its inception, NBB has donated more than $2.9 million to philanthropic causes. For every barrel of beer sold the prior year, NBB donates $1 to philanthropic causes within their distribution territory. The donations are divided between states in proportion to their percentage of overall sales. This is the company's way of staying local and giving back to the communities that support and purchase NBB products. In 2006, Arkansas, Arizona, California, Colorado, Idaho, Kansas, Missouri, Montana, Nebraska, Nevada, New Mexico, Oregon, Texas, Washington, and Wyoming all received funding. In 2008, NBB donated $490,000 in funds for philanthropic causes. It also participates in One Percent For The Planet, a philanthropic network to which NBB donates 1 percent of its profits.

Funding decisions are made by New Belgium's philanthropy committee, which is comprised of employees throughout the brewery including owners, employee-owners, area leaders, and production workers. New Belgium looks for nonprofit organizations that demonstrate creativity, diversity, and an innovative approach to their mission and objectives. The philanthropy committee also looks for groups that involve the community to reach their goals.

Additionally, NBB maintains a community bulletin board in its facility where it posts an array of community involvement activities and proposals. This community board allows tourists and employees to see the different ways they can help out the community, and it gives nonprofit organizations a chance to make their needs known. Organizations can even apply for grants through the New Belgium Brewing Company website, which has a link designated for this purpose. In 2009, the company hoped to award grants in the areas of water stewardship, sensible transportation and bike advocacy, sustainable agriculture, and youth environmental education.

NBB also sponsors a number of events, with a special focus on those that involve "human-powered" sports that cause minimal damage to the natural environment. Through event sponsorships, such as the Tour de Fat, NBB supports various environmental, social, and cycling nonprofit organizations. In the Tour de Fat, one participant hands over his or her car keys and vehicle title in exchange for an NBB commuter bike and trailer. The participant is then filmed for the world to see as he or she promotes sustainable transportation over driving. In addition, New Belgium has been supporting the National Multiple Sclerosis Society. NBB has helped by donating jerseys and by partnering with another organization to create a team for Pedal the Plains 2009. The team, known as Bike MS, will ride for a weekend to raise donations for the society. NBB also sponsored the Ride the Rockies bike tour, which donated the proceeds from beer sales to local nonprofit groups. The money raised from this annual event funds local projects, such as improving parks and bike trails. In the course of one year, New Belgium can be found at anywhere from 150 to 200 festivals and events across fifteen western states.

ORGANIZATIONAL SUCCESS

New Belgium Brewing Company's efforts to live up to its own high standards have paid off with numerous awards and a very loyal following. It was one of three winners of *Business Ethics* magazine's Business Ethics Awards for its "dedication to environmental excellence in every part of its innovative brewing process." Kim Jordan and Jeff Lebesch were named the recipients of the Rocky Mountain Region Entrepreneur of the Year Award for manufacturing, and NBB was listed in the *Wall Street Journal* as one of the fifteen best small workplaces. The company has also captured the award for best mid-sized brewing company of the year and best mid-sized brewmaster at the Great American Beer Festival. New Belgium has taken home medals for three different brews, Abbey Belgian Style Ale, Blue Paddle Pilsner, and LaFolie specialty ale. Additionally, the exemplary leadership of CEO Kim Lebesch was recognized as she won *ColoradoBiz* magazine's 2008 CEO of the year and was invited to meet then presidential-elect Barack Obama.

According to David Edgar, director of the Institute for Brewing Studies, "They've created a very positive image for their company in the beer-consuming public with smart decision-making." Although some members of society do not believe that a company whose major product is alcohol can be socially responsible, New Belgium has set out to prove that for those who make a choice to drink responsibly, the company can do everything possible to contribute to society. Its efforts to promote beer culture and the connoisseurship of beer have even led it to design a special "Worthy Glass," the shape of which is intended to retain foam, show off color, enhance visual presentation, and release aroma. New Belgium Brewing Company also promotes the responsible appreciation of beer through its participation in and support of the culinary arts. For instance, it frequently hosts New Belgium Beer Dinners, in which every course of the meal is served with a complementary culinary treat.

According to Greg Owsley, director of marketing, although the Fat Tire brand has a bloodline straight from the enterprise's ethical beliefs and practices, the firm's work is not done. The company must continually reexamine ethical, social, and environmental responsibilities. In 2004, New Belgium received the Environmental Protection Agency's regional Environmental Achievement Award. It was both an honor and a motivator for the company to continue its socially responsible goals. After all, there are still many ways for NBB to improve as a corporate citizen. For example, the manufacturing process is a fair distance from being zero waste or emission free. Although all electric power comes from renewable sources, the plant is still heated in part by using natural gas. Additionally, there will always be a need for more public dialog on avoiding alcohol abuse.

Practically speaking, the company has a never-ending to-do list. NBB must acknowledge that as its annual sales increase, the challenges for the brand to remain on a human scale and to continue to be culturally authentic will increase too. How to boldly grow the brand while maintaining its humble feel has always been a challenge. Additionally, reducing waste to an even greater extent will take lots of work on behalf of both managers and employees, creating the need for a collaborative process that will require the dedication of both parties toward sustainability.

Every six-pack of New Belgium Beer displays the phrase, "In this box is our labor of love. We feel incredibly lucky to be creating something fine that enhances people's lives." Although Jeff Lebesch has "semi-retired" from the company to focus on other interests, the founders of New Belgium hope this statement captures the spirit of the company. According to employee Dave Kemp, NBB's environmental concern and social

responsibility give it a competitive advantage because consumers want to believe in and feel good about the products they purchase. NBB's most important asset is its image—a corporate brand that stands for quality, responsibility, and concern for society. Defining itself as more than just a beer company, the brewer also sees itself as a caring organization that is concerned with all stakeholders, including the community, sustainability, and employees.

QUESTIONS

1. What environmental issues does the New Belgium Brewing Company work to address? How has NBB taken a strategic approach to addressing these issues? Why do you think the company has chosen to focus on environmental issues?

2. Are New Belgium's social initiatives indicative of strategic philanthropy? Why or why not?

3. Some segments of society vigorously contend that companies that sell alcoholic beverages and tobacco products cannot be socially responsible organizations because of the nature of their primary products. Do you believe that New Belgium Brewing Company's actions and initiatives are indicative of an ethical and socially responsible corporation? Why or why not?

SOURCES

Arnold, Katie, "Where to Apply Now," *Outside Online,* May 2008, http://outside.away.com/outside/culture/200805/best-companies-1.html, accessed September 8, 2009.

Asmus, Peter, "Goodbye Coal, Hello Wind," *Business Ethics* 13 (July/August 1999): 10–11.

Baun, Robert, "What's in a Name? Ask the Makers of Fat Tire," *[Fort Collins] Coloradoan,* October 8, 2000, pp. E1, E3.

"The Carbon Footprint of a 6-Pack of Fat Tire Amber Ale," New Belgium Brewing Blog, August 18, 2008, http://www.newbelgium.com/blog/post/carbon-footprint-6-pack-fat-tire-amber-ale, accessed September 8, 2009.

"Collabeeration," New Belgium, http://www.newbelgium.com/beerline/collabeeration, accessed September 8, 2009.

Deter, Stevi, "Fat Tire Amber Ale," The Net Net, www.thenetnet. com/reviews/fat.html, accessed September 8, 2009.

Dwyer, Robert F., and John F. Tanner Jr., *Business Marketing* (Boston: Irwin McGraw-Hill, 1999), p. 104.

Fera, Rae Ann, "Small Shops, Big Moves," *'boards*, January 1, 2005, http://www.boardsmag.com/articles/ magazine/20050101/smallshops.html?__b=yes, accessed September 9, 2009.

"Four Businesses Honored with Prestigious International Award for Outstanding Marketplace Ethics," Better Business Bureau, press release, September 23, 2002, http://www.bbb.org/us/ article/four-businesses-honored-with-prestigious-international- award-for-outstanding-marketplace-ethics-193, accessed September 9, 2009.

"GABF 2000 Awards," Reelbear.com, http://www.realbeer.com/ edu/gabf/gabf2000.php, accessed September 9, 2009.

Gordon, Julie, "Lebesch Balances Interests in Business, Community," *Coloradoan*, February 26, 2003.

Haiar, Nikole, "New Belgium Brewing Company Tour" November 20, 2000.

Hawkins, Del I., Roger J. Best, and Kenneth A. Coney, *Consumer Behavior: Building Marketing Strategy*, 8th ed. (Boston: Irwin McGraw-Hill, 2001).

Kemp, David, "Tour Connoisseur," New Belgium Brewing Company, personal interview by Nikole Haiar, November 21, 2000.

"Lips of Faith," New Belgium, http://www.newbelgium.com/ beerline/lips-of-faith, accessed September 8, 2009.

"New Belgium Brewing," MySpace, http://www.myspace.com/ follyyourfolly, accessed September 8, 2009.

"New Belgium Brewing Blog," New Belgium, http://www. newbelgium.com/blog/post/2008-sustainability-nonreport, accessed September 8, 2009.

New Belgium Brewing Company, Ft. Collins, CO, www. newbelgium.com, accessed September 8, 2009.

"New Belgium Brewing to Cut CO_2 Emissions by 25% Per Barrel," *Environmental Leader*, January 20, 2009, http:// www.environmentalleader.com/2009/01/20/new-belgium- brewing-to-cut-co2-emissions-by-25-per-barrel/, accessed September 8, 2009.

"New Belgium Brewing Wins Ethics Award," *Denver Business Journal*, January 2, 2003, http://denver.bizjournals.com/ denver/stories/2002/12/30/daily21.html, accessed September 8, 2009.

Owsley, Greg, "The Necessity for Aligning Brand with Corporate Ethics," in Sheb L. True, Linda Ferrell, and O. C. Ferrell, *Fulfilling Our Obligation, Perspectives on Teaching Business Ethics* (Kennesaw State University Press, 2005), pp. 128–132.

Raabe, Steve, "New Belgium Brewing Turns to Cans," denverpost.com, May 15, 2008, http://www.denverpost.com/ ci_9262005, accessed September 8, 2009.

"Recession-Proof Brewing," *Colorado Biz,* September 2009, pp. 62–64.

Reuteman, Rob, "REUTEMAN: Colorado Rides on Fat Tire to Beer Heights," *Rocky Mountain News,* November 24, 2007, http://www.rockymountainnews.com/news/2007/ nov/24/reuteman-colorado-rides-on-fat-tire-to-beer/, accessed September 9, 2009.

Simpson, Bryan, *New Belgium Brewing: Brand Building Through Advertising and Public Relations*, http://e-businessethics. com/NewBelgiumCases/newbelgiumbrewing.pdf, accessed September 8, 2009.

"South Dakota—Bike MS: Pedal the Plains 2009," *National Multiple Sclerosis Society*, http://main.nationalmssociety.org/ site/TR?pg=team&fr_id=10070&team_id=171995, accessed September 9, 2009.

"Sponsorship," New Belgium, http://www.newbelgium.com/ sponsorship, accessed September 9, 2009.

Spors, Kelly K., "Top Small Workplaces 2008," *Wall Street Journal*, February 22, 2009, http://online.wsj.com/article/ SB122347733961315417.html, accessed September 8, 2009.

"Sustainability," New Belgium website, http://www. newbelgium.com/sustainability.php, accessed September 8, 2009.

"A Tour of the New Belgium Brewery—Act One," LiveGreen blog, April 9, 2007, http://www.livegreensd.com/2007/04/ tour-of-new-belgium-brewery-act-one.html, accessed September 9, 2009.

"Trade Your Car for a Bike," New Belgium, http://www. newbelgium.com/trade, accessed September 8, 2009.

Tuttle, Andrea, *Ride the Rockies*, June 15–21, 2008, http://www. postnewsads.com/interactivekit/uploads/rtr/RideTheRockies. pdf, accessed September 9, 2009.

"2007 Sustainability Report," New Belgium, http://www. newbelgium.com/files/shared/07SustainabilityReportlow.pdf, accessed September 8, 2009.

NOTES

Chapter 1

1 Tricia Bisoux, "Playing by the Rules," *BizEd* (September–October 2005): 18–25; Doug Cameron, "Huntsman Posts Loss, Hints at Recovery," *Wall Street Journal*, May 9, 2009, p. B5; Huntsman LLC, http://www.huntsman.com, accessed May 10, 2009; Jon M. Huntsman, *Winners Never Cheat* (Philadelphia: Wharton School Publishing, 2005).

2 "How Business Rates: By the Numbers," *Business Week*, September 11, 2000, pp. 148–149.

3 "Conseco Seeks Protection," http://money.cnn.com/2002/12/18/news/companies/conseco/, accessed April 15, 2009; Janet Adamy, "Conseco Names Interim CEO; Says Net Fell 21% in First Quarter," *Wall Street Journal*, May 5, 2006, p. B5; Conseco Seeks Relief," http://www.forbes.com/2009/03/24/conseco-insurance-amend-markets-equity-default.html, accessed May 2, 2009.

4 Milton Friedman, *Capitalism and Freedom* (Chicago: University of Chicago Press, 1962).

5 Clive Crook, "Why Good Corporate Citizens Are a Public Menace," *National Journal*, April 24, 1999, p. 1087; Charles Handy, "What's a Business For?" *Harvard Business Review* 80 (December 2002): 49–55.

6 Nancy J. Miller and Terry L. Besser, "The Importance of Community Values in Small Business Strategy Formation: Evidence from Rural Iowa," *Journal of Small Business Management* 38 (January 2000): 68–85; James Knight and Mary Kate O'Riley, "Local Heroes," *Director* 55 (February 2002): 28.

7 "The Small Business Economy: A Report to the President 2005," U.S. Small Business Administration, http://www.sba.gov/advo/research/sb_econ2008.pdf, accessed April 15, 2009.

8 Shimizu Corporation, http://www.shimz.co.jp/english/index.html, accessed June 11, 2006.

9 "Corporate Awards and Recognition," Herman Miller Inc., http://www.hermanmiller.com/CDA/SSA/Awards/0,1582,a10-c21,00.html, accessed April 15, 2009; Journey Toward Sustainability," Herman Miller, http://www.hermanmiller.com/CDA/SSA/Category/0,1564,a10-c605,00.html, accessed April 15, 2009.

10 "The 1997 Cone/Roper Cause-Related Marketing Trends Report," *Business Ethics* 11 (March–April 1997): 14–16; Ronald Alsop, "Corporate Reputations Are Earned with Trust, Reliability, Study Shows," *Wall Street Journal*, September 23, 1999; http://interactive.wsj.com; Dale Kurschner, "5 Ways Ethical Busine$$ Creates Fatter Profit$," *Business Ethics* 10 (March–April 1996): 21.

11 Jim Carlton, "New Leaf: Once Targeted by Protestors, Home Depot Plays Green Role," *Wall Street Journal*, August 6, 2004, p. A1.

12 Ann E. Tenbrunsel, Zoe I. Barsness, and Paul M. Hirsch, "Sara Lee Corporation and Corporate Citizenship: Unity in Diversity," in *Corporate Global Citizenship*, ed. Noel M. Tichy, Andrew R. McGill, and Lynda St. Clair (San Francisco: New Lexington Press, 1997), pp. 197–213.

13 "Message to our Stakeholders," TOTO, "Annual Report 2008," p. 3, http://www.toto.co.jp/en/ir/annual/pdf/annu2008.pdf, accessed April 15, 2009.

14 Archie Carroll, "The Four Faces of Corporate Citizenship," *Business and Society Review*, January 1, 1998, p. 1; Naomi Gardberg and Charles Fombrun, "Corporate Citizenship: Creating Intangible Assets Across Institutional Environments," *Academy of Management Review* 31 (April 2006): 329–336

15 "Corruption Perceptions Index 2008," Transparency International, http://www.transparency.org/policy_research/surveys_indices/cpi/2008, accessed April 15, 2009.

16 "Judge Rules That Microsoft Violated U.S. Antitrust Laws," *Wall Street Journal*, April 3, 2000, http://interactive.wsj.com; Steven Levy, "Look, Ma, No Breaks," *Newsweek*, September 17, 2001, pp. 52–54; "Microsoft Begins Implementing Antitrust Settlement," *Computer & Online Industry Litigation Reporter*, November 19, 2002, p. 11.

17 "Code of Ethics," Direct Selling Association, http://www.dsa.org/ethics/, accessed April 15, 2009; "World Codes of Conduct for Direct Selling," World Federation of Direct Selling Associations, http://www.wfdsa.org/world_codes/, accessed April 1, 2009.

18 The Hitachi Foundation: 20 Years Strengthening Communities, http://www.hitachifoundation.org/pdfs/Hitachi20YearReport.pdf, accessed May 2, 2009.

19 Altman, "Transformed Corporate Community Relations," p. 43; Carroll, "The Four Faces of Corporate Citizenship," p. 1.

20 Feliza Mirasol, "Pfizer, Merck Point to Pharma's Fate," *Chemical Market Reporter*, January 9–15, 2006, p. 26; "Pfizer in $894 Million Drug Settlement," *New York Times*, October 18, 2008, p. 2.

21 Malcolm McIntosh, Deborah Leipziger, Keith Jones, and Gill Coleman, *Corporate Citizenship: Successful Strategies for Responsible Companies* (London: Financial Times Management, 2000); Linda S. Munilla and Morgan P. Miles, "The Corporate Social Responsibility Continuum as a Component of Stakeholder Theory," *Business and Society Review* 110 (December 2005): 371–387.

22 Betsy Morris and Patricia Sellers, "What Really Happened at Coke," *Fortune,* January 10, 2000, pp. 114–116; "America's Most Admired Companies," http://www.fortune.com/fortune/mostadmired/, accessed December 17, 2002; "The 100 Best Corporate Citizens for 2001," http://www.business-ethics.com/node/75, accessed April 15, 2009; "Global Most Admired Companies 2006," http://money.cnn.com/magazines/fortune/globalmostadmired/2006/top50/index.html, accessed April 15, 2009.

23 Charles Handy, "What's a Business For?" *Harvard Business Review* 80 (December 2002): 49–55.

24 R. E. Freeman, *Strategic Management: A Stakeholder Approach* (Boston: Pitman, 1984).

25 "Kingfisher Corporate Responsibility Report 2007/2008," http://www.kingfisher.com/managed_content/files/reports/cr_report_2008/index.asp, accessed April 15, 2009.

26 Edward S. Mason, "Introduction," in *The Corporation in Modern Society,* ed. Edward S. Mason (Cambridge, MA: Harvard University Press, 1959), pp. 1–24.

27 "About Benetton: Our Campaigns," http://press.benettongroup.com/ben_en/about/campaigns/list/, accessed April 15, 2009; Michael McCarthy and Lorrie Grant, "Sears Drops Benetton After Controversial Death Row Ads," *USA Today,* February 18, 2000, http://www.usatoday.com.

28 Isabelle Maignan and O. C. Ferrell, "Measuring Corporate Citizenship in Two Countries: The Case of the United States and France," *Journal of Business Ethics* 23 (February 2000): 283; Robert J. Samuelson, "R.I.P.: The Good Corporation," *Newsweek,* July 5, 1993, p. 41.

29 Charles W. Wootton and Christie L. Roszkowski, "Legal Aspects of Corporate Governance in Early American Railroads," *Business and Economic History* 28 (Winter 1999): 325–326.

30 Ralph Estes, *Tyranny of the Bottom Line* (San Francisco: Berrett-Koehler, 1996); David Finn, *The Corporate Oligarch* (New York: Simon & Schuster, 1969).

31 Marina v. N. Whitman, *New World, New Rules* (Boston: Harvard Business School Press, 1999).

32 Edward S. Mason, "Introduction," in *The Corporation in Modern Society,* ed. Mason, pp. 1–24.

33 Carl Kaysen, "The Corporation: How Much Power? What Scope?" in *The Corporation in Modern Society,* ed. Mason, pp. 85–105.

34 Whitman, *New World, New Rules.*

35 Ibid.

36 David M. Gordon, *Fat and Mean: The Corporate Squeeze of Working Americans and the Myth of Managerial "Downsizing"* (New York: Free Press, 1996).

37 Richard Leider, *The Power of Purpose: Creating Meaning in Your Life and Work* (San Francisco: Barrett-Koehler, 1997).

38 *The Economist,* "No More Business As Usual," http://www.economist.com/theworldin/displayStory.cfm?story_id=12494638&d=2009, accessed May 2, 2009.

39 Mark Lilla, "The Big Extract: Does Anyone Remember '68?" Guardian Editor (London), August 29, 1998, p. 12; Mark Lilla, "Still Living with '68," *New York Times Magazine,* August 16, 1998, p. 34.

40 Marjorie Kelly, "The Next Step for CSR: Economic Democracy," *Business Ethics* 16 (May–August 2002): 3–4.

41 Martin Wolf, "Comment and Analysis: The Big Lie of Global Inequality," *Financial Times,* February 9, 2000, p. 25.

42 Aaron Bernstein, "Too Much Corporate Power?" *Business Week,* September 11, 2000, pp. 144–158.

43 Bruce Horovitz, "Scandals Shake Public," *USA Today,* July 16, 2002, p. 1A.

44 "Public Trust Is Recovering," GlobeScan, Inc., http://www.globescan.com/news_archives/wef_trust_release.pdf, accessed April 15, 2009.

45 "Top 200: The Rise of Global Corporate Power," http://www.corpwatch.org/article.php?id=377, accessed April 15, 2009; Paul Magnusson, "Making a Federal Case Out of Overseas Abuses," *Business Week,* November 25, 2002, p. 78; "Unocal to Settle Rights Claims," http://www.corpwatch.com, accessed June 2, 2006.

46 M. N. Graham Dukes, "Accountability of the Pharmaceutical Industry," *The Lancet,* November 23, 2002, pp. 1682–1684; Elizabeth Olson, "Global Trade Negotiations Are Making Little Progress," *New York Times,* December 7, 2002, p. C3; Robert Pear, "Investigators Find Repeated Deception in Ads for Drugs," *New York Times,* December 4, 2002, p. A22.

47 John Dalla Costa, *The Ethical Imperative: Why Moral Leadership Is Good Business* (Reading, MA: Addison-Wesley, 1998).

48 "All About Nestlé: Business Principles," Nestlé, http://www.nestle.com/AllAbout/AllAboutNestle.htm, accessed April 15, 2009.

49 Lynda St. Clair, "Compaq Computer Corporation: Maximizing Environmental Conscientiousness Around the Globe," in *Corporate Global Citizenship,* ed. Tichy, McGill, and St. Clair, pp. 230–244.

50 S. A. Anwar, "APEC: Evidence and Policy Scenarios," *Journal of International Marketing and Marketing Research* 27 (October 2002): 141–153; Richard Feinberg, "Two Leading Lights of Humane Globalisation," *Singapore Straits Times,* February 21, 2000, p. 50.

51 Andreas Georg Scherer and Guido Palzaao, *Handbook of Research on Global Corporate Citizenship* (Cheltenham, UK: Edward Elgar, 2008).

52 Jonathan Levine, "Fear, Loathing and Opportunity: The Pollster's View of Global Citizenship," *The Voice of Corporate Citizenship,* May–June 2003, http://www.imakenews.com/cccbc/e_article000153082.cfm, accessed July 30, 2006.

53 Frederick Reichheld, *The Loyalty Effect* (Cambridge, MA: Harvard Business School, 1996); Jeffrey S. Harrison and R. Edward Freeman, "Stakeholders, Social Responsibility, and Performance: Empirical Evidence and Theoretical Perspectives," *Academy of Management Journal* 42 (October 1999): 479.

54 Stephen R. Covey, "Is Your Company's Bottom Line Taking a Hit?" *PRNewswire,* June 4, 1998, http://www.prnewswire.com; Terry W. Loe, "The Role of Ethical Climate in Developing Trust, Market Orientation and Commitment to Quality," unpublished Ph.D. dissertation, University of Memphis, 1996.

55 Ethics Resource Center, *2005 National Business Ethics Survey* (Washington, DC: Ethics Resource Center, 2005).

56 "The 1997 Cone/Roper Cause-Related Marketing Trends Report," *Business Ethics* 11 (March–April 1997): 14–16.

57 Rebecca Gardyn, "Philanthropy Post-Sept 11," *American Demographics* 24 (February 2002): 16–17; "The 1997 Cone/Roper Cause-Related Marketing Trends Report," p. 14.

58 Ronald Alsop, "Corporate Reputations Are Earned with Trust, Reliability, Study Shows," http://interactive.wsj.com.

59 Bernard J. Jaworski and Ajay K. Kohli, "Market Orientation: Antecedents and Consequences," *Journal of Marketing* 57 (July 1993): 10.

60 "About Hershey Foods," http://www.thehersheycompany.com/about/, accessed April 15, 2009; "Hershey Foods Philosophy and Values," Hershey Foods Corporation Videotape, 1990.

61 "2005 Loyalty in the Workplace," Walker Information, press release, November 21, 2005, http://walkerinfo.com/what/loyaltyreports/studies/employee05/newsrelease.cfm, accessed April 15, 2009.

62 John Galvin, "The New Business Ethics," *SmartBusinessMag.com,* June 2000, p. 97.

63 John A. Byrne, "Chainsaw," *Business Week,* October 18, 1999, pp. 128–149.

64 "Mutual Funds to Boycott Mitsubishi over Proposed Mexican Salt Plant," CNN, October 25, 1999, http://www.cnn.com.

65 David Rynecki, "Here Are 8 Easy Ways to Lose Your Shirt in Stocks," *USA Today,* June 26, 1998, p. 3B.

66 "Investment Club Numbers Decline; Crisis of Confidence Caused Many to Take Their Money and Run," *Investor Relations Business,* September 23, 2002, p. 1; Charles Jaffe, "Securities Industry Aims to Renew Trust; Leaders Face Challenge of Rebuilding Investor Confidence Amid Slump," *Boston Globe,* November 8, 2002, p. E1.

67 Isabelle Maignan, O. C. Ferrell, and G. Thomas Hult, "Corporate Citizenship: Antecedents and Business Benefits," *Journal of the Academy of Marketing Science* 24, no. 4 (1999): 455–469.

68 S. B. Graves and S. A. Waddock, "Institutional Owners and Corporate Social Performance: Maybe Not So Myopic After All," *Proceedings of the International Association for Business and Society,* San Diego, CA, 1993; Ronald M. Roman, Sefa Hayibor, and Bradley R. Agle, "The Relationship Between Social and Financial Performance," *Business and Society* 38 (March 1999); W. Gary Simpson and Theodor Kohers, "The Link Between Corporate Social and Financial Performance: Evidence from the Banking Industry," *Journal of Business Ethics* 35 (January 2002): 97–109; Curtis Verschoor and Elizabeth A. Murphy, "The Financial Performance of U.S. Firms and Those with Global Prominence: How Do the Best Corporate Citizens Rate?" *Business and Society Review* 107 (Fall 2002): 371–380; S. Waddock and S. Graves, "The Corporate Social Performance–Financial Performance Link," *Strategic Management Journal* 18 (1997): 303–319.

69 Chris C. Verschoor, "A Study of the Link Between a Corporation's Financial Performance and Its Commitment to Ethics," *Journal of Business Ethics* 31 (October 1998): 1509.

70 Shawn L. Berman, Andrew C. Wicks, Suresh Kotha, and Thomas M. Jones, "Does Stakeholder Orientation Matter? The Relationship Between Stakeholder Management Models and Firm Financial Performance," *Academy of Management Journal* 42 (October 1999): 502–503.

71 Roman, Hayibor, and Agle, "The Relationship Between Social and Financial Performance."

72 Melissa A. Baucus and David A. Baucus, "Paying the Payer: An Empirical Examination of Longer Term Financial Consequences of Illegal Corporate Behavior," *Academy of Management Journal* 40 (1997): 129–151.

73 Marc Orlitzky and Diane L. Swanson, *Toward Integrative Corporate Citizenship: Research Advances in Corporate Social Performance* (New York: Palgrave Macmillan, 2008).

74 K. J. Arrow, *The Limits of Organization* (New York: W. W. Norton, 1974), pp. 23, 26; D. C. North, *Institutions: Institutional Change, and Economic Performance* (Cambridge: Cambridge University Press, 1990).

75 Shelby D. Hunt, "Resource-Advantage Theory and the Wealth of Nations: Developing the Socio-Economic Research Tradition," *Journal of Socio-Economics* 26 (1997).

76 North, *Institutions,* p. 9.

77 L. E. Harrison, *Who Prospers? How Cultural Values Shape Economic and Political Success* (New York: Basic Books, 1992), p. 16.

78 Hunt, "Resource-Advantage Theory and the Wealth of Nations."

79 Ibid., pp. 351–352.

80 "Global Corruption Report 2008," Transparency International, http://www.transparency.org/publications/gcr, accessed April 15, 2009.

81 About Cummins, Inc., http://www.cummins.com/cmi/content.jsp?siteId=1&langId=1033&menuId=1&overviewId=0&menuIndex=0, accessed April 15, 2009; Cummins Sustainability Report, http://www.cummins.com/cmiweb/attachments/public/Global%20Citizenship/SustReport-Online-RevApril2009-v2.pdf, accessed April 15, 2009; "Cummins Receives Top Ranking in Corporate Governance," http://www.cummins.com/cmi/content.jsp?siteId=1&langId=1033&menuId=4&overviewId=15&dataId=2914&menuIndex=0, accessed May 2, 2009.

82 Jennifer Rewick, "Connecticut Attorney General Launches Probe of Priceline.com After Complaints," *Wall Street Journal,* October 2, 2000, p. E16.

83 "19th Annual Technical Excellence Awards," *PC Magazine,* November 19, 2002, http://www.pcmag.com, accessed December 20, 2002; Glenn R. Simpson, "Raytheon Offers Office Software for Snooping," *Wall Street Journal,* June 14, 2000, p. B1.

84 Julia Angwin, "Credit-Card Scams: The Devil E-stores," *Wall Street Journal,* September 19, 2000, pp. B1, B4; Michelle Delio, "Cops Bust Massive ID Theft Ring," Wired.com, November 25, 2002, http://www.wired.com/news/privacy/0,1848,56567,00.html, accessed April 15, 2009.

85 "Randstad included in Dow Jones Sustainability Index" http://www.ir.randstad.com/releasedetail.cfm?ReleaseID=143718, accessed May 3, 2009.

86 William B. Werther and David Chandler, "Strategic Corporate Social Responsibility as Global Brand Insurance," *Business Horizons* 48 (July–August 2005): 317–324.

Chapter 2

1 "Bono Mack, Lowey Introduce Bill to Improve the Health of Youth," *Drug Week,* May 22, 2009; Better Business Bureau, "The Children's Food and Beverage Industry Advertising Initiative in Action," http://www.bbb.org/us/storage/16/documents/CFBAI/ChildrenF&BInit_Sept21.pdf, accessed May 17, 2009; Sarah Ellison and Janet Adamy, "Panel Faults Food Packaging for Kid Obesity," *Dow Jones Reprints,* http://online.wsj.com/article/SB113387976454515095.html, accessed April 15, 2009; "Kaiser Family Foundation Releases New Report on Role of Media in Childhood Obesity," Washington Panel Discussion to Explore Role of Media/Policy Options, http://www.kff.org/entmedia/entmedia022404nr.cfm, accessed April 15, 2009; "More 'Healthy' Junk Food on the Horizon?" CNNMoney.com, http://money.cnn.com/2005/09/16/news/fortune500/healthy_food/index.htm, accessed April 15, 2009;

"A Ban on Soft Drinks in Schools?" CNNMoney.com, http://money.cnn.com/2005/12/07/news/fortune500/soda_schools/index.htm, accessed April 15, 2009.

2 Scott J. Reynolds, Frank C. Schultz, and David R. Hekman, "Stakeholder Theory and Managerial Decision-Making: Constraints and Implications of Balancing Stakeholder Interests," *Journal of Business Ethics* 64, no. 3 (March 2006): 285–301.

3 Vikas Anand, Blake E. Ashforth, and Mahendra Joshi, "Business as Usual: The Acceptance and Perpetuation of Corruption in Organizations," *Academy of Management Executive* 18, no. 2 (2004): 39–53.

4 D. L. Swanson and W. C. Frederick, "Denial and Leadership in Business Ethics Education," in *Business Ethics: New Challenges for Business Schools and Corporate Leaders*, ed. R. A. Peterson and O. C. Ferrell (New York: M. E. Sharpe, 2004).

5 American Productivity & Quality Center, *Community Relations: Unleashing the Power of Corporate Citizenship* (Houston, TX: American Productivity & Quality Center, 1998); Thomas Donaldson and Lee E. Preston, "The Stakeholder Theory of the Corporation: Concepts, Evidence and Implications," *Academy of Management Review* 29 (January 1995): 65–91; Jaan Elias and J. Gregory Dees, "The Normative Foundations of Business," Harvard Business School Publishing, June 10, 1997.

6 G. A. Steiner and J. F. Steiner, *Business, Government, and Society* (New York: Random House, 1988).

7 Milton Friedman, "Social Responsibility of Business Is to Increase Its Profits," *New York Times Magazine*, September 13, 1970, pp. 122–126.

8 "Business Leaders, Politicians and Academics Dub Corporate Irresponsibility 'An Attack on America from Within'," *Business Wire*, November 7, 2002, via America Online.

9 Adam Smith, *The Theory of Moral Sentiments*, Vol. 2 (New York: Prometheus, 2000).

10 Theodore Levitt, *The Marketing Imagination* (New York: Free Press, 1983).

11 Norman Bowie, "Empowering People as an End for Business," in *People in Corporations: Ethical Responsibilities and Corporate Effectiveness*, ed. Georges Enderle, Brenda Almond, and Antonio Argandona (Dordrecht, The Netherlands: Kluwer Academic Press, 1990), pp. 105–112.

12 Chris Marsden, "The New Corporate Citizenship of Big Business: Part of the Solution to Sustainability?" *Business and Society Review* 105 (Spring 2000): 9–25; James E. Post, Lee E. Preston, and Sybille Sachs, *Redefining the Corporation: Stakeholder Management and Organizational Wealth* (Stanford, CA: Stanford University Press, 2002).

13 1997 Cone/Roper Cause-Related Marketing Trends, in "Does It Pay to Be Ethical?" *Business Ethics* (March–April 1997): 15.

14 Isabelle Maignan, "Antecedents and Benefits of Corporate Citizenship: A Comparison of U.S. and French Businesses," unpublished Ph.D. dissertation, University of Memphis, 1997.

15 Adapted from Isabelle Maignan, O. C. Ferrell, and Linda Ferrell, "A Stakeholder Model for Implementing Social Responsibility in Marketing," *European Journal of Marketing* 39 (September–October 2005): 956–977.

16 Ibid.

17 Ibid.

18 Isabelle Maignan and O. C. Ferrell, "Corporate Social Responsibility: Toward a Marketing Conceptualization," *Journal of the Academy of Marketing Science* 32 (2004): 3–19.

19 Ibid.

20 David L. Schwartzkopf, "Stakeholder Perspectives and Business Risk Perception," *Journal of Business Ethics* 64, no. 4 (April 2006): 327–342.

21 Maignan and Ferrell, "Corporate Social Responsibility."

22 Amy Merrick, "Gap Report Says Factory Inspections Are Getting Better," *Wall Street Journal*, July 13, 2005, p. B10.

23 Maignan and Ferrell, "Corporate Social Responsibility."

24 This section is adapted from Isabelle Maignan, Bas Hillebrand, and Debbie Thorne McAlister, "Managing Socially Responsible Buying: How to Integrate Non-economic Criteria into the Purchasing Process," *European Management Journal* 20 (December 2002): 641–648.

25 Andrew L. Friedman and Samantha Miles, "Developing Stakeholder Theory," *Journal of Management Studies* 39 (January 2002): 1–21; Ronald K. Mitchell, Bradley R. Agle, and Donna J. Wood, "Toward a Theory of Stakeholder Identification and Salience: Defining the Principle of Who and What Really Counts," *Academy of Management Review* 22 (October 1997): 853–886.

26 Dana Frank, *Buy American: The Untold Story of Economic Nationalism* (Boston: Beacon Press, 1999); David Kaplan, "U.S. Goods Are Preferred, Says Poll," *Adweek* (June 24, 2002): 1.

27 Amitai Etzioni, *Modern Organizations* (Upper Saddle River, NJ: Prentice Hall, 1964).

28 Aaron Bernstein, "Too Much Corporate Power?" *Business Week* (September 11, 2000): 144–158.

29 Treasury Advisory Committee on International Child Labor Enforcement, "Notices," *Federal Register,* March 6, 2000, 65 FR 11831.

30 Andrew Ward, "McDonald's Eager for Talks with Critics," *Financial Times* (London), May 3, 2000, p. 3.

31 Mark C. Suchman, "Managing Legitimacy: Strategic and Institutional Approaches," *Academy of Management Review* 20 (July 1995): 571–610.

32 Brad Knickerbock, "Activists Step Up War to 'Liberate' Nature," *Christian Science Monitor* (January 20, 1999): 4.

33 Elliott Choueka, "Big Mac Fights Back," BBC Money Programme, July 8, 2005, http://news.bbc.co.uk/2/hi/business/4665205.stm, accessed April 15, 2009.

34 Joshua Kurlantzick, "Protestors Form Human Chain Outside ADB Meeting," *Agence France Presse*, May 8, 2000, via LEXIS®-NEXIS® Academic Universe.

35 "Diamond Trade Funding Wars," *African Business* 248 (November 1999): 28; James E. Post and Shawn L. Berman, "Global Corporate Citizenship in a Dot.com World," in *Perspectives on Corporate Citizenship,* ed. Jörg Andriof and Malcolm McIntosh (Sheffield, UK: Greenleaf Publishing, 2001), pp. 66–82; "Shaming the Sanctions-Busters," *Economist* (March 18, 2000): 47.

36 Ronald Alsop, "Corporate Reputations Are Earned with Trust, Reliability, Study Shows," *Wall Street Journal,* September 23, 1999, http://interactive.wsj.com; John F. Mahon, "Corporate Reputation: A Research Agenda Using Strategy and Stakeholder Literature," *Business and Society* 41 (December 2002): 415–445.

37 Scott Malone, "Corporate America's Reputation Plunges: Survey," http://www.reuters.com/article/ousiv/idUSTRE53R00220090428, accessed May 10, 2009.

38 Manto Gotsi and Alan Wilson, "Corporate Reputation Management: 'Living the Brand,'" *Management Decision* 39,

no. 2 (2001): 99–105; Jim Kartalia, "Technology Safeguards for a Good Corporate Reputation," *Information Executive* 3 (September 1999): 4; Prema Nakra, "Corporate Reputation Management: 'CRM' with a Strategic Twist?" *Public Relations Quarterly* 45 (Summer 2000): 35–42.

39 Jeanne Logsdon and Donna J. Wood, "Reputation as an Emerging Construct in the Business and Society Field: An Introduction," *Business and Society* 41 (December 2002): 265–270; "Putting a Price Tag to Reputation," Council of Public Relations Firms, http://www.prfirms.org, accessed December 20, 2002; Allen M. Weiss, Erin Anderson, and Deborah J. MacInnis, "Reputation Management as a Motivation for Sales Structure Decisions," *Journal of Marketing* 63 (October 1999): 74–89.

40 Christy Eidson and Melissa Master, "Who Makes the Call?" *Across the Board* 37 (March 2000): 16; Logsdon and Wood, "Reputation as an Emerging Construct in the Business and Society Field."

41 Alison Rankin Frost, "Brand vs. Reputation," *Communication World* 16 (February–March 1999): 22–25.

42 Glen Peters, *Waltzing with the Raptors: A Practical Roadmap to Protecting Your Company's Reputation* (New York: Wiley, 1999).

43 Green Mountain Coffee Annual Report 10-K, 2005, http://www.greenmountaincoffee.com, accessed April 15, 2009; Hoover Fact Sheet About Green Mountain Coffee http://www.hoovers.com/green-mountain-coffee-roasters,-inc./--ID__45721--/free-co-factsheet.xhtml, accessed April 15, 2009; "200 Best Small Companies in America," *Forbes Magazine*, October 8, 2008, http://www.forbes.com/2008/10/08/best-small-companies-ent-200smalls08-cz_kb_1008small_land.html, accessed April 15, 2009; "100 Best Corporate Citizens 2005," *Business Ethics* (Spring 2005): 22–23.

44 Much of this section is adapted from Lisa A. Mainiero, "Action or Reaction? Handling Businesses in Crisis After September 11," *Business Horizons* 45 (September–October 2002): 2–10; Robert R. Ulmer and Timothy L. Sellnow, "Consistent Questions of Ambiguity in Organizational Crisis Communication: Jack in the Box as a Case Study," *Journal of Business Ethics* 25 (May 2000): 143–155; Robert R. Ulmer and Timothy L. Sellnow, "Strategic Ambiguity and the Ethic of Significant Choices in the Tobacco Industry's Crisis Communication," *Communication Studies* 48, no. 3 (1997): 215–233; Timothy L. Sellnow and Robert R. Ulmer, "Ambiguous Argument as Advocacy in Organizational Crisis Communication," *Argumentation and Advocacy* 31, no. 3 (1995): 138–150; Peter V. Stanton, "Ten Communication Mistakes You Can Avoid When Managing a Crisis," *Public Relations Quarterly* 47 (Summer 2002): 19–22.

45 "Crisis Survival Tactics for HR," *HR Focus* 79 (April 2002): 1, 13; "Boss of IBM's Disaster Recovery Center Tells What He Learned from Last Week's Crisis," *InfoWorld.com,* http://www.infoworld.com/articles/hn/xml/01/09/19/010919hngordon.xml, accessed August 28, 2003.

46 Lynn Brewer, Robert Chandler, and O. C. Ferrell, *Managing Risks for Corporate Integrity: How to Survive an Ethical Misconduct Disaster* (Mason, OH: Texere/Thomson, 2006), pp. 2–3.

47 HealthSouth, http://www.healthsouth.com/medinfo/home/app/frame?2+article.jsp,0,091505_Scrushy_Press, accessed July 13, 2006.

48 Helen Shaw and Dave Cook, "Scrushy Acquitted on All Counts," *CFO.com*, June 28, 2005, http://www.cfo.com/article.cfm/4076776/c_4125234?f=todayinfinance_inside, accessed July 13, 2006.

49 HealthSouth Statement Regarding Scrushy Press Conference, http://www.healthsouth.com/medinfo/home/app/frame?2=article.jsp,0,091505_Scrushy_Press, accessed March 7, 2006.

50 Caroline E. Mayer, "Blockbuster Sued over Return Policy," *Washington Post,* February 19, 2005, http://www.washingtonpost.com/wp-dyn/articles/A36767-2005Feb18.html, accessed April 15, 2009.

51 Paul Argenti, "Crisis Communication: Lessons from 9/11," *Harvard Business Review* 80 (December 2002): 103–109; L. Paul Bremer, "Corporate Governance and Crisis Management," *Directors and Boards* 26 (Winter 2002): 16–20; Christine M. Pearson and Judith A. Clair, "Reframing Crisis Management," *Academy of Management Review* 23 (January 1998): 59–76.

52 "Disney World Ride Reopened," CBS News, July 14, 2005, http://www.cbsnews.com/stories/2005/07/13/national/main708906.shtml, accessed April 15, 2009.

53 Ibid.

54 Michael John Harker, "Relationship Marketing Defined?" *Marketing Intelligence and Planning* 17 (January 1999): 13–20; Robert M. Morgan and Shelby D. Hunt, "The Commitment-Trust Theory of Relationship Marketing," *Journal of Marketing* 58 (July 1994): 20–38.

55 "Hormel Plans Ahead with Oracle Internet Procurement," *Fortune,* May 1, 2000, p. S12.

56 Jörg Andriof and Sandra Waddock, "Unfolding Stakeholder Engagement," in *Unfolding Stakeholder Thinking: Theory, Responsibility and Engagement,* ed. Jörg Andriof, Sandra Waddock, Bryan Husted, and Sandra S. Rahman (Sheffield, UK: Greenleaf Publishing, 2002), pp. 19–42; James Coleman, "Social Capital in the Creation of Human Capital," *American Journal of Sociology* 94 (1988): S95–S120; Carrie R. Leana and Harry J. Van Buren III, "Organizational Social Capital and Employment Practices," *Academy of Management Review* 24 (July 1999): 538–555.

57 Chemical Manufacturers Association, *Improving Responsible Care Implementation, Enhancing Performance and Credibility* (Washington, DC: Chemical Manufacturers Association, 1993); "Details of Revamped *Responsible Care* Take Shape," *Chemical Week* (November 20, 2002): 33–39; Jennifer Howard, Jennifer Nash, and John Ehrenfeld, "Standard or Smokescreen? Implementation of a Voluntary Environmental Code," *California Management Review* 42 (Winter 2000): 63–82.

58 Adapted from Maignan, Ferrell, and Ferrell, "A Stakeholder Model for Implementing Social Responsibility in Marketing," pp. 956–977.

59 Marjorie Kelly, "*Business Ethics* 100 Best Corporate Citizens 2006," *Business Ethics* (Spring 2006): 20–25.

60 "Obesity Becomes Political Issue as Well as Cultural Obsession," Washington Wire, *Wall Street Journal*, March 3, 2006, http://www.wsj.com, accessed March 21, 2006.

61 "Readers on Health Care," *Wall Street Journal*, January 9, 2006, p. R3, http://www.wsj.com, accessed March 21, 2006.

62 "Corporate Social Responsibility at Starbucks," http://www.starbucks.com/aboutus/csr.asp, accessed April 15, 2009.

63 Stephanie Armour, "Maryland First to OK 'Wal-Mart Bill' Law Requires More Health Care Spending," *USA Today*, January 13, 2006, p. B1.

64 Kris Hudson, "Wal-Mart to Offer Improved Health-Care Benefits," *Wall Street Journal*, February 24, 2006, p. A2.

65 Michael Pirson and Deepak Malhotra, "Unconventional Insights for Managing Stakeholder Trust," *Sloan Management Review* 49 (Summer 2008): 42–50.

66 Jon Entine, "The Body Shop: Truth and Consequences," *Drug & Cosmetics Industry* 156 (February 1995): 54; Jon Entine, "Body Shop's Packaging Starts to Unravel," *Australian Financial Review,* December 18, 2002, p. 52.

67 Matthew Gitsham, "Cleaner, but Not Sparkling," *Ethical Corporation* (December 2005): 48–49.

68 Max B. E. Clarkson, "A Stakeholder Framework for Analyzing and Evaluating Corporate Social Performance," *Academy of Management Review* 20 (January 1995): 92–117.

69 Ibid., p. 109.

70 Ibid.

71 Ibid.

72 Ibid.

73 Jörg Andriof, "Managing Social Risk Through Stakeholder Partnership Building," unpublished Ph.D. dissertation, Warwick Business School, 2000; Jörg Andriof, "Patterns of Stakeholder Partnership Building," in *Perspectives on Corporate Citizenship*, ed. Andriof and McIntosh, pp. 215–238.

74 Nick Chaloner and David Brontzen, "How SABMiller Protects Its Biggest Asset—Its Reputation," *Strategic Communication Management* 6 (October–November 2002): 12–15.

Chapter 3

1 O. C. Ferrell, John Fraedrich, and Linda Ferrell, "Understanding the Importance of Business Ethics in the 2008–2009 Financial Crisis," preface to Business Ethics, updated 2009 edition (Mason, OH: South-Western Cengage Learning, 2009); Steven A. Holmes, "Fannie Mae Eases Credit to Aid Mortgage Lending," New York Times, September 30, 1999, http://www.nytimes.com/1999/09/30/business/fannie-mae-eases-credit-to-aid-mortgage-lending.html, accessed April 7, 2009; Associated Press, "Freddie Mac Pays Record $3.8 Million Fine," MSNBC, April 18, 2006, http://www.msnbc.msn.com/id/12373488/from/RSS/, accessed on April 8, 2009; Reuters, "Fannie Mae, Freddie Mac Subprime Restrictions Ease," CNBC, September 19, 2007, http://www.cnbc.com/id/20869608/, accessed April 8, 2009.

2 Rafael LaPorta and Florencio Lopez-de-Silanes, "Investor Protection and Corporate Governance," *Journal of Financial Economics* 58 (October–November 2000): 3–38.

3 *Dodge v. Ford Motor Co.,* 204 Mich. 459, 179 N.W. 668, 3 A.L.R. 413 (1919).

4 Alfred Marcus and Sheryl Kaiser, "Managing Beyond Compliance: The Ethical and Legal Dimensions of Corporate Responsibility" (Garfield Heights, OH: North Coast Publishers, 2006), p. 79.

5 Mauricio Guerrero, "Prosecutors Fight Stanford's Release," *New York Times*, June 26, 2009, http://www.nytimes.com/2009/06/27/business/27stanford.html?ref=business, accessed June 26, 2009.

6 Connie Bruck, "Angelo's Ashes," *New Yorker*, June 29, 2009, p. 48.

7 Ben W. Heineman Jr., "Are You a Good Corporate Citizen?" *Wall Street Journal,* June 28, 2005, http://online.wsj.com/article/0,,SB111991936947571125,00-search.html, accessed June 29, 2009.

8 "Saks Shareholders Call for Annual Director Election," Reuters, http://www.reuters.com/article/ousiv/idUSTRE5525DZ20090603, accessed June 3, 2009.

9 Erik Berglöf and Stijn Claessens, "Enforcement and Good Corporate Governance in Developing Countries and Transition Economies," *World Bank Research Observer,* February 21, 2006, http://wbro.oxfordjournals.org/cgi/content/full/21/1/123, accessed June 29, 2009; Darryl Reed, "Corporate Governance Reforms in Developing Countries," *Journal of Business Ethics* 37 (May 2002): 223–247.

10 Bryan W. Husted and Carlos Serrano, "Corporate Governance in Mexico," *Journal of Business Ethics* 37 (May 2002): 337–348.

11 Robert A. G. Monks, *Corporate Governance in the Twenty-First Century: A Preliminary Outline* (Portland, ME: LENS, 1996), available at http://www.lens-library.com/info/cg21.html.

12 McRitchie, "Ending the Wall Street Walk: Why Corporate Governance Now?" *Corporate Governance,* http://www.corpgov.net/forums/commentary/ending.html, accessed June 29, 2009.

13 David A. Cifrino and Garrison R. Smith, "NYSE and NASDAQ Propose to Review Corporate Governance Listing Standards," *Corporate Governance Advisor* 10 (November–December 2002): 18–25.

14 Jane J. Kim and Aaron Lucchetti, "Big Change in Store for Brokers in Obama's Oversight Overhaul," *Wall Street Journal,* June 19, 2009, http://online.wsj.com/article/SB124536973514629609.html?mod=googlenews_wsj, accessed June 26, 2009.

15 Timothy Devinney, "Is the Socially Responsible Corporation a Myth? The Good, the Bad, and the Ugly of Corporate Social Responsibility," *Academy of Management Perspectives* 23, no. 2 (May 2009): 44–56.

16 A. Demb and F. F. Neubauer, *The Corporate Board: Confronting the Paradoxes* (Oxford: Oxford University Press, 1992).

17 Sandy Shore, "Ex-Qwest Exec Settlement Said Collapsed," *Associated Press,* January 20, 2006, http://accounting.smartpros.com/x51431.xml, accessed July 1, 2009.

18 Bob Mook, "Former Qwest CEO Guilty on 19 Counts," *Business Journal News Service,* April 20, 2007, http://www.bizjournals.com/portland/stories/2007/04/16/daily54.html, accessed June 26, 2009.

19 Organisation for Economic Co-operation and Development, *The OECD Principles of Corporate Governance* (Paris: Organisation for Economic Co-operation and Development, 1999).

20 Wal-Mart Sustainability Progress Report, 2008, http://walmartstores.com/Sustainability/7951.aspx; Wal-Mart Stores, Inc., http://walmartstores.com, accessed June 2, 2009.

21 Edward A. Stolzenberg, "Governance Change for Public Hospitals," *Journal of Healthcare Management* 45 (September–October 2000): 347–350; Jeffrey A. Alexander, Bryan J. Weiner, and Richard J. Bogue, "Changes in the Structure, Composition, and Activity of Hospital Governing Boards, 1989–1997: Evidence from Two National Surveys," *Milbank Quarterly* 79 (May 2001): 253–279.

22 "Corporate Governance," International Finance Corporation: World Bank Group, http://www.ifc.org/corporategovernance, accessed June 29, 2009.

23 Clive Crook, "Why Good Corporate Citizens Are a Public Menace," *National Journal,* April 24, 1999, p. 1087.

24 Bank of America 2008 Annual Report, p. 16, http://media .corporate-ir.net/media_files/irol/71/71595/reports/2008_ AR.pdf, accessed July 1, 2009; "Bank of America Wins Top Environmental Leadership Award from California Governor," TradingMarkets.com, November 26, 2008, http://www.tradingmarkets.com/.site/news/Stock%20 News/2051715/, accessed April 26, 2009; "Bank of America Creates Environmental Banking Team," Jonathan Stempel, Reuters, February 12, 2008, http://www.reuters.com/article/ companyNewsAndPR/idUSN1225091020080212, accessed April 26, 2009; Greg Morcroft, "Citi Tells Clients to Buy Bank of America," Marketwatch, July 1, 2009, http://www .marketwatch.com/story/citi-adds-b-of-a-to-aggressive-growth- list, accessed July 1, 2009.

25 Joseph Major, "Citi's Board Seeks Revamp with ex-Finance Chiefs, Fed Official, *International Business Times,* http://www .ibtimes.com/articles/20090316/citi-calls-on-ex-finance-chiefs- former-fed-official-board.htm, accessed June 26, 2009.

26 Melvin A. Eisenberg, "Corporate Governance: The Board of Directors and Internal Control," *Cordoza Law Review* 19 (September–November 1997): 237.

27 National Association of Corporate Directors, http://www .nacdonline.org/, accessed June 26, 2009.

28 Heather Timmons, "Satyam Chief Admits Huge Fraud," *New York Times,* January 7, 2009, http://www.nytimes. com/2009/01/08/business/worldbusiness/08satyam.html, accessed June 26, 2009.

29 Louis Lavelle, "The Best and Worst Boards," *Business Week,* October 7, 2002, p. 104; McKinsey & Company, *McKinsey Director Opinion Survey on Corporate Governance, 2002,* http:// www.mckinsey.com/clientservice/organizationleadership/ser-vice/ corpgovernance/pdf/cg_survey.pdf, accessed June 29, 2009.

30 Harvey, L. Pitt, "Retaining Ethical Cultures During a Week Economy," *Compliance Week,* June 30, 2009, http://www. complianceweek.com/article/5468/retaining-ethical-cultures- during-a-weak-economy, accessed June 30, 2009.

31 Geoffrey Colvin, "CEO Knockdown," *Fortune,* April 4, 2005, http://money.cnn.com/magazines/fortune/fortune_ archive/2005/04/04/8255943/index.htm, accessed June 29, 2009.

32 Damian Paletta, Maya Jackson Randall, and Michael R. Crittenden, "Geithner Calls for Tougher Standards on Risk," *Wall Street Journal,* March 25, 2009, http://online.wsj.com/ article/SB123807231255147603.html, accessed June 11, 2009.

33 Adrian Cadbury, "What Are the Trends in Corporate Governance? How Will They Impact Your Company?" *Long Range Planning* 32 (January 1999): 12–19.

34 "How Shareholder Proposals Work," The Equality Project, http://www.equalityproject.org, accessed June 29, 2009; Barry Burr, "Shareholder Activism Hot in Poor Business Climate," *Pensions & Investments,* July 8, 2002, pp. 4, 32; Chuck Collins and Sam Pizzigati, "What Happened to the Crackdown on Executive Pay?" *Baltimore Sun,* June 24, 2009, http://www.baltimoresun.com/news/opinion/oped/bal-op. viewpoint24jun24,0,5021362.story, accessed June 29, 2009.

35 Lauren Tara LaCapra, "BofA's Board Shuffle an Ode to Stakeholders," *The Street,* June 22, 2009, http://www .thestreet.com/story/10523721/1/bofas-board-shuffle-an-ode- to-shareholders.html?cm_ven=GOOGLEFI, accessed June 30, 2009.

36 Peter D. Kinder, Steven D. Lyndenberg, and Amy L. Domini, *The Social Investment Almanac* (New York: Holt, 1992).

37 "Companies Fail Social Investors, Most Investors Value Corporate Responsibility, Few Are Satisfied," *Investor Relations Business,* August 6, 2001, pp. 1, 13; SocialFunds. com/Motley Fool, "Investor Survey on Corporate Responsibility," http://www.socialfunds.com/page.cgi/fool_ results.html, accessed June 29, 2009.

38 Ann Moore Odell, "New Survey Uncovers Discrepancies on Corporate Citizenship Issues," Social Funds Sustainability Investment News, January 29, 2008, http://www.socialfunds. com/page.cgi/fool_results.html, accessed June 29, 2009.

39 Susan Scherreik, "Following Your Conscience Is Just a Few Clicks Away," *Business Week,* May 13, 2002, pp. 116–118.

40 B. Langtry, "The Ethics of Shareholding," *Journal of Business Ethics* 37 (May 2002): 175–185.

41 R. Bruce Hutton, Louis D'Antonio, and Tommi Johnsen, "Socially Responsible Investing: Growing Issues and New Opportunities," *Business and Society* 37 (September 1998): 281–305.

42 Social Investment Forum, "2007 Report on Socially Responsible Investing Trends in the United States," http:// www.socialinvest.org/pdf/SRI_Trends_ExecSummary_2007. pdf, accessed June 29, 2009.

43 Social Investment Forum, "2007 Report."

44 "Biz Deans Talk—Business Management Education Blog," January 2, 2009, http://www.deanstalk.net/deanstalk/2009/01/ warren-buffetts.html, accessed May 27, 2009.

45 "Internal Auditors: Integral to Good Corporate Governance," *Internal Auditor* 59 (August 2002): 44–49.

46 Donna Kardos, "KPMG Is Sued Over New Century," *Wall Street Journal,* April 2, 2009, http://online.wsj.com/ article/SB123860415462378767.html, accessed June 11, 2009.

47 Eisenberg, "Corporate Governance."

48 Kathy Hoke, "Eyes Wide Open," *Business First–Columbus,* August 27, 1999, pp. 27–28.

49 Lynn Brewer, Robert Chandler, and O. C. Ferrell, *Managing Risks for Corporate Integrity: How to Survive an Ethical Misconduct Disaster* (Mason, OH: Texere/Thomson, 2006), p. 72.

50 Ray A. Goldberg, *Kraft General Foods: Risk Management Philosophy* (Boston: Harvard Business School Press, 1994).

51 Heather Timmons, "Financial Scandal at Outsourcing Company Rattles a Developing Country," *New York Times,* January 7, 2009, http://www.nytimes.com/ 2009/01/08/business/worldbusiness/08outsource.html?_ r=1&scp=1&sq=satyam%20riding%20a%20tiger&st=cse, accessed June 26, 2009.

52 Brewer, Chandler, and Ferrell, *Managing Risks for Corporate Integrity,* p. 75.

53 Ibid.

54 Jim Billington, "A Few Things Every Manager Ought to Know About Risk," *Harvard Management Update,* March 1997, pp. 10–11; Lee Puschaver and Robert G. Eccles, "In Pursuit of the Upside: The New Opportunity in Risk Management," *PW Review,* December 1996.

55 Scott Alexander, "Achieving Enterprisewide Privacy Compliance," *Insurance & Technology* 25 (November 2000): 53; M. Joseph Sirgy and Chenting Su, "The Ethics of Consumer Sovereignty in an Age of High Tech," *Journal of Business Ethics* 28 (November 2000): 1–14.

56 Phil Mattingly, "AIG Chief Goes Off Script, Says Employees Will Return Some of Bonus Money," Yahoo! News, March 18, 2009, http://news.yahoo.com/s/cq/20090318/pl_cq_ politics/politics3077969, accessed June 3, 2009.

57 Sarah Anderson, John Cavanaugh, Scott Kinger, and Liz Stanton, "Executive Excess 2008. How Average Taxpayers Subsidize Runaway Pay," *Institute for Policy Studies, United for a Fair Economy*, http://faireconomy.org/files/executive_excess_2008.pdf, accessed July 2, 2009.

58 "2009 Executive PayWatch," AFL–CIO, http://www.aflcio.org/corporatewatch/paywatch/, June 3, 2009.

59 Kara Scanell, "SEC Ready to Require More Pay Disclosures," *Wall Street Journal*, June 3, 2009, http://online.wsj.com/article/SB124397831899078781.html, accessed June 11, 2009.

60 Gary Strauss, "America's Corporate Meltdown," *USA Today,* June 27, 2002, pp. 1A, 2A.

61 Louis Lavelle, "CEO Pay, The More Things Change . . . ," *BusinessWeek,* October 16, 2000, http://www.businessweek.com/2000/00_42/b3703102.htm, accessed June 29, 2009.

62 "Measuring Corporate Governance Standards," *Asiamoney* 11 (December 2000–January 2001): 94–95.

63 Barbara Crutchfield George, Kathleen A. Lacey, and Jotta Birmele, "The 1998 OECD Convention," *American Business Law Journal* 37 (Spring 2000): 485–525; Ira Millstein, "Corporate Governance: The Role of Market Forces," *OECD Observer* (Summer 2000): 27–28; "About OECD," Organisation for Economic Co-operation and Development, http://www.oecd.org/pages/0,3417,en_36734052_36734103_1_1_1_1_1,00.html, accessed June 29, 2009.

64 Iceland's Collapse, *Wall Street Journal,* October 10, 2008, http://online.wsj.com/article/SB122357320328519651.html?mod=googlewsj, accessed June 26, 2009.

65 Fareed Zakaria, "A Capitalist Manifesto: Greed is Good (to a Point)," *Newsweek,* June 13, 2009, http://www.newsweek.com/id/201935, accessed June 26, 2009.

66 Adam M. Brandenburger and Barry J. Nalebuff, *Co-opetition: 1. A Revolutionary Mindset That Redefines Competition and Cooperation; 2. The Game Theory Strategy That's Changing the Game of Business* (New York: Doubleday, 1997).

67 Maher and Anderson, *Corporate Governance.*

68 Monks, *Corporate Governance in the Twenty-First Century.*

69 "Three Skills for Today's Leaders," *Harvard Management Update* 4 (November 1999): 11.

70 Catherine M. Daily, Dan R. Dalton, and Albert A. Cannella Jr., "Corporate Governance: A Decade of Dialogue and Data," *Academy of Management Review* 28 (July 2003): 371–382.

71 Carol Hymowitz, "How to Fix a Broken System," *Wall Street Journal,* February 24, 2003, pp. R1–R3.

72 Monks, *Corporate Governance in the Twenty-First Century.*

Chapter 4

1 Daniel Gross, "Remembering Bear Stearns?," *Newsweek,* April 2, 2009, http://www.newsweek.com/id/192113, accessed July 8, 2009; John Fraedrich, O. C. Ferrell, and Jennifer Jackson, *Banking Industry Meltdown: The Ethical and Financial Risk of Derivatives,* pp. 8–10.

2 David Goldman, "Obama Vows Antitrust Crackdown," *CNN Money,* May 11, 2009, http://money.cnn.com/2009/05/11/news/economy/antitrust/index.htm, accessed June 12, 2009.

3 Steve Lohr, "High-Tech Antitrust Cases: The Road Ahead," *New York Times,* May 13, 2009, http://bits.blogs.nytimes.com/2009/05/13/high-tech-antitrust-the-road-ahead/?scp=1&sq=high-tech%20antitrust&st=cse, accessed June 12, 2009.

4 Ronald A. Cass, "The EU's 'Nationalization by Regulation,'" *Wall Street Journal*, June 23, 2009, http://online.wsj.com.com/article/SB124571871033339547.html, accessed June 29, 2009.

5 Alistair Barr, "IRS Tries to Force UBS to Reveal US Tax Dodgers," Market Watch, February 19, 2009, http://www.marketwatch.com/story/ubs-kept-52000-secret-bank-accounts?print=true&dist=printMidSection, June 4, 2009.

6 Goran Mijuk, "Switzerland: Will Block UBS from Giving U.S. Client Data," *Wall Street Journal*, July 8, 2009, http://online.wsj.com/article/SB124704837562010835.html, accessed July 8, 2009.

7 "Welcome to BBB*OnLine*'s Consumer Safe Shopping Site," Better Business Bureau, http://www.bbb.org/online/consumer/default.aspx, accessed July 7, 2009.

8 "BBB*OnLine*: Why Your Business Should Participate," Better Business Bureau, http://www.bbb.org/us/bbb-online-business-accreditation/, accessed June 30, 2009.

9 Alan S. Blinder, *Keynesian Economics*. Library of Economics and Liberty, http://www.econlib.org/library/Enc/KeynesianEconomics.html, accessed June 1, 2009.

10 Robert L. Formaini, "Milton Friedman—Economist as Public Intellectual," *Economic Insights* 7, no. 2 (2002); Federal Reserve Bank of Dallas, http://www.dallasfed.org/research/ei/ei0202.html, accessed June 5, 2009.

11 Lisa Rein, "Electric Rates No Bright Spot for O'Malley as Election Nears," *Washington Post,* July 6, 2009, http://www.washingtonpost.com/wp-dyn/content/article/2009/07/05/AR2009070502697.html, accessed July 7, 2009.

12 Jennifer Levitz, "Laws Take on Financial Scams Against Seniors," *Wall Street Journal*, May 19, 2009, http://online.wsj.com/article/SB124269210323932723.html, accessed June 12, 2009.

13 Joan Lowy, "Airline Industry Changes Raise Safety Issues," Associated Press, May 16, 2009, http://www.google.com/hostednews/ap/article/ALeqM5htIO9mJZGmC7fdH6AC4-DQV5kd59wD9879S581, accessed June 4, 2009.

14 Amanda Kleha, "2008: The Year in Spam," *Official Google Enterprise Blog*, http://googleenterprise.blogspot.com/2009/01/2008-year-in-spam.html, accessed July 3, 2009.

15 "Sanford Wallace, MySpace Spam," *Chicago Tribune*, May 14, 2008, http://archives.chicagotribune.com/2008/may/14/business/chi-sanford-wallace-myspace-spam-080514-ht, accessed July 3, 2009.

16 S. Bono, A. Rubin, A. Stubblefield, and M. Green, "Security Through Legality," *Communications of the ACM* 49 (June 2006): 41–43.

17 "Sony BMG Music Settles Charges Its Music Fan Websites Violated the Children's Online Privacy Protection Act," *Federal Trade Commission*, December 11, 2008, http://www.ftc.gov/opa/2008/12/sonymusic.shtm, accessed July 3, 2009.

18 Julia Angwin, "How to Keep Kids Safe Online," *Wall Street Journal*, January 22, 2009, http://online.wsj.com/article/SB123238632055894993.html, accessed June 12, 2009.

19 "IC3 2008 Annual Report on Internet Crime Released," *Internet Crime Complaint Center*, March 31, 2008, http://www.ic3.gov/media/2009/090331.aspx, accessed July 3, 2009.

20 "Online Auction Fraud: Don't Let it Happen to You," *Federal Bureau of Investigation*, June 30, 2009, http://www.fbi.gov/page2/june09/auctionfraud_063009.html, accessed July 3, 2009.

21 "The Sherman Antitrust Act," Antitrust Case Browser, http://www.stolaf.edu/people/becker/antitrust/statutes/sherman.html, accessed July 5, 2009.

22 Ibid.

23 U.S. Department of Justice, "Antitrust Enforcement and the Consumer," http://www.usdoj.gov/atr/public/div_stats/211491.pdf, accessed July 5, 2009.

24 "Stanley Tools Settles 'Made in USA' Charges," *consumeraffairs.com*, June 11, 2006, http://www.consumeraffairs.com/news04/2006/06/ftc_stanley_works.html, accessed July 5, 2009.

25 "Doan's Pills Must Run Corrective Advertising: FTC," *Case Watch*, from May 27, 1999 FTC news release, http://www.casewatch.org/ftc/news/1999/doans.shtml, accessed July 5, 2009.

26 "FTC Announces Settlement with Bankrupt Web Site, Toysmart.com, Regarding Alleged Privacy Policy Violations," SmartPros, http://accounting.smartpros.com/x15465.xml, accessed July 5, 2009.

27 Kevin G. Hall, "How Obama's Plan Will Work," *Houston Chronicle*, June 18, 2009, D1, D4; Associated Press, "Frank Endorses Consumer-Protection Agency," *Wall Street Journal*, June 24, 2009, http://online.wsj.com/article/SB124585419323347729.html, accessed June 29, 2009; Steven Thomma and Kevin G. Hall, "End of an era in free market," *Houston Chronicle*, June 18, 2009, pp. A1, A8.

28 Jamie Dimon, "A Unified Bank Regulator Is a Good Start," *Wall Street Journal*, June 29, 2009, http://online.wsj.com/article/SB124605726587563517.htm, accessed June 29, 2009.

29 Jane J. Kim and Aaron Lucchetti, "Big Change in Store for Brokers in Obama's Oversight Overhaul," *Wall Street Journal*, June 19, 2009, http://online.wsj.com/article/SB124536973514629609.html?mod=googlenews_wsj, accessed June 29, 2009.

30 Sudeep Reddy, "A Personal-Finance Workout," *Wall Street Journal*, June 23, 2009, http://online.wsj.com/article/SB124570998785138771.html, accessed June 29, 2009.

31 Albert A. Foer and Robert H. Lande, "The Evolution of United States Antitrust Law: The Past, Present & (Possible) Future," *American Antitrust Institute*, October 20, 1999, http://www.antitrustinstitute.org/archives/files/64.pdf, accessed July 5, 2009.

32 Maria Bruno-Britz, "Visa and American Express Settle Legal Dispute," *Wall Street & Technology*, November 9, 2007, http://www.wallstreetandtech.com/news/showArticle.jhtml?articleID=202804267, accessed July 5, 2009.

33 "Feds Eye Book Scans by Google," *New York Post*, July 3, 2009, http://www.nypost.com/seven/07032009/business/feds_eye_book_scans_by_google_177463.htm, accessed July 3, 2009.

34 European Union, "Key Facts and Figures about Europe and the Europeans," http://europa.eu/abc/keyfigures/index_en.htm, accessed July 5, 2009.

35 Adam Cohen, "EU Plan for a New Market Watchdog Rattles U.K.," *Wall Street Journal*, June 18, 2009, http://online.wsj.com/article/SB124526378830024157.html, accessed July 1, 2009.

36 Theo Francis and Mark Scott, "Even Tougher Rules Across the Pond," *BusinessWeek*, July 6, 2009, p. 22.

37 Brandon Mitchener, "Global Antitrust Process May Get Simpler," *Wall Street Journal*, October 27, 2000, p. A17; Debbie Thorne LeClair, O. C. Ferrell, and Linda Ferrell, "Federal Sentencing Guidelines for Organizations: Legal, Ethical, and Public Policy Issues for International Marketing," *Journal of Public Policy and Marketing* 16 (Spring 1997): 30.

38 Veronique de Rugy and Melinda Warren, *Regulatory Agency Spending Reaches New Height: An Analysis of the U.S. Budget for Fiscal Years 2008 and 2009*, Washington University in St. Louis and the Mercatus Center at George Mason University, August 2008, http://www.mercatus.org/uploadedFiles/Mercatus/Publications/1-regulatoryagency20080807_wc-regulators_budget_09.pdf, accessed July 4, 2009.

39 William M. Pride and O. C. Ferrell, *Marketing: Concepts and Strategies*, 15th ed. (Boston: Houghton Mifflin, 2010), pp. 70–71; "BBB Structure," Better Business Bureau, http://www.bbb.org/us/BBB-Structure/, accessed July 4, 2009.

40 Jennifer Rewick, "Connecticut Attorney General Launches Probe of Priceline.com After Complaints," *Wall Street Journal*, October 2, 2000, p. B16.

41 "Overview of the SAFE Digital Identity and Signature Standard," *SAFE-BioPharma Association*, http://www.safe-biopharma.org/overview.htm, accessed July 5, 2009; "Global Regulatory: U.S. Food and Drug Administration," *SAFE-BioPharma Association*, http://www.safe-biopharma.org/globalregulatory.htm, accessed July 5, 2009.

42 Daniel Malan, "Corporate Citizens, Colonialists, Tourists or Activists? Ethical Challenges Facing South African Corporations in Africa," *Journal of Corporate Citizenship* 18 (Summer 2005): 49–60.

43 Joint Committee on the Organization of Congress, "Historical Overview," Organization of the Congress, December 1993, http://www.rules.house.gov/Archives/jcoc2.htm, accessed July 5, 2009; Joint Committee on the Organization of Congress, "Reorganization in the Modern Congress," Organization of the Congress, December 1993, http://www.rules.house.gov/Archives/jcoc2.htm; Marc A. Triebwasser, "Congressional Leadership and Reform: The Trends Toward Centralization and Decentralization," *American Politics*, http://www.polisci.ccsu.edu/trieb/Cong-9.html, accessed July 5, 2009; "Driving Mr. Gephardt," *Newsweek*, August 21, 2000, p. 48.

44 "About the FEC," Federal Election Commission, http://www.fec.gov/about.shtml, accessed July 5, 2009.

45 "A Brief History of Money and Politics," *Campaign Legal Center*, http://www.campaignfinanceguide.org/guide-35.html, accessed July 5, 2009.

46 Don Corney, Amy Borrus, and Jay Greene, "Microsoft's All Out Counterattack," *Business Week*, May 15, 2000, pp. 103–106.

47 Peter Eavis, "U.S. Reforms No Pushover for Banks," *Wall Street Journal*, June 22, 2009, http://online.wsj.com/article/SB124563161642335927.html, accessed June 29, 2009; Deborah Solomon and Damian Paletta, "U.S. Eyes Bank Pay Overhaul," *Wall Street Journal*, May 13, 2009, http://online.wsj.com/article/SB124215896684211987.html, accessed June 13, 2009.

48 Jake Sherman, "Legislators Framing Climate Bills Hold Energy Stock," *Wall Street Journal*, June 17, 2009, http://online.wsj.com/SB124519704993421187.html?mod=googlenews_wsj, accessed June 29, 2009.

49 John Fritze, "PACs Spent Record $416M on Federal Election," *USA Today*, March 2, 2009, http://www.usatoday.com/news/washington/2009-03-01-pacmoney_N.htm, accessed July 5, 2009.

50 "ELECTION FRAUD: Don't Commit a Campaign Crime," Federal Bureau of Investigation, December 18, 2007, http://www.fbi.gov/page2/dec07/electionfraud121807.html, accessed July 5, 2009.

51 Kara Scannell, "SEC Puts Rating Firms on Notice," *Wall Street Journal,* April 16, 2009, http://online.wsj.com/article/SB123980931135221355.html, accessed May 5, 2009.

52 Lynn Brewer, Robert Chandler, and O. C. Ferrell, *Managing Risks for Corporate Integrity: How to Survive an Ethical Misconduct Disaster* (Mason, OH: Texere/Thomson, 2006); United States Code Service (Lawyers Addition), 18 U.S.S.C. Appendix, Sentencing Guidelines for the United States Courts (Rochester, NY: Lawyers Cooperative Publishing, 1995), § 8A.1.

53 Peter Barnes and Joanna Ossinger, "Countrywide Ex-CEO Angelo Mozilo Charged with Fraud," *Fox Business,* June 4, 2009, http://www.foxbusiness.com/story/markets/countrywide-ceo-mozilo-charged-fraud/, accessed July 3, 2009.

54 Eric Lichtblau, "F.B.I. Looks Into 4 Firms at Center of the Economic Turmoil," *New York Times,* September 23, 2008, http://www.nytimes.com/2008/09/24/business/24inquiry.html?_r=1, accessed July 3, 2009.

55 *2008 Report to the Nation on Occupational Fraud and Abuse,* p. 4.

56 "Foley Study Reveals Continued High Cost of Being Public," Foley & Lardner LLP, http://www.foley.com/news/news_detail.aspx?newsid=3074, accessed June 12, 2009.

57 Amy Borrus, "Learning to Love Sarbanes-Oxley," *Business Week,* November 21, 2005, pp. 126–128.

58 "Sarbox and the Constitution," *Wall Street Journal,* May 20, 2009, accessed June 12, 2009.

Chapter 5

1 Salynn Boyles, "Kids' Cereals: Some Are 50% Sugar," WebMD, October 1, 2008, http://www.webmd.com/food-recipes/news/20081001/kids-cereals-some-are-50-percent-sugar, accessed July 8, 2009; sections adapted from a 2009 *Marketing and the Cereal Industry Case* written by Jennifer Mariani and Matt Schottmiller of the University of New Mexico.

2 "New US Consumer Survey Shows High Distrusts of Financial Services Companies," *Business Wire,* January 20, 2009, http://findarticles.com/p/articles/mi_m0EIN/is_2009_Jan_20/ai_n31202849/, accessed May 27, 2009.

3 "Ethics and Business Conduct: How the Ethics Process Works at Lockheed Martin," http://www.lockheedmartin.com/data/assets/corporate/documents/ethics/HowEthicsProcessWorks.pdf, accessed October 28, 2009.

4 "How Ethics Influence Future Profitability—Wal-Mart's Way," May 20, 2009, http://www.insideretailing.com.au/Default.aspx?articleId=5395&articleType=ArticleView&tabid=53, accessed June 3, 2009.

5 Mark Dolliver, "Corporate Reputation Hits a New Low," April 28, 2009, http://www.adweek.com/aw/content_display/data-center/research/e3i0dac803b1646d6af9cc89a12ad823619, accessed May 27, 2009.

6 "Caraco Pharmaceutical Laboratories, Ltd. Announces a Nationwide Voluntary Recall of All Lots of Digoxin Tablets Due to Size," FDA Product Recall, March 31, 2009, http://www.hipusa.com/downloads/digoxinrecall2009.pdf Variability," accessed May 27, 2009.

7 Greg Farrell, "Hunt Is on for Notebook That Scrushy Denies Exists," *USA Today,* June 12, 2003, p. B1.

8 Jay Reeves, "HealthSouth Reports Continuing Problems," Associated Press, March 17, 2006, http://www.highbeam.com/doc/1P1-120063167.html, accessed July 10, 2009.

9 Tracy Dalzell Walsh, "Shareholders Seek $2.8 Billion from Scrushy," Courthouse News Service, July 7, 2009, http://www.courthousenews.com/2009/07/07/Shareholders_Seek_$2_8_Billion_From_Scrushy.htm, accessed July 9, 2009.

10 Debbie Thorne McAlister and Robert Erffmeyer, "A Content Analysis of Outcomes and Responsibilities for Consumer Complaints to Third Party Organizations," *Journal of Business Research* 56 (April 2003): 341–352.

11 Roger Bate, "China's Bad Medicine," *Wall Street Journal,* May 5, 2009, http://online.wsj.com/article/SB124146383501884323.html, accessed June 10, 2009.

12 "Biz Deans Talk—Business Management Education Blog," January 2, 2009, http://www.deanstalk.net/deanstalk/2009/01/warren-buffetts.html, accessed May 27, 2009.

13 Barry Newman, "An Ad Professor Huffs Against Puffs, but It's a Quixotic Enterprise," *Wall Street Journal,* January 24, 2003, p. A1.

14 Tim Elfrink, "The Rise and Fall of the Stanford Financial Group," *Houston Press,* April 9, 2009, http://www.houstonpress.com/content/printVersion/1173931, accessed April 29, 2009; Steve Stecklow, "Hard Sell Drove Stanford's Rise and Fall," *Wall Street Journal,* April 3, 2009, http://online.wsj.com/article/SB123871796188984821.html, accessed April 29, 2009; Greg Barr, "Stanford Files Appeal in Bond Decision," *Houston Business Journal,* July 10, 2009, http://www.bizjournals.com/houston/stories/2009/07/06/daily52.html, accessed July 10, 2009.

15 Peter Lattman, "Boeing's Top Lawyer Spotlights Company's Ethical Lapses," *Wall Street Journal,* Law Blog, January 30, 2006, http://blogs.wsj.com/law/2006/01/31/boeings-top-lawyer-rips-into-his-company, accessed July 10, 2009.

16 Lisa Broadt, "Proposed Laws Could Send Firms to Court for 'Abusive' Behavior,'" *Washington Business Journal,* http://www.bizjournals.com/washington/stories/2008/09/29/smallb8.html, accessed February 2, 2009.

17 Charles Forelle, "EU Plans Fresh Strike on Microsoft," *Wall Street Journal,* May 30, 2009, http://online.wsj.com/article/SB124362706194767281.html, accessed June 4, 2009.

18 O. C. Ferrell, John Fraedrich, and Linda Ferrell, *Business Ethics,* 8th ed. (Boston: Houghton Mifflin).

19 Ibid.

20 Duff Wilson, "Harvard Medical Students in an Ethical Quandry," *New York Times,* March 2, 2009, http://www.nytimes.com/2009/03/03/business/03medschool.html?scp=3&sq=harvard%20medical&st=cse, accessed June 4, 2009.

21 "Panel Seeks Fuller Disclosure of Drug Company Payments," *Forbes,* April 27, 2009, http://www.forbes.com/feeds/hscout/2009/04/28/hscout626501.html, accessed June 4, 2009.

22 Brody Mullins, "Ethics Panel Probes Lawmakers' Travel to Caribbean Events," *Wall Street Journal,* June 26, 2009, p. A1.

23 Dionne Searcey, "U.S. Cracks Down on Corporate Bribes," *Wall Street Journal,* May 26, 2009, http://online.wsj.com/article/SB124329477230952689.html, accessed June 4, 2009.

24 "Co-workers Reporting Fraud," *USA Today,* Snapshot, October 3, 2002, p. 1D.

25 "5 Most Common Fraud Cases," E-Commerce Journal, http://www.ecommerce-journal.com/news/5_most_common_fraud_cases, accessed July 10, 2009.

26 Donna Kardos, "KPMG Is Sued Over New Century," *Wall Street Journal,* April 2, 2009, http://online.wsj.com/article/SB123860415462378767.html, accessed June 11, 2009.

27 Matt Kranz, "More Earnings Restatements on the Way," *USA Today,* October 25, 2002, p. 3B.

28 Tess Stynes, "WellCare Swings to Loss on Legal Costs, Investment Charges," *Wall Street Journal,* May 11, 2009, http://online.wsj.com/article/SB124204184849506371.html, accessed June 11, 2009.

29 Mark Maremont, "Pang Took $83 Million from Firm, Filings Say," *Wall Street Journal,* June 26, 2009, pp. A1, A4.

30 Press release, "Court Bars Global Marketing Group from Payment Processing," Federal Trade Commission, February 18, 2009, http://www.ftc.gov/opa/2009/02/gmg.shtm, accessed June 11, 2009.

31 *Gillette vs. Wilkinson Sword, Inc.,* 89-CV-3586, 1991 U.S. Dist. Lexis 21006, *6 (S.D.N.Y. January 9, 1991).

32 *Am. Council of Certified Pediatric Physicians & Surgeons v. Am. Bd. of Podiatric Surgery, Inc.,* 185 F.3d 606, 616 (6th Cir. 1999); *Johnson & Johnson-Merck Consumer Pharms. Co. v. Rhone-Poulene Rorer Pharms., Inc.,* 19 F.3d 125, 129–130 (3d Cir. 1994); *Coca-Cola Co. v. Tropicana Prods. Inc.,* 690 F.2d 312, 317 (2d Cir. 1982).

33 Jeff Bater, "FTC Says Companies Falsely Claim Cellphone Patches Provide False Protection," *Wall Street Journal,* February 21, 2002.

34 Archie B. Carroll, *Business and Society: Ethics and Stakeholder Management* (Cincinnati: South-Western, 1989), pp. 228–230.

35 "Netgear Settles Suit Over Speed Claims," *Wall Street Journal,* November 28, 2005, p. C5.

36 "Newsletter; Federal Trade Commission Report: ID Theft #1 Complaint," February 2005, http://www.machine-solution.com/_Article+FTC+ID+Theft.html, accessed July 10, 2009.

37 "Retail Theft and Inventory Shrinkage," *What You Need to Know About[[[…]]]Retail Industry,* http://retailindustry.about.com/library/weekly/02/aa021126a.htm, accessed February 6, 2003.

38 Daryl Koehn, "Consumer Fraud: The Hidden Threat," University of St. Thomas, *http://www.stthom.edu/Public/getFile.asp?File_Content_ID=488,* accessed July 10, 2009.

39 Annie Finnigan, "Different Strokes," *Working Woman,* April 2001, p. 44.

40 Mark H. Anderson, "Business Gets Stronger Hand in Age Cases," *Wall Street Journal,* June 18, 2009, http://online.wsj.com/article/SB124535060326328507.html, accessed July 10, 2009.

41 Sue Shellenberger, "Work & Family," *Wall Street Journal,* May 23, 2001, p. B1.

42 "What Is Affirmative Action?" HR Content Library, October 12, 2001, http://www.hrnext.com/content/view.cfm?articles_id=2007&subs_id=32, accessed July 10, 2009.

43 Ibid.

44 "Facts About Affirmative Action," National Partnership for Women and Families, http://www.nationalpartnership.org/site/DocServer/AffirmativeActionFacts.pdf?docID=861, accessed July 10, 2009.

45 Ibid.

46 *U.S. Equal Employment Opportunity Commission: An Overview* (Washington, DC: U.S. Equal Employment Opportunity Commission, 1997), http://www.ccoc.gov/overview.html.

47 See http://www.eeoc.gov/stats/harass.html for EEOC statistics.

48 Paula N. Rubin, "Civil Rights and Criminal Justice: Primer on Sexual Harassment Series: NIJ Research in Action," October 1995, http://www.ojp.usdoj.gov/nij/pubs-sum/156663.htm, accessed July 10, 2009.

49 Steve Stecklow, "Sexual-Harassment Cases Plague U.N.," *Wall Street Journal,* May 21, 2009, http://online.wsj.com/article/SB124233350385520879.html, accessed June 11, 2009.

50 U.S. Equal Employment Opportunity Commission, "Retaliation," http://www.eeoc.gov/types/retaliation.html, accessed May 1, 2006.

51 Glyn Moody, "G8 on Intellectual Monopolies: Not So Great," Computer World UK, July 10, 2009, http://www.computerworlduk.com/community/blogs/index.cfm?entryid=2345&blogid=14, accessed July 10, 2009.

52 "New National Poll: Nearly 40% of 'Ethically Prepared' Teens Believe Lying, Cheating, or Violence Necessary to Succeed," Junior Achievement/Deloitte Teen Ethics Survey, http://www.ja.org/about/releases/about/newsitem435.asp, accessed July 9, 2009.

53 "Teens Respect Good Business Ethics," *USA Today,* December 12, 2005, p. B1.

54 Marianne Jennings, "An Ethical Breach by Any Other Name," *Financial Engineering News,* January/February 2006.

55 Immanuel Kant, "Fundamental Principles of the Metaphysics of Morals," in *Problems of Moral Philosophy: An Introduction,* 2nd ed., ed. Paul W. Taylor (Encino, CA: Dickenson, 1972), p. 229.

56 Stefanie E. Naumann and Nathan Bennett, "A Case for Procedural Justice Climate: Development and Test of a Multilevel Model," *Academy of Management Journal* 43 (October 2000): 881–889.

57 Joel Brockner and P. A. Siegel, "Understanding the Interaction Between Procedural and Distributive Justice: The Role of Trust," in *Trust in Organizations: Frontiers of Theory and Research,* ed. R. M. Kramer and T. R. Tyler (Thousand Oaks, CA: Sage, 1995), pp. 390–413.

58 Debbie Thorne LeClair, O. C. Ferrell, and John Fraedrich, *Integrity Management: A Guide to Managing Legal and Ethical Issues in the Workplace* (Tampa, FL: University of Tampa Press, 1998), p. 37.

59 John Fraedrich and O. C. Ferrell, "Cognitive Consistency of Marketing Managers in Ethical Situations," *Journal of the Academy of Marketing Science* 20 (1992): 242–252.

60 This section was adapted from Ferrell, Fraedrich, and Ferrell, *Business Ethics,* pp. 106–109; and LeClair, Ferrell, and Fraedrich, *Integrity Management,* pp. 37–39.

61 Lawrence Kohlberg, "Stage and Sequence: The Cognitive Developmental Approach to Socialization," in *Handbook of Socialization Theory and Research,* ed. D. A. Goslin (Chicago: Rand McNally, 1969), pp. 347–480.

62 Suein L. Hwang, "The Executive Who Told Tobacco's Secrets," *Wall Street Journal,* November 28, 1995, pp. B1, B6.

63 Kohlberg, "Stage and Sequence," pp. 347–480.

64 Joseph W. Weiss, *Business Ethics: A Managerial, Stakeholder Approach* (Belmont, CA: Wadsworth, 1994), p. 13.

65 Carol Loomis, "Derivatives: The Risk That Still Won't Go Away," *Fortune,* June 6, 2009, pp. 55–60.

66 Amie Vaccaro, "The White Dog Café: A Study of Social Business and Mission-Aligned Exit," Greenbiz.com, April 24, 2009, http://www.greenbiz.com/blog/2009/04/24/white-dog-café, accessed July 9, 2009.

67 Ethics Resource Center, *2007 National Business Ethics Survey: An Inside View of Private Sector Ethics* (Washington, DC: Ethics Resource Center, 2005), p. 13.

68 O. C. Ferrell, Larry G. Gresham, and John Fraedrich, "A Synthesis of Ethical Decision Models for Marketing," *Journal of Macromarketing* 9 (Fall 1989): 58–59.

69 Michael S. James, "What Is Ethical?" ABCNews.com, February 21, 2003.

70 "Lack of Formal Ethics Program Connected to Workplace Problems: Survey Looks at Why People Sometimes Bend the Rules," PRNewswire, February 3, 1998.

71 Ethics Resource Center, *2007 National Business Ethics Survey,* p. 20.

72 Vault Editors, "Pens and Post-Its Among Most Pilfered Office Supplies, Says New Vault Survey," Vault.com, November 16, 2005, http://www.vault.com/nr/newsmain.jsp?nr_page=3&ch_id=420&article_id=25720773, accessed July 23, 2006.

73 Jeffrey L. Seglin, "Forewarned Is Forearmed? Not Always," *New York Times,* February 16, 2003, http://www.nytimes.com/2003/02/16/business/yourmoney/16ETHI.html; Barbara Ley Toffler, *Final Accounting: Ambition, Greed and the Fall of Arthur Andersen* (New York: Broadway Books, 2003).

74 Steve Lohr, "In Strategy Shift, G.E. Plans Lower-Cost Health Products," *New York Times,* May 8, 2009, p. B8.

75 Devin Leonard, "How Lehman Got its Real Estate Fix," *New York Times,* May 3, 2009, pp. B1, B6–B7.

76 Ferrell, Gresham, and Fraedrich, "A Synthesis of Ethical Decision Models for Marketing," pp. 58–59.

Chapter 6

1 Traci Watson, "Eco-Friendly Claims Go Unchecked," *USA Today,* June 22, 2009, p. A1; Collin Dunn, "Greenwash Watch: Pottery Barn's Eco Chic Collection," *Treehugger,* January 9, 2008, http://www.treehugger.com/files/2008/01/greenwash-watch-pottery-barn-eco-chic.php, accessed April 22, 2008; Staff Writer, "Pottery Barn's Eco Chic Line: Eco Friendly?," *Apartment Therapy Los Angeles,* January 7, 2008, http://www.apartmenttherapy.com/la/seating-sofas-armchairs/pottery-barns-eco-chic-line-ecofriendly-039690, accessed April 22, 2008; "The Seven Sins of Greenwashing," *Terrachoice,* http://sinsofgreenwashing.org/findings/the-seven-sins/, accessed April 22, 2008; Matthew Knight, "It's Not Easy Being Green," *CNN,* July 23, 2008, http://www.cnn.com/2008/TECH/science/07/16/greenwash/index.html, accessed April 22, 2008.

2 "A-Rod Steroids Report a Baseball Shocker," CBS News, February 7, 2009, http://www.cbsnews.com/stories/2009/02/07/national/main4782637.shtml, accessed July 9, 2009.

3 "62% of Americans Tell CEOs 'You're Not Doing Enough to Restore Trust and Confidence in American Business,'" Golin/Harris International, press release, June 20, 2002, http://www.golinharris.com/news/releases.asp?ID=3788.

4 "Wall Street's Entitlement Culture Hard to Shake," January 23, 2009, http://www.msnbc.msn.com/id/28817800/, accessed July 9, 2009.

5 "Forensic Leadership Message," KPMG Forensic Ethics Survey 2008–2009.

6 "How Am I Doing?" *Business Ethics,* Fall 2005, p. 11.

7 "The TI Commitment," 2008 Corporate Citizenship Report, http://www.ti.com/corp/docs/csr/corpgov/ethics/publication.shtml, accessed July 13, 2009.

8 The TI Quick Test, http://www.ti.com/corp/docs/company/citizen/ethics/quicktest.shtml, accessed July 9, 2009.

9 Mark S. Schwartz, "A Code of Ethics for Corporate Code of Ethics," *Journal of Business Ethics* 41 (2002): 37.

10 Ethics Resource Center, *2007 National Business Ethics Survey: An Inside Look of Private Sector Ethics* (Washington, DC: Ethics Resource Center), p. 19.

11 Wells Fargo Team Member Code of Ethics and Business Conduct, http://www.wellsfargo.com/downloads/pdf/about/team_member_code_of_ethics.pdf, accessed July 10, 2009.

12 "ECOA Sponsoring Partner Member L'Oreal Sponsors the First Law and Business Ethics Masters Degree," October 6, 2008, http://www.csrwire.com/press/press_release/19336-ECOA-Sponsoring-Partner-member-L-Oreal-Sponsors-the-first-Law-and-Business-Ethics-Masters-Degree-, accessed July 10, 2009.

13 About the ECOA. At a Glance, http://www.theecoa.org/AM/Template.cfm?Section=About, accessed July 14. 2009.

14 Alynda Wheat, "Keeping an Eye on Corporate America," *Fortune,* November 25, 2002, pp. 44–45.

15 Debbie Thorne LeClair and Linda Ferrell, "Innovation in Experiential Business Ethics Training," *Journal of Business Ethics* 23 (2000): 313–322.

16 "Ethics and Business Conduct," Boeing, http://www.boeing.com/companyoffices/aboutus/ethics/, accessed July 10, 2009. Courtesy of Boeing Business Services Company.

17 Janet Hankins, "The Best Hotlines," April 21, 2009, ethicaladvocate.blogspot.com/2009_04_01_archive.html, accessed July 10, 2009.

18 Janet Wiscombe, "Don't Fear Whistle-Blowers: With HR's Help, Principled Whistle-Blowers Can Be a Company's Salvation," *Workforce,* July 2002, http://www.findarticles.com, accessed February 7, 2003.

19 Steven Mufson, "Pickens Calls Off Plan for Vast Texas Wind Farm," *Washington Post,* July 8, 2009, http://www.washingtonpost.com/wp-dyn/content/article/2009/07/07/AR2009070702455.html?hpid=sec-business, accessed July 13, 2009; Based on *The Marketing of "The Pickens' Plan"* by Matthew Mazzei, 2009.

20 Allan Chernoff, Sr., "Madoff Whistleblower Blasts SEC," February 4, 2009, http://money.cnn.com/2009/02/04/news/newsmakers/madoff_whistleblower/index.htm, accessed July 10, 2009.

21 John W. Schoen, "Split CEO–Chairman Job, Says Panel," MSNBC.com, January 9, 2003, http://www.msnbc.com/news/857171.asp, accessed July 13, 2009.

22 Jathon Sapsford and Paul Beckett, "The Complex Goals and Unseen Cost of Whistle-Blowing," *Wall Street Journal,* November 25, 2002, pp. A1, A10.

23 Ethics Resource Center, *2007 National Business Ethics Survey,* p. 9.

24 Darren Dahl, "Learning to Love Whistleblowers," *Inc.,* March 2006, pp. 21–23.

25 "Fraud Study Says Whistleblowers Are the Most Common Means of Identifying Fraud, but This Comes at a High Personal Cost When Whistleblower Anonymity Is Not Maintained," February 2007, http://www.fulcruminquiry.com/Whistleblower_Fraud_Study.htm, accessed July 10, 2009.

26 John Kotter, *Leading Change* (Cambridge: Harvard Business School Press, 1995).

27 Ethics Resource Center, *2007 National Business Ethics Survey,*p. 18.

28 J. M. Burns, *Leadership* (New York: Harper & Row, 1985).

29 "WorldCom Chief Outlines Plans for Cost-Cuts, Layoffs," *Wall Street Journal,* January 15, 2003, http://online.wsj .com/article/SB1042561135669438224.html?mod=googlewsj, accessed July 13, 2009.

30 John R. P. French and Bertram Ravin, "The Bases of Social Power," in *Group Dynamics: Research and Theory,* ed. Dorwin Cartwright (Evanston, IL: Row, Peterson, 1962), pp. 607–623.

31 Lynn Brewer, Robert Chandler, and O. C. Ferrell, *Managing Risks for Corporate Integrity* (Mason, OH: Texere/Thomson, 2006), p. 35.

32 Susan Pulliam, "How Following Orders Can Harm Your Career," *CFO Magazine,* October 3, 2003, http://www.cfo .com/article.cfm/3010537/c_3036075, accessed July 12, 2009.

33 "Southwest Airlines Story Leads," http://www.swmedia.com/ swmedia/story_leads.html, accessed July 10, 2009.

34 Ferrell and Gresham, "A Contingency Framework for Understanding Ethical Decision-Making in Marketing."

35 Wiscombe, "Don't Fear Whistle-Blowers."

36 John Fraedrich and O. C. Ferrell, "Cognitive Consistency of Marketing Managers in Ethical Situations," *Journal of the Academy of Marketing Science* 20 (Summer 1992): 243–252.

Chapter 7

1 "Who We Are—About Shell," http://www.shell.com/home/ content/aboutshell/who_we_are/, accessed May 12, 2009; "BP, Sunoco & Shell Ranked Greenest Oil Companies in Sustainability Survey," http://www.treehugger.com/ files/2009/04/bp-sunoco-shell-greenest-oil-companies-sustainability-survey.php, accessed May 12, 2009; "Invest in Risavika," http://www.energiparken.no/doc/RISAVIKAeng_til_ nett.pdf, accessed March 24, 2009; "Shell Announces the Next Stage of Its European Refinery Rationalisation Program," http:// www.shell.com/home/Framework?siteId=media-en&FC2=/ media-en/html/iwgen/leftnavs/zzz_lhn2_9_0.html&FC3=/ media-en/html/iwgen/news_and_library/press_releases/1998/ dir_1998_pressrelease_index.html, accessed July 30, 2006.

2 Joanne B. Ciulla, *The Working Life: The Promise and Betrayal of Modern Work* (New York: Times Books, 2000).

3 Ciulla, *The Working Life;* Adriano Tilgher, *Work: What It Has Meant to Men Through the Ages,* trans. Dorothy Canfield Fisher (New York: Harcourt, Brace & World, 1958).

4 These facts are derived from Brenda Paik Sunoo, "Relying on Faith to Rebuild a Business," *Workforce* 78 (March 1999): 54–59.

5 Karen Sarkis, "Injured Workers File Claim with Malden Mills," *Occupational Hazards* 62 (February 2000): 16.

6 Sunoo, "Relying on Faith to Rebuild a Business"; Justin Pope, "Malden Mills Emerges from the Bankruptcy, Still Under Financial Cloud," *Houston Chronicle,* August 15, 2003, p. B1; Janet B. Rodie, "Textile World News," *Textile World* 152 (January 2002): 12; Polartec, "Corporate News," http://www.polartec.com/about/corporate.php, accessed March 24, 2009.

7 "Worldatwork Finds One-Third of Companies Downsized After 9/11," *Report on Salary Surveys* 2 (December 2002): 12; Stephanie Armour, "Companies Chisel Away at Workers' Benefits," *USA Today,* November 18, 2002, pp. 1B–3B; Lynn Gresham, "Winning the Talent War Requires a Fresh Benefits Approach," *Employee Benefit News,* April 15, 2006, p. 9.

8 Neil Conway and Rob B. Briner, *Understanding Psychological Contracts at Work* (London: Oxford University Press, 2006); Denise M. Rousseau, *Psychological Contracts in Organizations: Understanding Written and Unwritten Agreements* (Thousand Oaks, CA: Sage, 1995).

9 Jacqueline Coyle-Shapiro, "A Psychological Contract Perspective on Organizational Citizenship Behavior," *Journal of Organizational Behavior* 23 (December 2002): 927–946; William H. Turnley and Daniel C. Feldman, "The Impact of Psychological Contract Violations on Exit, Voice, Loyalty, and Neglect," *Human Relations* 52 (July 1999): 895–922.

10 Ibid.

11 Ans De Vos and Annelies Meganck, "What HR Managers Do Versus What Employees Value," *Personnel Review* 38 (2009): 45–60.

12 Kimberly D. Elsbach and Greg Elafson, "How the Packaging of Decision Explanations Affects Perceptions of Trustworthiness," *Academy of Management Journal* 43 (February 2000): 80–89; David E. Guest and Neil Conway, "Communicating the Psychological Contract: An Employer Perspective," *Human Resource Management Journal* 12, no. 2 (2002): 22–38.

13 Gillian Flynn, "Looking Back on 100 Years of Employment Law," *Workforce* 78 (November 1999): 74–77.

14 "A Guru Ahead of Her Time," *Nation's Business* 85 (May 1997): 24.

15 Steve Sayer, "Cleaning Up the Jungle," *Occupational Health & Safety* 66 (May 1997): 22.

16 Flynn, "Looking Back on 100 Years of Employment Law."

17 "Employee Relations in America," *IRS Employment Review* (March 1997): E7–E12; Roger LeRoy Miller and Gaylord A. Jentz, *Business Law Today* (Cincinnati, OH: West Legal Studies in Business, 2000).

18 C. Wright Mills, *White Collar: The American Middle Classes* (New York: Oxford University Press, 1951).

19 Ciulla, *The Working Life;* William H. Whyte, *The Organization Man* (New York: Simon & Schuster, 1956).

20 *Work in America: Report of a Special Task Force to the Secretary of Health, Education, and Welfare* (Cambridge, MA: MIT Press, 1973).

21 Ciulla, *The Working Life.*

22 Taina Savolainen, "Leadership Strategies for Gaining Business Excellence Through Total Quality Management: A Finnish Case Study," *Total Quality Management* 11 (March 2000): 211–226.

23 "Younger Employees Want Security," *USA Today,* October 3, 2001, p. 1B.

24 This section is adapted from Debbie Thorne LeClair, "The Ups and Downs of Rightsizing the Workplace," *ABACA Profile,* November–December 1999, p. 25.

25 Priti Pradhan Shah, "Network Destruction: The Structural Implications of Downsizing," *Academy of Management Journal* 43 (February 2000): 101–112; Steve Lohr, "Cutting Here, but Hiring Over There," *New York Times,* June 24, 2005, p. C3.

26 "GM Initiates Workforce Reduction," http://www.automotive-business-review.com/article_news.asp?guid=D377A0CA-263E-4FB9-9672-143E031737A0, accessed March 30, 2009; *New York Times Special Report: The Downsizing of America* (New York: Times Books, 1996); Victor B. Wayhan and Steve Werner, "The Impact of Workforce Reductions on Financial Performance: A Longitudinal Perspective," *Journal of Management* 26 (2000): 341–363.

27 Harry J. Van Buren III, "The Bindingness of Social and Psychological Contracts: Toward a Theory of Social Responsibility in Downsizing," *Journal of Business Ethics* 25 (January 2000): 205–219; Davis J. Flanagan and K. C. O'Saughnessy, "The Effects of Layoffs on Firm Reputation," *Journal of Management* (June 2005): 445.

28 Geoff Colvin, "Layoffs Cost More Than You Think," *Fortune* March 30, 2009, p. 24.

29 Steve Beigbeder, "Easing Workforce Reduction," *Risk Management* 47 (May 2000): 26–30; Matthew Camardella, "Legal Considerations of Workforce Reduction," *Employment Relations Today* 29 (Autumn 2002): 101–106.

30 U.S. Department of Labor, "The Worker Adjustment and Retraining Notification Act," http://www.doleta.gov/programs/factsht/warn.htm, accessed March 24, 2009.

31 Robert A. Nozar, "Nashville's Hot Job Market May Absorb Opryland Cuts," *Hotel and Motel Management* 214 (August 1999): 4, 40.

32 Angelo J. Kinicki, Gregory E. Prussia, and Francis M. McKee-Ryan, "A Panel Study of Coping with Involuntary Job Loss," *Academy of Management Journal* 43 (February 2000): 90–100.

33 Wayhan and Werner, "The Impact of Workforce Reductions on Financial Performance."

34 Nicholas Stein, "Winning the War to Keep Top Talent," *Fortune,* May 29, 2000, pp. 132–138.

35 Kathleen Melymuka, "Showing the Value of Brainpower," *Computerworld,* March 27, 2000, pp. 58–59; Milton Moskowitz and Robert Levering, "Best Companies to Work For: 10 Great Companies in Europe," *Fortune,* February 4, 2002, http://www.fortune.com/lists/bestcompanies/ten_great.html, accessed November 22, 2002.

36 Carlyn Kolker, "Survivor Blues," *American Lawyer* 24 (October 2002): 116–118; Susan Reynolds Fisher and Margaret A. White, "Downsizing in a Learning Organization," *Academy of Management Review* 25 (January≈2000): 244–251.

37 Susan Beck, "What to Do Before You Say 'You're Outta Here,'" *Business Week,* December 8, 1997, p. 6.

38 U.S. Department of Labor, Employment Law Guide, http://www.dol.gov/compliance/guide/index.htm, accessed August 17, 2009.

39 "Minimum Wage Laws in the States," U.S. Department of Labor, http://www.dol.gov/esa/minwage/america.htm, accessed March 19, 2006; Miller and Jentz, *Business Law Today.*

40 Flynn, "Looking Back on 100 Years of Employment Law."

41 Robert J. Nobile, "HR's Top 10 Legal Issues," *HR Focus* 74 (April 1997): 19–20.

42 Miller and Jentz, *Business Law Today.*

43 Flynn, "Looking Back on 100 Years of Employment Law."

44 Peter Elstrom, "Needed: A New Union for the New Economy," *Business Week,* September 4, 2000, p. 48; Tim Stentiford and David L. Young, "Case Study: Verizon Wireless Delivers on Its HR Web Site," *Employee Benefit Plan Review* 57 (November 2002): 43.

45 *The New OSHA: Reinventing Worker Safety and Health* (Washington, DC: U.S. Department of Labor, Occupational Safety and Health Administration, 1995), available at http://www.osha.gov/doc/outreachtraining/htmlfiles/newosha.html; Dana E. Corbin, "Speaking Their Language," *Occupational Health & Safety* 71 (July 2002): 32.

46 Judith N. Mottl, "Industry Fights OSHA's Proposed Ergonomic Rule," *Informationweek,* June 19, 2000, p. 122; Daniel R. Miller, "OSHA Goes Too Far with Ergonomics Rules," *National Underwriter,* May 8, 2000, p. 59; John D. Schulz, "Trucking Wants Out," *Traffic World,* May 29, 2000, pp. 21–22; Robin Suttell, "Healthy Work," *Buildings* 96 (October 2002): 56–58.

47 "Ergonomics Focus Makes Waterloo Ready, Not Reactive," http://www.deere.com/en_US/compinfo/envtsafety/innovation/waterloo_ergo.html, accessed April 19, 2006; "Waterloo Facility Earns Safety Award," http://www.deere.com/en_US/compinfo/csr/news/2009/04JFeb2009_waterloosafety.html, accessed March 24, 2009.

48 "Workplace Violence," Occupational Safety and Health Administration, http://www.osha.gov/SLTC/workplaceviolence/index.html, accessed August 17, 2009.

49 Karen Sarkis, "Workplace Violence Top Concern for Employers," *Occupational Hazards* 62 (June 2000): 23; Sarah J. Smith, "Workplace Violence," *Professional Safety* 47 (November 2002): 34–43.

50 *Fear and Violence in the Workplace: A Survey Documenting the Experiences of American Workers* (Minneapolis, MN: Northwestern National Life Insurance Company, 1993).

51 Cal/OSHA Guidelines for Workplace Security (State of California, 1995), available at http://www.dir.ca.gov/dosh/dosh%5Fpublications/worksecurity.html, accessed August 17, 2009.

52 Anonymous and Andrew R. Thomas, *Crisis in the Skies* (Amherst, NY: Prometheus, 2001); Irene Korn, "Emergency Training," *Successful Meetings* 51 (November 2002): 35; Steve Rubenstein, "Flight Attendants Fight 'Air Rage,'" *San Francisco Chronicle,* July 7, 2000, p. A2.

53 "Suspect in Honolulu Shooting Spree Faces First-Degree Murder Charges," CNN, November 3, 1999, http://www.cnn.com; "Xerox Hawaii Cited Unsafe in Connection with Mass Shooting," CNN, November 7, 2000, http://www.cnn.com.

54 Richard V. Denenberg and Mark Braverman, *The Violence-Prone Workplace: A New Approach to Dealing with Hostile, Threatening, and Uncivil Behavior* (Ithaca, NY: Cornell University Press, 1999); Robert Grossman, "Bulletproof Practices," *HR Magazine* 47 (November 2002): 34–42; Bill Merrick, "Make Work a Safe Place," *Credit Union Magazine* 66 (June 2000): 19.

55 Carrie Coolidge, "Risky Business," *Forbes,* January 6, 2003, p. 54; Todd Henneman, "Ignoring Signs of Violence Can Be Fatal, Costly Mistake," *Workforce Management,* February 27, 2006, p. 10; John Leming, "New Product Covers Losses Related to Workplace Violence," *Journal of Commerce,* April 6, 2000, p. 15.

56 "New Study Documents Sharp Rise in Pregnancy Discrimination Complaints Driven by Discrimination Against Women of Color," National Partnership for Women & Families, http://www.nationalpartnership.org/site/PageServer?pagename=newsroom_pr_PressRelease_081029, accessed March 25, 2009.

57 Judy Greenwald, "Employers Confront AIDS in Africa," *Business Insurance* 35 (July 23, 2001): 15; Michael T. Parker, "Fighting AIDS Stigma in the Workplace," *Business Mexico* 15 (August 2005): 43–44.

58 "What Affirmative Action Is (and What It Is Not)," National Partnership for Women & Families, http://www.nationalpartnership.org/site/DocServer/AffirmativeActionFacts.pdf?docID=861, accessed March 24, 2009.

59 Julio Faundez, *Affirmative Action: International Perspectives* (Geneva, Switzerland: International Labour Office, 1994).

60 "Facts About Sexual Harassment," U.S. Equal Employment Opportunity Commission, http://www.eeoc.gov/facts/fs-sex.html, accessed August 17, 2009.

61 Donald J. Petersen and Douglas P. Massengill, "Sexual Harassment Cases Five Years After *Meritor Savings Bank v. Vinson*," *Employee Relations Law Journal* 18 (Winter 1992–1993): 489–516.

62 Maria E. Conway, "Sexual Harassment Abroad," *Workforce* 77 (September 1998): 8–9.

63 "Code of Practice to Clamp Down on Sexual Harassment at Work," European Commission, http://europa.eu/scadplus/leg/en/cha/c10917b.htm, accessed March 24, 2009.

64 Robert D. Lee and Paul S. Greenlaw, "The Legal Evolution of Sexual Harassment," *Public Administration Review* 55 (July 1995): 357–364.

65 Ibid.

66 George D. Mesritz, "Hostile Environment Sexual Harassment Claims: When Once Is Enough," *Employee Relations Law Journal* 22 (Spring 1997): 79–85; Laura Hoffman Roppe, "*Harris v. Forklift Systems, Inc.*: Victory or Defeat?" *San Diego Law Review* 32 (Winter 1996): 321–342.

67 Joann Muller, "Ford: The High Cost of Harassment," *Business Week,* November 15, 1999, pp. 94–96.

68 "Mitsubishi Agrees to $34 Million Sexual Harassment Settlement," *Business Week,* June 15, 1998, pp. 1–3; Samuel Greengard, "Zero Tolerance: Making It Work," *Workforce* 78 (May 1999): 28–34.

69 Jonathan W. Dion, "Putting Employers on the Defense: The Supreme Court Develops a Consistent Standard Regarding an Employer's Liability for a Supervisor's Hostile Work Environment Sexual Harassment," *Wake Forest Law Review* 34 (Spring 1999): 199–227; Darlene Orlov and Michael T. Roumell, *What Every Manager Needs to Know About Sexual Harassment* (New York: AMACOM, 1999).

70 Joann Lublin, "Retaliation over Harassment Claims Takes Focus," *Wall Street Journal*, April 17, 2006, p. B4.

71 This section is adapted from Randy Chiu, Richard Tansey, Debbie Thorne, and Michael White, "Is Procedural Justice the Dominant Whistleblowing Motive Among Employees?" unpublished manuscript.

72 J. P. Near and M. P. Miceli, "Organizational Dissidence: The Case of Whistleblowing," *Journal of Business Ethics* 4 (January 1985): 1–16.

73 Greg Palast, *The Best Democracy Money Can Buy* (New York: Penguin Plume, 2004).

74 Ron Ruggles, "Education, Training Is Beneficial to Employees 'Knowing It All' About Industry," *Nation's Restaurant News,* October 16, 2000, pp. 80, 162; Rose French, "Cracker Barrel Launches Programs to Rebuild Image," *Marketing News,* July 15, 2005, p. 31.

75 Jill Schachner Chanen, "You Rang, Sir?" *ABA Journal* 86 (October 2000): 82–84.

76 Scott Westcott, "Good Bye and Good Luck," *Inc* 28 (April 2006): 40–41.

77 Betsy Cummings, "Training's Top Five," *Successful Meetings* 49 (October 2000): 67–73; Adam J. Grossberg, "The Effect of Formal Training on Employment Duration," *Industrial Relations* 39 (October 2000): 578–599; Kathryn Tyler, "Extending the Olive Branch," *HR Magazine* 47 (November 2002): 85–89.

78 "ASTD Highlights International Training Trends in Its 2002 International Comparisons Report," American Society for Training and Development, http://www1.astd.org/pressRoom/pdf/ICRreport.pdf, accessed April 23, 2006.

79 "Diversity: A 'New' Tool for Retention," *HR Focus* 77 (June 2000): 1, 14.

80 David Pollitt, "Diversity Is About More Than Observing the Letter of the Law," *Human Resource Management International Digest* 13 (2005): 37–40.

81 David P. Schulz, "Different Approaches to Approaching Differences," *Stores* 87 (April 2005): 98.

82 Marilyn Loden and Judith B. Rosener, *Workforce America! Managing Employee Diversity as a Vital Resource* (Burr Ridge, IL: Irwin/McGraw-Hill, 1991).

83 "Diversity Low Priority Reaps Low Numbers," *Editor & Publisher*, April 17, 2000, p. 16; Maryann Hammers, "Scripps Funds Media Diversity," *Workforce* 81 (December 2002): 16; Joe Strupp, "NAA: Diversity Under Review," *Editor & Publisher*, December 2, 2002, p. 6.

84 Ira Teinowitz, "Courting Change," *Advertising Age* 72 (May 14, 2001): 16–20.

85 New York Life, Diversity brochure, http://www.newyorklife.com/NYL2/pdf/diversity_broch.pdf, accessed April 20, 2006.

86 Rebecca Herwick, "Entrepreneurs, Hire the Disabled," http://www.usatoday.com/money/smallbusiness/2004-04-15-entre-3-apr_x.htm, accessed April 23, 2006.

87 "Verizon Named Private-Sector Employer of the Year by 'CAREERS & the disABLED' Magazine," news release, April 8, 2005, http://newscenter.verizon.com/, accessed April 20, 2006; "CAREERS & the disAbled Magazine Names Verizon's Thomas Boudrow Employee of the Year," http://www.tmcnet.com/usubmit/2009/03/12/4052868.htm, accessed March 18, 2009.

88 Phil Gorman, Teresa Nelson, and Alan Glassman, "The Millennial Generation: A Strategic Opportunity," *Organizational Analysis* 12, no. 3 (2004): 255–270; Ron Zemke, Claire Raines, and Bob Filipczak, *Generations at Work: Managing the Clash of Veterans, Boomers, Xers, and Nexters in Your Workplace* (New York: AMACOM, 2000).

89 Arthur P. Brief, Elizabeth Umphress, Joerg Dietz, Rebecca Butz, John Burrows, and Lotte Scholten, "Community Matters: Realistic Group Conflict Theory and the Impact of Diversity," *Academy of Management Journal* 48 (October 2005): 830–844.

90 Cora Daniels, "To Hire a Lumber Expert, Click Here," *Fortune*, April 3, 2000, pp. 267–270; Faye Wilson, "Implementing a Successful Corporate Diversity Plan," http://www.bna.com/bnabooks/ababna/eeo/2001/wilson.doc, accessed April 21, 2009.

91 Tyrone A. Holmes, "How to Connect Diversity to Performance," *Performance Improvement* 44 (May–June 2005): 13–17.

92 Robert D. Winsor and Ellen A. Ensher, "Choices Made in Balancing Work and Family: Following Two Women on a 16-Year Journey," *Journal of Management Inquiry* 9 (June 2000): 218–231.

93 Jeffrey R. Edwards and Nancy P. Rothbard, "Mechanisms Linking Work and Family," *Academy of Management Review* 25 (January 2000): 178–199.

94 Dalton Conley, *Elsewhere, USA* (New York: Pantheon Books, 2008).

95 Douglas M. McCracken, "Winning the Talent War for Women: Sometimes It Takes a Revolution," *Harvard Business Review* 78 (November–December 2000): 159–167; Sally Roberts, "Work/Life Programs No Longer a 'Woman's Issue,'" *Business Insurance*, August 8, 2005, pp. 3–4.

96 "DuPont," *Working Mother*, http://www.workingmother.com/dupont.html, accessed April 19, 2006.

97 Daniel Griffiths, "Japan's Workaholic Culture," *BBC News Online,* http://news.bbc.co.uk/1/low/world/asia-pacific/701458.stm, accessed March 21, 2006; Nik Paton, "Japan Cracks Down on Workaholic Culture," http://www.management-issues.com/display_page.asp?section=research&id=2939, accessed March 25, 2006; Rebecca Segall, "Japanese Killer," *Psychology Today* 33 (September–October 2000): 10–11.

98 Charles R. Stoner, Jennifer Robin, and Lori Russell-Chapin, "On the Edge: Perceptions and Responses to Life Imbalance," *Business Horizons* (July–August 2005): 48–54.

99 SAS, Annual Report, http://www.sas.com/corporate/report03/culture.html, accessed April 20, 2006; Thomas Watson, "Goodnight, Sweet Prince," *Canadian Business*, May 27, 2002, pp. 77–78.

100 E. Jeffrey Hill, Andrea Jackson, and Giuseppe Martinengo, "Twenty Years of Work and Family at International Business Machines Corporation," *American Behavioral Scientist* 49 (May 2006): 1165–1183.

101 Michael A. Verespej, "Balancing Act," *Industry Week,* May 15, 2000, pp. 81–85.

102 Booz Allen Hamilton, Work-Life Balance, http://www.boozallen.com/careers/a_great_place_to_work/work-life_balance, accessed August 17, 2009.

103 Texas Instruments, Work/Life Effectiveness, http://www.ti.com/recruit/docs/worklife.shtml, accessed April 19, 2006.

104 "The State of Knowledge Surrounding Employee Volunteering in the United States," Points of Light Foundation, http://www.pointsoflight.org/downloads/pdf/resources/research/StateOfKnowledge.pdf, accessed March 25, 2009.

105 William C. Symonds, "Sweating for Dollars," *Business Week*, September 19, 2005, pp. 88–90.

106 Alan J. Liddle, "McD Franchisees Make Online McStatement to Workers, Communities," *Nation's Restaurant News,* September 18, 2000, pp. 19, 94; McDonald's 2008 Corporate Social Responsibility Report, http://www.crmcdonalds.com/publish/csr/home/report.html, accessed March 25, 2009.

107 "Better Business Bureau Announces 2008 Local Torch Award Winners," http://images.smalldog.com/pressroom/PR_2008_BBB_torch.pdf, accessed March 18, 2009; "Small Dog Gives Pet Perk," CNNfn, July 10, 2000, http://www.cnnfn.com; T3, The Think Tank, http://www.t-3.com/company/culture#/culture, accessed March 18, 2009.

108 ENSR, "An Employer of Choice," http://www.ensr.aecom.com/Careers/48/27/index.html, accessed March 20, 2009; Roger E. Herman and Joyce L. Gioia, *How to Become an Employer of Choice* (Winchester, VA: Oakhill Press, 2000).

109 Ibid.; Da Joseph Kornik, "The Morale Majority," *Training* 43 (January 2006): 4.

110 "92.4% of Companies State ESOPs Are Good Business, Survey Reveals Positive Results for ESOP Companies," ESOP Association, http://www.esopassociation.org/media/media_EPS.asp, access March 18, 2009; "Employee-Owned Companies Abound on Fortune Magazine's Top 100 List for 2009," ESOP Association, http://www.esopassociation.org/media/media_fortune100_pressrelease.asp, accessed March 18, 2009; "Employee Ownership and Corporate Performance," ESOP Association, http://www.esopassociation.org/media/media_corporate.asp, accessed March 19, 2009; Jacquelyn Yates and Marjorie Kelly, "The Employee Ownership 100," *Business Ethics* 14 (September–October 2000), 12–19.

111 Kris Frieswick, "ESOPs: Split Personality," *CFO,* July 7, 2003, p. 1; Ronald Mano and E. Devon Deppe, "We Told You So: ESOPs Are Risky," *Ohio CPA Journal* 61 (July–September 2002): 67–68; Matthew Mouritsen, Ronald Mano, and E. Devon Deppe, "The ESOP Fable Revisited: Employees' Exposure to ESOPs and Enron's Exit," *Personal Financial Planning Monthly* 2 (May 2002): 27–31.

112 Lara Moroko and Mark D. Uncles, "Employer Branding," *Sloan Management Review*, March 23, 2009, http://sloanreview.mit.edu/business-insight/articles/2009/1/5118/employer-branding/, accessed April 14, 2009.

113 "The Nike Case and Corporate Self-Censorship," *Business & the Environment with ISO 14000 Updates* 15 (March 2004): 6–7; Isabelle Maignan, Bas Hillebrand, and Debbie Thorne McAlister, "Managing Socially Responsible Buying: How to Integrate Non-Economic Criteria into the Purchasing Process," *European Management Journal* 20 (December 2002): 641–648.

Chapter 8

1 "Winners and Losers," *Latin Trade* 13 (September 2005): 34; Rodrigo Amaral, "Americas: Mexico-Azteca Exports Winning Formula," *The Banker* (July 2008): 15; Banco Azteca, http://www.grupoelektra.com.mx/Business/BancoAzteca.aspx, accessed April 17, 2009; Theresa Braine, "Courting the Unbanked," *Business Mexico* 14–15, no. 12–1 (2005): 40–41; Lucy Conger, "A Bank for Mexico's Working Families," *New York Times,* December 31, 2002, p. W1; Geri Smith, "Buy a Toaster, Open a Bank Account," *Business Week*, January 13, 2003, p. 54.

2 "Whole Foods Market Reminds Consumers That How Their Food Tastes Has Everything to Do with How It Is Grown," *CSR Newswire,* January 3, 2003, http://www.csrwire.com/article.cgi/1494.html, accessed May 8, 2006; "Our Core Values," Whole Foods Market, http://www.wholefoodsmarket.com/company/corevalues.html, accessed July 7, 2009.

3 "International Buy Nothing Day," http://ecoplan.org/ibnd/, accessed April 17, 2009.

4 Consumers International, http://www.consumersinternational.org/, accessed April 17, 2009.

5 "World Consumer Rights Day," Consumers International, http://www.consumersinternational.org/Templates/Internal.asp?NodeID=95043, accessed April 17, 2009.

6 "Consumer Charter for Global Business," Consumers International, http://www.consumersinternational.org/Templates/Internal.asp?NodeID=95339&int1stParentNodeID=89647, accessed April 17, 2009.

7 "The Aggro of the Agora," *Economist*, January 14, 2006, p. 76; F. Knox, "The Doctrine of Consumer Sovereignty," *Review of Social Economy* 63 (September 2005): 383–394.

8 S. M. Solaiman, "Protection Through Administrative Enforcement of Disclosure Requirements in Prospectuses: Bangladeshi Laws Compared with Their Equivalents in India and Malaysia," *Journal of Financial Crime* 12 (August 2005): 260–293.

9 Lee E. Norrgard and Julia M. Norrgard, *Consumer Fraud: A Reference Handbook* (New York: ABC-Clio, 1998).

10 David M. Gardner, Jim Harris, and Junyong Kim, "The Fraudulent Consumer," in *Marketing and Public Policy Conference Proceedings,* ed. Gregory Gundlach, William Wilkie, and Patrick Murphy (Chicago: American Marketing Association, 1999), pp. 48–54.

11 Richard C. Hollinger, *2004 National Retail Security Survey,* 13th ed. (Gainesville: University of Florida, 2004); "Five Tools You Can Use to Prevent Online Fraud," Merchant Risk Council, https://www.merchantriskcouncil.org/, accessed May 21, 2009.

12 "ASA Bans Boots Anti-Cellulite Ads," *Soap, Perfumery & Cosmetics* 78 (October 2005): 5; Lisa McLaughlin, "Cloaking Cellulite," *Time,* May 24, 2004, p. 90; Christine Doyle, "How to Beat Cellulite—Part Two: Do Anti-Cellulite Creams, Lotions and Massage Really Work, or Do Women Just Like to Think They Do?" *Ottawa Citizen,* May 23, 2000, p. D8.

13 "Department of Consumers Affairs ID's Five Hot Issues Facing California Consumers in Today's Marketplace," California Department of Consumer Affairs, http://www.dca.ca.gov/publications/press_releases/2006/0206_cpw.shtml, accessed April 17, 2009.

14 "Bureau of Consumer Protection," Federal Trade Commission, http://www.ftc.gov/bcp/index.shtml, accessed April 17, 2009.

15 "Debt Management Operation Settles FTC Charges," U.S. Federal Trade Commission, http://www.ftc.gov/opa/2006/05/lighthouse.htm, accessed April 17, 2009.

16 "Consumer Affairs and Outreach Division," Federal Communications Commission, http://www.fcc.gov/cgb/cgb_offices.html#CPD, accessed April 17, 2009.

17 "Protecting Consumers," Iowa Attorney General, http://www.state.ia.us/government/ag/consumer/, accessed July 8, 2009.

18 State of Texas, Business & Commerce Code, "Chapter 17: Deceptive Trade Practices," http://www.statutes.legis.state.tx.us/SOTWDocs/BC/htm/BC.17.htm, accessed April 17, 2009.

19 Robert B. Downs, "Afterword," in Upton Sinclair, *The Jungle* (New York: New American Library, 1960).

20 "Manufacturers Pay $460,000 in Civil Penalties," *Consumer Product Litigation Reporter* 11 (June 2000): 15.

21 "2006 Fair Housing Month Statement from Assistant Secretary Kim Kendrick," U.S. Department of Housing and Urban Development, http://www.hud.gov/offices/fheo/FHMonth/fhm2006.cfm, accessed April 17, 2009; "The State of Fair Housing," U.S. Department of Housing and Urban Development, http://www.hud.gov/offices/fheo/library/FY2005_Annual_Report.pdf, accessed April 17, 2009.

22 Charles Fleming, "Politics & Economics: Financial Bias Simmers in Europe," *Wall Street Journal,* May 8, 2006, p. A8; "What Is Predatory Lending?," *Mortgage News Daily,* http://www.mortgagenewsdaily.com/mortgage_fraud/Predatory_Lending.asp, accessed July 7, 2009.

23 "Sweepstakes Giant Agrees to $34 Million Settlement," CNN.com, June 27, 2001, http://www.cnn.com/2001/LAW/06/26/sweepstakes.lawsuit/index.html, accessed April 17, 2009; Helen Rothschild and Roberta Ewald, "'You're a Guaranteed Winner': Composing 'You' in a Consumer Culture," *Journal of Business Communication* 40 (April 2003): 98–117.

24 John Eggerton, "FTC Declares Diet Claims Have No Weight," *Broadcasting & Cable,* November 25, 2002, p. 7; Federal Trade Commission, "A Reference Guide for Media on Bogus Weight Loss Claims," http://www.ftc.gov/bcp/conline/edcams/redflag/, accessed April 17, 2009.

25 Wine Institute, "Direct Wine Shipments," http://www.wineinstitute.org/programs/shipwine/main.htm, accessed July 7, 2009.

26 "Lemon Law Information and Sites," http://autopedia.com/html/HotLinks_LemonLaw.html, accessed April 17, 2009.

27 Michael Bradford, "New South Korean Law May Bring Increased Product Liability Claims," *Business Insurance,* April 22, 2002, pp. 29–30; Tom Chung, "When Products Cause User Damages," *Korea Herald,* January 12, 2005, p. 1.

28 "Roche Diagnostics Issues Worldwide Voluntary Recall," U.S. Food and Drug Administration, http://www.fda.gov/oc/po/firmrecalls/roche01_06.html, accessed May 9, 2006; Christine Gorman, "Diabetes Recall," *Time,* April 3, 2000, p. 94.

29 "17th, 18th and 19th Product Liability Lawsuits Dismissed Against TASER International," http://phx.corporate-ir.net/phoenix.zhtml?c=129937&p=irol-newsArticle&ID=859207&highlight=, May 22, 2006, press release, accessed April 17, 2009; Alex Berenson, "The Safety of Tasers Is Questioned Again," *New York Times,* May 25, 2006, p. C3.

30 "Regulatory Watch," *Business China,* February 27, 2006, p. 11.

31 Sandra N. Hurd, Peter Shears, and Frances E. Zollers, "Consumer Law," *Journal of Business Law* (May 2000): 262–277.

32 Irene M. Kunii, "Stand Up and Fight," *Business Week,* September 11, 2000, pp. 54–55.

33 Suk-ching Ho, "Executive Insights: Growing Consumer Power in China," *Journal of International Marketing* 9 (Spring 2001): 64–84.

34 Nigel Davis, "REACH Readiness Is Thrown into Focus," *Chemical News & Intelligence,* May 16, 2006, p. 1.

35 Kenneth J. Meier, E. Thomas Garman, and Lael R. Keiser, *Regulation and Consumer Protection: Politics, Bureaucracy and Economics* (Houston, TX: Dame Publications, 1998).

36 Allan Asher, "Going Global: A New Paradigm for Consumer Protection," *Journal of Consumer Affairs* 32 (Winter 1998): 183–203; Benet Middleton, "Consumerism: A Pragmatic Ideology," *Consumer Policy Review* 8 (November–December 1998): 213–217; Audhesh Paswan and Jhinuk Chowdhury, "Consumer Protection Issues and Non-governmental Organizations in a Developing Market," in *Developments in Marketing Science,* ed. Harlan E. Spotts and H. Lee Meadow (Coral Gables, FL: Academy of Marketing Science, 2000), pp. 171–176.

37 "On the Left: What Makes Ralph Run," *Business Week,* September 25, 2000, pp. 82, 86.

38 Paul N. Bloom and Stephen A. Greyser, "The Maturing of Consumerism," *Harvard Business Review* 59 (November–December 1981): 130–139.

39 Rhoda H. Karpatkin, "Toward a Fair and Just Marketplace for All Consumers: The Responsibilities of Marketing Professionals," *Journal of Public Policy and Marketing* 18 (Spring 1999): 118–123.

40 "Empowerment to the Consumer," *Marketing Week,* October 21, 1999, p. 3; Pierre M. Loewe and Mark S. Bonchek, "The Retail Revolution," *Management Review* 88 (April 1999): 38–44.

41 Jim Guest, "Grassroots Advocacy Is Still in Style," *Consumer Reports* 70 (August 2005): 5.

42 "Consumer Bill of Rights and Responsibilities: Report to the President of the United States," Advisory Commission on Consumer Protection and Quality in the Health Care Industry, November 1997, http://www.hcqualitycommission.gov/cborr/, accessed April 17, 2009; Mary Jane Fisher, "Pressure Mounts for Patient Rights Agreement," *National Underwriter/Life & Health Financial Services,* May 22, 2000, pp. 3–4; Michael Pretzer, "New Mind 'Patient Relations': Get Ready for 'Consumer Rights,'" *Medical Economics,* February 23, 1998, pp. 47–55.

43 "Comprehensive Consumer Rights Bill Addresses Bank Fees, Identity Theft," *Consumer Financial Services Law Report,* May 15, 2000, p. 2.

44 Nichole Christian, "Domino's Reaches Deal on Accusations of Bias," *New York Times,* June 7, 2000, p. A28; T. J. Degroat, "Domino's Revises Delivery Policy," DiversityInc., June 6, 2000, http://www.diversityinc.com.

45 Marianne Lavelle, "The States Take the Lead on Gun Control," *U.S. News & World Report,* April 17, 2000, p. 24.

46 Steve Jarvis, "They're Not Quitting," *Marketing News,* November 20, 2000, pp. 1, 9; Marianne Lavelle, "Big Tobacco Rises from the Ashes," *U.S. News & World Report,* November 13, 2000, p. 50; Nancy Shute, "Building a Better Butt," *U.S. News & World Report,* September 18, 2000, p. 66.

47 http://www.diversityinc.com; "Pirate's Booty: Too Good to Be True," *Washington Post,* February 19, 2002, p. F3; Paige Smoran, "Is Booty-licious Diet Food Part of a Large Conspiracy?" *Chicago Sun-Times,* April 18, 2002, p. 42.

48 A. Ben Oumlil and Alvin J. Williams, "Consumer Education Programs for Mature Consumers," *Journal of Services Marketing* 14, no. 3 (2000): 232–243; Lauren Paetsch, "URAC Accreditation Provides Benchmark for Health Information Web Sites," *Employee Benefit Plan Review* 56 (June 2002): 10–18.

49 Lyuba Pronina, "Top Firms Team Up to Create Consumer Telephone Hot Line," *Moscow Times,* November 29, 2000.

50 "Dispute Resolution Services," Better Business Bureau, http://www.bbb.org/us/Dispute-Resolution-Services/, accessed July 7, 2009.

51 Federal Trade Commission, *Privacy Online: Fair Information Practices in the Electronic Marketplace: A Federal Trade Commission Report to Congress* (Washington, DC: FTC, May 2000), also available at http://www.ftc.gov/reports/privacy2000/privacy2000.pdf, accessed April 17, 2009.

52 "CMC Properties," Better Business Bureau International Torch Award, http://www.bbb.org/torchaward/cmc.asp, accessed April 17, 2009; "Four Businesses Honored with Prestigious International Award for Outstanding Marketplace Ethics," *PR Newswire,* September 23, 2002, via LexisNexis.

53 Southwest Airlines, "Customer Service Commitment," http://www.southwest.com/about_swa/customer_service_commitment/customer_service_commitment.html, accessed April 17, 2009.

54 "Wal-Mart Bucks for Education," *Home Textiles Today,* June 5, 2000, p. 11; Mike France and Joann Muller, "A Site for Soreheads," *Business Week,* April 12, 1999, p. 86; Wendy Zellner, "Wal-Mart: Why an Apology Made Sense," *Business Week,* July 3, 2000, pp. 65–66; Wendy Zellner and Aaron Bernstein, "Up Against the Wal-Mart," *Business Week,* March 13, 2000, p. 76.

55 Damien McElroy, "Chinese Shun Toshiba in Anti-Japan Protests," *Sunday Telegraph* (London), June 4, 2000, p. 27.

56 Andy Altman-Ohr, "World Boycott of Transamerica Launched," *Jewish Bulletin News of Northern California,* January 21, 2000, http://www.angelfire.com/biz4/consumerama/transam.htm, accessed May 9, 2006.

57 "Home of the Casino Royale Boycott," http://www.danielcraigisnotbond.com/boycott_casino_royale.html, accessed April 17, 2009; Jamie Wienman, "Everything Old Is Young Again," *Maclean's,* May 8, 2006, p. 56.

58 "The 1997 Cone/Roper Cause-Related Marketing Trends Report," *Business Ethics* 12 (March–April 1997): 14–16.

59 Edwin R. Stafford and Cathy L. Hartman, "Environmentalist-Business Collaborations: Social Responsibility, Green Alliances, and Beyond," in *Advertising Research: The Internet, Consumer Behavior and Strategy,* ed. George Zinkhan (Chicago: American Marketing Association, 2000), pp. 170–192.

60 "David Lansky to Join the Markle Foundation," Markle Foundation, http://www.markle.org/resources/press_center/press_releases/2004/press_release_09282004.php, accessed April 17, 2009; Foundation for Accountability, "FACCT Legacy Documents," http://www.facct.org, accessed August 19, 2003.

61 D'Arcy Doran, "Village Women Paralyze Oil Giant in Nigeria," *Associated Press Worldstream,* July 12, 2002, via LexisNexis.

62 James L. Creighton, "The Utility as Civic Partner," *Public Utilities Fortnightly,* June 15, 2000, pp. 32–38; City of Redding, "Town Hall Meetings to Explain Utility Rate Increases," http://www.ci.redding.ca.us/cm/pressreleases/051209RMU-RatesTownhall.pdf, accessed July 7, 2009.

Chapter 9

1 Howard Rothman and Mary Scott, *Companies with a Conscience,* 3rd ed. (Denver, CO: MyersTempleton, 2004); "Chiefs Recognized Nationally for Their Community Commitment," Kansas City Chiefs, http://www.kcchiefs.com/news_article.asp?ID=Y8NTDBHEJFDYXR8NQH759NDS72, accessed April 17, 2009; "The Chiefs Way," Kansas City Chiefs, http://www.kcchiefs.com/chiefsway/, accessed May 19, 2009.

2 Merlino's Family Steakhouse, http://www.merlinossteakhouse.com/, accessed May 27, 2009.

3 American Productivity and Quality Center, *Community Relations: Unleashing the Power of Corporate Citizenship* (Houston, TX: American Productivity and Quality Center, 1998); Edmund M. Burke, *Corporate Community Relations: The Principle of the Neighbor of Choice* (Westport, CT: Praeger, 1999).

4 Bradley K. Googins, "Why Community Relations Is a Strategic Imperative," *Strategy & Business* (Third Quarter 1997): 14–16.

5 "We Build CommUnity," http://corporate.homedepot.com/wps/portal/!ut/p/.cmd/cs/.ce/7_0_A/.s/7_0_11N/_s.7_0_A/7_0_11N, accessed April 17, 2009.

6 "FedEx Community," http://www.fedex.com/us/about/responsibility/community/index.html, accessed April 17, 2009.

7 Business for Social Responsibility, "Community Involvement," http://www.bsr.org/resourcecenter/, accessed December 4, 2000; Sandra A. Waddock and Mary-Ellen Boyle, "The Dynamics of Change in Corporate Community Relations," *California Management Review* 37 (Summer 1995): 125–138; Barron Wells and Nelda Spinks, "Communicating with the Community," *Career Development International* 4, no. 2 (1999): 108–116.

8 "Cisco Systems, Grand Circle, and KaBOO! Win CECP Awards Honoring 'Excellence in Corporate Philanthropy,'" *Business Wire,* February 27, 2006, http://80-web.lexis-nexis.com.proxy.uwlib.uwyo.edu/universe/document?_m=ca22850a03, accessed April 22, 2006.

9 Alyson Warhurst, "The Future of Corporate Philanthopy," *Business Week,* December 9, 2008, p. 16.

10 Janelia Moreno, "More Casas for the Workers," *Houston Chronicle,* March 4, 2001, p. Business 1; "Delphi Mexico Careers," http://delphi.com/careers/international/mexico/, accessed July 11, 2009.

11 "Community Needs Assessment Survey Guide," Utah State University Extension, http://extension.usu.edu/files/uploads/surveyguide.pdf, accessed June 1, 2009.

12 Thomas A. Klein and Robert W. Nason, "Marketing and Development: Macromarketing Perspectives," in *Handbook of Marketing and Society,* ed. Paul N. Bloom and Gregory T. Gunlach (Thousand Oaks, CA: Sage, 2001), pp. 263–297.

13 BP Global, http://www.bp.com/bodycopyarticle.do?categoryId=1&contentId=7052055, accessed April 17, 2009.

14 FedEx St. Jude Classic, http://www.stjudeclassic.com/index.php?option=com_frontpage&Itemid=1, accessed June 1, 2009.

15 John Welbes, "Ford Layoffs Likely in July," http://www.twincities.com, March 1, 2006, http://www.twincities.com/mld.twincities/14034757.htm; Nicole Muehlhausen, "Nearly 800 Ford Plant Employees to Be Laid Off," http://kstp.com/article/stories/S680252.shtml?cat=206, accessed October 28, 2009.

16 Robert Jablon, "Squid Boat Companies Charged with Dumping," *Business Week Online,* May 9, 2006, http://www.businessweek.com/ap/financial news/d8hgii509.htm?campaign_id=search, accessed May 11, 2006.

17 Zellner and Bernstein, "Up Against the Wal-Mart," pp. 76–78.

18 David Kaplan, "Plant for Recycling Food Waste Planned," *Houston Chronicle,* February 13, 2001, p. Business 2; Rebecca Mowbray, "Turning Trash into Profits: An Entrepreneur's Plans to Turn Waste into Animal Feed Take the Community into Consideration," *Houston Chronicle,* August 1,1999, p. 4D.

19 Janicca Lee, "Daniels Fund Supporting Integrity and Ethics in Business," *UWYO Magazine,* 7, no. 4 (Spring 2006): 6.

20 New Belgium Brewing Company, Inc., http://www.newbelgium.com, accessed May 11, 2006.

21 Corporation for National and Community Service, "Volunteering in the United States," http://www.volunteeringinamerica.gov/newprofile.cfm, accessed July 11, 2009.

22 Corporate for National and Community Service, "Benefits of Volunteering," http://www.nationalservice.gov/about/volunteering/benefits.asp, accessed July 10, 2009.

23 "About Employee Volunteering," National Centre for Volunteering, http://www.volunteering.org.uk/WhatWeDo/Projects+and+initiatives/Employer+Supported+Volunteering/, accessed April 17, 2009.

24 Bill Leonard, "Supporting Volunteerism as Individual Americans Invest More Hours into Volunteer Activities," *HR Magazine,* June 6, 1998, p. 4; "TMMK Receives Volunteer Spirit Award," http://pressroom.toyota.com/pr/tms/tmmk-receives-volunteer-spirit-91301.aspx, accessed July 10, 2009.

25 "Vanderbilt Targets 100% Volunteerism," *Business Ethics,* Winter 2005, p. 10.

26 Sarah Townsend, "Euro Volunteering Year Will be 2011," *Third Sector,* February 10, 2009, p. 3.

27 Time Warner Cable, "Employee Engagement," http://www.timewarner.com/corp/citizenship/community/employee_engagement/index.html, accessed July 11, 2009.

28 Ingrid Murro Botero, "Charitable Giving Has 4 Big Benefits," *Business Journal of Phoenix,* January 1, 1999, http://www.bizjournals.com/phoenix/stories/1999/01/04/smallb3.html, accessed April 20, 2009.

29 "The Gift Shift," *Wall Street Journal,* November 25, 2005, pp. W1, W10.

30 Giving USA Foundation, "U.S. Charitable Giving Estimated to Be $307.65 Billion in 2008," http://www.givingusa.org/press_releases/gusa/GivingReaches300billion.pdf, accessed July 12, 2009.

31 "Money Woes May Close Russian Museum," *Associated Press Online,* November 24, 2000, via Comtex; "Our Partners," Moscow Center for Prison Reform, http://www.prison.org/english/mcprpart.htm, accessed April 20, 2009.

32 Diane Lindquist, "Drug Companies' Rx for the Bottom Line," *Industry Week,* September 7, 1998, p. 25.

33 Noel M. Tichy, Andrew R. McGill, and Lynda St. Clair, *Corporate Global Citizenship: Doing Business in the Public Eye* (San Francisco: New Lexington Press, 1997).

34 Michael E. Porter and Mark R. Kramer, "The Competitive Advantage of Corporate Philanthropy," *Harvard Business Review* 80 (December 2002): 56–68; Robbie Shell, "Breaking the Stereotypes of Corporate Philanthropy," *Wall Street Journal,* November 26, 2002, p. B2.

35 Reynold Levy, *Give and Take: A Candid Account of Corporate Philanthropy* (Boston: Harvard Business School Press, 1999); Noah's Bagels, http://www.noahs.com, accessed July 11, 2009.

36 Tichy, McGill, and St. Clair, *Corporate Global Citizenship.*

37 Jessica Stannard and Tamara Backer, "How Employee Volunteers Multiply Your Community Impact PART 2," *OnPhilanthropy.com,* December 29, 2005, http://www.onphilanthropy.com/articles/print.aspx?cid=760, accessed April 20, 2009.

38 "Corporate Citizen," Fuji Bank, http://www.mizuhofg.co.jp/english/investors/financial/annual/pdf/data9903a_fbk/ef_10.pdf, accessed April 20, 2009.

39 Curt Weeden, "Leave-Based Donation Programs," Contributions Academy, http://www.contributionsacademy.com/html/news.html, accessed November 5, 2001.

40 Ben & Jerry's, "Unilever Acquisition of Ben & Jerry's," http://benjerry.custhelp.com/cgi-bin/benjerry.cfg/php/enduser/std_adp.php?p_sid=oTybnf7i&p_lva=&p_faqid=136&p_created=955568704&p_sp=cF9zcmNoPSZwX2dyaWRzb3J0PSZwX3Jvd19jbnQ9MjI4JnBfcGFnZT0x&p_li=, accessed August 24, 2009.

41 Curt Weeden, *Corporate Social Investing* (San Francisco: Berrett-Koehler, 1998), pp. 116–123.

42 Avon, "Avon Breast Cancer Crusade," http://www
.avoncompany.com/women/avoncrusade, accessed July 12, 2009.

43 Tichy, McGill, and St. Clair, *Corporate Global Citizenship.*

44 Daniel Kadlec and Bruce Voorst, "The New World of Giving: Companies Are Doing More Good, and Demanding More Back," *Time,* May 5, 1997, pp. 62–66.

45 Kevin T. Higgins, "Marketing with a Conscience," *Marketing Management* 11 (July–August 2002): 12–15; P. Rajan Varadarajan and Anil Menon, "Cause-Related Marketing: A Coalignment of Marketing Strategy and Corporate Philanthropy," *Journal of Marketing* 52 (July 1988): 58–74.

46 Allyson L. Stewart-Allen, "Europe Ready for Cause-Related Campaigns," *Marketing News,* July 6, 1998, p. 9.

47 "Business in the Community, Awards for Excellence," http://www.bitc.org.uk/awards_for_excellence/index.html, accessed April 17, 2009; Sue Adkins, "Why Cause-Related Marketing Is a Winning Business Formula," *Marketing,* July 20, 2000, p. 18.

48 Steve Hoeffler and Kevin Lane Keller, "Building Brand Equity Through Corporate Societal Marketing," *Journal of Public Policy & Marketing* 21 (Spring 2002): 78–89; Sue Adkins and Nina Kowalska, "Consumers Put 'Causes' on the Shopping List," *M2 PressWire,* November 17, 1997.

49 Jennifer Mullen, "Performance-Based Corporate Philanthropy: How 'Giving Smart' Can Further Corporate Goals," *Public Relations Quarterly,* June 22, 1997, p. 42; Michal Strahilevitz, "The Effects of Prior Impressions of a Firm's Ethics on the Success of a Cause-Related Marketing Campaign," *Journal of Nonprofit & Public Sector Marketing* 11, no. 1: 77–92.

50 Stan Friedman and Charles Kouns, "Charitable Contribution: Reinventing Cause Marketing," *Brand Week,* October 27, 1997.

51 Nelson, *1001 Ways to Energize Employees.*

52 "How Strategic Philanthropy Builds Brands," Letter to *Harvard Business Review* responding to Michael Porter and Mark Kramer's article, "The Strategic Advantage of Corporate Philanthropy," available through *HBS Publishing,* http://www.holding.com/articles/philanthropy.html, accessed July 12, 2009.

53 "Corporate Philanthropy: Sony in America—Working Together to Make a Difference," http://www.sony.com/SCA/philanthropy.shtml, accessed April 17, 2009.

54 United Airlines, "Volunteerism," http://www.united.com/page/article/0,,1364,00.html, accessed July 12, 2009.

55 Rosenbluth and Peters, *Good Company.*

56 BE&K, "BE&K Awards," http://www.bek.com/news.asp?sectionId=3, accessed July 12, 2009.

57 "The Home Depot Announces $57 Million Investment to Support Gulf Coast Rebuilding Efforts," http://rhh.homedepot.com/pc.htm, accessed April 17, 2009.

58 "BT Bolsters Wealth of Responsibility Program," *Private Asset Management,* January 24, 2000, p. 7; "Wealth with Responsibility," Deutsche Bank, http://www.db.com/pwm/en/contact-subpage-north_america.html?7%3AWealth+with+Responsibility, accessed April 17, 2009.

59 Verizon Literacy Network, http://www.verizonreads.net/core/literacy.shtml, accessed July 12, 2009.

60 "Take Charge of Education," http://sites.target.com/site/en/corporate/page.jsp?contentId=PRD03-001825, accessed April 17, 2009.

61 Freeplay Energy, http://www.freeplayenergy.com/, accessed July 12, 2009.

62 BJC HealthCare, "Community Benefit Report," http://www.bjc.org/demoSite/2008Report/home.html, accessed July 12, 2009

63 Coca-Cola Company, "Environment," http://www.thecoca-colacompany.com/citizenship/environment.html, accessed May 20, 2009.

64 Alan Reder, *75 Best Business Practices for Socially Responsible Companies* (New York: Putnam, 1995); Merck, "The Merck Mectizan Donation Program," http://www.merck.com/cr/enabling_access/developing_world/mectizan/home.html, accessed April 17, 2009.

65 "Glasses Drive a Big Success," *Florida Times-Union,* May 10, 2003, p. K4; LensCrafters Charitable Giving—OneSight, http://www.lenscrafters.com/eyeglasses/7/about/onesight-charitable-giving, accessed July 12, 2009.

66 American Apparel and Footwear Association, http://www.apparelandfootwear.org/, accessed April 17, 2009.

67 Reder, *75 Best Business Practices for Socially Responsible Companies.*

68 3M "Recognition as a Sustainability Leader," http://solutions.3m.com/wps/portal/3M/en_US/global/sustainability/s/recognition/, accessed July 12, 2009.

69 Walker Information, *Corporate Philanthropy National Benchmark Study, Employee Report* (Chicago: Walker Information, 2002).

70 "For All Kids Foundation," http://www.forallkids.com/, accessed April 17, 2009.

71 Robert J. Williams and J. Douglas Barrett, "Corporate Philanthropy, Criminal Activity, and Firm Reputation: Is There a Link?" *Journal of Business Ethics* 26 (2000): 341–350.

72 Roger Bennett, "Corporate Philanthropy in France, Germany, and the UK," *International Marketing Review* 15 (June 1998): 469.

73 American Productivity and Quality Center, *Community Relations: Unleashing the Power of Corporate Citizenship* (Houston, TX: American Productivity and Quality Center, 1998).

74 John A. Byrne, "Chainsaw," *Business Week,* October 18, 1999, pp. 128–149.

75 Levy, *Give and Take.*

76 Weeden, *Corporate Social Investing.*

77 Reprinted with permission of the publisher. From *Corporate Social Investing,* copyright © 1998 by Curt Weeden, Berrett-Koehler Publishers, Inc., San Francisco, CA. All rights reserved. http://www.bkconnection.com, accessed October 28, 2009.

78 Walter W. Wymer Jr. and Sridhar Samu, "Dimensions of Business and Nonprofit Collaborative Relationships," *Journal of Nonprofit & Public Sector Marketing* 11, no. 1: 3–22.

79 John A. Byrne, "The New Face of Philanthropy," *Business Week,* December 2, 2002, pp. 82–86; Stephanie Strom, "Ground Zero: Charity; a Flood of Money, Then a Deluge of Scrutiny for Those Handing It Out," *New York Times,* September 11, 2002, p. B5; Panel on the Nonprofit Sector, "Principles for Good Governance and Ethical Practice: A Guide for Charities and Foundations," http://www.nonprofitpanel.org/Report/principles/Principles_Executive_Summary.pdf, accessed July 12, 2009.

80 Cathy Brisbois, "Ranking Disclosure: VanCity Savings & Credit Union, Canada," in *Building Corporate*

Accountability: The Emerging Practices in Social and Ethical Accounting, Auditing and Reporting, ed. Simon Zadek, Peter Pruzan, and Richard Evans (London: Earthscan Publications, 1997).

Chapter 10

1 "White Paper Discusses Achievements in Protecting Olympic IPR," http://www.chinaipr.gov.cn/news/headlines/255925.shtml, accessed August 9, 2009; "Handbags at Dawn," *Economist.com*, April 21, 2006, p. 1; "Silk Market Victory Could Open New Anti-Fake Front," *Managing Intellectual Property* (February 2006): 1; Geoffrey A. Fowler, "China's Logo Crackdown," *Wall Street Journal*, November 4, 2005, p. B1.

2 G. Elijah Dann and Neil Haddow, "Just Doing Business or Doing Just Business: Google, Microsoft, Yahoo! and the Business of Censoring China's Internet," *Journal of Business Ethics* 79 (May 2008): 219-234.

3 Kevin Bonsor, "How Electronic Ink Will Work," http://www.howstuffworks.com/e-ink1.htm, accessed August 1, 2009.

4 Robert Valdes, "How Broadband Over Powerlines Works," http://computer.howstuffworks.com/bpl.htm, accessed August 4, 2009.

5 Edward Taylor, "Supercomputers Speed Up Game," *Wall Street Journal*, April 14, 2006, p. C1.

6 Bill Saporito, "Get Ready for Class Warfare," January 13, 2003, http://www.cnn.com/2003/ALLPOLITICS/01/13/timep.classware.tm/index.html, accessed August 1, 2009.

7 Stacey Wells, "Across the Divide," Business2.com, December 12, 2000, pp. 186–204, http://www.business2.com/search?qt=Across+the+Divide&business2=on&expanded=, accessed September 11, 2003; Wayne Leighton, "Broadband Deployment and the Digital Divide: A Primer," *Policy Analysis*, http://www.cato.org/pubs/pas/pa410.pdf, accessed August 1, 2009.

8 Hispanic Association of Colleges and Universities, "MPC/Gateway and HACU Team Up to Help Bridge the Digital Divide," http://www.hacu.net/hacu/Gateway_EN.asp?SnID=2, accessed August 1, 2009.

9 "Charting the Future of the Net," MSNBC, July 7, 2000, http://www.msnbc.com, accessed August 8, 2006.

10 Semantic Web, http://semanticweb.org/wiki/Main_Page, accessed August 8, 2009; Leslie Walker, "The Lord of the Webs," *Washington Post*, January 30, 2003, p. E1.

11 "Technology and Economic Growth: Producing Real Results for the American People," The White House, http://clinton3.nara.gov/WH/EOP/OSTP/html/techgrow.html, accessed August 3, 2009.

12 Alan Greenspan, Remarks to the Economic Club of New York, Federal Reserve Board, New York, January 13, 2000.

13 Elana Varon, "The ABCs of B2B," http://dc.gzntax.gov.cn/k/2002-1/679970.html, accessed August 1, 2009.

14 Greenspan, Remarks to the Economic Club of New York.

15 "About Covisint," http://www.covisint.com/about/, accessed August 8, 2009; "Covisint Parts Exchange Officially Opens for Business," *Bloomberg Newswire*, December 11, 2000, via AOL.

16 Greenspan, Remarks to the Economic Club of New York.

17 Staples Contract Division, "Industry Awards," http://www.staplescontract.com/SNA/docs/industry-awards.asp, accessed August 8, 2009; Richard Karpinski, "Web Delivers Big Results for Staples," *B to B*, November 11, 2002, p. 14.

18 "IT Failing One in Four Small Businesses," http://smallbiztechnology.com/archive/2009/08/it-failing-one-in-four-small-b.html, accessed August 8, 2009.

19 U.S. Department of Education, "Digital Divide," http://www.ed.gov/Technology/digdiv.html, accessed August 9, 2009.

20 Anick Jesdanun, "Wiring Rural America," MSNBC, September 5, 2000, http://www.msnbc.com, accessed September 11, 2003.

21 Greenspan, Remarks to the Economic Club of New York.

22 Center for Advanced Purchasing Studies, "The Future of Purchasing and Supply: A Five and Ten Year Forecast," http://www.capsresearch.org/publications/pdfs-public/capsnapm1998es.pdf, accessed August 1, 2009.

23 Karen Thomas, "An Early Education in Tech Toys," *USA Today*, December 6, 2000, pp. 1D, 2D.

24 David Field, "Some E-ticket Fliers Can Print Boarding Passes on PC," *USA Today*, December 5, 2000, p. 12B.

25 Glenda Chui, "Mapping Goes Deep: Technology Points the Way to a Revolution in Cartography," *San Jose Mercury News*, September 12, 2000, p. 1F.

26 "Active Home Web Use by Country, May 2009," http://www.clickz.com/3634181, accessed August 1, 2009.

27 Internet Corporation for Assigned Names and Numbers, "Registry Listing," http://www.icann.org/en/registries/listing.html, accessed August 7, 2009.

28 William M. Pride and O. C. Ferrell, *Marketing: Concepts and Strategies*, 12th ed. (Boston: Houghton Mifflin, 2003), p. 493.

29 Julia Angwin, "Credit-Card Scams: The Devil E-stores," *Wall Street Journal*, September 19, 2000, pp. B1, B4.

30 Michael Pastore, "Fraud Continues to Haunt Online Retail," http://www.clickz.com/984441, accessed August 2, 2009.

31 Jim Carlton and Pui Wing Tam, "Online Auctioneers Face Growing Fraud Problem," *Wall Street Journal*, May 12, 2000, p. B2.

32 Michael Pastore, "Consumers Remain Confident in Online Auctions," http://www.clickz.com/578201, accessed August 2, 2009.

33 David H. Freedman, "Sleaze Bay," *Forbes ASAP*, November 27, 2000, pp. 134–140.

34 eBay Business, "Capital Equipment," http://pages.ebay.com/ebaybusiness/capital.html, accessed August 2, 2009; Steve Ulfelder, "Online auctions offer IT bargains, risks," *ComputerWorld*, http://www.computerworld.com/s/article/76944/Online_auctions_offer_IT_bargains_risks, accessed August 2, 2009.

35 "Online Auction Fraud," http://www.fbi.gov/page2/june09/auctionfraud_063009.htm, accessed August 8, 2009.

36 Eve M. Caudill and Patrick E. Murphy, "Consumer Online Privacy: Legal and Ethical Issues," *Journal of Public Policy & Marketing* 19 (Spring 2000): 7–12.

37 *Consumer Reports* WebWatch, "Leap of Faith: Using the Internet Despite the Dangers," http://www.consumerwebwatch.org/pdfs/princeton.pdf, accessed August 9, 2009.

38 http://www.peoplesearch.com, http://www.UsSearch.com, accessed August 2, 2009.

39 Federal Trade Commission, "Privacy Initiatives," http://www.ftc.gov/privacy/index.html, accessed August 2, 2009.

40 Diann Daniel, "Spam Grows, But Study Finds Users Equipped to Deal," http://www.cio.com/article/113202/Spam_Grows_But_Study_Finds_Users_Equipped_to_Deal, accessed August 9, 2009; Emil Protalinski, "Report: 81.5 Percent of All Emails

Sent in June Were Spam," http://arstechnica.com/security/
news/2008/07/report-81-5-percent-of-all-e-mails-sent-in-june-
were-spam.ars, accessed August 8, 2009.

41 Pride and Ferrell, *Marketing: Concepts and Strategies,*
pp. 600–601.

42 Federal Trade Commission, "2006 Identity Theft
Survey Report," http://www.ftc.gov/os/2007/11/
SynovateFinalReportIDTheft2006.pdf, accessed August 8,
2009; "Identity Theft Nightmare," *ABA Bank Compliance*, 23
(December 2002): 1.

43 Nancy Weil, "Report Prompts Investigation of Health-
Oriented Web Sites," CNN, April 3, 2000, http://edition.cnn
.com/2000/TECH/computing/04/03/yahoo.investigation.idg/
index.html, accessed August 2, 2009.

44 "FTC Gets Complaints About Amazon.com's New Privacy
Policy," *Wall Street Journal,* December 5, 2000, p. A10.

45 "CVS Caremark Settles FTC Charges," February 18, 2009,
http://www.ftc.gov/opa/2009/02/cvs.shtm, accessed August 8,
2009; Heather Green, "Commentary: Privacy—Don't Ask
Technology to Do the Job," *Business Week Online,* June 26,
2000, http://www.businessweek.com/2000/00_26/b3687091.
htm, accessed August 2, 2009.

46 "New Survey Shows Kids Disclose Private Details Online,"
World News Update, http://www.unitednewscanada.org/2000/
MayAug/wupdate.html, accessed August 2, 2009; Children's
Online Privacy Protection Act of 1998, http://www.ftc.gov/
ogc/coppa1.htm, accessed August 2, 2009.

47 Anne Reeks, "Electronic Sitters Evolve, but Some Still Beat
Others," *Houston Chronicle,* January 23, 2003, p. 3.

48 "Georgetown Internet Privacy Policy Survey," E-Center for
Business Ethics, http://www.e-businessethics.com/, accessed
August 2, 2009.

49 Customer Respect Group, "Telecommunications Report
Q1 2009," http://www.customerrespect.com/Insight/
Telecommunications_Q1_2009.html, accessed August 2, 2009.

50 "European Union Directive on Privacy," Banking & Financial
Services Policy Report, December 2002.

51 Thomas E. Weber, "Views on Protecting Privacy Diverse in
U.S. and Europe," *Wall Street Journal Interactive,* June 19,
2000, http://interactive.wsj.com, accessed September 11, 2003;
"The Trans-Atlantic Data Privacy Dispute," Knowledge@
Wharton, March 12, 2003, http://knowledge.wharton.upenn
.edu/article.cfm?articleid=726, accessed August 4, 2009.

52 "An Overview of Canada's New Private Sector Privacy
Law: The *Personal Information Protection and Electronic
Documents Act*," Privacy Commissioner of Canada, http://
www.priv.gc.ca/speech/2004/vs/vs_sp-d_040331_e.cfm,
accessed August 4, 2009.

53 "CSA Model Code for the Protection of Personal
Information," Media Awareness Network, http://www.media-
awareness.ca/english/resources/codes_guidelines/internet/
csa_private-code.cfm, accessed August 4, 2009.

54 "Privacy in Japan," E-Center for Business Ethics, http://www
.e-businessethics.com/privacyJA.htm, accessed August 2, 2009.

55 Lorrie Cranor, "No Quick Fixes for Protecting Online
Privacy," *Business Week Online,* March 14, 2000, http://www
.businessweek.com.

56 "Privacy in Russia," E-Center for Business Ethics, http://www.e-
businessethics.com/privacyRU.htm, accessed August 2, 2009.

57 "Customer Database Piracy Common in Russia,"
Communications Today, January 27, 2003, accessed via Lexis-
Nexis Academic Database.

58 Guy Chazan, "A High-Tech Folk Hero Challenges Russia's
Right to Snoop," *Wall Street Journal,* November 27, 2000,
p. A28.

59 International Association of Privacy Professionals, https://
www.privacyassociation.org/index.php, accessed July 31,
2009; Catherine Siskos, "In the Service of Guarding Secrets,"
Kiplinger's Personal Finance, February 2003, http://www
.encyclopedia.com/doc/1G1-96568034.html, accessed
October 28, 2009.

60 "TRUSTe.com," http://www.truste.com, accessed
August 2, 2009.

61 "Better Business Bureau Online," http://www.bbbonline.org,
accessed August 2, 2009.

62 Better Business Bureau, "Industry Self-Regulation Solutions,"
http://www.bbb.org/us/self-regulation/, accessed
August 2, 2009; "Better Business Bureau and PlanetFeedback
Will Help Companies Meet 'Whistleblower' Provision
of Recent Corporate Reform Legislation: Two trusted
organizations agree to create system for confidential reporting
of alleged misconduct," *PR Newswire,* December 11, 2002,
accessed via Lexis-Nexis Academic Database.

63 Federal Trade Commission, "FTC Announces Settlement with
Bankrupt Website, Toysmart.com, Regarding Alleged Privacy
Policy Violations," http://www.ftc.gov/opa/2000/07/toysmart2
.htm, accessed August 2, 2009.

64 ASIS International, "Trends in Proprietary Information Loss,"
http://www.asisonline.org/newsroom/surveys/spi2.pdf, accessed
August 8, 2009.

65 David G. McDonough, "But Can the WTO Really Sock It to
Software Pirates?" *Business Week Online,* March 9, 1999,
http://www.businessweek.com/bwdaily/dnflash/mar1999/
nf90309c.htm, accessed August 2, 2009.

66 "Study Finds PC Software Piracy Declining Emerging Markets,"
Computer & Internet Lawyer 23 (September 2006): 37–38.

67 McDonough, "But Can the WTO Really Sock It to Software
Pirates?"

68 Jim Duffy, "Cisco sues Huawei over intellectual property,"
Network World, January 23, 2003, IDGNews Service,
accessed via Lexis-Nexis Academic Database.

69 Rebecca Buckman, "Microsoft Steps Up Software Piracy
War," *Wall Street Journal,* August 2, 2000, p. B6.

70 "Microsoft Missing Out Unnecessarily on Billion Dollar
Revenues Due to Piracy," *Business Wire,* November 5, 2002,
accessed via Lexis-Nexis Academic Database.

71 Stephen Wildstrom, "Can Microsoft Stamp Out Piracy?"
Business Week Online, October 2, 2000, http://www.
businessweek.com/2000/00_40/b3701056.htm, accessed
August 2, 2009.

72 Rebecca Edelson and Adrienne D. Herman, "The Digital
Millennium Copyright Act: A Tool to Limit Liability for
Copyright Infringement and to Protect and Enforce
Copyrights on the Internet," Alschuler, Grossman, Stein, and
Kahan, LLP, http://www.agsk.com/print/index.html, accessed
September 11, 2003.

73 Elijah Cocks, "Internet Ruling: Hypertext Linking Does Not
Violate Copyright," Intellectual Property and Technology Forum,
Boston College Law School, Newton, MA, April 4, 2000.

74 William T. Neese and Charles R. McManis, "Summary Brief:
Law, Ethics and the Internet: How Recent Federal Trademark
Law Prohibits a Remedy Against 'Cyber-Squatters,'"
Proceedings from the Society of Marketing Advances,
November 4–7, 1998.

75 Neese and McManis, "Summary Brief: Law, Ethics and the Internet."

76 Martyn Williams, "Update: ICANN president calls for major overhaul," IDG News Service, February 25, 2002, accessed via Lexis-Nexis Academic Database.

77 Thomas A. Guida and Gerald J. Ferguson, "Strategy ICANN Arbitration vs. Federal Court: Choosing the Right Forum for Trademark Disputes," *Internet Newsletter,* November 7, 2002.

78 "ICANN Hears Concerns About Accountability, Control," http://www.pcworld.com/businesscenter/article/151736/icann_hears_concerns_about_accountability_control.html, accessed August 8, 2009; Rana Foorohar, "The Internet Splits Up; The Web changed the world. Politics is now changing it back," *Newsweek*, May 15, 2006, p. 1.

79 Arthur L. Caplan and Glenn McGee, "An Introduction to Bioethics," Bioethics.net, http://www.bioethics.net/articles.php?viewCat=3&articleId=1, accessed August 2, 2009.

80 Lucette Lagundo, "Drug Companies Face Assault on Prices," *Wall Street Journal,* May 11, 2000, p. B1.

81 Lisa Stansky, "Drug Makers Could Face Wave of Cases," *Connecticut Law Tribune,* January 24, 2003, pp. 123–128.

82 Lagundo, "Drug Companies Face Assault on Prices."

83 Biotechnology Industry Association, "Biotechnology Industry Facts," http://www.bio.org/speeches/pubs/er/statistics.asp, accessed August 8, 2009.

84 Biotechnology Industry Association, "Biotechnology Industry Facts."

85 GeneWatch UK, "Research Agendas and Patenting," http://www.genewatch.org/sub.shtml?als[cid]=396424, accessed August 2, 2009.

86 "Avon Foundation Continues Commitment to Breast Cancer Cause; Awards Nearly $30 Million in Grants to Thirteen Organizations," CDC Foundation, http://www.cdcfoundation.org/pr/2002/avon_foundation_continues_commitment_to_breast_cancer_cause.aspx, accessed August 2, 2009.

87 Marilynn Marchione, "Study suggests setback in effort to morph stem cells into insulin-producing pancreas cells," *Milwaukee Journal Sentinel,* January 17, 2003, p. B8.

88 John Leavitt, "What Will Human Clones Be Like?" *Connecticut Law Tribune,* January 24, 2003, p. 5.

89 Andy Coghlan, "Cloning Special Report: Cloning Without Embryos," *New Scientist,* January 29, 2000, p. 4.

90 Natasha McDowell, "Mini-Pig Clone Raises Transplant Hope," http://www.newscientist.com/article/dn3257, accessed August 2, 2009.

91 Rachel Nowak, "Australia OKs Human Embryo Research," http://www.newscientist.com/article/dn3149, accessed August 2, 2009.

92 Jacqueline Stensen, "Gene Patents Raise Concerns," MSNBC, http://www.msnbc.com, accessed September 11, 2003.

93 Rebecca S. Eisenberg, "How Can You Patent Genes?" *American Journal of Bioethics* 2 (Summer 2002): 3–11.

94 Sarah Lueck, "New Kits Let You Test Your Own Genes, but Interpreting Results Can Be Tricky," *Wall Street Journal,* May 24, 2005, p. D1.

95 "Conservation Ecology: Risks and Benefits of Genetically Modified Crops," http://www.ecologyandsociety.org/vol4/iss1/art13/, accessed August 2, 2009.

96 Bill Gates, "Will Frankenfood Feed the World?" June 11, 2000, http://www.microsoft.com/presspass/ofnote/06-11time.mspx, accessed August 2, 2009.

97 "Weighing the Future of Biotech Food," MSNBC, http://www.msnbc.com, accessed July 18, 2000.

98 Julia A. Moore and Gilbert Winham, "Let's not escalate the 'Frankenfood' war," http://www.csmonitor.com/2002/1220/p13s02-coop.html, accessed August 2, 2009.

99 "Green Groups Target Campbell Soup in GM Food Fight," GreenBiz.com, http://www.greenbiz.com/news/2000/07/20/green-groups-target-campbell-soup-gm-food-fight, accessed August 2, 2009.

100 "Conservation Ecology: Risks and Benefits of Genetically Modified Crops," http://www.ecologyandsociety.org/vol4/iss1/art13, accessed August 2, 2009.

101 Paul Magnusson, Ann Therese, and Kerry Capell, "Furor over Frankenfood," *Business Week,* October 18, 1999, pp. 50, 51; "Japan Asks That Imports of Corn Be StarLink-Free," *Wall Street Journal,* October 30, 2000, p. A26.

102 Peter Tyson, "Should We Grow GM Crops?" http://www.pbs.org/wgbh/harvest/exist/, accessed August 2, 2009.

103 Magnusson, Therese, and Capell, "Furor over Frankenfood."

104 "EU's anti-GM stance under threat," January 10, 2003, http://www.cnn.com/2003/WORLD/europe/01/10/biotech.us.europe/index.html, accessed August 2, 2009; "Conservation Ecology: Risks and Benefits of Genetically Modified Crops," http://www.ecologyandsociety.org/vol4/iss1/art13, accessed August 2, 2009.

105 "'Terminator' Victory a Small Step in Long War," CNN, October 7, 1999, http://www.cnn.com/NATURE/9910/07/terminator.victory.enn/index.html, accessed August 2, 2009.

106 "Viewpoints: Is Genetically Modified Food Safe to Eat?," PBS.org, http://www.pbs.org/wgbh/harvest/viewpoints/issafe.html, accessed August 4, 2009.

107 Fred Guterl, "The Fear of Food," Newsweek International, January 27, 2003, accessed via Lexis-Nexis Academic Database.

108 Greg Farrell, "Police Have Few Weapons Against Cyber-Criminals," USA Today, December 6, 2000, p. 5B; Edward Iwata and Kevin Johnson, "Computer Crime Outpacing Cybercops," USA Today, June 7, 2000, p. 1A.

109 Kevin Poulsen, "Feds seek public input on hacker sentencing," SecurityFocus, January 13, 2003, http://www.securityfocus.com/news/2028, accessed August 2, 2009.

110 Patrick Thibodeau, "Quick Study: The DMCA," ComputerWorld, December 2, 2002, http://www.computerworld.com/governmenttopics/government/legalissues/story/0,10801,76301,00.html, accessed August 2, 2009.

111 "Websense," http://www.websense.com/content/home.aspx, accessed August 2, 2009.

112 Mathis Thurman, "Proxy Server Serves to Block Porn-Surfing Slackers," *ComputerWorld*, http://www.computerworld.com/s/article/70567/Proxy_Server_Serves_to_Block_Porn-Surfing_Slackers, accessed August 2, 2009.

113 PriceWaterhouseCoopers, Information Security Breaches Survey 2006, http://www.berr.gov.uk/files/file28343.pdf, accessed August 2, 2009.

114 Lindsey Gerdes, "You Have 20 Minutes to Surf. Go," Business Week, December 26, 2005, p. 16.

115 Michael J. McCarthy, "Keystroke Loggers Save E-mail Rants, Raising Workplace Privacy Concerns," Wall Street Journal, March 7, 2000, http://interactive.wsj.com.

116 Julene Snyder, "Should Overworked Employees Be Allowed to Surf the Web on the Job?" CNN Online, May 11, 2000, http://www.cnn.com/2000/TECH/computing/05/11/job.surf.idg/, accessed August 2, 2009.

117 Roberta Fusaro, "Chief Privacy Officer: A Conversation with Richard Purcell," Harvard Business Review 78 (November–December 2000): 20–22.

118 Sheila M. J. Bonini, Lenny T. Mendonca, and Jeremy M. Oppenheim, "When Social Issues Become Strategic," The McKinsey Quarterly 2 (2006): 20.

Chapter 11

1 "Recession Caused Drop in Greenhouse Gas Emissions by Half in 2008," Little About, June 27, 2009, http://www.littleabout.com/news/20363,recession-caused-drop-greenhouse-gas-emissions-2008.html, accessed June 30, 2009; Sharon Begley, "The Recession's Green Lining," Newsweek. March 16, 2009, pp. 48–49; Quentin Hardy and Taylor Buley, "The Greening of Trade Wars," Forbes, April 27, 2009, pp. 26–27; Baikal Club, http://www.baikal-club.ru/eng/info/about/, accessed June 30, 2009.

2 Jeffrey Jones, "In the U.S., 28% Report Major Changes to Living Green," Gallup, April 18, 2008, http://www.gallup.com/poll/106624/US-28-Report-Major-Changes-Live-Green.aspx, accessed June 11, 2009.

3 PR Newswire, "Five Midwest Corporations Make EPA's Fortune 500 Green Power Challenge List," Reuters, January 29, 2008, http://www.reuters.com/article/pressRelease/idUS231156+29-Jan-2008+PRN20080129, accessed June 12, 2009.

4 "Air Quality," Office of Air Quality Planning and Standards, Environmental Protection Agency, http://www.epa.gov/oar/oaqps/cleanair.html, accessed June 30, 2009.

5 Christine Lagorio, "The Most Polluted Places on Earth," CBS News, June 6, 2007, http://www.cbsnews.com/stories/2007/06/06/eveningnews/main2895653.shtml, accessed June 30, 2009.

6 "The Plain English Guide to the Clean Air Act," Office of Air Quality Planning and Standards, Environmental Protection Agency, http://www.epa.gov/air/caa/peg/, accessed June 30, 2009.

7 "The Effects of Acid Rain," Environmental Protection Agency, http://www.epa.gov/acidrain/effects/index.html, accessed June 30, 2009.

8 "International Energy Outlook," Energy Information Administration, May 27, 2009, http://www.eia.doe.gov/oiaf/ieo/emissions.html, accessed June 30, 2009.

9 John M. Broder and Jonathan Ansfield, "China and U.S. Seek Truce on Greenhouse Gasses," New York Times, June 7, 2009, http://www.nytimes.com/2009/06/08/world/08treaty.html?ref=science, accessed June 30, 2009.

10 Jon Karl, Jake Tapper, and Kristina Wong, "Obama to Announce Stricter Emission Standards for Autos," ABC News, May 18, 2009, http://abcnews.go.com/Politics/story?id=7619781&page=1, accessed June 15, 2009; Stephen Power, "Obama Officials Urge Cap on Greenhouse Gases," Wall Street Journal, April 22, 2009, http://online.wsj.com/article/SB124041000623343693.html, accessed June 15, 2009.

11 Doyle Rice, "Earth's Temperature 8th Warmest on Record So Far in 2009," USA Today, April 16, 2009, http:// www.usatoday.com/weather/climate/2009-04-16-march-temperatures-emissions-reduction-study_N.htm, accessed June 30, 2009; John Ryden, "2008 Eighth Warmest Year on Record," Global Warming Examiner, January 19, 2009, http://www.examiner.com/x-325-Global-Warming-Examiner~y2009m1d19-2008-eight-warmest-year-on-record, accessed June 30, 2009.

12 "Climate Change Moves Border," Planet Ski, June 28, 2009, http://www.planetski.eu/news/535, accessed June 30, 2009.

13 "Hurricanes and Global Warming FAQs," Pew Center on Global Climate Change, http://www.pewclimate.org/hurricanes.cfm, accessed June 30, 2009.

14 Mark Alpert, "Protections for the Earth's Climate," Scientific American 293 (December 2005): 55.

15 Jim Tankersley, "EPA Gives California Emissions Waiver," Baltimore Sun, June 30, 2009, http://www.baltimoresun.com/features/green/bal-car-waiver-0630,0,3946031.story, accessed June 30, 2009.

16 "About Energy Star," Energy Star, http://www.energystar.gov/index.cfm?c=about.ab_index, accessed June 15, 2009.

17 United Nations Climate Change Conference 2009, http://en.cop15.dk/?gclid=CL2j0PjmspsCFRFMagod-EAyOg, accessed June 30, 2009.

18 Richard Harris, "Climate Change Bill Heads for House Vote," NPR, May 22, 2009, http://www.npr.org/templates/story/story.php?storyId=104436991, accessed June 3, 2009.

19 Stephan Power and Siobhan Hughes, "Farm Belt Lawmakers Challenge Climate Bill," Wall Street Journal, June 17, 2009, p. A4.

20 Joseph B. White, "Climate Fight Heads for New Round," Wall Street Journal, June 17, 2009, A14.

21 Mark Scott, "How Banks Will Pounce on Carbon Trading," BusinessWeek, June 8, 2009, p. 51.

22 Joseph B. White, "Climate Fight Heads for New Round."

23 "Firms Failing on Carbon Emissions," Microsoft Business and Industry, January 21, 2009, http://www.microsoft.com/uk/business/news/green-it/Firms-failing-on-carbon-emissions-18984719.mspx, accessed June 12, 2009.

24 "Pollution Causes 40 Percent of Deaths Worldwide, Study Finds," Science Daily, August 14, 2007, http://www.sciencedaily.com/releases/2007/08/070813162438.htm, accessed June 15, 2009.

25 "Great Lakes Areas of Concern," Environmental Protection Agency, June 25, 2009, http://www.epa.gov/glnpo/aoc/, accessed June 16, 2009.

26 "National Drinking Water Week is May 3–9," Centers for Disease Control and Prevention, http://www.cdc.gov/Features/DrinkingWater/, accessed June 15, 2009.

27 Pharmawater Investigation, Associated Press, http://hosted.ap.org/specials/interactives/_national/pharmawater_update/index.html, accessed June 30, 2009.

28 "Protecting the Clean Water Act," Audubon, http://www.audubon.org/campaign/cleanwateract.html, accessed June 17, 2009.

29 Managing Our Future Water Needs for Agriculture, Industry, Human Health, and the Environment, World Economic Forum, http://www.weforum.org/pdf/water/managing.pdf, accessed July 14, 2009.

30 Amit Srivasteva, "Communities Reject Coca-Cola in India," Crop Watch, July 10, 2003, http://www.corpwatch.org/article.php?id=7508, accessed July 14, 2009.

31 "Indoor Water Use in the United States," Environmental Protection Agency, http://www.epa.gov/watersense/pubs/indoor.htm, accessed August 20, 2009.

32 Susan Berfield, "There Will Be Water," *BusinessWeek,* June 23, 2008, p. 40; National Climatic Data Center, "Climate of 2008 Annual Review U.S. Drought," NOAA Satellite and Information Service, January 14, 2009, http://www.ncdc.noaa.gov/oa/climate/research/2008/ann/drought-summary.html, accessed June 17, 2009; "Water Sense," Environmental Protection Agency, http://www.epa.gov/watersense/news/archive/2008.htm, accessed June 17, 2009.

33 Robert Kunzig, "Drying of the West," *National Geographic,* February 2008, http://ngm.nationalgeographic.com/2008/02/drying-west/kunzig-text/1, accessed June 17, 2009.

34 Anoaneta Bezlova, "Environment—China: 'World Must Share Blame for Industrial Pollution,'" Interpress Service, April 12, 2009, http://www.ipsnews.net/news.asp?idnews=35554, accessed July 3, 2009.

35 Matthew Dalton, "European Farmers Turn to Biogas Plants," *Wall Street Journal,* June 18, 2009, http://online.wsj.com/article/SB124527861144324987.html, accessed July 3, 2009.

36 Ryan Knutson, "Electronics Firms Fight State Recycling Programs," *New York Times,* July 2, 2009, http://online.wsj.com/article/SB124648949162882917.html, accessed July 3, 2009.

37 Bryan Walsh, "Study: Economic Boost of Deforestation Is Short-Lived," *Time,* June 12, 2009, http://www.time.com/time/health/article/0,8599,1904174,00.html?iid=tsmodule, accessed July, 3, 2009.

38 Research and Resources, Rainforest Alliance, http://www.rainforest-alliance.org/resources.cfm?id=research_analyses, accessed July 3, 2009; Forest Stewardship Council, http://www.fsc.org, accessed July 3, 2009.

39 Jim Carleton, "Into the Woods," *Wall Street Journal,* June 15, 2009, http://online.wsj.com/article/SB10001424052970203771904574179372564159870.html, accessed July 3, 2009.

40 John William Uhler, Everglades National Park Information Page, http://www.everglades.national-park.com/info.htm#end, accessed June 19, 2009; "Saving the Everglades," Environment Florida, http://www.environmentflorida.org/preservation/saving-the-everglades, accessed June 19, 2009.

41 "The Red List: Wildlife in a Changing World," The International Union for Conservation of Nature, http://data.iucn.org/dbtw-wpd/edocs/RL-2009-001.pdf, accessed July 3, 2009.

42 "Earth Matters: Pollinator Decline Puts World Food Supply at Risk, Experts Warn," CNN, http://archives.cnn.com/2000/NATURE/05/05/pollinators.peril/, accessed July 3, 2009.

43 "Special Offering: Guatemala Santa Isabel," Peet's Coffee & Tea, http://www.peets.com/shop/coffee_detail.asp?rdir=1&id=1809&cid=1000040&cm_re=coffee-_-billboard-_-graphic, accessed July 14, 2009.

44 "Biotech Food Safe, but More Tests Needed, Study Suggests," *Coloradoan,* April 6, 2000, p. B3.

45 Karlene Lukovitz, "Whole Foods Adopts Non-GMO Verification," MediaPost News, July 8, 2009, http://www.mediapost.com/publications/?fa=Articles.showArticle&art_aid=109382, accessed July 14, 2009.

46 "Wal-Mart Says No to Milk from 'Juiced' Cows," Triple Pundit, March 28, 2008, http://www.triplepundit.com/pages/walmart-says-no.php, accessed July 14, 2009.

47 Miranda Hitti, "New Drug from Genetically Engineered Goat," MedicineNet.com, February 6, 2009, http://www.medicinenet.com/script/main/art.asp?articlekey=97520, accessed June 22, 2009.

48 "EPA's Mission, Goals, and Principles," *EPA Strategic Plan,* Office of the Chief Financial Officer, Environmental Protection Agency, http://www.epa.gov/ocfo/plan/plan.htm, accessed July 14, 2009.

49 "2009–2014 Strategic Plan Change Document," Environmental Protection Agency, September 2008, http://epa.gov/ocfo/plan/pdfs/strategic_plan_change_document_9-30-08.pdf, accessed July 14, 2009.

50 "About EPA," http://www.epa.gov/epahome/aboutepa.htm, accessed July 14, 2009.

51 "EPA Publishes Notice Identifying Hardrock Mining Industry for Financial Responsibility Requirements," EPA Newsroom, July 13, 2008, http://yosemite.epa.gov/opa/admpress.nsf/d0cf6618525a9efb85257359003fb69d/90a65f473216e941852575f2004807eb!OpenDocument, accessed July 14, 2009.

52 "The Plain English Guide to the Clean Air Act," http://www.epa.gov/air/caa/peg/, accessed July 14, 2009.

53 "Summary of the Endangered Species Act," Environmental Protection Agency, http://www.epa.gov/regulations/laws/esa.html, accessed July 14, 2009.

54 "Summary of Listed Species, Listed Populations and Recovery Plans as of Sat., 27 of June, 2009," *U.S. Fish and Wildlife Services Species Report,* http://ecos.fws.gov/tess_public/TESSBoxscore, accessed June 27, 2009.

55 "How Has the ESA Impacted America?" National Endangered Species Act Reform Coalition, http://www.nesarc.org/stories.htm, accessed July 14, 2009.

56 "Summary of the Toxic Substances Control Act," Environmental Protection Agency, http://www.epa.gov/regulations/laws/tsca.html, accessed July 14, 2009.

57 "Summary of the Clean Water Act," Environmental Protection Agency, http://www.epa.gov/regulations/laws/cwa.html, accessed July 14, 2009.

58 Michael McLaughlin, "One Big Problem—Save the Waves," *Fast Company,* December 19, 2007, http://www.fastcompany.com/online/32/waves.html, accessed July 14, 2009.

59 "Summary of the Pollution Prevention Act," Environmental Protection Agency, http://www.epa.gov/regulations/laws/ppa.html, accessed July 15, 2009.

60 "Food Quality Protection Act (FQPA)," Environmental Protection Agency, http://www.epa.gov/agriculture/lqpa.html, accessed July 15, 2009.

61 Associated Press, "Bush Signs $12.3 Billion Energy Bill into Law," MSNBC, August 8, 2005, http://www.msnbc.msn.com/id/8870039/, accessed June 22, 2009.

62 Josh Glasser, "T. Boone Pickens on Natural Gas: You Can't Beat it," *Fortune,* July 14, 2009, http://bigtech.blogs.fortune.cnn.com/2009/07/14/news/economy/pickens_natural_gas.fortune/?postversion=2009071415, accessed July 15, 2009.

63 "Local Press Release No. 2/2009 from Vestas Americas," Vestas, March 25, 2009, http://www.vestas.com/files//Filer/EN/Press_releases/Local/2009/AM_090325_LPMUK_02.pdf, accessed April 14, 2009; "Wind as a Modern Energy Source: The Vestas View," *PES: Europe,* pp. 50–52.

64 Hawley, "Clean-Energy Windmills a 'Dirty Business' for Farmers in Mexico," *USA Today,* June 17, 2009, pp. B1–B2.

65 "Geothermal Basics," and "Geothermal FAQS," U.S. Department of Energy Efficiency and Renewable Energy, http://www1.eere.energy.gov/geothermal/geothermal_basics.html, accessed June 24, 2009; "Geothermal," Institute for

Energy Research, 2009, http://www.instituteforenergyresearch.org/energy-overview/geothermal/, accessed June 24, 2009; John Lund, "Characteristics, Development and Utilization of Geothermal Resources," *GHC Bulletin,* June 2007, http://geoheat.oit.edu/bulletin/bull28-2/art1.pdf, accessed June 24, 2009; Ruggero Bertani, Enel, "World Geothermal Generation in 2007," *GHC Bulletin,* December 2007, http://geoheat.oit.edu/bulletin/bull28-3/art3.pdf, accessed June 24, 2009.

66 Melissa A. Schilling and Melissa Esmundo, "Technology S-Curves in Renewable Energy Alternatives: Analysis and Implications for Industry and Government," *Energy Policy* 3 (2009): 1767–1781.

67 "Solar Energy Grew at a Record Pace in 2008," *Energy Efficiency and Renewable Energy,* March 25, 2009, http://apps1.eere.energy.gov/news/news_detail.cfm?news_id=12362, accessed June 23, 2009.

68 "Press Release: Wal-Mart to Nearly Double Solar Energy Use in California," Wal-Mart Stores, Inc., April 22, 2009, http://walmartstores.com/FactsNews/NewsRoom/9091.aspx, accessed July 15, 2009.

69 "About BP Solar," BP, http://www.bp.com/sectiongenericarticle.do?categoryId=9071&contentId=7038231, accessed July 15, 2009.

70 "Showa Shell, Saudi Aramco to Form Solar Power JV," *Yahoo! Singapore News* via Reuters, June 24, 2009, http://sg.news.yahoo.com/rtrs/20090624/tbs-showashell-solar-7318940.html, accessed June 24, 2009.

71 Ulrike Dauer, "Firms Pursue Solar Power from Sahara," *Wall Street Journal,* July 14, 2009, http://online.wsj.com/article/SB124752067580934873.html?mod=googlenews_wsj, accessed July 15, 2009.

72 "Overview of Nuclear Energy," World Nuclear Association, http://world-nuclear.org/education/intro.htm, accessed June 24, 2009; Carl Behrens and Mark Holt, "Nuclear Power Plants: Vulnerability to Terrorist Attack," *CRS Report for Congress,* February 4, 2005, http://www.globalsecurity.org/military/library/report/crs/rs21131.pdf, accessed June 24, 2009.

73 World Nuclear Association, http://www.world-nuclear.org/info/inf41.html#govtRD, accessed June 24, 2009.

74 "Chevrolet Volt—GM's Concept Electric Vehicle Could Eliminate Trips to the Gas Station," *PR Domain,* January 7, 2007, http://www.prdomain.com/companies/G/GeneralMotors/newsreleases/20071838357.htm, accessed June 24, 2009.

75 "About," The Verenium Corporation, http://www.verenium.com/about.asp, accessed July 15, 2009.

76 "Hydroelectric Power Water Use," USGS, May 13, 2009, http://ga.water.usgs.gov/edu/wuhy.html, accessed June 24, 2009.

77 Stefan Ambec and Paul Lanoie, "Does It Pay to Be Green? A Systematic Overview," *Academy of Management Perspectives* 22, no. 4 (November 2008): 45–62.

78 Jim Hanas, "A World Gone Green," *Advertising Age,* June 19, 2007, http://www.greenmarketing.com/files/news/Advertising%20Age061807.pdf, accessed June 25, 2009.

79 Miguel Bustillo, "Wal-Mart Plans Environmental Labels for Products," *Wall Street Journal,* July 16, 2009, http://online.wsj.com/article/SB124766892562645475.html#mod=testMod, accessed July 16, 2009.

80 Stefan Ambec and Paul Lanoie, "Does It Pay to Be Green? A Systematic Overview."

81 "Sustainability," New Belgium Brewing, http://www.newbelgium.com/sustainability, accessed July 15, 2009.

82 "The EU Eco-Label," http://www.eco-label.com/default.htm, accessed July 15, 2009.

83 "Press Release: The Home Depot and Tembec Team Up," http://www.fscus.org/news/archive.php?article=276&, accessed July 15, 2009.

84 "The Seven Sins of Greenwashing," Terra Choice, http://sinsofgreenwashing.org/, accessed July 15, 2009.

85 "Eco-Friendly Product Claims Often Misleading," NPR, November 30, 2007, http://www.npr.org/templates/story/story.php?storyId=16754919, accessed June 25, 2009.

86 Paul Hawken and William McDonough, "Seven Steps to Doing Good Business," *Inc.,* November 1993, pp. 79–90, http://www.inc.com/magazine/19931101/3770.html, accessed September 11, 2003.

87 "Product Groups," *Caeran,* http://www.caeran.com/ProductGroups/product_groups.htm, accessed June 25, 2009.

88 Recycling, American Forest & Paper Association, http://www.afandpa.org/Recycling.aspx, accessed July 15, 2009.

89 "About WasteWise," http://www.epa.gov/waste/partnerships/wastewise/about.htm, accessed July 15, 2009.

90 Ana Campoy, "'Water Hog' Label Haunts Dallas," *Wall Street Journal,* July 15, 2009, http://online.wsj.com/article/SB124762034777142623.html, accessed July 15, 2009.

91 "Local Press Release No. 2/2009 from Vestas Americas," Vestas, March 25, 2009, http://www.vestas.com/files//Filer/EN/Press_releases/Local/2009/AM_090325_LPMUK_02.pdf, accessed April 14, 2009; "Wind as a Modern Energy Source: The Vestas View," *PES: Europe,* pp. 50–52; "About the Plan," *PickensPlan,* http://www.pickensplan.com/about/, accessed April 14, 2009; Scott DeCarlo, Project Editor, "The World's Best Companies," *Forbes,* April 27, 2009, pp. 102–112.

92 Daniel Fisher, "Chevron's $27 Billion Problem," *Forbes,* June 24, 2009, http://www.forbes.com/forbes/2009/0713/texaco-ecuador-pollution-chevrons-27-billion-problem.html, accessed July 15, 2009.

93 Jan Collins, "Being Green," *Business and Economic Review* 52 (January–March 2006): 3–7; "WasteWise Awards," *Business and the Environment* 17 (January 2006): 12–13; Herman Miller, "Environmental Advocacy," http://www.hermanmiller.com/About-Us/Environmental-Advocacy, accessed July 15, 2009; "Herman Miller Recognized for Sustainability," *Holland Sentinel,* July 7, 2009, http://www.hollandsentinel.com/business/x488829429/Herman-Miller-recognized-for-sustainability, accessed July 15, 2009.

94 "Voluntary Environmental Management Systems/ISO 14001: Frequently Asked Questions," Environmental Protection Agency, http://www.epa.gov/OWM/iso14001/isofaq.htm, accessed June 26, 2009.

95 Tim O'Brien, *Ford & ISO 14001: The Synergy Between Preserving the Environment and Rewarding Shareholders* (New York: McGraw-Hill, 2001); New Graph: Rhett A. Butler, "World Deforestation Rates and Forest Cover Statistics, 2000–2005," Mongabay.com, November 17, 2005, http://news.mongabay.com/2005/1115-forests.html, accessed June 18, 2009.

96 "History," Green Globe, http://www.greenglobeint.com/about/history/, accessed June 26, 2009; "About Us," Green Globe, http://www.greenglobecertification.com/about.html#, accessed June 26, 2009.

Chapter 12

1 "Exploring the Links Between International Business and Poverty Reduction: A Case Study of Unilever in Indonesia," Oxfam Great Britain, http://www.oxfam.org.uk/what_we_do/ issues/livelihoods/unilever.htm, accessed May 30, 2006; Oxfam International, http://www.oxfam.org, accessed June 11, 2006; Unilever, "Indonesia," http://www.unilever.com/sustainability/ economic/developing-emerging-markets/indonesia/, accessed July 12, 2009; United Nations, "The UN in Brief," http:// www.un.org/Overview/brief.html, accessed June 13, 2006.

2 Center for Cultural Intelligence, "What is Cultural Intelligence (CQ)?," http://www.cci.ntu.edu.sg/index.html, accessed August 15, 2009.

3 Mary Lou Egan and Marc Bendick, "Combining Multicultural Management and Diversity into One Course on Cultural Competence," *Academy of Management Learning and Education* 7, no. 3 (2008): 387–393.

4 P. Christopher Early and Elaine Mosakowski, "Cultural Intelligence," *Harvard Business Review* 82 (October 2004): 1–9.

5 Ibid.

6 Marieke K. de Mooj, *Consumer Behavior and Culture* (Thousand Oaks, CA: Sage, 2003).

7 Business Knowledge Source, "Overseas Manufacturing Pros and Cons," http://www.businessknowledgesource.com, accessed August 15, 2009.

8 Carrie Johnson, "U.S. Targets Overseas Bribery," *Washington Post*, December 5, 2007, p. D1.

9 Andrew Singer, "United Parcel Service Translates and Transports an Ethics Code Overseas," *Ethikos and Corporate Conduct Quarterly* (May/June 2001), http://www.singerpubs. com, accessed August 16, 2009.

10 Susan Raymond, "Global Philanthropy Part 2: Philanthropy in Latin America," http://www.onphilanthropy.com, March 6, 2008, accessed August 15, 2009.

11 "Global Sullivan Principles of Social Responsibility," http:// www.thesullivanfoundation.org/gsp/default.asp, accessed August 15, 2009.

12 Caux Round Table, "Global Governing Board," http://www .cauxroundtable.org, accessed August 16, 2009.

13 Mercer, "Engaging Employees to Drive Global Business Success, 2007," http://www.mercer.com/whatsworking, accessed August 14, 2009.

14 "Ethics in Toursim," World Tourism Organization, http:// www.world-tourism.org/code_ethics/eng.html, accessed August 16, 2009.

15 J. Brooke Hamilton, Stephen B. Knouse, and Vanessa Hill, "Google in China: A Manager-Friendly Heuristic Model for Resolving Cross-Cultural Ethical Conflicts" *Journal of Business Ethics* 86, no. 2 (2009): 143–157.

16 Fairtrade Labelling Organizations International, http://www .fairtrade.net/faqs.html?&no_cache=1, accessed August 13, 2009.

17 GreenAmerica, "Products and Producer Profiles," http://www .coopamerica.org/tools/print.cfm?page=/programs/fairtrade/ products, accessed August 13, 2009.

18 TransFair USA, "Fair Trade Certified Thriving in Tough U.S. Economy: Research Study and Sales Figures Show That Consumer Interest in Fair Trade Certified Remains Strong," April 16, 2009, http://www.transfairusa.org/content/about/pr/ pr_090416b.php, accessed August 13, 2009.

19 AccountAbility, "The State of Responsible Competitiveness 2007," http://www.accountability21.net/uploadedFiles/ publications/The%20State%20of%20Responsible%20 Competitiveness.pdf, accessed August 8, 2009.

20 Ibid.

21 Amartya Sen, *Development as Freedom* (New York: Random House, 1999).

22 United Nations Development Programme, "Johannesburg Summit Promotes Partnerships for Development," http://www .undp.org/dpa/frontpage archive/2002/september/5sept02/, accessed November 23, 2004.

23 United Nations, "Global Compact: Corporate Citizenship in the World Economy," http://www.unglobalcompact.org/docs/ news_events/8.1/GC_brochure_FINAL.pdf, accessed August 16, 2009.

24 Ananya Mukherjee Reed and Darryl Reed, "Partnerships for Development: Four Models of Business Involvement," *Journal of Business Ethics* 90, supplement 1 (May 2009): 3–37.

25 Uwafiokun Idemudia, "Oil Extraction and Poverty Reduction in the Niger Delta: A Critical Examination of Partnership Initiatives," *Journal of Business Ethics* 90, supplement 1 (May 2009): 91–116.

26 "Socialism in Reverse," *Wall Street Journal*, July 29, 2006, p. A10, accessed via ProQuest Database, August 14, 2009; FDI. net, "Privatization," http://www.fdi.net/spotlight/index .cfm?spid=8, accessed August 14, 2009.

27 William Finnegan, "Leasing the Rain," *The New Yorker*, April 8, 2002, http://www.newyorker.com/ archive/2002/04/08/020408fa_FACT1?printable=true, accessed August 14, 2009; Jim Shultz, "The Politics of Water in Bolivia," *The Nation*, January 28, 2005, http://www .thenation.com/doc/20050214/shultz/print, accessed August 14, 2009.

28 "About the Microcredit Summit Campaign," http://www .microcreditsummit.org/about/about_the_microcredit_summit_ campaign/, accessed August 17, 2009.

29 Grameen Bank, "The Nobel Peace Prize 2006," http://www .grameen-info.org/index.php?option=com_content&task=vie w&id=197&Itemid=197, accessed August 14, 2009; World Bank, "10 Years of World Bank Support for Microcredit in Bangladesh," http://web.worldbank.org, accessed August 14, 2009.

30 Fair Labor Association, http://www.fairlabor.org/news_ releases_a1.html, accessed August 14, 2009.

31 Self Employed Women's Association, http://www.sewa.org, accessed August 14, 2009.

32 Center for Global Development, "Commitment to Development Index, 2008," http://www.cgdev.org/section/ initiatives/_active/cdi/, accessed August 16, 2009.

INDEX

Page numbers followed by "f" indicate figures, those followed by "t" indicate tables, and those followed by "n" indicate source notes.